The Gospel of
Sri Ramakrishna

Originally recorded in Bengali
by M., a disciple of the Master

Sri Ramakrishna

The Gospel of
Sri Ramakrishna

*Translated into
English with an Introduction
by*

SWAMI NIKHILANANDA

NEW YORK

Ramakrishna-Vivekananda Center

The Gospel of Sri Ramakrishna

Ten Printing 2007

ISBN: 978 0-911206-01-2
ISBN: 0-911206-01-9

Library of Congress Catalog Card Number: 58–8948

Printed in the United States of America

FOREWORD

IN THE HISTORY of the arts genius is a thing of very rare occurrence. Rarer still, however, are the competent reporters and recorders of that genius. The world has had many hundreds of admirable poets and philosophers; but of these hundreds only a very few have had the fortune to attract a Boswell or an Eckermann.

When we leave the field of art for that of spiritual religion, the scarcity of competent reporters becomes even more strongly marked. Of the day-to-day life of the great theocentric saints and contemplatives we know, in the great majority of cases, nothing whatever. Many, it is true, have recorded their doctrines in writing, and a few, such as St Augustine, Suso and St Teresa, have left us autobiographies of the greatest value. But all doctrinal writing is in some measure formal and impersonal, while the autobiographer tends to omit what he regards as trifling matters and suffers from the further disadvantage of being unable to say how he strikes other people and in what way he affects their lives. Moreover, most saints have left neither writings nor self-portraits, and for a knowledge of their lives, their characters and their teachings, we are forced to rely upon the records made by their disciples who, in most cases, have proved themselves singularly incompetent as reporters and biographers. Hence the special interest attaching to this enormously detailed account of the daily life and conversations of Sri Ramakrishna.

"M", as the author modestly styles himself, was peculiarly qualified for his task. To a reverent love for his master, to a deep and experiential knowledge of that master's teaching, he added a prodigious memory for the small happenings of each day and a happy gift for recording them in an interesting and realistic way. Making good use of his natural gifts and of the circumstances in which he found himself, "M" produced a book unique, so far as my knowledge goes, in the literature of hagiography. No other saint has had so able and indefatigable a Boswell. Never have the small events of a contemplative's daily life been described with such a wealth of intimate detail. Never have the casual and unstudied utterances of a great religious teacher been set down with so minute a fidelity. To Western readers, it is true, this fidelity and this wealth of detail are sometimes a trifle disconcerting; for the social, religious and intellectual frames of reference within which Sri Ramakrishna did his thinking and expressed his feelings were entirely Indian. But after the first few surprises and bewilderments, we begin to find something peculiarly stimulating and instructive about the very strangeness and, to our eyes, the eccentricity of the man revealed to us in "M's" narrative. What a scholastic philosopher would call the "accidents" of Ramakrishna's life

v

were intensely Hindu and therefore, so far as we in the West are concerned, unfamiliar and hard to understand; its "essence", however, was intensely mystical and therefore universal. To read through these conversations in which mystical doctrine alternates with an unfamiliar kind of humour, and where discussions of the oddest aspects of Hindu mythology give place to the most profound and subtle utterances about the nature of Ultimate Reality, is in itself a liberal education in humility, tolerance and suspense of judgment. We must be grateful to the translator for his excellent version of a book so curious and delightful as a biographical document, so precious, at the same time, for what it teaches us of the life of the spirit.

ALDOUS HUXLEY

PREFACE

The Gospel of Sri Ramakrishna is the English translation of the *Sri Sri Ramakrishna Kathāmrita*, the conversations of Sri Ramakrishna with his disciples, devotees, and visitors, recorded by Mahendranath Gupta, who wrote the book under the pseudonym of "M." The conversations in Bengali fill five volumes, the first of which was published in 1897 and the last shortly after M.'s death in 1932. Sri Ramakrishna Math, Madras, has published in two volumes an English translation of selected chapters from the monumental Bengali work. I have consulted these while preparing my translation.

M., one of the intimate disciples of Sri Ramakrishna, was present during all the conversations recorded in the main body of the book and noted them down in his diary. They therefore have the value of almost stenographic records. In Appendix A are given several conversations which took place in the absence of M., but of which he received a first-hand record from persons concerned. The conversations will bring before the reader's mind an intimate picture of the Master's eventful life from March 1882 to April 24, 1886, only a few months before his passing away. During this period he came in contact chiefly with English-educated Bengalis; from among them he selected his disciples and the bearers of his message, and with them he shared his rich spiritual experiences.

I have made a literal translation, omitting only a few pages of no particular interest to English-speaking readers. Often literary grace has been sacrificed for the sake of literal translation. No translation can do full justice to the original. This difficulty is all the more felt in the present work, whose contents are of a deep mystical nature and describe the inner experiences of a great seer. Human language is an altogether inadequate vehicle to express supersensuous perception. Sri Ramakrishna was almost illiterate. He never clothed his thoughts in formal language. His words sought to convey his direct realization of Truth. His conversation was in a village patois. Therein lies its charm. In order to explain to his listeners an abstruse philosophy, he, like Christ before him, used with telling effect homely parables and illustrations, culled from his observation of the daily life around him.

The reader will find mentioned in this work many visions and experiences that fall outside the ken of physical science and even psychology. With the development of modern knowledge the border line between the natural and the supernatural is ever shifting its position. Genuine mystical experiences are not as suspect now as they were half a century ago. The words of Sri Ramakrishna have already exerted a tremendous influence in the land of his birth. Savants of Europe have found in his words the ring of universal truth.

But these words were not the product of intellectual cogitation; they were rooted in direct experience. Hence, to students of religion, psychology, and physical science, these experiences of the Master are of immense value for the understanding of religious phenomena in general. No doubt Sri Ramakrishna was a Hindu of the Hindus; yet his experiences transcended the limits of the dogmas and creeds of Hinduism. Mystics of religions other than Hinduism will find in Sri Ramakrishna's experiences a corroboration of the experiences of their own prophets and seers. And this is very important today for the resuscitation of religious values. The sceptical reader may pass by the supernatural experiences; he will yet find in the book enough material to provoke his serious thought and solve many of his spiritual problems.

There are repetitions of teachings and parables in the book. I have kept them purposely. They have their charm and usefulness, repeated as they were in different settings. Repetition is unavoidable in a work of this kind. In the first place, different seekers come to a religious teacher with questions of more or less identical nature; hence the answers will be of more or less identical pattern. Besides, religious teachers of all times and climes have tried, by means of repetition, to hammer truths into the stony soil of the recalcitrant human mind. Finally, repetition does not seem tedious if the ideas repeated are dear to a man's heart.

I have thought it necessary to write a rather lengthy Introduction to the book. In it I have given the biography of the Master, descriptions of people who came in contact with him, short explanations of several systems of Indian religious thought intimately connected with Sri Ramakrishna's life, and other relevant matters which, I hope, will enable the reader better to understand and appreciate the unusual contents of this book. It is particularly important that the Western reader, unacquainted with Hindu religious thought, should first read carefully the introductory chapter, in order that he may fully enjoy these conversations. Many Indian terms and names have been retained in the book for want of suitable English equivalents. Their meaning is given either in the Glossary or in the foot-notes. The Glossary also gives explanations of a number of expressions unfamiliar to Western readers. The diacritical marks are explained under Notes on Pronunciation.

In the Introduction I have drawn much material from the *Life of Sri Ramakrishna*, published by the Advaita Ashrama, Mayavati, India. I have also consulted the excellent article on Sri Ramakrishna by Swami Nirvedananda, in the second volume of the *Cultural Heritage of India*.

The book contains many songs sung either by the Master or by the devotees. These form an important feature of the spiritual tradition of Bengal and were for the most part written by men of mystical experience. For giving the songs their present form I am grateful to Mr. John Moffitt, Jr.

In the preparation of this manuscript I have received ungrudging help from several friends. Miss Margaret Woodrow Wilson and Mr. Joseph Campbell have worked hard in editing my translation. Mrs. Elizabeth Davidson has typed, more than once, the entire manuscript and rendered other valuable help. Mr. Aldous Huxley has laid me under a debt of gratitude by writing the Foreword. I sincerely thank them all.

In the spiritual firmament Sri Ramakrishna is a waxing crescent. Within one hundred years of his birth and fifty years of his death his message has spread across land and sea. Romain Rolland has described him as the fulfilment of the spiritual aspirations of the three hundred millions of Hindus for the last two thousand years. Mahatma Gandhi has written: "His life enables us to see God face to face. . . . Ramakrishna was a living embodiment of godliness." He is being recognized as a compeer of Krishna, Buddha, and Christ.

The life and teachings of Sri Ramakrishna have redirected the thoughts of the denationalized Hindus to the spiritual ideals of their forefathers. During the latter part of the nineteenth century his was the time-honoured role of the Saviour of the Eternal Religion of the Hindus. His teachings played an important part in liberalizing the minds of orthodox pundits and hermits. Even now he is the silent force that is moulding the spiritual destiny of India. His great disciple, Swami Vivekananda, was the first Hindu missionary to preach the message of Indian culture to the enlightened minds of Europe and America. The full consequence of Swami Vivekananda's work is still in the womb of the future.

May this translation of the first book of its kind in the religious history of the world, being the record of the direct words of a prophet, help stricken humanity to come nearer to the Eternal Verity of life and remove dissension and quarrel from among the different faiths! May it enable seekers of Truth to grasp the subtle laws of the supersensuous realm, and unfold before man's restricted vision the spiritual foundation of the universe, the unity of existence, and the divinity of the soul!

NIKHILANANDA

New York
Sri Ramakrishna's Birthday
February 1942

NOTES ON THE PRONUNCIATION OF
TRANSLITERATED SANSKRIT AND
VERNACULAR WORDS

a	has the sound of			*o* in *come.*
ā	” ” ”			” *a* in *far.*
e, ē	” ” ”			” *e* in *bed.*[1]
i	” ” ”			” *i* in *kin.*
ī	” ” ”			” *ee* in *feel.*
o	” ” ”			” *o* in *note.*
u	” ” ”			” *u* in *full.*

ai, ay	has the sound of			*oy* in *boy.*
ch	” ” ”			” *ch* in *church.*
ḍ	” ” ”			” hard *d* in English.
g	” ” ”			” *g* in *god.*
jn	” ” ”			” hard *gy* in English.[2]
ś	” ” ”			” *sh* in English.

sh may be pronounced as in English.
t and d are soft as in French.

Other consonants appearing in the transliterations are pronounced as in English.

Diacritical marks have generally not been used in proper names belonging to recent times or in modern and well-known geographical names.

Sri Ramakrishna is pronounced in Bengal as Śrī Rāmkrishna.

[1] Final *e* in proper names is mute.
[2] Jnāna is pronounced as *gyāna.*

CONTENTS

Contents

ter scolds Bankim — Devotees and the worldly-minded — Charity — The
sannyāsi's duty — The householder's duty — Difficulty of karmayoga —
Spirituality and book-learning — God and the world — Faith in guru —
Yearning for God-vision.

scolds Shyam Basu — Master's prayer — Pairs of opposites — Dr. Sarkar
on expressing feelings — Cause of Master's illness.

ILLUSTRATIONS

INTRODUCTION

INTRODUCTION

By Swami Nikhilananda

SRI RAMAKRISHNA, the God-man of modern India, was born at Kāmār-pukur. This village in the Hooghly District preserved during the last century the idyllic simplicity of the rural areas of Bengal. Situated far from the railway, it was untouched by the glamour of the city. It contained rice-fields, tall palms, royal banyans, a few lakes, and two cremation grounds. South of the village a stream took its leisurely course. A mango orchard dedicated by a neighbouring zemindar to the public use was frequented by the boys for their noonday sports. A highway passed through the village to the great temple of Jagannāth at Puri, and the villagers, most of whom were farmers and craftsmen, entertained many passing holy men and pilgrims. The dull round of the rural life was broken by lively festivals, the observance of sacred days, religious singing, and other innocent pleasures.

About his parents Sri Ramakrishna once said: "My mother was the personification of rectitude and gentleness. She did not know much about the ways of the world; innocent of the art of concealment, she would say what was in her mind. People loved her for her open-heartedness. My father, an orthodox brāhmin, never accepted gifts from the śudras. He spent much of his time in worship and meditation, and in repeating God's name and chanting His glories. Whenever in his daily prayers he invoked the Goddess Gāyatri, his chest flushed and tears rolled down his cheeks. He spent his leisure hours making garlands for the Family Deity, Raghuvir."

Khudiram Chattopadhyaya and Chandra Devi, the parents of Sri Rama-krishna, were married in 1799. At that time Khudiram was living in his ancestral village of Dereypore, not far from Kāmārpukur. Their first son, Ramkumar, was born in 1805, and their first daughter, Katyayani, in 1810. In 1814 Khudiram was ordered by his landlord to bear false witness in court against a neighbour. When he refused to do so, the landlord brought a false case against him and deprived him of his ancestral property. Thus dispossessed, he arrived, at the invitation of another landlord, in the quiet village of Kāmārpukur, where he was given a dwelling and about an acre of fertile land. The crops from this little property were enough to meet his family's simple needs. Here he lived in simplicity, dignity, and contentment.

Ten years after his coming to Kāmārpukur, Khudiram made a pilgrimage on foot to Rāmeśwar, at the southern extremity of India. Two years later was born his second son, whom he named Rameswar. Again in 1835, at the age of sixty, he made a pilgrimage, this time to Gayā. Here, from ancient times, Hindus have come from the four corners of India to discharge their

3

duties to their departed ancestors by offering them food and drink at the sacred footprint of the Lord Vishnu. At this holy place Khudiram had a dream in which the Lord Vishnu promised to be born as his son. And Chandra Devi, too, in front of the Śiva temple at Kāmārpukur, had a vision indicating the birth of a divine child. Upon his return the husband found that she had conceived.

It was on February 18, 1836, that the child, to be known afterwards as Ramakrishna, was born. In memory of the dream at Gayā he was given the name of Gadadhar, the "Bearer of the Mace", an epithet of Vishnu. Three years later a little sister was born.

BOYHOOD

Gadadhar grew up into a healthy and restless boy, full of fun and sweet mischief. He was intelligent and precocious and endowed with a prodigious memory. On his father's lap he learnt by heart the names of his ancestors and the hymns to the gods and goddesses, and at the village school he was taught to read and write. But his greatest delight was to listen to recitations of stories from Hindu mythology and the epics. These he would afterwards recount from memory, to the great joy of the villagers. Painting he enjoyed; the art of moulding images of the gods and goddesses he learnt from the potters. But arithmetic was his great aversion.

At the age of six or seven Gadadhar had his first experience of spiritual ecstasy. One day in June or July, when he was walking along a narrow path between paddy-fields, eating the puffed rice that he carried in a basket, he looked up at the sky and saw a beautiful, dark thunder-cloud. As it spread, rapidly enveloping the whole sky, a flight of snow-white cranes passed in front of it. The beauty of the contrast overwhelmed the boy. He fell to the ground, unconscious, and the puffed rice went in all directions. Some villagers found him and carried him home in their arms. Gadadhar said later that in that state he had experienced an indescribable joy.

Gadadhar was seven years old when his father died. This incident profoundly affected him. For the first time the boy realized that life on earth was impermanent. Unobserved by others, he began to slip into the mango orchard or into one of the cremation grounds, and he spent hours absorbed in his own thoughts. He also became more helpful to his mother in the discharge of her household duties. He gave more attention to reading and hearing the religious stories recorded in the Purānas. And he became interested in the wandering monks and pious pilgrims who would stop at Kāmārpukur on their way to Puri. These holy men, the custodians of India's spiritual heritage and the living witnesses of the ideal of renunciation of the world and all-absorbing love of God, entertained the little boy with stories from the Hindu epics, stories of saints and prophets, and also stories of their own adventures. He, on his part, fetched their water and fuel and served them in various ways. Meanwhile, he was observing their meditation and worship.

At the age of nine Gadadhar was invested with the sacred thread. This ceremony conferred upon him the privileges of his brāhmin lineage, including the worship of the Family Deity, Raghuvir, and imposed upon him the many strict disciplines of a brāhmin's life. During the ceremony of investiture he shocked his relatives by accepting a meal cooked by his nurse, a śudra woman. His father would never have dreamt of doing such a thing. But in a playful mood Gadadhar had once promised this woman that he would eat her food, and now he fulfilled his plighted word. The woman had piety and religious sincerity, and these were more important to the boy than the conventions of society.

Gadadhar was now permitted to worship Raghuvir. Thus began his first training in meditation. He so gave his heart and soul to the worship that the stone image very soon appeared to him as the living Lord of the Universe. His tendency to lose himself in contemplation was first noticed at this time. Behind his boyish light-heartedness was seen a deepening of his spiritual nature.

About this time, on the Śivarātri night, consecrated to the worship of Śiva, a dramatic performance was arranged. The principal actor, who was to play the part of Śiva, suddenly fell ill, and Gadadhar was persuaded to act in his place. While friends were dressing him for the role of Śiva—smearing his body with ashes, matting his locks, placing a trident in his hand and a string of rudrāksha beads around his neck—the boy appeared to become absent-minded. He approached the stage with slow and measured step, supported by his friends. He looked the living image of Śiva. The audience loudly applauded what it took to be his skill as an actor, but it was soon discovered that he was really lost in meditation. His countenance was radiant and tears flowed from his eyes. He was lost to the outer world. The effect of this scene on the audience was tremendous. The people felt blessed as by a vision of Śiva Himself. The performance had to be stopped, and the boy's mood lasted till the following morning.

Gadadhar himself now organized a dramatic company with his young friends. The stage was set in the mango orchard. The themes were selected from the stories of the *Rāmāyana* and the *Mahābhārata*. Gadadhar knew by heart almost all the roles, having heard them from professional actors. His favourite theme was the Vrindāvan episode of Krishna's life, depicting those exquisite love-stories of Krishna and the milkmaids and the cowherd boys. Gadadhar would play the parts of Rādhā or Krishna and would often lose himself in the character he was portraying. His natural feminine grace heightened the dramatic effect. The mango orchard would ring with the loud kirtan of the boys. Lost in song and merry-making, Gadadhar became indifferent to the routine of school.

In 1849 Ramkumar, the eldest son, went to Calcutta to improve the financial condition of the family.

Gadadhar was on the threshold of youth. He had become the pet of the women of the village. They loved to hear him talk, sing, or recite from the holy books. They enjoyed his knack of imitating voices. Their woman's instinct recognized the innate purity and guilelessness of this boy of clear skin, flowing hair, beaming eyes, smiling face, and inexhaustible fun. The pious elderly women looked upon him as Gopāla, the Baby Krishna, and the younger ones saw in him the youthful Krishna of Vrindāvan. He himself so idealized the love of the gopis for Krishna that he sometimes yearned to be born as a woman, if he must be born again, in order to be able to love Sri Krishna with all his heart and soul.

COMING TO CALCUTTA

At the age of sixteen Gadadhar was summoned to Calcutta by his elder brother Ramkumar, who wished assistance in his priestly duties. Ramkumar had opened a Sanskrit academy to supplement his income, and it was his intention gradually to turn his younger brother's mind to education. Gadadhar applied himself heart and soul to his new duty as family priest to a number of Calcutta families. His worship was very different from that of the professional priests. He spent hours decorating the images and singing hymns and devotional songs; he performed with love the other duties of his office. People were impressed with his ardour. But to his studies he paid scant attention.

Ramkumar did not at first oppose the ways of his temperamental brother. He wanted Gadadhar to become used to the conditions of city life. But one day he decided to warn the boy about his indifference to the world. After all, in the near future Gadadhar must, as a householder, earn his livelihood through the performance of his brāhminical duties; and these required a thorough knowledge of Hindu law, astrology, and kindred subjects. He gently admonished Gadadhar and asked him to pay more attention to his studies. But the boy replied spiritedly: "Brother, what shall I do with a mere bread-winning education? I would rather acquire that wisdom which will illumine my heart and give me satisfaction for ever."

BREAD-WINNING EDUCATION

The anguish of the inner soul of India found expression through these passionate words of the young Gadadhar. For what did his unsophisticated eyes see around him in Calcutta, at that time the metropolis of India and the centre of modern culture and learning? Greed and lust held sway in the higher levels of society, and the occasional religious practices were merely outer forms from which the soul had long ago departed. Gadadhar·had never seen anything like this at Kāmārpukur among the simple and pious villagers. The sādhus and wandering monks whom he had served in his boyhood had revealed to him an altogether different India. He had been impressed by their devotion and purity, their self-control and renunciation. He had learnt from them and from his own intuition that the ideal of life as taught by the ancient sages of India was the realization of God.

When Ramkumar reprimanded Gadadhar for neglecting a "bread-winning education", the inner voice of the boy reminded him that the legacy of his ancestors—the legacy of Rāmā, Krishna, Buddha, Śankara, Rāmānuja, Chaitanya—was not worldly security but the Knowledge of God. And these noble sages were the true representatives of Hindu society. Each of them was seated, as it were, on the crest of the wave that followed each successive trough in the tumultuous course of Indian national life. All demonstrated that the life current of India is spirituality. This truth was revealed to Gadadhar through that inner vision which scans past and future in one sweep, unobstructed by the barriers of time and space. But he was unaware of the history of the profound change that had taken place in the land of his birth during the previous one hundred years.

Hindu society during the eighteenth century had been passing through a period of decadence. It was the twilight of the Mussalmān rule. There were anarchy and confusion in all spheres. Superstitious practices dominated the religious life of the people. Rites and rituals passed for the essence of spirituality. Greedy priests became the custodians of heaven. True philosophy was supplanted by dogmatic opinions. The pundits took delight in vain polemics.

In 1757 English traders laid the foundation of British rule in India. Gradually the Government was systematized and lawlessness suppressed. The Hindus were much impressed by the military power and political acumen of the new rulers. In the wake of the merchants came the English educators, and social reformers, and Christian missionaries—all bearing a culture completely alien to the Hindu mind. In different parts of the country educational institutions were set up and Christian churches established. Hindu young men were offered the heady wine of the Western culture of the late eighteenth and early nineteenth centuries, and they drank it to the very dregs.

The first effect of the draught on the educated Hindus was a complete effacement from their minds of the time-honoured beliefs and traditions of Hindu society. They came to believe that there was no transcendental Truth. The world perceived by the senses was all that existed. God and religion were illusions of the untutored mind. True knowledge could be derived only from the analysis of nature. So atheism and agnosticism became the fashion of the day. The youth of India, taught in English schools, took malicious delight in openly breaking the customs and traditions of their society. They would do away with the caste-system and remove the discriminatory laws about food. Social reform, the spread of secular education, widow remarriage, abolition of early marriage—they considered these the panacea for the degenerate condition of Hindu society.

The Christian missionaries gave the finishing touch to the process of transformation. They ridiculed as relics of a barbarous age the images and rituals of the Hindu religion. They tried to persuade India that the teachings of her saints and seers were the cause of her downfall, that her Vedas, Purānas, and other scriptures were filled with superstition. Christianity, they maintained, had given the white races position and power in this world and assurance of happiness in the next; therefore Christianity was the best of all religions. Many intelligent young Hindus became converted. The man in the street was confused. The majority of the educated grew materialistic in their mental outlook. Everyone living near Calcutta or the other strongholds of Western culture, even those who attempted to cling to the orthodox traditions of Hindu society, became infected by the new uncertainties and the new beliefs.

But the soul of India was to be resuscitated through a spiritual awakening. We hear the first call of this renascence in the spirited retort of the young Gadadhar: "Brother, what shall I do with a mere bread-winning education?"

Ramkumar could hardly understand the import of his young brother's reply. He described in bright colours the happy and easy life of scholars in Calcutta society. But Gadadhar intuitively felt that the scholars, to use one of his own vivid illustrations, were like so many vultures, soaring high on the wings of their uninspired intellect, with their eyes fixed on the charnel-pit of greed and lust. So he stood firm and Ramkumar had to give way.

KĀLI TEMPLE AT DAKSHINESWAR

At that time there lived in Calcutta a rich widow named Rāni Rasmani, belonging to the śudra caste, and known far and wide not only for her business ability, courage, and intelligence, but also for her largeness of heart, piety, and devotion to God. She was assisted in the management of her vast property by her son-in-law Mathur Mohan.

In 1847 the Rāni purchased twenty acres of land at Dakshineswar, a village about four miles north of Calcutta. Here she created a temple garden and constructed several temples. Her Ishta, or Chosen Ideal, was the Divine Mother, Kāli.

The temple garden stands directly on the east bank of the Ganges. The northern section of the land and a portion to the east contain an orchard, flower gardens, and two small reservoirs. The southern section is paved with brick and mortar. The visitor arriving by boat ascends the steps of an imposing bathing-ghāt which leads to the chāndni, a roofed terrace, on either side of which stand in a row six temples of Śiva. East of the terrace and the Śiva temples is a large court, paved, rectangular in shape, and running north and south. Two temples stand in the centre of this court, the larger one, to the south and facing south, being dedicated to Kāli, and the smaller one, facing the Ganges, to Rādhākānta, that is, Krishna, the Consort of Rādhā. Nine domes with spires surmount the temple of Kāli, and before it stands the spacious nātmandir, or music hall, the terrace of which is supported by stately pillars. At the northwest and southwest corners of the temple compound are two nahabats, or music towers, from which music flows at different times of day, especially at sunup, noon, and sundown, when the worship is performed in the temples. Three sides of the paved courtyard—all except the west—are lined with rooms set apart for kitchens, store-rooms, dining-rooms, and quarters for the temple staff and guests. The chamber in the northwest angle, just beyond the last of the Śiva temples, is of special interest to us; for here Sri Ramakrishna was to spend a considerable part of his life. To the west of this chamber is a semicircular porch overlooking the river. In front of the porch runs a foot-path, north and south, and beyond the path is a large garden and, below the garden, the Ganges. The orchard to the north of the buildings contains the Panchavati, the banyan, and the bel-tree, associated with Sri Ramakrishna's spiritual practices. Outside and to the north of the temple compound proper is the kuthi, or bungalow, used by members of Rāni Rasmani's family visiting the garden. And north of the temple garden, separated from it by a high wall, is a powder-magazine belonging to the British Government.

ŚIVA

In the twelve Śiva temples are installed the emblems of the Great God of renunciation in His various aspects, worshipped daily with proper rites. Śiva requires few articles of worship. White flowers and bel-leaves and a little Ganges water offered with devotion are enough to satisfy the benign Deity and win from Him the boon of liberation.

RĀDHĀKĀNTA

The temple of Rādhākānta, also known as the temple of Vishnu, contains the images of Rādhā and Krishna, the symbol of union with God through ecstatic love. The two images stand on a pedestal facing the west. The floor is paved with marble. From the ceiling of the porch hang chandeliers protected from dust by coverings of red cloth. Canvas screens shield the images from the rays of the setting sun. Close to the threshold of the inner shrine is a small brass cup containing holy water. Devoted visitors reverently drink a few drops from the vessel.

KĀLI

The main temple is dedicated to Kālī, the Divine Mother, here worshipped as Bhavatāriṇi, the Saviour of the Universe. The floor of this temple also is paved with marble. The basalt image of the Mother, dressed in gorgeous gold brocade, stands on a white marble image of the prostrate body of Her Divine Consort, Śiva, the symbol of the Absolute. On the feet of the Goddess are, among other ornaments, anklets of gold. Her arms are decked with jewelled ornaments of gold. She wears necklaces of gold and pearls, a golden garland of human heads, and a girdle of human arms. She wears a golden crown, golden ear-rings, and a golden nose-ring with a pearl-drop. She has four arms. The lower left hand holds a severed human head and the upper grips a blood-stained sabre. One right hand offers boons to Her children; the other allays their fear. The majesty of Her posture can hardly be described. It combines the terror of destruction with the reassurance of motherly tenderness. For She is the Cosmic Power, the totality of the universe, a glorious harmony of the pairs of opposites. She deals out death, as She creates and preserves. She has three eyes, the third being the symbol of Divine Wisdom; they strike dismay into the wicked, yet pour out affection for Her devotees.

The whole symbolic world is represented in the temple garden—the Trinity of the Nature Mother (Kālī), the Absolute (Śiva), and Love (Rādhākānta), the Arch spanning heaven and earth. The terrific Goddess of the Tantra, the soul-enthralling Flute-Player of the *Bhāgavata*, and the Self-absorbed Absolute of the Vedas live together, creating the greatest synthesis of religions. All aspects of Reality are represented there. But of this divine household, Kālī is the pivot, the sovereign Mistress. She is Prakriti, the Procreatrix, Nature, the Destroyer, the Creator. Nay, She is something greater and deeper still for those who have eyes to see. She is the

Universal Mother, "my Mother" as Ramakrishna would say, the All-power-ful, who reveals Herself to Her children under different aspects and Divine Incarnations, the Visible God, who leads the elect to the Invisible Reality; and if it so pleases Her, She takes away the last trace of ego from created beings and merges it in the consciousness of the Absolute, the undifferen-tiated God. Through Her grace "the finite ego loses itself in the illimitable Ego—Ātman—Brahman".[1]

Rāni Rasmani spent a fortune for the construction of the temple garden and another fortune for its dedication ceremony, which took place on May 31, 1855.

Sri Ramakrishna—henceforth we shall call Gadadhar by this familiar name[2]—came to the temple garden with his elder brother Ramkumar, who was appointed priest of the Kāli temple. Sri Ramakrishna did not at first approve of Ramkumar's working for the śudra Rasmani. The example of their orthodox father was still fresh in Sri Ramakrishna's mind. He objected also to the eating of the cooked offerings of the temple, since, according to orthodox Hindu custom, such food can be offered to the Deity only in the house of a brāhmin. But the holy atmosphere of the temple grounds, the solitude of the surrounding wood, the loving care of his brother, the respect shown him by Rāni Rasmani and Mathur Babu, the living presence of the Goddess Kāli in the temple, and, above all, the proximity of the sacred Ganges, which Sri Ramakrishna always held in the highest respect, gradually overcame his disapproval, and he began to feel at home.

Within a very short time Sri Ramakrishna attracted the notice of Mathur Babu, who was impressed by the young man's religious fervour and wanted him to participate in the worship in the Kāli temple. But Sri Ramakrishna loved his freedom and was indifferent to any worldly career. The profession of the priesthood in a temple founded by a rich woman did not appeal to his mind. Further, he hesitated to take upon himself the responsibility for the ornaments and jewelry of the temple. Mathur had to wait for a suitable occasion.

At this time there came to Dakshineswar a youth of sixteen, destined to play an important role in Sri Ramakrishna's life. Hriday, a distant nephew[3] of Sri Ramakrishna, hailed from Sihore, a village not far from Kāmārpukur, and had been his boyhood friend. Clever, exceptionally energetic, and en-dowed with great presence of mind, he moved, as will be seen later, like a shadow about his uncle and was always ready to help him, even at the sacrifice of his personal comfort. He was destined to be a mute witness of many of the spiritual experiences of Sri Ramakrishna and the caretaker of his body during the stormy days of his spiritual practice. Hriday came to Dakshineswar in search of a job, and Sri Ramakrishna was glad to see him.

[1] Romain Rolland, *Prophets of the New India*, p. 11.

[2] No definite information is available as to the origin of this name. Most probably it was given by Mathur Babu, as Ramlal, Sri Ramakrishna's nephew, has said, quoting the authority of his uncle himself.

[3] Hriday's mother was the daughter of Sri Ramakrishna's aunt (Khudiram's sister). Such a degree of relationship is termed in Bengal that of a "distant nephew".

Unable to resist the persuasion of Mathur Babu, Sri Ramakrishna at last entered the temple service, on condition that Hriday should be asked to assist him. His first duty was to dress and decorate the image of Kāli.

One day the priest of the Rādhākānta temple accidentally dropped the image of Krishna on the floor, breaking one of its legs. The pundits advised the Rāni to install a new image, since the worship of an image with a broken limb was against the scriptural injunctions. But the Rāni was fond of the image, and she asked Sri Ramakrishna's opinion. In an abstracted mood, he said: "This solution is ridiculous. If a son-in-law of the Rāni broke his leg, would she discard him and put another in his place? Wouldn't she rather arrange for his treatment? Why should she not do the same thing in this case too? Let the image be repaired and worshipped as before." It was a simple, straightforward solution and was accepted by the Rāni. Sri Ramakrishna himself mended the break. The priest was dismissed for his carelessness, and at Mathur Babu's earnest request Sri Ramakrishna accepted the office of priest in the Rādhākānta temple.

SRI RAMAKRISHNA AS A PRIEST

Born in an orthodox brāhmin family, Sri Ramakrishna knew the formalities of worship, its rites and rituals. The innumerable gods and goddesses of the Hindu religion are the human aspects of the indescribable and incomprehensible Spirit, as conceived by the finite human mind. They understand and appreciate human love and emotion, help men to realize their secular and spiritual ideals, and ultimately enable men to attain liberation from the miseries of phenomenal life. The Source of light, intelligence, wisdom, and strength is the One alone from whom comes the fulfilment of desire. Yet, as long as a man is bound by his human limitations, he cannot but worship God through human forms. He must use human symbols. Therefore Hinduism asks the devotees to look on God as the ideal father, the ideal mother, the ideal husband, the ideal son, or the ideal friend. But the name ultimately leads to the Nameless, the form to the Formless, the word to the Silence, the emotion to the serene realization of Peace in Existence-Knowledge-Bliss Absolute. The gods gradually merge in the one God. But until that realization is achieved, the devotee cannot dissociate human factors from his worship. Therefore the Deity is bathed and clothed and decked with ornaments. He is fed and put to sleep. He is propitiated with hymns, songs, and prayers. And there are appropriate rites connected with all these functions. For instance, to secure for himself external purity, the priest bathes himself in holy water and puts on a holy cloth. He purifies the mind and the sense-organs by appropriate meditations. He fortifies the place of worship against evil forces by drawing around it circles of fire and water. He awakens the different spiritual centres of the body and invokes the Supreme Spirit in his heart. Then he transfers the Supreme Spirit to the image before him and worships the image, regarding it no longer as clay or stone, but as the embodiment of Spirit, throbbing with Life and Consciousness. After the worship the Supreme Spirit is recalled from the image to Its true sanctuary, the heart of the priest. The real devotee knows the absurdity of worshipping the Transcendental Reality with material articles—clothing That which pervades the whole universe and the beyond, putting on a pedestal That which cannot be limited by space, feeding That which is disembodied and incorporeal, singing before That whose glory the music of the spheres tries vainly to proclaim. But through these rites the devotee aspires to go ultimately beyond rites and rituals, forms and names, words and praise, and to realize God as the All-pervading Consciousness.

Hindu priests are thoroughly acquainted with the rites of worship, but few of them are aware of their underlying significance. They move their hands and limbs mechanically, in obedience to the letter of the scriptures, and repeat the holy mantras like parrots. But from the very beginning the inner meaning of these rites was revealed to Sri Ramakrishna. As he sat facing the image, a strange transformation came over his mind. While going through the prescribed ceremonies, he would actually find himself encircled by a wall of fire protecting him and the place of worship from unspiritual vibrations, or he would feel the rising of the mystic Kundalini through the different centres of the body. The glow on his face, his deep absorption, and the intense atmosphere of the temple impressed everyone who saw him worship the Deity.

Ramkumar wanted Sri Ramakrishna to learn the intricate rituals of the worship of Kāli. To become a priest of Kāli one must undergo a special form of initiation from a qualified guru, and for Sri Ramakrishna a suitable brāhmin was found. But no sooner did the brāhmin speak the holy word in his ear than Sri Ramakrishna, overwhelmed with emotion, uttered a loud cry and plunged into deep concentration.

Mathur begged Sri Ramakrishna to take charge of the worship in the Kāli temple. The young priest pleaded his incompetence and his ignorance of the scriptures. Mathur insisted that devotion and sincerity would more than compensate for any lack of formal knowledge and make the Divine Mother manifest Herself through the image. In the end, Sri Ramakrishna had to yield to Mathur's request. He became the priest of Kāli.

In 1856 Ramkumar breathed his last. Sri Ramakrishna had already witnessed more than one death in the family. He had come to realize how impermanent is life on earth. The more he was convinced of the transitory nature of worldly things, the more eager he became to realize God, the Fountain of Immortality.

THE FIRST VISION OF KĀLI

And, indeed, he soon discovered what a strange Goddess he had chosen to serve. He became gradually enmeshed in the web of Her all-pervading presence. To the ignorant She is, to be sure, the image of destruction; but he found in Her the benign, all-loving Mother. Her neck is encircled with a garland of heads, and Her waist with a girdle of human arms, and two of Her hands hold weapons of death, and Her eyes dart a glance of fire; but, strangely enough, Ramakrishna felt in Her breath the soothing touch of tender love and saw in Her the Seed of Immortality. She stands on the bosom of Her Consort, Śiva; it is because She is the Śakti, the Power, inseparable from the Absolute. She is surrounded by jackals and other un-holy creatures, the denizens of the cremation ground. But is not the Ultimate Reality above holiness and unholiness? She appears to be reeling under the spell of wine. But who would create this mad world unless under the influence of a divine drunkenness? She is the highest symbol of all the forces of nature, the synthesis of their antinomies, the Ultimate Divine in the form of woman. She now became to Sri Ramakrishna the only Reality, and the world became an unsubstantial shadow. Into Her worship he poured his soul. Before him She stood as the transparent portal to the shrine of Ineffable Reality.

The worship in the temple intensified Sri Ramakrishna's yearning for a living vision of the Mother of the Universe. He began to spend in medita-tion the time not actually employed in the temple service; and for this pur-pose he selected an extremely solitary place. A deep jungle, thick with underbrush and prickly plants, lay to the north of the temples. Used at one time as a burial ground, it was shunned by people even during the day-time for fear of ghosts. There Sri Ramakrishna began to spend the whole night in meditation, returning to his room only in the morning with eyes swollen as though from much weeping. While meditating, he would lay aside his cloth and his brāhminical thread. Explaining this strange conduct, he once said to Hriday: "Don't you know that when one thinks of God one should be freed from all ties? From our very birth we have the eight fetters of hatred, shame, lineage, pride of good conduct, fear, secretiveness, caste, and grief. The sacred thread reminds me that I am a brāhmin and therefore superior to all. When calling on the Mother one has to set aside all such ideas." Hriday thought his uncle was becoming insane.

As his love for God deepened, he began either to forget or to drop the formalities of worship. Sitting before the image, he would spend hours sing-ing the devotional songs of great devotees of the Mother, such as Kamalākānta and Rāmprasād. Those rhapsodical songs, describing the direct vision of God, only intensified Sri Ramakrishna's longing. He felt the pangs of a child separated from its mother. Sometimes, in agony, he would rub his face against the ground and weep so bitterly that people, thinking he had lost his earthly mother, would sympathize with him in his grief. Sometimes, in moments of scepticism, he would cry: "Art Thou true, Mother, or is it all fiction—mere poetry without any reality? If Thou dost exist, why do I not see Thee? Is religion a mere fantasy and art Thou only a figment of man's imagination?" Sometimes he would sit on the prayer carpet for two hours like an inert object. He began to behave in an abnormal manner, most of the time unconscious of the world. He almost gave up food; and sleep left him altogether.

But he did not have to wait very long. He has thus described his first vision of the Mother: "I felt as if my heart were being squeezed like a wet towel. I was overpowered with a great restlessness and a fear that it might not be my lot to realize Her in this life. I could not bear the separation from Her any longer. Life seemed to be not worth living. Suddenly my glance fell on the sword that was kept in the Mother's temple. I determined to put an end to my life. When I jumped up like a madman and seized it, suddenly the blessed Mother revealed Herself. The buildings with their different parts, the temple, and everything else vanished from my sight, leaving no trace whatsoever, and in their stead I saw a limitless, infinite, effulgent Ocean of Consciousness. As far as the eye could see, the shining billows were madly rushing at me from all sides with a terrific noise, to swallow me up! I was panting for breath. I was caught in the rush and collapsed, unconscious. What was happening in the outside world I did not know; but within me there was a steady flow of undiluted bliss, altogether new, and I felt the presence of the Divine Mother." On his lips when he regained consciousness of the world was the word "Mother".

GOD-INTOXICATED STATE

Yet this was only a foretaste of the intense experiences to come. The first glimpse of the Divine Mother made him the more eager for Her uninterrupted vision. He wanted to see Her both in meditation and with eyes open. But the Mother began to play a teasing game of hide-and-seek with him, intensifying both his joy and his suffering. Weeping bitterly during the moments of separation from Her, he would pass into a trance and then find Her standing before him, smiling, talking, consoling, bidding him be of good cheer, and instructing him. During this period of spiritual practice he had many uncommon experiences. When he sat to meditate, he would hear strange clicking sounds in the joints of his legs, as if someone were locking them up, one after the other, to keep him motionless; and at the conclusion of his meditation he would again hear the same sounds, this time unlocking them and leaving him free to move about. He would see flashes like a swarm of fire-flies floating before his eyes, or a sea of deep mist around him, with luminous waves of molten silver. Again, from a sea of translucent mist he would behold the Mother rising, first Her feet, then Her waist, body, face, and head, finally Her whole person; he would feel Her breath and hear Her voice. Worshipping in the temple, sometimes he would become exalted, sometimes he would remain motionless as stone, sometimes he would almost collapse from excessive emotion. Many of his actions, contrary to all tradition, seemed sacrilegious to the people. He would take a flower and touch it to his own head, body, and feet, and then offer it to the Goddess. Or, like a drunkard, he would reel to the throne of the Mother, touch Her chin by way of showing his affection for Her, and sing, talk, joke, laugh, and dance. Or he would take a morsel of food from the plate and hold it to Her mouth, begging Her to eat it, and would not be satisfied till he was convinced that She had really eaten. After the Mother had been put to sleep at night, from his own room he would hear Her ascending to the upper storey of the temple with the light steps of a happy girl, Her anklets jingling. Then he would discover Her standing with flowing hair, Her black form silhouetted against the sky of the night, looking at the Ganges or at the distant lights of Calcutta.

Naturally the temple officials took him for an insane person. His worldly well-wishers brought him to skilled physicians; but no medicine could cure his malady. Many a time he doubted his sanity himself. For he had been sailing across an uncharted sea, with no earthly guide to direct him. His only haven of security was the Divine Mother Herself. To Her he would pray: "I do not know what these things are. I am ignorant of mantras and the scriptures. Teach me, Mother, how to realize Thee. Who else can help me? Art Thou not my only refuge and guide?" And the sustaining presence of the Mother never failed him in his distress or doubt. Even those who criticized his conduct were greatly impressed with his purity, guilelessness, truthfulness, integrity, and holiness. They felt an uplifting influence in his presence.

It is said that samādhi, or trance, no more than opens the portal of the spiritual realm. Sri Ramakrishna felt an unquenchable desire to enjoy God in various ways. For his meditation he built a place in the northern wooded section of the temple garden. With Hriday's help he planted there five sacred trees. The spot, known as the Panchavati, became the scene of many of his visions.

As his spiritual mood deepened he more and more felt himself to be a child of the Divine Mother. He learnt to surrender himself completely to Her will and let Her direct him.

"O Mother," he would constantly pray, "I have taken refuge in Thee. Teach me what to do and what to say. Thy will is paramount everywhere and is for the good of Thy children. Merge my will in Thy will and make me Thy instrument."

His visions became deeper and more intimate. He no longer had to meditate to behold the Divine Mother. Even while retaining consciousness of the outer world, he would see Her as tangibly as the temples, the trees, the river, and the men around him.

On a certain occasion Mathur Babu stealthily entered the temple to watch the worship. He was profoundly moved by the young priest's devotion and sincerity. He realized that Sri Ramakrishna had transformed the stone image into the living Goddess.

Sri Ramakrishna one day fed a cat with the food that was to be offered to Kāli. This was too much for the manager of the temple garden, who considered himself responsible for the proper conduct of the worship. He reported Sri Ramakrishna's insane behaviour to Mathur Babu.

Sri Ramakrishna has described the incident: "The Divine Mother revealed to me in the Kāli temple that it was She who had become everything. She showed me that everything was full of Consciousness. The image was Consciousness, the altar was Consciousness, the water-vessels were Consciousness, the door-sill was Consciousness, the marble floor was Consciousness—all was Consciousness. I found everything inside the room soaked, as it were, in Bliss—the Bliss of God. I saw a wicked man in front of the Kāli temple; but in him also I saw the power of the Divine Mother vibrating. That was why I fed a cat with the food that was to be offered to the Divine Mother. I clearly perceived that all this was the Divine Mother—even the cat. The manager of the temple garden wrote to Mathur Babu saying that

I was feeding the cat with the offering intended for the Divine Mother. But Mathur Babu had insight into the state of my mind. He wrote back to the manager: 'Let him do whatever he likes. You must not say anything to him.'"

One of the painful ailments from which Sri Ramakrishna suffered at this time was a burning sensation in his body, and he was cured by a strange vision. During worship in the temple, following the scriptural injunctions, he would imagine the presence of the "sinner" in himself and the destruction of this "sinner". One day he was meditating in the Panchavati, when he saw come out of him a red-eyed man of black complexion, reeling like a drunkard. Soon there emerged from him another person, of serene countenance, wearing the ochre cloth of a sannyāsi and carrying in his hand a trident. The second person attacked the first and killed him with the trident. Thereafter Sri Ramakrishna was free of his pain.

About this time he began to worship God by assuming the attitude of a servant toward his master. He imitated the mood of Hanumān, the monkey chieftain of the *Rāmāyana*, the ideal servant of Rāma and traditional model for this self-effacing form of devotion. When he meditated on Hanumān his movements and his way of life began to resemble those of a monkey. His eyes became restless. He lived on fruits and roots. With his cloth tied around his waist, a portion of it hanging in the form of a tail, he jumped from place to place instead of walking. And after a short while he was blessed with a vision of Sītā, the divine consort of Rāma, who entered his body and disappeared there with the words, "I bequeath to you my smile."

Mathur had faith in the sincerity of Sri Ramakrishna's spiritual zeal, but began now to doubt his sanity. He had watched him jumping about like a monkey. One day, when Rāni Rasmani was listening to Sri Ramakrishna's singing in the temple, the young priest abruptly turned and slapped her. Apparently listening to his song, she had actually been thinking of a lawsuit. She accepted the punishment as though the Divine Mother Herself had imposed it; but Mathur was distressed. He begged Sri Ramakrishna to keep his feelings under control and to heed the conventions of society. God Himself, he argued, follows laws. God never permitted, for instance, flowers of two colours to grow on the same stalk. The following day Sri Ramakrishna presented Mathur Babu with two hibiscus flowers growing on the same stalk, one red and one white.

Mathur and Rāni Rasmani began to ascribe the mental ailment of Sri Ramakrishna in part, at least, to his observance of rigid continence. Thinking that a natural life would relax the tension of his nerves, they engineered a plan with two women of ill fame. But as soon as the women entered his room, Sri Ramakrishna beheld in them the manifestation of the Divine Mother of the Universe and went into samādhi uttering Her name.

HALADHARI

In 1858 there came to Dakshineswar a cousin of Sri Ramakrishna, Haladhari by name, who was to remain there about eight years. On account of Sri Ramakrishna's indifferent health, Mathur appointed this man to the

office of priest in the Kāli temple. He was a complex character, versed in
the letter of the scriptures, but hardly aware of their spirit. He loved to
participate in hair-splitting theological discussions and, by the measure of
his own erudition, he proceeded to gauge Sri Ramakrishna. An orthodox
brāhmin, he thoroughly disapproved of his cousin's unorthodox actions, but
he was not unimpressed by Sri Ramakrishna's purity of life, ecstatic love
of God, and yearning for realization.

One day Haladhari upset Sri Ramakrishna with the statement that God
is incomprehensible to the human mind. Sri Ramakrishna has described the
great moment of doubt when he wondered whether his visions had really
misled him: "With sobs I prayed to the Mother, 'Canst Thou have the heart
to deceive me like this because I am a fool?' A stream of tears flowed from
my eyes. Shortly afterwards I saw a volume of mist rising from the floor
and filling the space before me. In the midst of it there appeared a face
with flowing beard, calm, highly expressive, and fair. Fixing its gaze steadily
upon me, it said solemnly, 'Remain in bhāvamukha, on the threshold of
relative consciousness.' This it repeated three times and then it gently disappeared in the mist, which itself dissolved. This vision reassured me."

A garbled report of Sri Ramakrishna's failing health, indifference to
worldly life, and various abnormal activities reached Kāmārpukur and filled
the heart of his poor mother with anguish. At her repeated request he returned to his village for a change of air. But his boyhood friends did not
interest him any more. A divine fever was consuming him. He spent a great
part of the day and night in one of the cremation grounds, in meditation.
The place reminded him of the impermanence of the human body, of human
hopes and achievements. It also reminded him of Kāli, the Goddess of
destruction.

MARRIAGE AND AFTER

But in a few months his health showed improvement, and he recovered
to some extent his natural buoyancy of spirit. His happy mother was encouraged to think it might be a good time to arrange his marriage. The boy was
now twenty-three years old. A wife would bring him back to earth. And she
was delighted when her son welcomed her suggestion. Perhaps he saw in it
the finger of God.

Saradamani, a little girl of five, lived in the neighbouring village of
Jayrāmbāti. Even at this age she had been praying to God to make her character as stainless and fragrant as the white tuberose. Looking at the full
moon, she would say: "O God, there are dark spots even on the moon. But
make my character spotless." It was she who was selected as the bride for
Sri Ramakrishna.

The marriage ceremony was duly performed. Such early marriage in India
is in the nature of a betrothal, the marriage being consummated when the
girl attains puberty. But in this case the marriage remained for ever uncon-
summated. Sri Ramakrishna lived at Kāmārpukur about a year and a half
and then returned to Dakshineswar.

Hardly had he crossed the threshold of the Kāli temple when he found himself again in the whirlwind. His madness reappeared tenfold. The same meditation and prayer, the same ecstatic moods, the same burning sensation, the same weeping, the same sleeplessness, the same indifference to the body and the outside world, the same divine delirium. He subjected himself to fresh disciplines in order to eradicate greed and lust, the two great impediments to spiritual progress. With a rupee in one hand and some earth in the other, he would reflect on the comparative value of these two for the realization of God, and finding them equally worthless he would toss them, with equal indifference, into the Ganges. Women he regarded as the manifestations of the Divine Mother. Never even in a dream did he feel the impulses of lust. And to root out of his mind the idea of caste superiority, he cleaned a pariah's house with his long and neglected hair. When he would sit in meditation, birds would perch on his head and peck in his hair for grains of food. Snakes would crawl over his body, and neither would be aware of the other. Sleep left him altogether. Day and night, visions flitted before him. He saw the sannyāsi who had previously killed the "sinner" in him again coming out of his body, threatening him with the trident, and ordering him to concentrate on God. Or the same sannyāsi would visit distant places, following a luminous path, and bring him reports of what was happening there. Sri Ramakrishna used to say later that in the case of an advanced devotee the mind itself becomes the guru, living and moving like an embodied being.

Rāni Rasmani, the foundress of the temple garden, passed away in 1861. After her death her son-in-law Mathur became the sole executor of the estate. He placed himself and his resources at the disposal of Sri Ramakrishna and began to look after his physical comfort. Sri Ramakrishna later spoke of him as one of his five "suppliers of stores" appointed by the Divine Mother. Whenever a desire arose in his mind, Mathur fulfilled it without hesitation.

THE BRĀHMANI

There came to Dakshineswar at this time a brāhmin woman who was to play an important part in Sri Ramakrishna's spiritual unfoldment. Born in East Bengal, she was an adept in the Tāntrik and Vaishnava methods of worship. She was slightly over fifty years of age, handsome, and garbed in the orange robe of a nun. Her sole possessions were a few books and two pieces of wearing-cloth.

Sri Ramakrishna welcomed the visitor with great respect, described to her his experiences and visions, and told her of people's belief that these were symptoms of madness. She listened to him attentively and said: "My son, everyone in this world is mad. Some are mad for money, some for creature comforts, some for name and fame; and you are mad for God." She assured him that he was passing through the almost unknown spiritual experience described in the scriptures as mahābhāva, the most exalted rapture of divine love. She told him that this extreme exaltation had been described as manifesting itself through nineteen physical symptoms, including the shedding of tears, a tremor of the body, horripilation, perspiration, and a burning sensation. The Bhakti scriptures, she declared, had recorded only two instances of the experience, namely, those of Sri Rādhā and Sri Chaitanya.

Very soon a tender relationship sprang up between Sri Ramakrishna and the Brāhmani, she looking upon him as the Baby Krishna, and he upon her as mother. Day after day she watched his ecstasy during the kirtan and meditation, his samādhi, his mad yearning; and she recognized in him a power to transmit spirituality to others. She came to the conclusion that such things were not possible for an ordinary devotee, not even for a highly developed soul. Only an Incarnation of God was capable of such spiritual manifestations. She proclaimed openly that Sri Ramakrishna, like Sri Chaitanya, was an Incarnation of God.

When Sri Ramakrishna told Mathur what the Brāhmani had said about him, Mathur shook his head in doubt. He was reluctant to accept him as an Incarnation of God, an Avatār comparable to Rāma, Krishna, Buddha, and Chaitanya, though he admitted Sri Ramakrishna's extraordinary spirituality. Whereupon the Brāhmani asked Mathur to arrange a conference of scholars who should discuss the matter with her. He agreed to the proposal and the meeting was arranged. It was to be held in the nātmandir in front of the Kāli temple.

Two famous pundits of the time were invited: Vaishnavcharan, the leader of the Vaishnava society, and Gauri. The first to arrive was Vaishnavcharan, with a distinguished company of scholars and devotees. The Brāhmani, like a proud mother, proclaimed her view before him and supported it with quotations from the scriptures. As the pundits discussed the deep theological question, Sri Ramakrishna, perfectly indifferent to everything happening around him, sat in their midst like a child, immersed in his own thoughts, sometimes smiling, sometimes chewing a pinch of spices from a pouch, or again saying to Vaishnavcharan with a nudge: "Look here. Sometimes I feel like this, too." Presently Vaishnavcharan arose to declare himself in total agreement with the view of the Brāhmani. He declared that Sri Ramakrishna had undoubtedly experienced mahābhāva and that this was the certain sign of the rare manifestation of God in a man. The people assembled there, especially the officers of the temple garden, were struck dumb. Sri Ramakrishna said to Mathur, like a boy: "Just fancy, he too says so! Well, I am glad to learn that after all it is not a disease."

When, a few days later, Pundit Gauri arrived, another meeting was held, and he agreed with the view of the Brāhmani and Vaishnavcharan. To Sri Ramakrishna's remark that Vaishnavcharan had declared him to be an Avatār, Gauri replied: "Is that all he has to say about you? Then he has said very little. I am fully convinced that you are that Mine of Spiritual Power, only a small fraction of which descends on earth, from time to time, in the form of an Incarnation."

"Ah!" said Sri Ramakrishna with a smile, "you seem to have quite outbid Vaishnavcharan in this matter. What have you found in me that makes you entertain such an idea?"

Gauri said: "I feel it in my heart and I have the scriptures on my side. I am ready to prove it to anyone who challenges me."

"Well," Sri Ramakrishna said, "it is you who say so; but, believe me, I know nothing about it."

Thus the insane priest was by verdict of the great scholars of the day proclaimed a Divine Incarnation. His visions were not the result of an over-heated brain; they had precedent in spiritual history. And how did the proclamation affect Sri Ramakrishna himself? He remained the simple child of the Mother that he had been since the first day of his life. Years later, when two of his householder disciples openly spoke of him as a Divine Incarnation and the matter was reported to him, he said with a touch of sarcasm: "Do they think they will enhance my glory that way? One of them is an actor on the stage and the other a physician. What do they know about Incarnations? Why, years ago pundits like Gauri and Vaishnavcharan declared me to be an Avatār. They were great scholars and knew what they said. But that did not make any change in my mind."

Sri Ramakrishna was a learner all his life. He often used to quote a proverb to his disciples: "Friend, the more I live the more I learn." When the excitement created by the Brāhmani's declaration was over, he set him-self to the task of practising spiritual disciplines according to the traditional methods laid down in the Tantra and Vaishnava scriptures. Hitherto he had pursued his spiritual ideal according to the promptings of his own mind and heart. Now he accepted the Brāhmani as his guru and set foot on the tradi-tional highways.

TANTRA

According to the Tantra, the Ultimate Reality is Chit, or Consciousness, which is identical with Sat, or Being, and with Ānanda, or Bliss. This Ultimate Reality, Satchidānanda, Existence-Knowledge-Bliss Absolute, is identical with the Reality preached in the Vedas. And man is identical with this Reality; but under the influence of māyā, or illusion, he has for-gotten his true nature. He takes to be real a merely apparent world of subject and object, and this error is the cause of his bondage and suffering. The goal of spiritual discipline is the rediscovery of his true identity with the divine Reality.

For the achievement of this goal the Vedānta prescribes an austere nega-tive method of discrimination and renunciation, which can be followed by only a few individuals endowed with sharp intelligence and unshakable will-power. But Tantra takes into consideration the natural weakness of human beings, their lower appetites, and their love for the concrete. It combines philosophy with rituals, meditation with ceremonies, renunciation with enjoyment. The underlying purpose is gradually to train the aspirant to meditate on his identity with the Ultimate.

The average man wishes to enjoy the material objects of the world. Tantra bids him enjoy these, but at the same time discover in them the presence of God. Mystical rites are prescribed by which, slowly, the sense-objects become spiritualized and sense attraction is transformed into a love of God. So the very "bonds" of man are turned into "releasers". The very poison that kills is transmuted into the elixir of life. Outward renunciation is not necessary. Thus the aim of Tantra is to sublimate bhoga, or enjoyment, into yoga, or union with Consciousness. For, according to this philosophy, the world with all its manifestations is nothing but the sport of Śiva and Śakti, the Absolute and Its inscrutable Power.

The disciplines of Tantra are graded to suit aspirants of all degrees. Exercises are prescribed for people with "animal", "heroic", and "divine" outlooks. Certain of the rites require the presence of members of the opposite sex. Here the aspirant learns to look on woman as the embodiment of the Goddess Kāli, the Mother of the Universe. The very basis of Tantra is the Motherhood of God and the glorification of woman. Every part of a woman's body is to be regarded as incarnate Divinity. But the rites are extremely dangerous. The help of a qualified guru is absolutely necessary. An unwary devotee may lose his foothold and fall into a pit of depravity.

According to the Tantra, Śakti is the active creative force in the universe. Śiva, the Absolute, is a more or less passive principle. Further, Śakti is as inseparable from Śiva as fire's power to burn is from fire itself. Śakti, the Creative Power, contains in Its womb the universe, and therefore is the Divine Mother. All women are Her symbols. Kāli is one of Her several forms. The meditation on Kāli, the Creative Power, is the central discipline of the Tantra. While meditating, the aspirant at first regards himself as one with the Absolute and then thinks that out of that Impersonal Consciousness emerge two entities, namely, his own self and the living form of the Goddess. He then projects the Goddess into the tangible image before him and worships it as the Divine Mother.

Sri Ramakrishna set himself to the task of practising the disciplines of Tantra; and at the bidding of the Divine Mother Herself he accepted the Brāhmani as his guru. He performed profound and delicate ceremonies in the Panchavati and under the bel-tree at the northern extremity of the temple compound. He practised all the disciplines of the sixty-four principal Tantra books, and it took him never more than three days to achieve the result promised in any one of them. After the observance of a few preliminary rites, he would be overwhelmed with a strange divine fervour and would go into samādhi, where his mind would dwell in exaltation. Evil ceased to exist for him. The word "carnal" lost its meaning. The whole world and everything in it appeared as the līlā, the sport, of Śiva and Śakti. He beheld everywhere manifest the power and beauty of the Mother; the whole world, animate and inanimate, appeared to him as pervaded with Chit, Consciousness, and with Ānanda, Bliss.

He saw in a vision the Ultimate Cause of the universe as a huge luminous triangle giving birth every moment to an infinite number of worlds. He heard the Anāhata Śabda, the great sound Om, of which the innumerable sounds of the universe are only so many echoes. He acquired the eight supernatural powers of yoga, which make a man almost omnipotent, and these he spurned as of no value whatsoever to the Spirit. He had a vision of the divine Māyā, the inscrutable Power of God, by which the universe is created and sustained, and into which it is finally absorbed. In this vision he saw a woman of exquisite beauty, about to become a mother, emerging from the Ganges and slowly approaching the Panchavati. Presently she gave birth to a child and began to nurse it tenderly. A moment later she assumed a terrible aspect, seized the child with her grim jaws, and crushed it. Swallowing it, she re-entered the waters of the Ganges.

But the most remarkable experience during this period was the awakening of the Kundalini Śakti, the "Serpent Power". He actually saw the Power, at first lying asleep at the bottom of the spinal column, then waking up and ascending along the mystic Sushumnā canal and through its six centres, or lotuses, to the Sahasrāra, the thousand-petalled lotus in the top of the head. He further saw that as the Kundalini went upward the different lotuses bloomed. And this phenomenon was accompanied by visions and trances. Later on he described to his disciples and devotees the various movements of the Kundalini: the fishlike, birdlike, monkeylike, and so on. The awakening of the Kundalini is the beginning of spiritual consciousness, and its union with Śiva in the Sahasrāra, ending in samādhi, is the consummation of the Tāntrik disciplines.

About this time it was revealed to him that in a short while many devotees would seek his guidance.

VAISHNAVA DISCIPLINES

After completing the Tāntrik sādhanā Sri Ramakrishna followed the Brāhmani in the disciplines of Vaishnavism. The Vaishnavas are worshippers of Vishnu, the "All-pervading", the Supreme God, who is also known as Hari and Nārāyana. Of Vishnu's various Incarnations the two with the largest number of followers are Rāma and Krishna.

Vaishnavism is exclusively a religion of bhakti. Bhakti is intense love of God, attachment to Him alone; it is of the nature of bliss and bestows upon the lover immortality and liberation. God, according to Vaishnavism, cannot be realized through logic or reason; and, without bhakti, all penances, austerities, and rites are futile. Man cannot realize God by self-exertion alone. For the vision of God His grace is absolutely necessary, and this grace is felt by the pure of heart. The mind is to be purified through bhakti. The pure mind then remains for ever immersed in the ecstasy of God-vision. It is the cultivation of this divine love that is the chief concern of the Vaishnava religion.

There are three kinds of formal devotion: tāmasic, rājasic, and sāttvic. If a person, while showing devotion to God, is actuated by malevolence, arrogance, jealousy, or anger, then his devotion is tāmasic, since it is influenced by tamas, the quality of inertia. If he worships God from a desire for fame or wealth, or from any other worldly ambition, then his devotion is rājasic, since it is influenced by rajas, the quality of activity. But if a person loves God without any thought of material gain, if he performs his duties to please God alone and maintains toward all created beings the attitude of friendship, then his devotion is called sāttvic, since it is influenced by sattva, the quality of harmony. But the highest devotion transcends the three gunas, or qualities, being a spontaneous, uninterrupted inclination of the mind toward God, the Inner Soul of all beings; and it wells up in the heart of a true devotee as soon as he hears the name of God or mention of God's attributes. A devotee possessed of this love would not accept the happiness of heaven if it were offered him. His one desire is to love God under all conditions—in pleasure and pain, life and death, honour and dishonour, prosperity and adversity.

There are two stages of bhakti. The first is known as vaidhi-bhakti, or love of God qualified by scriptural injunctions. For the devotees of this stage are prescribed regular and methodical worship, hymns, prayers, the repetition of God's name, and the chanting of His glories. This lower bhakti in course of time matures into parā-bhakti, or supreme devotion, known also as prema, the most intense form of divine love. Divine love is an end in itself. It exists potentially in all human hearts, but in the case of bound creatures it is misdirected to earthly objects.

To develop the devotee's love for God, Vaishnavism humanizes God. God is to be regarded as the devotee's Parent, Master, Friend, Child, Husband, or Sweetheart, each succeeding relationship representing an intensification of love. These bhāvas, or attitudes toward God, are known as śānta, dāsya, sakhya, vātsalya, and madhur. The rishis of the Vedas, Hanumān, the cowherd boys of Vrindāvan, Rāma's mother Kausalyā, and Rādhikā, Krishna's sweetheart, exhibited, respectively, the most perfect examples of these forms. In the ascending scale the glories of God are gradually forgotten and the devotee realizes more and more the intimacy of divine communion. Finally he regards himself as the mistress of his Beloved, and no artificial barrier remains to separate him from his Ideal. No social or moral obligation can bind to the earth his soaring spirit. He experiences perfect union with the Godhead. Unlike the Vedāntist, who strives to transcend all varieties of the subject-object relationship, a devotee of the Vaishnava path wishes to retain both his own individuality and the personality of God. To him God is not an intangible Absolute, but the Purushottama, the Supreme Person.

While practising the discipline of the madhur bhāva, the male devotee often regards himself as a woman, in order to develop the most intense form of love for Sri Krishna, the only purusha, or man, in the universe. This assumption of the attitude of the opposite sex has a deep psychological significance. It is a matter of common experience that an idea may be cultivated to such an intense degree that every idea alien to it is driven from the mind. This peculiarity of the mind may be utilized for the subjugation of the lower desires and the development of the spiritual nature. Now, the idea which is the basis of all desires and passions in a man is the conviction of his indissoluble association with a male body. If he can inoculate himself thoroughly with the idea that he is a woman, he can get rid of the desires peculiar to his male body. Again, the idea that he is a woman may in turn be made to give way to another higher idea, namely, that he is neither man nor woman, but the Impersonal Spirit. The Impersonal Spirit alone can enjoy real communion with the Impersonal God. Hence the highest realization of the Vaishnava draws close to the transcendental experience of the Vedāntist.

A beautiful expression of the Vaishnava worship of God through love is to be found in the Vrindāvan episode of the *Bhāgavata*. The gopis, or milk-maids, of Vrindāvan regarded the six-year-old Krishna as their Beloved. They sought no personal gain or happiness from this love. They surrendered to Krishna their bodies, minds, and souls. Of all the gopis, Rādhikā, or Rādhā, because of her intense love for Him, was the closest to Krishna. She manifested mahābhāva and was united with her Beloved. This union represents, through sensuous language, a supersensuous experience.

Sri Chaitanya, also known as Gaurānga, Gorā, or Nimāi, born in Bengal in 1485 and regarded as an Incarnation of God, is a great prophet of the Vaishnava religion. Chaitanya declared the chanting of God's name to be the most efficacious spiritual discipline for the Kaliyuga.

Sri Ramakrishna, as the monkey Hanumān, had already worshipped God as his Master. Through his devotion to Kāli he had worshipped God as his Mother. He was now to take up the other relationships prescribed by the Vaishnava scriptures.

RĀMLĀLĀ

About the year 1864 there came to Dakshineswar a wandering Vaishnava monk, Jatadhari, whose Ideal Deity was Rāma. He always carried with him a small metal image of the Deity, which he called by the endearing name of Rāmlālā, the Boy Rāma. Toward this little image he displayed the tender affection of Kausalyā for her divine Son, Rāma. As a result of lifelong spiritual practice he had actually found in the metal image the presence of his Ideal. Rāmlālā was no longer for him a metal image, but the living God. He devoted himself to nursing Rāma, feeding Rāma, playing with Rāma, taking Rāma for a walk, and bathing Rāma. And he found that the image responded to his love.

Sri Ramakrishna, much impressed with his devotion, requested Jatadhari to spend a few days at Dakshineswar. Soon Rāmlālā became the favourite companion of Sri Ramakrishna too. Later on he described to the devotees how the little image would dance gracefully before him, jump on his back, insist on being taken in his arms, run to the fields in the sun, pluck flowers from the bushes, and play pranks like a naughty boy. A very sweet relationship sprang up between him and Rāmlālā, for whom he felt the love of a mother.

One day Jatadhari requested Sri Ramakrishna to keep the image and bade him adieu with tearful eyes. He declared that Rāmlālā had fulfilled his innermost prayer and that he now had no more need of formal worship. A few days later Sri Ramakrishna was blessed through Rāmlālā with a vision of Rāmachandra, whereby he realized that the Rāma of the *Rāmāyana*, the son of Daśaratha, pervades the whole universe as Spirit and Consciousness; that He is its Creator, Sustainer, and Destroyer; that, in still another aspect, He is the transcendental Brahman, without form, attribute, or name.

While worshipping Rāmlālā as the Divine Child, Sri Ramakrishna's heart became filled with motherly tenderness, and he began to regard himself as a woman. His speech and gestures changed. He began to move freely with the ladies of Mathur's family, who now looked upon him as one of their own sex. During this time he worshipped the Divine Mother as Her companion or handmaid.

IN COMMUNION WITH THE DIVINE BELOVED

Sri Ramakrishna now devoted himself to scaling the most inaccessible and dizzy heights of dualistic worship, namely, the complete union with Sri Krishna as the Beloved of the heart. He regarded himself as one of the gopis of Vrindāvan, mad with longing for her divine Sweetheart. At his request Mathur provided him with woman's dress and jewelry. In this love-pursuit, food and drink were forgotten. Day and night he wept bitterly. The yearning turned into a mad frenzy; for the divine Krishna began to play with him the old tricks He had played with the gopis. He would tease and taunt, now and then revealing Himself, but always keeping at a distance. Sri Ramakrishna's anguish brought on a return of the old physical symptoms: the burning sensation, an oozing of blood through the pores, a loosening of the joints, and the stopping of physiological functions.

The Vaishnava scriptures advise one to propitiate Rādhā and obtain her grace in order to realize Sri Krishna. So the tortured devotee now turned his prayer to her. Within a short time he enjoyed her blessed vision. He saw and felt the figure of Rādhā disappearing into his own body.

He said later on: "It is impossible to describe the heavenly beauty and sweetness of Rādhā. Her very appearance showed that she had completely forgotten herself in her passionate attachment to Krishna. Her complexion was a light yellow."

Now one with Rādhā, he manifested the great ecstatic love, the mahā-bhāva, which had found in her its fullest expression. Later Sri Ramakrishna said: "The manifestation in the same individual of the nineteen different kinds of emotion for God is called, in the books on bhakti, mahābhāva. An ordinary man takes a whole lifetime to express even a single one of these. But in this body [meaning himself] there has been a complete manifestation of all nineteen."

The love of Rādhā is the precursor of the resplendent vision of Sri Krishna, and Sri Ramakrishna soon experienced that vision. The enchanting form of Krishna appeared to him and merged in his person. He became Krishna; he totally forgot his own individuality and the world; he saw Krishna in himself and in the universe. Thus he attained to the fulfilment of the worship of the Personal God. He drank from the fountain of Immortal Bliss. The agony of his heart vanished forever. He realized Amrita, Immortality, beyond the shadow of death.

One day, listening to a recitation of the *Bhāgavata* on the verandah of the Rādhākānta temple, he fell into a divine mood and saw the enchanting form of Krishna. He perceived the luminous rays issuing from Krishna's Lotus Feet in the form of a stout rope, which touched first the *Bhāgavata* and then his own chest, connecting all three—God, the scripture, and the devotee. "After this vision", he used to say, "I came to realize that Bhagavān, Bhakta, and *Bhāgavata*—God, Devotee, and Scripture—are in reality one and the same."

VEDĀNTA

The Brāhmani was the enthusiastic teacher and astonished beholder of Sri Ramakrishna in his spiritual progress. She became proud of the achievements of her unique pupil. But the pupil himself was not permitted to rest; his destiny beckoned him forward. His Divine Mother would allow him no respite till he had left behind the entire realm of duality with its visions, experiences, and ecstatic dreams. But for the new ascent the old tender guides would not suffice. The Brāhmani, on whom he had depended for three years, saw her son escape from her to follow the command of a teacher with masculine strength, a sterner mien, a gnarled physique, and a virile voice. The new guru was a wandering monk, the sturdy Totapuri, whom Sri Ramakrishna learnt to address affectionately as Nangtā, the "Naked One", because of his total renunciation of all earthly objects and attachments, including even a piece of wearing-cloth.

Totapuri was the bearer of a philosophy new to Sri Ramakrishna, the non-dualistic Vedānta philosophy, whose conclusions Totapuri had experienced in his own life. This ancient Hindu system designates the Ultimate Reality as Brahman, also described as Satchidānanda, Existence-Knowledge-Bliss Absolute. Brahman is the only Real Existence. In It there is no time, no space, no causality, no multiplicity. But through māyā, Its inscrutable Power, time, space, and causality are created and the One appears to break into the many. The eternal Spirit appears as a manifold of individuals endowed with form and subject to the conditions of time. The Immortal becomes a victim of birth and death. The Changeless undergoes change. The sinless Pure Soul, hypnotized by Its own māyā, experiences the joys of heaven and the pains of hell. But these experiences based on the duality of the subject-object relationship are unreal. Even the vision of a Personal God is, ultimately speaking, as illusory as the experience of any other object. Man attains his liberation, therefore, by piercing the veil of māyā and rediscovering his total identity with Brahman. Knowing himself to be one with the Universal Spirit, he realizes ineffable Peace. Only then does he go beyond the fiction of birth and death; only then does he become immortal. And this is the ultimate goal of all religions—to dehypnotize the soul now hypnotized by its own ignorance.

The path of the Vedāntic discipline is the path of negation, "neti", in which, by stern determination, all that is unreal is both negated and renounced. It is the path of jnāna, knowledge, the direct method of realizing the Absolute. After the negation of everything relative, including the discriminating ego itself, the aspirant merges in the One without a Second, in the bliss of nirvikalpa samādhi, where subject and object are alike dissolved. The soul goes beyond the realm of thought. The domain of duality is transcended. Māyā is left behind with all its changes and modifications. The Real Man towers above the delusions of creation, preservation, and destruction. An avalanche of indescribable Bliss sweeps away all relative ideas of pain and pleasure, good and evil. There shines in the heart the glory of the Eternal Brahman, Existence-Knowledge-Bliss Absolute. Knower, knowledge, and known are dissolved in the Ocean of one eternal Consciousness; love, lover, and beloved merge in the unbounded Sea of supreme Felicity; birth, growth, and death vanish in infinite Existence. All doubts and misgivings are quelled for ever; the oscillations of the mind are stopped; the momentum of past actions is exhausted. Breaking down the ridge-pole of the tabernacle in which the soul has made its abode for untold ages, stilling the body, calming the mind, drowning the ego, the sweet joy of Brahman wells up in that superconscious state. Space disappears into nothingness, time is swallowed in eternity, and causation becomes a dream of the past. Only Existence is. Ah! Who can describe what the soul then feels in its communion with the Self?

Even when man descends from this dizzy height, he is devoid of ideas of "I" and "mine"; he looks on the body as a mere shadow, an outer sheath encasing the soul. He does not dwell on the past, takes no thought for the future, and looks with indifference on the present. He surveys everything in the world with an eye of equality; he is no longer touched by the infinite variety of phenomena; he no longer reacts to pleasure and pain. He remains unmoved whether he—that is to say, his body—is worshipped by the good or tormented by the wicked; for he realizes that it is the one Brahman that manifests Itself through everything. The impact of such an experience devastates the body and mind. Consciousness becomes blasted, as it were, with an excess of Light. In the Vedānta books it is said that after the experience of nirvikalpa samādhi the body drops off like a dry leaf. Only those who are born with a special mission for the world can return from this height to the valleys of normal life. They live and move in the world for the welfare of mankind. They are invested with a supreme spiritual power. A divine glory shines through them.

TOTAPURI

Totapuri arrived at the Dakshineswar temple garden toward the end of 1864. Perhaps born in the Punjab, he was the head of a monastery in that province of India and claimed leadership of seven hundred sannyāsis. Trained from early youth in the disciplines of the Advaita Vedānta, he looked upon the world as an illusion. The gods and goddesses of the dualistic worship were to him mere fantasies of the deluded mind. Prayers, ceremonies, rites, and rituals had nothing to do with true religion, and about these he was utterly indifferent. Exercising self-exertion and unshakable will-power, he had liberated himself from attachment to the sense-objects of the relative universe. For forty years he had practised austere discipline on the bank of the sacred Narmadā and had finally realized his identity with the Absolute. Thenceforward he roamed in the world as an unfettered soul, a lion free from the cage. Clad in a loin-cloth, he spent his days under the canopy of the sky alike in storm and sunshine, feeding his body on the slender pittance of alms. He had been visiting the estuary of the Ganges. On his return journey along the bank of the sacred river, led by the inscrutable Divine Will, he stopped at Dakshineswar.

Totapuri, discovering at once that Sri Ramakrishna was prepared to be a student of Vedānta, asked to initiate him into its mysteries. With the permission of the Divine Mother, Sri Ramakrishna agreed to the proposal. But Totapuri explained that only a sannyāsi could receive the teaching of Vedānta. Sri Ramakrishna agreed to renounce the world, but with the stipulation that the ceremony of his initiation into the monastic order be performed in secret, to spare the feelings of his old mother, who had been living with him at Dakshineswar.

On the appointed day, in the small hours of the morning, a fire was lighted in the Panchavati. Totapuri and Sri Ramakrishna sat before it. The flame played on their faces. "Ramakrishna was a small brown man with a short beard and beautiful eyes, long dark eyes, full of light, obliquely set and slightly veiled, never very wide open, but seeing half-closed a great distance both outwardly and inwardly. His mouth was open over his white teeth in a bewitching smile, at once affectionate and mischievous. Of medium height, he was thin to emaciation and extremely delicate. His temperament was high-strung, for he was supersensitive to all the winds of joy and sorrow, both moral and physical. He was indeed a living reflection of all that happened before the mirror of his eyes, a two-sided mirror, turned both out and in."[4] Facing him, the other rose like a rock. He was very tall and robust, a sturdy and tough oak. His constitution and mind were of iron. He was the strong leader of men.

In the burning flame before him Sri Ramakrishna performed the rituals of destroying his attachment to relatives, friends, body, mind, sense-organs, ego, and the world. The leaping flame swallowed it all, making the initiate free and pure. The sacred thread and the tuft of hair were consigned to the fire, completing his severance from caste, sex, and society. Last of all he burnt in that fire, with all that is holy as his witness, his desire for enjoyment here and hereafter. He uttered the sacred mantras giving assurance of safety and fearlessness to all beings, who were only manifestations of his own Self. The rites completed, the disciple received from the guru the loincloth and ochre robe, the emblems of his new life.

The teacher and the disciple repaired to the meditation room near by. Totapuri began to impart to Sri Ramakrishna the great truths of Vedānta.

"Brahman", he said, "is the only Reality, ever pure, ever illumined, ever free, beyond the limits of time, space, and causation. Though apparently divided by names and forms through the inscrutable power of māyā, that enchantress who makes the impossible possible, Brahman is really One and undivided. When a seeker merges in the beatitude of samādhi, he does not perceive time and space or name and form, the offspring of māyā. Whatever is within the domain of māyā is unreal. Give it up. Destroy the prison-house of name and form and rush out of it with the strength of a lion. Dive deep in search of the Self and realize It through samādhi. You will find the world of name and form vanishing into void, and the puny ego dissolving in Brahman-Consciousness. You will realize your identity with Brahman, Existence-Knowledge-Bliss Absolute." Quoting the Upanishad, Totapuri said: "That knowledge is shallow by which one sees or hears or knows

[4] Romain Rolland, *Prophets of the New India*, pp. 38-9.

another. What is shallow is worthless and can never give real felicity. But the Knowledge by which one does not see another or hear another or know another, which is beyond duality, is great, and through such Knowledge one attains the Infinite Bliss. How can the mind and senses grasp That which shines in the heart of all as the Eternal Subject?"

Totapuri asked the disciple to withdraw his mind from all objects of the relative world, including the gods and goddesses, and to concentrate on the Absolute. But the task was not easy even for Sri Ramakrishna. He found it impossible to take his mind beyond Kāli, the Divine Mother of the Universe. "After the initiation", Sri Ramakrishna once said, describing the event, "Nangtā began to teach me the various conclusions of the Advaita Vedānta and asked me to withdraw the mind completely from all objects and dive deep into the Ātman. But in spite of all my attempts I could not altogether cross the realm of name and form and bring my mind to the unconditioned state. I had no difficulty in taking the mind from all the objects of the world. But the radiant and too familiar figure of the Blissful Mother, the Embodiment of the essence of Pure Consciousness, appeared before me as a living reality. Her bewitching smile prevented me from passing into the Great Beyond. Again and again I tried, but She stood in my way every time. In despair I said to Nangtā: 'It is hopeless. I cannot raise my mind to the unconditioned state and come face to face with Ātman.' He grew excited and sharply said: 'What? You can't do it? But you have to.' He cast his eyes around. Finding a piece of glass he took it up and stuck it between my eyebrows. 'Concentrate the mind on this point!' he thundered. Then with stern determination I again sat to meditate. As soon as the gracious form of the Divine Mother appeared before me, I used my discrimination as a sword and with it clove Her in two. The last barrier fell. My spirit at once soared beyond the relative plane and I lost myself in samādhi."

Sri Ramakrishna remained completely absorbed in samādhi for three days. "Is it really true?" Totapuri cried out in astonishment. "Is it possible that he has attained in a single day what it took me forty years of strenuous practice to achieve? Great God! It is nothing short of a miracle!" With the help of Totapuri, Sri Ramakrishna's mind finally came down to the relative plane.

Totapuri, a monk of the most orthodox type, never stayed at a place more than three days. But he remained at Dakshineswar eleven months. He too had something to learn.

Totapuri had no idea of the struggles of ordinary men in the toils of passion and desire. Having maintained all through life the guilelessness of a child, he laughed at the idea of a man's being led astray by the senses. He was convinced that the world was māyā and had only to be denounced to vanish for ever. A born non-dualist, he had no faith in a Personal God. He did not believe in the terrible aspect of Kāli, much less in Her benign aspect. Music and the chanting of God's holy name were to him only so much nonsense. He ridiculed the spending of emotion on the worship of a Personal God.

KĀLI AND MĀYĀ

Sri Ramakrishna, on the other hand, though fully aware, like his guru, that the world is an illusory appearance, instead of slighting māyā, like an orthodox monist, acknowledged its power in the relative life. He was all love and reverence for māyā, perceiving in it a mysterious and majestic expression of Divinity. To him māyā itself was God, for everything was God. It was one of the faces of Brahman. What he had realized on the heights of the transcendental plane, he also found here below, everywhere about him, under the mysterious garb of names and forms. And this garb was a perfectly transparent sheath, through which he recognized the glory of the Divine Immanence. Māyā, the mighty weaver of the garb, is none other than Kāli, the Divine Mother. She is the primordial Divine Energy, Śakti, and She can no more be distinguished from the Supreme Brahman than can the power of burning be distinguished from fire. She projects the world and again withdraws it. She spins it as the spider spins its web. She is the Mother of the Universe, identical with the Brahman of Vedānta, and with the Ātman of Yoga. As eternal Lawgiver, She makes and unmakes laws; it is by Her imperious will that karma yields its fruit. She ensnares men with illusion and again releases them from bondage with a look of Her benign eyes. She is the supreme Mistress of the cosmic play, and all objects, animate and inanimate, dance by Her will. Even those who realize the Absolute in nirvikalpa samādhi are under Her jurisdiction as long as they still live on the relative plane.

Thus, after nirvikalpa samādhi, Sri Ramakrishna realized māyā in an altogether new role. The binding aspect of Kāli vanished from before his vision. She no longer obscured his understanding. The world became the glorious manifestation of the Divine Mother. Māyā became Brahman. The Transcendental Itself broke through the Immanent. Sri Ramakrishna discovered that māyā operates in the relative world in two ways, and he termed these "avidyāmāyā" and "vidyāmāyā". Avidyāmāyā represents the dark forces of creation: sensuous desires, evil passions, greed, lust, cruelty, and so on. It sustains the world system on the lower planes. It is responsible for the round of man's birth and death. It must be fought and vanquished. But vidyāmāyā is the higher force of creation: the spiritual virtues, the enlightening qualities, kindness, purity, love, devotion. Vidyāmāyā elevates man to the higher planes of consciousness. With the help of vidyāmāyā the devotee rids himself of avidyāmāyā; he then becomes māyātita, free of māyā. The two aspects of māyā are the two forces of creation, the two powers of Kāli; and She stands beyond them both. She is like the effulgent sun, bringing into existence and shining through and standing behind the clouds of different colours and shapes, conjuring up wonderful forms in the blue autumn heaven.

The Divine Mother asked Sri Ramakrishna not to be lost in the featureless Absolute but to remain in bhāvamukha, on the threshold of relative consciousness, the border line between the Absolute and the Relative. He was to keep himself at the "sixth centre" of Tantra, from which he could see not only the glory of the seventh, but also the divine manifestations of the Kundalini in the lower centres. He gently oscillated back and forth across the dividing line. Ecstatic devotion to the Divine Mother alternated with serene absorption in the Ocean of Absolute Unity. He thus bridged the gulf between the Personal and the Impersonal, the immanent and the transcendent aspects of Reality. This is a unique experience in the recorded spiritual history of the world.

TOTAPURI'S LESSON

From Sri Ramakrishna Totapuri had to learn the significance of Kāli, the Great Fact of the relative world, and of māyā, Her indescribable Power.

One day, when guru and disciple were engaged in an animated discussion about Vedānta, a servant of the temple garden came there and took a coal from the sacred fire that had been lighted by the great ascetic. He wanted it to light his tobacco. Totapuri flew into a rage and was about to beat the man. Sri Ramakrishna rocked with laughter. "What a shame!" he cried. "You are explaining to me the reality of Brahman and the illusoriness of the world; yet now you have so far forgotten yourself as to be about to beat a man in a fit of passion. The power of māyā is indeed inscrutable!" Totapuri was embarrassed.

About this time Totapuri was suddenly laid up with a severe attack of dysentery. On account of this miserable illness he found it impossible to meditate. One night the pain became excruciating. He could no longer concentrate on Brahman. The body stood in the way. He became incensed with its demands. A free soul, he did not at all care for the body. So he determined to drown it in the Ganges. Thereupon he walked into the river. But, lo! He walks to the other bank.[5] Is there not enough water in the Ganges? Standing dumbfounded on the other bank he looks back across the water. The trees, the temples, the houses, are silhouetted against the sky. Suddenly, in one dazzling moment, he sees on all sides the presence of the Divine Mother. She is in everything; She is everything. She is in the water; She is on land. She is the body; She is the mind. She is pain; She is comfort. She is knowledge; She is ignorance. She is life; She is death. She is everything that one sees, hears, or imagines. She turns "yea" into "nay", and "nay" into "yea". Without Her grace no embodied being can go beyond Her realm. Man has no free will. He is not even free to die. Yet, again, beyond the body and mind She resides in Her Transcendental, Absolute aspect. She is the Brahman that Totapuri had been worshipping all his life.

Totapuri returned to Dakshineswar and spent the remaining hours of the night meditating on the Divine Mother. In the morning he went to the Kāli temple with Sri Ramakrishna and prostrated himself before the image of the Mother. He now realized why he had spent eleven months at Dakshineswar. Bidding farewell to the disciple, he continued on his way, enlightened.

Sri Ramakrishna later described the significance of Totapuri's lessons:

[5] This version of the incident is taken from the biography of Sri Ramakrishna by Swami Saradananda, one of the Master's direct disciples.

"When I think of the Supreme Being as inactive—neither creating nor preserving nor destroying—, I call Him Brahman or Purusha, the Impersonal God. When I think of Him as active—creating, preserving, and destroying—, I call Him Śakti or Māyā or Prakriti, the Personal God. But the distinction between them does not mean a difference. The Personal and the Impersonal are the same thing, like milk and its whiteness, the diamond and its lustre, the snake and its wriggling motion. It is impossible to conceive of the one without the other. The Divine Mother and Brahman are one."

After the departure of Totapuri, Sri Ramakrishna remained for six months in a state of absolute identity with Brahman. "For six months at a stretch", he said, "I remained in that state from which ordinary men can never return; generally the body falls off, after three weeks, like a sere leaf. I was not conscious of day and night. Flies would enter my mouth and nostrils just as they do a dead body's, but I did not feel them. My hair became matted with dust."

His body would not have survived but for the kindly attention of a monk who happened to be at Dakshineswar at that time and who somehow realized that for the good of humanity Sri Ramakrishna's body must be preserved. He tried various means, even physical violence, to recall the fleeing soul to the prison-house of the body, and during the resultant fleeting moments of consciousness he would push a few morsels of food down Sri Ramakrishna's throat. Presently Sri Ramakrishna received the command of the Divine Mother to remain on the threshold of relative consciousness. Soon thereafter he was afflicted with a serious attack of dysentery. Day and night the pain tortured him, and his mind gradually came down to the physical plane.

COMPANY OF HOLY MEN AND DEVOTEES

From now on Sri Ramakrishna began to seek the company of devotees and holy men. He had gone through the storm and stress of spiritual disciplines and visions. Now he realized an inner calmness and appeared to others as a normal person. But he could not bear the company of worldly people or listen to their talk. Fortunately the holy atmosphere of Dakshineswar and the liberality of Mathur attracted monks and holy men from all parts of the country. Sādhus of all denominations—monists and dualists, Vaishnavas and Vedāntists, Śaktas and worshippers of Rāma—flocked there in ever increasing numbers. Ascetics and visionaries came to seek Sri Ramakrishna's advice. Vaishnavas had come during the period of his Vaishnava sādhanā, and Tāntriks when he practised the disciplines of Tantra. Vedāntists began to arrive after the departure of Totapuri. In the room of Sri Ramakrishna, who was then in bed with dysentery, the Vedāntists engaged in scriptural discussions, and, forgetting his own physical suffering, he solved their doubts by referring directly to his own experiences. Many of the visitors were genuine spiritual souls, the unseen pillars of Hinduism, and their spiritual lives were quickened in no small measure by the sage of Dakshineswar. Sri Ramakrishna in turn learnt from them anecdotes concerning the ways and the conduct of holy men, which he subsequently narrated to his devotees and disciples. At his request Mathur provided him with large stores of food-stuffs, clothes, and so forth, for distribution among the wandering monks.

Sri Ramakrishna had not read books, yet he possessed an encyclopedic knowledge of religions and religious philosophies. This he acquired from his contacts with innumerable holy men and scholars. He had a unique power of assimilation; through meditation he made this knowledge a part of his being. Once, when he was asked by a disciple about the source of his seemingly inexhaustible knowledge, he replied: "I have not read; but I have heard the learned. I have made a garland of their knowledge, wearing it round my neck, and I have given it as an offering at the feet of the Mother."

Sri Ramakrishna used to say that when the flower blooms the bees come to it for honey of their own accord. Now many souls began to visit Dakshineswar to satisfy their spiritual hunger. He, the devotee and aspirant, became the Master. Gauri, the great scholar who had been one of the first to proclaim Sri Ramakrishna an Incarnation of God, paid the Master a visit in 1870 and with the Master's blessings renounced the world. Narayan Shastri, another great pundit, who had mastered the six systems of Hindu philosophy and had been offered a lucrative post by the Mahārājā of Jaipur, met the Master and recognized in him one who had realized in life those ideals which he himself had encountered merely in books. Sri Ramakrishna initiated Narayan Shastri, at his earnest request, into the life of sannyās. Pundit Padmalochan, the court pundit of the Mahārājā of Burdwan, well known for his scholarship in both the Vedānta and the Nyāya systems of philosophy, accepted the Master as an Incarnation of God. Krishnakishore, a Vedāntist scholar, became devoted to the Master. And there arrived Viswanath Upadhyaya, who was to become a favourite devotee; Sri Rama-krishna always addressed him as "Captain". He was a high officer of the King of Nepal and had received the title of Colonel in recognition of his merit. A scholar of the *Gītā*, the *Bhāgavata*, and the Vedānta philosophy, he daily performed the worship of his Chosen Deity with great devotion. "I have read the Vedas and the other scriptures", he said. "I have also met a good many monks and devotees in different places. But it is in Sri Rama-krishna's presence that my spiritual yearnings have been fulfilled. To me he seems to be the embodiment of the truths of the scriptures."

The Knowledge of Brahman in nirvikalpa samādhi had convinced Sri Ramakrishna that the gods of the different religions are but so many readings of the Absolute, and that the Ultimate Reality could never be expressed by human tongue. He understood that all religions lead their devotees by dif-fering paths to one and the same goal. Now he became eager to explore some of the alien religions; for with him understanding meant actual experience.

ISLĀM

Toward the end of 1866 he began to practise the disciplines of Islām. Under the direction of his Mussalmān guru he abandoned himself to his new sādhanā. He dressed as a Mussalmān and repeated the name of Āllāh.

His prayers took the form of the Islāmic devotions. He forgot the Hindu gods and goddesses—even Kāli—and gave up visiting the temples. He took up his residence outside the temple precincts. After three days he saw the vision of a radiant figure, perhaps Mohammed. This figure gently approached him and finally lost himself in Sri Ramakrishna. Thus he realized the Mussalmān God. Thence he passed into communion with Brahman. The mighty river of Islām also led him back to the Ocean of the Absolute.

CHRISTIANITY

Eight years later, some time in November 1874, Sri Ramakrishna was seized with an irresistible desire to learn the truth of the Christian religion. He began to listen to readings from the Bible, by Sambhu Charan Mallick, a gentleman of Calcutta and a devotee of the Master. Sri Ramakrishna became fascinated by the life and teachings of Jesus. One day he was seated in the parlour of Jadu Mallick's garden house[6] at Dakshineswar, when his eyes became fixed on a painting of the Madonna and Child. Intently watching it, he became gradually overwhelmed with divine emotion. The figures in the picture took on life, and the rays of light emanating from them entered his soul. The effect of this experience was stronger than that of the vision of Mohammed. In dismay he cried out, "O Mother! What are You doing to me?" And, breaking through the barriers of creed and religion, he entered a new realm of ecstasy. Christ possessed his soul. For three days he did not set foot in the Kāli temple. On the fourth day, in the afternoon, as he was walking in the Panchavati, he saw coming toward him a person with beautiful large eyes, serene countenance, and fair skin. As the two faced each other, a voice rang out in the depths of Sri Ramakrishna's soul: "Behold the Christ, who shed His heart's blood for the redemption of the world, who suffered a sea of anguish for love of men. It is He, the Master Yogi, who is in eternal union with God. It is Jesus, Love Incarnate." The Son of Man embraced the Son of the Divine Mother and merged in him. Sri Ramakrishna realized his identity with Christ, as he had already realized his identity with Kāli, Rāma, Hanumān, Rādhā, Krishna, Brahman, and Mohammed. The Master went into samādhi and communed with the Brahman with attributes. Thus he experienced the truth that Christianity, too, was a path leading to God-Consciousness. Till the last moment of his life he believed that Christ was an Incarnation of God. But Christ, for him, was not the only Incarnation; there were others—Buddha, for instance, and Krishna.

ATTITUDE TOWARD DIFFERENT RELIGIONS

Sri Ramakrishna accepted the divinity of Buddha and used to point out the similarity of his teachings to those of the Upanishads. He also showed great respect for the Tirthankaras, who founded Jainism, and for the ten Gurus of Śikhism. But he did not speak of them as Divine Incarnations. He was heard to say that the Gurus of Śikhism were the reincarnations of King

---

[6] This expression is used throughout to translate the Bengali word denoting a rich man's country house set in a garden.

Janaka of ancient India. He kept in his room at Dakshineswar a small statue of Tirthankara Mahāvira and a picture of Christ, before which incense was burnt morning and evening.

Without being formally initiated into their doctrines, Sri Ramakrishna thus realized the ideals of religions other than Hinduism. He did not need to follow any doctrine. All barriers were removed by his overwhelming love of God. So he became a Master who could speak with authority regarding the ideas and ideals of the various religions of the world. "I have practised", said he, "all religions—Hinduism, Islām, Christianity—and I have also followed the paths of the different Hindu sects. I have found that it is the same God toward whom all are directing their steps, though along different paths. You must try all beliefs and traverse all the different ways once. Wherever I look, I see men quarrelling in the name of religion—Hindus, Mohammedans, Brāhmos, Vaishnavas, and the rest. But they never reflect that He who is called Krishna is also called Śiva, and bears the name of the Primal Energy, Jesus, and Āllāh as well—the same Rāma with a thousand names. A lake has several ghāts. At one the Hindus take water in pitchers and call it 'jal'; at another the Mussalmāns take water in leather bags and call it 'pāni'. At a third the Christians call it 'water'. Can we imagine that it is not 'jal', but only 'pāni' or 'water'? How ridiculous! The substance is One under different names, and everyone is seeking the same substance; only climate, temperament, and name create differences. Let each man follow his own path. If he sincerely and ardently wishes to know God, peace be unto him! He will surely realize Him."

In 1867 Sri Ramakrishna returned to Kāmārpukur to recuperate from the effect of his austerities. The peaceful countryside, the simple and artless companions of his boyhood, and the pure air did him much good. The villagers were happy to get back their playful, frank, witty, kind-hearted, and truthful Gadadhar, though they did not fail to notice the great change that had come over him during his years in Calcutta. His wife, Sarada Devi, now fourteen years old, soon arrived at Kāmārpukur. Her spiritual development was much beyond her age and she was able to understand immediately her husband's state of mind. She became eager to learn from him about God and to live with him as his attendant. The Master accepted her cheerfully both as his disciple and as his spiritual companion. Referring to the experiences of these few days, she once said: "I used to feel always as if a pitcher full of bliss were placed in my heart. The joy was indescribable."

PILGRIMAGE

On January 27, 1868, Mathur Babu with a party of some one hundred and twenty-five persons set out on a pilgrimage to the sacred places of northern India. At Vaidyanath in Behar, when the Master saw the inhabitants of a village reduced by poverty and starvation to mere skeletons, he requested his rich patron to feed the people and give each a piece of cloth. Mathur demurred at the added expense. The Master declared bitterly that he would not go on to Benares, but would live with the poor and share their miseries. He actually left Mathur and sat down with the villagers.

Whereupon Mathur had to yield. On another occasion, two years later, Sri Ramakrishna showed a similar sentiment for the poor and needy. He accompanied Mathur on a tour to one of the latter's estates at the time of the collection of rents. For two years the harvests had failed and the tenants were in a state of extreme poverty. The Master asked Mathur to remit their rents, distribute help to them, and in addition give the hungry people a sumptuous feast. When Mathur grumbled, the Master said: "You are only the steward of the Divine Mother. They are the Mother's tenants. You must spend the Mother's money. When they are suffering, how can you refuse to help them? You must help them." Again Mathur had to give in. Sri Ramakrishna's sympathy for the poor sprang from his perception of God in all created beings. His sentiment was not that of the humanist or philanthropist. To him the service of man was the same as the worship of God.

The party entered holy Benares by boat along the Ganges. When Sri Ramakrishna's eyes fell on this city of Śiva, where had accumulated for ages the devotion and piety of countless worshippers, he saw it to be made of gold, as the scriptures declare. He was visibly moved. During his stay in the city he treated every particle of its earth with utmost respect. At the Manikarnikā Ghāt, the great cremation ground of the city, he actually saw Śiva, with ash-covered body and tawny matted hair, serenely approaching each funeral pyre and breathing into the ears of the corpses the mantra of liberation; and then the Divine Mother removing from the dead their bonds. Thus he realized the significance of the scriptural statement that anyone dying in Benares attains salvation through the grace of Śiva. He paid a visit to Trailanga Swami, the celebrated monk, whom he later declared to be a real paramahamsa, a veritable image of Śiva.

Sri Ramakrishna visited Allāhābād, at the confluence of the Ganges and the Jamunā, and then proceeded to Vrindāvan and Mathurā, hallowed by the legends, songs, and dramas about Krishna and the gopis. Here he had numerous visions and his heart overflowed with divine emotion. He wept and said: "O Krishna! Everything here is as it was in the olden days. You alone are absent." He visited the great woman saint, Gangāmāyi, regarded by Vaishnava devotees as the reincarnation of an intimate attendant of Rādhā. She was sixty years old and had frequent trances. She spoke of Sri Ramakrishna as an incarnation of Rādhā. With great difficulty he was persuaded to leave her.

On the return journey Mathur wanted to visit Gayā, but Sri Ramakrishna declined to go. He recalled his father's vision at Gayā before his own birth and felt that in the temple of Vishnu he would become permanently absorbed in God. Mathur, honouring the Master's wish, returned with his party to Calcutta.

From Vrindāvan the Master had brought a handful of dust. Part of this he scattered in the Panchavati; the rest he buried in the little hut where he had practised meditation. "Now this place", he said, "is as sacred as Vrindāvan."

In 1870 the Master went on a pilgrimage to Nadiā, the birth-place of Sri Chaitanya. As the boat by which he travelled approached the sand-bank close to Nadiā, Sri Ramakrishna had a vision of the "two brothers", Sri Chaitanya and his companion Nityānanda, "bright as molten gold" and with haloes, rushing to greet him with uplifted hands. "There they come! There they come!" he cried. They entered his body and he went into a deep trance.

RELATION WITH HIS WIFE

In 1872 Sarada Devi paid her first visit to her husband at Dakshineswar. Four years earlier she had seen him at Kāmārpukur and had tasted the bliss of his divine company. Since then she had become even more gentle, tender, introspective, serious, and unselfish. She had heard many rumours about her husband's insanity. People had shown her pity in her misfortune. The more she thought, the more she felt that her duty was to be with him, giving him, in whatever measure she could, a wife's devoted service. She was now eighteen years old. Accompanied by her father, she arrived at Dakshineswar, having come on foot the distance of eighty miles. She had had an attack of fever on the way. When she arrived at the temple garden the Master said sorrowfully: "Ah! You have come too late. My Mathur is no longer here to look after you." Mathur had passed away the previous year.

The Master took up the duty of instructing his young wife, and this included everything from housekeeping to the Knowledge of Brahman. He taught her how to trim a lamp, how to behave toward people according to their differing temperaments, and how to conduct herself before visitors. He instructed her in the mysteries of spiritual life—prayer, meditation, japa, deep contemplation, and samādhi. The first lesson that Sarada Devi received was: "God is everybody's Beloved, just as the moon is dear to every child. Everyone has the same right to pray to Him. Out of His grace He reveals Himself to all who call upon Him. You too will see Him if you but pray to Him."

Totapuri, coming to know of the Master's marriage, had once remarked: "What does it matter? He alone is firmly established in the Knowledge of Brahman who can adhere to his spirit of discrimination and renunciation even while living with his wife. He alone has attained the supreme illumination who can look on man and woman alike as Brahman. A man with the idea of sex may be a good aspirant, but he is still far from the goal." Sri Ramakrishna and his wife lived together at Dakshineswar, but their minds always soared above the worldly plane. A few months after Sarada Devi's arrival Sri Ramakrishna arranged, on an auspicious day, a special worship of Kāli, the Divine Mother. Instead of an image of the Deity, he placed on the seat the living image, Sarada Devi herself. The worshipper and the worshipped went into deep samādhi and in the transcendental plane their souls were united. After several hours Sri Ramakrishna came down again to the relative plane, sang a hymn to the Great Goddess, and surrendered, at the feet of the living image, himself, his rosary, and the fruit of his life-long sādhanā. This is known in Tantra as the Shorasi Pujā, the "Adoration of Woman". Sri Ramakrishna realized the significance of the great statement of the Upanishad: "O Lord, Thou art the woman, Thou art the man; Thou art the boy, Thou art the girl; Thou art the old, tottering on their crutches. Thou pervadest the universe in its multiple forms."

By his marriage Sri Ramakrishna admitted the great value of marriage in man's spiritual evolution, and by adhering to his monastic vows he demonstrated the imperative necessity of self-control, purity, and continence, in the realization of God. By his unique spiritual relationship with his wife he proved that husband and wife can live together as spiritual companions. Thus his life is a synthesis of the ways of life of the householder and the monk.

THE "EGO" OF THE MASTER

In the nirvikalpa samādhi Sri Ramakrishna had realized that Brahman alone is real and the world illusory. By keeping his mind six months on the plane of the non-dual Brahman, he had attained to the state of the vijnāni, the knower of Truth in a special and very rich sense, who sees Brahman not only in himself and in the transcendental Absolute, but in everything of the world. In this state of vijnāna, sometimes, bereft of body-consciousness, he would regard himself as one with Brahman; sometimes, conscious of the dual world, he would regard himself as God's devotee, servant, or child. In order to enable the Master to work for the welfare of humanity, the Divine Mother had kept in him a trace of ego, which he described—according to his mood—as the "ego of Knowledge", the "ego of Devotion", the "ego of a child", or the "ego of a servant". In any case this ego of the Master, consumed by the fire of the Knowledge of Brahman, was an appearance only, like a burnt string. He often referred to this ego as the "ripe ego" in contrast with the ego of the bound soul, which he described as the "unripe" or "green" ego. The ego of the bound soul identifies itself with the body, relatives, possessions, and the world; but the "ripe ego", illumined by Divine Knowledge, knows the body, relatives, possessions, and the world to be unreal and establishes a relationship of love with God alone. Through this "ripe ego" Sri Ramakrishna dealt with the world and his wife. One day, while stroking his feet, Sarada Devi asked the Master, "What do you think of me?" Quick came the answer: "The Mother who is worshipped in the temple is the mother who has given birth to my body and is now living in the nahabat, and it is She again who is stroking my feet at this moment. Indeed, I always look on you as the personification of the Blissful Mother Kāli."

Sarada Devi, in the company of her husband, had rare spiritual experiences. She said: "I have no words to describe my wonderful exaltation of spirit as I watched him in his different moods. Under the influence of divine emotion he would sometimes talk on abstruse subjects, sometimes laugh, sometimes weep, and sometimes become perfectly motionless in samādhi. This would continue throughout the night. There was such an extraordinary divine presence in him that now and then I would shake with fear and wonder how the night would pass. Months went by in this way. Then one day he discovered that I had to keep awake the whole night lest, during my sleep, he should go into samādhi—for it might happen at any moment—, and so he asked me to sleep in the nahabat."

SUMMARY OF THE MASTER'S SPIRITUAL EXPERIENCES

We have now come to the end of Sri Ramakrishna's sādhanā, the period of his spiritual discipline. As a result of his supersensuous experiences he reached certain conclusions regarding himself and spirituality in general. His conclusions about himself may be summarized as follows:

First, he was an Incarnation of God, a specially commissioned person, whose spiritual experiences were for the benefit of humanity. Whereas it takes an ordinary man a whole life's struggle to realize one or two phases of God, he had in a few years realized God in all His phases.

Second, he knew that he had always been a free soul, that the various disciplines through which he had passed were really not necessary for his own liberation but were solely for the benefit of others. Thus the terms liberation and bondage were not applicable to him. As long as there are beings who consider themselves bound, God must come down to earth as an Incarnation to free them from bondage, just as a magistrate must visit any part of his district in which there is trouble.

Third, he came to foresee the time of his death. His words with respect to this matter were literally fulfilled.

About spirituality in general the following were his conclusions:

First, he was firmly convinced that all religions are true, that every doctrinal system represents a path to God. He had followed all the main paths and all had led him to the same goal. He was the first religious prophet recorded in history to preach the harmony of religions.

Second, the three great systems of thought known as Dualism, Qualified Non-dualism, and Absolute Non-dualism—Dvaita, Viśishtādvaita, and Advaita—he perceived to represent three stages in man's progress toward the Ultimate Reality. They were not contradictory but complementary and suited to different temperaments. For the ordinary man with strong attachment to the senses, a dualistic form of religion, prescribing a certain amount of material support, such as music and other symbols, is useful. A man of God-realization transcends the idea of worldly duties, but the ordinary mortal must perform his duties, striving to be unattached and to surrender the results to God. The mind can comprehend and describe the range of thought and experience up to the Viśishtādvaita, and no further. The Advaita, the last word in spiritual experience, is something to be felt in samādhi, for it transcends mind and speech. From the highest standpoint, the Absolute and Its manifestation are equally real—the Lord's Name, His Abode, and the Lord Himself are of the same spiritual Essence. Everything is Spirit, the difference being only in form.

Third, Sri Ramakrishna realized the wish of the Divine Mother that through him She should found a new Order, consisting of those who would uphold the universal doctrines illustrated in his life.

Fourth, his spiritual insight told him that those who were having their last birth on the mortal plane of existence and those who had sincerely called on the Lord even once in their lives must come to him.

During this period Sri Ramakrishna suffered several bereavements. The first was the death of a nephew named Akshay. After the young man's death Sri Ramakrishna said: "Akshay died before my very eyes. But it did not affect me in the least. I stood by and watched a man die. It was like a sword being drawn from its scabbard. I enjoyed the scene, and laughed and sang and danced over it. They removed the body and cremated it. But the next day as I stood there (*pointing to the southeast verandah of his room*), I felt a racking pain for the loss of Akshay, as if somebody were squeezing my heart like a wet towel. I wondered at it and thought that the Mother was teaching me a lesson. I was not much concerned even with my own body—much less with a relative. But if such was my pain at the loss of a nephew, how much more must be the grief of the householders at the loss of their near and dear ones!" In 1871 Mathur died, and some five years later Sambhu Mallick—who, after Mathur's passing away, had taken care of the Master's comfort. In 1873 died his elder brother Rameswar, and in 1876, his beloved mother. These bereavements left their imprint on the tender human heart of Sri Ramakrishna, albeit he had realized the immortality of the soul and the illusoriness of birth and death.

In March 1875, about a year before the death of his mother, the Master met Keshab Chandra Sen. The meeting was a momentous event for both Sri Ramakrishna and Keshab. Here the Master for the first time came into actual contact with a worthy representative of modern India.

BRĀHMO SAMĀJ

Keshab was the leader of the Brāhmo Samāj, one of the two great movements that, during the latter part of the nineteenth century, played an important part in shaping the course of the renascence of India. The founder of the Brāhmo movement had been the great Rājā Rammohan Roy (1774-1833). Though born in an orthodox brāhmin family, Rammohan Roy had shown great sympathy for Islām and Christianity. He had gone to Tibet in search of the Buddhist mysteries. He had extracted from Christianity its ethical system, but had rejected the divinity of Christ as he had denied the Hindu Incarnations. The religion of Islām influenced him, to a great extent, in the formulation of his monotheistic doctrines. But he always went back to the Vedas for his spiritual inspiration. The Brāhmo Samāj, which he founded in 1828, was dedicated to the "worship and adoration of the Eternal, the Unsearchable, the Immutable Being, who is the Author and Preserver of the Universe". The Samāj was open to all without distinction of colour, creed, caste, nation, or religion.

The real organizer of the Samāj was Devendranath Tagore (1817-1905), the father of the poet Rabindranath. His physical and spiritual beauty, aristocratic aloofness, penetrating intellect, and poetic sensibility made him the foremost leader of the educated Bengalis. These addressed him by the respectful epithet of Maharshi, the "Great Seer". The Maharshi was a Sanskrit scholar and, unlike Rājā Rammohan Roy, drew his inspiration entirely from the Upanishads. He was an implacable enemy of image worship and also fought to stop the infiltration of Christian ideas into the Samāj. He gave the movement its faith and ritual. Under his influence the

Brāhmo Samāj professed One Self-existent Supreme Being who had created the universe out of nothing, the God of Truth, Infinite Wisdom, Goodness, and Power, the Eternal and Omnipotent, the One without a Second. Man should love Him and do His will, believe in Him and worship Him, and thus merit salvation in the world to come.

By far the ablest leader of the Brāhmo movement was Keshab Chandra Sen (1838-1884). Unlike Rāja Rammohan Roy and Devendranath Tagore, Keshab was born of a middle-class Bengali family and had been brought up in an English school. He did not know Sanskrit and very soon broke away from the popular Hindu religion. Even at an early age he came under the spell of Christ and professed to have experienced the special favour of John the Baptist, Christ, and St. Paul. When he strove to introduce Christ to the Brāhmo Samāj, a rupture became inevitable with Devendranath. In 1868 Keshab broke with the older leader and founded the Brāhmo Samāj of India, Devendra retaining leadership of the first Brāhmo Samāj, now called the Ādi Samāj.

Keshab possessed a complex nature. When passing through a great moral crisis, he spent much of his time in solitude and felt that he heard the voice of God. When a devotional form of worship was introduced into the Brāhmo Samāj, he spent hours in singing kirtan with his followers. He visited England in 1870 and impressed the English people with his musical voice, his simple English, and his spiritual fervour. He was entertained by Queen Victoria. Returning to India, he founded centres of the Brāhmo Samāj in various parts of the country. Not unlike a professor of comparative religion in a European university, he began to discover, about the time of his first contact with Sri Ramakrishna, the harmony of religions. He became sympathetic toward the Hindu gods and goddesses, explaining them in a liberal fashion. Further, he believed that he was called by God to dictate to the world God's newly revealed law, the New Dispensation, the Navavidhān.

In 1878 a schism divided Keshab's Samāj. Some of his influential followers accused him of infringing the Brāhmo principles by marrying his daughter to a wealthy man before she had attained the marriageable age approved by the Samāj. This group seceded and established the Sādhāran Brāhmo Samāj, Keshab remaining the leader of the Navavidhān. Keshab now began to be drawn more and more toward the Christ ideal, though under the influence of Sri Ramakrishna his devotion to the Divine Mother also deepened. His mental oscillation between Christ and the Divine Mother of Hinduism found no position of rest. In Bengal and some other parts of India the Brāhmo movement took the form of unitarian Christianity, scoffed at Hindu rituals, and preached a crusade against image worship. Influenced by Western culture, it declared the supremacy of reason, advocated the ideals of the French Revolution, abolished the caste-system among its own members, stood for the emancipation of women, agitated for the abolition of early marriage, sanctioned the remarriage of widows, and encouraged various educational and social-reform movements. The immediate effect of the Brāhmo movement in Bengal was the checking of the proselytizing activities of the Christian missionaries. It also raised Indian culture in the estimation of its English masters. But it was an intellectual and eclectic religious ferment born of the necessity of the time. Unlike Hinduism, it was not founded on the deep inner experiences of sages and prophets. Its influence was confined to a comparatively few educated men and women of the country, and the vast masses of the Hindus remained outside it. It sounded monotonously only one of the notes in the rich gamut of the Eternal Religion of the Hindus.

ĀRYA SAMĀJ

The other movement playing an important part in the nineteenth-century religious revival of India was the Ārya Samāj. The Brāhmo Samāj, essentially a movement of compromise with European culture, tacitly admitted the superiority of the West. But the founder of the Ārya Samāj was a pugnacious Hindu sannyāsi who accepted the challenge of Islām and Christianity and was resolved to combat all foreign influence in India. Swami Dayananda (1824-1883) launched this movement in Bombay in 1875, and soon its influence was felt throughout western India. The Swami was a great scholar of the Vedas, which he explained as being strictly monotheistic. He preached against the worship of images and re-established the ancient Vedic sacrificial rites. According to him the Vedas were the ultimate authority on religion, and he accepted every word of them as literally true. The Ārya Samāj became a bulwark against the encroachments of Islām and Christianity, and its orthodox flavour appealed to many Hindu minds. It also assumed leadership in many movements of social reform. The caste-system became a target of its attack. Women it liberated from many of their social disabilities. The cause of education received from it a great impetus. It started agitation against early marriage and advocated the remarriage of Hindu widows. Its influence was strongest in the Punjab, the battle-ground of the Hindu and Islāmic cultures. A new fighting attitude was introduced into the slumbering Hindu society. Unlike the Brāhmo Samāj, the influence of the Ārya Samāj was not confined to the intellectuals. It was a force that spread to the masses. It was a dogmatic movement intolerant of those who disagreed with its views, and it emphasized only one way, the Ārya Samāj way, to the realization of Truth. Sri Ramakrishna met Swami Dayananda when the latter visited Bengal.

KESHAB CHANDRA SEN

Keshab Chandra Sen and Sri Ramakrishna met for the first time in the garden house of Jaygopal Sen at Belghariā, a few miles from Dakshineswar, where the great Brāhmo leader was staying with some of his disciples. In many respects the two were poles apart, though an irresistible inner attraction was to make them intimate friends. The Master had realized God as Pure Spirit and Consciousness, but he believed in the various forms of God as well. Keshab, on the other hand, regarded image worship as idolatry and gave allegorical explanations of the Hindu deities. Keshab was an orator and a writer of books and magazine articles; Sri Ramakrishna had a horror of lecturing and hardly knew how to write his own name. Keshab's fame spread

far and wide, even reaching the distant shores of England; the Master still
led a secluded life in the village of Dakshineswar. Keshab emphasized social
reforms for India's regeneration; to Sri Ramakrishna God-realization was
the only goal of life. Keshab considered himself a disciple of Christ and
accepted in a diluted form the Christian sacraments and Trinity; Sri Ramakrishna was the simple child of Kāli, the Divine Mother, though he too,
in a different way, acknowledged Christ's divinity. Keshab was a householder and took a real interest in the welfare of his children, whereas Sri
Ramakrishna was a paramahamsa and completely indifferent to the life of
the world. Yet, as their acquaintance ripened into friendship, Sri Ramakrishna and Keshab held each other in great love and respect. Years later,
at the news of Keshab's death, the Master felt as if half his body had become paralyzed. Keshab's concepts of the harmony of religions and the
Motherhood of God were deepened and enriched by his contact with Sri
Ramakrishna.

Sri Ramakrishna, dressed in a red-bordered dhoti, one end of which was
carelessly thrown over his left shoulder, came to Jaygopal's garden house
accompanied by Hriday. No one took notice of the unostentatious visitor.
Finally the Master said to Keshab, "People tell me you have seen God; so
I have come to hear from you about God." A magnificent conversation followed. The Master sang a thrilling song about Kāli and forthwith went into
samādhi. When Hriday uttered the sacred "Om" in his ears, he gradually
came back to consciousness of the world, his face still radiating a divine
brilliance. Keshab and his followers were amazed. The contrast between Sri
Ramakrishna and the Brāhmo devotees was very interesting. There sat this
small man, thin and extremely delicate. His eyes were illumined with an
inner light. Good humour gleamed in his eyes and lurked in the corners
of his mouth. His speech was Bengali of a homely kind with a slight, delightful stammer, and his words held men enthralled by their wealth of
spiritual experience, their inexhaustible store of simile and metaphor, their
power of observation, their bright and subtle humour, their wonderful
catholicity, their ceaseless flow of wisdom. And around him now were the
sophisticated men of Bengal, the best products of Western education, with
Keshab, the idol of young Bengal, as their leader.

Keshab's sincerity was enough for Sri Ramakrishna. Henceforth the two
saw each other frequently, either at Dakshineswar or at the temple of the
Brāhmo Samāj. Whenever the Master was in the temple at the time of
divine service, Keshab would request him to speak to the congregation. And
Keshab would visit the saint, in his turn, with offerings of flowers and
fruits.

OTHER BRĀHMO LEADERS

Gradually other Brāhmo leaders began to feel Sri Ramakrishna's influence. But they were by no means uncritical admirers of the Master. They
particularly disapproved of his ascetic renunciation and condemnation of
"woman and gold".[7] They measured him according to their own ideals of

[7] See foot-note, p. 82.

the householder's life. Some could not understand his samādhi and described it as a nervous malady. Yet they could not resist his magnetic personality.

Among the Brāhmo leaders who knew the Master closely were Pratap Chandra Mazumdar, Vijaykrishna Goswami, Trailokyanath Sannyal, and Shivanath Shastri.

Shivanath, one day, was greatly impressed by the Master's utter simplicity and abhorrence of praise. He was seated with Sri Ramakrishna in the latter's room when several rich men of Calcutta arrived. The Master left the room for a few minutes. In the mean time Hriday, his nephew, began to describe his samādhi to the visitors. The last few words caught the Master's ear as he entered the room. He said to Hriday: "What a mean-spirited fellow you must be to extol me thus before these rich men! You have seen their costly apparel and their gold watches and chains, and your object is to get from them as much money as you can. What do I care about what they think of me? (*Turning to the gentlemen*) No, my friends, what he has told you about me is not true. It was not love of God that made me absorbed in God and indifferent to external life. I became positively insane for some time. The sādhus who frequented this temple told me to practise many things. I tried to follow them, and the consequence was that my austerities drove me to insanity." This is a quotation from one of Shivanath's books. He took the Master's words literally and failed to see their real import.

Shivanath vehemently criticized the Master for his other-worldly attitude toward his wife. He writes: "Ramakrishna was practically separated from his wife, who lived in her village home. One day when I was complaining to some friends about the virtual widowhood of his wife, he drew me to one side and whispered in my ear: 'Why do you complain? It is no longer possible; it is all dead and gone.' Another day as I was inveighing against this part of his teaching, and also declaring that our program of work in the Brāhmo Samāj includes women, that ours is a social and domestic religion, and that we want to give education and social liberty to women, the·saint became very much excited, as was his way when anything against his settled conviction was asserted—a trait we so much liked in him—and exclaimed, 'Go, thou fool, go and perish in the pit that your women will dig for you.' Then he glared at me and said: 'What does a gardener do with a young plant? Does he not surround it with a fence, to protect it from goats and cattle? And when the young plant has grown up into a tree and it can no longer be injured by cattle, does he not remove the fence and let the tree grow freely?' I replied, 'Yes, that is the custom with gardeners.' Then he remarked, 'Do the same in your spiritual life; become strong, be full-grown; then you may seek them.' To which I replied, 'I don't agree with you in thinking that women's work is like that of cattle, destructive; they are our associates and helpers in our spiritual struggles and social progress'—a view with which he could not agree, and he marked his dissent by shaking his head. Then referring to the lateness of the hour he jocularly remarked, 'It is time for you to depart; take care, do not be late; otherwise *your woman* will not admit you into her room.' This evoked hearty laughter."

Pratap Chandra Mazumdar, the right-hand man of Keshab and an accomplished Brāhmo preacher in Europe and America, bitterly criticized Sri Ramakrishna's use of uncultured language and also his austere attitude toward his wife. But he could not escape the spell of the Master's personality. In the course of an article about Sri Ramakrishna, Pratap wrote in the "Theistic Quarterly Review": "What is there in common between him and me? I, a Europeanized, civilized, self-centred, semi-sceptical, so-called educated reasoner, and he, a poor, illiterate, unpolished, half-idolatrous, friendless Hindu devotee? Why should I sit long hours to attend to him, I, who have listened to Disraeli and Fawcett, Stanley and Max Müller, and a whole host of European scholars and divines? . . . And it is not I only, but dozens like me, who do the same. . . . He worships Śiva, he worships Kāli, he worships Rāma, he worships Krishna, and is a confirmed advocate of Vedāntic doctrines. . . . He is an idolater, yet is a faithful and most devoted meditator on the perfections of the One Formless, Absolute, Infinite Deity. . . . His religion is ecstasy, his worship means transcendental insight, his whole nature burns day and night with a permanent fire and fever of a strange faith and feeling. . . . So long as he is spared to us, gladly shall we sit at his feet to learn from him the sublime precepts of purity, unworldliness, spirituality, and inebriation in the love of God. . . . He, by his childlike bhakti, by his strong conceptions of an ever-ready Motherhood, helped to unfold it [God as our Mother] in our minds wonderfully. . . . By associating with him we learnt to realize better the divine attributes as scattered over the three hundred and thirty millions of deities of mythological India, the gods of the Purānas."

The Brāhmo leaders received much inspiration from their contact with Sri Ramakrishna. It broadened their religious views and kindled in their hearts the yearning for God-realization; it made them understand and appreciate the rituals and symbols of Hindu religion, convinced them of the manifestation of God in diverse forms, and deepened their thoughts about the harmony of religions. The Master, too, was impressed by the sincerity of many of the Brāhmo devotees. He told them about his own realizations and explained to them the essence of his teachings, such as the necessity of renunciation, sincerity in the pursuit of one's own course of discipline, faith in God, the performance of one's duties without thought of results, and discrimination between the Real and the unreal.

This contact with the educated and progressive Bengalis opened Sri Ramakrishna's eyes to a new realm of thought. Born and brought up in a simple village, without any formal education, and taught by the orthodox holy men of India in religious life, he had had no opportunity to study the influence of modernism on the thoughts and lives of the Hindus. He could not properly estimate the result of the impact of Western education on Indian culture. He was a Hindu of the Hindus, renunciation being to him the only means to the realization of God in life. From the Brāhmos he learnt that the new generation of India made a compromise between God and the world. Educated young men were influenced more by the Western philosophers than by their own prophets. But Sri Ramakrishna was not dismayed, for he saw in this, too, the hand of God. And though he expounded to the Brāhmos all his ideas about God and austere religious disciplines, yet he bade them accept from his teachings only as much as suited their tastes and temperaments.

THE MASTER'S YEARNING FOR HIS OWN DEVOTEES

Contact with the Brāhmos increased Sri Ramakrishna's longing to encounter aspirants who would be able to follow his teachings in their purest form. "There was no limit", he once declared, "to the longing I felt at that time. During the day-time I somehow managed to control it. The secular talk of the worldly-minded was galling to me, and I would look wistfully to the day when my own beloved companions would come. I hoped to find solace in conversing with them and relating to them my own realizations. Every little incident would remind me of them, and thoughts of them wholly engrossed me. I was already arranging in my mind what I should say to one and give to another, and so on. But when the day would come to a close I would not be able to curb my feelings. The thought that another day had gone by, and they had not come, oppressed me. When, during the evening service, the temples rang with the sound of bells and conch-shells, I would climb to the roof of the kuthi in the garden and, writhing in anguish of heart, cry at the top of my voice: 'Come, my children! Oh, where are you? I cannot bear to live without you.' A mother never longed so intensely for the sight of her child, nor a friend for his companions, nor a lover for his sweetheart, as I longed for them. Oh, it was indescribable! Shortly after this period of yearning the devotees[8] began to come."

In the year 1879 occasional writings about Sri Ramakrishna by the Brāhmos, in the Brāhmo magazines, began to attract his future disciples from the educated middle-class Bengalis, and they continued to come till 1884. But others, too, came, feeling the subtle power of his attraction. They were an ever shifting crowd of people of all castes and creeds: Hindus and Brāhmos, Vaishnavas and Śāktas, the educated with university degrees and the illiterate, old and young, mahārājās and beggars, journalists and artists, pundits and devotees, philosophers and the worldly-minded, jnānis and yogis, men of action and men of faith, virtuous women and prostitutes, office-holders and vagabonds, philanthropists and self-seekers, dramatists and drunkards, builders-up and pullers-down. He gave to them all, without stint, from his illimitable store of realization. No one went away empty-handed. He taught them the lofty knowledge of the Vedānta and the soul-melting love of the Purāna. Twenty hours out of twenty-four he would speak without rest or respite. He gave to all his sympathy and enlightenment, and he touched them with that strange power of the soul which could not but melt

---

[8] The word is generally used in the text to denote one devoted to God, a worshipper of the Personal God, or a follower of the path of love. A devotee of Sri Ramakrishna is one who is devoted to Sri Ramakrishna and follows his teachings. The word "disciple", when used in connexion with Sri Ramakrishna, refers to one who had been initiated into spiritual life by Sri Ramakrishna and who regarded him as his guru.

even the most hardened. And people understood him according to their powers of comprehension.

But he remained as ever the willing instrument in the hand of God, the child of the Divine Mother, totally untouched by the idea of being a teacher. He used to say that three ideas—that he was a guru, a father, and a master —pricked his flesh like thorns. Yet he was an extraordinary teacher. He stirred his disciples' hearts more by a subtle influence than by actions or words. He never claimed to be the founder of a religion or the organizer of a sect. Yet he was a religious dynamo. He was the verifier of all religions and creeds. He was like an expert gardener, who prepares the soil and removes the weeds, knowing that the plants will grow because of the inherent power of the seeds, producing each its appropriate flowers and fruits. He never thrust his ideas on anybody. He understood people's limitations and worked on the principle that what is good for one may be bad for another. He had the unusual power of knowing the devotees' minds, even their inmost souls, at the first sight. He accepted disciples with the full knowledge of their past tendencies and future possibilities. The life of evil did not frighten him, nor did religious squeamishness raise anybody in his estimation. He saw in everything the unerring finger of the Divine Mother. Even the light that leads astray was to him the light from God.

To those who became his intimate disciples the Master was a friend, companion, and playmate. Even the chores of religious discipline would be lightened in his presence. The devotees would be so inebriated with pure joy in his company that they would have no time to ask themselves whether he was an Incarnation, a perfect soul, or a yogi. His very presence was a great teaching; words were superfluous. In later years his disciples remarked that while they were with him they would regard him as a comrade, but afterwards would tremble to think of their frivolities in the presence of such a great person. They had convincing proof that the Master could, by his mere wish, kindle in their hearts the love of God and give them His vision.

Through all this fun and frolic, this merriment and frivolity, he always kept before them the shining ideal of God-Consciousness and the path of renunciation. He prescribed ascents steep or graded according to the powers of the climber. He permitted no compromise with the basic principles of purity. An aspirant had to keep his body, mind, senses, and soul unspotted; had to have a sincere love for God and an ever mounting spirit of yearning. The rest would be done by the Mother.

His disciples were of two kinds: the householders, and the young men, some of whom were later to become monks. There was also a small group of women devotees.

HOUSEHOLDER DEVOTEES

For the householders Sri Ramakrishna did not prescribe the hard path of total renunciation. He wanted them to discharge their obligations to their families. Their renunciation was to be mental. Spiritual life could not be acquired by flying away from responsibilities. A married couple should live like brother and sister after the birth of one or two children, devoting their time to spiritual talk and contemplation. He encouraged the householders, saying that their life was, in a way, easier than that of the monk, since it was more advantageous to fight the enemy from inside a fortress than in an open field. He insisted, however, on their repairing into solitude every now and then to strengthen their devotion and faith in God through prayer, japa, and meditation. He prescribed for them the companionship of sādhus. He asked them to perform their worldly duties with one hand, while holding to God with the other, and to pray to God to make their duties fewer and fewer so that in the end they might cling to Him with both hands. He would discourage in both the householders and the celibate youths any lukewarmness in their spiritual struggles. He would not ask them to follow indiscriminately the ideal of non-resistance, which ultimately makes a coward of the unwary.

FUTURE MONKS

But to the young men destined to be monks he pointed out the steep path of renunciation, both external and internal. They must take the vow of absolute continence and eschew all thought of greed and lust. By the practice of continence, aspirants develop a subtle nerve through which they understand the deeper mysteries of God. For them self-control is final, imperative, and absolute. The sannyāsis are teachers of men, and their lives should be totally free from blemish. They must not even look at a picture which may awaken their animal passions. The Master selected his future monks from young men untouched by "woman and gold" and plastic enough to be cast in his spiritual mould. When teaching them the path of renunciation and discrimination, he would not allow the householders to be anywhere near them.

RAM AND MANOMOHAN

The first two householder devotees to come to Dakshineswar were Ramchandra Dutta and Manomohan Mitra. A medical practitioner and chemist, Ram was sceptical about God and religion and never enjoyed peace of soul. He wanted tangible proof of God's existence. The Master said to him: "God really exists. You don't see the stars in the day-time, but that doesn't mean that the stars do not exist. There is butter in milk. But can anybody see it by merely looking at the milk? To get butter you must churn milk in a quiet and cool place. You cannot realize God by a mere wish; you must go through some mental disciplines." By degrees the Master awakened Ram's spirituality and the latter became one of his foremost lay disciples. It was Ram who introduced Narendranath to Sri Ramakrishna. Narendra was a relative of Ram.

Manomohan at first met with considerable opposition from his wife and other relatives, who resented his visits to Dakshineswar. But in the end the unselfish love of the Master triumphed over worldly affection. It was Manomohan who brought Rakhal to the Master.

SURENDRA

Suresh Mitra, a beloved disciple whom the Master often addressed as Surendra, had received an English education and held an important post in an English firm. Like many other educated young men of the time, he prided himself on his atheism and led a Bohemian life. He was addicted to drinking. He cherished an exaggerated notion about man's free will. A victim of mental depression, he was brought to Sri Ramakrishna by Ramchandra Dutta. When he heard the Master asking a disciple to practise the virtue of self-surrender to God, he was impressed. But though he tried thenceforth to do so, he was unable to give up his old associates and his drinking. One day the Master said in his presence, "Well, when a man goes to an undesirable place, why doesn't he take the Divine Mother with him?" And to Surendra himself Sri Ramakrishna said: "Why should you drink wine as wine? Offer it to Kāli, and then take it as Her prasād, as consecrated drink. But see that you don't become intoxicated; you must not reel and your thoughts must not wander. At first you will feel ordinary excitement, but soon you will experience spiritual exaltation." Gradually Surendra's entire life was changed. The Master designated him as one of those commissioned by the Divine Mother to defray a great part of his expenses. Surendra's purse was always open for the Master's comfort.

KEDAR

Kedarnath Chatterji was endowed with a spiritual temperament and had tried various paths of religion, some not very commendable. When he met the Master at Dakshineswar he understood the true meaning of religion. It is said that the Master, weary of instructing devotees who were coming to him in great numbers for guidance, once prayed to the Goddess Kāli: "Mother, I am tired of speaking to people. Please give power to Kedar, Girish, Ram, Vijay, and Mahendra to give them the preliminary instruction, so that just a little teaching from me will be enough." He was aware, however, of Kedar's lingering attachment to worldly things and often warned him about it.

HARISH

Harish, a young man in affluent circumstances, renounced his family and took shelter with the Master, who loved him for his sincerity, singleness of purpose, and quiet nature. He spent his leisure time in prayer and meditation, turning a deaf ear to the entreaties and threats of his relatives. Referring to his undisturbed peace of mind, the Master would say: "Real men are dead to the world though living. Look at Harish. He is an example." When one day the Master asked him to be a little kind to his wife, Harish said: "You must excuse me on this point. This is not the place to show kindness. If I try to be sympathetic to her, there is a possibility of my forgetting the ideal and becoming entangled in the world."

BHAVANATH

Bhavanath Chatterji visited the Master while he was still in his teens. His parents and relatives regarded Sri Ramakrishna as an insane person and tried their utmost to prevent him from becoming intimate with the Master. But the young boy was very stubborn and often spent nights at Dakshineswar. He was greatly attached to Narendra, and the Master encouraged their friendship. The very sight of him often awakened Sri Ramakrishna's spiritual emotion.

BALARAM BOSE

Balaram Bose came of a wealthy Vaishnava family. From his youth he had shown a deep religious temperament and had devoted his time to meditation, prayer, and the study of the Vaishnava scriptures. He was very much impressed by Sri Ramakrishna even at their first meeting. He asked Sri Ramakrishna whether God really existed and, if so, whether a man could realize Him. The Master said: "God reveals Himself to the devotee who thinks of Him as his nearest and dearest. Because you do not draw response by praying to Him once, you must not conclude that He does not exist. Pray to God, thinking of Him as dearer than your very self. He is much attached to His devotees. He comes to a man even before He is sought. There is none more intimate and affectionate than God." Balaram had never before heard God spoken of in such forceful words; every one of the words seemed true to him. Under the Master's influence he outgrew the conventions of the Vaishnava worship and became one of the most beloved of the disciples. It was at his home that the Master slept whenever he spent a night in Calcutta.

MAHENDRA OR M.

Mahendranath Gupta, known as "M.", arrived at Dakshineswar in February 1882. He belonged to the Brāhmo Samāj and was headmaster of the Vidyāsāgar High School at Śyāmbāzār, Calcutta. At the very first sight the Master recognized him as one of his "marked" disciples. Mahendra recorded in his diary Sri Ramakrishna's conversations with his devotees. These are the first directly recorded words, in the spiritual history of the world, of a man recognized as belonging in the class of Buddha and Christ. The present volume is a translation of this diary. Mahendra was instrumental, through his personal contacts, in spreading the Master's message among many young and aspiring souls.

NAG MAHĀSHAY

Durgacharan Nag, also known as Nag Mahāshay, was the ideal householder among the lay disciples of Sri Ramakrishna. He was the embodiment of the Master's ideal of life in the world, unstained by worldliness. In spite of his intense desire to become a sannyāsi, Sri Ramakrishna asked him to live in the world in the spirit of a monk, and the disciple truly carried out this injunction. He was born of a poor family and even during his boyhood often sacrificed everything to lessen the sufferings of the needy. He had married at an early age and after his wife's death had married a second time to obey his father's command. But he once said to his wife: "Love on the physical level never lasts. He is indeed blessed who can give his love to God with his whole heart. Even a little attachment to the body endures for several births. So do not be attached to this cage of bone and flesh. Take shelter at the feet of the Mother and think of Her alone. Thus your life here and hereafter will be ennobled." The Master spoke of him as a "blazing light". He received every word of Sri Ramakrishna in dead earnest. One day he heard the Master saying that it was difficult for doctors, lawyers, and brokers to make much progress in spirituality. Of doctors he said, "If the mind clings to the tiny drops of medicine, how can it conceive of the Infinite?" That was the end of Durgacharan's medical practice and he threw his chest of medicines into the Ganges. Sri Ramakrishna assured him that he would not lack simple food and clothing. He bade him serve holy men. On being asked where he would find real holy men, the Master said that the sādhus themselves would seek his company. No sannyāsi could have lived a more austere life than Durgacharan.

GIRISH GHOSH

Girish Chandra Ghosh was a born rebel against God, a sceptic, a Bohemian, a drunkard. He was the greatest Bengali dramatist of his time, the father of the modern Bengali stage. Like other young men he had imbibed all the vices of the West. He had plunged into a life of dissipation and had become convinced that religion was only a fraud. Materialistic philosophy he justified as enabling one to get at least a little fun out of life. But a series of reverses shocked him and he became eager to solve the riddle of life. He had heard people say that in spiritual life the help of a guru was imperative and that the guru was to be regarded as God Himself. But Girish was too well acquainted with human nature to see perfection in a man. His first meeting with Sri Ramakrishna did not impress him at all. He returned home feeling as if he had seen a freak at a circus; for the Master, in a semi-conscious mood, had inquired whether it was evening, though the lamps were burning in the room. But their paths often crossed, and Girish could not avoid further encounters. The Master attended a performance in Girish's Star Theatre. On this occasion, too, Girish found nothing impressive about him. One day, however, Girish happened to see the Master dancing and singing with the devotees. He felt the contagion and wanted to join them, but restrained himself for fear of ridicule. Another day Sri Ramakrishna was about to give him spiritual instruction, when Girish said: "I don't want to listen to instructions. I have myself written many instructions. They are of no use to me. Please help me in a more tangible way if you can." This pleased the Master and he asked Girish to cultivate faith.

As time passed, Girish began to learn that the guru is the one who silently unfolds the disciple's inner life. He became a steadfast devotee of the Master.

He often loaded the Master with insults, drank in his presence, and took liberties which astounded the other devotees. But the Master knew that at heart Girish was tender, faithful, and sincere. He would not allow Girish to give up the theatre. And when a devotee asked him to tell Girish to give up drinking, he sternly replied: "That is none of your business. He who has taken charge of him will look after him. Girish is a devotee of heroic type. I tell you, drinking will not affect him." The Master knew that mere words could not induce a man to break deep-rooted habits, but that the silent influence of love worked miracles. Therefore he never asked him to give up alcohol, with the result that Girish himself eventually broke the habit. Sri Ramakrishna had strengthened Girish's resolution by allowing him to feel that he was absolutely free.

One day Girish felt depressed because he was unable to submit to any routine of spiritual discipline. In an exalted mood the Master said to him: "All right, give me your power of attorney. Henceforth I assume responsibility for you. You need not do anything." Girish heaved a sigh of relief. He felt happy to think that Sri Ramakrishna had assumed his spiritual responsibilities. But poor Girish could not then realize that he also, on his part, had to give up his freedom and make of himself a puppet in Sri Ramakrishna's hands. The Master began to discipline him according to this new attitude. One day Girish said about a trifling matter, "Yes, I shall do this." "No, no!" the Master corrected him. "You must not speak in that egotistic manner. You should say, 'God willing, I shall do it.'" Girish understood. Thenceforth he tried to give up all idea of personal responsibility and surrender himself to the Divine Will. His mind began to dwell constantly on Sri Ramakrishna. This unconscious meditation in time chastened his turbulent spirit.

The householder devotees generally visited Sri Ramakrishna on Sunday afternoons and other holidays. Thus a brotherhood was gradually formed, and the Master encouraged their fraternal feeling. Now and then he would accept an invitation to a devotee's home, where other devotees would also be invited. Kirtan would be arranged and they would spend hours in dance and devotional music. The Master would go into trances or open his heart in religious discourses and in the narration of his own spiritual experiences. Many people who could not go to Dakshineswar participated in these meetings and felt blessed. Such an occasion would be concluded with a sumptuous feast.

But it was in the company of his younger devotees, pure souls yet unstained by the touch of worldliness, that Sri Ramakrishna took greatest joy. Among the young men who later embraced the householder's life were Narayan, Paltu, the younger Naren, Tejchandra, and Purna. These visited the Master sometimes against strong opposition from home.

PURNA

Purna was a lad of thirteen, whom Sri Ramakrishna described as an Iśvarakoti, a soul born with special spiritual qualities. The Master said that

Purna was the last of the group of brilliant devotees who, as he once had seen in a trance, would come to him for spiritual illumination. Purna said to Sri Ramakrishna during their second meeting, "You are God Himself incarnated in flesh and blood." Such words coming from a mere youngster proved of what stuff the boy was made.

MAHIMACHARAN AND PRATAP HAZRA

Mahimacharan and Pratap Hazra were two devotees outstanding for their pretentiousness and idiosyncrasies. But the Master showed them his unfailing love and kindness, though he was aware of their shortcomings. Mahimacharan Chakravarty had met the Master long before the arrival of the other disciples. He had had the intention of leading a spiritual life, but a strong desire to acquire name and fame was his weakness. He claimed to have been initiated by Totapuri and used to say that he had been following the path of knowledge according to his guru's instructions. He possessed a large library of English and Sanskrit books. But though he pretended to have read them, most of the leaves were uncut. The Master knew all his limitations, yet enjoyed listening to him recite from the Vedas and other scriptures. He would always exhort Mahima to meditate on the meaning of the scriptural texts and to practise spiritual discipline.

Pratap Hazra, a middle-aged man, hailed from a village near Kāmārpukur. He was not altogether unresponsive to religious feelings. On a moment's impulse he had left his home, aged mother, wife, and children, and had found shelter in the temple garden at Dakshineswar, where he intended to lead a spiritual life. He loved to argue, and the Master often pointed him out as an example of barren argumentation. He was hypercritical of others and cherished an exaggerated notion of his own spiritual advancement. He was mischievous and often tried to upset the minds of the Master's young disciples, criticizing them for their happy and joyous life and asking them to devote their time to meditation. The Master teasingly compared Hazra to Jatilā and Kutilā, the two women who always created obstructions in Krishna's sport with the gopis, and said that Hazra lived at Dakshineswar to "thicken the plot" by adding complications.

SOME NOTED MEN

Sri Ramakrishna also became acquainted with a number of people whose scholarship or wealth entitled them everywhere to respect. He had met, a few years before, Devendranath Tagore, famous all over Bengal for his wealth, scholarship, saintly character, and social position. But the Master found him disappointing; for, whereas Sri Ramakrishna expected of a saint complete renunciation of the world, Devendranath combined with his saint-liness a life of enjoyment. Sri Ramakrishna met the great poet Michael Madhusudan, who had embraced Christianity "for the sake of his stomach". To him the Master could not impart instruction, for the Divine Mother "pressed his tongue". In addition he met Mahārājā Jatindra Mohan Tagore, a titled aristocrat of Bengal; Kristodas Pal, the editor, social reformer, and patriot; Iswar Vidyāsāgar, the noted philanthropist and educator; Pundit

Shashadhar, a great champion of Hindu orthodoxy; Aswini Kumar Dutta, a headmaster, moralist, and leader of Indian Nationalism; and Bankim Chatterji, a deputy magistrate, novelist, and essayist, and one of the fashioners of modern Bengali prose. Sri Ramakrishna was not the man to be dazzled by outward show, glory, or eloquence. A pundit without discrimination he regarded as a mere straw. He would search people's hearts for the light of God, and if that was missing he would have nothing to do with them.

KRISTODAS PAL

The Europeanized Kristodas Pal did not approve of the Master's emphasis on renunciation and said: "Sir, this cant of renunciation has almost ruined the country. It is for this reason that the Indians are a subject nation today. Doing good to others, bringing education to the door of the ignorant, and above all, improving the material conditions of the country—these should be our duty now. The cry of religion and renunciation would, on the contrary, only weaken us. You should advise the young men of Bengal to resort only to such acts as will uplift the country." Sri Ramakrishna gave him a searching look and found no divine light within. "You man of poor understanding!" Sri Ramakrishna said sharply. "You dare to slight in these terms renunciation and piety, which our scriptures describe as the greatest of all virtues! After reading two pages of English you think you have come to know the world! You appear to think you are .omniscient. Well, have you seen those tiny crabs that are born in the Ganges just when the rains set in? In this big universe you are even less significant than one of those small creatures. How dare you talk of *helping* the world? The Lord will look to that. You haven't the power in you to do it." After a pause the Master continued: "Can you explain to me how you can work for others? I know what you mean by helping them. To feed a number of persons, to treat them when they are sick, to construct a road or dig a well—isn't that all? These are good deeds, no doubt, but how trifling in comparison with the vastness of the universe! How far can a man advance in this line? How many people can you save from famine? Malaria has ruined a whole province; what could you do to stop its onslaught? God alone looks after the world. Let a man first realize Him. Let a man get the authority from God and be endowed with His power; then, and then alone, may he think of doing good to others. A man should first be purged of all egotism. Then alone will the Blissful Mother ask him to work for the world." Sri Ramakrishna mistrusted philanthropy that presumed to pose as charity. He warned people against it. He saw in most acts of philanthropy nothing but egotism, vanity, a desire for glory, a barren excitement to kill the boredom of life, or an attempt to soothe a guilty conscience. True charity, he taught, is the result of love of God—service to man in a spirit of worship.

MONASTIC DISCIPLES

The disciples whom the Master trained for monastic life were the following:

Narendranath Dutta (Swami Vivekananda)

Rakhal Chandra Ghosh (Swami Brahmananda)

Gopal Chandra Ghosh (Swami Advaitananda)

Baburam Ghosh (Swami Premananda)

Taraknath Ghoshal (Swami Shivananda)

Jogindranath Choudhury (Swami Jogananda)

Sashibhushan Chakravarty (Swami Ramakrishnananda)

Saratchandra Chakravarty (Swami Saradananda)

Latu (Swami Adbhutananda)

Nitya Niranjan Sen (Swami Niranjanananda)

Kaliprasad Chandra (Swami Abhedananda)

Harinath Chattopadhyaya (Swami Turiyananda)

Sarada Prasanna (Swami Trigunatitananda)

Gangadhar Ghatak (Swami Akhandananda)

Subodh Ghosh (Swami Subodhananda)

Hariprasanna Chatterji (Swami Vijnanananda)

LATU

The first of these young men to come to the Master was Latu. Born of obscure parents, in Behar, he came to Calcutta in search of work and was engaged by Ramchandra Dutta as house-boy. Learning of the saintly Sri Ramakrishna, he visited the Master at Dakshineswar and was deeply touched by his cordiality. When he was about to leave, the Master asked him to take some money and return home in a boat or carriage. But Latu declared he had a few pennies and jingled the coins in his pocket. Sri Ramakrishna later requested Ram to allow Latu to stay with him permanently. Under Sri Ramakrishna's guidance Latu made great progress in meditation and was blessed with ecstatic visions, but all the efforts of the Master to give him a smattering of education failed. Latu was very fond of kirtan and other devotional songs but remained all his life illiterate.

RAKHAL

Even before Rakhal's coming to Dakshineswar, the Master had had visions of him as his spiritual son and as a playmate of Krishna at Vrindāvan. Rakhal was born of wealthy parents. During his childhood he developed wonderful spiritual traits and used to play at worshipping gods and goddesses. In his teens he was married to a sister of Manomohan Mitra, from whom he first heard of the Master. His father objected to his association with Sri Ramakrishna but afterwards was reassured to find that many celebrated people were visitors at Dakshineswar. The relationship between the Master and this beloved disciple was that of mother and child. Sri Ramakrishna allowed Rakhal many liberties denied to others. But he would not hesitate to chastise the boy for improper actions. At one time Rakhal felt a childlike jealousy because he found that other boys were receiving the Master's affection. He soon got over it and realized his guru as the Guru of the whole universe. The Master was worried to hear of his marriage, but was relieved to find that his wife was a spiritual soul who would not be a hindrance to his progress.

THE ELDER GOPAL

Gopal Chandra Ghosh came to Dakshineswar at a rather advanced age and was called the elder Gopal. He had lost his wife, and the Master assuaged his grief. Soon he renounced the world and devoted himself fully to meditation and prayer. Some years later Gopal gave the Master the ochre cloths with which the latter initiated several of his disciples into monastic life.

NARENDRA

To spread his message to the four corners of the earth Sri Ramakrishna needed a strong instrument. With his frail body and delicate limbs he could not make great journeys across wide spaces. And such an instrument was found in Narendranath Dutta, his beloved Naren, later known to the world as Swami Vivekananda. Even before meeting Narendranath, the Master had seen him in a vision as a sage, immersed in the meditation of the Absolute, who at Sri Ramakrishna's request had agreed to take human birth to assist him in his work.

Narendra was born in Calcutta on January 12, 1863, of an aristocratic kāyastha family. His mother was steeped in the great Hindu epics, and his father, a distinguished attorney of the Calcutta High Court, was an agnostic about religion, a friend of the poor, and a mocker at social conventions. Even in his boyhood and youth Narendra possessed great physical courage and presence of mind, a vivid imagination, deep power of thought, keen intelligence, an extraordinary memory, a love of truth, a passion for purity, a spirit of independence, and a tender heart. An expert musician, he also acquired proficiency in physics, astronomy, mathematics, philosophy, history, and literature. He grew up into an extremely handsome young man. Even as a child he practised meditation and showed great power of concentration. Though free and passionate in word and action, he took the vow of austere religious chastity and never allowed the fire of purity to be extinguished by the slightest defilement of body or soul.

As he read in college the rationalistic Western philosophers of the nineteenth century, his boyhood faith in God and religion was unsettled. He would not accept religion on mere faith; he wanted demonstration of God. But very soon his passionate nature discovered that mere Universal Reason was cold and bloodless. His emotional nature, dissatisfied with a mere abstraction, required a concrete support to help him in the hours of temptation. He wanted an external power, a guru, who by embodying perfection in the flesh would still the commotion of his soul. Attracted by the magnetic personality of Keshab, he joined the Brāhmo Samāj and became a singer in its choir. But in the Samāj he did not find the guru who could say that he had seen God.

In a state of mental conflict and torture of soul, Narendra came to Sri Ramakrishna at Dakshineswar. He was then eighteen years of age and had been in college two years. He entered the Master's room accompanied by some light-hearted friends. At Sri Ramakrishna's request he sang a few songs, pouring his whole soul into them, and the Master went into samādhi. A few minutes later Sri Ramakrishna suddenly left his seat, took Narendra by the hand, and led him to the screened verandah north of his room. They were alone. Addressing Narendra most tenderly, as if he were a friend of long acquaintance, the Master said: "Ah! You have come very late. Why have you been so unkind as to make me wait all these days? My ears are tired of hearing the futile words of worldly men. Oh, how I have longed to pour my spirit into the heart of someone fitted to receive my message!" He talked thus, sobbing all the time. Then, standing before Narendra with folded hands, he addressed him as Nārāyana, born on earth to remove the misery of humanity. Grasping Narendra's hand, he asked him to come again, alone, and very soon. Narendra was startled. "What is this I have come to see?" he said to himself. "He must be stark mad. Why, I am the son of Viswanath Dutta. How dare he speak this way to me?"

When they returned to the room and Narendra heard the Master speaking to others, he was surprised to find in his words an inner logic, a striking sincerity, and a convincing proof of his spiritual nature. In answer to Narendra's question, "Sir, have you seen God?" the Master said: "Yes, I have seen God. I have seen Him more tangibly than I see you. I have talked to Him more intimately than I am talking to you." Continuing, the Master said: "But, my child, who wants to see God? People shed jugs of tears for money, wife, and children. But if they would weep for God for only one day they would surely see Him." Narendra was amazed. These words he could not doubt. This was the first time he had ever heard a man saying that he had seen God. But he could not reconcile these words of the Master with the scene that had taken place on the verandah only a few minutes before. He concluded that Sri Ramakrishna was a monomaniac, and returned home rather puzzled in mind.

During his second visit, about a month later, suddenly, at the touch of the Master, Narendra felt overwhelmed and saw the walls of the room and everything around him whirling and vanishing. "What are you doing to me?" he cried in terror. "I have my father and mother at home." He saw his own ego and the whole universe almost swallowed in a nameless void. With a laugh the Master easily restored him. Narenda thought he might have been hypnotized, but he could not understand how a monomaniac could cast a spell over the mind of a strong person like himself. He returned home more confused than ever, resolved to be henceforth on his guard before this strange man.

But during his third visit Narendra fared no better. This time, at the Master's touch, he lost consciousness entirely. While he was still in that state, Sri Ramakrishna questioned him concerning his spiritual antecedents and whereabouts, his mission in this world, and the duration of his mortal life. The answers confirmed what the Master himself had known and inferred. Among other things, he came to know that Narendra was a sage who had already attained perfection, and that the day he learnt his real nature he would give up his body in yoga, by an act of will.

A few more meetings completely removed from Narendra's mind the last traces of the notion that Sri Ramakrishna might be a monomaniac or wily hypnotist. His integrity, purity, renunciation, and unselfishness were beyond question. But Narendra could not accept a man, an imperfect mortal, as his guru. As a member of the Brāhmo Samāj, he could not believe that a human intermediary was necessary between man and God. Moreover, he openly laughed at Sri Ramakrishna's visions as hallucinations. Yet in the secret chamber of his heart he bore a great love for the Master.

Sri Ramakrishna was grateful to the Divine Mother for sending him one who doubted his own realizations. Often he asked Narendra to test him as the money-changers test their coins. He laughed at Narendra's biting criticism of his spiritual experiences and samādhi. When at times Narendra's sharp words distressed him, the Divine Mother Herself would console him, saying: "Why do you listen to him? In a few days he will believe your every word." He could hardly bear Narendra's absences. Often he would weep bitterly for the sight of him. Sometimes Narendra would find the Master's love embarrassing; and one day he sharply scolded him, warning him that such infatuation would soon draw him down to the level of its object. The Master was distressed and prayed to the Divine Mother. Then he said to Narendra: "You rogue, I won't listen to you any more. Mother says that I love you because I see God in you, and the day I no longer see God in you I shall not be able to bear even the sight of you."

The Master wanted to train Narendra in the teachings of the non-dualistic Vedānta philosophy. But Narendra, because of his Brāhmo upbringing, considered it wholly blasphemous to look on man as one with his Creator. One day at the temple garden he laughingly said to a friend: "How silly! This jug is God! This cup is God! Whatever we see is God! And we too are God! Nothing could be more absurd." Sri Ramakrishna came out of his room and gently touched him. Spellbound, he immediately perceived that everything in the world was indeed God. A new universe opened around him. Returning home in a dazed state, he found there too that the food, the plate, the eater himself, the people around him, were all God. When he walked in the street, he saw that the cabs, the horses, the streams of people, the buildings, were all Brahman. He could hardly go about his day's business. His parents became anxious about him and thought him ill. And when the intensity of the experience abated a little, he saw the world as a dream. Walking in the public square, he would strike his head against the iron railings to know whether they were real. It took him a number of days to recover his normal self. He had a foretaste of the great experiences yet to come and realized that the words of the Vedānta were true.

At the beginning of 1884 Narendra's father suddenly died of heart-failure, leaving the family in a state of utmost poverty. There were six or seven mouths to feed at home. Creditors were knocking at the door. Relatives who had accepted his father's unstinted kindness now became enemies, some even bringing suit to deprive Narendra of his ancestral home. Actually starving and barefoot, Narendra searched for a job, but without success. He began to doubt whether anywhere in the world there was such a thing as unselfish sympathy. Two rich women made evil proposals to him and promised to put an end to his distress; but he refused them with contempt.

Narendra began to talk of his doubt of the very existence of God. His friends thought he had become an atheist and piously circulated gossip adducing unmentionable motives for his unbelief. His moral character was maligned. Even some of the Master's disciples partly believed the gossip, and Narendra told these to their faces that only a coward believed in God through fear of suffering or hell. But he was distressed to think that Sri Ramakrishna, too, might believe these false reports. His pride revolted. He said to himself: "What does it matter? If a man's good name rests on such slender foundations, I don't care." But later on he was amazed to learn that the Master had never lost faith in him. To a disciple who complained about Narendra's degradation, Sri Ramakrishna replied: "Hush, you fool! The Mother has told me it can never be so. I won't look at you if you speak that way again."

The moment came when Narendra's distress reached its climax. He had gone the whole day without food. As he was returning home in the evening he could hardly lift his tired limbs. He sat down in front of a house in sheer exhaustion, too weak even to think. His mind began to wander. Then, suddenly, a divine power lifted the veil over his soul. He found the solution of the problem of the coexistence of divine justice and misery, the presence of suffering in the creation of a blissful Providence. He felt bodily refreshed, his soul was bathed in peace, and he slept serenely.

Narendra now realized that he had a spiritual mission to fulfil. He resolved to renounce the world, as his grandfather had renounced it, and he came to Sri Ramakrishna for his blessing. But even before he had opened his mouth, the Master knew what was in his mind and wept bitterly at the thought of separation. "I know you cannot lead a worldly life," he said, "but for my sake live in the world as long as I live."

One day, soon after, Narendra requested Sri Ramakrishna to pray to the Divine Mother to remove his poverty. Sri Ramakrishna bade him pray to Her himself, for She would certainly listen to his prayer. Narendra entered the shrine of Kāli. As he stood before the image of the Mother, he beheld Her as a living Goddess, ready to give wisdom and liberation. Unable to ask Her for petty worldly things, he prayed only for knowledge and renunciation, love and liberation. The Master rebuked him for his failure to ask the Divine Mother to remove his poverty and sent him back to the temple. But Narendra, standing in Her presence, again forgot the purpose of his coming. Thrice he went to the temple at the bidding of the Master, and thrice he returned, having forgotten in Her presence why he had come. He was wondering about it when it suddenly flashed in his mind that this was all the work of Sri Ramakrishna; so now he asked the Master himself to remove his poverty, and was assured that his family would not lack simple food and clothing.

This was a very rich and significant experience for Narendra. It taught him that Śakti, the Divine Power, cannot be ignored in the world and that in the relative plane the need of worshipping a Personal God is imperative. Sri Ramakrishna was overjoyed with the conversion. The next day, sitting almost on Narendra's lap, he said to a devotee, pointing first to himself, then to Narendra: "I see I am this, and again that. Really I feel no difference. A stick floating in the Ganges seems to divide the water; but in reality the water is one. Do you see my point? Well, whatever is, is the Mother—isn't that so?" In later years Narendra would say: "Sri Ramakrishna was the only person who, from the time he met me, believed in me uniformly throughout. Even my mother and brothers did not. It was his unwavering trust and love for me that bound me to him for ever. He alone knew how to love. Worldly people only make a show of love for selfish ends."

TARAK

Others destined to be monastic disciples of Sri Ramakrishna came to Dakshineswar. Taraknath Ghoshal had felt from his boyhood the noble desire to realize God. Keshab and the Brāhmo Samāj had attracted him but proved inadequate. In 1882 he first met the Master at Ramchandra's house and was astonished to hear him talk about samādhi, a subject which always fascinated his mind. And that evening he actually saw a manifestation of that superconscious state in the Master. Tarak became a frequent visitor at Dakshineswar and received the Master's grace in abundance. The young boy often felt ecstatic fervour in meditation. He also wept profusely while meditating on God. Sri Ramakrishna said to him: "God favours those who can weep for Him. Tears shed for God wash away the sins of former births."

BABURAM

Baburam Ghosh came to Dakshineswar accompanied by Rakhal, his classmate. The Master, as was often his custom, examined the boy's physiognomy and was satisfied about his latent spirituality. At the age of eight Baburam had thought of leading a life of renunciation, in the company of a monk, in a hut shut out from the public view by a thick wall of trees. The very sight of the Panchavati awakened in his heart that dream of boyhood. Baburam was tender in body and soul. The Master used to say that he was pure to his very bones. One day Hazra in his usual mischievous fashion advised Baburam and some of the other young boys to ask Sri Ramakrishna for some spiritual powers and not waste their life in mere gaiety and merriment. The Master, scenting mischief, called Baburam to his side and said: "What can you ask of me? Isn't everything that I have already yours? Yes, everything I have earned in the shape of realizations is for the sake of you all. So get rid of the idea of begging, which alienates by creating a distance. Rather realize your kinship with me and gain the key to all the treasures."

NIRANJAN

Nitya Niranjan Sen was a disciple of heroic type. He came to the Master when he was eighteen years old. He was a medium for a group of spiritualists. During his first visit the Master said to him: "My boy, if you think always of ghosts you will become a ghost, and if you think of God you will become God. Now, which do you prefer?" Niranjan severed all connexions with the spiritualists. During his second visit the Master embraced him and said warmly: "Niranjan, my boy, the days are flitting away. When will you realize God? This life will be in vain if you do not realize Him. When will you devote your mind wholly to God?" Niranjan was surprised to see the Master's great anxiety for his spiritual welfare. He was a young man endowed with unusual spiritual parts. He felt disdain for worldly pleasures and was totally guileless, like a child. But he had a violent temper. One day, as he was coming in a country boat to Dakshineswar, some of his fellow passengers began to speak ill of the Master. Finding his protest futile, Niranjan began to rock the boat, threatening to sink it in mid stream. That silenced the offenders. When he reported the incident to the Master, he was rebuked for his inability to curb his anger.

JOGINDRA

Jogindranath, on the other hand, was gentle to a fault. One day, under circumstances very like those that had evoked Niranjan's anger, he curbed his temper and held his peace instead of threatening Sri Ramakrishna's abusers. The Master, learning of his conduct, scolded him roundly. Thus to each the fault of the other was recommended as a virtue. The guru was striving to develop, in the first instance, composure, and in the second, mettle. The secret of his training was to build up, by a tactful recognition of the requirements of each given case, the character of the devotee.

Jogindranath came of an aristocratic brāhmin family of Dakshineswar. His father and relatives shared the popular mistrust of Sri Ramakrishna's sanity. At a very early age the boy developed religious tendencies, spending two or three hours daily in meditation, and his meeting with Sri Ramakrishna deepened his desire for the realization of God. He had a perfect horror of marriage. But at the earnest request of his mother he had had to yield, and he now believed that his spiritual future was doomed. So he kept himself away from the Master.

Sri Ramakrishna employed a ruse to bring Jogindra to him. As soon as the disciple entered the room, the Master rushed forward to meet the young man. Catching hold of the disciple's hand, he said: "What if you have married? Haven't I too married? What is there to be afraid of in that?" Touching his own chest he said: "If this [meaning himself] is propitious, then even a hundred thousand marriages cannot injure you. If you desire to lead a householder's life, then bring your wife here one day, and I shall see that she becomes a real companion in your spiritual progress. But if you want to lead a monastic life, then I shall eat up your attachment to the world." Jogin was dumbfounded at these words. He received new strength, and his spirit of renunciation was re-established.

SASHI AND SARAT

Sashi and Sarat were two cousins who came from a pious brāhmin family of Calcutta. At an early age they had joined the Brāhmo Samāj and had come under the influence of Keshab Sen. The Master said to them at their first meeting: "If bricks and tiles are burnt after the trade-mark has been stamped on them, they retain the mark for ever. Similarly, man should be stamped with God before entering the world. Then he will not become attached to worldliness." Fully aware of the future course of their life, he asked them not to marry. The Master asked Sashi whether he believed in God with form or in God without form. Sashi replied that he was not even sure about the existence of God; so he could not speak one way or the other. This frank answer very much pleased the Master.

Sarat's soul longed for the all-embracing realization of the Godhead. When the Master inquired whether there was any particular form of God he wished to see, the boy replied that he would like to see God in all the living beings of the world. "But", the Master demurred, "that is the last word in realization. One cannot have it at the very outset." Sarat stated calmly: "I won't be satisfied with anything short of that. I shall trudge on along the path till I attain that blessed state." Sri Ramakrishna was very much pleased.

HARINATH

Harinath had led the austere life of a brahmachāri even from his early boyhood—bathing in the Ganges every day, cooking his own meals, waking before sunrise, and reciting the Gītā from memory before leaving bed. He found in the Master the embodiment of the Vedānta scriptures. Aspiring to be a follower of the ascetic Śankara, he cherished a great hatred for women. One day he said to the Master that he could not allow even small girls to come near him. The Master scolded him and said: "You are talking like a fool. Why should you hate women? They are the manifestations of the Divine Mother. Regard them as your own mother and you will never feel their evil influence. The more you hate them, the more you will fall into their snares." Hari said later that these words completely changed his attitude toward women.

The Master knew Hari's passion for Vedānta. But he did not wish any of his disciples to become a dry ascetic or a mere bookworm. So he asked Hari to practise Vedānta in life by giving up the unreal and following the Real. "But it is not so easy", Sri Ramakrishna said, "to realize the illusoriness of the world. Study alone does not help one very much. The grace of God is required. Mere personal effort is futile. A man is a tiny creature after all, with very limited powers. But he can achieve the impossible if he prays to God for His grace." Whereupon the Master sang a song in praise of grace. Hari was profoundly moved and shed tears. Later in life Hari achieved a wonderful synthesis of the ideals of the Personal God and the Impersonal Truth.

GANGADHAR

Gangadhar, Harinath's friend, also led the life of a strict brahmachāri, eating vegetarian food cooked by his own hands and devoting himself to the study of the scriptures. He met the Master in 1884 and soon became a member of his inner circle. The Master praised his ascetic habit and attributed it to the spiritual disciplines of his past life. Gangadhar became a close companion of Narendra.

HARIPRASANNA

Hariprasanna, a college student, visited the Master in the company of his friends Sashi and Sarat. Sri Ramakrishna showed him great favour by initiating him into spiritual life. As long as he lived, Hariprasanna remembered and observed the following drastic advice of the Master: "Even if a woman is pure as gold and rolls on the ground for love of God, it is dangerous for a monk ever to look at her."

KALI

Kaliprasad visited the Master toward the end of 1883. Given to the practice of meditation and the study of the scriptures, Kali was particularly interested in yoga. Feeling the need of a guru in spiritual life, he came to the Master and was accepted as a disciple. The young boy possessed a rational mind and often felt sceptical about the Personal God. The Master said to him: "Your doubts will soon disappear. Others, too, have passed through such a state of mind. Look at Naren. He now weeps at the names of Rādhā and Krishna." Kali began to see visions of gods and goddesses. Very soon these disappeared and in meditation he experienced vastness, infinity, and the other attributes of the Impersonal Brahman.

SUBODH

Subodh visited the Master in 1885. At the very first meeting Sri Ramakrishna said to him: "You will succeed. Mother says so. Those whom She sends here will certainly attain spirituality." During the second meeting the Master wrote something on Subodh's tongue, stroked his body from the navel to the throat, and said, "Awake, Mother! Awake." He asked the boy to meditate. At once Subodh's latent spirituality was awakened. He felt a current rushing along the spinal column to the brain. Joy filled his soul.

SARADA

One more young man, Sarada Prasanna by name, completes the small band of the Master's disciples later to embrace the life of the wandering monk. With the exception of the elder Gopal, all of them were in their teens or slightly over. They came from middle-class Bengali families, and most of them were students in school or college. Their parents and relatives had envisaged for them bright worldly careers. They came to Sri Ramakrishna with pure bodies, vigorous minds, and uncontaminated souls. All were born with unusual spiritual attributes. Sri Ramakrishna accepted them, even at first sight, as his children, relatives, friends, and companions. His magic touch unfolded them. And later each according to his measure reflected the life of the Master, becoming a torch-bearer of his message across land and sea.

WOMAN DEVOTEES

With his woman devotees Sri Ramakrishna established a very sweet relationship. He himself embodied the tender traits of a woman; he had dwelt on the highest plane of Truth, where there is not even the slightest trace of sex; and his innate purity evoked only the noblest emotion in men and women alike. His woman devotees often said: "We seldom looked on Sri Ramakrishna as a member of the male sex. We regarded him as one of us. We never felt any constraint before him. He was our best confidant." They loved him as their child, their friend, and their teacher. In spiritual discipline he advised them to renounce lust and greed and especially warned them not to fall into the snares of men.

GOPĀL MĀ

Unsurpassed among the woman devotees of the Master in the richness of her devotion and spiritual experiences was Aghoremani Devi, an orthodox brāhmin woman. Widowed at an early age, she had dedicated herself completely to spiritual pursuits. Gopāla, the Baby Krishna, was her Ideal Deity, whom she worshipped following the vātsalya attitude of the Vaishnava religion, regarding Him as her own child. Through Him she satisfied her unassuaged maternal love, cooking for Him, feeding Him, bathing Him, and putting Him to bed. This sweet intimacy with Gopāla won her the sobriquet of Gopāl Mā, or Gopāla's Mother. For forty years she had lived on the bank of the Ganges in a small, bare room, her only companions being a threadbare copy of the Rāmāyana and a bag containing her rosary. At the age of sixty, in 1884, she visited Sri Ramakrishna at Dakshineswar. During the second visit, as soon as the Master saw her, he said: "Oh, you have come! Give me something to eat." With great hesitation she gave him some ordinary sweets that she had purchased for him on the way. The Master ate them with relish and asked her to bring him simple curries or sweets prepared by her own hands. Gopāl Mā thought him a queer kind of monk, for, instead of talking of God, he always asked for food. She did not want to visit him again, but an irresistible attraction brought her back to the temple garden. She carried with her some simple curries that she had cooked herself.

One early morning at three o'clock, about a year later, Gopāl Mā was about to finish her daily devotions, when she was startled to find Sri Ramakrishna sitting on her left, with his right hand clenched, like the hand of the image of Gopāla. She was amazed and caught hold of the hand, whereupon the figure vanished and in its place appeared the real Gopāla, her Ideal Deity. She cried aloud with joy. Gopāla begged her for butter. She pleaded her poverty and gave Him some dry coconut candies. Gopāla sat on her lap, snatched away her rosary, jumped on her shoulders, and moved all about the room. As soon as the day broke she hastened to Dakshineswar like an insane woman. Of course Gopāla accompanied her, resting His head on her shoulder. She clearly saw His tiny ruddy feet hanging over her breast. She entered Sri Ramakrishna's room. The Master had fallen into samādhi. Like a child, he sat on her lap, and she began to feed him with butter, cream, and other delicacies. After some time he regained consciousness and returned to his bed. But the mind of Gopāla's Mother was still roaming in another plane. She was steeped in bliss. She saw Gopāla frequently entering the Master's body and again coming out of it. When she returned to her hut, still in a dazed condition, Gopāla accompanied her.

She spent about two months in uninterrupted communion with God, the Baby Gopāla never leaving her for a moment. Then the intensity of her vision was lessened; had it not been, her body would have perished. The Master spoke highly of her exalted spiritual condition and said that such vision of God was a rare thing for ordinary mortals. The fun-loving Master one day confronted the critical Narendranath with this simple-minded woman. No two could have presented a more striking contrast. The Master knew of Narendra's lofty contempt for all visions, and he asked the old lady to narrate her experiences to Narendra. With great hesitation she told him her story. Now and then she interrupted her maternal chatter to ask Narendra: "My son, I am a poor ignorant woman. I don't understand anything. You are so learned. Now tell me if these visions of Gopāla are true." As Narendra listened to the story he was profoundly moved. He said, "Yes, mother, they are quite true." Behind his cynicism Narendra, too, possessed a heart full of love and tenderness.

THE MARCH OF EVENTS

In 1881 Hriday was dismissed from service in the Kāli temple, for an act of indiscretion, and was ordered by the authorities never again to enter the garden. In a way the hand of the Divine Mother may be seen even in this. Having taken care of Sri Ramakrishna during the stormy days of his spiritual discipline, Hriday had come naturally to consider himself the sole guardian of his uncle. None could approach the Master without his knowledge. And he would be extremely jealous if Sri Ramakrishna paid attention to anyone else. Hriday's removal made it possible for the real devotees of the Master to approach him freely and live with him in the temple garden.

During the week-ends the householders, enjoying a respite from their office duties, visited the Master. The meetings on Sunday afternoons were of the nature of little festivals. Refreshments were often served. Professional musicians now and then sang devotional songs. The Master and the devotees sang and danced, Sri Ramakrishna frequently going into ecstatic moods. The happy memory of such a Sunday would linger long in the minds of the devotees. Those whom the Master wanted for special instruction he would ask to visit him on Tuesdays and Saturdays. These days were particularly auspicious for the worship of Kāli.

The young disciples destined to be monks, Sri Ramakrishna invited on week-days, when the householders were not present. The training of the householders and of the future monks had to proceed along entirely different lines. Since M. generally visited the Master on week-ends, the *Gospel of Sri Ramakrishna* does not contain much mention of the future monastic disciples.

Finally, there was a handful of fortunate disciples, householders as well as youngsters, who were privileged to spend nights with the Master in his room. They would see him get up early in the morning and walk up and down the room, singing in his sweet voice and tenderly communing with the Mother.

INJURY TO THE MASTER'S ARM

One day, in January 1884, the·Master was going toward the pine-grove when he went into a trance. He was alone. There was no one to support him or guide his footsteps. He fell to the ground and dislocated a bone in his left arm. This accident had a significant influence on his mind, the natural inclination of which was to soar above the consciousness of the body. The acute pain in the arm forced his mind to dwell on the body and on the world outside. But he saw even in this a divine purpose; for, with his mind compelled to dwell on the physical plane, he realized more than ever that he was an instrument in the hand of the Divine Mother, who had a mission to fulfil through his human body and mind. He also distinctly found that in the phenomenal world God manifests Himself, in an inscrutable way, through diverse human beings, both good and evil. Thus he would speak of God in the guise of the wicked, God in the guise of the pious, God in the guise of the hypocrite, God in the guise of the lewd. He began to take a special delight in watching the divine play in the relative world. Sometimes the sweet human relationship with God would appear to him more appealing than the all-effacing Knowledge of Brahman. Many a time he would pray: "Mother, don't make me unconscious through the Knowledge of Brahman. Don't give me Brahmajnāna, Mother. Am I not Your child, and naturally timid? I must have my Mother. A million salutations to the Knowledge of Brahman! Give it to those who want it." Again he prayed: "O Mother, let me remain in contact with men! Don't make me a dried-up ascetic. I want to enjoy Your sport in the world." He was able to taste this very rich divine experience and enjoy the love of God and the company of His devotees because his mind, on account of the injury to his arm, was forced to come down to the consciousness of the body. Again, he would make fun of people who proclaimed him as a Divine Incarnation, by pointing to his broken arm. He would say, "Have you ever heard of God breaking His arm?" It took the arm about five months to heal.

BEGINNING OF HIS ILLNESS

In April 1885 the Master's throat became inflamed. Prolonged conversation or absorption in samādhi, making the blood flow into the throat, would aggravate the pain. Yet when the annual Vaishnava festival was celebrated at Pānihāti, Sri Ramakrishna attended it against the doctor's advice. With a group of disciples he spent himself in music, dance, and ecstasy. The illness took a turn for the worse and was diagnosed as "clergyman's sore throat". The patient was cautioned against conversation and ecstasies. Though he followed the physician's directions regarding medicine and diet, he could neither control his trances nor withhold from seekers the solace of his advice. Sometimes, like a sulky child, he would complain to the Mother about the crowds, who gave him no rest day or night. He was overheard to say to Her: "Why do You bring here all these worthless people, who are like milk diluted with five times its own quantity of water? My eyes are almost destroyed with blowing the fire to dry up the water. My health is gone. It is beyond my strength. Do it Yourself, if You want it done. This (*pointing to his own body*) is but a perforated drum, and if you go on beating it day in and day out, how long will it last?"

But his large heart never turned anyone away. He said, "Let me be condemned to be born over and over again, even in the form of a dog, if I can be of help to a single soul." And he bore the pain, singing cheerfully, "Let the body be preoccupied with illness, but, O mind, dwell for ever in God's Bliss!"

One night he had a hemorrhage of the throat. The doctor now diagnosed the illness as cancer. Narendra was the first to break this heart-rending news to the disciples. Within three days the Master was removed to Calcutta for better treatment. At Balaram's house he remained a week until a suitable place could be found at Śyāmpukur, in the northern section of Calcutta. During this week he dedicated himself practically without respite to the instruction of those beloved devotees who had been unable to visit him oftener at Dakshineswar. Discourses incessantly flowed from his tongue, and he often went into samādhi. Dr. Mahendra Sarkar, the celebrated homeopath of Calcutta, was invited to undertake his treatment.

ŚYĀMPUKUR

In the beginning of September 1885 Sri Ramakrishna was moved to Śyāmpukur. Here Narendra organized the young disciples to attend the Master day and night. At first they concealed the Master's illness from their guardians; but when it became more serious they remained with him almost constantly, sweeping aside the objections of their relatives and devoting themselves whole-heartedly to the nursing of their beloved guru. These young men, under the watchful eyes of the Master and the leadership of Narendra, became the antaranga bhaktas, the devotees of Sri Ramakrishna's inner circle. They were privileged to witness many manifestations of the Master's divine powers. Narendra received instructions regarding the propagation of his message after his death.

The Holy Mother—so Sarada Devi had come to be affectionately known by Sri Ramakrishna's devotees—was brought from Dakshineswar to look after the general cooking and to prepare the special diet of the patient. The dwelling space being extremely limited, she had to adapt herself to cramped conditions. At three o'clock in the morning she would finish her bath in the Ganges and then enter a small covered place on the roof, where she spent the whole day cooking and praying. After eleven at night, when the visitors went away, she would come down to her small bedroom on the first floor to enjoy a few hours' sleep. Thus she spent three months, working hard, sleeping little, and praying constantly for the Master's recovery.

At Śyāmpukur the devotees led an intense life. Their attendance on the Master was in itself a form of spiritual discipline. His mind was constantly soaring to an exalted plane of consciousness. Now and then they would catch the contagion of his spiritual fervour. They sought to divine the meaning of this illness of the Master, whom most of them had accepted as an Incarnation of God. One group, headed by Girish with his robust optimism and great power of imagination, believed that the illness was a mere pretext to serve a deeper purpose. The Master had willed his illness in order to bring the devotees together and promote solidarity among them. As soon as this purpose was served, he would himself get rid of the disease. A second group thought that the Divine Mother, in whose hand the Master was an instrument, had brought about this illness to serve Her own mysterious ends. But the young rationalists, led by Narendra, refused to ascribe a super-natural cause to a natural phenomenon. They believed that the Master's body, a material thing, was subject, like all other material things, to physical laws. Growth, development, decay, and death were laws of nature to which the Master's body could not but respond. But though holding differing views, they all believed that it was to him alone that they must look for the attainment of their spiritual goal.

In spite of the physician's efforts and the prayers and nursing of the devotees, the illness rapidly progressed. The pain sometimes appeared to be unbearable. The Master lived only on liquid food, and his frail body was becoming a mere skeleton. Yet his face always radiated joy, and he con-tinued to welcome the visitors pouring in to receive his blessing. When cer-tain zealous devotees tried to keep the visitors away, they were told by Girish, "You cannot succeed in it; he has been born for this very purpose— to sacrifice himself for the redemption of others."

The more the body was devastated by illness, the more it became the habitation of the Divine Spirit. Through its transparency the gods and god-desses began to shine with ever increasing luminosity. On the day of the Kāli Pujā the devotees clearly saw in him the manifestation of the Divine Mother.

It was noticed at this time that some of the devotees were making an unbridled display of their emotions. A number of them, particularly among the householders, began to cultivate, though at first unconsciously, the art of shedding tears, shaking the body, contorting the face, and going into trances, attempting thereby to imitate the Master. They began openly to declare Sri Ramakrishna a Divine Incarnation and to regard themselves as his chosen people, who could neglect religious disciplines with impunity. Narendra's penetrating eye soon sized up the situation. He found out that some of these external manifestations were being carefully practised at home, while some were the outcome of malnutrition, mental weakness, or nervous debility. He mercilessly exposed the devotees who were pretending to have visions, and asked all to develop a healthy religious spirit. Narendra sang inspiring songs for the younger devotees, read with them the *Imitation of Christ* and the *Gītā*, and held before them the positive ideals of spirituality.

LAST DAYS AT COSSIPORE

When Sri Ramakrishna's illness showed signs of aggravation, the devotees, following the advice of Dr. Sarkar, rented a spacious garden house at Cossipore, in the northern suburbs of Calcutta. The Master was removed to this place on December 11, 1885.

It was at Cossipore that the curtain fell on the varied activities of the Master's life on the physical plane. His soul lingered in the body eight months more. It was the period of his great Passion, a constant crucifixion of the body and the triumphant revelation of the Soul. Here one sees the humanity and divinity of the Master passing and repassing across a thin border line. Every minute of those eight months was suffused with touching tenderness of heart and breath-taking elevation of spirit. Every word he uttered was full of pathos and sublimity.

It took the group only a few days to become adjusted to the new environment. The Holy Mother, assisted by Sri Ramakrishna's niece, Lakshmi Devi, and a few woman devotees, took charge of the cooking for the Master and his attendants. Surendra willingly bore the major portion of the expenses, other householders contributing according to their means. Twelve disciples were constant attendants of the Master: Narendra, Rakhal, Baburam, Niranjan, Jogin, Latu, Tarak, the elder Gopal, Kali, Sashi, Sarat, and the younger Gopal. Sarada, Harish, Hari, Gangadhar, and Tulasi visited the Master from time to time and practised sādhanā at home. Narendra, preparing for his law examination, brought his books to the garden house in order to continue his studies during the infrequent spare moments. He encouraged his brother disciples to intensify their meditation, scriptural studies, and other spiritual disciplines. They all forgot their relatives and their worldly duties.

Among the attendants Sashi was the embodiment of service. He did not practise meditation, japa, or any of the other disciplines followed by his brother devotees. He was convinced that service to the guru was the only religion for him. He forgot food and rest and was ever ready at the Master's bedside.

Pundit Shashadhar one day suggested to the Master that the latter could remove the illness by concentrating his mind on the throat, the scriptures having declared that yogis had power to cure themselves in that way. The Master rebuked the pundit. "For a scholar like you to make such a proposal!" he said. "How can I withdraw the mind from the Lotus Feet of God and turn it to this worthless cage of flesh and blood?" "For our sake at least", begged Narendra and the other disciples. "But", replied Sri Ramakrishna, "do you think I enjoy this suffering? I wish to recover, but that depends on the Mother."

NARENDRA: "Then please pray to Her. She must listen to you."

MASTER: "But I cannot pray for my body."

NARENDRA: "You must do it, for our sake at least."

MASTER: "Very well, I shall try."

A few hours later the Master said to Narendra: "I said to Her: 'Mother, I cannot swallow food because of my pain. Make it possible for me to eat a little.' She pointed you all out to me and said: 'What? You are eating enough through all these mouths. Isn't that so?' I was ashamed and could not utter another word." This dashed all the hopes of the devotees for the Master's recovery.

"I shall make the whole thing public before I go", the Master had said some time before. On January 1, 1886, he felt better and came down to the garden for a little stroll. It was about three o'clock in the afternoon. Some thirty lay disciples were in the hall or sitting about under the trees. Sri Ramakrishna said to Girish, "Well, Girish, what have you seen in me, that you proclaim me before everybody as an Incarnation of God?" Girish was not the man to be taken by surprise. He knelt before the Master and said with folded hands, "What can an insignificant person like myself say about the One whose glory even sages like Vyāsa and Vālmiki could not adequately measure?" The Master was profoundly moved. He said: "What more shall I say? I bless you all. Be illumined!" He fell into a spiritual mood. Hearing these words the devotees, one and all, became overwhelmed with emotion. They rushed to him and fell at his feet. He touched them all, and each received an appropriate benediction. Each of them, at the touch of the Master, experienced ineffable bliss. Some laughed, some wept, some sat down to meditate, some began to pray. Some saw light, some had visions of their Chosen Ideals, and some felt within their bodies the rush of spiritual power.

Narendra, consumed with a terrific fever for realization, complained to the Master that all the others had attained peace and that he alone was dissatisfied. The Master asked what he wanted. Narendra begged for samādhi, so that he might altogether forget the world for three or four days at a time. "You are a fool", the Master rebuked him. "There is a state even higher than that. Isn't it you who sing, 'All that exists art Thou'? First of all settle your family affairs and then come to me. You will experience a state even higher than samādhi."

The Master did not hide the fact that he wished to make Narendra his spiritual heir. Narendra was to continue the work after Sri Ramakrishna's passing. Sri Ramakrishna said to him: "I leave these young men in your charge. See that they develop their spirituality and do not return home." One day he asked the boys, in preparation for a monastic life, to beg their food from door to door without thought of caste. They hailed the Master's order and went out with begging-bowls. A few days later he gave the ochre cloth of the sannyāsi to each of them, including Girish, who was now second to none in his spirit of renunciation. Thus the Master himself laid the foundation of the future Ramakrishna Order of monks.

Sri Ramakrishna was sinking day by day. His diet was reduced to a minimum and he found it almost impossible to swallow. He whispered to M.: "I am bearing all this cheerfully, for otherwise you would be weeping. If you all say that it is better that the body should go rather than suffer this torture, I am willing." The next morning he said to his depressed disciples seated near the bed: "Do you know what I see? I see that God alone has become everything. Men and animals are only frameworks covered with skin, and it is He who is moving through their heads and limbs. I see that it is God Himself who has become the block, the executioner, and the victim for the sacrifice." He fainted with emotion. Regaining partial consciousness, he said: "Now I have no pain. I am very well." Looking at Latu he said: "There sits Latu resting his head on the palm of his hand. To me it is the Lord who is seated in that posture."

The words were tender and touching. Like a mother he caressed Narendra and Rakhal, gently stroking their faces. He said in a half whisper to M., "Had this body been allowed to last a little longer, many more souls would have been illumined." He paused a moment and then said: "But Mother has ordained otherwise. She will take me away lest, finding me guileless and foolish, people should take advantage of me and persuade me to bestow on them the rare gifts of spirituality." A few minutes later he touched his chest and said: "Here are two beings. One is She and the other is Her devotee. It is the latter who broke his arm, and it is he again who is now ill. Do you understand me?" After a pause he added: "Alas! To whom shall I tell all this? Who will understand me?" "Pain", he consoled them again, "is unavoidable as long as there is a body. The Lord takes on the body for the sake of His devotees."

Yet one is not sure whether the Master's soul actually was tortured by this agonizing disease. At least during his moments of spiritual exaltation—which became almost constant during the closing days of his life on earth—he lost all consciousness of the body, of illness and suffering. One of his attendants[9] said later on: "While Sri Ramakrishna lay sick he never actually suffered pain. He would often say: 'O mind! Forget the body, forget the sickness, and remain merged in Bliss.' No, he did not really suffer. At times he would be in a state when the thrill of joy was clearly manifested in his body. Even when he could not speak he would let us know in some way that there was no suffering, and this fact was clearly evident to all who watched him. People who did not understand him thought that his suffering was very great. What spiritual joy he transmitted to us at that time! Could such a thing have been possible if he had been suffering physically? It was during this period that he taught us again these truths: 'Brahman is always unattached. The three gunas are in It, but It is unaffected by them, just as the wind carries odour yet remains odourless.' 'Brahman is Infinite Being, Infinite Wisdom, Infinite Bliss. In It there exist no delusion, no misery, no disease, no death, no growth, no decay.' 'The Transcendental Being and the being within are one and the same. There is one indivisible Absolute Existence.'"

The Holy Mother secretly went to a Śiva temple across the Ganges to intercede with the Deity for the Master's recovery. In a revelation she was told to prepare herself for the inevitable end.

One day when Narendra was on the ground floor, meditating, the Master was lying awake in his bed upstairs. In the depths of his meditation Narendra felt as though a lamp were burning at the back of his head. Suddenly he lost consciousness. It was the yearned-for, all-effacing experience of nirvikalpa samādhi, when the embodied soul realizes its unity with the Absolute. After a very long time he regained partial consciousness but was unable to find his body. He could see only his head. "Where is my body?" he cried. The

[9] Latu, later known as Swami Adbhutananda.

elder Gopal entered the room and said, "Why, it is here, Naren!" But Narendra could not find it. Gopal, frightened, ran upstairs to the Master. Sri Ramakrishna only said: "Let him stay that way for a time. He has worried me long enough."

After another long period Narendra regained full consciousness. Bathed in peace, he went to the Master, who said: "Now the Mother has shown you everything. But this revelation will remain under lock and key, and I shall keep the key. When you have accomplished the Mother's work you will find the treasure again."

Some days later, Narendra being alone with the Master, Sri Ramakrishna looked at him and went into samādhi. Narendra felt the penetration of a subtle force and lost all outer consciousness. Regaining presently the normal mood, he found the Master weeping.

Sri Ramakrishna said to him: "Today I have given you my all and I am now only a poor fakir, possessing nothing. By this power you will do immense good in the world, and not until it is accomplished will you return." Henceforth the Master lived in the disciple.

Doubt, however, dies hard. After one or two days Narendra said to himself, "If in the midst of this racking physical pain he declares his Godhead, then only shall I accept him as an Incarnation of God." He was alone by the bedside of the Master. It was a passing thought, but the Master smiled. Gathering his remaining strength, he distinctly said, "He who was Rāma and Krishna is now, in this body, Ramakrishna—but not in your Vedāntic sense." Narendra was stricken with shame.

MAHĀSAMĀDHI

Sunday, August 15, 1886. The Master's pulse became irregular. The devotees stood by the bedside. Toward dusk Sri Ramakrishna had difficulty in breathing. A short time afterwards he complained of hunger. A little liquid food was put into his mouth; some of it he swallowed, and the rest ran over his chin. Two attendants began to fan him. All at once he went into samādhi of a rather unusual type. The body became stiff. Sashi burst into tears. But after midnight the Master revived. He was now very hungry and helped himself to a bowl of porridge. He said he was strong again. He sat up against five or six pillows, which were supported by the body of Sashi, who was fanning him. Narendra took his feet on his lap and began to rub them. Again and again the Master repeated to him, "Take care of these boys." Then he asked to lie down. Three times in ringing tones he cried the name of Kāli, his life's Beloved, and lay back. At two minutes past one there was a low sound in his throat and he fell a little to one side. A thrill passed over his body. His hair stood on end. His eyes became fixed on the tip of his nose. His face was lighted with a smile. The final ecstasy began. It was mahāsamādhi, total absorption, from which his mind never returned. Narendra, unable to bear it, ran downstairs.

Dr. Sarkar arrived the following noon and pronounced that life had departed not more than half an hour before. At five o'clock the Master's body was brought downstairs, laid on a cot, dressed in ochre clothes, and decorated with sandal-paste and flowers. A procession was formed. The passers-by wept as the body was taken to the cremation ground at the Barānagore Ghāt on the Ganges.

While the devotees were returning to the garden house, carrying the urn with the sacred ashes, a calm resignation came to their souls and they cried, "Victory unto the Guru!"

The Holy Mother was weeping in her room, not for her husband, but because she felt that Mother Kāli had left her. As she was about to put on the marks of a Hindu widow, in a moment of revelation she heard the words of faith, "I have only passed from one room to another."

The Gospel of
Sri Ramakrishna

MASTER AND DISCIPLE

IT WAS ON A SUNDAY in spring, a few days after Sri Ramakrishna's birthday, that M. met him the first time. Sri Ramakrishna lived at the Kālibāri, the temple garden of Mother Kāli, on the bank of the Ganges at Dakshineswar.

M., being at leisure on Sundays, had gone with his friend Sidhu to visit several gardens at Barānagore. As they were walking in Prasanna Bannerji's garden, Sidhu said: "There is a charming place on the bank of the Ganges where a paramahamsa lives. Should you like to go there?" M. assented and they started immediately for the Dakshineswar temple garden. They arrived at the main gate at dusk and went straight to Sri Ramakrishna's room. And there they found him seated on a wooden couch, facing the east. With a smile on his face he was talking of God. The room was full of people, all seated on the floor, drinking in his words in deep silence.

M. stood there speechless and looked on. It was as if he were standing where all the holy places met and as if Śukadeva himself were speaking the word of God, or as if Sri Chaitanya were singing the name and glories of the Lord in Puri with Rāmānanda, Swarup, and the other devotees.

Sri Ramakrishna said: "When, hearing the name of Hari or Rāma once, you shed tears and your hair stands on end, then you may know for certain that you do not have to perform such devotions as the sandhyā any more. Then only will you have a right to renounce rituals; or rather, rituals will drop away of themselves. Then it will be enough if you repeat only the name of Rāma or Hari, or even simply Om." Continuing, he said, "The sandhyā merges in the Gāyatri, and the Gāyatri merges in Om."

M. looked around him with wonder and said to himself: "What a beautiful place! What a charming man! How beautiful his words are! I have no wish to move from this spot." After a few minutes he thought, "Let me see the place first; then I'll come back here and sit down."

As he left the room with Sidhu, he heard the sweet music of the evening service arising in the temple from gong, bell, drum, and cymbal. He could hear music from the nahabat, too, at the south end of the garden. The sounds travelled over the Ganges, floating away and losing themselves in the distance. A soft spring wind was blowing, laden with the fragrance of flowers; the moon had just appeared. It was as if nature and man together were preparing for the evening worship. M. and Sidhu visited the twelve Śiva temples, the Rādhākānta temple, and the temple of Bhavatārini. And as M. watched the services before the images his heart was filled with joy.

On the way back to Sri Ramakrishna's room the two friends talked. Sidhu told M. that the temple garden had been founded by Rāni Rasmani. He said that God was worshipped there daily as Kāli, Krishna, and Śiva, and that within the gates many sādhus and beggars were fed. When they reached Sri Ramakrishna's door again, they found it shut, and Brindē, the maid, standing outside. M., who had been trained in English manners and would not enter a room without permission, asked her, "Is the holy man in?" Brindē replied, "Yes, he's in the room."

M: "How long has he lived here?"

BRINDĒ: "Oh, he has been here a long time."

M: "Does he read many books?"

BRINDĒ: "Books? Oh, dear no! They're all on his tongue."

M. had just finished his studies in college. It amazed him to hear that Sri Ramakrishna read no books.

M: "Perhaps it is time for his evening worship. May we go into the room? Will you tell him we are anxious to see him?"

BRINDĒ: "Go right in, children. Go in and sit down."

Entering the room, they found Sri Ramakrishna alone, seated on the wooden couch. Incense had just been burnt and all the doors were shut. As he entered, M. with folded hands saluted the Master. Then, at the Master's bidding, he and Sidhu sat on the floor. Sri Ramakrishna asked them: "Where do you live? What is your occupation? Why have you come to Barānagore?" M. answered the questions, but he noticed that now and then the Master seemed to become absent-minded. Later he learnt that this mood is called bhāva, ecstasy. It is like the state of the angler who has been sitting with his rod: the fish comes and swallows the bait, and the float begins to tremble; the angler is on the alert; he grips the rod and watches the float steadily and eagerly; he will not speak to anyone. Such was the state of Sri Ramakrishna's mind. Later M. heard, and himself noticed, that Sri Ramakrishna would often go into this mood after dusk, sometimes becoming totally unconscious of the outer world.

M: "Perhaps you want to perform your evening worship. In that case may we take our leave?"

SRI RAMAKRISHNA (still in ecstasy): "No—evening worship? No, it is not exactly that."

After a little conversation M. saluted the Master and took his leave. "Come again", Sri Ramakrishna said.

On his way home M. began to wonder: "Who is this serene-looking man who is drawing me back to him? Is it possible for a man to be great without being a scholar? How wonderful it is! I should like to see him again. He himself said, 'Come again.' I shall go tomorrow or the day after."

M.'s second visit to Sri Ramakrishna took place on the southeast verandah at eight o'clock in the morning. The Master was about to be shaved, the barber having just arrived. As the cold season still lingered he had put on a moleskin shawl bordered with red. Seeing M., the Master said: "So you have come. That's good. Sit down here." He was smiling. He stammered a little when he spoke.

SRI RAMAKRISHNA (*to M.*): "Where do you live?"

M: "In Calcutta, sir."

SRI RAMAKRISHNA: "Where are you staying here?"

M: "I am at Barānagore at my older sister's—Ishan Kavirāj's house."

SRI RAMAKRISHNA: "Oh, at Ishan's? Well, how is Keshab now? He was very ill."

M: "Indeed, I have heard so too, but I believe he is well now."

SRI RAMAKRISHNA: "I made a vow to worship the Mother with green coconut and sugar on Keshab's recovery. Sometimes, in the early hours of the morning, I would wake up and cry before Her: 'Mother, please make Keshab well again. If Keshab doesn't live, whom shall I talk with when I go to Calcutta?' And so it was that I resolved to offer Her the green coconut and sugar.

"Tell me, do you know of a certain Mr. Cook who has come to Calcutta? Is it true that he is giving lectures? Once Keshab took me on a steamer, and this Mr. Cook, too, was in the party."

M: "Yes, sir, I have heard something like that; but I have never been to his lectures. I don't know much about him."

SRI RAMAKRISHNA: "Pratap's brother came here. He stayed a few days. He had nothing to do and said he wanted to live here. I came to know that he had left his wife and children with his father-in-law. He has a whole brood of them! So I took him to task. Just fancy! He is the father of so many children! Will people from the neighbourhood feed them and bring them up? He isn't even ashamed that someone else is feeding his wife and children, and that they have been left at his father-in-law's house. I scolded him very hard and asked him to look for a job. Then he was willing to leave here.

"Are you married?"

M: "Yes, sir."

SRI RAMAKRISHNA (*with a shudder*): "Oh, Ramlal![1] Alas, he is married!"

Like one guilty of a terrible offence, M. sat motionless, his eyes fixed on the ground. He thought, "Is it such a wicked thing to get married?"

The Master continued, "Have you any children?"

M. this time could hear the beating of his own heart. He whispered in a trembling voice, "Yes, sir, I have children."

Very sadly Sri Ramakrishna said, "Ah me! He even has children!"

Thus rebuked M. sat speechless. His pride had received a blow. After a few minutes Sri Ramakrishna looked at him kindly and said affectionately: "You see, you have certain good signs. I know them by looking at a person's forehead, his eyes, and so on. Tell me, now, what kind of person is your wife? Has she spiritual attributes, or is she under the power of avidyā?"

[1] A nephew of Sri Ramakrishna, and a priest in the Kāli temple.

M: "She is all right. But I am afraid she is ignorant."

MASTER (*with evident displeasure*): "And you are a man of knowledge!"

M. had yet to learn the distinction between knowledge and ignorance. Up to this time his conception had been that one got knowledge from books and schools. Later on he gave up this false conception. He was taught that to know God is knowledge, and not to know Him, ignorance. When Sri Ramakrishna exclaimed, "And you are a man of knowledge!", M.'s ego was again badly shocked.

MASTER: "Well, do you believe in God with form or without form?"

M., rather surprised, said to himself: "How can one believe in God without form when one believes in God with form? And if one believes in God without form, how can one believe that God has a form? Can these two contradictory ideas be true at the same time? Can a white liquid like milk be black?"

M: "Sir, I like to think of God as formless."

MASTER: "Very good. It is enough to have faith in either aspect. You believe in God without form; that is quite all right. But never for a moment think that this alone is true and all else false. Remember that God with form is just as true as God without form. But hold fast to your own conviction."

The assertion that both are equally true amazed M.; he had never learnt this from his books. Thus his ego received a third blow; but since it was not yet completely crushed, he came forward to argue with the Master a little more.

M: "Sir, suppose one believes in God with form. Certainly He is not the clay image!"

MASTER (*interrupting*): "But why clay? It is an image of Spirit."

M. could not quite understand the significance of this "image of Spirit". "But, sir," he said to the Master, "one should explain to those who worship the clay image that it is *not* God, and that, while worshipping it, they should have God in view and not the clay image. One should not worship clay."

MASTER (*sharply*): "That's the one hobby of you Calcutta people—giving lectures and bringing others to the light! Nobody ever stops to consider how to get the light himself. Who are you to teach others?

"He who is the Lord of the Universe will teach everyone. He alone teaches us, who has created this universe; who has made the sun and moon, men and beasts, and all other beings; who has provided means for their sustenance; who has given children parents and endowed them with love to bring them up. The Lord has done so many things—will He not show people the way to worship Him? If they need teaching, then He will be the Teacher. He is our Inner Guide.

"Suppose there is an error in worshipping the clay image; doesn't God know that through it He alone is being invoked? He will be pleased with that very worship. Why should you get a headache over it? You had better try for knowledge and devotion yourself."

This time M. felt that his ego was completely crushed. He now said to himself: "Yes, he has spoken the truth. What need is there for me to teach others? Have I known God? Do I really love Him? 'I haven't room enough for myself in my bed, and I am inviting my friend to share it with me!' I know nothing about God, yet I am trying to teach others. What a shame! How foolish I am! This is not mathematics or history or literature, that one can teach it to others. No, this is the deep mystery of God. What he says appeals to me."

This was M.'s first argument with the Master, and happily his last.

MASTER: "You were talking of worshipping the clay image. Even if the image *is* made of clay, there is need for that sort of worship. God Himself has provided different forms of worship. He who is the Lord of the Universe has arranged all these forms to suit different men in different stages of knowledge.

"The mother cooks different dishes to suit the stomachs of her different children. Suppose she has five children. If there is a fish to cook, she prepares various dishes from it—pilau, pickled fish, fried fish, and so on—to suit their different tastes and powers of digestion.

"Do you understand me?"

M. (*humbly*): "Yes, sir. How, sir, may we fix our minds on God?"

MASTER: "Repeat God's name and sing His glories, and keep holy company; and now and then visit God's devotees and holy men. The mind cannot dwell on God if it is immersed day and night in worldliness, in worldly duties and responsibilities; it is most necessary to go into solitude now and then and think of God. To fix the mind on God is very difficult, in the beginning, unless one practises meditation in solitude. When a tree is young it should be fenced all around; otherwise it may be destroyed by cattle.

"To meditate, you should withdraw within yourself or retire to a secluded corner or to the forest. And you should always discriminate between the Real and the unreal. God alone is real, the Eternal Substance; all else is unreal, that is, impermanent. By discriminating thus, one should shake off impermanent objects from the mind."

M. (*humbly*): "How ought we to live in the world?"

MASTER: "Do all your duties, but keep your mind on God. Live with all—with wife and children, father and mother—and serve them. Treat them as if they were very dear to you, but know in your heart of hearts that they do not belong to you.

"A maidservant in the house of a rich man performs all the household duties, but her thoughts are fixed on her own home in her native village. She brings up her master's children as if they were her own. She even speaks of them as 'my Rama' or 'my Hari'. But in her own mind she knows very well that they do not belong to her at all.

"The tortoise moves about in the water. But can you guess where her thoughts are? There on the bank, where her eggs are lying. Do all your duties in the world, but keep your mind on God.

"If you enter the world without first cultivating love for God, you will be entangled more and more. You will be overwhelmed with its danger, its grief, its sorrows. And the more you think of worldly things, the more you will be attached to them.

"First rub your hands with oil and then break open the jack-fruit; otherwise they will be smeared with its sticky milk. First secure the oil of divine love, and then set your hands to the duties of the world.

"But one must go into solitude to attain this divine love. To get butter from milk you must let it set into curd in a secluded spot: if it is too much disturbed, milk won't turn into curd. Next, you must put aside all other duties, sit in a quiet 'spot, and churn the curd. Only then do you get butter.

"Further, by meditating on God in solitude the mind acquires knowledge, dispassion, and devotion. But the very same mind goes downward if it dwells in the world. In the world there is only one thought: 'woman and gold'.[2]

"The world is water and the mind milk. If you pour milk into water they become one; you cannot find the pure milk any more. But turn the milk into curd and churn it into butter. Then, when that butter is placed in water, it will float. So, practise spiritual discipline in solitude and obtain the butter of knowledge and love. Even if you keep that butter in the water of the world the two will not mix. The butter will float.

"Together with this, you must practise discrimination. 'Woman and gold' is impermanent. God is the only Eternal Substance. What does a man get with money? Food, clothes, and a dwelling-place—nothing more. You cannot realize God with its help. Therefore money can never be the goal of life. That is the process of discrimination. Do you understand?"

M: "Yes, sir. I recently read a Sanskrit play called *Prabodha Chandrodaya*. It deals with discrimination."

MASTER: "Yes, discrimination about objects. Consider—what is there in money or in a beautiful body? Discriminate and you will find that even the body of a beautiful woman consists of bones, flesh, fat, and other disagreeable things. Why should a man give up God and direct his attention to such things? Why should a man forget God for their sake?"

M: "Is it possible to *see* God?"

[2] The term "woman and gold", which has been used throughout in a collective sense, occurs again and again in the teachings of Sri Ramakrishna to designate the chief impediments to spiritual progress. This favourite expression of the Master, "kāminikānchan", has often been misconstrued. By it he meant only "lust and greed", the baneful influence of which retards the aspirant's spiritual growth. He used the word "kāmini", or "woman", as a concrete term for the sex instinct when addressing his man devotees. He advised women, on the other hand, to shun "man". "Kānchan", or "gold", symbolizes greed, which is the other obstacle to spiritual life.

Sri Ramakrishna never taught his disciples to hate any woman, or womankind in general. This can be seen clearly by going through all his teachings under this head and judging them collectively. The Master looked on all women as so many images of the Divine Mother of the Universe. He paid the highest homage to womankind by accepting a woman as his guide while practising the very profound spiritual disciplines of Tantra. His wife, known and revered as the Holy Mother, was his constant companion and first disciple. At the end of his spiritual practice he literally worshipped his wife as the embodiment of the Goddess Kāli, the Divine Mother. After his passing away the Holy Mother became the spiritual guide not only of a large number of householders, but also of many monastic members of the Ramakrishna Order.

MASTER: "Yes, certainly. Living in solitude now and then, repeating God's name and singing His glories, and discriminating between the Real and the unreal—these are the means to employ to see Him."

M: "Under what conditions does one see God?"

MASTER: "Cry to the Lord with an intensely yearning heart and you will certainly see Him. People shed a whole jug of tears for wife and children. They swim in tears for money. But who weeps for God? Cry to Him with a real cry."

The Master sang:

> Cry to your Mother Śyāmā with a real cry, O mind!
> And how can She hold Herself from you?
> How can Śyāmā stay away?
> How can your Mother Kālī hold Herself away?
>
> O mind, if you are in earnest, bring Her an offering
> Of bel-leaves and hibiscus flowers;
> Lay at Her feet your offering
> And with it mingle the fragrant sandal-paste of Love.

Continuing, he said: "Longing is like the rosy dawn. After the dawn out comes the sun. Longing is followed by the vision of God.

"God reveals Himself to a devotee who feels drawn to Him by the combined force of these three attractions: the attraction of worldly possessions for the worldly man, the child's attraction for its mother, and the husband's attraction for the chaste wife. If one feels drawn to Him by the combined force of these three attractions, then through it one can attain Him.

"The point is, to love God even as the mother loves her child, the chaste wife her husband, and the worldly man his wealth. Add together these three forces of love, these three powers of attraction, and give it all to God. Then you will certainly see Him.

"It is necessary to pray to Him with a longing heart. The kitten knows only how to call its mother, crying, 'Mew, mew!' It remains satisfied wherever its mother puts it. And the mother cat puts the kitten sometimes in the kitchen, sometimes on the floor, and sometimes on the bed. When it suffers it cries only, 'Mew, mew!' That's all it knows. But as soon as the mother hears this cry, wherever she may be, she comes to the kitten."

It was Sunday afternoon when M. came on his third visit to the Master. He had been profoundly impressed by his first two visits to this wonderful man. He had been thinking of the Master constantly, and of the utterly simple way he explained the deep truths of the spiritual life. Never before had he met such a man.

Sri Ramakrishna was sitting on the small couch. The room was filled with devotees,[3] who had taken advantage of the holiday to come to see the

---

[3] The word is generally used in the text to denote one devoted to God, a worshipper of the Personal God, or a follower of the path of love. A devotee of Sri Ramakrishna is one who is devoted to Sri Ramakrishna and follows his teachings.

Master. M. had not yet become acquainted with any of them; so he took his seat in a corner. The Master smiled as he talked with the devotees.

He addressed his words particularly to a young man of nineteen, named Narendranath,[4] who was a college student and frequented the Sādhāran Brāhmo Samāj. His eyes were bright, his words were full of spirit, and he had the look of a lover of God.

M. guessed that the conversation was about worldly men, who look down on those who aspire to spiritual things. The Master was talking about the great number of such people in the world, and about how to deal with them.

MASTER (*to Narendra*): "How do you feel about it? Worldly people say all kinds of things about the spiritually minded. But look here! When an elephant moves along the street, any number of curs and other small animals may bark and cry after it; but the elephant doesn't even look back at them. If people speak ill of you, what will you think of them?"

NARENDRA: "I shall think that dogs are barking at me."

MASTER (*smiling*): "Oh, no! You mustn't go that far, my child! (*Laughter.*) God dwells in all beings. But you may be intimate only with good people; you must keep away from the evil-minded. God is even in the tiger; but you cannot embrace the tiger on that account. (*Laughter.*) You may say, 'Why run away from a tiger, which is also a manifestation of God?' The answer to that is: 'Those who tell you to run away are also manifestations of God—and why shouldn't you listen to them?'

"Let me tell you a story. In a forest there lived a holy man who had many disciples. One day he taught them to see God in all beings and, knowing this, to bow low before them all. A disciple went to the forest to gather wood for the sacrificial fire. Suddenly he heard an outcry: 'Get out of the way! A mad elephant is coming!' All but the disciple of the holy man took to their heels. He reasoned that the elephant was also God in another form. Then why should he run away from it? He stood still, bowed before the animal, and began to sing its praises. The māhut of the elephant was shouting: 'Run away! Run away!' But the disciple didn't move. The animal seized him with its trunk, cast him to one side, and went on its way. Hurt and bruised, the disciple lay unconscious on the ground. Hearing what had happened, his teacher and his brother disciples came to him and carried him to the hermitage. With the help of some medicine he soon regained consciousness. Someone asked him, 'You knew the elephant was coming—why didn't you leave the place?' 'But', he said, 'our teacher has told us that God Himself has taken all these forms, of animals as well as men. Therefore, thinking it was only the elephant God that was coming, I didn't run away.' At this the teacher said: 'Yes, my child, it is true that the elephant God was coming; but the māhut God forbade you to stay there. Since all are mani-

---

The word "disciple", when used in connexion with Sri Ramakrishna, refers to one who had been initiated into spiritual life by Sri Ramakrishna and who regarded him as his guru.

[4] Subsequently world-famous as Swami Vivekananda.

festations of God, why didn't you trust the māhut's words? You should have heeded the words of the māhut God.' (*Laughter.*)

"It is said in the scriptures that water is a form of God. But some water is fit to be used for worship, some water for washing the face, and some only for washing plates or dirty linen. This last sort cannot be used for drinking or for a holy purpose. In like manner, God undoubtedly dwells in the hearts of all—holy and unholy, righteous and unrighteous; but a man should not have dealings with the unholy, the wicked, the impure. He must not be intimate with them. With some of them he may exchange words, but with others he shouldn't go even that far. He should keep aloof from such people."

A DEVOTEE: "Sir, if a wicked man is about to do harm, or actually does so, should we keep quiet then?"

MASTER: "A man living in society should make a show of tamas to protect himself from evil-minded people. But he should not harm anybody in anticipation of harm likely to be done him.

"Listen to a story. Some cowherd boys used to tend their cows in a meadow where a terrible poisonous snake lived. Everyone was on the alert for fear of it. One day a brahmachāri was going along the meadow. The boys ran to him and said: 'Revered sir, please don't go that way. A venomous snake lives over there.' 'What of it, my good children?' said the brahmachāri. 'I am not afraid of the snake. I know some mantras.' So saying, he continued on his way along the meadow. But the cowherd boys, being afraid, did not accompany him. In the mean time the snake moved swiftly toward him with upraised hood. As soon as it came near, he recited a mantra, and the snake lay at his feet like an earthworm. The brahmachāri said: 'Look here. Why do you go about doing harm? Come, I will give you a holy word. By repeating it you will learn to love God. Ultimately you will realize Him and so get rid of your violent nature.' Saying this, he taught the snake a holy word and initiated him into spiritual life. The snake bowed before the teacher and said, 'Revered sir, how shall I practise spiritual discipline?' 'Repeat that sacred word', said the teacher, 'and do no harm to anybody.' As he was about to depart, the brahmachāri said, 'I shall see you again.'

"Some days passed and the cowherd boys noticed that the snake would not bite. They threw stones at it. Still it showed no anger; it behaved as if it were an earthworm. One day one of the boys came close to it, caught it by the tail, and, whirling it round and round, dashed it again and again on the ground and threw it away. The snake vomited blood and became unconscious. It was stunned. It could not move. So, thinking it dead, the boys went their way.

"Late at night the snake regained consciousness. Slowly and with great difficulty it dragged itself into its hole; its bones were broken and it could scarcely move. Many days passed. The snake became a mere skeleton covered with a skin. Now and then, at night, it would come out in search of food. For fear of the boys it would not leave its hole during the day-time. Since receiving the sacred word from the teacher, it had given up doing harm to others. It maintained its life on dirt, leaves, or the fruit that dropped from the trees.

"About a year later the brahmachāri came that way again and asked after the snake. The cowherd boys told hĭm that it was dead. But he couldn't believe them. He knew that the snake would not die before attaining the fruit of the holy word with which it had been initiated. He found his way to the place and, searching here and there, called it by the name he had given it. Hearing the teacher's voice, it came out of its hole and bowed before him with great reverence. 'How are you?' asked the brahmachāri. 'I am well, sir', replied the snake. 'But', the teacher asked, 'why are you so thin?' The snake replied: 'Revered sir, you ordered me not to harm anybody. So I have been living only on leaves and fruit. Perhaps that has made me thinner.'

"The snake had developed the quality of sattva; it could not be angry with anyone. It had totally forgotten that the cowherd boys had almost killed it.

"The brahmachāri said: 'It can't be mere want of food that has reduced you to this state. There must be some other reason. Think a little.' Then the snake remembered that the boys had dashed it against the ground. It said: 'Yes, revered sir, now I remember. The boys one day dashed me violently against the ground. They are ignorant, after all. They didn't realize what a great change had come over my mind. How could they know I wouldn't bite or harm anyone?' The brahmachāri exclaimed: 'What a shame! You are such a fool! You don't know how to protect yourself. I asked you not to bite, but I didn't forbid you to hiss. Why didn't you scare them by hissing?'

"So you must hiss at wicked people. You must frighten them lest they should do you harm. But never inject your venom into them. One must not injure others.

"In this creation of God there is a variety of things: men, animals, trees, plants. Among the animals some are good, some bad. There are ferocious animals like the tiger. Some trees bear fruit sweet as nectar, and others bear fruit that is poisonous. Likewise, among human beings, there are the good and the wicked, the holy and the unholy. There are some who are devoted to God, and others who are attached to the world.

"Men may be divided into four classes: those bound by the fetters of the world, the seekers after liberation, the liberated, and the ever-free.

"Among the ever-free we may count sages like Nārada. They live in the world for the good of others, to teach men spiritual truth.

"Those in bondage are sunk in worldliness and forgetful of God. Not even by mistake do they think of God.

"The seekers after liberation want to free themselves from attachment to the world. Some of them succeed and others do not.

"The liberated souls, such as the sādhus and mahātmās, are not entangled in the world, in 'woman and gold'. Their minds are free from worldliness. Besides, they·always meditate on the Lotus Feet of God.

"Suppose a net has been cast into a lake to catch fish. Some fish are so clever that they are never caught in the net. They are like the ever-free. But most of the fish are entangled in the net. Some of them try to free themselves from it, and they are like those who seek liberation. But not all the fish that struggle succeed. A very few do jump out of the net, making a big splash in the water. Then the fishermen shout, 'Look! There goes a big one!' But most of the fish caught in the net cannot escape, nor do they make any effort to get out. On the contrary, they burrow into the mud with the net in their mouths and lie there quietly, thinking, 'We need not fear any more; we are quite safe here.' But the poor things do not know that the fishermen will drag them out with the net. These are like the men bound to the world.

"The bound souls are tied to the world by the fetters of 'woman and gold'. They are bound hand and foot. Thinking that 'woman and gold' will make them happy and give them security, they do not realize that it will lead them to annihilation. When a man thus bound to the world is about to die, his wife asks, 'You are about to go; but what have you done for me?' Again, such is his attachment to the things of the world that, when he sees the lamp burning brightly, he says: 'Dim the light. Too much oil is being used.' And he is on his death-bed!

"The bound souls never think of God. If they get any leisure they indulge in idle gossip and foolish talk, or they engage in fruitless work. If you ask one of them the reason, he answers, 'Oh, I cannot keep still; so I am making a hedge.' When time hangs heavy on their hands they perhaps start playing cards."

There was deep silence in the room.

A DEVOTEE: "Sir, is there no help, then, for such a worldly person?"

MASTER: "Certainly there is. From time to time he should live in the company of holy men, and from time to time go into solitude to meditate on God. Furthermore, he should practise discrimination and pray to God, 'Give me faith and devotion.' Once a person has faith he has achieved everything. There is nothing greater than faith.

(To Kedar) "You must have heard about the tremendous power of faith. It is said in the Purāna that Rāma, who was God Himself—the embodiment of Absolute Brahman—had to build a bridge to cross the sea to Ceylon. But Hanumān, trusting in Rāma's name, cleared the sea in one jump and reached the other side. He had no need of a bridge. (All laugh.)

"Once a man was about to cross the sea. Bibhishana wrote Rāma's name on a leaf, tied it in a corner of the man's wearing-cloth, and said to him: 'Don't be afraid. Have faith and walk on the water. But look here—the moment you lose faith you will be drowned.' The man was walking easily on the water. Suddenly he had an intense desire to see what was tied in his cloth. He opened it and found only a leaf with the name of Rāma written on it. 'What is this?' he thought. 'Just the name of Rāma!' As soon as doubt entered his mind he sank under the water.

"If a man has faith in God, then even if he has committed the most heinous sins—such as killing a cow, a brāhmin, or a woman—he will certainly be saved through his faith. Let him only say to God, 'O Lord, I will not repeat such an action', and he need not be afraid of anything."

When he had said this, the Master sang:

> If only I can pass away repeating Durgā's name,
> How canst Thou then, O Blessed One,
> Withhold from me deliverance,
> Wretched though I may be?
> I may have stolen a drink of wine, or killed a child unborn,
> Or slain a woman or a cow,
> Or even caused a brāhmin's death;
> But, though it all be true,
> Nothing of this can make me feel the least uneasiness;
> For through the power of Thy sweet name
> My wretched soul may still aspire
> Even to Brahmanhood.

Pointing to Narendra, the Master said: "You all see this boy. He behaves that way here. A naughty boy seems very gentle when with his father. But he is quite another person when he plays in the chāndni. Narendra and people of his type belong to the class of the ever-free. They are never entangled in the world. When they grow a little older they feel the awakening of inner consciousness and go directly toward God. They come to the world only to teach others. They never care for anything of the world. They are never attached to 'woman and gold'.

"The Vedas speak of the homā bird. It lives high up in the sky and there it lays its egg. As soon as the egg is laid it begins to fall; but it is so high up that it continues to fall for many days. As it falls it hatches, and the chick falls. As the chick falls its eyes open; it grows wings. As soon as its eyes open, it realizes that it is falling and will be dashed to pieces on touching the earth. Then it at once shoots up toward the mother bird high in the sky."

At this point Narendra left the room. Kedar, Prankrishna, M., and many others remained.

MASTER: "You see, Narendra excels in singing, playing on instruments, study, and everything. The other day he had a discussion with Kedar and tore his arguments to shreds. (All laugh.)

(To M.) "Is there any book in English on reasoning?"

M: "Yes, sir, there is. It is called Logic."

MASTER: "Tell me what it says."

M. was a little embarrassed. He said: "One part of the book deals with deduction from the general to the particular. For example: All men are mortal. Scholars are men. Therefore scholars are mortal. Another part deals with the method of reasoning from the particular to the general. For example: This crow is black. That crow is black. The crows we see everywhere are black. Therefore all crows are black. But there may be a fallacy in a conclusion arrived at in this way; for on inquiry one may find a white crow in some country. There is another illustration: If there is rain, there is or has been a cloud. Therefore rain comes from a cloud. Still another example: This man has thirty-two teeth. That man has thirty-two teeth. All the men we see have thirty-two teeth. Therefore men have thirty-two teeth. English logic deals with such inductions and deductions."

Sri Ramakrishna barely heard these words. While listening he became absent-minded. So the conversation did not proceed far.

When the meeting broke up, the devotees sauntered in the temple garden. M. went in the direction of the Panchavati. It was about five o'clock in the afternoon. After a while he returned to the Master's room. There, on the small north verandah, he witnessed an amazing sight.

Sri Ramakrishna was standing still, surrounded by a few devotees, and Narendra was singing. M. had never heard anyone except the Master sing so sweetly. When he looked at Sri Ramakrishna he was struck with wonder; for the Master stood motionless, with eyes transfixed. He seemed not even to breathe. A devotee told M. that the Master was in samādhi. M. had never before seen or heard of such a thing. Silent with wonder, he thought: "Is it possible for a man to be so oblivious of the outer world in the consciousness of God? How deep his faith and devotion must be to bring about such a state!"

Narendra was singing:

> Meditate, O my mind, on the Lord Hari,
> The Stainless One, Pure Spirit through and through.
> How peerless is the Light that in Him shines!
> How soul-bewitching is His wondrous form!
> How dear is He to all His devotees!
>
> Ever more beauteous in fresh-blossoming love
> That shames the splendour of a million moons,
> Like lightning gleams the glory of His form,
> Raising erect the hair for very joy.

The Master shuddered when this last line was sung. His hair stood on end, and tears of joy streamed down his cheeks. Now and then his lips parted in a smile. Was he seeing the peerless beauty of God, "that shames the splendour of a million moons"? Was this the vision of God, the Essence of Spirit? How much austerity and discipline, how much faith and devotion, must be necessary for such a vision!

The song went on:

> Worship His feet in the lotus of your heart;
> With mind serene and eyes made radiant
> With heavenly love, behold that matchless sight.

Again that bewitching smile. The body motionless as before, the eyes half shut, as if beholding a strange inner vision.

The song drew to a close. Narendra sang the last lines:

> Caught in the spell of His love's ecstasy,
> Immerse yourself for evermore, O mind,
> In Him who is Pure Knowledge and Pure Bliss.

The sight of the samādhi, and the divine bliss he had witnessed, left an indelible impression on M.'s mind. He returned home deeply moved. Now and then he could hear within himself the echo of those soul-intoxicating lines:

> Immerse yourself for evermore, O mind,
> In Him who is Pure Knowledge and Pure Bliss.

The next day, too, was a holiday for M. He arrived at Dakshineswar at three o'clock in the afternoon. Sri Ramakrishna was in his room; Narendra, Bhavanath, and a few other devotees were sitting on a mat spread on the floor. They were all young men of nineteen or twenty. Seated on the small couch, Sri Ramakrishna was talking with them and smiling.

No sooner had M. entered the room than the Master laughed aloud and said to the boys, "There! He has come again." They all joined in the laughter. M. bowed low before him and took a seat. Before this he had saluted the Master with folded hands, like one with an English education. But that day he learnt to fall down at his feet in orthodox Hindu fashion.

Presently the Master explained the cause of his laughter to the devotees. He said: "A man once fed a peacock with a pill of opium at four o'clock in the afternoon. The next day, exactly at that time, the peacock came back. It had felt the intoxication of the drug and returned just in time to have another dose." (*All laugh.*)

M. thought this a very apt illustration. Even at home he had been unable to banish the thought of Sri Ramakrishna for a moment. His mind was constantly at Dakshineswar and he had counted the minutes until he should go again.

In the mean time the Master was having great fun with the boys, treating them as if they were his most intimate friends. Peals of side-splitting laughter filled the room, as if it were a mart of joy. The whole thing was a revelation to M. He thought: "Didn't I see him only yesterday intoxicated with God? Wasn't he swimming then in the Ocean of Divine Love—a sight I had never seen before? And today the same person is behaving like an ordinary man! Wasn't it he who scolded me on the first day of my coming here? Didn't he admonish me, saying, 'And you are a man of knowledge!'? Wasn't it he who said to me that God with form is as true as God without form? Didn't he tell me that God alone is real and all else illusory? Wasn't it he who advised me to live in the world unattached, like a maidservant in a rich man's house?"

Sri Ramakrishna was having great fun with the young devotees; now and then he glanced at M. He noticed that M. sat in silence. The Master said to Ramlal: "You see, he is a little advanced in years, and therefore somewhat serious. He sits quiet while the youngsters are making merry." M. was then about twenty-eight years old.

The conversation drifted to Hanumān, whose picture hung on the wall in the Master's room.

Sri Ramakrishna said: "Just imagine Hanumān's state of mind. He didn't care for money, honour, creature comforts, or anything else. He longed only for God. When he was running away with the heavenly weapon that had been secreted in the crystal pillar, Mandodari began to tempt him with

various fruits so that he might come down and drop the weapon.[5] But he
couldn't be tricked so easily. In reply to her persuasions he sang this song:

> Am I in need of fruit?
> I have the Fruit that makes this life
> Fruitful indeed. Within my heart
> The Tree of Rāma grows,
> Bearing salvation for its fruit.
>
> Under the Wish-fulfilling Tree
> Of Rāma do I sit at ease,
> Plucking whatever fruit I will.
> But if you speak of fruit—
> No beggar, I, for common fruit.
> Behold, I go,
> Leaving a bitter fruit for you."

As Sri Ramakrishna was singing the song he went into samādhi. Again
the half-closed eyes and motionless body that one sees in his photograph.
Just a minute before, the devotees had been making merry in his company.
Now all eyes were riveted on him. Thus for the second time M. saw the
Master in samādhi.

After a long time the Master came back to ordinary consciousness. His
face lighted up with a smile, and his body relaxed; his senses began to function in a normal way. He shed tears of joy as he repeated the holy name
of Rāma. M. wondered whether this very saint was the person who a few
minutes earlier had been behaving like a child of five.

The Master said to Narendra and M., "I should like to hear you speak
and argue in English." They both laughed. But they continued to talk in
their mother tongue. It was impossible for M. to argue any more before the
Master. Though Sri Ramakrishna insisted, they did not talk in English.

At five o'clock in the afternoon all the devotees except Narendra and M.
took leave of the Master. As M. was walking in the temple garden, he
suddenly came upon the Master talking to Narendra on the bank of the
goose-pond. Sri Ramakrishna said to Narendra: "Look here. Come a little
more often. You are a new-comer. On first acquaintance people visit each
other quite often, as is the case with a lover and his sweetheart. (*Narendra
and M. laugh.*) So please come, won't you?"

Narendra, a member of the Brāhmo Samāj, was very particular about his
promises. He said with a smile, "Yes, sir, I shall try."

As they were returning to the Master's room, Sri Ramakrishna said to M.:
"When peasants go to market to buy bullocks for their ploughs, they can
easily tell the good from the bad by touching their tails. On being touched
there, some meekly lie down on the ground. The peasants recognize that
these are without mettle and so reject them. They select only those bullocks

[5] The story referred to here is told in the *Rāmāyana.* Rāvana had received a boon
as a result of which he could be killed only by a particular celestial weapon. This
weapon was concealed in a crystal pillar in his palace. One day Hanumān, in the
guise of an ordinary monkey, came to the palace and broke the pillar. As he was
running away with the weapon, he was tempted with fruit by Mandodari, Rāvana's
wife, so that he might give back the weapon. He soon assumed his own form and
sang the song given in the text.

that frisk about and show spirit when their tails are touched. Narendra is like a bullock of this latter class. He is full of spirit within."

The Master smiled as he said this, and continued: "There are some people who have no grit whatever. They are like flattened rice soaked in milk—soft and mushy. No inner strength!"

It was dusk. The Master was meditating on God. He said to M.: "Go and talk to Narendra. Then tell me what you think of him."

Evening worship was over in the temples. M. met Narendra on the bank of the Ganges and they began to converse. Narendra told M. about his studying in college, his being a member of the Brāhmo Samāj, and so on.

It was now late in the evening and time for M.'s departure; but he felt reluctant to go and instead went in search of Sri Ramakrishna. He had been fascinated by the Master's singing and wanted to hear more. At last he found the Master pacing alone in the nātmandir in front of the Kālī temple. A lamp was burning in the temple on either side of the image of the Divine Mother. The single lamp in the spacious nātmandir blended light and darkness into a kind of mystic twilight, in which the figure of the Master could be dimly seen.

M. had been enchanted by the Master's sweet music. With some hesitation he asked him whether there would be any more singing that evening. "No, not tonight", said Sri Ramakrishna after a little reflection. Then, as if remembering something, he added: "But I'm going soon to Balaram Bose's house in Calcutta. Come there and you'll hear me sing." M. agreed to go.

MASTER: "Do you know Balaram Bose?"

M: "No, sir. I don't."

MASTER: "He lives in Bosepārā."

M: "Well, sir, I shall find him."

As Sri Ramakrishna walked up and down the hall with M., he said to him: "Let me ask you something. What do you think of me?"

M. remained silent. Again Sri Ramakrishna asked: "What do you think of me? How many ānnās of knowledge of God have I?"

M: "I don't understand what you mean by 'ānnās'. But of this I am sure: I have never before seen such knowledge, ecstatic love, faith in God, renunciation, and catholicity anywhere."

The Master laughed.

M. bowed low before him and took his leave. He had gone as far as the main gate of the temple garden when he suddenly remembered something and came back to Sri Ramakrishna, who was still in the nātmandir. In the dim light the Master, all alone, was pacing the hall, rejoicing in the Self— as the lion lives and roams alone in the forest.

In silent wonder M. surveyed that great soul.

MASTER (to M.): "What makes you come back?"

M: "Perhaps the house you asked me to go to belongs to a rich man. They may not let me in. I think I had better not go. I would rather meet you here."

MASTER: "Oh, no! Why should you think that? Just mention my name. Say that you want to see me; then someone will take you to me."

M. nodded his assent and, after saluting the Master, took his leave.

IN THE COMPANY OF DEVOTEES

ABOUT EIGHT O'CLOCK in the morning Sri Ramakrishna went as planned to Balaram Bose's house in Calcutta. It was the day of the Dola-yātrā. Ram, Manomohan, Rakhal,[1] Nityagopal, and other devotees were with him. M., too, came, as bidden by the Master.

The devotees and the Master sang and danced in a state of divine fervour. Several of them were in an ecstatic mood. Nityagopal's chest glowed with the upsurge of emotion, and Rakhal lay on the floor in ecstasy, completely unconscious of the world. The Master put his hand on Rakhal's chest and said: "Peace. Be quiet." This was Rakhal's first experience of ecstasy. He lived with his father in Calcutta and now and then visited the Master at Dakshineswar. About this time he had studied a short while in Vidyāsāgar's school at Śyāmpukur.

When the music was over, the devotees sat down for their meal. Balaram stood there humbly, like a servant. Nobody would have taken him for the master of the house. M. was still a stranger to the devotees, having met only Narendra at Dakshineswar.

A few days later M. visited the Master at Dakshineswar. It was between four and five o'clock in the afternoon. The Master and he were sitting on the steps of the Śiva temples. Looking at the temple of Rādhākānta, across the courtyard, the Master went into an ecstatic mood.

Since his nephew Hriday's dismissal from the temple, Sri Ramakrishna had been living without an attendant. On account of his frequent spiritual moods he could hardly take care of himself. The lack of an attendant caused him great inconvenience.

Sri Ramakrishna was talking to Kāli, the Divine Mother of the Universe. He said: "Mother, everyone says, 'My watch alone is right.' The Christians, the Brāhmos, the Hindus, the Mussalmāns, all say, 'My religion alone is true.' But, Mother, the fact is that nobody's watch is right. Who can truly understand Thee? But if a man prays to Thee with a yearning heart, he can reach Thee, through Thy grace, by any path. Mother, show me some time how the Christians pray to Thee in their churches. But Mother, what will people say if I go in? Suppose they make a fuss! Suppose they don't

---

[1] A beloved disciple of the Master, later known as Swami Brahmananda.

93

allow me to enter the Kāli temple again! Well then, show me the Christian worship from the door of the church."

Another day the Master was seated on the small couch in his room, with his usual beaming countenance. M. arrived with Kalikrishna, who did not know where his friend M. was taking him. He had only been told: "If you want to see a grog-shop, then come with me. You will see a huge jar of wine there." M. related this to Sri Ramakrishna, who laughed about it. The Master said: "The bliss of worship and communion with God is the true wine, the wine of ecstatic love. The goal of human life is to love God. Bhakti is the one essential thing. To know God through jnāna and reasoning is extremely difficult."

Then the Master sang:

> Who is there that can understand what Mother Kāli is?
> Even the six darśanas are powerless to reveal Her. . . .

The Master said, again: "The one goal of life is to cultivate love for God, the love that the milkmaids, the milkmen, and the cowherd boys of Vrindāvan felt for Krishna. When Krishna went away to Mathurā, the cowherds roamed about weeping bitterly because of their separation from Him."

Saying this the Master sang, with his eyes turned upward:

> Just now I saw a youthful cowherd
> With a young calf in his arms;
> There he stood, by one hand holding
> The branch of a young tree.
> "Where are You, Brother Kānāi?" he cried;
> But "Kānāi" scarcely could he utter;
> "Kā" was as much as he could say.
> He cried, "Where are You, Brother?"
> And his eyes were filled with tears.

When M. heard this song of the Master's, laden with love, his eyes were moist with tears.

April 2, 1882

Sri Ramakrishna was sitting in the drawing-room of Keshab Chandra Sen's house in Calcutta; it was five o'clock in the afternoon. When Keshab was told of his arrival, he came to the drawing-room dressed to go out, for he was about to call on a sick friend. Now he cancelled his plan. The Master said to him: "You have so many things to attend to. Besides, you have to edit a newspaper. You have no time to come to Dakshineswar; so I have come to see you. When I heard of your illness I vowed green coconut and sugar to the Divine Mother for your recovery. I said to Her, 'Mother, if something happens to Keshab, with whom shall I talk in Calcutta?'"

Sri Ramakrishna spoke to Pratap and the other Brāhmo devotees. M. was seated near by. Pointing to him, the Master said to Keshab: "Will you please ask him why he doesn't come to Dakshineswar any more? He repeatedly tells me he is not attached to his wife and children." M. had been paying visits to the Master for about a month; his absence for a time from Dakshineswar called forth this remark. Sri Ramakrishna had asked M. to write to him, if his coming were delayed.

Pundit Samadhyayi was present. The Brāhmo devotees introduced him to Sri Ramakrishna as a scholar well versed in the Vedas and the other scriptures. The Master said, "Yes, I can see inside him through his eyes, as one can see the objects in a room through the glass door."

Trailokya sang. Suddenly the Master stood up and went into samādhi, repeating the Mother's name. Coming down a little to the plane of sense consciousness, he danced and sang:

> I drink no ordinary wine, but Wine of Everlasting Bliss,
> As I repeat my Mother Kāli's name;
> It so intoxicates my mind that people take me to be drunk!
> First my guru gives molasses for the making of the Wine;
> My longing is the ferment to transform it.
> Knowledge, the maker of the Wine, prepares it for me then;
> And when it is done, my mind imbibes it from the bottle of the
>   mantra,
> Taking the Mother's name to make it pure.
> Drink of this Wine, says Rāmprasād,[2] and the four fruits[3] of life
>   are yours.

The Master looked at Keshab tenderly, as if Keshab were his very own. He seemed to fear that Keshab might belong to someone else, that is to say, that he might become a worldly person. Looking at him, the Master sang again:

> We are afraid to speak, and yet we are afraid to keep still;
> Our minds, O Rādhā, half believe that we are about to lose you!
> We tell you the secret that we know—
> The secret whereby we ourselves, and others, with our help,
> Have passed through many a time of peril;
> Now it all depends on you.

Quoting the last part of the song, he said to Keshab: "That is to say, renounce everything and call on God. He alone is real; all else is illusory. Without the realization of God everything is futile. This is the great secret."

The Master sat down again and began to converse with the devotees. For a while he listened to a piano recital, enjoying it like a child. Then he was taken to the inner apartments, where he was served with refreshments and the ladies saluted him.

As the Master was leaving Keshab's house, the Brāhmo devotees accompanied him respectfully to his carriage.

[2] The author of the song. It is customary for writers of devotional songs in India to mention their names at the end of their songs.

[3] Dharma, artha, kāma, and moksha.

Sri Ramakrishna was seated with his devotees in the drawing-room of Prankrishna Mukherji's house in Calcutta; it was between one and two o'clock in the afternoon. Since Colonel Viswanath[4] lived in that neighbourhood, the Master intended to visit him before going to see Keshab at the Lily Cottage. A number of neighbours and other friends of Prankrishna had been invited to meet Sri Ramakrishna. They were all eager to hear his words.

MASTER: "God and His glory. This universe is His glory. People see His glory and forget everything. They do not seek God, whose glory is this world. All seek to enjoy 'woman and gold'. But there is too much misery and worry in that. This world is like the whirlpool of the Viśālākshi.[5] Once a boat gets into it there is no hope of its rescue. Again, the world is like a thorny bush: you have hardly freed yourself from one set of thorns before you find yourself entangled in another. Once you enter a labyrinth you find it very difficult to get out. Living in the world, a man becomes seared, as it were."

A DEVOTEE: "Then what is the way, sir?"

MASTER: "Prayer and the company of holy men. You cannot get rid of an ailment without the help of a physician. But it is not enough to be in the company of religious people only for a day. You should constantly seek it, for the disease has become chronic. Again, you can't understand the pulse rightly unless you live with a physician. Moving with him constantly, you learn to distinguish between the pulse of phlegm and the pulse of bile."

DEVOTEE: "What is the good of holy company?"

MASTER: "It begets yearning for God. It begets love of God. Nothing whatsoever is achieved in spiritual life without yearning. By constantly living in the company of holy men, the soul becomes restless for God. This yearning is like the state of mind of a man who has someone ill in the family. His mind is in a state of perpetual restlessness, thinking how the sick person may be cured. Or again, one should feel a yearning for God like the yearning of a man who has lost his job and is wandering from one office to another in search of work. If he is rejected at a certain place which has no vacancy, he goes there again the next day and inquires, 'Is there any vacancy today?'

"There is another way: earnestly praying to God. God is our very own. We should say to Him: 'O God, what is Thy nature? Reveal Thyself to me. Thou must show Thyself to me; for why else hast Thou created me?' Some Śikh devotees once said to me, 'God is full of compassion.' I said: 'But why should we call Him compassionate? He is our Creator. What is there to be wondered at if He is kind to us? Parents bring up their children. Do you call that an act of kindness? They must act that way.' Therefore we should force our demands on God. He is our Father and Mother, isn't

---

[4] The Resident of the Nepalese Government in Calcutta, and a devotee of the Master.

[5] A stream near Sri Ramakrishna's birth-place.

He? If the son demands his patrimony and gives up food and drink in order to enforce his demand, then the parents hand his share over to him three years before the legal time. Or when the child demands some pice from his mother, and says over and over again: 'Mother, give me a couple of pice. I beg you on my knees!'—then the mother, seeing his earnestness, and unable to bear it any more, tosses the money to him.

"There is another benefit from holy company. It helps one cultivate discrimination between the Real and the unreal. God alone is the Real, that is to say, the Eternal Substance, and the world is unreal, that is to say, transitory. As soon as a man finds his mind wandering away to the unreal, he should apply discrimination. The moment an elephant stretches out its trunk to eat a plaintain-tree in a neighbour's garden, it gets a blow from the iron goad of the driver."

A NEIGHBOUR: "Why does a man have sinful tendencies?"

MASTER: "In God's creation there are all sorts of things. He has created bad men as well as good men. It is He who gives us good tendencies, and it is He again who gives us evil tendencies."

NEIGHBOUR: "In that case we aren't responsible for our sinful actions, are we?"

MASTER: "Sin begets its own result. This is God's law. Won't you burn your tongue if you chew a chilli? In his youth Mathur[6] led a rather fast life; so he suffered from various diseases before his death.

"One may not realize this in youth. I have looked into the hearth in the kitchen of the Kāli temple when logs are being burnt. At first the wet wood burns rather well. It doesn't seem then that it contains much moisture. But when the wood is sufficiently burnt, all the moisture runs back to one end. At last water squirts from the fuel and puts out the fire.

"So one should be careful about anger, passion, and greed. Take, for instance, the case of Hanumān. In a fit of anger he burnt Ceylon. At last he remembered that Sītā was living in the aśoka grove. Then he began to tremble lest the fire should injure her."

NEIGHBOUR: "Why has God created wicked people?"

MASTER: "That is His will, His play. In His māyā there exists avidyā as well as vidyā. Darkness is needed too. It reveals all the more the glory of light. There is no doubt that anger, lust, and greed are evils. Why, then, has God created them? In order to create saints. A man becomes a saint by conquering the senses. Is there anything impossible for a man who has subdued his passions? He can even realize God, through His grace. Again, see how His whole play of creation is perpetuated through lust.

"Wicked people are needed too. At one time the tenants of an estate became unruly. The landlord had to send Golak Choudhury, who was a ruffian. He was such a harsh administrator that the tenants trembled at the very mention of his name.

"There is need of everything. Once Sītā said to her Husband: 'Rāma, it would be grand if every house in Ayodhyā were a mansion! I find many

---

[6] The son-in-law of Rāni Rasmani, and a great devotee of Sri Ramakrishna, whom he provided with all the necessaries of life at the temple garden.

houses old and dilapidated.' 'But, my dear,' said Rāma, 'if all the houses were beautiful ones, what would the masons do?' (*Laughter.*) God has created all kinds of things. He has created good trees, and poisonous plants and weeds as well. Among the animals there are good, bad, and all kinds of creatures—tigers, lions, snakes, and so on."

NEIGHBOUR: "Sir, is it ever possible to realize God while leading the life of a householder?"

MASTER: "Certainly. But as I said just now, one must live in holy company and pray unceasingly. One should weep for God. When the impurities of the mind are thus washed away, one realizes God. The mind is like a needle covered with mud, and God is like a magnet. The needle cannot be united with the magnet unless it is free from mud. Tears wash away the mud, which is nothing but lust, anger, greed, and other evil tendencies, and the inclination to worldly enjoyments as well. As soon as the mud is washed away, the magnet attracts the needle, that is to say, man realizes God. Only the pure in heart see God. A fever patient has an excess of the watery element in his system. What can quinine do for him unless that is removed?

"Why shouldn't one realize God while living in the world? But, as I said, one must live in holy company, pray to God, weeping for His grace, and now and then go into solitude. Unless the plants on a foot-path are protected at first by fences, they are destroyed by cattle."

NEIGHBOUR: "Then householders, too, will have the vision of God, won't they?"

MASTER: "Everybody will surely be liberated. But one should follow the instructions of the guru; if one follows a devious path, one will suffer in trying to retrace one's steps. It takes a long time to achieve liberation. A man may fail to obtain it in this life. Perhaps he will realize God only after many births. Sages like Janaka performed worldly duties. They performed them, bearing God in their minds, as a dancing-girl dances, keeping jars or trays on her head. Haven't you seen how the women in northwest India walk, talking and laughing while carrying water-pitchers on their heads?"

NEIGHBOUR: "You just referred to the instructions of the guru. How shall we find him?"

MASTER: "Anyone and everyone cannot be a guru. A huge timber floats on the water and can carry animals as well. But a piece of worthless wood sinks, if a man sits on it, and drowns him. Therefore in every age God incarnates Himself as the guru, to teach humanity. Satchidānanda alone is the guru.

"What is knowledge? And what is the nature of this ego? 'God alone is the Doer, and none else'—that is knowledge. I am not the doer; I am a mere instrument in His hand. Therefore I say: 'O Mother, Thou art the Operator and I am the machine. Thou art the Indweller and I am the house. Thou art the Driver and I am the carriage. I move as Thou movest me. I do as Thou makest me do. I speak as Thou makest me speak. Not I, not I, but Thou, but Thou.' "

From Prankrishna's house the Master went to Colonel Viswanath's and from there to the Lily Cottage.

VISIT TO VIDYĀSĀGAR

August 5, 1882

PUNDIT ISWAR CHANDRA VIDYĀSĀGAR was born in the village of Beer-singh, not far from Kāmārpukur, Sri Ramakrishna's birth-place. He was known as a great scholar, educator, writer, and philanthropist. One of the creators of modern Bengali, he was also well versed in Sanskrit grammar and poetry. His generosity made his name a household word with his countrymen, most of his income being given in charity to widows, orphans, indigent students, and other needy people. Nor was his compassion limited to human beings: he stopped drinking milk for years so that the calves should not be deprived of it, and he would not drive in a carriage for fear of causing discomfort to the horses. He was a man of indomitable spirit, which he showed when he gave up the lucrative position of principal of the Sanskrit College of Calcutta because of a disagreement with the authorities. His affection for his mother was especially deep. One day, in the absence of a ferry-boat, he swam a raging river at the risk of his life to fulfil her wish that he should be present at his brother's wedding. His whole life was one of utter simplicity. The title Vidyāsāgar, meaning "Ocean of Learning", was given him in recognition of his vast erudition.

Sri Ramakrishna had long wanted to visit Iswar Chandra Vidyāsāgar. Learning from M. that he was a teacher at Vidyāsāgar's school, the Master asked: "Can you take me to Vidyāsāgar? I should like very much to see him." M. told Iswar Chandra of Sri Ramakrishna's wish, and the pundit gladly agreed that M. should bring the Master, some Saturday afternoon at four o'clock. He only asked M. what kind of paramahamsa the Master was, saying, "Does he wear an ochre cloth?" M. answered: "No, sir. He is an unusual person. He wears a red-bordered cloth and polished slippers. He lives in a room in Rāni Rasmani's temple garden. In his room there is a couch with a mattress and mosquito net. He has no outer indication of holiness. But he doesn't know anything except God. Day and night he thinks of God alone."

On the afternoon of August 5 the Master left Dakshineswar in a hackney carriage, accompanied by Bhavanath, M., and Hazra. Vidyāsāgar lived in Bādurbāgan, in central Calcutta, about six miles from Dakshineswar. On the way Sri Ramakrishna talked with his companions; but as the carriage neared Vidyāsāgar's house his mood suddenly changed. He was overpowered with divine ecstasy. Not noticing this, M. pointed out the garden house where Rāja Rammohan Roy had lived. The Master was annoyed and said, "I don't care about such things now." He was going into an ecstatic state.

The carriage stopped in front of Vidyāsāgar's house. The Master alighted, supported by M., who then led the way. In the courtyard were many flowering plants. As the Master walked to the house he said to M., like a child, pointing to his shirt-button: "My shirt is unbuttoned. Will that offend Vidyāsāgar?" "Oh, no!" said M. "Don't be anxious about it. Nothing about you will be offensive. You don't have to button your shirt." He accepted the assurance simply, like a child.

Vidyāsāgar was about sixty-two years old, sixteen or seventeen years older than the Master. He lived in a two-storey house built in the English fashion, with lawns on all sides and surrounded by a high wall. After climbing the stairs to the second floor, Sri Ramakrishna and his devotees entered a room at the far end of which Vidyāsāgar was seated facing them, with a table in front of him. To the right of the table was a bench. Some friends of their host occupied chairs on the other two sides.

Vidyāsāgar rose to receive the Master. Sri Ramakrishna stood in front of the bench, with one hand resting on the table. He gazed at Vidyāsāgar, as if they had known each other before, and smiled in an ecstatic mood. In that mood he remained standing a few minutes. Now and then, to bring his mind back to normal consciousness, he said, "I shall have a drink of water."

In the mean time the young members of the household and a few friends and relatives of Vidyāsāgar had gathered around. Sri Ramakrishna, still in an ecstatic mood, sat on the bench. A young man, seventeen or eighteen years old, who had come to Vidyāsāgar to seek financial help for his education, was seated there. The Master sat down at a little distance from the boy, saying in an abstracted mood: "Mother, this boy is very much attached to the world. He belongs to Thy realm of ignorance."

Vidyāsāgar told someone to bring water and asked M. whether the Master would like some sweetmeats also. Since M. did not object, Vidyāsāgar himself went eagerly to the inner apartments and brought the sweets. They were placed before the Master. Bhavanath and Hazra also received their share. When they were offered to M., Vidyāsāgar said: "Oh, he is like one of the family. We needn't worry about him." Referring to a young devotee, the Master said to Vidyāsāgar: "He is a nice young man and is sound at the core. He is like the river Phalgu. The surface is covered with sand; but if you dig a little you will find water flowing underneath."

After taking some of the sweets, the Master, with a smile, began to speak to Vidyāsāgar. Meanwhile the room had become filled with people; some were standing and others were seated.

MASTER: "Ah! Today, at last, I have come to the ocean. Up till now I have seen only canals, marshes, or a river at the most. But today I am face to face with the sāgar, the ocean." (All laugh.)

VIDYĀSĀGAR (smiling): "Then please take home some salt water." (Laughter.)

MASTER: "Oh, no! Why salt water? You aren't the ocean of ignorance. You are the ocean of vidyā, knowledge. You are the ocean of condensed milk." (*All laugh.*)

VIDYĀSĀGAR: "Well, you may put it that way."

The pundit became silent. Sri Ramakrishna said: "Your activities are inspired by sattva. Though they are rājasic, they are influenced by sattva. Compassion springs from sattva. Though work for the good of others belongs to rajas, yet this rajas has sattva for its basis and is not harmful. Śuka and other sages cherished compassion in their minds to give people religious instruction, to teach them about God. You are distributing food and learning. That is good too. If these activities are done in a selfless spirit they lead to God. But most people work for fame or to acquire merit. Their activities are not selfless. Besides, you are already a siddha."[1]

VIDYĀSĀGAR: "How is that, sir?"

MASTER (*laughing*): "When potatoes and other vegetables are well cooked, they become soft and tender. And you possess such a tender nature! You are so compassionate!" (*Laughter.*)

VIDYĀSĀGAR (*laughing*): "But when the paste of kalāi pulse is boiled it becomes all the harder."

MASTER: "But you don't belong to that class. Mere pundits are like diseased fruit that becomes hard and will not ripen at all. Such fruit has neither the freshness of green fruit nor the flavour of ripe. Vultures soar very high in the sky, but their eyes are fixed on rotten carrion on the ground. The book-learned are reputed to be wise, but they are attached to 'woman and gold'. Like the vultures, they are in search of carrion. They are attached to the world of ignorance. Compassion, love of God, and renunciation are the glories of true knowledge."

Vidyāsāgar listened to these words in silence. The others, too, gazed at the Master and were attentive to every word he said.

Vidyāsāgar was very reticent about giving religious instruction to others. He had studied Hindu philosophy. Once, when M. had asked him his opinion of it, Vidyāsāgar had said, "I think the philosophers have failed to explain what was in their minds." But in his daily life he followed all the rituals of Hindu religion and wore the sacred thread of a brāhmin. About God he had once declared: "It is indeed impossible to know Him. What, then, should be our duty? It seems to me that we should live in such a way that, if others followed our example, this very earth would be heaven. Everyone should try to do good to the world."

Sri Ramakrishna's conversation now turned to the Knowledge of Brahman.

MASTER: "Brahman is beyond vidyā and avidyā, knowledge and ignorance. It is beyond māyā, the illusion of duality.

"The world consists of the illusory duality of knowledge and ignorance. It contains knowledge and devotion, and also attachment to 'woman and gold'; righteousness and unrighteousness; good and evil. But Brahman is unattached to these. Good and evil apply to the jīva, the individual soul, as

---

[1] Literally, "perfect" or "boiled"; the word is applied both to the perfected soul and to boiled things.

do righteousness and unrighteousness; but Brahman is not at all affected by them.

"One man may read the *Bhāgavata* by the light of a lamp, and another may commit a forgery by that very light; but the lamp is unaffected. The sun sheds its light on the wicked as well as on the virtuous.

"You may ask, 'How, then, can one explain misery and sin and unhappiness?' The answer is that these apply only to the jīva. Brahman is unaffected by them. There is poison in a snake; but though others may die if bitten by it, the snake itself is not affected by the poison.

"What Brahman is cannot be described. All things in the world—the Vedas, the Purānas, the Tantras, the six systems of philosophy—have been defiled, like food that has been touched by the tongue, for they have been read or uttered by the tongue. Only one thing has not been defiled in this way, and that is Brahman. No one has ever been able to say what Brahman is."

VIDYĀSĀGAR (*to his friends*): "Oh! That is a remarkable statement. I have learnt something new today."

MASTER: "A man had two sons. The father sent them to a preceptor to learn the Knowledge of Brahman. After a few years they returned from their preceptor's house and bowed low before their father. Wanting to measure the depth of their knowledge of Brahman, he first questioned the older of the two boys. 'My child,' he said, 'you have studied all the scriptures. Now tell me, what is the nature of Brahman?' The boy began to explain Brahman by reciting various texts from the Vedas. The father did not say anything. Then he asked the younger son the same question. But the boy remained silent and stood with eyes cast down. No word escaped his lips. The father was pleased and said to him: 'My child, you have understood a little of Brahman. What It is cannot be expressed in words.'

"Men often think they have understood Brahman fully. Once an ant went to a hill of sugar. One grain filled its stomach. Taking another grain in its mouth it started homeward. On its way it thought, 'Next time I shall carry home the whole hill.' That is the way shallow minds think. They don't know that Brahman is beyond one's words and thought. However great a man may be, how much can he know of Brahman? Śukadeva and sages like him may have been big ants; but even they could carry at the utmost eight or ten grains of sugar!

"As for what has been said in the Vedas and the Purānas, do you know what it is like? Suppose a man has seen the ocean, and somebody asks him, 'Well, what is the ocean like?' The first man opens his mouth as wide as he can and says: 'What a sight! What tremendous waves and sounds!' The description of Brahman in the sacred books is like that. It is said in the Vedas that Brahman is of the nature of Bliss—It is Satchidānanda.

"Śuka and other sages stood on the shore of this Ocean of Brahman and saw and touched the water. According to one school of thought they never plunged into it. Those who do, cannot come back to the world again.

"In samādhi one attains the Knowledge of Brahman—one realizes Brahman. In that state reasoning stops altogether, and man becomes mute. He has no power to describe the nature of Brahman.

"Once a salt doll went to measure the depth of the ocean. (*All laugh.*) It wanted to tell others how deep the water was. But this it could never do, for no sooner did it get into the water than it melted. Now who was there to report the ocean's depth?"

A DEVOTEE: "Suppose a man has obtained the Knowledge of Brahman in samādhi. Doesn't he speak any more?"

MASTER: "Śankarāchārya[2] retained the 'ego of Knowledge' in order to teach others. After the vision of Brahman a man becomes silent. He reasons about It as long as he has not realized It. If you heat butter in a pan on the stove, it makes a sizzling sound as long as the water it contains has not dried up. But when no trace of water is left the clarified butter makes no sound. If you put an uncooked cake of flour in that butter it sizzles again. But after the cake is cooked all sound stops. Just so, a man established in samādhi comes down to the relative plane of consciousness in order to teach others, and then he talks about God.

"The bee buzzes as long as it is not sitting on a flower. It becomes silent when it begins to sip the honey. But sometimes, intoxicated with the honey, it buzzes again.

"An empty pitcher makes a gurgling sound when it is dipped in water. When it fills up it becomes silent. (*All laugh.*) But if the water is poured from it into another pitcher, then you will hear the sound again. (*Laughter.*)

"The rishis of old attained the Knowledge of Brahman. One cannot have this so long as there is the slightest trace of worldliness. How hard the rishis laboured! Early in the morning they would go away from the hermitage, and would spend the whole day in solitude, meditating on Brahman. At night they would return to the hermitage and eat a little fruit or roots. They kept their minds aloof from the objects of sight, hearing, touch, and other things of a worldly nature. Only thus did they realize Brahman as their own inner consciousness.

"But in the Kaliyuga, man, being totally dependent on food for life, cannot altogether shake off the idea that he is the body. In this state of mind it is not proper for him to say, 'I am He.' When a man does all sorts of worldly things, he should not say, 'I am Brahman.' Those who cannot give up attachment to worldly things, and who find no means to shake off the feeling of 'I', should rather cherish the idea, 'I am God's servant; I am His devotee.' One can also realize God by following the path of devotion.

"The jnāni gives up his identification with worldly things, discriminating, 'Not this, not this'. Only then can he realize Brahman. It is like reaching the roof of a house by leaving the steps behind, one by one. But the vijnāni, who is more intimately acquainted with Brahman, realizes something more. He realizes that the steps are made of the same materials as the roof: bricks, lime, and brick-dust. That which is realized intuitively as Brahman, through the eliminating process of 'Not this, not this', is then found to have become

[2] One of the greatest philosophers of India.

the universe and all its living beings. The vijñāni sees that the Reality which is nirguna, without attributes, is also saguna, with attributes.

"A man cannot live on the roof a long time. He comes down again. Those who realize Brahman in samādhi come down also and find that it is Brahman that has become the universe and its living beings. In the musical scale there are the notes sā, re, gā, mā, pā, dhā, and ni; but one cannot keep one's voice on 'ni' a long time. The ego does not vanish altogether. The man coming down from samādhi perceives that it is Brahman that has become the ego, the universe, and all living beings. This is known as vijñāna.

"The path of knowledge leads to Truth, as does the path that combines knowledge and love. The path of love, too, leads to this goal. The way of love is as true as the way of knowledge. All paths ultimately lead to the same Truth. But as long as God keeps the feeling of ego in us, it is easier to follow the path of love.

"The vijñāni sees that Brahman is immovable and actionless, like Mount Sumeru. This universe consists of the three gunas—sattva, rajas, and tamas. They are in Brahman. But Brahman is unattached.

"The vijñāni further sees that what is Brahman is the Bhagavān, the Personal God. He who is beyond the three gunas is the Bhagavān, with His six supernatural powers. Living beings, the universe, mind, intelligence, love, renunciation, knowledge—all these are the manifestations of His power. (*With a laugh*) If an aristocrat has neither house nor property, or if he has been forced to sell them, one doesn't call him an aristocrat any more. (*All laugh.*) God is endowed with the six supernatural powers. If He were not, who would obey Him? (*All laugh.*)

"Just see how picturesque this universe is! How many things there are! The sun, moon, and stars; and how many varieties of living beings!—big and small, good and bad, strong and weak—some endowed with more power, some with less."

VIDYĀSĀGAR: "Has He endowed some with more power and others with less?"

MASTER: "As the All-pervading Spirit He exists in all beings, even in the ant. But the manifestations of His Power are different in different beings; otherwise, how can one person put ten to flight, while another can't face even one? And why do all people respect you? Have you grown a pair of horns? (*Laughter.*) You have more compassion and learning. Therefore people honour you and come to pay you their respects. Don't you agree with me?"

Vidyāsāgar smiled.

The Master continued: "There is nothing in mere scholarship. The object of study is to find means of knowing God and realizing Him. A holy man had a book. When asked what it contained, he opened it and showed that on all the pages were written the words 'Om Rāma', and nothing else.

"What is the significance of the *Gītā*? It is what you find by repeating the word ten times. It is then reversed into 'tāgi', which means a person who has renounced everything for God. And the lesson of the *Gītā* is: 'O man, renounce everything and seek God alone.' Whether a man is a monk or a householder, he has to shake off all attachment from his mind.

"Chaitanyadeva set out on a pilgrimage to southern India. One day he saw a man reading the *Gītā*. Another man, seated at a distance, was listening and weeping. His eyes were swimming in tears. Chaitanyadeva asked him, 'Do you understand all this?' The man said, 'No, revered sir, I don't understand a word of the text.' 'Then why are you crying?' asked Chaitanya. The devotee said: 'I see Arjuna's chariot before me. I see Lord Krishna and Arjuna seated in front of it, talking. I see this and I weep.'

"Why does a vijnāni keep an attitude of love toward God? The answer is that 'I-consciousness' persists. It disappears in the state of samādhi, no doubt, but it comes back. In the case of ordinary people the 'I' never disappears. You may cut down the aśwattha tree, but the next day sprouts shoot up. (*All laugh.*)

"Even after the attainment of Knowledge this 'I-consciousness' comes up, nobody knows from where. You dream of a tiger. Then you awake; but your heart keeps on palpitating! All our suffering is due to this 'I'. The cow cries, 'Hāmbā!', which means 'I'. That is why it suffers so much. It is yoked to the plough and made to work in rain and sun. Then it may be killed by the butcher. From its hide shoes are made, and also drums, which are mercilessly beaten. (*Laughter.*) Still it does not escape suffering. At last strings are made out of its entrails for the bows used in carding cotton. Then it no longer says, 'Hāmbā! Hāmbā!', 'I! I!', but 'Tuhu! Tuhu!', 'Thou! Thou!' Only then are its troubles over. O Lord, I am the servant; Thou art the Master. I am the child; Thou art the Mother.

"Once Rāma asked Hanumān, 'How do you look on Me?' And Hanumān replied: 'O Rāma, as long as I have the feeling of "I", I see that Thou art the whole and I am a part; Thou art the Master and I am Thy servant. But when, O Rāma, I have the knowledge of Truth, then I realize that Thou art I, and I am Thou.'

"The relationship of master and servant is the proper one. Since this 'I' must remain, let the rascal be God's servant.

" 'I' and 'mine'—these constitute ignorance. 'My house', 'my wealth', 'my learning', 'my possessions'—the attitude that prompts one to say such things comes of ignorance. On the contrary, the attitude born of Knowledge is: 'O God, Thou art the Master, and all these things belong to Thee. House, family, children, attendants, friends, are Thine.'

"One should constantly remember death. Nothing will survive death. We are born into this world to perform certain duties, like the people who come from the countryside to Calcutta on business. If a visitor goes to a rich man's garden, the superintendent says to him, 'This is our garden', 'This is our lake', and so forth. But if the superintendent is dismissed for some misdeed, he can't carry away even his mango-wood chest. He sends it secretly by the gate-keeper. (*Laughter.*)

"God laughs on two occasions. He laughs when the physician says to the patient's mother, 'Don't be afraid, mother; I shall certainly cure your boy.' God laughs, saying to Himself, 'I am going to take his life, and this man says he will save it!' The physician thinks he is the master, forgetting that God is the Master. God laughs again when two brothers divide their land with a string, saying to each other, 'This side is mine and that side is yours.' He laughs and says to Himself, 'The whole universe belongs to Me, but they say they own this portion or that portion.'

"Can one know God through reasoning? Be His servant, surrender yourself to Him, and then pray to Him.

(*To Vidyāsāgar, with a smile*) "Well, what is your attitude?"

VIDYĀSĀGAR (*smiling*): "Some day I shall confide it to you." (*All laugh.*)

MASTER (*laughing*): "God cannot be realized through mere scholarly reasoning."

Intoxicated with divine love, the Master sang:

> Who is there that can understand what Mother Kāli is?
> Even the six darśanas are powerless to reveal Her.
> It is She, the scriptures say, that is the Inner Self
> Of the yogi, who in Self discovers all his joy;
> She that, of Her own sweet will, inhabits every living thing.
>
> The macrocosm and microcosm rest in the Mother's womb;
> Now do you see how vast it is? In the Mulādhāra
> The yogi meditates on Her, and in the Sahasrāra:
> Who but Śiva has beheld Her as She really is?
> Within the lotus wilderness She sports beside Her Mate, the
> Swan.[3]
>
> When man aspires to understand Her, Rāmprasād must smile;
> To think of knowing Her, he says, is quite as laughable
> As to imagine one can swim across the boundless sea.
> But while my mind has understood, alas! my heart has not;
> Though but a dwarf, it still would strive to make a captive of
> the moon.

Continuing, the Master said: "Did you notice?

> The macrocosm and microcosm rest in the Mother's womb;
> Now do you see how vast it is?

"Again, the poet says:

> Even the six darśanas are powerless to reveal Her.

She cannot be realized by means of mere scholarship.

"One must have faith and love. Let me tell you how powerful faith is. A man was about to cross the sea from Ceylon to India. Bibhishana said to him: 'Tie this thing in a corner of your wearing-cloth, and you will cross the sea safely. You will be able to walk on the water. But be sure not to examine it, or you will sink.' The man was walking easily on the water of the sea—such is the strength of faith—when, having gone part of the way, he thought, 'What is this wonderful thing Bibhishana has given me, that I can walk even on the water?' He untied the knot and found only a leaf

---

[3] Śiva, the Absolute.

with the name of Rāma written on it. 'Oh, just this!' he thought, and instantly he sank.

"There is a popular saying that Hanumān jumped over the sea through his faith in Rāma's name, but Rāma Himself had to build a bridge

"If a man has faith in God, then he need not be afraid though he may have committed sin—nay, the vilest sin."

Then Sri Ramakrishna sang a song glorifying the power of faith:

> If only I can pass away repeating Durgā's name,
> How canst Thou then, O Blessed One,
> Withhold from me deliverance,
> Wretched though I may be? . . .

The Master continued: "Faith and devotion. One realizes God easily through devotion. He is grasped through ecstasy of love."

With these words the Master sang again:

> How are you trying, O my mind, to know the nature of God?
> You are groping like a madman locked in a dark room.
> He is grasped through ecstatic love; how can you fathom Him
>   without it?
> Only through affirmation, never negation, can you know Him;
> Neither through Veda nor through Tantra nor the six darśanas.
>
> It is in love's elixir only that He delights, O mind;
> He dwells in the body's inmost depths, in Everlasting Joy.
> And, for that love, the mighty yogis practise yoga from age to age;
> When love awakes, the Lord, like a magnet, draws to Him the soul.
>
> He it is, says Rāmprasād, that I approach as Mother;
> But must I give away the secret, here in the market-place?
> From the hints I have given, O mind, guess what that Being is!

While singing, the Master went into samādhi. He was seated on the bench, facing west, the palms of his hands joined together, his body erect and motionless. Everyone watched him expectantly. Vidyāsāgar, too, was speechless and could not take his eyes from the Master.

After a time Sri Ramakrishna showed signs of regaining the normal state. He drew a deep breath and said with a smile: "The means of realizing God are ecstasy of love and devotion—that is, one must love God. He who is Brahman is addressed as the Mother.

> He it is, says Rāmprasād, that I approach as Mother;
> But must I give away the secret, here in the market-place?
> From the hints I have given, O mind, guess what that Being is!

"Rāmprasād asks the mind only to guess the nature of God. He wishes it to understand that what is called Brahman in the Vedas is addressed by him as the Mother. He who is attributeless also has attributes. He who is Brahman is also Śakti. When thought of as inactive, He is called Brahman, and when thought of as the Creator, Preserver, and Destroyer, He is called the Primordial Energy, Kāli.

"Brahman and Śakti are identical, like fire and its power to burn. When we talk of fire we automatically mean also its power to burn. Again, the fire's power to burn implies the fire itself. If you accept the one you must accept the other.

"Brahman alone is addressed as the Mother. This is because a mother is an object of great love. One is able to realize God just through love. Ecstasy of feeling, devotion, love, and faith—these are the means. Listen to a song:

> As is a man's meditation, so is his feeling of love;
> As is a man's feeling of love, so is his gain;
> And faith is the root of all.
> If in the Nectar Lake of Mother Kāli's feet
> My mind remains immersed,
> Of little use are worship, oblations, or sacrifice.

"What is needed is absorption in God—loving Him intensely. The 'Nectar Lake' is the Lake of Immortality. A man sinking in It does not die, but becomes immortal. Some people believe that by thinking of God too much the mind becomes deranged; but that is not true. God is the Lake of Nectar, the Ocean of Immortality. He is called the 'Immortal' in the Vedas. Sinking in It, one does not die, but verily transcends death.

> Of little use are worship, oblations, or sacrifice.

If a man comes to love God, he need not trouble himself much about these activities. One needs a fan only as long as there is no breeze. The fan may be laid aside if the southern breeze blows. Then what need is there of a fan?

(To Vidyāsāgar) "The activities that you are engaged in are good. It is very good if you can perform them in a selfless spirit, renouncing egotism, giving up the idea that you are the doer. Through such action one develops love and devotion to God, and ultimately realizes Him.

"The more you come to love God, the less you will be inclined to perform action. When the daughter-in-law is with child, her mother-in-law gives her less work to do. As time goes by she is given less and less work. When the time of delivery nears, she is not allowed to do any work at all, lest it should hurt the child or cause difficulty at the time of birth.

"By these philanthropic activities you are really doing good to yourself. If you can do them disinterestedly, your mind will become pure and you will develop love of God. As soon as you have that love you will realize Him.

"Man cannot really help the world. God alone does that—He who has created the sun and the moon, who has put love for their children in parents' hearts, endowed noble souls with compassion, and holy men and devotees with divine love. The man who works for others, without any selfish motive, really does good to himself.

"There is gold buried in your heart, but you are not yet aware of it. It is covered with a thin layer of clay. Once you are aware of it, all these activities of yours will lessen. After the birth of her child, the daughter-in-law in the family busies herself with it alone. Everything she does is only for the child. Her mother-in-law doesn't let her do any household duties.

"Go forward. A wood-cutter once entered a forest to gather wood. A brahmachāri said to him, 'Go forward.' He obeyed the injunction and discovered some sandal-wood trees. After a few days he reflected, 'The holy man asked me to go forward. He didn't tell me to stop here.' So he went forward and found a silver-mine. After a few days he went still farther and discovered a gold-mine, and next, mines of diamonds and precious stones. With these he became immensely rich.

"Through selfless work, love of God grows in the heart. Then, through His grace, one realizes Him in course of time. God can be seen. One can talk to Him as I am talking to you."

In silent wonder they all sat listening to the Master's words. It seemed to them that the Goddess of Wisdom Herself, seated on Sri Ramakrishna's tongue, was addressing these words not merely to Vidyāsāgar, but to all humanity for its good.

It was nearly nine o'clock in the evening. The Master was about to leave.

MASTER (to Vidyāsāgar, with a smile): "The words I have spoken are really superfluous. You know all this; you simply aren't conscious of it. There are countless gems in the coffers of Varuna. But he himself isn't aware of them."

VIDYĀSĀGAR (with a smile): "You may say as you like."

MASTER (smiling): "Oh, yes. There are many wealthy people who don't know the names of all their servants, and are even unaware of many of the precious things in their houses." (All laugh.)

Everybody was delighted with the Master's conversation. Again addressing Vidyāsāgar, he said with a smile: "Please visit the temple garden some time—I mean the garden of Rasmani. It's a charming place."

VIDYĀSĀGAR: "Oh, of course I shall go. You have so kindly come here to see me, and shall I not return your visit?"

MASTER: "Visit me? Oh, never think of such a thing!"

VIDYĀSĀGAR: "Why, sir? Why do you say that? May I ask you to explain?"

MASTER (smiling): "You see, we are like small fishing-boats. (All smile.) We can ply in small canals and shallow waters and also in big rivers. But you are a ship. You may run aground on the way!" (All laugh.)

Vidyāsāgar remained silent. Sri Ramakrishna said with a laugh, "But even a ship can go there at this season."

VIDYĀSĀGAR (smiling): "Yes, this is the monsoon season." (All laugh.)

M. said to himself: "This is indeed the monsoon season of newly awakened love. At such times one doesn't care for prestige or formalities."

Sri Ramakrishna then took leave of Vidyāsāgar, who with his friends escorted the Master to the main gate, leading the way with a lighted candle in his hand. Before leaving the room, the Master prayed for the family's welfare, going into an ecstatic mood as he did so.

As soon as the Master and the devotees reached the gate, they saw an unexpected sight and stood still. In front of them was a bearded gentleman of fair complexion, aged about thirty-six. He wore his clothes like a Bengali, but on his head was a white turban tied after the fashion of the Sikhs. No sooner did he see the Master than he fell prostrate before him, turban and all.

When he stood up the Master said: "Who is this? Balaram? Why so late in the evening?"

BALARAM: "I have been waiting here a long time, sir."

MASTER: "Why didn't you come in?"

BALARAM: "All were listening to you. I didn't like to disturb you."

The Master got into the carriage with his companions.

VIDYĀSĀGAR (to M., softly): "Shall I pay the carriage hire?"

M: "Oh, don't bother, please. It is taken care of."

Vidyāsāgar and his friends bowed to Sri Ramakrishna, and the carriage started for Dakshineswar. But the little group, with the venerable Vidyāsāgar at their head holding the lighted candle, stood at the gate and gazed after the Master until he was out of sight.

ADVICE TO HOUSEHOLDERS

THE MASTER WAS CONVERSING with Kedar and some other devotees in his room in the temple garden. Kedar was a government official and had spent several years at Dacca, in East Bengal, where he had become a friend of Vijay Goswami. The two would spend a great part of their time together, talking about Sri Ramakrishna and his spiritual experiences. Kedar had once been a member of the Brāhmo Samāj. He followed the path of bhakti. Spiritual talk always brought tears to his eyes.

It was five o'clock in the afternoon. Kedar was very happy that day, having arranged a religious festival for Sri Ramakrishna. A singer had been hired by Ram, and the whole day passed in joy.

The Master explained to the devotees the secret of communion with God.

MASTER: "With the realization of Satchidānanda one goes into samādhi. Then duties drop away. Suppose I have been talking about the ostād and he arrives. What need is there of talking about him then? How long does the bee buzz around? So long as it isn't sitting on a flower. But it will not do for the sādhaka to renounce duties. He should perform his duties, such as worship, japa, meditation, prayer, and pilgrimage.

"If you see someone engaged in reasoning even after he has realized God, you may liken him to a bee, which also buzzes a little even while sipping honey from a flower."

The Master was highly pleased with the ostād's music. He said to the musician, "There is a special manifestation of God's power in a man who has any outstanding gift, such as proficiency in music."

MUSICIAN: "Sir, what is the way to realize God?"

MASTER: "Bhakti is the one essential thing. To be sure, God exists in all beings. Who, then, is a devotee? He whose mind dwells on God. But this is not possible as long as one has egotism and vanity. The water of God's grace cannot collect on the high mound of egotism. It runs down. I am a mere machine.

(*To Kedar and the other devotees*) "God can be realized through all paths. All religions are true. The important thing is to reach the roof. You can reach it by stone stairs or by wooden stairs or by bamboo steps or by a rope. You can also climb up by a bamboo pole.

"You may say that there are many errors and superstitions in another religion. I should reply: Suppose there are. Every religion has errors. Everyone thinks that his watch alone gives the correct time. It is enough to have yearning for God. It is enough to love Him and feel attracted to Him. Don't you know that God is the Inner Guide? He sees the longing of our heart and the yearning of our soul. Suppose a man has several sons. The older boys address him distinctly as 'Bābā' or 'Pāpā', but the babies can at best call him 'Bā' or 'Pā'. Now, will the father be angry with those who address him in this indistinct way? The father knows that they too are calling him, only they cannot pronounce his name well. All children are the same to the father. Likewise, the devotees call on God alone, though by different names. They call on one Person only. God is one, but His names are many."

Thursday, August 24, 1882

Sri Ramakrishna was talking to Hazra on the long northeast verandah of his room, when M. arrived. He saluted the Master reverently.

MASTER: "I should like to visit Iswar Chandra Vidyāsāgar a few times more. The painter first draws the general outlines and then puts in the details and colours at his leisure. The moulder first makes the image out of clay, then plasters it, then gives it a coat of whitewash, and last of all paints it with a brush. All these steps must be taken successively. Vidyāsāgar is fully ready, but his inner stuff is covered with a thin layer. He is now engaged in doing good works; but he doesn't know what is within himself. Gold is hidden within him. God dwells within us. If one knows that, one feels like giving up all activities and praying to God with a yearning soul."

So the Master talked with M.—now standing, now pacing up and down the long verandah.

MASTER: "A little spiritual discipline is necessary in order to know what lies within."

M: "Is it necessary to practise discipline all through life?"

MASTER: "No. But one must be up and doing in the beginning. After that one need not work hard. The helmsman stands up and clutches the rudder firmly as long as the boat is passing through waves, storms, high wind, or around the curves of a river; but he relaxes after steering through them. As soon as the boat passes the curves and the helmsman feels a favourable wind, he sits comfortably and just touches the rudder. Next he prepares to unfurl the sail and gets ready for a smoke. Likewise, the aspirant enjoys peace and calm after passing the waves and storms of 'woman and gold'.

"Some are born with the characteristics of the yogi; but they too should be careful. It is 'woman and gold' alone that is the obstacle; it makes them deviate from the path of yoga and drags them into worldliness. Perhaps they have some desire for enjoyment. After fulfilling their desire, they again direct their minds to God and thus recover their former state of mind, fit for the practise of yoga.

"Have you ever seen the spring trap for fish, called the 'satkā-kal'?"

M: "No, sir, I haven't seen it."

MASTER: "They use it in our part of the country. One end of a bamboo pole is fastened in the ground, and the other is bent over with a catch. From this end a line with a hook hangs over the water, with bait tied to the hook. When the fish swallows the bait, suddenly the bamboo jumps up and regains its upright position.

"Again, take a pair of scales, for example. If a weight is placed on one side, the lower needle moves away from the upper one. The lower needle is the mind, and the upper one, God. The meeting of the two is yoga.

"Unless the mind becomes steady there cannot be yoga. It is the wind of worldliness that always disturbs the mind, which may be likened to a candle-flame. If that flame doesn't move at all, then one is said to have attained yoga.

" 'Woman and gold' alone is the obstacle to yoga. Always analyse what you see. What is there in the body of a woman? Only such things as blood, flesh, fat, entrails, and the like. Why should one love such a body?

"Sometimes I used to assume a rājasic mood in order to practise renunciation. Once I had the desire to put on a gold-embroidered robe, wear a ring on my finger, and smoke a hubble-bubble with a long pipe. Mathur Babu procured all these things for me. I wore the gold-embroidered robe and said to myself after a while, 'Mind! This is what is called a gold-embroidered robe.' Then I took it off and threw it away. I couldn't stand the robe any more. Again I said to myself, 'Mind! This is called a shawl, and this a ring, and this, smoking a hubble-bubble with a long pipe.' I threw those things away once for all, and the desire to enjoy them never arose in my mind again."

It was almost dusk. The Master and M. stood talking alone near the door on the southeast verandah.

MASTER (to M.): "The mind of the yogi is always fixed on God, always absorbed in the Self. You can recognize such a man by merely looking at him. His eyes are wide open, with an aimless look, like the eyes of the mother bird hatching her eggs. Her entire mind is fixed on the eggs, and there is a vacant look in her eyes. Can you show me such a picture?"

M: "I shall try to get one."

As evening came on, the temples were lighted up. Sri Ramakrishna was seated on his small couch, meditating on the Divine Mother. Then he chanted the names of God. Incense was burnt in the room, where an oil lamp had been lighted. Sounds of conch-shells and gongs came floating on the air as the evening worship began in the temple of Kāli. The light of the moon flooded all the quarters. The Master again spoke to M.

MASTER: "Perform your duties in an unselfish spirit. The work that Vidyāsāgar is engaged in is very good. Always try to perform your duties without desiring any result."

M: "Yes, sir. But may I know if one can realize God while performing one's duties? Can 'Rāma' and 'desire' coexist? The other day I read in a Hindi couplet: 'Where Rāma is, there desire cannot be; where desire is, there Rāma cannot be.' "

MASTER: "All, without exception, perform work. Even to chant the name and glories of God is work, as is the meditation of the non-dualist on 'I am He'. Breathing is also an activity. There is no way of renouncing work altogether. So do your work, but surrender the result to God."

M: "Sir, may I make an effort to earn more money?"

MASTER: "It is permissible to do so to maintain a religious family. You may try to increase your income, but in an honest way. The goal of life is not the earning of money, but the service of God. Money is not harmful if it is devoted to the service of God."

M: "How long should a man feel obliged to do his duty toward his wife and children?"

MASTER: "As long as they feel pinched for food and clothing. But one need not take the responsibility of a son when he is able to support himself. When the young fledgling learns to pick its own food, its mother pecks it if it comes to her for food."

M: "How long must one do one's duty?"

MASTER: "The blossom drops off when the fruit appears. One doesn't have to do one's duty after the attainment of God, nor does one feel like doing it then.

"If a drunkard takes too much liquor he cannot retain consciousness. If he takes only two or three glasses, he can go on with his work. As you advance nearer and nearer to God, He will reduce your activities little by little. Have no fear.

"Finish the few duties you have at hand, and then you will have peace. When the mistress of the house goes to bathe after finishing her cooking and other household duties, she won't come back, however you may shout after her."

M: "Sir, what is the meaning of the realization of God? What do you mean by God-vision? How does one attain it?"

MASTER: "According to the Vaishnavas the aspirants and the seers of God may be divided into different groups. These are the pravartaka, the sādhaka, the siddha, and the siddha of the siddha. He who has just set foot on the path may be called a pravartaka. He may be called a sādhaka who has for some time been practising spiritual disciplines, such as worship, japa, meditation, and the chanting of God's name and glories. He may be called a siddha who has known from his inner experience that God exists. An analogy is given in the Vedānta to explain this. The master of the house is asleep in a dark room. Someone is groping in the darkness to find him. He touches the couch and says, 'No, it is not he.' He touches the window and says, 'No, it is not he.' He touches the door and says, 'No, it is not he.' This is known in the Vedānta as the process of 'Neti, neti', 'Not this, not this'. At last his hand touches the master's body and he exclaims, 'Here he is!' In other words, he is now conscious of the 'existence' of the master. He has found him, but he doesn't yet know him intimately.

"There is another type, known as the siddha of the siddha, the 'supremely perfect'. It is quite a different thing when one talks to the master intimately, when one knows God very intimately through love and devotion. A siddha has undoubtedly attained God, but the 'supremely perfect' has known God very intimately.

"But in order to realize God, one must assume one of these attitudes: śānta, dāsya, sakhya, vātsalya, or madhur.

"Śānta, the serene attitude. The rishis of olden times had this attitude toward God. They did not desire any worldly enjoyment. It is like the single-minded devotion of a wife to her husband. She knows that her husband is the embodiment of beauty and love, a veritable Madan.

"Dāsya, the attitude of a servant toward his master. Hanumān had this attitude toward Rāma. He felt the strength of a lion when he worked for Rāma. A wife feels this mood also. She serves her husband with all her heart and soul. A mother also has a little of this attitude, as Yaśodā had toward Krishna.

"Sakhya, the attitude of friendship. Friends say to one another, 'Come here and sit near me.' Śridāma and other friends sometimes fed Krishna with fruit, part of which they had already eaten, and sometimes climbed on His shoulders.

"Vātsalya, the attitude of a mother toward her child. This was Yaśodā's attitude toward Krishna. The wife, too, has a little of this. She feeds her husband with her very life-blood, as it were. The mother feels happy only when the child has eaten to his heart's content. Yaśodā would roam about with butter in her hand, in order to feed Krishna.

"Madhur, the attitude of a woman toward her paramour. Rādhā had this attitude toward Krishna. The wife also feels it for her husband. This attitude includes all the other four."

M: "When one sees God does one see Him with these eyes?"

MASTER: "God cannot be seen with these physical eyes. In the course of spiritual discipline one gets a 'love body', endowed with 'love eyes', 'love ears', and so on. One sees God with those 'love eyes'. One hears the voice of God with those 'love ears'. One even gets a sexual organ made of love."

At these words M. burst out laughing. The Master continued, unannoyed, "With this 'love body' the soul communes with God."

M. again became serious.

MASTER: "But this is not possible without intense love of God. One sees nothing but God everywhere when one loves Him with great intensity. It is like a person with jaundice, who sees everything yellow. Then one feels, 'I am verily He.'

"A drunkard, deeply intoxicated, says, 'Verily I am Kāli!' The gopis, intoxicated with love, exclaimed, 'Verily I am Krishna!'

"One who thinks of God, day and night, beholds Him everywhere. It is like a man's seeing flames on all sides after he has gazed fixedly at one flame for some time."

"But that isn't the real flame", flashed through M.'s mind.

Sri Ramakrishna, who could read a man's inmost thought, said: "One doesn't lose consciousness by thinking of Him who is all Spirit, all Consciousness. Shivanath once remarked that too much thinking about God confounds the brain. Thereupon I said to him, 'How can one become un-conscious by thinking of Consciousness?' "

M: "Yes, sir, I realize that. It isn't like thinking of an unreal object. How can a man lose his intelligence if he always fixes his mind on Him whose very nature is eternal Intelligence?"

MASTER (*with pleasure*): "It is through God's grace that you understand that. The doubts of the mind will not disappear without His grace. Doubts do not disappear without Self-realization.

"But one need not fear anything if one has received the grace of God. It is rather easy for a child to stumble if he holds his father's hand; but there can be no such fear if the father holds the child's hand. A man does not have to suffer any more if God, in His grace, removes his doubts and reveals Himself to him. But this grace descends upon him only after he has prayed to God with intense yearning of heart and practised spiritual disci-pline. The mother feels compassion for her child when she sees him running about breathlessly. She has been hiding herself; now she appears before the child."

"But why should God make us run about?" thought M.

Immediately Sri Ramakrishna said: "It is His will that we should run about a little. Then it is great fun. God has created the world in play, as it were. This is called Mahāmāyā, the Great Illusion. Therefore one must take refuge in the Divine Mother, the Cosmic Power Itself. It is She who has bound us with the shackles of illusion. The realization of God is possible only when those shackles are severed."

The Master continued: "One must propitiate the Divine Mother, the Primal Energy, in order to obtain God's grace. God Himself is Mahāmāyā, who deludes the world with Her illusion and conjures up the magic of creation, preservation, and destruction. She has spread this veil of ignorance before our eyes. We can go into the inner chamber only when She lets us pass through the door. Living outside, we see only outer objects, but not that Eternal Being, Existence-Knowledge-Bliss Absolute. Therefore it is stated in the Purāna that deities like Brahmā praised Mahāmāyā for the destruction of the demons Madhu and Kaitabha.

"Śakti alone is the root of the universe. That Primal Energy has two aspects: vidyā and avidyā. Avidyā deludes. Avidyā conjures up 'woman and gold', which casts the spell. Vidyā begets devotion, kindness, wisdom, and love, which lead one to God. This avidyā must be propitiated, and that is the purpose of the rites of Śakti worship.[1]

"The devotee assumes various attitudes toward Śakti in order to pro-pitiate Her: the attitude of a handmaid, a 'hero', or a child. A hero's attitude is to please Her even as a man pleases a woman through intercourse.

"The worship of Śakti is extremely difficult. It is no joke. I passed two years as the handmaid and companion of the Divine Mother. But my natural attitude has always been that of a child toward its mother. I regard the breasts of any woman as those of my own mother.

"Women are, all of them, the veritable images of Śakti. In northwest

[1] In this worship a woman is regarded as the representation of the Divine Mother.

India the bride holds a knife in her hand at the time of marriage; in Bengal, a nut-cutter. The meaning is that the bridegroom, with the help of the bride, who is the embodiment of the Divine Power, will sever the bondage of illusion. This is the 'heroic' attitude. I never worshipped the Divine Mother that way. My attitude toward Her is that of a child toward its mother.

"The bride is the very embodiment of Śakti. Haven't you noticed, at the marriage ceremony, how the groom sits behind like an idiot? But the bride— she is so bold!

"After attaining God one forgets His external splendour, the glories of His creation. One doesn't think of God's glories after one has seen Him. The devotee, once immersed in God's Bliss, doesn't calculate any more about outer things. When I see Narendra, I don't need to ask him: 'What's your name? Where do you live?' Where is the time for such questions? Once a man asked Hanumān which day of the fortnight it was. 'Brother,' said Hanumān, 'I don't know anything of the day of the week, or the fortnight, or the position of the stars. I think of Rāma alone.'"

October 16, 1882

It was Monday, a few days before the Durgā Pujā, the festival of the Divine Mother. Sri Ramakrishna was in a very happy state of mind, for Narendra was with him. Narendra had brought two or three young members of the Brāhmo Samāj to the temple garden. Besides these, Rakhal, Ramlal, Hazra, and M. were with the Master.

Narendra had his midday meal with Sri Ramakrishna. Afterwards a temporary bed was made on the floor of the Master's room so that the disciples might rest awhile. A mat was spread, over which was placed a quilt covered with a white sheet. A few cushions and pillows completed the simple bed. Like a child, the Master sat near Narendranath on the bed. He talked with the devotees in great delight. With a radiant smile lighting his face, and his eyes fixed on Narendra, he was giving them various spiritual teachings, interspersing these with incidents from his own life.

MASTER: "After I had experienced samādhi, my mind craved intensely to hear only about God. I would always search for places where they were reciting or explaining the sacred books, such as the *Bhāgavata*, the *Mahābhārata*, and the *Adhyātma Rāmāyana*. I used to go to Krishnakishore to hear him read the *Adhyātma Rāmāyana*.

"What tremendous faith Krishnakishore had! Once, while at Vrindāvan, he felt thirsty and went to a well. Near it he saw a man standing. On being asked to draw a little water for him, the man said: 'I belong to a low caste, sir. You are a brāhmin. How can I draw water for you?' Krishnakishore said: 'Take the name of Śiva. By repeating His holy name you will make yourself pure.' The low-caste man did as he was told, and Krishnakishore, orthodox brāhmin that he was, drank that water. What tremendous faith!

"Once a holy man came to the bank of the Ganges and lived near the bathing-ghāt at Āriādaha, not far from Dakshineswar. We thought of paying him a visit. I said to Haladhari: 'Krishnakishore and I are going to see a holy man. Will you come with us?' Haladhari' replied, 'What is the use of seeing a mere human body, which is no better than a cage of clay?' Haladhari was a student of the *Gītā* and Vedānta philosophy, and therefore referred to the holy man as a mere 'cage of clay'. I repeated this to Krishnakishore. With great anger he said: 'How impudent of Haladhari to make such a remark! How can he ridicule as a "cage of clay" the body of a man who constantly thinks of God, who meditates on Rāma, and has renounced all for the sake of the Lord? Doesn't he know that such a man is the embodiment of Spirit?' He was so upset by Haladhari's remarks that he would turn his face away from him whenever he met him in the temple garden, and stopped speaking to him.

"Once Krishnakishore asked me, 'Why have you cast off the sacred thread?' In those days of God-vision I felt as if I were passing through the great storm of Āswin,[2] and everything had blown away from me. No trace of my old self was left. I lost all consciousness of the world. I could hardly keep my cloth on my body, not to speak of the sacred thread! I said to Krishnakishore, 'Ah, you will understand if you ever happen to be as intoxicated with God as I was.'

"And it actually came to pass. He too passed through a God-intoxicated state, when he would repeat only the word 'Om' and shut himself up alone in his room. His relatives thought he was actually mad, and called in a physician. Ram Kavirāj of Nātāgore came to see him. Krishnakishore said to the physician, 'Cure me, sir, of my malady, if you please, but not of my Om.' (*All laugh.*)

"One day I went to see him and found him in a pensive mood. When I asked him about it, he said: 'The tax-collector was here. He threatened to dispose of my brass pots, my cups, and my few utensils, if I didn't pay the tax; so I am worried.' I said: 'But why should you worry about it? Let him take away your pots and pans. Let him arrest your body even. How will that affect you? For your nature is that of Kha!' (*Narendra and the others laugh.*) He used to say to me that he was the Spirit, all-pervading as the sky. He had got that idea from the *Adhyātma Rāmāyana.* I used to tease him now and then, addressing him as 'Kha'. Therefore I said to him that day, with a smile: 'You are Kha. Taxes cannot move you!'

"In that state of God-intoxication I used to speak out my mind to all. I was no respecter of persons. Even to men of position I was not afraid to speak the truth.

"One day Jatindra[3] came to the garden of Jadu Mallick. I was there too. I asked him: 'What is the duty of man? Isn't it our duty to think of God?' Jatindra replied: 'We are worldly people. How is it possible for us to achieve liberation? Even King Yudhisthira had to have a vision of hell.' This made me very angry. I said to him: 'What sort of man are you? Of all the incidents of Yudhisthira's life, you remember only his seeing hell. You don't remember his truthfulness, his forbearance, his patience, his discrimination, his

[2] The Master referred to the great cyclone of 1864.
[3] A titled aristocrat of Calcutta.

dispassion, his devotion to God.' I was about to say many more things, when
Hriday stopped my mouth. After a little while Jatindra left the place, saying
he had some other business to attend to.

"Many days later I went with Captain to see Rājā[4] Sourindra Tagore. As
soon as I met him, I said, 'I can't address you as "Rājā", or by any such title,
for I should be telling a lie.' He talked to me a few minutes, but even so
our conversation was interrupted by the frequent visits of Europeans and
others. A man of rājasic temperament, Sourindra was naturally busy with
many things. Jatindra, his eldest brother, had been told of my coming, but
he sent word that he had a pain in his throat and couldn't go out.

"One day, in that state of divine intoxication, I went to the bathing-ghāt
on the Ganges at Barānagore. There I saw Jaya Mukherji repeating the
name of God; but his mind was on something else. I went up and slapped
him twice on the cheeks.

"At one time Rāni Rasmani was staying in the temple garden. She came
to the shrine of the Divine Mother, as she frequently did when I worshipped
Kāli, and asked me to sing a song or two. On this occasion, while I was
singing, I noticed she was sorting the flowers for worship absent-mindedly.
At once I slapped her on the cheeks. She became quite embarrassed and
sat there with folded hands.

"Alarmed at this state of mind myself, I said to my cousin Haladhari:
'Just see my nature! How can I get rid of it?' After praying to the Divine
Mother for some time with great yearning, I was able to shake off this habit.

"When one gets into such a state of mind, one doesn't enjoy any conversation but that about God. I used to weep when I heard people talk
about worldly matters. When I accompanied Mathur Babu on a pilgrimage,
we spent a few days in Benares at Raja Babu's house. One day I was seated
in the drawing-room with Mathur Babu, Raja Babu, and others. Hearing
them talk about various worldly things, such as their business losses and so
forth,. I wept bitterly and said to the Divine Mother: 'Mother, where have
You brought me? I was much better off in the temple garden at Dakshineswar.
Here I am in a place where I must hear about "woman and gold". But at
Dakshineswar I could avoid it.' "

The Master asked the devotees, especially Narendra, to rest awhile, and
he himself lay down on the smaller couch.

Late in the afternoon Narendra sang. Rakhal, Latu,[5] M., Hazra, and
Priya, Narendra's Brāhmo friend, were present. The singing was accompanied by the drum:

> Meditate, O my mind, on the Lord Hari,
> The Stainless One, Pure Spirit through and through.
> How peerless is the light that in Him shines!
> How soul-bewitching is His wondrous form!
> How dear is He to all His devotees! . . .

[4] A title conferred on Sourindra by the Government of India. The word "rājā"
really means "ruler of a kingdom".
[5] A young disciple of the Master, who later became a monk under the name of
Swami Adbhutananda.

After this song Narendra sang:

> Oh, when will dawn for me that day of blessedness
> When He who is all Good, all Beauty, and all Truth,
> Will light the inmost shrine of my heart?
> When shall I sink at last, ever beholding Him,
> Into that Ocean of Delight?
> Lord, as Infinite Wisdom Thou shalt enter my soul,
> And my unquiet mind, made speechless by Thy sight,
> Will find a haven at Thy feet.
> In my heart's firmament, O Lord, Thou wilt arise
> As Blissful Immortality;
> And as, when the chakora beholds the rising moon,
> It sports about for very joy,
> So, too, shall I be filled with heavenly happiness
> When Thou appearest unto me.
>
> Thou One without a Second, all Peace, the King of Kings!
> At Thy beloved feet I shall renounce my life
> And so at last shall gain life's goal;
> I shall enjoy the bliss of heaven while yet on earth!
> Where else is a boon so rare bestowed?
> Then shall I see Thy glory, pure and untouched by stain;
> As darkness flees from light, so will my darkest sins
> Desert me at Thy dawn's approach.
> Kindle in me, O Lord, the blazing fire of faith
> To be the pole-star of my life;
> O Succour of the weak, fulfil my one desire!
> Then shall I bathe both day and night
> In the boundless bliss of Thy Love, and utterly forget
> Myself, O Lord, attaining Thee.

Narendra sang again:

> With beaming face chant the sweet name of God
> Till in your heart the nectar overflows.
> Drink of it ceaselessly and share it with all!
> If ever your heart runs dry, parched by the flames
> Of worldly desire, chant the sweet name of God,
> And heavenly love will moisten your arid soul.
>
> Be sure, O mind, you never forget to chant
> His holy name: when danger stares in your face,
> Call on Him, your Father Compassionate;
> With His name's thunder, snap the fetters of sin!
> Come, let us fulfil our hearts' desires
> By drinking deep of Everlasting Joy,
> Made one with Him in Love's pure ecstasy.

Now Narendra and the devotees began to sing kirtan, accompanied by the drum and cymbals. They moved round and round the Master as they sang:

> Immerse yourself for evermore, O mind,
> In Him who is Pure Knowledge and Pure Bliss.

Next they sang:

> Oh, when will dawn for me that day of blessedness
> When He who is all Good, all Beauty, and all Truth
> Will light the inmost shrine of my heart? . . .

At last Narendra himself was playing on the drums, and he sang with the Master, full of joy:

> With beaming face chant the sweet name of God . . .

When the music was over, Sri Ramakrishna held Narendra in his arms a long time and said, "You have made us so happy today!" The flood-gate of the Master's heart was open so wide, that night, that he could hardly contain himself for joy. It was eight o'clock in the evening. Intoxicated with divine love, he paced the long verandah north of his room. Now and then he could be heard talking to the Divine Mother. Suddenly he said in an excited voice, "What can you do to me?" Was the Master hinting that māyā was helpless before him, since he had the Divine Mother for his support?

Narendra, M., and Priya were going to spend the night at the temple garden. This pleased the Master highly, especially since Narendra would be with him. The Holy Mother,[6] who was living in the nahabat, had prepared the supper. Surendra[7] bore the greater part of the Master's expenses. The meal was ready, and the plates were set out on the southeast verandah of the Master's room.

Near the east door of his room Narendra and the other devotees were gossiping.

NARENDRA: "How do you find the young men nowadays?"

M: "They are not bad; but they don't receive any religious instruction."

NARENDRA: "But from my experience I feel they are going to the dogs. They smoke cigarettes, indulge in frivolous talk, enjoy foppishness, play truant, and do everything of that sort. I have even seen them visiting questionable places."

M: "I didn't notice such things during our student days."

NARENDRA: "Perhaps you didn't mix with the students intimately. I have even seen them talking with people of immoral character. Perhaps they are on terms of intimacy with them."

M: "It is strange indeed."

NARENDRA: "I know that many of them form bad habits. It would be proper if the guardians of the boys, and the authorities, kept their eyes on these matters."

They were talking thus when Sri Ramakrishna came to them and asked with a smile, "Well, what are you talking about?"

NARENDRA: "I have been asking M. about the boys in the schools. The conduct of students nowadays isn't all that it should be."

The Master became grave and said to M. rather seriously: "This kind of

---

[6] By this name Sri Ramakrishna's wife was known among his devotees.
[7] The name by which Sri Ramakrishna addressed Suresh Mitra, a beloved householder disciple.

conversation is not good. It isn't desirable to indulge in any talk but talk of God. You are their senior, and you are intelligent. You should not have encouraged them to talk about such matters."

Narendra was then about nineteen years old, and M. about twenty-eight. Thus admonished, M. felt embarrassed, and the others also fell silent.

While the devotees were enjoying their meal, Śri Ramakrishna stood by and watched them with intense delight. That night the Master's joy was very great.

After supper the devotees rested on the mat spread on the floor of the Master's room. They began to talk with him. It was indeed a mart of joy. The Master asked Narendra to sing the song beginning with the line: "In Wisdom's firmament the moon of Love is rising full."

Narendra sang, and other devotees played the drums and cymbals:

> In Wisdom's firmament the moon of Love is rising full,
> And Love's flood-tide, in surging waves, is flowing everywhere.
> O Lord, how full of bliss Thou art! Victory unto Thee!
>
> On every side shine devotees, like stars around the moon;
> Their Friend, the Lord All-merciful, joyously plays with them.
> Behold! the gates of paradise today are open wide.
>
> The soft spring wind of the New Day raises fresh waves of joy;
> Gently it carries to the earth the fragrance of God's Love,
> Till all the yogis, drunk with bliss, are lost in ecstasy.
>
> Upon the sea of the world unfolds the lotus of the New Day,
> And there the Mother sits enshrined in blissful majesty.
> See how the bees are mad with joy, sipping the nectar there!
>
> Behold the Mother's radiant face, which so enchants the heart
> And captivates the universe! About Her Lotus Feet
> Bands of ecstatic holy men are dancing in delight.
>
> What matchless loveliness is Hers! What infinite content
> Pervades the heart when She appears! O brothers, says Premdās,
> I humbly beg you, one and all, to sing the Mother's praise!

Sri Ramakrishna sang and danced, and the devotees danced around him.

When the song was over, the Master walked up and down the northeast verandah, where Hazra was seated with M. The Master sat down there. He asked a devotee, "Do you ever have dreams?"

DEVOTEE: "Yes, sir. The other day I dreamt a strange dream. I saw the whole world enveloped in water. There was water on all sides. A few boats were visible, but suddenly huge waves appeared and sank them. I was about to board a ship with a few others, when we saw a brāhmin walking over that expanse of water. I asked him, 'How can you walk over the deep?' The brāhmin said with a smile: 'Oh, there is no difficulty about that. There is a bridge under the water.' I said to him, 'Where are you going?' 'To Bhawāni-pur, the city of the Divine Mother', he replied. 'Wait a little', I cried. 'I shall accompany you.'"

MASTER: "Oh, I am thrilled to hear the story!"

DEVOTEE: "The brāhmin said: 'I am in a hurry. It will take you some time to get out of the boat. Good-bye. Remember this path and come after me.' "

MASTER: "Oh, my hair is standing on end! Please be initiated by a guru as soon as possible."

Shortly before midnight Narendra and the other devotees lay down on a bed made on the floor of the Master's room.

At dawn some of the devotees were up. They saw the Master, naked as a child, pacing up and down the room, repeating the names of the various gods and goddesses. His voice was sweet as nectar. Now he would look at the Ganges, now stop in front of the pictures hanging on the wall and bow down before them, chanting all the while the holy names in his sweet voice. He chanted: "Veda, Purāna, Tantra; Gītā, Gāyatri; Bhāgavata, Bhakta, Bhagavān." Referring to the *Gītā*, he repeated many times, "Tāgi, tāgi, tāgi."[8] Now and then he would say: "O Mother, Thou art verily Brahman, and Thou art verily Śakti. Thou art Purusha and Thou art Prakriti. Thou art Virāt. Thou art the Absolute, and Thou dost manifest Thyself as the Relative. Thou art verily the twenty-four cosmic principles."

In the mean time the morning service had begun in the temples of Kāli and Rādhākānta. Sounds of conch-shells and cymbals were carried on the air. The devotees came outside the room and saw the priests and servants gathering flowers in the garden for the divine service in the temples. From the nahabat floated the sweet melody of musical instruments, befitting the morning hours.

Narendra and the other devotees finished their morning duties and came to the Master. With a sweet smile on his lips Sri Ramakrishna was standing on the northeast verandah, close to his own room.

NARENDRA: "We noticed several sannyāsis belonging to the sect of Nānak in the Panchavati."

MASTER: "Yes, they arrived here yesterday. (*To Narendra*) I'd like to see you all sitting together on the mat."

As they sat there the Master looked at them with evident delight. He then began to talk with them. Narendra asked about spiritual discipline.

MASTER: "Bhakti, love of God, is the essence of all spiritual discipline. Through love one acquires renunciation and discrimination naturally."

NARENDRA: "Isn't it true that the Tantra prescribes spiritual discipline in the company of woman?"

MASTER: "That is not desirable. It is a very difficult path and often causes the aspirant's downfall. There are three such kinds of discipline. One may regard woman[9] as one's mistress or look on oneself as her handmaid or as her child. I look on woman as my mother. To look on oneself as her handmaid is also good; but it is extremely difficult to practise spiritual discipline looking on woman as one's mistress. To regard oneself as her child is a very pure attitude."

The sannyāsis belonging to the sect of Nānak entered the room and

---

[8] This word is formed by reversing the letters of "Gītā". "Tāgi" means "one who has renounced". Renunciation is the import of this sacred book.

[9] Woman is the symbol of the Divine Mother.

greeted the Master, saying, "Namo Nārāyanāya."[10] Sri Ramakrishna asked them to sit down.

MASTER: "Nothing is impossible for God. Nobody can describe His nature in words. Everything is possible for Him. There lived at a certain place two yogis who were practising spiritual discipline. The sage Nārada was passing that way one day. Realizing who he was, one of the yogis said: 'You have just come from God Himself. What is He doing now?' Nārada replied, 'Why, I saw Him making camels and elephants pass and repass through the eye of a needle.' At this the yogi said: 'Is that anything to wonder at? Everything is possible for God.' But the other yogi said: 'What? Making elephants pass through the eye of a needle—is that ever possible? You have never been to the Lord's dwelling-place.' "

At nine o'clock in the morning, while the Master was still sitting in his room, Manomohan arrived from Konnagar with some members of his family. In answer to Sri Ramakrishna's kind inquiries, Manomohan explained tnat he was taking them to Calcutta. The Master said: "Today is the first day of the Bengali month, an inauspicious day for undertaking a journey. I hope everything will be well with you." With a smile he began to talk of other matters.

When Narendra and his friends had finished bathing in the Ganges, the Master said to them earnestly: "Go to the Panchavati and meditate there under the banyan-tree. Shall I give you something to sit on?"

About half past ten Narendra and his Brāhmo friends were meditating in the Panchavati. After a while Sri Ramakrishna came to them. M., too, was present.

The Master said to the Brāhmo devotees: "In meditation one must be absorbed in God. By merely floating on the surface of the water, can you reach the gems lying at the bottom of the sea?"

Then he sang:

> Taking the name of Kāli, dive deep down, O mind,
> Into the heart's fathomless depths,
> Where many a precious gem lies hid.
> But never believe the bed of the ocean bare of gems
> If in the first few dives you fail;
> With firm resolve and self-control
> Dive deep and make your way to Mother Kāli's realm.
>
> Down in the ocean depths of heavenly Wisdom lie
> The wondrous pearls of Peace, O mind;
> And you yourself can gather them,
> If you but have pure love and follow the scriptures' rule.
> Within those ocean depths, as well,
> Six alligators[11] lurk—lust, anger, and the rest—
> Swimming about in search of prey.
> Smear yourself with the turmeric of discrimination;
> The very smell of it will shield you from their jaws.

[10] "Salutations to God." This is the way sādhus greet one another.
[11] The six passions: lust, anger, avarice, delusion, pride, and envy.

Upon the ocean bed lie strewn
Unnumbered pearls and precious gems;
Plunge in, says Rāmprasād, and gather up handfuls there!

Narendra and his friends came down from their seats on the raised platform of the Panchavati and stood near the Master. He returned to his room
with them. The Master continued: "When you plunge in the water of the
ocean, you may be attacked by alligators. But they won't touch you if your
body is smeared with turmeric. There are no doubt six alligators—lust, anger,
avarice, and so on—within you, in the 'heart's fathomless depths'. But protect yourself with the turmeric of discrimination and renunciation, and
they won't touch you.

"What can you achieve by mere lecturing and scholarship without discrimination and dispassion? God alone is real, and all else is unreal. God
alone is substance, and all else is nonentity. That is discrimination.

"First of all set up God in the shrine of your heart, and then deliver
lectures as much as you like. How will the mere repetition of 'Brahma'
profit you if you are not imbued with discrimination and dispassion? It is
the empty sound of a conch-shell.

"There lived in a village a young man named Padmalochan. People used
to call him 'Podo', for short. In this village there was a temple in a very
dilapidated condition. It contained no image of God. Aśwattha and other
plants sprang up on the ruins of its walls. Bats lived inside, and the floor
was covered with dust and the droppings of the bats. The people of the village had stopped visiting the temple. One day after dusk the villagers heard
the sound of a conch-shell from the direction of the temple. They thought
perhaps someone had installed an image in the shrine and was performing
the evening worship. One of them softly opened the door and saw Padmalochan standing in a corner, blowing the conch. No image had been set
up. The temple hadn't been swept or washed. And filth and dirt lay everywhere. Then he shouted to Podo:

You have set up no image here,
Within the shrine, O fool!
Blowing the conch, you simply make
Confusion worse confounded.
Day and night eleven bats
Scream there incessantly. . . .

"There is no use in merely making a noise if you want to establish the
Deity in the shrine of your heart, if you want to realize God. First of all
purify the mind. In the pure heart God takes His seat. One cannot bring
the holy image into the temple if the droppings of bats are all around. The
eleven bats are our eleven organs: five of action, five of perception, and the
mind.

"First of all invoke the Deity, and then give lectures to your heart's
content. First of all dive deep. Plunge to the bottom and gather up the
gems. Then you may do other things. But nobody wants to plunge. People
are without spiritual discipline and prayer, without renunciation and dis-

passion. They learn a few words and immediately start to deliver lectures. It is difficult to teach others. Only if a man gets a command from God, after realizing Him, is he entitled to teach."

Thus conversing, the Master came to the west end of the verandah. M. stood by his side. Sri Ramakrishna had repeated again and again that God cannot be realized without discrimination and renunciation. This made M. extremely worried. He had married and was then a young man of twenty-eight, educated in college in the Western way. Having a sense of duty, he asked himself, "Do discrimination and dispassion mean giving up 'woman and gold'?" He was really at a loss to know what to do.

M. (to the Master): "What should one do if one's wife says: 'You are neglecting me. I shall commit suicide.'?"

MASTER (in a serious tone): "Give up such a wife if she proves an obstacle in the way of spiritual life. Let her commit suicide or anything else she likes. The wife that hampers her husband's spiritual life is an ungodly wife."

Immersed in deep thought, M. stood leaning against the wall. Narendra and the other devotees remained silent a few minutes. The Master exchanged several words with them; then, suddenly going to M., he whispered in his ear: "But if a man has sincere love for God, then all come under his control —the king, wicked persons, and his wife. Sincere love of God on the husband's part may eventually help the wife to lead a spiritual life. If the husband is good, then through the grace of God the wife may also follow his example."

This had a most soothing effect on M.'s worried mind. All the while he had been thinking: "Let her commit suicide. What can I do?"

M. (to the Master): "This world is a terrible place indeed."

MASTER (to the devotees): "That is the reason Chaitanya said to his companion Nityānanda, 'Listen, brother, there is no hope of salvation for the worldly-minded.' "

On another occasion the Master had said to M. privately: "Yes, there is no hope for a worldly man if he is not sincerely devoted to God. But he has nothing to fear if he remains in the world after realizing God. Nor need a man have any fear whatever of the world if he attains sincere devotion by practising spiritual discipline now and then in solitude. Chaitanya had several householders among his devotees, but they were householders in name only, for they lived unattached to the world."

It was noon. The worship was over, and food offerings had been made in the temple. The doors of the temple were shut. Sri Ramakrishna sat down for his meal, and Narendra and the other devotees partook of the food offerings from the temple.

Sunday, October 22, 1882

It was the day of Vijayā, the last day of the celebration of the worship of Durgā, when the clay image is immersed in the water of a lake or river.

About nine o'clock in the morning M. was seated on the floor of the Master's room at Dakshineswar, near Sri Ramakrishna, who was reclining on the small couch. Rakhal was then living with the Master, and Narendra and Bhavanath visited him frequently. Baburam had seen him only once or twice.

MASTER: "Did you have any holiday during the Durgā Pujā?"

M: "Yes, sir. I went to Keshab's house every day for the first three days of the worship."

MASTER: "Is that so?"

M: "I heard there a very interesting interpretation of the Durgā Pujā."

MASTER: "Please tell me all about it."

M: "Keshab Sen held daily morning prayers in his house, lasting till ten or eleven. During these prayers he gave the inner meaning of the Durgā Pujā. He said that if anyone could realize the Divine Mother, that is to say, could install Mother Durgā in the shrine of his heart, then Lakshmi, Sarasvati, Kārtika, and Ganeśa[12] would come there of themselves. Lakshmi means wealth, Sarasvati knowledge, Kārtika strength, and Ganeśa success. By realizing the Divine Mother within one's heart, one gets all these without any effort whatever."

Sri Ramakrishna listened to the description, questioning M. now and then about the prayers conducted by Keshab. At last he said to M.: "Don't go hither and thither. Come here alone. Those who belong to the inner circle of my devotees will come only here. Boys like Narendra, Bhavanath, and Rakhal are my very intimate disciples. They are not to be thought lightly of. Feed[13] them one day. What do you think of Narendra?"

M: "I think very highly of him, sir."

MASTER: "Haven't you observed his many virtues? He is not only well versed in music, vocal and instrumental, but he is also very learned. Besides, he has controlled his passions and declares he will lead a celibate life. He has been devoted to God since his very boyhood.

"How are you getting along with your meditation nowadays? What aspect of God appeals to your mind—with form or without form?"

M: "Sir, now I can't fix my mind on God with form. On the other hand, I can't concentrate steadily on God without form."

MASTER: "Now you see that the mind cannot be fixed, all of a sudden, on the formless aspect of God. It is wise to think of God with form during the primary stages."

M: "Do you mean to suggest that one should meditate on clay images?"

MASTER: "Why clay? These images are the embodiments of Consciousness."

M: "Even so, one must think of hands, feet, and the other parts of the body. But again, I realize that the mind cannot be concentrated unless one meditates, in the beginning, on God with form. You have told me so. Well, God can easily assume different forms. May one meditate on the form of one's own mother?"

[12] According to Hindu mythology, Lakshmi and Sarasvati are the daughters, and Kārtika and Ganeśa the sons, of Durgā. Associated with the image of Durgā, they occupy positions on both sides of the Divine Mother.

[13] Feeding a holy man is considered a meritorious act.

MASTER: "Yes, the mother should be adored. She is indeed an embodiment of Brahman."

M. sat in silence. After a few minutes he asked the Master: "What does one feel while thinking of God without form? Isn't it possible to describe it?" After some reflection, the Master said, "Do you know what it is like?" He remained silent a moment and then said a few words to M. about one's experiences at the time of the vision of God with and without form.

MASTER: "You see, one must practise spiritual discipline to understand this correctly. Suppose there are treasures in a room. If you want to see them and lay hold of them, you must take the trouble to get the key and unlock the door. After that you must take the treasures out. But suppose the room is locked, and standing outside the door you say to yourself: 'Here I have opened the door. Now I have broken the lock of the chest. Now I have taken out the treasure.' Such brooding near the door will not enable you to achieve anything.

"You must practise discipline.

"The jnānis think of God without form. They don't accept the Divine Incarnation. Praising Sri Krishna, Arjuna said, 'Thou art Brahman Absolute.' Sri Krishna replied, 'Follow Me, and you will know whether or not I am Brahman Absolute.' So saying, Sri Krishna led Arjuna to a certain place and asked him what he saw there. 'I see a huge tree,' said Arjuna, 'and on it I notice fruits hanging like clusters of blackberries.' Then Krishna said to Arjuna, 'Come nearer and you will find that these are not clusters of blackberries, but clusters of innumerable Krishnas like Me, hanging from the tree.' In other words, Divine Incarnations without number appear and disappear on the tree of the Absolute Brahman.

"Kavirdās was strongly inclined to the formless God. At the mention of Krishna's name he would say: 'Why should I worship Him? The gopis would clap their hands while He performed a monkey dance.' (*With a smile*) But I accept God with form when I am in the company of people who believe in that ideal, and I also agree with those who believe in the formless God."

M. (*smiling*): "You are as infinite as He of whom we have been talking. Truly, no one can fathom your depth."

MASTER (*smiling*): "Ah! I see you have found it out. Let me tell you one thing. One should follow various paths. One should practise each creed for a time. In a game of satrancha a piece can't reach the centre square until it completes the circle; but once in the square it can't be overtaken by any other piece."

M: "That is true, sir."

MASTER: "There are two classes of yogis: the vahudakas and the kutichakas. The vahudakas roam about visiting various holy places and have not yet found peace of mind. But the kutichakas, having visited all the sacred places, have quieted their minds. Feeling serene and peaceful, they settle down in one place and no longer move about. In that one place they are happy; they don't feel the need of going to any sacred place. If one of them ever visits a place of pilgrimage, it is only for the purpose of new inspiration.

"I had to practise each religion for a time—Hinduism, Islām, Christianity. Furthermore, I followed the paths of the Śāktas, Vaishnavas, and Vedāntists. I realized that there is only one God toward whom all are travelling; but the paths are different.

"While visiting the holy places, I would sometimes suffer great agony. Once I went with Mathur to Raja Babu's drawing-room in Benares. I found that they talked there only of worldly matters—money, real estate, and the like. At this I burst into tears. I said to the Divine Mother, weeping: 'Mother! Where hast Thou brought me? I was much better off at Dakshineswar.' In Allāhābād I noticed the same things that I saw elsewhere—the same ponds, the same grass, the same trees, the same tamarind-leaves.

"But one undoubtedly finds inspiration in a holy place. I accompanied Mathur Babu to Vrindāvan. Hriday and the ladies of Mathur's family were in our party. No sooner did I see the Kāliyadaman Ghāt than a divine emotion surged up within me. I was completely overwhelmed. Hriday used to bathe me there as if I were a small child.

"In the dusk I would walk on the bank of the Jamunā when the cattle returned along the sandy banks from their pastures. At the very sight of those cows the thought of Krishna would flash in my mind. I would run along like a madman, crying: 'Oh, where is Krishna? Where is my Krishna?'

"I went to Śyāmakunda and Rādhākunda[14] in a palanquin and got out to visit the holy Mount Govardhan. At the very sight of the mount I was overpowered with divine emotion and ran to the top. I lost all consciousness of the world around me. The residents of the place helped me to come down. On my way to the sacred pools of Śyāmakunda and Rādhākunda, when I saw the meadows, the trees, the shrubs, the birds, and the deer, I was overcome with ecstasy. My clothes became wet with tears. I said: 'O Krishna! Everything here is as it was in the olden days. You alone are absent.' Seated inside the palanquin I lost all power of speech. Hriday followed the palanquin. He had warned the bearers to be careful about me.

"Gangāmāyi became very fond of me in Vrindāvan. She was an old woman who lived all alone in a hut near the Nidhuvan. Referring to my spiritual condition and ecstasy, she said, 'He is the very embodiment of Rādhā.' She addressed me as 'Dulāli'. When with her, I used to forget my food and drink, my bath, and all thought of going home. On some days Hriday used to bring food from home and feed me. Gangāmāyi also would serve me with food prepared by her own hands.

"Gangāmāyi used to experience trances. At such times a great crowd would come to see her. One day, in a state of ecstasy, she climbed on Hriday's shoulders.

"I didn't want to leave her and return to Calcutta. Everything was arranged for me to stay with her. I was to eat double-boiled rice, and we were to have our beds on either side of the cottage. All the arrangements had been made, when Hriday said: 'You have such a weak stomach. Who will look after you?' 'Why,' said Gangāmāyi, 'I shall look after him. I'll nurse him.' As Hriday dragged me by one hand and she by the other, I remem-

[14] Places near Mathurā associated with the episode of Krishna and Rādhā.

bered my mother, who was then living alone here in the nahabat of the temple garden. I found it impossible to stay away from her, and said to Gangāmāyi, 'No, I must go.' I loved the atmosphere of Vrindāvan."

About eleven o'clock the Master took his meal, the offerings from the temple of Kāli. After taking his noonday rest he resumed his conversation with the devotees. Every now and then he uttered the holy word "Om" or repeated the sacred names of the deities.

After sunset the evening worship was performed in the temples. Since it was the day of Vijayā, the devotees first saluted the Divine Mother and then took the dust[15] of the Master's feet.

Tuesday, October 24, 1882

It was three or four o'clock in the afternoon. The Master was standing near the shelf where the food was kept, when Balaram and M. arrived from Calcutta and saluted him. Sri Ramakrishna said to them with a smile: "I was going to take some sweets from the shelf, but no sooner did I put my hand on them than a lizard dropped on my body.[16] At once I removed my hand. (*All laugh.*)

"Oh, yes! One should observe all these things. You see, Rakhal is ill, and my limbs ache too. Do you know what's the matter? This morning as I was leaving my bed I saw[17] a certain person, whom I took for Rakhal. (*All laugh.*) Oh, yes! Physical features should be studied. The other day Narendra brought one of his friends, a man with only one good eye, though the other eye was not totally blind. I said to myself, 'What is this trouble that Narendra has brought with him?'

"A certain person comes here, but I can't eat any food that he brings. He works in an office at a salary of twenty rupees and earns another twenty by writing false bills. I can't utter a word in his presence, because he tells lies. Sometimes he stays here two or three days without going to his office. Can you guess his purpose? It is that I should recommend him to someone for a job somewhere else.

"Balaram comes from a family of devout Vaishnavas. His father, now an old man, is a pious devotee. He has a tuft of hair on his head, a rosary of tulsi beads round his neck, and a string of beads in his hand. He devotes his time to the repetition of God's name. He owns much property in Orissa and has built temples to Rādhā-Krishna in Kothār, Vrindāvan, and other places, establishing free guest-houses as well.

(*To Balaram*) "A certain person came here the other day. I understand he is the slave of that black hag of a wife. Why is it that people do not see God? It is because of the barrier of 'woman and gold'. How impudent he was to say to you the other day, 'A paramahamsa came to my father, who fed him with chicken curry!'[18]

[15] A form of reverent salutation in which one touches the feet of a superior with one's forehead.

[16] The dropping of a lizard on the body is considered an omen.

[17] Orthodox Hindus in Bengal believe that the first face seen in the morning indicates whether the day will bring good or evil.

[18] Orthodox Hindus are forbidden to eat chicken.

"In my present state of mind I can eat a little fish soup if it has been offered to the Divine Mother beforehand. I can't eat any meat, even if it is offered to the Divine Mother; but I taste it with the end of my finger lest She should be angry. (*Laughter.*)

"Well, can you explain this state of my mind? Once I was going from Burdwān to Kāmārpukur in a bullock-cart, when a great storm arose. Some people gathered near the cart. My companions said they were robbers. So I began to repeat the names of God, calling sometimes on Kāli, sometimes on Rāma, sometimes on Hanumān. What do you think of that?"

Was the Master hinting that God is one but is addressed differently by different sects?

MASTER (*to Balaram*): "Māyā is nothing but 'woman and gold'. A man living in its midst gradually loses his spiritual alertness. He thinks all is well with him. The scavenger carries a tub of night-soil on his head, and in course of time loses his repulsion to it. One gradually acquires love of God through the practice of chanting God's name and glories. (*To M.*) One should not be ashamed of chanting God's holy name. As the saying goes, 'One does not succeed so long as one has these three: shame, hatred, and fear.'

"At Kāmārpukur they sing kirtan very well. The devotional music is sung to the accompaniment of drums.

(*To Balaram*) "Have you installed any image at Vrindāvan?"

BALARAM: "Yes, sir. We have a grove where Krishna is worshipped."

MASTER: "I have been to Vrindāvan. The Nidhu Grove is very nice indeed."

THE MASTER AND KESHAB

October 27, 1882

IT WAS FRIDAY, the day of the Lakshmi Pujā. Keshab Chandra Sen had arranged a boat trip on the Ganges for Sri Ramakrishna.

About four o'clock in the afternoon the steamboat with Keshab and his Brāhmo followers cast anchor in the Ganges alongside the Kāli temple at Dakshineswar. The passengers saw in front of them the bathing-ghāt and the chāndni. To their left, in the temple compound, stood six temples of Śiva, and to their right another group of six Śiva temples. The white steeple of the Kāli temple, the tree-tops of the Panchavati, and the silhouette of pine-trees stood high against the blue autumn sky. The gardens between the two nahabats were filled with fragrant flowers, and along the bank of the Ganges were rows of flowering plants. The blue sky was reflected in the brown water of the river, the sacred Ganges, associated with the most ancient traditions of Āryan civilization. The outer world appeared soft and serene, and the hearts of the Brāhmo devotees were filled with peace.

Sri Ramakrishna was in his room talking with Vijay and Haralal. Some disciples of Keshab entered. Bowing before the Master, they said to him: "Sir, the steamer has arrived. Keshab Babu has asked us to take you there." A small boat was to carry the Master to the steamer. No sooner did he get into the boat than he lost outer consciousness in samādhi. Vijay was with him.

M. was among the passengers. As the boat came alongside the steamer, all rushed to the railing to have a view of Sri Ramakrishna. Keshab became anxious to get him safely on board. With great difficulty the Master was brought back to consciousness of the world and taken to a cabin in the steamer. Still in an abstracted mood, he walked mechanically, leaning on a devotee for support. Keshab and the others bowed before him, but he was not aware of them. Inside the cabin there were a few chairs and a table. He was made to sit on one of the chairs, Keshab and Vijay occupying two others. Some devotees were also seated, most of them on the floor, while many others had to stand outside. They peered eagerly through the door and windows. Sri Ramakrishna again went into deep samādhi and became totally unconscious of the outer world.

As the air in the room was stuffy because of the crowd of people, Keshab opened the windows. He was embarrassed to meet Vijay, since they had differed on certain principles of the Brāhmo Samāj and Vijay had separated himself from Keshab's organization, joining another society.

The Brāhmo devotees looked wistfully at the Master. Gradually he came back to sense consciousness; but the divine intoxication still lingered. He said to himself in a whisper: "Mother, why have You brought me here? They are hedged around and not free. Can I free them?" Did the Master find that the people assembled there were locked within the prison walls of the world? Did their helplessness make the Master address these words to the Divine Mother?

Sri Ramakrishna was gradually becoming conscious of the outside world. Nilmadhav of Ghāzipur and a Brāhmo devotee were talking about Pāvhāri Bābā. Another Brāhmo devotee said to the Master: "Sir, these gentlemen visited Pāvhāri Bābā. He lives in Ghāzipur. He is a holy man like yourself." The Master could hardly talk; he only smiled. The devotee continued, "Sir, Pāvhāri Bābā keeps your photograph in his room." Pointing to his body the Master said with a smile, "Just a pillow-case."

The Master continued: "But you should remember that the heart of the devotee is the abode of God. He dwells, no doubt, in all beings, but He especially manifests Himself in the heart of the devotee. A landlord may at one time or another visit all parts of his estate, but people say he is generally to be found in a particular drawing-room. The heart of the devotee is the drawing-room of God.

"He who is called Brahman by the jnānis is known as Ātman by the yogis and as Bhagavān by the bhaktas. The same brāhmin is called priest, when worshipping in the temple, and cook, when preparing a meal in the kitchen. The jnāni, sticking to the path of knowledge, always reasons about the Reality, saying, 'Not this, not this'. Brahman is neither 'this' nor 'that'; It is neither the universe nor its living beings. Reasoning in this way, the mind becomes steady. Then it disappears and the aspirant goes into samādhi. This is the Knowledge of Brahman. It is the unwavering conviction of the jnāni that Brahman alone is real and the world illusory. All these names and forms are illusory, like a dream. What Brahman is cannot be described. One cannot even say that Brahman is a Person. This is the opinion of the jnānis, the followers of Vedānta philosophy.

"But the bhaktas accept all the states of consciousness. They take the waking state to be real also. They don't think the world to be illusory, like a dream. They say that the universe is a manifestation of God's power and glory. God has created all these—sky, stars, moon, sun, mountains, ocean, men, animals. They constitute His glory. He is within us, in our hearts. Again, He is outside. The most advanced devotees say that He Himself has become all this—the twenty-four cosmic principles, the universe, and all living beings. The devotee of God wants to eat sugar, not to become sugar. (All laugh.)

"Do you know how a lover of God feels? His attitude is: 'O God, Thou art the Master, and I am Thy servant. Thou art the Mother, and I am Thy child.' Or again: 'Thou art my Father and Mother. Thou art the Whole, and I am a part.' He doesn't like to say, 'I am Brahman.'

"The yogi seeks to realize the Paramātman, the Supreme Soul. His ideal is the union of the embodied soul and the Supreme Soul. He withdraws his mind from sense-objects and tries to concentrate it on the Paramātman. Therefore, during the first stage of his spiritual discipline, he retires into solitude and with undivided attention practises meditation in a fixed posture.

"But the Reality is one and the same. The difference is only in name. He who is Brahman is verily Ātman, and again, He is the Bhagavān. He is Brahman to the followers of the path of knowledge, Paramātman to the yogis, and Bhagavān to the lovers of God."

The steamer had been going toward Calcutta; but the passengers, with their eyes fixed on the Master and their ears given to his nectar-like words, were oblivious of its motion. Dakshineswar, with its temples and gardens, was left behind. The paddles of the boat churned the waters of the Ganges with a murmuring sound. But the devotees were indifferent to all this. Spellbound, they looked on a great yogi, his face lighted with a divine smile, his countenance radiating love, his eyes sparkling with joy—a man who had renounced all for God and who knew nothing but God. Unceasing words of wisdom flowed from his lips.

MASTER: "The jnānis, who adhere to the non-dualistic philosophy of Vedānta, say that the acts of creation, preservation, and destruction, the universe itself and all its living beings, are the manifestations of Śakti, the Divine Power.[1] If you reason it out, you will realize that all these are as illusory as a dream. Brahman alone is the Reality, and all else is unreal. Even this very Śakti is unsubstantial, like a dream.

"But though you reason all your life, unless you are established in samādhi, you cannot go beyond the jurisdiction of Śakti. Even when you say, 'I am meditating', or 'I am contemplating', still you are moving in the realm of Śakti, within Its power.

"Thus Brahman and Śakti are identical. If you accept the one, you must accept the other. It is like fire and its power to burn. If you see the fire, you must recognize its power to burn also. You cannot think of fire without its power to burn, nor can you think of the power to burn without fire. You cannot conceive of the sun's rays without the sun, nor can you conceive of the sun without its rays.

"What is milk like? Oh, you say, it is something white. You cannot think of the milk without the whiteness, and again, you cannot think of the whiteness without the milk.

"Thus one cannot think of Brahman without Śakti, or of Śakti without Brahman. One cannot think of the Absolute without the Relative, or of the Relative without the Absolute.

"The Primordial Power is ever at play.[2] She is creating, preserving, and destroying in play, as it were. This Power is called Kāli. Kāli is verily Brahman, and Brahman is verily Kāli. It is one and the same Reality. When

[1] Known as māyā in the Vedānta philosophy.
[2] This idea introduces the elements of spontaneity and freedom in the creation.

we think of It as inactive, that is to say, not engaged in the acts of creation, preservation, and destruction, then we call It Brahman. But when It engages in these activities, then we call It Kāli or Śakti. The Reality is one and the same; the difference is in name and form.

"It is like water, called in different languages by different names, such as 'jal', 'pāni', and so forth. There are three or four ghāts on a lake. The Hindus, who drink water at one place, call it 'jal'. The Mussalmāns at another place call it 'pāni'. And the English at a third place call it 'water'. All three denote one and the same thing, the difference being in the name only. In the same way, some address the Reality as 'Allāh', some as 'God', some as 'Brahman', some as 'Kāli', and others by such names as 'Rāma', 'Jesus', 'Durgā', 'Hari'."

KESHAB (with a smile): "Describe to us, sir, in how many ways Kāli, the Divine Mother, sports in this world."

MASTER (with a smile): "Oh, She plays in different ways. It is She alone who is known as Mahā-Kāli, Nitya-Kāli, Śmaśāna-Kāli, Rakshā-Kāli, and Śyāmā-Kāli. Mahā-Kāli and Nitya-Kāli are mentioned in the Tantra philosophy. When there were neither the creation, nor the sun, the moon, the planets, and the earth, and when darkness was enveloped in darkness, then the Mother, the Formless One, Mahā-Kāli, the Great Power, was one with Mahā-Kāla, the Absolute.

"Śyāmā-Kāli has a somewhat tender aspect and is worshipped in the Hindu households. She is the Dispenser of boons and the Dispeller of fear. People worship Rakshā-Kāli, the Protectress, in times of epidemic, famine, earthquake, drought, and flood. Śmaśāna-Kāli is the embodiment of the power of destruction. She resides in the cremation ground, surrounded by corpses, jackals, and terrible female spirits. From Her mouth flows a stream of blood, from Her neck hangs a garland of human heads, and around Her waist is a girdle made of human hands.

"After the destruction of the universe, at the end of a great cycle, the Divine Mother garners the seeds for the next creation. She is like the elderly mistress of the house, who has a hotchpotch-pot in which she keeps different articles for household use. (All laugh.)

"Oh, yes! Housewives have pots like that, where they keep 'sea-foam',[3] blue pills, small bundles of seeds of cucumber, pumpkin, and gourd, and so on. They take them out when they want them. In the same way, after the destruction of the universe, my Divine Mother, the Embodiment of Brahman, gathers together the seeds for the next creation. After the creation the Primal Power dwells in the universe itself. She brings forth this phenomenal world and then pervades it. In the Vedas creation is likened to the spider and its web. The spider brings the web out of itself and then remains in it. God is the container of the universe and also what is contained in it.

"Is Kāli, my Divine Mother, of a black complexion? She appears black because She is viewed from a distance; but when intimately known She is no longer so. The sky appears blue at a distance; but look at it close by and you will find that it has no colour. The water of the ocean looks blue at a

[3] The Master perhaps referred to the cuttlefish bone found on the seashore. The popular belief is that it is hardened sea-foam.

distance, but when you go near and take it in your hand, you find that it is colourless."

The Master became intoxicated with divine love and sang:

> Is Kāli, my Mother, really black?
> The Naked One, of blackest hue,
> Lights the Lotus of the Heart. . . .

The Master continued: "Bondage and liberation are both of Her making. By Her māyā worldly people become entangled in 'woman and gold', and again, through Her grace they attain their liberation. She is called the Saviour, and the Remover of the bondage that binds one to the world."

Then the Master sang the following song[4] in his melodious voice:

> In the world's busy market-place, O Śyāmā, Thou art flying kites;
> High up they soar on the wind of hope, held fast by māyā's string.
> Their frames are human skeletons, their sails of the three gunas made;
> But all their curious workmanship is merely for ornament.
>
> Upon the kite-strings Thou hast rubbed the mānjā-paste[5] of worldliness,
> So as to make each straining strand all the more sharp and strong.
> Out of a hundred thousand kites, at best but one or two break free;
> And Thou dost laugh and clap Thy hands, O Mother, watching them!
>
> On favouring winds, says Rāmprasād, the kites set loose will speedily
> Be borne away to the Infinite, across the sea of the world.

The Master said: "The Divine Mother is always playful and sportive. This universe is Her play. She is self-willed and must always have Her own way. She is full of bliss. She gives freedom to one out of a hundred thousand."

A Brāhmo devotee: "But, sir, if She likes, She can give freedom to all. Why, then, has She kept us bound to the world?"

Master: "That is Her will. She wants to continue playing with Her created beings. In a game of hide-and-seek[6] the running about soon stops if in the beginning all the players touch the 'granny'. If all touch her, then how can the game go on? That displeases her. Her pleasure is in continuing the game. Therefore the poet said:

> Out of a hundred thousand kites, at best but one or two break free;
> And Thou dost laugh and clap Thy hands, O Mother, watching them!

[4] The allusion of this song is to the well-known kite-flying competitions in India. Several people fly their kites and try to cut one another's kite-strings. Whoever has his string cut loses his kite and quits the game.

[5] A glue of barley and powdered glass.

[6] The allusion is to the Indian game of hide-and-seek, in which the leader, known as the "granny", bandages the eyes of the players and hides herself. The players are supposed to find her. If any player can touch her, the bandage is removed from his eyes and he is released from the game.

"It is as if the Divine Mother said to the human mind in confidence, with a sign from Her eye, 'Go and enjoy the world.' How can one blame the mind? The mind can disentangle itself from worldliness if, through Her grace, She makes it turn toward Herself. Only then does it become devoted to the Lotus Feet of the Divine Mother."

Whereupon Sri Ramakrishna, taking upon himself, as it were, the agonies of all householders, sang a song complaining to the Divine Mother:

> Mother, this is the grief that sorely grieves my heart,
> That even with Thee for Mother, and though I am wide awake,
> There should be robbery in my house.
> Many and many a time I vow to call on Thee,
> Yet when the time for prayer comes round, I have forgotten.
> Now I see it is all Thy trick.
>
> As Thou hast never given, so Thou receivest naught;
> Am I to blame for this, O Mother? Hadst Thou but given,
> Surely then Thou hadst received;
> Out of Thine own gifts I should have given to Thee.
> Glory and shame, bitter and sweet, are Thine alone;
> This world is nothing but Thy play.
> Then why, O Blissful One, dost Thou cause a rift in it?
>
> Says Rāmprasād: Thou hast bestowed on me this mind,
> And with a knowing wink of Thine eye
> Bidden it, at the same time, to go and enjoy the world.
> And so I wander here forlorn through Thy creation,
> Blasted, as it were, by someone's evil glance,
> Taking the bitter for the sweet,
> Taking the unreal for the Real.

The Master continued: "Men are deluded through Her māyā and have become attached to the world.

> Says Rāmprasād: Thou hast bestowed on me this mind,
> And with a knowing wink of Thine eye
> Bidden it, at the same time, to go and enjoy the world."

BRĀHMO DEVOTEE: "Sir, can't we realize God without complete renunciation?"

MASTER (with a laugh): "Of course you can! Why should you renounce everything? You are all right as you are, following the middle path—like molasses partly solid and partly liquid. Do you know the game of nax?[7] Having scored the maximum number of points, I am out of the game. I can't enjoy it. But you are very clever. Some of you have scored ten points, some six, and some five. You have scored just the right number; so you are not out of the game like me. The game can go on. Why, that's fine! (All laugh.)

"I tell you the truth: there is nothing wrong in your being in the world. But you must direct your mind toward God; otherwise you will not succeed.

---

[7] In the Indian card-game of nax the object is to stay in the game by scoring under seventeen points. Anyone scoring seventeen points or more has to retire.

Do your duty with one hand and with the other hold to God. After the duty is over, you will hold to God with both hands.

"It is all a question of the mind. Bondage and liberation are of the mind alone. The mind will take the colour you dye it with. It is like white clothes just returned from the laundry. If you dip them in red dye, they will be red. If you dip them in blue or green, they will be blue or green. They will take only the colour you dip them in, whatever it may be. Haven't you noticed that, if you read a little English, you at once begin to utter English words: *Foot fut it mit?*[8] Then you put on boots and whistle a tune, and so on. It all goes together. Or, if a scholar studies Sanskrit, he will at once rattle off Sanskrit verses. If you are in bad company, then you will talk and think like your companions. On the other hand, when you are in the company of devotees, you will think and talk only of God.

"The mind is everything. A man has his wife on one side and his daughter on the other. He shows his affection to them in different ways. But his mind is one and the same.

"Bondage is of the mind, and freedom is also of the mind. A man is free if he constantly thinks: 'I am a free soul. How can I be bound, whether I live in the world or in the forest? I am a child of God, the King of Kings. Who can bind me?' If bitten by a snake, a man may get rid of its venom by saying emphatically, 'There is no poison in me.' In the same way, by repeating with grit and determination, 'I am not bound, I am free', one really becomes so—one really becomes free.

"Once someone gave me a book of the Christians. I asked him to read it to me. It talked about nothing but sin. (*To Keshab*) Sin is the only thing one hears of at your Brāhmo Samāj, too. The wretch who constantly says, 'I am bound, I am bound' only succeeds in being bound. He who says day and night, 'I am a sinner, I am a sinner' verily becomes a sinner.

"One should have such burning faith in God that one can say: 'What? I have repeated the name of God, and can sin still cling to me? How can I be a sinner any more? How can I be in bondage any more?'

"If a man repeats the name of God, his body, mind, and everything become pure. Why should one talk only about sin and hell, and such things? Say but once, 'O Lord, I have undoubtedly done wicked things, but I won't repeat them.' And have faith in His name."

Sri Ramakrishna became intoxicated with divine love and sang:

> If only I can pass away repeating Durgā's name,
> How canst Thou then, O Blessed One,
> Withhold from me deliverance,
> Wretched though I may be? . . .

Then he said: "To my Divine Mother I prayed only for pure love. I offered flowers at Her Lotus Feet and prayed to Her: 'Mother, here is Thy virtue, here is Thy vice. Take them both and grant me only pure love for Thee. Here is Thy knowledge, here is Thy ignorance. Take them both and grant me only pure love for Thee. Here is Thy purity, here is Thy impurity.

[8] The Master was merely mimicking the sound of English.

Take them both, Mother, and grant me only pure love for Thee. Here is Thy dharma, here is Thy adharma. Take them both, Mother, and grant me only pure love for Thee.'

(*To the Brāhmo devotees*) "Now listen to a song by Rāmprasād:

> Come, let us go for a walk, O mind, to Kāli, the Wish-fulfilling
> Tree,
> And there beneath It gather the four fruits of life.
> Of your two wives, Dispassion and Worldliness,
> Bring along Dispassion only, on your way to the Tree,
> And ask her son Discrimination about the Truth.
>
> When will you learn to lie, O mind, in the abode of Blessedness,
> With Cleanliness and Defilement on either side of you?
> Only when you have found the way
> To keep these wives contentedly under a single roof,
> Will you behold the matchless form of Mother Śyāmā.
>
> Ego and Ignorance, your parents, instantly banish from your sight;
> And should Delusion seek to drag you to its hole,
> Manfully cling to the pillar of Patience.
> Tie to the post of Unconcern the goats of Vice and Virtue,
> Killing them with the sword of Knowledge if they rebel.
>
> With the children of Worldliness, your first wife, plead from a
> goodly distance,
> And, if they will not listen, drown them in Wisdom's sea.
> Says Rāmprasād: If you do as I say,
> You can submit a good account, O mind, to the King of Death,
> And I shall be well pleased with you and call you my darling.

"Why shouldn't one be able to realize God in this world? King Janaka had such realization. Rāmprasād described the world as a mere 'framework of illusion'. But if one loves God's hallowed feet, then—

> This very world is a mansion of mirth;
> Here I can eat, here drink and make merry.
> Janaka's might was unsurpassed;
> What did he lack of the world or the Spirit?
> Holding to one as well as the other,
> He drank his milk from a brimming cup!

(*All laugh.*)

"But one cannot be a King Janaka all of a sudden. Janaka at first practised much austerity in solitude.

"Even if one lives in the world, one must go into solitude now and then. It will be of great help to a man if he goes away from his family, lives alone, and weeps for God even for three days. Even if he thinks of God for one day in solitude, when he has the leisure, that too will do him good. People shed a whole jug of tears for wife and children. But who cries for the Lord? Now and then one must go into solitude and practise spiritual discipline to realize God. Living in the world and entangled in many of its duties, the aspirant, during the first stage of spiritual life, finds many obstacles in the path of concentration. While the trees on the foot-path are young, they must be fenced around; otherwise they will be destroyed by cattle. The fence is necessary when the tree is young, but it can be taken away when the trunk is thick and strong. Then the tree won't be hurt even if an elephant is tied to it.

"The disease of worldliness is like typhoid. And there are a huge jug of water and a jar of savoury pickles in the typhoid patient's room. If you want to cure him of his illness, you must remove him from that room. The worldly man is like the typhoid patient. The various objects of enjoyment are the huge jug of water, and the craving for their enjoyment is his thirst. The very thought of pickles makes the mouth water; you don't have to bring them near. And he is surrounded with them. The companionship of woman is the pickles. Hence treatment in solitude is necessary.

"One may enter the world after attaining discrimination and dispassion. In the ocean of the world there are six alligators: lust, anger, and so forth. But you need not fear the alligators if you smear your body with turmeric before you go into the water. Discrimination and dispassion are the turmeric. Discrimination is the knowledge of what is real and what is unreal. It is the realization that God alone is the real and eternal Substance and that all else is unreal, transitory, impermanent. And you must cultivate intense zeal for God. You must feel love for Him and be attracted to Him. The gopis of Vrindāvan felt the attraction of Krishna. Let me sing you a song:

> Listen! The flute has sounded in yonder wood.
> There I must fly, for Krishna waits on the path.
> Tell me, friends, will you come along or no?
> To you my Krishna is merely an empty name;
> To me He is the anguish of my heart.
> You hear His flute-notes only with your ears,
> But, oh, I hear them in my deepest soul.
> I hear His flute calling: 'Rādhā, come out!
> Without you the grove is shorn of its loveliness.'"

The Master sang the song with tears in his eyes, and said to Keshab and the other Brāhmo devotees: "Whether you accept Rādhā and Krishna, or not, please do accept their attraction for each other. Try to create that same yearning in your heart for God. Yearning is all you need in order to realize Him."

Gradually the ebb-tide set in. The steamboat was speeding toward Calcutta. It passed under the Howrah Bridge and came within sight of the Botanical Garden. The captain was asked to go a little farther down the river. The passengers were enchanted with the Master's words, and most of them had no idea of time or of how far they had come.

Keshab began to serve some puffed rice and grated coconut. The guests held these in the folds of their wearing-cloths and presently started to eat. Everyone was joyful. The Master noticed, however, that Keshab and Vijay rather shrank from each other, and he was anxious to reconcile them.

MASTER (to Keshab): "Look here. There is Vijay. Your quarrel seems like the fight between Śiva and Rāma. Śiva was Rāma's guru. Though they fought with each other, yet they soon came to terms. But the grimaces of the ghosts, the followers of Śiva, and the gibberish of the monkeys, the followers of Rāma, would not come to an end! (*Loud laughter.*) Such quarrels take place even among one's own kith and kin. Didn't Rāma fight with His own sons, Lava and Kuśa? Again, you must have noticed how a mother and daughter, living together and having the same spiritual end in view, observe their religious fast separately on Tuesdays, each on her own account —as if the welfare of the mother were different from the welfare of the daughter. But what benefits the one benefits the other. In like manner, you have a religious society, and Vijay thinks he must have one too. (*Laughter.*) But I think all these are necessary. While Sri Krishna, Himself God Incarnate, played with the gopis at Vrindāvan, trouble-makers like Jatilā and Kutilā appeared on the scene. You may ask why. The answer is that the play does not develop without trouble-makers. (*All laugh.*) There is no fun without Jatilā and Kutilā. (*Loud laughter.*)

"Rāmānuja upheld the doctrine of Qualified Non-dualism. But his guru was a pure non-dualist. They disagreed with each other and refuted each other's arguments. That always happens. Still, to the teacher the disciple is his own."

All rejoiced in the Master's company and his words.

MASTER (*to Keshab*): "You don't look into people's natures before you make them your disciples, and so they break away from you.

"All men look alike, to be sure, but they have different natures. Some have an excess of sattva, others an excess of rajas, and still others an excess of tamas. You must have noticed that the cakes known as puli all look alike. But their contents are very different. Some contain condensed milk, some coconut kernel, and others mere boiled kalāi pulse. (*All laugh.*)

"Do you know my attitude? As for myself, I eat, drink, and live happily. The rest the Divine Mother knows. Indeed, there are three words that prick my flesh: 'guru', 'master', and 'father'.

"There is only one Guru, and that is Satchidānanda. He alone is the Teacher. My attitude toward God is that of a child toward its mother. One can get human gurus by the million. All want to be teachers. But who cares to be a disciple?

"It is extremely difficult to teach others. A man can teach only if God reveals Himself to him and gives the command. Nārada, Śukadeva, and sages like them had such a command from God, and Śankara had it too. Unless you have a command from God, who will listen to your words?

"Don't you know how easily the people of Calcutta get excited? The milk in the kettle puffs up and boils as long as the fire burns underneath. Take away the fuel and all becomes quiet. The people of Calcutta love sensations. You may see them digging a well at a certain place. They say they want water. But if they strike a stone they give up that place; they begin at another place. And there, perchance, they find sand; they give up the second place too. Next they begin at a third. And so it goes. But it won't do if a man only imagines that he has God's command.

"God does reveal Himself to man and speak. Only then may one receive

His command. How forceful are the words of such a teacher! They can move mountains. But mere lectures? People will listen to them for a few days and then forget them. They will never act upon mere words.

"At Kāmārpukur there is a small lake called the Hāldārpukur. Certain people used to befoul its banks every day. Others who came there in the morning to bathe would abuse the offenders loudly. But next morning they would find the same thing. The nuisance didn't stop. (*All laugh.*) The villagers finally informed the authorities about it. A constable was sent, who put up a notice on the bank which read: 'Commit no nuisance.' This stopped the miscreants at once. (*All laugh.*)

"To teach others, one must have a badge of authority; otherwise teaching becomes a mockery. A man who is himself ignorant starts out to teach others —like the blind leading the blind! Instead of doing good, such teaching does harm. After the realization of God one obtains an inner vision. Only then can one diagnose a person's spiritual malady and give instruction.

"Without the commission from God, a man becomes vain. He says to himself, 'I am teaching people.' This vanity comes from ignorance, for only an ignorant person feels that he is the doer. A man verily becomes liberated in life if he feels: 'God is the Doer. He alone is doing everything. I am doing nothing.' Man's sufferings and worries spring only from his persistent thought that he is the doer.

"You people speak of doing good to the world. Is the world such a small thing? And who are you, pray, to do good to the world? First realize God, see Him by means of spiritual discipline. If He imparts power, then you can do good to others; otherwise not."

A BRĀHMO DEVOTEE: "Then, sir, we must give up our activities until we realize God?"

MASTER: "No. Why should you? You must engage in such activities as contemplation, singing His praises, and other daily devotions."

BRĀHMO: "But what about our worldly duties—duties associated with our earning money, and so on?"

MASTER: "Yes, you can perform them too, but only as much as you need for your livelihood. At the same time, you must pray to God in solitude, with tears in your eyes, that you may be able to perform those duties in an unselfish manner. You should say to Him: 'O God, make my worldly duties fewer and fewer; otherwise, O Lord, I find that I forget Thee when I am involved in too many activities. I may think I am doing unselfish work, but it turns out to be selfish.' People who carry to excess the giving of alms, or the distributing of food among the poor, fall victims to the desire of acquiring name and fame.

"Sambhu Mallick once talked about establishing hospitals, dispensaries, and schools, making roads, digging public reservoirs, and so forth. I said to him: 'Don't go out of your way to look for such works. Undertake only those works that present themselves to you and are of pressing necessity—and those also in a spirit of detachment.' It is not good to become involved in many activities. That makes one forget God. Coming to the Kālighāt temple, some, perhaps, spend their whole time in giving alms to the poor. They have no time to see the Mother in the inner shrine! (*Laughter.*) First of all manage somehow to see the image of the Divine Mother, even by pushing through the crowd. Then you may or may not give alms, as you wish. You may give to the poor to your heart's content, if you feel that way. Work is only a means to the realization of God. Therefore I said to Sambhu, 'Suppose God appears before you; then will you ask Him to build hospitals and dispensaries for you?' (*Laughter.*) A lover of God never says that. He will rather say: 'O Lord, give me a place at Thy Lotus Feet. Keep me always in Thy company. Give me sincere and pure love for Thee.'

"Karmayoga is very hard indeed. In the Kaliyuga it is extremely difficult to perform the rites enjoined in the scriptures. Nowadays man's life is centred on food alone. He cannot perform many scriptural rites. Suppose a man is laid up with fever. If you attempt a slow cure with the old-fashioned indigenous remedies, before long his life may be snuffed out. He can't stand much delay. Nowadays the drastic 'D. Gupta'[9] mixture is appropriate. In the Kaliyuga the best way is bhaktiyoga, the path of devotion—singing the praises of the Lord, and prayer. The path of devotion alone is the religion for this age. (*To the Brāhmo devotees*) Yours also is the path of devotion. Blessed you are indeed that you chant the name of Hari and sing the Divine Mother's glories. I like your attitude. You don't call the world a dream, like the non-dualists. You are not Brahmajnānis like them; you are bhaktas, lovers of God. That you speak of Him as a Person is also good. You are devotees. You will certainly realize Him if you call on Him with sincerity and earnestness."

The boat cast anchor at Kayalāghāt and the passengers prepared to disembark. On coming outside they noticed that the full moon was up. The trees, the buildings, and the boats on the Ganges were bathed in its mellow light. A carriage was hailed for the Master, and M. and a few devotees got in with him. The Master asked for Keshab. Presently the latter arrived and inquired about the arrangements made for the Master's return to Dakshineswar. Then he bowed low and took leave of Sri Ramakrishna.

The carriage drove through the European quarter of the city. The Master enjoyed the sight of the beautiful mansions on both sides of the well lighted streets. Suddenly he said: "I am thirsty. What's to be done?" Nandalal, Keshab's nephew, stopped the carriage before the India Club and went upstairs to get some water. The Master inquired whether the glass had been well washed. On being assured that it had been, he drank the water.

As the carriage went along, the Master put his head out of the window and looked with childlike enjoyment at the people, the vehicles, the horses, and the streets, all flooded with moonlight. Now and then he heard European ladies singing at the piano. He was in a very happy mood.

The carriage arrived at the house of Suresh Mitra, who was a great devotee of the Master and whom he addressed affectionately as Surendra. He was not at home.

The members of the household opened a room on the ground floor for the Master and his party. The cab fare was to be paid. Surendra would

[9] A patent fever medicine containing a strong dose of quinine.

have taken care of it had he been there. The Master said to a devotee: "Why don't you ask the ladies to pay the fare? They certainly know that their master visits us at Dakshineswar. I am not a stranger to them." (*All laugh.*)

Narendra, who lived in that quarter of the city, was sent for. In the mean time Sri Ramakrishna and the devotees were invited to the drawing-room upstairs. The floor of the room was covered with a carpet and a white sheet. A few cushions were lying about. On the wall hung an oil painting especially painted for Surendra, in which Sri Ramakrishna was pointing out to Keshab the harmony of Christianity, Islām, Buddhism, Hinduism, and other religions. On seeing the picture Keshab had once said, "Blessed is the man who conceived the idea."

Sri Ramakrishna was talking joyously with the devotees, when Narendra arrived. This made the Master doubly happy. He said to his young disciple, "We had a boat trip with Keshab today. Vijay and many other Brāhmo devotees were there. (*Pointing to M.*) Ask him what I said to Keshab and Vijay about the mother and daughter observing their religious fast on Tuesdays, each on her own account, though the welfare of the one meant the welfare of the other. I also said to Keshab that trouble-makers like Jatilā and Kutilā were necessary to lend zest to the play. (*To M.*) Isn't that so?"

M: "Yes, sir. Quite so."

It was late. Surendra had not yet returned. The Master had to leave for the temple garden, and a cab was brought for him. M. and Narendra saluted him and took their leave. Sri Ramakrishna's carriage started for Dakshineswar through the moonlit streets.

THE MASTER WITH THE BRĀHMO
DEVOTEES (I)

October 28, 1882

IT WAS SATURDAY. The semi-annual Brāhmo festival, celebrated each autumn and spring, was being held in Benimadhav Pal's beautiful garden house at Sinthi, about three miles north of Calcutta. The house stood in a secluded place suited for contemplation. Trees laden with flowers, artificial lakes with grassy banks, and green arbours enhanced the beauty of the grounds. Just as the fleecy clouds were turning gold in the light of the setting sun, the Master arrived.

Many devotees had attended the morning devotions, and in the afternoon people from Calcutta and the neighbouring villages joined them. Shivanath, the great Brāhmo devotee whom the Master loved dearly, was one of the large gathering of members of the Brāhmo Samāj who had been eagerly awaiting Sri Ramakrishna's arrival.

When the carriage bringing the Master and a few devotees reached the garden house, the assembly stood up respectfully to receive him. There was a sudden silence, like that which comes when the curtain in a theatre is about to be rung up. People who had been conversing with one another now fixed their attention on the Master's serene face, eager not to lose one word that might fall from his lips.

At the sight of Shivanath the Master cried out joyously: "Ah! Here is Shivanath! You see, you are a devotee of God. The very sight of you gladdens my heart. One hemp-smoker feels very happy to meet another. Very often they embrace each other in an exuberance of joy."

The devotees burst out laughing.

MASTER: "Many people visit the temple garden at Dakshineswar. If I see some among the visitors indifferent to God, I say to them, 'You had better sit over there.' Or sometimes I say, 'Go and see the beautiful buildings.' (*Laughter.*)

"Sometimes I find that the devotees of God are accompanied by worthless people. Their companions are immersed in gross worldliness and don't enjoy spiritual talk at all. Since the devotees keep on, for a long time, talking with me about God, the others become restless. Finding it impossible to sit there

145

any longer, they whisper to their devotee friends: 'When shall we be going? How long will you stay here?' The devotees say: 'Wait a bit. We shall go after a little while.' Then the worldly people say in a disgusted tone: 'Well then, you can talk. We shall wait for you in the boat.' (*All laugh.*)

"Worldly people will never listen to you if you ask them to renounce everything and devote themselves whole-heartedly to God. Therefore Chaitanya and Nitāi, after some deliberation, made an arrangement to attract the worldly. They would say to such persons, 'Come, repeat the name of Hari, and you shall have a delicious soup of māgur fish and the embrace of a young woman.' Many people, attracted by the fish and the woman, would chant the name of God. After tasting a little of the nectar of God's hallowed name, they would soon realize that the 'fish soup' really meant the tears they shed for love of God, while the 'young woman' signified the earth. The embrace of the woman meant rolling on the ground in the rapture of divine love.

"Nitāi would employ any means to make people repeat Hari's name. Chaitanya said: 'The name of God has very great sanctity. It may not produce an immediate result, but one day it must bear fruit. It is like a seed that has been left on the cornice of a building. After many days the house crumbles, and the seed falls on the earth, germinates, and at last bears fruit.'

"As worldly people are endowed with sattva, rajas, and tamas, so also is bhakti characterized by the three gunas.

"Do you know what a worldly person endowed with sattva is like? Perhaps his house is in a dilapidated condition here and there. He doesn't care to repair it. The worship hall may be strewn with pigeon droppings and the courtyard covered with moss, but he pays no attention to these things. The furniture of the house may be old; he doesn't think of polishing it and making it look neat. He doesn't care for dress at all; anything is good enough for him. But the man himself is very gentle, quiet, kind, and humble; he doesn't injure anyone.

"Again, among the worldly there are people with the traits of rajas. Such a man has a watch and chain, and two or three rings on his fingers. The furniture of his house is all spick and span. On the walls hang portraits of the Queen, the Prince of Wales, and other prominent people; the building is whitewashed and spotlessly clean. His wardrobe is filled with a large assortment of clothes; even the servants have their livery, and all that.

"The traits of a worldly man endowed with tamas are sleep, lust, anger, egotism, and the like.

"Similarly, bhakti, devotion, has its sattva. A devotee who possesses it meditates on God in absolute secret, perhaps inside his mosquito net. Others think he is asleep. Since he is late in getting up, they think perhaps he has not slept well during the night. His love for the body goes only as far as appeasing his hunger, and that only by means of rice and simple greens. There is no elaborate arrangement about his meals, no luxury in clothes, and no display of furniture. Besides, such a devotee never flatters anybody for money.

"An aspirant possessed of rājasic bhakti puts a tilak[1] on his forehead and a necklace of holy rudrāksha beads, interspersed with gold ones, around his neck. (*All laugh.*) At worship he wears a silk cloth.

"A man endowed with tāmasic bhakti has burning faith. Such a devotee literally extorts boons from God, even as a robber falls upon a man and plunders his money. 'Bind! Beat! Kill!'—that is his way, the way of the dacoits."

Saying this, the Master began to sing in a voice sweet with rapturous love, his eyes turned upward:

> Why should I go to Gangā or Gayā, to Kāśi, Kānchi, or Prabhās,[2]
> So long as I can breathe my last with Kāli's name upon my lips?
> What need of rituals has a man, what need of devotions any more,
> If he repeats the Mother's name at the three holy hours?[3]
> Rituals may pursue him close, but never can they overtake him.
> Charity, vows, and giving of gifts do not appeal to Madan's[4] mind;
> The Blissful Mother's Lotus Feet are his whole prayer and sacrifice.
> Who could ever have conceived the power Her name possesses?
> Śiva Himself, the God of Gods, sings Her praise with His five
>   mouths!

The Master was beside himself with love for the Divine Mother. He sang with fiery enthusiasm:

> If only I can pass away repeating Durgā's name,
> How canst Thou then, O Blessed One,
> Withhold from me deliverance,
> Wretched though I may be? . . .

Then he said, "One must take the firm attitude: 'What? I have chanted the Mother's name. How can I be a sinner any more? I am Her child, heir to Her powers and glories.'

"If you can give a spiritual turn to your tamas, you can realize God with its help. Force your demands on God. He is by no means a stranger to you. He is indeed your very own.

"Again, you see, the quality of tamas can be used for the welfare of others. There are three classes of physicians: superior, mediocre, and inferior. The physician who feels the patient's pulse and just says to him, 'Take the medicine regularly' belongs to the inferior class. He doesn't care to inquire whether or not the patient has actually taken the medicine. The mediocre physician is he who in various ways persuades the patient to take the medicine, and says to him sweetly: 'My good man, how will you be cured unless you use the medicine? Take this medicine. I have made it for you myself.' But he who, finding the patient stubbornly refusing to take the medicine, forces it down his throat, going so far as to put his knee on the patient's

---

[1] A mark of sandal-paste or other material to denote one's religious affiliation.
[2] Five places of pilgrimage.
[3] Dawn, noon, and dusk.
[4] The author of the song.

chest, is the best physician. This is the manifestation of the tamas of the physician. It doesn't injure the patient; on the contrary, it does him good.

"Like the physicians, there are three types of religious teachers. The inferior teacher only gives instruction to the disciples but makes no inquiries about their progress. The mediocre teacher, for the good of the student, makes repeated efforts to bring the instruction home to him, begs him to assimilate it, and shows him love in many other ways. But there is a type of teacher who goes to the length of using force when he finds the student persistently unyielding; I call him the best teacher."

A BRĀHMO DEVOTEE: "Sir, has God forms or has He none?"

MASTER: "No one can say with finality that God is only 'this' and nothing else. He is formless, and again He has forms. For the bhakta He assumes forms. But He is formless for the jnāni, that is, for him who looks on the world as a mere dream. The bhakta feels that he is one entity and the world another. Therefore God reveals Himself to him as a Person. But the jnāni— the Vedāntist, for instance—always reasons, applying the process of 'Not this, not this'. Through this discrimination he realizes, by his inner perception, that the ego and the universe are both illusory, like a dream. Then the jnāni realizes Brahman in his own consciousness. He cannot describe what Brahman is.

"Do you know what I mean? Think of Brahman, Existence-Knowledge-Bliss Absolute, as a shoreless ocean. Through the cooling influence, as it were, of the bhakta's love, the water has frozen at places into blocks of ice. In other words, God now and then assumes various forms for His lovers and reveals Himself to them as a Person. But with the rising of the sun of Knowledge, the blocks of ice melt. Then one doesn't feel any more that God is a Person, nor does one see God's forms. What He is cannot be described. Who will describe Him? He who would do so disappears. He cannot find his 'I' any more.

"If one analyses oneself, one doesn't find any such thing as 'I'. Take an onion, for instance. First of all you peel off the red outer skin; then you find thick white skins. Peel these off one after the other, and you won't find anything inside.

"In that state a man no longer finds the existence of his ego. And who is there left to seek it? Who can describe how he feels in that state—in his own Pure Consciousness—about the real nature of Brahman? Once a salt doll went to measure the depth of the ocean. No sooner was it in the water than it melted. Now who was to tell the depth?

"There is a sign of Perfect Knowledge. Man becomes silent when It is attained. Then the 'I', which may be likened to the salt doll, melts in the Ocean of Existence-Knowledge-Bliss Absolute and becomes one with It. Not the slightest trace of distinction is left.

"As long as his self-analysis is not complete, man argues with much ado. But he becomes silent when he completes it. When the empty pitcher has been filled with water, when the water inside the pitcher becomes one with the water of the lake outside, no more sound is heard. Sound comes from the pitcher as long as the pitcher is not filled with water.

"People used to say in olden days that no boat returns after having once entered the 'black waters' of the ocean.

"All trouble and botheration come to an end when the 'I' dies. You may indulge in thousands of reasonings, but still the 'I' doesn't disappear. For people like you and me, it is good to have the feeling, 'I am a lover of God.'

"The Saguna Brahman is meant for the bhaktas. In other words, a bhakta believes that God has attributes and reveals Himself to men as a Person, assuming forms. It is He who listens to our prayers. The prayers that you utter are directed to Him alone. You are bhaktas, not jnānis or Vedāntists. It doesn't matter whether you accept God with form or not. It is enough to feel that God is a Person who listens to our prayers, who creates, preserves, and destroys the universe, and who is endowed with infinite power.

"It is easier to attain God by following the path of devotion."

BRĀHMO DEVOTEE: "Sir, is it possible for one to see God? If so, why can't we see Him?"

MASTER: "Yes, He can surely be seen. One can see His forms, and His formless aspect as well. How can I explain that to you?"

BRĀHMO DEVOTEE: "What are the means by which one can see God?"

MASTER: "Can you weep for Him with intense longing of heart? Men shed a jugful of tears for the sake of their children, for their wives, or for money. But who weeps for God? So long as the child remains engrossed with its toys, the mother looks after her cooking and other household duties. But when the child no longer relishes the toys, it throws them aside and yells for its mother. Then the mother takes the rice-pot down from the hearth, runs in haste, and takes the child in her arms."

BRĀHMO DEVOTEE: "Sir, why are there so many different opinions about the nature of God? Some say that God has form, while others say that He is formless. Again, those who speak of God with form tell us about His different forms. Why all this controversy?"

MASTER: "A devotee thinks of God as he sees Him. In reality there is no confusion about God. God explains all this to the devotee if the devotee only realizes Him somehow. You haven't set your foot in that direction. How can you expect to know all about God?

"Listen to a story. Once a man entered a wood and saw a small animal on a tree. He came back and told another man that he had seen a creature of a beautiful red colour on a certain tree. The second man replied: 'When I went into the wood, I also saw that animal. But why do you call it red? It is green.' Another man who was present contradicted them both and insisted that it was yellow. Presently others arrived and contended that it was grey, violet, blue, and so forth and so on. At last they started quarrelling among themselves. To settle the dispute they all went to the tree. They saw a man sitting under it. On being asked, he replied: 'Yes, I live under this tree and I know the animal very well. All your descriptions are true. Sometimes it appears red, sometimes yellow, and at other times blue, violet, grey, and so forth. It is a chameleon. And sometimes it has no colour at all. Now it has a colour, and now it has none.'

"In like manner, one who constantly thinks of God can know His real nature; he alone knows that God reveals Himself to seekers in various forms and aspects. God has attributes; then again He has none. Only the man who lives under the tree knows that the chameleon can appear in various colours, and he knows, further, that the animal at times has no colour at all. It is the others who suffer from the agony of futile argument.

"Kabir used to say, 'The formless Absolute is my Father, and God with form is my Mother.'

"God reveals Himself in the form which His devotee loves most. His love for the devotee knows no bounds. It is written in the Purāna that God assumed the form of Rāma for His heroic devotee, Hanumān.

"The forms and aspects of God disappear when one discriminates in accordance with the Vedānta philosophy. The ultimate conclusion of such discrimination is that Brahman alone is real and this world of names and forms illusory. It is possible for a man to see the forms of God, or to think of Him as a Person, only so long as he is conscious that he is a devotee. From the standpoint of discrimination this 'ego of a devotee' keeps him a little away from God.

"Do you know why images of Krishna or Kāli are three and a half cubits high? Because of distance. Again, on account of distance the sun appears to be small. But if you go near it you will find the sun so big that you won't be able to comprehend it. Why have images of Krishna and Kāli a dark-blue colour? That too is on account of distance, like the water of a lake, which appears green, blue, or black from a distance. Go near, take the water in the palm of your hand, and you will find that it has no colour. The sky also appears blue from a distance. Go near and you will see that it has no colour at all.

"Therefore I say that in the light of Vedāntic reasoning Brahman has no attributes. The real nature of Brahman cannot be described. But so long as your individuality is real, the world also is real, and equally real are the different forms of God and the feeling that God is a Person.

"Yours is the path of bhakti. That is very good; it is an easy path. Who can fully know the infinite God? and what need is there of knowing the Infinite? Having attained this rare human birth, my supreme need is to develop love for the Lotus Feet of God.

"If a jug of water is enough to remove my thirst, why should I measure the quantity of water in a lake? I become drunk on even half a bottle of wine—what is the use of my calculating the quantity of liquor in the tavern? What need is there of knowing the Infinite?

"The various states of mind of the Brahmajnāni are described in the Vedas. The path of knowledge is extremely difficult. One cannot obtain jnāna if one has the least trace of worldliness and the slightest attachment to 'woman and gold'. This is not the path for the Kaliyuga.

"The Vedas speak of seven planes where the mind dwells. When the mind is immersed in worldliness it dwells in the three lower planes—at the navel, the organ of generation, and the organ of evacuation. In that state the mind loses all its higher visions—it broods only on 'woman and gold'. The fourth plane of the mind is at the heart. When the mind dwells there, one has the first glimpse of spiritual consciousness. One sees light all around. Such a man, perceiving the divine light, becomes speechless with wonder and says: 'Ah! What is this? What is this?' His mind does not go downward to the objects of the world.

"The fifth plane of the mind is at the throat. When the mind reaches this, the aspirant becomes free from all ignorance and illusion. He does not enjoy talking or hearing about anything but God. If people talk about worldly things, he leaves the place at once.

"The sixth plane is at the forehead. When the mind reaches it, the aspirant sees the form of God day and night. But even then a little trace of ego remains. At the sight of that incomparable beauty of God's form, one becomes intoxicated and rushes forth to touch and embrace it. But one doesn't succeed. It is like the light inside a lantern. One feels as if one could touch the light, but one cannot on account of the pane of glass.

"In the top of the head is the seventh plane. When the mind rises there, one goes into samādhi. Then the Brahmajnāni directly perceives Brahman. But in that state his body does not last many days. He remains unconscious of the outer world. If milk is poured into his mouth, it runs out. Dwelling on this plane of consciousness, he gives up his body in twenty-one days. That is the condition of the Brahmajnāni. But yours is the path of devotion. That is a very good and easy path.

"Once a man said to me, 'Sir, can you teach me quickly the thing you call samādhi?' (All laugh.)

"After a man has attained samādhi all his actions drop away. All devotional activities, such as worship, japa, and the like, as well as all worldly duties, cease to exist for such a person. At the beginning there is much ado about work. As a man makes progress toward God, the outer display of his work becomes less and less—so much so that he cannot even sing the name and glories of God. (To Shivanath) As long as you were not here at the meeting, people talked a great deal about you and discussed your virtues. But no sooner did you arrive here than all that stopped. Now the very sight of you makes everyone happy. People now simply say, 'Ah! Here is Shivanath Babu.' All other talk about you has stopped.

"After attaining samādhi, I once went to the Ganges to perform tarpan. But as I took water in the palm of my hand, it trickled down through my fingers. Weeping, I said to Haladhari, 'Cousin, what is this?' Haladhari replied, 'It is called galitahasta[5] in the holy books.' After the vision of God, such duties as the performance of tarpan drop away.

"In the kirtan the devotee first sings, 'Nitāi āmār mātā hāti.'[6] As the devotional mood deepens, he simply sings, 'Hāti! Hāti!' Next, all he can sing is 'Hāti'. And last of all he simply sings, 'Hā!' and goes into samādhi. The man who has been singing all the while then becomes speechless.

"Again, at a feast given to the brāhmins one at first hears much noise of talking. When the guests sit on the floor with leaf-plates in front of them, much of the noise ceases. Then one hears only the cry, 'Bring some luchi!'

[5] Literally, "inert and benumbed hand".
[6] "My Nitāi dances like a mad elephant."

As they partake of the luchi and other dishes, three quarters of the noise subsides. When the curd, the last course, appears, one hears only the sound 'soop, soop' as the guests eat the curd with their fingers. Then there is practically no noise. Afterwards all retire to sleep, and absolute silence reigns.

"Therefore I say, at the beginning of religious life a man makes much ado about work, but as his mind dives deeper into God, he becomes less active. Last of all comes the renunciation of work, followed by samādhi.

"Generally the body does not remain alive after the attainment of samādhi. The only exceptions are such sages as Nārada, who keep their bodies alive in order to bring spiritual light to others. It is also true of Divine Incarnations, like Chaitanya. After the well is dug, one generally throws away the spade and the basket. But some keep them in order to help their neighbours. The great souls who retain their bodies after samādhi feel compassion for the suffering of others. They are not so selfish as to be satisfied with their own illumination. You are well aware of the nature of selfish people. If you ask them to spit at a particular place, they won't, lest it should do you good. If you ask them to bring a sweetmeat worth a cent from the store, they will perhaps lick it on the way back. (All laugh.)

"But the manifestations of Divine Power are different in different beings. Ordinary souls are afraid to teach others. A piece of worthless timber may itself somehow float across the water, but it sinks even under the weight of a bird. Sages like Nārada are like a heavy log of wood, which not only floats on the water but also can carry men, cows, and even elephants.

(To Shivanath and the other Brāhmo devotees) "Can you tell me why you dwell so much on the powers and glories of God? I asked the same thing of Keshab Sen. One day Keshab and his party came to the temple garden at Dakshineswar. I told them I wanted to hear how they lectured. A meeting was arranged in the paved courtyard above the bathing-ghāt on the Ganges, where Keshab gave a talk. He spoke very well. I went into a trance. After the lecture I said to Keshab, 'Why do you so often say such things as: "O God, what beautiful flowers Thou hast made! O God, Thou hast created the heavens, the stars, and the ocean!" and so on?' Those who love splendour themselves are fond of dwelling on God's splendour.

"Once a thief stole the jewels from the images in the temple of Rādhākānta. Mathur Babu entered the temple and said to the Deity: 'What a shame, O God! You couldn't save Your own ornaments.' 'The idea!' I said to Mathur. 'Does He who has Lakshmi for His handmaid and attendant ever lack any splendour? Those jewels may be precious to you, but to God they are no better than lumps of clay. Shame on you! You shouldn't have spoken so meanly. What riches can you give to God to magnify His glory?'

"Therefore I say, a man seeks the person in whom he finds joy. What need has he to ask where that person lives, the number of his houses, gardens, relatives, and servants, or the amount of his wealth? I forget everything when I see Narendra. Never, even unwittingly, have I asked him where he lived, what his father's profession was, or the number of his brothers.

"Dive deep in the sweetness of God's Bliss. What need have we of His infinite creation and unlimited glory?"

The Master sang:

> Dive deep, O mind, dive deep in the Ocean of God's Beauty;
> If you descend to the uttermost depths,
> There you will find the gem of Love.

> Go seek, O mind, go seek Vrindāvan in your heart,
> Where with His loving devotees
> Sri Krishna sports eternally.

> Light up, O mind, light up true wisdom's shining lamp,
> And let it burn with steady flame
> Unceasingly within your heart.

> Who is it that steers your boat across the solid earth?
> It is your guru, says Kubir;
> Meditate on his holy feet.

Sri Ramakrishna continued: "It is also true that after the vision of God the devotee desires to witness His līlā. After the destruction of Rāvana at Rāma's hands, Nikashā, Rāvana's mother, began to run away for fear of her life. Lakshmana said to Rāma: 'Revered Brother, please explain this strange thing to me. This Nikashā is an old woman who has suffered a great deal from the loss of her many sons, and yet she is so afraid of losing her own life that she is taking to her heels!' Rāma bade her come near, gave her assurance of safety, and asked her why she was running away. Nikashā answered: 'O Rāma, I am able to witness all this līlā of Yours because I am still alive. I want to live longer so that I may see the many more things You will do on this earth.' (*All laugh.*)

(*To Shivanath*) "I like to see you. How can I live unless I see pure-souled devotees? I feel as if they had been my friends in a former incarnation."

A BRĀHMO DEVOTEE: "Sir, do you believe in the reincarnation of the soul?"

MASTER: "Yes, they say there is something like that. How can we understand the ways of God through our small intellects? Many people have spoken about reincarnation; therefore I cannot disbelieve it. As Bhishma lay dying on his bed of arrows, the Pāndava brothers and Krishna stood around him. They saw tears flowing from the eyes of the great hero. Arjuna said to Krishna: 'Friend, how surprising it is! Even such a man as our grandsire Bhishma—truthful, self-restrained, supremely wise, and one of the eight Vasus—weeps, through māyā, at the hour of death.' Sri Krishna asked Bhishma about it. Bhishma replied: 'O Krishna, You know very well that this is not the cause of my grief. I am thinking that there is no end to the Pāndavas' sufferings, though God Himself is their charioteer.[7] A thought like this makes me feel that I have understood nothing of the ways of God, and so I weep.'"

It was about half past eight when the evening worship began in the prayer hall. Soon the moon rose in the autumn sky and flooded the trees and creepers of the garden with its light. After prayer the devotees began to sing. Sri Ramakrishna was dancing, intoxicated with love of God. The Brāhmo devotees danced around him to the accompaniment of drums and cymbals.

---

[7] Krishna, an Incarnation of God, was Arjuna's charioteer.

All appeared to be in a very joyous mood. The place echoed and re-echoed with God's holy name.

When the music had stopped, Sri Ramakrishna prostrated himself on the ground and, making salutations to the Divine Mother again and again, said: "Bhāgavata—Bhakta—Bhagavān! My salutations at the feet of the jnānis! My salutations at the feet of the bhaktas! I salute the bhaktas who believe in God with form, and I salute the bhaktas who believe in God without form. I salute the knowers of Brahman of olden times. And my salutations at the feet of the modern knowers of Brahman of the Brāhmo Samāj!"

Then the Master and the devotees enjoyed a supper of delicious dishes, which Benimadhav, their host, had provided.

Wednesday, November 15, 1882

Sri Ramakrishna, accompanied by Rakhal and several other devotees, came to Calcutta in a carriage and called for M. at the school where he was teaching. Then they all set out for the Maidān. Sri Ramakrishna wanted to see the Wilson Circus. As the carriage rolled along the crowded Chitpore Road, his joy was very great. Like a little child he leaned first out of one side of the carriage and then out of the other, talking to himself as if addressing the passers-by. To M. he said: "I find the attention of the people fixed on earthly things. They are all rushing about for the sake of their stomachs. No one is thinking of God."

They arrived at the circus. Tickets for the cheapest seats were purchased. The devotees took the Master to a high gallery, and they all sat on a bench. He said joyfully: "Ha! This is a good place. I can see the show well from here." There were exhibitions of various feats. A horse raced around a circular track over which large iron rings were hung at intervals. The circus rider, an Englishwoman, stood on one foot on the horse's back, and as the horse passed under the rings, she jumped through them, always alighting on one foot on the horse's back. The horse raced around the entire circle, and the woman never missed the horse or lost her balance.

When the circus was over, the Master and the devotees stood outside in the field, near the carriage. Since it was a cold night he covered his body with his green shawl.

Sri Ramakrishna said to M.: "Did you see how that Englishwoman stood on one foot on her horse, while it ran like lightning? How difficult a feat that must be! She must have practised a long time. The slightest carelessness and she would break her arms or legs; she might even be killed. One faces the same difficulty leading the life of a householder. A few succeed in it through the grace of God and as a result of their spiritual practice. But most people fail. Entering the world, they become more and more involved in it; they drown in worldliness and suffer the agonies of death. A few only, like Janaka, have succeeded, through the power of their austerity, in leading the spiritual life as householders. Therefore spiritual practice is extremely necessary; otherwise one cannot rightly live in the world."

The Master got into the carriage with the devotees and went to Balaram Bose's house. He was taken with his companions to the second floor. It was evening and the lamps were lighted. The Master described the feats he had seen at the circus. Gradually other devotees gathered, and soon he was engaged in spiritual talk with them.

The conversation turned to the caste-system. Sri Ramakrishna said: "The caste-system can be removed by one means only, and that is the love of God. Lovers of God do not belong to any caste. The mind, body, and soul of a man become purified through divine love. Chaitanya and Nityānanda scattered the name of Hari to everyone, including the pariah, and embraced them all. A brāhmin without this love is no longer a brāhmin. And a pariah with the love of God is no longer a pariah. Through bhakti an untouchable becomes pure and elevated."

Speaking of householders entangled in worldliness, the Master said: "They are like the silk-worm. They can come out of the cocoon of their worldly life if they wish. But they can't bear to; for they themselves have built the cocoon with great love and care. So they die there. Or they are like the fish in a trap. They can come out of it by the way they entered, but they sport inside the trap with other fish and hear the sweet sound of the murmuring water and forget everything else. They don't even make an effort to free themselves from the trap. The lisping of children is the murmur of the water, and the other fish are relatives and friends. Only one or two make good their escape by running away. They are the liberated souls."

The Master then sang:

> When such delusion veils the world, through Mahāmāyā's spell,
> That Brahmā is bereft of sense,
> And Vishnu loses consciousness,
> What hope is left for men?
>
> The narrow channel first is made, and there the trap is set;
> But open though the passage lies,
> The fish, once safely through the gate,
> Do not come out again.
>
> The silk-worm patiently prepares its closely spun cocoon;
> Yet even though a way leads forth,
> Encased within its own cocoon,
> The worm remains to die.

The Master continued: "Man may be likened to grain. He has fallen between the millstones and is about to be crushed. Only the few grains that stay near the peg escape. Therefore men should take refuge at the peg, that is to say, in God. Call on Him. Sing His name. Then you will be free. Otherwise you will be crushed by the King of Death."

The Master sang again:

> Mother! Mother! My boat is sinking, here in the ocean of this
> world;
> Fiercely the hurricane of delusion rages on every side!
> Clumsy is my helmsman, the mind; stubborn my six oarsmen, the
> passions;
> Into a pitiless wind
> I sailed my boat, and now it is sinking!

Split is the rudder of devotion; tattered is the sail of faith;
Into my boat the waters are pouring! Tell me, what shall I do?
For with my failing eyes, alas! nothing but darkness do I see.
Here in the waves I will swim,
O Mother, and cling to the raft of Thy name!

Mr. Viswas had been sitting in the room a long time; he now left. He had once been wealthy but had squandered everything in an immoral life. Finally he had become indifferent to his wife and children. Referring to Mr. Viswas, the Master said: "He is an unfortunate wretch. A householder has his duties to discharge, his debts to pay: his debt to the gods, his debt to his ancestors, his debt to the rishis, and his debt to wife and children. If a wife is chaste, then her husband should support her; he should also bring up their children until they are of age. Only a monk must not save; the bird and the monk do not provide for the morrow. But even a bird provides when it has young. It brings food in its bill for its chicks."

BALARAM: "Mr. Viswas now wants to cultivate the company of holy people."

MASTER (*with a smile*): "A monk's kamandalu goes to the four principal holy places[8] with him, but it still tastes bitter. Likewise, it is said that the Malaya breeze turns all trees into sandal-wood. But there are a few exceptions, such as the cotton-tree, the aśwattha, and the hog plum.

"Some frequent the company of holy men in order to smoke hemp. Many monks smoke it, and these householders stay with them, prepare the hemp, and partake of the prasād."

Thursday, November 16, 1882

The Master had come to Calcutta. In the evening he went to the house of Rajmohan, a member of the Brāhmo Samāj, where Narendra and some of his young friends used to meet and worship according to the Brāhmo ceremonies. Sri Ramakrishna wanted to see their worship. He was accompanied by M. and a few other devotees.

The Master was very happy to see Narendra and expressed a desire to watch the young men at their worship. Narendra sang and then the worship began. One of the young men conducted it. He prayed, "O Lord, may we give up everything and be absorbed in Thee!" Possibly the youth was inspired by the Master's presence and so talked of utter renunciation. Sri Ramakrishna remarked in a whisper, "Much likelihood there is of that!"

Rajmohan served the Master with refreshments.

Sunday, November 19, 1882

It was the auspicious occasion of the Jagaddhātri Pujā, the festival of the Divine Mother. Sri Ramakrishna was invited to Surendra's house in Calcutta; but first he went to the house of Manomohan in the neighbourhood.

The Master was seated in Manomohan's parlour. He said: "God very

---

[8] At the four cardinal points of India, namely, Kedārnāth in the Himālayas, Dwārakā in the west, Rāmeśwar in the south, and Puri in the east.

much relishes the bhakti of the poor and the lowly, just as the cow relishes fodder mixed with oil-cake. King Duryodhana showed Krishna the splendour of his wealth and riches, but Krishna accepted the hospitality of the poor Vidura. God is fond of His devotees. He runs after the devotee as the cow after the calf."

The Master sang:

> And, for that love, the mighty yogis practise yoga from age to age;
> When love awakes, the Lord, like a magnet, draws to Him the soul.

Then he said: "Chaitanya used to shed tears of joy at the very mention of Krishna's name. God alone is the real Substance; all else is illusory. Man can realize God if he wants to, but he madly craves the enjoyment of 'woman and gold'. The snake has a precious stone[9] in its head, but it is perfectly satisfied to eat a mere frog.

"Bhakti is the one essential thing. Who can ever know God through reasoning? I want love of God. What do I care about knowing His infinite glories? One bottle of wine makes me drunk. What do I care about knowing how many gallons there are in the grog-shop? One jar of water is enough to quench my thirst. I don't need to know the amount of water there is on earth."

Sri Ramakrishna arrived at Surendra's house. Many devotees had assembled there, including Surendra's elder brother, who was a judge.

MASTER (to Surendra's brother): "You are a judge. That is very good. But remember, everything happens through God's power. It is He who has given you your high position; that is how you became a judge. People think it is they who are great. The water from the roof flows through a spout that is shaped like a lion's head. It looks as if the lion were bringing the water out through its mouth. But look at the source of the water! A cloud gathers in the sky and rain falls on the roof; then the water flows through the pipe and at last comes out through the spout."

SURENDRA'S BROTHER: "The Brāhmo Samāj preaches the freedom of women and the abolition of the caste-system. What do you think about these matters?"

MASTER: "Men feel that way when they are just beginning to develop spiritual yearning. A storm raises clouds of dust, and one cannot distinguish between the different trees—the mango, the hog plum, and the tamarind. But after the storm blows over, one sees clearly. After the first storm of divine passion is quelled, one gradually understands that God alone is the Highest Good, the Eternal Substance, and that all else is transitory. One cannot grasp this without tapasyā and the company of holy men. What is the use of merely reciting the written parts for the drum? It is very difficult to put them into practice on the instrument. What can be accomplished by a mere lecture? It is austerity that is necessary. By that alone can one comprehend.

"You asked about caste distinctions. There is only one way to remove them, and that is by love of God. Lovers of God have no caste. Through this

[9] A folk belief in Bengal.

divine love the untouchable becomes pure, the pariah no longer remains a pariah. Chaitanya embraced all, including the pariahs.

"The members of the Brāhmo Samāj sing the name of Hari. That is very good. Through earnest prayer one receives the grace of God and realizes Him. God can be realized by means of all paths. The same God is invoked by different names."

SURENDRA'S BROTHER: "Sir, what do you think of Theosophy?"

MASTER: "I have heard that man can acquire superhuman powers through it and perform miracles. I saw a man who had brought a ghost under control. The ghost used to procure various things for his master. What shall I do with superhuman powers? Can one realize God through them? If God is not realized then everything becomes false."

November 1882

It was about four o'clock in the afternoon when Sri Ramakrishna arrived in Calcutta to attend the annual festival of the Brāhmo Samāj, which was to be celebrated at Manilal Mallick's house. Besides M. and other devotees of the Master, Vijay Goswami and a number of Brāhmos were present. Elaborate arrangements had been made to make the occasion a success. Vijay was to conduct the worship.

The kathak recited the life of Prahlāda from the Purāna. Its substance was as follows: Hiranyakaśipu, Prahlāda's father, was king of the demons. He bore great malice toward God and put his own son through endless tortures for leading a religious life. Afflicted by his father, Prahlāda prayed to God, "O God, please give my father holy inclinations."

At these words the Master wept. He went into an ecstatic mood. Afterwards he began to talk to the devotees.

MASTER: "Bhakti is the only essential thing. One obtains love of God by constantly chanting His name and singing His glories. Ah! What a devotee Shivanath is! He is soaked in the love of God, like a cheese-cake in syrup.

"One should not think, 'My religion alone is the right path and other religions are false.' God can be realized by means of all paths. It is enough to have sincere yearning for God. Infinite are the paths and infinite the opinions.

"Let me tell you one thing. God can be seen. The Vedas say that God is beyond mind and speech. The meaning of this is that God is unknown to the mind attached to worldly objects. Vaishnavcharan[10] used to say, 'God is known by the mind and intellect that are pure.' Therefore it is necessary to seek the company of holy men, practise prayer, and listen to the instruction of the guru. These purify the mind. Then one sees God. Dirt can be removed from water by a purifying agent. Then one sees one's reflection in it. One cannot see one's face in a mirror if the mirror is covered with dirt.

"After the purification of the heart one obtains divine love. Then one sees God, through His grace. One can teach others if one receives that command from God after seeing Him. Before that one should not 'lecture'. There is a song that says:

[10] A noted devotee of the Vaishnava sect and an admirer of Sri Ramakrishna.

You have set up no image here,
Within the shrine, O fool!
Blowing the conch, you simply make
Confusion worse confounded.

"You should first cleanse the shrine of your heart. Then you should install the Deity and arrange worship. As yet nothing has been done. What can you achieve by blowing the conch-shell[11] and simply making a loud noise?"

Vijay sat on a raised stool and conducted the worship according to the rules of the Brāhmo Samāj. Afterwards he sat by the Master.

MASTER (to Vijay): "Will you tell me one thing? Why did you harp so much on sin? By repeating a hundred times, 'I am a sinner', one verily becomes a sinner. One should have such faith as to be able to say, 'What? I have taken the name of God; how can I be a sinner?' God is our Father and Mother. Tell Him, 'O Lord, I have committed sins, but I won't repeat them.' Chant His name and purify your body and mind. Purify your tongue by singing God's holy name."

December 1882

In the afternoon Sri Ramakrishna was seated on the west porch of his room in the temple garden at Dakshineswar. Among others, Baburam, Ramdayal, and M. were present. These three were going to spend the night with the Master. M. intended to stay the following day also, for he was having his Christmas holidays. Baburam had only recently begun to visit the Master.

MASTER (to the devotees): "A man becomes liberated even in this life when he knows that God is the Doer of all things. Once Keshab came here with Sambhu Mallick. I said to him, 'Not even a leaf moves except by the will of God.' Where is man's free will? All are under the will of God. Nangtā was a man of great knowledge, yet even he was about to drown himself in the Ganges. He stayed here eleven months. At one time he suffered from stomach trouble. The excruciating pain made him lose control over himself, and he wanted to drown himself in the river. There was a long shoal near the bathing-ghāt. However far he went into the river, he couldn't find water above his knees. Then he understood everything[12] and came back. At one time I was very ill and was about to cut my throat with a knife. Therefore I say: 'O Mother, I am the machine and Thou art the Operator; I am the chariot and Thou art the Driver. I move as Thou movest me; I do as Thou makest me do.' "

The devotees sang kirtan in the Master's room:

Dwell, O Lord, O Lover of·bhakti,
In the Vrindāvan of my heart,
And my devotion unto Thee
Will be Thy Rādhā, dearly loved;

---

[11] The conch-shell is blown during the temple service.

[12] He realized that man is not free even to kill himself, that everything depends on the will of the Divine Mother. See Introduction, p. 31.

My body will be Nanda's home,
My tenderness will be Yaśodā,
My longing for deliverance
Will be Thy gentle gopi maids.

Lift the Govardhan of my sin
And slay my six unyielding passions,
Fierce as the demons sent by Kamśa!
Sweetly play the flute[13] of Thy grace,
Charming the milch cow of my mind;
Abide in the pasture of my soul.

Dwell by the Jamunā of my yearning,
Under the banyan of my hope,
For ever gracious to Thy servant;
And, if naught but the cowherds' love
Can hold Thee in Vrindāvan's vale,
Then, Lord, let Dāśarathi, too,
Become Thy cowherd and Thy slave.

Again they sang:

Sing, O bird that nestles deep within my heart!
Sing, O bird that sits on the Kalpa-Tree of Brahman!
Sing God's everlasting praise.
Taste, O bird, of the four fruits of the Kalpa-Tree,
Dharma, artha, kāma, moksha.
Sing, O bird, "He alone is the Comfort of my soul!"
Sing, O bird, "He alone is my life's enduring Joy!"
O thou wondrous bird of my life,
Sing aloud in my heart! Unceasingly sing, O bird!
Sing for evermore, even as the thirsty chātak
Sings for the raindrop from the cloud.

A devotee from Nandanbāgān entered the room with his friends. The Master looked at him and said, "Everything inside him can be seen through his eyes, as one sees the objects in a room through a glass door." This devotee and his brothers always celebrated the anniversary of the Brāhmo Samāj at their house in Nandanbāgān. Sri Ramakrishna had taken part in these festivals.

The evening worship began in the temples. The Master was seated on the small couch in his room, absorbed in meditation. He went into an ecstatic mood and said a little later: "Mother, please draw him to Thee. He is so modest and humble! He has been visiting Thee." Was the Master referring to Baburam, who later became one of his foremost disciples?

The Master explained the different kinds of samādhi to the devotees. The conversation then turned to the joy and suffering of life. Why did God create so much suffering?

M: "Once Vidyāsāgar said in a mood of pique: 'What is the use of calling on God? Just think of this incident: At one time Chenghiz Khan plundered

---

[13] A reference to Sri Krishna's pastoral life.

a country and imprisoned many people. The number of prisoners rose to about a hundred thousand. The commander of his army said to him: "Your Majesty, who will feed them? It is risky to keep them with us. It will be equally dangerous to release them. What shall I do?" Chenghiz Khan said: "That's true. What can be done? Well, have them killed." The order was accordingly given to cut them to pieces. Now, God saw this slaughter, didn't He? But He didn't stop it in any way. Therefore I don't need God, whether He exists or not. I don't derive any good from Him.' "

MASTER: "Is it possible to understand God's action and His motive? He creates, He preserves, and He destroys. Can we ever understand why He destroys? I say to the Divine Mother: 'O Mother, I do not need to understand. Please give me love for Thy Lotus Feet.' The aim of human life is to attain bhakti. As for other things, the Mother knows best. I have come to the garden to eat mangoes. What is the use of my calculating the number of trees, branches, and leaves? I only eat the mangoes; I don't need to know the number of trees and leaves."

Baburam, M., and Ramdayal slept that night on the floor of the Master's room.

It was an early hour of the morning, about two or three o'clock. The room was dark. Sri Ramakrishna was seated on his bed and now and then conversed with the devotees.

MASTER: "Remember that dayā, compassion, and māyā, attachment, are two different things. Attachment means the feeling of 'my-ness' toward one's relatives. It is the love one feels for one's parents, one's brother, one's sister, one's wife and children. Compassion is the love one feels for all beings of the world. It is an attitude of equality. If you see anywhere an instance of compassion, as in Vidyāsāgar, know that it is due to the grace of God. Through compassion one serves all beings. Māyā also comes from God. Through māyā God makes one serve one's relatives. But one thing should be remembered: māyā keeps us in ignorance and entangles us in the world, whereas dayā makes our hearts pure and gradually unties our bonds.

"God cannot be realized without purity of heart. One receives the grace of God by subduing the passions—lust, anger, and greed. Then one sees God. I tried many things in order to conquer lust.

"When I was ten or eleven years old and lived at Kāmārpukur, I first experienced samādhi. As I was passing through a paddy-field, I saw something and was overwhelmed. There are certain characteristics of God-vision. One sees light, feels joy, and experiences the upsurge of a great current in one's chest, like the bursting of a rocket."

The next day Baburam and Ramdayal returned·to Calcutta. M. spent the day and the night with the Master.

December 1882

It was afternoon. The Master was sitting in his room at Dakshineswar with M. and one or two other devotees. Several Mārwāri devotees arrived and saluted the Master. They requested Sri Ramakrishna to give them spiritual instruction. He smiled.

MASTER (*to the Mārwāri devotees*): "You see, the feeling of 'I' and 'mine' is the result of ignorance. But to say, 'O God, Thou art the Doer; all these belong to Thee' is the sign of Knowledge. How can you say such a thing as 'mine'? The superintendent of the garden says, 'This is my garden.' But if he is dismissed because of some misconduct, then he does not have the courage to take away even such a worthless thing as his mango-wood box. Anger and lust cannot be destroyed. Turn them toward God. If you must feel desire and temptation, then desire to realize God, feel tempted by Him. Discriminate and turn the passions away from worldly objects. When the elephant is about to devour a plaintain-tree in someone's garden, the mahut strikes it with his iron-tipped goad.

"You are merchants. You know how to improve your business gradually. Some of you start with a castor-oil factory. After making some money at that, you open a cloth shop. In the same way, one makes progress toward God. It may be that you go into solitude, now and then, and devote more time to prayer.

"But you must remember that nothing can be achieved except in its proper time. Some persons must pass through many experiences and perform many worldly duties before they can turn their attention to God; so they have to wait a long time. If an abscess is lanced before it is soft, the result is not good; the surgeon makes the opening when it is soft and has come to a head. Once a child said to its mother: 'Mother, I am going to sleep now. Please wake me up when I feel the call of nature.' 'My child,' said the mother, 'when it is time for that, you will wake up yourself. I shan't have to wake you.'"

The Mārwāri devotees generally brought offerings of fruit, candy, and other sweets for the Master. But Sri Ramakrishna could hardly eat them. He would say: "They earn their money by falsehood. I can't eat their offerings." He said to the Mārwāris: "You see, one can't strictly adhere to truth in business. There are ups and downs in business. Nānak once said, 'I was about to eat the food of unholy people, when I found it stained with blood.' A man should offer only pure things to holy men. He shouldn't give them food earned by dishonest means. God is realized by following the path of truth. One should always chant His name. Even while one is performing one's duties, the mind should be left with God. Suppose I have a carbuncle on my back. I perform my duties, but the mind is drawn to the carbuncle. It is good to repeat the name of Rāma. 'The same Rāma who was the son of King Daśaratha has created this world. Again, as Spirit, He pervades all beings. He is very near us; He is both within and without.'"

7

THE MASTER AND VIJAY GOSWAMI

IT WAS AFTERNOON. Sri Ramakrishna was sitting on his bed after a short noonday rest. Vijay, Balaram, M., and a few other devotees were sitting on the floor with their faces toward the Master. They could see the sacred river Ganges through the door. Since it was winter all were wrapped up in warm clothes. Vijay had been suffering from colic and had brought some medicine with him.

Vijay was a paid preacher in the Sādhāran Brāhmo Samāj, but there were many things about which he could not agree with the Samāj authorities. He came from a very noble family of Bengal noted for its piety and other spiritual qualities. Advaita Goswāmi, one of his remote ancestors, had been an intimate companion of Sri Chaitanya. Thus the blood of a great lover of God flowed in Vijay's veins. As an adherent of the Brāhmo Samāj, Vijay no doubt meditated on the formless Brahman; but his innate love of God, inherited from his distinguished ancestors, had merely been waiting for the proper time to manifest itself in all its sweetness. Thus Vijay was irresistibly attracted by the God-intoxicated state of Sri Ramakrishna and often sought his company. He would listen to the Master's words with great respect, and they would dance together in an ecstasy of divine love.

It was a week-day. Generally devotees came to the Master in large numbers on Sundays; hence those who wanted to have intimate talks with him visited him on week-days.

A boy named Vishnu, living in Āriādaha, had recently committed suicide by cutting his throat with a razor. The talk turned to him.

MASTER: "I felt very badly when I heard of the boy's passing away. He was a pupil in a school and he used to come here. He would often say to me that he couldn't enjoy worldly life. He had lived with some relatives in the western provinces and at that time used to meditate in solitude, in the meadows, hills, and forests. He told me he had visions of many divine forms.

"Perhaps this was his last birth. He must have finished most of his duties in his previous birth. The little that had been left undone was perhaps finished in this one.

"One must admit the existence of tendencies inherited from previous

163

births. There is a story about a man who practised the śava-sādhanā.[1] He worshipped the Divine Mother in a deep forest. First he saw many terrible visions. Finally a tiger attacked and killed him. Another man, happening to pass and seeing the approach of the tiger, had climbed a tree. Afterwards he got down and found all the arrangements for worship at hand. He performed some purifying ceremonies and seated himself on the corpse. No sooner had he done a little japa than the Divine Mother appeared before him and said: 'My child, I am very much pleased with you. Accept a boon from Me.' He bowed low at the Lotus Feet of the Goddess and said: 'May I ask You one question, Mother? I am speechless with amazement at Your action. The other man worked so hard to get the ingredients for Your worship and tried to propitiate You for such a long time, but You didn't condescend to show him Your favour. And I, who don't know anything of worship, who have done nothing, who have neither devotion nor knowledge nor love, and who haven't practised any austerities, am receiving so much of Your grace.' The Divine Mother said with a laugh: 'My child, you don't remember your previous births. For many births you tried to propitiate Me through austerities. As a result of those austerities all these things have come to hand, and you have been blessed with My vision. Now ask Me your boon.' "

A DEVOTEE: "I am frightened to hear of the suicide."

MASTER: "Suicide is a heinous sin, undoubtedly. A man who kills himself must return again and again to this world and suffer its agony.

"But I don't call it suicide if a person leaves his body after having the vision of God. There is no harm in giving up one's body that way. After attaining Knowledge some people give up their bodies. After the gold image has been cast in the clay mould, you may either preserve the mould or break it.

"Many years ago a young man of about twenty used to come to the temple garden from Barānagore; his name was Gopal Sen. In my presence he used to experience such intense ecstasy that Hriday had to support him for fear he might fall to the ground and break his limbs. That young man touched my feet one day and said: 'Sir, I shall not be able to see you any more. Let me bid you good-bye.' A few days later I learnt that he had given up his body.

"It is said that there are four classes of human beings: the bound, those aspiring after liberation, the liberated, and the ever-perfect.

"This world is like a fishing-net. Men are the fish, and God, whose māyā has created this world, is the fisherman. When the fish are entangled in the net, some of them try to tear through its meshes in order to get their liberation. They are like the men striving after liberation. But by no means all of them escape. Only a few jump out of the net with a loud splash, and then people say, 'Ah! There goes a big one!' In like manner, three or four men attain liberation. Again, some fish are so careful by nature that they are never caught in the net; some beings of the ever-perfect class, like Nārada,

---

[1] A religious practice prescribed by the Tantra, in which the aspirant uses a śava, or corpse, as his seat for meditation.

are never entangled in the meshes of worldliness. Most of the fish are trapped; but they are not conscious of the net and of their imminent death. No sooner are they entangled than they run headlong, net and all, trying to hide themselves in the mud. They don't make the least effort to get free. On the contrary, they go deeper and deeper into the mud. These fish are like the bound men. They are still inside the net, but they think they are quite safe there. A bound creature is immersed in worldliness, in 'woman and gold', having gone deep into the mire of degradation. But still he believes he is·quite happy and secure. The liberated, and the seekers after liberation, look on the world as a deep well. They do not enjoy it. Therefore, after the attainment of Knowledge, the realization of God, some give up their bodies. But such a thing is rare indeed.

"The bound creatures, entangled in worldliness, will not come to their senses at all. They suffer so much misery and agony, they face so many dangers, and yet they will not wake up.

"The camel loves to eat thorny bushes. The more it eats the thorns, the more the blood gushes from its mouth. Still it must eat thorny plants and will never give them up. The man of worldly nature suffers so much sorrow and affliction, but he forgets it all in a few days and begins his old life over again. Suppose a man has lost his wife or she has turned unfaithful. Lo! He marries again.

"Or take the instance of a mother: her son dies and she suffers bitter grief; but after a few days she forgets all about it. The mother, so overwhelmed with sorrow a few days before, now attends to her toilet and puts on her jewelry. A father becomes bankrupt through the marriage of his daughters, yet he goes on having children year after year. People are ruined by litigation, yet they go to court all the same. There are men who cannot feed the children they have, who cannot clothe them or provide decent shelter for them; yet they have more children every year.

"Again, the worldly man is like a snake trying to swallow a mole. The snake can neither swallow the mole nor give it up. The bound soul may have realized that there is no substance to the world—that the world is like a hog plum, only stone and skin—but still he cannot give it up and turn his mind to God.

"I once met a relative of Keshab Sen, fifty years old. He was playing cards. As if the time had not yet come for him to think of God!

"There is another characteristic of the bound soul. If you remove him from his worldly surroundings to a spiritual environment, he will pine away. The worm that grows in filth feels very happy there. It thrives in filth. It will die if you put it in a pot of rice."

All remained silent.

VIJAY: "What must the bound soul's condition of mind be in order to achieve liberation?"

MASTER: "He can free himself from attachment to 'woman and gold' if, by the grace of God, he cultivates a spirit of strong renunciation. What is this strong renunciation? One who has only a mild spirit of renunciation says, 'Well, all will happen in the course of time; let me now simply repeat the name of God.' But a man possessed of a strong spirit of renunciation feels restless for God, as the mother feels for her own child. A man of strong renunciation seeks nothing but God. He regards the world as a deep well and feels as if he were going to be drowned in it. He looks on his relatives as venomous snakes; he wants to fly away from them. And he does go away. He never thinks, 'Let me first make some arrangement for my family and then I shall think of God.' He has great inward resolution.

"Let me tell you a story about strong renunciation. At one time there was a drought in a certain part of the country. The farmers began to cut long channels to bring water to their fields. One farmer was stubbornly determined. He took a vow that he would not stop digging until the channel connected his field with the river. He set to work. The time came for his bath, and his wife sent their daughter to him with oil. 'Father,' said the girl, 'it is already late. Rub your body with oil and take your bath.' 'Go away!' thundered the farmer. 'I have too much to do now.' It was past midday, and the farmer was still at work in his field. He didn't even think of his bath. Then his wife came and said: 'Why haven't you taken your bath? The food is getting cold. You overdo everything. You can finish the rest tomorrow or even today after dinner.' The farmer scolded her furiously and ran at her, spade in hand, crying: 'What? Have you no sense? There's no rain. The crops are dying. What will the children eat? You'll all starve to death. I have taken a vow not to think of bath and food today before I bring water to my field.' The wife saw his state of mind and ran away in fear. Through a whole day's back-breaking labour the farmer managed by evening to connect his field with the river. Then he sat down and watched the water flowing into his field with a murmuring sound. His mind was filled with peace and joy. He went home, called his wife, and said to her, 'Now give me some oil and prepare me a smoke.' With serene mind he finished his bath and meal, and retired to bed, where he snored to his heart's content. The determination he showed is an example of strong renunciation.

"Now, there was another farmer who was also digging a channel to bring water to his field. His wife, too, came to the field and said to him: 'It's very late. Come home. It isn't necessary to overdo things.' The farmer didn't protest much, but put aside his spade and said to his wife, 'Well, I'll go home since you ask me to.' (*All laugh.*) That man never succeeded in irrigating his field. This is a case of mild renunciation.

"As without strong determination the farmer cannot bring water to his field, so also without intense yearning a man cannot realize God. (*To Vijay*) Why don't you come here now as frequently as before?"

VIJAY: "Sir, I wish to very much, but I am not free. I have accepted work in the Brāhmo Samāj."

MASTER: "It is 'woman and gold' that binds man and robs him of his freedom. It is woman that creates the need for gold. For woman one man becomes the slave of another, and so loses his freedom. Then he cannot act as he likes.

"The priests in the temple of Govindaji at Jaipur were celibates at first, and at that time they had fiery natures. Once the King of Jaipur sent for them, but they didn't obey him. They said to the messenger, 'Ask the king to come to see us.' After consultation, the king and his ministers arranged marriages for them. From then on the king didn't have to send for them. They would come to him of themselves and say: 'Your Majesty, we have come with our blessings. Here are the sacred flowers of the temple. Deign to accept them.' They came to the palace, for now they always wanted money for one thing or another: the building of a house, the rice-taking ceremony of their babies, or the rituals connected with the beginning of their children's education.

"There is the story of the twelve hundred neḍās[2] and thirteen hundred neḍis.[3] Virabhadra, the son of Nityānanda Goswāmi, had thirteen hundred 'shaven-headed' disciples. They attained great spiritual powers. That alarmed their teacher. 'My disciples have acquired great spiritual powers', thought Virabhadra. 'Whatever they say to people will come to pass. Wherever they go they may create alarming situations; for people offending them unwittingly will come to grief.' Thinking thus, Virabhadra one day called them to him and said, 'See me after performing your daily devotions on the bank of the Ganges.' These disciples had such a high spiritual nature that, while meditating, they would go into samādhi and be unaware of the river water flowing over their heads during the flood-tide. Then the ebb-tide would come and still they would remain absorbed in meditation.

"Now, one hundred of these disciples had anticipated what their teacher would ask of them. Lest they should have to disobey his injunctions, they had quickly disappeared from the place before he summoned them. So they did not go to Virabhadra with the others. The remaining twelve hundred disciples went to the teacher after finishing their meditation. Virabhadra said to them: 'These thirteen hundred nuns will serve you. I ask you to marry them.' 'As you please, revered sir', they said. 'But one hundred of us have gone away.' Thenceforth each of these twelve hundred disciples had a wife. Consequently they all lost their spiritual power. Their austerities did not have their original fire. The company of woman robbed them of their spirituality because it destroyed their freedom.

(*To Vijay*) "You yourself perceive how far you have gone down by being a servant of others. Again, one finds that people with many university degrees, scholars with their vast English education, accept service under their English masters and are daily trampled under their boots. The one cause of all this is woman. They have married and set up a 'gay fair' with their wives and children. Now they cannot go back, much as they would like to. Hence all these insults and humiliations, all this suffering from slavery.

"Once a man realizes God through intense dispassion, he is no longer attached to woman. Even if he must lead the life of a householder, he is free from fear of and attachment to woman. Suppose there are two magnets, one big and the other small. Which one will attract the iron? The big one,

[2] Literally, "shaven-headed". Among the Vaishnava devotees, those who renounce the world shave their heads.

[3] Vaishnava nuns.

of course. God is the big magnet. Compared to Him, woman is a small one. What can 'woman' do?"

A DEVOTEE: "Sir, shall we hate women then?"

MASTER: "He who has realized God does not look upon a woman with the eye of lust; so he is not afraid of her. He perceives clearly that women are but so many aspects of the Divine Mother. He worships them all as the Mother Herself.

(*To Vijay*) "Come here now and then. I like to see you very much."

VIJAY: "I have to do my various duties in the Brāhmo Samāj; that is why I can't always come here. But I shall visit you whenever I find it possible."

MASTER (*to Vijay*): "The task of a religious teacher is indeed difficult. One cannot teach men without a direct command from God. People won't listen to you if you teach without such authority. Such teaching has no force behind it. One must first of all attain God through spiritual discipline or some other means. Thus armed with authority from God, one can deliver lectures.

"After receiving the command from God, one can be a teacher and give lectures anywhere. He who receives authority from God also receives power from Him. Only then can he perform the difficult task of a teacher.

"An insignificant tenant was once engaged in a lawsuit with a big landlord. People realized that there was a powerful man behind the tenant. Perhaps another big landlord was directing the case from behind. Man is an insignificant creature. He cannot fulfil the difficult task of a teacher without receiving power direct from God."

VIJAY: "Don't the teachings of the Brāhmo Samāj bring men salvation?"

MASTER: "How is it ever possible for one man to liberate another from the bondage of the world? God alone, the Creator of this world-bewitching māyā, can save men from māyā. There is no other refuge but that great Teacher, Satchidānanda. How is it ever possible for men who have not realized God or received His command, and who are not strengthened with divine strength, to save others from the prison-house of the world?

"One day as I was passing the Panchavati on my way to the pine-grove, I heard a bullfrog croaking. I thought it must have been seized by a snake. After some time, as I was coming back, I could still hear its terrified croaking. I looked to see what was the matter, and found that a water-snake had seized it. The snake could neither swallow it nor give it up. So there was no end to the frog's suffering. I thought that had it been seized by a cobra it would have been silenced after three croaks at the most. As it was only a water-snake, both of them had to go through this agony. A man's ego is destroyed after three croaks, as it were, if he gets into the clutches of a real teacher. But if the teacher is an 'unripe' one, then both the teacher and the disciple undergo endless suffering. The disciple cannot get rid either of his ego or of the shackles of the world. If a disciple falls into the clutches of an incompetent teacher, he doesn't attain liberation."

VIJAY: "Sir, why are we bound like this? Why don't we see God?"

MASTER: "Māyā is nothing but the egotism of the embodied soul. This egotism has covered everything like a veil. 'All troubles come to an end when the ego dies.' If by the grace of God a man but once realizes that he is not the doer, then he at once becomes a jīvanmukta. Though living in the body, he is liberated. He has nothing else to fear.

"This māyā, that is to say, the ego, is like a cloud. The sun cannot be seen on account of a thin patch of cloud; when that disappears one sees the sun. If by the grace of the guru one's ego vanishes, then one sees God.

"Rāma, who is God Himself, was only two and a half cubits ahead of Lakshmana. But Lakshmana couldn't see Him because Sītā stood between them. Lakshmana may be compared to the jīva, and Sītā to māyā. Man cannot see God on account of the barrier of māyā. Just look: I am creating a barrier in front of my face with this towel. Now you can't see me, even though I am so near. Likewise, God is the nearest of all, but we cannot see Him on account of this covering of māyā.

"The jīva is nothing but the embodiment of Satchidānanda. But since māyā, or ego, has created various upādhis, he has forgotten his real Self.

"Each upādhi changes man's nature. If he wears a fine black-bordered cloth, you will at once find him humming Nidhu Babu's love-songs. Then playing-cards and a walking-stick follow. If even a sickly man puts on high boots, he begins to whistle and climbs the stairs like an Englishman, jumping from one step to another. If a man but holds a pen in his hand, he scribbles on any paper he can get hold of—such is the power of the pen!

"Money is also a great upādhi. The possession of money makes such a difference in a man! He is no longer the same person. A brāhmin used to frequent the temple garden. Outwardly he was very modest. One day I went to Konnagar with Hriday. No sooner did we get off the boat than we noticed the brāhmin seated on the bank of the Ganges. We thought he had been enjoying the fresh air. Looking at us, he said: 'Hello there, priest! How do you do?' I marked his tone and said to Hriday: 'The man must have got some money. That's why he talks that way.' Hriday laughed.

"A frog had a rupee, which he kept in his hole. One day an elephant was going over the hole, and the frog, coming out in a fit of anger, raised his foot, as if to kick the elephant, and said, 'How dare you walk over my head?' Such is the pride that money begets!

"One can get rid of the ego after the attainment of Knowledge. On attaining Knowledge one goes into samādhi, and the ego disappears. But it is very difficult to obtain such Knowledge.

"It is said in the Vedas that a man experiences samādhi when his mind ascends to the seventh plane. The ego can disappear only when one goes into samādhi. Where does the mind of a man ordinarily dwell? In the first three planes. These are at the organs of evacuation and generation, and at the navel. Then the mind is immersed only in worldliness, attached to 'woman and gold'. A man sees the light of God when his mind dwells in the plane of the heart. He sees the light and exclaims: 'Ah! What is this? What is this?' The next plane is at the throat. When the mind dwells there he likes to hear and talk only of God. When the mind ascends to the next plane, in the forehead, between the eyebrows, he sees the form of Satchidānanda and desires to touch and embrace It. But he is unable to do so. It is like the light in a lantern, which you can see but cannot touch. You feel as if you were touching the light, but in reality you are not. When the mind reaches the seventh plane, then the ego vanishes completely and the man goes into samādhi."

VIJAY: "What does a man see when he attains the Knowledge of Brahman after reaching the seventh plane?"

MASTER: "What happens when the mind reaches the seventh plane cannot be described.

"Once a boat enters the 'black waters' of the ocean, it does not return. Nobody knows what happens to the boat after that. Therefore the boat cannot give us any information about the ocean.

"Once a salt doll went to measure the depth of the ocean. No sooner did it enter the water than it melted. Now who could tell how deep the ocean was? That which could have told about its depth had melted. Reaching the seventh plane, the mind is annihilated; man goes into samādhi. What he feels then cannot be described in words.

"The 'I' that makes one a worldly person and attaches one to 'woman and gold' is the 'wicked I'. The intervention of this ego creates the difference between jīva and Ātman. Water appears to be divided into two parts if one puts a stick across it. But in reality there is only one water. It appears as two on account of the stick. This 'I' is the stick. Remove the stick and there remains only one water as before.

"Now, what is this 'wicked I'? It is the ego that says: 'What? Don't they know me? I have so much money! Who is wealthier than I?' If a thief robs such a man of only ten rupees, first of all he wrings the money out of the thief, then he gives him a good beating. But the matter doesn't end there: the thief is handed over to the police and is eventually sent to jail. The 'wicked I' says: 'What? Doesn't the rogue know whom he has robbed? To steal my ten rupees! How dare he?' "

VIJAY: "If without destroying the 'I' a man cannot get rid of attachment to the world and consequently cannot experience samādhi, then it would be wise for him to follow the path of Brahmajnāna to attain samādhi. If the 'I' persists in the path of devotion, then one should rather choose the path of knowledge."

MASTER: "It is true that one or two can get rid of the 'I' through samādhi; but these cases are very rare. You may indulge in thousands of reasonings, but still the 'I' comes back. You may cut the peepal-tree to the very root today, but you will notice a sprout springing up tomorrow. Therefore if the 'I' must remain, let the rascal remain as the 'servant I'. As long as you live, you should say, 'O God, Thou art the Master and I am Thy servant.' The 'I' that feels, 'I am the servant of God, I am His devotee' does not injure one. Sweet things cause acidity of the stomach, no doubt, but sugar candy is an exception.

"The path of knowledge is very difficult. One cannot obtain Knowledge unless one gets rid of the feeling that one is the body. In the Kaliyuga the life of man is centred on food. He cannot get rid of the feeling that he is the body and the ego. Therefore the path of devotion is prescribed for this cycle.

This is an easy path. You will attain God if you sing His name and glories and pray to Him with a longing heart. There is not the least doubt about it.

"Suppose you draw a line on the surface of water with a bamboo stick. The water appears to be divided into two parts; but the line doesn't remain for any length of time. The 'servant I' or the 'devotee I' or the 'child I' is only a line drawn with the ego and is not real."

VIJAY (to the Master): "Sir, you ask us to renounce the 'wicked I'. Is there any harm in the 'servant I'?"

MASTER: "The 'servant I'—that is, the feeling, 'I am the servant of God, I am the devotee of God'—does not injure one. On the contrary, it helps one to realize God."

VIJAY: "Well, sir, what becomes of the lust, anger, and other passions of one who keeps the 'servant I'?"

MASTER: "If a man truly feels like that, then he has only the semblance of lust, anger, and the like. If, after attaining God, he looks on himself as the servant or the devotee of God, then he cannot injure anyone. By touching the philosopher's stone a sword is turned into gold. It keeps the appearance of a sword but cannot injure.

"When the dry branch of a coconut palm drops to the ground, it leaves only a mark on the trunk indicating that once there was a branch at that place. In like manner, he who has attained God keeps only an appearance of ego; there remains in him only a semblance of anger and lust. He becomes like a child. A child has no attachment to the three gunas—sattva, rajas, and tamas. He becomes as quickly detached from a thing as he becomes attached to it. You can cajole him out of a cloth worth five rupees with a doll worth an ānnā, though at first he may say with great determination: 'No, I won't give it to you. My daddy bought it for me.' Again, all persons are the same to a child. He has no feeling of high and low in regard to persons. So he doesn't discriminate about caste. If his mother tells him that a particular man should be regarded as an elder brother, the child will eat from the same plate with him, though the man may belong to the low caste of a blacksmith. The child doesn't know hate, or what is holy or unholy.

"Even after attaining samādhi, some retain the 'servant ego' or the 'devotee ego'. The bhakta keeps this 'I-consciousness'. He says, 'O God, Thou art the Master and I am Thy servant; Thou art the Lord and I am Thy devotee.' He feels that way even after the realization of God. His 'I' is not completely effaced. Again, by constantly practising this kind of 'I-consciousness', one ultimately attains God. This is called bhaktiyoga.

"One can attain the Knowledge of Brahman, too, by following the path of bhakti. God is all-powerful. He may give His devotee Brahmajnāna also, if He so wills. But the devotee generally doesn't seek the Knowledge of the Absolute. He would rather have the consciousness that God is the Master and he the servant, or that God is the Divine Mother and he the child."

VIJAY: "But those who discriminate according to the Vedānta philosophy also realize Him in the end, don't they?"

MASTER: "Yes, one may reach Him by following the path of discrimination too: that is called jnānayoga. But it is an extremely difficult path. I have told you already of the seven planes of consciousness. On reaching the seventh plane the mind goes into samādhi. If a man acquires the firm knowledge that Brahman alone is real and the world illusory, then his mind merges in samādhi. But in the Kaliyuga the life of a man depends entirely on food. How can he have the consciousness that Brahman alone is real and the world illusory? In the Kaliyuga it is difficult to have the feeling, 'I am not the body, I am not the mind, I am not the twenty-four cosmic principles; I am beyond pleasure and pain, I am above disease and grief, old age and death.' However you may reason and argue, the feeling that the body is identical with the soul will somehow crop up from an unexpected quarter. You may cut a peepal-tree to the ground and think it is dead to its very root, but the next morning you will find a new sprout shooting up from the dead stump. One cannot get rid of this identification with the body; therefore the path of bhakti is best for the people of the Kaliyuga. It is an easy path.

"And, 'I don't want to become sugar; I want to eat it.' I never feel like saying, 'I am Brahman.' I say, 'Thou art my Lord and I am Thy servant.' It is better to make the mind go up and down between the fifth and sixth planes, like a boat racing between two points. I don't want to go beyond the sixth plane and keep my mind a long time in the seventh. My desire is to sing the name and glories of God. It is very good to look on God as the Master and oneself as His servant. Further, you see, people speak of the waves as belonging to the Ganges; but no one says that the Ganges belongs to the waves. The feeling, 'I am He', is not wholesome. A man who entertains such an idea, while looking on his body as the Self, causes himself great harm. He cannot go forward in spiritual life; he drags himself down. He deceives himself as well as others. He cannot understand his own state of mind.

"But it isn't any and every kind of bhakti that enables one to realize God. One cannot realize God without premā-bhakti. Another name for premā-bhakti is rāga-bhakti.[4] God cannot be realized without love and longing. Unless one has learnt to love God, one cannot realize Him.

"There is another kind of bhakti, known as vaidhi-bhakti, according to which one must repeat the name of God a fixed number of times, fast, make pilgrimages, worship God with prescribed offerings, make so many sacrifices, and so forth and so on. By continuing such practices a long time one gradually acquires rāga-bhakti. God cannot be realized until one has rāga-bhakti. One must love God. In order to realize God one must be completely free from worldliness and direct all of one's mind to Him.

"But some acquire rāga-bhakti directly. It is innate in them. They have it from their very childhood. Even at an early age they weep for God. An instance of such bhakti is to be found in Prahlāda. Vaidhi-bhakti is like moving a fan to make a breeze. One needs the fan to make the breeze. Similarly, one practises japa, austerity, and fasting, in order to acquire love of God. But the fan is set aside when the southern breeze blows of itself.

[4] Supreme love, which makes one attached only to God.

Such actions as japa and austerity drop away when one spontaneously feels love and attachment for God. Who, indeed, will perform the ceremonies enjoined in the scriptures, when mad with love of God?

"Devotion to God may be said to be 'green' so long as it doesn't grow into love of God; but it becomes 'ripe' when it has grown into such love.

"A man with 'green' bhakti cannot assimilate spiritual talk and instruction; but one with 'ripe' bhakti can. The image that falls on a photographic plate covered with black film[5] is retained. On the other hand, thousands of images may be reflected on a bare piece of glass, but not one of them is retained. As the object moves away, the glass becomes the same as it was before. One cannot assimilate spiritual instruction unless one has already developed love of God."

VIJAY: "Is bhakti alone sufficient for the attainment of God, for His vision?"

MASTER: "Yes, one can see God through bhakti alone. But it must be 'ripe' bhakti, premā-bhakti and rāga-bhakti. When one has that bhakti, one loves God even as the mother loves the child, the child the mother, or the wife the husband.

"When one has such love and attachment for God, one doesn't feel the attraction of māyā to wife, children, relatives, and friends. One retains only compassion for them. To such a man the world appears a strange land, a place where he has merely to perform his duties. It is like a man's having his real home in the country, but coming to Calcutta for work; he has to rent a house in Calcutta for the sake of his duties. When one develops love of God, one completely gets rid of one's attachment to the world and worldly wisdom.

"One cannot see God if one has even the slightest trace of worldliness. Match-sticks, if damp, won't strike fire though you rub a thousand of them against the match-box. You only waste a heap of sticks. The mind soaked in worldliness is such a damp match-stick. Once Sri Rādhā said to her friends that she saw Krishna everywhere—both within and without. The friends answered: 'Why, we don't see Him at all. Are you delirious?' Rādhā said, 'Friends, paint your eyes with the collyrium of divine love, and then you will see Him.'

(To Vijay) "It is said in a song of your Brāhmo Samāj:

O Lord, is it ever possible to know Thee without love,
However much one may perform worship and sacrifice?

"If the devotee but once feels this attachment and ecstatic love for God, this mature devotion and longing, then he sees God in both His aspects, with form and without form."

VIJAY: "How can one see God?"

MASTER: "One cannot see God without purity of heart. Through attachment to 'woman and gold' the mind has become stained—covered with dirt, as it were. A magnet cannot attract a needle if the needle is covered with mud. Wash away the mud and the magnet will draw it. Likewise, the dirt

[5] Silver nitrate.

of the mind can be washed away with the tears of our eyes. This stain is removed if one sheds tears of repentance and says, 'O God, I shall never again do such a thing.' Thereupon God, who is like the magnet, draws to Himself the mind, which is like the needle. Then the devotee goes into samādhi and obtains the vision of God.

"You may try thousands of times, but nothing can be achieved without God's grace. One cannot see God without His grace. Is it an easy thing to receive the grace of God? One must altogether renounce egotism; one cannot see God as long as one feels, 'I am the doer.' Suppose, in a family, a man has taken charge of the store-room; then if someone asks the master, 'Sir, will you yourself kindly give me something from the store-room?', the master says to him: 'There is already someone in the store-room. What can I do there?'

"God doesn't easily appear in the heart of a man who feels himself to be his own master. But God can be seen the moment His grace descends. He is the Sun of Knowledge. One single ray of His has illumined the world with the light of knowledge. That is how we are able to see one another and acquire varied knowledge. One can see God only if He turns His light toward His own face.

"The police sergeant goes his rounds in the dark of night with a lantern[6] in his hand. No one sees his face; but with the help of that light the sergeant sees everybody's face, and others, too, can see one another. If you want to see the sergeant, however, you must pray to him: 'Sir, please turn the light on your own face. Let me see you.' In the same way one must pray to God: 'O Lord, be gracious and turn the light of knowledge on Thyself, that I may see Thy face.'

"A house without light indicates poverty. So one must light the lamp of Knowledge in one's heart. As it is said in a song:

> Lighting the lamp of Knowledge in the chamber of your heart,
> Behold the face of the Mother, Brahman's Embodiment."

As Vijay had brought medicine with him, the Master asked a devotee to give him some water. He was indeed a fountain of infinite compassion. He had arranged for Vijay's boat fare, since the latter was too poor to pay it. Vijay, Balaram, M., and the other devotees left for Calcutta in a country boat.

Monday, January 1, 1883

At eight o'clock in the morning Sri Ramakrishna was seated on a mat spread on the floor of his room at Dakshineswar. Since it was a cold day, he had wrapped his body in his moleskin shawl. Prankrishna and M. were seated in front of him. Rakhal, too, was in the room. Prankrishna was a high government official and lived in Calcutta. Since he had had no offspring by his first wife, with her permission he had married a second time. By the second wife he had a son. Because he was rather stout, the Master addressed

---

[6] A reference to the lantern carried by the night-watch, which has dark glass on three sides.

him now and then as "the fat brāhmin". He had great respect for Sri Ramakrishna. Though a householder, Prankrishna studied the Vedānta and had
been heard to say: "Brahman alone is real and the world illusory. I am He."
The Master used to say to him: "In the Kaliyuga the life of a man depends
on food. The path of devotion prescribed by Nārada is best for this age."

A devotee had brought a basket of jilipi for the Master, which the latter
kept by his side. Eating a bit of the sweets, he said to Prankrishna with a
smile: "You see, I chant the name of the Divine Mother; so I get all these
good things to eat. (*Laughter.*) But She doesn't give such fruits as gourd or
pumpkin. She bestows the fruit of Amrita, Immortality—knowledge, love,
discrimination, renunciation, and so forth."

A boy six or seven years old entered the room. The Master himself became
like a child. He covered the contents of the basket with the palm of his
hand, as a child does to conceal sweets from another child lest the latter
should snatch them. Then he put the basket aside.

Suddenly the Master went into samādhi and sat thus a long time. His
body was transfixed, his eyes wide open and unwinking, his breathing hardly
perceptible. After a long time he drew a deep breath, indicating his return
to the world of sense.

MASTER (*to Prankrishna*): "My Divine Mother is not only formless,
She has forms as well. One can see Her forms. One can behold Her incomparable beauty through feeling and love. The Mother reveals Herself to Her
devotees in different forms.

"I saw Her yesterday. She was clad in a seamless ochre-coloured garment,
and She talked with me.

"She came to me another day as a Mussalmān girl six or seven years old.
She had a tilak on her forehead and was naked. She walked with me, joking
and frisking like a child.

"At Hriday's house I had a vision of Gaurānga. He wore a black-bordered
cloth.

"Haladhari used to say that God is beyond both Being and Non-being. I
told the Mother about it and asked Her, 'Then is the divine form an illusion?' The Divine Mother appeared to me in the form of Rati's mother and
said, 'Do thou remain in bhāva.'[7] I repeated this to Haladhari. Now and
then I forget Her command and suffer. Once I broke my teeth because I
didn't remain in bhāva. So I shall remain in bhāva unless I receive a revelation from heaven or have a direct experience to the contrary. I shall follow
the path of love. What do you say?"

PRANKRISHNA: "Yes, sir."

MASTER: "But why should I ask you about it? There is Someone within
me who does all these things through me. At times I used to remain in a
mood of Godhood and would enjoy no peace of mind unless I were being
worshipped.

[7] A rare state of divine exaltation, when the devotee, after realizing the Absolute,
remains in the borderland between the Absolute and the Relative; in this state he sees
that both the Absolute and the Relative, as the two aspects of the Godhead, are real.

"I am the machine and God is the Operator. I act as He makes me act. I speak as He makes me speak.

> Keep your raft, says Rāmprasād, afloat on the sea of life,
> Drifting up with the flood-tide, drifting down with the ebb.

"It is like the cast-off leaf before a gale; sometimes it is blown to a good place and sometimes into the gutter, according to the direction of the wind.

"As the weaver said in the story: 'The robbery was committed by the will of Rāma, I was arrested by the police by the will of Rāma, and again, by the will of Rāma, I was set free.'

"Hanumān once said to Rāma: 'O Rāma, I have taken refuge in Thee. Bless me that I may have pure devotion to Thy Lotus Feet and that I may not be caught in the spell of Thy world-bewitching māyā.'

"Once a dying bullfrog said to Rāma: 'O Rāma, when caught by a snake I cry for Your protection. But now I am about to die, struck by Your arrow. Hence I am silent.'

"I used to see God directly with these very eyes, just as I see you. Now I see divine visions in trance.

"After realizing God a man becomes like a child. One acquires the nature of the object one meditates upon. The nature of God is like that of a child. As a child builds up his toy house and then breaks it down, so God acts while creating, preserving, and destroying the universe. Further, as the child is not under the control of any guna, so God is beyond the three gunas—sattva, rajas, and tamas. That is why paramahamsas keep five or ten children with them, that they may assume their nature."

Sitting on the floor in the room was a young man from Āgarpārā about twenty-two years old. Whenever he came to the temple garden, he would take the Master aside, by a sign, and whisper his thoughts to him. He was a new-comer. That day he was sitting on the floor near the Master.

MASTER (to the young man): "A man can change his nature by imitating another's character. He can get rid of a passion like lust by assuming the feminine mood. He gradually comes to act exactly like a woman. I have noticed that men who take female parts in the theatre speak like women or brush their teeth like women while bathing. Come again on a Tuesday or Saturday.

(To Prankrishna) "Brahman and Śakti are inseparable. Unless you accept Śakti, you will find the whole universe unreal—'I', 'you', house, buildings, and family. The world stands solid because the Primordial Energy stands behind it. If there is no supporting pole, no framework can be made, and without the framework there can be no beautiful image of Durgā.

"Without giving up worldliness a man cannot awaken his spiritual consciousness, nor can he realize God. He cannot but be a hypocrite as long as he has even a trace of worldly desire. God cannot be realized without guilelessness.

> Cherish love within your heart; abandon cunning and deceit:
> Through service, worship, selflessness, does Rāma's blessed vision
> come.

Even those engaged in worldly activities, such as office work or business, should hold to the truth. Truthfulness alone is the spiritual discipline in the Kaliyuga."

PRANKRISHNA: "Yes, sir. It is said in the *Mahānirvāna Tantra*: 'O Goddess, this religion enjoins it upon one to be truthful, self-controlled, devoted to the welfare of others, unagitated, and compassionate.'"

MASTER: "Yes. But these ideas must be assimilated."

Sri Ramakrishna was sitting on the small couch. He was in an ecstatic mood and looked at Rakhal. Suddenly he was filled with the tender feeling of parental love toward his young disciple and spiritual child. Presently he went into samādhi. The devotees sat speechless, looking at the Master with wondering eyes.

Regaining partial consciousness, the Master said: "Why is my spiritual feeling kindled at the sight of Rakhal? The more you advance toward God, the less you will see of His glories and grandeur. The aspirant at first has a vision of the Goddess with ten arms;[8] there is a great display of power in that image. The next vision is that of the Deity with two arms; there are no longer ten arms holding various weapons and missiles. Then the aspirant has a vision of Gopāla, in which there is no trace of power. It is the form of a tender child. Beyond that there are other visions also. The aspirant then sees only Light.

"Reasoning and discrimination vanish after the attainment of God and communion with Him in samādhi. How long does a man reason and discriminate? As long as he is conscious of the manifold, as long as he is aware of the universe, of embodied beings, of 'I' and 'you'. He becomes silent when he is truly aware of Unity. This was the case with Trailanga Swami.[9]

"Have you watched a feast given to the brāhmins? At first there is a great uproar. But the noise lessens as their stomachs become more and more filled with food. When the last course of curd and sweets is served, one hears only the sound 'soop, soop' as they scoop up the curd in their hands. There is no other sound. Next is the stage of sleep—samādhi. There is no more uproar.

(*To M. and Prankrishna*) "Many people talk of Brahmajnāna, but their minds are always preoccupied with lower things: house, buildings, money, name, and sense pleasures. As long as you stand at the foot of the Monument,[10] so long do you see horses, carriages, Englishmen, and Englishwomen. But when you climb to its top, you behold the sky and the ocean stretching to infinity. Then you do not enjoy buildings, carriages, horses, or men. They look like ants.

"All such things as attachment to the world and enthusiasm for 'woman and gold' disappear after the attainment of the Knowledge of Brahman. Then comes the cessation of all passions. When the log burns, it makes a crackling noise and one sees the flame. But when the burning is over and

[8] The allusion is to the image of Durgā.

[9] A noted monk of Benares whom the Master once met. The Swami observed a vow of silence.

[10] A reference to the Ochterloney Monument in Calcutta.

only ash remains, then no more noise is heard. Thirst disappears with the destruction of attachment. Finally comes peace.

"The nearer you come to God, the more you feel peace. Peace, peace, peace—supreme peace! The nearer you come to the Ganges, the more you feel its coolness. You will feel completely soothed when you plunge into the river.

"But the universe and its created beings, and the twenty-four cosmic principles, all exist because God exists. Nothing remains if God is eliminated. The number increases if you put many zeros after the figure one; but the zeros don't have any value if the one is not there."

The Master continued: "There are some who come down, as it were, after attaining the Knowledge of Brahman—after samādhi—and retain the 'ego of Knowledge' or the 'ego of Devotion', just as there are people who, of their own sweet will, stay in the market-place after the market breaks up. This was the case with sages like Nārada. They kept the 'ego of Devotion' for the purpose of teaching men. Śankarāchārya kept the 'ego of Knowledge' for the same purpose.

"God cannot be realized if there is the slightest attachment to the things of the world. A thread cannot pass through the eye of a needle if the tiniest fibre sticks out.

"The anger and lust of a man who has realized God are only appearances. They are like a burnt string. It looks like a string, but a mere puff blows it away.

"God is realized as soon as the mind becomes free from attachment. Whatever appears in the Pure Mind is the voice of God. That which is Pure Mind is also Pure Buddhi; that, again, is Pure Ātman, because there is nothing pure but God. But in order to realize God one must go beyond dharma and adharma."

The Master sang in his melodious voice:

> Come, let us go for a walk, O mind, to Kāli, the Wish-fulfilling Tree,
> And there beneath It gather the four fruits of life. . . .

Sri Ramakrishna went out on the southeast verandah of his room and sat down. Prankrishna and the other devotees accompanied him. Hazra, too, was sitting there. The Master said to Prankrishna with a smile: "Hazra is not a man to be trifled with. If one finds the big dargāh here,[11] then Hazra is the smaller dargāh." All laughed at the Master's words. A certain gentleman, Navakumar by name, came to the door and stood there. At sight of the devotees he immediately left. "Oh! Egotism incarnate!" Sri Ramakrishna remarked.

About half past nine in the morning Prankrishna took leave of the Master. Soon afterwards a minstrel sang some devotional songs to the accompaniment of a stringed instrument. The Master was listening to the songs when Kedar Chatterji, a householder devotee, entered the room clad in his office clothes. He was a man of devotional temperament and cherished the

[11] Referring to himself.

attitude of the gopis of Vrindāvan. Words about God would make him weep.

The sight of Kedar awakened in the Master's mind the episode of Vrindāvan in Sri Krishna's life. Intoxicated with divine love, the Master stood up and sang, addressing Kedar:

> Tell me, friend, how far is the grove
> Where Krishna, my Beloved, dwells?
> His fragrance reaches me even here;
> But I am tired and can walk no farther. . . .

Sri Ramakrishna assumed the attitude of Sri Rādhā to Krishna and went into deep samādhi while singing the song. He stood there, still as a picture on canvas, with tears of divine joy running down his cheeks.

Kedar knelt before the Master. Touching his feet, he chanted a hymn:

> We worship the Brahman-Consciousness in the Lotus of the Heart,
> The Undifferentiated, who is adored by Hari, Hara, and Brahmā;
> Who is attained by yogis in the depths of their meditation;
> The Scatterer of the fear of birth and death,
> The Essence of Knowledge and Truth, the Primal Seed of the
>   world.

After a time the Master regained consciousness of the relative world. Soon Kedar took his leave and returned to his office in Calcutta.

At midday Ramlal brought the Master a plate of food that had been offered in the Kāli temple. Like a child he ate a little of everything.

Later in the afternoon several Mārwāri devotees entered the Master's room, where Rakhal and M. also were seated.

A MĀRWĀRI DEVOTEE: "Sir, what is the way?"

MASTER: "There are two ways. One is the path of discrimination, the other is that of love. Discrimination means to know the distinction between the Real and the unreal. God alone is the real and permanent Substance; all else is illusory and impermanent. The magician alone is real; his magic is illusory. This is discrimination.

"Discrimination and renunciation. Discrimination means to know the distinction between the Real and the unreal. Renunciation means to have dispassion for the things of the world. One cannot acquire them all of a sudden. They must be practised every day. One should renounce 'woman and gold' mentally at first. Then, by the will of God, one can renounce it both mentally and outwardly. It is impossible to ask the people of Calcutta to renounce all for the sake of God. One has to tell them to renounce mentally.

"Through the discipline of constant practice one is able to give up attachment to 'woman and gold'. That is what the Gītā says. By practice one acquires uncommon power of mind. Then one doesn't find it difficult to subdue the sense-organs and to bring anger, lust, and the like under control. Such a man behaves like a tortoise, which, once it has tucked in its limbs, never puts them out. You cannot make the tortoise put its limbs out again, though you chop it to pieces with an axe."

MĀRWĀRI DEVOTEE: "Revered sir, you just mentioned two paths. What is the other path?"

MASTER: "The path of bhakti, or zealous love of God. Weep for God in solitude, with a restless soul, and ask Him to reveal Himself to you.

> Cry to your Mother Śyāmā with a real cry, O mind!
> And how can She hold Herself from you?"

MĀRWĀRI DEVOTEE: "Sir, what is the meaning of the worship of the Personal God? And what is the meaning of God without form or attribute?"

MASTER: "As you recall your father by his photograph, so likewise the worship of the image reveals in a flash the nature of Reality.

"Do you know what God with form is like? Like bubbles rising on an expanse of water, various divine forms are seen to rise out of the Great Ākāśa of Consciousness. The Incarnation of God is one of these forms. The Primal Energy sports, as it were, through the activities of a Divine Incarnation.

"What is there in mere scholarship? God can be attained by crying to Him with a longing heart. There is no need to know many things.

"He who is an āchārya has to know different things. One needs a sword and shield to kill others; but to kill oneself, a needle or a nail-knife suffices.

"One ultimately discovers God by trying to know who this 'I' is. Is this 'I' the flesh, the bones, the blood, or the marrow? Is it the mind or the buddhi? Analysing thus, you realize at last that you are none of these. This is called the process of 'Neti, neti', 'Not this, not this'. One can neither comprehend nor touch the Ātman. It is without qualities or attributes.

"But, according to the path of devotion, God has attributes. To a devotee Krishna is Spirit, His Abode is Spirit, and everything about Him is Spirit."

The Mārwāri devotees saluted the Master and took their leave.

At the approach of evening Sri Ramakrishna went out to look at the sacred river. The lamp was lighted in his room. The Master chanted the hallowed name of the Divine Mother and meditated on Her. Then the evening worship began in the various temples. The sound of gongs, floating on the air, mingled with the murmuring voice of the river. Peace and blessedness reigned everywhere.

THE MASTER'S BIRTHDAY
CELEBRATION AT
DAKSHINESWAR

S RI RAMAKRISHNA arrived at Govinda Mukherji's house at Belghariā, near Calcutta. Besides Narendra, Ram, and other devotees, some of Govinda's neighbours were present. The Master first sang and danced with the devotees. After the kirtan they sat down. Many saluted the Master. Now and then he would say, "Bow before God."

"It is God alone", he said, "who has become all this. But in certain places— for instance, in a holy man—there is a greater manifestation than in others. You may say, there are wicked men also. That is true, even as there are tigers and lions; but one need not hug the 'tiger God'. One should keep away from him and salute him from a distance. Take water, for instance. Some water may be drunk, some may be used for worship, some for bathing, and some only for washing dishes."

A NEIGHBOUR: "Revered sir, what are the doctrines of Vedānta?"

MASTER: "The Vedāntist says, 'I am He.' Brahman is real and the world illusory. Even the 'I' is illusory. Only the Supreme Brahman exists.

"But the 'I' cannot be got rid of. Therefore it is good to have the feeling, 'I am the servant of God, His son, His devotee.'

"For the Kaliyuga the path of bhakti is especially good. One can realize God through bhakti too. As long as one is conscious of the body, one is also conscious of objects. Form, taste, smell, sound, and touch—these are the objects. It is extremely difficult to get rid of the consciousness of objects. And one cannot realize 'I am He' as long as one is aware of objects.

"The sannyāsi is very little conscious of worldly objects. But the house-holder is always engrossed in them. Therefore it is good for him to feel, 'I am the servant of God.' "

NEIGHBOUR: "Sir, we are sinners. What will happen to us?"

MASTER: "All the sins of the body fly away if one chants the name of God and sings His glories. The birds of sin dwell in the tree of the body. Singing the name of God is like clapping your hands. As, at a clap of the hands, the birds in the tree fly away, so do our sins disappear at the chanting of God's name and glories.

"Again, you find that the water of a reservoir dug in a meadow is evaporated by the heat of the sun. Likewise, the water of the reservoir of sin is dried up by the singing of the name and glories of God.

"You must practise it every day. The other day, at the circus, I saw a horse running at top speed, with an Englishwoman standing on one foot on its back. How much she must have practised to acquire that skill!

"Weep at least once to see God.

"These, then, are the two means: practice and passionate attachment to God, that is to say, restlessness of the soul to see Him."

Sri Ramakrishna began his midday meal with the devotees. It was about one o'clock. A devotee sang in the courtyard below:

> Awake, Mother! Awake! How long Thou hast been asleep
> In the lotus of the Mulādhāra!
> Fulfil Thy secret function, Mother:
> Rise to the thousand-petalled lotus within the head,
> Where mighty Śiva has His dwelling;
> Swiftly pierce the six lotuses
> And take away my grief, O Essence of Consciousness!

Hearing the song, Sri Ramakrishna went into samādhi; his whole body became still, and his hand remained touching the plate of food. He could eat no more. After a long time his mind came down partially to the plane of the sense world, and he said, "I want to go downstairs." A devotee led him down very carefully. Still in an abstracted mood, he sat near the singer. The song had ended. The Master said to him very humbly, "Sir, I want to hear the chanting of the Mother's name again."

The musician sang:

> Awake, Mother! Awake! How long Thou hast been asleep
> In the lotus of the Mulādhāra! . . .

The Master again went into ecstasy.

February 25, 1883

After his noon meal the Master conversed with the devotees. Ram, Kedar, Nityagopal, M., and others had arrived from Calcutta. Rakhal, Harish, Latu, and Hazra were living with the Master. Mr. Choudhury, who had three or four university degrees and was a government officer, was also present. He had recently lost his wife and had visited the Master several times for peace of mind.

MASTER (*to Ram and the other devotees*): "Devotees like Rakhal, Narendra, and Bhavanath may be called nityasiddha. Their spiritual consciousness has been awake since their very birth. They assume human bodies only to impart spiritual illumination to others.

"There is another class of devotees, known as kripāsiddha, that is to say, those on whom the grace of God descends all of a sudden and who at once attain His vision and Knowledge. Such people may be likened to a room that has been dark a thousand years, which, when a lamp is brought into it, becomes light immediately, not little by little.

"Those who lead a householder's life should practise spiritual discipline; they should pray eagerly to God in solitude. (*To Mr. Choudhury*) God cannot be realized through scholarship. Who, indeed, can understand the things of the Spirit through reason? No, all should strive for devotion to the Lotus Feet of God.

"Infinite are the glories of God! How little can you fathom them! Can you ever find out the meaning of God's ways?

"Bhishma was none other than one of the eight Vasus, but even he shed tears on his bed of arrows. He said: 'How astonishing! God Himself is the companion of the Pāndava brothers, and still there is no end to their troubles and sorrows!' Who can ever understand the ways of God?

"A man thinks, 'I have practised a little prayer and austerity; so I have gained a victory over others.' But victory and defeat lie with God. I have seen a prostitute dying in the Ganges and retaining consciousness[1] to the end."

MR. CHOUDHURY: "How can one see God?"

MASTER: "Not with these eyes. God gives one divine eyes; and only then can one behold Him. God gave Arjuna divine eyes so that he might see His Universal Form.[2]

"Your philosophy is mere speculation. It only reasons. God cannot be realized that way.

"God cannot remain unmoved if you have rāga-bhakti, that is, love of God with passionate attachment to Him. Do you know how fond God is of His devotees' love? It is like the cow's fondness for fodder mixed with oil-cake. The cow gobbles it down greedily.

"Rāga-bhakti is pure love of God, a love that seeks God alone and not any worldly end. Prahlāda had it. Suppose you go to a wealthy man every day, but you seek no favour of him; you simply love to see him. If he wants to show you favour, you say: 'No, sir. I don't need anything. I came just to see you.' Such is love of God for its own sake. You simply love God and don't want anything from Him in return."

Saying this, the Master sang:

> Though I[3] am never loath to grant salvation,
> I hesitate indeed to grant pure love.
> Whoever wins pure love surpasses all;
> He is adored by men;
> He triumphs over the three worlds. . . .

He continued, "The gist of the whole thing is that one must develop passionate yearning for God and practise discrimination and renunciation."

MR. CHOUDHURY: "Sir, is it not possible to have the vision of God without the help of a guru?"

[1] Dying in the Ganges while retaining full consciousness is considered by the Hindus an act of great spiritual merit and the result of pious living.

[2] An allusion to the eleventh chapter of the *Bhagavad Gītā*.

[3] The song represents Sri Krishna's words.

MASTER: "Satchidānanda Himself is the Guru. At the end of the śava-sādhanā, just when the vision of the Ishta is about to take place, the guru appears before the aspirant and says to him, 'Behold! There is your Ishta.' Saying this, the guru merges in the Ishta. He who is the guru is also the Ishta. The guru is the thread that leads to God. Women perform a ritualistic worship known as the 'Ananta-vrata', the object of worship being the Infinite. But actually the Deity worshipped is Vishnu. In Him are the 'infinite' forms of God.

(To Ram and the other devotees) "If you asked me which form of God you should meditate upon, I should say: Fix your attention on that form which appeals to you most; but know for certain that all forms are the forms of one God alone.

"Never harbour malice toward anyone. Śiva, Kāli, and Hari are but different forms of that One. He is blessed indeed who has known all as one.

> Outwardly he appears as Śiva's devotee,
> But in his heart he worships Kāli, the Blissful Mother,
> And with his tongue he chants aloud Lord Hari's name.

"The body does not endure without a trace of lust, anger, and the like. You should try to reduce them to a minimum."

Looking at Kedar, the Master said: "He is very nice. He accepts both the Absolute and the Relative. He believes in Brahman, but he.also accepts the gods and Divine Incarnations in human form."

In Kedar's opinion Sri Ramakrishna was such an Incarnation.

Looking at Nityagopal, the Master said to the devotees, "He is in a lofty mood.

(To Nityagopal) "Don't go there too often. You may go once in a while. She may be a devotee, but she is a woman too. Therefore I warn you.

"The sannyāsi must observe very strict discipline. He must not look even at the picture of a woman. But this rule doesn't apply to householders. An aspirant should not associate with a woman, even though she is very much devoted to God. A sannyāsi, even though he may have subdued his passions, should follow this discipline to set an example to householders.

"Worldly people learn renunciation by seeing the complete renunciation of a monk; otherwise they sink more and more. A sannyāsi is a world teacher."

Friday, March 9, 1883

About nine o'clock in the morning the Master was seated in his room with Rakhal, M., and a few other devotees. It was the day of the new moon. As usual with him on such days, Sri Ramakrishna entered again and again into communion with the Divine Mother. He said to the devotees: "God alone exists, and all else is unreal. The Divine Mother has kept all deluded by Her māyā. Look at men. Most of them are entangled in worldliness. They suffer so much, but still they have the same attachment to 'woman and gold'. The camel eats thorny shrubs, and blood gushes from its mouth; still it will eat thorns. While suffering pain at the time of delivery, a woman says, 'Ah! I shall never go to my husband again.' But afterwards she forgets.

"The truth is that no one seeks God. There are people who eat the prickly leaves of the pineapple and not the fruit."

DEVOTEE: "Sir, why has God put us in the world?"

MASTER: "The world is the field of action. Through action one acquires knowledge. The guru instructs the disciple to perform certain works and refrain from others. Again, he advises the pupil to perform action without desiring the result. The impurity of the mind is destroyed through the performance of duty. It is like getting rid of a disease by means of medicine, under the instruction of a competent physician.

"Why doesn't God free us from the world? Ah, He will free us when the disease is cured. He will liberate us from the world when we are through with the enjoyment of 'woman and gold'. Once a man registers his name in the hospital, he cannot run away. The doctor will not let him go away unless his illness is completely cured."

During these days Sri Ramakrishna's heart overflowed with motherly love like the love Yaśodā felt for Krishna. So he kept Rakhal with him. Rakhal felt toward the Master as a child feels toward its mother. He would sit leaning on the Master's lap as a young child leans on its mother while sucking her breast.

Rakhal was thus seated by the Master when a man entered the room and said that a high tide was coming in the Ganges. The Master and the devotees ran to the Panchavati to see it. At the sight of a boat being tossed by the tide, Sri Ramakrishna exclaimed: "Look! Look! I hope nothing happens to it."

They all sat in the Panchavati. The Master asked M. to explain the cause of the tide. M. drew on the ground the figures of the sun, moon, and earth and tried to explain gravitation, ebb-tide, flood-tide, new moon, full moon, eclipse, and so forth.

MASTER (to M.): "Stop it! I can't follow you. It makes me dizzy. My head is aching. Well, how can they know of things so far off?

"You see, during my childhood I could paint well; but arithmetic would make my head spin. I couldn't learn simple arithmetic."

Sri Ramakrishna returned to his room with the devotees. Looking at a picture of Yaśodā, on the wall, he said: "It is not well done. She looks like a garland-seller."

The Master enjoyed a nap after his noon meal. Adhar and other devotees gradually gathered. This was Adhar's first visit. He was a deputy magistrate and about thirty years old.

ADHAR (to the Master): "Sir, I have a question to ask. Is it good to sacrifice animals before the Deity? It certainly involves killing."

MASTER: "The śāstra prescribes sacrifice on special occasions. Such sacrifice is not harmful. Take, for instance, the sacrifice of a goat on the eighth day of the full or new moon.

"I am now in such a state of mind that I cannot watch a sacrifice. Also I cannot eat meat offered to the Divine Mother. Therefore I first touch my finger to it, then to my head, lest She should be angry with me.

"Again, in a certain state of mind I see God in all beings, even in an ant. At that time, if I see a living being die, I find consolation in the thought that it is the death of the body, the soul being beyond life and death.

"One should not reason too much; it is enough if one loves the Lotus Feet of the Mother. Too much reasoning throws the mind into confusion. You get clear water if you drink from the surface of a pool. Put your hand deeper and stir the water, and it becomes muddy. Therefore pray to God for devotion.

"Behind Dhruva's devotion there was desire. He practised austerities to gain his father's kingdom. But Prahlāda's love for God was motiveless—a love that sought no return."

A DEVOTEE: "How can one realize God?"

MASTER: "Through that kind of love. But one must force one's demand on God. One should be able to say: 'O God, wilt Thou not reveal Thyself to me? I will cut my throat with a knife.' This is the tamas of bhakti."

DEVOTEE: "Can one see God?"

MASTER: "Yes, *surely*. One can see both aspects of God—God with form and without form. One can see God with form, the Embodiment of Spirit. Again, God can be directly perceived in a man with a tangible form. Seeing an Incarnation of God is the same as seeing God Himself. God is born on earth as man in every age."

March 11, 1883

It was Sri Ramakrishna's birthday. Many of his disciples and devotees wanted to celebrate the happy occasion at the Dakshineswar temple garden.

From early morning the devotees streamed in, alone or in parties. After the morning worship in the temples sweet music was played in the nahabat. It was springtime. The trees, creepers, and plants were covered with new leaves and blossoms. The very air seemed laden with joy. And the hearts of the devotees were glad on this auspicious day.

M. arrived early in the morning and found the Master talking smilingly to Bhavanath, Rakhal, and Kalikrishna. M. prostrated himself before him.

MASTER (*to M.*): "I am glad you have come.

(*To the devotees*) "One cannot be spiritual as long as one has shame, hatred, or fear. Great will be the joy today. But those fools who will not sing or dance, mad with God's name, will never attain God. How can one feel any shame or fear when the names of God are sung? Now sing, all of you."

Bhavanath and his friend Kalikrishna sang:

> Thrice blessed is this day of joy!
> May all of us unite, O Lord,
> To preach Thy true religion here
> In India's holy land!
> Thou dwellest in each human heart;
> Thy name, resounding everywhere,

Fills the four corners of the sky.
Today Thy devotees proclaim
Thy boundless majesty.

We seek not wealth or friends or fame,
O Lord! No other hope is ours.
For Thee alone Thy devotees
Long with unflagging love.
Safe at Thy feet, what fear have we
Of death or danger? We have found
The Fount of Immortality.
To Thee the victory, O Lord!
To Thee the victory!

As Sri Ramakrishna listened to the song with folded hands, his mind soared to a far-off realm. He remained absorbed in meditation a long time. After a while Kalikrishna whispered something to Bhavanath. Then he bowed before the Master and rose. Sri Ramakrishna was surprised. He asked, "Where are you going?"

BHAVANATH: "He is going away on a little business."

MASTER: "What is it about?"

BHAVANATH: "He is going to the Barānagore Workingmen's Institute."

MASTER: "It's his bad luck. A stream of bliss will flow here today. He could have enjoyed it. But how unlucky!"

Sri Ramakrishna did not feel well; so he decided not to bathe in the Ganges. About nine o'clock a few jars of water were taken from the river, and with the help of the devotees he finished his bath on the verandah east of his room.

After bathing, the Master put on a new wearing-cloth, all the while chanting the name of God. Accompanied by one or two disciples he walked across the courtyard to the temple of Kāli, still chanting Her hallowed name. His eyes had an indrawn look, like that of a bird hatching her eggs.

On entering the temple, he prostrated himself before the image and worshipped the Divine Mother. But he did not observe any ritual of worship. Now he would offer flowers and sandal-paste at the feet of the image, and now he would put them on his own head. After finishing the worship in his own way, he asked Bhavanath to carry the green coconut that had been offered to the Mother. He also visited the images of Rādhā and Krishna in the Vishnu temple.

When the Master returned to his room, he found that other devotees had arrived, among them Ram, Nityagopal, and Kedar. They all saluted the Master, who greeted them cordially.

He asked Nityagopal, "Will you eat something now?" "Yes", the devotee answered. Nityagopal, who was twenty-three or twenty-four years old and unmarried, was like a child. His mind was always soaring in the spiritual realm. He visited the Master sometimes alone and sometimes in Ram's company. The Master had observed the spiritual state of his mind and had become very fond of him. He remarked now and then that Nityagopal was in the state of a paramahamsa.

After Nityagopal had finished eating, the Master took him aside and gave him various instructions.

A certain woman, about thirty-one years old and a great devotee, often visited Sri Ramakrishna and held him in high respect. She had been much impressed by Nityagopal's spiritual state and, looking upon him as her own son, often invited him to her house.

MASTER (to Nityagopal): "Do you go there?"

NITYAGOPAL (like a child): "Yes, I do. She takes me."

MASTER: "Beware, holy man! Go there once in a great while, but not frequently; otherwise you will slip from the ideal. Māyā is nothing but 'woman and gold'. A holy man must live away from woman. All sink there. 'Even Brahmā and Vishnu struggle for life in that whirlpool.' "

Nityagopal listened to these words attentively.

M. (to himself): "How strange! This young man has developed the state of a paramahamsa. That is what the Master says now and then. Is there still a possibility of his falling into danger in spite of his high spiritual state? What an austere rule is laid down for a sādhu! He may slip from his ideal by associating intimately with women. How can an ordinary man expect to attain liberation unless such a high ideal is set by holy men? The woman in question is very devout; but still there is danger. Now I understand why Chaitanya punished his disciple, the younger Haridās, so severely. In spite of his teacher's prohibition, Haridās conversed with a widow devotee. But he was a sannyāsi. Therefore Chaitanya banished him. What a severe punishment! How hard is the rule for one who has accepted the life of renunciation! Again, what love the Master cherishes for this devotee! He is warning him even now, lest he should run into danger in the future."

"Beware, holy man!" These words of the Master echoed in the hearts of the devotees, like the distant rumbling of thunder.

The Master went with the devotees to the northeast verandah of his room. Among them was a householder from the village of Dakshineswar, who studied Vedānta philosophy at home. He had been discussing Om with Kedar before the Master. He said, "This Eternal Word, the Anāhata Śabda, is ever present both within and without."

MASTER: "But the Word is not enough. There must be something indicated by the Word. Can your name alone make me happy? Complete happiness is not possible for me unless I see you."

DEVOTEE: "That Eternal Word itself is Brahman."

MASTER (to Kedar): "Oh, don't you understand? He upholds the doctrine of the rishis of olden times. They once said to Rāma: 'O Rāma, we know You only as the son of Daśaratha. Let sages like Bharadvāja worship You as God Incarnate. We want to realize Brahman, the Indivisible Existence-Knowledge-Bliss Absolute.' At these words Rāma smiled and went away."

KEDAR: "Those rishis could not recognize Rāma as an Incarnation of God. They must have been fools."

MASTER (seriously): "Please don't say such a thing. People worship God according to their tastes and temperaments. The mother cooks the same fish differently for her children, that each one may have what suits his stomach. For some she cooks the rich dish of pilau. But not all the children can digest it. For those with weak stomachs she prepares soup. Some, again, like fried fish or pickled fish. It depends on one's taste.

"The rishis followed the path of jnāna. Therefore they sought to realize Brahman, the Indivisible Existence-Knowledge-Bliss Absolute. But those who follow the path of devotion seek an Incarnation of God, to enjoy the sweetness of bhakti. The darkness of the mind disappears when God is realized. In the Purāna it is said that it was as if a hundred suns were shining when Rāma entered the court. Why, then, weren't the courtiers burnt up? It was because the brilliance of Rāma was not like that of a material object. As the lotus blooms when the sun rises, so the lotus of the heart of the people assembled in the court burst into blossom."

As the Master uttered these words, standing before the devotees, he suddenly fell into an ecstatic mood. His mind was withdrawn from external objects. No sooner did he say, "the lotus of the heart burst into blossom", than he went into deep samādhi. He stood motionless, his countenance beaming and his lips parted in a smile.

After a long time he returned to the normal consciousness of the world. He drew a long breath and repeatedly chanted the name of Rāma, every word showering nectar into the hearts of the devotees. The Master sat down, the others seating themselves around him.

MASTER (to the devotees): "Ordinary people do not recognize the advent of an Incarnation of God. He comes in secret. Only a few of His intimate disciples can recognize Him. That Rāma was both Brahman Absolute and a perfect Incarnation of God in human form was known only to twelve rishis. The other sages said to Him, 'Rāma, we know You only as Daśaratha's son.'

"Can everyone comprehend Brahman, the Indivisible Existence-Knowledge-Bliss Absolute? He alone has attained perfect love of God who, having reached the Absolute, keeps himself in the realm of the Relative in order to enjoy the divine līlā. A man can describe the ways and activities of the Queen[4] if he has previously visited her in England. Only then will his description of the Queen be correct. Sages like Bharadvāja adored Rāma and said: 'O Rāma, You are nothing but the Indivisible Satchidānanda. You have appeared before us as a human being, but You look like a man because You have shrouded Yourself with Your own māyā.' These rishis were great devotees of Rāma and had supreme love for God."

Presently some devotees from Konnagar arrived, singing kirtan to the accompaniment of drums and cymbals. As they reached the northeast verandah of Sri Ramakrishna's room, the Master joined in the music, dancing with them intoxicated with divine joy. Now and then he went into samādhi, standing still as a statue. While he was in one of these states of divine unconsciousness, the devotees put thick garlands of jasmine around his neck. The enchanting form of the Master reminded the devotees of Chaitanya, another Incarnation of God. The Master passed alternately

[4] Queen Victoria.

through three moods of divine consciousness: the inmost, when he completely lost all knowledge of the outer world; the semi-conscious, when he danced with the devotees in an ecstasy of love; and the conscious, when he joined them in loud singing. It was indeed a sight for the gods, to see the Master standing motionless in samādhi, with fragrant garlands hanging from his neck, his countenance beaming with love, and the devotees singing and dancing around him.

When it was time for his noon meal, Sri Ramakrishna put on a new yellow cloth and sat on the small couch. His golden complexion, blending with his yellow cloth, enchanted the eyes of the devotees.

After his meal Sri Ramakrishna rested a little on the small couch. Inside and outside his room crowded the devotees, among them Kedar, Suresh, Ram, Manomohan, Girindra, Rakhal, Bhavanath, and M. Rakhal's father was also present.

A Vaishnava goswāmi was seated in the room. The Master said to him: "Well, what do you say? What is the way?"

GOSWĀMI: "Sir, the chanting of God's name is enough. The scriptures emphasize the sanctity of God's name for the Kaliyuga."

MASTER: "Yes, there is no doubt about the sanctity of God's name. But can a mere name achieve anything, without the yearning love of the devotee behind it? One should feel great restlessness of soul for the vision of God. Suppose a man repeats the name of God mechanically, while his mind is absorbed in 'woman and gold'. Can he achieve anything? Mere muttering of magic words doesn't cure one of the pain of a spider or scorpion sting. One must also apply the smoke of burning cow-dung."[5]

GOSWĀMI: "But what about Ajāmila then? He was a great sinner; there was no sin he had not indulged in. But he uttered the name of Nārāyana on his death-bed, calling his son, who also had that name. And thus he was liberated."

MASTER: "Perhaps Ajāmila had done many spiritual things in his past births. It is also said that he once practised austerity; besides, those were the last moments of his life. What is the use of giving an elephant a bath? It will cover itself with dirt and dust again and become its former self. But if someone removes the dust from its body and gives it a bath just before it enters the stable, then the elephant remains clean.

"Suppose a man becomes pure by chanting the holy name of God, but immediately afterwards commits many sins. He has no strength of mind. He doesn't take a vow not to repeat his sins. A bath in the Ganges undoubtedly absolves one of all sins; but what does that avail? They say that the sins perch on the trees along the bank of the Ganges. No sooner does the man come back from the holy waters than the old sins jump on his shoulders from the trees. (All laugh.) The same old sins take possession of him again. He is hardly out of the water before they fall upon him.

"Therefore I say, chant the name of God, and with it pray to Him that you may have love for Him. Pray to God that your attachment to such

[5] A primitive medicine used by the villagers for scorpion bites.

transitory things as wealth, name, and creature comforts may become less and less every day.

(*To the goswāmi*) "With sincerity and earnestness one can realize God through all religions. The Vaishnavas will realize God, and so will the Śāktas, the Vedāntists, and the Brāhmos. The Mussalmāns and Christians will realize Him too. All will certainly realize God if they are earnest and sincere.

"Some people indulge in quarrels, saying, 'One cannot attain anything unless one worships our Krishna', or, 'Nothing can be gained without the worship of Kāli, our Divine Mother', or, 'One cannot be saved without accepting the Christian religion.' This is pure dogmatism. The dogmatist says, 'My religion alone is true, and the religions of others are false.' This is a bad attitude. God can be reached by different paths.

"Further, some say that God has form and is not formless. Thus they start quarrelling. A Vaishnava quarrels with a Vedāntist.

"One can rightly speak of God only after one has seen Him. He who has seen God knows really and truly that God has form and that He is formless as well. He has many other aspects that cannot be described.

"Once some blind men chanced to come near an animal that someone told them was an elephant. They were asked what the elephant was like. The blind men began to feel its body. One of them said the elephant was like a pillar; he had touched only its leg. Another said it was like a winnowing-fan; he had touched only its ear. In this way the others, having touched its tail or belly, gave their different versions of the elephant. Just so, a man who has seen only one aspect of God limits God to that alone. It is his conviction that God cannot be anything else.

(*To the goswāmi*) "How can you say that the only truth about God is that He has form? It is undoubtedly true that God comes down to earth in a human form, as in the case of Krishna. And it is true as well that God reveals Himself to His devotees in various forms. But it is also true that God is formless; He is the Indivisible Existence-Knowledge-Bliss Absolute. He has been described in the Vedas both as formless and as endowed with form. He is also described there both as attributeless and as endowed with attributes.

"Do you know what I mean? Satchidānanda is like an infinite ocean. Intense cold freezes the water into ice, which floats on the ocean in blocks of various forms. Likewise, through the cooling influence of bhakti, one sees forms of God in the Ocean of the Absolute. These forms are meant for the bhaktas, the lovers of God. But when the Sun of Knowledge rises, the ice melts; it becomes the same water it was before. Water above and water below, everywhere nothing but water. Therefore a prayer in the *Bhāgavata* says: 'O Lord, Thou hast form, and Thou art also formless. Thou walkest before us, O Lord, in the shape of a man; again, Thou hast been described in the Vedas as beyond words and thought.'

"But you may say that for certain devotees God assumes eternal forms. There are places in the ocean where the ice doesn't melt at all. It assumes the form of quartz."

KEDAR: "It is said in the *Bhāgavata* that Vyāsa asked God's forgiveness for his three transgressions. He said: 'O Lord, Thou art formless, but I have thought of Thee in my meditation as endowed with form; Thou art beyond speech, but I have sung Thee hymns; Thou art the All-pervading Spirit, but I have made pilgrimages to sacred places. Be gracious, O Lord, and forgive these three transgressions of mine.' "

MASTER: "Yes, God has form and He is formless too. Further, He is beyond both form and formlessness. No one can limit Him."

Rakhal's father was sitting in the room. At that time Rakhal was staying with the Master. After his mother's death his father had married a second time. Now and then he came to Dakshineswar because of Rakhal's being there. He did not raise much objection to his son's living with the Master. Being a wealthy man of the world, he was always involved in litigation. There were lawyers and deputy magistrates among Sri Ramakrishna's visitors. Rakhal's father found it profitable to cultivate their acquaintance, since he expected to be benefited by their counsels in worldly matters.

Now and then the Master cast a glance at Rakhal's father. It was his cherished desire that Rakhal should live with him permanently at Dakshineswar.

MASTER (*to Rakhal's father and the devotees*): "Ah, what a nice character Rakhal has developed! Look at his face and every now and then you will notice his lips moving. Inwardly he repeats the name of God, and so his lips move.

"Youngsters like him belong to the class of the ever-perfect. They are born with God-Consciousness. No sooner do they grow a little older than they realize the danger of coming in contact with the world. There is the parable of the homā bird in the Vedas. The bird lives high up in the sky and never descends to earth. It lays its egg in the sky, and the egg begins to fall. But the bird lives in such a high region that the egg hatches while falling. The fledgling comes out and continues to fall. But it is still so high that while falling it grows wings and its eyes open. Then the young bird perceives that it is dashing down toward the earth and will be instantly killed. The moment it sees the ground, it turns and shoots up toward its mother in the sky. Then its one goal is to reach its mother.

"Youngsters like Rakhal are like that bird. From their very childhood they are afraid of the world, and their one thought is how to reach the Mother, how to realize God.

"You may ask, 'How is it possible for these boys, born of worldly parents and living among the worldly-minded, to develop such knowledge and devotion?' It can be explained. If a pea falls into a heap of dung, it germinates into a pea-plant none the less. The peas that grow on that plant serve many useful purposes. Because it was sown in dung, will it produce another kind of plant?

"Ah, what a sweet nature Rakhal has nowadays! And why shouldn't it be so? If the yam is a good one, its shoots also become good. (*All laugh.*) Like father like son."

M. (*aside to Girindra*): "How well he has explained God with and without form! Do the Vaishnavas believe only in God with form?"

GIRINDRA: "Perhaps so. They are one-sided."

M: "Did you understand what he meant by the 'eternal form' of God? That 'quartz'? I couldn't grasp it well."

MASTER (*to M.*): "Well, what are you talking about?"

M. and Girindra smiled and remained silent.

Later in the afternoon the devotees were singing in the Panchavati, where the Master joined them. They sang together in praise of the Divine Mother:

> High in the heaven of the Mother's feet, my mind was soaring
>   like a kite,
> When came a blast of sin's rough wind that drove it swiftly toward
>   the earth.
> Māyā disturbed its even flight by bearing down upon one side,
> And I could make it rise no more.
> Entangled in the twisting string of love for children and for wife,
> Alas! my kite was rent in twain.
>
> It lost its crest of wisdom soon and downward plunged as I let it go;
> How could it hope to fly again, when all its top was torn away?
> Though fastened with devotion's cord, it came to grief in playing
>   here;
> Its six opponents[6] worsted it.
> Now Nareschandra rues this game of smiles and tears, and thinks
>   it better
> Never to have played at all.

The singing continued. Sri Ramakrishna danced with the devotees. They sang:

> The black bee of my mind is drawn in sheer delight
> To the blue lotus flower of Mother Śyāmā's feet,
> The blue flower of the feet of Kāli, Śiva's Consort;
> Tasteless, to the bee, are the blossoms of desire.
> My Mother's feet are black, and black, too, is the bee;
> Black is made one with black! This much of the mystery
> My mortal eyes behold, then hastily retreat.
> But Kamalākānta's hopes are answered in the end;
> He swims in the Sea of Bliss, unmoved by joy or pain.

The kirtan went on:

> O Mother, what a machine[7] is this that Thou hast made!
> What pranks Thou playest with this toy
> Three and a half cubits high!
> Hiding Thyself within, Thou holdest the guiding string;
> But the machine, not knowing it,
> Still believes it moves by itself.
> Whoever finds the Mother remains a machine no more;

[6] The six passions.
[7] The human body.

Yet some machines have even bound
The Mother Herself with the string of Love.

It was a very happy day for all.

The Master, accompanied by M., was coming back to his room, when he met Trailokya, a Brāhmo devotee, on the way. Trailokya bowed before the Master.

MASTER: "They are singing in the Panchavati. Won't you go there?"

TRAILOKYA: "What shall I do there?"

MASTER: "Why, you will enjoy the music."

TRAILOKYA: "I have been there already."

MASTER: "Well, well! That's good."

It was about six o'clock in the evening. The Master was sitting with the devotees on the southeast verandah of his room.

MASTER: "A holy man who has renounced the world will of course chant the name of God. That is only natural. He has no other duties to perform. If he meditates on God it shouldn't surprise anybody. On the other hand, if he fails to think of God or chant His holy name, then people will think ill of him.

"But it is a great deal to his credit if a householder utters the name of the Lord. Think of King Janaka. What courage he had, indeed! He fenced with two swords, the one of Knowledge and the other of work. He possessed the perfect Knowledge of Brahman and also was devoted to the duties of the world. An unchaste woman attends to the minutest duties of the world, but her mind always dwells on her paramour.

"The constant company of holy men is necessary. The holy man introduces one to God."

KEDAR: "Yes, sir. The great soul is born in the world for the redemption of humanity. He leads others to God, just as a locomotive engine takes along with it a long train of carriages. Or again, he is like a river or lake that quenches the thirst of many people."

The devotees were ready to return home. One by one they saluted the Master. At the sight of Bhavanath Sri Ramakrishna said: "Don't go away today. The very sight of you inspires me." Bhavanath had not yet entered into worldly life. A youth of twenty, he had a fair complexion and handsome features. He shed tears of joy on hearing the name of God. The Master looked on him as the embodiment of Nārāyana.

Thursday, March 29, 1883

The Master had taken a little rest after his noon meal, when a few devotees arrived from Calcutta, among them Amrita and the well-known singer of the Brāhmo Samāj, Trailokya.

Rakhal was not feeling well. The Master was greatly worried about him and said to the devotees: "You see, Rakhal is not well. Will soda-water help him? What am I to do now? Rakhal, please take the prasād from the Jagannāth temple."

Even as he spoke these words the Master underwent a strange transformation. He looked at Rakhal with the infinite tenderness of a mother and affectionately uttered the name of Govinda.[8] Did he see in Rakhal the manifestation of God Himself? The disciple was a young boy of pure heart who had renounced all attraction to lust and greed. And Sri Ramakrishna was intoxicated day and night with love of God. At the sight of Rakhal his eyes expressed the tender feelings of a mother, a love like that which had filled the heart of Mother Yaśodā at the sight of the Baby Krishna. The devotees gazed at the Master in wonder as he went into deep samādhi. As his soul soared into the realm of Divine Consciousness, his body became motionless, his eyes were fixed on the tip of his nose, and his breathing almost ceased.

An unknown Bengali, dressed in the ochre cloth of a monk, entered the room and sat on the floor. The Master's mind was coming down to the ordinary plane of consciousness. Presently he began to talk, though the spell of samādhi still lingered.

MASTER (*at the sight of the ochre cloth*): "Why this gerruā? Should one put on such a thing for a mere fancy? A man once said, 'I have exchanged the *Chandi* for a drum.' At first he used to sing the holy songs of the *Chandi*; now he beats the drum. (*All laugh.*)

"There are three or four varieties of renunciation. Afflicted with miseries at home, one may put on the ochre cloth of a monk; but that renunciation doesn't last long. Again, a man out of work puts on an ochre wearing-cloth and goes off to Benares. After three months he writes home: 'I have a job here. I shall come home in a few days. Don't worry about me.' Again, a man may have everything he wants. He lacks nothing, yet he does not enjoy his possessions. He weeps for God alone. That is real renunciation.

"No lie of any sort is good. A false garb, even though a holy one, is not good. If the outer garb does not correspond to the inner thought, it gradually brings ruin. Uttering false words or doing false deeds, one gradually loses all fear. Far better is the white cloth of a householder. Attachment to worldliness, occasional lapses from the ideal, and an outer garb of gerruā— how dreadful!

"It is not proper for a righteous person to tell a lie or do something false even in a dramatic performance. Once I went to Keshab's house to see the performance of a play called *Nava-Vrindāvan*. They brought something on the stage which they called the 'Cross'. Another actor sprinkled water, which they said was the 'Water of Peace'. I saw a third actor staggering and reeling in the role of a drunkard."

A BRĀHMO DEVOTEE: "It was K—."

MASTER: "It is not good for a devotee to play such parts. It is bad for the mind to dwell on such subjects for a long while. The mind is like white linen fresh from the laundry; it takes the colour in which you dip it. If it is associated with falsehood for a long time, it will be stained with falsehood.

"Another day I went to Keshab's house to see the play called *Nimāi-sannyās*.[9] Some flattering disciples of Keshab spoiled the whole performance.

---

[8] A name of Krishna. According to the Master, Rakhal, in one of his previous incarnations, had been a cowherd of Vrindāvan and an intimate companion of Sri Krishna.

[9] A play describing Sri Chaitanya's embracing of the monastic life.

One of them said to Keshab, 'You are the Chaitanya of the Kaliyuga.' Keshab pointed to me and asked with a smile, 'Then who is he?' I replied: 'Why, I am the servant of your servant. I am a speck of the dust of your feet.' Keshab had a desire for name and fame.

(*To Amrita and Trailokya*) "Youngsters like Narendra and Rakhal are ever-perfect. Every time they are born they are devoted to God. An ordinary man acquires a little devotion after austerities and a hard struggle. But these boys have love of God from the very moment of their birth. They are like the natural image of Śiva, which springs forth from the earth and is not set up by human hands.

"The ever-perfect form a class by themselves. Not all birds have crooked beaks. The ever-perfect are never attached to the world. There is the instance of Prahlāda.

"Ordinary people practise spiritual discipline and cultivate devotion to God; but they also become attached to the world and are caught in the glamour of 'woman and gold'. They are like flies, which sit on a flower or a sweetmeat and light on filth as well.

"But the ever-perfect are like bees, which light only on flowers and sip the honey. The ever-perfect drink only the Nectar of Divine Bliss. They are never inclined to worldly pleasures.

"The devotion of the ever-perfect is not like the ordinary devotion that one acquires as a result of strenuous spiritual discipline. Ritualistic devotion consists in repeating the name of God and performing worship in a prescribed manner. It is like crossing a rice-field in a roundabout way along the balk. Again, it is like reaching a near-by village by boat in a roundabout way along a winding river.

"One does not follow the injunctions of ceremonial worship when one develops rāga-bhakti, when one loves God as one's own. Then it is like crossing a rice-field after the harvest. You don't have to walk along the balk. You can go straight across the field in any direction.

"When the country is flooded deep with water, one doesn't have to follow the winding river. Then the fields are deep under water. You can row your boat straight to the village.

"Without this intense attachment, this passionate love, one cannot realize God."

AMRITA: "Sir, how do you feel in samādhi?"

MASTER: "You may have heard that the cockroach, by intently meditating on the bhramara, is transformed into a bhramara. Do you know how I feel then? I feel like a fish released from a pot into the water of the Ganges."

AMRITA: "Don't you feel at that time even a trace of ego?"

MASTER: "Yes, generally a little of it remains. However hard you may rub a grain of gold against a grindstone, still a bit of it always remains. Or again, take the case of a big fire; the ego is like one of its sparks. In samādhi I lose outer consciousness completely; but God generally keeps a little trace of ego in me for the enjoyment of divine communion. Enjoyment is possible only when 'I' and 'you' remain.

"Again, sometimes God effaces even that trace of 'I'. Then one experiences jaḍa samādhi or nirvikalpa samādhi. That experience cannot be described. A salt doll went to measure the depth of the ocean, but before it had gone far into the water it melted away. It became entirely one with the water of the ocean. Then who was to come back and tell the ocean's depth?"

ADVICE TO THE BRĀHMOS

SRI RAMAKRISHNA was visiting Balaram in Calcutta, with Narendra, Bhavanath, Rakhal, M., and others. Balaram, at the Master's bidding, had invited some of the young devotees to lunch. Sri Ramakrishna often said to him, "Feed them now and then; that will confer on you the merit of feeding holy men." The Master looked on his young disciples, yet untouched by "woman and gold", as veritable embodiments of God.

A few days earlier Sri Ramakrishna had been to Keshab's house with Narendra and Rakhal to see a performance of the play entitled *Nava-Vrindāvan*. Narendra had taken part in the performance, in which Keshab had played the role of Pāvhāri Bābā.

MASTER: "Keshab came on the stage in the role of a holy man and sprinkled the 'Water of Peace'. But I didn't like it. The idea of sprinkling such water on a theatrical stage after a performance!

"Another gentleman played the part of Sin. That is not good either. One should not commit sin; one should not even feign it."

The Master wanted to hear Narendra sing. The young disciple was not feeling well, but at the Master's earnest request he sang to the accompaniment of the tānpurā:

> Sing, O bird that nestles deep within my heart!
> Sing, O bird that sits on the Kalpa-Tree of Brahman!
> Sing God's everlasting praise. . . .

Then he sang:

> Brahman, Joy of the whole universe, Supreme Effulgence;
> God beginningless, Lord of the world, the very Life of life! . . .

And again:

> O King of Kings, reveal Thyself to me!
> I crave Thy mercy. Cast on me Thy glance!
> At Thy dear feet I dedicate my life,
> Seared in the fiery furnace of this world.
>
> My heart, alas, is deeply stained with sin;
> Ensnared in māyā, I am all but dead.

Compassionate Lord! Revive my fainting soul
With the life-giving nectar of Thy grace.

Narendra continued:

Upon the tray of the sky blaze bright
The lamps of sun and moon;
Like diamonds shine the glittering stars
To deck Thy wondrous form.
The sweet Malaya breeze blows soft,
For fragrant incense smoke;
The moving air sways to and fro
The fan before Thy holy face;
Like gleaming votive lights
The fresh and flowery groves appear.

How wonderful Thy worship is,
O Slayer of birth and death!
The sacred Om, from space arisen,
Is the resounding drum.
My mind craves nectar day and night
At Hari's Lotus Feet;
Oh, shower the waters of Thy grace
On thirsty Nānak, blessed Lord;
And may Thy hallowed name
Become his everlasting home!

He sang again:

In Wisdom's firmament the moon of Love is rising full,
And Love's flood-tide, in surging waves, is flowing everywhere.
O Lord, how full of bliss Thou art! Victory unto Thee! . . .

Then at the Master's bidding Bhavanath sang:

Where is a friend like Thee, O Essence of Mercy?
Where is another friend like Thee
To stand by me through pain and pleasure?
Who, among all my friends, forgives my failings,
Bringing me comfort for my grief,
Soothing my spirit in its terror?

Thou art the Helmsman who dost steer life's craft
Across the world's perilous sea;
Thy grace it is alone, O Lord,
That silences my raging passions' storm.
Thou pourest out the waters of peace
Upon my burning, penitent soul;
And Thine is the bosom that will shelter me
When every other friend I own
Deserts me in my dying hour.

Narendra said to the Master with a smile, referring to Bhavanath, "He has given up fish and betel-leaf."[1]

[1] Hindu religious aspirants often renounce these, since they are considered luxuries detrimental to spiritual progress.

MASTER: "Why so? What is the matter with fish and betel-leaf? They aren't harmful. The renunciation of 'woman and gold' is the true renunciation.

"Where is Rakhal?"

A DEVOTEE: "He is asleep, sir."

MASTER (*with a smile*): "Once a man went to a certain place to see a theatrical performance, carrying a mat under his arm. Hearing that it would be some time before the performance began, he spread the mat on the floor and fell asleep. When he woke up it was all over. (*All laugh.*) Then he returned home with the mat under his arm."

Ramdayal was very ill and lay in bed in another room. The Master went there to inquire about him.

About four o'clock in the afternoon some members of the Brāhmo Samāj arrived. The Master began to converse with them.

A BRĀHMO: "Sir, have you read the *Panchadaśi?*"

MASTER: "At first one should hear books like that and indulge in reasoning. But later on—

> Cherish my precious Mother Śyāmā
> Tenderly within, O mind;
> May you and I alone behold Her,
> Letting no one else intrude.

"One should hear the scriptures during the early stages of spiritual discipline. After attaining God there is no lack of knowledge. Then the Divine Mother supplies it without fail.

"A child spells out every word as he writes, but later on he writes fluently.

"The goldsmith is up and doing while melting gold. As long as the gold hasn't melted, he works the bellows with one hand, moves the fan with the other, and blows through a pipe with his mouth. But the moment the gold melts and is poured into the mould, he is relieved of all anxiety.

"Mere reading of the scriptures is not enough. A person cannot understand the true significance of the scriptures if he is attached to the world.

> Though with intense delight I learnt many poems and dramas,
> I have forgotten them all, entrapped in Krishna's love.

"Keshab enjoys the world and practises yoga as well. Living in the world, he directs his mind to God."

A devotee described the Convocation of Calcutta University, saying that the meeting looked like a forest of human heads.

MASTER: "The feeling of the Divine is awakened in me when I see a great crowd of people. Had I seen that meeting, I should have been overwhelmed with spiritual fervour."

Sunday, April 8, 1883

It was Sunday morning. The Master, looking like a boy, was seated in his room, and near him was another boy, his beloved disciple Rakhal. M.

entered and saluted the Master. Ramlal also was in the room, and Kishori, Manilal Mallick, and several other devotees gathered by and by.

Manilal Mallick, a business man, had recently been to Benares, where he owned a bungalow.

MASTER: "So you have been to Benares. Did you see any holy men there?"

MANILAL: "Yes, sir. I paid my respects to Trailanga Swami, Bhaskarananda, and others."

MASTER: "Tell us something about them."

MANILAL: "Trailanga Swami is living in the same temple where he lived before—on the Manikarnikā Ghāt, near the Benimādhav Minaret. People say he was formerly in a more exalted spiritual state. He could perform many miracles. Now he has lost much of that power."

MASTER: "That is the criticism of worldly people."

MANILAL: "Trailanga Swami keeps a strict vow of silence. Unlike him, Bhaskarananda is friendly with all."

MASTER: "Did you have any conversation with Bhaskarananda?"

MANILAL: "Yes, sir. We had a long talk. Among other things we discussed the problem of good and evil. He said to me: 'Don't follow the path of evil. Give up sinful thoughts. That is how God wants us to act. Perform only those duties that are virtuous.'"

MASTER: "Yes, that is also a path, meant for worldly-minded people. But those whose spiritual consciousness has been awakened, who have realized that God alone is real and all else illusory, cherish a different ideal. They are aware that God alone is the Doer and others are His instruments.

"Those whose spiritual consciousness has been awakened never make a false step. They do not have to reason in order to shun evil. They are so full of love of God that whatever action they undertake is a good action. They are fully conscious that they are not the doers of their actions, but mere servants of God. They always feel: 'I am the machine and He is the Operator. I do as He does through me. I speak as He speaks through me. I move as He moves me.'

"Fully awakened souls are beyond virtue and vice. They realize that it is God who does everything.

"There was a monastery in a certain place. The monks residing there went out daily to beg their food. One day a monk, while out for his alms, saw a landlord beating a man mercilessly. The compassionate monk stepped in and asked the landlord to stop. But the landlord was filled with anger and turned his wrath against the innocent monk. He beat the monk till he fell unconscious on the ground. Someone reported the matter to the monastery. The monks ran to the spot and found their brother lying there. Four or five of them carried him back and laid him on a bed. He was still unconscious. The other monks sat around him sad at heart; some were fanning him. Finally someone suggested that he should be given a little milk to drink. When it was poured into his mouth he regained consciousness. He opened his eyes and looked around. One of the monks said, 'Let us see whether he is fully conscious and can recognize us.' Shouting into his ear, he said,

'Revered sir, who is giving you milk?' 'Brother,' replied the holy man in a low voice, 'He who beat me is now giving me milk.'

"But one does not attain such a state of mind without the realization of God."

MANILAL: "Sir, what you have just said applies to a man of a very lofty spiritual state. I talked on such topics in a general way with Bhaskarananda."

MASTER: "Does he live in a house?"

MANILAL: "Yes, sir. He lives with a devotee."

MASTER: "How old is he now?"

MANILAL: "About fifty-five."

MASTER: "Did you talk about anything else?"

MANILAL: "I asked him how to cultivate bhakti. He said: 'Chant the name of God. Repeat the name of Rāma.'"

MASTER: "That is very good."

The worship was over in the temples and the bells rang for the food offerings in the shrines. As it was a summer noon the sun was very hot. The flood-tide began in the Ganges and a breeze came up from the south. Sri Ramakrishna was resting in his room after his meal.

The people of Basirhāt, Rakhal's birth-place, had been suffering from a severe drought during the summer months.

MASTER (to Manilal): "Rakhal says that the people in his native village have been suffering seriously from a scarcity of water. Why don't you build a reservoir there? That will do the people good. (Smiling) You have so much money; what will you do with all your wealth? But they say that telis² are very calculating." (All laugh.)

Manilal was truly a calculating man, though he suffered no lack of money. In later years he set up an endowment of twenty-five thousand rupees for the maintenance of poor students.

Manilal made no answer to these words of the Master about his caste characteristics. Later on, in the course of the conversation, he remarked casually: "Sir, you referred to a reservoir. You might as well have confined yourself to that suggestion. Why allude to the 'oil-man caste' and all that?"

Some of the devotees smiled to themselves. The Master laughed.

Presently a few elderly members of the Brāhmo Samāj arrived. The room was full of devotees. Sri Ramakrishna was sitting on his bed, facing the north. He kept smiling, and talked to the Brāhmo devotees in a joyous mood.

MASTER: "You talk glibly about prema. But is it such a commonplace thing? There are two characteristics of prema. First, it makes one forget the world. So intense is one's love of God that one becomes unconscious of outer things. Chaitanya had this ecstatic love; he 'took a wood for the sacred grove of Vrindāvan and the ocean for the dark waters of the Jamunā'. Second, one has no feeling of 'my-ness' toward the body, which is so dear to man. One wholly gets rid of the feeling that the body is the soul.

"There are certain signs of God-realization. The man in whom longing

² The oil-man caste to which Manilal belonged. It is a comparatively low caste in Hindu society in Bengal.

for God manifests its glories is not far from attaining Him. What are the glories of that longing? They are discrimination, dispassion, compassion for living beings, serving holy men, loving their company, chanting the name and glories of God, telling the truth, and the like. When you see those signs of longing in an aspirant, you can rightly say that for him the vision of God is not far to seek.

"The state of a servant's house will tell you unmistakably whether his master has decided to visit it. First, the rubbish and jungle around the house are cleared up. Second, the soot and dirt are removed from the rooms. Third, the courtyard, floors, and other places are swept clean. Finally the master himself sends various things to the house, such as a carpet, a hubble-bubble for smoking, and the like. When you see these things arriving, you conclude that the master will very soon come."

A DEVOTEE: "Sir, should one first practise discrimination to attain self-control?"

MASTER: "That is also a path. It is called the path of vichāra, reasoning. But the inner organs[3] are brought under control naturally through the path of devotion as well. It is rather easily accomplished that way. Sense pleasures appear more and more tasteless as love for God grows. Can carnal pleasure attract a grief-stricken man and woman the day their child has died?"

DEVOTEE: "How can I develop love for God?"

MASTER: "Repeat His name, and sins will disappear. Thus you will destroy lust, anger, the desire for creature comforts, and so on."

DEVOTEE: "How can I take delight in God's name?"

MASTER: "Pray to God with a yearning heart that you may take delight in His name. He will certainly fulfil your heart's desire."

So saying, the Master sang a song in his sweet voice, pleading with the Divine Mother to show Her grace to suffering men:

> O Mother, I have no one else to blame:
> Alas! I sink in the well these very hands have dug.
> With the six passions for my spade,
> I dug a pit in the sacred land of earth;
> And now the dark water of death gushes forth!
> How can I save myself, O my Redeemer?
>
> Surely I have been my own enemy;
> How can I now ward off this dark water of death?
> Behold, the waters rise to my chest!
> How can I save myself? O Mother, save me!
> Thou art my only Refuge; with Thy protecting glance
> Take me across to the other shore of the world.

The Master sang again:

> What a delirious fever is this that I suffer from!
> O Mother, Thy grace is my only cure.
> False pride is the fever that racks my wasted form;
> "I" and "mine" are my cry. Oh, what a wicked delusion!

[3] Mind (manas), intelligence (buddhi), mind-stuff (chitta), and ego (ahamkāra).

My quenchless thirst for wealth and friends is never-ceasing;
How, then, shall I sustain my life?
Talk about things unreal, this is my wretched delirium,
And I indulge in it always, O Giver of all good fortune!

My eyes in seeming sleep are closed, my stomach is filled
With the vile worms of cruelty.
Alas! I wander about absorbed in unmeaning deeds;
Even for Thy holy name I have no taste, O Mother!
I doubt that I shall ever be cured of this malady.

Then the Master said: " 'Even for Thy holy name I have no taste.' A typhoid patient has very little chance of recovery if he loses all taste for food; but his life need not be despaired of if he enjoys food even a little. That is why one should cultivate a taste for God's name. Any name will do—Durgā, Krishna, or Śiva. Then if, through the chanting of the name, one's attachment to God grows day by day, and joy fills the soul, one has nothing to fear. The delirium will certainly disappear; the grace of God will certainly descend.

" 'As is a man's feeling of love, so is his gain.' Once two friends were going along the street, when they saw some people listening to a reading of the Bhāgavata. 'Come, friend', said the one to the other. 'Let us hear the sacred book.' So saying he went in and sat down. The second man peeped in and went away. He entered a house of ill fame. But very soon he felt disgusted with the place. 'Shame on me!' he said to himself. 'My friend has been listening to the sacred word of Hari; and see where I am!' But the friend who had been listening to the Bhāgavata also became disgusted. 'What a fool I am!' he said. 'I have been listening to this fellow's blah-blah, and my friend is having a grand time.' In course of time they both died. The messenger of Death came for the soul of the one who had listened to the Bhāgavata and dragged it off to hell. The messenger of God came for the soul of the one who had been to the house of prostitution and led it up to heaven.

"Verily, the Lord looks into a man's heart and does not judge him by what he does or where he lives. 'Krishna accepts a devotee's inner feeling of love.'

"In the Kartābhajā sect, the teacher, while giving initiation, says to the disciple, 'Now everything depends on your mind.' According to this sect, 'He who has the right mind finds the right way and also achieves the right end.' It was through the power of his mind that Hanumān leapt over the sea. 'I am the servant of Rāma; I have repeated the holy name of Rāma. Is there anything impossible for me?'—that was Hanumān's faith.

"Ignorance lasts as long as one has ego. There can be no liberation so long as the ego remains. 'O God, Thou art the Doer and not I'—that is knowledge.

"By being lowly one can rise high. The chātak bird makes its nest on low ground, but it soars very high in the sky. Cultivation is not possible on high land; in low land water accumulates and makes cultivation possible.

"One must take the trouble to seek the company of holy persons. In his own home a man hears only worldly talk; the disease of worldliness has become chronic with him. The caged parrot sitting on its perch repeats, 'Rāma! Rāma!' But let it fly to the forest and it will squawk in its usual way.

"Mere possession of money doesn't make a nobleman. One sign of the mansion of a nobleman is that all the rooms are lighted. The poor cannot afford much oil, and consequently cannot have so many lights. This shrine of the body should not be left dark; one should illumine it with the lamp of Wisdom.

> Lighting the lamp of Knowledge in the chamber of your heart,
> Behold the face of the Mother, Brahman's Embodiment.

"Everyone can attain Knowledge. There are two entities: jīvātmā, the individual soul, and Paramātmā, the Supreme Soul. Through prayer all individual souls can be united to the Supreme Soul. Every house has a connection for gas, and gas can be obtained from the main storage-tank of the Gas Company. Apply to the Company, and it will arrange for your supply of gas. Then your house will be lighted.

"In some people spiritual consciousness has already been awakened; but they have special marks. They do not enjoy hearing or talking about anything but God. They are like the chātak, which prays for rain-water though the seven oceans, the Ganges, the Jamunā, and the rivers near it are all filled with water. It won't drink anything but rain-water, even though its throat is burning with thirst."

The Master wanted to hear a few songs. Ramlal and a brāhmin official of the temple garden sang:

> Dwell, O Lord, O Lover of bhakti,
> In the Vrindāvan of my heart,
> And my devotion unto Thee
> Will be Thy Rādhā, dearly loved. . . .

And again:

> The dark cloud of the summer storm fades into nothingness,
> When, flute in hand and a smile on His lips,
> Lighting the world with His loveliness,
> Krishna, the Dark One, appears.

> His dazzling yellow robe outgleams even the lightning's glare;
> A wreath of wild-flowers interwoven
> Gently swings from His youthful breast
> And softly kisses His feet.

> See, there He stands, the Lord of life, the Moon of Nanda's line,
> Outshining all the moons in heaven
> And with the splendour of His rays
> Flooding the Jamunā's bank!

> He stands there, stealing the maidens' hearts; He lures them from
>   hearth and home.
> Krishna enters my own heart's shrine,
> And with His flute-note steals away
> My wisdom, life, and soul.

To whom shall Gangā Nārāyana pour out his tale of woe?
Ah, friend, you might have understood
Had you but gone to the Jamunā's bank
To fill your water-jar!

Again they sang:

High in the heaven of the Mother's feet, my mind was soaring
like a kite,
When came a blast of sin's rough wind that drove it swiftly toward
the earth. . . .

MASTER (*to the devotees*): "As the tiger devours other animals, so does the 'tiger of zeal for the Lord' eat up lust, anger, and the other passions. Once this zeal grows in the heart, lust and the other passions disappear. The gopis of Vrindāvan had that state of mind because of their zeal for Krishna.

"Again, this zeal for God is compared to collyrium. Rādhā said to her friends, 'I see Krishna everywhere.' They replied, 'Friend, you have painted your eyes with the collyrium of love; that is why you see Krishna everywhere.'

"They say that when your eyes are painted with collyrium made from the ashes of a frog's head you see snakes everywhere.

"They are indeed bound souls who constantly dwell with 'woman and gold' and do not think of God even for a moment. How can you expect noble deeds of them? They are like mangoes pecked by a crow, which may not be offered to the Deity in the temple, and which even men hesitate to eat.

"Bound souls, worldly people, are like silk-worms. The worms can cut through their cocoons if they want, but having woven the cocoons themselves, they are too much attached to them to leave them. And so they die there.

"Free souls are not under the control of 'woman and gold'. There are some silk-worms that cut through the cocoon they have made with such great care. But they are few and far between.

"It is māyā that deludes. Only a few become spiritually awakened and are not deluded by the spell of māyā. They do not come under the control of 'woman and gold'.

"There are two classes of perfect .souls: those who attain perfection through spiritual practice, and those who attain it through the grace of God. Some farmers irrigate their fields with great labour. Only then can they grow crops. But there are some who do not have to irrigate at all; their fields are flooded by rain. They don't have to go to the trouble of drawing water. One must practise spiritual discipline laboriously, in order to avoid the clutches of māyā. Those who attain liberation through the grace of God do not have to labour. But they are few indeed.

"Then there is the class of the ever-perfect. They are born in each life with their spiritual consciousness already awakened. Think of a spring whose outlet is obstructed. While looking after various things in the garden, the plumber accidentally clears it and the water gushes out. Yet people are amazed to see the first manifestations of an ever-perfect soul's zeal for God. They say, 'Where was all this devotion and renunciation and love?' "

The conversation turned to the spiritual zeal of devotees, as illustrated in the earnestness of the gopis of Vrindāvan. Ramlal sang:

> Thou art my All in All, O Lord!—the Life of my life, the Essence
> of essence;
> In the three worlds I have none else but Thee to call my own.
> Thou art my peace, my joy, my hope; Thou my support, my
> wealth, my glory;
> Thou my wisdom and my strength.

> Thou art my home, my place of rest; my dearest friend, my next of
> kin;
> My present and my future, Thou; my heaven and my salvation.
> Thou art my scriptures, my commandments; Thou art my ever
> gracious Guru;
> Thou the Spring of my boundless bliss.

> Thou art the Way, and Thou the Goal; Thou the Adorable One,
> O Lord!
> Thou art the Mother tender-hearted; Thou the chastising Father;
> Thou the Creator and Protector; Thou the Helmsman who dost
> steer
> My craft across the sea of life.

MASTER (*to the devotees*): "Ah! What a beautiful song!—'Thou art my All in All.' "

Ramlal sang again, this time describing the pangs of the gopis on being separated from their beloved Krishna:[4]

> Hold not, hold not the chariot's wheels!
> Is it the wheels that make it move?
> The Mover of its wheels is Krishna,
> By whose will the worlds are moved. . . .

The Master went into deep samādhi. His body was motionless; he sat with folded hands as in his photograph. Tears of joy flowed from the corners of his eyes. After a long time his mind came down to the ordinary plane of consciousness. He mumbled something, of which only a word now and then could be heard by the devotees in the room. He was saying: "Thou art I, and I am Thou—Thou eatest—Thou—I eat! . . . What is this confusion Thou hast created?"

Continuing, the Master said: "I see everything like a man with jaundiced eyes! I see Thee alone everywhere. O Krishna, Friend of the lowly! O Eternal Consort of my soul! O Govinda!"

As he uttered the words "Eternal Consort of my soul" and "Govinda", the Master again went into samàdhi. There was complete silence in the

---

[4] When Krishna mounted His chariot to go away to Mathurā, the gopis clung to the wheels and would not let the chariot move.

room. The eager and unsatiated eyes of the devotees were fixed on the Master, a God-man of infinite moods.

Adhar Sen arrived with several of his friends. He was a deputy magistrate, about thirty years old. This was his second visit to the Master. He was accompanied by his friend Saradacharan, who was extremely unhappy because of the death of his eldest son. A retired deputy inspector of schools, Saradacharan devoted himself to meditation and prayer. Adhar had brought his friend to the Master for consolation in his afflicted state of mind.

Coming down from samādhi, the Master found the eyes of the devotees fixed on him. He muttered to himself, still in an abstracted mood.

Then, addressing the devotees, Sri Ramakrishna said: "The spiritual wisdom of worldly people is seen only on rare occasions. It is like the flame of a candle. No, it is rather like a single ray of the sun passing through a chink in a wall. Worldly people chant the name of God, but there is no zeal behind it. It is like children's swearing by God, having learnt the word from the quarrels of their aunts.

"Worldly people have no grit. If they succeed in an undertaking, it is all right, but if they don't succeed, it scarcely bothers them at all. When they need water they begin to dig a well. But as soon as they strike a stone they give up digging there and begin at another place. Perhaps they come to a bed of sand. Finding nothing but sand, they give that place up too. How can they succeed in getting water unless they continue to dig persistently where they started?

"Man reaps the harvest of his own past actions. Hence you read in the song:

O Mother, I have no one else to blame:
Alas! I sink in the well these very hands have dug.

" 'I' and 'mine'—that is ignorance. By discriminating you will realize that what you call 'I' is really nothing but Ātman. Reason it out. Are you the body or the flesh or something else? At the end you will know that you are none of these. You are free from attributes. Then you will realize that you have never been the doer of any action, that you have been free from virtue and faults alike, that you are beyond righteousness and unrighteousness.

"From ignorance a man says, 'This is gold and this is brass.' But a man of Knowledge says, 'It is all gold.'

"Reasoning stops when one sees God. But there are instances of people who have realized God and who still continue to reason. Again, there are people who, even after having seen God, chant His name with devotion and sing His glories.

"How long does a child cry? So long as it is not sucking at its mother's breast. As soon as it is nursed it stops crying. Then the child feels only joy. Joyously it drinks the milk from its mother's breast. But it is also true that, while drinking, the child sometimes plays and laughs.

"It is God alone who has become everything. But in man He manifests Himself the most. God is directly present in the man who has the pure heart of a child and who laughs and cries and dances and sings in divine ecstasy."

By this time Sri Ramakrishna had become better acquainted with Adhar, who related the cause of his friend's grief. The Master sang, as if to himself:

To arms! To arms, O man! Death storms your house in battle array!
Bearing the quiver of knowledge, mount the chariot of devotion;
Bend the bow of your tongue with the bow-string of love,
And aim at him the shaft of Mother Kāli's holy name.
Here is a ruse for the fray: You need no chariot or charioteer;
Fight your foe from the Ganges' bank, and he is easily slain.

Then he said: "What can you do? Be ready for Death. Death has entered the house. You must fight him with the weapon of God's holy name. God alone is the Doer. I say: 'O Lord, I do as Thou doest through me. I speak as Thou speakest through me. I am the machine and Thou art the Operator. I am the house and Thou art the Indweller. I am the engine and Thou art the Engineer.' Give your power of attorney to God. One doesn't come to grief through letting a good man assume one's responsibilities. Let His will be done.

"But isn't your grief for your son only natural? The son is one's own self reborn. Lakshmana ran to Rāvana when the latter fell dead on the battle-field. Looking at Rāvana's body, he found that every one of his bones was full of holes. Thereupon he said to Rāma: 'O Rāma, glory be to Your arrows! There is no spot in Rāvana's body that they have not pierced.' 'Brother,' replied Rāma, 'the holes you see in his bones are not from My arrows. Grief for his sons has pierced them through and through. These holes are the marks of his grief. It has penetrated his very bones.'

"But house, wife, and children are all transitory; they have only a momentary existence. The palm-tree alone is real. One or two fruits have dropped off. Why lament?

"God is engaged in three kinds of activity: creation, preservation, and destruction. Death is inevitable. All will be destroyed at the time of dissolution. Nothing will remain. At that time the Divine Mother will gather up the seeds for the future creation, even as the elderly mistress of the house keeps in her hotchpotch-pot little bags of cucumber seeds, 'sea-foam', blue pills, and other miscellaneous things. The Divine Mother will take Her seeds out again at the time of the new creation."

Sri Ramakrishna began to talk with Adhar on the verandah north of his room.

MASTER (to Adhar): "You are a deputy magistrate. Remember that you have obtained your position through the grace of God. Do not forget Him, but remember that all men must one day walk down the same path.[5] We stay in the world only a couple of days.

"This world is our field of activity. We are born here to perform certain duties. People have their homes in the country but come to Calcutta to work.

"It is necessary to do a certain amount of work. This is a kind of discipline. But one must finish it speedily. While melting gold, the goldsmith uses

[5] Adhar Sen passed away eighteen months after this conversation. At the news of his death the Master wept before the Mother a long time. Adhar was a great devotee of Sri Ramakrishna, who referred to him as his own relative.

everything—the bellows, the fan, and the pipe—so that he may have the hot fire he needs to melt the metal. After the melting is over, he relaxes and asks his attendant to prepare a smoke for him. All this time his face has been hot and perspiring; but now he can smoke.

"One must have stern determination; then alone is spiritual practice possible. One must make a firm resolve.

"There is great power in the seed of God's name. It destroys ignorance. A seed is tender, and the sprout soft; still it pierces the hard ground. The ground breaks and makes way for the sprout.

"The mind becomes very much distracted if one lives long in the midst of 'woman and gold'. Therefore one must be very careful. But monks do not have much to fear. The real sannyāsi lives away from 'woman and gold'. Therefore through the practice of spiritual discipline he can always fix his mind on God.

"True sannyāsis, those who are able to devote their minds constantly to God, are like bees, which light only on flowers and sip their honey. Those who live in the world, in the midst of 'woman and gold', may direct their attention to God; but sometimes their minds dwell also on 'woman and gold'. They are like common flies, which light on a piece of candy, then on a sore or filth.

"Always keep your mind fixed on God. In the beginning you must struggle a little; later on you will enjoy your pension."

Sunday, April 15, 1883

Surendra, a beloved lay disciple of the Master, had invited him to his house on the auspicious occasion of the Annapurnā Pujā. It was about six o'clock when Sri Ramakrishna arrived there with some of his devotees. The image of the Divine Mother had been installed in the worship hall. At Her feet lay hibiscus flowers and vilwa-leaves; from Her neck hung a garland of flowers. Sri Ramakrishna entered the hall and bowed down before the image. Then he went to the open courtyard, where he sat on a carpet, surrounded by his devotees and disciples. A few bolsters lay on the carpet, which was covered with a white linen sheet. He was asked to lean against one of these, but he pushed it aside.

MASTER (*to the devotees*): "To lean against a bolster![6] You see, it is very difficult to give up vanity. You may discriminate, saying that the ego is nothing at all; but still it comes, nobody knows from where. A goat's legs jerk for a few moments even after its head has been cut off. Or perhaps you are frightened in a dream; you shake off sleep and are wide awake, but still you feel your heart palpitating. Egotism is exactly like that. You may drive it away, but still it appears from somewhere. Then you look sullen and say: 'What! I have not been shown proper respect!'"

KEDAR: "'One should be lowlier than a straw and patient as a tree.'"

MASTER: "As for me, I consider myself as a speck of the dust of the devotee's feet."

Vaidyanath arrived. He was a well-educated man, a lawyer of the High

[6] Rich and aristocratic persons seeking comfort generally sit in this fashion.

Court of Calcutta. With folded hands he saluted the Master and took his seat at one side.

SURENDRA (*to the Master*): "He is one of my relatives."

MASTER: "Yes, I see he has a nice nature."

SURENDRA: "He has come here because he wants to ask you a question or two."

MASTER (*to Vaidyanath*): "All that you see is the manifestation of God's Power. No one can do anything without this Power. But you must remember that there is not an equal manifestation of God's Power in all things. Vidyāsāgar once asked me whether God endowed some with greater power than others. I said to him: 'If there are no greater and lesser manifestations of His Power, then why have we taken the trouble to visit you? Have you grown two horns?' So it stands to reason that God exists in all beings as the All-pervasive Power; but the manifestations of His Power are different in different beings."

VAIDYANATH: "Sir, I have a doubt. People speak of free will. They say that a man can do either good or evil according to his will. Is it true? Are we really free to do whatever we like?"

MASTER: "Everything depends on the will of God. The world is His play. He has created all these different things—great and small, strong and weak, good and bad, virtuous and vicious. This is all His māyā, His sport. You must have observed that all the trees in a garden are not of the same kind.

"As long as a man has not realized God, he thinks he is free. It is God Himself who keeps this error in man. Otherwise sin would have multiplied. Man would not have been afraid of sin, and there would have been no punishment for it.

"But do you know the attitude of one who has realized God? He feels: 'I am the machine, and Thou, O Lord, art the Operator. I am the house and Thou art the Indweller. I am the chariot and Thou art the Driver. I move as Thou movest me; I speak as Thou makest me speak.'

(*To Vaidyanath*): "It is not good to argue. Isn't that so?"

VAIDYANATH: "Yes, sir. The desire to argue disappears when a man attains wisdom."

The Master, out of his stock of a dozen English words, said, "Thank you!" in the most charming way, and all laughed.

MASTER (*to Vaidyanath*): "You will make spiritual progress. People don't trust a man when he speaks about God. Even if a great soul affirms that he has seen God, still the average person will not accept his words. He says to himself, 'If this man has really seen God, then let him show Him to me.' But can a man learn to feel a person's pulse in one day? He must go about with a physician for many days; only then can he distinguish the different pulses. He must be in the company of those with whom the examination of the pulse has become a regular profession.

"Can anyone and everyone pick out a yarn of a particular count? If you are in that trade, you can distinguish in a moment a forty-count thread from a forty-one."

The kirtan was about to begin. Some Vaishnavas were seated on one side with their mridangas and cymbals. A drummer began to play on his instrument preparatory to the singing. The sweet and melodious sound of the mridanga filled the courtyard, calling to mind the ecstatic kirtan of Sri Gaurānga. The Master passed into a deep spiritual state. Now and then he looked at the drummer and said, "Ah! Ah! My hair is all standing on end."

The singers asked what kind of song they should sing. The Master said humbly, "Something about Gaurānga, if you please."

The kirtan began. They sang about the celestial beauty of Sri Gaurānga:

> The beauty of Gaurānga's face
> Glows brighter than the brightest gold;
> His smile illumines all the world.
> Who cares for even a million moons
> Shining in the blue autumn sky?

The chief musician added improvised lines as they sang: "O friend, his face shines like the full moon!" "But it does not wane nor has it any stain." "It illumines the devotee's heart." Again he improvised: "His face is bathed with the essence of a million moons."

At these words the Master went into deep samādhi. After a short while he regained consciousness of the sense world. Then he suddenly stood up, overpowered by his spiritual mood, and sang improvised lines with the professionals, thinking himself to be a milkmaid of Vrindāvan gone mad with the beauty of Sri Krishna's form: "Whose fault is it—my mind's or His beauty's?" "In the three worlds I see nothing but my beloved Krishna."

The Master danced and sang. All remained spellbound as they watched. The chief musician sang the words of a gopi: "O flute, pray stop. Can you not go to sleep?" One of the musicians added a new line: "How can. it sleep? It rests on Krishna's lips."

The Master sat down. The music went on. They sang, assuming the mood of Rādhā: "My eyes are blinded. My ears are deaf. I have lost the power of smell. All my senses are paralysed. But, alas, why am I left alone?"

Finally the musicians sang of the union of Rādhā and Krishna:

> Rādhā and Krishna are joined at last in the Nidhu Grove of
>   Vrindāvan;
> Incomparable their beauty, and limitless their love!
> The one half shines like yellow gold, the other like bluest sapphire;
> Round the neck, on one side, a wild-flower garland hangs,
> And, on the other, there swings a necklace of precious gems.
> A ring of gold adorns one ear, a ring of shell the other;
> Half of the brow is bright as the blazing midday sun,
> The other softly gleams with the glow of the rising moon.
> Upon one half of the head a graceful peacock feather stands,
> And, from the other half, there hangs a braid of hair.

As the music came to a close the Master said, "Bhāgavata—Bhakta— Bhagavān", and bowed low to the devotees seated on all sides. He touched with his forehead the ground made holy by the singing of the sacred music.

It was now about half past nine in the evening. Surendra entertained the

Master and the devotees with a sumptuous feast. When it was time to take leave of their host, the Master, the devotees, and Surendra entered the worship hall and stood before the image.

SURENDRA (*to the Master*): "No one has sung anything about the Divine Mother today."

MASTER (*pointing to the image*): "Ah! Look at the beauty of the hall. The light of the Divine Mother seems to have lighted the whole place. Such a sight fills the heart with joy. Grief and desire for pleasure disappear.

"But can one not see God as formless Reality? Of course one can. But not if one has the slightest trace of worldliness. The rishis of olden times renounced everything and then contemplated Satchidānanda, the Indivisible Brahman.

"The Brahmajnānis of modern times[7] sing of God as 'immutable, homogeneous'. It sounds very dry to me. It seems as if the singers themselves don't enjoy the sweetness of God's Bliss. One doesn't want a refreshing drink made with sugar candy if one is satisfied with mere coarse treacle.

"Just see how happy you are, looking at this image of the Deity. But those who always cry after the formless Reality do not get anything. They realize nothing either inside or outside."

The Master sang a song to the Divine Mother:

> O Mother, ever blissful as Thou art,
> Do not deprive Thy worthless child of bliss!
> My mind knows nothing but Thy Lotus Feet.
> The King of Death scowls at me terribly;
> Tell me, Mother, what shall I say to him?
>
> It was my heart's desire to sail my boat
> Across the ocean of this mortal life,
> O Durgā, with Thy name upon my lips.
> I never dreamt that Thou wouldst drown me here
> In the dark waters of this shoreless sea.
>
> Both day and night I swim among its waves,
> Chanting Thy saving name; yet even so
> There is no end, O Mother, to my grief.
> If I am drowned this time, in such a plight,
> No one will ever chant Thy name again.

Again he sang:

> Repeat, O mind, my Mother Durgā's hallowed name!
> Whoever treads the path, repeating "Durgā! Durgā!",
> Śiva Himself protects with His almighty trident.
> Thou art the day, O Mother! Thou art the dusk and the night.
> Sometimes Thou art man, and sometimes woman art Thou.
> Thou mayest even say to me: "Step aside! Go away!"
> Yet I shall cling to Thee, O Durgā! Unto Thy feet
> As Thine anklets I shall cling, making their tinkling sound.

[7] A reference to the members of the Brāhmo Samāj.

Mother, when as the Kite[8] Thou soarest in the sky,
There, in the water beneath, as a minnow I shall be swimming;
Upon me Thou wilt pounce, and pierce me through with Thy claws.
Thus, when the breath of life forsakes me in Thy grip,
Do not deny me the shelter of Thy Lotus Feet!

The Master saluted the divine image. As he came down the steps, he called softly to Rakhal: "Where are my shoes? Are they missing?"

As the Master got into the carriage, Surendra and the other devotees bowed down before him. Then the carriage started for Dakshineswar. The moon still lighted the streets.

[8] According to Hindu mythology the Divine Mother at one time took the form of a bird similar to the kite.

THE MASTER WITH THE BRĀHMO
DEVOTEES (II)

April 22, 1883

S RI RAMAKRISHNA paid a visit to Benimadhav Pal's garden house at Sinthi, near Calcutta, on the occasion of the semi-annual festival of the Brāhmo Samāj. Many devotees of the Samāj were present and sat around the Master. Now and then some of them asked him questions.

A BRĀHMO DEVOTEE: "Sir, what is the way?"

MASTER: "Attachment to God, or, in other words, love for Him. And secondly, prayer."

BRĀHMO DEVOTEE: "Which one is the way—love or prayer?"

MASTER: "First love, and then prayer."

The Master sang:

> Cry to your Mother Śyāmā with a real cry, O mind!
> And how can She hold Herself from you?
> How can Śyāmā stay away? . . .

Continuing, the Master said: "And one must always chant the name and glories of God and pray to Him. An old metal pot must be scrubbed every day. What is the use of cleaning it only once? Further, one must practise discrimination and renunciation; one must be conscious of the unreality of the world."

BRĀHMO: "Is it good to renounce the world?"

MASTER: "Not for all. Those who have not yet come to the end of their enjoyments should not renounce the world. Can one get drunk on two ānnās' worth of wine?"

BRĀHMO: "Then should they lead a worldly life?"

MASTER: "Yes, they should try to perform their duties in a detached way. Before you break the jack-fruit open, rub your hands with oil, so that the sticky milk will not smear them. The maidservant in a rich man's house performs all her duties, but her mind dwells on her home in the country. This is an example of doing duty in a detached way. You should renounce the world only in mind. But a sannyāsi should renounce the world both inwardly and outwardly."

BRĀHMO: "What is the meaning of the 'end of enjoyments'?"

215

MASTER: "I mean the enjoyment of 'woman and gold'. It is risky to put a typhoid patient in a room where pitchers of water and jugs of pickled tamarind are kept. Most people don't feel any longing for God unless they have once passed through the experience of wealth, name, fame, creature comforts, and the like, that is to say, unless they have seen through these enjoyments."

BRĀHMO: "Who is really bad, man or woman?"

MASTER: "As there are women endowed with vidyāśakti, so also there are women with avidyāśakti. A woman endowed with spiritual attributes leads a man to God, but a woman who is the embodiment of delusion makes him forget God and drowns him in the ocean of worldliness.

"This universe is created by the Mahāmāyā[1] of God. Mahāmāyā contains both vidyāmāyā, the illusion of knowledge, and avidyāmāyā, the illusion of ignorance. Through the help of vidyāmāyā one cultivates such virtues as the taste for holy company, knowledge, devotion, love, and renunciation. Avidyāmāyā consists of the five elements and the objects of the five senses—form, flavour, smell, touch, and sound. These make one forget God."

BRĀHMO: "If the power of avidyā is the cause of ignorance, then why has God created it?"

MASTER: "That is His play. The glory of light cannot be appreciated without darkness. Happiness cannot be understood without misery. Knowledge of good is possible because of knowledge of evil.

"Further, the mango grows and ripens on account of the covering skin. You throw away the skin when the mango is fully ripe and ready to be eaten. It is possible for a man to attain gradually to the Knowledge of Brahman because of the covering skin of māyā. Māyā in its aspects of vidyā and avidyā may be likened to the skin of the mango. Both are necessary."

BRĀHMO: "Sir, is it good to worship God with form, an image of the Deity made of clay?"

MASTER: "You do not accept God with form. That is all right. The image is not meant for you. For you it is good to deepen your feeling toward your own Ideal. From the worshippers of the Personal God you should learn their yearning—for instance, Sri Krishna's attraction for Rādhā. You should learn from the worshippers of the Personal God their love for their Chosen Ideal. When the believers in the Personal God worship the images of Kālī and Durgā, with what feeling they cry from the depths of their souls, 'Mother! O Mother!' How much they love the Deity! You should accept that feeling. You don't have to accept the image."

BRĀHMO: "How does one cultivate the spirit of dispassion? Why don't all attain it?"

MASTER: "Dispassion is not possible unless there is satiety through enjoyment. You can easily cajole a small child with candies or toys. But after eating the candies and finishing its play, it cries, 'I want to go to my mother.' Unless you take the child to its mother, it will throw away the toy and scream at the top of its voice."

The members of the Brāhmo Samāj are opposed to the traditional guru

[1] The inscrutable Power of Illusion.

system of orthodox Hinduism. Therefore the Brāhmo devotee asked the Master about it.

BRĀHMO: "Is spiritual knowledge impossible without a guru?"

MASTER: "Satchidānanda alone is the Guru. If a man in the form of a guru awakens spiritual consciousness in you, then know for certain that it is God the Absolute who has assumed that human form for your sake. The guru is like a companion who leads you by the hand. After the realization of God, one loses the distinction between the guru and the disciple. 'That creates a very difficult situation; there the guru and the disciple do not see each other.'[2] It was for this reason that Janaka said to Śukadeva, 'Give me first my teacher's fee if you want me to initiate you into the Knowledge of Brahman.' For the distinction between the teacher and the disciple ceases to exist after the disciple attains to Brahman. The relationship between them remains as long as the disciple does not see God."

It was dusk. Some of the Brāhmo devotees said to the Master, "Perhaps it is time for your evening devotions."

MASTER: "No, it isn't exactly that. One should pass through these disciplines in the beginning. Later one doesn't need the rituals of formal worship or to follow the injunctions."

After dusk the preacher of the Brāhmo Samāj conducted the service from the pulpit. The service was interspersed with recitations from the Upanishads and the singing of Brāhmo songs.

After the service the Master and the preacher conversed.

MASTER: "Well, it seems to me that both the formless Deity and God with form are real. What do you say?"

PREACHER: "Sir, I compare the formless God to the electric current, which is not seen with the eyes but can be felt."

MASTER: "Yes, both are true. God with form is as real as God without form. Do you know what describing God as being formless only is like? It is like a man's playing only a monotone on his flute, though it has seven holes. But on the same instrument another man plays different melodies. Likewise, in how many ways the believers in a Personal God enjoy Him! They enjoy Him through many different attitudes: the serene attitude, the attitude of a servant, a friend, a mother, a husband, or a lover.

"You see, the thing is somehow or other to get into the Lake of the Nectar of Immortality. Suppose one person gets into It by propitiating the Deity with hymns and worship, and you are pushed into It. The result will be the same. Both of you will certainly become immortal.

"I give the Brāhmos the illustration of water and ice. Satchidānanda is like an endless expanse of water. The water of the great ocean in cold regions freezes into blocks of ice. Similarly, through the cooling influence of divine love, Satchidānanda assumes forms for the sake of the bhaktas. The rishis had the vision of the supersensuous Spirit-form and talked with It. But devotees acquire a 'love body', and with its help they see the Spirit-form of the Absolute.

[2] Because the aspirant realizes, at that time, the oneness of existence and hence does not perceive the separate existence of the teacher.

"It is also said in the Vedas that Brahman is beyond mind and words. The heat of the sun of Knowledge melts the ice-like form of the Personal God. On attaining the Knowledge of Brahman and communing with It in nirvikalpa samādhi, one realizes Brahman, the Infinite, without form or shape and beyond mind and words.

"The nature of Brahman cannot be described. About It one remains silent. Who can explain the Infinite in words? However high a bird may soar, there are regions higher still. What do you say?"

PREACHER: "Yes, sir, it is so stated in the Vedānta philosophy."

MASTER: "Once a salt doll went to the ocean to measure its depth. But it could not come back to give a report. According to one school of thought, sages like Śukadeva saw and touched the Ocean of Brahman, but did not plunge into It.

"Once I said to Vidyāsāgar, 'Everything else but Brahman has been polluted, as it were, like food touched by the tongue.' In other words, no one has been able to describe what Brahman is. A thing once uttered by the tongue becomes polluted. Vidyāsāgar, great pundit though he was, was highly pleased with my remarks.

"It is said that there are places near Kedār[3] that are covered with eternal snow; he who climbs too high cannot come back. Those who have tried to find out what there is in the higher regions, or what one feels there, have not come back to tell us about it.

"After having the vision of God man is overpowered with bliss. He becomes silent. Who will speak? Who will explain?

"The king lives beyond seven gates. At each gate sits a man endowed with great power and glory. At each gate the visitor asks, 'Is this the king?' The gate-keeper answers, 'No. Not this, not this.' The visitor passes through the seventh gate and becomes overpowered with joy. He is speechless. This time he doesn't have to ask, 'Is this the king?' The mere sight of him removes all doubts."

PREACHER: "Yes, sir, it is so described in Vedānta."

MASTER: "When the Godhead is thought of as creating, preserving, and destroying, It is known as the Personal God, Saguna Brahman, or the Primal Energy, Ādyāśakti. Again, when It is thought of as beyond the three gunas, then It is called the Attributeless Reality, Nirguna Brahman, beyond speech and thought; this is the Supreme Brahman, Parabrahman.

"Under the spell of God's māyā man forgets his true nature. He forgets that he is heir to the infinite glories of his Father. This divine māyā is made up of three gunas. And all three are robbers; for they rob man of all his treasures and make him forget his true nature. The three gunas are sattva, rajas, and tamas. Of these, sattva alone points the way to God. But even sattva cannot take a man to God.

"Let me tell you a story. Once a rich man was passing through a forest, when three robbers surrounded him and robbed him of all his wealth. After snatching all his possessions from him, one of the robbers said: 'What's the good of keeping the man alive? Kill him.' Saying this, he was about to

[3] A high peak in the Himālayas, which is a place of pilgrimage for the Hindus.

strike their victim with his sword, when the second robber interrupted and said: 'There's no use in killing him. Let us bind him fast and leave him here. Then he won't be able to tell the police.' Accordingly the robbers tied him with a rope, left him, and went away.

"After a while the third robber returned to the rich man and said: 'Ah! You're badly hurt, aren't you? Come, I'm going to release you.' The third robber set the man free and led him out of the forest. When they came near the highway, the robber said, 'Follow this road and you will reach home easily.' 'But you must come with me too', said the man. 'You have done so much for me. We shall all be happy to see you at our home.' 'No,' said the robber, 'it is not possible for me to go there. The police will arrest me.' So saying, he left the rich man after pointing out his way.

"Now, the first robber, who said: 'What's the good of keeping the man alive? Kill him', is tamas. It destroys. The second robber is rajas, which binds a man to the world and entangles him in a variety of activities. Rajas makes him forget God. Sattva alone shows the way to God. It produces virtues like compassion, righteousness, and devotion. Again, sattva is like the last step of the stairs. Next to it is the roof. The Supreme Brahman is man's own abode. One cannot attain the Knowledge of Brahman unless one transcends the three gunas."

PREACHER: "You have given us a fine talk, sir."

MASTER (*with a smile*): "Do you know the nature of devotees? When one devotee meets another, he says, 'Let me speak and you listen; and when you speak I shall listen.' You are a preacher and teach so many people! You are a steamship, and I am a mere fishing-boat." (*All laugh.*)

Wednesday, May 2, 1883

About five o'clock in the afternoon Sri Ramakrishna arrived at the temple of the Brāhmo Samāj in Nandanbāgān, accompanied by M., Rakhal, and a few other devotees. At first the Master sat in the drawing-room on the ground floor, where the Brāhmo devotees gradually assembled. Rabindranath Tagore and a few other members of the Tagore family were present on this occasion.

Sri Ramakrishna was asked to go to the worship hall on the second floor. A dais had been built on the eastern side of the room. There were a few chairs and a piano in the hall. The Brāhmo worship was to begin at dusk.

As soon as the Master entered the worship hall he bowed low before the dais. Having taken his seat, he said to M. and the other devotees, "Narendra once asked me, 'What good is there in bowing before the Brāhmo Samāj temple?' The sight of the temple recalls to my mind God alone; then God-Consciousness is kindled in my mind. God is present where people talk about Him. One feels there the presence of all the holy places. Places of worship recall God alone to my mind.

"Once a devotee was overwhelmed with ecstasy at the sight of a bāblā-tree. The idea flashed in his mind that the handle of the axe used in the garden of the temple of Rādhākānta was made from the wood of the bāblā. Another devotee had such devotion for his guru that he would be overwhelmed with divine feeling at the sight of his guru's neighbours. Krishna-consciousness would be kindled in Rādhā's mind at the sight of a cloud, a blue dress,[4] or a painting of Krishna. She would become restless and cry like a mad person, 'Krishna, where art Thou?' "

GHOSAL: "But madness is not desirable."

MASTER: "What do you mean? Was Rādhā's madness the madness that comes from brooding over worldly objects and makes one unconscious? One attains that madness by meditating on God. Haven't you heard of love-madness and knowledge-madness?"

A BRĀHMO DEVOTEE: "How can one realize God?"

MASTER: "By directing your love to Him and constantly reasoning that God alone is real and the world illusory. The aśwattha tree alone is permanent; its fruit is transitory."

BRĀHMO: "We have passions like anger and lust. What shall we do with these?"

MASTER: "Direct the six passions to God. The impulse of *lust* should be turned into the desire to have intercourse with Ātman. Feel *angry* at those who stand in your way to God. Feel *greedy* for Him. If you must have the feeling of *I and mine*, then associate it with God. Say, for instance, 'My Rāma, my Krishna.' If you must have *pride*, then feel like Bibhishana, who said, 'I have touched the feet of Rāma with my head; I will not bow this head before anyone else.' "

BRĀHMO: "If it is God that makes me do everything, then I am not responsible for my sins."

MASTER (*with a smile*): "Yes, Duryodhana also said that. 'O Krishna, I do what Thou, seated in my heart, makest me do.' If a man has the firm conviction that God alone is the Doer and he is His instrument, then he cannot do anything sinful. He who has learnt to dance correctly never makes a false step. One cannot even believe in the existence of God until one's heart becomes pure."

Sri Ramakrishna looked at the devotees assembled in the worship hall and said: "It is very good to gather in this way, now and then, and think of God and sing His name and glories. But the worldly man's yearning for God is momentary. It lasts as long as a drop of water on a red-hot frying-pan."

The worship was about to begin, and the big hall was filled with Brāhmo devotees. Some of the Brāhmo ladies sat on chairs, with music books in their hands. The songs of the Brāhmo Samāj were sung to the accompaniment of harmonium and piano. Sri Ramakrishna's joy was unbounded. The invocation was followed by a prayer, and then the worship began. The āchāryas, seated on the platform, recited from the Vedas:

> Om. Thou art our Father. Give us right knowledge; do not destroy us! We bow to Thee.

The Brāhmo devotees chanted in chorus with the āchāryas:

> Om. Brahman is Truth, Knowledge, Infinity. It shines as Bliss and

[4] Krishna had a dark-blue complexion.

Immortality. Brahman is Peace, Blessedness, and the One without a Second; It is pure and unstained by sin.

The āchāryas chanted in praise of God:

Om. O Reality, Cause of the Universe, we bow to Thee!

Then the āchāryas chanted their prayer together:

From the unreal lead us to the Real; from darkness lead us to Light; from death lead us to Immortality. Reach us through and through, O Rudra, and protect us evermore with Thy Compassionate Face.

As Sri Ramakrishna heard these hymns, he went into a spiritual mood. After this an āchārya read a paper.

The worship was over. Most of the devotees went downstairs or to the courtyard for fresh air while the refreshments were being made ready. It was about nine o'clock in the evening. The hosts were so engrossed with the other invited guests that they forgot to pay any attention to Sri Ramakrishna.

MASTER (to Rakhal and the other devotees): "What's the matter? Nobody is paying any attention to us!"

RAKHAL (angrily): "Sir, let us leave here and go to Dakshineswar."

MASTER (with a smile): "Keep quiet! The carriage hire is three rupees and two ānnās. Who will pay that? Stubbornness won't get us anywhere. You haven't a penny, and you are making these empty threats! Besides, where shall we find food at this late hour of the night?"

After a long time dinner was announced. The devotees were asked to take their seats. The Master, with Rakhal and the others, followed the crowd to the second floor. No room could be found for him inside the hall. Finally, with great difficulty, a place was found for him in a dusty corner. A brāhmin woman served some curry, but Sri Ramakrishna could not eat it. He ate luchi with salt and took some sweets.

There was no limit to the Master's kindness. The hosts were mere youngsters; how could he be displeased with them, even though they did not show him proper respect? Further, it would have been inauspicious for the household if a holy man had left the place without taking food. Finally, the feast had been prepared in the name of God.

Sri Ramakrishna got into a carriage: but who was to pay the hire? The hosts could not be found. Referring to this incident afterwards, the Master said to the devotees, jokingly: "The boys went to our hosts for the carriage hire. First they were put out, but at last they managed to get together three rupees. Our hosts refused to pay the extra two ānnās and said, 'No, that will do.'"

Sunday, May 13, 1883

The Master paid a visit to the Hari-Bhakti-Pradāyini Sabhā of Kānshāripāra, in Calcutta, on the anniversary day of that religious society.

Kirtan and other forms of devotional music had been arranged for the occasion. The songs centred round the Vrindāvan episode of Sri Krishna's life. The theme was Rādhā's pique because of Sri Krishna's having visited Chandrāvali, another of the gopis of Vrindāvan. Rādhā's friends tried to console her and said to her: "Why are you piqued? It seems you are not thinking of Krishna's happiness, but only of your own." Rādhā said to them: "I am not angry at His going to Chandrāvali's grove. But why should He go there? She doesn't know how to take care of Him."

May 20, 1883

The following Sunday a kirtan was arranged at the house of Ram, one of the Master's householder devotees. Sri Ramakrishna graced the occasion with his presence. The musicians sang about Rādhā's pangs at her separation from Krishna:

> Rādhā said to her friends: "I have loved to see Krishna from my childhood. My finger-nails are worn off from counting the days on them till I shall see Him. Once He gave me a garland. Look, it has withered, but I have not yet thrown it away. Alas! Where has the Moon of Krishna risen now? Has that Moon gone away from my firmament, afraid of the Rāhu[5] of my pique? Alas! Shall I ever see Krishna again? O my beloved Krishna, I have never been able to look at You to my heart's complete satisfaction. I have only one pair of eyes; they blink and so hinder my vision. And further, on account of streams of tears I could not see enough of my Beloved. The peacock feather on the crown of His head shines like arrested lightning. The peacocks, seeing Krishna's dark-cloud complexion, would dance in joy, spreading their tails. O friends, I shall not be able to keep my life-breath. After my death, place my body on a branch of the dark tamāla tree and inscribe on my body Krishna's sweet name."

The Master said: "God and His name are identical; that is the reason Rādhā said that. There is no difference between Rāma and His holy name."

May 27, 1883

Sri Ramakrishna was in his room at Dakshineswar, conversing with the devotees. It was about nine o'clock in the morning.

MASTER (*to M. and the other devotees*): "It is not good to harbour malice. The Śāktas, the Vaishnavas, and the Vedāntists quarrel among themselves. That is not wise. Padmalochan was court pundit of the Mahārājā of Burdwān. Once at a meeting the pundits were discussing whether Śiva was superior to Brahmā, or Brahmā to Śiva. Padmalochan gave an appropriate reply. 'I don't know anything about it', said he. 'I haven't talked either to Śiva or to Brahmā.'

"If people feel sincere longing, they will find that all paths lead to God. But one should have nishthā, single-minded devotion. It is also described as chaste and unswerving devotion to God. It is like a tree with only one trunk shooting straight up. Promiscuous devotion is like a tree with five branches.

[5] A monster in Hindu mythology, said to cause the eclipse by devouring the sun and the moon.

Such was the single-minded devotion of the gopis to Krishna that they didn't care to look at anyone but the Krishna they had seen at Vrindāvan—the Shepherd Krishna, bedecked with a garland of yellow wild-flowers and wearing a peacock feather on His crest. At the sight of Krishna at Mathurā with a turban on His head and dressed in royal robes, the gopis pulled down their veils. They would not look at His face. 'Who is this man?' they said. 'Should we violate our chaste love for Krishna by talking to him?'

"The devotion of the wife to her husband is also an instance of unswerving love. She feeds her brothers-in-law as well, and looks after their comforts, but she has a special relationship with her husband. Likewise, one may have that single-minded devotion to one's own religion; but one should not on that account hate other faiths. On the contrary, one should have a friendly attitude toward them."

The Master bathed in the Ganges and then went to the Kāli temple with M. He sat before the image and offered flowers at the feet of the Divine Mother. Now and then he put flowers on his own head and meditated.

After a long time he stood up. He was in a spiritual mood and danced before the image, chanting the name of Kāli. Now and again he said: "O Mother! O Destroyer of suffering! O Remover of grief and agony!" Was he teaching people thus to pray to the Mother of the Universe with a yearning heart, in order to get rid of the suffering inevitable in physical life?

Sri Ramakrishna returned to his room and sat on the west porch. Rakhal, M., Nakur Vaishnav, and other devotees were with him. Nakur had been known to the Master for about twenty-five years. He was a devotee of Gaurānga and had a small shop which Sri Ramakrishna had often visited when he first came to Calcutta from Kāmārpukur.

Still overpowered with divine ecstasy, the Master sang:

> O Kāli, my Mother full of Bliss! Enchantress of the almighty Śiva!
> In Thy delirious joy Thou dancest, clapping Thy hands together!
> Eternal One! Thou great First Cause, clothed in the form of the
>   Void!
> Thou wearest the moon upon Thy brow.
> Where didst Thou find Thy garland of heads before the universe
>   was made?
>
> Thou art the Mover of all that move, and we are but Thy helpless
>   toys;
> We move alone as Thou movest us and speak as through us Thou
>   speakest.
> But worthless Kamalākānta says, fondly berating Thee:
> Confoundress! With Thy flashing sword
> Thoughtlessly Thou hast put to death my virtue and my sin alike!

He sang again:

> Mother, Thou art our sole Redeemer,
> Thou the Support of the three gunas,
> Higher than the most high.
> Thou art compassionate, I know,
> Who takest away our bitter grief.

Sandhyā art Thou, and Gāyatri;
Thou dost sustain this universe.
Mother, the Help art Thou
Of those that have no help but Thee,
O Eternal Beloved of Śiva!

Thou art in earth, in water Thou;
Thou liest at the root of all.
In me, in every creature,
Thou hast Thy home; though clothed with form,
Yet art Thou formless Reality.

The Master sang a few more songs in praise of the Divine Mother. Then he said to the devotees: "It is not always best to tell householders about the sorrows of life. They want bliss. Those who suffer from chronic poverty can go without food for a day or two. But it is not wise to talk about the sorrows and miseries of life to those who suffer if their food is delayed a few minutes. Vaishnavcharan used to say: 'Why should one constantly dwell on sin? Be merry!' "

While the Master was resting after his midday meal, Manohor Goswami, a singer of kirtan, arrived. He sang about the ecstatic love of Gaurānga and the divine episode of Vrindāvan. The Master was absorbed in a deep spiritual mood. He tore off his shirt and said, to the melody of the kirtan, assuming the attitude of Rādhā: "O Krishna, my Beloved! O friends, bring Krishna to me. Then you will be real friends. Or take me to Him, and I will be your slave for ever."

The musician sat spellbound at Sri Ramakrishna's ecstasy; then he said with folded hands, "Won't you please rid me of my worldliness?"

MASTER: "You are like the holy man who went about the city after first finding a lodging. You are a sweet person and express many sweet ideas."

MUSICIAN: "Sir, I am like the bullock that only carries the bag of sugar but cannot taste it. Alas, I myself do not enjoy the sweetness of divine bliss."

The melodious music went on, and all were filled with joy.

Saturday, June 2, 1883

Sri Ramakrishna had been invited to visit the homes of his devotees Balaram, Adhar, and Ram in Calcutta. Devotional music had been arranged by Adhar and Ram. The Master was accompanied in the carriage by Rakhal, M., and others.

As they drove along, Sri Ramakrishna said to the devotees: "You see, sin flies away when love of God grows in a man's heart, even as the water of the reservoir dug in a meadow dries up under the heat of the sun. But one cannot love God if one feels attracted to worldly things, to 'woman and gold'. Merely taking the vow of monastic life will not help a man if he is attached to the world. It is like swallowing your own spittle after spitting it out on the ground."

After a few minutes the Master continued: "The members of the Brāhmo

Samāj do not accept God with form. Narendra says that God with form is a mere idol. He says further: 'What? He[6] still goes to the Kāli temple!' "

Sri Ramakrishna and his party arrived at Balaram's house. Yajnanath of Nandanbāgān came to invite the Master to his house at four o'clock in the afternoon. Sri Ramakrishna agreed to go if he felt well. After Yajnanath's departure the Master went into an ecstatic mood. He said to the Divine Mother: "Mother, what is all this? Stop! What are these things Thou art showing to me? What is it that Thou dost reveal to me through Rakhal and others? The form is disappearing. But, Mother, what people call 'man' is only a pillow-case, nothing but a pillow-case. Consciousness is Thine alone.

"The modern Brahmajnānis have not tasted Thy sweet bliss. Their eyes look dry and so do their faces. They won't achieve anything without ecstatic love of God.

"Mother, once I asked Thee to give me a companion just like myself. Is that why Thou hast given me Rakhal?"

The Master went to Adhar's house, where arrangements were being made for the kirtan. Many devotees and neighbours had gathered in Adhar's drawing-room, anxious to listen to the Master's words.

MASTER (to the devotees): "Both worldliness and liberation depend on God's will. It is God alone who has kept man in the world in a state of ignorance; and man will be free when God, of His own sweet will, calls him to Himself. It is like the mother calling the child at meal-time, when he is out playing. When the time comes for setting a man free, God makes him seek the company of holy men. Further, it is God who makes him restless for spiritual life."

A NEIGHBOUR: "What kind of restlessness, sir?"

MASTER: "Like the restlessness of a clerk who has lost his job. He makes the round of the offices daily and asks whether there is any vacancy. When that restlessness comes, man longs for God. A fop, seated comfortably with one leg over the other, chewing betel-leaf and twirling his moustaches—a carefree dandy—, cannot attain God."

NEIGHBOUR: "Can one get this longing for God through frequenting the company of holy men?"

MASTER: "Yes, it is possible. But not for a confirmed scoundrel. A sannyāsi's kamandalu, made of bitter gourd, travels with him to the four great places of pilgrimage but still does not lose its bitterness."

The kirtan began. The musician sang of Sri Krishna's life in Vrindāvan:

RĀDHĀ: "Friend, I am about to die. Give me back my Krishna."

FRIEND: "But, Rādhā, the cloud of Krishna was ready to burst into rain. It was yourself who blew it away with the strong wind of your pique. You are certainly not happy to see Krishna happy; or why were you piqued?"

RĀDHĀ: "But this pride was not mine. My pride has gone away with Him who made me proud."

After the music Sri Ramakrishna conversed with the devotees.

[6] Referring to the Master.

MASTER: "The gopis worshipped Kātyāyani in order to be united with Sri Krishna. Everyone is under the authority of the Divine Mother, Mahāmāyā, the Primal Energy. Even the Incarnations of God accept the help of māyā to fulfil their mission on earth. Therefore they worship the Primal Energy. Don't you see how bitterly Rāma wept for Sītā? 'Brahman weeps, ensnared in the meshes of māyā.'

"Vishnu incarnated Himself as a sow in order to kill the demon Hiranyāksha. After killing the demon, the sow remained quite happy with her young ones. Forgetting her real nature, she was suckling them very contentedly. The gods in heaven could not persuade Vishnu to relinquish His sow's body and return to the celestial regions. He was absorbed in the happiness of His beast form. After consulting among themselves, the gods sent Śiva to the sow. Śiva asked the sow, 'Why have you forgotten yourself?' Vishnu replied through the sow's body, 'Why, I am quite happy here.' Thereupon with a stroke of his trident Śiva destroyed the sow's body, and Vishnu went back to heaven."

From Adhar's house Sri Ramakrishna went to Ram's house. Ramchandra Dutta, one of the chief householder disciples of the Master, lived in Calcutta. He had been one of the first to announce the Master as an Incarnation of God. The Master had visited his house a number of times and unstintingly praised the devotion and generosity of this beloved disciple. A few of the Master's disciples made Ram's house virtually their own dwelling-place.

Ram had arranged a special festival to celebrate the Master's visit. The small courtyard was nicely decorated. A kathak, seated on a raised platform, was reciting from the *Bhāgavata* when the Master arrived. Ram greeted him respectfully and seated him near the reader. The disciple was extremely happy. The kathak was in the midst of the story of King Harischandra.

The great King Harischandra of the Purāna was the embodiment of generosity. No one ever went away from him empty-handed. Now, the sage Viśwāmitra, wanting to test the extent of the king's charity, extracted from him a promise to grant any boon that he might ask. Then the sage asked for the gift of the sea-girt world, of which Harischandra was king. Without the slightest hesitation the king gave away his kingdom. Then Viśwāmitra demanded the auxiliary fee, which alone makes charity valid and meritorious.

The kathak continued his recitation:

> Viśwāmitra said to the king: "O King, you have given away the entire world, which was your kingdom. It now belongs to me; you cannot claim any place here. But you may live in Benares, which belongs to Śiva. I shall lead you there with your wife Śaibyā, and Rohitāśva, your son. There you can procure the auxiliary fee that you owe me." The royal family, accompanied by the sage, reached Benares and visited the temple of Śiva.

At the very mention of Śiva, the Master went into spiritual mood and repeated the holy name several times indistinctly.

The kathak continued:

> The king could not procure the fee and was compelled to sell Śaibyā, his royal consort, to a brāhmin. With her went Prince Rohitāśva. But since even that was not enough to redeem his pledge to the sage, Harischandra sold himself to an untouchable who kept a cremation ground. He was ordered to supervise the cremations.
>
> One day, while plucking flowers for his brāhmin master, Prince Rohitāśva was bitten by a venomous snake and that very night died. The cruel brāhmin would not leave his bed to help the poor mother cremate the body. The night was dark and stormy. Lightning rent the black clouds. Śaibyā started for the cremation ground alone, carrying the body of her son in her arms. Smitten with fear and overpowered with grief, the queen filled heaven and earth with her wailing. Arriving at the cremation ground, she did not recognize her husband, who demanded the usual fee for the cremation. Śaibyā was penniless and wept bitterly at her unending misfortunes. The impenetrable darkness was illumined only by the terrible flames of the cremation pyres. Above her the thunder roared, and before her the uncouth guardian of the cremation ground demanded his fee. She who had once been queen of the world sat there with her only child dead and cold on her lap.

The devotees burst into tears and loudly lamented this tragic episode of a royal life. And what was the Master doing? He was listening to the recital with rapt attention. Tear-drops appeared in his eyes and he wiped them away.

The kathak continued:

> When the queen, wailing bitterly, uttered the name of her husband, Harischandra at once recognized his wife and son. Then the two wept for the dead prince. Yet in all these misfortunes the king never once uttered a word of regret for his charity.
>
> Finally the sage Viśwāmitra appeared and told them that he had only wanted to put the king's charitable impulses to a crucial test. Then, through his spiritual power, the sage brought the prince back to life and returned to the king his lost kingdom.

Sri Ramakrishna asked the kathak to recite the episode of Uddhava, the friend and devotee of Krishna.

At the request of Krishna, Uddhava had gone to Vrindāvan to console the cowherds and the gopis, who were sore at heart because of their separation from their beloved Krishna.

The kathak said:

> When Uddhava arrived at Vrindāvan, the gopis and cowherd boys ran to him eagerly and asked him: "How is our Krishna? Has He forgotten us altogether? Doesn't He even speak our names?" So saying, some of them wept. Others accompanied him to various places in Vrindāvan still filled with Krishna's sweet memory. They said: "Here it was that Krishna lifted up Mount Govardhan, and here He killed the demons sent by the evil-minded Kamśa. In this meadow He tended His cows; here on the bank of the Jamunā He sported with the gopis. Here

He played with the cowherd boys, and here in these groves He met the gopis secretly." Uddhava said to them: "Why are you so grief-stricken at Krishna's absence? He resides in all beings as their indwelling Spirit. He is God Himself, and nothing can exist without God." "But", said the gopis, "we do not understand all that. We can neither read nor write. We know only our Krishna of Vrindāvan, who played with us here in so many ways." Uddhava said: "Krishna is God Himself. By meditating on Him, man escapes from birth and death in the world and attains liberation." The gopis said: "We do not understand big words like 'liberation'. We want to see the Krishna of our hearts."

The Master listened to the story from the *Bhāgavata* with great attention and said at last, "Yes, the gopis were right."

Then he sang:

> Though I[7] am never loath to grant salvation,
> I hesitate indeed to grant pure love.
> Whoever wins pure love surpasses all;
> He is adored by men;
> He triumphs over the three worlds.

> Listen, Chandrāvali![8] I shall tell you of love:
> Mukti a man may gain, but rare is bhakti.
> Solely for pure love's sake did I become
> King Vali's door-keeper
> Down in his realm in the nether world.[9]

> Alone in Vrindāvan can pure love be found;
> Its secret none but the gopas and gopis know.
> For pure love's sake I dwelt in Nanda's house;
> Taking him as My father,
> I carried his burdens on My head.

The Master said to the kathak: "The gopis had ecstatic love, unswerving and single-minded devotion to one ideal. Do you know the meaning of devotion that is not loyal to one ideal? It is devotion tinged with intellectual knowledge. It makes one feel: 'Krishna has become all these. He alone is the Supreme Brahman. He is Rāma, Śiva, and Śakti.' But this element of knowledge is not present in ecstatic love of God. Once Hanumān came to Dwārakā and wanted to see Sītā and Rāma. Krishna said to Rukmini, His queen, 'You had better assume the form of Sītā; otherwise there will be no escape from the hands of Hanumān.'[10]

"Once the Pāndava brothers performed the Rājasuya sacrifice. All the kings placed Yudhisthira on the royal throne and bowed low before him in homage. But Bibhishana, the King of Ceylon, said, 'I bow down to Nārāyana and to none else.' At these words the Lord Krishna bowed down to

---

[7] The song represents Sri Krishna's words.

[8] One of the gopis of Vrindāvan.

[9] An allusion to the story of Vali, narrated in the Purāna. He was punished by the Lord for his excessive charity and was condemned to rule over the nether world. But he succeeded in extracting from the Lord the boon that He would be his door-keeper.

[10] Because Rāma and Sītā were Hanumān's Chosen Ideals.

Yudhisthira. Only then did Bibhishana prostrate himself, crown and all, before him.

"Do you know what devotion to one ideal is like? It is like the attitude of a daughter-in-law in the family. She serves all the members of the family—her brothers-in-law, father-in-law, husband, and so forth—, bringing them water to wash their feet, fetching their towels, arranging their seats, and the like; but with her husband she has a special relationship.

"There are two elements in this ecstatic love: 'I-ness' and 'my-ness'. Yaśodā used to think: 'Who would look after Gopāla if I did not? He will fall ill if I do not serve Him.' She did not look on Krishna as God. The other element is 'my-ness'. It means to look on God as one's own—'my Gopāla'. Uddhava said to Yaśodā: 'Mother, your Krishna is God Himself. He is the Lord of the Universe and not a common human being.' 'Oh!' exclaimed Yaśodā. 'I am not asking you about your Lord of the Universe. I want to know how my Gopāla fares. Not the Lord of the Universe, but my Gopāla.'

"How faithful to Krishna the gopis were! After many entreaties to the door-keeper, the gopis entered the royal court in Mathurā, where Krishna was seated as king. The door-keeper took them to Him; but at the sight of King Krishna wearing the royal turban, the gopis bent down their heads and said among themselves: 'Who is this man with a turban on his head? Should we violate our chaste love for Krishna by talking to him? Where is our beloved Krishna with the yellow robe and the bewitching crest with the peacock feather?'

"Did you observe the single-minded love of the gopis for Krishna? The ideal of Vrindāvan is unique. I am told that the people of Dwārakā worship Krishna, the companion of Arjuna, but reject Rādhā."

A DEVOTEE: "Which is the better, ecstatic love or love mixed with knowledge?"

MASTER: "It is not possible to develop ecstatic love of God unless you love Him very deeply and regard Him as your very own.

"Listen to a story. Once three friends were going through a forest, when a tiger suddenly appeared before them. 'Brothers,' one of them exclaimed, 'we are lost!' 'Why should you say that?' said the second friend. 'Why should we be lost? Come, let us pray to God.' The third friend said: 'No. Why should we trouble God about it? Come, let us climb this tree.'

"The friend who said, 'We are lost!' did not know that there is a God who is our Protector. The friend who asked the others to pray to God was a jnāni. He was aware that God is the Creator, Preserver, and Destroyer of the world. The third friend, who didn't want to trouble God with prayers and suggested climbing the tree, had ecstatic love of God. It is the very nature of such love that it makes a man think himself stronger than his Beloved. He is always alert lest his Beloved should suffer. The one desire of his life is to keep his Beloved from even being pricked in the foot by a thorn."

Ram served the Master and the devotees with delicious sweets.

WITH THE DEVOTEES AT
DAKSHINESWAR (I)

ABOUT NINE O'CLOCK in the morning the devotees began to arrive at the temple garden. Sri Ramakrishna was sitting on the porch of his room facing the Ganges. M., who had spent the previous night with the Master, sat near him. Balaram and several other devotees were present. Rakhal lay on the floor, resting his head on the Master's lap. For the past few days the Master had been regarding Rakhal as the Baby Krishna.

Seeing Trailokya[1] passing on his way to the Kāli temple, Sri Ramakrishna asked Rakhal to get up. Trailokya bowed to the Master.

MASTER (*to Trailokya*): "Was there no yātrā performance last night?"[2]

TRAILOKYA: "No, sir. We couldn't conveniently arrange it."

MASTER: "What is done is done. But please see that this doesn't happen again. The traditions of the temple should be properly observed."

Trailokya gave a suitable reply and went on his way. After a while Ram Chatterji, the priest of the Vishnu temple, came up to Sri Ramakrishna.

MASTER: "Well, Ram, I told Trailokya that the yātrā performance should not be omitted again. Was I right in saying that?"

RAM: "What of it, sir? Of course you were right. The traditions should be observed."

The Master asked Balaram to stay for his midday meal. Before the meal Sri Ramakrishna described to the devotees the days of his God-intoxication. Rakhal, M., Ramlal, and a few others were present.

MASTER: "Now and then Hazra comes forward to teach me. He says to me, 'Why do you think so much about the youngsters?' One day, as I was going to Balaram's house in a carriage, I felt greatly troubled about it. I said to the Divine Mother: 'Mother, Hazra admonishes me for worrying about Narendra and the other young boys. He asks me why I forget God and think about these youngsters.' No sooner did this thought arise in my mind

---

[1] The son of Mathur and grandson of Rāni Rasmani. He had become proprietor of the temple in 1871.

[2] A special worship of the Divine Mother had taken place that night in the Kāli temple. On similar occasions in previous years the proprietors of the temple had arranged the performance of the yātrā.

than the Divine Mother revealed to me in a flash that it is She Herself who has become man. But She manifests Herself most clearly through a pure soul. At this vision I went into samādhi. Afterwards I felt angry with Hazra. I said to myself, 'That rascal made me miserable.' Then I thought: 'But why should I blame the poor man? How is he to know?'

"I know these youngsters to be Nārāyana Himself. At my first meeting with Narendra I found him completely indifferent to his body. When I touched his chest with my hand, he lost consciousness of the outer world. Regaining consciousness, Narendra said: 'Oh, what have you done to me? I have my father and mother at home!' The same thing happened at Jadu Mallick's house. As the days passed I longed more and more to see him. My heart yearned for him. One day at that time I said to Bholanath:[3] 'Can you tell me why I should feel this way? There is a boy called Narendra, of the kāyastha caste. Why should I feel so restless for him?' Bholanath said: 'You will find the explanation in the Mahābhārata. On coming down to the plane of ordinary consciousness, a man established in samādhi enjoys himself in the company of sāttvic people. He feels peace of mind at the sight of such men.' When I heard this my mind was set at ease. Now and then I would sit alone and weep for the sight of Narendra.

"Oh, what a state of mind I passed through! When I first had that experience, I could not perceive the coming and going of day or night. People said I was insane. What else could they say? They made me marry. I was then in a state of God-intoxication. At first I felt worried about my wife. Then I thought she too would eat and drink and live like me.

"I visited my father-in-law's house. They arranged a kirtan. It was a great religious festival, and there was much singing of God's holy name. Now and then I would wonder about my future. I would say to the Divine Mother, 'Mother, I shall take my spiritual experiences to be real if the landlords of the country show me respect.' They too came of their own accord and talked with me.

"Oh, what an ecstatic state it was! Even the slightest suggestion would awaken my spiritual consciousness. I worshipped the 'Beautiful' in a girl fourteen years old. I saw that she was the personification of the Divine Mother. At the end of the worship I bowed before her and offered a rupee at her feet. One day I witnessed a Rāmlīlā performance. I saw the performers to be the actual Sītā, Rāma, Lakshmana, Hanumān, and Bibhishana. Then I worshipped the actors and actresses who played those parts.

"At that time I used to invite maidens here and worship them. I found them to be embodiments of the Divine Mother Herself.

"One day I saw a woman in blue standing near the bakul-tree. She was a prostitute. But she instantly kindled in me the vision of Sītā. I forgot the woman. I saw that it was Sītā herself on her way to meet Rāma after her rescue from Rāvana in Ceylon. For a long time I remained in samādhi, unconscious of the outer world.

"Another day I had gone to the Maidān in Calcutta for fresh air. A great crowd had assembled there to watch a balloon ascension. Suddenly I saw an

[3] A clerk at the Dakshineswar temple garden.

English boy leaning against a tree. As he stood there his body was bent in three places. The vision of Krishna came before me in a flash. I went into samādhi.

"Once, at Sihore, I fed the cowherd boys. I put sweetmeats into their hands. I saw that these boys were actually the cowherd boys of Vrindāvan, and I partook of the sweetmeats from their hands.

"At that time I was almost unconscious of the outer world. Mathur Babu kept me at his Jānbāzār mansion a few days. While living there I regarded myself as the handmaid of the Divine Mother. The ladies of the house didn't feel at all bashful with me. They felt as free before me as women feel before a small boy or girl. I used to escort Mathur's daughter to her husband's chamber with the maidservant.

"Even now the slightest thing awakens God-Consciousness in me. Rakhal used to repeat the name of God half aloud. At such times I couldn't control myself. It would rouse my spiritual consciousness and overwhelm me."

Sri Ramakrishna went on describing the different experiences he had had while worshipping the Divine Mother as Her handmaid. He said: "Once I imitated a professional woman singer for a man singer. He said my acting was quite correct and asked me where I had learnt it." The Master repeated his imitation for the devotees, and they burst into laughter.

After his noon meal the Master took a short rest. Manilal Mallick, an old member of the Brāhmo Samāj, entered the room and sat down after saluting the Master, who was still lying on his bed. Manilal asked him questions now and then, and the Master, still half asleep, answered with a word or two. Manilal said that Shivanath admired Nityagopal's spiritual state. The Master asked in a sleepy tone what they thought of Hazra.

Then Sri Ramakrishna sat up on his bed and told Manilal about Bhavanath's devotion to God.

MASTER: "Ah, what an exalted state he is in! He has hardly begun to sing about God before his eyes fill with tears. The very sight of Harish made him ecstatic. He said that Harish was very lucky. He made the remark because Harish was spending a few days here, now and then, away from his home."

Sri Ramakrishna asked M., "Well, what is the cause of bhakti? Why should the spiritual feeling of young boys like Bhavanath be awakened?" M. remained silent.

MASTER: "The fact is, all men may look alike from the outside, but some of them have fillings of 'condensed milk'. Cakes may have fillings of condensed milk or powdered black grams, but they all look alike from the outside. The desire to know God, ecstatic love of Him, and such other spiritual qualities are the 'condensed milk'."

Sri Ramakrishna spoke reassuringly to the devotees.

MASTER (to M.): "Some think: 'Oh, I am a bound soul. I shall never acquire knowledge and devotion.' But if one receives the guru's grace, one has nothing to fear. Once a tigress attacked a flock of goats. As she sprang on her prey, she gave birth to a cub and died. The cub grew up in the company of the goats. The goats ate grass and the cub followed their example.

They bleated; the cub bleated too. Gradually it grew to be a big tiger. One day another tiger attacked the same flock. It was amazed to see the grass-eating tiger. Running after it, the wild tiger at last seized it, whereupon the grass-eating tiger began to bleat. The wild tiger dragged it to the water and said: 'Look at your face in the water. It is just like mine. Here is a little meat. Eat it.' Saying this, it thrust some meat into its mouth. But the grass-eating tiger would not swallow it and began to bleat again. Gradually, however, it got the taste for blood and came to relish the meat. Then the wild tiger said: 'Now you see there is no difference between you and me. Come along and follow me into the forest.'

"So there can be no fear if the guru's grace descends on one. He will let you know who you are and what your real nature is.

"If the devotee practises spiritual discipline a little, the guru explains everything to him. Then the disciple understands for himself what is real and what is unreal. God alone is real, and the world is illusory.

"One night a fisherman went into a garden and cast his net into the lake in order to steal some fish. The owner heard him and surrounded him with his servants. They brought lighted torches and began to search for him. In the mean time the fisherman smeared his body with ashes and sat under a tree, pretending to be a holy man. The owner and his men searched a great deal but could not find the thief. All they saw was a holy man covered with ashes, meditating under a tree. The next day the news spread in the neighbourhood that a great sage was staying in the garden. People gathered there and saluted him with offerings of fruit, flowers, and sweets. Many also offered silver and copper coins. 'How strange!' thought the fisherman. 'I am not a genuine holy man, and still people show such devotion to me. I shall certainly realize God if I become a true sādhu. There is no doubt about it.'

"If a mere pretence of religious life can bring such spiritual awakening, you can imagine the effect of real sādhanā. In that state you will surely realize what is real and what is unreal. God alone is real, and the world is illusory."

One of the devotees said to himself: "Is the world unreal, then? The fisherman, to be sure, renounced worldly life. What, then, will happen to those who live in the world? Must they too renounce it?" Sri Ramakrishna, who could see into a man's innermost thought, said very tenderly: "Suppose an office clerk has been sent to jail. He undoubtedly leads a prisoner's life there. But when he is released from jail, does he cut capers in the street? Not at all. He gets a job as a clerk again and goes on working as before. Even after attaining Knowledge through the guru's grace, one can very well live in the world as a jīvanmukta." Thus did Sri Ramakrishna reassure those who were living as householders.

MANILAL: "Sir, where shall I meditate on God when I perform my daily worship?"

MASTER: "Why, the heart is a splendid place. Meditate on God there."

Manilal, a member of the Brāhmo Samāj, believed in a formless God. Addressing him, the Master said: "Kabir used to say: 'God with form is my Mother, the formless God my Father. Whom should I blame? Whom should

I adore? The two sides of the scales are even.' During the day-time Haladhari used to meditate on God with form, and at night on the formless God. Whichever attitude you adopt, you will certainly realize God if you have firm faith. You may believe in God with form or in God without form, but your faith must be sincere and whole-hearted. Sambhu Mallick used to come on foot from Bāghbāzār to his garden house at Dakshineswar. One day a friend said to him: 'It is risky to walk such a long distance. Why don't you come in a carriage?' At that Sambhu's face turned red and he exclaimed: 'I set out repeating the name of God! What danger can befall me?' Through faith alone one attains everything. I used to say, 'I shall take all this[4] to be true if I meet a certain person or if a certain officer of the temple garden talks to me.' What I would think of would invariably come to pass."

M. had studied English logic. In the chapters on fallacies he had read that only superstitious people believed in the coincidence of morning dreams with actual events. Therefore he asked the Master, "Was there never any exception?"

MASTER: "No. At that time everything happened that way. I would repeat the name of God and believe that a certain thing would happen, and it would invariably come to pass. (To Manilal) But you must remember, unless one is guileless and broad-minded, one cannot have such faith. Bony people, the hollow-eyed, the cross-eyed—people with physical traits like those cannot easily acquire faith. What can a man do if there are evil omens on all sides?"

It was dusk. The maidservant entered the room and burnt incense. Manilal and some other devotees left for Calcutta. M. and Rakhal were in the room. The Master was seated on his small couch absorbed in meditation on the Divine Mother. There was complete silence.

After a time Bhagavati, an old maidservant of the temple proprietor, entered the room and saluted the Master from a distance. Sri Ramakrishna bade her sit down. The Master had known her for many years. In her younger days she had lived a rather immoral life; but the Master's compassion was great. Soon he began to converse with her.

MASTER: "Now you are pretty old. Have you been feeding the Vaishnavas and holy men, and thus spending your money in a noble way?"

BHAGAVATI (smiling): "How can I say that?"[5]

MASTER: "Have you been to Vrindāvan, Benares, and the other holy places?"

BHAGAVATI (shrinkingly): "How can I say that?—I have built a bathing-place, and my name is inscribed there on a slab."

MASTER: "Indeed!"

BHAGAVATI: "Yes, sir. My name, 'Srimati Bhagavati Dasi', is written there."

MASTER (with a smile): "How nice!"

Emboldened by the Master's words, Bhagavati approached and saluted him, touching his feet. Like a man stung by a scorpion, Sri Ramakrishna stood up and cried out, "Govinda! Govinda!" A big jar of Ganges water stood

---

[4] His spiritual experiences.

[5] She meant "yes". In India it is customary not to mention one's meritorious deeds.

in a corner of the room. He hurried there, panting, and washed with the holy water the spot the maidservant had touched. The devotees in the room were amazed to see this incident. Bhagavati sat as if struck dead.

Sri Ramakrishna consoled her and said in a very kindly tone, "You should salute me from a distance." In order to relieve her mind of all embarrassment, the Master said tenderly, "Listen to a few songs."

The Master then sang about the Divine Mother:

> The black bee of my mind is drawn in sheer delight
> To the blue lotus flower of Mother Śyāmā's feet. . . .

Then he sang:

> High in the heaven of the Mother's feet, my mind was soaring like
>   a kite,
> When came a gust of sin's rough wind that drove it swiftly toward
>   the earth. . . .

Again:

> Dwell, O mind, within yourself;
> Enter no other's home.
> If you but seek there, you will find
> All you are searching for.
>
> God, the true Philosopher's Stone,
> Who answers every prayer,
> Lies hidden deep within your heart,
> The richest gem of all.
>
> How many pearls and precious stones
> Are scattered all about
> The outer court that lies before
> The chamber of your heart!

Tuesday, June 5, 1883

Rakhal and Hazra were staying with the Master in the temple garden at Dakshineswar. M., too, had been there since the previous Sunday. As it was a week-day there were only a few devotees in the room. Generally people gathered there in large numbers on Sundays or holidays.

It was afternoon. Sri Ramakrishna was telling the devotees about his experiences during his God-intoxicated state.

MASTER (*to M.*): "Oh, what a state I passed through! At that time I didn't eat my meals here. I would enter the house of a brāhmin in the village or at Barānagore or at Āriādaha. Generally it would be past meal-time. I would just sit down there without saying a word. If the members of the household asked me why I had come, I would simply say, 'I want something to eat.' Now and then I would go, uninvited of course, to Ram Chatterji's house at Ālambāzār or to the Choudhurys at Dakshineswar. But I didn't relish the food at the Choudhurys' house.

"One day I begged Mathur to take me to Devendra Tagore's house. I said: 'Devendra chants the name of God. I want to see him. Will you take me there?' Mathur Babu was a very proud man. How could one expect him to go to another man's house uninvited? At first he hesitated. But then he said: 'All right. Devendra and I were fellow students. I will take you to him.'

"Another day I learnt of a good man named Dina Mukherji, living at Bāghbāzār near the bridge. He was a devotee. I asked Mathur to take me there. Finding me insistent, he took me to Dina's house in a carriage. It was a small place. The arrival of a rich man in a big carriage embarrassed the inmates. We too were embarrassed. That day Dina's son was being invested with the sacred thread. The house was crowded, and there was hardly any place for Dina to receive us. We were about to enter a side room, when someone cried out: 'Please don't go into that room. There are ladies there.' It was really a distressing situation. Returning, Mathur Babu said, 'Father, I shall never listen to you again.' I laughed.

"Oh, what a state I passed through! Once Kumar Singh gave a feast to the sādhus and invited me too. I found a great many holy men assembled there. When I sat down for the meal, several sādhus asked me about myself. At once I felt like leaving them and sitting alone. I wondered why they should bother about all that. The sādhus took their seats. I began to eat before they had started. I heard several of them remark, 'Oh! What sort of man is this?' "

It was about five o'clock in the afternoon. Sri Ramakrishna was sitting on the steps of his verandah. Hazra, Rakhal, and M. were near him. Hazra had the attitude of a Vedāntist: "I am He."

MASTER (to Hazra): "Yes, all one's confusion comes to an end if one only realizes that it is God who manifests Himself as the atheist and the believer, the good and the bad, the real and the unreal; that it is He who is present in waking and in sleep; and that He is beyond all these.

"There was a farmer to whom an only son was born when he was rather advanced in age. As the child grew up, his parents became very fond of him. One day the farmer was out working in the fields, when a neighbour told him that his son was dangerously ill—indeed, at the point of death. Returning home he found the boy dead. His wife wept bitterly, but his own eyes remained dry. Sadly the wife said to her neighbours, 'Such a son has passed away, and he hasn't even one tear to shed!' After a long while the farmer said to his wife: 'Do you know why I am not crying? Last night I dreamt I had become a king, and the father of seven princes. These princes were beautiful as well as virtuous. They grew in stature and acquired wisdom and knowledge in the various arts. Suddenly I woke up. Now I have been wondering whether I should weep for those seven children or this one boy.' To the jnānis the waking state is no more real than the dream state.

"God alone is the Doer. Everything happens by His will."

HAZRA: "But it is very difficult to understand that. Take the case of the sādhu of Bhukailās. How people tortured him and, in a way, killed him! They had found him in samādhi. First they buried him, then they put him under water, and then they branded him with a hot iron. Thus they brought him back to consciousness of the world. But in the end the sādhu died as a result of these tortures. He undoubtedly suffered at the hands of men, though, as you say, he died by the will of God."

MASTER: "Man must reap the fruit of his own karma. But as far as the death of that holy man is concerned, it was brought about by the will of God. The kavirājs prepare makaradhvaja[6] in a bottle. The bottle is covered with clay and heated in the fire. The gold inside the bottle melts and combines with the other ingredients, and the medicine is made. Then the physicians break the bottle carefully and take out the medicine. When the medicine is made, what difference does it make whether the bottle is preserved or broken? So people think that the holy man was killed. But perhaps his inner stuff had been made. After the realization of God, what difference does it make whether the body lives or dies?

"The sādhu of Bhukailās was in samādhi. There are many kinds of samādhi. My own spiritual experiences tally with the words I heard from a sādhu of Hrishikesh. Sometimes I feel the rising of the spiritual current inside me, as though it were the creeping of an ant. Sometimes it feels like the movement of a monkey jumping from one branch to another. Again, sometimes it feels like a fish swimming in water. Only he who experiences it knows what it is like. In samādhi one forgets the world. When the mind comes down a little, I say to the Divine Mother: 'Mother, please cure me of this. I want to talk to people.'

"None but the Iśvarakotis can return to the plane of relative consciousness after attaining samādhi. Some ordinary men attain samādhi through spiritual discipline; but they do not come back. But when God Himself is born as a man, as an Incarnation, holding in His hand the key to others' liberation, then for the welfare of humanity the Incarnation returns from samādhi to consciousness of the world."

M. (to himself): "Does the Master hold in his hand the key to man's liberation?"

HAZRA: "The one thing needful is to please God. What does it matter whether an Incarnation of God exists or not?"

It was the day of the new moon. Gradually night descended and dense darkness enveloped the trees and the temples. A few lights shone here and there in the temple garden. The black sky was reflected in the waters of the Ganges.

The Master went to the verandah south of his room. A spiritual mood was the natural state of his mind. The dark night of the new moon, associated with the black complexion of Kāli, the Divine Mother, intensified his spiritual exaltation. Now and then he repeated "Om" and the name of Kāli. He lay down on a mat and whispered to M.

MASTER: "Yes, God can be seen. X— has had a vision of God. But don't tell anyone about it. Tell me, which do you like better, God with form, or the formless Reality?"

M: "Sir, nowadays I like to think of God without form. But I am also

[6] An Indian medicine made of mercury and sulphur, in the preparation of which gold acts as a catalytic agent.

beginning to understand that it is God alone who manifests Himself through different forms."

MASTER: "Will you take me in a carriage some day to Mati Seal's garden house at Belgharia? When you throw puffed rice into the lake there, the fish come to the surface and eat it. Ah! I feel so happy to see them sport in the water. That will awaken your spiritual consciousness too. You will feel as if the fish of the human soul were playing in the Ocean of Satchidananda. In the same manner, I go into an ecstatic mood when I stand in a big meadow. I feel like a fish released from a bowl into a lake.

"Spiritual discipline is necessary in order to see God. I had to pass through very severe discipline. How many austerities I practised under the bel-tree! I would lie down under it, crying to the Divine Mother, 'O Mother, reveal Thyself to me.' The tears would flow in torrents and soak my body."

M: "You practised so many austerities, but people expect to realize God in a moment! Can a man build a wall simply by moving his finger around his home?"

MASTER (with a smile): "Amrita says that one man lights a fire and ten bask in its heat. I want to tell you something else. It is good to remain on the plane of the Līlā after reaching the Nitya."

M: "You once said that one comes down to the plane of the Līlā in order to enjoy the divine play."

MASTER: "No, not exactly that. The Līlā is real too.

"Let me tell you something. Whenever you come here, bring a trifle with you.[7] Perhaps I shouldn't say it; it may look like egotism. I also told Adhar Sen that he should bring a pennyworth of something with him. I asked Bhavanath to bring a pennyworth of betel-leaf. Have you noticed Bhavanath's devotion? Narendra and he seem like man and woman. He is devoted to Narendra. Bring Narendra here with you in a carriage, and also bring some sweets with you. It will do you good.

"Knowledge and love—both are paths leading to God. Those who follow the path of love have to observe a little more outer purity. But the violation of this by a man following the path of knowledge cannot injure him. It is destroyed in the fire of knowledge. Even a banana tree is burnt up when it is thrown into a roaring fire.

"The jnānis follow the path of discrimination. Sometimes it happens that, discriminating between the Real and the unreal, a man loses his faith in the existence of God. But a devotee who sincerely yearns for God does not give up his meditation even though he is invaded by atheistic ideas. A man whose father and grandfather have been farmers continues his farming even though he doesn't get any crop in a year of drought."

Lying on the mat and resting his head on a pillow, Sri Ramakrishna continued the conversation. He said to M: "My legs are aching. Please stroke them gently." Thus, out of his infinite compassion, the Master allowed his disciple to render him personal service.

[7] The Hindu scriptures command the householder to visit a holy man with suitable presents.

June 8, 1883

It was a summer day. The evening service in the Kāli temple was over. Sri Ramakrishna stood before the image of the Divine Mother and waved the fan a few minutes.

Ram, Kedar Chatterji, and Tarak arrived from Calcutta with flowers and sweets. Kedar was about fifty years old. At first he had frequented the Brāhmo Samāj and joined other religious sects in his search for God, but later on he had accepted the Master as his spiritual guide. He was an accountant in a government office and lived in a suburb of Calcutta.

Tarak was a young man of twenty-four. His wife had died shortly after their marriage. He hailed from the village of Bārāsat not far from Calcutta. His father, a highly spiritual soul, had visited Sri Ramakrishna many times. Tarak often went to Ram's house and used to go to Dakshineswar in the company of Ram and Nityagopal. He worked in a business firm, but his attitude toward the world was one of utter indifference.

As Sri Ramakrishna came out of the temple, he saw Ram, Kedar, M., Tarak, and other devotees standing outside. He showed his affection for Tarak by touching his chin. He was very happy to see him.

Returning to his room, the Master sat on the floor in an ecstatic mood, with his legs stretched before him. Ram and Kedar decorated his feet with flowers and garlands. The Master was in samādhi.

Kedar believed in certain queer practices of a religious sect to which he had once belonged. He held the Master's big toe in his hand, believing that in this way the Master's spiritual power would be transmitted to him. As Sri Ramakrishna regained partial consciousness, he said, "Mother, what can he do to me by holding my toe?" Kedar sat humbly with folded hands. Still in an ecstatic mood, the Master said to Kedar: "Your mind is still attracted by 'woman and gold'. What is the use of saying you don't care for it? Go forward. Beyond the forest of sandal-wood there are many more things: mines of silver, gold, diamonds, and other precious stones. Having a glimpse of spirituality, don't think you have attained everything." The Master was again in an ecstatic mood. He said to the Divine Mother, "Mother, take him away." At these words Kedar's throat dried up. In a frightened tone he said to Ram, "What is the Master saying?"

At the sight of Rakhal, Sri Ramakrishna was again overpowered with a spiritual mood. He said to his beloved disciple: "I have been here many days. When did you come?"

Was the Master hinting that he was an Incarnation of God, and Rakhal his divine companion, a member of the inner circle of devotees?

Sunday, June 10, 1883

The Master was sitting in his room with Rakhal, M., Latu, Kishori, Ramlal, Hazra, and other devotees. It was about ten o'clock in the morning.

Describing his early life, Sri Ramakrishna said to them: "During my younger days the men and women of Kāmārpukur were equally fond of me. They loved to hear me sing. I could imitate other people's gestures and conversation, and I used to entertain them that way. The women would put aside things for me to eat. No one distrusted me. Everybody took me in as one of the family.

"But I was like a happy pigeon. I used to frequent only happy families. I would run away from a place where I saw misery and suffering.

"One or two young boys of the village were my close friends. I was very intimate with some of them; but now they are totally immersed in worldliness. A few of them visit me here now and then and say, 'Goodness! He seems to be just the same as he was in the village school!' While I was at school, arithmetic would throw me into confusion, but I could paint very well and could also model small images of the deities.

"I loved to visit the free eating-places maintained for holy men and the poor, and would watch them for hours.

"I loved to hear the reading of sacred books such as the *Rāmāyana* and *Bhāgavata*. If the readers had any affectations, I could easily imitate them and would entertain others with my mimicry.

"I understood the behaviour of women very well and imitated their words and intonations. I could easily recognize immoral women. Immoral widows part their hair in the middle and perform their toilet with great care. They have very little modesty. The way they sit is so different! But let's not talk of worldly things any more."

The Master asked Ramlal to sing. Ramlal sang:

> Who is this terrible Woman, dark as the sky at midnight?
> Who is this Woman dancing over the field of battle,
> Like a blue lotus that floats on a crimson sea of blood?
> Who is She, clad alone in the Infinite for a garment,
> Rolling Her three great eyes in frenzy and savage fury?
> Under the weight of Her tread the earth itself is trembling!
> Śiva, Her mighty Husband, who wields the fearful trident,
> Lies like a lifeless corpse beneath Her conquering feet.

The next song described the grief of Mandodari at the death of her husband Rāvana. As he listened to it the Master shed tears of sorrow and said: "Once, when I entered the pine-grove over there, I heard the boatmen on the Ganges singing that song and wept bitterly for a long time. I had to be brought back to my room."

Ramlal sang about the love of the gopis for Sri Krishna. Akrura was about to drive Sri Krishna in a chariot from Vrindāvan to Mathurā. The gopis would not let Him go. Some held the wheels of the chariot; some lay down in front of it. They blamed Akrura, not knowing that Sri Krishna was leaving them of His own will. Akrura was explaining this to the gopis.

Ramlal sang:

> Hold not, hold not the chariot's wheels!
> Is it the wheels that make it move?
> The Mover of its wheels is Krishna,
> By whose will the worlds are moved. . . .

About the gopis, the Master said: "What deep love, what ecstatic devotion they had for Krishna! Rādhā painted the picture of Sri Krishna with her own hand, but did not paint His legs lest He should run away to Mathurā! I used to sing these songs very often during my boyhood. I could reproduce the whole drama from memory."

After his meal Sri Ramakrishna sat on the couch. He had not yet found time to rest. The devotees began to assemble. One party arrived from Manirāmpur and another from Belgharīā. Some of the devotees said, "We have disturbed your rest."

MASTER: "Oh, no! What you say applies only to a rājasic man. About him people say, 'Ah, now he will enjoy his sleep.' "

The devotees from Manirāmpur asked the Master how to realize God.

MASTER: "You must practise spiritual discipline a little. It will not do simply to say that milk contains butter. You must let the milk set into curd and then churn it. Only then can you get butter from it. Spiritual aspirants must go into solitude now and then. After acquiring love of God in solitude, they may live in the world. If one is wearing a pair of shoes, one can easily walk over thorns.

"The most important thing is faith.

> As is a man's meditation, so is his feeling of love;
> As is a man's feeling of love, so is his gain;
> And faith is the root of all.

If one has faith one has nothing to fear."

A DEVOTEE: "Sir, is it necessary to have a guru?"

MASTER: "Yes, many need a guru. But a man must have faith in the guru's words. He succeeds in spiritual life by looking on his guru as God Himself. Therefore the Vaishnavas speak of Guru, Krishna, and Vaishnava.[8]

"One should constantly repeat the name of God. The name of God is highly effective in the Kaliyuga. The practice of yoga is not possible in this age, for the life of a man depends on food. Clap your hands while repeating God's name, and the birds of your sin will fly away.

"One should always seek the company of holy men. The nearer you approach the Ganges, the cooler the breeze will feel. Again, the nearer you go to a fire, the hotter the air will feel.

"But one cannot achieve anything through laziness and procrastination. People who desire worldly enjoyment say about spiritual progress: 'Well, it will all happen in time. We shall realize God some time or other.'

"I said to Keshab Sen: 'When a father sees that his son has become restless for his inheritance, he gives him his share of the property even three years before the legal time. A mother keeps on cooking while the baby is in bed sucking its toy. But when it throws the toy away and cries for her, she puts down the rice-pot and takes the baby in her arms and nurses it.' I said all this to Keshab.

"It is said that, in the Kaliyuga, if a man can weep for God one day and one night, he sees Him.

---

[8] The Master meant that the guru, Krishna, and the Vaishnava were to be equally revered. One should honour the Vaishnava because God dwells in his heart.

"Feel piqued at God and say to Him: 'You have created me. Now You must reveal Yourself to me.' Whether you live in the world or elsewhere, always fix your mind on God. The mind soaked in worldliness may be compared to a wet match-stick. You won't get a spark, however much you may rub it. Ekalavya placed the clay image of Drona, his teacher, in front of him and thus learnt archery.[9]

"Go forward. The wood-cutter, following the instructions of the holy man, went forward and found in the forest sandal-wood and mines of silver and gold; and going still farther, he found diamonds and other precious stones.

"The ignorant are like people living in a house with clay walls. There is very little light inside, and they cannot see outside at all. But those who enter the world after attaining the Knowledge of God are like people living in a house made of glass. For them both inside and outside are light. They can see things outside as well as inside.

"Nothing exists except the One. That One is the Supreme Brahman. So long as He keeps the 'I' in us, He reveals to us that it is He who, as the Primal Energy, creates, preserves, and destroys the universe.

"That which is Brahman is also the Primal Energy. Once a king asked a yogi to impart Knowledge to him in one word. The yogi said, 'All right; you will get Knowledge in one word.' After a while a magician came to the king. The king saw the magician moving two of his fingers rapidly and heard him exclaim, 'Behold, O King! Behold.' The king looked at him amazed when, after a few minutes, he saw the two fingers becoming one. The magician moved that one finger rapidly and said, 'Behold, O King! Behold.' The implication of the story is that Brahman and the Primal Energy at first appear to be two. But after attaining the Knowledge of Brahman one does not see the two. Then there is no differentiation; it is One, without a second—Advaita—non-duality."

The Master was very happy to see a musician who had come with the devotees from Belghariā. Some time before, Sri Ramakrishna had gone into an ecstatic mood on hearing his devotional music. At the Master's request the musician sang a few songs, one of which described the awakening of the Kundalini and the six centres:

> Awake, Mother! Awake! How long Thou hast been asleep
> In the lotus of the Mulādhāra!
> Fulfil Thy secret function, Mother:
> Rise to the thousand-petalled lotus within the head,
> Where mighty Śiva has His dwelling;
> Swiftly pierce the six lotuses
> And take away my grief, O Essence of Consciousness!

[9] The story is in the *Mahābhārata*. Drona refused to teach Ekalavya archery because the latter belonged to a low caste. Thereupon Ekalavya went to the forest and practised archery before the clay image of Drona, whom he regarded as his teacher. In course of time he became an expert archer. When Drona discovered that he excelled even Arjuna, Drona's most beloved disciple, in this art, he asked Ekalavya to give him his thumb as the teacher's fee. By carrying out this order, Ekalavya demonstrated his spirit of self-sacrifice and also his love for his teacher.

MASTER: "The song speaks of the Kundalini's passing through the six centres. God is both within and without. From within He creates the various states of mind. After passing through the six centres, the jīva goes beyond the realm of māyā and becomes united with the Supreme Soul. This is the vision of God.

"One cannot see God unless māyā steps aside from the door. Rāma, Lakshmana, and Sītā were walking together. Rāma was in front, Sītā walked in the middle, and Lakshmana followed them. But Lakshmana could not see Rāma because Sītā was between them. In like manner, man cannot see God because māyā is between them. (*To Mani Mallick*) But māyā steps aside from the door when God shows His grace to the devotee. When the visitor stands before the door, the door-keeper says to the master, 'Sir, command us, and we shall let him pass.'

"There are two schools of thought: the Vedānta and the Purāna. According to the Vedānta this world is a 'framework of illusion', that is to say, it is all illusory, like a dream. But according to the Purāna, the books of devotion, God Himself has become the twenty-four cosmic principles. Worship God both within and without.

"As long as God keeps the awareness of 'I' in us, so long do sense-objects exist; and we cannot very well speak of the world as a dream. There is fire in the hearth; therefore the rice and pulse and potatoes and the other vegetables jump about in the pot. They jump about as if to say: 'We are here! We are jumping!' This body is the pot. The mind and intelligence are the water. The objects of the senses are the rice, potatoes, and other vegetables. The 'I-consciousness' identified with the senses says, 'I am jumping about.' And Satchidānanda is the fire.

"Hence the Bhakti scriptures describe this very world as a 'mansion of mirth'. Rāmprasād sang in one of his songs, 'This world is a framework of illusion.' Another devotee gave the reply, 'This very world is a mansion of mirth.' As the saying goes, 'The devotee of Kāli, free while living, is full of Eternal Bliss.' The bhakta sees that He who is God has also become māyā. Again, He Himself has become the universe and all its living beings. The bhakta sees God, māyā, the universe, and the living beings as one. Some devotees see everything as Rāma: it is Rāma alone who has become everything. Some see everything as Rādhā and Krishna. To them it is Krishna alone who has become the twenty-four cosmic principles. It is like seeing everything green through green glasses.

"But the Bhakti scriptures admit that the manifestations of Power are different in different beings. It is Rāma who has become everything, no doubt; but He manifests Himself more in some than in others. There is one kind of manifestation of Rāma in the Incarnation of God, and another in men. Even the Incarnations are conscious of the body. Embodiment is due to māyā. Rāma wept for Sītā. But the Incarnation of God puts a bandage over His eyes by His own will, like children playing blindman's buff. The children stop playing when their mother calls them. It is quite different, however, with the ordinary man. The cloth his eyes are bandaged with is fastened to his back with screws, as it were. There are eight fetters. Shame, hatred, fear, caste, lineage, good conduct, grief, and secretiveness—these are the eight fetters. And they cannot be unfastened without the help of a guru."

A DEVOTEE: "Sir, please bless us."

MASTER: "God is in all beings. But you must apply to the Gas Company. It will connect the storage-tank with the pipe in your house.

"One must pray earnestly. It is said that one can realize God by directing to Him the combined intensity of three attractions, namely, the child's attraction for the mother, the husband's attraction for the chaste wife, and the attraction of worldly possessions for the worldly man.

"There are certain signs by which you can know a true devotee of God. His mind becomes quiet as he listens to his teacher's instruction, just as the poisonous snake is quieted by the music of the charmer. I don't mean the cobra. There is another sign. A real devotee develops the power of assimilating instruction. An image cannot be impressed on bare glass, but only on glass stained with a black solution, as in photography. The black solution is devotion to God. There is a third sign of a true devotee. The true devotee has controlled his senses. He has subdued his lust. The gopis were free from lust.

"You are talking about your leading a householder's life. Suppose you are a householder. It rather helps in the practice of spiritual discipline. It is like fighting from inside a fort. The Tāntriks sometimes use a corpse in their religious rites. Now and then the dead body frightens them by opening its mouth. That is why they keep fried rice and grams near them, and from time to time they throw some of the grains into the corpse's mouth. Thus pacifying the corpse, they repeat the name of the Deity without any worry. Likewise, the householder should pacify his wife and the other members of his family. He should provide them with food and other necessities. Thus he removes the obstacles to his practice of spiritual discipline.

"Those who still have a few worldly experiences to enjoy should lead a householder's life and pray to God. That is why Nityānanda allowed the worldly to enjoy catfish soup and the warm embrace of a young woman while repeating God's name.

"But it is quite different with genuine sannyāsis. A bee lights on flowers and on nothing else. To the chātak all water except rain is tasteless. It will drink no other water, but looks up agape for the rain that falls when the star Svāti is in the ascendant. It drinks only that water. A real sannyāsi will not enjoy any kind of bliss except the Bliss of God. The bee lights only on flowers. The real monk is like a bee, whereas the householder devotee is like a common fly, which lights on a festering sore as well as on a sweetmeat.

"You have taken so much trouble to come here. You must be seeking God. But almost everyone is satisfied simply by seeing the garden. Only one or two look for its owner. People enjoy the beauty of the world; they do not seek its Owner.

(Pointing to the singer) "A little while ago he sang a song describing the six centres. These are dealt with in Yoga. There are two kinds of yoga: hathayoga and rājayoga. The hathayogi practises physical exercises. His goal is to acquire supernatural powers: longevity and the eight psychic powers. These are his aims. But the aim of rājayoga is the attainment of devotion, ecstatic love, knowledge, and renunciation. Of these two, rājayoga is the better.

"There is much similarity between the seven 'planes' described in the Vedānta and the six 'centres' of Yoga. The first three planes of the Vedas may be compared to the first three Yogic centres, namely, Mulādhāra, Svādhisthāna, and Manipura. With ordinary people the mind dwells in these three planes, at the organs of evacuation and generation and at the navel. When the mind ascends to the fourth plane, the centre designated in Yoga as Anāhata, it sees the individual soul as a flame. Besides, it sees light. At this the aspirant cries: 'Ah! What is this? Ah! What is this?'

"When the mind rises to the fifth plane, the aspirant wants to hear only about God. This is the Viśuddha centre of Yoga. The sixth plane and the centre known by the yogi as Ājnā are one and the same. When the mind rises there, the aspirant sees God. But still there is a barrier between God and the devotee. It is like the barrier of glass in a lantern, which keeps one from touching the light. King Janaka used to give instruction about Brahma-jnāna from the fifth plane. Sometimes he dwelt on the fifth plane, and sometimes on the sixth.

"After passing the six centres the aspirant arrives at the seventh plane. Reaching it, the mind merges in Brahman. The individual soul and the Supreme Soul become one. The aspirant goes into samādhi. His conscious-ness of the body disappears. He loses the knowledge of the outer world. He does not see the manifold any more. His reasoning comes to a stop.

"Trailanga Swami once said that because a man reasons he is conscious of multiplicity, of variety. Attaining samādhi, one gives up the body in twenty-one days. Spiritual consciousness is not possible without the awaken-ing of the Kundalini.

"A man who has realized God shows certain characteristics. He becomes like a child or a madman or an inert thing or a ghoul. Further, he is firmly convinced that he is the machine and God is its Operator, that God alone is the Doer and all others are His instruments. As some Śikh devotees once said to me, even the leaf moves because of God's will. One should be aware that everything happens by the will of Rāma. The weaver said: 'The price of the cloth, by the will of Rāma, is one rupee six ānnās. By the will of Rāma the robbery was committed. By the will of Rāma the robbers were arrested. By the will of Rāma I too was arrested by the police. And at last, by the will of Rāma, I was released.'"

It was dusk. Sri Ramakrishna had had no rest since his midday meal. He had talked unceasingly to the devotees about God. At last the visitors took their leave and went home.

Friday, June 15, 1883

It was a holiday on account of the Hindu religious festival Dasaharā. Among the devotees who visited Sri Ramakrishna at Dakshineswar that day were Adhar, M., and Rakhal's father. Rakhal's father's father-in-law was also present. All were seated on the floor of the Master's room.

Rakhal's father's father-in-law was a devotee of God. He asked the Master, "Sir, can one realize God while leading the life of a householder?"

MASTER (*with a smile*): "Why not? Live in the world like a mudfish. The mudfish lives in the mud but itself remains unstained. Or live in the world like a loose woman. She attends to her household duties, but her mind is always on her sweetheart. Do your duties in the world, fixing your mind on God. But this is extremely difficult. I said to the members of the Brāhmo Samāj: 'Suppose a typhoid patient is kept in a room where there are jars of pickles and pitchers of water. How can you expect the patient to recover? The very thought of spiced pickles brings water to one's mouth.' To a man, woman is like that pickle. The craving for worldly things, which is chronic in man, is like the patient's craving for water. There is no end to this craving. The typhoid patient says, 'I shall drink a whole pitcher of water.' The situation is very difficult. There is so much confusion in the world. If you go this way, you are threatened with a shovel; if you go that way, you are threatened with a broomstick; again, in another direction, you are threatened with a shoe-beating. Besides, one cannot think of God unless one lives in solitude. The goldsmith melts gold to make ornaments. But how can he do his work well if he is disturbed again and again? Suppose you are separating rice from bits of husk. You must do it all by yourself. Every now and then you have to take the rice in your hand to see how clean it is. But how can you do your work well if you are called away again and again?"

A DEVOTEE: "What then is the way, sir?"

MASTER: "There *is* a way. One succeeds if one develops a strong spirit of renunciation. Give up at once, with determination, what you know to be unreal. Once, when I was seriously ill, I was taken to the physician Gangaprasad Sen. He said to me: 'I shall give you a medicine, but you mustn't drink any water. You may take pomegranate juice.' Everyone wondered how I could live without water; but I was determined not to drink it. I said to myself: 'I am a paramahamsa and not a goose. I shall drink only milk.'[10]

"You have to spend a few days in solitude. If you but touch the 'granny'[11] you are safe. Turn yourself into gold and then live wherever you please. After realizing God and divine love in solitude, one may live in the world as well. (*To Rakhal's father*) That is why I ask the youngsters to stay with me; for they will develop love of God by staying here a few days. After that they can very well lead the life of a householder."

DEVOTEE: "If God is responsible for everything, then why should people speak of good and evil, virtue and vice? One commits sin also by the will of God, isn't that so?"

ANOTHER DEVOTEE: "How can we understand the will of God?"

MASTER: "There is no doubt that virtue and vice exist in the world; but

---

[10] A paramahamsa is one belonging to the highest order of monks; the word also means "swan". There is a popular tradition in India that a swan can separate the milk from a mixture of milk and water. It is said that a secretion of acid turns the milk into curd, which the swan eats, leaving the water.

[11] An allusion to the game of hide-and-seek. See foot-note 6, p. 136.

God Himself is unattached to them. There may be good and bad smells in the air, but the air is not attached to them. The very nature of God's creation is that good and evil, righteousness and unrighteousness, will always exist in the world. Among the trees in the garden one finds mango and jack-fruit, and hog plum too. Haven't you noticed that even wicked men are needed? Suppose there are rough tenants on an estate; then the landlord must send a ruffian to control them."

The conversation again turned to the life of the householder.

MASTER (*to the devotees*): "You see, by leading a householder's life a man needlessly dissipates his mental powers. The loss he thus incurs can be made up if he takes to monastic life. The first birth is a gift of the father; then comes the second birth, when one is invested with the sacred thread. There is still another birth at the time of being initiated into monastic life. The two obstacles to spiritual life are 'woman' and 'gold'. Attachment to 'woman' diverts one from the way leading to God. Man doesn't know what it is that causes his downfall. Once, while going to the Fort,[12] I couldn't see at all that I was driving down a sloping road; but when the carriage went inside the Fort, I realized how far down I had come. Alas! Women keep men deluded. Captain says, 'My wife is full of wisdom.' The man possessed by a ghost does not realize it. He says, 'Why, I am all right!' "

The devotees listened to these words in deep silence.

MASTER: "It is not lust alone that one should be afraid of in the life of the world. There is also anger. Anger arises when obstacles are placed in the way of desire."

M: "At meal-time, sometimes a cat stretches out its paw to take the fish from my plate. But I cannot show any resentment."

MASTER: "Why? You may even beat it once in a while. What's the harm? A worldly man should hiss, but he shouldn't pour out his venom. He mustn't actually injure others. But he should make a show of anger to protect himself from enemies. Otherwise they will injure him. But a sannyāsi need not even hiss."

A DEVOTEE: "I find it is extremely difficult for a householder to realize God. How few people can lead the life you prescribe for them! I haven't found any."

MASTER: "Why should that be so? I have heard of a deputy magistrate named Pratap Singh. He is a great man. He has many virtues: compassion and devotion to God. He meditates on God. Once he sent for me. Certainly there are people like him.

"The practice of discipline is absolutely necessary. Why shouldn't a man succeed if he practises sādhanā? But he doesn't have to work hard if he has real faith—faith in his guru's words. Once Vyāsa was about to cross the Jamunā, when the gopis also arrived there, wishing to go to the other side. But no ferry-boat was in sight. They said to Vyāsa, 'Revered sir, what shall we do now?' 'Don't worry', said Vyāsa. 'I will take you across. But I am very hungry. Have you anything for me to eat?' The gopis had plenty of milk, cream, and butter with them. Vyāsa ate it all. Then the gopis asked, 'Well,

[12] A reference to the fort in Calcutta.

sir, what about crossing the river?' Vyāsa stood on the bank of the Jamunā and said, 'O Jamunā, if I have not eaten anything today, then may your waters part so that we may all walk to the other side.' No sooner did the sage utter these words than the waters of the Jamunā parted. The gopis were speechless with wonder. 'He ate so much just now,' they said to themselves, 'and he says, "If I have not eaten anything . . ." ! ' Vyāsa had the firm conviction that it was not himself, but the Nārāyana who dwelt in his heart, that had partaken of the food.

"Śankarāchārya was a Brahmajnāni, to be sure. But at the beginning he too had the feeling of differentiation. He didn't have absolute faith that everything in the world is Brahman. One day as he was coming out of the Ganges after his bath, he saw an untouchable, a butcher, carrying a load of meat. Inadvertently the butcher touched his body. Śankara shouted angrily, 'Hey there! How dare you touch me?' 'Revered sir,' said the butcher, 'I have not touched you, nor have you touched me. The Pure Self cannot be the body nor the five elements nor the twenty-four cosmic principles.' Then Śankara came to his senses. Once Jadabharata was carrying King Rahugana's palanquin and at the same time giving a discourse on Self-Knowledge. The king got down from the palanquin and said to Jadabharata, 'Who are you, pray?' The latter answered, 'I am *Not this, not this*—I am the Pure Self.' He had perfect faith that he was the Pure Self.

" 'I am He', 'I am the Pure Self'—that is the conclusion of the jnānis. But the bhaktas say, 'The whole universe is the glory of God.' Who would recognize a wealthy man without his power and riches? But it is quite different when God Himself, gratified by the aspirant's devotion, says to him, 'You are the same as Myself.' Suppose a king is seated in his court, and his cook enters the hall, sits on the throne, and says, 'O King, you and I are the same!' People will certainly call him a madman. But suppose one day the king, pleased with the cook's service, says to him: 'Come, sit beside me. There is nothing wrong in that. There is no difference between you and me.' Then, if the cook sits on the throne with the king, there is no harm in it. It is not good for ordinary people to say, 'I am He'. The waves belong to the water. Does the water belong to the waves?

"The upshot of the whole thing is that, no matter what path you follow, yoga is impossible unless the mind becomes quiet. The mind of a yogi is under his control; he is not under the control of his mind. When the mind is quiet the prāna stops functioning. Then one gets kumbhaka. One may have the same kumbhaka through bhaktiyoga as well: the prāna stops functioning through love of God too. In the kirtan the musician sings, 'Nitāi āmār mātā hāti!'[13] Repeating this, he goes into a spiritual mood and cannot sing the whole sentence. He simply sings, 'Hāti! Hāti!' When the mood deepens he sings only, 'Hā! Hā!' Thus his prāna stops through ecstasy, and kumbhaka follows.

"Suppose a man is sweeping a courtyard with his broom, and another man comes and says to him: 'Hello! So-and-so is no more. He is dead.' Now,

[13] "My Nitāi dances like a mad elephant!"

if the dead person was not related to the sweeper, the latter goes on with his work, remarking casually: 'Ah! That's too bad. He is dead. He was a good fellow.' The sweeping goes on all the same. But if the dead man was his relative, then the broom drops from his hand. 'Ah!' he exclaims, and he too drops to the ground. His prāna has stopped functioning. He can neither work nor think. Haven't you noticed, among women, that if one of them looks at something or listens to something in speechless amazement, the other women say to her, 'What? Are you in ecstasy?' In this instance, too, the prāna has stopped functioning, and so she remains speechless, with mouth agape.

"It will not do merely to repeat, 'I am He, I am He.' There are certain signs of a jnāni. Narendra has big protruding eyes. (*Pointing to a devotee*) He also has good eyes and forehead.

"All men are by no means on the same level. It is said that there are four classes of men: the bound, the struggling, the liberated, and the ever-free. It is also not a fact that all men have to practise spiritual discipline. There are the ever-free and those who achieve perfection through spiritual discipline. Some realize God after much spiritual austerity, and some are perfect from their very birth. Prahlāda is an example of the ever-free.

"Eternally perfect sages like Prahlāda also practise meditation and prayer. But they have realized the *fruit*, God-vision, even before their spiritual practice. They are like gourds and pumpkins, which grow fruit first and then flowers.

(*Looking at Rakhal's father*) "Even though an eternally perfect soul is born in a low family, still he retains his innate perfection. He cannot do anything else. A pea germinating in a heap of cow-dung still grows into a pea-plant.

"God has given to some greater power than to others. In one man you see it as the light of a lamp, in another, as the light of a torch. One word of Vidyāsāgar's revealed to me the utmost limit of his intelligence. When I told him of the different manifestations of God's Power in different beings, he said to me, 'Sir, has God then given greater power to some than to others?' At once I said: 'Yes, certainly He has. If there are not different degrees of manifestation of His Power, then why should your name be known far and wide? You see, we have come to you after hearing of your knowledge and compassion. You haven't grown two horns, have you?' With all his fame and erudition, Vidyāsāgar said such a childish thing as 'Has God given greater power to some than to others?' The truth is that when the fisherman draws his net, he first catches big fish like trout and carp; then he stirs up the mud with his feet, and small fish come out—minnows, mud-fish, and so on. So also, unless a man knows God, 'minnows' and the like gradually come out from within him. What can one achieve through mere scholarship?"

Sunday, June 17, 1883

Sri Ramakrishna was resting in his room in the temple garden at Dakshineswar. It was afternoon. Adhar and M. arrived and saluted the

Master. A Tāntrik devotee also came in. Rakhal, Hazra, and Ramlal were staying with Sri Ramakrishna.

MASTER (*to the devotees*): "Why shouldn't one be able to attain spirituality, living the life of a householder? But it is extremely difficult. Sages like Janaka entered the world after attaining Knowledge. But still the world is a place of terror. Even a detached householder has to be careful. Once Janaka bent down his head at the sight of a bhairavi. He shrank from seeing a woman. The bhairavi said to him: 'Janaka, I see you have not yet attained Knowledge. You still differentiate between man and woman.'

"If you move about in a room filled with soot, you will soil your body, however slightly, no matter how clever you may be. I have seen householder devotees filled with spiritual emotion while performing their daily worship wearing their silk clothes. They maintain that attitude even until they take their refreshments after the worship. But afterwards they become their old selves again. They display their rājasic and tāmasic natures.

"Sattva begets bhakti. Even bhakti has three aspects: sattva, rajas, and tamas. The sattva of bhakti is pure sattva. When a devotee acquires it he doesn't direct his mind to anything but God. He pays only as much attention to his body as is absolutely necessary for its protection.

"But a paramahamsa is beyond the three gunas. Though they exist in him, yet they are practically non-existent. Like a child, he is not under the control of any of the gunas. That is why paramahamsas allow small children to come near them—in order to assume their nature.

"Paramahamsas may not lay things up; but this rule does not apply to householders. They must provide for their families."

TĀNTRIK DEVOTEE: "Is a paramahamsa aware of virtue and vice?"

MASTER: "Keshab Sen also asked that question. I said to him, 'If I explain that to you, then you won't be able to keep your society together.' 'In that case we had better stop here', said Keshab.

"Do you know the significance of virtue and vice? A paramahamsa sees that it is God who gives us evil tendencies as well as good tendencies. Haven't you noticed that there are both sweet and bitter fruits? Some trees give sweet fruit, and some bitter or sour. God has made the mango-tree, which yields sweet fruit, and also the hog plum, which yields sour fruit."

TĀNTRIK: "Yes, sir. That is true. On the hill-top one sees extensive rose gardens, reaching as far as the eye can see."

MASTER: "The paramahamsa realizes that all these—good and bad, virtue and vice, real and unreal—are only the glories of God's māyā. But these are very deep thoughts. One realizing this cannot keep an organization together or anything like that."

TĀNTRIK: "But the law of karma exists, doesn't it?"

MASTER: "That also is true. Good produces good, and bad produces bad. Don't you get the hot taste if you eat chillies? But these are all God's līlā, His play."

TĀNTRIK: "Then what is the way for us? We shall have to reap the result of our past karma, shall we not?"

MASTER: "That may be so. But it is different with the devotees of God. Listen to a song:

> O mind, you do not know how to farm!
> Fallow lies the field of your life.
> If you had only worked it well,
> How rich a harvest you might reap!
> Hedge it about with Kāli's name
> If you would keep your harvest safe;
> This is the stoutest hedge of all,
> For Death himself cannot come near it.
>
> Sooner or later will dawn the day
> When you must forfeit your precious field;
> Gather, O mind, what fruit you may.
> Sow for your seed the holy name
> Of God that your guru has given to you,
> Faithfully watering it with love;
> And if you should find the task too hard,
> Call upon Rāmprasād for help.

He sang again:

> I have securely blocked the way by which the King of Death will
>   come;
> Henceforward all my doubts and fears are set at naught for ever.
> Śiva Himself is standing guard at the nine doorways of my house,[14]
> Which has one Pillar[15] for support, and three ropes[16] to secure it.
> The Lord has made His dwelling-place the thousand-petalled
>   lotus flower
> Within the head, and comforts me with never-ceasing care.

The Master continued: "Anyone who dies in Benares, whether a brāhmin or a prostitute, will become Śiva. When a man sheds tears at the name of Hari, Kāli, or Rāma, then he has no further need of the sandhyā and other rites. All actions drop away of themselves. The fruit of action does not touch him."

Again the Master sang:

> As is a man's meditation, so is his feeling of love;
> As is a man's feeling of love, so is his gain;
> And faith is the root of all.
> If in the Nectar Lake of Mother Kāli's feet
> My mind remains immersed,
> Of little use are worship, oblations, or sacrifice.

He sang another song:

> Why should I go to Gangā or Gayā, to Kāśi, Kānchi, or Prabhās,
> So long as I can breathe my last with Kāli's name upon my
>   lips? . . .

[14] The body with its nine apertures, such as eyes, ears, nose, mouth, etc.
[15] Brahman.
[16] The three gunas.

Then he said, "When a man merges himself in God, he can no longer retain wicked or sinful tendencies."

TĀNTRIK: "You have said rightly that he keeps only the 'Knowledge ego'."

MASTER: "Yes, he keeps only the 'Knowledge ego', the 'devotee ego', the 'servant ego', and the 'good ego'. His 'wicked ego' disappears."

TĀNTRIK: "Today you have destroyed many of our doubts."

MASTER: "All doubts disappear when one realizes the Self.

"Assume the tāmasic aspect of bhakti. Say with force: 'What? I have uttered the names of Rāma and Kāli. How can I be in bondage any more? How can I be affected by the law of karma?'"

The Master sang:

> If only I can pass away repeating Durgā's name,
> How canst Thou then, O Blessed One,
> Withhold from me deliverance,
> Wretched though I may be?
> I may have stolen a drink of wine, or killed a child unborn,
> Or slain a woman or a cow,
> Or even caused a brāhmin's death;
> But, though it all be true,
> Nothing of this can make me feel the least uneasiness;
> For through the power of Thy sweet name
> My wretched soul may still aspire
> Even to Brahmanhood.

The Master continued: "Faith! Faith! Faith! Once a guru said to his pupil, 'Rāma alone has become everything.' When a dog began to eat the pupil's bread, he said to it: 'O Rāma, wait a little. I shall butter Your bread.' Such was his faith in the words of his guru.

"Worthless people do not have any faith. They always doubt. But doubts do not disappear completely till one realizes the Self.

"In genuine love of God there is no desire. Only through such love does one speedily realize God. Attainment of supernatural powers and so on— these are desires. Krishna once said to Arjuna: 'Friend, you cannot realize God if you acquire even one of the eight supernatural powers. They will only add a little to your power.'"

TĀNTRIK: "Sir, why don't the rituals of Tantra bear fruit nowadays?"

MASTER: "It is because people cannot practise them with absolute correctness and devotion."

In conclusion the Master said: "Love of God is the one essential thing. A true lover of God has nothing to fear, nothing to worry about. He is aware that the Divine Mother knows everything. The cat handles the mouse one way, but its own kitten a very different way."

THE FESTIVAL AT PĀNIHĀTI

SRI RAMAKRISHNA had been invited to the great religious festival at Pānihāti, near Calcutta. This "Festival of the Flattened Rice" was inaugurated by Raghunāth Dās, a disciple of Sri Chaitanya. It is said that Raghunāth used to run away from home, secretly practise his devotions, and enjoy the bliss of spiritual ecstasy. One day Nityānanda said to him: "Thief! You run away from home and enjoy the love of God all alone. You hide it from us. I shall punish you today. You must arrange a religious festival and entertain the devotees with flattened rice." Since then the festival has been annually celebrated at Pānihāti by the Vaishnavas. Thousands of the followers of Sri Chaitanya participate in it. Its chief feature is the singing of the names and glories of God, and the dancing of the devotees in religious fervour. The centre of the festivity is the temple of Rādhā-Krishna, built on the bank of the Ganges.

The Master had been invited to the festival by Mani Sen, who was the custodian of the temple. Ram, M., Rakhal, Bhavanath, and a few other disciples went with the Master in a carriage. On his way to Pānihāti Sri Ramakrishna was in a light mood and joked with the youngsters. But as soon as the carriage reached the place of the festival, the Master, to the utter amazement of the devotees, shot into the crowd. He joined the kirtan party of Navadvip Goswami, Mani Sen's guru, and danced, totally forgetting the world. Every now and then he stood still in samādhi, carefully supported by Navadvip Goswami for fear he might fall to the ground. Thousands of devotees were gathered together for the festival. Wherever one looked there was a forest of human heads. The crowd seemed to become infected by the Master's divine fervour and swayed to and fro, chanting the name of God, until the very air seemed to reverberate with it. Drums, cymbals, and other instruments produced melodious sounds. The atmosphere became intense with spiritual fervour. The devotees felt that Gaurānga himself was being manifested in the person of Sri Ramakrishna. Flowers were showered from all sides on his feet and head. The shouting of the name of Hari was heard even at a distance, like the rumbling of the ocean.

Sri Ramakrishna entered by turn into all the moods of ecstasy. In deep samādhi he stood still, his face radiating a divine glow. In the state of partial consciousness he danced, sometimes gently and sometimes with the vigour of a lion. Again, regaining consciousness of the world, he sang, himself leading the chorus:

> Behold, the two brothers[1] have come, who weep while chanting
>   Hari's name,
> The brothers who dance in ecstasy and make the world dance in
>   His name!
> Behold them, weeping themselves, and making the whole world
>   weep as well,
> The brothers who, in return for blows, offer to sinners Hari's love.
> Behold them, drunk with Hari's love, who make the world drunk
>   as well!
> Behold, the two brothers have come, who once were Kānāi and
>   Balāi of Braja,
> They who would steal the butter out of the pots of the gopi maids.
> Behold, the two have come, who shatter all the rules of caste,
> Embracing everyone as brother, even the outcaste shunned by men;
> Who lose themselves in Hari's name, making the whole world mad;
> Who are none other than Hari Himself, and chant His hallowed
>   name!
> Behold them, who saved from their sinful ways the ruffians Jagāi
>   and Mādhāi,[2]
> They who cannot distinguish between a friend and an enemy!
> Behold the two brothers, Gaur and Nitāi, who come again to save
>   mankind.

Again the Master sang:

> See how all Nadiā is shaking
> Under the waves of Gaurānga's love! . . .

The crowd, with the Master in the centre, surged toward the temple of Rādhā-Krishna. Only a small number could enter. The rest stood outside the portal and jostled with one another to have a look at Sri Ramakrishna. In a mood of intoxication he began to dance in the courtyard of the shrine. Every now and then his body stood transfixed in deep samādhi. Hundreds of people around him shouted the name of God, and thousands outside caught the strain and raised the cry with full-throated voices. The echo travelled over the Ganges, striking a note in the hearts of people in the boats on the holy river, and they too chanted the name of God.

When the kirtan was over, Mani Sen took Sri Ramakrishna and Navadvip Goswami into a room and served them with refreshments. Afterwards Ram, M., and the other devotees were also served with the prasād.

In the afternoon, the Master was sitting in Mani Sen's drawing-room with the devotees. Navadvip was also near him. Mani offered the carriage hire to Sri Ramakrishna. Pointing to Ram and the others, the Master said: "Why

---

[1] Gaurānga and Nityānanda.
[2] At one time Nityānanda was beaten by the ruffians Jagāi and Mādhāi, who later were converted to spiritual life by his love.

should they accept it from you? They earn money." He became engaged in conversation with Navadvip.

MASTER: "Bhakti matured becomes bhāva. Next is mahābhāva, then prema, and last of all is the attainment of God. Gaurānga experienced the states of mahābhāva and prema. When prema is awakened, a devotee completely forgets the world; he also forgets his body, which is so dear to a man. Gaurānga experienced prema. He jumped into the ocean, thinking it to be the Jamunā. The ordinary jīva does not experience mahābhāva or prema. He goes only as far as bhāva. But Gaurānga experienced all three states. Isn't that so?"

NAVADVIP: "Yes, sir, that is true. The inmost state, the semi-conscious state, and the conscious state."

MASTER: "In the inmost state he would remain in samādhi, unconscious of the outer world. In the semi-conscious state he could only dance. In the conscious state he chanted the name of God."

Navadvip introduced his son to the Master. The young man was a student of the scriptures. He saluted Sri Ramakrishna.

NAVADVIP: "He studies the scriptures at home. Previously one hardly saw a copy of the Vedas in this country. Max Müller has translated them; so people can now read these books."

MASTER: "Too much study of the scriptures does more harm than good. The important thing is to know the essence of the scriptures. After that, what is the need of books? One should learn the essence and then dive deep in order to realize God.

"The Divine Mother has revealed to me the essence of the Vedānta. It is that Brahman alone is real and the world illusory. The essence of the Gītā is what you get by repeating the word ten times. The word becomes reversed. It is then 'tāgi', which refers to renunciation. The essence of the Gītā is: 'O man, renounce everything and practise spiritual discipline for the realization of God.' "

NAVADVIP: "But how can we persuade our minds to renounce?"

MASTER: "You are a goswāmi. It is your duty to officiate as priest in the temple. You cannot renounce the world; otherwise, who would look after the temple and its services? You have to renounce mentally.

"It is God Himself who has kept you in the world to set an example to men. You may resolve in your mind a thousand times to renounce the world, but you will not succeed. God has given you such a nature that you must perform your worldly duties.

"Krishna said to Arjuna: 'What do you mean, you will not fight? By your mere will you cannot desist from fighting. Your very nature will make you fight.' "

At the mere mention of Krishna and Arjuna the Master went into samādhi. In the twinkling of an eye his body became motionless and his eyeballs transfixed, while his breathing could scarcely be noticed. At this sudden transformation Navadvip and his son and the other devotees looked at the Master in mute wonder.

Regaining partial consciousness, he said to Navadvip: "Yoga and bhoga.

You goswāmis have both. Now your only duty is to call on God and pray to Him sincerely: 'O God, I don't want the glories of Thy world-bewitching māyā. I want Thee alone!' God dwells in all beings, undoubtedly. That being the case, who may be called His devotee? He who dwells in God, he who has merged his mind and life and innermost soul in God."

The Master returned to the sense plane. Referring to his samādhi, he said to Navadvip: "Some say that this state of mine is a disease. I say to them, 'How can one become unconscious by thinking of Him whose Consciousness has made the whole world conscious?' "

Mani Sen said good-bye to the invited brāhmins and Vaishnavas with suitable gifts of money. He offered five rupees to Sri Ramakrishna. The latter said that he could not possibly accept any money. But Mani insisted. The Master then asked him in the name of his guru not to press him. Mani requested him again to accept the offering. Sri Ramakrishna asked M., in a distressed voice, whether he should take the money. The disciple made a vehement protest and said, "No, sir. By no means."

Friends of Mani Sen gave the money to Rakhal, requesting him to buy some mangoes and sweets for the Master. Sri Ramakrishna said to M.: "I have definitely said to Mani that I would not accept the money. I feel free now. But Rakhal has accepted it. His is now the responsibility."

Sri Ramakrishna, accompanied by the devotees, took a carriage to return to Dakshineswar. They were going to pass the temple garden of Mati Seal on the way. For a long time the Master had been asking M. to take him to the reservoir in the garden in order that he might teach him how to meditate on the formless God. There were tame fish in the reservoir. Nobody harmed them. Visitors threw puffed rice and other bits of food into the water, and the big fish came in swarms to eat the food. Fearlessly the fish swam in the water and sported there joyously.

Coming to the reservoir, the Master said to M.: "Look at the fish. Meditating on the formless God is like swimming joyfully like these fish, in the Ocean of Bliss and Consciousness."

Monday, June 25, 1883

Sri Ramakrishna was at Balaram Bose's house in Calcutta. Rakhal and M. were seated near him. The Master was in ecstasy. He conversed with the devotees in an abstracted mood.

MASTER: "Let me assure you that a man can realize his Inner Self through sincere prayer. But to the extent that he has the desire to enjoy worldly objects, his vision of the Self becomes obstructed."

M: "Yes, sir. You always ask us to plunge into God."

MASTER (joyously): "Yes! That's it. Let me tell you that the realization of Self is possible for all, without any exception."

M: "That is true, sir. But God is the Doer. He works through different beings in different ways, according to their capacity to manifest the Divine. God gives to some full spiritual consciousness, and others He keeps in ignorance."

MASTER: "No, that is not so. One should pray to God with a longing heart. God certainly listens to prayer if it is sincere. There is no doubt about it."

A DEVOTEE: "Yes, sir. There is this 'I-consciousness' in us; therefore we must pray."

MASTER (to M.): "A man should reach the Nitya, the Absolute, by following the trail of the Līlā, the Relative. It is like reaching the roof by the stairs. After realizing the Absolute, he should climb down to the Relative and live on that plane in the company of devotees, charging his mind with the love of God. This is my final and most mature opinion.

"God has different forms, and He sports in different ways. He sports as Iśvara, deva, man, and the universe. In every age He descends to earth in human form, as an Incarnation, to teach people love and devotion. There is the instance of Chaitanya. One can taste devotion and love of God only through His Incarnations. Infinite are the ways of God's play, but what I need is love and devotion. I want only the milk. The milk comes through the udder of the cow. The Incarnation is the udder."

Was Sri Ramakrishna hinting that he was an Incarnation of God? Did he suggest that those who saw him saw God? Did he thus speak about himself when speaking of Chaitanya?

It was a hot day in June 1883. Sri Ramakrishna was sitting on the steps of the Śiva temples in the temple garden. M. arrived with ice and other offerings and sat down on the steps after saluting the Master.

MASTER (to M.): "The husband of Mani Mallick's granddaughter was here. He read in a book[3] that God could not be said to be quite wise and omniscient; otherwise, why should there be so much misery in the world? As regards death, it would be much better to kill a man all at once, instead of putting him through slow torture. Further, the author writes that if he himself were the Creator, he would have created a better world."

M. listened to these words in surprise and made no comment.

MASTER (to M.): "Can a man ever understand God's ways? I too think of God sometimes as good and sometimes as bad. He has kept us deluded by His great illusion. Sometimes He wakes us up and sometimes He keeps us unconscious. One moment the ignorance disappears, and the next moment it covers our mind. If you throw a brick-bat into a pond covered with moss, you get a glimpse of the water. But a few moments later the moss comes dancing back and covers the water.

"One is aware of pleasure and pain, birth and death, disease and grief, as long as one is identified with the body. All these belong to the body alone, and not to the Soul. After the death of the body, perhaps God carries one to a better place. It is like the birth of the child after the pain of delivery. Attaining Self-Knowledge, one looks on pleasure and pain, birth and death, as a dream.

"How little we know! Can a one-seer pot hold ten seers of milk? If ever a salt doll ventures into the ocean to measure its depth, it cannot come back and give us the information. It melts into the water and disappears."

[3] The autobiography of John Stuart Mill.

At dusk the evening service began in the different temples. The Master was sitting on the small couch in his room, absorbed in contemplation of the Divine Mother. Several devotees also were there. M. was going to spend the night with the Master.

A little later Sri Ramakrishna began to talk to a devotee privately, on the verandah north of his room. He said: "It is good to meditate in the small hours of the morning and at dawn. One should also meditate daily after dusk." He instructed the devotee about meditation on the Personal God and on the Impersonal Reality.

After a time he sat on the semicircular porch west of his room. It was about nine o'clock.

MASTER: "Those who come here will certainly have all their doubts removed. What do you say?"

M: "That is true, sir."

A boat was moving in the Ganges, far away from the bank. The boatman began to sing. The sound of his voice floating over the river reached the Master's ears, and he went into a spiritual mood. The hair on his body stood on end. He said to M., "Just feel my body." M. was greatly amazed. He thought: "The Upanishads describe Brahman as permeating the universe and the ether. Has that Brahman, as sound, touched the Master's body?"

After a time Sri Ramakrishna began to converse again.

MASTER: "Those who come here must have been born with good tendencies. Isn't that true?"

M: "It is true, sir."

MASTER: "Adhar must have good tendencies."

M: "That goes without saying."

MASTER: "A guileless man easily realizes God. There are two paths: the path of righteousness and the path of wickedness. One should follow the path of righteousness."

M: "That is true, sir. If a thread has a single fibre sticking out, it cannot pass through the eye of a needle."

MASTER: "If a man finds a hair in the food he is chewing, he spits out the entire morsel."

M: "But you say that the man who has realized God cannot be injured by evil company. A blazing fire burns up even a plantain-tree."

Saturday, July 14, 1883

Sri Ramakrishna arrived at Adhar's house in Calcutta. Rakhal, M., and other devotees were with the Master. Adhar had arranged to have Rajnarayan, the famous singer, and his party, recite the *Chandi*.

Rajnarayan began the recital in the worship hall. He sang:

> I have surrendered my soul at the fearless feet of the Mother;
> Am I afraid of Death any more? . . .

As the Master listened, he became filled with divine fervour and joined the musicians. Now and then he improvised an appropriate line. Suddenly he went into samādhi and stood still.

The singer sang again:

> Who is the Woman yonder who lights the field of battle?
> Darker Her body gleams even than the darkest storm-cloud,
> And from Her teeth there flash the lightning's blinding flames!
> Dishevelled Her hair is flying behind as She rushes about,
> Undaunted in this war between the gods and the demons.
> Laughing Her terrible laugh, She slays the fleeing asuras,
> And with Her dazzling flashes She bares the horror of war.
>
> How beautiful on Her brow the drops of moisture appear!
> About Her dense black hair the bees are buzzing in swarms;
> The moon has veiled its face, beholding this Sea of Beauty.
> Tell me, who can She be, this Sorceress? Wonder of wonders!
> Śiva Himself, like a corpse, lies vanquished at Her feet.
> Kamalākānta has guessed who She is, with the elephant's gait;
> She is none other than Kāli, Mother of all the worlds.

Sri Ramakrishna was in deep samādhi.

Saturday, July 21, 1883

It was about four o'clock in the afternoon when Sri Ramakrishna, with Ramlal and one or two other devotees, started from Dakshineswar for Calcutta in a carriage. As the carriage passed the gate of the Kāli temple, they met M. coming on foot with four mangoes in his hand. The carriage stopped and M. saluted the Master. Sri Ramakrishna was going to visit some of his devotees in Calcutta.

MASTER (*to M., with a smile*): "Come with us. We are going to Adhar's house."

M. got joyfully into the carriage. Having received an English education, he did not believe in the tendencies inherited from previous births. But he had admitted a few days before that it was on account of Adhar's good tendencies from past births that he showed such great devotion to the Master. Later on he had thought about this subject and had discovered that he was not yet completely convinced about inherited tendencies. He had come to Dakshineswar that day to discuss the matter with Sri Ramakrishna.

MASTER: "Well, what do you think of Adhar?"

M: "He has great yearning for God."

MASTER: "Adhar, too, speaks very highly of you."

M. remained silent awhile and then began to speak of past tendencies.

M: "I haven't much faith in rebirth and inherited tendencies. Will that in any way injure my devotion to God?"

MASTER: "It is enough to believe that all is possible in God's creation. Never allow the thought to cross your mind that your ideas are the only true ones, and that those of others are false. Then God will explain everything.

"What can a man understand of God's activities? The facets of God's creation are infinite. I do not try to understand God's actions at all. I have heard that everything is possible in God's creation, and I always bear that in mind. Therefore I do not give a thought to the world, but meditate on

God alone. Once Hanumān was asked, 'What day of the lunar month is it?' Hanumān said: 'I don't know anything about the day of the month, the position of the moon and stars, or any such things. I think of Rāma alone.'

"Can one ever understand the work of God? He is so near; still it is not possible for us to know Him. Balarāma did not realize that Krishna was God."

M: "That is true, sir."

MASTER: "God has covered all with His māyā. He doesn't let us know anything. Māyā is 'woman and gold'. He who puts māyā aside to see God, can see Him. Once, when I was explaining God's actions to someone, God suddenly showed me the lake at Kāmārpukur. I saw a man removing the green scum and drinking the water. The water was clear as crystal. God revealed to me that Satchidānanda is covered by the scum of māyā. He who puts the green scum aside can drink the water.

"Let me tell you a very secret experience. Once I had entered the wood near the pine-grove, and was sitting there, when I had a vision of something like the hidden door of a chamber. I couldn't see the inside of the chamber. I tried to bore a hole in the door with a nail-knife, but did not succeed. As I bored, the earth fell back into the hole and filled it. Then suddenly I made a very big opening."

Uttering these words, the Master remained silent. After a time he said: "These are very profound words. I feel as if someone were pressing my mouth. . . . I have seen with my own eyes that God dwells even in the sexual organ. I saw Him once in the sexual intercourse of a dog and a bitch.

"The universe is conscious on account of the Consciousness of God. Sometimes I find that this Consciousness wriggles about, as it were, even in small fish."

The carriage came to the crossing at Shovābāzār in Calcutta. The Master continued, saying, "Sometimes I find that the universe is saturated with the Consciousness of God, as the earth is soaked with water in the rainy season.

"Well, I see so many visions, but I never feel vain about them."

M. (with a smile): "That you should speak of vanity, sir!"

MASTER: "Upon my word, I don't feel vanity even in the slightest degree."

M: "There once lived a man in Greece, Socrates by name. A voice from heaven said that he was wise among men. Socrates was amazed at this revelation. He meditated on it a long time in solitude and then realized its significance. He said to his friends, 'I alone of all people have understood that I do not know anything.' But every man believes he is wise. In reality all are ignorant."

MASTER: "Now and then I think, 'What is it I know that makes so many people come to me?' Vaishnavcharan was a great pundit. He used to say to me: 'I can find in the scriptures all the things you talk about. But do you know why I come to you? I come to hear them from your mouth.'"

M: "All your words tally with the scriptures. Navadvip Goswami also said that the other day at the festival at Pānihāti. You told us that day that by repeating the word 'Gītā' a number of times one reverses it and it becomes 'tāgi', which refers to renunciation. Renunciation is the essence of the

Gītā. Navadvip Goswami supported your statement from the grammatical standpoint."

MASTER: "Have you found anyone else resembling me—any pundit or holy man?"

M: "God has created you with His own hands, whereas He has made others by machine. All others He has created according to law."

MASTER (*laughing, to Ramlal and the other devotees*): "Listen to what he is saying!"

Sri Ramakrishna laughed for some time, and said at last, "Really and truly I have no pride—no, not even the slightest bit."

M: "Knowledge does us good in one respect at least; it makes us feel that we do not know anything, that we are nothing."

MASTER: "Right you are! I am nothing. I am nobody.

"Do you believe in English astronomy?"

M: "It is possible to make new discoveries by applying the laws of Western astronomy. Observing the irregular movement of Uranus, the astronomers looked through their telescopes and discovered Neptune shining in the sky. They can also foretell eclipses."

MASTER: "Yes, that is so."

The carriage drove on. They were approaching Adhar's house. Sri Ramakrishna said to M., "Dwell in the truth and you will certainly realize God."

M: "You said the other day to Navadvip Goswami: 'O God, I want Thee. Please do not delude me with Thy world-bewitching māyā. I want to realize Thee.'"

MASTER: "Yes, one should be able to say that from one's innermost soul."

Sri Ramakrishna arrived at Adhar's house and took a seat in the parlour. Ramlal, Adhar, M., and the other devotees sat near him. Rakhal was staying with his father in Calcutta.

MASTER (*to Adhar*): "Didn't you let Rakhal know that I was coming?"

ADHAR: "Yes, sir. I have sent him word."

Finding that the Master was eager to see Rakhal, Adhar at once sent his carriage to fetch him. Adhar had been yearning to see the Master that day, but he had not definitely known that Sri Ramakrishna was coming.

ADHAR: "You haven't been here for a long time. I prayed to God today that you might come. I even shed tears."

The Master was pleased and said with a smile, "You don't mean that!"

It was dusk and the lamps were lighted. Sri Ramakrishna saluted the Divine Mother with folded hands and sat quietly absorbed in meditation. Then he began to chant the names of God in his sweet voice: "Govinda! Govinda! Satchidānanda! Hari! Hari!" Every word he uttered showered nectar on the ears of the devotees.

Ramlal sang in praise of Kāli, the Divine Mother:

> Thy name, I have heard, O Consort of Śiva, is the destroyer of
> our fear,
> And so on Thee I cast my burden: Save me! Save me, O kindly
> Mother!

Out of Thy womb the world is born, and Thou it is that dost
pervade it.
Art Thou Kāli? Art Thou Rādhā? Who can ever rightly say?

Mother, in every living creature Thou dost have Thy dwelling-
place;
As Kundalini Thou dost live in the lotus of the Mulādhāra.
Above it lies the Svādhisthāna, where the four-petalled lotus
blooms;
There also Thou dost make Thy home, O mystic power of
Kundalini,
In the four petals of that flower, and in Vajrāsana's six petals.
At the navel is Manipura, the blue ten-petalled lotus flower;
Through the pathway of Sushumnā, Thou dost ascend and enter
there.
O Lady of the lotuses, in lotus blossoms Thou dost dwell!

Beyond them lies the Lake of Nectar, in the region of the heart,
Where the twelve-petalled lotus flower enchants the eye with
scarlet flame.
When Thou dost open it, O Mother, touching it with Thy Lotus
Feet,
The age-long darkness of the heart instantly scatters at Thy sight.
Above, in the throat, is the sixteen-petalled lotus flower, of smoky
hue;
Within the petals of this flower there lies concealed a subtle space,
Transcending which, one sees at length the universe in Space
dissolve.
And higher yet, between the eyebrows, blossoms the lotus of two
petals,
Where the mind of man remains a prisoner and past controlling;
From this flower the mind desires to watch the sportive play of life.

Highest of all, within the head, the soul-enthralling centre is,
Where shines the thousand-petalled lotus, Mahādeva's dwelling-
place.
Having ascended to His throne, O Spouse of Śiva, sit beside Him!
Thou art the Primal Power, O Mother! She whose senses are
controlled;
The yogis meditate on Thee as Umā, great Himālaya's daughter.

Thou who art the Power of Śiva! Put to death my ceaseless
cravings;
Grant that I never fall again into the ocean of this world.
Mother, Thou art the Primal Power, Thou the five cosmic prin-
ciples;
Who can ever hope to know Thee, who art beyond all principles?
Only for Thy bhaktas' sake dost Thou assume Thy various forms;
But when Thy devotee's five senses merge in the five elements,
Mother, it is Thyself alone that he beholds as formless Truth.

As Ramlal sang the lines:

Above, in the throat, is the sixteen-petalled lotus flower, of smoky
hue;

Within the petals of this flower there lies concealed a subtle space,
Transcending which, one sees at length the universe in Space
dissolve,

the Master said to M.: "Listen. This is known as the vision of Satchidānanda,
the Formless Brahman. The Kundalini, rising above the Viśuddha chakra,
enables one to see everything as ākāśa."

M: "Yes, sir."

MASTER: "One attains the Absolute by going beyond the universe and its
created beings conjured up by māyā. By passing beyond the Nāda one goes
into samādhi. By repeating 'Om' one goes beyond the Nāda and attains
samādhi."

Adhar served Sri Ramakrishna with fruits and sweets. The Master left for
Jadu Mallick's house.

Sri Ramakrishna entered the room in Jadu's house where the Divine
Mother was worshipped. He stood before the image, which had been decorated with flowers, garlands, and sandal-paste, and which radiated a heavenly
beauty and splendour. Lights were burning before the pedestal. A priest was
seated before the image. The Master asked one of his companions to offer a
rupee in the shrine, according to the Hindu custom.

Sri Ramakrishna stood a long time with folded hands before the blissful
image, the devotees standing behind him. Gradually he went into samādhi,
his body becoming motionless and his eyes fixed.

With a long sigh he came back to the world of the senses and said, still
intoxicated with divine fervour, "Mother, good-bye." But he could not leave
the place. He remained standing there. Addressing Ramlal, he said: "Please
sing that song. Then I shall be all right."

Ramlal sang:

O Mother, Consort of Śiva, Thou hast deluded this world. . . .

The Master went to the drawing-room with the devotees. Every now and
then he said, "O Mother, please dwell in my heart!" Jadu was sitting in the
drawing-room with his friends. The Master sat down, still in an ecstatic
mood, and sang:

O Mother, ever blissful as Thou art,
Do not deprive Thy worthless child of bliss! . . .

Finishing the song, he said to Jadu, still in a state of divine fervour: "Well,
sir, what shall I sing? Shall I sing 'Mother, am I Thine eight-months child'?"
He sang:

Mother, am I Thine eight-months child?[4] Thy red eyes cannot
    frighten me!
My riches are Thy Lotus Feet, which Śiva holds upon His breast;
Yet, when I seek my heritage, I meet with excuses and delays.
A deed of gift I hold in my heart, attested by Thy Husband Śiva;
I shall sue Thee, if I must, and with a single point shall win.

[4] A premature child is generally weak and fearful.

If Thou dost oppose me, Thou wilt learn what sort of mother's
   son I am.
This bitterly contested suit between the Mother and Her son—
What sport it is! says Rāmprasād. I shall not cease tormenting Thee
Till Thou Thyself shalt yield the fight and take me in Thine arms
   at last.

Coming down nearly to a normal state, the Master said, "I shall take some of the Divine Mother's prasād." Then he ate a little of it.

Jadu Mallick was sitting near him with several friends, among whom were a few of his flatterers.

MASTER (with a smile): "Well, why do you keep these buffoons with you?"

JADU (with a smile): "Suppose they are. Won't you redeem them?"

MASTER (smiling): "The water of the Ganges cannot purify a wine-jar."

Jadu had promised the Master that he would arrange a recital of the Chandi in his house. Some time had elapsed, but he had not yet kept his promise.

MASTER: "Well, what about the recital of the Chandi?"

JADU: "I have been busy with many things; I haven't been able to arrange it."

MASTER: "How is that? A man gives his word and doesn't take it back! 'The words of a man are like the tusks of the elephant: they come out but do not go back.' A man must be true to his word. What do you say?"

JADU (with a smile): "You are right."

MASTER: "You are a shrewd man. You do a thing after much calculation. You are like the brāhmin who selects a cow that eats very little, supplies plenty of dung, and gives much milk." (All laugh.)

After a time he said to Jadu: "I now understand your nature. It is half warm and half cold. You are devoted to God and also to the world."

The Master and his devotees were served by Jadu with sweets and fruit, and then the party left for the home of Khelat Ghosh.

Khelat Ghosh's house was a big mansion, but it looked deserted. As the Master entered the house he fell into an ecstatic mood. M., Ramlal, and a few other devotees were with him. Their host was Khelat Ghosh's brother-in-law. He was an old man, a Vaishnava. His body was stamped with the name of God, according to the Vaishnava custom, and he carried in his hand a small bag containing his rosary. He had visited the Master, now and then, at Dakshineswar. But most of the Vaishnavas held narrow religious views; they criticized the Vedāntists and the followers of the Śiva cult. Sri Ramakrishna soon began to speak.

MASTER: "It is not good to feel that one's own religion alone is true and all others are false. God is one only, and not two. Different people call on Him by different names: some as Āllāh, some as God, and others as Krishna, Śiva, and Brahman. It is like the water in a lake. Some drink it at one place and call it 'jal', others at another place and call it 'pāni', and still others at a third place and call it 'water'. The Hindus call it 'jal', the Christians 'water', and the Mussalmāns 'pāni'. But it is one and the same thing. Opinions are but paths. Each religion is only a path leading to God, as rivers come from different directions and ultimately become one in the one ocean.

"The Truth established in the Vedas, the Purānas, and the Tantras is but one Satchidānanda. In the Vedas It is called Brahman, in the Purānas It is called Krishna, Rāma, and so on, and in the Tantras It is called Śiva. The one Satchidānanda is called Brahman, Krishna, and Śiva."

The devotees were silent.

A VAISHNAVA DEVOTEE: "Sir, why should one think of God at all?"

MASTER: "If a man really has that knowledge,[5] then he is indeed liberated though living in a body.

"Not all, by any means, believe in God. They simply talk. The worldly-minded have heard from someone that God exists and that everything happens by His will; but it is not their inner belief.

"Do you know what a worldly man's idea of God is like? It is like the children's swearing by God when they quarrel. They have heard the word while listening to their elderly aunts quarrelling.

"Is it possible for all to comprehend God? God has created the good and the bad, the devoted and the impious, the faithful and the sceptical. The wonders that we see all exist in His creation. In one place there is more manifestation of His Power, in another less. The sun's light is better reflected by water than by earth, and still better by a mirror. Again, there are different levels among the devotees of God: superior, mediocre, and inferior. All this has been described in the Gītā."

VAISHNAVA: "True, sir."

MASTER: "The inferior devotee says, 'God exists, but He is very far off, up there in heaven.' The mediocre devotee says, 'God exists in all beings as life and consciousness.' The superior devotee says: 'It is God Himself who has become everything; whatever I see is only a form of God. It is He alone who has become māyā, the universe, and all living beings. Nothing exists but God.'"

VAISHNAVA: "Does anyone ever attain that state of mind?"

MASTER: "One cannot attain it unless one has seen God. But there are signs that a man has had the vision of God. A man who has seen God sometimes behaves like a madman: he laughs, weeps, dances, and sings. Sometimes he behaves like a child, a child five years old—guileless, generous, without vanity, unattached to anything, not under the control of any of the gunas, always blissful. Sometimes he behaves like a ghoul: he doesn't differentiate between things pure and things impure; he sees no difference between things clean and things unclean. And sometimes he is like an inert thing, staring vacantly: he cannot do any work; he cannot strive for anything."

Was the Master making a veiled reference to his own states of mind?

MASTER (to the Vaishnava devotee): "The feeling of 'Thee and Thine' is the outcome of Knowledge; 'I and mine' comes from ignorance. Knowledge makes one feel: 'O God, Thou art the Doer and I am Thy instrument.

[5] The knowledge that God exists within and without and everywhere. In that case, thinking of God is superfluous.

O God, to Thee belongs all—body, mind, house, family, living beings, and the universe. All these are Thine. Nothing belongs to me.'

"An ignorant person says, 'Oh, God is there—very far off.' The man of Knowledge knows that God is right here, very near, in the heart; that He has assumed all forms and dwells in all hearts as their Inner Controller."

Sunday, July 22, 1883

Taking advantage of the holiday, many householder devotees visited Sri Ramakrishna in his room at the Dakshineswar temple garden. The young devotees, mostly students, generally came on week-days. Sometimes the Master asked his intimate disciples to come on a Tuesday or a Saturday, days that he considered very auspicious for special religious instruction. Adhar, Rakhal, and M. had come from Calcutta in a hired carriage.

Sri Ramakrishna had enjoyed a little rest after his midday meal. The room had an atmosphere of purity and holiness. On the walls hung pictures of gods and goddesses, among them one of Christ rescuing the drowning Peter. Outside the room were plants laden with fragrant flowers, and the Ganges could be seen flowing toward the south. The Master was seated on the small couch, facing the north, and the devotees sat on mats and carpets spread on the floor. All eyes were directed toward him. Mani Mallick, an old Brāhmo devotee about sixty-five years of age, came to pay his respects to the Master. He had returned a few months earlier from a pilgrimage to Benares and was recounting his experiences to Sri Ramakrishna.

MANI MALLICK: "A monk whom I met in Benares said that no religious experience is possible without the control of the sense-organs. Nothing could be achieved by merely crying, 'God! God!' "

MASTER: "Do you understand the views of teachers like him? According to them, one must first practise spiritual discipline: self-restraint, self-control, forbearance, and the like. Their aim is to attain Nirvāna. They are followers of Vedānta. They constantly discriminate, saying, 'Brahman alone is real, and the world illusory.' But this is an extremely difficult path. If the world is illusory, then you too are illusory. The teacher who gives the instruction is equally illusory. His words, too, are as illusory as a dream.

"But this experience is beyond the reach of the ordinary man. Do you know what it is like? If you burn camphor nothing remains. When wood is burnt at least a little ash is left. Finally, after the last analysis, the devotee goes into samādhi. Then he knows nothing whatsoever of 'I', 'you', or the universe.

"Padmalochan was a man of deep wisdom. He had great respect for me, though at that time I constantly repeated the name of the Divine Mother. He was the court pundit of the Mahārājā of Burdwan. Once he came to Calcutta and went to live in a garden house near Kāmārhāti. I felt a desire to see him and sent Hriday there to learn if the pundit had any vanity. I was told that he had none. Then I met him. Though a man of great knowledge and scholarship, he began to weep on hearing me sing Rāmprasād's devotional songs. We talked together a long while; conversation with nobody else gave me such satisfaction. He said to me, 'Give up the desire for the company of devotees; otherwise people of all sorts will come to you and make you deviate from your spiritual ideal.' Once he entered into a controversy, by correspondence, with Utshavānanda, Vaishnavcharan's guru. He told me an interesting incident. Once a meeting was called to decide which of the two deities, Śiva or Brahmā, was the greater. Unable to come to any decision, the pundits at last referred the matter to Padmalochan. With characteristic guilelessness he said: 'How do I know? Neither I nor any of my ancestors back to the fourteenth generation have seen Śiva or Brahmā.' About the renunciation of 'woman and gold', he said to me one day: 'Why have you given up those things? Such distinctions as "This is money and that is clay" are the outcome of ignorance.' What could I say to that? I replied: 'I don't know all these things, my dear sir. But for my part, I cannot relish such things as money and the like.'

"There was a pundit who was tremendously vain. He did not believe in the forms of God. But who can understand the inscrutable ways of the Divine? God revealed Himself to him as the Primal Power. This vision made the pundit unconscious for a long time. After regaining partial consciousness he uttered only the sound 'Kā! Kā! Kā!' He could not fully pronounce 'Kāli'."

A DEVOTEE: "Sir, you met Pundit Vidyāsāgar. What did you think of him?"

MASTER: "Vidyāsāgar has both scholarship and charity, but he lacks inner vision. Gold lies hidden within him. Had he but found it out, his activities would have been reduced; finally they would have stopped altogether. Had he but known that God resides in his heart, his mind would have been directed to God in thought and meditation. Some persons must perform selfless work a long time before they can practise dispassion and direct their minds to the spiritual ideal and at last be absorbed in God.

"The activities that Vidyāsāgar is engaged in are good. Charity is very noble. There is a great deal of difference between dayā, compassion, and māyā, attachment. Dayā is good, but not māyā. Māyā is love for one's relatives—one's wife, children, brother, sister, nephew, father, and mother. But dayā is the same love for all created beings without any distinction."

M: "Is dayā also a bondage?"

MASTER: "Yes, it is. But that concept is something far beyond the ordinary man. Dayā springs from sattva. Sattva preserves, rajas creates, and tamas destroys. But Brahman is beyond the three gunas. It is beyond Prakriti.

"None of the three gunas can reach Truth; they are like robbers, who cannot come to a public place for fear of being arrested. Sattva, rajas, and tamas are like so many robbers.

"Listen to a story. Once a man was going through a forest, when three robbers fell upon him and robbed him of all his possessions. One of the robbers said, 'What's the use of keeping this man alive?' So saying, he was about to kill him with his sword, when the second robber interrupted him, saying: 'Oh, no! What is the use of killing him? Tie him hand and foot and leave him here.' The robbers bound his hands and feet and went away.

After a while the third robber returned and said to the man: 'Ah, I am sorry. Are you hurt? I will release you from your bonds.' After setting the man free, the thief said: 'Come with me. I will take you to the public highway.' After a long time they reached the road. Then the robber said: 'Follow this road. Over there is your house.' At this the man said: 'Sir, you have been very good to me. Come with me to my house.' 'Oh, no!' the robber replied. 'I can't go there. The police will know it.'

"This world itself is the forest. The three robbers prowling here are sattva, rajas, and tamas. It is they that rob a man of the Knowledge of Truth. Tamas wants to destroy him. Rajas binds him to the world. But sattva rescues him from the clutches of rajas and tamas. Under the protection of sattva, man is rescued from anger, passion, and the other evil effects of tamas. Further, sattva loosens the bonds of the world. But sattva also is a robber. It cannot give him the ultimate Knowledge of Truth, though it shows him the road leading to the Supreme Abode of God. Setting him on the path, sattva tells him: 'Look yonder. There is your home.' Even sattva is far away from the Knowledge of Brahman.

"What Brahman is cannot be described. Even he who knows It cannot talk about It. There is a saying that a boat, once reaching the 'black waters' of the ocean, cannot come back.

"Once four friends, in the course of a walk, saw a place enclosed by a wall. The wall was very high. They all became eager to know what was inside. One of them climbed to the top of the wall. What he saw on looking inside made him speechless with wonder. He only cried, 'Ah! Ah!' and dropped in. He could not give any information about what he saw. The others, too, climbed the wall, uttered the same cry, 'Ah! Ah!', and jumped in. Now who could tell what was inside?

"Sages like Jadabharata and Dattātreya, after realizing Brahman, could not describe It. A man's 'I' completely disappears when he goes into samādhi after attaining the Knowledge of Brahman. That is why Rāmprasād sang, addressing his mind:

> If you should find the task too hard,
> Call upon Rāmprasād for help.

The mind must completely merge itself in Knowledge. But that is not enough. 'Rāmprasād', that is, the principle of 'I', must vanish too. Then alone does one get the Knowledge of Brahman."

A DEVOTEE: "Sir, is it possible then that Śukadeva did not have the ultimate Knowledge?"

MASTER: "According to some people, Śukadeva only saw and touched the Ocean of Brahman; he did not dive into It. That is why he could return to the world and impart religious instruction. According to others, he returned to the world of name and form, after attaining the Knowledge of Brahman, for the purpose of teaching others. He had to recite the *Bhāgavata* to King Parikshit and had to teach people in various ways; therefore God did not destroy his 'I' altogether. God kept in him the 'ego of Knowledge'."

DEVOTEE: "Can one keep up an organization after attaining the Knowledge of Brahman?"

MASTER: "Once I talked to Keshab Sen about the Knowledge of Brahman. He asked me to explain it further. I said, 'If I proceed further, then you won't be able to preserve your organization and following.' 'Then please stop here!' replied Keshab. (*All laugh.*) But still I said to Keshab: ' "I" and "mine" indicate ignorance. Without ignorance one cannot have such a feeling as "I am the doer; these are my wife, children, possessions, name and fame".' Thereupon Keshab said, 'Sir, if one gave up the "I", nothing whatsoever would remain.' I reassured him and said: 'I am not asking you to give up all of the "I". You should give up only the "unripe I". The "unripe I" makes one feel: "I am the doer. These are my wife and children. I am a teacher." Renounce this "unripe I" and keep the "ripe I", which will make you feel that you are the servant of God, His devotee, and that God is the Doer and you are His instrument.' "

DEVOTEE: "Can the 'ripe I' form an organization?"

MASTER: "I said to Keshab Sen that the 'I' that says, 'I am a leader, I have formed this party, I am teaching people', is the 'unripe I'. It is very difficult to preach religion. It is not possible to do so without receiving the commandment of God. The permission of God is necessary. Śukadeva had a command from God to recite the *Bhāgavata*. If, after realizing God, a man gets His command and becomes a preacher or teacher, then that preaching or teaching does no harm. His 'I' is not 'unripe'; it is 'ripe'.

"I asked Keshab to give up this 'unripe I'. The ego that feels, 'I am the servant of God and lover of God' does not injure one. I said to him: 'You have been constantly talking of your organization and your followers. But people also go away from your organization.' Keshab answered: 'It is true, sir. After staying in it several years, people go to another organization. What is worse, on deserting me they abuse me right and left.' 'Why don't you study their nature?' I said. 'Is there any good in making anybody and everybody a disciple?'

"I said to Keshab further: 'You should accept the Divine Mother, the Primal Energy. Brahman is not different from Its Śakti. What is Brahman is also Śakti. As long as a man remains conscious of the body, he is conscious of duality. It is only when a man tries to describe what he sees that he finds duality.' Keshab later on recognized Kālī.

"One day when Keshab was here with his disciples, I said to him that I would like to hear him preach. He delivered a lecture in the chāndni. Then we all sat by the bathing-ghat and had a long conversation. I said to him: 'It is Bhagavān alone who in one form appears as bhakta, and in another as the *Bhāgavata*. Please repeat "Bhāgavata—Bhakta—Bhagavān".' Keshab and his disciples repeated the words. Then I asked him to repeat 'Guru—Krishna —Vaishnava'. Thereupon Keshab said: 'Sir, I should not go so far now. People will say that I have become an orthodox Hindu.'

"It is extremely difficult to go beyond the three gunas. One cannot reach that state without having realized God. Man dwells in the realm of māyā. Māyā does not permit him to see God. It has made him a victim of ignorance.

"Once Hriday brought a bull-calf here. I saw, one day, that he had tied it with a rope in the garden, so that it might graze there. I asked him, 'Hriday, why do you tie the calf there every day?' 'Uncle,' he said, 'I am going to send this calf to our village. When it grows strong I shall yoke it to the plough.' As soon as I heard these words I was stunned to think: 'How inscrutable is the play of the divine māyā! Kāmārpukur and Sihore[6] are so far away from Calcutta! This poor calf must go all that way. Then it will grow, and at length it will be yoked to the plough. This is indeed the world! This is indeed māyā!' I fell down unconscious. Only after a long time did I regain consciousness."

It was three or four o'clock in the afternoon. M. found Sri Ramakrishna seated on the couch in an abstracted mood. After some time he heard him talking to the Divine Mother. The Master said, "O Mother, why hast Thou given him only a particle?" Remaining silent a few moments, he added: "I understand it, Mother. That little bit will be enough for him and will serve Thy purpose. That little bit will enable him to teach people."

Did the Master thus transmit spiritual powers to his disciples? Did he thus come to know that his disciples, after him, would go out into the world as teachers of men?

Rakhal was in the room. Sri Ramakrishna was still in a state of partial consciousness when he said to Rakhal: "You were angry with me, weren't you? Do you know why I made you angry? There was a reason. Only then would the medicine work. The surgeon first brings an abscess to a head. Only then does he apply a herb so that it may burst and dry up."

After a pause he went on: "Yes, I have found Hazra to be like a piece of dry wood. Then why does he live here? This has a meaning too. The play is enlivened by the presence of trouble-makers like Jatilā and Kutilā.

(To M.) "One must accept the forms of God. Do you know the meaning of the image of Jagaddhātri? She is the Bearer of the Universe. Without Her support and protection the universe would fall from its place and be destroyed. The Divine Mother, Jagaddhātri, reveals Herself in the heart of one who can control the mind, which may be compared to an elephant."

RAKHAL: "The mind is a mad elephant."

MASTER: "Therefore the lion, the carrier of the Divine Mother, keeps it under control."[7]

It was dusk. The evening service began in the temples. Sri Ramakrishna was chanting the names of the gods and goddesses. He was seated on the small couch, with folded hands, and became absorbed in contemplation of the Divine Mother. The world outside was flooded with moonlight, and the devotees inside the Master's room sat in silence and looked at his serene face.

In the mean time Govinda of Belghariā and some of his friends had entered the room. Sri Ramakrishna was still in a semi-conscious state. After a few

[6] Hriday's birth-place.
[7] In the image of Jagaddhātri, the lion, Her carrier, is seen keeping an elephant under control.

minutes he said to the devotees: "Tell me your doubts. I shall explain everything."

Govinda and the other devotees looked thoughtful.

GOVINDA: "Revered sir, why does the Divine Mother have a black complexion?"[8]

MASTER: "You see Her as black because you are far away from Her. Go near and you will find Her devoid of all colour. The water of a lake appears black from a distance. Go near and take the water in your hand, and you will see that it has no colour at all. Similarly, the sky looks blue from a distance. But look at the atmosphere near you; it has no colour. The nearer you come to God, the more you will realize that He has neither name nor form. If you move away from the Divine Mother, you will find Her blue, like the grass-flower. Is Śyāmā male or female? A man once saw the image of the Divine Mother wearing a sacred thread.[9] He said to the worshipper: 'What? You have put the sacred thread on the Mother's neck!' The worshipper said: 'Brother, I see that you have truly known the Mother. But I have not yet been able to find out whether She is male or female; that is why I have put the sacred thread on Her image.'

"That which is Śyāmā is also Brahman. That which has form, again, is without form. That which has attributes, again, has no attributes. Brahman is Śakti; Śakti is Brahman. They are not two. These are only two aspects, male and female, of the same Reality, Existence-Knowledge-Bliss Absolute."

GOVINDA: "What is the meaning of 'yogamāyā'?"

MASTER: "It signifies the yoga, or union, of Purusha[10] and Prakriti.[11] Whatever you perceive in the universe is the outcome of this union. Take the image of Śiva and Kāli. Kāli stands on the bosom of Śiva; Śiva lies under Her feet like a corpse; Kāli looks at Śiva. All this denotes the union of Purusha and Prakriti. Purusha is inactive; therefore Śiva lies on the ground like a corpse. Prakriti performs all Her activities in conjunction with Purusha. Thus She creates, preserves, and destroys. That is also the meaning of the conjoined images of Rādhā and Krishna. On account of that union, again, the images are slightly inclined toward each other.

"To denote this union, Sri Krishna wears a pearl in His nose, Rādhā a blue stone in hers. Rādhā has a fair complexion, bright as the pearl. Sri Krishna's is blue. For this reason Rādhā wears the blue stone. Further, Krishna's apparel is yellow, and Rādhā's blue.

"Who is the best devotee of God? It is he who sees, after the realization of Brahman, that God alone has become all living beings, the universe, and the twenty-four cosmic principles. One must discriminate at first, saying 'Not this, not this', and reach the roof. After that one realizes that the steps are made of the same materials as the roof, namely, brick, lime, and brick-dust. The devotee realizes that it is Brahman alone that has become all these—the living beings, the universe, and so on.

[8] A reference to the image of Kāli.

[9] The images of male deities only are invested with the sacred thread.

[10] The male aspect of Reality; the Soul, or Absolute.

[11] The female aspect of Reality; Primordial Nature, or Power.

"Mere dry reasoning—I spit on it! I have no use for it! (*The Master spits on the ground.*)

"Why should I make myself dry through mere reasoning? May I have unalloyed love for the Lotus Feet of God as long as the consciousness of 'I' and 'you' remains with me!

(*To Govinda*) "Sometimes I say, 'Thou art verily I, and I am verily Thou.' Again I feel, 'Thou art Thou.' Then I do not find any trace of 'I'. It is Śakti alone that becomes flesh as God Incarnate. According to one school of thought, Rāma and Krishna are but two waves in the Ocean of Absolute Bliss and Consciousness.

"Chaitanya, Consciousness, is awakened after Advaita-jnāna, the Knowledge of the non-dual Brahman. Then one perceives that God alone exists in all beings as Consciousness. After this realization comes Ānanda, Bliss. Advaita, Chaitanya, and Nityānanda.[12]

(*To M.*) "Let me ask you not to disbelieve in the forms of God. Have faith in God's forms. Meditate on that form of God which appeals to your mind.

(*To Govinda*) "The fact is that one does not feel the longing to know or see God as long as one wants to enjoy worldly objects. The child forgets everything when he plays with his toys. Try to cajole him away from play with a sweetmeat; you will not succeed. He will eat only a bit of it. When he relishes neither the sweetmeat nor his play, then he says, 'I want to go to my mother.' He doesn't care for the sweetmeat any more. If a man whom he doesn't know and has never seen says to the child, 'Come along; I shall take you to your mother', the child follows him. The child will go with anyone who will carry him to his mother.

"The soul becomes restless for God when one is through with the enjoyment of worldly things. Then a person has only one thought—how to realize God. He listens to whatever anyone says to him about God."

M. (*to himself*): "Alas! The soul becomes restless for God only when one is through with the enjoyment of worldly things."

August 18, 1883

Sri Ramakrishna was at Balaram Bose's house in Calcutta. He was explaining the mystery of Divine Incarnation to the devotees.

MASTER: "In order to bring people spiritual knowledge, an Incarnation of God lives in the world in the company of devotees, cherishing an attitude of love for God. It is like going up and coming down the stairs after having once reached the roof. In order to reach the roof, other people should follow the path of devotion, as long as they have not attained Knowledge and become free of desire. The roof can be reached only when all desires are done away with. The shopkeeper does not go to bed before finishing his accounts. He goes to sleep only when his accounts are finished.

(*To M.*) "A man will certainly succeed if he will take the plunge. Success is sure for such a man.

[12] Non-duality, Consciousness, and Eternal Bliss.

"Well, what do you think of the worship conducted by Keshab, Shivanath, and the other Brāhmo leaders?"

M: "They are satisfied, as you say, with describing the garden, but they seldom speak of seeing the Master of the garden. Describing the garden is the beginning and end of their worship."

MASTER: "You are right. Our only duty is to seek the Master of the garden and speak to Him. The only purpose of life is to realize God."

Sri Ramakrishna then went to Adhar's house. After dusk he sang and danced in Adhar's drawing-room. M., Rakhal, and other devotees were present. After the music he sat down, still in an ecstatic mood. He said to Rakhal: "This religious fervour[13] is not like rain in the rainy season, which comes in torrents and goes in torrents. It is like an image of Śiva that has not been set up by human hands but is a natural one that has sprung up, as it were, from the bowels of the earth. The other day you left Dakshineswar in a temper. I prayed to the Divine Mother to forgive you."

The Master was still in an abstracted mood and said to Adhar, "My son, meditate on the Deity whose name you chanted." With these words he touched Adhar's tongue with his finger and wrote something on it. Did the Master thereby impart spirituality to Adhar?

[13] Referring to himself.

THE MASTER AND M.

IT WAS SUNDAY, the first day after the full moon. Sri Ramakrishna was resting after his noon meal. The midday offering had been made in the temples, and the temple doors were closed.

In the early afternoon the Master sat up on the small couch in his room. M. prostrated himself before him and sat on the floor. The Master was talking to him on the philosophy of Vedānta.

MASTER (*to M.*): "Self-Knowledge is discussed in the *Ashtāvakra Samhitā*. The non-dualists say, 'Soham', that is, 'I am the Supreme Self.' This is the view of the sannyāsis of the Vedāntic school. But this is not the right attitude for householders, who are conscious of doing everything themselves. That being so, how can they declare, 'I am That, the actionless Supreme Self'? According to the non-dualists the Self is unattached. Good and bad, virtue and vice, and the other pairs of opposites, cannot in any way injure the Self, though they undoubtedly afflict those who have identified themselves with their bodies. Smoke soils the wall, certainly, but it cannot in any way affect ākāśa, space. Following the Vedāntists of this class, Krishnakishore used to say, 'I am Kha', meaning ākāśa. Being a great devotee, he could say that with some justification; but it is not becoming for others to do so.

"But to feel that one is a free soul is very good. By constantly repeating, 'I am free, I am free', a man verily becomes free. On the other hand, by constantly repeating, 'I am bound, I am bound', he certainly becomes bound to worldliness. The fool who says only, 'I am a sinner, I am a sinner', verily drowns himself in worldliness. One should rather say: 'I have chanted the name of God. How can I be a sinner? How can I be bound?'

(*To M.*) "You see, I am very much depressed today. Hriday has written me that he is very ill. Why should I feel dejected about it? Is it because of māyā or dayā?"

M. could not find suitable words for a reply, and remained silent.

MASTER: "Do you know what māyā is? It is attachment to relatives—parents, brother and sister, wife and children, nephew and niece. Dayā means love for all created beings. Now what is this, my feeling about Hriday? Is it māyā or dayā? But Hriday did so much for me: he served me

274

had almost stopped. With unwinking eyes he sat motionless as a picture on a canvas. His mind had dived deep into the Ocean of God's Beauty.

Narendra left the room and went to the east verandah, where Hazra was seated on a blanket, with a rosary in his hand. They fell to talking. Other devotees arrived. The Master came down from samādhi and looked around. He could not find Narendra. The tānpurā was lying on the floor. He noticed that the earnest eyes of the devotees were riveted on him.

MASTER (referring to Narendra): "He has lighted the fire. Now it doesn't matter whether he stays in the room or goes out.

(To Captain and the other devotees) "Attribute to yourselves the bliss of God-Consciousness; then you too will experience ineffable joy. The bliss of God-Consciousness always exists in you. It is only hidden by the veiling and projecting power of māyā.[2] The less you are attached to the world, the more you love God."

CAPTAIN: "The farther you proceed toward your home in Calcutta, the farther you leave Benares behind. Again, the farther you proceed toward Benares, the farther behind you leave your home."

MASTER: "As Rādhā advanced toward Krishna, she could smell more and more of the sweet fragrance of His body. The nearer you approach to God, the more you feel His love. As the river approaches the ocean it increasingly feels the flow of the tides.

"The jnāni experiences God-Consciousness within himself; it is like the upper Ganges, flowing in only one direction. To him the whole universe is illusory, like a dream; he is always established in the Reality of Self. But with the lover of God the case is different. His feeling does not flow in only one direction. He feels both the ebb-tide and the flood-tide of divine emotion. He laughs and weeps and dances and sings in the ecstasy of God. The lover of God likes to sport with Him. In the Ocean of God-Consciousness he sometimes swims, sometimes goes down, and sometimes rises to the surface—like pieces of ice in the water. (Laughter.)

"The jnāni seeks to realize Brahman. But the ideal of the bhakta is the Personal God—a God endowed with omnipotence and with the six treasures. Yet Brahman and Śakti are, in fact, not different. That which is the Blissful Mother is, again, Existence-Knowledge-Bliss Absolute. They are like the gem and its lustre. When one speaks of the lustre of the gem, one thinks of the gem; and again, when one speaks of the gem, one refers to its lustre. One cannot conceive of the lustre of the gem without thinking of the gem, and one cannot conceive of the gem without thinking of its lustre.

"Existence-Knowledge-Bliss Absolute is one, and one only. But It is associated with different limiting adjuncts on account of the different degrees of Its manifestation. That is why one finds various forms of God. The devotee sings, 'O my Divine Mother, Thou art all these!' Wherever you see actions, like creation, preservation, and dissolution, there is the manifestation of Śakti. Water is water whether it is calm or full of waves and bubbles. The Absolute alone is the Primordial Energy, which creates, preserves, and

---

[2] The veiling power of māyā hides the Reality; the projecting power of māyā creates the names and forms of the manifold universe.

destroys. Thus it is the same 'Captain', whether he remains inactive or performs his worship or pays a visit to the Governor General. Only we designate
him by different names at different times."

CAPTAIN: "Yes, sir, that is so."

MASTER: "I said those words to Keshab Sen."

CAPTAIN: "Keshab is not an orthodox Hindu. He adopts manners and
customs according to his own whim. He is a well-to-do gentleman and not
a holy man."

MASTER (to the other devotees): "Captain forbids me to go to see Keshab."

CAPTAIN: "But, sir, you act as you will. What can I do?"

MASTER (sharply): "Why shouldn't I go to see Keshab? You feel at ease
when you go to the Governor General's house,[3] and for money at that. Keshab
thinks of God and chants His name. Isn't it you who are always saying
that God Himself has become the universe and all its living beings? Doesn't
God dwell in Keshab also?"

With these words the Master left the room abruptly and went to the northeast verandah. Captain and the other devotees remained, waiting for his
return. M. accompanied the Master to the verandah, where Narendra was
talking with Hazra. Sri Ramakrishna knew that Hazra always indulged in
dry philosophical discussions. Hazra would say: "The world is unreal, like
a dream. Worship, food offerings to the Deity, and so forth, are only hallucinations of the mind. The aim of spiritual life is to meditate on one's
own real Self." Then he would repeat, "I am He." But, with all that, he had
a soft corner in his heart for money, material things, and people's attention.

Sri Ramakrishna smiled and said to Hazra and Narendra, "Hello! What
are you talking about?"

NARENDRA (smiling): "Oh, we are discussing a great many things. They
are rather too deep for others."

MASTER (with a smile): "But Pure Knowledge and Pure Love are one
and the same thing. Both lead the aspirants to the same goal. The path of
love is much the easier."

Narendra quoted a song:

> O Mother, make me mad with Thy love!
> What need have I of knowledge or reason?

Narendra said to M. that he had been reading a book by Hamilton, who
wrote: "A learned ignorance is the end of philosophy and the beginning of
religion."

MASTER (to M.): "What does that mean?"

Narendra explained the sentence in Bengali. The Master beamed with
joy and said in English, "Thank you! Thank you!" Everyone laughed at the
charming way he said these words. They knew that his English vocabulary
consisted of only half a dozen words.

It was almost dusk when most of the devotees, including Narendra, took
leave of the Master. Sri Ramakrishna went out and looked at the Ganges

[3] According to orthodox Hindu custom, an Englishman is a mlechchha, one outside
the pale of Hindu society. The touch of a mlechchha pollutes a Hindu.

for a few minutes from the west porch. Two priests were bathing in preparation for the evening worship. Young men of the village were strolling in
the garden or standing on the concrete embankment, gazing at the murmuring river. Others, perhaps more thoughtful, were walking about in the
solitude of the Panchavati.

It became dark. The maidservant lighted the lamp in Sri Ramakrishna's
room and burnt incense. The evening worship began in the twelve temples
of Śiva and in the shrines of Krishna and Kāli.

As it was the first day after the full moon, the moonlight soon flooded the
tops of the trees and temples, and touched with silver the numberless waves
of the sacred river.

The Master returned to his room. After bowing to the Divine Mother, he
clapped his hands and chanted the sweet names of God. A number of holy
pictures hung on the walls of the room. Among others, there were pictures
of Dhruva, Prahlāda, Kāli, Rādhā-Krishna, and the coronation of Rāma.
The Master bowed low before the pictures and repeated the holy names.
Then he repeated the holy words, "Brahma—Ātmā—Bhagavān; Bhāgavata—
Bhakta—Bhagavān; Brahma—Śakti, Śakti—Brahma; Veda, Purāna, Tantra,
Gītā, Gāyatri." Then he said: "I have taken refuge at Thy feet, O Divine
Mother; not I, but Thou. I am the machine and Thou art the Operator",
and so on.

While the Master was meditating in this fashion on the Divine Mother,
a few devotees, coming in from the garden, gathered in his room. Sri Ramakrishna sat down on the small couch. He said to the devotees: "Narendra,
Bhavanath, Rakhal, and devotees like them belong to the group of the
nityasiddhas; they are eternally free. Religious practice on their part is superfluous. Look at Narendra. He doesn't care about anyone. One day he was
going with me in Captain's carriage. Captain wanted him to take a good seat,
but Narendra didn't even look at him. He is independent even of me. He
doesn't tell me all he knows, lest I should praise his scholarship before
others. He is free from ignorance and delusion. He has no bonds. He is a
great soul. He has many good qualities. He is expert in music, both as a
singer and player, and is also a versatile scholar. Again, he keeps his passions
under control and says that he will never marry. There is a close friendship
between Narendra and Bhavanath; they are just like man and woman.
Narendra doesn't come here very often. That is good, for I am overwhelmed
by his presence."

Monday, August 20, 1883

Sri Ramakrishna was sitting on his bed, inside the mosquito net, meditating. It was about eight o'clock in the evening. M. was sitting on the floor
with his friend Hari Babu. Hari, a young man of twenty-eight, had lost his
wife about eleven years before and had not married a second time. He was
much devoted to his parents, brothers, and sisters.

Hazra was living at Dakshineswar. Rakhal lived with the Master, though
now and then he stayed at Adhar's house. Narendra, Bhavanath, Adhar, M.,
Ram, Manomohan, and other devotees visited the Master almost every week.

Hriday, Sri Ramakrishna's nephew, was ill in his home in the country. The Master was worried about him. One of the devotees had sent him a little money, but the Master did not know it.

When Sri Ramakrishna came out of the mosquito net and sat on the small couch, the devotees saluted him.

MASTER (to M.): "I was meditating inside the net. It occurred to me that meditation, after all, was nothing but the imagining of a form, and so I did not enjoy it. One gets satisfaction if God reveals Himself in a flash. Again, I said to myself, 'Who is it that meditates, and on whom does he meditate?' "

M: "Yes, sir. You said that God Himself has become everything—the universe and all living beings. Even he who meditates is God."

MASTER: "What is more, one cannot meditate unless God wills it. One can meditate when God makes it possible for one to do so. What do you say?"

M: "True, sir. You feel like that because there is no 'I' in you. When there is no ego, one feels like that."

MASTER: "But it is good to have a trace of ego, which makes it possible for a man to feel that he is the servant of God. As long as a man thinks that it is he who is doing his duties, it is very good for him to feel that God is the Master and he God's servant. When one is conscious of doing work, one should establish with God the relationship of servant and Master."

M. was always reflecting on the nature of the Supreme Brahman.

MASTER (to M.): "Like the ākāsa, Brahman is without any modification. It has become manifold because of Sakti. Again, Brahman is like fire, which itself has no colour. The fire appears white if you throw a white substance into it, red if you throw a red, black if you throw a black. The three gunas —sattva, rajas, and tamas—belong to Sakti alone. Brahman Itself is beyond the three gunas. What Brahman is cannot be described. It is beyond words. That which remains after everything is eliminated by the Vedāntic process of 'Not this, not this', and which is of the nature of Bliss, is Brahman.

"Suppose the husband of a young girl has come to his father-in-law's house and is seated in the drawing-room with other young men of his age. The girl and her friends are looking at them through the window. Her friends do not know her husband and ask her, pointing to one young man, 'Is that your husband?' 'No', she answers, smiling. They point to another young man and ask if he is her husband. Again she answers no. They repeat the question, referring to a third, and she gives the same answer. At last they point to her husband and ask, 'Is he the one?' She says neither yes nor no, but only smiles and keeps quiet. Her friends realize that he is her husband.

"One becomes silent on realizing the true nature of Brahman.

(To M.) "Well, why do I talk so much?"

M: "You talk in order to awaken the spiritual consciousness of the devotees. You once said that when an uncooked luchi is dropped into boiling ghee it makes a sizzling noise."

The Master began to talk to M. about Hazra.

MASTER: "Do you know the nature of a good man? He never troubles

others. He doesn't harass people. The nature of some people is such that when they go to a feast they want special seats. A man who has true devotion to God never makes a false step, never gives others trouble for nothing.

"It is not good to live in the company of bad people. A man should stay away from them and thus protect himself. (*To M.*) Isn't that so?"

M: "Yes, sir. The mind sinks far down in the company of the wicked. But it is quite different with a hero, as you say."

MASTER: "How is that?"

M: "When a fire is feeble it goes out when even a small stick is thrown into it; but a blazing fire is not affected even if a plantain-tree is thrown into it. The tree itself is burnt to ashes."

The Master asked M. about his friend Hari Babu.

M: "He has come here to pay you his respects. He lost his wife long ago."

MASTER (*to Hari*): "What kind of work do you do?"

M: "Nothing in particular. But at home he takes good care of his parents and his brothers and sisters."

MASTER (*with a smile*): "How is that? You are like 'Elder, the pumpkin-cutter'. You are neither a man of the world nor a devotee of God. That is not good. You must have seen the sort of elderly man who lives in a family and is always ready, day or night, to entertain the children. He sits in the parlour and smokes the hubble-bubble. With nothing in particular to do, he leads a lazy life. Now and again he goes to the inner court and cuts a pumpkin; for, since women do not cut pumpkins, they send the children to ask him to come and do it. That is the extent of his usefulness—hence his nickname, 'Elder, the pumpkin-cutter'.

"You must do 'this' as well as 'that'. Do your duties in the world, and also fix your mind on the Lotus Feet of the Lord. Read books of devotion like the *Bhāgavata* or the life of Chaitanya when you are alone and have nothing else to do."

It was about ten o'clock. Sri Ramakrishna finished a light supper of farina pudding and one or two luchis. After saluting him, M. and his friend took their leave.

Friday, September 7, 1883

Sri Ramakrishna and M. were talking in the Master's room at half past seven in the evening. No one else was present.

MASTER: "The other day I went to Calcutta. As I drove along the streets in the carriage, I observed that everyone's attention was fixed on low things. Everyone was brooding over his stomach and running after nothing but food. Everyone's mind was turned to 'woman and gold'. I saw only one or two with their attention fixed on higher things, with their minds turned to God."

M: "The present age has aggravated this stomach-worry. Trying to imitate the English, people have turned their attention to more luxuries; therefore their wants have also increased."

MASTER: "What do the English think about God?"

M: "They believe in a formless God."

MASTER: "That is also one of our beliefs."

For a time Master and disciple remained silent. Then Sri Ramakrishna began to describe his experiences of Brahman.

MASTER: "One day I had the vision of Consciousness, non-dual and indivisible. At first it had been revealed to me that there were innumerable men, animals, and other creatures. Among them there were aristocrats, the English, the Mussalmāns, myself, scavengers, dogs, and also a bearded Mussalmān with an earthenware tray of rice in his hand. He put a few grains of rice into everybody's mouth. I too tasted a little.

"Another day I saw rice, vegetables, and other food-stuff, and filth and dirt as well, lying around. Suddenly the soul came out of my body and, like a flame, touched everything. It was like a protruding tongue of fire and tasted everything once, even the excreta. It was revealed to me that all these are one Substance, the non-dual and indivisible Consciousness.

"Another day[4] it was revealed to me that I had devotees—my intimate companions, my very own. Thereafter I would climb to the roof of the kuthi as soon as the bells and the conch-shells of the evening service sounded in the temples, and cry out with a longing heart: 'Oh, where are you all? Come here! I am dying to see you!'

(To M.) "Well, what do you think of these visions?"

M: "God sports through you. This I have realized, that you are the instrument and God is the Master. God has created other beings as if with a machine, but yourself with His own hands."

MASTER: "Well, Hazra says that after the vision of God one acquires the six divine powers."

M: "Those who seek pure love don't want powers."

MASTER: "Perhaps Hazra was a poor man in his previous life, and that is why he wants so much to see the manifestation of power. He wants to know what I talk about with the cook. He says to me: 'You don't have to talk to the cook. I shall talk to the manager of the temple myself and see that you get everything you want.' (M. laughs aloud.) He talks to me that way and I say nothing."

M: "Many a time you have said that a devotee who loves God for the sake of love does not care to see God's powers. A true devotee wants to see God as Gopāla.[5] In the beginning God becomes the magnet, and the devotee the needle. But in the end the devotee himself becomes the magnet, and God the needle; that is to say, God becomes small to His devotee."

MASTER: "Yes, it is just like the sun at dawn. You can easily look at that sun. It doesn't dazzle the eyes; rather it satisfies them. God becomes tender for the sake of His devotees. He appears before them, setting aside His powers."

Both remained silent for some time.

M: "Why should your visions not be real? If they are unreal, then the

[4] This happened before any of the Master's intimate disciples came to him.

[5] The Baby Krishna, bereft of all divine powers.

world is still more unreal; for there is only one mind that is the instrument of perception. Your pure mind sees those visions, and our ordinary minds see worldly objects."

MASTER: "I see that you have grasped the idea of unreality. Well, tell me what you think of Hazra."

M: "Oh, I don't know." (*The Master laughs.*)

MASTER: "Well, do you find me to be like anybody else?"

M: "No, sir."

MASTER: "Like any other paramahamsa?"

M: "No, sir. You can't be compared to anybody else."

MASTER (*smiling*): "Have you heard of a tree called the 'achina'?"[6]

M: "No, sir."

MASTER: "There is a tree called by that name. But nobody knows what it is."

M: "Likewise, it is not possible to recognize you. The more a man understands you, the more uplifted he will be."

M. was silent. He said to himself: "The Master referred to 'the sun at dawn' and 'the tree unrecognizable by man'. Did he mean an Incarnation of God? Is this the play of God through man? Is the Master himself an Incarnation? Was this why he cried to the devotees from the roof of the kuthi: 'Where are you? Come to me!'?"

Sri Ramakrishna was sitting on the steps of the southeast verandah of the Kāli temple. Rakhal, M., and Hazra were with him. He talked lightheartedly about his boyhood days.

When it was dusk he returned to his room and sat down on the small couch. Soon he went into samādhi and in that state began to talk to the Divine Mother. He said: "Mother, what is all this row about? Shall I go there? I shall go if You take me." The Master was to go to a devotee's house. Was it for this that he was asking the Divine Mother's permission?

Again he spoke to Her, perhaps praying about an intimate disciple: "Mother, please make him stainless. Well, Mother, why have You given him only a particle?" Remaining silent a moment, he said: "Oh, I see. That will be enough for Your work."

In the same state he said, addressing the devotees: "That which is Brahman is verily Śakti. I address That, again, as the Mother. I call It Brahman when It is inactive, and Śakti when It creates, preserves, and destroys. It is like water, sometimes still and sometimes covered with waves. The Incarnation of God is a part of the līlā of Śakti. The purpose of the Divine Incarnation is to teach man ecstatic love for God. The Incarnation is like the udder of the cow, the only place milk is to be got. God incarnates Himself as man. There is a great accumulation of divinity in an Incarnation, like the accumulation of fish in a deep hollow in a lake."

Some of the devotees wondered, "Is Sri Ramakrishna an Incarnation of God, like Krishna, Chaitanya, and Christ?"

[6] Literally, "unrecognizable".

Sunday, September 9, 1883

Sri Ramakrishna had finished his midday meal and was sitting on the small couch. Rakhal, M., and Ratan were sitting on the floor. Ratan was the steward of Jadu Mallick's garden house and was devoted to the Master. Now and then Ram Chatterji and Hazra passed in or out of the room. It was about two o'clock.

Ratan told the Master that a yātrā performance by Nilkantha had been arranged in Jadu Mallick's house in Calcutta.

RATAN (*to the Master*): "You must go. The date has been set."

MASTER: "That's good. I want to go. Nilkantha sings with great devotion."

A DEVOTEE: "That is true, sir."

MASTER: "Tears flow from his eyes as he sings. (*To Ratan*) I am thinking of spending the night in Calcutta when I go to see the yātrā."

RATAN: "That will be fine."

Ram Chatterji and the other devotees asked Ratan about a theft in Jadu Mallick's house.

RATAN: "Yes, the golden sandals of the Deity were stolen from the shrine room in Jadu Babu's house. It has created an uproar. They are going to try to discover the thief by means of a 'charmed plate'. Everybody will sit in one room, and the plate will move in the direction of the man who stole the sandals."

MASTER (*with a smile*): "How does the plate move? By itself?"

RATAN: "No. A man presses it to the ground."

A DEVOTEE: "It is a kind of sleight of hand. It is a clever trick."

MASTER: "The real cleverness is the cleverness by which one realizes God. That trick is the best of all tricks."

As the conversation went on, several Bengali gentlemen entered the room and, after saluting the Master, sat down. One of them was already known to Sri Ramakrishna. These gentlemen followed the cult of Tantra. The Master knew that one of them indulged in immoral acts in the name of religion. The Tantra rituals, under certain conditions, allow the mixing of men and women devotees. But Sri Ramakrishna regarded all women, even prostitutes, as manifestations of the Divine Mother. He addressed them all as "Mother".

MASTER (*with a smile*): "Where is Achalananda? My ideal is different from that of Achalananda and his disciples. As for myself, I look on all women as my mother."

The visiting gentlemen sat silent.

MASTER: "Every woman is a mother to me. Achalananda used to stay here now and then. He would drink a great deal of consecrated wine. Hearing about my attitude toward women, he stubbornly justified his own views. He insisted again and again: 'Why should you not recognize the attitude of a "hero" toward women? Won't you admit the injunctions of Śiva? Śiva Himself is the author of the Tantra, which prescribes various disciplines, including the "heroic".' I said to him: 'But, my dear sir, I don't know. I don't like these ideas. To me every woman is a mother.'

"Achalananda did not support his own children. He said to me, 'God will support them.' I said nothing. But this is the way I felt about it: 'Who will support your children? I hope your renunciation of wife and children is not a way of earning money. People will think you are a holy man because you have renounced everything; so they will give you money. In that way you will earn plenty of money.'

"Spiritual practice with a view to winning a lawsuit and earning money, or to helping others win in court and acquire property, shows a very mean understanding.

"Money enables a man to get food and drink, build a house, worship the Deity, serve devotees and holy men, and help the poor when he happens to meet them. These are the good uses of money. Money is not meant for luxuries or creature comforts or for buying a position in society.

"People practise various Tāntrik disciplines to acquire supernatural powers. How mean such people are! Krishna said to Arjuna, 'Friend, by acquiring one of the eight siddhis you may add a little to your power, but you will not be able to realize Me.' One cannot get rid of māyā as long as one exercises supernatural powers. And māyā begets egotism.

"Body and wealth are impermanent. Why go to so much trouble for their sakes? Just think of the plight of the hathayogis. Their attention is fixed on one ideal only—longevity. They do not aim at the realization of God at all. They practise such exercises as washing out the intestines, drinking milk through a tube, and the like, with that one aim in view.

"There was once a goldsmith whose tongue suddenly turned up and stuck to his palate. He looked like a man in samādhi. He became completely inert and remained so a long time. People came to worship him. After several years, his tongue suddenly returned to its natural position, and he became conscious of things as before. So he went back to his work as a goldsmith. (All laugh.)

"These are physical things and have nothing to do with God. There was a man who knew eighty-two postures and talked big about yoga-samādhi. But inwardly he was drawn to 'woman and gold'. Once he found a bank-note worth several thousand rupees. He could not resist the temptation, and swallowed it, thinking he would get it out somehow later on. The note was got out of him all right, but he was sent to jail for three years. In my guilelessness I used to think that the man had made great spiritual progress. Really, I say it upon my word!

"Mahendra Pal of Sinthi once gave Ramlal five rupees. Ramlal told me about it after he had gone. I asked him what the gift was for, and Ramlal said that it was meant for me. I thought it might enable me to pay off some of my debt for milk. That night I went to bed and, if you will believe me, I suddenly woke up with a pain. I felt as if a cat were scratching inside my chest. I at once went to Ramlal and asked him: 'For whom did Mahendra give this money? Was it for your aunt?'[7] 'No,' said Ramlal, 'it is meant for you.' I said to him, 'Go and return the money at once, or I shall have no peace of mind.' Ramlal returned the money early in the morning and I felt relieved.

[7] Referring to the Holy Mother, Sri Ramakrishna's wife.

"Once a rich man came here and said to me: 'Sir, you must do something so that I may win my lawsuit. I have heard of your reputation and so I have come here.' 'My dear sir,' I said to him, 'you have made a mistake. I am not the person you are looking for; Achalananda is your man.'

"A true devotee of God does not care for such things as wealth or health. He thinks: 'Why should I practise spiritual austerities for creature comforts, money, or name and fame? These are all impermanent. They last only a day or two.'"

The visiting gentlemen took leave of the Master after saluting him. When they had departed, Sri Ramakrishna smiled and said to M., "You can never make a thief listen to religion. (*All laugh.*)

"Well, what do you think of Narendra?"

M: "He is splendid."

MASTER: "Yes. His intelligence is as great as his learning. Besides, he is gifted in music, both as a singer and player. Then too, he has control over his passions. He says he will never marry."

M: "You once said that one who constantly talks of his sin really becomes a sinner; he cannot extricate himself from sin. But if a man has firm faith that he is the son of God, then he makes rapid strides in spiritual life."

MASTER: "Yes, faith. What tremendous faith Krishnakishore had! He used to say: 'I have spoken the name of God once. That is enough. How can I remain a sinner? I have become pure and stainless.' One day Haladhari said: 'Even Ajāmila had to perform austerities to gratify God. Can one receive the grace of God without austerities? What will one gain by speaking the name of Nārāyana only once?' At these remarks Krishnakishore's anger knew no bounds. The next time he came to this garden to pick flowers he wouldn't even look at Haladhari.

"Haladhari's father was a great devotee. At bathing-time he would stand waist-deep in the water and meditate on God, uttering the sacred mantra; then the tears would flow from his eyes.

"One day a holy man came to the bathing-place on the Ganges at Āriādaha. We talked about seeing him. Haladhari said, 'What shall we gain by seeing the body of a man, a mere cage made of the five elements?' Krishnakishore heard about it and said: 'What? Did Haladhari ask what would be gained by visiting a holy man? By repeating the name of Krishna or Rāma a man transforms his physical body into a spiritual body. To such a man everything is the embodiment of Spirit. To him Krishna is the embodiment of Spirit, and His sacred Abode is the embodiment of Spirit.' He also said, 'A man who utters the name of Krishna or Rāma even once reaps the result of a hundred sandhyās.'

"One of his sons chanted the name of Rāma on his death-bed. Krishnakishore said, 'He has nothing to worry about; he has chanted the name of Rāma.' But now and then he wept. After all, it was the death of his own son.

"Nothing whatsoever is achieved by the performance of worship, japa, and devotions, without faith. Isn't that so?"

M: "Yes, sir. That is true."

MASTER: "I see people coming to the Ganges to bathe. They talk their heads off about everything under the sun. The widowed aunt says: 'Without me they cannot perform the Durgā Pujā. I have to look after even the smallest detail. Again, I have to supervise everything when there is a marriage festival in the family, even the bed of the bride and groom.' "

M: "Why should we blame them? How else will they pass the time?"

MASTER (*with a smile*): "Some people have their shrine rooms in their attics. The women arrange the offerings and flowers and make the sandalpaste. But, while doing so, they never say a word about God. The burden of the conversation is: 'What shall we cook today? I couldn't get good vegetables in the market. That curry was delicious yesterday. That boy is my cousin. Hello there! Have you that job still? Don't ask me how I am. My Hari is no more.' Just fancy! They talk of such things in the shrine room at the time of worship!"

M: "Yes, sir, it is so in the majority of cases. As you say, can one who has passionate yearning for God continue formal worship and devotions for long?"

Sri Ramakrishna and M. were now conversing alone.

M: "Sir, if it is God Himself who has become everything, then why do people have so many different feelings?"

MASTER: "Undoubtedly God exists in all beings as the All-pervading Spirit, but the manifestations of His Power are different in different beings. In some places there is a manifestation of the power of Knowledge; in others, of the power of ignorance. In some places there is a greater manifestation of power than in others. Don't you see that among human beings there are cheats and gamblers, to say nothing of men who are like tigers. I think of them as the 'cheat God', the 'tiger God'."

M. (*with a smile*): "We should salute them from a distance. If we go near the 'tiger God' and embrace him, he may devour us."

MASTER: "He and His Power, Brahman and Its Power—nothing else exists but this. In a hymn to Rāma, Nārada said: 'O Rāma, You are Śiva, and Sītā is Bhagavati; You are Brahmā, and Sītā is Brahmāni; You are Indra, and Sītā is Indrāni; You are Nārāyana, and Sītā is Lakshmi. O Rāma, You are the symbol of all that is masculine, and Sītā of all that is feminine.' "

M: "Sir, what is the Spirit-form of God like?"

Sri Ramakrishna reflected a moment and said softly: "Shall I tell you what it is like? It is like water. . . . One understands all this through spiritual discipline.

"Believe in the form of God. It is only after attaining Brahmajnāna that one sees non-duality, the oneness of Brahman and Its Śakti. Brahman and Śakti are identical, like fire and its power to burn. When a man thinks of fire, he must also think of its power to burn. Again, when he thinks of the power to burn, he must also think of fire. Further, Brahman and Śakti are like milk and its whiteness, water and its wetness.

"But there is a stage beyond even Brahmajnāna. After jnāna comes vijnāna. He who is aware of knowledge is also aware of ignorance. The sage Vaśishtha was stricken with grief at the death of his hundred sons. Asked by Lakshmana why a man of knowledge should grieve for such a reason, Rāma said, 'Brother, go beyond both knowledge and ignorance.' He who has knowledge has ignorance also. If a thorn has entered your foot, get another thorn and with its help take out the first; then throw away the second also."

M: "Should one throw away both knowledge and ignorance?"

MASTER: "Yes. That is why one should acquire vijnāna. You see, he who is aware of light is also aware of darkness. He who is aware of happiness is also aware of suffering. He who is aware of virtue is also aware of vice. He who is aware of good is also aware of evil. He who is aware of holiness is also aware of unholiness. He who is aware of 'I' is also aware of 'you'.

"What is vijnāna? It is knowing God in a special way. The awareness and conviction that fire exists in wood is jnāna, knowledge. But to cook rice on that fire, eat the rice, and get nourishment from it is vijnāna. To know by one's inner experience that God exists is jnāna. But to talk to Him, to enjoy Him as Child, as Friend, as Master, as Beloved, is vijnāna. The realization that God alone has become the universe and all living beings is vijnāna.

"According to one school of thought, God cannot be seen. Who sees whom? Is God outside you, that you can see Him? One sees only oneself. Having once entered the 'black waters' of the ocean, the ship does not come back and so cannot describe what it experiences."

M: "It is true, sir. As you say, having climbed to the top of the monument, one becomes unaware of what is below: horses and carriages, men and women, houses, shops and offices, and so on."

MASTER: "I don't go to the Kāli temple nowadays. Is that an offence? At one time Narendra used to say, 'What? He still goes to the Kāli temple!'"

M: "Every day you are in a new state of mind. How can you ever offend God?"

MASTER: "Someone said to Sen, about Hriday: 'He is very ill. Please bring two pieces of cloth and a couple of shirts for him. We will send them to his village.' Sen offered only two rupees. How do you explain that? He has so much money, and yet he is so miserly! What do you say to that?"

M: "Those who seek God cannot behave that way—I mean those whose goal is the attainment of Knowledge."

MASTER: "God alone is the Reality and all else is unreal."

Saturday, September 22, 1883

Sri Ramakrishna was seated in the drawing-room of Adhar's house in Calcutta, with Rakhal, Adhar, M., Ishan, and other devotees. Many gentlemen of the neighbourhood were also present. It was afternoon.

The Master was very fond of Ishan. He had been a superintendent in the Accountant General's office, and later on his children also occupied high government positions. One of them was a class-mate of Narendra. Ishan's purse was always open for the poor and needy. When he retired from service, he devoted his time to spiritual practices and charity. He often visited Sri Ramakrishna at Dakshineswar.

MASTER (*to Ishan*): "Please tell us the story of the boy who posted the letter."

ISHAN (*with a smile*): "A boy once heard that God is our Creator. So he wrote a letter to God, setting forth his prayers, and posted it. The address he put on the envelope was 'Heaven'."

MASTER (*with a smile*): "Did you hear that story? One succeeds in spiritual life when one develops a faith like that boy's. (*To Ishan*) Tell us about the renunciation of activities."

ISHAN: "After the attainment of God, religious duties such as the sandyhā drop away. One day some people were sitting on the bank of the Ganges performing the sandyhā. But one of them abstained from it. On being asked the reason, he said: 'I am observing aśoucha. I cannot perform the sandyhā ceremony.[8] In my case the defilement is due to both a birth and a death. My mother, Ignorance, is dead, and my son, Self-Knowledge, has been born.' "

MASTER: "Tell us, also, how caste distinctions drop away when one attains Self-Knowledge."

ISHAN: "Śankarāchārya was once climbing the steps after finishing his bath in the Ganges, when he saw just in front of him an untouchable who had a pack of dogs with him. 'You have touched me!' said Śankara. 'Revered sir,' said the pariah, 'I have not touched you, nor have you touched me. The Self is the Inner Ruler of all beings and cannot be contaminated. Is there any difference between the sun's reflection in wine and its reflection in the Ganges?' "

MASTER (*with a smile*): "And about harmony: how one can realize God through all paths."

ISHAN (*smiling*): "Both Hari and Hara are derived from the same root.[9] The difference is only in the pratyaya.[10] In reality, He who is Hari is also Hara. If a man has faith in God, then it doesn't matter whom he worships."

MASTER: "And please tell us also how the heart of the sādhu is the greatest of all."

ISHAN: "This earth is the largest thing we see anywhere around us. But larger than the earth is the ocean, and larger than the ocean is the sky. But Vishnu, the Godhead, has covered earth, sky, and the nether world with one of His feet. And that foot of Vishnu is enshrined in the sādhu's heart. Therefore the heart of a holy man is the greatest of all."

The devotees were delighted with Ishan's words.

Ishan intended to retire to a solitary place and practise a special discipline of the Gāyatri, through which Brahman is invoked. But the Master said that the Knowledge of Brahman was not possible without the complete destruction of worldliness. Further, he said that it was impossible for a man

---

[8] Aśoucha is a temporary defilement caused by the birth or death of a blood relative. A man observing aśoucha cannot perform the sandyhā, or daily worship.

[9] The root "hri", from which both words are derived. Further, Hari and Hara are two manifestations of the same Godhead. Hari is a name of Vishnu, the Ideal Deity of the Vaishnavas, and Hara a name of Śiva, the Ideal Deity of the Śaivas.

[10] There is a pun on this word, which means both "faith" and "inflection".

totally to withdraw his mind from the objects of the senses in the Kaliyuga, when his life was dependent on food. That is why the Master discouraged people from attempting the Vedic worship of Brahman and asked them to worship Śakti, the Divine Mother, who is identical with Brahman.

MASTER (to Ishan): "Why do you waste your time simply repeating 'Neti, neti'? Nothing whatsoever can be specified about Brahman, except that It exists.

"Whatever we see or think about is the manifestation of the glory of the Primordial Energy, the Primal Consciousness. Creation, preservation, and destruction, living beings and the universe, and further, meditation and the meditator, bhakti and prema—all these are manifestations of the glory of that Power.

"But Brahman is identical with Its Power. On returning from Ceylon, Hanumān praised Rāma, saying: 'O Rāma, You are the Supreme Brahman, and Sītā is Your Śakti. You and She are identical.' Brahman and Śakti are like the snake and its wriggling motion. Thinking of the snake, one must think of its wriggling motion, and thinking of its wriggling motion, one must think of the snake. Or they are like milk and its whiteness. Thinking of milk, one has to think of its colour, that is, whiteness, and thinking of the whiteness of milk, one has to think of milk itself. Or they are like water and its wetness. Thinking of water, one has to think of its wetness, and thinking of the wetness of water, one has to think of water.

"This Primal Power, Mahāmāyā, has covered Brahman. As soon as the covering is withdrawn, one realizes: 'I am what I was before', 'I am Thou; Thou art I'.

"As long as that covering remains, the Vedāntic formula 'I am He', that is, man is the Supreme Brahman, does not rightly apply. The wave is part of the water, but the water is not part of the wave. As long as that covering remains, one should call on God as Mother. Addressing God, the devotee should say, 'Thou art the Mother and I am Thy child; Thou art the Master and I am Thy servant.' It is good to have the attitude of the servant toward the master. From this relationship of master and servant spring up other attitudes: the attitude of serene love for God, the attitude of friend toward friend, and so forth. When the master loves his servant, he may say to him, 'Come, sit by my side; there is no difference between you and me.' But if the servant comes forward of his own will to sit by the master, will not the master be angry?

"God's play on earth as an Incarnation is the manifestation of the glory of the Chitśakti, the Divine Power. That which is Brahman is also Rāma, Krishna, and Śiva."

ISHAN: "Yes, sir. Both Hari and Hara are derived from the same root. The difference lies only in the pratyaya."

MASTER: "Yes, there is only One without a second. The Vedas speak of It as 'Om Satchidānanda Brahma', the Purānas as 'Om Satchidānanda Krishna', and the Tantra as 'Om Satchidānanda Śiva'.

"The Chitśakti, as Mahāmāyā, has deluded all with ignorance. It is said in the *Adhyātma Rāmāyana* that when the rishis saw Rāma, they prayed to Him in these words only: 'O Rāma, please do not delude us with Your world-bewitching māyā.'"

ISHAN: "What is this māyā?"

MASTER: "Whatever you see, think, or hear is māyā. In a word, 'woman and gold' is the covering of māyā.

"There is no harm in chewing betel-leaf, eating fish, smoking, or rubbing the body with oil. What will one achieve by renouncing only these things? The one thing needful is the renunciation of 'woman and gold'. That renunciation is the real and supreme renunciation. Householders should go into solitude now and then, to practise spiritual discipline in order to cultivate devotion to God; they should renounce mentally. But the sannyāsi should renounce both mentally and physically.

"I once said to Keshab, 'How can a typhoid patient be cured if he remains in a room where a pitcher of water and a jar of pickles are kept?' Now and then one should live in solitude."

A DEVOTEE: "Sir, what do you think of the Navavidhān? It seems to me like a hotchpotch of everything."

MASTER: "Some say it is a modern thing. That sets me wondering: 'Then is the God of the Brāhmo Samāj a new God?' The Brāhmos speak of their cult as the Navavidhān, as a New Dispensation. Well, it may be so. Who knows? There are six systems of philosophy; so perhaps it is like one of these.

"But do you know where those who speak of the formless God make their mistake? It is where they say that God is formless only, and that those who differ with them are wrong.

"But I know that God is both with and without form. And He may have many more aspects. It is possible for Him to be everything.

(*To Ishan*) "The Chitśakti, Mahāmāyā, has become the twenty-four cosmic principles. One day as I was meditating, my mind wandered away to Rashke's house. He is a scavenger. I said to my mind, 'Stay there, you rogue!' The Divine Mother revealed to me that the men and women in this house were mere masks; inside them was the same Divine Power, Kundalini, that rises up through the six spiritual centres of the body.

"Is the Primal Energy man or woman? Once at Kāmārpukur I saw the worship of Kāli in the house of the Lahas. They put a sacred thread[11] on the image of the Divine Mother. One man asked, 'Why have they put the sacred thread on the Mother's person?' The master of the house said: 'Brother, I see that you have rightly understood the Mother. But I do not yet know whether the Divine Mother is male or female.'

"It is said that Mahāmāyā swallowed Śiva. When the six centres in Her were awakened, Śiva came out through Her thigh. Then Śiva created the Tantra philosophy.

"Take refuge in the Chitśakti, the Mahāmāyā."

ISHAN: "Please bestow your grace on me."

MASTER: "Say to God with a guileless heart, 'O God, reveal Thyself to

[11] See foot-note 9, p. 271.

me.' And weep. Pray to God, 'O God, keep my mind away from "woman and gold".' And dive deep. Can a man get pearls by floating or swimming on the surface? He must dive deep.

"One must get instruction from a guru. Once a man was looking for a stone image of Śiva. Someone said to him: 'Go to a certain river. There you will find a tree. Near it is a whirlpool. Dive into the water there, and you will find the image of Śiva.' So I say that one must get instruction from a teacher."

ISHAN: "That is true, sir."

MASTER: "It is Satchidānanda that comes to us in the form of the guru. If a man is initiated by a human guru, he will not achieve anything if he regards his guru as a mere man. The guru should be regarded as the direct manifestation of God. Only then can the disciple have faith in the mantra given by the guru. Once a man has faith he achieves all. The śudra Ekalavya learnt archery in the forest before a clay image of Drona. He worshipped the image as the living Drona; that by itself enabled him to attain mastery in archery.

"Don't mix intimately with brāhmin pundits. Their only concern is to earn money. I have seen brāhmin priests reciting the *Chandi* while performing the swastyayana. It is hard to tell whether they are reading the sacred book or something else. They turn half the pages without reading them. (*All laugh.*)

"A nail-knife suffices to kill oneself. One needs sword and shield to kill others. That is the purpose of the śāstras.

"One doesn't really need to study the different scriptures. If one has no discrimination, one doesn't achieve anything through mere scholarship, even though one studies all the six systems of philosophy. Call on God, crying to Him secretly in solitude. He will give all that you need."

Sri Ramakrishna had heard that Ishan was building a house on the bank of the Ganges for the practice of spiritual discipline. He asked Ishan eagerly: "Has the house been built? Let me tell you that the less people know of your spiritual life, the better it will be for you. Devotees endowed with sattva meditate in a secluded corner or in a forest, or withdraw into the mind. Sometimes they meditate inside the mosquito net."

Now and then Ishan invited Hazra to his house. Hazra had a craze for outward purity. Sri Ramakrishna often discouraged him in this.

MASTER (*to Ishan*): "Let me tell you another thing. Don't be over-fastidious about outward purity. Once a sādhu felt very thirsty. A water-carrier was carrying water in his skin water-bag, and offered the water to the holy man. The sādhu asked if the skin was clean. The carrier said: 'Revered sir, my skin bag is perfectly clean. But inside *your skin* are all sorts of filthy things. That is why I can ask you to drink water from my skin. It won't injure you.' By 'your skin', the carrier meant the body, the belly, and so forth.

"Have faith in the name of God. Then you won't need even to go to holy places."

Sri Ramakrishna sang, intoxicated with divine fervour:

> Why should I go to Gangā or Gayā, to Kāśi, Kānchi, or Prabhās,
> So long as I can breathe my last with Kāli's name upon my
> lips? . . .

Ishan remained silent.

MASTER (to Ishan): "Tell me if you have any more doubts."

ISHAN: "You said everything when you spoke of faith."

MASTER: "God can be realized by true faith alone. And the realization is hastened if you believe everything about God. The cow that picks and chooses its food gives milk only in dribblets, but if she eats all kinds of plants, then her milk flows in torrents.

"Once I heard a story. A man heard the command of God that he should see his Ideal Deity in a ram. He at once believed it. It is God who exists in all beings.

"A guru said to his disciple, 'It is Rāma alone who resides in all bodies.' The disciple was a man of great faith. One day a dog snatched a piece of bread from him and started to run away. He ran after the dog, with a jar of butter in his hand, and cried again and again: 'O Rāma, stand still a minute. That bread hasn't been buttered.'

"What tremendous faith Krishnakishore had! He used to say, 'By chanting "Om Krishna, Om Rāma", one gets the result of a million sandhyās.' Once he said to me secretly, 'I don't like the sandhyā and other devotions any more; but don't tell anyone.'

"Sometimes I too feel that way. The Mother reveals to me that She Herself has become everything. One day I was coming from the pine-grove toward the Panchavati. A dog followed me. I stood still for a while near the Panchavati. The thought came to my mind that the Mother might say something to me through that dog.

"You were absolutely right when you said that through faith alone one achieves all."

ISHAN: "But we are householders."

MASTER: "What if you are? Through His grace even the impossible becomes possible. Rāmprasād sang, 'This world is a mere framework of illusion.' Another man composed a song by way of reply:

> This very world is a mansion of mirth;
> Here I can eat, here drink and make merry.
> Janaka's might was unsurpassed;
> What did he lack of the world or the Spirit?
> Holding to one as well as the other,
> He drank his milk from a brimming cup!

"One should first realize God through spiritual discipline in solitude, and then live in the world. Only then can one be a King Janaka. What can you achieve otherwise?

"Further, take the case of Śiva. He has everything—Kārtika, Ganeśa, Lakshmi, and Sarasvati. Still, sometimes He dances in a state of divine fervour, chanting the name of Rāma, and sometimes He is absorbed in samādhi."

INSTRUCTION TO VAISHNAVAS
AND BRĀHMOS

Sunday, September 23, 1883

SRI RAMAKRISHNA was sitting in his room at Dakshineswar with Rakhal, M., and other devotees. Hazra sat on the porch outside. The Master was conversing with the devotees.

MASTER (*to a devotee*): "Narendra doesn't like even you, nowadays. (*To M.*) Why didn't he come to see me at Adhar's house?

"How versatile Narendra is! He is gifted in singing, in playing on instruments, and ·in studies. He is independent and doesn't care about anybody. The other day he was returning to Calcutta with Captain in his carriage. Captain begged Narendra to sit beside him, but he took a seat opposite. He didn't even look at Captain.

"What can a man achieve through mere scholarship? What is needed is prayer and spiritual discipline. Gauri of Indesh was both a scholar and a devotee. He was a worshipper of the Divine Mother. Now and then he would be overpowered with spiritual fervour. When he chanted a hymn to the Mother, the pundits would seem like earth-worms beside him. I too would be overcome with ecstasy.

"At first he was a bigoted worshipper of Śakti. He used to pick up tulsi-leaves[1] with a couple of sticks, so as not to touch them with his fingers. (*All laugh.*) Then he went home. When he came back he didn't behave that way any more. He gave remarkable interpretations of Hindu mythology. He would say that the ten heads of Rāvana represented the ten organs. Kumbhakarna was the symbol of tamas, Rāvana of rajas, and Bibhishana of sattva. That was why Bibhishana obtained favour with Rāma."

After the Master's midday meal, while he was resting, Ram, Tarak,[2] and some other devotees arrived from Calcutta.

Nityagopal, Tarak, and several others were staying with Ram, a householder disciple of the Master. Nityagopal was always in an exalted spiritual mood. Tarak's mind, too, was always indrawn; he seldom exchanged words

---

[1] These leaves are sacred to Vishnu. The bigoted worshipper of Śakti hates everything associated with Vishnu, and *vice versa*.

[2] A monastic disciple of the Master, known later as Swami Shivananda.

with others. Ram looked after their physical needs. Rakhal now and then spent a few days at Adhar's house.

RAM (*to the Master*): "We have been taking lessons on the drum."

MASTER (*to Ram*): "Nityagopal too?"

RAM: "No, sir. He plays a little."

MASTER: "And Tarak?"

RAM: "He knows a good deal."

MASTER: "Then he won't keep his eyes on the ground so much. If the mind is much directed to something else, it doesn't dwell deeply on God."

RAM: "I have been studying the drum only to accompany the kirtan."

MASTER (*to M.*): "I hear that you too are taking singing lessons. Is that so?"

M: "No, sir. I just open my mouth now and then."

MASTER: "Have you practised that song: 'O Mother, make me mad with Thy love'? If you have, please sing it. The song expresses my ideal perfectly."

The conversation turned to Hazra's hatred for certain people, which Sri Ramakrishna did not like.

MASTER (*to the devotees*): "I used frequently to visit a certain house at Kāmārpukur. The boys of the family were of my age. The other day they came here and spent two or three days with me. Their mother, like Hazra, used to hate people. Then something happened to her foot, and gangrene set in. On account of the foul smell, no one could enter her room. I told the incident to Hazra and asked him not to hate anyone."

Toward evening, as Sri Ramakrishna was standing in the northwest corner of the courtyard, he went into samādhi. In those days the Master remained almost always in an ecstatic state. He would lose consciousness of the world at the slightest suggestion from outside. But for scant conversation with visiting devotees, he remained in an indrawn mood and was unable to perform his daily worship and devotions.

Coming down to the relative world, he began to talk to the Divine Mother, still standing where he was. "O Mother," he said, "worship has left me, and japa also. Please see, Mother, that I do not become an inert thing. Let my attitude toward God be that of the servant toward the master. O Mother, let me talk about Thee and chant Thy holy name. I want to sing Thy glories. Give me a little strength of body that I may move about, that I may go to places where Thy devotees live, and sing Thy name."

In the morning Sri Ramakrishna had been to the Kāli temple to offer flowers at the Mother's feet.

Continuing, the Master said: "O Mother, I offered flowers at Thy feet this morning. I thought: 'That is good. My mind is again going back to formal worship.' Then why do I feel like this now? Why art Thou turning me into a sort of inert thing?"

The moon had not yet risen. It was a dark night. The Master, still in an abstracted mood, sat on the small couch in his room and continued his talk with the Divine Mother. He said: "Why this special discipline of the Gāyatri? Why this jumping from this roof to that? . . . Who told him to do it? Perhaps he is doing it of his own accord. . . . Well, he will practise a little of that discipline."

The previous day Sri Ramakrishna had discouraged Ishan· about Vedic worship, saying that it was not suitable for the Kaliyuga. He had asked Ishan to worship God as the Divine Mother.

The Master said to M., "Are these all my fancies, or are they real?" M. remained silent with wonder at the Master's intimate relationship with the Divine Mother. He thought She must be within us as well as without. Indeed She must be very near us; or why should the Master speak to Her in a whisper?

Wednesday, September 26, 1883

There were very few devotees with the Master, for most of them came on Sundays. Rakhal and Latu were living with him the greater part of the time. M. arrived in the afternoon and found the Master seated on the small couch. The conversation turned to Narendra.

MASTER (*to M.*): "Have you seen Narendra lately? (*With a smile*) He said of me: 'He still goes to the Kāli temple. But he will not when he truly understands.' His people are very much dissatisfied with him because he comes here now and then. The other day he came here in a hired carriage, and Surendra paid for it. Narendra's aunt almost had a row with Surendra about it."

The Master left the couch and went to the northeast verandah, where Hazra, Kishori, Rakhal, and a few other devotees were sitting.

MASTER (*to M.*): "How is it that you are here today? Have you no school?"

M: "Our school closed today at half past one."

MASTER: "Why so early?"

M: "Vidyāsāgar visited the school. He owns the school. So the boys get a half holiday whenever he comes."

MASTER: "Why doesn't Vidyāsāgar keep his word? 'If one who holds to truth and looks on woman as his mother does not realize God, then Tulsi is a liar.'[3] If a man holds to truth he will certainly realize God. The other day Vidyāsāgar said he would come here and visit me. But he hasn't kept his word.

"There is a big difference between a scholar and a holy man. The mind of a mere scholar is fixed on 'woman and gold', but the sādhu's mind is on the Lotus Feet of Hari. A scholar says one thing and does another. But it is quite a different matter with a sādhu. The words and actions of a man who has given his mind to the Lotus Feet of God are altogether different. In Benares I saw a young sannyāsi who belonged to the sect of Nānak. He was the same age as you. He used to refer to me as the 'loving monk'. His sect has a monastery in Benares. I was invited there one day. I found that the mohant was like a housewife. I asked him, 'What is the way?' 'For the Kaliyuga,' he said, 'the path of devotion as enjoined by Nārada.' He was reading a book. When the reading was over, he recited: 'Vishnu is in water,

[3] A quotation from the sayings of Tulsidās, a great sage and poet.

Vishnu is on land, Vishnu is on the mountain top; the whole world is pervaded by Vishnu.' At the end he said, 'Peace! Peace! Abiding Peace!'

"One day he was reading the *Gītā*. He was so strict about his monastic rules that he would not read a holy book looking at a worldly man. So he turned his face toward me and his back on Mathur, who was also present. It was this holy man who told me of Nārada's path of devotion as suited to the people of the Kaliyuga."

M: "Are not sādhus of his class followers of the Vedānta?"

MASTER: "Yes, they are. But they also accept the path of devotion. The fact is that in the Kaliyuga one cannot wholly follow the path laid down in the Vedas. Once a man said to me that he would perform the puraścharana of the Gāyatri. I said: 'Why don't you do that according to the Tantra? In the Kaliyuga the discipline of Tantra is very efficacious.'

"It is extremely difficult to perform the rites enjoined in the Vedas. Further, at the present time people lead the life of slaves.[4] It is said that those who serve others for twelve years or so become slaves. They acquire the traits of those they serve. While serving their masters they acquire the rajas, the tamas, the spirit of violence, the love of luxury, and the other traits of their masters. Not only do they serve their masters, but they also enjoy a pension after their term of service is over.

"Once a Vedāntic monk came here. He used to dance at the sight of a cloud. He would go into an ecstasy of joy over a rain-storm. He would get very angry if anyone went near him when he meditated. One day I came to him while he was meditating, and that made him very cross. He discriminated constantly, 'Brahman alone is real and the world is illusory.' Since the appearance of diversity is due to māyā, he walked about with a prism from a chandelier in his hand. One sees different colours through the prism; in reality there is no such thing as colour. Likewise, nothing exists, in reality, except Brahman. But there is an appearance of the manifold because of māyā, egoism. He would not look at an object more than once, lest he should be deluded by māyā and attachment. He would discriminate, while taking his bath, at the sight of birds flying in the sky. He knew grammar. He stayed here for three days. One day he heard the sound of a flute near the embankment and said that a man who had realized Brahman would go into samādhi at such a sound."

While talking about the monk, the Master showed his devotees the manners and movements of a paramahamsa: the gait of a child, face beaming with laughter, eyes swimming in joy, and body completely naked. Then he again took his seat on the small couch and poured out his soul-enthralling words.

MASTER (*to M.*): "I learnt Vedānta from Nangtā: 'Brahman alone is real; the world is illusory.' The magician performs his magic. He produces a mango-tree which even bears mangoes. But this is all sleight of hand. The magician alone is real."

M: "It seems that the whole of life is a long sleep. This much I understand, that we are not seeing things rightly. We perceive the world with a

---

[4] Perhaps the Master was referring to the foreign rule in India.

mind by which we cannot comprehend even the nature of the sky. So how can our perceptions be correct?"

MASTER: "There is another way of looking at it. We do not see the sky rightly. It looks as if the sky were touching the ground at the horizon. How can a man see correctly? His mind is delirious, like the mind of a typhoid patient."

The Master sang in his sweet voice:

What a delirious fever is this that I suffer from!
O Mother, Thy grace is my only cure. . . .

Continuing, the Master said: "Truly it is a state of delirium. Just see how worldly men quarrel among themselves. No one knows what they quarrel about. Oh, how they quarrel! 'May such and such a thing befall you!' How much shouting! How much abuse!"

M: "I said to Kishori: 'The box is empty; there is nothing inside. But two men pull at it from either side, thinking the box contains money.' Well, the body alone is the cause of all this mischief, isn't it? The jnānis see all this and say to themselves, 'What a relief one feels when this pillow-case of the body drops off.' "

The Master and M. went toward the Kāli temple.

MASTER: "Why should you say such things? This world may be a 'framework of illusion', but it is also said that it is a 'mansion of mirth'. Let the body remain. One can also turn this world into a mansion of mirth."

M: "But where is unbroken bliss in this world?"

MASTER: "Yes, where is it?"

Sri Ramakrishna stood in front of the shrine of Kāli and prostrated himself before the Divine Mother. M. followed him. Then the Master sat on the lower floor in front of the shrine room, facing the blissful image, and leaned against a pillar of the nātmandir. He wore a red-bordered cloth, part of which was on his shoulder and back. M. sat by his side.

M: "Since there is no unbroken happiness in the world, why should one assume a body at all? I know that the body is meant only to reap the results of past action. But who knows what sort of action it is performing now? The unfortunate part is that we are being crushed."

MASTER: "If a pea falls into filth, it grows into a pea-plant none the less."

M: "But still there are the eight bonds."

MASTER: "They are not eight bonds, but eight fetters. But what if they are? These fetters fall off in a moment, by the grace of God. Do you know what it is like? Suppose a room has been kept dark a thousand years. The moment a man brings a light into it, the darkness vanishes. Not little by little. Haven't you seen the magician's feat? He takes a string with many knots, and ties one end to something, keeping the other in his hand. Then he shakes the string once or twice, and immediately all the knots come undone. But another man cannot untie the knots however he may try. All the knots of ignorance come undone in the twinkling of an eye, through the guru's grace.

"Well, can you tell me why Keshab Sen has changed so much lately? He used to come here very often. He learnt here how to bow low before a holy man. One day I told him that one should not salute a holy man as he had been doing. Harish says rightly: 'All the cheques must be approved here. Only then will they be cashed in the bank.' " (*Laughter.*)

M. listened to these words breathlessly. He began to realize that Satchidānanda, in the form of the guru, passes the "cheque".

MASTER: "Do not reason. Who can ever know God? I have heard it from Nangtā, once for all, that this whole universe is only a fragment of Brahman.

"Hazra is given to too much calculation. He says, 'This much of God has become the universe and this much is the balance.' My head aches at his calculations. I know that I know nothing. Sometimes I think of God as good, and sometimes as bad. What can I know of Him?"

M: "It is true, sir. Can anyone ever know God? Each thinks, with his little bit of intelligence, that he has understood all of God. As you say, an ant went to a sugar hill and, finding that one grain of sugar filled its stomach, thought that the next time it would take the entire hill into its hole."

MASTER: "Who can ever know God? I don't even try. I only call on Him as Mother. Let Mother do whatever She likes. I shall know Her if it is Her will; but I shall be happy to remain ignorant if She wills otherwise. My nature is that of a kitten. It only cries, 'Mew, mew!' The rest it leaves to its mother. The mother cat puts the kitten sometimes in the kitchen and sometimes on the master's bed. The young child wants only his mother. He doesn't know how wealthy his mother is, and he doesn't even want to know. He knows only, 'I have a mother; why should I worry?' Even the child of the maidservant knows that he has a mother. If he quarrels with the son of the master, he says: 'I shall tell my mother. I have a mother.' My attitude, too, is that of a child."

Suddenly Sri Ramakrishna caught M.'s attention and said, touching his own chest: "Well, there must be something here. Isn't that so?"

M. looked wonderingly at the Master. He said to himself: "Does the Mother Herself dwell in the Master's heart? Is it the Divine Mother who has assumed this human body for the welfare of humanity?"

Sri Ramakrishna was praying to the Divine Mother: "O Mother! O Embodiment of Om! Mother, how many things people say about Thee! But I don't understand any of them. I don't know anything, Mother. I have taken refuge at Thy feet. I have sought protection in Thee. O Mother, I pray only that I may have pure love for Thy Lotus Feet, love that seeks no return. And Mother, do not delude me with Thy world-bewitching māyā. I seek Thy protection. I have taken refuge in Thee."

The evening worship in the temples was over. Sri Ramakrishna was again seated in his room with M.

M. had been visiting the Master for the past two years and had received his grace and blessings. He had been told that God was both with form and without form, that He assumed forms for the sake of His devotees. To the worshipper of the formless God, the Master said: "Hold to your conviction, but remember that all is possible with God. He has form, and again, He is formless. He can be many things more."

MASTER (to M.): "You have accepted an ideal, that of God without form—isn't that so?"

M: "Yes, sir. But I also believe what you say—that all is possible with God. It is quite possible for God to have forms."

MASTER: "Good. Remember further that, as Consciousness, He pervades the entire universe of the living and non-living."

M: "I think of Him as the consciousness in conscious beings."

MASTER: "Stick to that ideal now. There is no need of tearing down and changing one's attitude. You will gradually come to realize that the consciousness in conscious beings is the Consciousness of God. He alone is Consciousness.

"Let me ask you one thing. Do you feel attracted to money and treasures?"

M: "No, sir. But I think of earning money in order to be free from anxiety, to be able to think of God without worry."

MASTER: "Oh, that's perfectly natural."

M: "Is it greed? I don't think so."

MASTER: "You are right. Otherwise, who will look after your children? What will become of them if you feel that you are not the doer?"

M: "I have heard that one cannot attain Knowledge as long as one has the consciousness of duty. Duty is like the scorching sun."

MASTER: "Keep your present attitude. It will be different when the consciousness of duty drops away of itself."

They remained silent a few minutes.

M: "To enter the world after attaining partial knowledge! Why, it is like dying in full consciousness, as in cholera!"

MASTER: "Oh, Rām! Rām!"

The idea in M.'s mind was that just as a cholera patient feels excruciating pain at the time of death, because of retaining consciousness, so also a jnāni with partial knowledge must feel extremely miserable leading the life of the world, which he knows to be illusory.

M: "People who are completely ignorant are like typhoid patients, who remain unconscious at the time of death and so do not feel the pain."

MASTER: "Tell me, what does one attain through money? Jaygopal Sen is such a wealthy man; but he complains that his children don't obey him."

M: "Is poverty the only painful thing in the world? There are the six passions besides. Then disease and grief."

MASTER: "And also name and fame, the desire to win people's recognition. Well, what do you think my attitude is?"

M: "It is like that of a man just awakened from sleep. He becomes aware of himself. You are always united with God."

MASTER: "Do you ever dream of me?"

M: "Yes, sir. Many times."

MASTER: "How? Did you dream of me as giving you instruction?"

M. remained silent.

MASTER: "If you ever see me instructing you, then know that it is Satchidānanda Himself that does so."

M. related his dream experiences to Sri Ramakrishna, who listened to them attentively.

MASTER (*to M.*): "That is very good. Don't reason any more. You are a follower of Śakti."

Wednesday, October 10, 1883

Adhar had invited the Master to come to his house on the occasion of the Durgā Pujā festival. It was the third day of the worship of the Divine Mother. When Sri Ramakrishna arrived at Adhar's house, he found Adhar's friend Sarada, Balaram's father, and Adhar's neighbours and relatives waiting for him.

The Master went into the worship hall to see the evening worship. When it was over, he remained standing there in an abstracted mood and sang in praise of the Divine Mother:

> Out of my deep affliction rescue me, O Redeemer!
> Terrified by the threats of the King of Death am I!
> Left to myself, I shall perish soon;
> Save me, oh, save me now, I pray!
>
> Mother of all the worlds! Thou, the Support of mankind!
> Thou, the Bewitcher of all, the Mother of all that has life!
> Vrindāvan's charming Rādhā art Thou,
> Dearest playmate of Braja's Beloved.
>
> Blissful comrade of Krishna, well-spring of Krishna's līlā,
> Child of Himālaya, best of the gopis, beloved of Govinda!
> Sacred Gangā, Giver of moksha!
> Śakti! The universe sings Thy praise.
>
> Thou art the Spouse of Śiva, the Ever-blessed, the All;
> Sometimes Thou takest form and sometimes art absolute.
> Eternal Beloved of Mahādeva,
> Who can fathom Thine infinite glories?

The Master went to Adhar's drawing-room on the second floor and took a seat, surrounded by the guests. Still in a mood of divine fervour, he said: "Gentlemen, I have eaten. Now go and enjoy the feast." Was the Master hinting that the Divine Mother had partaken of Adhar's offering? Did he identify himself with the Divine Mother and therefore say, "I have eaten"?

Then, addressing the Divine Mother, he continued: "Shall I eat, O Mother? Or will You eat? O Mother, the very Embodiment of the Wine of Divine Bliss!" Did the Master look on himself as one with the Divine Mother? Had the Mother incarnated Herself as the Son to instruct mankind in the ways of God? Was this why the Master said, "I have eaten"?

In that state of divine ecstasy Sri Ramakrishna saw the six centres in his body, and the Divine Mother dwelling in them. He sang a song to that effect.

Again he sang:

My mind is overwhelmed with wonder,
Pondering the Mother's mystery;
Her very name removes
The fear of Kāla, Death himself;
Beneath Her feet lies Mahā-Kāla.

Why should Her hue be kāla, black?
Many the forms of black, but She
Appears astoundingly black;
When contemplated in the heart,
She lights the lotus that blossoms there.

Her form is black, and She is named
Kāli, the Black One. Blacker than black
Is She! Beholding Her,
Man is bewitched for evermore;
No other form can he enjoy.

In wonderment asks Rāmprasād:
Where dwells this Woman so amazing?
At Her mere name, his mind
Becomes at once absorbed in Her,
Though he has never yet beheld Her.

The fear of the devotees flies away if they but seek shelter at the feet
of the Divine Mother. Was that why the Master sang the following song?

I have surrendered my soul at the fearless feet of the Mother;
Am I afraid of Death any more?
Unto the tuft of hair on my head
Is tied the almighty mantra, Mother Kāli's name.
My body I have sold in the market-place of the world
And with it have bought Sri Durgā's name.

Deep within my heart I have planted the name of Kāli,
The Wish-fulfilling Tree of heaven;
When Yama, King of Death, appears,
To him I shall open my heart and show it growing there.
I have cast out from me my six unflagging foes;[5]
Ready am I to sail life's sea,
Crying, "To Durgā, victory!"

Sarada was stricken with grief on account of his son's death. So Adhar
had taken him to Dakshineswar to visit the Master. Sarada was a devotee
of Sri Chaitanya. Sri Ramakrishna looked at him and was inspired with the
ideal of Gaurānga.

He sang:[6]

Why has My body turned so golden? It is not time for this to be:
Many the ages that must pass, before as Gaurānga I appear.
Here in the age of Dwāpara My sport is not yet at an end;
How strange this transformation is!

---

[5] The six passions.
[6] The song represents the words of Gaurānga in the mood of Krishna. Gaurānga,
who had a golden complexion, is regarded as an Incarnation of Krishna.

The peacock glistens, all of gold; and golden, too, the cuckoo
    gleams!
Everything around Me here has turned to gold! Naught else
    appears
But gold, whichever way I look.
What can it mean, this miracle, that everything I see is gold?

Ah, I can guess its meaning now:
Rādhā has come to Mathurā,[7] and that is why My skin is gold.
For she is like the bhramara,[8] and so has given Me her hue.
Dark blue My body was but now; yet in the twinkling of an eye
It turned to gold. Have I become Rādhā by contemplating her?

I cannot imagine where I am—in Mathurā or Navadvip.
But how could this have come to pass?
Not yet is Balarāma born as Nitāi, nor has Nārada
Become Śrivās, nor Yaśodā as Mother Sachi yet returned.
Then why should I, among them all, alone assume a golden face?
Not yet is Father Nanda born as Jagannāth;[9] then why should I
Be thus transmuted into gold?
Perhaps because in Mathurā sweet Rādhā has appeared, My skin
Has borrowed Gaurānga's golden hue.

Sri Ramakrishna sang again, still overpowered with the ideal of Gaurānga:

Surely Gaurānga is lost in a state of blissful ecstasy;
In an exuberance of joy, he laughs and weeps and dances and
    sings.
He takes a wood for Vrindāvan, the Ganges for the blue Jamunā;
Loudly he sobs and weeps. Yet, though he is all gold without,
He is all black within—black with the blackness of Krishna!

The Master continued to sing, assuming the attitude of a woman devotee
infatuated with love for Gaurānga:

Why do my neighbours raise such a scandal?
Why do they cast aspersions upon me
Simply because of Gaurānga?
How can they understand my feelings?
How can I ever explain?
Can I ever explain at all?
Alas, to whom shall I explain it?
Ah, but they make me die of shame!

Once on a time, at the house of Śrivās,
Gorā was loudly singing the kirtan,
When, on the ground of the courtyard,
Falling, he rolled in an ecstasy.
I, who was standing near him,
Seeing him where he lay entranced,

---

[7] The capital of Krishna's kingdom, where He lived after leaving Vrindāvan.

[8] According to a Hindu legend, the cockroach, by intently meditating upon the
bhramara, becomes transformed into the latter.

[9] Sachi and Jagannāth were Gaurānga's parents; Yaśodā and Nanda were Krishna's
parents.

Was suddenly lost to outward sense,
Until the wife of Śrivās revived me.

Another day, in the bhaktas' procession,
Gorā was sweetly singing the kirtan;
Clasping the outcastes to him,
He softened the unbelievers' hearts.
Through Nadiā's market-place
He chanted Lord Hari's holy name.
I followed the throng, and from close by
Caught a glimpse of his golden feet.

Once by the Ganges' bank he stood,
His body bright as the sun and moon,
Charming all with his beauty.
I too had come, to fetch some water,
And, as I looked from one side,
My water-jar slipped and fell to the ground.
My sister-in-law, the gossip, saw me,
And now she is spreading it everywhere.

Balaram's father was a Vaishnava; hence the Master also sang of the divine love of the gopis for their beloved Krishna:

I have not found my Krishna, O friend! How cheerless my home
     without Him!
Ah, if Krishna could only be the hair upon my head,
Carefully I should braid it then, and deck it with bakul-flowers;
Carefully I should fashion the braids out of my Krishna-hair.
Krishna is black, and black is my hair; black would be one with
     black!

Ah, if Krishna could only be the ring I wear in my nose,
Always from my nose He would hang, and my two lips could touch
     Him.
But it can never be, alas! Why should I idly dream?
Why should Krishna care at all to be the ring in my nose?

Ah, if Krishna could only be the bracelets on my arms,
Always He would cling to my wrists, and proudly I should walk,
Shaking my bracelets to make them sound, shaking my arms to
     show them;
Down the king's highway I should walk, wearing my Krishn
     bracelets.

Balaram's father was a wealthy man with estates in different parts of Orissa. An orthodox member of the Vaishnava sect, he had built temples and arranged for distribution of food to the pilgrims at various holy places. He had been spending the last years of his life in Vrindāvan. The Vaishnavas, for the most part, are bigoted in their religious views. Some of them harbour malicious feelings toward the followers of the Tantra and Vedānta. But Sri Ramakrishna never encouraged such a narrow outlook. According to his teachings, through earnestness and yearning all lovers of God will ultimately reach the same goal. The Master began the conversation in order to broaden the religious views of Balaram's father.

MASTER (*to M.*): "Once I thought, 'Why should I be one-sided?' Therefore I was initiated into Vaishnavism in Vrindāvan and took the garb of a Vaishnava monk. I spent three days practising the Vaishnava discipline. Again, at Dakshineswar I was initiated into the mystery of Rāma worship. I painted my forehead with a long mark and put on a string with a diamond round my neck. But after a few days I gave them up.

"A certain man had a tub. People would come to him to have their clothes dyed. The tub contained a solution of dye. Whatever colour a man wanted for his cloth, he would get by dipping the cloth in the tub. One man was amazed to see this and said to the dyer, 'Please give me the dye you have in your tub.'"

Was the Master hinting that people professing different religions would come to him and have their spiritual consciousness awakened according to their own ideals?

MASTER (*to Balaram's father*): "Don't read books any more. But you may read books on devotion, such as the life of Chaitanya.

"The whole thing is to love God and taste His sweetness. He is sweetness and the devotee is its enjoyer. The devotee drinks the sweet Bliss of God. Further, God is the lotus and the devotee the bee. The devotee sips the honey of the lotus.

"As a devotee cannot live without God, so also God cannot live without His devotee. Then the devotee becomes the sweetness, and God its enjoyer. The devotee becomes the lotus, and God the bee. It is the Godhead that has become these two in order to enjoy Its own Bliss. That is the significance of the episode of Rādhā and Krishna.[10]

"At the beginning of spiritual life the devotee should observe such rites as pilgrimage, putting a string of beads around his neck, and so forth. But outward ceremonies gradually drop off as he attains the goal, the vision of God. Then his only activity is the repetition of God's name, and contemplation and meditation on Him.

"The pennies equivalent to sixteen rupees make a great heap. But sixteen silver coins do not look like such a big amount. Again, the quantity becomes much smaller when you change the sixteen rupees into one gold mohur. And if you change the gold into a tiny piece of diamond, people hardly notice it."

Orthodox Vaishnavas insist on the outer insignia of religion. They criticize any devotee who does not wear these marks. Was that why the Master said that, after the vision of God, a devotee becomes indifferent to outer marks, giving up formal worship when the goal of spiritual life is attained?

MASTER (*to Balaram's father*): "The Kartābhajās group the devotees into four classes: the pravartaka, the sādhaka, the siddha, and the siddha of the siddha. The pravartaka, the beginner, puts the mark of his religion on his

[10] According to one school of the Vaishnava religion, the Supreme God Himself became Rādhā and Krishna in order to enjoy the bliss of their mutual communion.

forehead, wears a string of beads around his neck, and observes other outer conventions. The sādhaka, the struggling devotee, does not care so much for elaborate rites. An example of this class is the Bāul. The siddha, the perfect, firmly believes that God exists. The siddha of the siddha, the supremely perfect, like Chaitanya, not only has realized God but also has become intimate with Him and talks with Him all the time. This is the last limit of realization.

"There are many kinds of spiritual aspirants. Those endowed with sattva perform their spiritual practices secretly. They look like ordinary people, but they meditate inside the mosquito net.

"Aspirants endowed with rajas exhibit outward pomp—a string of beads around the neck, a mark on the forehead, an ochre robe, a silk cloth, a rosary with a gold bead, and so on. They are like stall-keepers advertising their wares with signboards.

"All religions and all paths call upon their followers to pray to one and the same God. Therefore one should not show disrespect to any religion or religious opinion. It is God alone who is called Satchidānanda Brahman in the Vedas, Satchidānanda Krishna in the Purānas, and Satchidānanda Śiva in the Tantras. It is one and the same Satchidānanda.

"There are different sects of Vaishnavas. That which is called Brahman in the Vedas is called Ālekh-Niranjan by one Vaishnava sect. 'Ālekh' means That which cannot be pointed out or perceived by the sense-organs. According to this sect, Rādhā and Krishna are only two bubbles of the Ālekh.

"According to the Vedānta,[11] there is no Incarnation of God. The Vedāntists say that Rāma and Krishna are but two waves in the Ocean of Satchidānanda.

"In reality there are not two. There is only One. A man may call on God by any name; if he is sincere in his prayer he will certainly reach Him. He will succeed if he has longing."

As Sri Ramakrishna spoke these words to the devotees, he was overwhelmed with divine fervour. Coming down to partial consciousness of the world, he said to Balaram's father, "Are you the father of Balaram?"

All sat in silence. Balaram's aged father was silently telling his beads.

MASTER (to M. and the others): "Well, these people practise so much japa and go to so many sacred places, but why are they like this? Why do they make no progress? In their case it seems as if the year consists of eighteen months.

"Once I said to Harish: 'What is the use of going to Benares if one does not feel restless for God? And if one feels that longing, then this very place is Benares.'

"They make so many pilgrimages and repeat the name of God so much, but why do they not realize anything? It is because they have no longing for God. God reveals Himself to the devotee if only he calls upon Him with a longing heart.

"At the beginning of a yātrā performance much light-hearted restlessness

[11] A reference to the Advaita Vedānta.

is to be observed on the stage. At that time one does not see Krishna. Next the sage Nārada enters with his flute and sings longingly, 'O Govinda! O my Life! O my Soul!' Then Krishna can no longer remain away and appears with the cowherd boys."

Tuesday, October 16, 1883

Sri Ramakrishna was in his room with Rakhal, Balaram's father, Beni Pal, M., Mani Mallick, Ishan, Kishori, and other devotees.

MASTER: "Liberal-minded devotees accept all the forms of God: Krishna, Kāli, Śiva, Rāma, and so on."

BALARAM'S FATHER: "Yes, sir. It is like a woman's recognizing her husband, whatever clothes he wears."

MASTER: "But again, there is a thing called nishthā, single-minded devotion. When the gopis went to Mathurā they saw Krishna with a turban on His head. At this they pulled down their veils and said, 'Who is this man? Where is *our* Krishna with the peacock feather on His crest and the yellow cloth on His body?' Hanumān also had that unswerving devotion. He came to Dwārakā in the cycle of Dwāpara. Krishna said to Rukmini, His queen, 'Hanumān will not be satisfied unless he sees the form of Rāma.' So, to please Hanumān, Krishna assumed the form of Rāma.

"But, my dear sir, I am in a peculiar state of mind. My mind constantly descends from the Absolute to the Relative, and again ascends from the Relative to the Absolute.

"The attainment of the Absolute is called the Knowledge of Brahman. But it is extremely difficult to acquire. A man cannot acquire the Knowledge of Brahman unless he completely rids himself of his attachment to the world. When the Divine Mother was born as the daughter of King Himālaya, She showed Her various forms to Her father. The king said, 'I want to see Brahman.' Thereupon the Divine Mother said: 'Father, if that is your desire, then you must seek the company of holy men. You must go into solitude, away from the world, and now and then live in holy company.'

"The manifold has come from the One alone, the Relative from the Absolute. There is a state of consciousness where the many disappears, and the One, as well; for the many must exist as long as the One exists. Brahman is without comparison. It is impossible to explain Brahman by analogy. It is between light and darkness. It is Light, but not the light that we perceive, not material light.

"Again, when God changes the state of my mind, when He brings my mind down to the plane of the Relative, I perceive that it is He who has become all these—the Creator, māyā, the living beings, and the universe.

"Again, sometimes He shows me that He has created the universe and all living beings. He is the Master, and the universe His garden.

" 'He is the Master, and the universe and all its living beings belong to Him'—that is Knowledge. And, 'I am the doer', 'I am the guru', 'I am the father'—that is ignorance. 'This is my house; this is my family; this is my wealth; these are my relatives'—this also is ignorance."

BALARAM'S FATHER: "That is true, sir."

MASTER: "As long as you do not feel that God is the Master, you must come back to the world, you must be born again and again. There will be no rebirth when you can truly say, 'O God, Thou art the Master.' As long as you cannot say, 'O Lord, Thou alone art real', you will not be released from the life of the world. This going and coming, this rebirth, is inevitable. There will be no liberation. Further, what can you achieve by saying, 'It is mine'? The manager of an estate may say, 'This is our garden; these are our couches and furniture.' But when he is dismissed by the master, he hasn't the right to take away even a chest of worthless mango-wood given to him for his use.

"The feeling of 'I and mine' has covered the Reality. Because of this we do not see Truth. Attainment of Chaitanya, Divine Consciousness, is not possible without the knowledge of Advaita, Non-duality. After realizing Chaitanya one enjoys Nityananda, Eternal Bliss. One enjoys this Bliss after attaining the state of a paramahamsa.

"Vedanta does not recognize the Incarnation of God. According to it, Chaitanyadeva is only a bubble of the non-dual Brahman.

"Do you know what the vision of Divine Consciousness is like? It is like the sudden illumination of a dark room when a match is struck.

"The Incarnation of God is accepted by those who follow the path of bhakti. A woman belonging to the Kartabhaja sect observed my condition and remarked: 'You have inner realization. Don't dance and sing too much. Ripe grapes must be preserved carefully in cotton. The mother-in-law lessens her daughter-in-law's activities when the daughter-in-law is with child. One characteristic of God-realization is that the activities of a man with such realization gradually drop away. Inside this man [meaning Sri Ramakrishna] is the real Jewel.'

"Watching me eat, she remarked, 'Sir, are you yourself eating, or are you feeding someone else?'

"The feeling of ego has covered the Truth. Narendra once said, 'As the "I" of man recedes, the "I" of God approaches.' Kedar says, 'The more clay there is in the jar, the less water it holds.'

"Krishna said to Arjuna: 'Brother, you will not realize Me if you possess even one of the eight siddhis.' These give only a little power. With healing and the like one may do only a little good to others. Isn't that true?

"Therefore I prayed to the Divine Mother for pure love only, a love that does not seek any return. I never asked for occult powers."

While talking thus, Sri Ramakrishna went into samadhi. He sat there motionless, completely forgetful of the outer world. Then, coming down to the sense world, he sang:

> Ah, friend! I have not found Him yet, whose love has driven me
> mad. . . .

At the Master's request, Ramlal sang a song describing how Chaitanya embraced the monastic life:

Oh, what a vision I have beheld in Keshab Bhārati's[12] hut!
Gorā, in all his matchless grace,
Shedding tears in a thousand streams!
Like a mad elephant
He dances in ecstasy and sings,
Drunk with an overwhelming love.

Rolling flat upon the ground and swimming in his tears,
He weeps and shouts Lord Hari's name,
Piercing the very heavens with his cries,
Loud as a lion's roar;
Then most humbly he begs men's love,
To feel himself the servant of God.

Shorn of his locks, he has put on the yogi's ochre robe;
Even the hardest heart must melt
To see his pure and heavenly love.
Smitten by man's deep woe,
He has abandoned everything
And pours out love unstintingly.

Oh, would that Premdās were his slave and, passing from
  door to door,
Might sing Gaurānga's endless praise!

The Master asked Mani Mallick to quote the words of Tulsidās to the
effect that one who had developed love of God could not observe caste
distinctions.

MANI: " 'The throat of the chātak bird is pierced with thirst. All around
are the waters of the Ganges, the Jamunā, the Saraju, and of innumerable
other rivers and lakes; but the bird will not touch any of these. It only looks
up expectantly for the rain that falls when the star Svāti is in the ascendant.' "

MASTER: "That means that love for the Lotus Feet of God is alone real,
and all else illusory."

MANI: "Tulsi also said: 'At the touch of the philosopher's stone, the
eight metals become gold. Likewise all castes, even the butcher and the untouchable, become pure by repeating Hari's name. Without Hari's name the
people of the four castes are but butchers.' "

MASTER: "The hide that the scriptures forbid one to touch can be taken
inside the temple after it has been tanned.

"Man becomes pure by repeating the name of God. Therefore one should
practise the chanting of God's name. I said to Jadu Mallick's mother: 'In
the hour of death you will think only of worldly things—of family, children,
executing the will, and so forth. The thought of God will not come to your
mind. The way to remember God in the hour of death is to practise, now,
the repetition of His name and the chanting of His glories. If one keeps up
this practice, then in the hour of death one will repeat the name of God.
When the cat pounces upon the bird, the bird only squawks and does not
say, 'Rāma, Rāma, Harē-Krishna'.

"It is good to prepare for death. One should constantly think of God and

[12] The monastic teacher of Sri Chaitanya.

chant His name in solitude during the last years of one's life. If the elephant is put into the stable after its bath it is not soiled again by dirt and dust."

Balaram's father, Mani Mallick, and Beni Pal were all elderly mèn. Did the Master give this instruction especially for their benefit?

MASTER: "Why do I ask you to think of God and chant His name in solitude? Living in the world day and night, one suffers from worries. Haven't you noticed brother killing brother for a foot of land? The Śikhs said to me, 'The cause of all worry and confusion is these three: land, woman, and money.'

"You are leading a householder's life. Why should you be afraid of the world? When Rāma said to Daśaratha that He was going to renounce the world, it worried His father, and the king sought counsel of Vaśishtha. Vaśishtha said to Rāma: 'Rāma, why should You give up the world? Reason with me. Is this world outside God? What is there to renounce and what is there to accept? Nothing whatever exists but God. It is Brahman alone that appears as Iśvara, māyā, living beings, and the universe.'"

BALARAM'S FATHER: "It is very difficult, sir."

MASTER: "The aspirant, while practising spiritual discipline, looks upon the world as a 'framework of illusion'. Again, after the attainment of Knowledge, the vision of God, this very world becomes to him a 'mansion of mirth'.

"It is written in the books of the Vaishnavas: 'God can be attained through faith alone; reasoning pushes Him far away.' Faith alone!

"What faith Krishnakishore had! At Vrindāvan a low-caste man drew water for him from a well. Krishnakishore said to him, 'Repeat the name of Śiva.' After the man had repeated the name of Śiva, Krishnakishore unhesitatingly drank the water. He used to say, 'If a man chants the name of God, does he need to spend money any more for the atonement of his sins? How foolish!' He was amazed to see people worshipping God with the sacred tulsi-leaf in order to get rid of their illnesses. At the bathing-ghat here he said to us, 'Please bless me, that I may pass my days repeating Rāma's holy name.' Whenever I went to his house he would dance with joy at the sight of me. Rāma said to Lakshmana, 'Brother, whenever you find people singing and dancing in the ecstasy of divine love, know for certain that I am there.' Chaitanya is an example of such ecstatic love. He laughed and wept and danced and sang in divine ecstasy. He was an Incarnation. God incarnated Himself through Chaitanya."

Sri Ramakrishna sang a song describing the divine love of Chaitanya. Then Balaram's father, Mani Mallick, Beni Pal, and several other devotees took leave of the Master.

In the evening, devotees from Kānsāritolā, Calcutta, arrived. The Master danced and sang with them in a state of divine fervour. After dancing, he went into a spiritual mood and said, "I shall go part of the way myself." Kishori came forward to massage his feet, but the Master did not allow anyone to touch him.

Ishan arrived. The Master was seated, still in a spiritual mood. After a

while he became engaged in talk with Ishan. It was Ishan's desire to practise
the puraścharana of the Gāyatri.

MASTER (*to Ishan*): "Follow your own intuition. I hope there is no more
doubt in your mind. Is there any? The path of the Vedas is not meant for
the Kaliyuga. The path of Tantra is efficacious."

ISHAN: "I have almost resolved to perform an atonement ceremony."

MASTER: "Do you mean to say that one cannot follow the path of Tantra?
That which is Brahman is also Śakti, Kāli.

> Knowing the secret that Kāli is one with the highest Brahman,
> I have discarded, once for all, both righteousness and sin."

ISHAN: "It is mentioned in a hymn in the *Chandi* that Brahman alone is
the Primal Energy. Brahman is identical with Śakti."

MASTER: "It will not do simply to express that idea in words. Only when
you assimilate it will all be well with you.

"When the heart becomes pure through the practice of spiritual discipline,
then one rightly feels that God alone is the Doer. He alone has become mind,
life, and intelligence. We are only His instruments.

> Thou it is that holdest the elephant in the mire;
> Thou, that helpest the lame man scale the loftiest hill.

"When your heart becomes pure, then you will realize that it is God who
makes us perform such rites as the puraścharana.

> Thou workest Thine own work; men only call it theirs.

"All doubts disappear after the realization of God. Then the devotee meets
the favourable wind. He becomes free from worry. He is like the boatman
who, when the favourable wind blows, unfurls the sail, holds the rudder
lightly, and enjoys a smoke."

Ishan took his leave and Sri Ramakrishna talked with M. No one else was
present. He asked M. what he thought of Narendra, Rakhal, Adhar, and
Hazra, and whether they were guileless. "And", asked the Master, "what do
you think of me?"

M. said: "You are simple and at the same time deep. It is extremely difficult to understand you."

Sri Ramakrishna laughed.

November 26, 1883

It was the day of the annual festival of the Sinduriāpatti Brāhmo Samāj.
The ceremony was to be performed in Manilal Mallick's house. The worship
hall was beautifully decorated with flowers, wreaths, and evergreens, and
many devotees were assembled, eagerly awaiting the worship. Their enthusiasm had been greatly heightened by the news that Sri Ramakrishna was
going to grace the occasion with his presence. Keshab, Vijay, Shivanath, and
other leaders of the Brāhmo Samāj held him in high respect. His God-
intoxicated state of mind, his intense love of spiritual life, his burning faith,
his intimate communion with God, and his respect for women, whom he

regarded as veritable manifestations of the Divine Mother, together with the unsullied purity of his character, his complete renunciation of worldly talk, his love and respect for all religious faiths, and his eagerness to meet devotees of all creeds, attracted the members of the Brāhmo Samāj to him. Devotees came that day from far-off places to join the festival, for it would give them a chance to get a glimpse of the Master and listen to his inspiring talk.

Sri Ramakrishna arrived at the house before the worship began, and became engaged in conversation with Vijaykrishna Goswami and the other devotees. The lamps were lighted and the divine service was about to begin.

The Master asked if Shivanath would come to the festival. A Brāhmo devotee said that he had other important things to do and was not coming.

MASTER: "I feel very happy when I see Shivanath. He always seems to be absorbed in the bliss of bhakti. Further, a man who is respected by so many surely possesses some divine power. But he has one great defect: he doesn't keep his word. Once he said to me that he would come to Dakshineswar, but he neither came nor sent me word. That is not good. It is said that truthfulness alone constitutes the spiritual discipline of the Kaliyuga. If a man clings tenaciously to truth he ultimately realizes God. Without this regard for truth, one gradually loses everything. If by chance I say that I will go to the pine-grove, I must go there even if there is no further need of it, lest I lose my attachment to truth. After my vision of the Divine Mother, I prayed to Her, taking a flower in my hands: 'Mother, here is Thy knowledge and here is Thy ignorance. Take them both, and give me only pure love. Here is Thy holiness and here is Thy unholiness. Take them both, Mother, and give me pure love. Here is Thy good and here is Thy evil. Take them both, Mother, and give me pure love. Here is Thy righteousness and here is Thy unrighteousness. Take them both, Mother, and give me pure love.' I mentioned all these, but I could not say: 'Mother, here is Thy truth and here is Thy falsehood. Take them both.' I gave up everything at Her feet but could not bring myself to give up truth."

Soon the service began according to the rules of the Brāhmo Samāj. The preacher was seated on the dais. After the opening prayer he recited holy texts of the Vedas and was joined by the congregation in the invocation to the Supreme Brahman. They chanted in chorus: "Brahman is Truth, Knowledge, and Infinity. It shines as Bliss and Immortality. Brahman is Peace, Blessedness, the One without a Second; It is pure and unstained by sin." The minds of the devotees were stilled, and they closed their eyes in meditation.

The Master went into deep samādhi. He sat there transfixed and speechless. After some time he opened his eyes, looked around, and suddenly stood up with the words "Brahma! Brahma!" on his lips. Soon the devotional music began, accompanied by drums and cymbals. In a state of divine fervour the Master began to dance with the devotees. Vijay and the other Brāhmos danced around him. The guests and the devotees were enchanted. Many of them drank the sweet bliss of God's name and forgot the world. The happiness of the material world appeared bitter to them, at least for the time being.

After the kirtan all sat around the Master, eager to hear his words.

MASTER: "It is difficult to lead the life of a householder in a spirit of detachment. Once Pratap[13] said to me: 'Sir, we follow the example of King Janaka. He led the life of a householder in a detached spirit. We shall follow him.' I said to him: 'Can one be like King Janaka by merely wishing it? How many austerities he practised in order to acquire divine knowledge! He practised the most intense form of asceticism for many years and only then returned to the life of the world.'

"Is there, then, no hope for householders? Certainly there is. They must practise spiritual discipline in solitude for some days. Thus they will acquire knowledge and devotion. Then it will not hurt them to lead the life of the world. But when you practise discipline in solitude, keep yourself entirely away from your family. You must not allow your wife, son, daughter, mother, father, sister, brother, friends, or relatives near you. While thus practising discipline in solitude, you should think: 'I have no one else in the world. God is my all.' You must also pray to Him, with tears in your eyes, for knowledge and devotion.

"If you ask me how long you should live in solitude away from your family, I should say that it would be good for you if you could spend even one day in such a manner. Three days at a time are still better. One may live in solitude for twelve days, a month, three months, or a year, according to one's convenience and ability. One hasn't much to fear if one leads the life of a householder after attaining knowledge and devotion.

"If you break a jack-fruit after rubbing your hands with oil, then its sticky milk will not smear your hands. While playing the game of hide-and-seek, you are safe if you but once touch the 'granny'. Be turned into gold by touching the philosopher's stone. After that you may remain buried underground a thousand years; when you are taken out you will still be gold.

"The mind is like milk. If you keep the mind in the world, which is like water, then the milk and water will get mixed. That is why people keep milk in a quiet place and let it set into curd, and then churn butter from it. Likewise, through spiritual discipline practised in solitude, churn the butter of knowledge and devotion from the milk of the mind. Then that butter can easily be kept in the water of the world. It will not get mixed with the world. The mind will float detached on the water of the world."

Vijay had just returned from Gayā, where he had spent a long time in solitude and holy company. He had put on the ochre robe of a monk and was in an exalted state of mind, always indrawn. He was sitting before the Master with his head bent down, as if absorbed in some deep thought.

Casting his benign glance on Vijay, the Master said: "Vijay, have you found your room?

"Let me tell you a parable: Once two holy men, in the course of their wanderings, entered a city. One of them, with wondering eyes and mouth agape, was looking at the market-place, the stalls, and the buildings, when he met his companion. The latter said: 'You seem to be filled with wonder at the city. Where is your baggage?' He replied: 'First of all I found a room.

[13] Pratap Chandra Mazumdar, a celebrated leader of the Brāhmo Samāj.

I put my things in it, locked the door, and felt totally relieved. Now I am going about the city enjoying all the fun.'

"So I am asking you, Vijay, if you have found your room. (*To M. and the others*) You see, the spring in Vijay's heart has been covered all these days. Now it is open.

(*To Vijay*) "Well, Shivanath is always in trouble and turmoil. He has to write for magazines and perform many other duties. Worldly duties bring much worry and anxiety along with them.

"It is narrated in the *Bhāgavata* that the Avadhuta had twenty-four gurus, one of whom was a kite. In a certain place the fishermen were catching fish. A kite swooped down and snatched a fish. At the sight of the fish, about a thousand crows chased the kite and made a great noise with their cawing. Whichever way the kite flew with the fish, the crows followed it. The kite flew to the south and the crows followed it there. The kite flew to the north and still the crows followed after it. The kite went east and west, but with the same result. As the kite began to fly about in confusion, lo, the fish dropped from its mouth. The crows at once let the kite alone and flew after the fish. Thus relieved of its worries, the kite sat on the branch of a tree and thought: 'That wretched fish was at the root of all my troubles. I have now got rid of it and therefore I am at peace.'

"The Avadhuta learnt this lesson from the kite, that as long as a man has the fish, that is, worldly desires, he must perform actions and consequently suffer from worry, anxiety, and restlessness. No sooner does he renounce these desires than his activities fall away and he enjoys peace of soul.

"But work without any selfish motive is good. It does not create any worry. But it is very difficult to be totally unselfish. We may think that our work is selfless, but selfishness comes, unknown to us, from no one knows where. But if a man has already undergone great spiritual discipline, then as a result of it he may be able to do work without any selfish motive. After the vision of God a man can easily do unselfish work. In most cases action drops away after the attainment of God. Only a few, like Nārada, work to bring light to mankind.

"The Avadhuta accepted a bee as another teacher. Bees accumulate their honey by days of hard labour. But they cannot enjoy their honey, for a man soon breaks the comb and takes it away. The Avadhuta learnt this lesson from the bees, that one should not lay things up. Sādhus should depend one hundred per cent on God. They must not gather for the morrow. But this does not apply to the householder. He must bring up his family; therefore it is necessary for him to provide. Birds and monks do not hoard. Yet birds also hoard after their chicks are hatched: they collect food in their beaks for their young ones.

"Let me tell you one thing, Vijay. Don't trust a sādhu if he keeps bag and baggage with him and a bundle of clothes with many knots. I have seen such sādhus under the banyan tree in the Panchavati. Two or three of them were seated there. One was picking over lentils, some were sewing their clothes, and all were gossiping about a feast they had enjoyed in a rich man's house. They said among themselves, 'That rich man spent a hundred thousand rupees on the feast and fed the sādhus sumptuously with cake, sweets, and many such delicious things.' " (*All laugh.*)

VIJAY: "It is true, sir. I have seen such sādhus at Gayā. They are called the lotāwalla sādhus[14] of Gayā."

MASTER (*to Vijay*): "When love of God is awakened, work drops away of itself. If God makes some men work, let them work. It is now time for you to give up everything. Renounce all and say, 'O mind, may you and I alone behold the Mother, letting no one else intrude.' "

Saying this, Sri Ramakrishna began to sing in his soul-enthralling voice:

> Cherish my precious Mother Śyāmā
> Tenderly within, O mind;
> May you and I alone behold Her,
> Letting no one else intrude.
>
> O mind, in solitude enjoy Her,
> Keeping the passions all outside;
> Take but the tongue, that now and again
> It may cry out, "O Mother! Mother!"
>
> Suffer no breath of base desire
> To enter and approach us there,
> But bid true knowledge stand on guard,
> Alert and watchful evermore.

The Master said to Vijay: "Surrender yourself completely to God, and set aside all such things as fear and shame. Give up such feelings as, 'What will people think of me if I dance in the ecstasy of God's holy name?' The saying, 'One cannot have the vision of God as long as one has these three— shame, hatred, and fear', is very true. Shame, hatred, fear, caste, pride, secretiveness, and the like are so many bonds. Man is free when he is liberated from all these.

"When bound by ties one is jīva, and when free from ties one is Śiva. Prema, ecstatic love of God, is a rare thing.

"First of all one acquires bhakti. Bhakti is single-minded devotion to God, like the devotion a wife feels for her husband. It is very difficult to have unalloyed devotion to God. Through such devotion one's mind and soul merge in Him.

"Then comes bhāva, intense love. Through bhāva a man becomes speechless. His nerve currents are stilled. Kumbhaka comes by itself. It is like the case of a man whose breath and speech stop when he fires a gun.

"But prema, ecstatic love, is an extremely rare thing. Chaitanya had that love. When one has prema one forgets all outer things. One forgets the world. One even forgets one's own body, which is so dear to a man."

The Master began to sing:

> Oh, when will dawn the blessed day
> When tears of joy will flow from my eyes
> As I repeat Lord Hari's name?
> Oh, when will dawn the blessed day

[14] Sādhus carrying water-pots.

When all my craving for the world
Will vanish straightway from my heart,
And with the thrill of His holy name
All of my hair will stand on end?
Oh, when will dawn that blessed day?

So the talk of divine things was proceeding, when some invited Brāhmo devotees entered the room. There were among them a few pundits and high government officials.

Sri Ramakrishna had said that bhāva stills the nerve currents of the devotee. He continued: "When Arjuna was about to shoot at the target, the eye of a fish, his eyes were fixed on the eye of the fish, and on nothing else. He didn't even notice any part of the fish except the eye. In such a state the breathing stops and one experiences kumbhaka.

"Another characteristic of God-vision is that a great spiritual current rushes up along the spine and goes toward the brain. If then the devotee goes into samādhi, he sees God."

Looking at the Brāhmo devotees who had just arrived, the Master said: "Mere pundits, devoid of divine love, talk incoherently. Pundit Samadhyayi once said, in the course of his sermon: 'God is dry. Make Him sweet by your love and devotion.' Imagine! To describe Him as dry, whom the Vedas declare as the Essence of Bliss! It makes one feel that the pundit didn't know what God really is. That was why his words were so incoherent.

"A man once said, 'There are many horses in my uncle's cow-shed.' From that one could know that the man had no horses at all. No one keeps a horse in a cow-shed.

"Some people pride themselves on their riches and power—their wealth, honour, and social position. But these are only transitory. Nothing will remain with you in death.

"There is a song that runs:

Remember this, O mind! Nobody is your own:
Vain is your wandering in this world.
Trapped in the subtle snare of māyā as you are,
Do not forget the Mother's name.

Only a day or two men honour you on earth
As lord and master; all too soon
That form, so honoured now, must needs be cast away,
When Death, the Master, seizes you.

Even your beloved wife, for whom, while yet you live,
You fret yourself almost to death,
Will not go with you then; she too will say farewell,
And shun your corpse as an evil thing.

"One must not be proud of one's money. If you say that you are rich, then one can remind you that there are richer men than you, and others richer still, and so on. At dusk the glow-worm comes out and thinks that it lights the world. But its pride is crushed when the stars appear in the sky. The stars feel that they give light to the earth. But when the moon rises the stars fade in shame. The moon feels that the world smiles at its light and that it lights the earth. Then the eastern horizon becomes red, and the sun rises. The moon fades and after a while is no longer seen.

"If wealthy people would think that way, they would get rid of their pride in their wealth."

Manilal had provided a sumptuous feast in celebration of the festival. He entertained the Master and the other guests with great love and attention. It was late at night when they returned to their homes.

LAST VISIT TO KESHAB

AT TWO O'CLOCK in the afternoon, M. was pacing the foot-path of
the Circular Road in front of the Lily Cottage, where Keshab
Chandra Sen lived. He was eagerly awaiting the arrival of Sri Ramakrishna. Keshab's illness had taken a serious turn, and there was very little
chance of his recovery. Since the Master loved Keshab dearly, he was coming
from Dakshineswar to pay him a visit.

On the east side of the Circular Road was Victoria College, where the
ladies of Keshab's Brāhmo Samāj and their daughters received their education.
To the north of the college was a spacious garden house inhabited by an
English family. M. noticed that there was a commotion in the house and
wondered what was going on. Presently a hearse arrived with the drivers
dressed in black, and the members of the household appeared, looking very
sad. There had been a death in the family.

"Whither does the soul go, leaving behind this mortal body?" Pondering
the age-old question, M. waited, watching the carriages that came from the
north.

About five o'clock a carriage stopped in front of the Lily Cottage and Sri
Ramakrishna got out with Latu and several other devotees, including Rakhal.
He was received by Keshab's relatives, who led him and the devotees upstairs
to the verandah south of the drawing-room. The Master seated himself
on a couch.

After a long wait he became impatient to see Keshab. Keshab's disciples
said that he was resting and would be there presently. Sri Ramakrishna
became more and more impatient and said to Keshab's disciples: "Look here,
what need is there of his coming to me? Why can't I go in and see him?"

PRASANNA (*humbly*): "Sir, he will come in a few minutes."

MASTER: "Go away! It is you who are making all this fuss. Let me go in."

Prasanna began to talk about Keshab in order to divert the Master's
attention. He said: "Keshab is now an altogether different person. Like
you, sir, he talks to the Divine Mother. He hears what the Mother says,
and laughs and cries."

When he was told that Keshab talked to the Divine Mother and laughed
and cried, the Master became ecstatic. Presently he went into samādhi.

It was winter and the Master was wearing a green flannel coat with a shawl thrown over it. He sat straight, with his eyes fixed, deep in ecstasy. A long time passed in this way. There was no indication of his returning to the normal plane of consciousness.

Gradually it became dark. Lamps were lighted in the drawing-room, where the Master was now to go. While he was slowly coming down to the plane of ordinary consciousness, he was taken there, though with great difficulty. The room was well furnished. At the sight of the furniture, the Master muttered to himself, "These things were necessary before, but of what use are they now?" Seeing Rakhal, he said, "Oh, hello! Are you here?" Then, seating himself on a couch, he again lost consciousness of the outer world, and, looking around as if seeing someone, he said: "Hello, Mother! I see that You too have come. How You are showing off in Your Benares sāri! Don't bother me now, please. Sit down and be quiet."

The Master was in a state of intense divine intoxication. In the well-lighted room the Brāhmo devotees sat around the Master; Latu, Rakhal, and M. remained near him. He was saying to himself, still filled with divine fervour: "The body and the soul! The body was born and it will die. But for the soul there is no death. It is like the betel-nut. When the nut is ripe it does not stick to the shell. But when it is green it is difficult to separate it from the shell. After realizing God, one does not identify oneself any more with the body. Then one knows that body and soul are two different things."

At this moment Keshab entered the room. He came through the east door. Those who remembered the man who had preached in the Town Hall or the Brāhmo Samāj temple were shocked to see this skeleton covered with skin. He could hardly stand. He walked holding to the wall for support. With great difficulty he sat down in front of the couch. In the mean time Sri Ramakrishna had got down from the couch and was sitting on the floor. Keshab bowed low before the Master and remained in that position a long time, touching the Master's feet with his forehead. Then he sat up. Sri Ramakrishna was still in a state of ecstasy. He muttered to himself. He talked to the Divine Mother.

Raising his voice, Keshab said: "I am here, sir. I am here." He took Sri Ramakrishna's left hand and stroked it gently. But the Master was in deep samādhi, completely intoxicated with divine love. A stream of words came from his lips as he talked to himself, and the devotees listened to him spellbound.

MASTER: "As long as a man associates himself with upādhis, so long he sees the manifold, such as Keshab, Prasanna, Amrita, and so on; but on attaining Perfect Knowledge he sees only one Consciousness everywhere. The same Perfect Knowledge, again, makes him realize that the one Consciousness has become the universe and its living beings and the twenty-four cosmic principles. But the manifestations of Divine Power are different in different beings. It is He, undoubtedly, who has become everything; but in some cases there is a greater manifestation than in others.

"Vidyāsāgar once asked me, 'Can it be true that God has endowed some with greater power and some with less?' I replied: 'If that were not so, how is it that one.man may be stronger than fifty? If that were not the case, again, how is it that we have all come here to see you?'

"The soul through which God sports is endowed with His special power. The landlord may reside in any part of his estate, but he is generally to be found in a particular drawing-room. The devotee is God's drawing-room. God loves to sport in the heart of His devotee. It is there that His special power is manifest.

"What is the sign of such a devotee? When you see a man doing great works, you may know that God's special power is manifested through him.

"The Primordial Power and the Supreme Brahman are identical. You can never think of the one without the other. They are like the gem and its brilliance. One cannot think of the brilliance without the gem, or of the gem without its brilliance. Again, it is like the snake and its wriggling motion. One cannot think of the wriggling motion without the snake, or of the snake without its wriggling motion.

"It is the Primordial Power that has become the universe and its living beings and the twenty-four cosmic principles. It is a case of involution and evolution.[1]

"Why do I feel so restless for Rakhal, Narendra, and the other youngsters? Hazra once asked me, 'When will you think of God if you are always anxious about these boys?' (*Keshab and the others smile.*) That worried me greatly. I prayed to the Divine Mother: 'Mother, see what a fix I am in! Hazra scolds me because I worry about these young men.' Afterwards I asked Bholanath about it. He said to me that such a state of mind is described in the *Mahābhārata*. How else will a man established in samādhi occupy his mind in the phenomenal world, after coming down from samādhi? That is why he seeks the company of devotees endowed with sattva. I gave a sigh of relief when Bholanath told me of the *Mahābhārata*.

"Hazra is not to blame. During the period of struggle one should follow the method of discrimination—'Not this, not this'—and direct the whole mind to God. But the state of perfection is quite different. After reaching God one reaffirms what formerly one denied. To extract butter you must separate it from the buttermilk. Then you discover that butter and buttermilk are intrinsically related to one another. They belong to the same stuff. The butter is not essentially different from the buttermilk, nor the buttermilk essentially different from the butter. After realizing God one knows definitely that it is He who has become everything. In some objects He is manifested more clearly, and in others less clearly.

"When a flood comes from the ocean, all the land is deep under water. Before the flood, the boat could have reached the ocean only by following the winding course of the river. But after the flood, one can row straight to the ocean. One need not take a roundabout course. After the harvest has been reaped, one need not take the roundabout course along the balk of the field. One can cross the field at any point.

[1] That is to say, before the creation, the universe and its living beings and the twenty-four cosmic principles lie involved in the Primordial Power, and after the creation these gradually evolve from It.

"After the realization of God, He is seen in all beings. But His greater manifestation is in man. Again, among men, God manifests Himself more clearly in those devotees who are sāttvic, in those who have no desire whatever to enjoy 'woman and gold'. Where can a man of samādhi rest his mind, after coming down from the plane of samādhi? That is why he feels the need of seeking the company of pure-hearted devotees, endowed with sattva and free from attachment to 'woman and gold'. How else could such a person occupy himself in the relative plane of consciousness?

"He who is Brahman is the Ādyaśakti, the Primal Energy. When inactive He is called Brahman, the Purusha; He is called Śakti, or Prakriti, when engaged in creation, preservation, and destruction. These are the two aspects of Reality: Purusha and Prakriti. He who is the Purusha is also Prakriti. Both are the embodiment of Bliss.

"If you are aware of the Male Principle, you cannot ignore the Female Principle. He who is aware of the father must also think of the mother. (Keshab laughs.) He who knows darkness also knows light. He who knows night also knows day. He who knows happiness also knows misery. You understand this, don't you?"

KESHAB: "Yes, sir. I do."

MASTER: "My Mother! Who is my Mother? Ah, She is the Mother of the Universe. It is She who creates and preserves the world, who always protects Her children, and who grants whatever they desire: dharma, artha, kāma, moksha. A true son cannot live away from his mother. The mother knows everything. The child only eats, drinks, and makes merry; he doesn't worry himself about the things of the world."

KESHAB: "Yes, sir. It is quite true."

While talking, Sri Ramakrishna regained the normal consciousness of the world. With a smile on his face he conversed with Keshab. The roomful of men watched them eagerly, and listened to their words. Everybody was amazed to find that neither Keshab nor the Master inquired about each other's health. They talked only of God.

MASTER (to Keshab): "Why do the members of the Brāhmo Samāj dwell so much on God's glories? Is there any great need of repeating such things as 'O God, Thou hast created the moon, the sun, and the stars'? Most people are filled with admiration for the garden only. How few care to see its owner! Who is greater, the garden or its owner?

"After a few drinks at a tavern, do I care to know how many gallons of wine are stored there? One bottle is enough for me.

"When I met Narendra, I never asked him: 'Who is your father? How many houses does he own?'

"Shall I tell you the truth? Man loves his own riches, and so he thinks that God loves His, too. He thinks that God will be pleased if we glorify His riches. Once Sambhu said to me, 'Please bless me, that I may die leaving my riches at the Lotus Feet of God.' I answered: 'These are riches only to you. What riches can you offer God? To Him these are mere dust and straw.'

"Once a thief broke into the temple of Vishnu and robbed the image of its jewels. Mathur Babu and I went to the temple to see what was the matter. Addressing the image, Mathur said bitterly: 'What a shame, Lord! You are so worthless! The thief took all the ornaments from Your body, and You couldn't do a thing about it.' Thereupon I said to Mathur: 'Shame on you! How improper your words are! To God, the jewels you talk so much about are only lumps of clay. Lakshmi, the Goddess of Fortune, is His Consort. Do you mean to say that He should spend sleepless nights because a thief has taken your few rupees? You mustn't say such things.'

"Can one ever bring God under control through wealth? He can be tamed only through love. What does He want? Certainly not wealth! He wants from His devotees love, devotion, feeling, discrimination, and renunciation.

"One looks on God exactly according to one's own inner feeling. Take, for instance, a devotee with an excess of tamas. He thinks that the Divine Mother eats goat. So he slaughters one for Her. Again, the devotee endowed with rajas cooks rice and various other dishes for the Mother. But the sāttvic devotee doesn't make any outer show of his worship. People don't even know he is worshipping. If he has no flowers, he worships God with mere Ganges water and the leaves of the bel-tree. His food offering to the Deity consists of sweetened puffed rice or a few candies. Occasionally he cooks a little rice pudding for the Deity.

"There is also another class of devotees, those who are beyond the three gunas. They have the nature of a child. Their worship consists in chanting God's name—just His name.

(To Keshab, with a smile) "Why is it that you are ill? There is a reason for it. Many spiritual feelings have passed through your body; therefore it has fallen ill. At the time an emotion is aroused, one understands very little about it. The blow that it delivers to the body is felt only after a long while. I have seen big steamers going by on the Ganges, at the time hardly noticing their passing. But oh, my! What a terrific noise is heard after a while, when the waves splash against the banks! Perhaps a piece of the bank breaks loose and falls into the water.

"An elephant entering a hut creates havoc within and ultimately shakes it down. The elephant of divine emotion enters the hut of this body and shatters it to pieces.

"Do you know what actually happens? When a house is on fire, at first a few things inside burn. Then comes the great commotion. Just so, the fire of Knowledge at first destroys such enemies of spiritual life as passion, anger, and so forth. Then comes the turn of ego. And lastly a violent commotion is seen in the physical frame.

"You may think that everything is going to be over. But God will not release you as long as the slightest trace of your illness is left. You simply cannot leave the hospital if your name is registered there. As long as the illness is not perfectly cured, the doctor won't give you a permit to go. Why did you register your name in the hospital at all?" (All laugh.)

Keshab laughed again and again at the Master's allusion to the hospital. Then Sri Ramakrishna spoke of his own illness. (To Keshab) "Hriday used to say, 'Never before have I seen such ecstasy for God, and never before have I seen such illness.' I was then seriously ill with stubborn diarrhoea. It was as if millions of ants were gnawing at my brain. But all the same, spiritual talk went on day and night. Dr. Rama of Natagore was called in to see me. He found me discussing spiritual truth. 'What a madman!' he said. 'Nothing is left of him but a few bones, and still he is reasoning like that!' "

MASTER (to Keshab): "All depends on God's will.

> O Mother, all is done after Thine own sweet will;
> Thou art in truth self-willed, Redeemer of mankind!
> Thou workest Thine own work; men only call it theirs.

"In order to take full advantage of the dew, the gardener removes the soil from the Basra rose down to the very root. The plant thrives better on account of the moisture. Perhaps that is why you too are being shaken to the very root. (Keshab and the Master laugh.) It may be that you will do tremendous things when you come back.

"Whenever I hear that you are ill I become extremely restless. After hearing of your last illness I used to weep to the Divine Mother in the small hours of the morning. I prayed to Her, 'O Mother, if anything happens to Keshab, with whom, then, shall I talk in Calcutta?' Coming to Calcutta, I offered fruits and sweets to the Divine Mother with a prayer for your well-being."

The devotees were deeply touched to hear of Sri Ramakrishna's love for Keshab and his longing for the Brāhmo leader.

MASTER: "But this time, to tell the truth, I didn't feel anxious to that extent. Only for two or three days did I feel a little worried."

Keshab's venerable mother came to the east door of the room, the same door through which Keshab had entered. Umanath said aloud to the Master, "Sir, here is mother saluting you."

Sri Ramakrishna smiled. Umanath said again, "Mother asks you to bless Keshab that he may be cured of his illness."

MASTER (to Keshab's mother): "Please pray to the Divine Mother, who is the Bestower of all bliss. She will take away your troubles.

(To Keshab) "Don't spend long hours in the inner apartments. You will sink down and down in the company of women. You will feel better if you hear only talk of God."

The Master uttered these words in a serious voice and then began to laugh like a boy. He said to Keshab, "Let me see your hand." He weighed it playfully, like a child. At last he said: "No, your hand is light. Hypocrites have heavy hands." (All laugh.)

Umanath again said to the Master from the door, "Mother asks you to bless Keshab."

MASTER (gravely): "What can I do? God alone blesses all. 'Thou workest Thine own work; men only call it theirs.'

"God laughs on two occasions. He laughs when two brothers divide land between them. They put a string across the land and say to each other, 'This side is mine, and that side is yours.' God laughs and says to Himself, 'Why, this whole universe is Mine; and about a little clod they say, "This side is mine, and that side is yours"!'

"God laughs again when the physician says to the mother weeping bitterly because of her child's desperate illness: 'Don't be afraid, mother. I shall cure your child.' The physician does not know that no one can save the child if God wills that he should die." (*All are silent.*)

Just then Keshab was seized with a fit of coughing, which lasted for a long time. The sight of his suffering made everyone sad. He became exhausted and could stay no longer. He bowed low before the Master and left the room, holding to the wall as before.

Some refreshments had been arranged for the Master. Keshab's eldest son was seated near him. Amrita introduced the boy and requested Sri Ramakrishna to bless him. The Master said, "It is not given to me to bless anyone." With a sweet smile he stroked the boy's body gently.

AMRITA (*with a smile*): "All right, then do as you please."

MASTER (*to the devotees*): "I cannot say such a thing as 'May you be healed.' I never ask the Divine Mother to give me the power of healing. I pray to Her only for pure love.

"Is Keshab a small person? He is respected by all, seekers after wealth as well as holy men. Once I visited Dayananda, who was then staying at a garden house. I saw he was extremely anxious about Keshab's coming; he went out every few minutes to see whether he had arrived. I learnt later on that Keshab had made an appointment with him that day. Keshab, I understood, had no faith in the sacrifices and the deities mentioned in the Vedas. Referring to this, Dayananda said: 'Why, the Lord has created so many things. Could He not make deities as well?'"

Continuing, the Master said: "Keshab is free from the pride of a small-minded religious teacher. To many people he has said, 'If you have any doubts, go there[2] to have them solved.' It is my way, too, to say: 'What shall I do with people's respect? Let Keshab's virtues increase a millionfold.' Keshab is certainly a great man. Everyone respects him, seekers after wealth as well as holy men." Thus did Sri Ramakrishna praise Keshab before the latter's disciples.

After partaking of the refreshments the Master was ready to leave. The Brāhmo devotees accompanied him to the cab, which was standing in the street. While coming down the stairs the Master noticed that there was no light on the ground floor. He said to Amrita and Keshab's other disciples: "These places should be well lighted. A house without light becomes stricken with poverty. Please see that it doesn't happen again."

Then Sri Ramakrishna left for Dakshineswar with one or two devotees.

On his way to Dakshineswar from Keshab's cottage Sri Ramakrishna stopped at Jaygopal Sen's house. It was about seven o'clock in the evening.

[2] To Sri Ramakrishna.

In the drawing-room Jaygopal's relatives and neighbours had gathered. Vaikuntha, Jaygopal's brother, said to the Master: "Sir, we are worldly people. Please give us some advice."

MASTER: "Do your duty to the world after knowing God. With one hand hold to the Lotus Feet of the Lord and with the other do your work."

VAIKUNTHA: "Is the world unreal?"

MASTER: "Yes, it is unreal as long as one has not realized God. Through ignorance man forgets God and speaks always of 'I' and 'mine'. He sinks down and down, entangled in māyā, deluded by 'woman and gold'. Māyā robs him of his knowledge to such an extent that he cannot find the way of escape, though such a way exists.

"Listen to a song:

> When such delusion veils the world, through Mahāmāyā's spell,
> That Brahmā is bereft of sense
> And Vishnu loses consciousness,
> What hope is left for men? . . .

"You all know from your experience how impermanent the world is. Look at it this way. How many people have come into the world and again passed away! People are born and they die. This moment the world is and the next it is not. It is impermanent. Those you think to be your very own will not exist for you when you close your eyes in death. Again, you see people who have no immediate relatives, and yet for the sake of a grandson they will not go to Benares to lead a holy life. 'Oh, what will become of my Haru then?' they argue.

> The narrow channel first is made, and there the trap is set;
> But open though the passage lies,
> The fish, once safely through the gate,
> Do not come out again.
>
> Yet even though a way leads forth,
> Encased within its own cocoon,
> The worm remains to die.

This kind of world is illusory and impermanent."

A NEIGHBOUR: "Why, sir, should one hold to God with one hand and to the world with the other? Why should one even stretch out one hand to hold to the world, if it is impermanent?"

MASTER: "The world is not impermanent if one lives there after knowing God. Listen to another song:

> O mind, you do not know how to farm!
> Fallow lies the field of your life.
> If you had only worked it well,
> How rich a harvest you might reap!
> Hedge it about with Kāli's name
> If you would keep your harvest safe;
> This is the stoutest hedge of all,
> For Death himself cannot come near it. . . .

"Did you listen to the song?

> Hedge it about with Kāli's name
> If you would keep your harvest safe.

Surrender yourself to God and you will achieve everything.

> This is the stoutest hedge of all,
> For Death himself cannot come near it.

"Yes, it is a strong hedge indeed. If you but realize God, you won't see the world as unsubstantial. He who has realized God knows that God Himself has become the world and all living beings. When you feed your child, you should feel that you are feeding God. You should look on your father and mother as veritable manifestations of God and the Divine Mother, and serve them as such. If a man enters the world after realizing God, he does not generally keep up physical relations with his wife. Both of them are devotees; they love to talk only of God and pass their time in spiritual conversation. They serve other devotees of God, for they know that God alone has become all living beings; and, knowing this, they devote their lives to the service of others."

NEIGHBOUR: "But, sir, such a husband and wife are not to be found anywhere."

MASTER: "Yes, they can be found, though they may be very rare. Worldly people cannot recognize them. In order to lead such a life both husband and wife must be spiritual. It is possible to lead such a life if both of them have tasted the Bliss of God. God's special grace is necessary to create such a couple; otherwise there will always be misunderstanding between them. In that case the one has to leave the other. Life becomes very miserable if husband and wife do not agree. The wife will say to her husband day and night: 'Why did my father marry me to such a person? I can't get enough to eat or to feed my children. I haven't clothes enough to cover my body or to give to my children. I haven't received a single piece of jewelry from you. How happy you have made me! Ah! You keep your eyes closed and mutter the name of God! Now do give up all these crazy ideas.'"

DEVOTEE: "There are such obstacles, certainly. Besides, the children may be disobedient. There is no end of difficulties. Now, sir, what is the way?"

MASTER: "It is extremely difficult to practise spiritual discipline and at the same time lead a householder's life. There are many handicaps: disease, grief, poverty, misunderstanding with one's wife, and disobedient, stupid, and stubborn children. I don't have to give you a list of them.

"But still there is a way out. One should pray to God, going now and then into solitude, and make efforts to realize Him."

NEIGHBOUR: "Must one leave home then?"

MASTER: "No, not altogether. Whenever you have leisure, go into solitude for a day or two. At that time don't have any relations with the outside world and don't hold any conversation with worldly people on worldly affairs. You must live either in solitude or in the company of holy men."

NEIGHBOUR: "How can one recognize a holy man?"

MASTER: "He who has surrendered his body, mind, and innermost self to God is surely a holy man. He who has renounced 'woman and gold' is surely a holy man. He is a holy man who does not regard woman with the eyes of a worldly person. He never forgets to look upon a woman as his mother, and to offer her his worship if he happens to be near her. The holy man constantly thinks of God and does not indulge in any talk except about spiritual things. Furthermore, he serves all beings, knowing that God resides in everybody's heart. These, in general, are the signs of a holy man."

NEIGHBOUR: "Must one always live in solitude?"

MASTER: "Haven't you seen the trees on the foot-path along a street? They are fenced around as long as they are very young; otherwise cattle destroy them. But there is no longer any need of fences when their trunks grow thick and strong. Then they won't break even if an elephant is tied to them. Just so, there will be no need for you to worry and fear if you make your mind as strong as a thick tree-trunk. First of all try to acquire discrimination. Break the jack-fruit open only after you have rubbed your hands with oil; then its sticky milk won't smear them."

NEIGHBOUR: "What is discrimination?"

MASTER: "Discrimination is the reasoning by which one knows that God alone is real and all else is unreal. Real means eternal, and unreal means impermanent. He who has acquired discrimination knows that God is the only Substance and all else is non-existent. With the awakening of this spirit of discrimination a man wants to know God. On the contrary, if a man loves the unreal—such things as creature comforts, name, fame, and wealth—, then he doesn't want to know God, who is of the very nature of Reality. Through discrimination between the Real and the unreal one seeks to know God.

"Listen to a song:

> Come, let us go for a walk, O mind, to Kāli, the Wish-fulfilling
> Tree,
> And there beneath It gather the four fruits of life.
> Of your two wives, Dispassion and Worldliness,
> Bring along Dispassion only, on your way to the Tree,
> And ask her son Discrimination about the Truth. . . .

"By turning the mind within oneself one acquires discrimination, and through discrimination one thinks of Truth. Then the mind feels the desire to 'go for a walk to Kāli, the Wish-fulfilling Tree.' Reaching that Tree, that is to say, going near to God, you can without any effort gather four fruits, namely, dharma, artha, kāma, and moksha. Yes, after realizing God, one can also get, if one so desires, dharma, artha, and kāma, which are necessary for leading the worldly life."

NEIGHBOUR: "Then why should one call the world māyā?"

MASTER: "As long as one has not realized God, one should renounce the world, following the process of 'Neti, neti'. But he who has attained God knows that it is God who has become all this. Then he sees that

God, māyā, living beings, and the universe form one whole. God includes the universe and its living beings. Suppose you have separated the shell, flesh, and seeds of a bel-fruit and someone asks you the weight of the fruit. Will you leave aside the shell and the seeds, and weigh only the flesh? Not at all. To know the real weight of the fruit, you must weigh the whole of it—the shell, the flesh, and the seeds. Only then can you tell its real weight. The shell may be likened to the universe, and the seeds to living beings. While one is engaged in discrimination one says to oneself that the universe and the living beings are non-Self and unsubstantial. At that time one thinks of the flesh alone as the substance, and the shell and seeds as unsubstantial. But after discrimination is over, one feels that all three parts of the fruit together form a unity. Then one further realizes that the stuff that has produced the flesh of the fruit has also produced the shell and seeds. To know the real nature of the bel-fruit one must know all three.

"It is the process of evolution and involution. The world, after its dissolution, remains involved in God; and God, at the time of creation, evolves as the world. Butter goes with buttermilk, and buttermilk goes with butter. If there is a thing called buttermilk, then butter also exists; and if there is a thing called butter, then buttermilk also exists. If the Self exists, then the non-Self must also exist.

"The phenomenal world belongs to that very Reality to which the Absolute belongs; again, the Absolute belongs to that very Reality to which the phenomenal world belongs. He who is realized as God has also become the universe and its living beings. One who knows the Truth knows that it is He alone who has become father and mother, child and neighbour, man and animal, good and bad, holy and unholy, and so forth."

NEIGHBOUR: "Then is there no virtue and no sin?"

MASTER: "They both exist and do not exist. If God keeps the ego in a man, then He keeps in him the sense of differentiation and also the sense of virtue and sin. But in a rare few He completely effaces the ego, and these go beyond virtue and sin, good and bad. As long as a man has not realized God, he retains the sense of differentiation and the knowledge of good and bad. You may say: 'Virtue and sin are the same to me. I am doing only as God bids me.' But you know in your heart of hearts that those are mere words. No sooner do you commit an evil deed than you feel a palpitation in your heart. Even after God has been realized, He keeps in the mind of the devotee, if He so desires, the feeling of the 'servant ego'. In that state the devotee says, 'O God, Thou art the Master and I am Thy servant.' Such a devotee enjoys only spiritual talk and spiritual deeds. He does not enjoy the company of ungodly people. He does not care for any work that is not of a holy nature. So you see that God keeps the sense of differentiation even in such a devotee."

NEIGHBOUR: "You ask us, sir, to live in the world after knowing God. Can God really be known?"

MASTER: "God cannot be known by the sense-organs or by this mind;

but He can be known by the pure mind, the mind that is free from worldly desires."

NEIGHBOUR: "Who can know God?"

MASTER: "Right. Who can really know Him? But as for us, it is enough to know as much of Him as we need. What need have I of a whole well of water? One jar is more than enough for me. An ant went to a sugar hill. Did it need the entire hill? A grain or two of sugar was more than enough."

NEIGHBOUR: "Sir, we are like typhoid patients. How can we be satisfied with one jar of water? We feel like knowing the whole of God."

MASTER: "That's true. But there is also medicine for typhoid."

NEIGHBOUR: "What is that medicine, sir?"

MASTER: "The company of holy men, repeating the name of God and singing His glories, and unceasing prayer. I prayed to the Divine Mother: 'Mother, I don't seek knowledge. Here, take Thy knowledge, take Thy ignorance. Give me only pure love for Thy Lotus Feet.' I didn't ask for anything else.

"As is the disease, so must the remedy be. The Lord says in the *Gītā*: 'O Arjuna, take refuge in Me. I shall deliver you from all sins.' Take shelter at His feet. He will give you right understanding. He will take entire responsibility for you. Then you will get rid of the typhoid. Can one ever know God with such a mind as this? Can one pour four seers of milk into a one-seer pot? Can we ever know God unless He lets us know Him? Therefore I say, take shelter in God. Let Him do whatever He likes. He is self-willed. What power is there in a man?"

WITH THE DEVOTEES AT
DAKSHINESWAR (II)

S
RI RAMAKRISHNA was seated on the small couch in his room with Adhar, Manomohan, Rakhal, M., Harish, and other devotees. It was about two o'clock in the afternoon. The Master was describing to them the exalted state of Sri Chaitanya.

MASTER: "Chaitanya experienced three states of mind. First, the conscious state, when his mind dwelt on the gross and the subtle. Second, the semi-conscious state, when his mind entered the causal body and was absorbed in the bliss of divine intoxication. Third, the inmost state, when his mind was merged in the Great Cause.

"This agrees very well with the five koshas, or 'sheaths', described in the Vedānta. The gross body corresponds to the annamayakosha and the prānamayakosha, the subtle body to the manomayakosha and the vijnānamayakosha, and the causal body to the ānandamayakosha. The Mahākārana, the Great Cause, is beyond the five sheaths. When Chaitanya's mind merged in That, he would go into samādhi. This is called the nirvikalpa or jaḍa samādhi.

"While conscious of the outer world, Chaitanya sang the name of God; while in the state of partial consciousness, he danced with the devotees; and while in the inmost state of consciousness, he remained absorbed in samādhi."

M. (*to himself*): "Is the Master hinting at the different states of his own mind? There is much similarity between Chaitanya and the Master."

MASTER: "Chaitanya was Divine Love incarnate. He came down to earth to teach people how to love God. One achieves everything when one loves God. There is no need of hathayoga."

A DEVOTEE: "Sir, what is hathayoga like?"

MASTER: "A man practising hathayoga dwells a great deal on his body. He washes his intestines by means of a bamboo tube through his anus. He draws ghee and milk through his sexual organ. He learns how to manipulate his tongue by performing exercises. He sits in a fixed posture and now and then levitates. All these are actions of prāna. A magician was performing his feats when his tongue turned up and clove to the roof of his mouth.

Immediately his body' became motionless. People thought he was dead. He was buried and remained many years in the grave. After a long time the grave somehow broke open. Suddenly the man regained consciousness of the world and cried out, 'Come delusion! Come confusion!'¹ (*All laugh.*) All these are actions of prāna.

"The Vedāntists do not accept hathayoga. There is also rājayoga. Rājayoga describes how to achieve union with God through the mind—by means of discrimination and bhakti. This yoga is good. Hathayoga is not good. The life of a man in the Kaliyuga is dependent on food."

Sri Ramakrishna was standing in the road by the side of the nahabat. He was on his way to his room, having come from the pine-grove. He saw M. seated on the verandah of the nahabat, behind the fence, absorbed in meditation.

MASTER: "Hello! You are here? You will get results very soon. If you practise a little, then someone will come forward to help you."

M. looked up at the Master, startled; he remained sitting on the floor.

MASTER: "The time is ripe for you. The mother bird does not break the shell of the egg until the right time arrives. What I told you is indeed your Ideal."

Sri Ramakrishna again mentioned to M. his spiritual Ideal.

MASTER: "It is not necessary for all to practise great austerity. But I went through great suffering. I used to lie on the ground with my head resting on a mound for a pillow. I hardly noticed the passing of the days. I only called on God and wept, 'O Mother! O Mother!' "

M. had been visiting Sri Ramakrishna for the past two years. Since he had been educated along English lines, he had acquired a fondness for Western philosophy and science, and had liked to hear Keshab and other scholars lecture. Sri Ramakrishna would address him now and then as the "Englishman". Since coming to Sri Ramakrishna, M. had lost all relish for lectures and for books written by English scholars. The only thing that appealed to him now was to see the Master day and night, and hear the words that fell from his blessed lips. M. constantly dwelt on certain of Sri Ramakrishna's sayings. The Master had said, "One can certainly see God through the practice of spiritual discipline", and again, "The vision of God is the only goal of human life."

MASTER (*to M.*): "If you practise only a little, someone will come forward to tell you the right path. Observe the ekādaśi.

"You are my very own, my relative; otherwise, why should you come here so frequently? While listening to the kirtan, I had a vision of Rakhal in the midst of Sri Krishna's companions in Vrindāvan. Narendra belongs to a very high level. Hirananda² too; how childlike his nature is! What a sweet disposition he has! I want to see him too.

¹ Magicians, while performing their feats, cry in this way in order to cast a spell on the spectators.
² A devotee of the Master from Sindh.

"Once I saw the companions of Chaitanya, not in a trance but with these very eyes. Formerly I was in such an exalted state of mind that I could see all these things with my naked eyes; but now I see them in samādhi. I saw the companions of Chaitanya with these naked eyes. I think I saw you there, and Balaram too. You must have noticed that when I see certain people I jump up with a start. Do you know why? A man feels that way when he sees his own people after a long time.

"I used to pray to the Mother, crying: 'Mother, if I do not find the devotees I'll surely die. Please bring them to me immediately.' In those days whatever desire arose in my mind would come to pass. I planted a tulsi-grove in the Panchavati in order to practise japa and meditation. I wanted very much to fence it around with bamboo sticks. Soon afterwards a bundle of bamboo sticks and some string were carried by the flood-tide of the Ganges right in front of the Panchavati. A temple servant noticed them and joyfully told me.

"In that state of divine exaltation I could no longer perform the formal worship. 'Mother,' I said, 'who will look after me? I haven't the power to take care of myself. I want to listen only to talk about Thee. I want to feed Thy devotees. I want to give a little help to those whom I chance to meet. How will all that be possible, Mother? Give me a rich man to stand by me.' That is why Mathur Babu did so much to serve me.

"I said further, 'Certainly I shall not have any children, Mother. But it is my desire that a boy with sincere love for God should always remain with me. Give me such a boy.' That is the reason Rakhal came here. Those whom I think of as my own are part and parcel of me."

The Master started again for the Panchavati accompanied by M. No one else was with them. Sri Ramakrishna with a smile narrated to him various incidents of the past years of his life.

MASTER: "You see, one day I saw a strange figure covering the whole space from the Kāli temple to the Panchavati. Do you believe this?"

M. remained silent with wonder. He plucked one or two leaves from a branch in the Panchavati and put them in his pocket.

MASTER: "See there—that branch has been broken. I used to sit under it."

M: "I took a young twig from that tree—I have it at home."

MASTER (with a smile): "Why?"

M: "I feel happy when I look at it. After all this is over, this place will be considered very holy."

MASTER (smiling): "What kind of holy place? Like Pānihāti?"

Almost every year, for some time past, the Master had been attending the religious festival at Pānihāti.

It was evening. Sri Ramakrishna was sitting on the small couch in his room, absorbed in meditation on the Divine Mother. The evening worship in the temples began, with the music of gong and conch-shell. M. was going to spend the night with the Master.

After a time Sri Ramakrishna asked M. to read from the *Bhaktamāla*, a book about the Vaishnava saints.

M. read:

> There was a king named Jayamal who loved Krishna with all his heart. He followed with unfailing devotion all the rites and ceremonies associated with the adoration of Krishna, whom he worshipped under the name of Śyāmalasundara. Completely satisfied with his own Ideal Deity, he never directed his attention to any other god or goddess. One of the inflexible rules of his devotions was to worship the Deity daily till almost midday. He would never deviate from this practice, even at the risk of his wealth or his kingdom. Learning this secret, an enemy king invaded the kingdom during the morning hours. Jayamal's soldiers could not fight without his command; so they watched the invasion silently. Slowly the enemy surrounded the moat of the capital; yet Jayamal did not come out of his shrine room. His mother came to him and wept bitterly, trying to persuade the king to fight. He said to her calmly: "Why are you worried? Śyāmalasundara gave me this kingdom. What can I do if He has decided to take it away? On the other hand, none will be able to do me harm if He protects me. Our own efforts are vain!"
>
> And actually, in the mean time, Śyāmalasundara, the Deity Himself, had taken the king's horse from the stable and had ridden fully armed to the field. Alone He faced the hostile king and alone destroyed his army. Having crushed the enemy forces, the Deity returned to the temple and fastened the horse near by.
>
> Jayamal, on completing his worship, came out and discovered the horse there, panting and covered with sweat. "Who has been riding my horse?" he demanded. "Who brought it to the temple?" The officers declared they knew nothing about it. In a pensive mood the king proceeded to the battle-field with his army and there found the enemy, with the exception of their leader, lying dead. He was staring uncomprehendingly at the scene, when the enemy king approached, worshipped him, and said: "Please permit me to tell you something. How could I fight? You have a warrior who could conquer the entire world. I do not want your wealth or your kingdom; indeed, I will gladly give you my own, if you will tell me about that Blue Warrior, your friend. No sooner did I turn my eyes on him than he cast a spell on my heart and soul."
>
> Jayamal then realized it had been none other than Śyāmalasundara that had appeared on the battle-field. The enemy king understood too. He worshipped Jayamal and through his blessings received Krishna's grace.

MASTER: "Do you believe all that? Do you believe Krishna rode on that horse and killed Jayamal's enemies?"

M: "I believe that Jayamal, Krishna's devotee, prayed to Him with a yearning heart. But I don't know whether the enemy really saw Him coming to the battle-field on a horse. Krishna might have come there riding the horse, but I do not know whether they really saw Him."

MASTER (*with a smile*): "The book contains nice stories about devotees. But it is one-sided. Also, it abuses those who differ with its views."

The following morning the Master and M. were talking in the garden. M: "Then I shall stay here."

MASTER: "Well, you all come here so often. What does it mean? People visit a holy man once at the most. But you all come here so often. What is the significance of that?"

M. remained silent. The Master himself gave the reply.

MASTER: "Could you come here unless you belonged to my inner circle? That means you all are my own relatives, my own people—like father and son, brother and sister.

"I do not tell you everything. If I did, would you come here any more?

"Once Śukadeva went to Janaka to be instructed in the Knowledge of Brahman. Janaka said, 'First give me my fee.' 'But', said Śukadeva, 'why should I give you the fee before receiving the instruction?' Janaka laughed and said: 'Will you be conscious of guru and disciple after attaining Brahma-jnāna? That is why I asked you to give me the fee first.'"

It was night. The moon rose, flooding all the quarters with its silvery light. M. was walking alone in the garden of the temple. On one side of the path stood the Panchavati, the bakul-grove, the nahabat, and the Master's room, and on the other side flowed the Ganges, reflecting millions of broken moons on its rippling surface.

M. said to himself: "Can one really see God? The Master says it is possible. He says that, if one makes a little effort, then someone comes forward and shows the way. Well, I am married. I have children. Can one realize God in spite of all that?"

M. reflected awhile and continued his soliloquy: "Surely one can. Otherwise, why should the Master say so? Why shouldn't it be possible through the grace of God?

"Here is the world around me—the sun, moon, stars, living beings, and the twenty-four cosmic principles. How did they come into existence? Who is their Creator? What am I to Him? Life is indeed vain without this knowledge.

"Sri Ramakrishna is certainly the best of men. In all my life I have not seen another great soul like him. He must have seen God. Otherwise, how could he talk with God day and night, addressing Him so intimately as 'Mother'? Otherwise, how could he love God so intimately? Such is his love for God that he forgets the outer world. He goes into samādhi and remains like a lifeless thing. Again, in the ecstasy of that love, he laughs and cries and dances and sings."

Friday, December 14, 1883

At nine o'clock in the morning Sri Ramakrishna was standing on the southeast verandah near the door of his room, with Ramlal by his side. Rakhal and Latu were moving about. M. arrived and prostrated himself before the Master. Sri Ramakrishna said to him affectionately: "You have come. That's very good. Today is an auspicious day."

It was the last day of the Bengali month and the day of the full moon. M. was going to spend a few days with the Master practising spiritual discipline. The Master had said to him, "If an aspirant practises a little spiritual discipline, then someone comes forward to help him."

The Master had said to M: "You should not eat every day at the guest-house of the Kāli temple. The guest-house is intended to supply free food to monks and the destitute. Bring your own cook with you." M. had accordingly done so. The Master arranged a place for the man to cook and he asked Ramlal to speak to the milkman about milk.

A little later Ramlal began to read from the *Adhyātma Rāmāyana*. The Master and M. listened while he read:

> Rāma had married Sītā after breaking the great bow of Śiva. On the way to Ayodhyā with His bride, Rāma was confronted by the warrior sage Paraśurāma, who was about to make trouble for Him. Paraśurāma threw a bow at Rāma and challenged Him to string it. Daśaratha, Rāma's father, was seized with fear. With a smile, Rāma took the bow in His left hand and strung it. Then, twanging the bow-string, He fixed an arrow and asked Paraśurāma where to shoot it. That curbed the pride of the warrior sage. Prostrating himself before Rāma, Paraśurāma worshipped Him as the Supreme Brahman.

As Sri Ramakrishna listened to Paraśurāma's hymn, he went into a spiritual mood and now and then chanted the name of Rāma in his melodious voice.

Then the Master asked Ramlal to read about Guhaka. Ramlal read:

> Guhaka, the pariah, was chief of the untouchables and an intimate friend of Rāma. When Rāma, Sītā, and Lakshmana were starting into the forest to redeem Daśaratha's pledge, Guhaka ferried them across the river. Rāma embraced Guhaka tenderly and told him He was going to spend fourteen years in exile, wearing the bark of trees and eating the herbs, fruits, and roots that grew in the woods. He promised to visit Guhaka again on His way back to Ayodhyā after the period of exile was over. The pariah king waited patiently. But when the fourteenth year had run out and Rāma had not returned, Guhaka lighted a funeral pyre. He was on the point of entering it when Hanumān arrived as Rāma's messenger. In a celestial chariot Rāma and Sītā soon appeared, and Guhaka's joy was unbounded.

After the midday meal Sri Ramakrishna lay down on his bed to rest. M. was seated on the floor. Presently Dr. Shyama and a few devotees arrived. The Master sat up on the bed and began to converse with them.

MASTER: "It is by no means necessary for a man always to be engaged in his duties. Actions drop away when one realizes God, as the flower drops of itself when the fruit appears.

"He who has realized God no longer performs religious duties such as the sandhyā. In his case the sandhyā merges in the Gāyatri. When that happens, it is enough for a person to repeat just the Gāyatri mantra. Then the Gāyatri merges in Om. After that one no longer chants even the Gāyatri; it is enough then to chant simply Om. How long should a man practise such devotions as the sandhyā? As long as he does not feel a thrill in his body and shed tears of joy while repeating the name of Rāma or of Hari. People worship God to win money or a lawsuit. That is not good."

A DEVOTEE: "We find that everyone strives after money. Even Keshab Sen married his daughter to a prince."

MASTER: "Keshab's case is quite different. God provides everything for a genuine devotee, even without his making any effort. The son of a real king gets his monthly allowance. I am not talking of lawyers and men of that sort, who go through suffering in order to earn money, and who become slaves of others to that end. I am speaking of a real prince. A true devotee has no desire. He does not care for money. Money comes to him of itself. The Gītā describes such a devotee as 'content with what comes to him without effort'. A good brāhmin, without any personal motive, can accept food even from the house of an untouchable. He does not desire it; it comes of its own accord."

A DEVOTEE: "Sir, how should one live in the world?"

MASTER: "Live in the world as the mudfish lives in the mud. One develops love of God by going away from the world into solitude, now and then, and meditating on God. After that one can live in the world unattached. The mud is there, and the fish has to live in it, but its body is not stained by the mud. Such a man can lead the life of a householder in a spirit of detachment."

The Master noticed that M. was listening to his words with great attention.

MASTER (looking at M.): "One can realize God if one feels intense dispassion for worldly things. A man with such dispassion feels that the world is like a forest on fire. He regards his wife and children as a deep well. If he really feels that kind of dispassion, he renounces home and family. It is not enough for him to live in the world in a spirit of detachment.

"'Woman and gold' alone is māyā. If māyā is once recognized, it feels ashamed of itself and takes to flight. A man put on a tiger skin and tried to frighten another man. But the latter said: 'Ah! I have recognized you! You are our Harē.' At that the man dressed in the skin went away smiling to frighten someone else.

"All women are the embodiments of Śakti. It is the Primal Power that has become women and appears to us in the form of women. It is said in the Adhyātma Rāmāyana that Nārada and others praised Rāma, saying: 'O Rāma, Thou alone art all that we see as male, and Sītā, all that we see as female. Thou art Indra, and Sītā is Indrāni; Thou art Śiva, and Sītā is Śivāni; Thou art man, and Sītā is woman. What more need I say? Thou alone dost exist wherever there is a male, and Sītā wherever there is a female.'

(To the devotees) "One cannot renounce by the mere wish. There are prārabdha karma—inherited tendencies—and the like. Once a yogi said to a king, 'Live with me in the forest and think of God.' The king replied: 'That I cannot very well do. I could live with you, but I still have the desire for enjoyment. If I live in this forest, perhaps I shall create a kingdom even here. I still have desires.'

"Natabar Panja used to look after his cows in this garden during his boyhood. He had many desires. Hence he has established a castor-oil factory and earned a great deal of money. He has a prosperous castor-oil business at Ālambāzār.

"There is one sect that prescribes spiritual discipline in company with women. I was once taken to the women belonging to the Kartābhajā sect. They all sat around me. I addressed them as 'mother'. At that they whispered among themselves: 'He is still a pravartaka. He doesn't know the way.' According to that sect the pravartaka is the beginner. Then comes the sādhaka, the struggling aspirant, and last of all the siddha of the siddha, the supremely perfect. A woman walked over to Vaishnavcharan and sat near him. Asked about it, he answered, 'She feels just like a young girl.' One quickly strays from the religious path by looking on woman as wife. But to regard her as mother is a pure attitude."

Some of the devotees took leave of the Master, saying that they were going to visit the temple of Kāli and several of the other temples.

M. went walking alone in the Panchavati and other places in the temple garden. He thought about the Master's assurance that God can be easily realized, and about his exhortation to lead a life of intense renunciation, and his saying that māyā, when recognized, takes to flight.

At half past three in the afternoon M. again entered the Master's room and sat on the floor. A teacher from the Broughton Institution had come with several students to pay a visit to Sri Ramakrishna. They were conversing together. Now and then the teacher asked questions. The conversation was about the worship of images.

MASTER (to the teacher): "What is wrong with image worship? The Vedānta says that Brahman manifests Itself where there is 'Existence, Light, and Love'. Therefore nothing exists but Brahman.

"How long do small girls play with their dolls? As long as they are not married and do not live with their husbands. After marriage they put the dolls away in a box. What further need is there of worshipping the image after the vision of God?"

The Master glanced at M. and said: "One attains God when one feels yearning for Him. An intense restlessness is needed. Through it the whole mind goes to God.

"A man had a daughter who became a widow when she was very young. She had never known her husband. She noticed the husbands of other girls and said one day to her father, 'Where is my husband?' The father replied: 'Govinda[3] is your husband. He will come to you if you call Him.' At these words the girl went to her room, closed the door, and cried to Govinda, saying: 'O Govinda, come to me! Show Yourself to me! Why don't You come?' God could not resist the girl's piteous cry and appeared before her.

"One must have childlike faith—and the intense yearning that a child

[3] A name of Krishna.

feels to see its mother. That yearning is like the red sky in the east at dawn. After such a sky the sun must rise. Immediately after that yearning one sees God.

"Let me tell you the story of a boy named Jatila. He used to walk to school through the woods, and the journey frightened him. One day he told his mother of his fear. She replied: 'Why should you be afraid? Call Madhusudana.'[4] 'Mother,' asked the boy, 'who is Madhusudana?' The mother said, 'He is your Elder Brother.' One day after this, when the boy again felt afraid in the woods, he cried out, 'O Brother Madhusudana!' But there was no response. He began to weep aloud: 'Where are You, Brother Madhusudana? Come to me. I am afraid.' Then God could no longer stay away. He appeared before the boy and said: 'Here I am. Why are you frightened?' And so saying He took the boy out of the woods and showed him the way to school. When He took leave of the boy, God said: 'I will come whenever you call Me. Do not be afraid.' One must have this faith of a child, this yearning.

"A brāhmin used to worship his Family Deity daily with food offerings. One day he had to go away on business. As he was about to leave the house, he said to his young son: 'Give the offering to the Deity today. See that God is fed.' The boy offered food in the shrine, but the image remained silent on the altar. It would neither talk nor eat. The boy waited a long time, but still the image did not move. But the boy firmly believed that God would come down from His throne, sit on the floor, and partake of the food. Again and again he prayed to the Deity, saying: 'O Lord, come down and eat the food. It is already very late. I cannot sit here any longer.' But the image did not utter a word. The boy burst into tears and cried: 'O Lord, my father asked me to feed You. Why won't You come down? Why won't You eat from my hands?' The boy wept for some time with a longing soul. At last the Deity, smiling, came down from the altar and sat before the meal and ate it. After feeding the Deity, the boy came out of the shrine room. His relatives said: 'The worship is over. Now bring away the offering.' 'Yes,' said the boy, 'the worship is over. But God has eaten everything.' 'How is that?' asked the relatives. The boy replied innocently, 'Why, God has eaten the food.' They entered the shrine and were speechless with wonder to see that the Deity had really eaten every bit of the offering."

Late in the afternoon Sri Ramakrishna was talking to M. They were standing on the south side of the nahabat. Since it was winter the Master was wrapped in his woolen shawl.

MASTER: "Where will you sleep? In the hut in the Panchavati?"

M: "Won't they let me have the room on the upper floor of the nahabat?"

M. selected the nahabat because he had a poetic temperament. From there he could see the sky, the Ganges, the moonlight, and the flowers in the garden.

MASTER: "Oh, they'll let you have it. But I suggested the Panchavati

---

[4] A name of Krishna.

because so much contemplation and meditation have been practised[5] there
and the name of God has been chanted there so often."

It was evening. Incense was burning in the Master's room. He was sitting
on the small couch, absorbed in meditation. M. was sitting on the floor with
Rakhal, Latu, and Ramlal.

The Master said to M., "The sum and substance of the whole thing is to
cultivate devotion for God and love Him." At Sri Ramakrishna's request
Ramlal sang a few songs, the Master himself singing the first line of each.
Ramlal sang:

> Oh, what a vision I have beheld in Keshab Bhārati's hut!
> Gorā, in all his matchless grace,
> Shedding tears in a thousand streams!
> Like a mad elephant
> He dances in ecstasy and sings,
> Drunk with an overwhelming love. . . .

Then he sang:

> Though I[6] am never loath to grant salvation,
> I hesitate indeed to grant pure love.
> Whoever wins pure love surpasses all;
> He is adored by men;
> He triumphs over the three worlds. . . .

Sri Ramakrishna said to Ramlal, "Sing that one—'Gaur and Nitāi, ye
blessed brothers'." Ramlal began the song and the Master joined him:

> Gaur and Nitāi, ye blessed brothers!
> I have heard how kind you are,
> And therefore I have come to you.
> When I visited Benares,
> Śiva, Lord of Kāśi, told me
> Of the Parabrahman's birth,
> As man, in Mother Sachi's home.
> O Brahman, Thee I recognize!
> Many a sādhu have I seen,
> But never one so kind as you.
>
> Once at Braja you were born
> As Kānāi and Balāi, His brother;
> Now, once more, in Nadiā,
> As Gaur and Nitāi do you appear,
> Hiding the shapes that then you wore.
> In Braja's pastures running freely,
> Once you frolicked; now, for play,
> You roll on the ground in Nadiā,
> Chanting aloud Lord Hari's name.

[5] During the period of his sādhanā Sri Ramakrishna practised spiritual discipline
in the hut in the Panchavati.
[6] The song represents Sri Krishna's words.

Laughing, shouting, once you played
At Braja with your cowherd friends;
And now you chant Lord Hari's name.

O Gaur, how cleverly you hide
The dark-blue form[7] you wore at Braja!
But your slanting eyes betray you.
Through the blessing of your name
The sinner is set free, they say;
And so my soul is filled with hope.
Now with eager heart I hasten
To your feet: Lord! I implore you,
Keep me safe within their shadow.

You redeemed Jagāi and Mādhāi,
Wretched sinners though they were;
I pray you, do the same for me.
I have heard that you embrace
All men as brothers, even the outcaste,
Whispering in the ears of all
Lord Hari's life-renewing name.

Late at night M. sat alone in the nahabat. The sky, the river, the garden, the steeples of the temples, the trees, and the Panchavati were flooded with moonlight. Deep silence reigned everywhere, broken only by the melodious murmuring of the Ganges. M. was meditating on Sri Ramakrishna.

At three o'clock in the morning M. left his seat. He proceeded toward the Panchavati as Sri Ramakrishna had suggested. He did not care for the nahabat any more and resolved to stay in the hut in the Panchavati.

Suddenly he heard a distant sound, as if someone were wailing piteously, "Oh, where art Thou, Brother Madhusudana?" The light of the full moon streamed through the thick foliage of the Panchavati, and as he proceeded he saw at a distance one of the Master's disciples sitting alone in the grove, crying helplessly, "Oh, where art Thou, Brother Madhusudana?"

Silently M. watched him.

Saturday, December 15, 1883

M. had been staying at Dakshineswar with Sri Ramakrishna. The Master was sitting in his room, listening to the life of Prahlāda, which Ramlal was reading from the *Bhaktamāla*. M. was sitting on the floor. Rakhal, Latu, and Harish were also in the room, and Hazra was on the verandah. While listening to the story of Prahlāda's love for God, Sri Ramakrishna went into an ecstatic mood.

Hiranyakaśipu, the king of the demons and father of Prahlāda, had put his son to endless torture to divert the boy's mind·from the love of God. But through divine grace all the king's attempts to kill Prahlāda were ineffective. At last God appeared, assuming the form of Nrisimha, the Man-lion, and killed Hiranyakaśipu. The gods were frightened at the rage and roaring of the Man-lion and thought that the destruction of the world was imminent.

[7] An allusion to Krishna's dark-blue complexion; Gaurānga's complexion was golden.

They sent Prahlāda to pacify the Deity. The boy sang a hymn to Him in words of love, and the Man-lion, moved by affection, licked Prahlāda's body.

Still in an ecstatic mood, the Master said, "Ah! Ah! What love for the devotee!" The Master went into deep samādhi. He sat there motionless. A tear-drop could be seen at the corner of each of his eyes.

The Master came down to the plane of the sense world and spoke to M., expressing his abhorrence for those who, while practising spiritual discipline, enjoyed sex-life.

MASTER: "Aren't you ashamed of yourself? You have children, and still you enjoy intercourse with your wife. Don't you hate yourself for thus leading an animal life? Don't you hate yourself for dallying with a body which contains only blood, phlegm, filth, and excreta? He who contemplates the Lotus Feet of God looks on even the most beautiful woman as mere ash from the cremation ground. To enjoy a body which will not last and which consists of such impure ingredients as intestines, bile, flesh, and bone! Aren't you ashamed of yourself?"

M. sat there silently, hanging his head in shame.

MASTER: "A man who has tasted even a drop of God's ecstatic love looks on 'woman and gold' as most insignificant. He who has tasted syrup made from sugar candy regards a drink made from treacle as a mere trifle. One gradually obtains that love for God if one but prays to Him with a yearning heart and always chants His name and glories."

The Master was in an ecstasy of love. He began to dance about the room and sing:

> Who is singing Hari's name upon the sacred Ganges' bank?
> Is it Nitāi that has come, the giver of heavenly love? . . .

It was ten o'clock in the morning. Ramlal had finished the daily worship in the Kāli temple. The Master went to the temple accompanied by M. Entering the shrine, the Master sat before the image. He offered a flower or two at the feet of the Divine Mother. Then he put a flower on his own head and began to meditate. He sang a song to the Divine Mother:

> Thy name, I have heard, O Consort of Śiva, is the destroyer of
>   our fear,
> And so on Thee I cast my burden: Save me! Save me, O kindly
>   Mother! . . .

Sri Ramakrishna returned from the Kāli temple and sat on the southeast verandah of his room. He ate some refreshments which had been offered at the temple, and the devotees also received a share.

Rakhal sat by the Master and read about Lord Erskine from *Self-Help* by Smiles.

MASTER (*to M.*): "What does the book say?"

M: "It says that Lord Erskine performed his duty without desiring any result for himself. Disinterested duty."

MASTER: "That is very good. But the characteristic of a man of Perfect Knowledge is that he doesn't keep a single book with him. He carries all his

Knowledge on the tip of his tongue. There's the instance of Śukadeva. Books—I mean the scriptures—contain a mixture of sand and sugar. The sādhu takes the sugar, leaving aside the sand. He takes only the essence."

Vaishnavcharan, the musician, arrived and sang a few devotional songs.

M. spent the night in the nahabat.

Sunday, December 16, 1883

Sri Ramakrishna was seated with M. on the semicircular porch of his room at about ten o'clock in the morning. The fragrance of gardenias, jasmines, oleanders, roses, and other flowers filled the air. The Master was singing, looking at M:

> Thou must save me, sweetest Mother! Unto Thee I come for
>   refuge,
> Helpless as a bird imprisoned in a cage.
> I have done unnumbered wrongs, and aimlessly I roam about,
> Misled by māyā's spell, bereft of wisdom's light,
> Comfortless as a mother cow whose calf has wandered far away.

MASTER: "But why? Why should I live like a 'bird imprisoned in a cage'? Fie! For shame!"

As the Master said these words he went into an ecstatic mood. His body became motionless and his mind stopped functioning; tears streamed down his cheeks. After a while he said, "O Mother, make me like Sītā, completely forgetful of everything—body and limbs—, totally unconscious of hands, feet, and sense-organs—only the one thought in her mind, 'Where is Rāma?' "

Was the Master inspired by the ideal of Sītā to teach M. the yearning that a devotee should feel for God? Sītā's very life was centred in Rāma. Completely absorbed in the thought of Rāma, Sītā forgot even the body, which is so dear to all.

At four o'clock in the afternoon Mr. Mukherji, a relative of Prankrishna, arrived in the company of a brāhmin well versed in the scriptures.

MUKHERJI: "I am very happy to meet you, sir."

MASTER: "God dwells in all beings. He is the gold in all. In some places it is more clearly manifest than in others. God dwells in the worldly-minded, no doubt, but He is hidden there, like gold under deep layers of clay."

MUKHERJI: "Sir, what is the difference between worldly and other-worldly things?"

MASTER: "While striving for the realization of God, the aspirant has to practise renunciation, applying the logic of 'Neti, neti'—'Not this, not this'. But after attaining the vision of God, he realizes that God alone has become all things.

"At one time Rāma was overpowered by the spirit of renunciation. Daśaratha, worried at this, went to the sage Vasishtha and begged him to persuade Rāma not to give up the world. The sage came to Rāma and found him in a gloomy mood. The fire of intense renunciation had been raging in the Prince's mind. Vasishtha said: 'Rāma, why should You renounce the world? Is the world outside God? Reason with me.' Rāma realized that the world had evolved from the Supreme Brahman. So He said nothing.

"Buttermilk is made from the same substance as butter. One who realizes this knows that butter goes with buttermilk and buttermilk with butter. After separating the butter with great effort—that is to say, after attaining Brahmajnāna—you will realize that as long as butter exists, buttermilk also must exist. Wherever there is butter there must be buttermilk as well. As long as one feels that Brahman exists, one must also be aware that the universe, living beings, and the twenty-four cosmic principles exist as well.

"What Brahman is cannot be described in words. Everything has been polluted, like food that has touched the tongue—that is, everything has been described in words. But no one has been able to describe Brahman. It is therefore unpolluted. I said this to Vidyāsāgar and he was delighted.

"But the Knowledge of Brahman cannot be realized if the aspirant is worldly-minded even in the slightest degree. He succeeds in acquiring this Knowledge only when his mind is totally free from 'woman and gold'. Pārvati once said to Her father, 'Father, seek the company of holy men if you want the Knowledge of Brahman.' "

Addressing Mr. Mukherji, Sri Ramakrishna said: "You are rich, and still you call on God. That is very good indeed. It is said in the Gītā that those who fall from the path of yoga are born in their next birth as devotees of God in rich families."

Mr. Mukherji quoted the line from the Gītā.

MASTER: "God, if He so desires, can keep a jnāni in the world too. The world and all living beings have been created by His will. But He is self-willed."

MUKHERJI (with a smile): "How can God have any will? Does He lack anything?"

MASTER (with a smile): "What's wrong in that? Water is water whether it is still or in waves. The snake is a snake whether it is coiled up motionless or wriggles along. A man is the same man whether sitting still or engaged in action.

"How can you eliminate from the Reality the universe and its living beings? If you do that, It will lack Its full weight. You cannot find out the total weight of the bel-fruit if you eliminate the seeds and shell.

"Brahman is unattached. One finds good and bad smells in the air, but the air itself is untainted. Brahman and Śakti are identical. It is the Primordial Power that has become the world and all living beings."

MUKHERJI: "Why does one deviate from the path of yoga?"

MASTER: "As the saying goes: 'In my mother's womb I was in a state of yoga; coming into the world, I have eaten its clay. The midwife has cut one shackle, the navel cord; but how shall I cut the shackle of māyā?'

"Māyā is nothing but 'woman' and 'gold'. A man attains yoga when he has freed his mind from these two. The Self—the Supreme Self—is the magnet; the individual self is the needle. The individual self experiences the state of yoga when it is attracted by the Supreme Self to Itself. But the magnet cannot attract the needle if the needle is covered with clay; it can draw the needle only when the clay is removed. The clay of 'woman' and 'gold' must be removed."

MUKHERJI: "How can one remove it?"

MASTER: "Weep for God with a longing heart. Tears shed for Him will wash away the clay. When you have thus freed yourself from impurity, you will be attracted by the magnet. Only then will you attain yoga."

MUKHERJI: "Priceless words!"

MASTER: "If a man is able to weep for God, he will see Him. He will go into samādhi. Perfection in yoga is samādhi. A man achieves kumbhaka without any yogic exercise if he but weeps for God. The next stage is samādhi.

"There is another method—that of meditation. In the Sahasrāra, Śiva manifests Himself in a special manner. The aspirant should meditate on Him. The body is like a tray; the mind and buddhi are like water. The Sun of Satchidānanda is reflected in this water. Meditating on the reflected sun, one sees the Real Sun through the grace of God.

"But the worldly man must constantly live in the company of holy men. It is necessary for all, even for sannyāsis. But it is especially necessary for the householder. His disease has become chronic because he has to live constantly in the midst of 'woman and gold'."

MUKHERJI: "Yes, sir. The disease has indeed become chronic."

MASTER: "Give God the power of attorney. Let Him do whatever He wants. Be like a kitten and cry to Him with a fervent heart. The mother cat puts the kitten wherever she wants to. The kitten doesn't know anything. It is left sometimes on the bed and sometimes near the hearth."

MUKHERJI: "It is good to read sacred books like the Gītā."

MASTER: "But what will you gain by mere reading? Some have heard of milk, some have seen it, and there are some, besides, who have drunk it. God can indeed be seen; what is more, one can talk to Him.

"The first stage is that of the beginner. He studies and hears. Second is the stage of the struggling aspirant. He prays to God, meditates on Him, and sings His name and glories. The third stage is that of the perfect soul. He has seen God, realized Him directly and immediately in his inner Consciousness. Last is the stage of the supremely perfect, like Chaitanya. Such a devotee establishes a definite relationship with God, looking on Him as his Son or Beloved."

M., Rakhal, Jogin, Latu, and the other devotees were entranced by these words of divine realization.

Mr. Mukherji and his friend were taking leave of the Master. After saluting him, they stood up. The Master also stood up to show them courtesy.

MUKHERJI (smiling): "That you should stand up or sit down!"

MASTER (smiling): "But what's the harm? Water is water whether it is placid or in waves. I am like a cast-off leaf in the wind. The wind blows that leaf wherever it lists. I am the machine and God is its Operator."

Mr. Mukherji and his friend left the room. M. thought: "According to the Vedānta all is like a dream. Are all these—the ego, the universe, and the living beings—unreal then?"

M. had studied a little of the Vedānta. He also had read the German philosophers, such as Kant and Hegel, whose writings are only a faint echo of the Vedānta. But Sri Ramakrishna did not arrive at his conclusions by reasoning, as do ordinary scholars. It was the Divine Mother of the Universe who revealed the Truth to him. These were the thoughts that passed through M.'s mind.

A little later Sri Ramakrishna and M. were conversing on the porch west of the Master's room. No one else was there. It was a late winter afternoon, and the sun had not yet gone below the horizon.

M: "Is the world unreal?"

MASTER: "Why should it be unreal? What you are asking is a matter for philosophical discussion.

"In the beginning, when a man reasons following the Vedāntic method of 'Not this, not this', he realizes that Brahman is not the living beings, not the universe, not the twenty-four cosmic principles. All these things become like dreams to him. Then comes the affirmation of what has been denied, and he feels that God Himself has become the universe and all living beings.

"Suppose you are climbing to the roof by the stairs. As long as you are aware of the roof, you are also aware of the stairs. He who is aware of the high is also aware of the low. But after reaching the roof you realize that the stairs are made of the same materials—brick, lime, and brick-dust—as the roof.

"Further, I have given the illustration of the bel-fruit. Both changeability and unchangeability belong to one and the same Reality.

"The ego cannot be done away with. As long as 'I-consciousness' exists, living beings and the universe must also exist. After realizing God, one sees that it is He Himself who has become the universe and the living beings. But one cannot realize this by mere reasoning.

"Śiva has two states of mind. First, the state of samādhi, when He is transfixed in the Great Yoga. He is then Ātmārāma, satisfied in the Self. Second, the state when He descends from samādhi and keeps a trace of ego. Then He dances about, chanting, 'Rāma, Rāma!'"

Did the Master describe Śiva to hint at his own state of mind?

It was evening. Sri Ramakrishna was meditating on the Divine Mother and chanting Her holy name. The devotees also went off to solitary places and meditated on their Chosen Ideals. Evening worship began at the temple garden in the shrines of Kāli, Rādhā-Krishna, and Śiva.

It was the second day of the dark fortnight of the moon. Soon the moon rose in the sky, bathing temples, trees, flowers, and the rippling surface of the Ganges in its light. The Master was sitting on the couch and M. on the floor. The conversation turned to the Vedānta.

MASTER (to M.): "Why should the universe be unreal? That is a speculation of the philosophers. After realizing God, one sees that it is God Himself who has become the universe and all living beings.

"The Divine Mother revealed to me in the Kāli temple that it was She who had become everything. She showed me that everything was full of Consciousness. The Image was Consciousness, the altar was Consciousness, the water-vessels were Consciousness, the door-sill was Consciousness, the marble floor was Consciousness—all was Consciousness.

"I found everything inside the room soaked, as it were, in Bliss—the Bliss of Satchidānanda. I saw a wicked man in front of the Kāli temple; but in him also I saw the Power of the Divine Mother vibrating.

"That was why I fed a cat with the food that was to be offered to the Divine Mother. I clearly perceived that the Divine Mother Herself had become everything—even the cat. The manager of the temple garden wrote to Mathur Babu saying that I was feeding the cat with the offering intended for the Divine Mother. But Mathur Babu had insight into the state of my mind. He wrote back to the manager: 'Let him do whatever he likes. You must not say anything to him.'

"After realizing God, one sees all this aright—that it is He who has become the universe, living beings, and the twenty-four cosmic principles. But what remains when God completely effaces the ego cannot be described in words. As Rāmprasād said in one of his songs, 'Then alone will you know whether you are good or I am good!' I get into even that state now and then.

"A man sees a thing in one way through reasoning and in an altogether different way when God Himself shows it to him."

Monday, December 17, 1883

It was about eight o'clock in the morning. Sri Ramakrishna was in his room with M., when Dr. Madhu arrived and sat down beside the Master on the small couch. He was an elderly man and full of wit. He used to visit the Master when the latter felt indisposed.

MASTER: "The whole thing in a nutshell is that one must develop ecstatic love for Satchidānanda. What kind of love? How should one love God? Gauri used to say that one must become like Sītā to understand Rāma; like Bhagavati, the Divine Mother, to understand Bhagavān, Śiva. One must practise austerity, as Bhagavati did, in order to attain Śiva. One must cultivate the attitude of Prakriti in order to realize Purusha—the attitude of a friend, a handmaid, or a mother.

"I saw Sītā in a vision. I found that her entire mind was concentrated on Rāma. She was totally indifferent to everything—her hands, her feet, her clothes, her jewels. It seemed that Rāma had filled every bit of her life and she could not remain alive without Rāma."

M: "Yes, sir. She was mad with love for Rāma."

MASTER: "Mad! That's the word. One must become mad with love in order to realize God. But that love is not possible if the mind dwells on 'woman and gold'. Sex-life with a woman! What happiness is there in that? The realization of God gives ten million times more happiness. Gauri used to say that when a man attains ecstatic love of God all the pores of the skin, even the roots of the hair, become like so many sexual organs, and in every pore the aspirant enjoys the happiness of communion with the Ātman.

"One must call on God with a longing heart. One must learn from the guru how God can be realized. Only if the guru himself has attained Perfect Knowledge can he show the way.

"A man gets rid of all desires when he has Perfect Knowledge. He becomes like a child five years old. Sages like Dattātreya and Jaḍabharata had the nature of a child."

M: "One hears about them. But there were many others like them that the world doesn't hear about."

MASTER: "Yes. The jnāni gets rid of all desire. If any is left, it does not hurt him. At the touch of the philosopher's stone the sword is transformed into gold. Then that sword cannot do any killing. Just so, the jnāni keeps only a semblance of anger and passion. They are anger and passion only in name and cannot injure him."

M: "Yes, sir. The jnāni goes beyond the three gunas, as you say. He is not under the control of any of the gunas—sattva, rajas, or tamas. All these three are so many robbers, as it were."

MASTER: "Yes, one must assimilate that."

M: "In this world there are perhaps not more than three or four men of Perfect Knowledge."

MASTER: "Why do you say that? One sees many holy men and sannyāsis in the monasteries of upper India."

M: "Well, I too can become a sannyāsi like one of those."

The Master fixed his gaze on M. and said, "By renouncing everything?"

M: "What can a man achieve unless he gets rid of māyā? What will a man gain by merely being a sannyāsi, if he cannot subdue māyā?"

Both remained silent a few minutes.

M: "Sir, what is the nature of the divine love transcending the three gunas?"

MASTER: "Attaining that love, the devotee sees everything full of Spirit and Consciousness. To him 'Krishna is Consciousness, and His sacred Abode is also Consciousness'. The devotee, too, is Consciousness. Everything is Consciousness. Very few people attain such love."

DR. MADHU: "The love transcending the three gunas means, in other words, that the devotee is not under the control of any of the gunas."

MASTER (smiling): "Yes, that's it. He becomes like a child five years old, not under the control of any of the gunas."

The Master was resting after his noon meal. Mani Mallick arrived and saluted him. Sri Ramakrishna remained lying on the couch and said a word or two to Mani.

MANI: "I hear you visited Keshab Sen."

MASTER: "Yes. How is he now?"

MANI: "He hasn't recovered to any extent from his illness."

MASTER: "I found him to be very rājasic. I had to wait a long time before I could see him."

The Master sat up on the couch and continued his conversation with the devotees.

MASTER (to M.): "I became mad for Rāma. I used to walk about carrying an image of Rāmlālā[8] given to me by a monk. I bathed it, fed it, and laid it down to sleep. I carried it wherever I went. I became mad for Rāmlālā."

[8] A brass image of the Boy Rāma.

M. AT DAKSHINESWAR (I)

SRI RAMAKRISHNA was seated in his room with his devotees. He spoke highly of Devendranath Tagore's love of God and renunciation, and then said, pointing to Rakhal and the other young devotees, "Devendra is a good man; but blessed indeed are those young aspirants who, like Śukadeva, practise renunciation from their very boyhood and think of God day and night without being involved in worldly life.

"The worldly man always has some desire or other, though at times he shows much devotion to God. Once Mathur Babu was entangled in a lawsuit. He said to me in the shrine of Kāli, 'Sir, please offer this flower to the Divine Mother.' I offered it unsuspectingly, but he firmly believed that he would attain his objective if I offered the flower.

"What devotion Rati's mother had! How often she used to come here and how much she served me! She was a Vaishnava. One day she noticed that I ate the food offered at the Kāli temple, and that stopped her coming. Her devotion to God was one-sided. It isn't possible to understand a person right away."

It was a winter morning, and the Master was sitting near the east door of his room, wrapped in his moleskin shawl. He looked at the sun and suddenly went into samādhi. His eyes stopped blinking and he lost all consciousness of the outer world. After a long time he came down to the plane of the sense world. Rakhal, Hazra, M., and other devotees were seated near him.

MASTER (*to Hazra*): "The state of samādhi is certainly inspired by love. Once, at Śyāmbāzār, they arranged a kirtan at Natavar Goswami's house. There I had a vision of Krishna and the gopis of Vrindāvan. I felt that my subtle body was walking at Krishna's heels.

"I went into samādhi when similar devotional songs were sung at the Hari Sabhā in Jorāshānko in Calcutta. That day they feared I might give up the body."

After the Master had finished his bath, he again spoke of the ecstatic love of the gopis. He said to M. and the other devotees: "One should accept the fervent attachment of the gopis to their beloved Krishna. Sing songs like this:

348

Tell me, friend, how far is the grove
Where Krishna, my Beloved, dwells?
His fragrance reaches me even here;
But I am tired and can walk no farther."

Again he sang:

I am not going home, O friend,
For there it is hard for me to chant my Krishna's name. . . .

Sri Ramakrishna had vowed to offer green coconut and sugar to Siddheśvari, the Divine Mother, for Rakhal's welfare. He asked M. whether he would pay for the offerings.

That afternoon the Master, accompanied by M., Rakhal, and some other devotees, set out in a carriage for the temple of Siddheśvari in Calcutta. On the way the offerings were purchased. On reaching the temple, the Master asked the devotees to offer the fruit and sugar to the Divine Mother. They saw the priests and their friends playing cards in the temple. Sri Ramakrishna said: "To play cards in a temple! One should think of God here."

From the temple the Master went to Jadu Mallick's house. Jadu was surrounded by his admirers, well-dressed dandies. He welcomed the Master.

MASTER (*with a smile*): "Why do you keep so many clowns and flatterers with you?"

JADU (*smiling*): "That you may liberate them." (*Laughter.*)

MASTER: "Flatterers think that the rich man will loosen his purse-strings for them. But it is very difficult to get anything from him. Once a jackal saw a bullock and would not give up his company. The bullock roamed about and the jackal followed him. The jackal thought: 'There hang the bullock's testicles. Some time or other they will drop to the ground and I shall eat them.' When the bullock slept on the ground, the jackal lay down too, and when the bullock moved about, the jackal followed him. Many days passed in this way, but the bullock's testicles still clung to his body. The jackal went away disappointed. (*All laugh.*) That also happens to flatterers."

Jadu and his mother served refreshments to Sri Ramakrishna and the devotees.

Wednesday, December 19, 1883

It was nine o'clock in the morning. Sri Ramakrishna was talking to M. near the bel-tree at Dakshineswar. This tree, under which the Master had practised the most austere sādhanā, stood in the northern end of the temple garden. Farther north ran a high wall, and just outside was the government magazine. West of the bel-tree was a row of tall pines that rustled in the wind. Below the trees flowed the Ganges, and to the south could be seen the sacred grove of the Panchavati. The dense trees and underbrush hid the temples. No noise of the outside world reached the bel-tree.

MASTER (*to M.*): "But one cannot realize God without renouncing 'woman and gold'."

M: "Why? Did not Vaśishtha say to Rāma, 'O Rāma, You may renounce the world if the world is outside God'?"

MASTER (smiling): "He said that to Rāma so that Rāma might destroy Rāvana. Rāma accepted the life of a householder and married to fulfil that mission."

M. stood there like a log, stunned and speechless.

Sri Ramakrishna went to the Panchavati on his way back to his room. M. accompanied him. It was then about ten o'clock.

M: "Sir, is there no spiritual discipline leading to realization of the Impersonal God?"

MASTER: "Yes, there is. But the path is extremely difficult. After intense austerities the rishis of olden times realized God as their innermost consciousness and experienced the real nature of Brahman. But how hard they had to work! They went out of their dwellings in the early morning and all day practised austerities and meditation. Returning home at nightfall, they took a light supper of fruit and roots.

"But an aspirant cannot succeed in this form of spiritual discipline if his mind is stained with worldliness even in the slightest degree. The mind must withdraw totally from all objects of form, taste, smell, touch, and sound. Only thus does it become pure. The Pure Mind is the same as the Pure Ātman. But such a mind must be altogether free from 'woman and gold'. When it becomes pure, one has another experience. One realizes: 'God alone is the Doer, and I am His instrument.' One does not feel oneself to be absolutely necessary to others either in their misery or in their happiness.

"Once a wicked man beat into unconsciousness a monk who lived in a monastery. On regaining consciousness he was asked by his friends, 'Who is feeding you milk?' The monk said, 'He who beat me is now feeding me.'"

M: "Yes, sir. I know that story."

MASTER: "It is not enough to know it. One must assimilate its meaning. It is the thought of worldly objects that prevents the mind from going into samādhi. One becomes established in samādhi when one is completely rid of worldliness. It is possible for me to give up the body in samādhi; but I have a slight desire to enjoy the love of God and the company of His devotees. Therefore I pay a little attention to my body.

"There is another kind of samādhi, called unmanā samādhi. One attains it by suddenly gathering the dispersed mind. You understand what that is, don't you?"

M: "Yes, sir."

MASTER: "Yes. It is the sudden withdrawal of the dispersed mind to the Ideal. But that samādhi does not last long. Worldly thoughts intrude and destroy it. The yogi slips down from his yoga.

"At Kāmārpukur I have seen the mongoose living in its hole up in the wall. It feels snug there. Sometimes people tie a brick to its tail; then the pull of the brick makes it come out of its hole. Every time the mongoose tries to be comfortable inside the hole, it has to come out because of the pull of the brick. Such is the effect of brooding on worldly objects that it makes the yogi stray from the path of yoga.

"Worldly people may now and then experience samādhi. The lotus blooms, no doubt, when the sun is up; but its petals close again when the sun is covered by a cloud. Worldly thought is the cloud."

M: "Isn't it possible to develop both jnāna and bhakti by the practice of spiritual discipline?"

MASTER: "Through the path of bhakti a man may attain them both. If it is necessary, God gives him the Knowledge of Brahman. But a highly qualified aspirant may develop both jnāna and bhakti at the same time. Such is the case with the Iśvarakotis—Chaitanya for example. But the case of ordinary devotees is different.

"There are five kinds of light: the light of a lamp, the light of various kinds of fire, the light of the moon, the light of the sun, and lastly the combined light of the sun and the moon. Bhakti is the light of the moon, and jnāna the light of the sun.

"Sometimes it is seen that the sun has hardly set when the moon rises in the sky. In an Incarnation of God one sees, at the same time, the sun of Knowledge and the moon of Love.

"Can everyone, by the mere wish, develop Knowledge and Love at the same time? It depends on the person. One bamboo is more hollow than another. Is it possible for all to comprehend the nature of God? Can a one-seer pot hold five seers of milk?"

M: "But what about the grace of God? Through His grace a camel can pass through the eye of a needle."

MASTER: "But is it possible to obtain God's grace just like that? A beggar may get a penny, if he asks for it. But suppose he asks you right off for his train fare. How about that?"

M. stood silent. The Master, too, remained silent. Suddenly he said: "Yes, it is true. Through the grace of God some may get both jnāna and bhakti."

M. saluted the Master and went back to the bel-tree.

At midday, finding that M. had not yet returned, Sri Ramakrishna started toward the bel-tree; but on reaching the Panchavati he met M. carrying his prayer carpet and water-jug. M. saluted the Master.

Sri Ramakrishna said to M: "I was coming to look for you. Because of your delay I thought you might have scaled the wall and run away. I watched your eyes this morning and felt apprehensive lest you should go away like Narayan Shastri. Then I said to myself: 'No, he won't run away. He thinks a great deal before doing anything.'"

The same night the Master talked to M., Rakhal, Latu, Harish, and a few other devotees.

MASTER (to M.): "Some people give a metaphysical interpretation of the Vrindāvan episode of Sri Krishna's life. What do you say about it?"

M: "There are various opinions. What if there are? You have told us the story of Bhishmadeva's weeping, on his bed of arrows, because he could not understand anything of God's ways.

"Again, you have told us that Hanumān used to say: 'I don't know any thing about the day of the week, the position of the stars, and so forth. I only meditate on Rāma.'

"Further, you have said to us that in the last analysis there are two things only: Brahman and Its Power. You have also said that, after the attainment of Brahmajnāna, a man realizes these two to be One, the One that has no two."

MASTER: "Yes, that is true. Your ideal is to reach the goal. You may reach it by going either through a thorny forest or along a good road.

"Diverse opinions certainly exist. Nangtā used to say that the monks could not be feasted because of the diversity of their views. Once a feast was arranged for the sannyāsis. Monks belonging to many sects were invited. Everyone claimed that his sect should be fed first, but no conclusion could be arrived at. At last they all went away and the food had to be given to the prostitutes."

M: "Totapuri was indeed a great soul."

MASTER: "But Hazra says he was an ordinary man. There's no use in discussing these things. Everyone says that his watch alone gives the correct time.

"You see, Narayan Shastri developed a spirit of intense renunciation. He was a great scholar. He gave up his wife and went away. A man attains yoga when he completely effaces 'woman and gold' from his mind. With some, the characteristics of the yogi are well marked.

"I shall have to tell you something of the six centres. The mind of the yogi passes through these, and he realizes God through His grace. Have you heard of the six centres?"

M: "These are the 'seven planes' of the Vedānta."

MASTER: "Not the Vedānta, but the Vedas. Do you know what the six centres are like? They are the 'lotuses' in the subtle body. The yogis see them. They are like the fruits and leaves of a wax tree."

M: "Yes, sir. The yogis can perceive them. I have read that there is a kind of glass through which a tiny object looks very big. Likewise, through yoga one can see those subtle lotuses."

Following Sri Ramakrishna's direction, M. spent the night in the hut at the Panchavati. In the early hours of the morning he was singing alone:

> I am without the least benefit of prayer and austerity, O Lord!
> I am the lowliest of the lowly; make me pure with Thy hallowed
> 　　touch.
> One by one I pass my days in hope of reaching Thy Lotus Feet,
> But Thee, alas, I have not found. . . .

Suddenly M. glanced toward the window and saw the Master standing there. Sri Ramakrishna's eyes became heavy with tears as M. sang the line:

> I am the lowliest of the lowly; make me pure with Thy hallowed
> 　　touch.

M. sang again:

> I shall put on the ochre robe and ear-rings made of conch-shell;
> Thus, in the garb of a yogini, from place to place I shall wander,
> Till I have found my cruel Hari. . . .

M. saw that the Master was walking with Rakhal.

Friday, December 21, 1883

In the morning the Master and M. were conversing alone under the bel-tree. The Master told him many secrets of spiritual discipline, exhorting him to renounce "woman and gold". He further said that the mind at times becomes one's guru.

After his midday meal the Master went to the Panchavati wearing a beautiful yellow robe. Two or three Vaishnava monks were there, clad in the dress of their sect.

In the afternoon a monk belonging to the sect of Nānak arrived. He was a worshipper of the formless God. Sri Ramakrishna asked him to meditate as well on God with form. The Master said to him: "Dive deep; one does not get the precious gems by merely floating on the surface. God is without form, no doubt; but He also has form. By meditating on God with form one speedily acquires devotion; then one can meditate on the formless God. It is like throwing a letter away, after learning its contents, and then setting out to follow its instructions."

Saturday, December 22, 1883

Rakhal, Harish, M., and Latu had been staying with Sri Ramakrishna at Dakshineswar. About nine o'clock in the morning the Master was sitting with them on the southeast verandah of his room, when Balaram's father and Devendra Ghosh of Śyāmpukur arrived.

A DEVOTEE: "Sir, how does one obtain love for God?"

MASTER: "Go forward. The king dwells beyond the seven gates. You can see him only after passing through all the gates.

"At the time of the installation of Annapurnā at Chānak, I said to Dwarika Babu: 'Large fish live in the deep water of a big lake. Throw some spiced bait into the water; then the fish will come, attracted by its smell; now and then they will make the water splash. Devotion and ecstatic love are like the spiced bait.

"God sports in the world as man. He incarnates Himself as man—as in the case of Krishna, Rāma, and Chaitanya. Once I said to Keshab: 'The greatest manifestation of God is in man. There are small holes in the balk of a field, where crabs and fish accumulate in the rainy season. If you want to find them you must seek them in the holes. If you seek God, you must seek Him in the Incarnations.'

"The Divine Mother of the Universe manifests Herself through this three-and-a-half cubit man. There is a song that says:

> O Mother, what a machine is this that Thou hast made!
> What pranks Thou playest with this toy
> Three and a half cubits high! . . .

"One needs spiritual practice in order to know God and recognize Divine Incarnations. Big fish live in the large lake, but to see them one must throw spiced bait in the water. There is butter in milk, but one must churn the milk to get it. There is oil in mustard-seed, but one must press the seed to extract the oil."

DEVOTEE: "Has God form, or is He formless?"

MASTER: "Wait, wait! First of all you must go to Calcutta; then only will you know where the Maidān, the Asiatic Society, and the Bengal Bank are located. If you want to go to the brāhmin quarter of Khardaha, you must first of all go to Khardaha.

"Why should it not be possible to practise the discipline of the formless God? But it is very difficult to follow that path. One cannot follow it without renouncing 'woman and gold'. There must be complete renunciation, both inner and outer. You cannot succeed in this path if you have the slightest trace of worldliness.

"It is easy to worship God with form. But it is not as easy as all that.

"One should not discuss the discipline of the Impersonal God or the path of knowledge with a bhakta. Through great effort perhaps he is just cultivating a little devotion. You will injure it if you explain away everything as a mere dream.

"Kabir was a worshipper of the Impersonal God. He did not believe in Śiva, Kāli, or Krishna. He used to make fun of them and say that Kāli lived on the offerings of rice and banana, and that Krishna danced like a monkey when the gopis clapped their hands. (All laugh.)

"One who worships God without form perhaps sees at first the deity with ten arms, then the deity with four arms, then the Baby Krishna with two arms. At last he sees the Indivisible Light and merges in It.

"It is said that sages like Dattātreya and Jaḍabharata did not return to the relative plane after having the vision of Brahman. According to some people, Śukadeva tasted only a drop of that Ocean of Brahman-Consciousness. He saw and heard the rumbling of the waves of that Ocean, but he did not dive into It.

"A brahmachāri once said to me, 'One who goes beyond Kedār cannot keep his body alive.' Likewise, a man cannot preserve his body after attaining Brahmajnāna.[1] The body drops off in twenty-one days.

"There was an infinite field beyond a high wall. Four friends tried to find out what was beyond the wall. Three of them, one after the other, climbed the wall, saw the field, burst into loud laughter, and dropped to the other side. These three could not give any information about the field. Only the fourth man came back and told people about it. He is like those who retain their bodies, even after attaining Brahmajnāna, in order to teach others. Divine Incarnations belong to this class.

"Pārvati was born as the daughter of King Himālaya. After Her birth She revealed to the king Her various divine forms. The father said: 'Well,

---

[1] In the case of an ordinary aspirant the body drops off after he attains the Knowledge of Brahman, but this is not so in the case of a Divine Incarnation, because He is born with a special mission to teach mankind.

Daughter, You have shown me all these forms. That is nice. But You have another aspect, which is Brahman. Please show me that.' 'Father,' replied Pārvati, 'if you seek the Knowledge of Brahman, then renounce the world and live in the company of holy men.' But King Himālaya insisted. Thereupon Pārvati revealed Her Brahman-form, and immediately the king fell down unconscious.

"All that I have just said belongs to the realm of reasoning. Brahman alone is real and the world illusory—that is reasoning. And everything but Brahman is like a dream. But this is an extremely difficult path. To one who follows it even the divine play in the world becomes like a dream and appears unreal; his 'I' also vanishes. The followers of this path do not accept the Divine Incarnation. It is a very difficult path. The lovers of God should not hear much of such reasoning.

"That is why God incarnates Himself as man and teaches people the path of devotion. He exhorts people to cultivate self-surrender to God. Following the path of devotion, one realizes everything through His grace—both Knowledge and Supreme Wisdom.

"God sports in this world. He is under the control of His devotee. 'Syāmā, the Divine Mother, is Herself tied by the cord of the love of Her devotee.'

"Sometimes God becomes the magnet and the devotee the needle, and sometimes the devotee becomes the magnet and God the needle. The devotee attracts God to him. God is the Beloved of His devotee and is under his control.

"According to one school, the gopis of Vrindāvan, like Yaśodā, had believed in the formless God in their previous births; but they did not derive any satisfaction from this belief. That is why later on they enjoyed so much bliss in the company of Sri Krishna in the Vrindāvan episode of His life. One day Krishna said to the gopis: 'Come along. I shall show you the Abode of the Eternal. Let us go to the Jamunā for a bath.' As they dived into the water of the river, they at once saw Goloka. Next they saw the Indivisible Light. Thereupon Yaśodā exclaimed: 'O Krishna, we don't care for these things any more. We would like to see You in Your human form. I want to take You in my arms and feed You.'

"So the greatest manifestation of God is through His Incarnations. The devotee should worship and serve an Incarnation of God as long as He lives in a human body. 'At the break of day He disappears into the secret chamber of His House.'

"Not all, by any means, can recognize an Incarnation of God. Assuming a human body, the Incarnation falls a victim to disease, grief, hunger, thirst, and all such things, like ordinary mortals. Rāma wept for Sītā. 'Brahman weeps, entrapped in the snare of the five elements.'

"It is said in the Purāna that God, in His Incarnation as the Sow, lived happily with His young ones even after the destruction of Hiranyāksha.[2] As the Sow, He nursed them and forgot all about His abode in heaven. At

[2] According to Hindu mythology, God incarnated Himself as a sow in order to save the world from the iniquities of the demon Hiranyāksha.

last Śiva killed the sow body with his trident, and God, laughing aloud, went to His own abode."

In the afternoon Bhavanath arrived. Rakhal, M., Harish, and other devotees were in the room.

MASTER (*to Bhavanath*): "To love an Incarnation of God—that is enough. Ah, what ecstatic love the gopis had for Krishna!"

Sri Ramakrishna began to sing, assuming the attitude of the gopis:

> O Krishna! You are the Soul of my soul. . . .

Then he sang:

> I am not going home, O friend,
> For there it is hard for me to chant my Krishna's name. . . .

And again:

> O Friend, that day I stood at my door as You were going to the woods. . . .

Continuing, the Master said: "When Krishna suddenly disappeared in the act of dancing and playing with the gopis, they were beside themselves with grief. Looking at a tree, they said: 'O tree, you must be a great hermit. You must have seen Krishna. Otherwise, why do you stand there motionless, as if absorbed in samādhi?' Looking at the earth covered with green grass, they said: 'O earth, you must have seen Krishna. Otherwise, why does your hair stand on end? You must have enjoyed the thrill of His touch.' Looking at the mādhavi creeper, they said, 'O mādhavi, give us back our Mādhava!' The gopis were intoxicated with ecstatic love for Krishna. Akrura came to Vrindāvan to take Krishna and Balarāma to Mathurā. When they mounted the chariot, the gopis clung to the wheels. They would not let the chariot move."

Saying this, Sri Ramakrishna sang, assuming the attitude of Akrura:

> Hold not, hold not the chariot's wheels!
> Is it the wheels that make it move?
> The Mover of its wheels is Krishna,
> By whose will the worlds are moved. . . .

MASTER: " 'Is it the wheels that make it move?' 'By whose will the worlds are moved.' 'The driver moves the chariot at his Master's bidding.' I feel deeply touched by these lines."

Sunday, December 23, 1883

At nine o'clock in the morning Sri Ramakrishna was seated on the southwest porch of his room, with Rakhal, Latu, M., Harish, and some other devotees. M. had now been nine days with the Master at Dakshineswar. Earlier in the morning Manomohan had arrived from Konnagar on his way to Calcutta. Hazra, too, was present.

A Vaishnava was singing. Referring to one of the songs, Sri Ramakrishna said: "I didn't enjoy that song very much. The songs of the earlier writers seem to me to have more of the right spirit. Once I sang for Nangtā at the Panchavati: 'To arms! To arms, O man! Death storms your house in battle array.' I sang another: 'O Mother, I have no one else to blame: Alas! I sink in the well these very hands have dug.'

"Nangtā, the Vedāntist, was a man of profound knowledge. The song moved him to tears though he didn't understand its meaning. Padmalochan also wept when I sang the songs of Rāmprasād about the Divine Mother. And he was truly a great pundit."

After the midday meal Sri Ramakrishna rested a few minutes in his room. M. was sitting on the floor. The Master was delighted to hear the music that was being played in the nahabat. He then explained to M. that Brahman alone has become the universe and all living beings.

MASTER: "Referring to a certain place, someone once said to me: 'Nobody sings the name of God there. It has no holy atmosphere.' No sooner did he say this than I perceived that it was God alone who had become all living beings. They appeared as countless bubbles or reflections in the Ocean of Satchidānanda.

"Again, I find sometimes that living beings are like so many pills made of Indivisible Consciousness. Once I was on my way to Burdwan from Kāmārpukur. At one place I ran to the meadow to see how living beings are sustained. I saw ants crawling there. It appeared to me that every place was filled with Consciousness."

Hazra entered the room and sat on the floor.

MASTER: "Again, I perceive that living beings are like different flowers with various layers of petals. They are also revealed to me as bubbles, some big, some small."

While describing in this way the vision of different divine forms, the Master went into an ecstatic state and said, "I have become! I am here!" Uttering these words he went into samādhi. His body was motionless. He remained in that state a long time and then gradually regained partial consciousness of the world. He began to laugh like a boy and pace the room. His eyes radiated bliss as if he had seen a wondrous vision. His gaze was not fixed on any particular object, and his face beamed with joy. Still pacing the room, the Master said: "I saw the paramahamsa who stayed under the banyan tree walking thus with just such a smile. Am I too in that state of mind?"

He sat on the small couch and engaged in conversation with the Divine Mother.

MASTER: "I don't even care to know. Mother, may I have pure love for Thy Lotus Feet!

(To M.) "One attains this state immediately after freeing oneself of all grief and desire.

(To the Divine Mother) "Mother, Thou hast done away with my worship. Please see, Mother, that I don't give up all desire. Mother, the paramahamsa is but a child. Doesn't a child need a mother? Therefore Thou art the Mother and I am the child. How can the child live without the Mother?"

Sri Ramakrishna was talking to the Divine Mother in a voice that would have melted even a stone. Again he addressed Her, saying: "Mere knowledge of Advaita! I spit on it! Thou dost exist as long as Thou dost keep the ego in me. The paramahamsa is but a child. Doesn't a child need a mother?"

M. sat there speechless and looked at the divine manifestation in the Master. He said to himself: "The Master is an ocean of mercy that knows no motive. He has kept himself in the state of a paramahamsa that he might, as teacher, awaken the spiritual consciousness of myself and other earnest souls."

M. further thought: "The Master says, 'Advaita—Chaitanya—Nityā-nanda'; that is to say, through the knowledge of the Non-dual Brahman one attains Consciousness and enjoys Eternal Bliss. The Master has not only attained the knowledge of non-duality but is in a state of Eternal Bliss. He is always drunk with ecstatic love for the Mother of the Universe."

With folded hands Hazra looked at the Master and said every now and then: "How blessed you are! How blessed you are!"

MASTER (to Hazra): "But you have hardly any faith; you simply live here to add to the play, like Jatilā and Kutilā."

In the afternoon M. paced the temple garden alone. He was deeply absorbed in the thought of the Master and was pondering the Master's words concerning the attainment of the exalted state of the paramahamsa, after the elimination of grief and desire. M. said to himself: "Who is this Sri Ramakrishna, acting as my teacher? Has God embodied Himself for our welfare? The Master himself says that no one but an Incarnation can come down to the phenomenal plane from the state of nirvikalpa samādhi."

Monday, December 24, 1883

At eight o'clock in the morning Sri Ramakrishna and M. were talking together in the pine-grove at the northern end of the temple garden. This was the eleventh day of M.'s stay with the Master.

It was winter. The sun had just risen. The river was flowing north with the tide. Not far off could be seen the bel-tree where the Master had practised great spiritual austerities. Sri Ramakrishna faced the east as he talked to his disciple and told him about the Knowledge of Brahman.

MASTER: "The formless God is real, and equally real is God with form. Nangtā used to instruct me about the nature of Satchidānanda Brahman. He would say that It is like an infinite ocean—water everywhere, to the right, left, above, and below. Water enveloped in water. It is the Water of the Great Cause, motionless. Waves spring up when It becomes active. Its activities are creation, preservation, and destruction.

"Again, he used to say that Brahman is where reason comes to a stop. There is the instance of camphor. Nothing remains after it is burnt—not even a trace of ash.

"Brahman is beyond mind and speech. A salt doll entered the ocean to measure its depth; but it did not return to tell others how deep the ocean was. It melted in the ocean itself.

"The rishis once said to Rāma: 'O Rāma, sages like Bharadvāja may very well call you an Incarnation of God, but we cannot do that. We adore the

Word-Brahman.[3] We do not want the human form of God.' Rāma smiled and went away, pleased with their adoration.

"But the Nitya and the Līlā are the two aspects of the same Reality. As I have said before, it is like the roof and the steps leading to it. The Absolute plays in many ways: as Iśvara, as the gods, as man, and as the universe. The Incarnation is the play of the Absolute as man. Do you know how the Absolute plays as man? It is like the rushing down of water from a big roof through a pipe; the power of Satchidānanda—nay, Satchidānanda Itself—descends through the conduit of a human form as water descends through the pipe. Only twelve sages, Bharadvāja and the others, recognized Rāma as an Incarnation of God. Not everyone can recognize an Incarnation.

"It is God alone who incarnates Himself as man to teach people the ways of love and knowledge. Well, what do you think of me?

"Once my father went to Gayā. There Raghuvir said to him in a dream, 'I shall be born as your son.' Thereupon my father said to Him: 'O Lord, I am a poor brāhmin. How shall I be able to serve You?' 'Don't worry about it', Raghuvir replied. 'It will be taken care of.'

"My sister, Hriday's mother, used to worship my feet with flowers and sandal-paste. One day I placed my foot on her head and said to her, 'You will die in Benares.'

"Once Mathur Babu said to me: 'Father, there is nothing inside you but God. Your body is like an empty shell. It may look from outside like a pumpkin, but inside there is nothing—neither flesh nor seed. Once I saw you as someone moving with a veil on.'

(To M.) "I am shown everything beforehand. Once I saw Gaurānga and his devotees singing kirtan in the Panchavati. I think I saw Balaram there and you too.

"I wanted to know the experiences of Gaurānga and was shown them at Śyāmbāzār in our native district. A crowd gathered; they even climbed the trees and the walls; they stayed with me day and night. For seven days I had no privacy whatever. Thereupon I said to the Divine Mother, 'Mother, I have had enough of it.'

"I am at peace now. I shall have to be born once more. Therefore I am not giving all knowledge to my companions. (With a smile) Suppose I give you all knowledge; will you then come to me again so willingly?

"I recognized you on hearing you read the Chaitanya Bhāgavat.[4] You are my own. The same substance, like father and son. All of you are coming here again. When you pull one part of the kalmi creeper, all the branches come toward you. You are all relatives—like brothers. Suppose Rakhal, Harish, and the others had gone to Puri, and you were there too. Would you live separately?

"Before you came here, you didn't know who you were. Now you will know. It is God who, as the guru, makes one know.

"Nangtā told the story of the tigress and the herd of goats. Once a tigress attacked a herd of goats. A hunter saw her from a distance and killed her.

[3] Om, the symbol of Brahman.
[4] A life of Chaitanya.

The tigress was pregnant and gave birth to a cub as she expired. The cub began to grow in the company of the goats. At first it was nursed by the she-goats, and later on, as it grew bigger, it began to eat grass and bleat like the goats. Gradually the cub became a big tiger; but still it ate grass and bleated. When attacked by other animals, it would run away, like the goats. One day a fierce-looking tiger attacked the herd. It was amazed to see a tiger in the herd eating grass and running away with the goats at its approach. It left the goats and caught hold of the grass-eating tiger, which began to bleat and tried to run away. But the fierce tiger dragged it to the water and said: 'Now look at your face in the water. You see, you have the pot-face of a tiger; it is exactly like mine.' Next it pressed a piece of meat into its mouth. At first the grass-eating tiger refused to eat the meat. Then it got the taste of the meat and relished it. At last the fierce tiger said to the grass-eater: 'What a disgrace! You lived with the goats and ate grass like them!' And the other was really ashamed of itself.

"Eating grass is like enjoying 'woman and gold'. To bleat and run away like a goat is to behave like an ordinary man. Going away with the new tiger is like taking shelter with the guru, who awakens one's spiritual consciousness, and recognizing him alone as one's relative. To see one's face rightly is to know one's real Self."

Sri Ramakrishna stood up. There was silence all around, disturbed only by the gentle rustling of the pine-needles and the murmuring of the Ganges. The Master went to the Panchavati and then to his room, talking all the while with M. The disciple followed him, fascinated. At the Panchavati Sri Ramakrishna touched with his forehead the raised platform around the banyan-tree. This was the place of his intense spiritual discipline, where he had wept bitterly for the vision of the Divine Mother, where he had held intimate communion with Her, and where he had seen many divine forms.

The Master and M. passed the cluster of bakul-trees and came to the nahabat. Hazra was there. The Master said to him: "Don't eat too much, and give up this craze for outer cleanliness. People with a craze do not attain Knowledge. Follow conventions only as much as necessary. Don't go to excess." The Master entered his room and sat on the couch.

Sri Ramakrishna was resting after his midday meal when Surendra, Ram, and other devotees arrived from Calcutta. It was about one o'clock. While M. was strolling alone under the pine-trees, Harish came there and told him that the Master wanted him in his room. Someone was going to read from the Śiva Samhitā, a book containing instructions about yoga and the six centres.

M. entered the room and saluted the Master. The devotees were seated on the floor, but no one was reading the book. Sri Ramakrishna was talking to the devotees.

MASTER: "The gopis cherished ecstatic love for Krishna. There are two elements in such love: 'I-ness' and 'my-ness'. 'I-ness' is the feeling that Krishna will be ill if 'I' do not serve Him. In this attitude the devotee does not look upon his Ideal as God.

" 'My-ness' is to feel that the Beloved is 'my' own. The gopis had such a feeling of 'my-ness' toward Krishna that they would place their subtle bodies under His feet lest His soles should get hurt.

"Yaśodā remarked: 'I don't understand your Chintāmani Krishna. To me He is simply Gopāla.' The gopis also said: 'Oh, where is Krishna, our Beloved? Where is Krishna, our Sweetheart?' They were not conscious of His being God.

"It is like a small child saying 'my daddy'. If someone says to the child, 'No, he is not your daddy', the child says, 'Yes, he is my daddy.'

"God, incarnating Himself as man, behaves exactly like a man. That is why it is difficult to recognize an Incarnation. When God becomes man, He is exactly like man. He has the same hunger, thirst, disease, grief, and sometimes even fear. Rāma was stricken with grief for Sītā. Krishna carried on His head the shoes and wooden stool of His father Nanda.

"In the theatre, when an actor comes on the stage in the role of a holy man, he behaves like one, and not like the actor who is taking the part of the king. He plays his own role.

"Once an impersonator dressed himself as a world-renouncing monk. Pleased with the correctness of his disguise, some rich people offered him a rupee. He did not accept the money but went away shaking his head. Afterwards he removed his disguise and appeared in his usual dress. Then he said to the rich people, 'Please give me the rupee.' They replied: 'Why, you went away refusing our present. Why do you ask for it now?' The man said: 'But then I was in the role of a holy man. I could not accept money.' Likewise, when God becomes man He behaves exactly like a man.

"At Vrindāvan one sees many places associated with Krishna's life."

SURENDRA: "We were there during the holidays. Visitors were continually pestered for money. The priests and others asked for it continually. We told them that we were going to leave for Calcutta the next day, but we fled from Vrindāvan that very night."

MASTER: "What is that? Shame! You said you would leave the place the next day and ran away that very day. What a shame!"

SURENDRA (embarrassed): "Here and there we saw the bābājis in the woods practising spiritual discipline in solitude."

MASTER: "Did you give them anything?"

SURENDRA: "No, sir."

MASTER: "That was not proper of you. One should give something to monks and devotees. Those who have the means should help such persons when they meet them.

"I went to Vrindāvan with Mathur Babu. The moment I came to the Dhruva Ghāt[5] at Mathurā, in a flash I saw Vasudeva crossing the Jamunā with Krishna in his arms.

"One evening I was taking a stroll on the beach of the river. There were small thatched huts on the beach and big plum-trees. It was the 'cow-dust' hour. The cows were returning from the pasture, raising dust with their

---

[5] A bathing-place in the Jamunā, where, according to tradition, Vasudeva, the father of Krishna, crossed the river carrying the new-born child through a stormy night.

hoofs. I saw them fording the river. Then came some cowherd boys crossing the river with their cows. No sooner did I behold this scene than I cried out, 'O Krishna, where are You?' and became unconscious.

"I wanted to visit Śyāmakunda and Rādhākunda; so Mathur Babu sent me there in a palanquin. We had a long way to go. Food was put in the palanquin. While going over the meadow I was overpowered with emotion and wept: 'O Krishna, I find everything the same; only You are not here. This is the very meadow where You tended the cows.' Hriday followed me on foot. I was bathed in tears. I couldn't ask the bearers to stop the palanquin.

"At Śyāmakunda and Rādhākunda I saw the holy men living in small mud huts. Facing away from the road lest their eyes should fall on men, they were engaged in spiritual discipline. One should visit the 'Twelve Grove'.

"I went into samādhi at the sight of the image of Bankuvihāri. In that state I wanted to touch it. I did not want to visit Govindaji twice. At Mathurā I dreamt of Krishna as the cowherd boy. Hriday and Mathur Babu had the same dream.

(To Surendra) "You have both—yoga and bhoga. There are different classes of sages: the brahmarshi, the devarshi, and the rājarshi. Śukadeva is an example of the brahmarshi. He didn't keep even one book with him. An example of the devarshi is Nārada. Janaka was a rājarshi, devoted to selfless work.

"The devotee of the Divine Mother attains dharma and moksha. He enjoys artha and kāma as well. Once I saw you in a vision as the child of the Divine Mother. You have both—yoga and bhoga; otherwise your countenance would look dry.

"The man who renounces all looks dry. Once I saw a devotee of the Divine Mother at the bathing-ghat on the Ganges. He was eating his meal and at the same time worshipping the Mother. He looked on himself as the Mother's child.

"But it isn't good to have much money. I find that Jadu Mallick is drowned in worldliness. It is because he has too much money. Nabin Niyogi, too, has both yoga and bhoga. I saw him and his son waving the fan before the image of the Divine Mother at the time of the Durgā Pujā."

SURENDRA: "Sir, why can't I meditate?"

MASTER: "You remember God and think of Him, don't you?"

SURENDRA: "Yes, sir. I go to sleep repeating the word 'Mother'."

MASTER: "That is very good. It will be enough if you remember God and think of Him."

Sri Ramakrishna had taken Surendra's responsibilities on himself. Why should Surendra worry about anything?

It was evening. The Master was sitting on the floor of his room with the devotees. He was talking to them about yoga and the six centres. These are described in the Śiva Samhitā.

MASTER: "Idā, Pingalā, and Sushumnā are the three principal nerves. All the lotuses are located in the Sushumnā. They are formed of Consciousness,

like a tree made of wax—the branches, twigs, fruits, and so forth all of wax.
The Kundalini lies in the lotus of the Mulādhāra. That lotus has four
petals. The Primordial Energy resides in all bodies as the Kundalini. She
is like a sleeping snake coiled up—'of the form of a sleeping snake, having
the Mulādhāra for Her abode'. (*To M.*) The Kundalini is speedily awakened if one follows the path of bhakti. God cannot be seen unless She is
awakened. Sing earnestly and secretly in solitude:

Waken, O Mother! O Kundalini, whose nature is Bliss Eternal!
Thou art the serpent coiled in sleep, in the lotus of the Mulādhāra.

"Rāmprasād achieved perfection through singing. One obtains the vision
of God if one sings with yearning heart."

M: "Grief and distress of mind disappear if one has these experiences
but once."

MASTER: "That is true. Distress of mind disappears for ever. I shall tell
you a few things about yoga. But you see, the mother bird doesn't break
the shell until the chick inside the egg is matured. The egg is hatched in
the fullness of time. It is necessary to practise some spiritual discipline. The
guru no doubt does everything for the disciple; but at the end he makes
the disciple work a little himself. When cutting down a big tree, a man cuts
almost through the trunk; then he stands aside for a moment, and the tree
falls down with a crash.

"The farmer brings water to his field through a canal from the river. He
stands aside when only a little digging remains to be done to connect the
field with the water. Then the earth becomes soaked and falls of itself, and
the water of the river pours into the canal in torrents.

"A man is able to see God as soon as he gets rid of ego and other limitations. He sees God as soon as he is free from such feelings as 'I am a scholar',
'I am the son of such and such a person', 'I am wealthy', 'I am honourable',
and so forth.

" 'God alone is real and all else unreal; the world is illusory'—that is discrimination. One cannot assimilate spiritual instruction without discrimination.

"Through the practice of spiritual discipline one attains perfection, by the
grace of God. But one must also labour a little. Then one sees God and
enjoys bliss. If a man hears that a jar filled with gold is buried at a certain
place, he rushes there and begins to dig. He sweats as he goes on digging.
After much digging he feels the spade strike something. Then he throws
away the spade and looks for the jar. At the sight of the jar he dances for
joy. Then he takes up the jar and pours out the gold coins. He takes them
into his hand, counts them, and feels the ecstasy of joy. Vision—touch—
enjoyment. Isn't it so?"

M: "Yes, sir."

The Master was silent a moment and then went on.

MASTER: "Those who are my own will come here even if I scold them.
Look at Narendra's nature! At first he used to abuse my Mother Kāli very
much. One day I said to him sharply, 'Rascal! Don't come here any more.'

He slowly left the room and prepared a smoke. He who is one's own will not be angry even if scolded. What do you say?"

M: "That is true, sir."

MASTER: "Narendra is perfect from his very birth. He is devoted to the ideal of the formless God."

M. (smiling): "Whenever he comes here he brings along great excitement."

Sri Ramakrishna smiled and said, "Yes, excitement indeed."

The following day was Tuesday, the ekādaśi day of the lunar fortnight. It was eleven o'clock in the morning and the Master had not yet taken his meal. M., Rakhal, and other devotees were sitting in the Master's room.

MASTER (to M.): "One should fast on the eleventh day of the lunar fortnight. That purifies the mind and helps one to develop love of God. Isn't that so?"

M: "Yes, sir."

MASTER: "But you may take milk and puffed rice. Don't you think so?"

M. AT DAKSHINESWAR (II)

SRI RAMAKRISHNA, accompanied by Manilal Mallick, M., and several other devotees, was in a carriage on his way to Ram's new garden. The garden, which Ram had recently purchased, was next to Surendra's. Ram adored the Master as an Incarnation of God. He visited Sri Ramakrishna frequently at Dakshineswar. Manilal Mallick was a member of the Brāhmo Samāj. The Brāhmos do not believe in Divine Incarnations.

MASTER (to Manilal): "In order to meditate on God, one should try at first to think of Him as free from upādhis, limitations. God is beyond upādhis. He is beyond speech and mind. But it is very difficult to achieve perfection in this form of meditation.

"But it is easy to meditate on an Incarnation—God born as man. Yes, God in man. The body is a mere covering. It is like a lantern with a light burning inside, or like a glass case in which one sees precious things."

Arriving at the garden, the Master got out of the carriage and accompanied Ram and the other devotees to the sacred tulsi-grove. Standing near it, he said: "How nice! It is a fine place. You can easily meditate on God here."

Sri Ramakrishna sat down in the house, which stood to the south of the lake. Ram offered him a plate of fruit and sweets which he enjoyed with the devotees. After a short time he went around the garden.

Next Sri Ramakrishna proceeded toward Surendra's garden. He walked on foot a little distance and saw a sādhu sitting on a couch under a tree. At once he went up to the holy man and joyfully began a conversation with him.

MASTER: "To which order of monks do you belong? Have you any title—Giri, Puri, or the like?"

SĀDHU: "People call me a paramahamsa."

MASTER: "That is good. 'I am Śiva'—that is a good attitude. But I must tell you something else. The process of creation, preservation, and destruction that is going on day and night is due to Śakti, the Power of God. This Primal Power and Brahman are one and the same. Śakti cannot exist without Brahman, just as waves cannot exist without water. There cannot be any instrumental music without an instrument.

"As long as God keeps us in His relative world, so long we feel that there are two. If one accepts Śakti, one accepts Brahman as well. If one is aware of night, one is also aware of day. If one is aware of knowledge, one is also aware of ignorance.

"But there is another state in which God reveals to His devotee that Brahman is beyond both knowledge and ignorance. It cannot be described in words. What exists, exists."

After a pleasant conversation with the sādhu, the Master returned to the carriage, the holy man walking with him. Sri Ramakrishna looked upon him as a friend of long acquaintance, and they walked arm in arm.

The Master arrived at Surendra's garden. The very first thing he talked about was the sādhu.

MASTER: "He is a very nice man. (*To Ram*) Bring him to Dakshineswar when you come. He is really a good man. There is a line in a song to the effect that a man cannot recognize a holy person unless he is holy himself.

"The sādhu believes in God without form. That is good. God is both formless and endowed with form. He is many things more. The Absolute and the Relative belong to one and the same Reality. What is beyond speech and mind is born in the flesh, assuming various forms and engaging in various activities. From that one Om have sprung 'Om Śiva', 'Om Kāli', and 'Om Krishna'. Suppose the master of a house has sent out a small boy of the family to invite people to a feast. All look on the boy with great fondness and affection because he is the son or grandson of a prominent man."

The Master took refreshments at Surendra's garden house and then set out for Dakshineswar with the devotees.

Thursday, December 27, 1883

The temple garden was filled with the sweet music of the dawn service, which mingled with the morning melody from the nahabat. Leaving his bed, Sri Ramakrishna chanted the names of God in sweet tones. Then he bowed before the pictures of the different deities in his room and went to the west porch to salute the Ganges.

Some of the devotees who had spent the night at the temple garden came to the Master's room and bowed before him. Rakhal was staying with the Master, and Baburam had come the previous evening. M. had been staying there two weeks.

Sri Ramakrishna said to M.: "I have been invited to Ishan's this morning. Baburam will accompany me, and you too." M. made ready to go with the Master.

At eight o'clock the carriage hired for the Master stood waiting in front of the nahabat. On all sides plants and trees were in flower, and the river sparkled in the sunlight of the bright winter's day. The Master bowed once more before the pictures. Then, still chanting the name of the Divine Mother, he got into the carriage, followed by M. and Baburam. The devotees took with them Sri Ramakrishna's woolen shawl, woolen cap, and small bag of spices.

Sri Ramakrishna was very happy during the trip and enjoyed it like a child. About nine o'clock the carriage stopped at the door of Ishan's house.

Ishan and his relatives greeted the Master and led him to the parlour on the first floor. Shrish, Ishan's son, was introduced to Sri Ramakrishna. The young man practised law at Alipur. He had been a brilliant student, having stood first in two of the university examinations, but he was extremely modest.

MASTER (to Shrish): "What is your profession?"

SHRISH: "I am practising law at Alipur."

MASTER (to M.): "For such a man to be a lawyer! (To Shrish) Well, have you any questions to ask? Perhaps you want to know how to live unattached in the world. Isn't that so?"

SHRISH: "Under the pressure of duties people do many unrighteous things in the world. Further, some are engaged in good work, and some in evil. Is this due to their actions in previous births? Is that why they act this way?"

MASTER: "How long should a man perform his duties? As long as he has not attained God. Duties drop away after the realization of God. Then one goes beyond good and evil. The flower drops off as soon as the fruit appears. The flower serves the purpose of begetting the fruit.

"How long should a devotee perform daily devotions such as the sandhyā? As long as his hair does not stand on end and his eyes do not shed tears at the name of God. These things indicate that the devotee has realized God. From these one knows that he has attained pure love of God. Realizing God one goes beyond virtue and vice.

> I bow my head, says Prasād, before desire and liberation;
> Knowing the secret that Kāli is one with the highest Brahman,
> I have discarded, once for all, both righteousness and sin.

"The more you advance toward God, the less He will give you worldly duties to perform."

SHRISH: "It is extremely difficult to proceed toward God while leading the life of a householder."

MASTER: "Why so? What about the yoga of practice? At Kāmārpukur I have seen the women of the carpenter families selling flattened rice. Let me tell you how alert they are while doing their business. The pestle of the husking-machine that flattens the paddy constantly falls into the hole of the mortar. The woman turns the paddy in the hole with one hand and with the other holds her baby on her lap as she nurses it. In the mean time customers arrive. The machine goes on pounding the paddy, and she carries on her bargains with the customers. She says to them, 'Pay the few pennies you owe me before you take anything more.' You see, she has all these things to do at the same time—nurse the baby, turn the paddy as the pestle pounds it, take the flattened rice out of the hole, and talk to the buyers. This is called the yoga of practice. Fifteen parts of her mind out of sixteen are fixed on the pestle of the husking-machine, lest it should pound her hand. With only one part of her mind she nurses the baby and talks to the buyers. Likewise, he who leads the life of a householder should devote fifteen parts of his mind to God; otherwise he will face ruin and fall into the clutches of

Death. He should perform the duties of the world with only one part of his mind.

"A man may lead the life of a householder after attaining Knowledge. But he must attain Knowledge first. If the milk of the mind is kept in the water of the world, they get mixed. Therefore he should turn the milk into curd and extract butter from it by churning it in solitude; then he may keep the butter in the water of the world. Therefore, you see, spiritual discipline is necessary. When the aśwattha tree is a mere sapling, it must be enclosed by a fence; otherwise the cattle will eat it. But the fence may be taken away when the trunk grows thick and strong. Then even an elephant tied to the tree cannot harm it.

"Therefore at the beginning the aspirant should go into solitude now and then. Spiritual discipline is necessary. You want to eat rice; suppose you sit down somewhere and say, 'Wood contains fire and fire cooks rice.' Can saying it cook the rice? You must get two pieces of wood and by rubbing them together bring out the fire.

"By eating siddhi one becomes intoxicated and feels happy. But suppose you haven't eaten the stuff or done anything else with it; you simply sit down somewhere and mutter, 'Siddhi! siddhi!' Will that intoxicate you or make you happy?

"You may learn a great deal from books; but it is all futile if you have no love for God and no desire to realize Him. A mere pundit, without discrimination and renunciation, has his attention fixed on 'woman and gold'. The vulture soars very high but its eyes are fixed on the charnel-pit.

"That alone is Knowledge through which one is able to know God. All else is futile. Well, what is your idea about God?"

SHRISH: "Sir, I feel that there is an All-knowing Person. We get an indication of His Knowledge by looking at His creation. Let me give an illustration. God has made devices to keep fish and other aquatic animals alive in cold regions. As water grows colder, it gradually shrinks. But the amazing thing is that, just before turning into ice, the water becomes light and expands. In the freezing cold, fish can easily live in the water of a lake: the surface of the lake may be frozen, but the water below is all liquid. If a very cold breeze blows, it is obstructed by the ice. The water below remains warm."

MASTER: "That God exists may be known by looking at the universe. But it is one thing to hear of God, another thing to see God, and still another thing to talk to God. Some have heard of milk, some have seen it, and some, again, have tasted it. You feel happy when you see milk; you are nourished and strengthened when you drink it. You will get peace of mind only when you have seen God. You will enjoy bliss and gain strength only when you have talked to Him."

SHRISH: "We do not have time to pray to God."

MASTER (with a smile): "That is true. Nothing comes to pass except at the right time. Going to bed, a child said to his mother, 'Mother, please wake me up when I feel the call of nature.' 'My son,' said the mother, 'that urge itself will wake you up. I don't have to wake you.'

"It is all decided beforehand by God what each one shall receive. A mother-in-law used to measure rice with a dish for her daughters-in-law. But it was not enough for them. One day the dish was broken and that made the girls happy. But the mother-in-law said to them, 'Children, you may shout and dance, but I can measure the rice with the palm of my hand.'

(To Shrish): "Surrender everything at the feet of God. What else can you do? Give Him the power of attorney. Let Him do whatever He thinks best. If you rely on a great man, he will never injure you.

"It is no doubt necessary to practise spiritual discipline; but there are two kinds of aspirants. The nature of the one kind is like that of the young monkey, and the nature of the other kind is like that of the kitten. The young monkey, with great exertion, somehow clings to its mother. Likewise, there are some aspirants who think that in order to realize God they must repeat His name a certain number of times, meditate on Him for a certain period, and practise a certain amount of austerity. An aspirant of this kind makes his own efforts to catch hold of God. But the kitten, of itself, cannot cling to its mother. It lies on the ground and cries, 'Mew, mew!' It leaves everything to its mother. The mother cat sometimes puts it on a bed, sometimes on the roof behind a pile of wood. She carries the kitten in her mouth hither and thither. The kitten doesn't know how to cling to the mother. Likewise, there are some aspirants who cannot practise spiritual discipline by calculating about japa or the period of meditation. All that they do is cry to God with yearning hearts. God hears their cry and cannot keep Himself away. He reveals Himself to them."

At noon the host wished to feed the Master and the devotees. Sri Ramakrishna was smilingly pacing the room. Now and then he exchanged a few words with the musician.

MUSICIAN: "It is God alone who is both the 'instrument' and the 'cause'. Duryodhana said to Krishna: 'O Lord, Thou art seated in my heart. I act as Thou makest me act.'"

MASTER (with a smile): "Yes, that is true. It is God alone who acts through us. He is the Doer, undoubtedly, and man is His instrument. But it is also true that an action cannot fail to produce its result. Your stomach will certainly burn if you eat hot chilli. It is God who has ordained that chilli will burn your stomach. If you commit a sin, you must bear its fruit. But one who has attained perfection, realized God, cannot commit sin. An expert singer cannot sing a false note. A man with a trained voice sings the notes correctly: sā, re, gā, mā, pā, dhā, ni."

The meal was ready. The Master and the devotees went to the inner court, where they were treated to a generous feast.

About three o'clock in the afternoon the Master was seated again in Ishan's drawing-room with M. and Shrish. He resumed his conversation with Shrish.

MASTER: "What is your attitude toward God? 'I am He', or 'Master and servant'? For the householder it is very good to look on God as the Master. The householder is conscious of doing the duties of life himself. Under such conditions how can he say, 'I am He'? To him who says, 'I am He' the world appears to be a dream. His mind, his body, even his ego, are dreams to him. Therefore he cannot perform worldly duties. So it is very good for the householder to look on himself as the servant and on God as the Master.

"Hanumān had the attitude of a servant. He said to Rāma: 'O Rāma, sometimes I meditate on You as the whole and on myself as the part. Sometimes I feel that You are the Master and I am the servant. But when I have the Knowledge of Reality, I see that I am You and You are I.'

"In the state of Perfect Knowledge one may feel, 'I am He'; but that is far beyond the ordinary man's experience."

SHRISH: "That is true, sir. The attitude of a servant relieves a man of all his worries. The servant depends entirely upon his master. A dog is devoted to its master. It depends upon him and is at peace."

MASTER: "Well, what suits your taste—God with form or the formless Reality? But to tell you the truth, He who is formless is also endowed with form. To His bhaktas He reveals Himself as having a form. It is like a great ocean, an infinite expanse of water, without any trace of shore. Here and there some of the water has been frozen. Intense cold has turned it into ice. Just so, under the cooling influence, so to speak, of the bhakta's love, the Infinite appears to take a form. Again, the ice melts when the sun rises; it becomes water as before. Just so, one who follows the path of knowledge —the path of discrimination—does not see the form of God any more. To him everything is formless. The ice melts into formless water with the rise of the Sun of Knowledge. But mark this: form and formlessness belong to one and the same Reality."

At dusk the Master was ready to start for Dakshineswar. He stood on the south porch of the drawing-room, talking to Ishan. Someone remarked that the chanting of God's holy name did not always produce results. Ishan said: "How can you say that? The seeds of an aswattha tree are no doubt tiny, but in them lie the germs of big trees. It may take a very long time for them to grow."

"Yes, yes!" said the Master. "It takes a long time to see the effect."

Next to Ishan's was his father-in-law's house. Sri Ramakrishna stood at the door of this house, ready to get into the carriage. Ishan and his friends stood around to bid him adieu. Sri Ramakrishna said to Ishan: "You are living in the world as a mudfish lives in the mud. It lives in the mud but its body is not stained.

"There are both vidyā and avidyā in this world of māyā. Who may be called a paramahamsa? He who, like a swan, can take the milk from a mixture of milk and water, leaving aside the water. He who, like an ant, can take the sugar from a mixture of sugar and sand, leaving aside the sand."

It was evening. The Master stopped at Ram's house on his way to Dakshineswar. He was taken to the drawing-room and there he engaged in conversation with Mahendra Goswami. Mahendra belonged to the Vaishnava sect and was Ram's neighbour. Sri Ramakrishna was fond of him.

MASTER: "The worshippers of Vishnu and the worshippers of Śakti will all ultimately reach one and the same goal; the ways may be different. The true Vaishnavas do not criticize the Śāktas."

Goswami (*smiling*): "Śiva and Pārvati are our Father and Mother."

Sri Ramakrishna, out of his stock of a dozen English words, said sweetly, "Thank you!" Then he added, "Yes, Father and Mother!"

Goswami: "Besides, it is a sin to criticize anyone, especially a devotee of God. All sins may be forgiven, but not the sin of criticizing a devotee."

Master: "But this idea of sin does not by any means affect all. For instance, the Iśvarakotis, such as Incarnations of God, are above sin. Sri Chaitanya is an example.

"A child, walking on a narrow ridge and holding to his father, may slip into the ditch. But that can never happen if the father holds the child by the hand.

"Listen. I prayed to the Divine Mother for pure love. I said to Her: 'Here is Thy righteousness, here is Thy unrighteousness. Take them both and give me pure love for Thee. Here is Thy purity, here is Thy impurity. Take them both and give me pure love for Thee. O Mother, here is Thy virtue, here is Thy vice. Take them both and give me pure love for Thee.' "

Goswami: "Yes, sir. That is right."

Master: "You should undoubtedly bow before all views. But there is a thing called unswerving devotion to one ideal. True, you should salute everyone. But you must love one ideal with your whole soul. That is unswerving devotion.

"Hanumān could not take delight in any other form than that of Rāma. The gopis had such single-minded love for the cowherd Krishna of Vrindāvan that they did not care to see the turbaned Krishna of Dwārakā.

"A wife may serve her husband's brothers by fetching water, or in other ways, but she cannot serve them in the way she does her husband. With him she has a special relationship."

Ram treated the Master to sweets. Sri Ramakrishna was ready to start for Dakshineswar. He put on his woolen shawl and cap, and got into the carriage with M. and the other devotees. Ram and his friends saluted the Master.

Saturday, December 29, 1883

It was the day of the new moon, auspicious for the worship of the Divine Mother. At one o'clock in the afternoon Sri Ramakrishna got into a carriage to visit the temple of Kāli at Kālighāt. He intended to stop at Adhar's house on the way, since Adhar was to accompany him to the temple. While the carriage was waiting near the north porch of the Master's room, M. went to the Master and said, "Sir, may I also go with you?"

Master: "Why?"

M: "I should like to visit my home in Calcutta."

Sri Ramakrishna reflected a moment and said: "Must you go home? Why? You are quite all right here."

M. wanted to see his people a few hours, but evidently the Master did not approve.

Sunday, December 30, 1883

At three o'clock in the afternoon, while M. was walking up and down under a tree, a devotee came to him and said that the Master had sent for him. M. went to Sri Ramakrishna's room and found a number of devotees there. He saluted the Master.

Ram, Kedar, and others had arrived from Calcutta. Ram had brought with him the Vedāntist monk whom the Master had visited near his garden a few days earlier. On that occasion Sri Ramakrishna had asked him to bring the sādhu to Dakshineswar.

The monk was sitting on the small couch with the Master. They were talking happily in Hindusthāni.

MASTER: "What do you feel about all this?"

MONK: "It is all like a dream."

MASTER: "Brahman alone is real and the world illusory. Well, sir, what is Brahman?"

MONK: "Brahman is the Sound. It is Om."

MASTER: "But there must be something indicated by the sound. Isn't that so?"

MONK: "That Itself is the thing indicated as well as the indicator."

At these words Sri Ramakrishna went into samādhi and sat motionless. The monk and the devotees looked wonderingly at him in his ecstatic condition. Kedar said to the monk: "Look at him, sir. This is samādhi."

The monk had read of samādhi but had never seen it before. After a few minutes the Master began gradually to come down to the normal plane of consciousness. He said to the Divine Mother: "Mother, I want to be normal. Please don't make me unconscious. I should like to talk to the sādhu about Satchidānanda. Mother, I want to be merry talking about Satchidānanda."

The monk was amazed to see the Master's condition and to hear these words. Sri Ramakrishna said to him: "Please do away with your 'I am He'. Let us now keep 'I' and 'Thou' to enjoy the fun."

A little later the Master was walking in the Panchavati with Ram, Kedar, M., and the other devotees.

MASTER (*to Kedar, with a smile*): "What did you think of the sādhu?"

KEDAR: "It is all dry knowledge. The pot has just been put on the fire, but as yet there is no rice in it."

MASTER: "That may be true. But he has renounced everything. He who has renounced the world has already made great progress. The sādhu belongs to the stage of the beginner. Nothing can be achieved without the realization of God. When a man is intoxicated with ecstatic love of God, he doesn't take delight in anything else. Then—

> Cherish my precious Mother Śyāma
> Tenderly within, O mind;
> May you and I alone behold Her,
> Letting no one else intrude."

Kedar repeated the words of a song in keeping with the Master's feeling:

> How shall I open my heart, O friend?
> It is forbidden me to speak.
> I am about to die, for lack of a kindred soul
> To understand my misery. . . .

Sri Ramakrishna returned to his room. About four o'clock the door of the Kāli temple was opened, and the Master walked to the temple with the monk; M. accompanied them. Entering the inner chamber, the Master prostrated himself reverently before the image. The monk, with folded hands, also bowed his head repeatedly before Kāli.

MASTER: "What do you think of Kāli?"

MONK (*with devotion*): "Kāli is supreme."

MASTER: "Kāli and Brahman are identical. Is that not so?"

MONK: "As long as one's mind is turned to the outer world, one must accept Kāli. As long as a man sees the outer world, and discriminates between good and evil, he must accept good and reject evil. To be sure, all names and forms are illusory; but as long as the mind sees the outer world, the aspirant must give up woman. The ideas of good and evil are applied to one who is still a student on the path; otherwise he will stray from the path of righteousness."

Thus conversing, the Master and the monk returned from the temple.

MASTER (*to M.*): "Did you notice that the sādhu bowed before Kāli?"

M: "Yes, sir."

Monday, December 31, 1883

At four o'clock in the afternoon the Master was sitting in his room with M., Rakhal, Latu, Harish, and other devotees.

Addressing M. and Balaram, the Master said: "Haladhari followed the path of knowledge. Day and night he used to study the Upanishads, the *Adhyātma Rāmāyana*, and similar books on Vedānta. He would turn up his nose at the mention of the forms of God. Once I ate from the leaf-plates of the beggars. At this Haladhari said to me, 'How will you be able to marry your children?' I said: 'You rascal! Shall I ever have children? May your mouth that repeats words from the *Gītā* and the Vedānta be blighted!' Just fancy! He declared that the world was illusory and, again, would meditate in the temple of Vishnu with turned-up nose."

In the evening Balaram and the other devotees returned to Calcutta. The Master remained in his room, absorbed in contemplation of the Divine Mother. After a while the sweet music of the evening worship in the temples was heard.

A little later the Master began to talk to the Mother in a tender voice that touched the heart of M., who was seated on the floor. After repeating, "Hari Om! Hari Om! Om!", the Master said: "Mother, don't make me unconscious with the Knowledge of Brahman. Mother, I don't want Brahmajnāna. I want to be merry. I want to play." Again he said: "Mother, I don't know the Vedānta; and Mother, I don't even care to know. The Vedas and the Vedānta remain so far below when Thou art realized, O Divine Mother!" Then he said: "O Krishna, I shall say to Thee, 'Eat, my Child! Take this, my Child!' O Krishna, I shall say to Thee, 'My Child, Thou hast assumed this body for my sake.' "

Wednesday, January 2, 1884

Rakhal, Latu, Harish, Ramlal, and M. had been staying with Sri Ramakrishna at the temple garden. About three o'clock in the afternoon M. found the Master on the west porch of his room engaged in conversation with a Tāntrik devotee. The Tāntrik was wearing an ochre cloth. Sri Ramakrishna asked M. to sit by his side. Perhaps the Master intended to instruct him through his talk with the Tāntrik devotee. Mahima Chakravarty had sent the latter to the Master.

MASTER (*to the Tāntrik*): "It is a part of the Tāntrik discipline to drink wine from a human skull. This wine is called 'kārana'. Isn't that so?"

TĀNTRIK: "Yes, sir."

MASTER: "But I cannot touch wine at all."

TĀNTRIK: "You have spontaneous Divine Bliss. One who enjoys that Bliss wants nothing else."

MASTER: "I don't care for japa and austerity. But I have constant remembrance and consciousness of God.

"Tell me, when they speak of the six centres, what do they mean?"

TĀNTRIK: "These are like different holy places. In each of the centres dwell Śiva and Śakti. One cannot see them with the physical eyes. One cannot take them out by cutting open the body."

M. listened silently to the conversation. Looking at him, the Master asked the Tāntrik devotee, "Can a man attain perfection without the help of a vija mantra, a sacred word from the guru?"

TĀNTRIK: "Yes, he can if he has faith—faith in the words of the guru."

The Master turned to M. and said, drawing his attention, "Faith!"

After the Tāntrik devotee had taken his leave, Jaygopal Sen, a member of the Brāhmo Samāj, arrived. The Master talked with him.

MASTER (*to Jaygopal*): "One should not harbour malice toward any person or any opinion. The believers in the formless God and the worshippers of God with form are all, without exception, going toward God alone. The jnāni, the yogi, the bhakta—all, without exception, are seeking Him alone. The follower of the path of knowledge calls Him 'Brahman'. The yogi calls Him 'Ātman' or 'Paramātman'. The bhakta calls Him 'Bhagavān'. Further, it is said that there is the Eternal Lord and His Eternal Servant."

JAYGOPAL: "How can we know that all paths are true?"

MASTER: "A man can reach God if he follows one path rightly. Then he can learn about all the other paths. It is like reaching the roof by some means or other. Then one is able to climb down by the wooden or stone stairs, by a bamboo pole, or even by a rope.

"A devotee can know everything when God's grace descends on him. If you but realize Him, you will be able to know all about Him. You should somehow meet the master of a house and become acquainted with him; then he himself will tell you how many houses he owns and all about his gardens and government securities."

JAYGOPAL: "How does one receive the grace of God?"

MASTER: "Constantly you have to chant the name and glories of God and give up worldly thoughts as much as you can. With the greatest effort you may try to bring water into your field for your crops, but it may all leak out through holes in the ridges. Then all your efforts to bring the water by digging a canal will be futile.

"You will feel restless for God when your heart becomes pure and your mind free from attachment to the things of the world. Then alone will your prayer reach God. A telegraph wire cannot carry messages if it has a break or some other defect.

"I used to cry for God all alone, with a longing heart. I used to weep, 'O God, where art Thou?' Weeping thus, I would lose all consciousness of the world. My mind would merge in the Mahāvāyu.

"How can one attain yoga? By completely renouncing attachment to worldly things. The mind must be pure and without blemish, like the telegraph wire that has no defect.

"One must not cherish any desire whatever. The devotion of a man who has any desire is selfish. But desireless devotion is love for its own sake. You may love me or not, but I love you: this is love for its own sake.

"The thing is that one must love God. Through intense love one attains the vision of Him. The attraction of the husband for the chaste wife, the attraction of the child for its mother, the attraction of worldly possessions for the worldly man—when a man can blend these three into one, and direct it all to God, then he gets the vision of God."

Jaygopal was a man of the world. Was this why the Master gave instruction suited to him?

At eight o'clock that evening the Master was sitting in his room with Rakhal and M. It was the twenty-first day of M.'s stay with Sri Ramakrishna. The Master had forbidden him to indulge in reasoning.

MASTER (to Rakhal): "It is not good to reason too much. First comes God, and then the world. Realize God first; then you will know all about His world. (To M. and Rakhal) If first one is introduced to Jadu Mallick, then one can know everything about him—the number of his houses, gardens, government securities, and so on. For this reason the rishi Nārada advised Vālmiki[1] to repeat the word 'mara'. 'Ma' means God, and 'rā' the world. First comes God, and then the world. Krishnakishore said that the word 'marā' is a holy mantra because it was given to Vālmiki by the rishi. 'Ma' means God, and 'rā' the world.

[1] The author of the *Rāmāyaṇa*. It is said that this sage had lived the life of a highwayman. Coming in contact with Nārada, he became eager to lead a spiritual life. Nārada asked him to chant the holy name of Rāma as a spiritual discipline; but on account of the sinful tendency of his mind, Vālmiki could not utter the holy word. He was then advised to repeat the word 'marā', the reverse of 'Rāma'. Through yearning and earnestness the heart of the robber became purified, and it was then possible for him to chant Rāma's name. As a result he attained perfection.

"Therefore, like Vālmiki, one should at first renounce everything and cry to God in solitude with a longing heart. The first thing necessary is the vision of God; then comes reasoning—about the scriptures and the world.

(*To M.*) "That is why I have been telling you not to reason any more. I came from the pine-grove to say that to you. Through too much reasoning your spiritual life will be injured; you will at last become like Hazra. I used to roam at night in the streets, all alone, and cry to the Divine Mother, 'O Mother, blight with Thy thunderbolt my desire to reason!' Tell me that you won't reason any more."

M: "Yes, sir. I won't reason any more."

MASTER: "Everything can be achieved through bhakti alone. Those who want the Knowledge of Brahman will certainly achieve that also by following the trail of bhakti.

"Can a man blessed with the grace of God ever lack Knowledge? At Kāmārpukur I have seen grain-dealers measuring paddy. As one heap is measured away another heap is pushed forward to be measured. The Mother supplies the devotees with the 'heap' of Knowledge.

"After attaining God, one looks on a pundit as mere straw and dust. Padmalochan said to me: 'What does it matter if I accompany you to a meeting at the house of a fisherman?[2] With you I can dine even at the house of a pariah.'

"Everything can be realized simply through love of God. If one is able to love God, one does not lack anything. Kārtika and Ganeśa[3] were seated near Bhagavati, who had a necklace of gems around Her neck. The Divine Mother said to them, 'I will present this necklace to him who is the first to go around the universe.' Thereupon Kārtika, without losing a moment, set out on the peacock, his carrier. Ganeśa, on the other hand, in a leisurely fashion went around the Divine Mother and prostrated himself before Her. He knew that She contained within Herself the entire universe. The Divine Mother was pleased with him and put the necklace around his neck. After a long while Kārtika returned and found his brother seated there with the necklace on.

"Weeping, I prayed to the Mother: 'O Mother, reveal to me what is contained in the Vedas and the Vedānta. Reveal to me what is in the Purāna and the Tantra.' One by one She has revealed all these to me.

"Yes, She has taught me everything. Oh, how many things She has shown me! One day She showed me Śiva and Śakti everywhere. Everywhere I saw the communion of Śiva and Śakti. Śiva and Śakti existing in all living things—men, animals, trees, plants. I saw Them in the communion of all male and female elements.

"Another day I was shown heaps of human heads, mountain high. Nothing else existed, and I was seated alone in their midst.

"Still another day She showed me an ocean. Taking the form of a salt doll, I was going to measure its depth. While doing this, through the grace of the guru I was turned to stone. Then I saw a ship and at once got into it.

[2] A reference to Mathur Babu, who belonged to the fisherman caste. The orthodox brāhmin refuses to set foot in the house of a fisherman, who belongs to a low caste.

[3] The two sons of Bhagavati, the Divine Mother.

The helmsman was the guru. I hope you pray every day to Satchidānanda, who is the Guru. Do you?"

M: "Yes, sir."

MASTER: "The guru was the helmsman in that boat. I saw that 'I' and 'you' were two different things. Again I jumped into the ocean, and was changed into a fish. I found myself swimming joyfully in the Ocean of Satchidānanda.

"These are all deep mysteries. What can you understand through reasoning? You will realize everything when God Himself teaches you. Then you will not lack any knowledge."

Friday, January 4, 1884

Sri Ramakrishna was sitting in his room. M. was still staying with the Master, devoting his time to the practice of spiritual discipline. He had been spending a great part of each day in prayer and meditation under the bel-tree, where the Master had performed great austerities and had seen many wonderful visions of God.

MASTER (*to M.*): "Don't reason any more. In the end, reasoning only injures the aspirant. One should assume a particular attitude toward God while praying to Him—the attitude of friend or servant or son or 'hero'.

"I assume the attitude of a child. To me every woman is my mother. The divine Māyā, seeing this attitude in an aspirant, moves away from his path out of sheer shame.

"The attitude of 'hero' is extremely difficult. The Śāktas and the Bāuls among the Vaishnavas follow it, but it is very hard to keep one's spiritual life pure in that attitude. One can assume other attitudes toward God as well—the attitude in which the devotee serenely contemplates God as the Creator, the attitude of service to Him, the attitude of friendship, the attitude of motherly affection, or the attitude of conjugal love. The conjugal relationship, the attitude of a woman to het husband or sweetheart, contains all the rest—serenity, service, friendship, and motherly affection. (*To M.*) Which one of these appeals to your mind?"

M: "I like them all."

MASTER: "When one attains perfection one takes delight in all these relationships. In that state a devotee has not the slightest trace of lust. The holy books of the Vaishnavas speak of Chandidās and the washerwoman. Their love was entirely free from lust.

"In that state a devotee looks on himself as a woman. He does not regard himself as a man. Sanātana Goswāmi refused to see Mirābāi because she was a woman. Mirā informed him that at Vrindāvan the only man was Krishna and that all others were His handmaids. 'Was it right of Sanātana to think of himself as a man?' Mirā inquired."

At dusk M. was sitting at the Master's feet. Sri Ramakrishna had been told that Keshab's illness had taken a turn for the worse. He was talking about Keshab and incidentally about the Brāhmo Samāj.

MASTER (*to M.*): "Do they only give lectures in the Brāhmo Samāj? Or do they also meditate? I understand that they call their service in the temple 'upāsanā'.

"Keshab at one time thought a great deal of Christianity and the Christian views. At that time, and even before, he belonged to Devendranath Tagore's organization."

M: "Had Keshab Babu come here from the very beginning, he would not have been so preoccupied with social reform. He would not have been so busy with the abolition of the caste system, widow remarriage, inter-caste marriage, women's education, and such social activities."

MASTER: "Keshab now believes in Kāli as the Embodiment of Spirit and Consciousness, the Primal Energy. Besides, he repeats the holy name of the Mother and chants Her glories.

"Do you think the Brāhmo Samāj will develop in the future into a sort of social-reform organization?"

M: "The soil of this country is different. Only what is true survives here."

MASTER: "Yes, that is so. The Sanātana Dharma, the Eternal Religion declared by the rishis, will alone endure. But there will also remain some sects like the Brāhmo Samāj. Everything appears and disappears through the will of God."

Earlier in the afternoon several devotees from Calcutta had visited the Master and had sung many songs. One of the songs contained the following idea: "O Mother, You have cajoled us with red toys. You will certainly come running to us when we throw them away and cry ourselves hoarse for You."

MASTER (to M.): "How well they sang about the red toys!"

M: "Yes, sir. You once told Keshab about the red toys."

MASTER: "Yes. I also told him about the Chidākāśa, the Inner Consciousness, and about many other things. Oh, how happy we were! We used to sing and dance together."

Saturday, January 5, 1884

It was the twenty-third day of M.'s stay with Sri Ramakrishna. M. had finished his midday meal about one o'clock and was resting in the nahabat when suddenly he heard someone call his name three or four times. Coming out, he saw Sri Ramakrishna calling to him from the verandah north of his room.

M. saluted the Master and they conversed on the south verandah.

MASTER: "I want to know how you meditate. When I meditated under the bel-tree I used to see various visions clearly. One day I saw in front of me money, a shawl, a tray of sandesh, and two women. I asked my mind, 'Mind, do you want any of these?' I saw the sandesh to be mere filth. One of the women had a big ring in her nose. I could see both their inside and outside—entrails, filth, bone, flesh, and blood. The mind did not want any of these—money, shawl, sweets, or women. It remained fixed at the Lotus Feet of God.

"A small balance has two needles, the upper and the lower. The mind is the lower needle. I was always afraid lest the mind should move away from the upper needle—God. Further, I would see a man always sitting by me with a trident in his hand. He threatened to strike me with it if the lower needle moved away from the upper one.

"But no spiritual progress is possible without the renunciation of 'woman and gold'. I renounced these three: land, wife, and wealth. Once I went to the Registry Office to register some land, the title of which was in the name of Raghuvir. The officer asked me to sign my name; but I didn't do it, because I couldn't feel that it was 'my' land. I was shown much respect as the guru of Keshab Sen. They presented me with mangoes, but I couldn't carry them home. A sannyāsi cannot lay things up.

"How can one expect to attain God without renunciation? Suppose one thing is placed upon another; how can you get the second without removing the first?

"One must pray to God without any selfish desire. But selfish worship, if practised with perseverance, is gradually turned into selfless worship. Dhruva practised tapasyā to obtain his kingdom, but at last he realized God. He said, 'Why should a man give up gold if he gets it while searching for glass beads?'

"God can be realized when a man acquires sattva. Householders engage in philanthropic work, such as charity, mostly with a motive. That is not good. But actions without motives are good. Yet it is very difficult to leave motives out of one's actions.

"When you realize God, will you pray to Him, 'O God, please grant that I may dig reservoirs, build roads, and found hospitals and dispensaries'? After the realization of God all such desires are left behind.

"Then mustn't one perform acts of compassion, such as charity to the poor? I do not forbid it. If a man has money, he should give it to remove the sorrows and sufferings that come to his notice. In such an event the wise man says, 'Give the poor something.' But inwardly he feels: 'What can I do? God alone is the Doer. I am nothing.'

"The great souls, deeply affected by the sufferings of men, show them the way to God. Śankarāchārya kept the 'ego of Knowledge' in order to teach mankind. The gift of knowledge and devotion is far superior to the gift of food. Therefore Chaitanyadeva distributed bhakti to all, including the outcaste. Happiness and suffering are the inevitable characteristics of the body. You have come to eat mangoes. Fulfil that desire. The one thing needful is jnāna and bhakti. God alone is Substance; all else is illusory.

"It is God alone who does everything. You may say that in that case man may commit sin. But that is not true. If a man is firmly convinced that God alone is the Doer and that he himself is nothing, then he will never make a false step.

"It is God alone who has planted in man's mind what the 'Englishman'[4] calls free will. People who have not realized God would become engaged in more and more sinful actions if God had not planted in them the notion of free will. Sin would have increased if God had not made the sinner feel that he alone was responsible for his sin.

"Those who have realized God are aware that free will is a mere appear-

---

[4] Sri Ramakrishna used this word to denote Europeans in general, and also those whose ways and thoughts were largely influenced by Western ideas.

ance. In reality man is the machine and God its Operator, man is the carriage and God its Driver."

It was about four o'clock. Rakhal and several other devotees were listening to a kirtan by M. in the hut at the Panchavati. Rakhal went into a spiritual mood while listening to the devotional song. After a while the Master came to the Panchavati accompanied by Baburam and Harish. Other devotees followed.

RAKHAL: "How well he [referring to M.] sang kirtan for us! He made us all very happy."

The Master sang in an ecstatic mood:

O friends, how great is my relief
To hear you chanting Krishna's name! . . .

To the devotees he said, "Always sing devotional songs." Continuing, he said: "To love God and live in the company of the devotees: that is all. What more is there?" He said, again: "When Krishna went to Mathurā, Yaśodā came to Rādhā, who was absorbed in meditation. Afterwards Rādhā said to Yaśodā: 'I am the Primordial Energy. Ask a boon of Me.' 'What other boon shall I ask of You?' said Yaśodā. 'Only bless me that I may serve God with my body, mind, and tongue; that I may behold His devotees with these eyes, that I may meditate on Him with this mind, and that I may chant His name and glories with this tongue.'

"But those who are firmly established in God may do as well without the devotees. This is true of those who feel the presence of God both within and without. Sometimes they don't enjoy the devotees' company. You don't whitewash a wall inlaid with mother of pearl—the lime won't stick."

The Master returned presently from the Panchavati, talking to M.

MASTER: "You have the voice of a woman. Can't you practise a song such as this?—

Tell me, friend, how far is the grove
Where Krishna, my Beloved, dwells?

(To M., pointing to Baburam) "You see, my own people have become strangers; Ramlal and my other relatives seem to be foreigners. And strangers have become my own. Don't you notice how I tell Baburam to go and wash his face? The devotees have become relatives.

(Looking at the Panchavati) "I used to sit there. In course of time I became mad. That phase also passed away. Kāla, Śiva, is Brahman. That which sports with Kāla is Kāli, the Primal Energy. Kāli moves even the Immutable"

Saying this, the Master sang:

My mind is overwhelmed with wonder,
Pondering the Mother's mystery;
Her very name removes
The fear of Kāla, Death himself;
Beneath Her feet lies Mahā-Kāla. . . .

Then he said to M.: "Today is Saturday.[5] Go to the temple of Kāli."

[5] Saturday and Tuesday are regarded as auspicious days for the worship of the Divine Mother.

As the Master came to the bakul-tree he spoke to M. again: "Chidātmā and Chitśakti. The Purusha is the Chidātmā and Prakriti is the Chitśakti. Sri Krishna is the Chidātmā and Sri Rādhā the Chitśakti. The devotees are so many forms of the Chitśakti. They should think of themselves as companions or handmaids of the Chitśakti, Sri Rādhā. This is the whole gist of the thing."

After dusk Sri Ramakrishna went to the Kāli temple and was pleased to see M. meditating there.

The evening worship was over in the temples. The Master returned to his room and sat on the couch, absorbed in meditation on the Divine Mother. M. sat on the floor. There was no one else in the room.

The Master was in samādhi. He began to come gradually down to the normal plane. His mind was still filled with the consciousness of the Divine Mother. In that state he was speaking to Her like a small child making importunate demands on his mother. He said in a piteous voice: "Mother, why haven't You revealed to me that form of Yours, the form that bewitches the world? I pleaded with You so much for it. But You wouldn't listen to me. You act as You please."

The voice in which these words were uttered was very touching.

He went on: "Mother, one needs faith. Away with this wretched reasoning! Let it be blighted! One needs faith—faith in the words of the guru, childlike faith. The mother says to her child, 'A ghost lives there', and the child is firmly convinced that the ghost is there. Again, the mother says to the child, 'A bogy man is there', and the child is sure of it. Further, the mother says, pointing to a man, 'He is your elder brother', and the child believes that the man is one hundred and twenty-five per cent his brother. One needs faith. But why should I blame them, Mother? What can they do? It is necessary to go through reasoning once. Didn't You see how much I told him about it the other day? But it all proved useless."

The Master was weeping and praying to the Mother in a voice choked with emotion. He prayed to Her with tearful eyes for the welfare of the devotees: "Mother, may those who come to You have all their desires fulfilled! But please don't make them give up everything at once, Mother. Well, You may do whatever You like in the end. If You keep them in the world, Mother, then please reveal Yourself to them now and then. Otherwise, how will they live? How will they be encouraged if they don't see You once in a while? But You may do whatever You like in the end."

The Master was still in the ecstatic mood. Suddenly he said to M: "Look here, you have had enough of reasoning. No more of it. Promise that you won't reason any more."

M. (with folded hands): "Yes, sir. I won't."

MASTER: "You have had enough of it. When you came to me the first time, I told you your spiritual Ideal. I know everything about you, do I not?"

M. (with folded hands): "Yes, sir."

MASTER: "Yes, I know everything: what your Ideal is, who you are, your inside and outside, the events of your past lives, and your future. Do I not?"

M. (*with folded hands*): "Yes, sir."

MASTER: "I scolded you on learning that you had a son. Now go home and live there. Let them know that you belong to them. But you must remember in your heart of hearts that you do not belong to them nor they to you."

M. sat in silence. The Master went on instructing him.

MASTER: "You have now learnt to fly. But keep your loving relationship with your father. Can't you prostrate yourself before him?"

M. (*with folded hands*): "Yes, sir. I can."

MASTER: "What more shall I say to you? You know everything. You understand, don't you?"

M. sat there without uttering a word.

MASTER: "You have understood, haven't you?"

M: "Yes, sir, I now understand a little."

MASTER: "No, you understand a great deal. Rakhal's father is pleased about his staying here."

M. remained with folded hands.

MASTER: "Yes, what you are thinking will also come to pass."

Sri Ramakrishna now came down to the normal state of mind. Rakhal and Ramlal entered the room. At the Master's bidding Ramlal sang:

> Who is the Woman yonder who lights the field of battle?
> Darker Her body gleams even than the darkest storm-cloud
> And from Her teeth there flash the lightning's blinding flames! . . .

He sang again:

> Who is this terrible Woman, dark as the sky at midnight?
> Who is this Woman dancing over the field of battle? . . .

MASTER: "The Divine Mother and the earthly mother. It is the Divine Mother who exists in the form of the universe and pervades everything as Consciousness. The earthly mother gives birth to this body. I used to go into samādhi uttering the word 'Mā'. While repeating the word I would draw the Mother of the Universe to me, as it were, like the fishermen casting their net and after a while drawing it in. When they draw in the net they find big fish inside it.

"Gauri once said that one attains true Knowledge when one realizes the identity of Kālī and Gaurānga.[6] That which is Brahman is also Śakti, Kālī. It is That, again, which, assuming the human form, has become Gaurānga."

At the Master's request, Ramlal sang again, this time about Gaurānga.

MASTER (*to M.*): "The Nitya and the Līlā are the two aspects of the Reality. God plays in the world as man for the sake of His devotees. They can love God only if they see Him in a human form; only then can they show their affection for Him as their Brother, Sister, Father, Mother, or Child.

"It is just for this love of the devotees that God contracts Himself into a human form and descends on earth to play His līlā."

[6] An uncompromising hostility exists between the devotees of Kālī and the devotees of Gaurānga

THE MASTER AND HIS INJURED
ARM

Saturday, February 2, 1884

IT WAS THREE O'CLOCK in the afternoon. Sri Ramakrishna had been conversing with Rakhal, Mahimacharan, Hazra, and other devotees, when M.
entered the room and saluted him. He brought with him splint, pad, and
lint to bandage the Master's injured arm.

One day, while going toward the pine-grove, Sri Ramakrishna had fallen
near the railing and dislocated a bone in his left arm. He had been in an
ecstatic mood at the time and no one had been with him.

MASTER (to M.): "Hello! What was ailing you? Are you quite well now?"

M: "Yes, sir, I am all right now."

MASTER (to Mahima): "Well, if I am the machine and God is its
Operator, then why should this have happened to me?"

The Master was sitting on the couch, listening to the story of Mahimacharan's pilgrimage. Mahima had visited several holy places twelve years
before.

MAHIMA: "I found a brahmachāri in a garden at Sicrole in Benares. He
said he had been living there for twenty years but did not know its owner.
He asked me if I worked in an office. On my answering in the negative, he
said, 'Then are you a wandering holy man?' I saw a sādhu on the bank of
the Narmadā. He repeated the Gāyatri mentally. It so thrilled him that the
hair on his body stood on end. And when he repeated the Gāyatri and Om
aloud, it thrilled those who sat near him and caused their hair to stand on
end."

The Master was in the mood of a child. Being hungry he said to M.,
"What have you brought for me?" Looking at Rakhal he went into samādhi.

He was gradually coming down to the normal plane. To bring his mind
back to the consciousness of the body, he said: "I shall eat some jilipi. I shall
drink some water."

Weeping like a child, he said to the Divine Mother: "O Brahmamayi!
O Mother! Why hast Thou done this to me? My arm is badly hurt. (To
the devotees) Will I be all right again?" They consoled him, as one would
a child, and said: "Surely. You will be quite well again."

MASTER (*to Rakhal*): "You aren't to blame for it, though you are living here to look after me; for even if you had accompanied me, you certainly wouldn't have gone up to the railing."

The Master again went into a spiritual mood and said: "Om! Om! Om! Mother, what is this that I am saying? Don't make me unconscious, Mother, with the Knowledge of Brahman. Don't give me Brahmajnāna. I am but Thy child. I am easily worried and frightened. I want a Mother. A million salutations to the Knowledge of Brahman! Give it to those who seek it. O Ānandamayi! O Blissful Mother!"

Uttering loudly the word "Ānandamayi", he burst into tears and said:

> Mother, this is the grief that sorely grieves my heart,
> That even with Thee for Mother, and though I am wide awake,
> There should be robbery in my house.

Again he said to the Divine Mother: "What wrong have I done, Mother? Do I ever do anything? It is Thou, Mother, who doest everything. I am the machine and Thou art its Operator.

(*To Rakhal, smiling*) "See that you don't fall! Don't be piqued and cheat yourself."

Again addressing the Mother, Sri Ramakrishna said: "Do I weep because I am hurt? Not at all.

> Mother, this is the grief that sorely grieves my heart,
> That even with Thee for Mother, and though I am wide awake,
> There should be robbery in my house."

The Master was again talking and laughing, like a child who, though ailing, sometimes forgets his illness and laughs and plays about.

MASTER (*to the devotees*): "It will avail you nothing unless you realize Satchidānanda. There is nothing like discrimination and renunciation. The worldly man's devotion to God is momentary—like a drop of water on a red-hot frying-pan. Perchance he looks at a flower and exclaims, 'Ah, what a wonderful creation of God!'

"One must be restless for God. If a son clamours persistently for his share of the property, his parents consult with each other and give it to him even though he is a minor. God will certainly listen to your prayers if you feel restless for Him. Since He has begotten us, surely we can claim our inheritance from Him. He is our own Father, our own Mother. We can force our demand on Him. We can say to Him, 'Reveal Thyself to me or I shall cut my throat with a knife!'"

Sri Ramakrishna taught the devotees how to call on the Divine Mother.

MASTER: "I used to pray to Her in this way: 'O Mother! O Blissful One! Reveal Thyself to me. Thou must!' Again, I would say to Her: 'O Lord of the lowly! O Lord of the universe! Surely I am not outside Thy universe. I am bereft of knowledge. I am without discipline. I have no devotion. I know nothing. Thou must be gracious and reveal Thyself to me.'"

Thus the Master taught the devotees how to pray. They were deeply touched. Tears filled Mahimacharan's eyes.

Sri Ramakrishna looked at him and sang:

> Cry to your Mother Śyāmā with a real cry, O mind!
> And how can She hold Herself from you?
> How can Śyāmā stay away? . . .

Several devotees arrived from Shibpur. Since they had come from a great distance the Master could not disappoint them. He told them some of the essentials of spiritual life.

MASTER: "God alone is real, and all else illusory. The garden and its owner. God and His splendour. But people look at the garden only. How few seek out the owner!"

A DEVOTEE: "Sir, what is the way?"

MASTER: "Discrimination between the Real and the unreal. One should always discriminate to the effect that God alone is real and the world unreal. And one should pray with sincere longing."

DEVOTEE: "But, sir, where is our leisure for these things?"

MASTER: "Those who have the time must meditate and worship. But those who cannot possibly do so must bow down whole-heartedly to God twice a day. He abides in the hearts of all; He knows that worldly people have many things to do. What else is possible for them? You don't have time to pray to God; therefore give Him the power of attorney. But all is in vain unless you attain God and see Him."

ANOTHER DEVOTEE: "Sir, to see you is the same as to see God."

MASTER: "Don't ever say that again. The waves belong to the Ganges, not the Ganges to the waves. A man cannot realize God unless he gets rid of all such egotistic ideas as 'I am such an important man' or 'I am so and so'. Level the mound of 'I' to the ground by dissolving it with tears of devotion."

DEVOTEE: "Why has God put us in the world?"

MASTER: "To perpetuate His creation. It is His will, His māyā. He has deluded man with 'woman and gold'."

DEVOTEE: "Why has He deluded us? Why has He so willed?"

MASTER: "If but once He should give man a taste of divine joy, then man would not care to lead a worldly life. The creation would come to an end.

"The grain-dealer stores rice in huge bags in his warehouse. Near them he puts some puffed rice in a tray. This is to keep the rats away. The puffed rice tastes sweet to the rats and they nibble at it all night; they do not seek the rice itself. But just think! One seer of rice yields fourteen seers of puffed rice. How infinitely superior is the joy of God to the pleasure of 'woman and gold'! To one who thinks of the beauty of God, the beauty of even Rambhā and Tilottamā[1] appears as but the ashes of a funeral pyre."

DEVOTEE: "Why do we not feel intense restlessness to realize Him?"

MASTER: "A man does not feel restless for God until all his worldly desires are satisfied. He does not remember the Mother of the Universe until his share of the enjoyment of 'woman and gold' is completed. A child absorbed in play does not seek his mother. But after his play is over, he says, 'Mother! I must go to my mother.' Hriday's son was playing with the pigeons, calling

[1] Two celestial dancing-girls of exquisite beauty.

to them, 'Come! Ti, ti!' When he had had enough of play he began to cry. Then a stranger came and said: 'Come with me. I will take you to your mother.' Unhesitatingly he climbed on the man's shoulders and was off.

"Those who are eternally free do not have to enter worldly life. Their desire for enjoyment has been satisfied with their very birth."

At five o'clock in the afternoon Dr. Madhusudan arrived. While he prepared the bandage for the Master's arm, Sri Ramakrishna laughed like a child and said, "You are the Madhusudan[2] of both this world and the next!"

DR. MADHUSUDAN (smiling): "I only labour under the weight of my name."

MASTER (smiling): "Why, is the name a trifling thing? God is not different from His name. Satyabhama tried to balance Krishna with gold and precious stones, but could not do it. Then Rukmini put a tulsi-leaf with the name of Krishna on the scales. That balanced the Lord."

The doctor was ready to bandage the Master's arm. A bed was spread on the floor and the Master, laughing, lay down upon it. He said, intoning the words: "Ah! This is Radha's final stage. But Brinde says, 'Who knows what is yet to be?'"

The devotees were sitting around the Master. He sang:

The gopis all were gathered about the shore of the lake.

Sri Ramakrishna laughed and the devotees laughed with him.

After his arm was bandaged he said: "I haven't very much faith in your Calcutta physicians. When Sambhu became delirious, Dr. Sarvadhikari said: 'Oh, it is nothing. It is just grogginess from the medicine. And a little while after, Sambhu[3] breathed his last."

It was evening and the worship in the temples was over. A few minutes later Adhar arrived from Calcutta to see the Master. Mahimacharan, Rakhal, and M. were in the room.

ADHAR: "How are you?"

MASTER (affectionately): "Look here. How my arm hurts! (Smiling) You don't have to ask how I am!"

Adhar sat on the floor with the devotees. The Master said to him, "Please stroke here gently." Adhar sat on the end of the couch and gently stroked Sri Ramakrishna's feet.

The Master conversed with Mahimacharan.

MASTER: "It will be very good if you can practise unselfish love for God. A man who has such love says: 'O Lord, I do not seek salvation, fame, wealth, or cure of disease. None of these do I seek. I want only Thee.' Many are the people who come to a rich man with various desires. But if someone comes to him simply out of love, not wanting any favour, then the rich man feels attracted to him. Prahlada had this unselfish love, this pure love for God without any worldly end."

Mahimacharan sat silent. The Master turned to him.

[2] Also a name of Krishna.
[3] Sambhu Mallick died in 1877.

MASTER: "Now let me tell you something that will agree with your mood. According to the Vedānta one has to know the real nature of one's own Self. But such knowledge is impossible without the renunciation of ego. The ego is like a stick that seems to divide the water in two. It makes you feel that you are one and I am another. When the ego disappears in samādhi, then one knows Brahman to be one's own inner consciousness.

"One must renounce the 'I' that makes one feel, 'I am Mahima Chakravarty', 'I am a learned man', and so on. But the 'ego of Knowledge' does not injure one. Śankarāchārya retained the 'ego of Knowledge' in order to teach mankind.

"One cannot obtain the Knowledge of Brahman unless one is extremely cautious about women. Therefore it is very difficult for those who live in the world to get such Knowledge. However clever you may be, you will stain your body if you live in a sooty room. The company of a young woman evokes lust even in a lustless man.

"But it is not so harmful for a householder who follows the path of knowledge to enjoy conjugal happiness with his own wife now and then. He may satisfy his sexual impulse like any other natural impulse. Yes, you may enjoy a sweetmeat once in a while. (*Mahimacharan laughs.*) It is not so harmful for a householder.

"But it is extremely harmful for a sannyāsi. He must not look even at the portrait of a woman. A monk enjoying a woman is like a man swallowing the spittle he has already spat out. A sannyāsi must not sit near a woman and talk to her, even if she is intensely pious. No, he must not talk to a woman even though he may have controlled his passion.

"A sannyāsi must renounce both 'woman' and 'gold'. As he must not look even at the portrait of a woman, so also he must not touch gold, that is to say, money. It is bad for him even to keep money near him, for it brings in its train calculation, worry, insolence, anger, and such evils. There is an instance in the sun: it shines brightly; suddenly a cloud appears and hides it.

"That is why I didn't agree to the Mārwāri's depositing money for me with Hriday. I said: 'No, I won't allow even that. If I keep money near me, it will certainly raise clouds.'

"Why all these strict rules for a sannyāsi? It is for the welfare of mankind as well as for his own good. A sannyāsi may himself lead an unattached life and may have controlled his passion, but he must renounce 'woman and gold' to set an example to the world.

"A man will have the courage to practise renunciation if he sees one hundred per cent renunciation in a sannyāsi. Then only will he try to give up 'woman and gold'. If a sannyāsi does not set this example, then who will?

"One may lead a householder's life after realizing God. It is like churning butter from milk and then keeping the butter in water. Janaka led the life of a householder after attaining Brahmajnāna.

"Janaka fenced with two swords, the one of jnāna and the other of karma. The sannyāsi renounces action; therefore he fences with one sword only, that of knowledge. A householder, endowed with knowledge like

Janaka's, can enjoy fruit both from the tree and from the ground. He can serve holy men, entertain guests, and do other things like that. I said to the Divine Mother, 'O Mother, I don't want to be a dry sādhu.'

"After attaining Brahmajnāna one does not have to discriminate even about food. The rishis of olden times, endowed with the Knowledge of Brahman and having experienced divine bliss, ate everything, even pork.

(To Mahima) "Generally speaking there are two kinds of yoga: karma-yoga and manoyoga, that is to say, union with God through work and through the mind.

"There are four stages of life: brahmacharya, gārhasthya, vānaprastha, and sannyās. During the first three stages a man has to perform his worldly duties. The sannyāsi carries only his staff, water-pot, and begging-bowl. He too may perform certain nityakarma, but his mind is not attached to it; he is not conscious of doing such work. Some sannyāsis perform nityakarma to set an example to the world. If a householder or a man belonging to the other stages of life performs action without attachment, then he is united with God through such action.

"In the case of a paramahamsa, like Śukadeva, all karmas—all pujā, japa, tarpan, sandhyā, and so forth—drop away. In this state a man communes with God through the mind alone. Sometimes he may be pleased to perform outward activities for the welfare of mankind. But his recollection and contemplation of God remain uninterrupted."

It was about eight o'clock in the evening. Sri Ramakrishna asked Mahima-charan to recite a few hymns from the scriptures. Mahima read the first verse of the *Uttara Gītā*, describing the nature of the Supreme Brahman:

> He, Brahman, is one, partless, stainless, and beyond the ether;
> Without beginning or end, unknowable by mind or intelligence.

Finally he came to the seventh verse of the third chapter, which reads:

> The twice-born[4] worships the Deity in fire,
> The munis contemplate Him in the heart,
> Men of limited wisdom see Him in the image,
> And the yogis who have attained samesightedness
> Behold Him everywhere.

No sooner did the Master hear the words "the yogis who have attained samesightedness" than he stood up and went into samādhi, his arm supported by the splint and bandage. Speechless, the devotees looked at this yogi who had himself attained the state of samesightedness.

After a long time the Master regained consciousness of the outer world and took his seat. He asked Mahima to recite verses describing the love of God. The latter recited from the *Nārada Pancharātra*:

> What need is there of penance if God is worshipped with love?
> What is the use of penance if God is not worshipped with love?

4 A man belonging to the brāhmin, kshatriya, or vaiśya caste, who has his second or spiritual birth at the time of his investiture with the sacred thread.

What need is there of penance if God is seen within and without?
What is the use of penance if God is not seen within and without?

O Brahman! O my child! Cease from practising further penances.
Hasten to Śankara, the Ocean of Heavenly Wisdom;
Obtain from Him the love of God, the pure love praised by devotees,
Which snaps in twain the shackles that bind you to the world.

MASTER: "Ah! Ah!"

On hearing these verses the Master was about to go again into an ecstatic mood, but he restrained himself with effort.

Mahima read from the *Yatipanchaka*:

I am She, the Divine Mother, in whom the illusion of the universe of animate and inanimate things is seen, as in magic, and in whom the universe shines, being the play of Her mind. I am She, the Embodiment of Consciousness, who is the Self of the universe, the only Existence, Knowledge, and Bliss.

When the Master heard the line, "I am She, the Embodiment of Consciousness", he said with a smile, "Whatever is in the microcosm is also in the macrocosm."

Next Mahima read the Six Stanzas on Nirvāna:

Om. I am neither mind, intelligence, ego, nor chitta,
Neither ears nor tongue nor the senses of smell and sight;
Nor am I ether, earth, fire, water, or air:
I am Pure Knowledge and Bliss: I am Śiva! I am Śiva!

I am neither the prāna, nor the five vital breaths,
Neither the seven elements of the body nor its five sheaths,
Nor hands nor feet nor tongue, nor the organs of sex and voiding:
I am Pure Knowledge and Bliss: I am Śiva! I am Śiva!

Neither loathing nor liking have I, neither greed nor delusion;
No sense have I of ego or pride, neither dharma nor moksha;
Neither desire of the mind nor object for its desiring:
I am Pure Knowledge and Bliss: I am Śiva! I am Śiva!

Neither right nor wrongdoing am I, neither pleasure nor pain,
Nor the mantra, the sacred place, the Vedas, the sacrifice;
Neither the act of eating, the eater, nor the food:
I am Pure Knowledge and Bliss: I am Śiva! I am Śiva!

Death or fear I have none, nor any distinction of caste;
Neither father nor mother nor even a birth have I;
Neither friend nor comrade, neither disciple nor guru:
I am Pure Knowledge and Bliss: I am Śiva! I am Śiva!

I have no form or fancy; the All-pervading am I;
Everywhere I exist, yet I am beyond the senses;
Neither salvation am I, nor anything that may be known:
I am Pure Knowledge and Bliss: I am Śiva! I am Śiva!

Each time Mahima repeated: "I am Śiva! I am Śiva!", the Master rejoined with a smile: "Not I! Not I! Thou art Knowledge Absolute."

Mahima read a few more verses and also a description of the six psychic centres of the body. He said that in Benares he had witnessed the death of a yogi in the state of yoga.

MAHIMA: "There are fine passages in the *Rāma Gītā*."

MASTER: "You are speaking of the *Rāma Gītā*. Then you must be a staunch Vedāntist. How many books of that kind the sādhus used to read here!"

Mahima recited the description of Om:

It is like the unceasing flow of oil, like the long peal of a bell.

About the characteristics of samādhi he read: "The man established in samādhi sees the upper region filled with Ātman, the nether region filled with Ātman, the middle region filled with Ātman. He sees all filled with Ātman."

Adhar and Mahima saluted the Master and departed.

At noon the following day, after his midday meal, Sri Ramakrishna was sitting on the small couch, when Ram, Surendra, and a few other devotees arrived from Calcutta. They were worried about the Master's injured arm. The arm was bandaged. M. was present.

MASTER (*to the devotees*): "The Mother has put me in such a state of mind that I cannot hide anything from anyone. Mine is the condition of a child. Rakhal doesn't understand it. He covers my injured arm, wrapping my body with a cloth lest others should see my injury and criticize me. He took Dr. Madhu aside and reported my illness. But I shouted and said: 'Hello! Where are you, Madhusudan? Come and see. My arm is broken!'

"I used to sleep in the same room with Mathur and his wife. They took care of me as if I were their own child. I was then passing through a state of divine madness. Mathur would ask me, 'Father, do you hear our conversation?' 'Yes', I would reply.

"Once Mathur's wife became suspicious of his movements and said to him, 'If you go anywhere, he[5] must accompany you.' One day Mathur went to a certain place and asked me to wait downstairs. He returned after half an hour and said to me: 'Come, father, let us go now. The carriage is waiting.' When Mathur's wife asked me about it, I reported the thing correctly. I said to her: 'We went to a certain house. He told me to stay downstairs and himself went upstairs. He came down after half an hour and we left the place.' Of course she understood the thing in her own way.

"A partner of Mathur's estate used to take fruits and vegetables stealthily from the temple garden. When the other partners asked me about it, I told them the exact truth."

Sunday, February 24, 1884

Sri Ramakrishna was resting in his room after his midday meal, and Mani Mallick was sitting on the floor beside him, when M. arrived. M. saluted

[5] The Master.

the Master and sat down beside Mani. The Master's injured arm was bandaged.

MASTER (*to M.*): "How did you come?"

M: "I came as far as Ālambāzār in a carriage and from there I walked."

MANILAL: "Oh, he is so hot!"

MASTER (*with a smile*): "This makes me think that all these are not mere fancies of my brain. Otherwise why should these 'Englishmen' take so much trouble to come here?"

Sri Ramakrishna began to talk to them about his health and his injured arm.

MASTER: "Now and then I become impatient about my arm. I show it to this or that man and ask him whether I shall get well again. That makes Rakhal angry. He doesn't understand my mood. Now and then I say to myself, 'Let him go away.' Again I say to the Mother: 'Mother, where will he go? Why should he burn himself in the frying-pan of the world?'

"This childlike impatience of mine is nothing new. I used to ask Mathur Babu to feel my pulse and tell me whether I was ill.

"Well, where then is my faith in God? Once I was going to Kāmārpukur in a bullock-cart, when several persons came up to the cart with clubs in their hands. They looked like highwaymen. I began to chant the names of the gods. Sometimes I repeated the names of Rāma and Durgā, and sometimes 'Om Tat Sat', so that in case one failed another would work.

(*To M.*) "Can you tell me why I am so impatient?"

M: "Your mind, sir, is always absorbed in samādhi. You have kept a fraction of it on your body for the welfare of the devotees. Therefore you feel impatient now and then for your body's safety."

MASTER: "That is true. A little of the mind is attached to the body. It wants to enjoy the love of God and the company of the devotees."

Mani Mallick told the Master about an exhibition that was being held in Calcutta. He described a beautiful image of Yaśodā with the Baby Krishna on her lap. Sri Ramakrishna's eyes filled with tears. On hearing about Yaśodā, the embodiment of maternal love, his spiritual consciousness was kindled and he wept.

MANILAL: "If you were not unwell, you could visit the exhibition in the Maidān."

MASTER (*to M. and the others*): "I shan't be able to see everything even if I go. Perhaps my eyes will fall on some certain thing and I shall become unconscious. Then I shall not be able to see the rest. I was taken to the Zoological Garden. I went into samādhi at the sight of the lion, for the carrier[6] of the Mother awakened in my mind the consciousness of the Mother Herself. In that state who could see the other animals? I had to return home after seeing only the lion. Hence Jadu Mallick's mother first suggested that I should go to the exhibition and then said I should not."

Mani Mallick, about sixty-five years old, had been a member of the Brāhmo Samāj for many years, and Sri Ramakrishna gave him instruction that would agree with his mood.

[6] In Hindu mythology the lion is the carrier of Durgā, the Divine Mother.

MASTER: "Pundit Jaynarayan had very liberal views. I visited him once and liked his attitude. But his sons wore high boots. He told me he intended to go to Benares and live there, and at last he carried out his intention; for later on he did live in Benares and die there. When one grows old one should retire, like Jaynarayan, and devote oneself to the thought of God. What do you say?"

MANILAL: "True, sir. I don't relish the worries and troubles of the world."

MASTER: "Gauri used to worship his wife with offerings of flowers. All women are manifestations of the Divine Mother. (*To Manilal*) Please tell them that little story of yours."

MANILAL (*smiling*): "Once several men were crossing the Ganges in a boat. One of them, a pundit, was making a great display of his erudition, saying that he had studied various books—the Vedas, the Vedānta, and the six systems of philosophy. He asked a fellow passenger, 'Do you know the Vedānta?' 'No, revered sir.' 'The Sāmkhya and the Pātanjala?' 'No, revered sir.' 'Have you read no philosophy whatsoever?' 'No, revered sir.' The pundit was talking in this vain way and the passenger sitting in silence, when a great storm arose and the boat was about to sink. The passenger said to the pundit, 'Sir, can you swim?' 'No', replied the pundit. The passenger said, 'I don't know the Sāmkhya or the Pātanjala, but I can swim.'"

MASTER (*smiling*): "What will a man gain by knowing many scriptures? The one thing needful is to know how to cross the river of the world. God alone is real, and all else illusory.

"While Arjuna was aiming his arrow at the eye of the bird, Drona asked him: 'What do you see? Do you see these kings?' 'No, sir', replied Arjuna. 'Do you see me?' 'No.' 'The tree?' 'No.' 'The bird on the tree?' 'No.' 'What do you see then?' 'Only the eye of the bird.'

"He who sees only the eye of the bird can hit the mark. He alone is clever who sees that God is real and all else is illusory. What need have I of other information? Hanumān once remarked: 'I don't know anything about the phase of the moon or the position of the stars. I only contemplate Rāma.'

(*To M.*) "Please buy a few fans for our use here.

(*To Manilal*) "Look here, pay a visit to his [meaning M.'s] father. The sight of a devotee will inspire you.

(*To M.*) "Since my arm was injured a deep change has come over me. I now delight only in the Naralīlā, the human manifestation of God. Nitya and Līlā. The Nitya is the Indivisible Satchidānanda, and the Līlā, or Sport, takes various forms, such as the Līlā as God, the Līlā as the deities, the Līlā as man, and the Līlā as the universe.

"Vaishnavcharan used to say that one has attained Perfect Knowledge if one believes in God sporting as man. I wouldn't admit it then. But now I realize that he was right. Vaishnavcharan liked pictures of man expressing tenderness and love.

(*To Manilal*) "It is God Himself who is sporting in the form of man. It is He alone who has become Mani Mallick. The Śikhs teach: 'Thou art Satchidānanda.'

"Now and then man catches a glimpse of his real Self and becomes speechless with wonder. At such times he swims in an ocean of joy. It is like suddenly meeting a dear relative. (*To M.*) The other day as I was coming here in a carriage, I felt like that at the sight of Baburam. When Śiva realizes His own Self, He dances about in joy exclaiming, 'What am I! What am I!'

"The same thing has been described in the *Adhyātma Rāmāyana*. Nārada said, 'O Rāma, all men are Thy forms, and it is Sītā who has become all women.' On looking at the actors in the Rāmlīlā, I felt that Nārāyana Himself had taken these human forms. The genuine and the imitation appeared to be the same.

"Why do people worship virgins? All women are so many forms of the Divine Mother. But Her manifestation is greatest in pure-souled virgins.

(*To M.*) "Why do I become impatient when I am ill? Because the Mother has placed me in the state of a child. The child depends entirely on its mother. The child of the maidservant, when he quarrels with the child of the master, says, 'I shall tell my mother.'

"I was taken to Rādhābāzar to be photographed. It had been arranged that I should go to Rajendra Mitra's house that day. I heard that Keshab would be there. I planned to tell them certain things, but I forgot it all when I went to Rādhābāzar. I said: 'O Mother, Thou wilt speak. What shall I say?'

"I have not the nature of a jnāni. He considers himself great. He says, 'What? How can I be ill?'

"Koar Singh once said to me, 'You still worry about your body.' But it is my nature to believe that my Mother knows everything. It was She who would speak at Rajendra Mitra's house. Hers are the only effective words. One ray of light from the Goddess of Wisdom stuns a thousand scholars.

"The Mother has kept me in the state of a bhakta, a vijnāni. That is why I joke with Rakhal and the others. Had I been in the condition of a jnāni I couldn't do that.

"In this state I realize that it is the Mother alone who has become everything. I see Her everywhere. In the Kāli temple I found that the Mother Herself had become everything—even the wicked, even the brother of Bhagavat Pundit.

"Once I was about to scold Ramlal's mother, but I had to restrain myself. I saw her to be a form of the Divine Mother. I worship virgins because I see in them the Divine Mother. My wife strokes my feet, but I salute her afterwards.

"You salute me by touching my feet. But had Hriday been here, who would have dared to touch them? He wouldn't have allowed anyone to do it. I have to return your salutes because the Mother has placed me in a state in which I see God in everything.

"You see, one cannot exclude even a wicked person. A tulsi-leaf, however dry or small, can be used for worship in the temple."

Sunday, March 2, 1884

Sri Ramakrishna was sitting on the small couch in his room, listening to devotional music by Trailokya Sannyal of the Brāhmo Samāj. He had not yet recovered from the effects of the injury to his arm, which was still supported by a splint. Many devotees, including Narendra, Surendra, and M., were sitting on the floor.

Narendra's father, a lawyer of the High Court of Calcutta, had passed away suddenly. He had not been able to make provision for the family, which consequently faced grave financial difficulties. The members of the family sometimes had to go without food. Narendra was therefore passing his days in great anxiety.

Trailokya sang about the Divine Mother:

> O Mother, I hide myself in Thy loving bosom;
> I gaze at Thy face and cry out, "Mother! Mother!"
> I sink in the Sea of Bliss and am lost to sense
> In yoga-sleep; I gaze with unwinking eyes
> Upon Thy face, powerless to turn away.
> O Mother, I am terrified by this world;
> My spirit trembles and cries out in fear.
> Keep me, sweet Mother, in Thy loving bosom;
> Cover me with the spreading skirt of Thy love.

The Master shed tears of love and cried out, "Ah me! Ah me!"

Trailokya sang again:

> O Lord, Destroyer of my shame! Who but Thyself can save
> The honour of Thy devotee?
> Thou art the Ruler of my soul, my very life's Support,
> And I am Thy slave for evermore. . . .

He continued:

> Seeking a shelter at Thy feet,
> I have for ever set aside
> My pride of caste and race, O Lord,
> And turned my back on fear and shame.
> A lonely pilgrim on life's way,
> Where shall I go for succour now?
> For Thy sake, Lord, I bear men's blame;
> They rail at me with bitter words
> And hate me for my love of Thee.
> Both friends and strangers use me ill.
>
> Thou art the Guardian of my name;
> Thou mayest save or slay me, Lord!
> Upon the honour of Thy servant
> Rests, O Lord, Thy name as well;
> Thou art the Ruler of my soul,
> The glow of love within my heart;
> Do with me as it pleases Thee!

Once more he sang:

> Lord, Thou hast taken me from home and made me captive with
>   Thy love;
> Shield me for ever at Thy feet, O Thou Beloved One!
> Upon the Nectar of Thy love, feed me both day and night,
> And save Premdās, who is Thy slave.

The Master again shed tears of joy. He sang some lines from a song of Rāmprasād:

> Glory and shame, bitter and sweet, are Thine alone;
> This world is nothing but Thy play.
> Then why, O Blissful One, dost Thou cause a rift in it?

Addressing Trailokya, the Master said: "Ah! How touching your songs are! They are genuine. Only he who has gone to the ocean can fetch its water."

Trailokya sang again:

> Thou it is that dancest, Lord, and Thou that singest the song;
> Thou it is that clappest Thy hands in time with the music's beat;
> But man, who is an onlooker merely, foolishly thinks it is he.
>
> Though but a puppet, man becomes a god if he moves with Thee;
> Thou art the Mover of the machine, the Driver of the car;
> But man is weighted down with woe, dreaming that he is free.
>
> Thou art the Root of everything, Thou the Soul of our souls;
> Thou art the Master of our hearts; through Thine unbounded grace
> Thou turnest even the meanest sinner into the mightiest saint.

The singing came to an end. The Master engaged in conversation with the devotees.

MASTER: "God alone is the Master, and again, He is the Servant. This attitude indicates Perfect Knowledge. At first one discriminates, 'Not this, not this', and feels that God alone is real and all else is illusory. Afterwards the same person finds that it is God Himself who has become all this—the universe, māyā, and the living beings. First negation and then affirmation. This is the view held by the Purānas. A vilwa-fruit, for instance, includes flesh, seeds, and shell. You get the flesh by discarding the shell and seeds. But if you want to know the weight of the fruit, you cannot find it if you discard the shell and seeds. Just so, one should attain Satchidānanda by negating the universe and its living beings. But after the attainment of Satchidānanda one finds that Satchidānanda Itself has become the universe and the living beings. It is of one substance that the flesh and the shell and seeds are made, just like butter and buttermilk.

"It may be asked, 'How has Satchidānanda become so hard?' This earth does indeed feel very hard to the touch. The answer is that blood and semen are thin liquids, and yet out of them comes such a big creature as man. Everything is possible for God. First of all reach the indivisible Satchidānanda, and then, coming down, look at the universe. You will then find that everything is Its manifestation. It is God alone who has become everything. The world by no means exists apart from Him.

"All elements finally merge in ākāśa. Again, at the time of creation, ākāśa evolves into mahat and mahat into ahamkāra. In this way the whole world-system is evolved. It is the process of involution and evolution. A devotee of God accepts everything. He accepts the universe and its created beings as well as the indivisible Satchidānanda.

"But the yogi's path is different. He does not come back after reaching the Paramātman, the Supreme Soul. He becomes united with It.

"The 'partial knower' limits God to one object only. He thinks that God cannot exist in anything beyond that.

"There are three classes of devotees. The lowest one says, 'God is up there.' That is, he points to heaven. The mediocre devotee says that God dwells in the heart as the 'Inner Controller'. But the highest devotee says: 'God alone has become everything. All that we perceive is so many forms of God.' Narendra used to make fun of me and say: 'Yes, God has become all! Then a pot is God, a cup is God!' (*Laughter.*)

"All doubts disappear when one sees God. It is one thing to hear of God, but quite a different thing to see Him. A man cannot have one hundred per cent conviction through mere hearing. But if he beholds God face to face, then he is wholly convinced.

"Formal worship drops away after the vision of God. It was thus that my worship in the temple came to an end. I used to worship the Deity in the Kāli temple. It was suddenly revealed to me that everything is Pure Spirit. The utensils of worship, the altar, the door-frame—all Pure Spirit. Men, animals, and other living beings—all Pure Spirit. Then like a madman I began to shower flowers in all directions. Whatever I saw I worshipped.

"One day, while worshipping Śiva, I was about to offer a bel-leaf on the head of the image, when it was revealed to me that this Virāt, this Universe, itself is Śiva. After that my worship of Śiva through the image came to an end. Another day I had been plucking flowers, when it was revealed to me that the flowering plants were so many bouquets."

TRAILOKYA: "Ah! How beautiful is God's creation!"

MASTER: "Oh no, it is not that. It was revealed to me in a flash. I didn't calculate about it. It was shown to me that each plant was a bouquet adorning the Universal Form of God. That was the end of my plucking flowers. I look on man in just the same way. When I see a man, I see that it is God Himself who walks on earth, as it were, rocking to and fro, like a pillow floating on the waves. The pillow moves with the waves. It bobs up and down.

"The body has, indeed, only a momentary existence. God alone is real. Now the body exists, and now it does not. Years ago, when I had been suffering terribly from indigestion, Hriday said to me, 'Do ask the Mother to cure you.' I felt ashamed to speak to Her about my illness. I said to Her: 'Mother, I saw a skeleton in the Asiatic Society Museum. It was pieced together with wires into a human form. O Mother, please keep my body together a little, like that, so that I may sing Thy name and glories.'

"Why this desire to live? After Rāvana's death Rāma and Lakshmana entered his capital and saw Nikashā, his old mother, running away. Lakshmana was surprised at this and said to Rāma, 'All her children are dead, but still life attracts her so much!' Rāma called Nikashā to His side and said: 'Don't be afraid. Why are you running away?' She replied: 'Rāma, it was not fear that made me flee from You. I have been able to see all these wondrous actions of Yours simply because I am alive. I shall see many more things like these if I continue to live. Hence I desire to live.'

"Without desires the body cannot live. (*Smiling*) I had one or two desires. I prayed to the Mother, 'O Mother, give me the company of those who have renounced "woman and gold".' I said further: 'I should like to enjoy the society of Thy jnānis and bhaktas. So give me a little strength that I may walk hither and thither and visit those people.' But She did not give me the strength to walk."

TRAILOKYA (*smiling*): "Have all the desires been fulfilled?"

MASTER (*smiling*): "No, there are still a few left. (*All laugh.*)

"The body is really impermanent. When my arm was broken I said to the Mother, 'Mother, it hurts me very much.' At once She revealed to me a carriage and its driver. Here and there a few screws were loose. The carriage moved as the driver directed it. It had no power of its own.

"Why then do I take care of the body? It is to enjoy God, to sing His name and glories, and to go about visiting His jnānis and bhaktas."

Narendra was sitting on the floor in front of the Master.

MASTER (*to Trailokya and the other devotees*): "The joys and sorrows of the body are inevitable. Look at Narendra. His father is dead, and his people have been put to extreme suffering. He can't find any way out of it. God places one sometimes in happiness and sometimes in misery."

TRAILOKYA: "Revered sir, God will be gracious to Narendra."

MASTER (*with a smile*): "But when? It is true that no one starves at the temple of Annapurnā in Benares; but some must wait for food till evening.

"Once Hriday asked Sambhu Mallick for some money. Sambhu held the views of 'Englishmen' on such matters. He said to Hriday: 'Why should I give you money? You can earn your livelihood by working. Even now you are earning something. The case of a very poor person is different. The purpose of charity is fulfilled if one gives money to the blind or the lame.' Thereupon Hriday said: 'Sir, please don't say that. I don't need your money. May God help me not to become blind or deaf or extremely poor! I don't want you to give, and I don't want to receive.' "

The Master spoke as if piqued because God had not yet shown His kindness to Narendra. Now and then he cast an affectionate glance at his beloved disciple.

NARENDRA: "I am now studying the views of the atheists."

MASTER: "There are two doctrines: the existence and the non-existence of God. Why don't you accept the first?"

SURENDRA: "God is just. He must look after His devotees."

MASTER: "It is said in the scriptures that only those who have been charitable in their former births get money in this life. But to tell you the truth, this world is God's māyā. And there are many confusing things in this realm of māyā. One cannot comprehend them.

"The ways of God are inscrutable indeed. Bhishma lay on his bed of arrows. The Pāndava brothers visited him in Krishna's company. Presently Bhishma burst into tears. The Pāndavas said to Krishna: 'Krishna, how amazing this is! Our grandsire Bhishma is one of the eight Vasus. Another man as wise as he is not to be found. Yet even he is bewildered by māyā and weeps at death.' 'But', said Krishna, 'Bhishma isn't weeping on that account. You may ask him about it.' When asked, Bhishma said: 'O Krishna, I am unable to understand anything of the ways of God. God Himself is the constant companion of the Pāndavas, and still they have no end of trouble. That is why I weep. When I reflect on this, I realize that one cannot understand anything of God's ways.'

"God has revealed to me that only the Paramātman, whom the Vedas describe as the Pure Soul, is as immutable as Mount Sumeru, unattached, and beyond pain and pleasure. There is much confusion in this world of His māyā. One can by no means say that 'this' will come after 'that' or 'this' will produce 'that'."

SURENDRA (smiling): "If by giving away money in a previous birth one gets wealth in this life, then we should all give away money now."

MASTER: "Those who have money should give it to the poor and needy. (To Trailokya) Jaygopal Sen is well-to-do. He should be charitable. That he is not so is to his discredit. There are some who are miserly even though they have money. There is no knowing who will enjoy their money afterwards.

"Jaygopal came here the other day. He drove over here in a carriage. The lamps were broken, the horse seemed to have been returned from the charnel-house, and the coachman looked as if he had just been discharged from the Medical College Hospital. And he brought me two rotten pomegranates!" (All laugh.)

SURENDRA: "Jaygopal Babu belongs to the Brāhmo Samāj. I understand that now there is not one worth-while man in Keshab's organization. Vijay Goswami, Shivanath, and other notables have organized the Sādhāran Brāhmo Samāj."

MASTER (smiling): "Govinda Adhikari, it is said, would not keep good actors in his theatre lest they should claim a share of the profit. (All laugh.)

"The other day I saw a disciple of Keshab. A theatrical performance was being given in Keshab's house, and I saw the disciple dancing on the stage with a child in his arms. I understand that this man delivers 'lectures'. He had better lecture to himself."

Trailokya sang:

> Upon the Sea of Blissful Awareness waves of ecstatic love arise:
> Rapture divine! Play of God's Bliss!
> Oh, how enthralling!
> Wondrous waves of the sweetness of God, ever new and ever
>   enchanting,
> Rise on the surface, ever assuming
> Forms ever fresh.
> Then once more in the Great Communion all are merged, as the
>   barrier walls
> Of time and space dissolve and vanish:
> Dance then, O mind!
> Dance in delight, with hands upraised, chanting Lord Hari's holy
>   name.

Sri Ramakrishna requested Trailokya to sing the song beginning, "O Mother, make me mad with Thy love".

Trailokya sang:

O Mother, make me mad with Thy love!
What need have I of knowledge or reason?
Make me drunk with Thy love's Wine;
O Thou who stealest Thy bhaktas' hearts,
Drown me deep in the Sea of Thy love!
Here in this world, this madhouse of Thine
Some laugh, some weep, some dance for joy:
Jesus, Buddha, Moses, Gaurānga,
All are drunk with the Wine of Thy love.
O Mother, when shall I be blessed
By joining their blissful company?

RULES FOR HOUSEHOLDERS AND MONKS

SRI RAMAKRISHNA was sitting in his room at Dakshineswar with many devotees. Among them were Mani Mallick, Mahendra Kavirāj, Balaram, M., Bhavanath, Rakhal, Latu, and Harish. The Master's injured arm was in a splint. In spite of the injury he was constantly absorbed in samādhi or instructing the devotees.

Mani Mallick and Bhavanath referred to the exhibition which was then being held near the Asiatic Museum. They said: "Many mahārājās have sent precious articles to the exhibition—gold couches and the like. It is worth seeing."

MASTER (to the devotees, with a smile): "Yes, you gain much by visiting those things. You realize that those articles of gold and the other things sent by mahārājās are mere trash. That is a great gain in itself. When I used to go to Calcutta with Hriday, he would show me the Viceroy's palace and say: 'Look, uncle! There is the Viceroy's palace with the big columns.' The Mother revealed to me that they were merely clay bricks laid one on top of another.

"God and His splendour. God alone is real; the splendour has but a two-days existence. The magician and his magic. All become speechless with wonder at the magic, but it is all unreal. The magician alone is real. The rich man and his garden. People see only the garden; they should look for its rich owner."

MANI MALLICK (to the Master): "What a big electric light they have at the exhibition! It makes us think how great He must be who has made such an electric light."

MASTER (to Mani): "But according to one view it is He Himself who has become everything. Even those who say that are He. It is Satchidānanda Itself that has become all—the Creator, māyā, the universe, and living beings."

The conversation turned to the museum.

MASTER (to the devotees): "I visited the museum once. I was shown fossils. A whole animal has become stone! Just see what an effect has been

400

produced by company! Likewise, by constantly living in the company of a holy man one verily becomes holy."

MANI (*smiling*): "Had you visited the exhibition only once, we could receive instruction for ten or fifteen years."

MASTER (*with a smile*): "How so? You mean illustrations?"

BALARAM: "No, you shouldn't go. Your arm won't heal if you go here and there."

MASTER: "I should like to have two pictures. One of a yogi seated before a lighted log, and another of a yogi smoking hemp and the charcoal blazing up as he pulls. Such pictures kindle my spiritual consciousness, as an imitation fruit awakens the idea of a real one.

"The obstacle to yoga is 'woman and gold'. Yoga is possible when the mind becomes pure. The seat of the mind is between the eyebrows; but its look is fixed on the navel and the organs of generation and evacuation, that is to say, on 'woman and gold'. But through spiritual discipline the same mind looks upward.

"What are the spiritual disciplines that give the mind its upward direction? One learns all this by constantly living in holy company. The rishis of olden times lived either in solitude or in the company of holy persons; therefore they could easily renounce 'woman and gold' and 'fix their minds on God. They had no fear nor did they mind the criticism of others.

"In order to be able to renounce, one must pray to God for the will-power to do so. One must immediately renounce what one feels to be unreal. The rishis had this will-power. Through it they controlled the sense-organs. If the tortoise once tucks in its limbs, you cannot make it bring them out even by cutting it into four pieces.

"The worldly man is a hypocrite. He cannot be guileless. He professes to love God, but he is attracted by worldly objects. He doesn't give God even a very small part of the love he feels for 'woman and gold'. But he says that he loves God. (*To Mani Mallick*) Give up hypocrisy."

MANI: "Regarding whom, God or man?"

MASTER: "Regarding everything—man as well as God. One must not be a hypocrite.

"How guileless Bhavanath is! After his marriage he came to me and asked, 'Why do I feel so much love for my wife?' Alas, he is so guileless!

"Isn't it natural for a man to love his wife? This is due to the world-bewitching māyā of the Divine Mother of the Universe. A man feels about his wife that he has no one else in the world so near and dear; that she is his very own in life and death, here and hereafter.

"Again, how much a man suffers for his wife! Still he believes that there is no other relative so near. Look at the sad plight of a husband. Perhaps he earns twenty rupees a month and is the father of three children. He hasn't the means to feed them well. His roof leaks, but he hasn't the wherewithal to repair it. He cannot afford to buy new books for his son. He cannot invest his son with the sacred thread. He begs a few pennies from his different friends.

"But a wife endowed with spiritual wisdom is a real partner in life. She greatly helps her husband to follow the religious path. After the birth of one or two children they live like brother and sister. Both of them are devotees of God—His servant and His handmaid. Their family is a spiritual family. They are always happy with God and His devotees. They know that God alone is their own, from everlasting to everlasting. They are like the Pāndava brothers; they do not forget God in happiness or in sorrow.

"The longing of the worldly-minded for God is momentary, like a drop of water on a red-hot frying-pan. The water hisses and dries up in an instant. The attention of the worldly-minded is directed to the enjoyment of worldly pleasure. Therefore they do not feel yearning and restlessness for God.

"People may observe the ekādaśi in three ways. First, the 'waterless' ekādaśi—they are not permitted to drink even a drop of water. Likewise, an all-renouncing religious mendicant completely gives up all forms of enjoyment. Second, while observing the ekādaśi they take milk and sandesh. Likewise, a householder devotee keeps in his house simple objects of enjoyment. Third, while observing the ekādaśi they eat luchi and chakkā. They eat their fill. They keep a couple of loaves soaking in milk, which they will eat later on.[1]

"A man practises spiritual discipline, but his mind is on 'woman and gold'—it is turned toward enjoyment. Therefore, in his case, the spiritual discipline does not produce the right result.

"Hazra used to practise much japa and austerity here. But in the country he has his wife, children, and land. Therefore along with his spiritual discipline he carried on the business of a broker. Such people cannot be true to their word. One moment they say they will give up fish, but the next moment they break their vow.

"Is there anything that a man will not do for money? He will even compel a brāhmin or a holy man to carry a load.

"In my room sweets would turn bad; still I could not give them away to the worldly-minded. I could accept dirty water from others, but not even touch the jar of a worldly person.

"At the sight of rich people Hazra would call them to him. He would give them long lectures. He would say to them: 'You see Rakhal and the other youngsters. They do not practise any spiritual discipline. They simply wander about merrily.'

"A man may live in a mountain cave, smear his body with ashes, observe fasts, and practise austere discipline; but if his mind dwells on worldly objects, on 'woman and gold', I say, 'Shame on him!' But I say that a man is blessed indeed who eats, drinks, and roams about, but who keeps his mind free from 'woman and gold'.

(*Pointing to Mani Mallick*) "There is no picture of a holy man at his house. Divine feeling is awakened through such pictures."

MANILAL: "Yes, there is. In one room there is a picture of a pious Christian woman engaged in prayer. There is another picture in which a man holds

---

[1] This observance is an ekādaśi in name only, since the observer fills his stomach with delicious food. By avoiding rice and a few cooked articles, he keeps to the letter of the law.

to the Hill of Faith; below is an ocean of immeasurable depth. If he gives up his hold on faith, he will drop into the bottomless water. There is still a third picture. Several virgins are keeping vigil, feeding their lamps with oil in expectation of the Bridegroom. A sleeping virgin is by their side. She will not behold the Bridegroom when He arrives. God is described here as the Bridegroom."

MASTER (smiling): "That's very nice."

MANILAL: "I have other pictures too—one of the 'Tree of Faith' and another of 'Sin and Virtue'."

MASTER (to Bhavanath): "Those are good pictures. Go to his house and see them."

The Master remained silent a few minutes.

MASTER: "Now and then I reflect on these ideas and find that I do not like them. In the beginning of spiritual life a man should think about sin and how to get rid of it. But when, through the grace of God, devotion and ecstatic love are awakened in his heart, then he altogether forgets virtue and sin. Then he leaves the scriptures and their injunctions far behind. Thoughts of repentance and penance do not bother him at all.

"It is like going to your destination along a winding river. This requires great effort and a long time. But when there is a flood all around, then you can go straight to your destination in a short time. Then you find the land lying under water deep as a bamboo pole.

"In the beginning of spiritual life one goes by a roundabout way. One has to suffer a great deal. But the path becomes very easy when ecstatic love is awakened in the heart. It is like going over the paddy-field after the harvest is over. You may then walk in any direction. Before the harvest you had to go along the winding balk, but now you can walk in any direction. There may be stubble in the field, but you will not be hurt by it if you walk with your shoes on. Just so, an aspirant does not suffer if he has discrimination, dispassion, and faith in the guru's words."

MANILAL (to the Master): "Well, what is the rule for concentration? Where should one concentrate?"

MASTER: "The heart is a splendid place. One can meditate there or in the Sahasrāra. These are rules for meditation given in the scriptures. But you may meditate wherever you like. Every place is filled with Brahman-Consciousness. Is there any place where It does not exist? Nārāyana, in Vali's presence, covered with two steps the heavens, the earth, and the interspaces.[2] Is there then any place left uncovered by God? A dirty place is as holy as the bank of the Ganges. It is said that the whole creation is the Virāt, the Universal Form of God.

"There are two kinds of meditation, one on the formless God and the other on God with form. But meditation on the formless God is extremely

[2] A reference to a story in the *Bhāgavata*. King Vali was proud of his charity. God appeared before him in the form of a dwarf and asked him for the space that He could cover with three steps. Vali granted the boon. With two steps the Lord covered the earth, the heavens, and the interspaces. Vali was forced to place his own head before the Lord for the third step. This curbed his pride.

difficult. In that meditation you must wipe out all that you see or hear. You contemplate only the nature of your Inner Self. Meditating on His Inner Self, Śiva dances about. He exclaims, 'What am I! What am I!' This is called the 'Śiva yoga'. While practising this form of meditation, one directs one's look to the forehead. It is meditation on the nature of one's Inner Self after negating the world, following the Vedāntic method of 'Neti, neti'.

"There is another form of meditation known as the 'Vishnu yoga'. The eyes are fixed on the tip of the nose. Half the look is directed inward and the other half outward. This is how one meditates on God with form. Sometimes Śiva meditates on God with form, and dances. At that time he exclaims, 'Rāma! Rāma!' and dances about."

Sri Ramakrishna then explained the sacred Word "Om" and the true Knowledge of Brahman and the state of mind after the attainment of Brahmajnāna.

MASTER: "The sound Om is Brahman. The rishis and sages practised austerity to realize that Sound-Brahman. After attaining perfection one hears the sound of this eternal Word rising spontaneously from the navel.

" 'What will you gain', some sages ask, 'by merely hearing this sound?' You hear the roar of the ocean from a distance. By following the roar you can reach the ocean. As long as there is the roar, there must also be the ocean. By following the trail of Om you attain Brahman, of which the Word is the symbol. That Brahman has been described by the Vedas as the ultimate goal. But such vision is not possible as long as you are conscious of your ego. A man realizes Brahman only when he feels neither 'I' nor 'you', neither 'one' nor 'many'.

"Think of the sun and of ten jars filled with water. The sun is reflected in each jar. At first you see one real sun and ten reflected ones. If you break nine of the jars, there will remain only the real sun and one reflection. Each jar represents a jīva. Following the reflection one can find the real sun. Through the individual soul one can reach the Supreme Soul. Through spiritual discipline the individual soul can get the vision of the Supreme Soul. What remains when the last jar is broken cannot be described.

"The jīva at first remains in a state of ignorance. He is not conscious of God, but of the multiplicity. He sees many things around him. On attaining Knowledge he becomes conscious that God dwells in all beings. Suppose a man has a thorn in the sole of his foot. He gets another thorn and takes out the first one. In other words, he removes the thorn of ajnāna, ignorance, by means of the thorn of jnāna, knowledge. But on attaining vijnāna, he discards both thorns, knowledge and ignorance. Then he talks intimately with God day and night. It is no mere vision of God.

"He who has merely heard of milk is 'ignorant'. He who has seen milk has 'knowledge'. But he who has drunk milk and been strengthened by it has attained vijnāna."

Thus the Master described his own state of mind to the devotees. He was indeed a vijnāni.

MASTER (to the devotees): "There is a difference between a sādhu endowed with jnāna and one endowed with vijnāna. The jnāni sādhu has a certain way of sitting. He twirls his moustache and asks the visitor, 'Well, sir! Have you any question to ask?' But the man who always sees God and talks to Him intimately has an altogether different nature. He is sometimes like an inert thing, sometimes like a ghoul, sometimes like a child, and sometimes like a madman.

"When he is in samādhi, he becomes unconscious of the outer world and appears inert. He sees everything to be full of Brahman-Consciousness; therefore he behaves like a ghoul. He is not conscious of the holy and the unholy. He does not observe any formal purity. To him everything is Brahman. He is not aware of filth as such. Even rice and other cooked food after a few days become like filth.

"Again, he is like a madman. People notice his ways and actions and think of him as insane. Or sometimes he is like a child—no bondage, no shame, no hatred, no hesitation, or the like.

"One reaches this state of mind after having the vision of God. When a boat passes by a magnetic hill, its screws and nails become loose and drop out. Lust, anger, and the other passions cannot exist after the vision of God.

"Once a thunderbolt struck the Kāli temple. I noticed that it flattened the points of the screws.

"It is no longer possible for the man who has seen God to beget children and perpetuate the creation. When a grain of paddy is sown it grows into a plant; but a grain of boiled paddy does not germinate.

"He who has seen God retains his 'I' only in name. No evil can be done by that 'I'. It is a mere appearance, like the mark left on the coconut tree by its branch. The branch has fallen off. Only the mark remains.

"I said to Keshab Sen, 'Give up the ego that makes you feel, "I am the doer; I am teaching people."' Keshab said to me, 'Sir, then I cannot keep the organization.' Thereupon I said to him, 'Give up the "wicked ego".' One doesn't have to renounce the ego that makes one feel, 'I am the servant of God; I am His devotee.' One doesn't develop the 'divine ego' as long as one retains the 'wicked ego'. If a man is in charge of the store-room, the master of the house doesn't feel responsible for it.

(To the devotees) "You see, my nature is changing on account of this injury to my arm. It is being revealed to me that there is a greater manifestation of God in man than in other created beings. God is telling me, as it were: 'I dwell in men. Be merry with men.'. Among men God manifests Himself in a still greater degree in pure-souled devotees. That is why I feel great longing for Narendra, Rakhal, and other such youngsters.

"One often sees small holes along the edge of a lake. Fish and crabs accumulate there. Just so, there is a greater accumulation of divinity in man. It is said that man is greater than the śālagrām. Man is Nārāyana Himself. If God can manifest Himself through an image, then why not through man also?

"God is born as man for the purpose of sporting as man. Rāma, Krishna, and Chaitanya are examples. By meditating on an Incarnation of God one meditates on God Himself."

Bhagavan Das, a Brāhmo devotee, arrived.

MASTER (to Bhagavan Das): "The Eternal Religion, the religion of the rishis, has been in existence from time out of mind and will exist eternally. There exist in this Sanātana Dharma all forms of worship—worship of God with form and worship of the Impersonal Deity as well. It contains all paths —the path of knowledge, the path of devotion, and so on. Other forms of religion, the modern cults, will remain for a few days and then disappear."

March 23, 1884

Sri Ramakrishna was sitting in his room after his midday meal, with Rakhal, Ram, and some other devotees. He was not quite well. The injured arm was still bandaged.

But in spite of his illness, his room was a veritable mart of joy and he the centre of it. Devotees thronged there daily to see the Master. Spiritual talk went on incessantly, and the very air of the room vibrated with bliss. Sometimes the Master would sing the name and glories of God, and sometimes he would go into samādhi, the devotees being amazed at the ease with which the Master freed himself from the consciousness of the body.

RAM: "There is talk of Narendra's marrying Mr. R. Mitra's daughter. Narendra has been offered a large dowry."

MASTER (smiling): "Yes, Narendra may thus become a leader of society or something like that. He will be an outstanding man, whatever career he follows."

The Master did not much encourage the conversation about Narendra.

MASTER (to Ram): "Well, can you tell me why I become so impatient when I am ill? Sometimes I ask this man and sometimes that man how I may be cured. You see, one must either believe everyone or no one at all.

"It is God Himself who has become the physicians. Therefore one must believe all of them. But one cannot have faith in them if one thinks of them as mere men.

"Sambhu was fearfully delirious. Dr. Sarvadhikari said that the delirium was due to the strong medicine. Haladhari asked the doctor to feel his pulse. The doctor said: 'Let me see your eyes. Oh, it is an enlargement of the spleen!' Haladhari said he had nothing of the sort. But Dr. Madhu gives good medicine."

RAM: "The medicine by itself does no good, though it greatly helps nature."

MASTER: "If that is so, why does opium cause constipation?"

Ram referred to Keshab Sen's death.

RAM: "You were quite right. You said that a gardener uncovers the roots of a good rose-plant so that it may absorb the dew and grow stronger and healthier. The words of a holy man have been fulfilled."

MASTER: "I don't know about that. I wasn't calculating when I said it. It is you who say that."

RAM: "The Brāhmos have published something about you in their magazine."

MASTER: "Published about me? Why? Why should they write now? I eat and drink and make merry. I don't know anything else.

"I once asked Keshab, 'Why have you written about me?' He said that it would bring people here. But man cannot teach by his own power. One cannot conquer ignorance without the power of God.

"At one time two men were engaged to wrestle. One of them was Hanumān Singh and the other a Mussalmān from the Punjab. The Mussalmān was a strong, stout man. He had eaten lustily of butter and meat for fifteen days before the day of the wrestling-match, and even on that day. All thought he would be the victor. Hanumān Singh, on the other hand, clad in a dirty cloth, had eaten sparingly for some days before the day of the match and devoted himself to repeating the holy name of Mahāvir.[3] On the day of the match he observed a complete fast. All thought that he would surely be defeated. But it was he who won, while the man who had feasted for fifteen days lost the fight.

"What is the use of printing and advertising? He who teaches men gets his power from God. None but a man of renunciation can teach others. I am the greatest of all fools!" (All laugh.)

A DEVOTEE: "Then how is it that the Vedas and the Vedānta, and many things besides, come out of your mouth?"

MASTER (smiling): "During my boyhood I could understand what the sādhus read at the Lahas' house at Kāmārpukur, although I would miss a little here and there. If a pundit speaks to me in Sanskrit I can follow him, but I cannot speak it myself.

"To realize God is the one goal of life. While aiming his arrow at the mark, Arjuna said, 'I see only the eye of the bird and nothing else—not the kings, not the trees, not even the bird itself.'

"The realization of God is enough for me. What does it matter if I don't know Sanskrit?

"The grace of God falls alike on all His children, learned and illiterate—whoever longs for Him. The father has the same love for all his children. Suppose a father has five children. One calls him 'Bābā', some 'Bā', and some 'Pā'. These last cannot pronounce the whole word. Does the father love those who address him as 'Bābā' more than those who call him 'Pā'? The father knows that these last are simply too young to say 'Bābā' correctly.

"Since this injury to my arm a change has been coming over my mind. I have been feeling much inclined to the Naralīlā. It is God Himself who plays about as human beings. If God can be worshipped through a clay image, then why not through a man?

"Once a merchant was shipwrecked. He floated to the shore of Ceylon, where Bibhishana was the king of the monsters. Bibhishana ordered his servants to bring the merchant to him. At the sight of him Bibhishana was overwhelmed with joy and said: 'Ah! He looks like my Rāma. The same human form!' He adorned the merchant with robes and jewels, and worshipped him. When I first heard this story, I felt such joy that I cannot describe it.

[3] Mahāvir, or Hanumān, is the patron deity of wrestlers.

"Vaishnavcharan said to me, 'If a person looks on his beloved as his Ishta, he finds it very easy to direct his mind to God.' The men and women of a particular sect[4] at Syāmbāzār, near Kāmārpukur, say to each other, 'Whom do you love?' 'I love so-and-so.' 'Then know him to be your God.' When I heard this, I said to them: 'That is not my way. I look on all women as my mother.' I found out that they talked big but led immoral lives. The women then asked me if they would have salvation. 'Yes,' I said, 'if you are absolutely faithful to one man and look on him as your God. But you cannot be liberated if you live with five men.'"

RAM: "I understand that Kedar Babu has recently visited the Kartābhajās' place."

MASTER: "He gathers honey from various flowers. (To Ram, Nityagopal, and the others) If a devotee believes one hundred per cent that his Chosen Ideal is God, then he attains God and sees Him.

"People of bygone generations had tremendous faith. What faith Haladhari's father had! Once he was on the way to his daughter's house when he noticed some beautiful flowers and vilwa-leaves. He gathered them for the worship of the Family Deity and walked back five or six miles to his own house.

"Once a theatrical troupe in the village was enacting the life of Rāma. When Kaikeyi asked Rāma to go into exile in the forest, Haladhari's father, who had been watching the performance, sprang up. He went to the actor who played Kaikeyi, crying out, 'You wretch!', and was about to burn the actor's face with a torch. He was a very pious man. After finishing his ablutions he would stand in the water and meditate on the Deity, reciting the invocation: 'I meditate on Thee, of red hue and four faces', while tears streamed down his cheeks.

"When my father walked along the lanes of the village wearing his wooden sandals, the shopkeepers would stand up out of respect and say, 'There he comes!' When he bathed in the Hāldārpukur, the villagers would not have the courage to get into the water. Before bathing they would inquire if he had finished his bath.

"When my father chanted the name of Raghuvir, his chest would turn* crimson. This also happened to me. When I saw the cows at Vrindāvan returning from the pasture, I was transported into a divine mood and my body became red.

"Very strong was the faith of the people in those days. One hears that God used to dance then, taking the form of Kāli, while the devotee clapped his hands keeping time."

A hathayogi was staying in the hut at the Panchavati. Ramprasanna, the son of Krishnakishore of Āriādaha, and several other men had become his devotees. The yogi needed twenty-five rupees a month for his milk and

[4] The reference is to certain minor sects of Vaishnavism, such as the Kartābhajā and the Navarasika, which teach that men and women should live together in the relationship of love. Gradually they should idealize their love by looking upon each other as divine, eventually realizing that their physical love is also the love of God. This is very difficult to realize.

opium; so Ramprasanna had requested Sri Ramakrishna to speak to his devotees about the yogi and get some money. The Master said to several devotees: "A hathayogi has come to the Panchavati. Go and visit him. See what sort of man he is."

A young man of twenty-seven or twenty-eight, known as Thākur Dādā, entered the room with a few friends and saluted the Master. He lived at Barānagore and was the son of a brāhmin pundit. He was practising the kathakatā[5] in order to earn money to meet his family's expenses. At one time he had been seized with the spirit of renunciation and had gone away from his family. Even now he practised spiritual discipline at home.

MASTER: "Have you come on foot? Where do you live?"

DĀDĀ: "Yes, sir, I have walked from home. I live at Barānagore."

MASTER: "Have you come here for any particular purpose?"

DĀDĀ: "I have come here to visit you. I pray to God. But why do I suffer now and then from worries? For a few days I feel very happy. Why do I feel restless afterwards?"

MASTER: "I see. Things have not been fitted quite exactly. The machine works smoothly if the mechanic fits the cogs of the wheels correctly. In your case there is an obstruction somewhere."

DĀDĀ: "Yes, sir. That must be so."

MASTER: "Are you initiated?"

DĀDĀ: "Yes, sir."

MASTER: "Do you have faith in your mantra?"

A friend of Thākur Dādā said that the latter could sing well. The Master asked him to sing.

Thākur Dādā sang:

> I shall become a yogi and dwell in Love's mountain cave;
> I shall be lost in yoga beside the Fountain-head of Bliss.
> I shall appease my hunger for Knowledge with the fruit of Truth;
> I shall worship the feet of God with the flower of Dispassion.
>
> I shall not seek a well to slake the burning thirst of my heart,
> But I shall draw the water of Peace into the jar of my soul.
> Drinking the glorious Nectar of Thy blessed Lotus Feet,
> I shall both laugh and dance and weep and sing on the heights of Joy.

MASTER: "Ah, what a nice song! 'Fountain-head of Bliss'! 'Fruit of Truth'! 'Laugh and dance and weep and sing'! Your song tastes very sweet to me. Why should you worry?

"Pleasure and pain are inevitable in the life of the world. One suffers now and then from a little worry and trouble. A man living in a room full of soot cannot avoid being a little stained."

DĀDĀ: "Please tell me what I should do now."

MASTER: "Chant the name of Hari morning and evening, clapping your hands. Come once more when my arm is healed a bit."

Mahimacharan entered the room and saluted the Master. Sri Ramakrishna

[5] The recital of stories from religious books, with appropriate music.

said to him: "Ah! He has sung a nice song. Please sing it again." Thākur Dādā repeated the song.

MASTER (to Mahima): "Please recite that verse, the one about devotion to Hari."

Mahimacharan recited, quoting from the Nārada Pancharātra:

> What need is there of penance if God is worshipped with love?
> What is the use of penance if God is not worshipped with love?
> What need is there of penance if God is seen within and without?
> What is the use of penance if God is not seen within and without?

MASTER: "Recite that part also—'Obtain from Him the love of God'."
Mahima recited:

> O Brahman! O my child! Cease from practising further penances.
> Hasten to Śankara, the Ocean of Heavenly Wisdom;
> Obtain from Him the love of God, the pure love praised by devotees,
> Which snaps in twain the shackles that bind you to the world.

MASTER: "Yes, Śankara will bestow the love of God."

MAHIMA: "One who is free from bondage is the eternal Śiva."

MASTER: "Shame, hatred, fear, hesitation—these are the shackles. What do you say?"

MAHIMA: "Yes, sir. And also the desire to conceal, and shrinking before praise."

MASTER: "There are two signs of knowledge. First, an unshakable buddhi. No matter how many sorrows, afflictions, dangers, and obstacles one may be faced with, one's mind does not undergo any change. It is like the blacksmith's anvil, which receives constant blows from the hammer and still remains unshaken. And second, manliness—very strong grit. If lust and anger injure a man, he must renounce them once for all. If a tortoise once tucks in its limbs, it won't put them out again though you may cut it into four pieces. (To Thākur Dādā and the others) There are two kinds of renunciation: intense and feeble. Feeble renunciation is a slow process; one moves in a slow rhythm. Intense renunciation is like the sharp edge of a razor. It cuts the bondage of māyā easily and at once.

"One farmer labours for days to bring water from the lake to his field. But his efforts are futile because he has no grit. Another farmer, after labouring for two or three days, takes a vow and says, 'I will bring water into my field today, and not till then will I go home.' He puts aside all thought of his bath or his meal. He labours the whole day and feels great joy when in the evening he finds water entering his field with a murmuring sound. Then he goes home and says to his wife: 'Now give me some oil. I shall take my bath.' After finishing his bath and his meal he lies down to sleep with a peaceful mind.

"A certain woman said to her husband: 'So-and-so has developed a spirit of great dispassion for the world, but I don't see anything of the sort in you. He has sixteen wives. He is giving them up one by one.' The husband, with a towel on his shoulder, was going to the lake for his bath. He said to his wife: 'You are crazy! He won't be able to give up the world. Is it ever possible to renounce bit by bit? I can renounce. Look! Here I go.' He didn't stop even to settle his household affairs. He left home just as he was, the towel on his shoulder, and went away. That is intense renunciation.

"There is another kind of renunciation, called 'markatavairāgya', 'monkey renunciation'. A man, harrowed by distress at home, puts on an ochre robe and goes away to Benares. For many days he does not send home any news of himself. Then he writes to his people: 'Don't be worried about me. I have got a job here.'

"There is always trouble in family life. The wife may be disobedient. Perhaps the husband earns only twenty rupees a month. He hasn't the means to perform the 'rice-eating ceremony' for his baby. He cannot educate his son. The house is dilapidated. The roof leaks and he hasn't the money to repair it.

"Therefore when the youngsters come here I ask them whether they have anyone at home. (*To Mahima*) Why should householders renounce the world? What great troubles the wandering monks pass through! The wife of a certain man said to him: 'You want to renounce the world? Why? You will have to beg morsels from eight different homes. But here you get all your food at one place. Isn't that nice?'

"Wandering monks, while searching for a sadāvrata,[6] may have to go six miles out of their way. I have seen them travelling along the regular road after their pilgrimage to Puri and making a detour to find an eating-place.

"You are leading a householder's life. That is very good. It is like fighting from a fort. There are many disadvantages in fighting in an open field. So many dangers, too. Bullets may hit you.

"But one should spend some time in solitude and attain Knowledge. Then one can lead the life of a householder. Janaka lived in the world after attaining Knowledge. When you have gained it, you may live anywhere. Then nothing matters."

MAHIMA: "Sir, why does a man become deluded by worldly objects?"

MASTER: "It is because he lives in their midst without having realized God. Man never succumbs to delusion after he has realized God. The moth no longer enjoys darkness if it has once seen the light.

"To be able to realize God, one must practise absolute continence. Sages like Śukadeva are examples of an urdhvaretā.[7] Their chastity was absolutely unbroken. There is another class, who previously have had discharges of semen but who later on have controlled them. A man controlling the seminal fluid for twelve years develops a special power. He grows a new inner nerve called the nerve of memory. Through that nerve he remembers all, he understands all.

"Loss of semen impairs the strength. But it does not injure one if one loses it in a dream. That semen one gets from food. What remains after nocturnal discharge is enough. But one must not know a woman.

[6] An eating-place where food is supplied free to monks and beggars.
[7] A man of unbroken and complete continence.

"The semen that remains after nocturnal discharge is very 'refined'. The Lahas kept jars of molasses in their house. Every jar had a hole in it. After a year they found that the molasses had crystallized like sugar candy. The unnecessary watery part had leaked out through the hole.

"A sannyāsi must absolutely renounce woman. You are already involved; but that doesn't matter.

"A sannyāsi must not look even at the picture of a woman. But this is too difficult for an ordinary man. Sā, re, gā, mā, pā, dhā, ni are the seven notes of the scale. It is not possible to keep your voice on 'ni' a long time.

"To lose semen is extremely harmful for a sannyāsi. Therefore he must live so carefully that he will not have to see the form of a woman. He must keep himself away from a woman even if she is a devotee of God. It is injurious for him to look even at the picture of a woman. He will lose semen in a dream, if not in the waking state.

"A sannyāsi may have control over his senses, but to set an example to mankind he should not talk with women. He must not talk to one very long, even if she is a devotee of God.

"Living as a sannyāsi is like observing the ekādaśi without drinking even a drop of water. There are two other ways of observing the day. You may eat fruit or take luchi and curry. With the luchi and curry you may also take slices of bread soaked in milk. (All laugh.)

(Smiling) "Absolute fasting is not possible for you.

"Once I saw Krishnakishore eating luchi and curry on an ekādaśi day. I said to Hriday, 'Hridu, I want to observe Krishnakishore's ekādaśi!' (All laugh.) And so I did one day. I ate my fill. The next day I had to fast." (Laughter.)

The devotees who had gone to the Panchavati to visit the hathayogi came back.

Master (addressing them): "Well, what do you think of him? I dare say you have measured him with your own tape."

Sri Ramakrishna saw that very few of the devotees were willing to give money to the hathayogi.

Master: "You don't like a sādhu if you have to give him money. Rajendra Mitra draws a salary of eight hundred rupees a month. He had been to Allāhābād to see the kumbhamelā. I asked him, 'Well, what kind of sādhus did you see at the fair?' Rajendra said: 'I didn't find any very great sādhu there. I noticed one, it is true. But even he accepted money.'

"I say to myself, 'If no one gives money to a sādhu, then how will he feed himself?' There is no collection plate here; therefore all come. And I say to myself: 'Alas! They love their money. Let them have it.'"

The Master rested awhile. A devotee sat on the end of the small couch and gently stroked his feet. The Master said to him softly: "That which is formless again has form. One should believe in the forms of God also. By meditating on Kāli the aspirant realizes God as Kāli. Next he finds that the form merges in the Indivisible Absolute. That which is the Indivisible Sat-chidānanda is verily Kāli."

Sri Ramakrishna was sitting on the semicircular porch west of his room, talking with Mahima and other devotees about the hathayogi. The talk drifted to Ramprasanna, the son of Krishnakishore. The Master was fond of the young man.

MASTER: "Ramprasanna roams about aimlessly. The other day he came here and sat in the room, but he did not speak a word. He pressed his nostrils with his fingers, practising prānāyāma. I offered him something to eat, but he wouldn't take it. On another occasion I had asked him to sit by me. He squatted on the floor placing one leg upon the other. He was rather discourteous to Captain. I weep at his mother's suffering.

(To Mahima) "Ramprasanna asked me to speak to you about the hatha-yogi. The yogi's daily expenses are six and a half ānnās. But he won't tell you about it himself."

MAHIMA: "Who will listen to him even if he does?"

Mani Sen of Pānihāti entered the room with several friends, one of whom was a physician. Mani asked the Master about his injured arm. The doctor did not approve of the medicine prescribed by Pratap Mazumdar. The Master said to him: "Why should you say that? Pratap is no fool."

Suddenly Latu cried out, "Oh! The medicine bottle has dropped and broken."

It was not yet dusk. The Master, seated on the couch, was talking to M. Mahimacharan was on the semicircular porch engaged in a loud discussion of the scriptures with the physician friend of Mani Sen. Sri Ramakrishna heard it and with a smile said to M.: "There! He is delivering himself. That is the characteristic of rajas. It stimulates the desire to 'lecture' and to show off one's scholarship. But sattva makes one introspective. It makes one hide one's virtues. But I must say that Mahima is a grand person. He takes such delight in spiritual talk."

Adhar entered the room, saluted the Master, and sat by M.'s side. He had not come for the past few days.

MASTER: "Hello! Why haven't you come all these days?"

ADHAR: "Sir, I have been busy with so many things. I had to attend a conference of the school committee and various other meetings."

MASTER: "So you completely lost yourself in schools and meetings and forgot everything else?"

ADHAR: "Everything else was hidden away in a corner of my mind. How is your arm?"

MASTER: "Just look. It is not yet healed. I have been taking medicine prescribed by Pratap."

After a time the Master suddenly said to Adhar: "Look here. All these are unreal—meetings, school, office, and everything else. God alone is the Substance, and all else is illusory. One should worship God with one's whole mind."

Adhar sat without speaking a word.

MASTER: "All else is illusory. This moment the body is and the next moment it is not. One must make haste to worship God.[8]

"But you don't have to renounce everything. Live in the world the way

[8] A few months after this conversation Adhar died.

the tortoise does. The tortoise roams about in the water but keeps its eggs on land. Its whole mind is on the eggs.

"What a nice state of mind Captain has developed! He looks like a rishi when he is seated to perform worship. He performs the ārati with lighted camphor and recites beautiful hymns. When he rises from his seat after finishing the worship, his eyes are swollen from emotion, as if bitten by ants. Besides, he always devotes himself to the study of the sacred books, such as the *Gītā* and the *Bhāgavata*. Once I used one or two English words before him, and that made him angry. He said, 'English-educated people are profane.'"

After a while Adhar said humbly to the Master: "Sir, you haven't been to our place for a long time. The drawing-room smells worldly and everything else appears to be steeped in darkness."

The Master was deeply touched by these words of his devotee. He suddenly stood up and blessed M. and Adhar in an ecstatic mood, touching their heads and hearts. In a voice choked with love the Master said: "I look upon you as Nārāyana Himself. You are indeed my own."

Mahimacharan entered the room.

MASTER (*to Mahima*): "What I said about aspirants practising continence is true. Without chastity one cannot assimilate these teachings.

"Once a man said to Chaitanya: 'You give the devotees so much instruction. Why don't they make much progress?' Chaitanya said: 'They dissipate their powers in the company of women. That is why they cannot assimilate spiritual instruction. If one keeps water in a leaky jar, the water escapes little by little through the leak.'"

Mahima and the other devotees remained silent. After a time Mahima said, "Please pray to God for us that we may acquire the necessary strength."

MASTER: "Be on your guard even now. It is difficult, no doubt, to check the torrent in the rainy season. But a great deal of water has gone out. If you build the embankment now it will stand."

A DAY AT DAKSHINESWAR

Saturday, April 5, 1884

IT WAS ABOUT EIGHT O'CLOCK in the morning when M. arrived at the temple garden and found Sri Ramakrishna seated on the small couch in his room. A few devotees were sitting on the floor. The Master was talking to them. Prankrishna Mukherji was there.

Prankrishna belonged to an aristocratic family and lived in the northern part of Calcutta. He held a high post in an English business firm. He was very much devoted to Sri Ramakrishna and, though a householder, derived great pleasure from the study of Vedānta philosophy. He was a frequent visitor at the temple garden. Once he invited the Master to his house in Calcutta and held a religious festival. Every day, early in the morning, he bathed in the holy water of the Ganges. Whenever it was convenient, he would come to Dakshineswar in a hired country boat.

That morning he had hired a boat and invited M. to accompany him to Dakshineswar. The boat had hardly left shore when the river became choppy. M. had become frightened and begged Prankrishna to put him back on land. In spite of assurances, M. had kept saying: "You must put me ashore. I shall walk to Dakshineswar." And so M. came on foot and found Sri Ramakrishna talking to Prankrishna and the others.

MASTER (to Prankrishna): "But there is a greater manifestation of God in man. You may ask, 'How is it possible for God to be incarnated as a man who suffers from hunger, thirst, and the other traits of an embodied being, and perhaps also from disease and grief?' The reply is, 'Even Brahman weeps, entrapped in the snare of the five elements.'

"Don't you know how Rāma had to weep, stricken with grief for Sītā? Further, it is said that the Lord incarnated Himself as a sow in order to kill the demon Hiranyāksha. Hiranyāksha was eventually killed, but God would not go back to His abode in heaven. He enjoyed His sow's life. He had given birth to several young ones and was rather happy with them. The gods said among themselves: 'What does this mean? The Lord doesn't care to return to heaven!' They all went to Śiva and laid the matter before him. Śiva came down and urged the Lord to leave the sow body and return to heaven. But the sow only suckled her young ones. (Laughter.) Then Śiva destroyed the sow body with his trident, and the Lord came out laughing aloud and went back to His own abode."

PRANKRISHNA (to the Master): "Sir, what is the Anāhata sound?"

MASTER: "It is a spontaneous sound constantly going on by itself. It is the sound of the Pranava, Om. It originates in the Supreme Brahman and is heard by yogis. People immersed in worldliness do not hear it. A yogi alone knows that this sound originates both from his navel and from the Supreme Brahman resting on the Ocean of Milk."[1]

PRANKRISHNA: "Sir, what is the nature of the life after death?"

MASTER: "Keshab Sen also asked that question. As long as a man remains ignorant, that is to say, as long as he has not realized God, so long will he be born. But after attaining Knowledge he will not have to come back to this earth or to any other plane of existence.

"The potter puts his pots in the sun to dry. Haven't you noticed that among them there are both baked and unbaked ones? When a cow happens to walk over them, some of the pots get broken to pieces. The broken pots that are already baked, the potter throws away, since they are of no more use to him. But the soft ones, though broken, he gathers up. He makes them into a lump and out of this forms new pots. In the same way, so long as a man has not realized God, he will have to come back to the Potter's hand, that is, he will have to be born again and again.

"What is the use of sowing a boiled paddy grain? It will never bring forth a shoot. Likewise, if a man is boiled in the fire of Knowledge, he will not be used for new creation. He is liberated.

"According to the Purānas, the bhakta and the Bhagavān are two separate entities. 'I' am one and 'You' are another. The body is a plate, as it were, containing the water of mind, intelligence, and ego. Brahman is like the sun. It is reflected in the water. Therefore the devotee sees the divine form.

"According to the Vedānta, Brahman alone is real and all else is māyā, dreamlike and unsubstantial. The ego, like a stick, lies across the Ocean of Satchidānanda. (To M.) Listen to what I am saying. When this ego is taken away, there remains only one undivided Ocean of Satchidānanda. But as long as the stick of ego remains, there is an appearance of two: here is one part of the water and there another part. Attaining the Knowledge of Brahman one is established in samādhi. Then the ego is effaced.

"But Sankarāchārya retained the 'ego of Knowledge'[2] in order to teach

[1] According to Hindu mythology, after the dissolution of the universe and before the next creation, the Supreme Lord rests on the Ocean of the Great Cause, also called the "Ocean of Milk".

[2] The ego illumined and purified by the Knowledge of God. Following the method of discrimination, the jnāni, in samādhi, merges his ego in Brahman. Thereafter he may come down to the relative plane with an appearance of individuality, but even then he is always conscious of his identity with Brahman. This apparent ego is called the "ego of Knowledge". A bhakta, following the path of love, realizes his eternal relationship with God. He too keeps an appearance of individuality on the relative plane. This ego has none of the characteristics of the worldly ego and is called the "ego of Devotion". The two egos here described refer to the same state of realization.

men. (*To Prankrishna*) But there are signs that distinguish the man of Knowledge. Some people think they have Knowledge. What are the characteristics of Knowledge? A jnāni cannot injure anybody. He becomes like a child. If a steel sword touches the philosopher's stone, it is transformed into gold. Gold can never cut. It may seem from the outside that a jnāni also has anger or egotism, but in reality he has no such thing.

"From a distance a burnt string lying on the ground may look like a real one; but if you come near and blow at it, it disappears altogether. The anger and egotism of a jnāni are mere appearances; they are not real.

"A child has no attachment. He makes a play house, and if anyone touches it, he will jump about and cry. The next moment he himself will break it. This moment he may be very attached to his cloth. He says: 'My daddy has given it to me. I won't part with it.' But the next moment you can cajole him away from it with a toy. He will go away with you, leaving the cloth behind.

"These are the characteristics of a jnāni. Perhaps he has many luxuries at home—couch, chairs, paintings, and equipage. But any day he may leave all these and go off to Benares.

"According to Vedānta the waking state, too, is unreal. Once a wood-cutter lay dreaming, when someone woke him up. Greatly annoyed, he said: 'Why have you disturbed my sleep? I was dreaming that I was a king and the father of seven children. The princes were becoming well versed in letters and military arts. I was secure on my throne and ruled over my subjects. Why have you demolished my world of joy?' 'But that was a mere dream', said the other man. 'Why should that bother you?' 'Fool!' said the wood-cutter. 'You don't understand. My becoming a king in the dream was just as real as is my being a wood-cutter. If being a wood-cutter is real, then being a king in a dream is real also.'"

Prankrishna always talked about jnāna. Was this why the Master described the state of the jnāni? Now he proceeded to describe the state of the vijnāni.

MASTER: "Jnāna is the realization of Self through the process of 'Neti, neti', 'Not this, not this'. One goes into samādhi through this process of elimination and realizes the Ātman.

"But vijnāna means Knowledge with a greater fullness. Some have heard of milk, some have seen milk, and some have drunk milk. He who has merely heard of it is 'ignorant'. He who has seen it is a jnāni. But he who has drunk it has vijnāna, that is to say, a fuller knowledge of it. After having the vision of God one talks to Him as if He were an intimate relative. That is vijnāna.

"First of all you must discriminate, following the method of 'Neti, neti': 'He is not the five elements, nor the sense-organs, nor the mind, nor the intelligence, nor the ego. He is beyond all these cosmic principles.' You want to climb to the roof; then you must eliminate and leave behind all the steps, one by one. The steps are by no means the roof. But after reaching the roof you find that the steps are made of the same materials—brick, lime, and brick-dust—as the roof. It is the Supreme Brahman that has become the universe and its living beings and the twenty-four cosmic principles. That which is Ātman has become the five elements. You may ask why the earth is so hard, if it has come out of Ātman? All is possible through the will of God. Don't you see that bone and flesh are made from blood and semen? How hard 'sea-foam'[3] becomes!

"After attaining vijnāna one can live in the world as well. Then one clearly realizes that God Himself has become the universe and all living beings, that He is not outside the world.

(To Prankrishna) "The fact is that one must have the 'spiritual eye'. You will develop that eye as soon as your mind becomes pure. Take for instance the Kumāri Pujā. I worshipped a virgin. The girl, to be sure, had all her human imperfections; still I regarded her as the Divine Mother Herself.

"On one side is the wife and on the other the son. Love is bestowed on both, but in different ways. Therefore it comes to this, that everything depends upon the mind. The pure mind acquires a new attitude. Through that mind one sees God in this world. Therefore one needs spiritual discipline.

"Yes, spiritual discipline is necessary. You should know that a man becomes easily attached to a woman. A woman naturally loves a man, and a man also naturally loves a woman. Therefore both fall speedily from their spiritual ideal. But it also must be said that there is a great advantage in leading the life of a householder. In case of urgent necessity a man may live with his wife.

(Smiling) "Well, M., why are you smiling?"

M. (to himself): "The Master makes this much allowance for householders since they cannot renounce everything. Is complete and absolute continence impossible for a householder?"

The hathayogi who had been living in the Panchavati entered the room. He was in the habit of taking milk and opium. He did not eat rice or other food and had no money to buy the milk and opium. The Master had talked with him in the Panchavati. The hathayogi had told Rakhal to ask the Master to make some provision for him, and Sri Ramakrishna had promised to speak about it to the visitors from Calcutta.

HATHAYOGI (to the Master): "What did you say to Rakhal about me?"

MASTER: "I said that I would ask some rich visitors to help you. But— (to Prankrishna) you, perhaps, do not like these yogis?"

Prankrishna remained silent. The hathayogi left the room and the conversation went on.

MASTER (to Prankrishna and the others): "If a man leads a householder's life he must have unflagging devotion to truth. God can be realized through truth alone. Formerly I was very particular about telling the truth, though now my zeal has abated a little. If I said, 'I shall bathe', then I would get into the water of the Ganges, recite the mantra, and sprinkle a little water over my head. But still there would remain some doubt in me as to whether my bath was complete. Once I went to Ram's house in Calcutta. I hap-

[3] The Master perhaps referred to the cuttle-bone found on the seashore. The popular belief is that it is hardened foam.

pened to say, 'I shall not take any luchi.' When I sat down for the meal I felt hungry. But I had said I would not eat the luchi; so I had to fill my stomach with sweets. (*All laugh.*)

"But my zeal for truthfulness has abated a little now. Once I said I would go to the pine-grove, but then I felt I had no particular urge to go. What was to be done? I asked Ram[4] about it. He said I didn't have to go. Then I reasoned to myself: 'Well, everyone is Nārāyana. So Ram, too, is Nārāyana. Why shouldn't I listen to him? The elephant is Nārāyana no doubt, but the māhut is Nārāyana too. Since the māhut asked me not to go near the elephant, then why shouldn't I obey him?' Through reasoning like this my zeal for truthfulness is slightly less strong now than before.

"I find a change coming over me. Years ago Vaishnavcharan said to me, 'One attains Perfect Knowledge when one sees God in man.' Now I see that it is God alone who is moving about in various forms: as a holy man, as a cheat, as a villain. Therefore I say, 'Nārāyana in the guise of the sādhu, Nārāyana in the guise of the cheat, Nārāyana in the guise of the villain, Nārāyana in the guise of the lecher.'

"Now my problem is how I can feed all of you. I want to feed everyone. So I keep one at a time with me and feed him."

Prankrishna (*looking at M. and smiling*): "A fine man, indeed! (*To the Master*) He would not let us go till we put him ashore."

MASTER (*smiling*): "Why? What happened?"

PRANKRISHNA: "He was in our boat. Seeing that the river was slightly rough, he insisted on being put ashore. (*To M.*) How did you come?"

M. (*smiling*): "On foot."

Sri Ramakrishna laughed.

PRANKRISHNA (*to the Master*): "Sir, I am thinking now of giving up my work. One who is involved in activity cannot accomplish anything. (*Pointing to his companion*) I am training him to do my work. After I resign, he will relieve me. Work has become intolerable."

MASTER: "Yes, work is very troublesome. It is now good for you to meditate on God for a few days in solitude. No doubt you say that you would like to give up your work. Captain said the same thing. Worldly people talk that way; but they don't succeed in carrying out their intention.

"There are many pundits who speak words of wisdom. But they merely talk; they don't live up to them. They are like vultures, which soar very high but keep their gaze fixed on the charnel-pit. What I mean is that these pundits are attached to the world, to 'woman and gold'. If I hear that pundits are practising discrimination and dispassion, then I fear them. Otherwise I look upon them as mere goats and dogs."

Prankrishna saluted the Master and took his leave. He said to M., "Will you come with us?"

M: "No, sir! Catch me going with you again! Good-bye."

Prankrishna laughed and said, "I see you won't come in the boat."

M. took a little stroll near the Panchavati and bathed in the river. Then he went to the temples of Rādhākānta and Kāli and prostrated himself be-

[4] Ram Chatterji, the priest in the Rādhākānta temple.

fore the images. He said to himself: "I have heard that God has no form. Then why do I bow before these images? Is it because Sri Ramakrishna believes in gods and goddesses with form? I don't know anything about God, nor do I understand Him. The Master believes in images; then why shouldn't I too, who am so insignificant a creature, accept them?"

M. looked at the image of Kāli. He saw that the Divine Mother holds in Her two left hands a man's severed head and a sword. With Her two right hands She offers boons and reassurance to Her devotees. In one aspect She is terrible, and in another She is the ever affectionate Mother of Her devotees. The two ideals are harmonized in Her. She is compassionate and affectionate to Her devotees, to those who are submissive and helpless. It is also true that She is terrible, the "Consort of Death". She alone knows why She assumes two aspects at the same time.

M. remembered this interpretation of Kāli given by the Master. He said to himself, "I have heard that Keshab accepted Kāli in Sri Ramakrishna's presence. Is this, as Keshab used to say, the Goddess, all Spirit and Consciousness, manifesting Herself through a clay image?"

M. returned to the Master's room and sat on the floor. Sri Ramakrishna offered him some fruit and sweets to eat. On account of trouble in the family, M. had recently rented a house in another section of Calcutta near his school, his father and brothers continuing to live in the ancestral home. But Sri Ramakrishna wanted him to return to his own home, since a joint family affords many advantages to one leading a religious life. Once or twice the Master had spoken to M. to this effect, but unfortunately he had not yet returned to his family. Sri Ramakrishna referred to the matter again.

MASTER: "Tell me that you are going to your ancestral home."

M: "I can never persuade myself to enter that place."

MASTER: "Why? Your father is making over the whole house."

M: "I have suffered too much there. I can by no means make up my mind to go there."

MASTER: "Whom do you fear?"

M: "All of them."

MASTER (seriously): "Isn't that like your being afraid to get into the boat?"

The midday worship and the offering of food in the temples were over. The bells, gongs, and cymbals of the ārati were being played, and the temple garden was filled with joyful activity. Beggars, sādhus, and guests hurried to the guest-house for the noonday meal, carrying leaf or metal plates in their hands. M. also took some of the prasād from the Kāli temple.

Sri Ramakrishna had been resting awhile after his meal when several devotees, including Ram and Girindra, arrived. They sat down after saluting the Master. The conversation turned to the New Dispensation Church of Keshab Chandra Sen.

RAM (to the Master): "Sir, I don't think the Navavidhān has done people any good. If Keshab Babu himself was a genuine man, why are his disciples left in such a plight? I don't think there is anything at all in the New Dispensation. It is like rattling some potsherds in a room and then locking it up. People may take it to be the jingling of coins, but inside there is nothing but potsherds. Outsiders don't know what is inside."

MASTER: "There must be some substance in it. Otherwise, why should so many people respect Keshab? Why isn't Shivanath honoured as much as Keshab? Such a thing cannot happen without the will of God.

"But a man cannot act as an āchārya without renouncing the world. People won't respect him. They will say: 'Oh, he is a worldly man. He secretly enjoys "woman and gold" himself but tells us that God alone is real and the world unsubstantial, like a dream.' Unless a man renounces everything his teachings cannot be accepted by all. Some worldly people may follow him. Keshab led the life of a householder; hence his mind was directed to the world also. He had to safeguard his family interests. That is why he left his affairs in such good order though he delivered so many religious lectures. What an aristocratic man he married his daughter to! Inside Keshab's inner apartments I saw many big bedsteads. All these things gradually come to one who leads a householder's life. The world is indeed a place for enjoyment."

RAM: "Keshab Sen inherited those bedsteads when his ancestral property was divided. And for Keshab to take part in the division of property! Whatever you may say, sir, Vijay Babu told me that Keshab had said to him, 'I am a partial manifestation of Christ and Gaurānga. I suggest that you declare yourself as Advaita.'[5] Do you know what else he said? He said that you too were a follower of the New Dispensation." (All laugh.)

MASTER (laughing): "Who knows? But as for myself, I don't even know what the term 'New Dispensation' means." (Laughter.)

RAM: "Keshab's disciples say that he was the first to harmonize jnāna and bhakti."

MASTER (in surprise): "How is that? What then of the Adhyātma Rāmāyana? It is written there that, while praying to Rāma, Nārada said: 'O Rāma, Thou art the Supreme Brahman described in the Vedas. Thou dwellest with us as a man; Thou appearest as a man. In reality Thou art not a man; Thou art that Supreme Brahman.' Rāma said: 'Nārada, I am very much pleased with you. Accept a boon from Me.' Nārada replied: 'What boon shall I ask of Thee? Grant me pure love for Thy Lotus Feet, and may I never be deluded by Thy world-bewitching māyā!' The Adhyātma Rāmāyana is full of such statements regarding jnāna and bhakti."

The conversation turned to Amrita, a disciple of Keshab.

RAM: "Amrita Babu seems to be in very bad shape."

MASTER: "Yes, he looked very ill when I saw him the other day."

RAM: "Sir, let me tell you about the lectures of the New Dispensation. While the drum is being played, the members cry out, 'Victory unto Keshab!' You say that 'dal'[6] grows only in a stagnant pool. So Amrita said one day in the course of his sermon: 'The holy man[7] has no doubt said that

---

[5] An intimate companion of Gaurānga.
[6] The word has the double meaning of "sedge" and "sect".
[7] Referring to Sri Ramakrishna.

'dal' grows in a stagnant pool. But, brothers, we want 'dal', we want a sect. Really and truly, I tell you that we want a sect.' "

MASTER: "What nonsense! Shame on him! What kind of sermon is that?"

The conversation drifted to the desire of some people for praise.

MASTER: "They took me to Keshab's house to see a performance of the *Nimāi-sannyās*. I heard, that day, someone speaking of Keshab and Pratap as Chaitanya and Nityānanda. Prasanna asked me, 'Who are you then?' Keshab looked at me to see what I would say. I said to him, 'I am the servant of your servant, the dust of the dust of your feet.' Keshab said with a smile, 'You can't catch him!' "

RAM: "Sometimes Keshab used to say you were John the Baptist."

A DEVOTEE: "But Keshab also said you were the Chaitanya of the *nineteenth century* [said in English]."

MASTER: "What does that mean?"

DEVOTEE: "That Chaitanya has been incarnated again in the present century of the Christian era, and that you are he."

MASTER (*absent-mindedly*): "What of it? Can you tell me now how my arm can be cured? This arm is worrying me so much."

They talked about Trailokya's music. Trailokya sang devotional songs in Keshab's Brāhmo Samāj.

MASTER: "Ah! How nice his songs are!"

RAM: "Do you think they are genuine?"

MASTER: "Yes, they are. Otherwise, why should I be so drawn to them?"

RAM: "He has composed his songs by borrowing your ideas. While conducting the worship Keshab Sen described your feelings and realizations, and Trailokya Babu composed songs accordingly. Take this song, for instance:

> There is an overflow of Joy in the market-place of Love;
> See how the Lord sports with His own in the ecstasy of Bliss!

He saw you enjoying divine bliss in the company of devotees and wrote songs like this."

MASTER (*with a smile*): "Stop! Don't torment me any more. Why should I be involved in all this?" (*All laugh.*)

GIRINDRA: "The Brāhmos say that the Paramahamsadeva has no *faculty for organization* [said in English]."

MASTER: "What does that mean?"

M: "That you don't know how to lead a sect; that your intellect is rather dull. They say things like that." (*All laugh.*)

MASTER (*to Ram*): "Now tell me why my arm was hurt. Stand up and deliver a lecture on that. (*Laughter.*)

"The Brāhmos insist that God is formless. Suppose they do. It is enough to call on Him with sincerity of heart. If the devotee is sincere, then God, who is the Inner Guide of all, will certainly reveal to the devotee His true nature.

"But it is not good to say that what we ourselves think of God is the only truth and what others think is false; that because we think of God as formless, therefore He is formless and cannot have any form; that because we think of God as having form, therefore He has form and cannot be formless. Can a man really fathom God's nature?

"This kind of friction exists between the Vaishnavas and the Śāktas. The Vaishnava says, 'My Keśava is the only Saviour', whereas the Śākta insists, 'My Bhagavati is the only Saviour.'

"Once I took Vaishnavcharan to Mathur Babu. Now, Vaishnavcharan was a very learned Vaishnava and an orthodox devotee of his sect. Mathur, on the other hand, was a devotee of the Divine Mother. They were engaged in a friendly discussion when suddenly Vaishnavcharan said, 'Keśava is the only Saviour.' No sooner did Mathur hear this than his face became red with anger and he blurted out, 'You rascal!' (All laugh.) He was a Śākta. Wasn't it natural for him to say that? I gave Vaishnavcharan a nudge.

"I see people who talk about religion constantly quarrelling with one another. Hindus, Mussalmāns, Brāhmos, Śāktas, Vaishnavas, Śaivas, all quarrel with one another. They haven't the intelligence to understand that He who is called Krishna is also Śiva and the Primal Śakti, and that it is He, again, who is called Jesus and Āllāh. 'There is only one Rāma and He has a thousand names.'

"Truth is one; only It is called by different names. All people are seeking the same Truth; the variance is due to climate, temperament, and name. A lake has many ghāts. From one ghāt the Hindus take water in jars and call it 'jal'. From another ghāt the Mussalmāns take water in leather bags and call it 'pāni'. From a third the Christians take the same thing and call it 'water'. (All laugh.) Suppose someone says that the thing is not 'jal' but 'pāni', or that it is not 'pāni' but 'water', or that it is not 'water' but 'jal'. It would indeed be ridiculous. But this very thing is at the root of the friction among sects, their misunderstandings and quarrels. This is why people injure and kill one another, and shed blood, in the name of religion. But this is not good. Everyone is going toward God. They will all realize Him if they have sincerity and longing of heart.

(To M.) "This is for you. All scriptures—the Vedas, the Purānas, the Tantras—seek Him alone and no one else, only that one Satchidānanda. That which is called Satchidānanda Brahman in the Vedas is called Satchidānanda Śiva in the Tantra. Again it is He alone who is called Satchidānanda Krishna in the Purānas."

The Master was told that now and then Ram cooked his own food at home.

MASTER (to M.): "Do you too cook your own meals?"

M: "No, sir."

MASTER: "You may try it. With your meals take a little clarified butter made from cow's milk. That will purify your body and mind."

A long conversation ensued about Ram's household affairs. Ram's father was a devout Vaishnava and worshipped Krishna daily at home. He had married a second time when Ram was quite young. Both the father and the stepmother lived with Ram at Ram's house. But Ram was never happy with his stepmother, and this sometimes created a misunderstanding between himself and his father.

They were talking about this when Ram said, "My father has gone to the dogs!"

MASTER (to the devotees): "Did you hear that? The father has gone to the dogs and the son is all right!"

RAM: "There is no peace when my stepmother comes home. There is always some trouble or other. Our family is about to break up. So I say, let her live with her father."

GIRINDRA (to Ram): "Why don't you too keep your wife at her father's home?" (Laughter.)

MASTER (smiling): "Are husband and wife like earthen pots or jars, that you may keep the pot in one place and the lid in another? Śiva in one place and Śakti in another?"

RAM: "Sir, we are quite happy. But when she comes the family is broken up. If such is the case—"

MASTER: "Then build them a separate home. That will be a different thing. You will defray their monthly expenses. How worthy of worship one's parents are! Rakhal asked me if he could take the food left on his father's plate. 'What do you mean?' I said. 'What have you become that you cannot?' But it is also true that good people won't give anyone, even a dog, the food from their plates."

GIRINDRA: "Sir, suppose one's parents are guilty of a terrible crime, a heinous sin?"

MASTER: "What if they are? You must not renounce your mother even if she commits adultery. The woman guru of a certain family became corrupt. The members of the family said that they would like to make the son of the guru their spiritual guide. But I said: 'How is that? Will you accept the shoot and give up the yam? Suppose she is corrupt; still you must regard her as your Ishta. "Though my guru visits the tavern, still to me he is the holy Nityānanda." '

"Are father and mother mere trifles? No spiritual practice will bear fruit unless they are pleased. Chaitanya was intoxicated with the love of God. Still, before taking to the monastic life, for how many days did he try to persuade his mother to give him her permission to become a monk! He said to her: 'Mother, don't worry. I shall visit you every now and then.'

(To M., reproachfully) "And let me say this to you. Your father and mother brought you up. You yourself are the father of several children. Yet you have left home with your wife. You have cheated your parents. You have come away with your wife and children, and you feel you have become a holy man. Your father doesn't need any money from you; otherwise I should have cried, 'Shame on you!' "

Everybody in the room became grave and remained silent.

MASTER: "A man has certain debts to pay: his debts to the gods and rishis, and his debts to mother, father, and wife. He cannot achieve anything without paying the debt he owes to his parents. A man is indebted to his wife as well. Harish has renounced his wife and is living here. If he had left her unprovided for, then I should have called him an abominable wretch.

"After attaining Knowledge you will regard that very wife as the manifestation of the Divine Mother Herself. It is written in the *Chandi*, 'The Goddess dwells in all beings as the Mother.' It is She who has become your mother.

"All the women you see are only She, the Divine Mother. That is why I cannot rebuke even Brindē, the maidservant. There are people who spout verses from the scriptures and talk big, but in their conduct they are quite different. Ramprasanna is constantly busy procuring opium and milk for the hathayogi. He says that Manu enjoins it upon man to serve the sādhu. But his old mother hasn't enough to eat. She walks to the market to buy her own groceries. It makes me very angry.

"But here you have to consider another thing. When a man is intoxicated with ecstatic love of God, then who is his father or mother or wife? His love of God is so intense that he becomes mad with it. Then he has no duty to perform. He is free from all debts. What is this divine intoxication? In this state a man forgets the world. He also forgets his own body, which is so dear to all. Chaitanya had this intoxication. He plunged into the ocean not knowing that it was the ocean. He dashed himself again and again on the ground. He was not aware of hunger, of thirst, or of sleep. He was not at all conscious of any such thing as his body."

All at once Sri Ramakrishna exclaimed, "Ah, Chaitanya!" and stood up.

MASTER (*to the devotees*): "Chaitanya means 'Undivided Consciousness'. Vaishnavcharan used to say that Gaurānga was like a bubble in the Ocean of Undivided Consciousness.

(*To the elder Gopal*[8]) "Do you intend to go on a pilgrimage now?"

GOPAL: "Yes, sir. I should like to wander about a little."

RAM (*to Gopal*): "He [meaning the Master] says that one becomes a kutichaka after being a vahudaka. The sādhu that visits many holy places is called a vahudaka. He whose craving for travel has been satiated and who sits down in one place is called a kutichaka.

"He also tells us a parable. Once a bird sat on the mast of a ship. When the ship sailed through the mouth of the Ganges into the 'black waters' of the ocean, the bird failed to notice the fact. When it finally became aware of the ocean, it left the mast and flew north in search of land. But it found no limit to the water and so returned. After resting awhile it flew south. There too it found no limit to the water. Panting for breath the bird returned to the mast. Again, after resting awhile, it flew east and then west. Finding no limit to the water in any direction, at last it settled down on the mast of the ship."

MASTER (*to the elder Gopal and the other devotees*): "As long as a man feels that God is 'there', he is ignorant. But he attains Knowledge when he feels that God is 'here'.

"A man wanted a smoke. He went to a neighbour's house to light his charcoal. It was the dead of night and the household was asleep. After he

[8] A monastic disciple of the Master, known later as Swami Advaitananda.

had knocked a great deal, someone came down to open the door. At sight of the man he asked, 'Hello! What's the matter?' The man replied: 'Can't you guess? You know how fond I am of smoking. I have come here to light my charcoal.' The neighbour said: 'Ha! Ha! You are a fine man indeed! You took the trouble to come and do all this knocking at the door! Why, you have a lighted lantern in your hand!' (*All laugh.*)

"What a man seeks is very near him. Still he wanders about from place to place."

RAM: "Sir, I now realize why a guru asks some of his disciples to visit the four principal holy places of the country. Once having wandered about, the disciple discovers that it is the same here as there. Then he returns to the guru. All this wandering is only to create faith in the guru's words."

After this conversation had come to an end, Sri Ramakrishna extolled Ram's virtues.

MASTER (*to the devotees*): "How many fine qualities Ram possesses! How many devotees he serves and looks after! (*To Ram*) Adhar told me that you showed him great kindness."

Adhar, a beloved householder devotee of the Master, had recently arranged some religious music at his house. The Master and many devotees had been present. But Adhar had forgotten to invite Ram, who was a very proud man and had complained about it to his friends. So Adhar had gone to Ram's house to express his regret for the mistake.

RAM: "It wasn't really Adhar's mistake. I have come to know that Rakhal is to blame. Rakhal was given charge—"

MASTER: "You mustn't find fault with Rakhal. He's a mere child. Even now you can bring out his mother's milk by squeezing his throat."

RAM: "Sir, why should you speak that way? It was such an occasion!"

MASTER: (*interrupting*): "Adhar simply didn't remember to invite you. He is absent-minded. The other day he went with me to Jadu Mallick's house. As we took our leave, I said to him, 'You haven't offered anything to the Goddess in the chapel.' 'Sir,' he said, 'I didn't know one should.'

(*To Ram*) "Suppose he didn't invite you to his house. Why such a fuss about going to a place where the name of the Lord was sung? One may go unasked to participate in religious music. One doesn't have to be invited."

22

ADVICE TO AN ACTOR

SRI RAMAKRISHNA was sitting on the small couch in his room. Rakhal, M., and several other devotees were present. A special worship of Kāli had been performed in the temple the previous night. In connexion with the worship a theatrical performance of the *Vidyāsundar* had been staged in the nātmandir. The Master had watched a part of it that morning. The actors came to his room to pay him their respects. The Master, in a happy mood, became engaged in conversation with a fair-complexioned young man who had taken the part of Vidyā and played his part very well.

MASTER (*to the actor*): "Your acting was very good. If a person excels in singing, music, dancing, or any other art, he can also quickly realize God provided he strives sincerely.

"Just as you practise much in order to sing, dance, and play on instruments, so one should practise the art of fixing the mind on God. One should practise regularly such disciplines as worship, japa, and meditation.

"Are you married? Any children?"

ACTOR: "Yes, sir. I had a girl who died. Another child has been born."

MASTER: "Ah! A death and a birth, and all so quickly! You are so young! There is a saying: 'My husband died just after our marriage. There are so many nights for me to weep!' You are no doubt realizing the nature of worldly happiness. The world is like a hog plum. The hog plum has only pit and skin, and after eating it you suffer from colic.

"You are an actor in the theatre. That's fine. But it is a very painful profession. You are young now; so you have a full, round face. Afterwards there will be hollows in your cheeks. Almost all actors become like that; they get hollow cheeks and big bellies. (*Laughter.*)

"Why did I stay to watch your performance? I found the rhythm, the music, and the melody all correct. Then the Divine Mother showed me that it was God alone who acted in the performance in the roles of the players."

ACTOR: "Sir, what is the difference between lust and desire?"

MASTER: "Lust is like the root of the tree, and desires are branches and twigs.

"One cannot completely get rid of the six passions: lust, anger, greed, and the like. Therefore one should direct them to God. If you must have desire and greed, then you should desire love of God and be greedy to attain Him. If you must be conceited and egotistic, then feel conceited and egotistic thinking that you are the servant of God, the child of God.

"A man cannot see God unless he gives his whole mind to Him. The mind is wasted on 'woman and gold'. Take your own case. You have children and are occupied with the theatre. The mind cannot be united with God on account of these different activities.

"As long as there is bhoga, there will be less of yoga. Furthermore, bhoga begets suffering. It is said in the *Bhāgavata* that the Avadhuta chose a kite as one of his twenty-four gurus. The kite had a fish in its beak; so it was surrounded by a thousand crows. Whichever way it flew with the fish, the crows pursued it crying, 'Caw! Caw!' When all of a sudden the fish dropped from its beak, the crows flew after the fish, leaving the kite alone.

"The 'fish' is the object of enjoyment. The 'crows' are worries and anxiety. Worries and anxiety are inevitable with enjoyment. No sooner does one give up enjoyment than one finds peace.

"What is more, money itself becomes a source of trouble. Brothers may live happily, but they get into trouble when the property is divided. Dogs lick one another's bodies; they are perfectly friendly. But when the householder throws them a little food, they get into a scrap.

"Come here now and then. (*Pointing to M. and the others*) They come here on Sundays and other holidays."

ACTOR: "We have holidays for three months, during the rainy and harvest seasons. It is our good fortune to be able to visit you. On our way to Dakshineswar we heard of two persons—yourself and Jnanarnava."

MASTER: "Be on friendly terms with your brothers. It looks well. You must have noticed in your theatrical performance that if four singers sing each in a different way, the play is spoiled."

ACTOR: "Yes, sir. Many birds are trapped in a net; if they all fly together and drag the net in one direction, then many of them may be saved. But that doesn't happen if they try to fly in different directions.

"One also sees in a theatrical performance a person keeping a pitcher of water on his head and at the same time dancing about."

MASTER: "Live in the world but keep the pitcher steady on your head; that is to say, keep the mind firmly on God.

"I once said to the sepoys from the barracks: 'Do your duty in the world but remember that the "pestle of death" will some time smash your hand. Be alert about it.'

"In Kāmārpukur I have seen the women of carpenter families making flattened rice with a husking-machine. One woman kicks the end of the wooden beam, and another woman, while nursing her baby, turns the paddy in the mortar dug in the earth. The second woman is always alert lest the pestle of the machine should fall on her hand. With the other hand she fries the soaked paddy in a pan. Besides, she is talking with customers; she says: 'You owe us so much money. Please pay it before you go.' Likewise, do your different duties in the world, fixing your mind on God. But practice is necessary, and one should also be alert. Only in this way can one safeguard both—God and the world."

ACTOR: "Sir, what is the proof that the soul is separate from the body?"

MASTER: "Proof? God can be seen. By practising spiritual discipline one sees God, through His grace. The rishis directly realized the Self. One cannot know the truth about God through science. Science gives us information only about things perceived by the senses, as for instance: this material mixed with that material gives such and such a result, and that material mixed with this material gives such and such a result.

"For this reason a man cannot comprehend spiritual things with his ordinary intelligence. To understand them he must live in the company of holy persons. You learn to feel the pulse by living with a physician."

ACTOR: "Yes, sir. Now I understand."

MASTER: "You must practise tapasyā. Only then can you attain the goal. It will avail you nothing even if you learn the texts of the scriptures by heart. You cannot become intoxicated by merely saying 'siddhi' over and over. You must swallow some.

"One cannot explain the vision of God to others. One cannot explain conjugal happiness to a child five years old."

ACTOR: "How does one realize the Ātman?"

Just then Rakhal was about to take his meal in the Master's room. He hesitated at the sight of so many people. During those days the Master looked on Rakhal as Gopāla and on himself as Mother Yaśodā.

MASTER (to Rakhal): "Why don't you eat? Let the people stand aside if you wish it. (To a devotee) Keep some ice for Rakhal. (To Rakhal) Do you intend to go to Vanhooghly? Don't go in this sun."

Rakhal sat down to his meal. Sri Ramakrishna again spoke to the actor.

MASTER: "Why didn't all of you take your meal from the kitchen of the Kāli temple? That would have been nice."

ACTOR: "All of us don't have the same opinion about food; so our food is cooked separately. All don't like to eat in the guest-house."

While Rakhal was taking his meal, the Master and the devotees sat on the porch and continued their conversation.

MASTER (to the actor): "You asked me about Self-realization. Longing is the means of realizing Ātman. A man must strive to attain God with all his body, with all his mind, and with all his speech. Because of an excess of bile one gets jaundice. Then one sees everything as yellow; one perceives no colour but yellow. Among you actors, those who take only the roles of women acquire the nature of a woman; by thinking of woman your ways and thoughts become womanly. Just so, by thinking day and night of God one acquires the nature of God.

"The mind is like white linen just returned from the laundry. It takes on the colour you dip it in."

ACTOR: "But it must first be sent to the laundry."

MASTER: "Yes. First is the purification of the mind. Afterwards, if you direct the mind to the contemplation of God, it will be coloured by God-

Consciousness. Again, if you direct the mind to worldly duties, such as the acting of a play, it will be coloured by worldliness."

Sri Ramakrishna had rested on his bed only a few minutes when Hari,[1] Narayan, Narendra Bannerji, and other devotees arrived from Calcutta and saluted him. Narendra Bannerji was the son of the professor of Sanskrit at the Presidency College of Calcutta. Because of friction with other members of the family, he had rented a separate house where he lived with his wife and children. Narendra was a very simple and guileless man. He practised spiritual discipline and, at the time of meditation, heard various sounds— the sound of a gong, and so on. He had travelled in different parts of India and he visited the Master now and then.

Narayan was a schoolboy sixteen or seventeen years old. He often visited the Master, who was very fond of him.

Hari lived with his brothers at their Bāghbāzār house. He had studied up to the matriculation class in the General Assembly Institution. Then he had given up his studies and devoted his time at home to the contemplation of God, the reading of the scriptures, and the practice of yoga. He also visited the Master now and then. Sri Ramakrishna often sent for Hari when he went to Balaram's house in Bāghbāzār.

MASTER (to the devotees): "I have heard a great deal about Buddha. He is one of the ten Incarnations of God.[2] Brahman is immovable, immutable, inactive, and of the nature of Consciousness. When a man merges his buddhi, his intelligence, in Bodha, Consciousness, then he attains the Knowledge of Brahman; he becomes buddha, enlightened.

"Nangtā used to say that the mind merges in the buddhi, and the buddhi in Bodha, Consciousness.

"The aspirant does not attain the Knowledge of Brahman as long as he is conscious of his ego. The ego comes under one's control after one has obtained the Knowledge of Brahman and seen God. Otherwise the ego cannot be controlled. It is difficult to catch one's own shadow. But when the sun is overhead, the shadow is within a few inches of the body."

A DEVOTEE: "What is the vision of God like?"

MASTER: "Haven't you seen a theatrical performance? The people are engaged in conversation, when suddenly the curtain goes up. Then the entire mind of the audience is directed to the play. The people don't look at other things any longer. Samādhi is to go within oneself like that. When the curtain is rung down, people look around again. Just so, when the curtain of māyā falls, the mind becomes externalized.

(To Narendra Bannerji) "You have travelled a great deal. Tell us something about the sādhus."

Narendra told the story of two yogis in Bhutan who used to drink daily a pound of the bitter juice of neem-leaves. He had also visited the hermitage of a holy man on the bank of the Narmadā. At the sight of the Bengali

---

[1] A monastic disciple of the Master, later known as Swami Turiyananda.
[2] Hindu mythology speaks of ten Incarnations of God.

Babu dressed in European clothes, the sādhu had remarked, "He has a knife hidden under his clothes, next to his belly."

MASTER: "One should keep pictures of holy men in one's room. That constantly quickens divine ideas."

BANNERJI: "I have your picture in my room; also the picture of a sādhu living in the mountains, blowing on a piece of lighted charcoal in a bowl of hemp."[3]

MASTER: "It is true that one's spiritual feelings are awakened by looking at the picture of a sādhu. It is like being reminded of the custard-apple by looking at an imitation one, or like stimulating the desire for enjoyment by looking at a young woman. Therefore I tell you that you should constantly live in the company of holy men.

(To Bannerji) "You know very well the suffering of the world. You suffer whenever you accept enjoyment. As long as the kite kept the fish in its beak, it was tormented by the flock of crows.

"One finds peace of mind in the company of holy men. The alligator remains under water a long time. But every now and then it rises to the surface and breathes with a deep wheezing noise. Then it gives a sigh of relief."

ACTOR: "Revered sir, what you have just said about enjoyment is very true. One ultimately courts disaster if one prays to God for enjoyment. Various desires come to the mind and by no means all of them are good. God is the Kalpataru, the Wish-fulfilling Tree. A man gets whatever he asks of God. Suppose it comes to his mind: 'God is the Kalpataru. Well, let me see if a tiger will appear before me.' Because he thinks of the tiger, it really appears and devours him."

MASTER: "Yes, you must remember that the tiger comes. What more shall I tell you? Keep your mind on God. Don't forget Him. God will certainly reveal Himself to you if you pray to Him with sincerity. Another thing. Sing the name of God at the end of each performance. Then the actors, the singers, and the audience will go home with the thought of God in their minds."

The actors saluted the Master and took their leave.

Two ladies, devotees of Sri Ramakrishna, entered the room and saluted the Master. They had been fasting in preparation for this visit. They were sisters-in-law, the wives of two brothers, and were twenty-two or twenty-three years old. They were mothers of children. Both of them had their faces covered with veils.

MASTER (to the ladies): "Worship Śiva. This worship is described in a book called the Nityakarma. Learn the rituals from it. In order to perform the worship of God you will be preoccupied for a long time with such religious duties as plucking flowers, making sandal-paste, polishing the utensils of worship, and arranging offerings. As you perform these duties your mind will naturally be directed to God. You will get rid of meanness, anger, jealousy, and so forth. When you two sisters talk to each other, always talk about spiritual matters.

[3] Many wandering monks smoke Indian hemp.

"The thing is somehow to unite the mind with God. You must not forget Him, not even once. Your thought of Him should be like the flow of oil, without any interruption. If you worship with love even a brick or stone as God, then through His grace you can see Him.

"Remember what I have just said to you. One should perform such worship as the Śiva Pujā. Once the mind has become mature, one doesn't have to continue formal worship for long. The mind then always remains united with God; meditation and contemplation become a constant habit of mind."

ELDER SISTER-IN-LAW: "Will you please give us some instruction?"

MASTER (affectionately): "I don't give initiation. If a guru gives initiation he must assume responsibility for the disciple's sin and suffering. The Divine Mother has placed me in the state of a child. Perform the Śiva Pujā as I told you. Come here now and then. We shall see what happens later on through the will of God. I asked you to chant the name of Hari at home. Are you doing that?"

ELDER SISTER-IN-LAW: "Yes."

MASTER: "Why have you fasted? You should take your meal before you come here. Women are but so many forms of my Divine Mother. I cannot bear to see them suffer. You are all images of the Mother of the Universe. Come here after you have eaten, and you will feel happy."

Saying this, Sri Ramakrishna asked Ramlal to give the ladies some food. They were given fruit, sweets, drinks, and other offerings from the temple.

The Master said: "You have eaten something. Now my mind is at peace. I cannot bear to see women fast."

It was about five o'clock in the afternoon. Sri Ramakrishna was sitting on the steps of the Śiva temples. Adhar, Dr. Nitai, M., and several other devotees were with him.

MASTER (to the devotees): "I want to tell you something. A change has been coming over my nature."

The Master came down a step and sat near the devotees. It seemed that he intended to communicate some of his deeper experiences to them.

MASTER: "You are devotees. I have no hesitation in telling you this. Nowadays I don't see the Spirit-form of God. He is revealed to me in human form. It is my nature to see the form of God, to touch and embrace Him. God is saying to me, 'You have assumed a body; therefore enjoy God through His human forms.'

"God no doubt dwells in all, but He manifests Himself more through man than through other beings. Is man an insignificant thing? He can think of God, he can think of the Infinite, while other living beings cannot. God exists in other living beings—animals, plants, nay, in all beings—, but He manifests Himself more through man than through these others. Fire exists in all beings, in all things; but its presence is felt more in wood. Rāma said to Lakshmana: 'Look at the elephant, brother. He is such a big animal, but he cannot think of God.'

"But in the Incarnation there is a greater manifestation of God than in other men. Rāma said to Lakshmana, 'Brother, if you see in a man ecstatic love of God, if he laughs, weeps, and dances in divine ecstasy, then know for certain that I dwell in him.'"

The Master remained silent. After a few minutes he resumed the conversation.

MASTER: "Keshab Sen used to come here frequently. As a result he changed a great deal. Of late he became quite a remarkable man. Many a time he came here with his party; but he also wanted to come alone. In the earlier years of his life Keshab didn't have much opportunity to live in the company of holy men.

"I visited him at his house in Coolootola Street. Hriday was with me. We were shown into the room where Keshab was working. He was writing something. After a long while he put aside his pen, got off his chair, and sat on the floor with us. But he didn't salute us or show us respect in any other way.

"He used to come here now and then. One day in a spiritual mood I said to him: 'One should not sit before a sādhu with one leg over the other. That increases one's rajas.' As soon as he and his friends would arrive, I would salute them before they bowed to me. Thus they gradually learnt to salute a holy man, touching the ground with their foreheads.

"I said to Keshab: 'Chant the name of Hari. In the Kaliyuga one should sing the name and glories of God.' After that they began to sing the name of God with drums and cymbals.[4]

"Do you know how my faith in the name of Hari was all the more strengthened? Holy men, as you know, frequently visit the temple garden. Once a sādhu from Multan arrived. He was waiting for a party going to Gangāsāgar. (Pointing to M.) The sādhu was of his age. It was he who said to me, 'The way to realize God in the Kaliyuga is the path of bhakti as prescribed by Nārada.'

"One day Keshab came here with his followers. They stayed till ten at night. We were all seated in the Panchavati. Pratap and several others said they would like to spend the night here. Keshab said: 'No, I must go. I have some work to do.' I laughed and said: 'Can't you sleep without the smell of your fish-basket? Once a fishwife was a guest in the house of a gardener who raised flowers. She came there with her empty basket, after selling fish in the market, and was asked to sleep in a room where flowers were kept. But, because of the fragrance of the flowers, she couldn't get to sleep for a long time. Her hostess saw her condition and said, "Hello! Why are you tossing from side to side so restlessly?" The fishwife said: "I don't know, friend. Perhaps the smell of the flowers has been disturbing my sleep. Can you give me my fish-basket? Perhaps that will put me to sleep."

* For some years before meeting the Master, Keshab and his followers had been singing the name of "Brahma" to the accompaniment of drums and cymbals. After meeting Sri Ramakrishna in 1875, Keshab showed particular devotion to the singing of the names of Hari and the Divine Mother. [Foot-note by M. in the Bengali *Gospel of Sri Ramakrishna*, vol. v, p. 113.]

The basket was brought to her. She sprinkled water on it and set it near her nose. Then she fell sound asleep and snored all night.'

"At this story the followers of Keshab burst into loud laughter.

"Keshab conducted the prayer that evening at the bathing-ghāt on the river. After the worship I said to him: 'It is God who manifests Himself, in one aspect, as the scriptures; therefore one should worship the sacred books, such as the Vedas, the Purānas, and the Tantras. In another aspect He has become the devotee. The heart of the devotee is God's drawing-room. One can easily find one's master in the drawing-room. Therefore, by worshipping His devotee, one worships God Himself.'

"Keshab and his followers listened to my words with great attention. It was a full-moon night. The sky was flooded with light. We were seated in the open court at the top of the stairs leading to the river. I said, 'Now let us all chant, "Bhāgavata—Bhakta—Bhagavān." ' All chanted in unison, 'Bhāgavata—Bhakta—Bhagavān.' Next I said to them, 'Say, "Brahman is verily Śakti; Śakti is verily Brahman." ' Again they chanted in unison, 'Brahman is verily Śakti; Śakti is verily Brahman.' I said to them: 'He whom you address as Brahma is none other than She whom I call Mother. Mother is a very sweet name.'

"Then I said to them, 'Say, "Guru—Krishna—Vaishnava." '5 At this Keshab said: 'We must not go so far, sir. If we do that, then all will take us for orthodox Vaishnavas.'

"I used to tell Keshab now and then: 'He whom you address as Brahma is none other than She whom I call Śakti, the Primal Energy. It is called Brahman in the Vedas when It transcends speech and thought and is without attributes and action. I call It Śakti, Ādyāśakti, and so forth, when I find It creating, preserving, and destroying the universe.'

"I said to Keshab: 'It is extremely difficult to realize God while leading a worldly life. How can a typhoid patient be cured if he is kept in a room where tamarind, pickle, and jars of water are kept? Therefore one should go into solitude now and then to practise spiritual discipline. When the trunk of a tree becomes thick and strong, an elephant can be tied to it; but a young sapling is eaten by cattle.' That is why Keshab would say in his lectures, 'Live in the world after being strengthened in spiritual life.'

(To the devotees) "You see, Keshab was a great scholar. He lectured in English. Many people honoured him. Queen Victoria herself talked to him. But when Keshab came here he would be bare-bodied and bring some fruit, as one should when visiting a holy man. He was totally free from egotism.

(To Adhar) "You are a scholar and a deputy magistrate, but with all that you are hen-pecked. Go forward. Beyond the forest of sandal-wood there are many more valuable things: silver-mines, gold-mines, diamonds, and other gems. The wood-cutter was chopping wood in the forest; the brahma-chāri said to him, 'Go forward.' "

Sri Ramakrishna came down from the steps of the Śiva temples and went

---

5 The Master meant that the guru, Krishna, and the Vaishnava were to be equally revered. One should honour the Vaishnava because God dwells in his heart.

to his own room through the courtyard. The devotees were with him. Just then Ram Chatterji came and said that the Holy Mother's attendant had had an attack of cholera.

RAM (to the Master): "I told you about it at ten o'clock this morning, but you didn't pay any attention to me."

MASTER: "What could I do?"

RAM: "Yes, what could you do! But there were Rakhal, Ramlal, and others. Even they didn't pay any attention."

M: "Kishori has gone to Ālambāzār to get medicine."

MASTER: "Alone? Where will he get medicine?"

M: "Yes, alone. He will get it at Ālambāzār."

MASTER (to M.): "Tell the nurse what to do if the illness takes a turn for the worse or if the patient feels better."

M: "Yes, sir."

The ladies mentioned before saluted the Master and were about to take their leave. Sri Ramakrishna again said to them: "Perform the Śiva Pujā according to my instruction. And have something to eat before you come here. Otherwise I shall feel unhappy. Come another day."

Sri Ramakrishna sat down on the porch west of his room. Narendra Bannerji, Hari, M., and others sat by his side. The Master knew about Narendra's family difficulties.

MASTER: "You see, all these sufferings are 'because of a piece of loin-cloth'.[6] A man takes a wife and begets children; therefore he must secure a job. The sādhu is worried about his loin-cloth, and the householder about his wife. Further, the householder may not live on good terms with his relatives; so he must live separately with his wife. (With a laugh) Chaitanya once said to Nityānanda: 'Listen to me, brother. A man entangled in worldliness can never be free.' "

M. (to himself): "Perhaps the Master is referring to the world of avidyā. It is the world of avidyā that entangles a householder."

M. was still living in a separate house with his wife, on account of a misunderstanding with the other members of his family.

MASTER (to Bannerji, pointing to M.): "He also lives in a separate house. You two will get along very well. Once two men happened to meet. One said to the other, 'Who are you?' 'Oh, I am away from my country', was the other's reply. The second man then asked the first, 'And who are you,

---

[6] A reference to the following story, which Sri Ramakrishna often told his devotees: There was a sannyāsi whose only possession was two pairs of loin-cloths. One day a mouse nibbled at one piece. So the holy man kept a cat to protect his loin-cloths from the mouse. Then he had to keep a cow to supply milk for the cat. Later he had to engage a servant to look after the cow. Gradually the number of his cows multiplied. He acquired pastures and farm land. He had to engage a number of servants. Thus he became, in course of time, a sort of landlord. And, last of all, he had to take a wife to look after his big household. One day, one of his friends, another monk, happened to visit him and was surprised to see his altered circumstances. When asked the reason, the holy man said, "It is all for the sake of a piece of loin-cloth!"

pray?' 'Oh, I am away from my beloved', was the answer. Both were in the same plight; so they got along very well. (*All laugh.*)

"But one need not have any fear if one takes refuge in God. God protects His devotee."

HARI: "Well, why does it take many people such a long time to realize Him?"

MASTER: "The truth is that a man doesn't feel restless for God unless he is finished with his enjoyments and duties. The physician says, referring to the patient: 'Let a few days pass first. Then a little medicine will do him good.'

"Nārada said to Rāma: 'Rāma, You are passing Your time in Ayodhyā. How will Rāvana be killed? You have taken this human body for that purpose alone.' Rāma replied: 'Nārada, let the right time come. Let Rāvana's past actions begin to bear fruit. Then everything will be made ready for his death.'"

HARI: "Why is there so much suffering in the world?"

MASTER: "This world is the līlā of God. It is like a game. In this game there are joy and sorrow, virtue and vice, knowledge and ignorance, good and evil. The game cannot continue if sin and suffering are altogether eliminated from the creation.

"In the game of hide-and-seek one must touch the 'granny' in order to be free. But the 'granny' is never pleased if she is touched at the very outset. It is God's wish that the play should continue for some time. Then—

> Out of a hundred thousand kites, at best but one or two break free;
> And Thou dost laugh and clap Thy hands, O Mother, watching
> them!

In other words, after the practice of hard spiritual discipline, one or two have the vision of God, through His grace, and are liberated. Then the Divine Mother claps Her hands in joy and exclaims, 'Bravo! There they go!'"

HARI: "But this play of God is our death."

MASTER (*smiling*): "Please tell me who *you* are. God alone has become all this—māyā, the universe, living beings, and the twenty-four cosmic principles. 'As the snake I bite, and as the charmer I cure.' It is God Himself who has become both vidyā and avidyā. He remains deluded by the māyā of avidyā, ignorance. Again, with the help of the guru, He is cured by the māyā of vidyā, Knowledge.

"Ignorance, Knowledge, and Perfect Wisdom. The jnāni sees that God alone exists and is the Doer, that He creates, preserves, and destroys. The vijnāni sees that it is God who has become all this.

"After attaining mahābhāva and prema one realizes that nothing exists but God. Bhakti pales before bhāva. Bhāva ripens into mahābhāva and prema.

(*To Bannerji*) "Do you still hear that gong-like sound at the time of meditation?"

BANNERJI: "Yes, sir. Every day. Besides, I have visions of God's form. Do such things stop after the mind has once experienced them?"

MASTER: "True. Once the wood catches fire, it cannot be put out. (*To the devotees*) He knows many things about faith."

BANNERJI: "I have too much faith."

MASTER: "Bring the women of your family with those of Balaram's."

BANNERJI: "Who is Balaram?"

MASTER: "Don't you know Balaram? He lives at Bosepārā."

Sri Ramakrishna loved guileless people. Narendra Bannerji was absolutely guileless. The Master loved Niranjan[7] because he, too, was without guile.

MASTER (*to M.*): "Why do I ask you to see Niranjan? It is to find out if he is truly guileless."

Sunday, May 25, 1884

Sri Ramakrishna was sitting on the cement platform that encircled the trunk of the old banyan-tree in the Panchavati. Vijay, Surendra, Bhavanath, Rakhal, and other devotees were present, a few of them sitting with the Master on the platform, the rest on the ground below. The devotees had thought of celebrating the Master's birthday, which had had to be put off because of his illness. Since Sri Ramakrishna now felt much better, the devotees wanted to have the celebration that day. A woman musician, a famous singer of kirtan, was going to entertain them with devotional songs.

It was one o'clock in the afternoon. M. had been looking for Sri Ramakrishna in the Master's room. When he did not find him there, he went to the Panchavati and eagerly asked the devotees, "Where is he?" He was standing right in front of the Master but in his excitement did not notice him. The devotees laughed loudly. A moment later M. saw Sri Ramakrishna and felt very much embarrassed. He prostrated himself before the Master, who sat there facing the south and smiling happily. Kedar and Vijay were sitting at his left. These two devotees had had a misunderstanding recently when Kedar had cut off his connexion with the Brāhmo Samāj.

MASTER (*to M., with a smile*): "You see how I have united them?"

The Master had brought a mādhavi creeper from Vrindāvan in the year 1868 and had planted it in the Panchavati. The creeper had grown big and strong. Some children were jumping and swinging from it. The Master observed them and laughed. He said: "They are like young monkeys. They will not give up swinging even though they sometimes fall to the ground." Noticing that Surendra was standing before him, the Master said to him affectionately: "Come up and sit with us on the platform. Then you can dangle your feet comfortably." Surendra went up and took his seat. Bhavanath had his coat on. Surendra said to him, "Are you going to England?"

MASTER (*smiling*): "God is our England. Now and then I used to leave off my clothes and joyfully roam about naked. Once Sambhu said to me: 'It is very comfortable to walk about naked. That is why you do it. Once I did it myself.'"

[7] A young disciple of the Master, who later became a monk under the name of Swami Niranjanananda.

SURENDRA: "On returning from the office, as I put away my coat and trousers, I say to the Divine Mother, 'O Mother, how tightly You have bound me to the world!'"

MASTER: "There are eight fetters with which man is bound: shame, hatred, fear, pride of caste, hesitation, the desire to conceal, and so forth."

Sri Ramakrishna sang:

> Mother, this is the grief that sorely grieves my heart,
> That even with Thee for Mother, and though I am wide awake,
> There should be robbery in my house. . . .

He continued:

> In the world's busy market-place, O Śyāmā, Thou art flying kites;
> High up they soar on the wind of hope, held fast by māyā's string.
> Their frames are human skeletons, their sails of the three gunas
>   made;
> But all their curious workmanship is merely for ornament.
>
> Upon the kite-strings Thou hast rubbed the mānjā-paste of worldliness,
> So as to make each straining strand all the more sharp and strong.
> Out of a hundred thousand kites, at best but one or two break free;
> And Thou dost laugh and clap Thy hands, O Mother, watching
>   them!
>
> On favouring winds, says Rāmprasād, the kites set loose will
>   speedily
> Be borne away to the Infinite, across the sea of the world.

MASTER: "'Māyā's string' means wife and children.

> Upon the kite-strings Thou hast rubbed the mānjā-paste of worldliness.

'Worldliness' means 'woman and gold'.

"The three gunas—sattva, rajas, and tamas—have men under their control. They are like three brothers. As long as sattva exists, it calls on rajas for help; and rajas can get help from tamas. The three gunas are so many robbers. Tamas kills and rajas binds. Sattva no doubt releases man from his bondage, but it cannot take him to God."

VIJAY (smiling): "It is because sattva, too, is a robber."

MASTER (smiling): "True. Sattva cannot take man to God, but it shows him the way."

BHAVANATH: "These are wonderful words indeed."

MASTER: "Yes, this is a lofty thought."

Listening to these words of the Master, the devotees felt very happy.

MASTER: "'Woman and gold' is the cause of bondage. 'Woman and gold' alone constitutes samsāra, the world. It is 'woman and gold' that keeps one from seeing God. (Holding the towel in front of his face) Do you see my face any more? Of course not. The towel hides it. No sooner is the covering of 'woman and gold' removed than one attains Chidānanda, Consciousness and Bliss.

"Let me tell you something. He who has renounced the pleasure of a wife has verily renounced the pleasure of the world. God is very near to such a person."

The devotees listened to these words in silence.

MASTER (*to Kedar, Vijay, and the other devotees*): "He who has renounced the pleasure of a wife has verily renounced the pleasure of the world. It is 'woman and gold' that hides God. You people have such imposing moustaches, and yet you too are involved in 'woman and gold'. Tell me if it isn't true. Search your heart and answer me."

VIJAY: "Yes, it is true."

Kedar remained silent.

MASTER: "I see that all are under the control of woman. One day I went to Captain's house. From there I was to go to Ram's house. So I said to Captain, 'Please give me my carriage hire.' He asked his wife about it. She too held back and said: 'What's the matter? What's the matter?' At last Captain said, 'Ram will take care of it.' You see, the *Gītā*, the *Bhāgavata*, and the Vedānta all bow before a woman! (*All laugh.*)

"A man leaves his money, his property, and everything in the hands of his wife. But he says with affected simplicity, 'I have such a nature that I cannot keep even two rupees with me.'

"A man went to an office in search of a job. There were many vacancies, but the manager did not grant his request. A friend said to the applicant, 'Appeal to Golapi, and you will get the job.' Golapi was the manager's mistress.

"Men do not realize how far they are dragged down by women. Once I went to the Fort in a carriage, feeling all the while that I was going along a level road. At last I found that I had gone four storeys down. It was a sloping road.

"A man possessed by a ghost does not know he is under the ghost's control. He thinks he is quite normal."

VIJAY (*smiling*): "But he can be cured by an exorcist if he finds one."

In answer to Vijay Sri Ramakrishna only said, "That depends on the will of God." Then he went on with his talk about women.

MASTER: "Everyone I talk to says, 'Yes, sir, my wife is good.' Nobody says that his wife is bad. (*All laugh.*) Those who constantly live with 'woman and gold' are so infatuated with it that they don't see things properly. Chess-players oftentimes cannot see the right move for their pieces on the board. But those who watch the game from a distance can understand the moves more accurately.

"Woman is the embodiment of māyā. In the course of his hymn to Rāma, Nārada said: 'O Rāma, all men are parts of Thee. All women are parts of Sītā, the personification of Thy māyā. Please deign to grant that I may have pure love for Thy Lotus Feet and that I may not be deluded by Thy world-bewitching māyā. I do not want any other favour than that.' "

Surendra's younger brother and his nephews were present. The brother worked in an office and one of the nephews was studying law.

MASTER (*to Surendra's relatives*): "My advice to you is not to become attached to the world. You see, Rakhal now understands what is knowledge and what is ignorance. He can discriminate between the Real and the unreal. So I say to him: 'Go home. You may come here once in a while and spend a day or two with me.'

"Have a friendly relationship with one another. That will be for your good and make you all happy. In a theatre the performance goes well only if the musicians sing with one voice. And that also gladdens the hearts of the audience.

"Do your worldly duties with a part of your mind and direct most of it to God. A sādhu should think of God with three quarters of his mind and with one quarter should do his other duties. He should be very alert about spiritual things. The snake is very sensitive in its tail. Its whole body reacts when it is hurt there. Similarly, the whole life of a sādhu is affected when his spirituality is touched."

Sri Ramakrishna was going to the pine-grove and asked Gopal of Sinthi to take his umbrella to his room. Arrangements had been made in the Panchavati for the kirtan. When the Master had returned and taken his seat again among the devotees, the musician began her song. Suddenly there came a rain-storm. The Master went back to his room with the devotees, the musician accompanying them to continue her songs there.

MASTER (to Gopal): "Have you brought the umbrella?"

GOPAL: "No, sir. I forgot all about it while listening to the music."

The umbrella had been left in the Panchavati and Gopal hurried to fetch it.

MASTER: "I am generally careless, but not to that extent. Rakhal also is very careless. Referring to the date of an invitation, he says 'the eleventh' instead of 'the thirteenth'. And Gopal—he belongs in a herd of cows!"[8]

The musician sang a song about the monastic life of Chaitanya. Now and then she improvised lines: "He will not look upon a woman; for that is against the sannyāsi's duty." "Eager to take away men's sorrows, he will not look upon a woman." "For the Lord's birth as Sri Chaitanya otherwise would be in vain."

The Master stood up, as he heard about Chaitanya's renunciation, and went into samādhi. The devotees put garlands of flowers around his neck. Bhavanath and Rakhal supported his body lest he should fall on the ground. Vijay, Kedar, Ram, M., Latu, and the other devotees stood around him in a circle, recalling one of the scenes of Chaitanya's kirtan.

The Master gradually came down to the sense plane. He was talking to Krishna, now and then uttering the word "Krishna". He could not say it very distinctly because of the intensity of his spiritual emotion. He said: "Krishna! Krishna! Krishna! Krishna Satchidānanda! Nowadays I do not see Your form. Now I see You both inside me and outside. I see that it is You who have become the universe, all living beings, the twenty-four cosmic principles, and everything else. You alone have become mind, intelligence, everything. It is said in the 'Hymn of Salutation to the Guru': 'I bow down

[8] There is a pun on the word "Gopal", which means also "herd of cows".

to the Guru by whose grace I have realized Him who pervades the indivisible universe of the animate and the inanimate.'

"You alone are the Indivisible. Again, it is You who pervade the universe of the animate and the inanimate. You are verily the manifold universe; again, You alone are its basis. O Krishna! You are my life. O Krishna! You are my mind. O Krishna! You are my intelligence. O Krishna! You are my soul. O Govinda! You are my life-breath. You are my life itself."

Vijay was also in an ecstatic mood. The Master asked him, "My dear sir, have you too become unconscious?" "No, sir", said Vijay humbly.

The music went on. The musician was singing about the blinding love of God. As she improvised the lines:

> O Beloved of my soul! Within the chamber of my heart
> I would have kept You day and night!

the Master again went into samādhi. His injured arm rested on Bhavanath's shoulder.

Sri Ramakrishna partly regained outer consciousness. The musician improvised:

> Why should one who, for Thy sake, has given up everything
> Endure so much of suffering?

The Master bowed to the musician and sat down to listen to the music. Now and then he became abstracted. When the musician stopped singing, Sri Ramakrishna began to talk to the devotees.

MASTER (*to Vijay and the others*): "What is prema? He who feels it, this intense and ecstatic love of God, not only forgets the world but forgets even the body, which is so dear to all. Chaitanya experienced it."

The Master explained this to the devotees by singing a song describing the ecstatic state of prema:

> Oh, when will dawn the blessed day
> When tears of joy will flow from my eyes
> As I repeat Lord Hari's name? . . .

The Master began to dance, and the devotees joined him. He caught M. by the arm and dragged him into the circle. Thus dancing, Sri Ramakrishna again went into samādhi. Standing transfixed, he looked like a picture on canvas. Kedar repeated the following hymn to bring his mind down from the plane of samādhi:

> We worship the Brahman-Consciousness in the Lotus of the Heart,
> The Undifferentiated, who is adored by Hari, Hara, and Brahmā;
> Who is attained by yogis in the depths of their meditation;
> The Scatterer of the fear of birth and death,
> The Essence of Knowledge and Truth, the Primal Seed of the world.

Sri Ramakrishna gradually came back to the plane of normal consciousness. He took his seat and chanted the names of God: "Om Satchidānanda! Govinda! Govinda! Govinda! Yogamāyā! Bhāgavata—Bhakta—Bhagavān!"

The Master took dust from the place where the kirtan had been sung and touched it to his forehead.

A little later Sri Ramakrishna was sitting on the semicircular porch facing the Ganges, the devotees sitting by his side. Now and then the Master would exclaim, "Ah, Krishnachaitanya!"[9]

MASTER (to Vijay and the others): "There has been much chanting of the Lord's name in the room. That is why the atmosphere has become so intense."

BHAVANATH: "Words of renunciation, too."

The Master said, "Ah, how thrilling!" Then he sang about Gaurānga and Nityānanda:

Gorā bestows the Nectar of prema;
Jar after jar he pours it out,
And still there is no end!
Sweetest Nitāi is summoning all;
Beloved Gorā bids them come;
Shāntipur is almost drowned,
And Nadiā[10] is flooded with prema!

MASTER (to Vijay and the others): "The musician sang rightly: 'A sannyāsi must not look at a woman.' This is the sannyāsi's dharma. What a lofty ideal!"

VIJAY: "Yes indeed, sir."

MASTER: "Others learn from the sannyāsi's example. That is why such strict rules are prescribed for him. A sannyāsi must not look even at the portrait of a woman. What a strict rule! The slaughtering of a black goat is prescribed for the worship of the Divine Mother; but a goat with even a slight wound cannot be offered. A sannyāsi must not only not have intercourse with woman; he must not even talk to her."

VIJAY: "Young Haridās talked with a pious woman. For that reason Chaitanya banished him from his presence."

MASTER: "A sannyāsi associated with 'woman and gold' is like a beautiful damsel with a bad odour. The odour makes her beauty useless.

"Once a Mārwāri devotee wanted to give me some money. Mathur wanted to deed me some land. But I couldn't accept either.

"The rules for the life of a sannyāsi are very strict indeed. If a man takes the garb of a sannyāsi, he must act exactly like one. Haven't you noticed in the theatre that the man who takes the part of the king acts like a king, and the man who takes the part of a minister acts like a minister?

"But on attaining the state of the paramahamsa one becomes like a child. A child five years old doesn't know the difference between a man and a woman. But even a paramahamsa must be careful, so as not to set a bad example to others."

Referring to Keshab's association with "woman and gold", which had hin-

---

[9] One of the names of Gaurānga.

[10] Shāntipur and Nadiā are places associated with Chaitanya.

dered his work as a spiritual teacher, Sri Ramakrishna said to Vijay, "He—do you understand?"

VIJAY: "Yes, sir."

MASTER: "He couldn't achieve very much because he wanted to satisfy both God and the world."

VIJAY: "Chaitanya said to Nityānanda: 'Nitāi, I shall not be able to do the people any good unless I renounce the world. All will imitate me and want to lead the life of a householder. No one will try to direct his whole mind to the Lotus Feet of God, renouncing "woman and gold".' "

MASTER: "Yes. Chaitanyadeva renounced the world to set an example to mankind.

"The sannyāsi must renounce 'woman and gold' for his own welfare. Even if he is unattached, and consequently not in danger, still, in order to set an example to others, he must not keep 'woman and gold' near him. The sannyāsi, the man of renunciation, is a world teacher. It is his example that awakens the spiritual consciousness of men."

It was nearly dusk. The devotees saluted the Master and took their leave.

FESTIVAL AT SURENDRA'S HOUSE

SRI RAMAKRISHNA arrived in the morning at the garden house of Surendra, one of his beloved householder disciples, in the village of Kānkurgāchi near Calcutta. Surendra had invited him and a large number of the devotees to a religious festival.

Occasions like this were a source of great happiness and rejoicing to the Master's devotees. He was then seen at his best. He joined with the others in devotional music and in chanting the names of God, frequently going into ecstasy. He poured out his entire soul in inspired talk, explaining the various phases of God-Consciousness. The impressions of such a festival lingered in the minds of all for many days.

The devotees stood in rows inside the big hall of the garden house to hear the music sung by the professional singers. The floor of the room was covered with a carpet over which was spread a white sheet; a few bolsters, pillows, and cushions lay here and there.

The musicians were singing of the episodes in the life of Sri Krishna especially associated with His divine love for the gopis of Vrindāvan. This was a theme which always appealed to the Master and would throw him into ecstatic moods.

Krishna, God Incarnate, lived the years of His boyhood in Vrindāvan as a cowherd. He tended His cows on the green meadows along the bank of the Jamunā and played His flute. The milkmaids could not resist the force of His divine attraction. At the sound of His flute they would leave their household duties and go to the bank of the sacred river. Their love for Krishna destroyed their attachment to worldly things. Neither the threats of their relatives nor the criticism of others could make them desist from seeking the company of Krishna. In the love of the gopis for Krishna there was not the slightest trace of worldliness. It was the innate attraction of God for pure souls, as of the magnet for iron. The author of the *Bhāgavata* has compared this love to the all-consuming love of a woman for her beloved. Before the onrush of that love all barriers between man and God are swept away. The devotee surrenders himself completely to his Divine Beloved and in the end becomes one with Him.

Rādhā was the foremost of the gopis, and Krishna's chief playmate. She

444

felt an indescribable longing for union with Him. A moment's separation from Krishna would rend her heart and soul. During many a moonlit night Krishna would dance with Rādhā and the gopis in the sacred groves of Vrindāvan, and on such occasions the gopis would experience the highest religious ecstasy. At the age of eleven Krishna was called to be the king of Mathurā. He left the gopis, promising them, however, His divine vision whenever they concentrated on Him in their hearts.

For centuries and centuries the lovers of God in India have been worshipping the Divine by recreating in themselves the yearning of the gopis for Krishna. Many of the folk-songs of India have as their theme this sweet episode of Krishna's life. Sri Chaitanya revived this phase of Hindu religious life by his spiritual practice and his divine visions. In his ecstatic music Chaitanya assumed the role of Rādhā and manifested the longing to be united with Krishna. For a long period Sri Ramakrishna also worshipped God as his beloved Krishna, looking on himself as one of the gopis or as God's handmaid.

At Surendra's garden house the kirtan had begun early in the morning. The musicians were singing about the love of Krishna and Rādhā for each other. The Master was frequently in samādhi. The room was crowded with devotees, among them Bhavanath, Niranjan, Rakhal, Surendra, Ram, and M., and many members of the Brāhmo Samāj.

In accordance with the custom, the kirtan had begun with an introductory song about Gaurānga. Gaurānga embraces monastic life. He is being consumed with longing for a vision of Krishna. He leaves Navadvip and goes away as a wandering monk to seek out his Beloved. His devotees, unable to bear the pangs of separation, weep bitterly and beg Gaurānga to return.

The musician sang:

O Gaur, come back to Nadiā!

Next the musician sang about the anguish of Rādhā at her separation from Krishna. When Sri Ramakrishna heard the song he suddenly stood up. Assuming the mood of Rādhā, he sang in a voice laden with sorrow, improvising the words: "O friend, either bring my beloved Krishna here or take me to Him." Thus singing, he completely lost himself in Rādhā and could not continue the song. He became speechless, his body motionless, his eyes half closed, his mind totally unconscious of the outer world. He was in deep samādhi.

After a long time he regained normal consciousness and said in the same heart-rending voice: "O friend, take me to my beloved Krishna and make me your bondslave. I shall be your handmaid for ever. O friend, it was you who taught me how to love Krishna. O Krishna! O Beloved of my soul!"

The professional musicians continued their song. They took the part of Rādhā and sang as if she were talking to her friend: "O friend, I shall not go again to the Jamunā to draw water. Once I beheld my beloved Friend under the kadamba tree. Whenever I pass it I am overwhelmed."

The Master again became abstracted. Heaving a deep sigh he said, "Ah me! Ah me!"

The song went on. Rādhā says:

> Even the desire for Krishna's presence
> Has cooled and refreshed my feverish body.

Now and then the musicians improvised lines to the music, continuing in the attitude of Rādhā: "O friends, you can wait. Show me Krishna, my Beloved." Again: "Do not bother about my ornaments. I have lost my most precious Ornament." And again: "Alas! I have fallen on evil days. My happy days are over." And finally: "This unhappy time lingers so long!"

Sri Ramakrishna improvised a line himself: "Are not better times yet in sight for me?" The musicians then improvised: "Such a long time has passed! Are not better times yet in sight for me?"

The musicians sang Rādhā's words to a friend:

> O friend, I am dying! Surely I die.
> The anguish of being kept apart
> From Krishna is more than I can bear.
> Alas! to whom then shall I leave
> My priceless Treasure?[1] When I am dead,
> I beg you, do not burn my body;
> Do not cast it into the river.
> See that it is not given to the flames;
> Do not cast it into the water.
> In this body I played with Krishna.
>
> Bind my lifeless form, I beg you,
> To the black tamāla's branches;
> Tie it to the tamāla tree.
> Touching tamāla it touches black.
> Krishna is black, and black is tamāla;
> Black is the colour that I love.
> From earliest childhood I have loved it.
> To the black Krishna my body belongs;
> Let it not lie apart from black!

Rādhā reaches her last extremity. She faints away.

> Rādhā has fallen to the·ground;
> She lies there lost to outward sense,
> Repeating her precious Krishna's name,
> And straightway closes both her eyes.
> Ah, has the drama reached its end?
> What ails you, O delight of Krishna?
> Only a moment ago you spoke.
>
> Her friends, anointing Rādhā's form
> With cool and soothing sandal-paste,
> Attempt to bring her back to earth.
> Some of them weep in bitter grief;
> They cannot bear to see her die.
> Some sprinkle water on her face;

[1] Krishna.

> Perhaps she will revive again!
> But, oh, can water give back life
> To one who dies of Krishna's love?

Rādhā's friends chant Krishna's sweet name in her ears. This brings her back to partial consciousness. She looks at the black tamāla tree and thinks that Krishna stands before her.

> Krishna's name restores her life;
> Once more her two eyes gaze around,
> But Krishna's face she cannot see.
> Alas, how bitterly she weeps!
> "Where is my Krishna? Where is He
> Whose name you chanted in my ears?
> Bring Him but once before me here!"

> Seeing the black tamāla tree,
> She stares at it and cries aloud:
> "There is His crest! I see it clearly!
> There is my Krishna's lovely crest!"
> But only a peacock did she see,
> Whose glistening feathers she mistook
> For the gay feather on Krishna's crest.

Krishna has gone to Mathurā to assume His royal duties. He has discarded His cowherd's dress and flute and put on the royal regalia. Rādhā's friends, after a hurried consultation, send a gopi to Mathurā as messenger. She meets a woman of that city, of her own age, who asks her where she comes from.

Rādhā's friend says: "I don't have to call Krishna. He Himself will come to me." But none the less she follows the woman of Mathurā and goes to Krishna's palace. In the street she weeps, overcome with grief, and prays to Krishna: "O Hari, where are You? O Life of the gopis! O Enchanter of our hearts! O Beloved of Rādhā! O Hari, Remover of Your devotees' shame! Come to us once more! With great pride I said to the people of Mathurā that You Yourself would come to me. Please do not humiliate me."

> In scorn says the woman of Mathurā:
> "Oh, you are only a simple milkmaid!
> How can you go to see our King,
> Our Krishna, in your beggar's rags?
> Behind seven doors His chamber stands.
> You cannot enter. How can you go?
> I die of shame to see your boldness.
> Tell me, how will you manage to enter?"

> Says the gopi: "Krishna! Beloved!
> Soul of the gopis! Oh, where are You?
> Come to me here and save my life.
> Where are You, adorable Soul of the gopis?
> Come to me, Lord of Mathurā!
> And save the life of Your sorrowing handmaid.
> Ah, where are You, Beloved of Rādhā?
> Lord of our hearts and Friend of our souls!

O Hari, Destroyer of our shame!
O priceless Treasure of the gopis!
Come to Your handmaid and save her honour."

Thus the messenger weeps and cries out for Krishna.

When the musicians sang, "Where are You, adorable Soul of the gopis?" the Master went into samādhi. As the music neared its end the musicians sang louder. Sri Ramakrishna was on his feet, again in deep samādhi. Regaining partial consciousness, he said in a half articulate voice, "Kitna! Kitna!" He was too much overwhelmed to utter Krishna's name distinctly.

The kirtan was coming to a close. At the reunion of Rādhā and Krishna the Master sang with the musicians, composing the lines himself:

Behold, there Rādhā stands by Krishna;
On His bosom she reclines.
Behold her standing at His left,
Like a golden creeper twining
Round a black tamāla tree!

As the music came to a close the Master led the chorus. All chanted together to the accompaniment of drums and cymbals: "Victory to Rādhā and Krishna! Hallowed be the names of Rādhā and Krishna!" The devotees felt a surge of divine emotion and danced around the Master. He too danced in an ecstasy of joy. The names of God echoed and re-echoed in the house and garden.

After the music the Master sat with the devotees. Just then Niranjan arrived and prostrated himself before him. At the very sight of this beloved disciple the Master stood up, with beaming eyes and smiling face, and said: "You have come too! (To M.) You see, this boy is absolutely guileless. One cannot be guileless without a great deal of spiritual discipline in previous births. A hypocritical and calculating mind can never attain God.

"Don't you see that God incarnates Himself only in a family where innocence exists? How guileless Daśaratha was! So was Nanda, Krishna's father. There is a saying: 'Ah, how innocent a man he is! He is just like Nanda.'

(To Niranjan) "I feel as if a dark veil has covered your face. It is because you have accepted a job in an office. One must keep accounts there. Besides, one must attend to many other things, and that always keeps the mind in a state of worry. You are serving in an office like other worldly people; but there is a slight difference, in that you are earning money for the sake of your mother. One must show the highest respect to one's mother, for she is the very embodiment of the Blissful Mother of the Universe. If you had accepted the job for the sake of wife and children, I should have said: 'Fie upon you! Shame! A thousand shames!'

(To Mani Mallick, pointing to Niranjan) "Look at this boy. He is absolutely guileless. But he has one fault: he is slightly untruthful nowadays. The other day he said that he would visit me again very soon, but he didn't come. (To Niranjan) That is why Rakhal asked you why you didn't come to see me while you were at Āriādaha, so near Dakshineswar."

NIRANJAN: "I was there only a couple of days."

MASTER (*to Niranjan, pointing to M.*) "He is the headmaster of a school. At my bidding he went to see you. (*To M.*) Did you send Baburam to me the other day?"

The Master went to an adjoining room and began to talk with some devotees there.

MASTER (*to M.*): "Ah! How wonderful was the yearning of the gopis for Krishna! They were seized with divine madness at the very sight of the black tamāla tree. Separation from Krishna created such a fire of anguish in Rādhā's heart that it dried up even the tears in her eyes! Her tears would disappear in steam. There were other times when nobody could notice the depth of her feeling. People do not notice the plunge of an elephant in a big lake."

M: "Yes, sir, that is true. Chaitanya, too, experienced a similar feeling. He mistook a forest for the sacred grove of Vrindāvan, and the dark water of the ocean for the blue Jamunā."

MASTER: "Ah! If anyone has but a particle of such prema! What yearning! What love! Rādhā possessed not only one hundred per cent of divine love, but one hundred and twenty-five per cent. This is what it means to be intoxicated with ecstatic love of God. The sum and substance of the whole matter is that a man must love God, must be restless for Him. It doesn't matter whether you believe in God with form or in God without form. You may or may not believe that God incarnates Himself as man. But you will realize Him if you have that yearning. Then He Himself will let you know what He is like. If you must be mad, why should you be mad for the things of the world? If you must be mad, be mad for God alone."

Presently Sri Ramakrishna returned to the main hall of the house. A big pillow was placed near him for his use. Before touching it he said, "Om Tat Sat."[2] Perhaps the pillow had been used by many worldly people, and that was why he purified it in this way. Bhavanath, M., and other devotees sat near him. It was getting late, but there was no indication that the meal was going to be served. The Master became impatient, like a child, and said: "I don't see any sign of food. What's the matter? Where is Narendra?"

A DEVOTEE (*with a smile*): "Sir, Ram Babu is the manager of the feast. He is superintending everything."

MASTER (*laughing*): "Oh, Ram is the manager! Then we know what to expect."

A DEVOTEE: "Things like this always happen when he is the supervisor." (*All laugh.*)

MASTER (*to the devotees*): "Where is Surendra? What a nice disposition he has now! He is very outspoken; he isn't afraid to speak the truth. He is unstinting in his liberality. No one that goes to him for help comes away empty-handed. (*To M.*) You went to Bhagavan Das.[3] What sort of man is he?"

---

[2] A sacred formula of the Hindu religion, meaning, "The Lord is the only Reality."

[3] A great Vaishnava devotee.

M: "He is very old now. I saw him at Kālnā. It was night. He lay on a carpet and a devotee fed him with food that had been offered to God. He can hear only if one speaks loudly into his ear. Hearing me mention your name he said, 'You have nothing to worry about.'"

BHAVANATH (to M.): "You haven't been to Dakshineswar for a long time. The Master asked me about you and said one day, 'Has M. lost all taste for this place?'"

Bhavanath laughed as he said these words. The Master heard their conversation and said to M. in a loving voice: "Yes, that is true. Why haven't you been to Dakshineswar for such a long time?" M. could only stammer some lame excuses.

Just then Mahimacharan arrived. He lived at Cossipore near Calcutta. Mahimacharan held the Master in great respect and was a frequent visitor at the temple garden. He was a man of independent means, having inherited some ancestral property. He devoted his time to religious thought and to the study of the scriptures. He was a man of some scholarship, having studied many books, both Sanskrit and English.

MASTER (to Mahima): "What is this? I see a steamship here. (All laugh.) We expect here a small boat at the most, but a real steamship has arrived. But then I know. It's the rainy season!" (Laughter.)

The Master was conversing with Mahimacharan. He asked him: "Isn't feeding people a kind of service to God? God exists in all beings as fire. To feed people is to offer oblations to that Indwelling Spirit. But then one shouldn't feed the wicked, I mean people who are entangled in gross worldliness or who have committed heinous crimes like adultery. Even the ground where such people sit becomes impure to a depth of seven cubits. Once Hriday fed a number of people at his native place. A good many of them were wicked. I said to Hriday: 'Look here. If you feed such people I shall leave your house at once.' (To Mahima) I hear that you used to feed people; but now you don't give any such feasts. Is it because your expenses have gone up?" (Laughter.)

The meal was to be served on the south verandah of the house. Leaf-plates were being placed on the floor. The Master said to Mahimacharan: "Please go there and see what they are doing. You may help them a little in serving the food. But I shouldn't ask you." Mahimacharan said: "Let them bring in the food. I shall see." Hemming and hawing, he went toward the kitchen, but presently he came back.

Sri Ramakrishna and the devotees enjoyed the meal greatly. Afterwards he rested awhile. About two o'clock in the afternoon Pratap Chandra Mazumdar of the Brāhmo Samāj arrived. He was a co-worker of Keshab Chandra Sen and had been to Europe and America in connection with the Brāhmo missionary work. He greeted Sri Ramakrishna, and the Master, too, bowed before him with his usual modesty. They were soon engaged in conversation.

PRATAP: "I have been to Darjeeling recently for a change of air."

MASTER: "But your health hasn't much improved. What are you suffering from?"

PRATAP: "The same illness that Keshab died of."

They began to talk about Keshab. Pratap said: "Even in boyhood he showed non-attachment to worldly things, seldom making merry with other boys. He was a student in the Hindu College. At that time he became friendly with Satyendra and through him made the acquaintance of his father, Devendranath Tagore. Keshab cultivated bhakti and at the same time practised meditation. At times he would be so much overcome with divine love that he would become unconscious. The main purpose of his life was to introduce religion among householders."

The conversation next turned to a certain Mārhāttā lady.

PRATAP: "Some women of our country have been to England. This Mārhāttā lady, who is very scholarly, also visited England. Later she embraced Christianity. Have you heard her name, sir?"

MASTER: "No. But from what you say it seems to me that she has a desire for name and fame. That kind of egotism is not good. The feeling 'I am the doer' is the outcome of ignorance. But the feeling that God does everything is due to knowledge. God alone is the Doer; all others are mere instruments in His hands.

"The misfortune that befalls a man on account of his egotism can be realized if you only think of the condition of the calf. The calf says, 'Hāmmā! Hāmmā!', that is, 'I! I!' And just look at its misfortune! At times it is yoked to the plough and made to work in the field from sunup to sundown, rain or shine. Again, it may be slaughtered by the butcher. In that case the flesh is eaten and the skin tanned into hide. From the hide shoes are made. People put on these shoes and walk on the rough ground. Still that is not the end of its misfortunes. Drums are made from its skin and mercilessly beaten with sticks. At last its entrails are made into strings for the bow used in carding cotton. When used by the carder the string gives the sound 'Tuhu! Tuhu!', 'Thou! Thou!'—that is, 'It is Thou, O Lord! It is Thou!' It no longer says, 'Hāmmā! Hāmmā!', 'I! I!' Only then does the calf's trouble come to an end, and it is liberated. It doesn't return to the world of action.

"Likewise, when the embodied soul says: 'O God, I am not the doer; Thou art the Doer. I am the machine and Thou art its Operator', only then does its suffering of worldly life come to an end; only then does it obtain liberation. It no longer has to be reborn in this world of action."

A DEVOTEE: "How can a man get rid of his ego?"

MASTER: "You cannot get rid of it until you have realized God. If you find a person free from ego, then know for certain that he has seen God."

DEVOTEE: "What, sir, are the signs of God-vision?"

MASTER: "Yes, there are such signs. It is said in the *Bhāgavata* that a man who has seen God behaves sometimes like a child, sometimes like a ghoul, sometimes like an inert thing, and sometimes like a madman.

"The man who has seen God becomes like a child. He is beyond the three gunas; he is unattached to any of them. He behaves like a ghoul, for he maintains the same attitude toward things holy and unholy. Again, like a madman, he sometimes laughs and sometimes weeps. Now he dresses himself like a dandy and the next moment he goes entirely naked and roams about with his cloth under his arm. Therefore he seems to be a lunatic. Again, at times he sits motionless like an inert thing."

DEVOTEE: "Does the ego disappear altogether after the realization of God?"

MASTER: "Yes, sometimes God totally effaces the ego of His devotee, as in the state of samādhi. But in many cases He keeps a trace of ego. But that doesn't injure anybody. It is like the ego of a child. A five-year-old child no doubt says 'I', but that ego doesn't harm anybody. At the touch of the philosopher's stone, steel is turned into gold; the steel sword becomes a sword of gold. The gold sword has the form of a sword, no doubt, but it cannot injure anybody. One cannot cut anything with a gold sword.

(To Pratap) "You have been to England. Tell us what you saw there."

PRATAP: "The English people worship what you call 'gold'. Of course, there are also some good people in England, those who live an unattached life. But generally one finds there a great display of rajas in everything. I saw the same thing in America."

MASTER (to Pratap): "It is not in England alone that one sees attachment to worldly things. You see it everywhere. But remember that work is only the first step in spiritual life. God cannot be realized without sattva—love, discrimination, kindness, and so on. It is the very nature of rajas to involve a man in many worldly activities. That is why rajas degenerates into tamas. If a man is entangled in too many activities he surely forgets God. He becomes more and more attached to 'woman and gold'.

"But it is not possible for you to give up work altogether. Your very nature will lead you to it whether you like it or not. Therefore the scriptures ask you to work in a detached spirit, that is to say, not to crave the work's results. For example, you may perform devotions and worship, and practise austerities, but your aim is not to earn people's recognition or to increase your merit.

"To work in such a spirit of detachment is known as karmayoga. But it is very difficult. We are living in the Kaliyuga, when one easily becomes attached to one's actions. You may think you are working in a detached spirit, but attachment creeps into the mind from nobody knows where. You may worship in the temple or arrange a grand religious festival or feed many poor and starving people. You may think you have done all this without hankering after the results. But unknown to yourself the desire for name and fame has somehow crept into your mind. Complete detachment from the results of action is possible only for one who has seen God."

A DEVOTEE: "Then what is the way for those who have not seen God? Must they give up all the duties of the world?"

MASTER: "The best path for this age is bhaktiyoga, the path of bhakti prescribed by Nārada: to sing the name and glories of God and pray to Him with a longing heart, 'O God, give me knowledge, give me devotion, and reveal Thyself to me!' The path of karma is extremely difficult. Therefore one should pray: 'O God, make my duties fewer and fewer; and may I, through Thy grace, do the few duties that Thou givest me without any attachment to their results! May I have no desire to be involved in many activities!'

"It is not possible to give up work altogether. Even to think or to meditate is a kind of work. As you develop love for God, your worldly activities become fewer and fewer of themselves. And you lose all interest in them. Can one who has tasted a drink made of sugar candy enjoy a drink made of ordinary molasses?"

A DEVOTEE: "The English people always exhort us to be active. Isn't action the aim of life then?"

MASTER: "The aim of life is the attainment of God. Work is only a preliminary step; it can never be the end. Even unselfish work is only a means; it is not the end.

"Sambhu Mallick once said to me, 'Please bless me, sir, that I may spend all my money for good purposes, such as building hospitals and dispensaries, making roads, and digging wells.' I said to him: 'It will be good if you can do these things in a spirit of detachment. But that is very difficult. Whatever you may do, you must always remember that the aim of this life of yours is the attainment of God and not the building of hospitals and dispensaries. Suppose God appeared before you and said to you, "Accept a boon from Me." Would you then ask Him, "O God, build me some hospitals and dispensaries"? Or would you not rather pray to Him: "O God, may I have pure love at Your Lotus Feet! May I have Your uninterrupted vision!"? Hospitals, dispensaries, and all such things are unreal. God alone is real and all else unreal. Furthermore, after realizing God one feels that He alone is the Doer and we are but His instruments. Then why should we forget Him and destroy ourselves by being involved in too many activities? After realizing Him, one may, through His grace, become His instrument in building many hospitals and dispensaries.'

"Therefore I say again that work is only the first step. It can never be the goal of life. Devote yourself to spiritual practice and go forward. Through practice you will advance more and more in the path of God. At last you will come to know that God alone is real and all else is illusory, and that the goal of life is the attainment of God.

"Once upon a time a wood-cutter went into a forest to chop wood. There suddenly he met a brahmachāri. The holy man said to him, 'My good man, go forward.' On returning home the wood-cutter asked himself, 'Why did the brahmachāri tell me to go forward?' Some time passed. One day he remembered the brahmachāri's words. He said to himself, 'Today I shall go deeper into the forest.' Going deep into the forest, he discovered innumerable sandal-wood trees. He was very happy and returned with cart-loads of sandal-wood. He sold them in the market and became very rich.

"A few days later he again remembered the words of the holy man to go forward. He went deeper into the forest and discovered a silver-mine near a river. This was even beyond his dreams. He dug out silver from the mine and sold it in the market. He got so much money that he didn't even know how much he had.

"A few more days passed. One day he thought: 'The brahmachāri didn't ask me to stop at the silver-mine; he told me to go forward.' This time he went to the other side of the river and found a gold-mine. Then he exclaimed: 'Ah, just see! This is why he asked me to go forward.'

"Again, a few days afterwards, he went still deeper into the forest and found heaps of diamonds and other precious gems. He took these also and became as rich as the god of wealth himself.

"Therefore I say that, whatever you may do, you will find better and better things if only you go forward. You may feel a little ecstasy as the result of japa, but don't conclude from this that you have achieved everything in spiritual life. Work is by no means the goal of life. Go forward, and then you will be able to perform unselfish work. But again I say that it is most difficult to perform unselfish work. Therefore with love and longing in your heart pray to God: 'O God, grant me devotion at Thy Lotus Feet and reduce my worldly duties. Please grant me the boon that the few duties I must do may be done in a detached spirit.' If you go still farther you will realize God. You will see Him. In time you will converse with Him."

Next the conversation turned to the quarrels among the members of the Brāhmo Samāj. They had had a misunderstanding about the right to preach in the temple after Keshab's death.

MASTER (to Pratap): "I hear that some members of the Samāj have quarrelled with you about the altar. But they are most insignificant persons—mere nobodies.

(To the devotees): "People like Pratap and Amrita are like good conch-shells, which give out a loud sound. And the rest, about whom you hear so much, don't give out any sound at all." (All laugh.)

PRATAP: "Speaking of sounds, even such a worthless thing as a mango-stone makes a sound!"[4]

MASTER (to Pratap): "One can very well understand the inner feeling of a teacher of your Brāhmo Samāj by hearing his preaching. Once I went to a meeting of a Hari Sabhā. The preacher of the day was a pundit named Samadhyayi. And can you imagine what he said? He said in the course of his sermon: 'God is dry. We must make Him sweet and fresh with our love and devotion.' I was stunned to hear these words. Then I was reminded of a story. A boy once said: 'At my uncle's house there are many horses. Oh, yes! His whole cow-shed is full of them.' Now if it was really a cow-shed, then horses could not be kept there. Possibly he had only cows. What did people think on hearing such an incoherent statement? They believed that there were surely no such animals as horses in the shed." (Laughter.)

A DEVOTEE: "True, sir, there were not only no horses, but possibly there were also no cows!" (Laughter.)

MASTER: "Just fancy, to describe God, who is of the very nature of Love and Bliss, as dry! It only proves that the man has never experienced what God is like.

(To Pratap) "Let me tell you something. You are a learned and intelligent and serious-minded soul. Keshab and you were like the two brothers, Gaur and Nitāi. You have had enough of lectures, arguments, quarrels,

[4] The split stone of a mango, about to sprout, makes a sound when one blows through it.

discussions, and dissensions. Can such things interest you any more? Now gather your whole mind and direct it to God. Plunge deep into God."

PRATAP: "Yes, sir, you are right. That is surely my only duty now. But I am doing all these things only to perpetuate Keshab's name."

MASTER (*with a smile*): "No doubt you say now that you are doing all this to keep his name alive; but in a few days you won't feel that way. Listen to a story. A man had built a house on a hill. It was only a mud hut, but he had built it with great labour. A few days after, there came a violent storm and the hut began to rock. The man became very anxious to save it and prayed to the god of the winds, 'O god of the winds, please don't wreck the house!' But the god of the winds paid no heed to his prayer. The house was about to crash. Then he thought of a trick. He remembered that Hanumān was the son of the god of the winds. At once he cried out with great earnestness: 'O revered sir, please don't pull down the house. It belongs to Hanumān. I beseech you to protect it.' But still the house continued to shake violently. Nobody seemed to listen to his prayer. He repeated many times, 'Oh, this house belongs to Hanumān!' But the fury of the wind did not abate. Then he remembered that Hanumān was the devoted servant of Rāma, whose younger brother was Lakshmana. Desperately the man prayed, crying aloud, 'Oh, this house belongs to Lakshmana!' But that also failed to help matters. So the man cried out as a last resort: 'This is Rāma's house. Don't break it down, O god of the winds! I beseech you most humbly.' But this too proved futile, and the house began to crash down. Whereupon the man, who now had to save his own life, rushed out of it with the curse: 'Let it go! This is the devil's own hut!'

(*To Pratap*): "You don't have to perpetuate Keshab's name. Remember that he achieved all his success through the will of God. Through the divine will his work was established, and through the divine will it is disintegrating. What can you do about it? Now it is your bounden duty to give your entire mind to God, to plunge deep into the Ocean of His Love."

Saying these words the Master sang in his sweet voice:

> Dive deep, O mind, dive deep in the Ocean of God's Beauty;
> If you descend to the uttermost depths,
> There you will find the gem of Love.
>
> Go seek, O mind, go seek Vrindāvan in your heart,
> Where with His loving devotees
> Sri Krishna sports eternally.
>
> Light up, O mind, light up true wisdom's shining lamp,
> And let it burn with steady flame
> Unceasingly within your heart.
>
> Who is it that steers your boat across the solid earth?
> It is your guru, says Kubir;
> Meditate on his holy feet.

The Master continued, addressing Pratap: "Did you listen to the song? You have had enough of lectures and quarrels. Now dive deep into the Ocean of God. There is no fear of death from plunging into this Ocean, for this is the Ocean of Immortality. Don't think that this will make you lose your head. Never for a moment harbour the idea that by thinking too much of God one becomes insane. Once I said to Narendra—"

PRATAP: "Who is Narendra, sir?"

MASTER: "Oh, never mind. There is a young man of that name. I said to Narendra: 'Look here, my boy. God is the Ocean of Bliss. Don't you want to plunge into this Ocean? Suppose there is a cup of syrup and you are a fly. Where will you sit to sip the syrup?' Narendra said, 'I will sit on the edge of the cup and stick my head out to drink it.' 'Why?' said I. 'Why should you sit on the edge?' He replied, 'If I go far into the syrup, I shall be drowned and lose my life.' Then I said to him: 'But, my child, there is no such fear in the Ocean of Satchidānanda. It is the Ocean of Immortality. By plunging into It a man does not die; he becomes immortal. Man does not lose his consciousness by being mad about God.

(To the devotees) "The feeling of 'I' and 'mine' is ignorance. People say that Rāni Rasmani built the Kāli temple; but nobody says it was the work of God. They say that such and such a person established the Brāhmo Samāj; but nobody says it was founded through the will of God. This feeling, 'I am the doer', is ignorance. On the contrary, the idea, 'O God, Thou art the Doer and I am only an instrument; Thou art the Operator and I am the machine', is Knowledge. After attaining Knowledge a man says: 'O God, nothing belongs to me—neither this house of worship nor this Kāli temple nor this Brāhmo Samāj. These are all Thine. Wife, son, and family do not belong to me. They are all Thine.'

"To love these objects, regarding them as one's own, is māyā. But to love all things is dayā, compassion. To love only the members of the Brāhmo Samāj or of one's own family is māyā; to love one's own countrymen is māyā. But to love the people of all countries, to love the members of all religions, is dayā. Such love comes from love of God, from dayā.

"Māyā entangles a man and turns him away from God. But through dayā one realizes God. Sages like Sukadeva and Nārada always cherished dayā in their hearts."

PRATAP: "Revered sir, are those who live with you making progress in spiritual life?"

MASTER: "I tell people that there is nothing wrong in the life of the world. But they must live in the world as a maidservant lives in her master's house. Referring to her master's house, she says, 'That is our house.' But her real home is perhaps in a far-away village. Pointing out her master's house to others, she says, no doubt, 'This is our house', but in her heart she knows very well that it doesn't belong to her and that her own house is in a far-away village. She brings up her master's son and says, 'My Hari has grown very naughty', or 'My Hari doesn't like sweets.' Though she repeats, 'My Hari' with her lips, yet she knows in her heart that Hari doesn't belong to her, that he is her master's son.

"Thus I say to those who visit me: 'Why don't you live in the world? There is no harm in that. But always keep your mind on God. Know for certain that house, family, and property are not yours. They are God's. Your real home is in God.' Also I ask them to pray always with a longing heart for love of God's Lotus Feet."

Again the conversation turned to the English people. A devotee said, "Sir, I understand that nowadays the pundits of England do not believe in the existence of God."

PRATAP: "However they may talk, I don't believe that any of them is a real atheist. Many of them have had to admit that there is a great power behind the activities of the universe."

MASTER: "Well, that is enough. They believe in Śakti, don't they? Then why should they be atheists?"

PRATAP: "They also believe in the moral government of the universe."

Pratap was now about to take leave of the Master.

MASTER (to Pratap): "What more shall I say to you? My only request is that you do not involve yourself in quarrels and dissensions any more. Another thing. It is 'woman and gold' that keeps men away from God. That is the barrier. Don't you find that everyone has nothing but praise for his own wife? (All laugh.) A wife may be good or bad; but if you ask her husband about her he will always say, 'Oh, she is very good—'"

At this point Pratap bade the Master good-bye. He did not wait to hear the end of Sri Ramakrishna's words about the renunciation of "woman and gold". Those burning words touched the hearts of the devotees and were carried away on the wind through the gently rustling leaves in the garden.

A few minutes later Mani Mallick said to Sri Ramakrishna: "Sir, it is time for you to leave for Dakshineswar. Today Keshab's mother and the other ladies of his family are going to the temple garden to visit you. They will be hurt if they do not find you there."

Keshab had passed away only a few months before. His old mother and his other relatives wanted to visit the Master.

MASTER (to Mani Mallick): "Don't hurry me, please. I didn't sleep well. I can't rush. They are going to Dakshineswar. What am I to do about it? They will stroll in the garden and enjoy it thoroughly."

After resting a little the Master was ready to leave for Dakshineswar. He was thinking of Surendra's welfare. He visited the different rooms, softly chanting the holy name of God. Suddenly he stood still and said: "I didn't eat any luchi at meal-time. Bring me a little now." He ate only a crumb and said: "There is much meaning in my asking for the luchi. If I should remember that I hadn't eaten any at Surendra's house, then I should want to come back for it." (All laugh.)

MANI MALLICK: "That would have been nice. Then we too should have come with you."

The devotees laughed.

Friday, June 20, 1884

It was dusk. Sri Ramakrishna was sitting in his room, absorbed in contemplation of the Divine Mother. Now and then he was chanting Her name. Rakhal, Adhar, M., and several other devotees were with him.

After a while the evening worship began in the temples. Adhar left the room to see the worship. Sri Ramakrishna and M. conversed.

MASTER: "Tell me, does Baburam intend to continue his studies? I said to him, 'Continue your studies to set an example to others.' After Sītā had been set free, Bibhishana refused to become king of Ceylon. Rāma said to him: 'You should become king to open the eyes of the ignorant. Otherwise they will ask you what you have gained as a result of serving Me. They will be pleased to see you acquire the kingdom.'

"I noticed the other day that Baburam, Bhavanath, and Harish have a feminine nature. In a vision I saw Baburam as a goddess with a necklace around her neck and with woman companions about her. He has received something in a dream. His body is pure. Only a very little effort will awaken his spiritual consciousness.

"You see, I am having some difficulty about my physical needs. It will be nice if Baburam lives with me. The nature of these attendants of mine is undergoing a change. Latu is always tense with spiritual emotion. He is about to merge himself in God. Rakhal is getting into such a spiritual mood that he can't do anything even for himself. I have to get water for him. He isn't of much service to me.

"Among the youngsters Baburam and Niranjan are rather exceptional. If other boys come in the future, they will, it seems to me, receive instruction and then go away.

"But I don't want Baburam to tear himself away from his family. It may make trouble at home. (Smiling) When I ask him, 'Why don't you come?', he says, 'Why not make me come?'. He looks at Rakhal and weeps. He says, 'Rakhal is very happy here.'

"Rakhal now lives here as one of the family. I know that he will never again be attached to the world. He says that worldly enjoyments have become tasteless to him. His wife came here on her way to Konnagar. She is fourteen. He too was asked to go to Konnagar, but he didn't go. He said, 'I don't like merriment and gaiety.'

"What do you think of Niranjan?"

M: "He is very handsome."

MASTER: "No, I am not asking about his looks. He is guileless. One can easily realize God if one is free from guile. Spiritual instruction produces quick results in a guileless heart. Such a heart is like well cultivated land from which all the stones have been removed. No sooner is the seed sown than it germinates. The fruit also appears quickly.

"Niranjan will not marry. It is 'woman and gold' that causes entanglement. Isn't that so?"

M: "Yes, sir."

MASTER: "What will one gain by renouncing betel-leaf and tobacco? The real renunciation is the renunciation of 'woman and gold'.

"I came to know in an ecstatic mood that, though Niranjan had accepted a job in an office, he would not be stained by it. He is earning money for his mother. There is no harm in that.

"The work you are doing won't injure you either. What you are doing is good. Suppose a clerk is sent to jail; he is shut up there and chained, and at last he is released. Does he cut capers after his release? Of course not. He works again as a clerk. It is not your intention to accumulate money. You only want to support your family. Otherwise, where will they go?"

M: "I shall be relieved if someone takes charge of them."

MASTER: "That is true. But now do 'this' as well as 'that'."[5]

M: "It is great luck to be able to renounce everything."

MASTER: "That is true. But people act according to their inherent tendencies. You have a few more duties to perform. After these are over you will have peace. Then you will be released. A man cannot easily get out of the hospital once his name is registered there. He is discharged only when he is completely cured.

"The devotees who come here may be divided into two groups. One group says, 'O God, give me liberation.' Another group, belonging to the inner circle, doesn't talk that way. They are satisfied if they can know two things: first, who I[6] am; second, who they are and what their relationship to me is. You belong to this second group; otherwise . . .

"Bhavanath, Baburam, and a few others have a feminine nature. Harish sleeps in a woman's cloth. Baburam says that he too likes the womanly attitude. So I am right. Bhavanath also is like that. But Narendra, Rakhal, and Niranjan have a masculine nature.

"Please tell me one thing. What is the significance of my having hurt my arm? Once my teeth were broken while I was in a state of ecstasy. It is the arm this time."

Seeing M. silent, the Master himself continued the conversation.

MASTER: "My arm was broken in order to destroy my ego to its very root. Now I cannot find my ego within myself any more. When I search for it I see God alone. One can never attain God without completely getting rid of the ego. You must have noticed that the chātak bird has its nest on the ground but soars up very high.

"Captain says I haven't acquired any occult powers because I eat fish. I tremble with fear lest I should acquire those powers. If I should have them, then this place would be turned into a hospital or a dispensary. People would flock here and ask me to cure their illness. Is it good to have occult powers?"

M: "No, sir. You have said to us that a man cannot realize God if he possesses even one of the eight occult powers."

MASTER: "Right you are. Only the small-minded seek them. If one asks something of a rich man, one no longer receives any favour from him. The rich man doesn't allow such a person to ride in the same carriage with him. Even if he does, he doesn't allow the man to sit near him. Therefore love without any selfish motive is best.

"God with form and the formless God are both equally true. What do you say? One cannot keep one's mind on the formless God a long time. That is why God assumes form for His devotees.

"Captain makes a nice remark in this connexion. He says that when a

[5] That is to say, both worldly duty and spiritual practice.
[6] Referring to himself.

bird gets tired of soaring very high it perches on a tree and rests. First is the formless God, and then comes God with form.

"I shall have to go to your house once. I saw in a vision that the houses of Adhar, Balaram, and Surendra were so many 'places for our forgathering. But it makes no difference to me whether they come here or not."

M: "That's right. Why shouldn't it be so? One must feel misery if one feels happiness. But you are beyond both."

MASTER: "Yes. Further, I think of the magician and his magic. The magician alone is real. His magic is illusory, like a dream. I realized this when I heard the *Chandi* recited. Sumbha and Nisumbha[7] were scarcely born when I learnt that they both were dead."

M: "Yes, sir. Once I was going to Kālnā with Gangadhar in a steamer. A country boat struck our ship and sank with twenty or twenty-five passengers. They all disappeared in the water, like foam churned up by the steamer.

"May I ask you one thing? Does a man watching magic really feel compassion when he sees suffering in the performance? Does he feel, at that time, any sense of responsibility? One thinks of compassion only when one feels responsibility. Isn't that so?"

MASTER: "A jnāni sees everything at once—God, māyā, the universe, and living beings. He sees that vidyāmāyā, avidyāmāyā, the universe, and all living beings exist and at the same time do not exist. As long as he is conscious of 'I', he is conscious of 'others' too. Nothing whatsoever exists after he cuts through the whole thing with the sword of jnāna. Then even his 'I' becomes as unreal as the magic of the magician."

M. was reflecting on these words, when the Master said: "Do you know what it is like? It is as if there were a flower with twenty-five layers of petals, and you cut them all with one stroke.

"The idea of responsibility! Goodness gracious! Men like Sankarāchārya and Sukadeva kept the 'ego of Knowledge'. It is not for man to show compassion, but for God. One feels compassion as long as one has the 'ego of Knowledge'. And it is God Himself who has become the 'ego of Knowledge'.

"You may feel a thousand times that it is all magic; but you are still under the control of the Divine Mother. You cannot escape Her. You are not free. You must do what She makes you do. A man attains Brahmajnāna only when it is given to him by the Ādyāsakti, the Divine Mother. Then alone does he see the whole thing as magic; otherwise not.

"As long as the slightest trace of ego remains, one lives within the jurisdiction of the Ādyāsakti. One is under Her sway. One cannot go beyond Her.

"With the help of the Ādyāsakti, God sports as an Incarnation. God, through His Sakti, incarnates Himself as man. Then alone does it become possible for the Incarnation to carry on His work. Everything is due to the Sakti of the Divine Mother.

"When anyone asked the former manager of the temple garden a great favour, the manager would say, 'Come after two or three days.' He must ask the proprietor's permission.

---

[7] Two demons mentioned in the *Chandi*, who were killed by the Divine Mother.

"God will incarnate Himself as Kalki at the end of the Kaliyuga. He will be born as the son of a brāhmin. Suddenly and unexpectedly a sword and horse will come to him. . . ."

Adhar returned to the Master's room after watching the evening worship in the temples.

MASTER (*to Adhar and the others*): "Bhuvan was here and brought me twenty-five Bombay mangoes and some sweets. She said to me, 'Will you eat a mango?' I said, 'My stomach is heavy today.' And to tell you the truth, I am feeling uncomfortable after eating a few of the sweets."

Bhuvanmohini was a nurse who used to visit Sri Ramakrishna now and then. The Master could not eat the food offerings of everyone, especially of physicians and nurses. It was because they accepted money from the sick in spite of the suffering of these people.

MASTER: "Keshab Sen's mother, sisters, and other relatives came here; so I had to dance a little. I had to entertain them. What else could I do? They were so grief-stricken!"

PUNDIT SHASHADHAR

Wednesday, June 25, 1884

IT WAS THE DAY of the Rathayātrā, the Car Festival of the Hindus. At Ishan's invitation Sri Ramakrishna went to his house in Calcutta. For some time the Master had had a desire to meet Pundit Shashadhar Tarkachudāmani, who had been staying with one of Ishan's neighbours. So it was decided that he would visit the pundit in the afternoon.

A few devotees, including Hazra, accompanied the Master to Ishan's house. Ishan had invited one or two brāhmin scholars and a devotee who followed the Tāntrik method of worship. Shrish and Ishan's other sons were also present.

The Master noticed that the Tāntrik worshipper had a vermilion mark on his forehead, and smilingly said, "I see he is branded."

After a while M. and Narendra arrived and bowed before Sri Ramakrishna. The Master had previously informed M. that he would be at Ishan's house.

The Master joked about the delay in serving their meal. One of the scholars quoted a Sanskrit verse about the anxiety created in people's minds by the pangs of hunger. Proceeding to explain the verse he said: "The study of philosophy is indeed edifying, but poetry is more fascinating than philosophy. People listening to good poems think of the study of philosophy —Vedānta, Nyāya, Sāmkhya, and so forth—as dry and insipid. Again, music is more attractive than poetry. Music melts even a heart of stone. But a beautiful woman has an even greater attraction for a man's heart than music. Such a woman, passing by, diverts a man's attention from both poetry and music. But when a man feels the pangs of hunger, everything else—poetry, music, and woman—appears as of no consequence. Thus hunger is the most arresting thing."

The Master remarked with a smile, "The pundit is witty."

Soon Narendra began to sing. A few moments later the Master went upstairs for a little rest. M. and Shrish accompanied him. M. introduced Shrish to the Master, saying: "He is a scholar and a man of peaceful nature. We were fellow students in our boyhood. Now he is a lawyer."

MASTER: "It is a pity that such a man should practise law."

M: "Yes, sir. It was a mistake on his part."

MASTER: "I know a few lawyers. One of them shows me great respect. He is a straightforward man. (*To Shrish*) What is your idea about the most essential thing in life?"

SHRISH: "God exists and He alone does everything. But the attributes we ascribe to Him are not the right ones. How can a man conceive of Him? His nature is infinite."

MASTER: "What need is there of your counting the number of trees and branches in an orchard? You have come to the orchard to eat mangoes. Do that and be happy. The aim of human birth is to love God. Realize that love and be at peace.

"Suppose you have entered a tavern for a drink. Is it necessary for you to know how many gallons of wine there are in the tavern? One glass is enough for you. What need is there of your knowing the infinite qualities of God? You may discriminate for millions of years about God's attributes and still you will not know them."

The Master remained silent a few minutes. A brāhmin pundit came into the room.

MASTER (*to M.*): "There is no substance whatsoever in the worldly life. The members of Ishan's family are good; so he has some peace here. Suppose his sons had been lewd, disobedient, and addicted to drink and other vices. Then there would have been no end to his troubles. One very seldom comes across such a religious family, in which all the members are devoted to God. I have seen only two or three such families. Generally one finds quarrels, misunderstanding, jealousy, and friction. Besides, there are disease, grief, and poverty in the world. Seeing this condition, I prayed to the Divine Mother, 'O Mother, turn my mind at once from the world to God.'

"Look at Narendra's troubles. His father is dead and the members of his family are starving. He has been trying his utmost to secure a position, but he has not yet found one. Just see how unsettled his mind is!

(*To M.*) "You used to come to Dakshineswar very frequently. But why have you become such a rare visitor? Perhaps you have become particularly friendly with your wife. Is it true? Why should I blame you? The influence of 'woman and gold' is everywhere. Therefore I pray, 'O Divine Mother, please don't make me a worldly man if I am to be born again in a human body.'"

BRĀHMIN SCHOLAR: "Why should you say that, sir? The scriptures extol the life of a householder."

MASTER: "Yes, that is true. But it is very difficult to lead the true life of a householder. (*To M.*) How wrong of us! They are singing, especially Narendra, and we have left the room."

About four o'clock in the afternoon the Master left in a carriage for the house where Pundit Shashadhar was staying. As soon as Sri Ramakrishna got into the carriage he went into samādhi. His physical frame was very tender as a result of the austerities he had undergone during the long years of his spiritual discipline and his constant absorption in God-Consciousness. The Master would suffer from the slightest physical discomfort and even from the vibration of worldly thoughts around him. Once Keshab Chandra Sen had said that Sri Ramakrishna, Christ, and Sri Chaitanya belonged to a delicate species of humanity that should be kept in a glass case and protected from the vulgar contact of the world.

It was the rainy season, and a fine drizzle of rain had made the road muddy. The sky was overcast. The devotees followed the carriage on foot. As the carriage stopped in front of the house, the host and his relatives welcomed the Master and took him upstairs to the drawing-room. There the Master met the pundit.

Pundit Shashadhar, a man of fair complexion and no longer young, had a string of rudrāksha beads around his neck. He was one of the renowned Sanskrit scholars of his time—a pillar of orthodox Hinduism, which had reasserted itself after the first wave of Christianity and Western culture had passed over Hindu society. His clear exposition of the Hindu scriptures, his ringing sincerity, and his stirring eloquence had brought back a large number of the educated young Hindus of Bengal to the religion of their forefathers.

The pundit saluted the Master with reverence. Narendra, Rakhal, Ram, Hazra, and M., who had come with the Master, seated themselves in the room as near the Master as they could, anxious not to miss one of his words.

At the sight of the pundit the Master again went into samādhi. After a while, still remaining in that state, he looked at the pundit and said with a smile, "Very well, very well." Then, addressing the pundit, the Master said, "Tell me how you give lectures."

PUNDIT: "Sir, I try to explain the teachings of the Hindu scriptures."

MASTER: "For the Kaliyuga the path of devotion described by Nārada is best. Where can people find time now to perform their duties according to the scriptural injunctions? Nowadays the decoctions of roots and herbs of the orthodox Hindu physicians cannot be given to a fever patient. By the time that kind of medicine begins its slow process of curing, the patient is done for. Therefore only a drastic medicine like the allopathic 'fever mixture' is effective now. You may ask people to practise scriptural rites and rituals; but, when prescribing the rituals, remove the 'head and tail'.[1] I tell people not to bother about the elaborate rituals of the sandhyā as enjoined in the scriptures. I say that it will be enough for them to repeat the Gāyatri alone. If you must give instruction about scriptural ceremonies, do so only to a very few, like Ishan.

"You may deliver thousands of lectures, but they won't make the slightest impression on worldly people. Can one drive a nail into a stone wall? The point of the nail will sooner break than make a dent in the stone. What will you gain by striking the tough skin of the crocodile with a sword? The sādhu's water-bowl, made from the shell of a bitter gourd, may visit the four principal holy places of India with its owner, but it will still remain as bitter as ever. Your lectures are not helping worldly people very much; and

[1] The non-essential parts. The allusion is to the head and tail of fish, which are non-essential.

you will realize this by and by. The calf cannot stand on its legs all at once. Now it drops to the ground and now it stands up. So it learns to stand firmly on its legs and walk.

"You cannot distinguish a lover of God from a worldly person. It isn't your fault, of course. When the first onrush of the gale shakes the trees, it is impossible to distinguish one tree from another—the mango from the tamarind, for instance.

"Without having realized God one cannot give up rituals altogether. How long should one practise the sandhyā and other forms of ritualistic worship? As long as one does not shed tears of joy at the name of God and feel a thrill in one's body. You will know that your ritualistic worship has come to an end when your eyes become filled with tears as you repeat 'Om Rāma'. Then you do not have to continue your sandhyā or other rituals.

"When the fruit appears the blossom drops off. Love of God is the fruit, and rituals are the blossom. When the daughter-in-law of the house becomes pregnant, she cannot do much work. Her mother-in-law gradually lessens her duties in the house. When her time arrives she does practically nothing. And after the child is born her only work is to play with it. She doesn't do any household duties at all. The sandhyā merges in the Gāyatri, the Gāyatri in Om, and Om in samādhi. It is like the sound of a bell: t—a—m. The yogi, by following in the trail of the sound Om, gradually merges himself in the Supreme Brahman. His sandhyā and other ritualistic duties disappear in samādhi. Thus the duties of the jnāni come to an end."

As the Master talked of samādhi, he himself went into that state. His face radiated a heavenly light. Bereft of outer consciousness, he could not utter another word. His gaze was indrawn and transfixed in communion with the Self. After a long time the Master began to recognize the world around him and said, like a child, "I shall have a drink of water." Whenever after samādhi the Master asked for a drink of water, his devotees knew that he was gradually becoming conscious of the outer world.

Still lingering in the state of ecstasy, he said to the Divine Mother: "O Mother, the other day You showed me Pundit Iswar Chandra Vidyāsāgar. Then I told You that I should like to see another pundit, and so You have brought me here."

Looking at the pundit, he said: "My child, add a little more to your strength. Practise spiritual discipline a few days more. You have hardly set your foot on the tree, yet you expect to lay hold of a big cluster of fruit. But, of course, you are doing all this for the welfare of others." With these words he bowed his head before the pundit.

The Master continued: "When I first heard about you, I inquired whether you were merely erudite or whether you had discrimination and renunciation. A pundit who doesn't know how to discriminate between the Real and the unreal is no pundit at all.

"There is no harm in teaching others if the preacher has a commission from the Lord. Nobody can confound a preacher who teaches people after having received the command of God. Getting a ray of light from the goddess of learning, a man becomes so powerful that before him big scholars seem mere earthworms.

"When the lamp is lighted the moths come in swarms. They don't have to be invited. In the same way, the preacher who has a commission from God need not invite people to hear him. He doesn't have to announce the time of his lectures. He possesses such irresistible attraction that people come to him of their own accord. People of all classes, even kings and aristocrats, gather around him. They say to him: 'Revered sir, what can we offer you? Here are mangoes, sweets, money, shawls, and other things. What will you be pleased to accept?' In that case I say to them: 'Go away. I don't care for these. I don't want anything.'

"Does the magnet say to the iron, 'Come near me?' That is not necessary. Because of the attraction of the magnet, the iron rushes to it.

"Such a preacher may not be a scholarly person, but don't conclude from that that he has any lack of wisdom. Does book-learning make one wise? He who has a commission from God never runs short of wisdom. That wisdom comes from God; it is inexhaustible. At Kāmārpukur I have seen people measuring grain. It lies in a heap. One man keeps pushing grain from the heap toward another man, who weighs it on a scales. So the man who weighs doesn't run short of grain. It is the same with the preacher who has received a commission from God. As he teaches people, the Divine Mother Herself supplies him with fresh knowledge from behind. That knowledge never comes to an end.

"Can a preacher ever lack knowledge if but once he is favoured with a benign glance from the Divine Mother? Therefore I ask you whether you have received any commission from God."

HAZRA: "Oh yes, he must have it. (*To the pundit*) Isn't it true, sir?"

PUNDIT: "Commission? No, sir, I am afraid I haven't received any such thing."

HOST: "He may not have received the commission, but he preaches from a sense of duty."

MASTER: "What will a man accomplish by mere lectures without the commission from God? Once a Brāhmo preacher said in the course of his sermon, 'Friends, how much I used to drink!' and so on. Hearing this the people began to whisper among themselves: 'What is this fool saying? He used to drink!' Now these words produced a very unfavourable effect. This shows that preaching cannot bring a good result unless it comes from a good man.

"A high government official from Barisāl once said to me, 'Sir, if you begin the work of preaching, I too shall gird my loins.' I told him the story of people's dirtying the bank of the Hāldārpukur and of its being stopped only when a constable, armed with authority from the government, put up a notice prohibiting it.

"So I say, a worthless man may talk his head off preaching, and yet he will produce no effect. But people will listen to him if he is armed with a badge of authority from God. One cannot teach others without the commission from God. A teacher of men must have great power. There's many a

Hanumanpuri[2] in Calcutta. It is with them that you will have to wrestle. *(Pointing to the people assembled there)* These are mere sheep!

"Chaitanyadeva was an Incarnation of God. How little is left of what he accomplished—not to speak of a lecturer who preaches without authority from God! What good will a lecturer do?

"Therefore I say to you, dive deep in God-Consciousness."

Saying this, the Master began to sing in an ecstasy of love for God:

> Dive deep, O mind, dive deep in the Ocean of God's Beauty;
> If you descend to the uttermost depths,
> There you will find the gem of Love. . . .

The Master continued: "One does not die if one sinks in this Ocean. This is the Ocean of Immortality. Once I said to Narendra: 'God is the Ocean of Bliss. Tell me if you want to plunge into It. Just imagine there is some syrup in a cup and that you have become a fly. Now tell me where you will sit to sip the syrup.' Narendra answered: 'I will sit on the edge of the cup and stretch out my neck to drink, because I am sure to die if I go far into the cup.' Then I said to him: 'But my child, this is the Ocean of Satchidānanda. There is no fear of death in It. This is the Ocean of Immortality. Only ignorant people say that one should not have an excess of devotion and divine love. How foolish! Can there be any excess of divine love?'

(To the pundit) "Therefore I say to you, dive into the Ocean of Satchidānanda. Nothing will ever worry you if you but realize God. Then you will get His commission to teach people.

"There are innumerable pathways leading to the Ocean of Immortality. The essential thing is to reach the Ocean. It doesn't matter which path you follow. Imagine that there is a reservoir containing the Elixir of Immortality. You will be immortal if a few drops of the Elixir somehow get into your mouth. You may get into the reservoir either by jumping into it, or by being pushed into it from behind, or by slowly walking down the steps. The effect is one and the same. You will become immortal by tasting a drop of that Elixir.

"Innumerable are the ways that lead to God. There are the paths of jnāna, of karma, and of bhakti. If you are sincere, you will attain God in the end, whichever path you follow. Roughly speaking, there are three kinds of yoga: jnānayoga, karmayoga, and bhaktiyoga.

"What is jnānayoga? The jnāni seeks to realize Brahman. He discriminates, saying, 'Not this, not this'. He discriminates, saying, 'Brahman is real and the universe illusory.' He discriminates between the Real and the unreal. As he comes to the end of discrimination, he goes into samādhi and attains the Knowledge of Brahman.

"What is karmayoga? Its aim is to fix one's mind on God by means of work. That is what you are teaching. It consists of breath-control,[3] concentration, meditation, and so on, done in a spirit of detachment. If a householder performs his duties in the world in a spirit of detachment, surrender-

---

[2] A noted wrestler of the time.
[3] Breathing exercises as prescribed in rājayoga.

ing the results to God and with devotion to God in his heart, he too may be said to practise karmayoga. Further, if a person performs worship, japa, and other forms of devotion, surrendering the results to God, he may be said to practise karmayoga. Attainment of God alone is the aim of karmayoga.

"What is bhaktiyoga? It is to keep the mind on God by chanting His name and glories. For the Kaliyuga the path of devotion is easiest. This is indeed the path for this age.

"The path of karma is very difficult. First of all, as I have just said, where will one find the time for it nowadays? Where is the time for a man to perform his duties as enjoined in the scriptures? Man's life is short in this age. Further, it is extremely difficult to perform one's duties in a spirit of detachment, without craving the result. One cannot work in such a spirit without first having realized God. Attachment to the result somehow enters the mind, though you may not be aware of it.

"To follow jnānayoga in this age is also very difficult. First, a man's life depends entirely on food. Second, he has a short span of life. Third, he can by no means get rid of body-consciousness; and the Knowledge of Brahman is impossible without the destruction of body-consciousness. The jnāni says: 'I am Brahman; I am not the body. I am beyond hunger and thirst, disease and grief, birth and death, pleasure and pain.' How can you be a jnāni if you are conscious of disease, grief, pain, pleasure, and the like? A thorn enters your flesh, blood flows from the wound, and you suffer very badly from the pain; but nevertheless if you are a jnāni you must be able to say: 'Why, there is no thorn in my flesh at all. Nothing is the matter with me.'

"Therefore bhaktiyoga is prescribed for this age. By following this path one comes to God more easily than by following the others. One can undoubtedly reach God by following the paths of jnāna and karma, but they are very difficult paths.

"Bhaktiyoga is the religion for this age. But that does not mean that the lover of God will reach one goal and the philosopher and worker another. It means that if a person seeks the Knowledge of Brahman he can attain It by following the path of bhakti, too. God, who loves His devotee, can give him the Knowledge of Brahman if He so desires.

"But the bhakta wants to realize the Personal God endowed with form and talk to Him. He seldom seeks the Knowledge of Brahman. But God, who does everything at His pleasure, can make His devotee the heir to His infinite glories if it pleases Him. He gives His devotee both the Love of God and the Knowledge of Brahman. If one is able somehow to reach Calcutta, one can see the Maidān and the museum and other places too. The thing is how to reach Calcutta.

"By realizing the Divine Mother of the Universe, you will get Knowledge as well as Devotion. You will get both. In bhāva samādhi you will see the form of God, and in nirvikalpa samādhi you will realize Brahman, the Absolute Existence-Knowledge-Bliss. In nirvikalpa samādhi ego, name, and form do not exist.

"A lover of God prays to the Divine Mother: 'O Mother, I am very much afraid of selfish actions. Such actions have desires behind them, and if I perform them I shall have to reap their fruit. But it is very difficult to work in a detached spirit. I shall certainly forget Thee, O Mother, if I involve myself in selfish actions. Therefore I have no use for them. May my actions, O Divine Mother, be fewer every day till I attain Thee. May I perform, without attachment to the results, only what action is absolutely necessary for me. May I have great love for Thee as I go on with my few duties. May I not entangle myself in new work so long as I do not realize Thee. But I shall perform it if I receive Thy command. Otherwise not.' "

PUNDIT: "How far did you go in visiting the sacred places?"

MASTER: "Oh, I visited a few places. (*With a smile*) But Hazra went farther and also climbed higher. He visited Hrishikesh, but I didn't go so far or so high.

"You must have noticed kites and vultures soaring very high in the sky; but their eyes are always fixed on the charnel-pits. Do you know the meaning of 'charnel-pits'? It is 'woman and gold'.

"What is the use of making pilgrimages if you can attain love of God remaining where you are? I have been to Benares and noticed the same trees there as here. The same green tamarind-leaves!

"Pilgrimage becomes futile if it does not enable you to attain love of God. Love of God is the one essential and necessary thing. Do you know the meaning of 'kites and vultures'? There are many people who talk big and who say that they have performed most of the duties enjoined in the scriptures. But with all that their minds are engrossed in worldliness and deeply preoccupied with money, riches, name, fame, creature comforts, and such things."

PUNDIT: "It is true, sir. Going on a pilgrimage is like seeking diamonds and gems, while discarding the precious stone that is worn by Nārāyana Himself on His breast."

MASTER: "I want you to remember this. You may impart thousands of instructions to people, but they will not bear fruit except in proper time. On going to bed, a child said to his mother, 'Mother, please wake me up when I feel the call of nature.' The mother said: 'Don't worry about it, my child. That call will wake you up itself.' (*All laugh.*) One feels yearning for God at the proper time.

"There are three classes of physicians. The physicians of one class feel the patient's pulse and go away, merely prescribing medicine. As they leave the room they simply ask the patient to take the medicine. They are the poorest class of physicians. Likewise, there are teachers who only give instruction, but do not stop to see whether their teachings have produced a good or bad effect. They do not think at all about the disciple.

"There are physicians of another class, who prescribe medicine and ask the patient to take it. If the patient is unwilling to follow their directions, they reason with him. They are the mediocre physicians. Likewise, there are mediocre teachers. They give instruction to the student and, further, try to persuade him in various ways to follow the instruction.

"Lastly, there are the physicians of the highest class. If the patient does not respond to their gentle persuasion, they even exert force upon him. If necessary, they press their knees on the patient's chest and force the medicine down his throat. Likewise, there are teachers of the highest class, who even exert force to direct the mind of the pupil toward God."

PUNDIT: "Sir, if there are such superior teachers as you have described, then why should you say that one does not get the Knowledge of God until the right time comes?"

MASTER: "You are right. But what will the physician do if the medicine runs out of the patient's mouth and doesn't reach his stomach? In such a case even the best physician can't do anything.

"The teacher should judge the fitness of the student before giving him instruction. But you don't discriminate in your instruction. When a young man comes to me for instruction, first of all I ask him about his relatives at home. Suppose he has lost his father; suppose his father has left some debts for him. How can such a person direct his mind to God? Are you listening to me?"

PUNDIT: "Yes, sir. I am paying attention to every word."

MASTER: "One day some Sikh soldiers came to the temple garden at Dakshineswar. I met them in front of the Kāli temple. One of them referred to God as very compassionate. 'Indeed!' I said. 'Is that true? But how do you know?' He answered, 'Because, sir, God gives us food and takes every care of us.' I said: 'Why should that surprise you? God is the Father of us all. Who will look after the child if the father doesn't? Do you mean to say that the people of the neighbouring village should look after the child?"

NARENDRA: "Then shouldn't we call God kind?"

MASTER: "Have I forbidden you to? What I mean is that God is our very own. He is not a stranger to us."

PUNDIT: "Priceless words!"

MASTER (to Narendra): "I listened to your singing, but I didn't enjoy it. So I left the room. Your mind is now set on seeking a job, and therefore your song sounded dull."

Narendra flushed. He felt ashamed of himself and remained silent.

The Master asked for a drink of water. A glass of water had been placed near him, but he could not take it. He asked for some fresh water. Later it was found that a man of immoral character had touched the first glass.

PUNDIT (to Hazra): "You live in his company day and night. You must be very happy."

MASTER (with a smile): "This is indeed a great occasion for me. Today I have seen the crescent moon of the second day of the bright fortnight. (All laugh.) Do you know why I referred to the moon of the second day? Sītā once said to Rāvana, 'You are the full moon and Rāma is the crescent moon of the second day of the bright fortnight.' Rāvana did not understand the meaning of these words. He thought Sītā was flattering him and became exceedingly happy. But Sītā meant that Rāvana had reached the fullest limit of his power and prosperity, and that thenceforth he would wane like the full moon. Rāma, on the other hand, was like the moon of the second day. He would wax day by day."

The Master was about to take his leave. The pundit and his friends bowed low before him.

It was not yet dusk, and Sri Ramakrishna returned to Ishan's house with the devotees. The Master took his seat in the drawing-room with Ishan and his sons, a pundit, and a few devotees.

MASTER (smiling, to Ishan): "I said to Pundit Shashadhar: 'You have hardly set your foot on the tree, and yet you aspire to lay hold of a big bunch of fruit. First of all practise some spiritual discipline. Then you may teach others.'"

ISHAN: "Every preacher thinks that he enlightens others. The glow-worm also may think that it illumines the world. Imagining this to be the glow-worm's feeling, someone said to it: 'O glow-worm, how can you bring light to the world? You only reveal the intensity of the darkness.'"

MASTER (with a smile): "But Shashadhar is not just a scholar. He also has a little discrimination and dispassion."

A pundit who was present said to Sri Ramakrishna, "You are indeed a great soul."

MASTER: "You may say that about sages like Nārada, Prahlāda, or Śukadeva. I am like your son.

"Of course, in one sense your words are true. It is said that in one respect the devotee of God is greater than God Himself, because he carries God in his heart. (All rejoice.) It is said in the Vaishnava books: 'A devotee regards himself as a higher, and God as a lower, being.' Yaśodā, the mother of Krishna, was about to fetter Krishna, who was God Incarnate, with chains! She believed that no one but herself could take care of Krishna.

"Sometimes God acts as the magnet and the devotee as the needle. God attracts the devotee to Himself. Again, sometimes the devotee acts as the magnet and God as the needle. Such is the attraction of the devotee that God comes to him, unable to resist his love."

The Master was about to leave for Dakshineswar. Ishan and the other devotees stood around him while he gave Ishan various words of advice.

MASTER: "A devotee who can call on God while living a householder's life is a hero indeed. God thinks: 'He who has renounced the world for My sake will surely pray to Me. He must serve Me. Is there anything very remarkable about it? People will cry shame on him if he fails to do so. But he is blessed indeed who prays to Me in the midst of his worldly duties. He is trying to find Me, overcoming a great obstacle—pushing away, as it were, a huge block of stone weighing a ton. Such a man is a real hero.'"

PUNDIT: "You are right, sir. The scripture says the same thing. There is in the Mahābhārata the story of the 'pious hunter' and the 'chaste woman'. Once a hermit was disturbed in his meditation by a crow. When he cast an angry glance at the bird, it was reduced to ashes. The hermit said to himself: 'I have destroyed the crow by a mere glance. I must have made great progress in spiritual life.' One day he went to a woman's house to beg his food. She was devoted to her husband and served him day and night; she provided him with water to wash his feet and even dried them with her hair. When the hermit knocked at her door for alms, she was serving her husband

and could not open the door at once. The hermit, in a fit of anger, began to curse her. The chaste woman answered from the inner apartments: 'I am not your crow. Wait a few minutes, sir. After finishing my service to my husband I shall give you my attention.' The hermit was very much surprised to find that this simple woman was aware of his having burnt the crow to ashes. He wanted her to give him spiritual instruction. At her bidding he went to the 'pious hunter' at Benares. This hunter sold meat, but he also served his parents day and night as embodiments of God. The hermit said to himself in utter amazement: 'Why, he is a butcher and a worldly man! How can he give me the Knowledge of Brahman?' But the hunter was a knower of Brahman and had acquired divine knowledge through the performance of his worldly duties. The hermit was illumined by the instruction of the 'pious hunter'."

The Master was about to take his leave. He was standing at the door of the next house, where Ishan's father-in-law lived. Ishan and the other devotees stood by the Master. They were waiting to bid him good-bye. Sri Ramakrishna said to Ishan: "Live in the world like an ant. The world contains a mixture of truth and untruth, sugar and sand. Be an ant and take the sugar.

"Again, the world is a mixture of milk and water, the bliss of God-Consciousness and the pleasure of sense-enjoyment. Be a swan and drink the milk, leaving the water aside.

"Live in the world like a waterfowl. The water clings to the bird, but the bird shakes it off. Live in the world like a mudfish. The fish lives in the mud, but its skin is always bright and shiny.

"The world is indeed a mixture of truth and make-believe. Discard the make-believe and take the truth."

Sri Ramakrishna got into the carriage and left for Dakshineswar.

ADVICE TO PUNDIT SHASHADHAR

SRI RAMAKRISHNA was in his room, sitting on a mat spread on the floor. Pundit Shashadhar and a few devotees were with him on the mat, and the rest sat on the bare floor. Surendra, Baburam, M., Harish, Latu, Hazra, and others were present. It was about four o'clock in the afternoon.

Sri Ramakrishna had met Pundit Shashadhar six days before in Calcutta, and now the pundit had come to Dakshineswar to visit the Master. Bhudar Chattopadhyaya and his elder brother, the pundit's hosts, were with him.

The pundit was a follower of the path of jnāna. The Master was explaining this path to him. He said: "Nityā and Līlā are the two aspects of one and the same Reality. He who is the Indivisible Satchidānanda has assumed different forms for the sake of His Līlā." As he described the nature of the Ultimate Reality the Master every now and then became unconscious in samādhi. While he talked he was intoxicated with spiritual fervour. He said to the pundit: "My dear sir, Brahman is immutable and immovable, like Mount Sumeru. But He who is 'immovable' can also 'move'."

The Master was in ecstasy. He began to sing in his melodious voice:

> Who is there that can understand what Mother Kāli is?
> Even the six darśanas are powerless to reveal Her. . . .

He went on:

> Is Mother merely a simple woman, born as others are born?
> Only by chanting Her holy name
> Does Śiva survive the deadly poison.[1]

> She it is who creates the worlds, She who preserves and destroys,
> With a mere wink of Her wondrous eyes;
> She holds the universe in Her womb.

> Seeking a shelter at Her feet, the gods themselves feel safe;
> And Mahādeva, God of Gods,
> Lies prostrate underneath Her feet.

[1] An allusion to the poison that appeared when the ocean was churned by the gods and demons. Śiva drank it out of kindness to others, and the poison remained in His throat, giving it a blue colour. Therefore Śiva is known as the "god with a blue throat".

Again he sang:

> Is Mother only Śiva's wife? To Her must needs bow down
> The all-destroying King of Death!
> Naked She roams about the world, slaying Her demon foes,
> Or stands erect on Śiva's breast.
> Her feet upon Her Husband's form! What a strange wife She makes!
> My Mother's play, declares Prasād, shatters all rules and laws:
> Strive hard for purity, O mind,
> And understand my Mother's ways.

And again:

> I drink no ordinary wine, but Wine of Everlasting Bliss,
> As I repeat my Mother Kāli's name;
> It so intoxicates my mind that people take me to be drunk! . . .

And again:

> Can everyone have the vision of Śyāmā? Is Kāli's treasure for
> everyone?
> Oh, what a pity my foolish mind will not see what is true!
> Even with all His penances, rarely does Śiva Himself behold
> The mind-bewitching sight of Mother Śyāmā's crimson feet.
>
> To him who meditates on Her the riches of heaven are poor indeed;
> If Śyāmā casts Her glance on him, he swims in Eternal Bliss.
> The prince of yogis, the king of the gods, meditate on Her feet in
> vain;
> Yet worthless Kamalākānta yearns for the Mother's blessed feet!

The Master's ecstatic mood gradually relaxed. He stopped singing and
sat in silence. After a while he got up and sat on the small couch.

Pundit Shashadhar was charmed with his singing. Very humbly he said
to Sri Ramakrishna, "Are you going to sing any more?"

A little later the Master sang again:

> High in the heaven of the Mother's feet, my mind was soaring like
> a kite,
> When came a blast of sin's rough wind that drove it swiftly toward
> the earth. . . .

Then he sang:

> Once for all, this time, I have thoroughly understood;
> From One[2] who knows it well, I have learnt the secret of bhāva.
> A man has come to me from a country where there is no night,
> And now I cannot distinguish day from night any longer;
> Rituals and devotions have all grown profitless for me.
>
> My sleep is broken; how can I slumber any more?
> For now I am wide awake in the sleeplessness of yoga.
> O Divine Mother, made one with Thee in yoga-sleep[3] at last,
> My slumber I have lulled asleep for evermore.

[2] God, whom the poet worshipped as the Divine Mother.
[3] Samādhi, which makes one appear asleep.

I bow my head, says Prasād, before desire and liberation;
Knowing the secret that Kāli is one with the highest Brahman,
I have discarded, once for all, both righteousness and sin.

Sri Ramakrishna continued:

I have surrendered my soul at the fearless feet of the Mother;
Am I afraid of Death any more?
Unto the tuft of hair on my head
Is tied the almighty mantra, Mother Kāli's name.
My body I have sold in the market-place of the world
And with it have bought Sri Durgā's name.

As Sri Ramakrishna sang the line, "And with it have bought Sri Durgā's name", the tears flowed from Pundit Shashadhar's eyes. The Master went on with the song:

Deep within my heart I have planted the name of Kāli,
The Wish-fulfilling Tree of heaven;
When Yama, King of Death, appears,
To him I shall open my heart and show it growing theιe.
I have cast out from me my six unflagging foes;[4]
Ready am I to sail life's sea,
Crying, "To Durgā, victory!"

Again he sang:

Dwell, O mind, within yourself;
Enter no other's home.
If you but seek there, you will find
All you are searching for. . . .

And again:

Though I[5] am never loath to grant salvation,
I hesitate indeed to grant pure love.
Whoever wins pure love surpasses all;
He is adored by men;
He triumphs over the three worlds. . . .

The pundit had studied the Vedas and the other scriptures. He loved to discuss philosophy. The Master, seated on the couch, cast his benign look on the pundit and gave him counsel through parables.

MASTER (to the pundit): "There are many scriptures like the Vedas. But one cannot realize God without austerity and spiritual discipline. 'God cannot be found in the six systems, the Vedas, or the Tantra.'

"But one should learn the contents of the scriptures and then act according to their injunctions. A man lost a letter. He couldn't remember where he had left it. He began to search for it with a lamp. After two or three people had searched, the letter was at last found. The message in the letter was: 'Please send us five seers of sandesh and a piece of wearing-cloth.' The man

---

[4] The six passions.
[5] The song represents Sri Krishna's words.

read it and then threw the letter away. There was no further need of it; now all he had to do was to buy the five seers of sandesh and the piece of cloth.

"Better than reading is hearing, and better than hearing is seeing. One understands the scriptures better by hearing them from the lips of the guru or of a holy man. Then one doesn't have to think about their non-essential part. Hanumān said: 'Brother, I don't know much about the phase of the moon or the position of the stars. I just contemplate Rāma.'

"But seeing is far better than hearing. Then all doubts disappear. It is true that many things are recorded in the scriptures; but all these are useless without the direct realization of God, without devotion to His Lotus Feet, without purity of heart. The almanac forecasts the rainfall of the year. But not a drop of water will you get by squeezing the almanac. No, not even one drop.

"How long should one reason about the texts of the scriptures? So long as one does not have direct realization of God. How long does the bee buzz about? As long as it is not sitting on a flower. No sooner does it light on a flower and begin to sip honey than it keeps quiet.

"But you must remember another thing. One may talk even after the realization of God. But then one talks only of God and of Divine Bliss. It is like a drunkard's crying, 'Victory to the Divine Mother!' He can hardly say anything else on account of his drunkenness. You can notice, too, that a bee makes an indistinct humming sound after having sipped the honey from a flower.

"The jnāni reasons about the world through the process of 'Neti, neti', 'Not this, not this'. Reasoning in this way, he at last comes to a state of Bliss, and that is Brahman. What is the nature of a jnāni? He behaves according to scriptural injunctions.

"Once I was taken to Chānak and saw some sādhus there. Several of them were sewing. (All laugh.) At the sight of us they threw aside their sewing. They sat straight, crossing their legs, and conversed with us. (All laugh.)

"But jnānis will not talk about spiritual things without being asked. They will inquire, at first, about such things as your health and your family.

"But the nature of the vijnāni is different. He is unconcerned about anything. Perhaps he carries his wearing-cloth loose under his arm, like a child; or perhaps the cloth has dropped from his body altogether.

"The man who knows that God exists is called a jnāni. A jnāni is like one who knows beyond a doubt that a log of wood contains fire. But a vijnāni is he who lights the log, cooks over the fire, and is nourished by the food. The eight fetters have fallen from the vijnāni. He may keep merely the appearance of lust, anger, and the rest."

PUNDIT: " 'The knots of his heart are cut asunder; all his doubts are destroyed.' "

MASTER: "Yes. Once a ship sailed into the ocean. Suddenly its iron joints, nails, and screws fell out. The ship was passing a magnetic hill, and so all its iron was loosened.

"I used to go to Krishnakishore's house. Once, when I was there, he said to me, 'Why do you chew betel-leaf?' I said: 'It is my sweet pleasure. I shall chew betel-leaf, look at my face in the mirror, and dance naked among a thousand girls.'[6] Krishnakishore's wife scolded him and said: 'What have you said to Ramakrishna? You don't know how to talk to people.'

"In this state, passions like lust and anger are burnt up, though nothing happens to the physical body. It looks just like any other body; but the inside is all hollow and pure."

A DEVOTEE: "Does the body remain even after the realization of God?"

MASTER: "The body survives with some so that they may work out their prārabdha karma or work for the welfare of others. By bathing in the Ganges a man gets rid of his sin and attains liberation. But if he happens to be blind, he doesn't get rid of his blindness. Of course, he escapes future births, which would otherwise be necessary for reaping the results of his past sinful karma. His present body remains alive as long as its momentum[7] is not exhausted; but future births are no longer possible. The wheel moves as long as the impulse that has set it in motion lasts. Then it comes to a stop. In the case of such a person, passions like lust and anger are burnt up. Only the body remains alive to perform a few actions."

PUNDIT: "That is called samskāra."

MASTER: "The vijnāni always sees God. That is why he is so indifferent about the world. He sees God even with his eyes open. Sometimes he comes down to the Līlā from the Nitya, and sometimes he goes up to the Nitya from the Līlā."

PUNDIT: "I don't understand that."

MASTER: "The jnāni reasons about the world through the process of 'Neti, neti', and at last reaches the Eternal and Indivisible Satchidānanda. He reasons in this manner: 'Brahman is not the living beings; It is neither the universe nor the twenty-four cosmic principles.' As a result of such reasoning he attains the Absolute. Then he realizes that it is the Absolute that has become all this—the universe, its living beings, and the twenty-four cosmic principles.

"Milk sets into curd, and the curd is churned into butter. After extracting the butter one realizes that butter is not essentially different from buttermilk and buttermilk not essentially different from butter. The bark of a tree goes with the pith and the pith goes with the bark."

PUNDIT (smiling, to Bhudar): "Did you understand that? It is very difficult."

MASTER: "If there is butter, there must be buttermilk also. If you think of butter, you must also think of buttermilk along with it; for there cannot be any butter without buttermilk. Just so, if you accept the Nitya, you must also accept the Līlā. It is the process of negation and affirmation. You realize the Nitya by negating the Līlā. Then you affirm the Līlā, seeing in it the manifestation of the Nitya. One attains this state after realizing Reality in

---

[6] Because the Master was a vijnāni.

[7] The momentum of the actions of his previous birth, which has given rise to his present body.

both aspects: Personal and Impersonal. The Personal is the embodiment of Chit, Consciousness; and the Impersonal is the Indivisible Satchidānanda.

"Brahman alone has become everything. Therefore to the vijnāni this world is a 'mansion of mirth'. But to the jnāni it is a 'framework of illusion'. Rāmprasād described the world as a 'framework of illusion'. Another man said to him by way of retort:

> This very world is a mansion of mirth;
> Here I can eat, here drink and make merry.
> O physician,[8] you are a fool!
> You see only the surface of things.
> Janaka's might was unsurpassed;
> What did he lack of the world or the Spirit?
> Holding to one as well as the other,
> He drank his milk from a brimming cup!

"The vijnāni enjoys the Bliss of God in a richer way. Some have heard of milk, some have seen it, and some have drunk it. The vijnāni has drunk milk, enjoyed it, and been nourished by it."

The Master remained silent a few moments and then asked Pundit Shashadhar to have a smoke. The pundit went to the southeast verandah to smoke. Soon he came back to the room and sat on the floor with the devotees. Seated on the small couch, the Master continued the conversation.

MASTER (to the pundit): "Let me tell you something. There are three kinds of ānanda, joy: the joy of worldly enjoyment, the joy of worship, and the Joy of Brahman. The joy of worldly enjoyment is the joy of 'woman and gold', which people always enjoy. The joy of worship one enjoys while chanting the name and glories of God. And the Joy of Brahman is the joy of God-vision. After experiencing the joy of God-vision the rishis of olden times went beyond all rules and conventions.

"Chaitanyadeva used to experience three spiritual states: the inmost, the semi-conscious, and the conscious. In the inmost state he would see God and go into samādhi. He would be in the state of jada samādhi. In the semi-conscious state he would be partially conscious of the outer world. In the conscious state he could sing the name and glories of God."

HAZRA (to the pundit): "So your doubts are now solved."

MASTER (to the pundit): "What is samādhi? It is the complete merging, of the mind in God-Consciousness. The jnāni experiences jada samādhi, in which no trace of 'I' is left. The samādhi attained through the path of bhakti is called 'chetana samādhi'. In this samādhi there remains the consciousness of 'I'—the 'I' of the servant-and-Master relationship, of the lover-and-Beloved relationship, of the enjoyer-and-Food relationship. God is the Master; the devotee is the servant. God is the Beloved; the devotee is the lover. God is the Food, and the devotee is the enjoyer. 'I don't want to be sugar. I want to eat it.'"

PUNDIT: "What will happen if God dissolves all of the 'I', if He changes the enjoyer himself into sugar?"

MASTER (smiling): "Come, come! Tell me what is in your mind. But

[8] Rāmprasād belonged to the physician caste.

don't the scriptures mention Nārada, Sanaka, Sanātana, Sananda, and Sanatkumāra?"

PUNDIT: "Yes, sir. They do."

MASTER: "Though they were jnānis, yet they kept the 'I' of the bhakta. Haven't you read the *Bhāgavata*?"

PUNDIT: "I have read only part of it, not the whole."

MASTER: "Pray to God. He is full of compassion. Will He not listen to the words of His devotee? He is the Kalpataru. You will get whatever you desire from Him."

PUNDIT: "I haven't thought deeply about these things before. But now I understand."

MASTER: "God keeps a little of 'I' in His devotee even after giving him the Knowledge of Brahman. That 'I' is the 'I of the devotee', the 'I of the jnāni'. Through that 'I' the devotee enjoys the infinite play of God.

"The pestle[9] was almost worn out with rubbing. Only a little was left. That fell into the underbrush and brought about the destruction of the lunar race, the race of the Yadus. The vijnāni retains the 'I of the devotee', the 'I of the jnāni', in order to taste the Bliss of God and teach people.

"The rishis of old had timid natures. They were easily frightened. Do you know their attitude? It was this: 'Let me somehow get my own salvation; who cares for others?' A hollow piece of drift-wood somehow manages to float; but it sinks if even a bird sits on it. But Nārada and sages of his kind are like a huge log that not only can float across to the other shore but can carry many animals and other creatures as well. A steamship itself crosses the ocean and also carries people across.

"Teachers like Nārada belong to the class of the vijnāni. They were much more courageous than the other rishis. They are like an expert satrancha-player. You must have noticed how he shouts, as he throws the dice: 'What do I want? Six? No, five! Here is five!' And every time he throws the dice he gets the number he wants. He is such a clever player! And while playing he even twirls his moustaches.

"A mere jnāni trembles with fear. He is like an amateur satrancha-player. He is anxious to move his pieces somehow to the safety zone, where they won't be overtaken by his opponent. But a vijnāni isn't afraid of anything. He has realized both aspects of God: Personal and Impersonal. He has talked with God. He has enjoyed the Bliss of God.

"It is a joy to merge the mind in the Indivisible Brahman through contemplation. And it is also a joy to keep the mind on the Līlā, the Relative, without dissolving it in the Absolute.

"A mere jnāni is a monotonous person. He always analyses, saying: 'It is not this, not this. The world is like a dream.' But I have 'raised both my hands'. Therefore I accept everything.

"Listen to a story. Once a woman went to see her weaver friend. The weaver, who had been spinning different kinds of silk thread, was very

[9] The story is told in the *Mahābhārata* of how the relatives of Krishna quarrelled over a fragment of a pestle and exterminated themselves by fighting with one another.

happy to see her friend and said to her: 'Friend, I can't tell you how happy I am to see you. Let me get you some refreshments.' She left the room. The woman looked at the threads of different colours and was tempted. She hid a bundle of thread under one arm. The weaver returned presently with the refreshments and began to feed her guest with great enthusiasm. But, looking at the thread, she realized that her friend had taken a bundle. Hitting upon a plan to get it back, she said: 'Friend, it is so long since I have seen you. This is a day of great joy for me. I feel very much like asking you to dance with me.' The friend said, 'Sister, I am feeling very happy too.' So the two friends began to dance together. When the weaver saw that her friend danced without raising her hands, she said: 'Friend, let us dance with both hands raised. This is a day of great joy.' But the guest pressed one arm to her side and danced raising only the other. The weaver said: 'How is this, friend? Why should you dance with only one hand raised? Dance with me raising both hands. Look at me. See how I dance with both hands raised.' But the guest still pressed one arm to her side. She danced with the other hand raised and said with a smile, 'This is all I know of dancing.' "

The Master continued: "I don't press my arm to my side. Both my hands are free. I am not afraid of anything. I accept both the Nitya and the Līlā, both the Absolute and the Relative.

"I said to Keshab Sen that he would not be able to realize God without renouncing the ego. He said, 'Sir, in that case I should not be able to keep my organization together.' Thereupon I said to him: 'I am asking you to give up the "unripe ego", the "wicked ego". But there is no harm in the "ripe ego", the "child ego", the "servant ego", the "ego of Knowledge".'

"The worldly man's ego, the 'ignorant ego', the 'unripe ego', is like a thick stick. It divides, as it were, the water of the Ocean of Satchidānanda. But the 'servant ego', the 'child ego', the 'ego of Knowledge', is like a line on the water. One clearly sees that there is only one expanse of water. The dividing line makes it appear that the water has two parts, but one clearly sees that in reality there is only one expanse of water.

"Śankarāchārya kept the 'ego of Knowledge' in order to teach people. God keeps in many people the 'ego of a jnāni' or the 'ego of a bhakta' even after they have attained Brahmajnāna. Hanumān, after realizing God in both His Personal and His Impersonal aspect, cherished toward God the attitude of a servant, a devotee. He said to Rāma: 'O Rāma, sometimes I think that You are the whole and I am a part of You. Sometimes I think that You are the Master and I am Your servant. And sometimes, Rāma, when I contemplate the Absolute, I see that I am You and You are I.'

"Yaśodā became grief-stricken at being separated from Krishna, and called on Rādhā. Rādhā saw Yaśodā's suffering and revealed herself to her as the divine Śakti, which was her real nature. She said to Yaśodā: 'Krishna is Chidātmā, Absolute Consciousness, and I am Chitśakti, the Primal Power. Ask a boon of Me.' Yaśodā said: 'I don't want Brahmajnāna. Please grant me only this: that I may see the form of Gopāla in my meditation; that I may always have the company of Krishna's devotees; that I may always serve the devotees of God; that I may always chant God's name and glories.'

"Once the gopis felt a great desire to see the forms of the Lord. So Krishna asked them to dive into the water of the Jamunā. No sooner did they dive into the water than they all arrived at Vaikuntha. There they saw the form of the Lord endowed with His six celestial splendours. But they did not like it. They said to Krishna: 'We want to see Gopāla and serve Him. Please grant us that boon alone. We don't want anything else.'

"Before His departure for Mathurā, Krishna wanted to give the Knowledge of Brahman to the gopis. He said to them: 'I dwell both inside and outside all beings. Why should you see only one form of Mine?' The gopis cried in chorus: 'O Krishna, do You want to go away from us? Is that why You are instructing us in Brahmajnāna?'

"Do you know the attitude of the gopis? It is this: 'We are Rādhā's and Rādhā is ours.' "[10]

A DEVOTEE: "Does this 'I' of the devotee never disappear altogether?"

MASTER: "Yes, it disappears at times. Then one attains the Knowledge of Brahman and goes into samādhi. I too lose it, but not for all the time. In the musical scale there are seven notes: sā, re, gā, mā, pā, dhā, and ni. But one cannot keep one's voice on 'ni' a long time. One must bring it down again to the lower notes. I pray to the Divine Mother, 'O Mother, do not give me Brahmajnāna.' Formerly believers in God with form used to visit me a great deal. Then the modern Brahmajnānis[11] began to arrive. During that period I used to remain unconscious in samādhi most of the time. Whenever I regained consciousness, I would say to the Divine Mother, 'O Mother, please don't give me Brahmajnāna.' "

PUNDIT: "Does God listen to our prayers?"

MASTER: "God is the Kalpataru, the Wish-fulfilling Tree. You will certainly get whatever you ask of Him. But you must pray standing near the Kalpataru. Only then will your prayer be fulfilled. But you must remember another thing. God knows our inner feeling. A man gets the fulfilment of the desire he cherishes while practising sādhana. As one thinks, so one receives. A magician was showing his tricks before a king. Now and then he exclaimed: 'Come confusion! Come delusion! O King, give me money! Give me clothes!' Suddenly his tongue turned upward and clove to the roof of his mouth. He experienced kumbhaka. He could utter neither word nor sound, and became motionless. People thought he was dead. They built a vault of bricks and buried him there in that posture. After a thousand years someone dug into the vault. Inside it people found a man seated in samādhi. They took him for a holy man and worshipped him. When they shook him his tongue was loosened and regained its normal position. The magician became conscious of the outer world and cried, as he had a thousand years

---

[10] The ideal of the gopis was not to merge themselves in God-Consciousness, but to keep their individuality in order to enjoy the communion of Rādhā and Krishna. They regarded themselves as the companions of Rādhā.

[11] The members of the Brāhmo Samāj, who believed in the formless Brahman.

before: 'Come confusion! Come delusion! O King, give me money! Give me clothes!'

"I used to weep, praying to the Divine Mother, 'O Mother, destroy with Thy thunderbolt my inclination to reason.'"

PUNDIT: "Then you too had an inclination to reason?"

MASTER: "Yes, once."

PUNDIT: "Then please assure us that we shall get rid of that inclination too. How did you get rid of yours?"

MASTER: "Oh, somehow or other."

Sri Ramakrishna was silent awhile. Then he went on with his conversation.

MASTER: "God is the Kalpataru. One should pray standing near It. Then one will get whatever one desires.

"How many things God has created! Infinite is His universe. But what need have I to know about His infinite splendours? If I must know these, let me first realize Him. Then God Himself will tell me all about them. What need have I to know how many houses and how many government securities Jadu Mallick possesses? All that I need is somehow to converse with Jadu Mallick. I may succeed in seeing him by jumping over a ditch or through a petition or after being pushed about by his gate-keeper. Once I get a chance to talk to him, then he himself will tell me all about his possessions if I ask him. If one becomes acquainted with the master, then one is respected by his officers too. (*All laugh.*)

"There are some who do not care to know the splendours of God. What do I care about knowing how many gallons of wine there are in the tavern? One bottle is enough for me. Why should I desire the knowledge of God's splendours? I am intoxicated with the little wine I have swallowed.

"Both bhaktiyoga and jnanayoga are paths by which you can realize God. Whatever path you may follow, you will certainly realize Him. The path of bhakti is an easy one. The path of knowledge and discrimination is very difficult. Why should one reason so much to know which path is the best? I talked about this with Vijay for many days. Once I told him about a man who used to pray, 'O God, reveal to me who and what You are.'

"The path of knowledge and discrimination is difficult indeed. Pārvati, the Divine Mother, revealed Her various forms to Her father and said, 'Father, if you want Brahmajnāna, then live in the company of holy men.'

"Brahman cannot be described in words. It is said in the *Rāma Gītā* that Brahman has only been indirectly hinted at by the scriptures. When one speaks about the 'cowherd village on the Ganges', one indirectly states that the village is situated on the *bank* of the Ganges.

"Why shouldn't a man be able to realize the formless Brahman? But it is extremely difficult. He cannot if he has even the slightest trace of worldliness. He can be directly aware of Brahman in his inmost consciousness only when he renounces all sense-objects—form, taste, smell, touch, and sound—and only when his mind completely stops functioning. And then, too, he knows only this much of Brahman—that It exists."

Quoting from an Upanishad, the pundit said, "It is to be experienced only as Existence."

MASTER: "In order to realize God a devotee should make use of a particular attitude—the attitude of a 'hero' or a friend or a handmaid or a child."

MANI MALLICK: "Only then can one feel attached to God."

MASTER: "For many days I cherished the feeling that I was a companion of the Divine Mother. I used to say: 'I am the handmaid of Brahmamayi, the Blissful Mother. O companions of the Divine Mother, make me the Mother's handmaid! I shall go about proudly, saying, "I am Brahmamayi's handmaid!"' '

"Some souls realize God without practising any spiritual discipline. They are called nityasiddha, *eternally* perfect. Those who have realized God through austerity, japa, and the like, are called sādhanasiddha, perfect through *spiritual discipline*. Again, there are those called kripāsiddha, perfect through *divine grace*. These last may be compared to a room kept dark a thousand years, which becomes light the moment a lamp is brought in.

"There is also a class of devotees, the hathātsiddha, that is to say, those who have *suddenly* attained God-vision. Their case is like that of a poor boy who has suddenly found favour with a rich man. The rich man marries his daughter to the boy and along with her gives him land, house, carriage, servants, and so forth.

"There is still another class of devotees, the svapnasiddha, who have had the vision of God in a *dream*."

SURENDRA (*smiling*): "Let us go to sleep then. We shall wake and find ourselves babus, aristocrats."

MASTER (*tenderly*): "You are already a babu. When the letter 'a' is joined to the letter 'ka', 'ka' becomes 'kā'. It is futile to add another 'a'. If you add it, you will still have the same 'kā'. (*All laugh.*)

"The nityasiddha is in a class apart. He is like arani wood.[12] A little rubbing produces fire. You can get fire from it even without rubbing. The nityasiddha realizes God by practising slight spiritual discipline and sometimes without practising any at all. But he does practise spiritual discipline after realizing God. He is like the gourd or pumpkin vine—first fruit, then flower."

The pundit smiled at this illustration.

MASTER: "There is the instance of Prahlāda. He was a nityasiddha. While writing the letter 'ka' he shed a stream of tears."[13]

The Master was pleased with the pundit's humility. He praised him to the devotees.

MASTER: "He has such a nice nature. You find no difficulty in driving a nail into a mud wall. But its point breaks if you try to drive it against a stone; and still it will not pierce it. There are people whose spiritual consciousness is not at all awakened even though they hear about God a thou-

[12] A piece of wood used for kindling the sacred fire by friction.
[13] Because the latter "ka" reminded Prahlāda of Krishna, his Ideal Deity.

sand times. They are like a crocodile, on whose hide you cannot make any impression with a sword."

PUNDIT: "But one can hurt a crocodile by throwing a spear into its belly." (*All laugh.*)

MASTER (*smiling*): "What good is there in reading a whole lot of scriptures? What good is there in the study of philosophy? What is the use of talking big? In order to learn archery one should first aim at a banana tree, then at a reed, then at a wick, and last at a flying bird. At the beginning one should concentrate on God with form.

"Then there are devotees who are beyond the three gunas. They are eternally devoted to God, like Nārada. These devotees behold Krishna as Chinmaya, all Spirit, His Abode as Chinmaya, His devotee as Chinmaya. To them God is eternal, His Abode is eternal, His devotee is eternal.

"Those who reason and speculate following the process of 'Neti, neti' do not accept the Incarnation of God. Hazra says well that Divine Incarnation is only for the bhakta, and not for the jnāni, because the jnāni is quite contented with his ideal, 'I am He'."

Sri Ramakrishna and the devotees remained silent awhile. The pundit resumed the conversation.

PUNDIT: "Sir, how does one get rid of callousness? Laughter makes me think of muscles and nerves. Grief makes me think of the nervous system."

MASTER (*smiling*): "That is why Narayan Shastri used to say, 'The harmful effect of the study of the scriptures is that it encourages reasoning and arguing.'"

PUNDIT: "Is there no way for us then?"

MASTER: "Yes, there is the path of discrimination. In a song occurs the line: 'Ask her son Discrimination about the Truth.'

"The way lies through discrimination, renunciation, and passionate yearning for God. Unless a man practises discrimination, he cannot utter the right words. One time, after expounding religion at great length, Pundit Samadhyayi said, 'God is dry.' He reminded me of the man who once said, 'My uncle's cow-shed is full of horses.' Now, does anyone keep horses in a cowshed? (*With a smile*) You have become like a chānābarā[14] fried in butter. Now it will be good for you, and for others as well, if you are soaked in syrup a few days. Just a few days."

PUNDIT (*smiling*): "The sweetmeat is over-fried. It has become charred."

MASTER (*with a laugh*): "No! No! It is brown as a cockroach. Just the right colour."

HAZRA: "The sweetmeat is well cooked. It has become spongy. Now it will soak up the syrup nicely."

MASTER: "You see, there is no need to read too much of the scriptures. If you read too much you will be inclined to reason and argue. Nangtā used to teach me thus: What you get by repeating the word 'Gītā' ten times is the essence of the book. In other words, if you repeat 'Gītā' ten times it is reversed into 'tāgi', which indicates renunciation.

[14] A Bengali sweetmeat made from cheese, first fried in butter and then soaked in syrup.

"Yes, the way to realize God is through discrimination, renunciation, and yearning for Him. What kind of yearning? One should yearn for God as the cow, with yearning heart, runs after its calf."

PUNDIT: "The same thing is said in the Vedas: 'O God, we call on Thee as the cow lows for the calf.' "

MASTER: "Add your tears to your yearning. And if you can renounce everything through discrimination and dispassion, then you will be able to see God. That yearning brings about God-intoxication, whether you follow the path of knowledge or the path of devotion. The sage Durvāsā was mad with the Knowledge of God.

"There is a great deal of difference between the knowledge of a householder and that of an all-renouncing sannyāsi. The householder's knowledge is like the light of a lamp, which illumines only the inside of a room. He cannot see anything, with the help of such knowledge, except his own body and his immediate family. But the knowledge of the all-renouncing monk is like the light of the sun. Through that light he can see both inside and outside the room. Chaitanyadeva's knowledge had the brilliance of the sun —the sun of Knowledge. Further, he radiated the soothing light of the moon of Devotion. He was endowed with both—the Knowledge of Brahman and ecstatic love of God.

(*To the pundit*) "One can attain spiritual consciousness through both affirmation and negation. There is the positive path of love and devotion, and there is the negative path of knowledge and discrimination. You are preaching the path of knowledge. But that creates a very difficult situation: there the guru and the disciple do not see each other. Śukadeva went to Janaka for instruction about the Knowledge of Brahman. Janaka said to him: 'You must pay me the guru's fee beforehand. When you attain the Knowledge of Brahman you won't pay me the fee, because the knower of Brahman sees no difference between the guru and the disciple.'

"Both negation and affirmation are ways to realize one and the same goal. Infinite are the opinions and infinite are the ways. But you must remember one thing. The injunction is that the path of devotion described by Nārada is best suited to the Kaliyuga. According to this path, first comes bhakti; then bhāva, when bhakti is mature. Higher than bhāva are mahābhāva and prema. An ordinary mortal does not attain mahābhāva and prema. He who has achieved these has realized the goal, that is to say, has attained God."

PUNDIT: "In expounding religion one has to use a great many words."

MASTER: "While preaching, eliminate the 'head and tail', that is to say, emphasize only the essentials."

The pundit and Mani Mallick became engaged in conversation. Mani was a member of the Brāhmo Samāj. The pundit argued vehemently about the good and bad sides of the Samāj. Sri Ramakrishna was seated on the small couch and looked on, smiling. Presently he remarked: "This is the tāmasic aspect of sattva, the attitude of a hero. This is necessary. One should not hold one's tongue at the sight of injustice and untruth. Suppose a bad woman wants to drag you from the path of righteousness. You must then assume the heroic attitude and say: 'What? You witch! You dare injure my spiritual life? I shall cut your body in two right now.'"

With a smile Sri Ramakrishna said to the pundit: "Mani Mallick has been following the tenets of the Brāhmo Samāj a long time. You can't convert him to your views. Is it an easy thing to destroy old tendencies? Once there lived a very pious Hindu who always worshipped the Divine Mother and chanted Her name. When the Mussalmāns conquered the country, they forced him to embrace Islām. They said to him: 'You are now a Mussalmān. Say "Āllāh". From now on you must repeat only the name of Āllāh.' With great difficulty he repeated the word 'Āllāh', but every now and then blurted out 'Jagadambā'.[15] At that the Mussalmāns were about to beat him. Thereupon he said to them: 'I beseech you! Please do not kill me. I have been trying my utmost to repeat the name of Āllāh, but our Jagadambā has filled me up to the throat. She pushes out your Āllāh.' (All laugh.)

(To the pundit) "Please don't say anything to Mani Mallick. You must know that there are different tastes. There are also different powers of digestion. God has made different religions and creeds to suit different aspirants. By no means all are fit for the Knowledge of Brahman. Therefore the worship of God with form has been provided.

"The mother brings home a fish for her children. She curries part of the fish, part she fries, and with another part she makes pilau. By no means all can digest the pilau. So she makes fish soup for those who have weak stomachs. Further, some want pickled or fried fish. There are different temperaments. There are differences in the capacity to comprehend."

All sat in silence. Sri Ramakrishna said to the pundit, "Go and visit the temples and take a stroll in the garden." It was about half past five in the afternoon. The pundit left the room with his friends and several of the devotees.

After a while the Master went with M. toward the bathing-ghāt on the Ganges. He said to M., "Baburam now says, 'What shall I gain by study?'" On the bank of the river he met the pundit and said to him, "Aren't you going to the Kāli temple?" The pundit said: "Yes, sir. Let us go together."

With a smiling face Sri Ramakrishna proceeded to the temple through the courtyard. He said to the pundit, "Listen to a song."

He sang:

> Is Kāli, my Mother, really black?
> The Naked One, of blackest hue,
> Lights the Lotus of the Heart. . . .

As he was going through the courtyard, he quoted to the pundit from a song:

> Lighting the lamp of Knowledge in the chamber of your heart,
> Behold the face of the Mother, Brahman's Embodiment.

They came to the temple. Sri Ramakrishna saluted the Divine Mother, touching the ground with his forehead.

[15] "The Mother of the Universe", a name of the Divine Mother.

Red hibiscus flowers and vilwa-leaves adorned the Mother's feet. Her three eyes radiated love for Her devotees. Two of Her hands were raised as if to give them boons and reassurance; the other two hands held symbols of death. She was clothed in a sāri of Benares silk and was decked with ornaments.

Referring to the image, one of the party remarked, "I heard it was made by the sculptor Nabin." The Master answered: "Yes, I know. But to me She is the Embodiment of Spirit."

As Sri Ramakrishna was coming back to his room with the devotees, he said to Baburam, "Come with us." M. also joined them.

It was dusk. The Master was sitting on the semicircular porch west of his room. Baburam and M. sat near him. He was in a mood of partial ecstasy.

Rakhal was not then living with Sri Ramakrishna, and therefore the Master was having difficulties about his personal service. Several devotees lived with him, but he could not bear the touch of everyone during his spiritual moods. He hinted to Baburam: "Do stay with me. It will be very nice. In this mood I cannot allow others to touch me."

The pundit entered the Master's room after visiting the temples. The Master said to him from the porch, "Take some refreshments." The pundit said that he had not yet performed his evening devotions. At once Sri Ramakrishna stood up and sang in an exalted mood:

> Why should I go to Gangā or Gayā, to Kāsi, Kānchi, or Prabhās,
> So long as I can breathe my last with Kāli's name upon my lips?
> What need of rituals has a man, what need of devotions any more,
> If he repeats the Mother's name at the three holy hours? . . .

Intoxicated with ecstatic love, the Master said: "How long should one perform devotions? So long as one's mind does not merge in God while repeating Om."

PUNDIT: "Then let me eat the refreshments. I shall perform the devotions later on."

MASTER: "No, I don't want to obstruct the current of your life. It is not good to renounce anything before the proper time arrives. When the fruit ripens, the flower drops off of itself. One shouldn't forcibly tear off the green branch of a coconut tree. That injures the tree."

Surendra was about to leave. He invited his friends into his carriage. The Master, still in an ecstatic mood, said, "Don't take more people than your horse can draw." Surendra took leave of Sri Ramakrishna. The pundit left the room to perform his worship. M. and Baburam saluted the Master. They were about to leave for Calcutta. Sri Ramakrishna was still in an ecstatic mood.

MASTER (to M.): "I cannot utter a word now. Stay a few minutes."

M. again took his seat and waited for the Master's command. Sri Ramakrishna motioned to Baburam to take a seat and asked him to fan him a little. M. also took part in rendering this personal service to the Master.

MASTER (to M., tenderly): "Why don't you come here so frequently now?"

M: "Not for any special reason. I have been rather busy at home."

MASTER: "Yesterday I came to know Baburam's inner nature. That is why I have been trying so hard to persuade him to live with me. The mother bird hatches the egg in proper time. Boys like Baburam are pure in heart. They have not yet fallen into the clutches of 'woman and gold'. Isn't that so?"

M: "It is true, sir. They are still stainless."

MASTER: "They are like a new pot. Milk kept in it will not turn sour."

M: "Yes, sir."

MASTER: "I need Baburam here. I pass through certain spiritual states when I need someone like him. He says he must not, all at once, live with me permanently, for it will create difficulties. His relatives will make trouble. I am asking him to come here Saturdays and Sundays."

The pundit entered the room with his friends. He had finished his devotions and was ready to eat the refreshments. One of his companions asked the Master: "Shall we succeed in spiritual life? Please tell us what our way is."

MASTER: "You all have the yearning for liberation. If an aspirant has yearning, that is enough for him to realize God. Don't eat any food of the śrāddha ceremony.[16] Live in the world like an unchaste woman. She performs her household duties with great attention, but her mind dwells day and night on her paramour. Perform your duties in the world but keep your mind always fixed on God."

The pundit finished eating his refreshments.

MASTER (to the pundit): "You have read the Gītā, no doubt. It says that there is a special power of God in the man who is honoured and respected by all."

The pundit quoted the verse from the Gītā.

MASTER: "You surely possess divine power."

PUNDIT: "Shall I labour with perseverance to finish the task that I have accepted?"

Sri Ramakrishna forced himself, as it were, to say, "Yes." He soon changed the conversation.

MASTER: "One cannot but admit the manifestation of power. Vidyāsāgar once asked me, 'Has God given more power to some than to others?' I said to him: 'Certainly. Otherwise, how can one man kill a hundred? If there is no special manifestation of power, then why is Queen Victoria so much honoured and respected? Don't you admit it?' He agreed with me."

The pundit and his friends saluted the Master and were about to take their leave. Sri Ramakrishna said to the pundit: "Come again. One hemp-smoker rejoices in the company of another hemp-smoker. They even embrace each other. But they hide at the sight of people not of their own kind. A cow licks the body of her calf; but she threatens a strange cow with her horns." (All laugh.)

The pundit left the room. With a smile the Master said: "He has become 'diluted' even in one day. Did you notice how modest he was? And he accepted everything I said."

[16] Offering of food and drink to deceased relatives, especially ancestors.

Moonlight flooded the semicircular porch. Sri Ramakrishna was still seated there. M. was about to leave.

MASTER (*tenderly*): "Must you go now?"

M: "Yes, sir. Let me say good-bye."

MASTER: "I have been thinking of visiting the houses of the devotees. I want to visit yours also. What do you say?"

M: "That will be very fine."

Thursday, July 3, 1884

Sri Ramakrishna was sitting in Balaram Bose's house in Calcutta. It was the day of the "Return Car Festival". The Lord of the Universe was worshipped in Balaram's house as Jagannāth. There was a small car in the house for use during the Car Festival.

Balaram's father was a pious Vaishnava who devoted most of his time to prayer and meditation in his garden house at Vrindāvan. He also studied devotional books and enjoyed the company of devotees. Balaram had brought his father to Calcutta to meet the Master.

Sri Ramakrishna was in a very happy mood. Seated near him were Ram, Balaram, Balaram's father, M., Manomohan, and several young devotees. He was conversing with them.

MASTER (*to Balaram's father and the others*): "The *Bhaktamāla* is one of the Vaishnava books. It is a fine book. It describes the lives of the various Vaishnava devotees. But it is one-sided. At one place the author found peace of mind only after compelling Bhagavati, the Divine Mother, to take Her initiation according to the Vaishnava discipline.

"Once I spoke highly of Vaishnavcharan to Mathur and persuaded him to invite Vaishnavcharan to his house. Mathur welcomed him with great courtesy. He fed his guest from silver plates. Then do you know what happened? Vaishnav said in front of Mathur, 'You will achieve nothing whatsoever in spiritual life unless you accept Krishna as your Ideal.' Mathur was a follower of the Śākta cult and a worshipper of the Divine Mother. At once his face became crimson. I nudged Vaishnavcharan.

"I understand that the *Bhāgavata* also contains some statements like that. I hear that it is said there that trying to cross the ocean of the world without accepting Krishna as the Ideal Deity is like trying to cross a great sea by holding to the tail of a dog. Each sect magnifies its own view.

"The Śāktas, too, try to belittle the Vaishnavas. The Vaishnavas say that Krishna alone is the Helmsman to take one across the ocean of the world. The Śāktas retort: 'Oh, yes! We agree to that. Our Divine Mother is the Empress of the Universe. Why should She bother about a ferry-boat? Therefore She has engaged that fellow Krishna for the purpose.' (*All laugh.*)

"Besides, how vain people are about their own sects! There are weavers in the villages near Kāmārpukur. Many of them are Vaishnavas and like to talk big. They say: 'Which Vishnu does he worship? The Preserver? Oh, we wouldn't touch him!' Or: 'Which Siva are you talking about? We accept the Ātmārāma Śiva.' Or again, 'Please explain to us which Hari you worship.' They spin their yarn and indulge in talk like that.

"Rati's mother, Rāni Katyayani's favourite confidante, is a follower of Vaishnavcharan. She is a bigoted Vaishnava. She used to visit me very frequently, and none could outdo her in devotion. One day she noticed me eating the prasād from the Kāli temple. Since then I haven't seen even her shadow.

"He is indeed a real man who has harmonized everything. Most people are one-sided. But I find that all opinions point to the One. All views—the Śākta, the Vaishnava, the Vedānta—have that One for their centre. He who is formless is, again, endowed with form. It is He who appears in different forms. 'The attributeless Brahman is my Father. God with attributes is my Mother. Whom shall I blame? Whom shall I praise? The two pans of the scales are equally heavy.'

"He who is described in the Vedas is also described in the Tantras and the Purānas. All of them speak about the one Satchidānanda. The Nitya and the Līlā are the two aspects of the one Reality. It is described in the Vedas as 'Om Satchidānanda Brahman', in the Tantras as 'Om Satchidānanda Śiva', the ever-pure Śiva, and in the Purānas as 'Om Satchidānanda Krishna'. All the scriptures, the Vedas, the Purānas, and the Tantras, speak only of one Satchidānanda. It is stated in the Vaishnava scriptures that it is Krishna Himself who has become Kāli."

Sri Ramakrishna went to the porch for a few minutes and then returned. As he was going out, Vishvamvhar's daughter, six or seven years old, saluted him. On returning to the room, the Master began talking to the little girl and her companions, who were of the same age.

THE CHILD (to the Master): "I saluted you and you didn't even notice it."

MASTER (smiling): "Did you? I really didn't notice."

CHILD: "Then wait. I want to salute you again—the other foot too."

Sri Ramakrishna laughed and sat down. He returned the salute and bowed to the child, touching the ground with his forehead. He asked her to sing. The child said, "I swear I don't sing." When the Master pressed her again, she said, "Should you press me when I said 'I swear'?" The Master was very happy with the children and sang light and frivolous songs to entertain them. He sang:

> Come, let me braid your hair,
> Lest your husband should scold you
> When he beholds you!

The children and the devotees laughed.

MASTER (to the devotees): "The paramahamsa is like a five-year-old child. He sees everything filled with Consciousness. At one time I was staying at Kāmārpukur when Shivaram[17] was four or five years old. One day he was trying to catch grasshoppers near the pond. The leaves were moving. To stop their rustling he said to the leaves: 'Hush! Hush! I want to catch a grasshopper.' Another day it was stormy. It rained hard. Shivaram was with me inside the house. There were flashes of lightning. He wanted to open the door and go out. I scolded him and stopped him, but still he peeped out

[17] A nephew of the Master.

now and then. When he saw the lightning he exclaimed, 'There, uncle! They are striking matches again!'

"The paramahamsa is like a child. He cannot distinguish between a stranger and a relative. He isn't particular about worldly relationships. One day Shivaram said to me, 'Uncle, are you my father's brother or his brother-in-law?'

"The paramahamsa is like a child. He doesn't keep any track of his whereabouts. He sees everything as Brahman. He is indifferent to his own movements. Shivaram went to Hriday's house to see the Durgā Pujā. He slipped out of the house and wandered away. A passer-by saw the child, who was then only four years old, and asked, 'Where do you come from?' He couldn't say much. He only said the word 'hut'. He was speaking of the big hut in which the image of the Divine Mother was being worshipped. The stranger asked him further, 'Whom are you living with?' He only said the word 'brother'.

"Sometimes the paramahamsa behaves like a madman. When I experienced that divine madness I used to worship my own sexual organ as the Śiva-phallus. But I can't do that now. A few days after the dedication of the temple at Dakshineswar, a madman came there who was really a sage endowed with the Knowledge of Brahman. He had a bamboo twig in one hand and a potted mango-plant in the other, and was wearing torn shoes. He didn't follow any social conventions. After bathing in the Ganges he didn't perform any religious rites. He ate something that he carried in a corner of his wearing-cloth. Then he entered the Kāli temple and chanted hymns to the Deity. The temple trembled. Haladhari was then in the shrine. The madman wasn't allowed to eat at the guest-house, but he paid no attention to this slight. He searched for food in the rubbish heap where the dogs were eating crumbs from the discarded leaf-plates. Now and then he pushed the dogs aside to get his crumbs. The dogs didn't mind either. Haladhari followed him and asked: 'Who are you? Are you a purnajnāni?'[18] The madman whispered, 'Sh! Yes, I am a purnajnāni.' My heart began to palpitate as Haladhari told me about it. I clung to Hriday. I said to the Divine Mother, 'Mother, shall I too have to pass through such a state?' We all went to see the man. He spoke words of great wisdom to us but behaved like a madman before others. Haladhari followed him a great way when he left the garden. After passing the gate he said to Haladhari: 'What else shall I say to you? When you no longer make any distinction between the water of this pool and the water of the Ganges, then you will know that you have Perfect Knowledge.' Saying this he walked rapidly away."

Sri Ramakrishna began to talk with M. Other devotees, too, were present.

MASTER (to M.): "How do you feel about Shashadhar?"

M: "He is very nice."

MASTER: "He is very intelligent, isn't he?"

M: "Yes, sir. He is very erudite."

MASTER: "According to the Gītā there is a power of God in one who is respected and honoured by many. But Shashadhar has still a few things to do.

---

[18] A perfect knower of Brahman.

What will he accomplish with mere scholarship? He needs to practise some austerity. It is necessary to practise some spiritual discipline.

"Gauri Pundit practised austerity. When he chanted a hymn to the Divine Mother, the other pundits would seem no more than earthworms.

"Narayan Shastri was not merely a scholar, either. He practised sādhanā as well. He studied for twenty-five years without a break. Nyāya alone, he studied for seven years. Still he would go into ecstasy while repeating the name of Śiva. The King of Jaipur wanted to make him his court pundit, but Narayan refused. He used to spend much time here. He had a great desire to go to the Vaśishtha Āśrama to practise tapasyā. He often spoke to me about it, but I forbade him to go there. At that he said: 'Who knows when I shall die? When shall I practise sādhanā? Any day I may crack.' After much insistence on his part I let him go. Some say that he is dead, that he died while practising austerity. Others say that he is still alive and that they saw him off on a railway train.

"Before meeting Keshab, I asked Narayan Shastri to visit him and tell me what he thought of him. Narayan reported that Keshab was an adept in japa. He knew astrology and remarked that Keshab had been born under a good star. Then I went to visit Keshab in the garden house at Belgharia. Hriday was with me. The moment I saw Keshab, I said: 'Of all the people I see here, he alone has dropped his tail. He can now live on land as well as in water, like a frog.'

"Keshab sent three members of the Brāhmo Samāj to the temple garden at Dakshineswar to test me. Prasanna was one of them. They were commissioned to watch me day and night, and to report to Keshab. They were in my room and intended to spend the night there. They constantly uttered the word 'Dayāmaya'[19] and said to me: 'Follow Keshab Babu. That will do you good.' I said, 'I believe in God with form.' Still they went on with their exclamations of 'Dayāmaya!' Then a strange mood came over me. I said to them, 'Get out of here!' I didn't allow them to spend the night in my room. So they slept on the verandah. Captain also spent the night in the temple garden the first time he visited me.

"Michael[20] visited the temple garden when Narayan Shastri was living with me. Dwarika Babu, Mathur's eldest son, brought him here. The owners of the temple garden were about to get into a lawsuit with the English proprietors of the neighbouring powder magazine; so they wanted Michael's advice. I met him in the big room next to the manager's office. Narayan Shastri was with me. I asked Narayan to talk to him. Michael couldn't talk very well in Sanskrit. He made mistakes. Then they talked in the popular dialect. Narayan Shastri asked him his reason for giving up the Hindu religion. Pointing to his stomach, Michael said, 'It was for this.' Narayan said, 'What shall I say to a man who gives up his religion for his belly's sake?' Thereupon Michael asked me to say something. I said: 'I don't know

[19] "The Compassionate One." The Brāhmos are fond of using this name for God, whom they believe to be formless and yet personal and endowed with attributes.

[20] Michael Madhusudan Dutt, a lawyer, and one of the greatest of Bengali poets. He was a convert to Christianity.

why, but I don't feel like saying anything. Someone seems to be pressing my tongue.' "

MANOMOHAN: "Mr. Choudhury will not come. He said: 'That fellow Shashadhar from Faridpur will be there. I shall not go.' "

Mr. Choudhury had obtained his Master's degree from Calcutta University. He drew a salary of three or four hundred rupees. After the death of his first wife he had felt intense dispassion for the world, but after some time he had married again. He frequently visited the Master at the temple garden.

MASTER: "How mean of him! He is vain of his scholarship. Besides, he has married a second time. He looks on the world as a mere mud-puddle.

(*To the devotees*) "This attachment to 'woman and gold' makes a man small-minded. When I first saw Haramohan he had many good traits. I longed to see him. He was then seventeen or eighteen years old. I used to send for him every now and then, but he wouldn't come. He is now living away from the family with his wife. He had been living with his uncle before. That was very good. He had no worldly troubles. Now he has a separate home and does the marketing for his wife daily. The other day he came to Dakshineswar. I said to him: 'Go away. Leave this place. I don't even feel like touching you.' "

Sri Ramakrishna went to the inner apartments to see the Deity. He offered some flowers. The ladies of Balaram's family were pleased to see him.

The Master came back to the drawing-room and said: "The worldly-minded practise devotions, japa, and austerity only by fits and starts. But those who know nothing else but God repeat His name with every breath. Some always repeat mentally, 'Om Rāma'. Even the followers of the path of knowledge repeat, 'Soham', 'I am He'. There are others whose tongues are always moving, repeating the name of God. One should remember and think of God constantly."

Pundit Shashadhar entered the room with one or two friends and saluted the Master.

MASTER (*smiling*): "We are like the bridesmaids waiting near the bed for the arrival of the groom."

The pundit laughed. The room was filled with devotees, among them Dr. Pratap and Balaram's father. The Master continued his talk.

MASTER (*to Shashadhar*): "The first sign of knowledge is a peaceful nature, and the second is absence of egotism. You have both. There are other indications of a jnāni. He shows intense dispassion in the presence of a sādhu, is a lion when at work, for instance, when he lectures, and is full of wit before his wife. (*All laugh.*)

"But the nature of the vijnāni is quite different, as was the case with Chaitanyadeva. He acts like a child or a madman or an inert thing or a ghoul. While in the mood of a child, he sometimes shows childlike guilelessness, sometimes the frivolity of adolescence, and sometimes, while instructing others, the strength of a young man."

PUNDIT: "By what kind of bhakti does one realize God?"

MASTER: "Three kinds of bhakti are found, according to the nature of the man: sāttvic bhakti, rājasic bhakti, and tāmasic bhakti.

"Sāttvic bhakti is known to God alone. It makes no outward display. A man with such devotion loves privacy. Perhaps he meditates inside the mosquito net, where nobody sees him. When this kind of devotion is awakened, one hasn't long to wait for the vision of God. The appearance of the dawn in the east shows that the sun will rise before long.

"A man with rājasic bhakti feels like making a display of his devotion before others. He worships the Deity with 'sixteen ingredients',[21] enters the temple wearing a silk cloth, and puts around his neck a string of rudrāksha beads interspersed here and there with beads of gold and ruby.

"A man with tāmasic bhakti shows the courage and boisterousness of a highway robber. A highway robber goes on his expedition openly, shouting, 'Kill! Plunder!' He isn't afraid even of eight police inspectors. The devotee with tāmasic bhakti also shouts like a madman: 'Hara! Hara! Vyom! Vyom![22] Victory to Kāli!' He has great strength of mind and burning faith.

"A Śākta has such faith. He says: 'What? I have uttered once the name of Kāli and of Durgā! I have uttered once the name of Rāma! Can there be any sin in me?'

"The Vaishnavas have a very humble and lowly attitude. (*Looking at Balaram's father*) They tell their rosary and whine and whimper: 'O Krishna, be gracious to us! We are wretched! We are sinners!'

"A man should have such fiery faith as to be able to say, 'I have uttered the name of God; how can I be a sinner?' Imagine a man repeating the name of Hari day and night and at the same time saying that he is a sinner!"

So saying, Sri Ramakrishna became overwhelmed with divine ecstasy and sang:

> If only I can pass away repeating Durgā's name,
> How canst Thou then, O Blessed One,
> Withhold from me deliverance,
> Wretched though I may be?
> I may have stolen a drink of wine, or killed a child unborn,
> Or slain a woman or a cow,
> Or even caused a brāhmin's death;
> But, though it all be true,
> Nothing of this can make me feel the least uneasiness;
> For through the power of Thy sweet name
> My wretched soul may still aspire
> Even to Brahmanhood.

He sang again:

> Behold my Mother playing with Śiva, lost in an ecstasy of joy!
> Drunk with a draught of celestial wine, She reels, and yet She
>   does not fall.

[21] As prescribed in the books of Hindu ritual.
[22] By such loud exclamations a devotee of Śiva invokes his Ideal Deity.

Erect She stands on Śiva's bosom, and the earth trembles under
    Her tread;
She and Her Lord are mad with frenzy, casting aside all fear and
    shame!

Pundit Shashadhar was weeping. Vaishnavcharan, the musician, sang:

O tongue, always repeat the name of Mother Durgā!
Who but your Mother Durgā will save you in distress?
Thou art the heavens and the earth, and Thou the nether world;
From Thee have the twelve Gopālas and Hari and Śiva sprung.
The ten Embodiments of Divine Śakti art Thou,
And Thou the ten Avatārs: this time, save me Thou must!
The moving and the unmoving, the gross and the subtle, art Thou;
Creation and preservation art Thou, and the last dissolution.
Thou art the Primal Root of this manifold universe;
The Mother of the three worlds, their only Saviour, art Thou;
Thou art the Śakti of all, and Thou Thine own Śakti, too.

As the Master listened to the last few lines, he went into an ecstatic **mood.**
The Master himself sang:[23]

O Mother, for Yaśodā Thou wouldst dance, when she called Thee
    her precious "Blue Jewel":[24]
Where hast Thou hidden that lovely form, O terrible Śyāmā?
Dance that way once for me, O Mother! Throw down Thy sword
    and take the flute;
Cast off Thy garland of heads, and wear Thy wild-flower garland.
If without Śiva Thou canst not dance, then let Balarāma be Thy
    Śiva.
Dance, O Śyāmā, as Thou didst dance when Thou wast Krishna!

Mother, play on Thy flute again, once so full of delight for the
    gopis;
Play again on Thy magic flute, which called the cattle in from the
    pasture,
Stopping the Jamunā's murmuring flow and turning it backward.

Hot in the sky the sun would burn, when Yaśodā, restless for her
    Krishna,
Fondly would call: "Here, my Gopāla! Cream and butter—eat
    them, my Darling!"
And she would comb His long black hair and carefully braid it.

Bending Thy supple body, Mother, both at the neck, the waist,
    and the knee,
Thou didst dance with Thy friend Śridāma, while Thy two anklets
    played the music:
Tā-thaiā! Tā-thaiā! Tā-tā! Thaiā-thaiā!
Hearing their captivating sound, the gopis would rush there.

Again Pundit Shashadhar shed tears of love.
Sri Ramakrishna came down to consciousness of the world. Pointing to

[23] This song signifies the oneness of Krishna and Kāli.
[24] A pet name of the Baby Krishna.

Shashadhar, he said to M., "Why don't you prod him?" He wanted M. or some other devotee to ask Shashadhar a question.

RAMDAYAL (to Shashadhar): "The scriptures speak of Brahman's form as a projection of mind. Who is it that projects?"

SHASHADHAR: "It is Brahman Itself that does so. It is no projection of a man's mind."

PRATAP: "Why does Brahman project the form?"

MASTER: "You ask why? Brahman doesn't act in consultation with others. It is Brahman's pleasure. Brahman is self-willed. Why should we try to know the reason for Brahman's acting this way or that? You have come to the orchard to eat mangoes. Eat the mangoes. What is the good of calculating how many trees there are in the orchard, how many thousands of branches, and how many millions of leaves? One cannot realize Truth by futile arguments and reasoning."

PRATAP: "Shouldn't we reason any more then?"

MASTER: "I am asking you not to indulge in futile reasoning. But reason, by all means, about the Real and the unreal, about what is permanent and what is transitory. You must reason when you are overcome by lust, anger, or grief."

SHASHADHAR: "That is different. It is called reasoning based on discrimination."

MASTER: "Yes, discrimination between the Real and the unreal."

All sat in silence. Again the Master spoke, addressing the pundit.

MASTER: "Formerly many great men used to come here."

SHASHADHAR: "You mean rich people?"

MASTER: "No. Great scholars."

In the mean time the small car of Jagannāth had been brought to the verandah. Inside the car were the images of Krishna, Balarāma, and Subhadrā. They were adorned with flowers, garlands, jewelry, and yellow apparel. Balaram was a sāttvic worshipper: there was no outward grandeur in his worship. Outsiders did not even know of this Car Festival at his house. The Master and the devotees went to the verandah. Sri Ramakrishna pulled the car by the rope. Then he began to sing:

> See how all Nadiā is shaking
> Under the waves of Gaurānga's love. . . .

He sang again:

> Behold, the two brothers[25] have come, who weep while chanting
> Hari's name,
> The brothers who, in return for blows, offer to sinners Hari's
> love. . . .

Sri Ramakrishna danced with the devotees. The musician and his party joined the Master in the music and dancing. Soon the whole verandah was filled with people. The ladies witnessed this scene of joy from an adjoining

[25] Gaurānga and Nityānanda.

room. It appeared as if Chaitanya himself were dancing with his devotees, intoxicated with divine love.

It was not yet dusk. Sri Ramakrishna returned to the drawing-room with the devotees.

MASTER (to Shashadhar): "This is called bhajanānanda, the bliss of devotees in the worship of God. Worldly people keep themselves engrossed in the joy of sensuous objects, of 'woman and gold'. Through worship devotees receive the grace of God, and then His vision. Then they enjoy Brahmānanda, the Bliss of Brahman."

Shashadhar and the devotees listened to these words with rapt attention.

SHASHADHAR (humbly): "Sir, please tell us what kind of yearning gives one this blissful state of mind."

MASTER: "One feels restless for God when one's soul longs for His vision. The guru said to the disciple: 'Come with me. I shall show you what kind of longing will enable you to see God.' Saying this, he took the disciple to a pond and pressed his head under the water. After a few moments he released the disciple and asked, 'How did you feel?' The disciple answered: 'Oh, I felt as if I were dying! I was longing for a breath of air.' "

SHASHADHAR: "Yes! Yes! That's it. I understand it now."

MASTER: "To love God is the essence of the whole thing. Bhakti alone is the essence. Nārada said to Rāma, 'May I always have pure love for Your Lotus Feet; and may I not be deluded by Your world-bewitching māyā!' Rāma said to him, 'Ask for some other boon.' 'No,' said Nārada, 'I don't want anything else. May I have love for Your Lotus Feet. This is my only prayer.' "

Pundit Shashadhar was ready to leave. Sri Ramakrishna asked a devotee to bring a carriage for the pundit.

SHASHADHAR: "Don't trouble yourself. I shall walk."

MASTER (smiling): "Oh, how can that be? 'You are beyond the reach of even Brahmā's meditation.' "

SHASHADHAR: "There is no particular need of my going just now. The only thing is that I shall have to perform my sandhyā."

MASTER: "The Divine Mother has taken away my sandhyā and other devotions. The purpose of the sandhyā is to purify body and mind. I am no longer in that state."

The Master sang the following lines of a song:

> When will you learn to lie, O mind, in the abode of Blessedness,
> With Cleanliness and Defilement on either side of you?
> Only when you have found the way
> To keep these wives contentedly under a single roof,
> Will you behold the matchless form of Mother Śyāmā.

Pundit Shashadhar saluted the Master and went away.

RAM: "I visited Shashadhar yesterday. You asked me to."

MASTER: "Did I? I don't remember. But it is nice that you went."

RAM: "The editor of a newspaper[26] was abusing you."

[26] The *Indian Empire*.

MASTER: "Suppose he was. What does it matter?"

RAM: "Please listen. Then I began to talk to the editor about you. He wanted to hear more and wouldn't let me go."

It was dusk. Sri Ramakrishna began to chant the names of the Divine Mother, Krishna, Rāma, and Hari. The devotees sat in silence. The Master chanted the names in such sweet tones that the hearts of the devotees were deeply touched. That day Balaram's house was like Navadvip when Chaitanya lived there. On the verandah it was like Navadvip, and in the parlour it was like Vrindāvan.

That same night Sri Ramakrishna was to go to Dakshineswar. Balaram took him into the inner apartments and served him with refreshments. The ladies of the family saluted the Master.

The devotees were singing kirtan in the drawing-room, awaiting the Master's coming. Presently Sri Ramakrishna came and joined the singers.

The kirtan went on:

> Behold, my Gorā is dancing! With the devotees
> He dances in Śrivās's courtyard, singing the kirtan.
> Gorā says to all, "Repeat the name of Hari!"
> He looks at Gadādhar, and from his red eyes
> Are flowing tears of love over his golden body.

The Master improvised the lines:

> Gorā is dancing in the kirtan:
> There he dances, Sachi's darling!
> There he dances, my Gaurānga!
> There he dances, my soul's beloved!

FESTIVAL AT ADHAR'S HOUSE

SRI RAMAKRISHNA was sitting in his room in the temple garden at Dakshineswar after his midday meal. A party of Bāuls from Shibpur, several devotees from Bhawānipur, Balaram, and M. were in the room. Rakhal, Latu, and Harish were then living with the Master. They too were present.

The Master began the conversation by addressing the Bāul musicians from Shibpur.

MASTER: "Yoga is not possible if the mind dwells on 'woman and gold'. The mind of a worldly man generally moves among the three lower centres: those at the navel, at the sexual organ, and at the organ of evacuation. After great effort and spiritual practice the Kundalini is awakened. According to the yogis there are three nerves in the spinal column: Idā, Pingalā, and Sushumnā. Along the Sushumnā are six lotuses, or centres, the lowest being known as the Mulādhāra. Then come successively Svādhisthāna, Manipura, Anāhata, Viśuddha, and Ājnā. These are the six centres. The Kundalini, when awakened, passes through the lower centres and comes to the Anāhata, which is at the heart. It stays there. At that time the mind of the aspirant is withdrawn from the three lower centres. He feels the awakening of Divine Consciousness and sees Light. In mute wonder he sees that radiance and cries out: 'What is this? What is this?'

"After passing through the six centres, the Kundalini reaches the thousand-petalled lotus known as the Sahasrāra, and the aspirant goes into samādhi.

"According to the Vedas these centres are called 'bhumi', 'planes'. There are seven such planes. The centre at the heart corresponds to the fourth plane of the Vedas. According to the Tantra there is in this centre a lotus called Anāhata, with twelve petals.

"The centre known as Viśuddha is the fifth plane. This centre is at the throat and has a lotus with sixteen petals. When the Kundalini reaches this plane, the devotee longs to talk and hear only about God. Conversation on worldly subjects, on 'woman and gold', causes him great pain. He leaves a place where people talk of these matters.

"Then comes the sixth plane, corresponding to the centre known as Ājnā. This centre is located between the eyebrows and it has a lotus with two petals. When the Kundalini reaches it, the aspirant sees the form of God. But still there remains a slight barrier between the devotee and God. It is like a light inside a lantern. You may think you have touched the light, but in reality you cannot because of the barrier of glass.

"And last of all is the seventh plane, which, according to Tantra, is the centre of the thousand-petalled lotus. When the Kundalini arrives there, the aspirant goes into samādhi. In that lotus dwells Satchidānanda Śiva, the Absolute. There Kundalini, the awakened Power, unites with Śiva. This is known as the union of Śiva and Śakti.

"When the Kundalini rises to the Sahasrāra and the mind goes into samādhi, the aspirant loses all consciousness of the outer world. He can no longer retain his physical body. If milk is poured into his mouth, it runs out again. In that state the life-breath lingers for twenty-one days and then passes out. Entering the 'black waters' of the ocean, the ship never comes back. But the Iśvarakotis, such as the Incarnations of God, can come down from this state of samādhi. They can descend from this exalted state because they like to live in the company of devotees and enjoy the love of God. God retains in them the 'ego of Knowledge' or the 'ego of Devotion' so that they may teach men. Their minds move between the sixth and the seventh planes. They run a boat-race back and forth, as it were, between these two planes.

"After attaining samādhi some souls of their own accord keep the 'ego of Knowledge'. But that ego does not create any attachment. It is like a line drawn on the water.

"Hanumān kept the 'servant ego' after realizing God in both His Personal and His Impersonal aspects. He thought of himself as the servant of God. The great sages, such as Nārada, Sanaka, Sananda, Sanātana, and Sanat-kumāra, after attaining the Knowledge of Brahman, kept the 'servant ego' and the 'ego of Devotion'. They are like big steamships, which not only cross the ocean themselves but carry many passengers to the other shore.

"There are two classes of paramahamsas, one affirming the formless Reality and the other affirming God with form. Trailanga Swami believed in the formless Reality. Paramahamsas like him care for their own good alone; they feel satisfied if they themselves attain the goal.

"But those paramahamsas who believe in God with form keep the love of God even after attaining the Knowledge of Brahman, so that they may teach spiritual truth to others. They are like a pitcher brimful of water. Part of the water may be poured into another pitcher. These perfected souls describe to others the various spiritual disciplines by which they have realized God. They do this only to teach others and to help them in spiritual life. With great effort men dig a well for drinking-water, using spades and baskets for the purpose. After the digging is over, some throw the spades and other implements into the well, not needing them any more. But some put them away near the well, so that others may use them.

"Some eat mangoes secretly and remove all trace of them by wiping their mouths with a towel. But some share the fruit with others. There are sages who, even after attaining Knowledge, work to help others and also to enjoy the Bliss of God in the company of devotees. 'I want to eat sugar. I don't want to be sugar.'

"The gopis of Vrindāvan, too, attained the Knowledge of Brahman; but they were not seeking It. They wanted to enjoy God, looking on themselves as His mother, His friend, His handmaid, or His lover."

The Bāuls from Shibpur began to sing to the accompaniment of a stringed instrument. A line in the first song was:

> We are sinners: redeem us, O merciful Lord!

MASTER (*to the devotees*): "It is the attitude of a beginner to worship God out of fear. Please sing about God-realization—songs expressing divine joy.

(*To Rakhal*) "How well they sang that song the other day at Nabin Niyogi's house: 'Be drunk, O mind, be drunk with the Wine of Heavenly Bliss'! While singing religious songs one should not constantly refer to one's worries. One should rather feel joyous and ecstatic as one chants God's name."

A DEVOTEE: "Sir, won't you sing?"

MASTER: "What shall I sing? Well, I may sing when the spirit moves me."

After a few minutes the Master began to sing. His eyes were turned upward. He sang:

> Behold the waves of Gorā's ecstatic love;
> Under them all the universe lies submerged!
> And in his love I, too, long to be drowned.
> O friend, Gaurānga's love has swallowed me;
> Who else feels for our misery like Gaurānga,
> Dragging us from the mire of worldliness?

He sang again:

> Dive deep, O mind, dive deep in the Ocean of God's Beauty;
> If you descend to the uttermost depths,
> There you will find the gem of Love. . . .

Then he sang about the Divine Mother:

> Can everyone have the vision of Śyāmā? Is Kāli's treasure for
>   everyone?
> Oh, what a pity my foolish mind will not see what is true! . . .

He continued:

> The black bee of my mind is drawn in sheer delight
> To the blue lotus flower of Mother Śyāmā's feet. . . .

And again:

> O Mother, what a machine[1] is this that Thou hast made!
> What pranks Thou playest with this toy
> Three and a half cubits high! . . .

[1] The human body.

As Sri Ramakrishna sang the last song he went into samādhi. The devotees sat speechless, gazing at his radiant figure. After some time he regained partial consciousness of the world and began to talk to the Divine Mother.

The Master said, "Mother, please come down from up there." Did he feel his mind still lingering in the seventh plane of consciousness, the thousand-petalled lotus of the Sahasrāra?

"Please do come down", he said. "Don't torment me that way. Be still, Mother, and sit down.

"O Mother, everybody's future is determined by the tendencies of his previous births. What shall I say to these people? Nothing can be achieved without discrimination and renunciation."

Sri Ramakrishna had now regained full consciousness of the world, and he continued: "There are many kinds of renunciation. One of them may be called 'markatavairāgya', 'monkey renunciation'. It is a false renunciation stimulated by the afflictions of the world. That renunciation doesn't last long. Then there is real renunciation. A man with everything in the world, lacking nothing, feels all to be unreal.

"It is not possible to acquire renunciation all at once. The time factor must be taken into account. But it is also true that a man should hear about it. When the right time comes, he will say to himself, 'Oh yes, I heard about this.'

"You must also remember another thing. By constantly hearing about renunciation one's desire for worldly objects gradually wears away. One should take rice-water in small doses to get rid of the intoxication of liquor. Then one gradually becomes normal.

"An aspirant entitled to the Knowledge of God is very rare. It is said in the *Gītā* that one in thousands desires to know God, and again, that among thousands who have such a desire, only one is able to know Him."

A devotee quoted the text from the *Gītā*.

MASTER: "As your attachment to the world diminishes, your spiritual knowledge will increase. Attachment to the world means attachment to 'woman and gold'.

"It is not given to everybody to feel prema, ecstatic love of God. Chaitanya experienced it. An ordinary man can at the most experience bhāva. Only the Iśvarakotis, such as Divine Incarnations, experience prema. When prema is awakened the devotee not only feels the world to be unreal, but forgets even the body, which everyone loves so intensely.

"In a Persian book it is said that inside the skin is the flesh, inside the flesh the bone, inside the bone the marrow, and so on, but that prema is the innermost of all. One becomes soft and tender through prema. On account of this prema, Krishna became tribhanga.[2]

"Prema is the rope by which you can tether God, as it were. Whenever you want to see Him you have merely to pull the rope. Whenever you call Him, He will appear before you.

"The mature stage of bhakti is bhāva. When one attains it one remains

[2] Literally, "bent in three places". The usual standing figure of Krishna is bent in three places, namely, the neck, the waist, and the knees.

speechless, thinking of Satchidānanda. The feeling of an ordinary man can go only that far. When bhāva ripens it becomes mahābhāva. Prema is the last. You know the difference between a green mango and a ripe one. Unalloyed love of God is the essential thing. All else is unreal.

"Once Rāma was pleased with the prayer of Nārada and told him to ask for a boon. Nārada prayed for pure love and said further, 'O Rāma, please grant that I may not be deluded by Thy world-bewitching māyā.' Rāma said: 'That is all right. But ask for something else.' Nārada replied: 'I don't want anything else. I pray only for pure love.'

"How can a devotee attain such love? First, the company of holy men. That awakens śraddhā, faith in God. Then comes nishthā, single-minded devotion to the Ideal. In that stage the devotee does not like to hear anything but talk about God. He performs only those acts that please God. After nishthā comes bhakti, devotion to God; then comes bhāva. Next mahābhāva, then prema, and last of all the attainment of God Himself. Only for Iśvarakotis, such as the Incarnations, is it possible to have mahābhāva or prema.

"The knowledge of a worldly person, the knowledge of a devotee, and the Knowledge of an Incarnation are by no means of the same degree. The knowledge of a worldly person is like the light of an oil lamp, which shows only the inside of a room. Through such knowledge he eats and drinks, attends to household duties, protects his body, brings up his children, and so on.

"The knowledge of a devotee is like the light of the moon, which illumines objects both inside and outside a room. But such light does not enable him to see a distant or a very minute object.

"The Knowledge of an Incarnation of God is like the light of the sun. Through that light the Incarnation sees everything, inside and outside, big and small.

"The mind of a worldly person is, no doubt, like muddy water; but it can be made clear by a purifying agent. Discrimination and renunciation are the purifying agent."

The Master spoke to the devotees from Shibpur.

MASTER: "Have you any questions to ask?"

A DEVOTEE: "We have listened to your words."

MASTER: "Yes, it is good to listen to these things. But nothing will happen except at the right time. What can quinine do for a fever patient when he runs a high temperature? Only when his temperature comes down through the use of 'fever mixture' or a purgative should quinine be prescribed. There are patients who get rid of their fever even without quinine. A child said to his mother, when he was put to bed, 'Mother, please wake me up when I feel the call of nature.' The mother said: 'My child, I shall not have to wake you. The urge itself will wake you.'

"Different kinds of people come here. Some come by boat with the devotees. But they do not enjoy spiritual talk. They keep nudging their friends and whispering: 'When shall we leave here? When are we going?' If the friends show no sign of getting up, they say, 'We would rather wait for you in the boat.'

"Those who have a human body for the first time need the experience of sense enjoyments. Spiritual consciousness is not awakened unless certain duties have been performed."

The Master was going to the pine-grove. With a smile he said to M., on the semicircular porch, "Well, what do you think of my state of mind?"

M. (smiling): "On the surface you are very simple, but inwardly very deep. It is extremely difficult to understand you."

MASTER (smiling): "True. It is like the cement floor of a house. People see only the outer surface and do not know how many materials there are under it."

It was about four o'clock in the afternoon. Balaram and several other devotees got into a country boat to return to Calcutta. It was ebb-tide in the Ganges. A gentle breeze was blowing from the south, covering the bosom of the sacred river with ripples. M. looked at the scene a long time. As the boat disappeared in the direction of Calcutta, he came back to the Master.

Sri Ramakrishna was going to the pine-grove. A beautiful, dark rain-cloud was to be seen in the northwest. The Master asked M.: "Do you think it will rain? Please bring my umbrella." M. brought the umbrella. Reaching the Panchavati, the Master said to Latu, who also accompanied him, "Why do you look so sickly?"

LATU: "I can hardly eat anything."

MASTER: "Is that the only reason? It is also a bad time of the year. Are you meditating too much? (To M.) I have a request to make of you. Please tell Baburam to stay with me a day or two during Rakhal's absence. Otherwise I shall feel very unhappy."

M: "Yes, sir. I shall tell him."

Sri Ramakrishna asked M. whether he thought that Baburam was guileless.

Presently the Master left them, going in the direction of the pine-trees. After a few minutes M. and Latu, standing in the Panchavati, saw the Master coming back toward them. Behind him the sky was black with the rain-cloud. Its reflection in the Ganges made the water darker. The disciples felt that the Master was God Incarnate, a Divine Child five years old, radiant with the smile of innocence and purity. Around him were the sacred trees of the Panchavati under which he had practised spiritual discipline and had beheld visions of God. At his feet flowed the sacred river Ganges, the destroyer of man's sins. The presence of this God-man charged the trees, shrubs, flowers, plants, and temples with spiritual fervour and divine joy.

Sri Ramakrishna returned to his room and sat on the small couch. He began to praise a medicine that a certain brahmachāri had prepared for him. Referring to this man, Hazra said: "He is now entangled in many worldly anxieties. What a shame! Look at Nabai Chaitanya of Konnagar. Though a householder, he has put on a red cloth."

MASTER: "What shall I say? I clearly see that it is God Himself who has assumed all these human forms. Therefore I cannot take anybody to task."

HAZRA: "Narendra is again involved in a lawsuit."

MASTER: "He doesn't believe in Śakti, the Divine Mother. If one assumes a human body, one must recognize Her."

HAZRA: "Narendra says: 'If I believed in Śakti, all would follow me. Therefore I cannot.'"

MASTER: "But it is not good for him to go to the extreme of denying the Divine Mother. He is now under Śakti's jurisdiction. Even a judge, while giving evidence in a case, comes down and stands in the witness-box. (*To M.*) "Have you seen Narendra lately?"

M: "Not during the last few days."

MASTER: "See him and bring him here in a carriage. (*To Hazra*) "Well, what is his relation to this [meaning himself]?"

HAZRA: "He expects help from you."

MASTER: "And what about Bhavanath? Would he come here so frequently if he didn't have good tendencies? What about Harish and Latu? They always meditate. Why is that?"

HAZRA: "That's right. Why should they devote all their time to meditation? It is quite a different thing for them to stay here to attend to your personal needs."

MASTER: "Possibly you are right. Perhaps others may take their place now."

Hazra left the room, leaving the Master alone with M.

MASTER: "Does what I say in the state of ecstasy attract people?"

M: "Oh, yes. Very much."

MASTER: "What do people think of me? Do they think anything in particular about me when they see me in that condition?"

M: "We feel in you a wonderful synthesis of knowledge, love, and renunciation, and on the surface a natural spontaneity. Many divine experiences have passed, like huge steamboats, through the deep of your inner consciousness; still you maintain outwardly this utter simplicity. Many cannot understand it, but a few are attracted by this state alone."

MASTER: "There is a sect of Vaishnavas known as the Ghoshpárá, who describe God as the 'Sahaja', the 'Simple One'. They say further that a man cannot recognize this 'Simple One' unless he too is simple. (*To M.*) Have I any ego?"

M: "Yes, sir. A little. You have kept it to preserve your body, and to enjoy divine love in the company of the devotees and impart spiritual knowledge to them. Further, you have kept this trace of ego by praying to the Divine Mother for it."

MASTER: "No. I have not kept it. It is God Himself who has left it in me. Can you tell me how I appear in the state of samādhi?"

M: "As you said a little while ago, you see the form of God when your mind rises to the 'sixth plane'. When you speak after that, your mind comes down to the 'fifth plane'."

MASTER: "It is God who does all these things. I do not know anything."

M: "That is why you attract people so much. Sir, I have a question to ask. There are two opinions in the scriptures. According to one Purāna, Krishna is Chidātmā, the Absolute, and Rādhā is Chitśakti, Its Divine Power; but according to another, Krishna Himself is Kāli, the Primordial Energy."

MASTER: "This second view is held in the *Devi Purāna*. According to it,

Kālī Herself has become Krishna. But what difference does it make? God is infinite, and infinite are the ways to reach Him."

M. remained speechless with wonder for a few moments and then said: "Oh, now I understand. As you say, the important thing is to climb to the roof. Our goal will be achieved if we can accomplish it by following any of the means—a rope or a pole."

MASTER: "It is through the grace of God that you have understood that. Without His grace doubt is never cleared up.

"The important thing is somehow to cultivate devotion to God and love for Him. What is the use of knowing many things? It is enough to cultivate love of God by following any of the paths. When you have this love, you are sure to attain God. Afterwards, if it is necessary, God will explain everything to you and tell you about the other paths as well. It is enough for you to develop love of God. You have no need of many opinions and discussions. You have come to the orchard to eat mangoes. Enjoy them to your heart's content. You don't need to count the branches and leaves on the trees. It is wise to follow the attitude of Hanumān: 'I do not know the day of the week, the phase of the moon, or the position of the stars; I only contemplate Rāma.' "

M: "I now desire that my activities may be much reduced and that I may devote myself greatly to God."

MASTER: "Ah! Certainly your desire will be fulfilled. But a jnāni can live unattached in the world."

M: "True, sir. But one needs special power to lead an unattached life."

MASTER: "That is also true. But perhaps you wanted the worldly life. Krishna had been enshrined in Rādhā's heart; but Rādhā wanted to sport with Him in human form. Hence all the episodes of Vrindāvan. Now you should pray to God that your worldly duties may be reduced. And you will achieve the goal if you renounce mentally."

M: "But mental renunciation is prescribed for those who cannot give up the world outwardly. For superior devotees total renunciation is enjoined —both outer and inner."

Sri Ramakrishna was silent a few minutes and then resumed the conversation.

MASTER: "How did you like what I said about renunciation a little while ago?"

M: "Very much, sir."

MASTER: "Tell me, what is the meaning of renunciation?"

M: "Renunciation does not mean simply dispassion for the world. It means dispassion for the world and also longing for God."

MASTER: "You are right. You no doubt need money for your worldly life; but don't worry too much about it. The wise course is to accept what comes of its own accord. Don't take too much trouble to save money. Those who surrender their hearts and souls to God, those who are devoted to Him and have taken refuge in Him, do not worry much about money. As they earn, so they spend. The money comes in one way and goes out the other. This is what the *Gītā* describes as 'accepting what comes of its own accord'."

The Master referred to Haripada and said, "He came here the other day."

M: "He knows how to sing the stories of the Purāna. He sings melodiously about the life of Prahlāda and the nativity of Sri Krishna."

MASTER: "Is that so? That day I looked into his eyes. They had an inward look. I asked him whether he meditated a great deal, but he sat with his eyes cast down and didn't answer. Then I said to him, 'Look here, don't strain yourself too much.'"

It was now dusk. Sri Ramakrishna, as was usual with him during this part of the day, chanted the names of God and turned his mind to contemplation. Soon the moon rose in the sky. The temples, courtyards, and trees were bathed in its silvery light, and millions of broken moons played on the rippling surface of the Ganges. Rakhal and M. were with the Master in his room.

MASTER (to M.): "Baburam says, 'Oh, the worldly life! God forbid!'"

M: "His opinion is based on mere hearsay. What does he know of the world? He is a mere child."

MASTER: "Yes, that is true. Have you noticed Niranjan? He is utterly artless."

M: "Yes, sir. His very appearance attracts people. How expressive his eyes are!"

MASTER: "Not only his eyes, but his entire person. His relatives proposed that he marry. At this he said, 'Why are you going to drown me?' (With a smile) Tell me this. People say that a man finds great pleasure in the company of his wife after the hard work of the day."

M: "That is no doubt true of those who think that way. (To Rakhal, with a smile) We are now being examined. This is a leading question."

Both Rakhal and M. were married.

MASTER (with a smile): "A mother says, 'I shall heave a sigh of relief if I can procure a "shade-tree"[3] for my son. He will rest in its shade when scorched by the heat of the world.'"

M: "True, sir. But there are parents and parents. A father who is spiritually illumined doesn't give his children in marriage. If he does, his is a fine spirituality!"

Adhar Sen arrived from Calcutta and saluted the Master. After a few minutes he went to the temple of Kāli, where M. followed him.

A little later M. was sitting at the bathing-ghat on the Ganges. The flood-tide had just set in. As he listened to the waters lapping against the bank, many pictures of Sri Ramakrishna's divine life flitted before his mind: the Master's deep samādhi, his constant ecstasy, his joy in the love of God, his untiring discourse on spiritual life, his genuine love for the devotees, and, above all, his childlike simplicity. Who was this man? Was it God who had embodied Himself on earth for the sake of His devotees?

Adhar and M. returned to the Master's room. Adhar had been to Chittagong, in East Bengal, on official duty. He was telling the Master about his visit to the Chandranāth Hills and Sītākunda, sacred places of Chittagong.

[3] The word means "wife".

ADHAR: "Near Sītākunda I visited a well where I saw fire in the water. It is always burning on the water with leaping tongues."

MASTER: "How is that possible?"

ADHAR: "The water contains phosphorus."

Presently Ram Chatterji entered the room. The Master said some kind words about him to Adhar.

MASTER: "Ram's presence in the temple garden has relieved us of many anxieties. He searches out Harish, Latu, and the others at meal-time. Very often they are absorbed in meditation in some corner of the temple garden. It is Ram who sees that they eat at the proper time."

Saturday, September 6, 1884

About three o'clock in the afternoon Sri Ramakrishna was seated in Adhar's parlour on the second floor. Narendra, the Mukherji brothers, Bhavanath, M., Hazra, and other devotees were with the Master.

Arrangements were being made for Narendra to sing: While he was tuning the tānpurā, one of the strings snapped, and the Master exclaimed, "Oh! What have you done?" Narendra then tuned the drums. The Master said to him, "You are beating that drum, and I feel as if someone were slapping my cheek."

Referring to the kirtan, Narendra said: "There is not much rhythm in the kirtan. That's why it is so popular and people love it so much."

MASTER: "How silly! People like it because it is so tender and full of pathos."

Narendra sang:

Sweet is Thy name, O Refuge of the humble!
It falls like sweetest nectar on our ears
And comforts us, Beloved of our souls! . . .

He sang again:

O Lord, must all my days pass by so utterly in vain?
Down the path of hope I gaze with longing, day and night.
Thou art the Lord of all the worlds, and I but a beggar here;
How can I ask of Thee to come and dwell within my heart?
My poor heart's humble cottage door is standing open wide;
Be gracious, Lord, and enter there but once, and quench its thirst!

MASTER (to Hazra, smiling): "That was the first song he sang for me."

Narendra sang one or two more songs. Then Vaishnavcharan sang, describing the grief of the gopis at the sight of Krishna as king of Mathurā:

O Hari, how shall we know You now?
In Mathurā's royal splendour You have forgotten us. . . .

MASTER: "Won't you sing that one—'O vīnā, sing Lord Hari's name'?"

Vaishnavcharan sang:

O vīnā, sing Lord Hari's name!
Without the blessing of His feet

You cannot know the final Truth.
The name of Hari slays all grief:
Sing Hari's name! Sing Krishna's name!
If only Hari shows His grace,
Then I shall never be distressed.
O vīnā, sing His name but once;
No earthly gem is half so rare.
Govinda says: In vain my days
Have passed. No longer may I float
Here in life's trackless ocean waste!

While listening to the song, the Master became abstracted. Saying "Ah me! Ah me!", he went into samādhi. The devotees were sitting around him, their eyes riveted on him. The room was filled with people.

The musician sang again. As he improvised new lines describing ecstatic love of God, the Master stood up and danced. He himself improvised lines and sang them with outstretched arms. Soon he went into samādhi and sat down, with his head resting on the bolster in front of him. The musician was also carried away with emotion and sang new songs. Sri Ramakrishna again stood up and began to dance. The devotees could not control themselves. They too danced with the Master. While dancing, Sri Ramakrishna every now and then went into deep samādhi. When he was in the deepest samādhi he could not utter a word and his whole body remained transfixed. The devotees danced encircling him. After a while, regaining partial consciousness, he danced with the strength of a lion, intoxicated with ecstatic love. But even then he could not utter a word. Finally, regaining more of the consciousness of the world, he sang again, improvising the lines. An intense spiritual atmosphere was created in Adhar's parlour. At the sound of the loud music a large crowd had gathered in the street.

Sri Ramakrishna danced a long time in the company of the devotees. When he resumed his seat, still tinged with the lingering glow of divine fervour, he asked Narendra to sing "O Mother, make me mad with Thy love".

Narendra sang:

O Mother, make me mad with Thy love!
What need have I of knowledge or reason? . . .

MASTER: "And that one—'Upon the Sea of Blissful Awareness'."
Narendra sang:

Upon the Sea of Blissful Awareness waves of ecstatic love arise:
Rapture divine! Play of God's Bliss!
Oh, how enthralling! . . .

MASTER: "And that one too—'In Wisdom's firmament'. Perhaps it is too long. Do you think so? All right, sing it slowly."
Narendra sang:

In Wisdom's firmament the moon of Love is rising full,
And Love's flood-tide, in surging waves, is flowing everywhere.
O Lord, how full of bliss Thou art! Victory unto Thee! . . .

MASTER: "And won't you sing that one—'The Wine of Heavenly Bliss'?"
Narendra sang:

> Be drunk, O mind, be drunk with the Wine of Heavenly Bliss!
> Roll on the ground and weep, chanting Hari's sweet name!
> Fill the arching heavens with your deep lion roar,
> Singing Hari's sweet name! With both your arms upraised,
> Dance in the name of Hari and give His name to all.
> Swim by day and by night in the bliss of Hari's love;
> Slay desire with His name, and blessed be your life!

The Master improvised, "Be drunk with prema and weep, chanting Hari's sweet name." And, "Be mad with divine fervour and weep, chanting His name."

Sri Ramakrishna and the devotees rested awhile. Narendra said to the Master in a low voice, "Will you kindly sing that one?"

MASTER: "My voice has become a little hoarse."

After a few minutes he asked Narendra, "Which one?"

NARENDRA: " 'Gaur, whose beauty delights the world.' "

Sri Ramakrishna sang, describing the beauty of Sri Chaitanya:

> Who has brought Gaur to Nadiā—
> Gaur, whose beauty delights the world?
> His face, covered with ringlets of hair,
> Shines like lightning against a dark cloud. . . .

Again he sang, this time about the grief of a gopi at her separation from Sri Krishna:

> I have not found my Krishna, O friend! How cheerless my home
>   without Him!
> Ah, if Krishna could only be the hair upon my head,
> Carefully I should braid it then, and deck it with bakul-flowers;
> Carefully I should fashion the braids out of my Krishna-hair.
> Krishna is black, and black is my hair; black would be one with
>   black.
>
> Ah, if Krishna could only be the ring I wear in my nose,
> Always from my nose He would hang, and my two lips could
>   touch Him.
> But it can never be, alas! Why should I idly dream?
> Why should Krishna care at all to be the ring in my nose?
>
> Ah, if Krishna could only be the bracelets on my arms,
> Always He would cling to my wrists, and proudly I should walk,
> Shaking my bracelets to make them sound, shaking my arms to
>   show them;
> Down the king's highway I should walk, wearing my Krishna-
>   bracelets.

The music was over. The Master began to talk with the devotees.

MASTER (smiling): "Hazra danced."

NARENDRA: "Yes, a little."

MASTER: "A little?"

NARENDRA: "Yes. His belly danced too." (*All laugh.*)

Pundit Shashadhar's host had been thinking of inviting the Master for dinner.

MASTER: "I have heard that his host is not an honest man. He is immoral."

NARENDRA: "That is why you didn't drink the water he touched. It happened the first day you met Shashadhar at his house. How did you come to know he was immoral?"

MASTER (*smiling*): "Hazra knows of another instance. It happened at Sihore in Hriday's house."

HAZRA: "The man was a Vaishnava. He came with me to see you [meaning Sri Ramakrishna]. As soon as he sat in front of you, you turned your back on him."

MASTER: "We learnt later that he led an immoral life. (*To Narendra*) You used to say, at first, that these were all hallucinations."

NARENDRA: "How was I to know? Now I see that you are always right."

Adhar had prepared a feast for the Master and the devotees, and now he invited them to the meal. The Master said to the Mukherji brothers: "What? Won't you eat?" They said humbly, "Please excuse us."

MASTER: "But why? You are doing everything else. Why this hesitation only about eating the meal?"

Adhar was a low-caste Hindu. Therefore some of the Master's brāhmin devotees hesitated to eat at his house. They came to their senses at last when they saw Sri Ramakrishna himself eating.

It was about nine o'clock. The Master was resting in the drawing-room with the devotees. He would soon leave for Dakshineswar.

The Mukherji brothers had arranged with a singer of kirtan to entertain the Master the following day. Ram was taking singing-lessons from this musician. Sri Ramakrishna asked Narendra to come to Dakshineswar to hear the kirtan.

MASTER (*to Narendra*): "Come tomorrow, won't you?"

NARENDRA: "I shall try, sir."

MASTER: "You can bathe there and also take your meal. (*Pointing to M.*) He may dine there too. (*To M.*) Are you quite well now? I hope you are not on a diet."

M: "No, sir. I shall come."

Nityagopal was living at Vrindāvan. Chunilal had returned from Vrindāvan only a few days before, and the Master inquired about Nityagopal.

As Sri Ramakrishna was about to leave, M. saluted him, touching the Master's feet with his forehead. The Master said to him tenderly: "Then I shall see you tomorrow. Narendra! Bhavanath! Please come tomorrow." Then with several devotees he set out for Dakshineswar.

The other devotees returned home in the moonlit night, cherishing in their hearts the Master's ecstatic music and dancing.

27

AT DAKSHINESWAR

I T WAS ABOUT ELEVEN O'CLOCK. The Master was sitting in his room at Dakshineswar. He had not yet taken his midday meal.

Arrangements had been made with the musician Shyamdas to enter-
tain the Master and the devotees with his kirtan. Baburam, M., Manomohan,
Bhavanath, Kishori, Chunilal, Haripada, the Mukherji brothers, Ram,
Surendra, Tarak, Niranjan, and others arrived at the temple garden. Latu,
Harish, and Hazra were staying with the Master.

When M. saluted Sri Ramakrishna, the Master asked: "Where is Narendra? Isn't he coming?" M. told him that Narendra could not come.

A brāhmin devotee was reading to the Master from a book of devotional
songs by Rāmprasād. Sri Ramakrishna asked him to continue. The brāhmin
read a song, the first line of which was: "O Mother, put on Thy clothes."

MASTER: "Stop, please! These ideas are outlandish and bizarre. Read
something that will awaken bhakti."

The brāhmin read:

> Who is there that can understand what Mother Kāli is?
> Even the six darśanas are powerless to reveal Her. . . .

MASTER (to M.): "I got a pain because I lay too long on one side while
in samādhi yesterday at Adhar's house; so now I'll take Baburam with me
when I visit the houses of the devotees. He is a sympathetic soul."

With these words the Master sang:

> How shall I open my heart, O friend?
> It is forbidden me to speak.
> I am about to die, for lack of a kindred soul
> To understand my misery.
>
> Simply by looking in his eyes,
> I find the beloved of my heart;
> But rare is such a soul, who swims in ecstatic bliss
> On the high tide of heavenly love.

MASTER: "The Bāuls sing songs like that. They also sing another kind of
song:

> Stay your steps, O wandering monk!
> Stand there with begging-bowl in hand,
> And let me behold your radiant face.

"According to the Śakti cult the siddha is called a koul, and according to the Vedānta, a paramahamsa. The Bāuls call him a sāi. They say, 'No one is greater than a sāi.' The sāi is a man of supreme perfection. He doesn't see any differentiation in the world. He wears a necklace, one half made of cow bones and the other of the sacred tulsi-plant. He calls the Ultimate Truth 'Ālekh', the 'Incomprehensible One'. The Vedas call It 'Brahman'. About the jīvas the Bāuls say, 'They come from Ālekh and they go unto Ālekh.' That is to say, the individual soul has come from the Unmanifest and goes back to the Unmanifest. The Bāuls will ask you, 'Do you know about the wind?' The 'wind' means the great current that one feels in the subtle nerves, Iḍā, Pingalā, and Sushumnā, when the Kundalini is awakened. They will ask you further, 'In which station are you dwelling?' According to them there are six 'stations', corresponding to the six psychic centres of Yoga. If they say that a man dwells in the 'fifth station', it means that his mind has climbed to the fifth centre, known as the Viśuddha chakra. (*To M.*) At that time he sees the Formless."

Saying this the Master sang:

> Within the petals of this flower there lies concealed a subtle space,
> Transcending which, one sees at length the universe in Space
> dissolve.

"Once a Bāul came here. I asked him, 'Have you finished the task of "refining the syrup"? Have you taken the pot off the stove?' The more you boil the juice of sugar-cane, the more it is refined. In the first stage of boiling it is simply the juice of the sugar-cane. Next it is molasses, then sugar, then sugar candy, and so on. As it goes on boiling, the substances you get are more and more refined.

"When does a man take the pot off the stove? That is, when does a man come to the end of his sādhanā? He comes to the end when he has acquired complete mastery over his sense-organs. His sense-organs become loosened and powerless, as the leech is loosened from the body when you put lime on its mouth. In that state a man may live with a woman, but he does not feel any lust for her.

"Many of the Bāuls follow a 'dirty' method of spiritual discipline. It is like entering a house through the back door by which the scavengers come.

"One day I was taking my meal when a Bāul devotee arrived. He asked me, 'Are you yourself eating, or are you feeding someone else?' The meaning of his words was that the siddha sees God dwelling within a man. The siddhas among the Bāuls will not talk to persons of another sect; they call them 'strangers'.

"The Bāuls designate the state of perfection as the 'sahaja', the 'natural' state. There are two signs of this state. First, a perfect man will not 'smell of Krishna'. Second, he is like the bee that lights on the lotus but does not sip the honey. The first means that he keeps all his spiritual feelings within himself. He doesn't show outwardly any sign of spirituality. He doesn't even utter the name of Hari. The second means that he is not attached to woman. He has completely mastered his senses.

"The Bāuls do not like the worship of an image. They want a living man. That is why one of their sects is called the Kartābhajā. They worship the kartā, that is to say, the guru, as God.

"You see how many opinions there are about God. Each opinion is a path. There are innumerable opinions and innumerable paths leading to God."

BHAVANATH: "Then what should we do?"

MASTER: "You must stick to one path with all your strength. A man can reach the roof of a house by stone stairs or a ladder or a rope-ladder or a rope or even by a bamboo pole. But he cannot reach the roof if he sets foot now on one and now on another. He should firmly follow one path. Likewise, in order to realize God a man must follow one path with all his strength.

"But you must regard other views as so many paths leading to God. You should not feel that your path is the only right path and that other paths are wrong. You mustn't bear malice toward others.

"Well, to what path do I belong? Keshab Sen used to say to me: 'You belong to our path. You are gradually accepting the ideal of the formless God.' Shashadhar says that I belong to his path. Vijay, too, says that I belong to his—Vijay's—path."

Sri Ramakrishna walked toward the Panchavati with M. and a few other devotees. It was midday and time for the flood-tide in the Ganges.

They waited in the Panchavati to see the bore of the tide.

MASTER (to the devotees): "The ebb-tide and flood-tide are indeed amazing. But notice one thing. Near the sea you see ebb-tide and flood-tide in a river, but far away from the sea the river flows in one direction only. What does this mean? Try to apply its significance to your spiritual life. Those who live very near God feel within them the currents of bhakti, bhāva, and the like. In the case of a few—the Iśvarakotis, for instance—one sees even mahābhāva and prema.

(To M.) "What is the explanation of the ebb-tide and flood-tide?"

M: "According to Western astronomy, they are due to the attraction of the sun and the moon."

In order to explain it, M. drew figures on the earth and began to show the Master the movement of the earth, the sun, and the moon. The Master looked at the figures for a minute and said: "Stop, please! It gives me a headache."

Presently the tide came up the Ganges. They heard the sound of the rushing water. The tide struck the bank of the river and flowed toward the north. Sri Ramakrishna looked at it intently and exclaimed like a child: "Look at that boat! I wonder what is going to happen to it."

The Master and M. sat down for a while in the Panchavati, Sri Ramakrishna placing his umbrella on the cement platform. The conversation turned to Narayan. The boy was a student. Sri Ramakrishna looked upon him as Nārāyana, God Himself, and was very fond of him.

MASTER: "Have you noticed Naran's[1] nature? He can mix with all, old and young. One cannot do this without a special power. Besides, all love him. Is he really artless?"

M: "I think so."

MASTER: "I understand that he goes to your place. Is that so?"

M: "Yes, sir. He has visited me once or twice."

MASTER: "Will you give him a rupee? Or shall I ask Kali[2] about it?"

M: "Very well, sir. I shall give him the money."

MASTER: "That's fine. It is good to help those who yearn for God. Thus one makes good use of one's money. What will you gain by spending everything on your family?"

Kishori had several children. His salary was too small to support his family. Sri Ramakrishna said to M.: "Naran said he would get a job for Kishori. Please remind him of it."

The Master walked away in the direction of the pine-grove. Returning to the Panchavati, he said to M.: "Please ask someone to spread a mat outside my room. I shall lie down a few minutes. I am coming presently."

When the Master returned to his room, he could not find his umbrella and exclaimed: "You have all forgotten the umbrella! The busybody doesn't see a thing even when it is very near him. A man went to a friend's house to light the charcoal for his smoke, though all the time he had a lighted lantern in his hand. Another man looked everywhere for his towel. Finally he discovered that it had been on his shoulder all the time."

It was about one o'clock in the afternoon. The Master ate the prasād from the Kāli temple. Then he wanted to rest awhile, but the devotees were still sitting in his room. They were asked to go out, and then the Master lay down. He said to Baburam, "Come here; sit near me." Baburam answered, "I am preparing betel-leaf." The Master said, "Put your betel-leaf aside."

The devotees sat under the bakul-tree in the Panchavati. Tarak, who had just returned from Vrindāvan, told them stories of his visit.

A little later Sri Ramakrishna was seated again on his couch, the devotees sitting on the floor. Shyamdas was singing with his party. He sang of the gopis' grief at their separation from Sri Krishna:

> Dry as a desert seemed the happy lake to them:
> The chātak died of thirst, gazing toward the clouds.

The Master became somewhat abstracted, but the musician could not create a spiritual atmosphere. Sri Ramakrishna asked Nabai of Konnagar to sing a kirtan. Nabai was Manomohan's uncle. He lived on the bank of the Ganges, devoting his time to prayer and meditation, and was a frequent visitor of Sri Ramakrishna at Dakshineswar.

Nabai began the kirtan in a loud voice. The Master left the couch and began to dance. Immediately Nabai and other devotees began to dance around him. The atmosphere became intense with spiritual fervour.

[1] Short for Narayan, a young disciple of the Master.
[2] A devotee of the Master.

After the kirtan, Sri Ramakrishna resumed his seat. With great feeling he began to sing of the Divine Mother, his eyes turned upward:

> O Mother, ever blissful as Thou art,
> Do not deprive Thy worthless child of bliss!
> My mind knows nothing but Thy Lotus Feet.
> The King of Death scowls at me terribly;
> Tell me, Mother, what shall I say to him? . . .

He sang again:

> As is a man's meditation, so is his feeling of love;
> As is a man's feeling of love, so is his gain;
> And faith is the root of all. . . .

He continued:

> This world, O Mother, is Thy madhouse! What can I say of all
>   Thy virtues?
> Setting aside Thine elephant, Thou roamest about on foot;
> Putting off Thy gems and pearls, O Self-willed Mother,
> Thou dost adorn Thy comely neck with a garland of human heads.
> Now Thou must rescue Rāmprasād out of the forest of this world.

Again he sang:

> Why should I go to Gangā or Gayā, to Kāśi, Kānchi, or Prabhās,
> So long as I can breathe my last with Kāli's name upon my
>   lips? . . .

And again:

> Dwell, O mind, within yourself;
> Enter no other's home.
> If you but seek there, you will find
> All you are searching for. . . .

And then:

> The black bee of my mind is drawn in sheer delight
> To the blue lotus flower of Mother Śyāmā's feet. . . .

And then:

> Cherish my precious Mother Śyāmā
> Tenderly within, O mind;
> May you and I alone behold Her,
> Letting no one else intrude. . . .

As the Master sang this last song he stood up. He was almost intoxicated with divine love. Again and again he said to the devotees, "Cherish my precious Mother Śyāmā tenderly within." Then he danced and sang:

> Is Kāli, my Mother, really black?
> The Naked One, of blackest hue,
> Lights the Lotus of the Heart. . . .

The Master reeled as he sang. Niranjan came forward to hold him. The Master said to him softly, "Don't touch me, you rascal!" Seeing the Master dance, the devotees stood up. He caught hold of M.'s hand and said: "Don't be foolish! Dance!"

Sri Ramakrishna resumed his seat, still charged with divine ecstasy. Coming down a little to the normal state, he said: "Om! Om! Om! Om! Om! Om Kāli!" Again he said, "Let me have a smoke." Many of the devotees stood around. Mahimacharan was fanning him. The Master asked him to sit down and recite from the scriptures. Mahimacharan recited from the *Mahānirvāna Tantra*:

> Om. I bow to Thee, the Everlasting Cause of the world;
> I bow to Thee, Pure Consciousness, the Soul that sustains the
>   whole universe.
> I bow to Thee, who art One without duality, who dost bestow
>   liberation;
> I bow to Thee, Brahman, the all-pervading Attributeless Reality.
>
> Thou alone art the Refuge, the only Object of adoration;
> Thou art the only Cause of the universe, the Soul of everything
>   that is;
> Thou alone art the world's Creator, Thou its Preserver and
>   Destroyer;
> Thou art the immutable Supreme Lord, the Absolute; Thou art
>   unchanging Consciousness.
>
> Dread of the dreadful! Terror of the terrible!
> Refuge of all beings! Purity of purifiers!
> Thou alone dost rule over those in the high places,
> Supreme over the supreme, the Protector of protectors.
>
> Almighty Lord, who art made manifest as the Form of all, yet art
>   Thyself unmanifest and indestructible;
> Thou who art imperceptible to the senses, yet art the very Truth;
> Incomprehensible, imperishable, all-pervading, hidden, and with-
>   out form;
> O Lord! O Light of the Universe! Protect us from harm.
>
> On that One alone we meditate; that One is the sole object of our
>   worship;
> To That alone, the non-dual Witness of the Universe, we bow.
> In that One who alone exists and who is our sole eternal Support,
>   we seek refuge,
> The self-dependent Lord, the Vessel of Safety in the ocean of
>   existence.

Sri Ramakrishna listened to the hymn with folded hands. After it was sung he saluted Brahman. The devotees did likewise.

Adhar arrived from Calcutta and bowed down before the Master.

MASTER (to M.): "We have had such joy today! How much joy Hari's name creates! Is it not so?"

M: "Yes, sir."

Mahimacharan was a student of philosophy. That day he too had chanted the name of Hari and danced during the kirtan. This made the Master very happy.

It was about dusk. Many of the devotees took their leave. A lamp was lighted in Sri Ramakrishna's room and incense was burnt. After some time the moon came out, flooding the sky with its light.

Sri Ramakrishna was sitting on his couch. He was in a spiritual mood, absorbed in contemplation of the Divine Mother. Now and then he chanted Her hallowed name. Adhar was sitting on the floor. M. and Niranjan, too, were there. Sri Ramakrishna began to talk to Adhar.

MASTER: "What! You have come just now! We have had so much kirtan and dancing. Shyamdas began the kirtan. He is Ram's music teacher. But I didn't enjoy his singing very much; I didn't feel like dancing. Later I heard about his character. I was told that he had as many mistresses as there are hairs on a man's head.

"Didn't you get the job?"

Adhar held the post of deputy magistrate, a government post that carried with it great prestige. He earned three hundred rupees a month. He had applied for the office of vice-chairman of the Calcutta Municipality. The salary attached to this office was one thousand rupees. In order to secure it, Adhar had interviewed many influential people in Calcutta.

MASTER (to M. and Niranjan): "Hazra said to me, 'Please pray to the Divine Mother for Adhar, that he may secure the job.' Adhar made the same request to me. I said to the Mother: 'O Mother, Adhar has been visiting You. May he get the job if it pleases You.' But at the same time I said to Her: 'How small-minded he is! He is praying to You for things like that and not for Knowledge and Devotion.'

(To Adhar) "Why did you dance attendance on all those small-minded people? You have seen so much; you have heard so much! 'After reading the entire Rāmāyana, to ask whose wife Sītā is!' "

ADHAR: "A man cannot but do these things if he wants to lead a householder's life. You haven't forbidden us to, have you?"

MASTER: "Nivritti alone is good, and not pravritti.[3] Once, when I was in a God-intoxicated state, I was asked to go to the manager of the Kāli temple to sign the receipt for my salary.[4] They all do it here. But I said to the manager: 'I cannot do that. I am not asking for any salary. You may give it to someone else if you want.' I am the servant of God alone. Whom else shall I serve? Mallick noticed the late hours of my meals and arranged for a cook. He gave me one rupee for a month's expenses. That embarrassed me. I had to run to him whenever he sent for me. It would have been quite a different thing if I had gone to him of my own accord.

"In leading the worldly life one has to humour mean-minded people and do many such things. After the attainment of my exalted state, I noticed how things were around me and said to the Divine Mother, 'O Mother,

[3] Nivritti and pravritti mean, respectively, inwardness of the mind and its inclination to outer enjoyment.

[4] Sri Ramakrishna was then acting as the salaried priest of the Kāli temple.

please change the direction of my mind right now, so that I may not have to flatter rich people.'

(*To Adhar*) "Be satisfied with the job you have. People hanker after a post paying fifty or a hundred rupees, and you are earning three hundred rupees! You are a deputy magistrate. I saw a deputy magistrate at Kāmār-pukur. His name was Ishwar Ghoshal. He had a turban on his head. Men's very bones trembled before him. I remember having seen him during my boyhood. Is a deputy magistrate a person to be trifled with?

"Serve him whom you are already serving. The mind becomes soiled by serving but one master. And to serve five masters!

"Once a woman became attached to a Mussalman and invited him to her room. But he was a righteous person; he said to her that he wanted to use the toilet and must go home to get his water-jar for water. The woman offered him her own, but he said: 'No, that will not do. I shall use the jar to which I have already exposed myself. I cannot expose myself before a new one.' With these words he went away. That brought the woman to her senses. She understood that a new water-jar, in her case, signified a paramour."

Narendra was in straitened circumstances on account of his father's unexpected death. He had been seeking a job to maintain his mother, brothers, and sisters. He had served a few days as headmaster of the Vidyāsāgar School at Bowbāzār.

ADHAR: "May I ask if Narendra would accept a job?"

MASTER: "Yes, he would. He has his mother, brothers, and sisters to support."

ADHAR: "Well, Narendra can support his family with fifty or with a hundred rupees. Will he try for a hundred?"

MASTER: "Worldly people think highly of their wealth. They feel that there is nothing like it. Sambhu said, 'It is my desire to leave all my property at the Lotus Feet of God.' But does God care for money? He wants from His devotees knowledge, devotion, discrimination, and renunciation.

"After the theft of the jewelry from the temple of Rādhākānta, Mathur Babu said: 'O God, You could not protect Your own jewelry! What a shame!' Once he wanted to give me an estate and consulted Hriday about it. I overheard the whole thing from the Kāli temple and said to him: 'Please don't harbour any such thought. It will injure me greatly.'"

ADHAR: "I can tell you truthfully, sir, that not more than six or seven persons like you have been born since the creation of the world."

MASTER: "How so? There certainly are people who have given up everything for God. As soon as a man gives up his wealth, people come to know about him. But it is also true that there are others unknown to people. Are there not such holy men in upper India?"

ADHAR: "I know of at least one such person in Calcutta. He is Devendranath Tagore."

MASTER: "What did you say? Who has enjoyed the world as much as he? Once I visited him at his house with Mathur Babu. I saw that he had many young children. The family physician was there writing out prescriptions.

If, after having eight children, a man doesn't think of God, then who will? If, after enjoying so much wealth, Devendranath hadn't thought of God, then people would have cried shame upon him."

NIRANJAN: "But he paid off all his father's debts."

MASTER: "Keep quiet! Don't torment me any more. Do you call anyone a man who doesn't pay off his father's debts if he is able to? But I admit that Devendranath is infinitely greater than other worldly men, who are sunk in their worldliness. They can learn much from him.

"There is an ocean of difference between a real all-renouncing devotee of God and a householder devotee. A real sannyāsi, a real devotee who has renounced the world, is like a bee. The bee will not light on anything but a flower. It will not drink anything but honey. But a devotee leading the worldly life is like a fly. The fly sits on a festering sore as well as on a sweetmeat. One moment he enjoys a spiritual mood, and the next moment he is beside himself with the pleasure of 'woman and gold'.

"A devotee who has really and truly renounced all for God is like the chātak bird. It will drink only the rain-water that falls when the star Svāti is in the ascendant. It will rather die of thirst than touch any other water, though all around there may lie seven oceans and rivers full to the brim with water. An all-renouncing devotee will not touch 'woman and gold'. He will not keep 'woman and gold' near him lest he should feel attached."

ADHAR: "But Chaitanya, too, enjoyed the world."

MASTER (amazed): "What? What did he enjoy in the world?"

ADHAR: "Scholarship! Honour!"

MASTER: "It was honour in the sight of others, but nothing to him. Whether you—a deputy magistrate—or this youngster Niranjan honours me, it is all the same to me. And I tell you this truthfully: the idea of controlling a wealthy man never enters my mind. Surendra once said, rather condescendingly, that Rakhal's father could sue me for letting Rakhal[5] stay with me. When I heard this from Manomohan, I said: 'Who is this Surendra? How does he dare make a remark like that? He keeps a carpet and pillow here and gives me some money. Is that his excuse for daring to make such an impudent remark?' "

ADHAR: "I understand that he gives ten rupees a month. Isn't that so?"

MASTER: "That covers two months' expenses. The devotees stay here and he gives the money for their service. It is he who earns the merit. What is that to me? Is it for my personal gain that I love Narendra, Rakhal, and the others?"

M: "Your love for them is like a mother's for her children."

MASTER: "But even behind the mother's love lies her hope that the children will support her later on. But I love these youngsters because I see in them Nārāyana Himself. These are not mere words.

(To Adhar) "Listen. There is no scarcity of moths when the lamp is lighted. When God is realized, He Himself provides everything for His devotees. He sees that they do not lack anything. When God is enshrined in the heart, many people come forward to offer their services.

[5] Rakhal was then a minor.

"Once a young sannyāsi went to a householder to beg his food. He had lived as a monk from his very birth; he knew nothing of worldly matters. A young daughter of the householder came out to give him alms. He turned to her mother and said, 'Mother, has this girl abscesses on her chest?' The mother said: 'No, my child. God has given her breasts to nurse her child when she becomes a mother.' Thereupon the sannyāsi said: 'Then why should I worry about myself? Why should I beg my food? He who has created me will certainly feed me.'

"Listen. If a woman renounces everything for her paramour, she can say to him, if need be, 'You wretch! I shall sit on your chest and devour you.'

"Nangtā told me of a certain king who gave a feast to the sādhus, using plates and tumblers of gold. I noticed in the monasteries at Benares with what great respect the abbots were treated. Many wealthy up-country people stood before them with folded hands, ready to obey their commands. But a true sādhu, a man who has really renounced everything, seeks neither a gold plate nor honour. God sees that he lacks nothing. God gives the devotee everything that is needed for realizing Him.

(*To Adhar*) "You are an executive officer. What shall I say to you? Do whatever you think best. I am an illiterate person."

ADHAR (*smiling, to the devotees*): "Now he is examining me."

MASTER (*smiling*): "Dispassion alone is good. Don't you see, I didn't sign the receipt for my salary? God alone is real and all else is illusory."

Hazra entered the room and sat with the devotees on the floor. Hazra repeated now and then, "Soham! Soham!", "I am He! I am He!" To Latu and other devotees he often said: "What does one gain by worshipping God with offerings? That is merely giving Him things that are His already." He had said this once to Narendra.

The Master spoke to him.

MASTER: "I explained to Latu who the object of the devotee's worship is."

HAZRA: "The devotee really prays to his own Self."

MASTER: "What you say is a very lofty thought. The aim of spiritual discipline, of chanting God's name and glories, is to realize just that. A man attains everything when he discovers his true Self in himself. The object of sādhanā is to realize that. That also is the purpose of assuming a human body. One needs the clay mould as long as the gold image has not been cast; but when the image is made, the mould is thrown away. The body may be given up after the realization of God.

"God is not only inside us; He is both inside and outside. The Divine Mother showed me in the Kāli temple that everything is Chinmaya, the Embodiment of Spirit; that it is She who has become all this—the image, myself, the utensils of worship, the door-sill, the marble floor. Everything is indeed Chinmaya.

"The aim of prayer, of spiritual discipline, of chanting the name and glories of God, is to realize just that. For that alone a devotee loves God. These youngsters[6] are on a lower level; they haven't yet reached a high

[6] Referring to Latu and the others.

spiritual state. They are following the path of bhakti. Please don't tell them such things as 'I am He'."

Like the mother bird brooding over her chicks, Sri Ramakrishna was alert to protect his devotees.

Adhar and Niranjan went out on the porch to take refreshments. Presently they returned to the room.

ADHAR (smiling): "We talked about so many things. (Pointing to M.) But he didn't utter a word."

MASTER: "In Keshab's organization there was a young man with four university degrees. He laughed when he saw people arguing with me. He said: 'To argue with him! How silly!' I saw him again, later on, at one of Keshab's meetings. But then he did not have the same bright complexion."

Sri Ramakrishna sat on the floor for his supper. It was a light meal of a little farina pudding and one or two luchis that had been offered in the Kāli temple. M. and Latu were in the room. The devotees had brought various sweets for the Master. He touched a sandesh and asked Latu, "Who is the rascal that brought this?" He took it out of the cup and left it on the ground. He said to Latu and M.: "I know all about him. He is immoral."

LATU: "Shall I give you this sweet?"

MASTER: "Kishori brought it."

LATU: "Will it suit you?"

MASTER (smiling): "Yes."

M. had received an English education. Sri Ramakrishna said to him: "It is not possible for me to eat things offered by anyone and everyone. Do you believe this?"

M: "Gradually I shall have to believe all these things."

MASTER: "Yes, that is so."

After finishing the meal Sri Ramakrishna washed his mouth. He said to M., "Then will you give the rupee to Naran?" "Yes," said M., "certainly I will."

The moon rose in the clear autumn sky and was reflected in the river. It was ebb-tide in the Ganges and the river flowed south toward the sea.

Sunday, September 14, 1884

Sri Ramakrishna was sitting in his room with Narendra, Bhavanath, the Mukherji brothers, and other devotees. Rakhal was staying with Balaram at Vrindāvan and was laid up with an attack of fever. Narendra was preparing himself for his coming law examination.

About eleven o'clock Jnan Babu arrived. He was a government official and had received four university degrees.

MASTER (at the sight of Jnan Babu): "Well! Well! This sudden awakening of 'knowledge'!"[7]

JNAN (smiling): "You must admit, sir, that one sees the awakening of knowledge as a result of very good fortune."

MASTER (smiling): "You are Jnān. Then why should you have ajnān,

7 "Jnān" means "knowledge".

ignorance? Oh, I understand. Where there is knowledge there is also ignorance. The sage Vaśishtha was endowed with great knowledge and still he wept at the death of his sons. Therefore I ask you to go beyond both knowledge and ignorance. The thorn of ignorance has pierced the sole of a man's foot. He needs the thorn of knowledge to take it out. Afterwards he throws away both thorns. The jnāni says, 'This world is a "framework of illusion".' But he who is beyond both knowledge and ignorance describes it as a 'mansion of mirth'. He sees that it is God Himself who has become the universe, all living beings, and the twenty-four cosmic principles.

"A man can live in the world after attaining God. Then he can lead the life of detachment. In the country I have seen the women of the carpenter families making flattened rice with a husking-machine. With one hand one of them turns the paddy in the hole and with the other she holds a nursing child. At the same time she talks with the buyer. She says to him: 'You owe me two ānnās. Pay it before you go.' But seventy-five per cent of the woman's mind is on her hand lest it should be crushed by the pestle of the husking-machine.

"A man should do his worldly duties with only twenty-five per cent of his mind, devoting the rest to God."

Referring to Pundit Shashadhar, the Master said to the devotees, "I found him monotonous—engaged in the dry discussion of philosophy.

"He alone who, after reaching the Nitya, the Absolute, can dwell in the Līlā, the Relative, and again climb from the Līlā to the Nitya, has ripe knowledge and devotion. Sages like Nārada cherished love of God after attaining the Knowledge of Brahman. This is called vijnāna.

"Mere dry knowledge is like an ordinary rocket: it bursts into a few sparks and then dies out. But the Knowledge of sages like Nārada and Śukadeva is like a good rocket: for a while it showers balls of different colours, and then it stops; again it throws out new balls, and again it stops; and thus it goes on. Those sages had prema for God. Prema is the rope by which one can reach Satchidānanda."

The Master finished his midday meal and rested a few minutes. Bhavanath, M., the Mukherji brothers, Hazra, and several other devotees sat down under the bakul-tree and began to converse. The Master stopped there awhile on his way to the pine-grove.

HAZRA (to the younger Gopal): "Please prepare a smoke for him [meaning the Master]."

MASTER (smiling): "Why don't you admit that you want it?" (All laugh.)

MUKHERJI (to Hazra): "You must have learnt much wisdom from him [meaning the Master]."

MASTER (smiling): "No, he has been wise like this from his boyhood." (All laugh.)

Presently Sri Ramakrishna returned from the pine-grove. The devotees noticed that he was in an ecstatic mood and was reeling like a drunkard. After reaching his room he regained the normal state.

Many devotees gathered in the room. Among them was a new-comer, a sādhaka from Konnagar, who looked over fifty years of age and seemed to have great vanity of scholarship.

The Master stood in the middle of the room and suddenly said to M., "He came here—Naran."

Narendra was engaged in a discussion with Hazra and a few others on the verandah. They could be heard from the room.

MASTER (referring to Narendra): "The chatterbox! But he is now much worried about his family."

M: "Yes, sir, it is true."

MASTER: "Once he said that he would look upon adversity as his good fortune. Isn't that so?"

M: "He has great strength of mind."

A DEVOTEE: "Does he lack strength in anything?"

Pointing to the sādhaka from Konnagar, a devotee said to the Master: "Sir, he has come to visit you. He has some questions to ask." The sādhaka was seated erect, his chin up.

SĀDHAKA: "Sir, what is the way?"

MASTER: "Faith in the guru's words. One attains God by following the guru's instructions step by step. It is like reaching an object by following the trail of a thread."

SĀDHAKA: "Is it possible to see God?"

MASTER: "He is unknowable by the mind engrossed in worldliness. One cannot attain God if one has even a trace of attachment to 'woman and gold'. But He is knowable by the pure mind and the pure intelligence—the mind and intelligence that have not the slightest trace of attachment. Pure Mind, Pure Intelligence, Pure Ātman, are one and the same thing."

SĀDHAKA: "But the scriptures say, 'From Him words and mind return baffled.' He is unknowable by mind and words."

MASTER: "Oh, stop! One cannot understand the meaning of the scriptures without practising spiritual discipline. What will you gain by merely uttering the word 'siddhi'?[8] The pundits glibly quote the scriptures; but what will that accomplish? A man does not become intoxicated even by rubbing siddhi on his body; he must swallow it. What is the use of merely repeating, 'There is butter in the milk'? Turn the milk into curd and churn it. Only then will you get butter."

SĀDHAKA: "You talk about churning butter. But you too are quoting the scriptures."

MASTER: "What will one gain by merely quoting or hearing the scriptures? One must assimilate them. The almanac makes a forecast of the rainfall for the year, but you won't get a drop by squeezing its pages."

SĀDHAKA: "You talk about churning butter. Have you done it yourself?"

MASTER: "You don't have to bother about what I have or haven't done. Besides, it is very difficult to explain these things to others. Suppose someone asks you, 'What does ghee taste like?' Your answer will be, 'Ghee tastes like ghee.'

"To understand these things one needs to live with holy men, just as to

[8] Indian hemp.

understand the pulse of bile,[9] of phlegm, and so on, one needs to live with a physician."

SĀDHAKA: "There are some people who are irritated by others' company."

MASTER: "That happens only after the attainment of Knowledge, after the realization of God. Shouldn't a beginner live in the company of holy men?"

The sādhaka sat in silence a few moments. Then he said with some irritation: "Please tell me whether you have realized God either directly or intuitively. You may answer me if you are able, or you may keep silent if you wish." The Master said with a smile: "What shall I say? One can only give a hint."

SĀDHAKA: "Then tell us that much."

Narendra was going to sing. He said, "No one has brought a pākhoāj."

THE YOUNGER GOPAL: "Mahimacharan has one."

MASTER (interrupting): "No, we don't want anything of his here."

A devotee from Konnagar sang a song. Every now and then Sri Ramakrishna glanced at the sādhaka. The singer and Narendra became engaged in a furious discussion about musical technique. The sādhaka said to the singer, "What is the use of such discussions?" Referring to another man who had joined in the discussion, Sri Ramakrishna said to the sādhaka, "Why didn't you scold him, too?" It could be seen that the sādhaka was not on friendly terms with his companions from Konnagar.

Narendra sang:

> O Lord, must all my days pass by so utterly in vain?
> Down the path of hope I gaze with longing, day and night. . . .

The sādhaka closed his eyes in meditation as he listened to the song. It was four o'clock in the afternoon. The rays of the setting sun fell on his body. Sri Ramakrishna quickly opened an umbrella and placed it near the door so that the sun might not disturb the sādhaka.

Narendra sang again:

> How shall I call on Thee, O Lord, with such a stained and worldly
>   mind?
> Can a straw remain unharmed, cast in a pit of flaming coals?
> Thou, all goodness, art the fire, and I, all sin, am but a straw:
> How shall I ever worship Thee?
>
> The glory of Thy name, they say, redeems those even past
>   redeeming;
> Yet, when I chant Thy sacred name, alas! my poor heart quakes
>   with fright.
> I spend my life a slave to sin; how can I find a refuge, then,
> O Lord, within Thy holy way?
>
> In Thine abounding kindliness, rescue Thou this sinful wretch;
> Drag me off by the hair of my head and give me shelter at Thy
>   feet.

[9] According to orthodox Hindu medicine, phlegm, bile, and wind are the three humours that control physical health. A physician can determine their condition by feeling the patient's pulse.

Again he sang:

> Sweet is Thy name, O Refuge of the humble!
> It falls like sweetest nectar on our ears
> And comforts us, Beloved of our souls!
> The priceless treasure of Thy name alone
> Is the abode of Immortality,
> And he who chants Thy name becomes immortal.
> Falling upon our ears, Thy holy name
> Instantly slays the anguish of our hearts,
> Thou Soul of our souls, and fills our hearts with bliss!

As Narendra sang the line, "And he who chants Thy name becomes immortal", the Master went into samādhi. At first his fingers, especially the thumbs, began to tremble. The devotees from Konnagar had never seen the Master in samādhi. Seeing him silent, they were about to leave the room. Bhavanath said to them: "Why are you going away? This is his samādhi." The devotees resumed their places.

Narendra sang:

> I have laboured day and night
> To make Thy seat within my heart;
> Wilt Thou not be kind to me,
> O Lord of the World, and enter there?

Sri Ramakrishna, still in the ecstatic mood, came down from his couch to the floor and sat by Narendra. The beloved disciple sang again:

> In Wisdom's firmament the moon of Love is rising full,
> And Love's flood-tide, in surging waves, is flowing everywhere.
> O Lord, how full of bliss Thou art! Victory unto Thee! . . .

As Narendra sang the last line, Sri Ramakrishna stood up, still absorbed in samādhi.

After a long time the Master regained partial consciousness of the world and sat down on the mat. Narendra finished his singing, and the tānpurā was put back in its place. The Master was still in a spiritual mood and said: "Mother, tell me what this is. They want someone to extract the butter for them and hold it to their mouths. They won't throw the spiced bait into the lake. They won't even hold the fishing-rod. Someone must catch the fish and put it into their hands! How troublesome! Mother, I won't listen to any more argument. The rogues force it on me. What a bother! I shall shake it off. God is beyond the Vedas and their injunctions. Can one realize Him by studying the scriptures, the Vedas, and the Vedānta? (To Narendra) Do you understand this? The Vedas give only a hint."

Narendra wanted the tānpurā again. The Master said, "I want to sing." He was still in an ecstatic mood and sang:

> Mother, this is the grief that sorely grieves my heart,
> That even with Thee for Mother, and though I am wide awake,
> There should be robbery in my house. . . .

The Master said, "Mother, why do You make me argue?" He sang again:

> Once for all, this time, I have thoroughly understood;
> From One who knows it well, I have learnt the secret of
> bhāva. . . .

The Master said, "I am quite conscious." But he was still groggy with divine fervour. He sang once more:

> I drink no ordinary wine, but Wine of Everlasting Bliss,
> As I repeat my Mother Kāli's name;
> It so intoxicates my mind that people take me to be drunk! . . .

Sri Ramakrishna had said, "Mother, I won't listen to any more argument." Narendra sang:

> O Mother, make me mad with Thy love!
> What need have I of knowledge or reason? . . .

Sri Ramakrishna said with a smile: "O Mother, make me mad! God cannot be realized through knowledge and reasoning, through the arguments in the scriptures." He had been pleased with the singing of the musician from Konnagar and said to him humbly: "Please sing about the Divine Mother. Please—one song."

MUSICIAN: "You must excuse me, sir."

MASTER (*bowing with folded hands*): "No, sir. I can enforce this demand."

Saying this, Sri Ramakrishna sang a few lines from a kirtan, assuming the attitude of a gopi:

> Rādhā has every right to say it;
> She has kept awake for Krishna.
> She has stayed awake all night,
> And she has every right to be piqued.

Then he said to the musician: "My dear sir, you are a child of the Divine Mother. She dwells in all beings. Therefore I have every right to enforce my demand. A farmer said to his guru, 'I shall get my mantra from you by beating you, if I have to.' "

MUSICIAN (*smiling*): "By a shoe-beating?"

MASTER (*smiling*): "No! I won't go that far."

Again in an abstracted mood Sri Ramakrishna said: "The beginner, the struggling, the perfect, and the supremely perfect. Which are you—perfect or supremely perfect? Come along! Sing for us."

The musician complied. He sang just a melody.

MASTER: "My dear sir, that too makes me happy."

The musician then sang a song. When the music was over, the devotees from Konnagar saluted the Master and took their leave. The sādhaka bowed before him with folded hands and said, "Holy man, let me say good-bye."

Sri Ramakrishna, still in an ecstatic mood, was talking to the Divine Mother.

MASTER: "Mother, is it You or I? Do I do anything? No, no! It is You.

Was it You who heard the arguments all this time, or was it I? No, not I. It was You."

Sri Ramakrishna became conscious of the outer world and began to converse with Narendra, Bhavanath, and the other devotees. They were talking about the sādhaka.

BHAVANATH (smiling): "What kind of man is he?"

MASTER: "He is a tāmasic devotee."

BHAVANATH: "He can certainly recite Sanskrit verses."

MASTER: "Once I said to a man about a sādhu: 'He is a rājasic sādhu. Why should one give him food and other presents?' At this another sādhu taught me a lesson by saying to me: 'Don't say that. There are three classes of holy men: sāttvic, rājasic, and tāmasic.' Since that day I have respected holy men of all classes."

NARENDRA (smiling): "What? Is it like the 'elephant God'? All, indeed, are God."

MASTER (smiling): "It is God Himself who sports in the world as both vidyā and avidyā. Therefore I salute both. It is written in the *Chandi*: 'The Divine Mother is the good fortune of the blessed and the ill fortune of the unlucky.' (To Bhavanath) Is that mentioned in the *Vishnu Purāna?*"

BHAVANATH (smiling): "I don't know, sir. The devotees from Konnagar did not understand your samādhi and were about to leave the room."

MASTER: "Who was it that asked them to remain?"

BHAVANATH (smiling): "It was I."

MASTER: "My child, you are equally good in bringing people here and in driving them away."

The conversation turned to the argument that Narendra had had with the musician from Konnagar.

MUKHERJI: "Narendra didn't spare him."

MASTER: "That's right. One needs such grit. This is called the influence of tamas on sattva. Must a man listen to everything another man says? Should one say to a prostitute, 'All right, you may do whatever you like'? Must one listen to her? At one time Rādhā was piqued. A friend said, 'Her ego has been roused.' Brindē, another friend, said: 'Whose is this ego? Her ego belongs to Krishna alone. She is proud in the pride of Krishna.'"

The conversation turned to the glory of God's name.

BHAVANATH: "I feel such relief while chanting the name of Hari."

MASTER: "He who relieves us of sin is Hari. He relieves us of our three afflictions in the world. Chaitanya preached the glory of Hari's name; so it must be good. You see, he was such a great scholar, and an Incarnation too. Since *he* preached that name, it must be good. (Smiling) Once some peasants were invited to a feast. They were asked if they would eat a preparation of hog plum. They answered: 'You may give it to us if the gentlemen have eaten it. If *they* enjoyed it, then it must be good.' (All laugh.)

(To the Mukherji brothers) "I should like to visit Shivanath. I won't have to hire a carriage if you take me in yours."

MUKHERJI: "All right, sir, we shall set a day."

MASTER (*to the devotees*): "Do you think the Brāhmos will like me? They criticize those who believe in God with form."

Mahendra Mukherji wanted to go on a pilgrimage. He told Sri Ramakrishna so.

MASTER (*smiling*): "How is that? Do you want to go when the sprout of divine love has hardly come up? First comes the sprout, then the tree, then the fruit. We are so happy to have you here to talk to."

MAHENDRA: "I feel like visiting the holy places a little. I shall return soon."

It was about five o'clock in the afternoon. Sri Ramakrishna left his room. The devotees were walking in the garden. Many of them were about to leave.

The Master was conversing with Hazra on the north verandah. They were talking of Narendra's frequent visits to Annada, the eldest son of the Guhas.

HAZRA: "I hear that Annada is now practising austerity. He lives on very little food and eats rice once every four days."

MASTER: "Is that so? 'Who knows? One may realize God even by means of a religious garb.'"

HAZRA: "Narendra sang the āgamani."[10]

MASTER (*eagerly*): "How did he sing it?"

Kishori stood close by. The Master said to him, "Are you well?"

A little later the Master was standing on the west porch. Since it was autumn, he had put on a flannel shirt dyed with ochre. He asked Narendra, "Is it true that you[11] sang the āgamani?"

Accompanied by Narendra and M., Sri Ramakrishna walked to the embankment of the Ganges.

Narendra sang the āgamani:

> Tell me, my Umā, how have you fared, alone in the Stranger's[12]
>   house?
> People speak so much ill of us! Alas, I die of shame!
> My Son-in-law smears His body with ashes from the funeral pyre
> And roams about in great delight;
> You too, along with Him, cover with ash your golden skin.
> He begs the food that He eats! How can I bear it, being your
>   mother?
> This time, when He returns to claim you, I shall say to Him,
> "My daughter Umā is not at home."

[10] A class of songs invoking Durgā, the Divine Mother. According to Hindu mythology Durgā, or Umā, is the daughter of King Himālaya. She was married, against the will of Her parents, to Śiva, who roams in the cremation ground in the company of ghosts, smearing His body with ashes and living on alms. According to the terms of the marriage, Durgā was allowed to stay with Her parents three days each year. The Hindu women of Bengal look on Durgā as their own daughter. On the first day of the Durgā Pujā they sing the āgamani to welcome the Divine Mother. The song is full of the tenderness and affection of a mother for her daughter who is returning home from her husband's house after a long time.

[11] As a member of the Brāhmo Samāj, Narendra at that time did not believe in the gods and goddesses of the Hindu religion.

[12] Śiva, Umā's Husband.

Sri Ramakrishna stood listening to the song and went into samādhi. The sun was still above the horizon as the Master stood on the embankment in the ecstatic mood. On one side' of him was the Ganges, flowing north with the flood-tide. Behind him was the flower garden. To his right one could see the nahabat and the Panchavati. Narendra stood by his side and sang. Gradually the darkness of evening fell upon the earth.

After Narendra and several other devotees had saluted the Master and left for Calcutta, Sri Ramakrishna returned to his room. He was absorbed in meditation on the Divine Mother and was chanting Her holy name.

Jadu Mallick had arrived at his garden house next to the Kāli temple. He sent for the Master. Adhar, too, had arrived from Calcutta, and he saluted Sri Ramakrishna. The Master asked Latu to light the lantern and accompany him to Jadu's garden.

MASTER (to M.): "Why didn't you bring Naran with you?"

M: "Shall I come with you?"

MASTER: "Do you want to come? Adhar and the others are here. All right, you may come. Will the Mukherjis also come with us? (To the Mukherjis) Come along. Then we can leave Jadu Mallick quickly."

The Master went to Jadu's drawing-room. It was a well furnished room, with everything spick and span. The lamps were lighted. Jadu was sitting with his friends and was playing with the children. Servants were in attendance. Smiling, Jadu welcomed Sri Ramakrishna, but he did not get up. He treated the Master as a friend of long acquaintance.

Jadu was a devotee of Gaurānga. He had just seen a performance of Gaurānga's life at the Star Theatre and told the Master about it. The Master listened to his account joyfully and played with the children. M. and the Mukherji brothers sat near him. In the course of the conversation Sri Ramakrishna told Jadu that Adhar had not been able to secure the post of vice-chairman of the Calcutta Municipality. Jadu said that Adhar was still young and could try for it again. At his request the Master sang a few songs about Gaurānga.

After the music was over, the Mukherjis were about to take their leave. The Master, too, was ready to go, but he was in an ecstatic mood. On coming to the porch he went into samādhi. The gate-keeper of the garden house was a pious man. Now and then he invited the Master to his house and fed him. Sri Ramakrishna stood there in samādhi, and the gate-keeper fanned him with a large fan. Ratan, the manager of the garden house, saluted the Master, and Sri Ramakrishna, returning to the consciousness of the relative world, greeted the manager and the gate-keeper, saying, "Nārāyana". Then, accompanied by the devotees, he went back to the temple garden through the main gate.

MASTER (to the Mukherjis, pointing to M.): "Please visit him often."

MUKHERJI (smiling): "Yes, henceforth he will be our teacher."

MASTER: "It is the nature of the hemp-smoker to make merry in the company of another hemp-smoker. He will not talk even to an āmir, but he will embrace a wretched hemp-smoker if he happens to meet one." (All laugh.)

It was about nine o'clock. The Mukherji brothers saluted the Master and went away. Adhar and M. sat on the floor in the Master's room while he talked to Adhar about Rakhal.

Rakhal was staying in Vrindāvan with Balaram. The Master had learnt from a letter about Rakhal's illness. He was so worried about him that two or three days earlier he had wept before Hazra like a child. Adhar had sent a registered letter to Rakhal but had received no reply.

MASTER (*to Adhar*): "Naran has received a letter from Vrindāvan. Why haven't you received a reply to yours?"

ADHAR: "I haven't yet heard from Vrindāvan."

MASTER: "M. has also received a letter from Vrindāvan."

They began to talk of Sri Ramakrishna's seeing a play, at the Star Theatre, about the life of Gaurānga.

MASTER (*smiling*): "Jadu told me that one could see the play very well from a one-rupee seat.[13] Very cheap! Once we were talking about going to Pānihāti. Jadu wanted me to go in a country boat with a whole crowd of passengers. (*All laugh.*)

"Formerly he liked to hear a little about God. But I don't see Jadu much nowadays. He is always surrounded by flatterers. They have spoiled him. He is a man of a very calculating nature. I would no sooner set foot in his house than he would ask me, 'How much is the carriage hire?'[14] I would say: 'You don't have to bother about it. You may give two and a half rupees.' That would keep him quiet." (*All laugh.*)

It was late. Adhar was about to depart. The Master asked M. to bring Naran with him.

[13] In spite of his great wealth, Jadu Mallick was very miserly.

[14] It is customary for a householder in India to pay the carriage hire of a holy man when the latter visits his house.

AT THE STAR THEATRE (I)

I T WAS MAHĀLAYĀ, a sacred day of the Hindus, and the day of the new
moon. At two o'clock in the afternoon Sri Ramakrishna was sitting in his
room with Mahendra Mukherji, Priya Mukherji, M., Baburam, Harish,
Kishori, and Latu. Some were sitting on the floor, some standing, and others
moving about. Hazra was sitting on the porch. Rakhal was still at Vrindāvan
with Balaram.

MASTER (to the devotees): "I was at Captain's house in Calcutta. It was
very late when I returned. What a sweet nature Captain has! What devotion!
He performs the ārati before the image. First he waves a lamp with three
lights, then a lamp with one light, and last of all he waves burning camphor.
When performing the worship he does not speak. Once he motioned to me
to take my seat. During the worship his eyes become swollen from spiritual
emotion. They look as if they have been stung by wasps. He cannot sing,
but he chants hymns beautifully. In his mother's presence he sits on a lower
level; she sits on a high stool.

"His father was a hāvildār in the English army. He would hold a gun with
one hand and with the other worship Śiva. His servant made a clay image
of Śiva for him. He wouldn't even touch water before performing the worship.
He earned six thousand rupees a year.

"Captain sends his mother to Benares now and then. Twelve or thirteen
servants attend her there; it is very expensive. Captain knows the Vedānta,
the Gītā, and the Bhāgavata by heart. He says that the educated gentlemen
of Calcutta follow the ways of the mlechchhas.

"In his earlier years he practised hathayoga. That is why he strokes my
head gently when I am in samādhi. His wife worships the Deity in another
form—that of Gopāla. This time I didn't find her so miserly. She too knows
the Gītā and other scriptures. What devotion they have!

"They cooked a goat curry. Captain said they could eat it for fifteen days,
but she said, 'No, no! Only seven days.' But I liked the taste of it. They
serve a very small quantity of each dish, but nowadays they give me good
portions since I eat more than they do. After the meal either Captain or his
wife fans me.

"They are very pious souls and show great respect to holy men. The peo-

ple of upper India are greatly devoted to sādhus. The sons and nephews of
the Jung Bāhādur of Nepal once visited the temple garden; before me they
showed great respect and humility. Once a young girl of Nepal came to see
me with Captain. She was a great devotee, and unmarried; she knew the
whole of the *Gītagovinda* by heart. Dwarika Babu[1] and the others wanted
to hear her music. When she sang the *Gītagovinda*, Dwarika Babu was
profoundly moved and wiped the tears from his eyes with his handkerchief.
She was asked why she was not married. She said: 'I am the handmaid of
God. Whom else shall I serve?' Her people respect her as a goddess, as
the scriptures enjoin.

(*To Mahendra Mukherji and the others*) "I shall feel very happy to know
that you are being benefited by your visits here. (*To M.*) Why do people
come here? I don't know much of reading and writing."

M: "God's power is in you. That is why there is such power of attraction. It is the Divine Spirit that attracts."

MASTER: "Yes, this is the attraction of Yogamāyā, the Divine Śakti. She
casts the spell. God performs all His līlā through the help of Yogamāyā.

"The love of the gopis was like the attachment of a woman to her paramour. They were intoxicated with ecstatic love for Sri Krishna. A woman
cherishing illicit love is not very keen about her own husband. If she is told
that her husband has come, she will say: 'What if he has? There is food in
the kitchen. He can help himself.' But if she is told of the arrival of a
stranger—jovial, handsome, and witty—she will run to see him and peep at
him from behind a screen.

"You may raise an objection and say: 'We have not seen God. How can
we feel attracted to Him as the gopis felt attracted to Krishna?' But it is
possible. 'I do not know Him. I have only heard His name, and that has
fixed my mind upon Him.' "

A DEVOTEE: "Sir, what is the significance of Sri Krishna's stealing the
gopis' clothes?"

MASTER: "There are eight fetters that bind a person to the world. The
gopis were free from all but one: shame. Therefore Krishna freed them from
that one, too, by taking away their clothes. On attaining God one gets rid of
all fetters. (*To Mahendra Mukherji and the others*) By no means all
people feel attracted to God. There are special souls who feel so. To love
God one must be born with good tendencies. Otherwise, why should you
alone of all the people of Bāghbāzār come here? You can't expect anything
good in a dunghill. The touch of the Malaya breeze turns all trees into
sandal-wood, no doubt. But there are a few exceptions—the banyan, the
cotton-tree, and the aśwattha, for example.

(*To the Mukherji brothers*) "You are well off. If a man slips from the
path of yoga, then he is reborn in a prosperous family and starts again his
spiritual practice for the realization of God."

MAHENDRA: "Why does one slip from the path of yoga?"

MASTER: "While thinking of God the aspirant may feel a craving for
material enjoyment. It is this craving that makes him slip from the path. In

[1] A son of Mathur Babu.

his next life he will be born with the spiritual tendencies that he failed to translate into action in his present life."

MAHENDRA: "Then what is the way?"

MASTER: "No salvation is possible for a man as long as he has desire, as long as he hankers for worldly things. Therefore fulfil all your desires regarding food, clothes, and sex. (*Smiling*) What do you say about the last one? Legitimate or illegitimate? (*M. and Mahendra laugh.*)

"It is not good to cherish desires and hankerings. For that reason I used to fulfil whatever desires came to my mind. Once I saw some coloured sweetmeats at Burrabāzār and wanted to eat them. They brought me the sweets and I ate a great many. The result was that I fell ill.

"In my boyhood days, while bathing in the Ganges, I saw a boy with a gold ornament around his waist. During my state of divine intoxication I felt a desire to have a similar ornament myself. I was given one, but I couldn't keep it on very long. When I put it on, I felt within my body the painful uprush of a current of air. It was because I had touched gold to my skin. I wore the ornament a few moments and then had to put it aside. Otherwise I should have had to tear it off.

"I once felt a desire to eat the famous sweetmeats of different cities. (*All laugh.*) I had a desire to hear Sambhu's musical recital of the *Chandi*. After fulfilling that desire I wanted to hear the same thing by Rajnarayan. That desire also was satisfied.

"At that time many holy men used to visit the temple garden. A desire arose in my mind that there should be a separate store-room to supply them with their provisions. Mathur Babu arranged for one. The sādhus were given food-stuffs, fuel, and the like from that store-room.

"Once the idea came to me to put on a very expensive robe embroidered with gold and to smoke a silver hubble-bubble. Mathur Babu sent me the new robe and the hubble-bubble. I put on the robe. I also smoked the hubble-bubble in various fashions. Sometimes I smoked it reclining this way, and sometimes that way, sometimes with head up, and sometimes with head down. Then I said to myself, 'O mind, this is what they call smoking a silver hubble-bubble.' Immediately I renounced it. I kept the robe on my body a few minutes longer and then took it off. I began to trample it underfoot and spit on it, saying: 'So this is an expensive robe! But it only increases man's rajas.'"

Rakhal had been staying at Vrindāvan with Balaram. At first he had written excited letters praising the holy place. He had written to M.: "It is the best of all places. Please come here. The peacocks dance around, and one always hears and sees religious music and dancing. There is an unending flow of divine bliss." But then Rakhal had been laid up with an attack of fever. Sri Ramakrishna was very much worried about him and vowed to worship the Divine Mother for his recovery. So he began to talk about Rakhal.

MASTER: "Rakhal had his first religious ecstasy while sitting here massaging my feet. A *Bhāgavata* scholar had been expounding the sacred book in the room. As Rakhal listened to his words, he shuddered every now and then. Then he became altogether still.

"His second ecstasy was at Balaram Bose's house. In that state he could not keep himself sitting upright; he lay flat on the floor. Rakhal belongs to the realm of the Personal God. He leaves the place if one talks about the Impersonal.

"I have taken a vow to worship the Divine Mother when he recovers. You see, he has renounced his home and relatives and completely surrendered himself to me. It was I who sent him to his wife now and then. He still had a little desire for enjoyment.

(*Pointing to M.*) "Rakhal has written him from Vrindāvan that it is a grand place—the peacocks dance around. Now let the peacocks take care of him. He has really put me in a fix.

"Rakhal has been staying with Balaram at Vrindāvan. Ah, what a nice nature Balaram has! It is only for my sake that he doesn't go to Orissa, where his family owns an estate. His brother stopped his monthly allowance and wrote to him: 'Come and stay with us here. Why should you waste so much money in Calcutta?' But he didn't listen. He has been living in Calcutta because he wants to see me. What devotion to God! He is busy day and night with his worship. His gardener is always making garlands of flowers for the Deity. He has decided to spend four months a year at Vrindāvan to reduce his expenses. He gets a monthly allowance of two hundred rupees.

"Why am I so fond of the youngsters? They are still untouched by 'woman and gold'. I find that they belong to the class of the nityasiddhas, the ever-perfect.

"When Narendra first came here he was dressed in dirty clothes; but his eyes and face betokened some inner stuff. At that time he did not know many songs. He sang one or two: 'Let us go back once more, O mind, to our own abode!' and 'O Lord, must all my days pass by so utterly in vain?'.

"Whenever he came here, I would talk only with him, though the room was filled with people. He would say to me, 'Please talk to them', and then I would talk with the others.

"I became mad for the sight of him and wept for him in Jadu Mallick's garden house. I wept here, too, holding Bholanath's hand. Bholanath said, 'Sir, you shouldn't behave that way for a mere kāyastha boy.' One day the 'fat brāhmin'[2] said to me about Narendra, with folded hands, 'Sir, he has very little education; why should you be so restless for him?'

"Bhavanath and Narendra are a pair. They are like man and woman. So I asked Bhavanath to rent a house near Narendra's. Both of them belong to the realm of the formless Reality.

"I forbid the youngsters to spend a long time with women or visit them too frequently. Haripada has fallen into the clutches of a woman of the Ghoshpārā sect. She shows maternal feeling for him; but Haripada is a child and doesn't understand its real meaning. The women of that sect act that way when they see young boys. I understand that Haripada lies on her lap and that she feeds him with her own hands. I shall tell him that this is

[2] A nickname for Prankrishna, a devotee of the Master.

not good. This very maternal feeling leads to a downfall. The women of that sect practise spiritual discipline in the company of men; they regard men as Krishna. A teacher of that sect asks a woman devotee, 'Have you found your Krishna?' and she says, 'Yes, I have found my Krishna.'

"The other day that woman came here. I watched the way she looked around and I didn't approve of it. I said to her, 'You may treat Haripada any way you like, but don't have any wrong feeling for him.'

"The youngsters are now in the stage of sādhanā. They are aspirants. For them the only thing now is renunciation. A sannyāsi must not look even at the portrait of a woman. I say to them: 'Don't sit beside a woman and talk to her, even if she is a devotee. You may say a word or two to her, standing.' Even a perfect soul must follow this precept for his own protection and also to set an example to others. When women come to me, I too say to them after a few minutes, 'Go and visit the temples.' If they don't get up, I myself leave the room. Others will learn from my example.

"Can you tell me why all these youngsters, and you people, too, visit me? There must be something in me; or why should you all feel such a pull, such attraction?

"Once I visited Hriday's house at Sihore. From there I was taken to Śyāmbāzār. I had a vision of Gaurānga before I entered the village, and I realized that I should meet Gaurānga's devotees there. For seven days and nights I was surrounded by a huge crowd of people. Such attraction! Nothing but kirtan and dancing day and night. People stood in rows on the walls and even were in the trees.

"I stayed at Natavar Goswami's house. It was crowded day and night. In the morning I would run away to the house of a weaver for a little rest. There too I found that people would gather after a few minutes. They carried drums and cymbals with them, and the drum constantly played: 'Tākuti! Tākuti!' We would have our meal at three in the afternoon.

"The rumour spread everywhere that a man had arrived who died[3] seven times and came back to life again. Hriday would drag me away from the crowd to a paddy-field for fear I might have an attack of heat apoplexy. The crowd would follow us there like a line of ants. Again the cymbals and the never-ending 'Tākuti! Tākuti!' of the drums. Hriday scolded them and said: 'Why do you bother us like this? Have we never heard kirtan?'

"The Vaishnava priests of the village came and almost started a quarrel. They thought I would take their share of the fees from the devotees. But soon they discovered that I didn't touch a piece of cloth or even a thread. Someone remarked that I was a Brahmajñāni. So the Vaishnava pundits wanted to test me. One said, 'Why hasn't he beads, and a mark on his forehead?' Another of them replied, 'They have dropped from him, as the dry branch from a coconut tree.' It was there that I learnt this illustration of the dry branch of a coconut tree. The upādhis, limitations, drop when one attains Knowledge.

"People came thronging from distant villages. They even spent the night there. At Śyāmbāzār I learnt the meaning of divine attraction. When God

[3] Referring to the Master's samādhi.

incarnates Himself on earth He attracts people through the help of Yoga-māyā, His Divine Power. People become spellbound."

It was about three o'clock in the afternoon. The Master had been conversing with the Mukherji brothers and the other devotees, when Radhika Goswami, a Vaishnava scholar, arrived and bowed before him. This was his first visit to the Master. Radhika Goswami took a seat.

MASTER: "Are you a descendant of Advaita?"[4]

GOSWAMI: "Yes, sir."

At this the Master saluted him with folded hands.

MASTER: "You are descended from Advaita Goswāmi. You must have inherited some of his traits. A sweet-mango tree produces only sweet mangoes and not sour ones. Of course, it happens that some trees produce large mangoes and some small; that depends on the soil. Isn't that true?"

GOSWAMI (humbly): "Sir, what do I know?"

MASTER: "Whatever you may say, others will not let you off so easily. Brāhmins, however imperfect they may be, are worshipped by all on account of their having been born in the lines of great sages. (To M.) Tell us the story of the śamkhachila."[5]

M. sat in silence.

MASTER: "If one of your ancestors was a great soul, he will certainly pull you up, however unworthy you may be. When King Duryodhana and his brothers were taken captive by the gandharvas, Yudhisthira released them in spite of the fact that King Duryodhana was his enemy and had banished him to the forest.

"Besides, one must show respect to the religious garb. Even the mere garb recalls to mind the real object. Chaitanya once dressed an ass in a religious garb and then prostrated himself before it.

"Why do people bow before a śamkhachila? When Kamśa was about to kill the Divine Mother, She flew away taking the form of a śamkhachila.[6] So even now people salute the bird.

[4] An intimate companion of Sri Chaitanya.

[5] A bird similar to the kite.

[6] The following story is recorded in connexion with the birth of Sri Krishna: Kamśa, the king of Mathurā, was the very personification of evil. His god-fearing sister Devaki was married to Vasudeva. When Kamśa came to know that a son of Devaki would be his slayer, and that his sister was already expecting a child, he was about to kill her. But he spared her life on her promise to deliver her child to him as soon as it was born. Both Vasudeva and Devaki were kept in prison under a strong guard. In the prison seven sons were born to Devaki, one after another, and they were all slain by the evil Kamśa. The eighth child was Sri Krishna. Immediately after His birth, Vasudeva, through divine help, took Him across the Jamunā river to the village of Gokula, where Nanda and his wife Yaśodā lived. To them had just been born a daughter, who was an Incarnation of the Divine Power. Sri Krishna was exchanged for the girl, who was then delivered to Kamśa as the new-born child of Devaki. Kamśa was about to kill her when she flew into the sky in the form of a bird, the śamkhachila, remarking that Kamśa's slayer was growing up at Gokula. This is why the śamkhachila is held in respect. Eventually Sri Krishna killed Kamśa.

"An Englishman arrived at the cantonment of Chānak. The sepoys saluted him. Koar Singh explained to me: 'India is under the rule of the English. Therefore one should salute an Englishman.'

"The Śāktas follow the Tantra, and the Vaishnavas the Purāna. There is no harm for the Vaishnavas in speaking publicly of their spiritual practices. But the Śāktas maintain secrecy about theirs. For this reason it is difficult to understand a Śākta.

(*To Goswami*) "You are all good people. How much japa you practise! How much you chant the name of Hari!"

GOSWAMI (*humbly*): "Oh, no! We do very little. I am a great sinner."

MASTER (*smiling*): "You have humility. That is good. But there is also another way: 'I chant the name of Hari. How can I be a sinner?' He who constantly repeats: 'I am a sinner! I am a wretch!' verily becomes a sinner. What lack of faith! A man chants the name of God so much, and still he talks of sin!"

Radhika Goswami listened to these words in amazement.

MASTER: "At Vrindāvan I myself put on the garb of the Vaishnavas and wore it for fifteen days. (*To the devotees*) I have practised the disciplines of all the paths, each for a few days. Otherwise I should have found no peace of mind. (*Smiling*) I have practised all the disciplines; I accept all paths. I respect the Śāktas, the Vaishnavas, and also the Vedāntists. Therefore people of all sects come here. And every one of them thinks that I belong to his school. I also respect the modern Brahmajnānis.[7]

"A man had a tub of dye. Such was its wonderful property that people could dye their clothes any colour they wanted by merely dipping them in it. A clever man said to the owner of the tub, 'Dye my cloth the colour of your dye-stuff.' (*All laugh.*)

"Why should I be one-sided? The idea that the people of a particular sect will not come to me does not frighten me. I don't care a bit whether people come to me or not. The thought of keeping anyone under my control never crosses my mind. Adhar Sen asked me to ask the Divine Mother for a big position for him, but he didn't get it. If that makes him think differently about me, what do I care?

"Once at Keshab's house I found myself in a new mood. The Brāhmos always speak of the Impersonal; therefore I said to the Divine Mother in an ecstatic mood: 'Mother, please don't come here. They don't believe in Your forms.' "

Radhika Goswami listened to these words of the Master against sectarianism and remained silent.

MASTER (*smiling*): "Vijay[8] is in a wonderful state of mind nowadays. He falls to the ground while chanting the name of Hari. He devotes himself to kirtan, meditation, and other spiritual practices till four in the morning. He now puts on an ochre robe and prostrates himself before the images of God. Once he accompanied me to Gadādhar's[9] schoolhouse. I pointed out

---

[7] The members of the Brāhmo Samāj.

[8] Vijaykrishna Goswami. Though born in a Vaishnava family, he became a member of the Brāhmo Samāj. Later he returned to the worship of the Personal God.

[9] A celebrated Vaishnava saint.

the place where Gadādhar used to meditate. At once Vijay prostrated himself there. Again he fell prostrate before the picture of Chaitanyadeva."

GOSWAMI: "What about the image of Rādhā-Krishna?"

MASTER: "He prostrated himself there too. Vijay also follows all the conventions of religious life."

GOSWAMI: "He can now be accepted in Vaishnava society."

MASTER: "People's opinions don't count for much with him."

GOSWAMI: "I don't mean that. By accepting him Vaishnava society will honour itself."

MASTER: "He respects me very much. But it is difficult to reach him. One day he is called to Dacca, the next day to some other place. He is always busy. His presence has created great trouble in the Sādhāran Brāhmo Samāj."[10]

GOSWAMI: "Why so, sir?"

MASTER: "The Brāhmos tell him: 'You mix with people who worship God with form. You are an idolater.' Vijay is liberal and straightforward. Unless a man is guileless, he doesn't receive the grace of God."

Sri Ramakrishna talked to the Mukherji brothers. Mahendra, the elder, had his own business. Priyanath, the younger, had been an engineer. After making some provision for himself, he had given up his job. Mahendra was thirty-five or thirty-six years old. The brothers had homes both in the country and in Calcutta.

MASTER (smiling): "Don't sit idle simply because your spiritual consciousness has been awakened a little. Go forward. Beyond the forest of sandalwood there are other and more valuable things—silver-mines, gold-mines, and so on."

PRIYA (smiling): "Sir, our legs are in chains. We cannot go forward."

MASTER: "What if the legs are chained? The important thing is the mind. Bondage is of the mind, and freedom also is of the mind.

"Listen to a story. There were two friends. One went into a house of prostitution and the other to hear a recital of the Bhāgavata. 'What a shame!' thought the first. 'My friend is hearing spiritual discourse, but just see what I have slipped down to!' The second friend said to himself: 'Shame on me! My friend is having a good time, but how stupid I am!' After death the soul of the first was taken to Vaikuntha by the messenger of Vishnu, while that of the second was taken to the nether world of Yama."

PRIYA: "But the mind is not under my control."

MASTER: "How is that? There is such a thing as abhyāsayoga, yoga through practice. Keep up the practice and you will find that your mind will follow in whatever direction you lead it. The mind is like a white cloth just returned from the laundry. It will be red if you dip it in red dye and blue if you dip it in blue. It will have whatever colour you dip it in.

(To Goswami) "Have you anything to ask?"

GOSWAMI: "No, sir. I am satisfied that I have seen you and have been listening to your words."

[10] Vijay and several of his friends, on account of a disagreement with Keshab, seceded from Keshab's organization and founded the Sādhāran Brāhmo Samāj.

MASTER: "Go and visit the temples."

GOSWAMI (*very humbly*): "Won't you please sing something about Sri Chaitanya?"

The Master complied. He sang:

> Why has My body turned so golden? It is not time for this to be:
> Many the ages that must pass, before as Gaurānga I appear! . . .

Again:

> Gorā gazes at Vrindāvan and tears stream from his eyes;
> In an exuberance of joy, he laughs and weeps and dances and sings.
> He takes a wood for Vrindāvan, the ocean for the blue Jamunā;
> He rolls on the ground for love of Hari.

After singing, the Master went on with the conversation.

MASTER (*to Goswami*): "I have sung these songs to suit your Vaishnava temperament. But I must sing differently when the Śāktas or others come.

"Here[11] people of all sects come—Vaishnavas, Śāktas, Kartābhajās, Vedāntists, and also members of the modern Brāhmo Samāj. Therefore one finds here all ideals and attitudes. It is by the will of God that different religions and opinions have come into existence. God gives to different people what they can digest. The mother does not give fish pilau to all her children. All cannot digest it; so she prepares simple fish soup for some. Everyone cherishes his own special ideal and follows his own nature.

"They provide various images for the Bāroāri[12] because people of different sects assemble at it. You see there images of Rādhā-Krishna, Śiva-Durgā, and Sītā-Rāma—different images in different places. A crowd gathers before each image. The Vaishnavas spend most of their time before the image of Rādhā-Krishna, the Śāktas before Śiva-Durgā, and the devotees of Rāma before Sītā-Rāma.

"But it is quite different with those who are not spiritually minded at all. In the Bāroāri one sees another image also—a prostitute beating her paramour with a broomstick. Those people stand there with gaping mouths and cry to their friends: 'What are you looking at over there? Come here! Look at this!' " (*All laugh.*)

Radhika Goswami saluted the Master and took his leave.

It was about five o'clock. The Master was on the semicircular west porch. Baburam, Latu, the Mukherji brothers, M., and some other devotees were with him.

MASTER (*to M. and the others*): "Why should I be one-sided? The goswāmis belong to the Vaishnava school and are very bigoted. They think that their opinion alone is right and all other opinions are wrong. My words have hit him hard. (*Smiling*) One must strike the elephant on the head with the goad; that is the elephant's most sensitive spot."

Then Sri Ramakrishna told a few naughty jokes for the young men.

MASTER (*to the devotees*): "I don't give the youngsters a pure vegetarian

[11] Referring to himself.

[12] A religious festival, the cost of which is borne by the whole community.

diet: now and then I give them a little water smelling of fish. Otherwise, why should they come?"

The Mukherji brothers left the porch. They went to the garden for a stroll.

MASTER (to M.): "I wonder whether the Mukherjis have taken offence at my jokes?"

M: "Why should they? Captain said that you are like a child. After realizing God a man becomes childlike."

MASTER: "Yes, and sometimes he behaves like a boy, and sometimes like a young man. As a boy he is very light-hearted. He may use frivolous language. As a young man he is like a roaring lion while teaching others. You had better explain my state of mind to the Mukherjis."

M: "I don't have to do that. Haven't they the sense to see it?"

Again the Master became light-hearted with the boys. Then he said to one of the devotees: "Today is the new moon. Go to the Kāli temple in the evening."[13]

It was dusk. They heard the sound of gongs, cymbals, and other instruments used in the evening service in the temples. The Master said to Baburam, "Come with me to the Kāli temple." He and Baburam went toward the temple, accompanied by M. At the sight of Harish sitting on the porch, the Master said: "What is this? Is he in ecstasy?"

Going through the courtyard, the Master and the devotees stopped a minute in front of the Rādhākānta temple to watch the worship. Then they proceeded to the shrine of Kāli. With folded hands the Master prayed to the Divine Mother: "O Mother! O Divine Mother! O Brahmamayi!"

Reaching the raised platform in front of the shrine, he bowed low before the image. The ārati was going on. He entered the shrine and fanned the image.

The evening worship was over. The devotees bowed before the Deity. It was the night of the new moon. The Master was in a spiritual mood. Gradually his mood deepened into intense ecstasy. He returned to his room, reeling like a drunkard and holding to Baburam's hand.

A lamp was lighted on the west porch. The Master sat there a few minutes, chanting: "Hari Om! Hari Om! Hari Om!" and other mystic syllables of the Tantra. Presently he returned to his room and sat on the small couch, facing the east. He was still completely absorbed in divine fervour. He said to the Divine Mother: "Mother, that I should first speak and You then act— oh, that's nonsense! What is the meaning of talk? It is nothing but a sign. One man says, 'I shall eat.' Again, another says, 'No! I won't hear of it.' Well, Mother, suppose I had said I would not eat; wouldn't I still feel hungry? Is it ever possible that You should listen only when one prays aloud and not when one feels an inner longing? You are what You are. Then why do I speak? Why do I pray? I do as You make me do. Oh, what confusion! Why do You make me reason?"

As Sri Ramakrishna was thus talking to God, the devotees listened wonderstruck to his words. The Master's eyes fell upon them.

[13] The night of the new moon is especially auspicious for the worship of the Divine Mother.

MASTER (*to the devotees*): "One must inherit good tendencies to realize God. One must have done something, some form of tapasyā, either in this life or in another.

"When Draupadi's[14] clothes were being taken off, she cried earnestly, praying to God. God revealed Himself to her and said: 'Try to remember whether you have ever made a gift of a cloth to anyone. Then your modesty will be preserved.' Draupadi replied: 'Yes, I remember now. Once a rishi was taking his bath when his loin-cloth was carried away by the current. I tore off half my cloth and gave it to him.' Thereupon the Lord said, 'Then you have nothing to fear.'"

M. was sitting on the small foot-rug.

MASTER (*to M.*): "You have understood what I said."

M: "Yes, sir. You spoke about inherent tendencies."

MASTER: "Repeat what I said."

M. repeated the story of Draupadi.

Hazra entered the room. He had been living with Sri Ramakrishna in the temple garden for the past two years and had first met the Master in 1880 at Sihore in the house of Hriday, the Master's nephew. Hazra's native village was near Sihore, and he owned some property there. He had a wife and children and also some debts. From youth he had felt a spirit of renunciation and sought the company of holy men and devotees. The Master had asked him to live with him at Dakshineswar and looked after his necessities. Hazra's mind was a jumble of undigested religious moods. He professed the path of knowledge and disapproved of Sri Ramakrishna's attitude of bhakti and his longing for the young devotees. Now and then he thought of the Master as a great soul, but again he slighted him as an ordinary human being. He spent much of his time in telling his beads, and he criticized Rakhal and the other young men for their indifference to the practice. He was a strong advocate of religious conventions and rules of conduct, and made a fad of them. He was about thirty-eight years old.

As Hazra came in, the Master became a little abstracted and in that mood began to talk.

MASTER (*to Hazra*): "What you are doing is right in principle, but the application is not quite correct. Don't find fault with anyone, not even with an insect. As you pray to God for devotion, so also pray that you may not find fault with anyone."

HAZRA: "Does God listen to our prayer for bhakti?"

MASTER: "Surely. I can assure you of that a hundred times. But the prayer must be genuine and earnest. Do worldly-minded people weep for God as they do for wife and children? At Kāmārpukur the wife of a certain man fell ill. The man thought she would not recover; he began to tremble and was about to faint. Who feels that way for God?"

Hazra was about to take the dust of the Master's feet.

MASTER (*shrinking*): "What is this?"

---

[14] The wife of the five Pāndava brothers. In order to humiliate her in the court, Duryodhana ordered her clothes to be taken off.

HAZRA: "Why should I not take the dust of his feet who has so kindly kept me with him?"

MASTER: "Satisfy God and everyone will be satisfied. 'If He is pleased the world is pleased.' Once the Lord ate a few greens from Draupadi's cooking-pot and said, 'Ah, I am satisfied.' Immediately the whole world and all its living beings were satisfied; they felt as if they had eaten their fill. But was the world satisfied or did it feel that way when the rishis ate their food?

(To Hazra) "A perfect soul, even after attaining Knowledge, practises devotions or observes religious ceremonies to set an example to others. I go to the Kāli temple and I bow before the holy pictures in my room; therefore others do the same. Further, if a man has become habituated to such ceremonies, he feels restless if he does not observe them.

"One day I saw a sannyāsi under the banyan-tree. He had put the śālagrām on the same carpet with his guru's sandals. He was worshipping them. I said to him, 'If you have attained Knowledge to that extent,[15] then why such formal worship at all?' He replied: 'What difference does it make? Since I do everything else, why not this too? Sometimes I offer the flowers at the guru's feet and sometimes to God.'

"One cannot renounce work as long as one has a body. As long as there is mud at the bottom of the lake, bubbles will be produced.

(To Hazra) "If there is knowledge of one, there is also knowledge of many. What will you achieve by mere study of the scriptures? The scriptures contain a mixture of sand and sugar, as it were. It is extremely difficult to separate the sugar from the sand. Therefore one should learn the essence of the scriptures from the teacher or from a sādhu. Afterwards what does one care for books?

(To the devotees) "Gather all the information and then plunge in. Suppose a pot has dropped in a certain part of a lake. Locate the spot and dive there.

"One should learn the essence of the scriptures from the guru and then practise sādhanā. If one rightly follows spiritual discipline, then one directly sees God. The discipline is said to be rightly followed only when one plunges in. What will a man gain by merely reasoning about the words of the scriptures? Ah, the fools! They reason themselves to death over information about the path. They never take the plunge. What a pity!

"You may say, even though you dive deep you are still in danger of sharks and crocodiles, of lust and anger. But dive after rubbing your body with turmeric powder; then sharks and crocodiles will not come near you. The turmeric is discrimination and renunciation.

(To the devotees) "God made me pass through the disciplines of various paths. First according to the Purāna, then according to the Tantra. I also followed the disciplines of the Vedas. At first I practised sādhanā in the Panchavati. I made a grove of tulsi-plants and used to sit inside it and meditate. Sometimes I cried with a longing heart, 'Mother! Mother!' Or again, 'Rāma! Rāma!'

"While repeating the name of Rāma, I sometimes assumed the attitude of

[15] That is to say, realization of the identity of the guru and God.

Hanumān and fixed a tail to the lower end of my backbone. I was in a God-intoxicated state. At that time I used to put on a silk robe and worship the Deity. What joy I experienced in that worship!

"I practised the discipline of the Tantra under the bel-tree. At that time I could see no distinction between the sacred tulsi and any other plant. In that state I sometimes ate the leavings from a jackal's meal,[16] food that had been exposed the whole night, part of which might have been eaten by snakes or other creatures. Yes, I ate that stuff.

"Sometimes I rode on a dog and fed him with luchi, also eating part of the bread myself. I realized that the whole world was filled with God alone. One cannot have spiritual realization without destroying ignorance; so I would assume the attitude of a tiger and devour ignorance.

"While practising the disciplines of the Vedas, I became a sannyāsi. I used to lie down in the chāndni and say to Hriday: 'I am a sannyāsi. I shall take my meals here.'[17]

"I vowed to the Divine Mother that I would kill myself if I did not see God. I said to Her: 'O Mother, I am a fool. Please teach me what is contained in the Vedas, the Purānas, the Tantras, and the other scriptures.' The Mother said to me, 'The essence of the Vedānta is that Brahman alone is real and the world illusory.' The Satchidānanda Brahman described in the Vedas is the Satchidānanda Śiva of the Tantra and the Satchidānanda Krishna of the Purāna. The essence of the *Gītā* is what you get by repeating the word ten times. It is reversed into 'tāgi', which indicates renunciation.

"After the realization of God, how far below lie the Vedas, the Vedānta, the Purāna, the Tantra! (*To Hazra*) I cannot utter the word 'Om' in samādhi. Why is that? I cannot say 'Om' unless I come down very far from the state of samādhi.

"I had all the experiences that one should have, according to the scriptures, after one's direct perception of God. I behaved like a child, like a madman, like a ghoul, and like an inert thing.

"I saw the visions described in the scriptures. Sometimes I saw the universe filled with sparks of fire. Sometimes I saw all the quarters glittering with light, as if the world were a lake of mercury. Sometimes I saw the world as if made of liquid silver. Sometimes, again, I saw all the quarters illumined as if with the light of Roman candles. So you see my experiences tally with those described in the scriptures.

"It was revealed to me further that God Himself has become the universe and all its living beings and the twenty-four cosmic principles. It is like the process of evolution and involution.[18]

"Oh, what a state God kept me in at that time! One experience would hardly be over before another overcame me. It was like the movement of the husking-machine: no sooner is one end down than the other goes up.

[16] In a certain form of Tāntrik worship, food is offered to the jackals, the companions of the Goddess Kāli.

[17] The chāndni is an open portico in the temple garden with steps descending to the Ganges. According to the orthodox Hindu tradition, a monk is forbidden to live in a house.

[18] That is to say, God Himself evolves as the universe, at the time of creation, and names and forms are involved back into God, at the time of dissolution.

"I would see God in meditation, in the state of samādhi, and I would see the same God when my mind came back to the outer world. When looking at this side of the mirror I would see Him alone, and when looking on the reverse side I saw the same God."

The devotees listened to these words with rapt attention.

(To the Mukherji brothers) "Captain is now really in the state of the sādhaka. That the mere possession of wealth should create attachment is by no means true. Sambhu Mallick used to say to Hriday, 'Hridu, I have packed my things and am ready for the journey.' I said to him: 'God forbid! Why do you say such ominous words?' 'No', replied Sambhu. 'Please bless me that I may cast aside all these possessions and go to God.'

"God's devotees have nothing to fear. They are His own. He always stands by them. Once Duryodhana and his brothers were imprisoned by the gandharvas. It was Yudhisthira who freed them. Yudhisthira said, 'If our relatives are placed in such a plight, then it is our disgrace.'"

It was about nine o'clock in the evening. The Mukherji brothers were ready to return to Calcutta. The Master left his seat and began to pace the room and the porch. He could hear the kirtan sung in the Vishnu temple. A devotee said that Harish and Latu were in the singing party.

Sri Ramakrishna and the devotees went to the Vishnu temple and saluted the Deity. The brāhmins belonging to the staff of the temple garden, and also the priests, the cooks, and the servants, were singing the kirtan. He stood there a few minutes and encouraged the singers. On the way back to his room he remarked to the devotees, "You see, some of them polish the metal utensils and some go to houses of prostitution."

The Master returned to his room and took his seat. Presently the singers came and bowed low before him. The Master said to them: "One should perspire, dancing and singing the name of God, as people do earning money. I had thought of joining you in the dancing; but I found that you did everything very well. You had flavoured the curry with all the seasoning. What could I add? It will be nice if you sing devotional songs that way now and then."

The Mukherji brothers saluted the Master. Their carriage was ready near the verandah north of the room. The Master stood facing the north. On his left was the Ganges; in front of him were the nahabat, the garden, and the kuthi; and to his right was the road leading to the gate. The night was dark, and a devotee had brought a lantern to show the visitors their way. One by one the devotees bowed and took the dust of the Master's feet. The carriage seemed too heavily loaded for the horses. The Master said, "Aren't there too many people in the carriage?"

Sri Ramakrishna remained standing. As the carriage rolled away, the devotees looked back at the Master's face beaming with compassion and love.

Sunday, September 21, 1884

A large number of devotees were in Sri Ramakrishna's room, among them Ram, Mahendra Mukherji, M., and Chunilal. Chunilal had just returned from Vrindāvan, where he had gone with Rakhal and Balaram. The two latter were still there. Nityagopal also was staying there. The Master began to talk with Chunilal about Vrindavan.

MASTER: "How is Rakhal?"

CHUNI: "He is quite well now, sir."

MASTER: "Isn't Nityagopal coming back?"

CHUNI: "He was still there when I left."

MASTER: "Who will bring your family back?"

CHUNI: "Balaram Babu told me he would arrange it with some reliable person. He didn't mention any name."

Sri Ramakrishna then spoke to Mahendra Mukherji about Narayan, a school-boy sixteen or seventeen years old, who often visited the Master and was very dear to him.

MASTER: "He is quite guileless, isn't he?"

The very uttering of the word "guileless" filled the Master with great joy.

MAHENDRA: "Yes, sir. Completely guileless."

MASTER: "His mother came here the other day. I was a little frightened to see that she was a proud woman. That day she found that Captain, you, and many others, too, visited me. Then she must have realized that she and her son were not the only people to come here. (All laugh.) There was some sugar candy in the room and she remarked that it was good. That made her feel there was no scarcity of food here. I happened to tell Baburam, in front of her, to keep some sweets for himself and Naran. Ganu's mother said that Naran always bothered his mother for the boat hire to come here. His mother said to me, 'Please ask Naran to consent to marry.' I replied, 'All that depends on one's fate.' Why should I interfere? (All laugh.) Naran is indifferent to his studies. His mother said, 'Please ask him to pay a little more attention.' So I said to Naran, 'Attend to your studies.' Then his mother said, 'Please tell him seriously.' (All laugh.)

(To Chunilal) "Why doesn't Gopal come here?"

CHUNILAL: "He has been suffering from dysentery."

MASTER: "Is he taking any medicine?"

Sri Ramakrishna was planning to go to a performance of the *Chaitanyalīlā* at the Star Theatre. Mahendra Mukherji was to take him to Calcutta in his carriage. They were talking about choosing good seats. Some suggested that one could see the performance well from the one-rupee gallery. Ram said, "Oh, no! I shall engage a box for him." The Master laughed. Some of the devotees said that public women took part in the play. They took the parts of Nimāi, Nitāi, and others.

MASTER (to the devotees): "I shall look upon them as the Blissful Mother Herself. What if one of them acts the part of Chaitanya? An imitation custard-apple reminds one of the real fruit. Once, while going along a road, a devotee of Krishna noticed some bāblā-trees. Instantly his mind was thrown into ecstasy. He remembered that the wood of bāblā-trees was used for the handles of the spades that the garden of the temple of Śyāmasundar[19] was dug with. The trees instantly reminded him of Krishna. I was once taken to the Maidān in Calcutta to see a balloon go up. There I noticed a

[19] A name of Krishna.

young English boy leaning against a tree, with his body bent in three places. It at once brought before me the vision of Krishna[20] and I went into samādhi.

"Once Chaitanyadeva was passing through a village. Someone told him that the body of the drum used in the kirtan was made from the earth of that village, and at once he went into ecstasy.

"Rādhā could not control herself at the sight of a cloud or the blue throat of a peacock. It would at once awaken in her mind the thought of Krishna, and she would go into ecstasy."

The Master was silent a few moments and then resumed the conversation.

MASTER: "Rādhā had attained mahābhāva. There was no desire behind the ecstatic love of the gopis. A true lover does not seek anything from God. He prays only for pure love. He doesn't want any powers or miracles.

"It is very troublesome to possess occult powers. Nangtā taught me this by a story. A man who had acquired occult powers was sitting on the seashore when a storm arose. It caused him great discomfort; so he said, 'Let the storm stop.' His words could not remain unfulfilled. At that moment a ship was going full sail before the wind. When the storm ceased abruptly the ship capsized and sank. The passengers perished and the sin of causing their death fell to the man. And because of that sin he lost his occult powers and went to hell.

"Once upon a time a sādhu acquired great occult powers. He was vain about them. But he was a good man and had some austerities to his credit. One day the Lord, disguised as a holy man, came to him and said, 'Revered sir, I have heard that you have great occult powers.' The sādhu received the Lord cordially and offered him a seat. Just then an elephant passed by. The Lord, in the disguise of the holy man, said to the sādhu, 'Revered sir, can you kill this elephant if you like?' The sādhu said, 'Yes, it is possible.' So saying, he took a pinch of dust, muttered some mantras over it, and threw it at the elephant. The beast struggled awhile in pain and then dropped dead. The Lord said: 'What power you have! You have killed the elephant!' The sādhu laughed. Again the Lord spoke: 'Now can you revive the elephant?' 'That too is possible', replied the sādhu. He threw another pinch of charmed dust at the beast. The elephant writhed about a little and came back to life. Then the Lord said: 'Wonderful is your power. But may I ask you one thing? You have killed the elephant and you have revived it. But what has that done for you? Do you feel uplifted by it? Has it enabled you to realize God?' Saying this the Lord vanished.

"Subtle are the ways of dharma. One cannot realize God if one has even the least trace of desire. A thread cannot pass through the eye of a needle if it has the smallest fibre sticking out.

"Krishna said to Arjuna, 'Friend, if you want to realize Me, you will not succeed if you have even one of the eight occult powers.' This is the truth. Occult power is sure to beget pride, and pride makes one forget God.

"Once a cross-eyed rich man came here. He said to me: 'You are a paramahamsa. That is good. You must perform a swastyayana ceremony for

[20] Images of Krishna are usually bent in three parts of the body, namely, the neck, the waist, and the knees.

me.' What a small-minded person he was! He called me a paramahamsa and yet wanted me to perform that ceremony. To secure welfare by means of the swastyayana is to exercise occult power.

"An egotistic person cannot realize God. Do you know what egotism is like? It is like a high mound, where rain-water cannot collect: the water runs off. Water collects in low land. There seeds sprout and grow into trees. Then the trees bear fruit.

"Therefore I say to Hazra, 'Never think that you alone have true understanding and that others are fools.' One must love all. No one is a stranger. It is Hari alone who dwells in all beings. Nothing exists without Him.

"The Lord said to Prahlāda, 'Ask a boon of Me.' 'I have seen You', replied Prahlāda. 'That is enough. I don't need anything else.' But the Lord insisted. Thereupon Prahlāda said, 'If You must give me a boon, let it be that those who have tortured me may not have to suffer punishment.' The meaning of those words is that it was God who tortured Prahlāda in the form of his persecutors, and, if they suffered punishment, it would really be God who suffered.

"Rādhā was mad with prema, ecstatic love of God. But there is also the madness of bhakti. Hanumān's was such. When he saw Sītā entering the fire he was going to kill Rāma. Then, too, there is the madness of Knowledge. I once saw a jnāni behaving like a madman. He came here very soon after the temple garden was dedicated. People said he belonged to the Brāhmo Sabhā of Rammohan Roy. He had a torn shoe on one foot, a stick in one hand, and a potted mango-plant in the other. After a dip in the Ganges he went to the Kāli temple where Haladhari was seated. With great fervour he began to chant a hymn to the Divine Mother. Then he went up to a dog, held it by the ear, and ate some of its food. The dog didn't mind. Just at that time I too was about to experience the state of divine madness. I threw my arm around Hriday's neck and said, 'Oh, Hridē! Shall I too fall into that plight?'

"I became mad. Narayan Shastri came here and saw me roaming about with a bamboo pole on my shoulder. He said to the people, 'Ah, he is mad!' In that state I could not observe any caste restrictions. The wife of a low-caste man used to send me cooked greens, and I ate them.

"I touched my head and lips with the leaf-plates from which the beggars ate their food in the guest-house of the Kāli temple. Thereupon Haladhari said to me: 'What have you done? You have taken the food left by beggars. How will you marry off your children?'[21] These words aroused my anger. Haladhari was my cousin, older than myself. But could that restrain me? I said to him: 'You wretch! Isn't it you who take pride in the study of the Gītā and the Vedānta? Isn't it you who teach people that Brahman alone is real and the world illusory? And yet you imagine that I shall beget children! May your mouth that recites from the Gītā be blighted!'

(To M.) "You see, mere study of books avails nothing. One may recite

[21] According to the rules of Hindu society, brāhmins lose their caste by eating food left or touched by people of a lower caste.

the written part for the drum glibly from memory, but to play the drum is exceedingly difficult."

The Master continued with the description of his divine madness:

"Once, for a few days, I was out on an excursion with Mathur Babu in his house-boat. We took the trip for a change of air. During that trip we visited Navadvip. One day I saw the boatmen cooking their meal and stood and watched them. Mathur said to me, 'What are you doing there?' I replied with a smile, 'The boatmen are cooking, and their food looks very good.' Mathur felt that I might ask the boatmen to give me a portion of their food; so he said: 'Come away! Come away!'

"But I cannot do such a thing now. I am no longer in that mood. Now the food must be cooked by a brāhmin observing ceremonial purity, and be offered to the Deity; then only can I eat it.

"Oh, what moods I passed through! At Kāmārpukur I said to Chine Sankhari and the other chums of my boyhood days, 'Oh, I fall at your feet and beg of you to utter the name of Hari.' I was about to prostrate myself before them all. Thereupon Chine said, 'This is the first outburst of your divine love; so you don't see any distinction between one man and another.' When the storm breaks and raises the dust, then mango and tamarind trees look the same. One cannot distinguish the one from the other."

A DEVOTEE: "How can a householder keep on with his worldly duties if he is overwhelmed by such bhakti-madness or Love-madness or Knowledge-madness?"

MASTER (looking at him): "There are two kinds of yogis, the 'revealed' and the 'hidden'. The householder may be a 'hidden' yogi. None recognizes him. The householder should renounce mentally, not outwardly."

RAM: "You talk as if you were consoling children. A householder may be a jnāni but never a vijnāni."

MASTER: "He may become a vijnāni in the end. But it is not good to force oneself into renunciation."

RAM: "Keshab Sen used to say: 'Why do people go to him so much? One day he will sting them and they will flee from him.'"

MASTER: "Why should I sting people? I say to people: 'Do this as well as that. Do your worldly duties and call on God as well.' I don't ask them to renounce everything. (With a smile) One day Keshab was delivering a lecture. He said, 'O Lord, grant us that we may dive into the river of divine love and go straight to the Ocean of Satchidānanda.' The ladies were seated behind the screen. I said to Keshab, 'How can you all dive once for all?' Pointing to the ladies, I said: 'Then what would happen to them? Every now and then you must return to dry land. You must dive and rise alternately.' Keshab and the others laughed.

"Hazra says to me, 'You love most those endowed with rajas, those who have great wealth and name and fame.' If that is so, then why do I love people like Harish and Noto?[22] Why do I love Narendra? He can't even afford salt to season his roast banana!"

Sri Ramakrishna left his room and went toward the pine-grove talking

[22] Referring to Latu.

with M. A devotee followed them with water and towel. The Master was talking about his intended visit to the Star Theatre. He said to M.: "What Ram says applies to rājasic people. What is the use of reserving an expensive seat?"

About five o'clock that afternoon Sri Ramakrishna was on his way to Calcutta. M., Mahendra Mukherji, and a few other devotees accompanied him in Mahendra's carriage. Thinking of God, the Master soon went into an ecstatic mood. After a long time he regained consciousness of the world. He observed: "That fellow Hazra dares teach me! The rascal!" After a short pause he said, "I shall drink some water." He often made such remarks in order to bring his mind down to the sense plane.

MAHENDRA (to M.): "May I get some refreshments for him?"

M: "No, he won't eat anything now."

MASTER (still in ecstatic mood): "I shall eat."

Mahendra took the Master to his flour-mill located at Hāthibāgān. After a little rest Sri Ramakrishna was to go to the theatre. Mahendra did not care to take him to his own house, for the Master was not well acquainted with his father. Priyanath, Mahendra's second brother, was also a devotee of the Master.

Sri Ramakrishna was sitting on a cot over which a carpet had been spread, and was engaged in spiritual talk.

MASTER (to M. and the others): "Once, while listening to the various incidents of the life of Chaitanya, Hazra said that these were manifestations of Śakti, and that Brahman, the All-pervasive Spirit, had nothing to do with them. But can there be Śakti without Brahman? Hazra wants to nullify the teachings of this place.[23]

"I have realized that Brahman and Śakti are identical, like water and its wetness, like fire and its power to burn. Brahman dwells in all beings as the Bibhu, the All-pervasive Consciousness, though Its manifestation is greater in some places than in others. Hazra says, further, that anyone who realizes God must also acquire God's supernatural powers; that he possesses these powers, though he may or may not use them."

M: "Yes, one must have control over these supernatural powers!" (All laugh.)

MASTER (smiling): "Yes, one must have them in one's grasp! How mean! He who has never enjoyed power and riches becomes impatient for them. But a true devotee never prays to God for them."

Sri Ramakrishna washed his face. A smoke was prepared for him. He said to M.: "Is it dusk now? If it is, I won't smoke. During the twilight hour of the dusk you should give up all other activities and remember God." Saying this he looked at the hairs on his arm. He wanted to see whether he could count them. If he could not, it would be dusk.

About half past eight in the evening the carriage with the Master and the devotees drew up in front of the Star Theatre on Beadon Street. He was accompanied by M., Baburam, Mahendra, and two or three others. They

[23] Referring to himself.

were talking about engaging seats, when Girish Chandra Ghosh, the manager of the theatre, accompanied by several officials, came out to the carriage, greeted the Master, and took him and the party upstairs. Girish had heard of the Master and was very glad to see him at the theatre. The Master was conducted to one of the boxes. M. sat next to him; Baburam and one or two devotees sat behind.

The hall was brilliantly lighted. The Master looked down at the pit and saw that it was crowded. The boxes also were full. For every box there was a man to fan those who occupied it. Sri Ramakrishna was filled with joy and said to M., with his childlike smile: "Ah, it is very nice here! I am glad to have come. I feel inspired when I see so many people together. Then I clearly perceive that God Himself has become everything."

M: "It is true, sir."

MASTER: "How much will they charge us here?"

M: "They won't take anything. They are very happy that you have come to the theatre."

MASTER: "It is all due to the grace of the Divine Mother."

The *Chaitanyalīlā* was about to be performed. It was a play about the early life of Sri Chaitanya, who was also known as Nimāi, Gaur, Gorā, and Gaurānga. The curtain rose; the attention of the audience was fixed on the stage.

> The first scene depicts a council of Sin and the Six Passions. On a forest path behind them walk Viveka, Vairāgya, and Bhakti, engaged in conversation.
>
> Bhakti says to her companions: "Gaurānga is born in Nadiā. Therefore the vidyādharis,[24] the munis, and the rishis have come down to earth in disguise to pay their respects to him."
>
> She sings:
>
> > Blest indeed is the earth! Gorā is born in Nadiā!
> > Behold the vidyādharis, coming in chariots to adore him;
> > Behold the munis and rishis, who come, allured by the
> >   spell of Love.
>
> The vidyādharis, munis, and rishis sing a hymn to Gaurānga and adore him as an Incarnation of God.

Sri Ramakrishna watched the scene and was overpowered with divine ecstasy. He said to M.: "Look at it! Ah! Ah!"

> *Sages:*   O Keśava, bestow Thy grace
> >   Upon Thy luckless servants here!
> >   O Keśava, who dost delight
> >   To roam Vrindāvan's glades and groves!
>
> *Goddesses:* O Mādhava, our mind's Bewitcher!
> >   Sweet One, who dost steal our hearts,
> >   Sweetly playing on Thy flute!

[24] Demigoddesses.

Chorus: Chant, O mind, the name of Hari,
Sing aloud the name of Hari,
Praise Lord Hari's name!

Sages: O Thou Eternal Youth of Braja,
Tamer of fierce Kāliya,
Slayer of the afflicted's fear!

Goddesses: Beloved with the arching eyes
And crest with arching peacock feather,
Charmer of Sri Rādhā's heart!

Sages: Govardhan's mighty Lifter, Thou,
All garlanded with sylvan flowers!
O Dāmodara, Kamśa's Scourge!

Goddesses: O Dark One, who dost sport in bliss
With sweet Vrindāvan's gopi maids.

Chorus: Chant, O mind, the name of Hari,
Sing aloud the name of Hari,
Praise Lord Hari's name!

As the vidyādharis sang the lines,

Beloved with the arching eyes
And crest with arching peacock feather!

the Master went into deep samādhi. The orchestra played on, but he was
not aware of the outer world.

Another scene: A guest has arrived at the house of Jagannāth Misra,
Nimāi's father. The boy Nimāi plays about, singing with his friends,
in a happy mood:[25]

Tell Me, where is My blessed Vrindāvan?
Where is Mother Yaśodā?
Where Father Nanda and Brother Balāi?
Where My twin cows, black and white?
Tell Me, where is My magic flute?
My friends Sudāma and Sridāma?
Where My Jamunā's bank, My banyan?
Where My beloved gopi maids?
Where is Rādhā, queen of My heart?

The guest closes his eyes while offering food to the Lord. Nimāi
runs to him and eats the food from the plate. The guest recognizes
Nimāi as an Incarnation of God and seeks to please him with the
Hymn of the Ten Incarnations. Before taking leave of Gaurānga's
parents he sings:

Glory to Gorā, the Source of Bliss!
Hail Gaurānga, Redeemer of earth!
Help of the helpless, Life of the living,
Slayer of fear in the hearts of the fearful!
Age after age we see Thy play —

[25] In this song Gaurānga identifies himself with Krishna.

New sports unfolding, moods ever new;
New waves rolling, new tales to be told.

Thou who bearest the whole world's burden,
Shower on us the nectar of Love!
Take away our grief and affliction:
Thou in Love's pleasure-cave dost dwell.
Hope of the suffering! Chastiser of sin!
Scourge of the wicked! Victory to Thee!

Listening to the hymn, the Master was thrilled with ecstasy.

The next scene is at Navadvip on the bank of the Ganges. After bathing in the holy water, the brāhmin men and women engage in worship by the riverside. As they close their eyes, Nimāi steals their food offerings and begins to eat them. A brāhmin loses his temper and says: "You scapegrace! You rascal! You are taking away my offering for Vishnu. Ruin will seize you!" Nimāi holds on to the offering and is about to run away. Many of the women love him dearly and cannot bear to have him go away. They call to him: "Return, O Nimāi! Come back, O Nimāi!" Nimāi turns a deaf ear to them.

One of the women, however, knows the irresistible charm that will bring him back. She loudly chants the name of Hari. Immediately he repeats the name of Hari and comes back.

M. was seated beside the Master. Sri Ramakrishna could not control himself. He cried out, "Ah!" and shed tears of love. He said to Baburam and M.: "Don't make a fuss if I fall into an ecstatic mood or go into samādhi. Then the worldly people will take me for a cheat."

Another scene: Nimāi is invested with the sacred thread of the brāhmins. He puts on the traditional ochre robe of the sannyāsi. Mother Sachi and the women of the neighbourhood stand about while he begs for alms, singing:

Drop a morsel of food, I pray, into my begging-bowl;
Alone I roam, a new-made yogi, on the highways of the world.
People of Braja, you I love, and so, time and again,
I come to you; at hunger's call I beg my food from door to door.
The sun is low, and I must seek my home on the Jamunā's bank;
Into its waters fall my tears, as onward murmuring it flows.

The onlookers leave the stage. Nimāi stands alone. The gods, in the guise of brāhmin men and women, sing his praises.

Men: Thy body gleams like liquid moonlight;
Thou hast put on man's dwarfish form.
O Lord, Thee we salute!

Women: Bewitcher of the gopis' hearts,
Thou roamest in the shady groves
About Vrindāvan's vale.

Nimāi: Hail Sri Rādhā! Glory to Rādhā!

Men: The youths of Braja are Thy friends;
Thou curbest haughty Madan's[26] pride.

[26] The god of love in Hindu mythology.

Women: Thy love has made the gopis mad;
In ecstasy the Jamunā thrills.

Men: Nārāyana, Deluder of demons!
Refuge of the fear-stricken gods!

Women: O Lover of Braja, Thou dost beg
The love of Braja's comely maidens!

Nimāi: Hail Sri Rādhā! Glory to Rādhā!

Listening to the music, the Master went into samādhi. The curtain fell and the orchestra played on.

A new scene: Śrivās and other devotees are engaged in conversation in front of Advaita's house. Mukunda sings:

Sleep no more! How long will you lie
In māyā's slumber locked, O mind?
Who are you? Why have you been born?
Forgotten is your own true Self.
O mind, unclose your eyes at last
And wake yourself from evil dreams;
A fool you are to bind yourself
So to the passing shows of life,
When in you lives Eternal Bliss.
Come out of the gloom, O foolish mind!
Come out and hail the rising Sun!

Sri Ramakrishna praised the voice of the singer highly.

Another scene: Nimāi is staying at home. Śrivās comes to visit him. First he meets Sachi. The mother weeps and says: "My son doesn't attend to his household duties. My eldest son, Viswarupa, has renounced the world, and my heart has ached ever since. Now I fear that Nimāi will follow in his steps."

Nimāi arrives. Sachi says to Śrivās: "Look at him. Tears run down his cheeks and breast. Tell, tell me how I can free him from these notions."

At the sight of Śrivās, Nimāi clings to his feet and says, with eyes full of tears: "Ah me! Revered sir, I have not yet attained devotion to Krishna. Futile is this wretched life! Tell me, sir, where is Krishna? Where shall I find Krishna? Give me the dust of your feet with your blessing, that I may realize the Blue One with the garland of wild-flowers hanging about His neck."

Sri Ramakrishna looked at M. He was eager to say something but he could not. His voice was choked with emotion; the tears ran down his cheeks; with unmoving eyes he watched Nimāi clinging to Śrivās's feet and saying, "Sir, I have not yet attained devotion to Krishna."

Nimāi has opened a school, but he cannot teach the students any longer. Gangādās, his former teacher, comes to persuade him to direct his attention to his worldly duties. He says to Śrivās: "Listen, Śrivās! We are brāhmins, too, and devoted to the worship of Vishnu. But you people are ruining Nimāi's worldly prospects."

MASTER (*to M.*): "That is the advice of the worldly-wise: Do 'this' as well as 'that'. When the worldly man teaches spirituality he always advises a compromise between the world and God."

M: "Yes, sir. That is true."

Gangādās continues his argument with Nimāi. He says: "Nimāi, undoubtedly you are versed in the scriptures. Reason with me. Explain to me if any other duty is superior to worldly duties. You are a householder. Why disregard the duties of a householder and follow others' duties?"

MASTER (*to M.*): "Did you notice? He's trying to persuade Nimāi to make a compromise."

M: "Yes, sir."

Nimāi says to Gangādās: "I am not wilfully indifferent to a householder's duties. On the contrary, it is my desire to hold to all sides. But, revered sir, I don't know what it is that draws me on. I don't know what to do. I want to cling to the shore but I cannot. My soul wanders away. I am helpless. My soul constantly wants to plunge headlong into the boundless Ocean."

MASTER: "Ah me!"

The scene changes: Nityānanda has arrived at Navadvip. After a search he meets Nimāi, who, in turn, has been seeking him. When they meet, Nimāi says to him: "Blessed is my life! Fulfilled is my dream! You visited me in a dream and then disappeared."

The Master said in a voice choked with emotion, "Nimāi said he had seen him in a dream."

Nimāi is in an ecstatic mood and becomes engaged in conversation with Advaita, Śrivās, Haridās, and other devotees. Nitāi sings a song suited to Nimāi's mood:

> Where is Krishna? Where is my Krishna?
> He is not in the grove, dear friends.
> Give me Krishna! Bring me my Krishna!
> Rādhā's heart knows naught but Him.

At this song Sri Ramakrishna went into samādhi. He remained in that state a long time. The orchestra played on. Gradually his mind came down to the relative plane. In the mean time a young man of Khardaha, born in the holy family of Nityānanda, had entered the box. He was standing behind the Master's chair. Sri Ramakrishna was filled with delight at the sight of him. He held his hand and talked to him affectionately. Every now and then he said: "Please sit down here. Your very presence awakens my spiritual feeling." He played tenderly with the young man's hands and lovingly stroked his face.

After he had left, Sri Ramakrishna said to M.: "He is a great scholar. His father is a great devotee of God. When I go to Khardaha to visit Śyāmasundar, the father entertains me with sacred offerings such as one cannot buy even for a hundred rupees. This young man has good traits. A little shaking will awaken his inner spirit. At the sight of him my spiritual mood is aroused. I should have been overwhelmed with ecstasy if he had stayed here a little longer."

> The curtain rises: Nityānanda is walking in a procession on the public road with his companions, chanting the name of Hari. He meets two ruffians, Jagāi and Mādhāi, who are sworn enemies of all religious people. Mādhāi strikes Nitāi with a piece of broken pottery. Nitāi is hurt and bleeds profusely, but he pays no heed, inebriated as he is with the love of God.

Sri Ramakrishna was in an ecstatic mood.

> Nitāi embraces both Jagāi and Mādhāi, and sings a song to the two ruffians:

> > Jagāi! Mādhāi! Oh, come and dance,
> > Chanting Hari's name with fervour!
> > What does it matter that you struck me?
> > Dance, dear friends, in Hari's name!
> > Sing the name of our Beloved:
> > He will embrace you in love's rapture!
> > Let the heavens resound with His name!
> > You have not tasted true emotion:
> > Weep as you chant the name of Hari,
> > And you will see the Moon of your soul.
> > Hari's name would I lovingly give you;
> > Nitāi calls you to share His love.

> Nimāi speaks to Sachi of his desire to enter the monastic life. His mother faints and falls to the ground.

At this point many in the audience burst into tears. Sri Ramakrishna remained still and looked intently at the stage. A single tear appeared in the corner of each eye. The performance was over.

Sri Ramakrishna was about to enter a carriage. A devotee asked him how he had enjoyed the play. The Master said with a smile, "I found the representation the same as the real."

The carriage proceeded toward Mahendra's mill. Suddenly Sri Ramakrishna went into an ecstatic mood and murmured to himself in loving tones: "O Krishna! O Krishna! Krishna is knowledge! Krishna is soul! Krishna is mind! Krishna is life! Krishna is body!" He continued: "O Govinda, Thou art my life! Thou art my soul!"

The carriage reached the mill. Mahendra fed the Master tenderly with various dishes. M. sat by his side. Affectionately he said to M., "Here, eat a little." He put some sweets in his hands.

With Mahendra and a few other devotees, Sri Ramakrishna left in the carriage for the Dakshineswar temple garden. The Master was in a happy mood. He sang a song about Gaurānga and Nitāi. M. sang with him:

> > Gaur and Nitāi, ye blessed brothers!
> > I have heard how kind you are,
> > And therefore I have come to you. . . .

The Master and Mahendra talked about the latter's intended pilgrimage.

MASTER (*smiling*): "The divine love in you is barely a sprout now. Why should you let it wither? But come back very soon. Many a time I have thought of visiting your place. At last I have done it. I am so happy."

MAHENDRA: "My life is indeed blessed, sir."

MASTER: "You were already blessed. Your father is also a good man. I saw him the other day. He has faith in the *Adhyātma Rāmāyana*."

MAHENDRA: "Please bless me that I may have love for God."

MASTER: "You are generous and artless. One cannot realize God without sincerity and simplicity. God is far, far away from the crooked heart."

Near Śyāmbāzār, Mahendra bade the Master good-bye, and the carriage continued on its way.

THE DURGĀ PUJĀ FESTIVAL

SRI RAMAKRISHNA had come to Calcutta. It was the first day of the Durgā Pujā, the great religious festival, and the Hindus of the metropolis were celebrating it. The Master intended to visit the image of the Divine Mother at Adhar's house. He also wanted to see Shivanath, the Brāhmo devotee.

It was about midday. Umbrella in hand, M. was pacing the foot-path in front of the Brāhmo Samāj temple. Two hours had passed but the Master had not yet appeared. Now and then M. sat down on the steps of Dr. Mahalnavish's dispensary and watched the joy and mirth of the people, young and old, who were celebrating the Pujā.

A little after three the Master's carriage drove up. As soon as Sri Ramakrishna stepped out he saluted the temple of the Brāhmo Samāj with folded hands. Hazra and a few other devotees were with him. M. bowed before the Master and took the dust of his feet. The Master told him that he was going to Shivanath's house. A few minutes later several members of the Brāhmo Samāj came and took him to Shivanath's. But Shivanath was not at home. Shortly afterwards Vijay Goswami, Mahalnavish, and several other Brāhmo leaders greeted the Master and took him inside the Brāhmo temple.

Sri Ramakrishna was in a happy mood. He was given a seat below the altar. There the Brāhmo devotees sang their devotional music. Vijay and the Brāhmo devotees sat in front of the Master.

MASTER (*to Vijay, with a smile*): "I was told that you had put up a 'signboard' here that people belonging to other faiths are not allowed to come in. Narendra, too, said to me: 'You shouldn't go to the Brāhmo Samāj. You had better visit Shivanath's house.'

"But I say that we are all calling on the same God. Jealousy and malice need not be. Some say that God is formless, and some that God has form. I say, let one man meditate on God with form if he believes in form, and let another meditate on the formless Deity if he does not believe in form. What I mean is that dogmatism is not good. It is not good to feel that my religion alone is true and other religions are false. The correct attitude is this: My religion is right, but I do not know whether other religions are right or wrong, true or false. I say this because one cannot know the true nature of

God unless one realizes Him. Kabir used to say: 'God with form is my Mother, the Formless is my Father. Which shall I blame? Which shall I praise? The two pans of the scales are equally heavy.'

"Hindus, Mussalmāns, Christians, Śaktas, Śaivas, Vaishnavas, the Brahmajnānis of the time of the rishis, and you, the Brahmajnānis of modern times, all seek the same object. A mother prepares dishes to suit the stomachs of her children. Suppose a mother has five children and a fish is bought for the family. She doesn't cook pilau or kāliā for all of them. All have not the same power of digestion; so she prepares a simple stew for some. But she loves all her children equally.

"Do you know my attitude? I love all the preparations of fish. I have a womanly nature. (All laugh.) I feel myself at home with every dish—fried fish, fish cooked with turmeric powder, pickled fish. And further, I equally relish rich preparations like fish-head, kāliā, and pilau. (All laugh.)

"Do you know what the truth is? God has made different religions to suit different aspirants, times, and countries. All doctrines are only so many paths; but a path is by no means God Himself. Indeed, one can reach God if one follows any of the paths with whole-hearted devotion. Suppose there are errors in the religion that one has accepted; if one is sincere and earnest, then God Himself will correct those errors. Suppose a man has set out with a sincere desire to visit Jagannāth at Puri and by mistake has gone north instead of south; then certainly someone meeting him on the way will tell him: 'My good fellow, don't go that way. Go to the south.' And the man will reach Jagannāth sooner or later.

"If there are errors in other religions, that is none of our business. God, to whom the world belongs, takes care of that. Our duty is somehow to visit Jagannāth. (To the Brāhmos) The view you hold is good indeed. You describe God as formless. That is fine. One may eat a cake with icing, either straight or sidewise. It will taste sweet either way.

"But dogmatism is not good. You have no doubt heard the story of the chameleon. A man entered a wood and saw a chameleon on a tree. He reported to his friends, 'I have seen a red lizard.' He was firmly convinced that it was nothing but red. Another person, after visiting the tree, said, 'I have seen a green lizard.' He was firmly convinced that it was nothing but green. But the man who lived under the tree said: 'What both of you have said is true. But the fact is that the creature is sometimes red, sometimes green, sometimes yellow, and sometimes has no colour at all.'

"God has been described in the Vedas as both with attributes and without. You describe Him as without form only. That is one-sided. But never mind. If you know one of His aspects truly, you will be able to know His other aspects too. God Himself will tell you all about them. (Pointing to two or three Brāhmo devotees) Those who come to your Samāj know both this gentleman and that."

Vijay still belonged to the Sādhāran Brāhmo Samāj. He was a salaried preacher of that organization but could not obey all its rules and regulations. He mixed with those who believed in God with form. This was creating a misunderstanding between him and the Brāhmo authorities. Many Brāhmos disapproved of his conduct. The Master suddenly looked at Vijay and began to talk to him.

MASTER (to Vijay, smiling): "I understand that they have been finding fault with you for mixing with those who believe in God with form. Is that true? He who is a devotee of God must have an understanding that cannot be shaken under any conditions. He must be like the anvil in a blacksmith's shop. It is constantly being struck by the hammer; still it is unshaken. Bad people may abuse you very much and speak ill of you; but you must bear with them all if you sincerely seek God. Isn't it possible to think of God in the midst of the wicked? Just think of the rishis of ancient times. They used to meditate on God in the forest, surrounded on all sides by tigers, bears, and other ferocious beasts. Wicked men have the nature of tigers and bears. They will pursue you to do you an injury.

"One must be careful about these few things. First, an influential man who has much money and many men under his control. He can injure you if he wants; you must be careful while talking to him; perhaps you may have to approve what he says. Second, a dog. When it chases you or barks at you, you must stand still, talk to it gently, and pacify it. Third, a bull. If it runs after you with lowered horns, you must calm it with a gentle voice. Fourth, a drunkard. If you arouse his anger, he will abuse you, naming fourteen generations of your family. You should say to him: 'Hello uncle! How are you?' Then he will be mightily pleased and sit by you and smoke.

"In the presence of a wicked person I become alert. If such a man asks me whether I have a pipe for smoking, I say, 'Yes, I have.' Some people have the nature of a snake: they will bite you without warning. You have to discriminate a great deal in order to avoid the bite; otherwise your passion will be stirred up to such an extent that you will feel like doing injury in return. The companionship of a holy man is greatly needed now and then. It enables one to discriminate between the Real and the unreal."

VIJAY: "I have no time, sir. I am entangled in my duties here."

MASTER: "You are a religious teacher. Others have holidays, but not so a religious teacher. When the manager of an estate brings order to one part of it, the landlord sends him to another part. So you have no leisure." (All laugh.)

VIJAY (with folded hands): "Sir, please give me your blessing."

MASTER: "Now you are talking like an ignorant person. It is God alone who blesses."

VIJAY: "Revered sir, please give us some instruction."

The Master glanced around the Brāhmo temple and said with a smile, "This is nice too—a mixture of crystals and syrup.[1] There are crystals, and there is syrup too.

---

[1] That is to say, a mixture of worldly and spiritual ideals. The allusion is to the practice of keeping molasses in an earthen jar with a small hole at the bottom; the watery part slowly leaks out and crystals are formed inside.

"I have scored too many points and am therefore out of the game. (*All laugh.*) Do you know the game called 'nax'? It is a game of cards, and anyone scoring above seventeen is out of the game. Those who score fewer points —say five, seven, or ten—are clever. I have scored too many and am out of the game.

"Once Keshab Sen gave a lecture at his house. I was present. Many people were there. The ladies were seated behind the screen. Keshab, in the course of his talk, said, 'O God, please bless us that we may dive and disappear altogether in the river of bhakti.' I said to Keshab with a smile: 'If you disappear altogether in the river of bhakti, then what will be the fate of those behind the screen? By all means dive into the river, but you had better come back to dry land now and then. Don't disappear in the river altogether.' At these words Keshab and the others burst out laughing.

"Never mind. One can realize God in the world, too, if only one is sincere. 'I' and 'mine'—that is ignorance. But, 'O God! Thou and Thine'— that is knowledge.

"Live in the world like a maidservant in a rich man's house. She performs all the household duties, brings up her master's child, and speaks of him as 'my Hari'. But in her heart she knows quite well that neither the house nor the child belongs to her. She performs all her duties, but just the same her mind dwells on her native place. Likewise, do your worldly duties but fix your mind on God. And know that house, family, and son do not belong to you; they are God's. You are only His servant.

"I ask people to renounce mentally. I do not ask them to give up the world. If one lives in the world unattached and seeks God with sincerity, then one is able to attain Him.

(*To Vijay*) "There was a time when I too would meditate on God with my eyes closed.[2] Then I said to myself: 'Does God exist only when I think of Him with my eyes closed? Doesn't He exist when I look around with my eyes open?' Now, when I look around with my eyes open, I see that God dwells in all beings. He is the Indwelling Spirit of all—men, animals and other living beings, trees and plants, sun and moon, land and water.

"Why do I seek Shivanath? He who meditates on God for many days has substance in him, has divine power in him. Further, he who sings well, plays well on a musical instrument, or has mastered any one art, has in him real substance and the power of God. This is the view of the *Gītā*. It is said in the *Chandi* that he who is endowed with physical beauty has in him substance and the power of God. (*To Vijay*) Ah, what a beautiful nature Kedar has! No sooner does he come to me than he bursts into tears. His eyes are always red and swim in tears, like a chānābarā in syrup."

VIJAY: "At Dacca he is constantly talking about you. He is always eager to see you."

Sri Ramakrishna was about to depart. The Brāhmo devotees bowed low before him and he returned their salute. Then, getting into the carriage, he set out for Adhar's house to see the image of the Divine Mother.

[2] An allusion to the Brāhmo way of meditating on God.

Sunday, September 28, 1884

It was the day of the Mahāshtami, the most auspicious day of the worship of Durgā, the Divine Mother. At Adhar's invitation Sri Ramakrishna had come to Calcutta to see the holy image at his house. Before going there he went to Ram's. Many devotees, including Narendra, Baburam, M., Niranjan, Vijay, Kedar, Ram, and Surendra, were present. Balaram and Rakhal were still at Vrindāvan.

MASTER (*looking at Vijay and Kedar, with a smile*): "This is a nice reunion today. You two have the same spiritual mood. (*To Vijay*) Well, what about Shivanath? Did you—?"

VIJAY: "Yes, sir, he heard that you had been to his house. I haven't seen him, but I sent him word. He knows about it."

MASTER (*to Vijay and the others*): "Four desires have come into my mind. I shall eat fish curry cooked with egg-plant. I shall visit Shivanath. The devotees will repeat the name of Hari over their beads, and I shall watch them. And the Tāntrik devotees will drink consecrated wine, eight ānnās' worth, on the ashtami[3] day, and I shall watch them and salute them."

Narendra was seated in front of the Master. He was about twenty-two years old. While Sri Ramakrishna was talking thus his eyes fell upon his beloved disciple. At once the Master stood up and went into samādhi. He placed one foot on Narendra's knee. He was in a deep spiritual mood, his eyes unblinking, his mind completely unconscious of the outer world. After a long time he came down to the relative plane of consciousness; but he still appeared dazed, for the intoxication of divine bliss had not altogether left him. Speaking to himself in that ecstatic state, he repeated the name of God. He said: "Satchidānanda! Satchidānanda! Satchidānanda! Shall I repeat that? No, it is the day of the Divine Mother, the Giver of the bliss of divine inebriation. O Mother, full of the bliss of divine inebriation! Sā, re, gā, mā, pā, dhā, ni. It is not good to keep the voice on 'ni'. It is not possible to keep it there very long. I shall keep it on the next lower note.

"There are different planes of consciousness: the gross, the subtle, the causal, and the Great Cause. Entering the Mahākārana, the Great Cause, one becomes silent; one cannot utter a word.

"But an Iśvarakoti, after attaining the Great Cause, can come down again to the lower planes. Incarnations of God, and others like them, belong to the class of the Iśvarakotis. They climb up, and they can also come down. They climb to the roof, and they can come down again by the stairs and move about on a lower floor. It is a case of negation and affirmation.[4] There is, for instance, the seven-storey palace of a king. Strangers have access only to the lower apartments; but the prince, who knows the palace to be his own, can move up and down from floor to floor. There is a kind of rocket that throws out sparks in one pattern and then seems to go out. After a

[3] The eighth day of either half of the lunar month, an auspicious day for the followers of Tantra.
[4] That is to say, the aspirant at first negates the world on account of its not being God; but after divine realization he accepts the same world as the manifestation of God Himself.

moment it makes another pattern, and then still another. There is no end to
the patterns it can make. But there is another kind of rocket that, when it
is lighted, makes only a dull sound, throws out a few sparks, and then goes out
altogether. Like this second kind, an ordinary jīva, after much spiritual effort,
can go to a higher plane; but he cannot come down to tell others his experiences. After much effort he may go into samādhi; but he cannot climb
down from that state or tell others what he has seen there.

"There is a class of devotees, the nityasiddhas, the ever-perfect. From their
very birth they seek God. They do not enjoy anything of the world. The
Vedas speak of the homā bird. It lives very high in the sky. There the
mother bird lays her egg. She lives so high that the egg falls for many days.
While falling it is hatched. The chick continues to fall. That also goes on for
many days. In the mean time the chick develops eyes. Coming near the
earth, it becomes conscious of the world. It realizes it will meet certain death
if it hits the ground. Then it gives a shrill cry and shoots up toward its
mother. The earth means death, and it frightens the young bird; it then
seeks its mother. She dwells high up in the sky, and the young bird shoots
straight up in that direction. It doesn't look anywhere else."

"Those who are born as the companions of an Incarnation of God are
eternally perfect. For some of them that birth is the last.

(To Vijay) "You have both—yoga and bhoga. King Janaka also had yoga
and bhoga. Therefore he is called a rājarshi, both king and seer. Nārada was
a devarshi, and Śukadeva a brahmarshi. Yes, Śukadeva was a brahmarshi.
He was not a mere jnāni; he was the very embodiment of Jnāna, Divine
Knowledge. Whom do I call a jnāni? A man who has attained Knowledge
and has done so after much effort. Śukadeva was the very image of Knowledge, in other words, a form of concentrated Knowledge. He attained
Knowledge spontaneously, without any labour."

Saying this, Sri Ramakrishna came down to the normal mood. Then he
talked freely with the devotees. The Master asked Kedar to sing.

Kedar sang:

> How shall I open my heart, O friend?
> It is forbidden me to speak.
> I am about to die, for lack of a kindred soul
> To understand my misery. . . .

Kedar sang several other songs. After the music the Master again talked
to the devotees. Nandalal, Keshab's nephew, was also present with a few
Brāhmo friends. They were sitting near the Master.

MASTER (to Vijay and the other devotees): "A man brought a bottle of
consecrated wine for me; but I couldn't even touch it."

VIJAY: "Ah!"

MASTER: "I become intoxicated at the mere thought of God. I don't have
to take any wine. I feel drunk at the very sight of the charanāmrita.[5] I feel as
if I had drunk five bottles of liquor. When a person attains such a state he
cannot help discriminating about food."

[5] The water in which the image of the Deity is bathed; it is considered very sacred.

NARENDRA: "As regards food, one should take whatever comes."

MASTER: "What you say applies only to a particular state of the aspirant's mind. No food can harm a jnāni. According to the Gītā, the jnāni himself does not eat; his eating is an offering to the Kundalini. But that does not apply to a bhakta. The present state of my mind is such that I cannot eat any food unless it is first offered to God by a brāhmin priest. Formerly my state of mind was such that I would enjoy inhaling the smell of burning corpses, carried by the wind from the other side of the Ganges. It tasted very sweet to me. But nowadays I cannot eat food touched by anybody and everybody. No, I cannot. But once in a while I do. One day I was taken to see a performance of a play at Keshab's house. They gave me luchi and curries to eat. I didn't know whether the food was handed to me by a washerman or a barber; but I ate quite a little. (All laugh.) Rakhal had asked me to eat.

(To Narendra) "With you it is all right. You are in 'this' as well as in 'that'.[6] You can eat everything now. (To the devotees) Blessed is he who feels longing for God, though he eats pork. But shame on him whose mind dwells on 'woman and gold', though he eats the purest food—boiled vegetables, rice, and ghee.

"Once I had a desire to eat dāl cooked in a blacksmith's house. From my childhood I had heard the blacksmiths say, 'Do the brāhmins know how to cook?' I ate the dāl, but it smelt of the blacksmith. (All laugh.)

"I received the Āllāh mantra[7] from Govinda Rai. Rice was cooked for me with onions[8] in the kuthi. I ate some. I ate curry in Mani Mallick's garden house, but I felt a kind of repulsion to it.

"When I went to Kāmārpukur, Ramlal's father was frightened. He thought I might eat at any and every house. He was frightened to think I might be expelled from the caste; so I couldn't stay long. I came away.

"Both the Vedas and the Purānas describe pure food and conduct. But what the Vedas and the Purānas ask people to shun as impure is extolled by the Tantra as good.

"Oh, what a state of mind I passed through! I would open my mouth, touching, as it were, heaven and the nether world with my jaws, and utter the word 'Mā'. I felt that I had seized the Mother, like a fisherman dragging fish in his net. Let me recite a song:

> This time I shall devour Thee utterly, Mother Kāli!
> For I was born under an evil star,
> And one so born becomes, they say, the eater of his mother.
> Thou must devour me first, or I myself shall eat Thee up;
> One or the other it must be.
>
> I shall besmear my hands with black,[9] and with black my face;
> With black I shall besmear the whole of my body.
> And when Death seizes me, with black I shall besmear his face.

[6] That is to say, Narendra was attentive both to the world and to the spiritual life.
[7] The Master was referring to his initiation into Islām.
[8] The Mussalmāns generally relish onions, which are forbidden to orthodox brāhmins.
[9] Black is the colour of Kāli's complexion.

O Mother, I shall eat Thee up but not digest Thee;
I shall install Thee in my heart
And make Thee offerings with my mind.

You may say that by eating Kāli I shall embroil myself
With Kāla,[10] Her Husband, but I am not afraid;
Braving His anger, I shall chant my Mother's name.
To show the world that Rāmprasād is Kāli's rightful son,
Come what may, I shall eat Thee up—Thee and Thy retinue—
Or lose my life attempting it.

"I almost became mad—such was my longing for God."
Narendra began to sing:

O Mother, make me mad with Thy love!
What need have I of knowledge or reason? . . .

Listening to the song, the Master again went into samādhi. Coming down to the normal plane, he assumed the attitude of Girirāni[11] and sang the āgamani. He sang, intoxicated with divine love:

Tell me, my Umā, how have you fared, alone in the Stranger's house? . . .

He said to the devotees, "Today is the Mahāshtami. The Mother has come; that is why I feel such an awakening of spiritual emotion."

KEDAR: "Lord, you are here. Are you different from the Divine Mother?"

Sri Ramakrishna looked in another direction and sang in an absent-minded mood:

Ah, friend! I have not found Him yet, whose love has driven me mad. . . .

Again he became ecstatic and sang of the Divine Mother. As he sang, Vijay suddenly stood up crying the name of Hari. Sri Ramakrishna, full of divine love, began to dance with Vijay and the other devotees.

The music was over. The Master, Vijay, Narendra, and the other devotees sat down. All eyes were fixed on Sri Ramakrishna, who began conversing with the devotees. He asked about their health. Kedar spoke to him humbly in a soft, sweet voice. Narendra, Chunilal, Ram, M., and Harish were sitting by the Master.

KEDAR (humbly): "How can I get rid of my dizziness?"

MASTER (tenderly): "One gets that. I have had it myself. Use a little almond oil. I have heard that it cures dizziness."

KEDAR: "I shall, sir."

MASTER (to Chunilal): "Hello! How is everything?"

CHUNILAL: "Everything is all right with us now. Balaram Babu and Rakhal are well at Vrindāvan."

MASTER: "Why have you sent so many sweetmeats? (To Harish) Wait a day or two before coming to Dakshineswar. You are not well. You may fall

[10] Śiva, the Absolute.
[11] Consort of King Himālaya and mother of Umā.

ill again there. (*To Narayan, tenderly*) Sit here. Sit by me. Come to Dak-shineswar tomorrow and have your meal there. (*Pointing to M.*) Come with him. (*To M.*) What do you say?"

M. wanted to accompany Sri Ramakrishna to Dakshineswar that very day. He became thoughtful.

Surendra stood near Sri Ramakrishna. He was in the habit of drinking and often went to excess. This had worried the Master greatly, but he had not asked Surendra to give up drinking altogether. He had said to him: "Look here, Surendra! Whenever you drink wine, offer it beforehand to the Divine Mother. See that your brain doesn't become clouded and that you don't reel. The more you think of the Divine Mother, the less you will like to drink. The Mother is the Giver of the bliss of divine inebriation. Realizing Her, one feels a natural bliss."

The Master looked at Surendra and said, "You have had a drink." With these words he went into samādhi.

It was dusk. Regaining partial consciousness, the Master sang:

> Behold my Mother playing with Śiva, lost in an ecstasy of joy!
> Drunk with a draught of celestial wine, She reels, and yet She
>   does not fall. . . .

Then he chanted the name of Hari, clapping his hands occasionally. In a sweet voice he said: "Hari! Hari! O mind, chant the name of Hari! Sing the name of Hari!" Then he chanted: "Rāma! Rāma Rāma! Rāma!"

Now the Master began to pray: "O Rāma! O Rāma! I am without devotion and austerity, without knowledge and love; I have not performed any religious rites. O Rāma, I have taken refuge in Thee; I have taken shelter at Thy feet. I do not want creature comforts; I do not seek name and fame. O Rāma, I do not crave the eight occult powers; I do not care for a hundred occult powers! I am Thy servant. I have taken refuge in Thee. Grant, O Rāma, that I may have pure love for Thy Lotus Feet; that I may not be deluded by Thy world-bewitching māyā! O Rāma, I have taken refuge in Thee."

As the Master prayed all eyes were turned toward him. Hearing his piteous voice, few could restrain their tears.

Ramchandra Dutta came in and stood near him.

MASTER: "Where have you been, Ram?"

RAM: "I was upstairs, sir."

Ram had been making arrangements for feeding the devotees on the roof of the house.

MASTER (*to Ram, with a smile*): "Isn't it better to stay down below than to be high up? Water accumulates in low land but flows down from a high mound."

RAM (*with a smile*): "That is true, sir."

Supper was ready on the roof. Sri Ramakrishna and the devotees were taken there and sumptuously fed. Later the Master went to Adhar's house with M., Niranjan, and others. The Divine Mother was being worshipped there. It had been Adhar's earnest prayer that on this sacred day Sri Ramakrishna might bless his house with his presence.

Monday, September 29, 1884

It was the third day of the Durgā Pujā. The Master had been awake in his room at Dakshineswar since early morning. The morning worship in the Kāli temple was over and the orchestra had played the morning melodies in the nahabat. Brāhmins and gardeners, basket in hand, were plucking flowers for the worship of the Divine Mother. Bhavanath, Baburam, Niranjan, and M. had spent the night at Dakshineswar, sleeping on the porch of the Master's room. As soon as they awoke they saw Sri Rāmakrishna dancing in an ecstatic mood. He was chanting: "Victory to Mother Durgā! Hallowed be the name of Durgā!" He was naked and looked like a child as he chanted the name of the Blissful Mother. After a few moments he said: "Oh, the bliss of divine ecstasy! Oh, the bliss of divine drunkenness!" Then he repeatedly chanted the name of Govinda: "O Govinda! My life! My soul!"

The devotees sat on their beds and with unwinking eyes watched Sri Rāmakrishna's spiritual mood. Hazra was living at the temple garden. Latu was also living there to render the Master personal service. Rakhal was still at Vrindāvan. Narendra visited Sri Rāmakrishna now and then. He was expected that day.

The devotees washed their faces. The Master took his seat on a mat on the north verandah. Bhavanath and M. sat beside him. Other devotees were coming in and out of the room.

MASTER (*to Bhavanath*): "The truth is that ordinary men cannot easily have faith. But an Iśvarakoti's faith is spontaneous. Prahlāda burst into tears while writing the letter 'ka'.[12] It reminded him of Krishna. It is the nature of jīvas to doubt. They say yes, no doubt, but—

"Hazra can never be persuaded to believe that Brahman and Śakti, that Śakti and the Being endowed with Śakti, are one and the same. When the Reality appears as Creator, Preserver, and Destroyer, we call It Śakti; when It is inactive, we call It Brahman. But really It is one and the same thing— indivisible. Fire naturally brings to mind its power to burn; and the idea of burning naturally brings to mind the idea of fire. It is impossible to think of the one without the other.

"So I prayed to the Divine Mother: 'O Mother! Hazra is trying to upset the views of this place.[13] Either give him right understanding or take him from here.' The next day he came to me and said, 'Yes, I agree with you.' He said that God exists everywhere as All-pervading Consciousness."

BHAVANATH (*smiling*): "Did what Hazra said really make you suffer so much?"

MASTER: "You see, I am now in a different mood. I can't shout and carry on heated discussions with people. I am not in a mood now to argue and quarrel with Hazra. Hriday said to me at Jadu Mallick's garden house,

[12] The first consonant of the Sanskrit alphabet.
[13] "This place" refers to the Master himself.

'Uncle, don't you want to keep me with you?'[14] 'No,' I said, 'I am no longer in a mood to get into heated arguments with you.'

"What is knowledge and what is ignorance? A man is ignorant so long as he feels that God is far away. He has knowledge when he knows that God is here and everywhere.

"When a man has true knowledge he feels that everything is filled with Consciousness. At Kāmārpukur I used to talk to Shibu,[15] who was then a lad four or five years old. When the clouds rumbled and lightning flashed, Shibu would say to me: 'There, uncle! They're striking matches again!' (*All laugh.*) One day I noticed him chasing grasshoppers by himself. The leaves rustled in the near-by trees. 'Hush! Hush!' he said to the leaves. 'I want to catch the grasshoppers.' He was a child and saw everything throbbing with consciousness. One cannot realize God without the faith that knows no guile, the simple faith of a child.

"Ah, what a state of mind I passed through! One day something bit me while I was sitting in the grass. I was afraid it might have been a snake, and I didn't know what to do. I had heard that if a snake bites you again immediately after its first bite, it takes back its own venom. At once I set out to discover the hole so that I might let the snake bite me again. While I was searching, a man said to me, 'What are you doing?' After listening to my story, he said, 'But the snake must bite in the very same place it has bitten before.' Thereupon I went away. Perhaps I had been bitten by a scorpion or some other insect.

"I had heard from Ramlal that the autumn chill was good for one's health. Ramlal had quoted a verse to support it. One day, as I was returning from Calcutta in a carriage, I stuck my head out of the window so that I might get all the chill. Then I fell ill." (*All laugh.*)

Sri Ramakrishna entered his room and sat down. His legs were a little swollen. He asked the devotees to feel his legs and see whether or not the pressure of their fingers made dimples. Dimples did appear with the pressure, but the devotees said that it was nothing.

MASTER (*to Bhavanath*): "Please ask Mahendra of Sinthi to see me. I shall feel better if he reassures me."

BHAVANATH (*with a smile*): "You have great faith in medicine. But we haven't so much."

MASTER: "It is God who, as the doctor, prescribes the medicine. It is He who, in one form, has become the physician. Dr. Gangaprasad asked me not to drink water at night. I regarded his statement as the words of the Vedas. I look upon him as the physician of heaven."

Hazra entered the room and sat down. The Master talked awhile about different things and then said to Hazra: "You see, many people were at Ram's house yesterday. Vijay, Kedar, and others were there. But why did I

---

[14] Hriday, the Master's nephew, had taken care of him for many years. During the latter part of his stay at Dakshineswar he had treated the Master harshly and often spoken rudely to him. Finally he had incurred the displeasure of the temple authorities. He was driven out and was not allowed to set foot in the temple garden again.

[15] Shivaram, a nephew of the Master.

feel so deeply stirred at the sight of Narendra? I found that Kedar belonged to the realm of Divine Inebriation."

Presently Narendra arrived, and Sri Ramakrishna was exceedingly happy. Narendra saluted the Master and began to talk with Bhavanath and others in the room. M. was seated near by. A long mat was spread on the floor. While talking, Narendra lay on it flat on his stomach. The Master looked at him and suddenly went into samādhi. He sat on Narendra's back in an ecstatic mood.

Bhavanath sang:

> O Mother, ever blissful as Thou art,
> Do not deprive Thy worthless child of bliss! . . .

Sri Ramakrishna came down from the plane of samādhi. He sang:

> Repeat, O mind, my Mother Durgā's hallowed name!
> O Gauri! O Nārāyani! to Thee I bow.
> Thou art the day, O Mother! Thou art the dusk and the night.
> As Rāma Thou drawest the bow, as Krishna Thou playest the flute;
> As Kāli all-terrible, Thou hast silenced Śiva, Thy Lord.
> The ten Embodiments[16] of Divine Śakti art Thou,
> And Thou the ten Avatārs: this time save me Thou must!
> With flowers and vilwa-leaves did Yaśodā worship Thee,
> And Thou didst bless her by placing Krishna, the Child, in her arms.
> Wherever I chance to live, O Mother, in forest or grove,
> May my mind, day and night, dwell at Thy Lotus Feet;
> Whether at last I die a natural or sudden death,
> Oh, may my tongue repeat Durgā's name at the end!
> Thou mayest send me away, O Mother, but where shall I go?
> Tell me, Mother, where else shall I hear so sweet a name?
> Thou mayest even say to me: "Step aside! Go away!"
> Yet I shall cling to Thee, O Durgā! Unto Thy feet
> As Thine anklets I shall cling, making their tinkling sound.
> When, O Mother, Thou sittest at mighty Śiva's side,
> Then I shall cry from Thy feet, "Victory unto Śiva!"
> Mother, when as the Kite[17] Thou soarest in the sky,
> There, in the water beneath, as a minnow I shall be swimming;
> Upon me Thou wilt pounce, and pierce me through with Thy claws.
> Thus, when the breath of life forsakes me in Thy grip,
> Do not deny me the shelter of Thy Lotus Feet!
> From the world's bondage free me, O Spouse of the Absolute!
> Thy two feet are my boat to cross this world's dark sea.
> Thou art the heavens and the earth, and Thou the nether world;
> From Thee have the twelve Gopālas and Hari and Brahmā sprung.
> Whoever treads the path, repeating "Durgā! Durgā!"
> Śiva Himself protects with His almighty trident.

[16] The Mahāvidyās, or Powers, of the Divine Mother.
[17] According to Hindu mythology the Divine Mother at one time took the form of a bird similar to the kite.

Hazra was sitting on the northeast verandah counting the beads of his rosary. The Master went and sat in front of him, taking the rosary in his own hands.

MASTER (to Hazra): "You see, I cannot use the rosary. No, perhaps I can. Yes, I can with my left hand. But I cannot repeat the name of God with it."

With these words Sri Ramakrishna tried to perform a little japa. But hardly had he begun when he went into samādhi. He sat in that state a long time, still holding the rosary in his hand. The devotees looked at him with wonder in their eyes. Hazra also watched the Master without uttering a word. After a long time Sri Ramakrishna regained consciousness of the outer world and said that he was hungry. He often said such things to bring his mind down to the normal plane. M. was going to bring something for him to eat. The Master said, "No, I shall first go to the Kāli temple."

He went across the cement courtyard toward the Kāli temple. On the way he bowed with folded hands to the twelve Śiva temples. On the left was the temple of Rādhākānta. He went there first and bowed before the image. Then he entered the Kāli temple and saluted the Mother. Sitting on a carpet, he offered flowers at the Mother's holy feet. He also placed a flower on his own head. While returning from the temple he asked Bhavanath to carry the green coconut offered at the temple, and the charanāmrita. Coming back to his room, accompanied by M. and Bhavanath, he saluted Hazra, who cried out in dismay: "What are you doing, sir? What is this?" The Master said, "Why should you say it is wrong?" Hazra often argued with the Master, declaring that God dwelt in all beings and that everybody could attain Brahmajnāna through sādhanā. He had an exaggerated idea of his own spiritual progress.

It was about noon. The gong and the bells announced the worship and offering in the various temples. The brāhmins, the Vaishnavas, and the beggars went to the guest-house to have their midday meal. The devotees of the Master were also to partake of the sacred offerings. He asked them to go to the guest-house. To Narendra he said: "Won't you take your meal in my room? All right. Narendra and I will eat here." Bhavanath, Baburam, M., and the other devotees went to the guest-house.

After his meal Sri Ramakrishna rested a few minutes. The devotees were on the verandah engaged in light conversation. He soon joined them and was happy in their company. It was about two o'clock. All were still sitting on the verandah, when suddenly Bhavanath appeared in the garb of a brahmachāri, dressed in an ochre cloth, kamandalu in hand, his face beaming with smiles.

MASTER (with a smile): "That is his inner feeling. Therefore he has dressed himself as a brahmachāri."

NARENDRA: "He has put on the garb of a brahmachāri; let me put on the garb of a Tāntrik worshipper."

HAZRA: "Then you will have to follow the Tāntrik rituals, with women, wine, and so on."

Sri Ramakrishna did not encourage the conversation. Indeed, he made fun of it.

Suddenly the Master began to dance in an ecstatic mood. He sang:

> Mother, Thou canst not trick me any more,
> For I have seen Thy crimson Lotus Feet. . . .

The Master said: "Ah, how wonderfully Rajnarayan sings about the Divine Mother! He sings and dances that way. The music of Nakur Āchārya at Kāmārpukur is also wonderful. Ah, how beautiful his singing and dancing are!"

A sādhu was staying at the Panchavati. But he was a hot-tempered man; he scolded and cursed everyone. He came to the Master's room wearing wooden sandals and asked the Master, "Can I get fire here?" Sri Ramakrishna saluted him and stood with folded hands as long as he remained in the room.

When he had left, Bhavanath said to the Master with a laugh, "What great respect you showed the sādhu!"

MASTER (smiling): "You see, he too is Nārāyana, though full of tamas. This is the way one should please people who have an excess of tamas. Besides, he is a sādhu."

The devotees were engaged in a game of golokdhām.[18] Hazra joined them. The Master stood by, watching them play. M. and Kishori reached "heaven". Sri Ramakrishna bowed before them and said, "Blessed are you two brothers." He said to M., aside, "Don't play any more." Hazra fell into "hell". The Master said: "What's the matter with Hazra? Again!" No sooner had Hazra got out of "hell" than he fell into it again. All burst into laughter. Latu, at the first throw of the dice, went to "heaven" from "earth". He began to cut capers of joy. "See Latu's joy!" said the Master. "He would have been terribly sad if he hadn't achieved this. (Aside to the devotees) This too has a meaning. Hazra is so vain that he thinks he will triumph over all even in this game. This is the law of God, that He never humiliates a righteous person. Such a man is victorious everywhere."

Sri Ramakrishna was sitting on the small couch in his room. Narendra, Baburam, Bhavanath, and M. were sitting on the floor. Narendra referred to various religious sects—the Ghoshpārā, Panchanāmi, and others. Sri Ramakrishna described their views and condemned their immoral practices. He said that they could not follow the right course of spiritual discipline, but enjoyed sensuous pleasures in the name of religion.

MASTER (to Narendra): "You need not listen to these things. The bhairavas and the bhairavis of the Tāntrik sect also follow this kind of discipline. While in Benares I was taken to one of their mystic circles. Each bhairava had a bhairavi with him. I was asked to drink the consecrated wine, but I said I couldn't touch wine. They drank it. I thought perhaps they would then practise meditation and japa. But nothing of the sort. They began to dance. I was afraid they might fall into the Ganges: the circle had been

---

[18] A game in which the player tries to get to "heaven" by passing through different "planes"; but on each false step he falls into a particular "hell".

made on its bank. It is very honourable for husband and wife to assume the roles of bhairava and bhairavi.

(*To Narendra and the others*) "Let me tell you this. I regard woman as my mother; I regard myself as her son. This is a very pure attitude. There is no danger in it. To look on woman as a sister is also not bad. But to assume the attitude of a 'hero', to look on woman as one's mistress, is the most difficult discipline. Tarak's father followed this discipline. It is very difficult. In this form of sādhanā one cannot always maintain the right attitude.

"There are various paths to reach God. Each view is a path. It is like reaching the Kāli temple by different roads. But it must be said that some paths are clean and some dirty. It is good to travel on a clean path.

"Many views, many paths—and I have seen them all. But I don't enjoy them any more; they all quarrel.

"No one else is here, and you are my own people. Let me tell you something. I have come to the final realization that God is the Whole and I am a part of Him, that God is the Master and I am His servant. Furthermore, I think every now and then that He is I and I am He."

The devotees listened to these words in deep silence.

BHAVANATH (*humbly*): "I feel disturbed if I have a misunderstanding with someone. I feel that in that case I am not able to love all."

MASTER: "Try at the outset to talk to him and establish a friendly relationship with him. If you fail in spite of your efforts, then don't give it another thought. Take refuge in God. Meditate on Him. There is no use in giving up God and feeling depressed from thinking about others."

BHAVANATH: "Great souls, such as Christ and Chaitanya, have admonished us to love all beings."

MASTER: "Love you must, because God dwells in all beings. But salute a wicked person from a distance. You speak of Chaitanya? He also used to restrain his spiritual feeling in the presence of unsympathetic people. At Śrivās's house he put Śrivās's mother-in-law out of the room, dragging her out by the hair."

BHAVANATH: "It was not he but others who did it."

MASTER: "Could the others have done it without his approval? What can be done? Suppose a man cannot make another love him; must he worry about it day and night? Must I waste my mind, which should be given to God, on useless things? I say: 'O Mother, I don't want Narendra, Bhavanath, Rakhal, or anybody. I seek Thee alone. What shall I do with man?'

> When the Blissful Mother comes to my house, how much of the
> Chandi I shall hear!
> How many monks will come here, and how many yogis with
> matted locks!

"When I attain God I shall attain everything. I renounced gold and silver, saying, 'Rupee is clay and clay is rupee; gold is clay and clay is gold.' With these words I threw gold, silver, and clay into the Ganges. Then I was afraid at the thought that Mother Lakshmi might be angry with me because

I had treated Her wealth with contempt; that She might even stop my meals. So I prayed to the Divine Mother, 'O Mother, I want Thee and nothing else.' I knew that by realizing Her I should get everything."

BHAVANATH (smiling): "This is the shrewd calculation of a business man."

MASTER (smiling): "Yes, that is so. Once the Lord was pleased with a certain devotee. He appeared before him and said: 'I am very much pleased with your austerities. Ask a boon of Me.' The devotee said, 'O Lord, if You are gracious enough to give me a boon, then please grant that I may eat from gold plates with my grandchildren.' One boon covered many things— wealth, children, and grandchildren." (All laugh.)

Hazra was sitting on the verandah.

MASTER: "Do you know what Hazra wants? He wants money. His family is in distress; he has debts. He thinks that God will give him money because he devotes himself to japa and meditation."

A DEVOTEE: "Can't God fulfil a devotee's desire?"

MASTER: "If it is His sweet will. But God doesn't take entire responsibility for a devotee unless the devotee is completely intoxicated with ecstatic love for Him. At a feast it is only a child whom one takes by the hand and seats at his place. Who does that with older people? Not until a man thinks so much of God that he cannot look after himself does God take on his responsibilities. Hazra doesn't inquire about his family. His son said to Ramlal: 'Please ask father to come home. We shall not ask anything of him.' These words almost brought tears to my eyes. Hazra's mother said to Ramlal: 'Please ask Pratap[19] to come home just once. Also ask your uncle[20] to request him to come home.' I told him about it, but he didn't listen to me.

"Is a mother to be trifled with? Before becoming a sannyāsi Chaitanyadeva worked hard to persuade his mother to let him renounce home. Mother Sachi said that she would kill Keshab Bhārati.[21] Chaitanyadeva did his utmost to persuade her. He said: 'Mother, I shall not renounce home if you won't let me. But if you compel me to lead a householder's life, I shall die. And, mother, even if I go away as a sannyāsi, you will be able to see me whenever you desire. I shall stay near you. I shall see you every now and then.' Only when Chaitanya explained it to her thus did she give her permission. Nārada could not go to the forest to practise austerity as long as his mother was alive. He had to take care of her. After her death he went away to realize God.

"When I went to Vrindāvan I felt no desire to return to Calcutta. It was arranged that I should live with Gangāmā.[22] Everything was settled. My bed was to be on one side and Gangāmā's on the other. I resolved not to go back to Calcutta. I said to myself, 'How long must I eat a kaivarta's[23] food?' 'No,' said Hriday to me, 'let us go to Calcutta.' He pulled me by one hand and Gangāmā pulled me by the other. I felt an intense desire to live at

[19] Hazra.
[20] The Master.
[21] The guru who initiated Chaitanya into monastic life.
[22] A great woman saint of Vrindāvan.
[23] A reference to the proprietors of the Dakshineswar temple, who belonged to the fisherman caste, considered low in Hindu society.

Vrindāvan. But just then I remembered my mother. That completely changed everything. She was old. I said to myself: 'My devotion to God will take to its wings if I have to worry about my mother. I would rather live with her. Then I shall have peace of mind and be able to meditate on God.'

(*To Narendra*) "Why don't you say a few words to Hazra about going home? The other day he said to me, 'Yes, I shall go home and stay there three days.' But now he has forgotten all about it.

(*To the devotees*) "We have talked about filthy things—Ghoshpārā and things like that. Govinda! Govinda! Govinda! Now chant the name of Hari. Let there be a dish of rice pudding and sweets after the ordinary lentils."

Narendra began to sing:

> Fasten your mind, O man, on the Primal Purusha,
> Who is the Cause of all causes,
> The Stainless One, the Beginningless Truth.
> As Prāna He pervades the infinite universe;
> The man of faith beholds Him,
> Living, resplendent, the Root of all.
> Beyond the senses, eternal, the Essence of Consciousness,
> He shines in the cave of the heart,
> Adorned with Holiness, Wisdom, and Love;
> By meditating on Him, man is delivered from grief.
>
> Of countenance ever serene,
> An inexhaustible Ocean of Virtue,
> None can fathom His depths; yet freely, of His own grace,
> Does He reveal Himself
> To those who come to His feet for shelter,
> Merciful since they are helpless and He is the Ever-forgiving,
> The Giver of happiness,
> The Ready Help in the sea of our woe.
>
> Unswervingly just, bestowing the fruits of our deeds, good and ill,
> Yet is He the Fount of Compassion,
> The Ocean of Mercy brimming with Love;
> Even to hear of His glory suffuses the eyes with tears.
> Gaze on His face and be blest:
> Your heart is hungry for Him, O man!
> Bright with unspeakable beauty, peerless and without stain,
> No words can ever describe Him;
> Be as a beggar before His gate
> And worship Him day and night, beseeching Him for His grace.

He sang again:

> In Wisdom's firmament the moon of Love is rising full,
> And Love's flood-tide, in surging waves, is flowing everywhere.
> O Lord, how full of bliss Thou art! Victory unto Thee!
>
> On every side shine devotees, like stars around the moon;
> Their Friend, the Lord All-merciful, joyously plays with them.
> Behold! the gates of paradise today are open wide. . . .

Sri Ramakrishna was dancing in a circle. The devotees joined him. They all sang and danced. Their bliss was indescribable. The Master sang about the Divine Mother:

> Behold my Mother playing with Śiva, lost in an ecstasy of joy! . . .

Sri Ramakrishna was highly pleased because M. had joined in the music. He said to M., with a smile, "The atmosphere would have been more intense with divine fervour if a drum had accompanied the music and played: 'Tāk tāk tā dhinā! Dāk dāk dā dhinā!'"

It was dusk when the kirtan was finished.

Wednesday, October 1, 1884

Sri Ramakrishna had set out from Dakshineswar for Adhar's house in Calcutta. Narayan and Gangadhar were with him. In the carriage, in an ecstatic mood, he said: "Shall I count the beads? How shameful that would be! This emblem of Śiva has sprung from the bowels of the earth; it is self-created and not set up by man's hands."

They arrived at Adhar's house, where many devotees, including Kedar, Baburam, and Vijay, had assembled. Vaishnavcharan, the musician, was present. At the Master's behest, Adhar heard Vaishnavcharan's music daily after his return from the office.

When the Master entered Adhar's drawing-room the devotees stood up to receive him. Kedar and Vijay saluted him, and the Master asked Narayan and Baburam to salute Kedar and Vijay. He asked Kedar and Vijay to bless Narayan and Baburam that they might have devotion to God. Pointing to Narayan he said, "He is utterly guileless." The eyes of the devotees were fixed on the two boys.

MASTER (*to Kedar and the other devotees*): "It is good that I have met you all here; otherwise perhaps you would have come to the Kāli temple to see me. Through the will of God, however, we have met here."

KEDAR (*with folded hands*): "The will of God! It is all your will."

Sri Ramakrishna smiled. Vaishnavcharan began a kirtan about Rādhā and Krishna. When the music was nearing its end, with the union of Rādhā and Krishna, the Master began to dance with ecstatic fervour. The devotees danced and sang around him. After the music they all sat down. The Master said to Vijay, referring to Vaishnavcharan, "He sings very well." He asked the musician to sing the song about Sri Chaitanya, beginning with the line, "The beautiful Gaurānga, the youthful dancer, fair as molten gold."

When the song was over, the Master asked Vijay, "How did you like it?"

VIJAY: "Wonderful."

Sri Ramakrishna also sang a song about Sri Chaitanya, M. joining him. Then Vaishnavcharan sang another song:

> O my flute, sing Hari's name!
> You cannot know the highest Truth
> Without Lord Hari's grace.
> His name removes our bitter grief;
> Repeat the name of Hari, then,
> Repeat Sri Krishna's holy name!

If He bestows His grace on me,
No longer shall I be afraid
Of this unfriendly world;
Sing then Lord Hari's name, my flute!
Our only treasure is His name.

Govinda says: Behold, my days
Are passing by in vain;
In the world's deep and shoreless sea,
Oh, let me not be drowned!

Vaishnavcharan sang again, this time about Mother Durgā:

O tongue, always repeat the name of Mother Durgā;
Who but your Mother Durgā will save you in distress? . . .

The Master and the musician sang again and again the following lines from the song:

The moving and the unmoving, the gross and the subtle, art Thou;
Creation and preservation art Thou, and the last dissolution.
Thou art the Primal Root of this manifold universe;
The Mother of the three worlds, their only Saviour, art Thou;
Thou art the Śakti of all, and Thou Thine own Śakti, too.

Kedar and several devotees stood up. They were about to return home. Kedar saluted the Master and bade him good-bye.

MASTER: "Should you go away without bidding Adhar good-bye? Wouldn't that be an act of discourtesy?"

KEDAR: " 'When God is pleased, the world is pleased.' You are staying; so in a sense we are all staying. I am not feeling well. Besides, I am a little nervous about my social conventions.[24] Once before I had trouble with our community."

VIJAY (pointing to the Master): "Should we go away and leave him here?"

Just then Adhar came in to take the Master to the dining-room, for the meal was ready. Sri Ramakrishna stood up and said, addressing Kedar and Vijay: "Come. Come with me." They followed him and partook of the dinner together with the other devotees.

After dinner they all returned to the drawing-room, where the devotees sat around the Master. Kedar said to him with folded hands, "Please forgive me for hesitating to eat here." Perhaps the thought had come to his mind that he should not have hesitated, since the Master himself had no scruples about eating at Adhar's house.

Kedar worked at Dacca. Many devotees brought offerings of sweets and other food for him. Referring to this, Kedar said to the Master: "People want to give me food. What should I do? Lord, what is your command in this matter?"

MASTER: "One can eat food even from an untouchable if the untouchable is a devotee of God. After spending seven years in a God-intoxicated state

---

[24] Adhar belonged to a lower caste. Kedar, a brāhmin, could not dine with him or eat at his home.

at Dakshineswar, I visited Kāmārpukur. Oh, what a state of mind I was in at that time! Even a prostitute fed me with her own hands. But I cannot allow that now."

Kedar was about to take his leave.

KEDAR (*in a low voice*): "Lord, please transmit power to me. Many people come to me. What do I know?"

MASTER: "Everything will be all right. One gets along well if one is sincerely devoted to God."

Yogendra, the editor of a Bengali paper, the *Bangavāsi*, entered the room. The conversation turned to the Personal God and God without form.

MASTER: "God has form; again, He is formless. How many aspects He has! We cannot comprehend Him. Why should we say that God is formless only?"

YOGENDRA: "That is the one amazing thing about the Brāhmo Samāj. There even a boy twelve years old sees God as formless. The members of the Ādi Samāj[25] do not object very much to God with form. They are allowed to attend ritualistic worship if it takes place in respectable families."

MASTER (*smiling*): "How nicely he has put it! Even a boy sees the formless God!"

ADHAR: "Shivanath Babu does not believe in God's forms."

VIJAY: "That is his mistake. (*Pointing to the Master*) As he says, the chameleon assumes different colours—now this colour, now that. Only the man who lives under the tree knows the animal's true colour.

"While meditating I saw images of gods painted on a canvas. How many gods! How many different things they said! I said to myself: 'I shall go to the Master. He will explain it all to me.'"

MASTER: "You saw correctly."

KEDAR: "God assumes forms for the sake of His devotees. Through ecstatic love a devotee sees God with form. Dhruva had a vision of the Lord. He said: 'Why don't Your ear-rings move?' The Lord said, 'They will move if you move them.'"

MASTER: "One must accept everything: God with form and God without form. While meditating in the Kāli temple I noticed Ramani, a prostitute. I said, 'Mother, I see that Thou art in that form too.' Therefore I say one must accept everything. One does not know when or how God will reveal Himself."

The Master sang:

A mendicant has come to us, ever absorbed in divine moods. . . .

VIJAY: "God has infinite power. Can He not reveal Himself in any form He chooses? Man is a speck of dust, and he dares come to a conclusion about God. How amazing!"

MASTER: "A man reads a little of the *Gitā*, the *Bhāgavata*, or the Vedānta and thinks he has understood everything. Once an ant went to a hill of sugar. One grain of sugar filled its stomach, and it was returning home with another grain in its mouth. On the way it said to itself, 'Next time I go, I shall bring home the whole hill.' " (*All laugh.*)

[25] A branch of the Brāhmo Samāj.

THE MASTER IN VARIOUS MOODS

SRI RAMAKRISHNA was sitting in his room at Dakshineswar. Latu, Ramlal, Harish, and Hazra were living with him at the temple garden. Baburam spent a day or two with him now and then.

Manilal Mallick, Priya Mukherji and his relative Hari, a bearded Brāhmo devotee from Shibpur, and several Mārwāri devotees from Calcutta were in the Master's room. Manilal was an old member of the Brāhmo Samāj.

MASTER (*to Manilal and the others*): "It is wise to salute a person mentally. What need is there of touching his feet? Mental salutation doesn't embarrass anybody.

"The attitude that my religion alone is right and all other religions are false is not good. I see that God Himself has become all these: men, images, and śālagrām. I see one alone in all these; I do not see two. I see only one.

"Many people think that their opinion alone is right and others' opinions are wrong; that they alone have won and others have lost. But a person who has gone forward may be detained by some slight obstacle, and someone who has been lagging behind may then steal a march on him. In the game of golokdhām one may advance a great deal, but still somehow one's piece may fail to reach the goal.

"Triumph or defeat is in the hands of God. We cannot understand His ways. You must have noticed that the green coconut remains high in the tree and is exposed to the sun, but still its milk is cool. On the other hand the pāniphal[1] remains in the water, but when eaten it heats the body.

"Look at the body of man. The head is the root, and it is at the top."

MANILAL: "What then is our duty?"

MASTER: "To remain somehow united with God. There are two ways: karmayoga and manoyoga. Householders practise yoga through karma, the performance of duty. There are four stages of life: brahmacharya, gārhasthya, vānaprastha, and sannyās. Sannyāsis must renounce those karmas which are performed with special ends in view; but they should perform the daily obligatory karmas, giving up all desire for results. Sannyāsis are united with God by such karmas as the acceptance of the staff, the receiving of alms, going on pilgrimage, and the performance of worship and japa.

---

[1] A kind of aquatic fruit.

"It doesn't matter what kind of action you are engaged in. You can be united with God through any action provided that, performing it, you give up all desire for its result.

"There is the other path: manoyoga. A yogi practising this discipline doesn't show any outward sign. He is inwardly united with God. Take Jaḍabharata and Śukadeva, for instance. There are many other yogis of this class, but these two are well known. They shave neither hair nor beard.

"All actions drop away when a man reaches the stage of the paramahamsa. He always remembers the ideal and meditates on it. He is always united with God in his mind. If he ever performs an action it is to teach men.

"A man may be united with God either through action or through inwardness of thought, but he can know everything through bhakti. Through bhakti one spontaneously experiences kumbhaka. The nerve currents and breathing calm down when the mind is concentrated. Again, the mind is concentrated when the nerve currents and breathing calm down. Then the buddhi, the discriminating power, becomes steady. The man who achieves this state is not himself aware of it.

"One can attain everything through bhaktiyoga. I wept before the Mother and prayed, 'O Mother, please tell me, please reveal to me, what the yogis have realized through yoga and the jnānis through discrimination.' And the Mother has revealed everything to me. She reveals everything if the devotee cries to Her with a yearning heart. She has shown me everything that is in the Vedas, the Vedānta, the Purānas, and the Tantra."

MANILAL: "And what about hathayoga?"

MASTER: "The hathayogis identify themselves with their bodies. They practise internal washing and similar disciplines, and devote themselves only to the care of the body. Their ideal is to increase longevity. They serve the body day and night. That is not good.

"What is your duty? You should renounce 'woman and gold' mentally. You cannot look on the world as crow-droppings.

"The goswāmis are householders. Therefore I said to them: 'You have your duties in the temple; how can you renounce the world? You cannot explain away the world as māyā.'

"Chaitanyadeva said that the duties of householders were kindness to living beings, service to the Vaishnavas, and the chanting of God's holy name.

"Keshab Sen once said about me: 'Now he asks us to hold to both—God and the world. But one day he will sting us.' No, that is not true. Why should I sting?"

MANI MALLICK: "But, sir, you do."

MASTER (smiling): "How so? You are a householder. Why should you renounce?

"But the renunciation of the world is needful for those whom God wants to be teachers of men. One who is an āchārya should give up 'woman and gold'; otherwise people will not take his advice. It is not enough for him to renounce only mentally; he should also renounce outwardly. Only then will his teaching bear fruit. Otherwise people will think, 'Though he asks us to give up "woman and gold", he enjoys them himself in secret.'

"A physician prescribed medicine for a patient and said to him, 'Come another day and I'll give you directions about diet.' The physician had several jars of molasses in his room that day. The patient lived very far away. He visited the physician later and the physician said to him: 'Be careful about your food. It is not good for you to eat molasses.' After the patient left, another person who was there said to the physician: 'Why did you give him all the trouble of coming here again? You could very well have given him the instructions the first day.' The physician replied with a smile: 'There is a reason. I had several jars of molasses in my room that day. If I had asked the patient then to give up molasses, he would not have had faith in my words. He would have thought: "He has so many jars of molasses in his room, he must eat some of it. Then molasses can't be so bad." Today I have hidden the jars. Now he will have faith in my words.'

"I have seen the āchārya of the Ādi Brāhmo Samāj. I understand that he has married for the second or third time. He has grown-up children. And such men are teachers! If they say, 'God is real and all else illusory', who will believe them? You can very well understand who will be their disciples.

"Like teacher, like disciple. Even if a sannyāsi renounces 'woman and gold' mentally, but lives with them outwardly, he cannot be a teacher of men. People will say that he enjoys 'molasses' secretly.

"Once Mahendra Kavirāj of Sinthi gave five rupees to Ramlal. I didn't know about it. When Ramlal told me about the money, I asked him, 'For whom was the money given?' He said it was for me. At first I thought that I should use it to pay what I owed for my milk. But will you believe me? I had slept only a little while when I suddenly woke up writhing with pain, as if a cat were scratching my chest. I went to Ramlal and asked him again, 'Was the money given for your aunt?'[2] 'No', Ramlal answered. Thereupon I said to him, 'Go at once and return the money.' Ramlal gave it back the next day.

"Do you know how it looks for a sannyāsi to accept money or to be attached to an object of temptation? It is as if a brāhmin widow who had practised continence and lived on simple boiled rice and vegetables and milk for many years, were suddenly to accept an untouchable as her paramour. (*All look stunned.*)

"There was a low-caste woman named Bhagi Teli in our part of the country. She had many disciples and devotees. Finding that she, a śudra, was being saluted by people, the landlord became jealous and engaged a wicked man to tempt her. He succeeded in corrupting her and all her spiritual practice came to nothing. A fallen sannyāsi is like that.

"You are leading householders' lives. It is necessary for you to live in the company of holy men. First of all, the company of holy men; then śraddhā, faith in God.

"How can people have reverence and faith in God if the holy men do not sing His name and glories? People respect a man if they know that in his family there have been royal ministers for three generations.

(*To M.*) "Even if one has attained Knowledge, one must still constantly

[2] The Holy Mother, his wife.

practise God-Consciousness. Nangtā used to say: 'What is the use of polishing the outside of a metal pot one day only? If you don't polish it regularly it will get tarnished again.' I shall have to go to your house some time. If I know your house I can meet other devotees there. Please go to see Ishan some time.

(To Manilal) "Keshab Sen's mother came here the other day. The young boys of her family sang the name of Hari. She went around them clapping her hands. I noticed she was not very much stricken with grief over Keshab's death. She observed the fast of ekādasi here and counted her beads. I was pleased to see her devotion to God."

MANILAL: "Ramkamal Sen, Keshab Babu's grandfather, was a devotee of God. He used to sit in a tulsi-grove and repeat God's holy name. Pyarimohan, Keshab's father, was also a Vaishnava devotee."

MASTER: "The son could not have been so devoted to God if the father had not been like that. Look at Vijay. His father would become unconscious of the world in divine ecstasy while reading the *Bhāgavata*. Vijay can hardly control his emotion: while uttering Hari's name, he sometimes stands up from his seat. The forms of God that Vijay sees nowadays are all real. Speaking about the different aspects of God, formless and with form, Vijay said that God sometimes appears with attributes and sometimes without attributes. He gave the example of the chameleon, which sometimes turns red, sometimes blue, sometimes green, and sometimes remains colourless.

"Vijay is really guileless. One cannot realize God without being guileless and liberal-minded. Yesterday Vijay was at Adhar Sen's house. He behaved as if it were his own place and those who lived there his own people. One cannot be guileless and liberal-minded unless one is free from worldliness."

Then the Master sang:

> You will attain that priceless Treasure when your mind is free
> from stain. . . .

He continued: "You cannot make a pot without first carefully preparing the clay. The pot will crack if the clay contains particles of sand or stone. That is why the potter first prepares the clay by removing the sand and stones.

"If a mirror is covered with dirt, it won't reflect one's face. A man cannot realize his true Self unless his heart is pure. You will find guilelessness wherever God incarnates Himself as man. Nandaghosh, Daśaratha, Vasudeva—all of them were guileless.

"The Vedānta says that a man does not even desire to know God unless he has a pure mind. One cannot be guileless and liberal-minded without much tapasyā or unless it is one's last birth."

Sri Ramakrishna was worrying, like a child, because he thought his legs were slightly swollen. Mahendra Kavirāj of Sinthi entered the room and saluted the Master.

MASTER (to the devotees): "Yesterday I said to Naran, 'Just press your leg and see if there is any dimple.' He pressed it and there was one. Then I gave a sigh of relief. (*To Mukherji*) Will you please press your leg? Is there any dimple?"

MUKHERJI: "Yes, sir."

MASTER: "Ah, what a relief!"

MANI MALLICK: "Why should you worry about it, sir? Please take your bath in the river. Why should you take medicine?"

MASTER: "No, sir. You have strong blood. Your case is different. The Divine Mother has placed me in the state of a child. One day I was bitten by something in the jungle. I had heard people say that, in case of snake-bite, the poison would come out if the snake bit again. So I put my hand in a hole and waited. A man passing by said to me: 'What are you doing? You will get rid of the poison only if the snake bites again in the same place. You will not be cured if the snake bites another part of your body.'

"I was told that the autumn dew was good. One day, while coming from Calcutta, I stuck my head out of the carriage and exposed it to the damp air. (*All laugh.*)

(*To Mahendra of Sinthi*) "That pundit from Sinthi is very good. He holds a title for his scholarship. He respects me. I said to him, 'You have read a great deal; but give up the vanity that you are a scholar.' That made him very happy. I discussed Vedānta with him.

(*To M.*) "That which is Pure Ātman is unattached. Māyā, or avidyā, is in It. In māyā there are three gunas: sattva, rajas, and tamas. These three gunas also exist in the Pure Ātman. But Ātman Itself is unattached. If you throw a blue pill into the fire, you will see a blue flame. If you throw a red pill, you will see a red flame. But fire itself has no colour of its own.

"If you put a blue pill in water, the water will turn blue. Again, if you put alum in that water, it will regain its natural colour.

"A butcher was carrying a load of meat when he touched Śankara. Śankara exclaimed: 'What! You have touched me!' The butcher replied: 'Venerable sir, neither have you touched me nor have I touched you. You are Pure Ātman, unattached.' Jadabharata said the same thing to King Rahugana.

"The Pure Ātman is unattached, and one cannot see It. If salt is mixed with water, one cannot see the salt with the eyes.

"That which is the Pure Ātman is the Great Cause, the Cause of the cause. The gross, the subtle, the causal, and the Great Cause. The five elements are gross. Mind, buddhi, and ego are subtle. Prakriti, the Primal Energy, is the cause of all these. Brahman, Pure Ātman, is the Cause of the cause.

This Pure Atman alone is our real nature. What is jnāna? It is to know one's own Self and keep the mind in It. It is to know the Pure Atman.

"How long should a man perform his duties? As long as he identifies himself with the body, in other words, as long as he thinks he is the body. That is what the *Gītā* says. To think of the body as the Ātman is ajnāna, ignorance.

(*To the bearded Brāhmo devotee from Shibpur*) "Are you a Brāhmo?"

DEVOTEE: "Yes, sir."

MASTER (*smiling*): "I can recognize a worshipper of the Formless by looking at his face and eyes. Please dive a little deeper. One doesn't get the gem by floating on the surface. As for myself, I accept all—the formless God and God with form."

The Mārwāri devotees from Burrabāzar entered the room and saluted the Master. He began to praise them.

MASTER (*to the devotees*): "Ah! They are real devotees of God. They visit temples, sing hymns to God, and eat prasād. And the gentleman whom they have made their priest this year is learned in the *Bhāgavata*."

MĀRWĀRI DEVOTEE: "Who is this 'I' that says, 'O Lord, I am Thy servant'?"

MASTER: "This is the liṅgaśarira, or embodied soul. It consists of manas, buddhi, chitta, and ahamkāra."

DEVOTEE: "Who is the embodied soul?"

MASTER: "It is the Ātman bound by the eight fetters. And what is the chitta? It is the 'I-consciousness' that says, 'Aha!'"

DEVOTEE: "Revered sir, what happens after death?"

MASTER: "According to the *Gītā*, one becomes afterwards what one thinks of at the time of death. King Bharata thought of his deer and became a deer in his next life. Therefore one must practise sādhanā in order to realize God. If a man thinks of God day and night, he will have the same thought in the hour of death."

DEVOTEE: "Why don't we feel dispassion toward worldly objects?"

MASTER: "Because of māyā. Through māyā one feels the Real to be the unreal and the unreal to be the Real. The Real means That which is eternal, the Supreme Brahman; and the unreal means that which is non-eternal, that is to say, the world."

DEVOTEE: "We read the scriptures. Why is it that we can't assimilate them?"

MASTER: "What will one accomplish by mere reading? One needs spiritual practice—austerity. Call on God. What is the use of merely repeating the word 'siddhi'? One must eat a little of it.

"The hand bleeds when it touches a thorny plant. Suppose you bring such a plant and repeat, sitting near it: 'There! The plant is burning.' Will that burn the plant? This world is like the thorny plant. Light the fire of Knowledge and with it set the plant ablaze. Only then will it be burnt up.

"One must labour a little while at the stage of sādhanā. Then the path becomes easy. Steer the boat around the curves of the river and then let it go with the favourable wind.

"As long as you live inside the house of māyā, as long as there exists the cloud of māyā, you do not see the effect of the Sun of Knowledge. Come outside the house of māyā, give up 'woman and gold', and then the Sun of Knowledge will destroy ignorance. A lens cannot burn paper inside the house. If you stand outside, then the rays of the sun fall on the lens and the paper burns. Again, the lens cannot burn the paper if there is a cloud. The paper burns when the cloud disappears.

"The darkness of the mind is destroyed only when a man stands a little apart from 'woman and gold' and, thus standing apart, practises a little austerity and spiritual discipline. Then only does the cloud of his ego and ignorance vanish. Then only does he attain the Knowledge of God. This 'woman and gold' is the only cloud that hides the Sun of Knowledge.

(*To the Mārwāri devotee*) "The rules for a sannyāsi are extremely hard. He cannot have the slightest contact with 'woman and gold'. He must not accept money with his own hands, and he must not even allow it to be left near him.

"Lakshminarayan Mārwāri, a Vedāntist, used to come here very often. One day he saw a dirty sheet on my bed and said: 'I shall invest ten thousand rupees in your name. The interest will enable you to pay your expenses.' The moment he uttered these words, I fell unconscious, as if struck by a stick. Regaining consciousness I said to him: 'If you utter such words again, you had better not come here. It is impossible for me to touch money. It is also impossible for me to keep it near me.' He was a very clever fellow. He said: 'Then you too have the idea of acceptance and rejection. In that case you haven't attained Perfect Knowledge.' 'My dear sir,' I said, 'I haven't yet gone that far.' (*All laugh.*) Lakshminarayan then wanted to leave the money with Hriday. I said to him: 'That will not do. If you leave it with Hriday, then I shall instruct him to spend it as I wish. If he does not comply, I shall be angry. The very contact of money is bad. No, you can't leave it with Hriday.' Won't an object kept near a mirror be reflected in it?"

DEVOTEE: "Revered sir, is a man liberated only when he dies on the bank of the Ganges?"

MASTER: "It is the Knowledge of God alone that gives liberation. The jnāni will certainly attain liberation wherever he may die, whether in the charnel-pit or on the bank of the Ganges. But the bank of the Ganges is prescribed for a bound soul."

DEVOTEE: "Revered sir, why does a man dying in Benares become liberated?"

MASTER: "A person dying in Benares sees the vision of Śiva. Śiva says to him: 'This is My aspect with form, My embodiment in māyā. I assume this form for the sake of the devotees. Now look. I am merging in the indivisible Satchidānanda!' Uttering these words, Śiva withdraws His form and enables the dying person to see Brahman.

"The Purānas say that even a chandāla endowed with love of God achieves liberation. According to this school the name of God is enough to liberate a soul. There is no need of such things as worship, sacrifice, the discipline of Tantra, and the recitation of mantras.

"But the teachings of the Vedas are different. According to the Vedas none but a brāhmin can be liberated. Further, the worship is not accepted by the gods unless the mantras are recited correctly. One must perform sacrifice, worship, and so on, according to scriptural injunction. But where is the time in the Kaliyuga to perform the Vedic rituals? Therefore in the Kaliyuga the path of devotion prescribed by Nārada is best. The path of karma is very difficult. Karma becomes a cause of bondage unless it is performed in a spirit of detachment. Further, the life of man nowadays depends on food. He has no time to observe the rituals enjoined by the scriptures. The patient dies if he tries to cure his fever by taking the decoction of herbs prescribed by the orthodox native physicians. Therefore he should take a modern 'fever mixture'.

"According to Nārada the devotee should sing the name and glories of God. The path of karma is not the right one for the Kaliyuga. Bhaktiyoga is the right path. Do your duties in the world as long as you need them to reap the fruit of the actions of your past lives. But you must develop love for God and be passionately attached to Him. The singing of the name and glories of God destroys the effect of past action.

"You don't have to perform duties all your life. As you develop unalloyed love and longing for God, your duties become fewer and fewer. After the realization of God they completely drop away. When the young daughter-in-law is pregnant, her mother-in-law lessens her duties. After the birth of the child she doesn't have to do any household work."

Several young men from the village of Dakshineswar entered the room and saluted Sri Ramakrishna. It was about four o'clock in the afternoon. They sat down and began to talk with the Master.

YOUNG MAN: "Sir, what is Knowledge?"

MASTER: "It is to know that God is the only Reality and that all else is unreal. That which is the Real is also called Brahman. It has another name: Kāla, Time. There is a saying, 'O brother, how many things come into being in Time and disappear in Time!'

"That which sports with Kāla is called Kāli. She is the Primal Energy. Kāla and Kāli, Brahman and Śakti, are indivisible.

"That Brahman, of the nature of Reality, is eternal. It exists in past, present, and future. It is without beginning or end. It cannot be described in words. The utmost that can be said of Brahman is that It is of the very nature of Intelligence and Bliss.

"The world is illusory; Brahman alone is real. The world is of the nature of magic. The magician is real but his magic is unreal."

YOUNG MAN: "If the world is of the nature of illusion—magic—then why doesn't one get rid of it?"

MASTER: "It is due to the samskāras, inborn tendencies. Repeated births in this world of māyā make one believe that māyā is real.

"Let me tell you how powerful inborn tendencies are. A prince had, in a previous birth, been the son of a washerman. While playing with his chums in his incarnation as the prince, he said to them: 'Stop those games. I will show you a new one. I shall lie on my belly, and you will beat the clothes on my back as the washerman does, making a swishing sound.'

"Many youngsters come here. But only a few long for God. These few are born with a spiritual tendency. They shudder at the talk of marriage. Niranjan has said from boyhood that he will not marry.

"More than twenty years ago two young men used to come here from Barānagore. One was named Govinda Pal and the other Gopal Sen. They had been devoted to God since boyhood. The very mention of marriage would frighten them. Gopal used to have bhāva samādhi. He would shrink from worldly people, as a mouse from a cat. One day he saw the boys of the Tagore family strolling in the garden. He shut himself in the kuthi lest he should have to talk with them.

"Gopal went into samādhi in the Panchavati. In that state he said to me, touching my feet: 'Let me go. I cannot live in this world any more. You have a long time to wait. Let me go.' I said to him, in an ecstatic mood, 'You must come again.' 'Very well, I will', he said. A few days later Govinda came to me. 'Where is Gopal?' I asked him. He said, 'He has passed away.'

"What are the other youngsters about? Money, house, carriage, clothes, and finally marriage. These are the things that keep them busy. If they want to marry, at the outset they make inquiries about the girl. They want to find out for themselves whether she is beautiful.

"There is a person who speaks much ill of me. He is always criticizing me for loving the youngsters. I love only those who are born with good tendencies, pure souls with longing for God, who do not pay any attention to money, creature comforts, and such things.

"If married people develop love for God, they will not be attached to the world. Hirananda is married. What if he is? He will not be much attached to the world."

Hirananda, a member of the Brāhmo Samāj, was a native of Sindh. He had met the Master in Calcutta and become devoted to him.

Manilal, the Mārwāri devotees, the Brāhmo devotees from Shibpur, and the young men from Dakshineswar saluted Sri Ramakrishna and took their leave.

It was evening. Lamps were lighted on the south and west verandahs. A lamp was lighted in the Master's room also, and incense was burnt. He was repeating the name of the Divine Mother, absorbed in contemplation of Her. After a while he talked again to the devotees. There was still some time before the evening worship in the temples.

MASTER (to M.): "What need of the sandhyā has a man who thinks of God day and night?

> What need of rituals has a man, what need of devotions any more,
> If he repeats the Mother's name at the three holy hours?
> Rituals may pursue him close, but never can they overtake him.
> Charity, vows, and giving of gifts do not appeal to Madan's mind;
> The Blissful Mother's Lotus Feet are his whole prayer and sacrifice.

"The sandhyā merges in the Gāyatri, the Gāyatri in Om. A man is firmly established in spiritual life when he goes into samādhi on uttering 'Om' only once.

"There is a sādhu in Hrishikesh who gets up early in the morning and stands near a great waterfall. He looks at it the whole day and says to God: 'Ah, You have done well! Well done! How amazing!' He doesn't practise any other form of japa or austerity. At night he returns to his hut.

"What need is there even to bother one's head about whether God is formless or has a form? It is enough for a man to pray to Him, alone in solitude, weeping, 'O God, reveal Yourself to me as You are.'

"God is both inside and outside. It is He who dwells inside us. Therefore the Vedas say, 'Tattvamasi—That thou art.' God is also outside us. He appears manifold through māyā; but in reality He alone exists. Therefore before describing the various names and forms of God, one should say, 'Om Tat Sat.'[3]

"It is one thing to learn about God from the scriptures, and quite another to see Him. The scriptures only give hints. Therefore to read a great many scriptures is not necessary. It is much better to pray to God in solitude.

"It isn't necessary to read all of the Gītā. One can get the essence of the Gītā by repeating the word ten times. It becomes reversed and is then 'tāgi'. The essence of the book is: 'O man, renounce everything and worship God.' "

The Master went into an ecstatic mood while watching the evening worship of Kāli in the company of the devotees. He was in no condition even to salute the image. Very carefully he returned to his room with the devotees and sat down; he was still in an ecstatic mood. He spoke to them while in that state.

In the room was Hari, a young man about twenty years of age, who was a relative of the Mukherjis and very much devoted to the Master. He was married. At that time he was living with the Mukherjis and looking for a job.

MASTER (to Hari, in an ecstatic mood): "Take your initiation after getting your mother's permission. (To Priya, referring to Hari) I couldn't give him the mantra though I said I would initiate him. I don't initiate people. Continue with your own meditation and japa as you have been doing."

PRIYA: "Yes, sir."

MASTER: "And I am saying this to you in this state of my mind. Believe my words. You see, there is no show or deceit here. I just said to the Divine Mother in my ecstatic mood, 'O Mother, may those who come here [referring to himself] through sincere attraction obtain perfection!' "

Mahendra Kavirāj of Sinthi was seated on the verandah conversing with Ramlal, Hazra, and others. The Master called to him from his room. M. went out quickly and brought Mahendra in.

MASTER (to Mahendra): "Sit down and listen to my words."

Mahendra was a little embarrassed. He sat down.

MASTER (to the devotees): "God can be served in different ways. An ecstatic lover of God enjoys Him in different ways. Sometimes he says, 'O God, You are the lotus and I am the bee', and sometimes, 'You are the Ocean of Satchidānanda and I am the fish.' Sometimes, again, the lover of God says, 'I am Your dancing-girl.' He dances and sings before Him. He thinks of himself sometimes as the friend of God and sometimes as His handmaid. He looks on God sometimes as a child, as did Yaśodā, and sometimes as husband or sweetheart, as did the gopis.

[3] "Om. That alone is the Reality."

"Sometimes Balarāma looked on Krishna as a friend; sometimes he would think he was Krishna's umbrella or carpet. He served Krishna in all possible ways."

Was Sri Ramakrishna hinting at his own state of mind while thus describing the different attitudes of a lover of God?

Next he described Chaitanya's three spiritual moods.

MASTER: "Chaitanyadeva used to experience three moods. In the inmost mood he would be absorbed in samādhi, unconscious of the outer world. In the semi-conscious mood he would dance in ecstasy but could not talk. In the conscious mood he would sing the glories of God.

(To the devotees) "You are listening to my words. Try to assimilate them. When worldly people sit before a sādhu, for the time being they completely hide all worldly thoughts and ideas. But once away from the holy man they let them out again. You have seen a pigeon eating dried peas. You think he has digested them, but he keeps them in his crop. You can feel them there.

"At dusk put aside all duties and pray to God. One is reminded of Him by darkness. At the approach of darkness one thinks: 'I could see everything a moment ago. Who has brought about this change?' The Mussalmāns put aside all activities and say their prayers at the appointed times."

MUKHERJI: "Revered sir, is it good to practise japa?"

MASTER: "Yes. One attains God through japa. By repeating the name of God secretly and in solitude one receives divine grace. Then comes His vision. Suppose there is a big piece of timber lying under water and fastened to the land with a chain; by proceeding along the chain, link by link, you will at last touch the timber.

"Higher than worship is japa, higher than japa is meditation, higher than meditation is bhāva, and higher than bhāva are mahābhāva and prema. Chaitanyadeva had prema. When one attains prema one has the rope to tie God."

Hazra entered the room.

MASTER (to Hazra): "Love of God, when it is intense and spontaneous, is called rāga-bhakti. Vaidhi-bhakti, formal devotion, depends on scriptural injunctions. It comes and it goes. But rāga-bhakti is like a stone emblem of Śiva that has sprung up out of the bowels of the earth. One cannot find its root; they say the root goes as far as Benares. Only an Incarnation of God and His companions attain rāga-bhakti."

HAZRA: "Ah me!"

MASTER: "One day I was returning from the pine-grove, when I saw you telling your beads. I said to the Divine Mother: 'Mother, what a small-minded fellow he is! He lives here and still he practises japa with a rosary! Whoever comes here [referring to himself] will have his spiritual consciousness awakened all at once; he won't have to bother much about japa. Go to Calcutta and you will find thousands telling their beads—even the prostitutes.'

(To M.) "Please bring Naran here in a carriage. I am making the same request to Mukherji. I shall give Naran something to eat when he comes. There is great significance in feeding boys like him."

Saturday, October 4, 1884

It was the day of the first full moon after the Durgā Pujā. Sri Rama-krishna arrived at the Calcutta house of Nabin Sen, the elder brother of Keshab Chandra Sen. On the previous Thursday Keshab's mother had begged the Master to pay her a visit in Calcutta.

The Master seated himself in a room on the upper floor of the house. With him were Baburam, Kishori, and a few other devotees. Nandalal and Keshab's other nephews, Keshab's mother, and other relatives of his, waited on the Master. It had been arranged to have devotional music performed in the room. M. was sitting in a room downstairs, listening to the kirtan.

Sri Ramakrishna said to the Brāhmo devotees: "The world is impermanent. One should constantly remember death." Then he sang:

> Remember this, O mind! Nobody is your own:
> Vain is your wandering in this world.
> Trapped in the subtle snare of māyā as you are,
> Do not forget the Mother's name. . . .

The Master said to the devotees: "Dive deep. What will you gain by merely floating on the surface? Renounce everything for a few days, retire into solitude, and call on God with all your soul."

The Master sang:

> Dive deep, O mind, dive deep in the Ocean of God's Beauty;
> If you descend to the uttermost depths,
> There you will find the gem of Love. . . .

At Sri Ramakrishna's request the Brāhmo devotees sang:

> Thou art my All in All, O Lord!—the Life of my life, the Essence
>   of essence;
> In the three worlds I have none else but Thee to call my own.
> Thou art my peace, my joy, my hope; Thou my support, my
>   wealth, my glory;
> Thou my wisdom and my strength. . . .

The Master sang again:

> O Mother, for Yaśodā Thou wouldst dance, when she called
>   Thee her precious "Blue Jewel":
> Where hast Thou hidden that lovely form, O terrible Śyāmā? . . .

The Brāhmo devotees also sang to the accompaniment of cymbals and drums:

> O Mother, how deep is Thy love for men!
> Mindful of it, I weep for joy.
> Almost from the day of my birth
> I have transgressed Thine every law,
> And still Thou lookest on me with love,
> Comforting me with sweetest words.
> Mindful of it, I weep for joy.
> O Mother, the burden of Thy love

Is far too great for me to bear;
My soul gives a heart-piercing cry
At Thy love's touch. To Thee I come,
Seeking a refuge at Thy feet.

They again sang of the Divine Mother:

O Mother, Thou my Inner Guide, ever awake within my heart!
Day and night Thou holdest me in Thy lap.
Why dost Thou show such tenderness to this unworthy child of
    Thine?

Ah! It seems Thou art mad with love: now caressing, now with
    strong grasp
Holding me firm, Thou givest me to drink
Thy nectar, pouring in my ears Thy words of loving tenderness.

Unceasing is Thy love for me, a love that cannot see my faults;
Whenever I am in danger, Thou dost save me.
Saviour of sinners! I know the truth: I am my Mother's and She is
    mine.

Now I shall listen to Her alone, and follow the path of righteous-
    ness;
Drinking the milk that flows from my Mother's breasts,
I shall be strong and sing with joy: "Hail, O Mother! Brahman
    Eternal!"

The Master and the Brāhmo devotees sang several songs about Hari and
Gaurānga.

Sunday, October 5, 1884

Sri Ramakrishna was sitting in his room after the midday meal, with M.,
Hazra, the elder Kali, Baburam, Ramlal, Hari, and others. Some of them
sat on the floor and some stood about. On the previous day the Master had
visited Keshab's mother at her Calcutta house and had made her happy with
his devotional songs.

Hazra had been living with the Master at Dakshineswar a long time. He
was a little conceited about his knowledge and even criticized the Master
now and then before others. Again, he would sit on the verandah of the
Master's room and tell his beads with apparent concentration. He spoke
slightingly of Chaitanya as a "modern Incarnation". He would say: "God
gives not only pure devotion but also wealth. He has no lack of it. By attaining God one obtains the eight occult powers as well." Hazra had a small
debt to clear up, about one thousand rupees. He had incurred it for the
building of his house and was worried about paying it.

The elder Kali had a position in an office, from which he received a small
salary. He had a large family to maintain. He was devoted to the Master
and visited him now and then, even absenting himself from the office.

KALI (*to Hazra*): "You go about criticizing people; you are like a touch-
stone, testing what is pure gold and what is impure. Why do you speak so
much ill of others?"

HAZRA: "Whatever I say, I say to him [meaning Sri Ramakrishna] alone."

MASTER: "That is so."

Hazra began to explain Tattvajnāna.

HAZRA: "The meaning of Tattvajnāna is the knowledge of the existence of the twenty-four tattvas, or cosmic principles."

He was wrong about the meaning of the word.

A DEVOTEE: "What are they?"

HAZRA: "The five elements, the six passions, the five organs of perception, the five organs of action, and so forth."

M. (to the Master, smiling): "He says that the six passions are included in the twenty-four cosmic principles."

MASTER (smiling): "Listen to him! Notice how he explains Tattvajnāna! The word really means 'knowledge of Self'. The word 'Tat' means the Supreme Self, and the word 'tvam', the embodied soul. One attains Supreme Knowledge, Tattvajnāna, by realizing the identity of the embodied soul and the Supreme Self."

After a few minutes Hazra left the room and sat on the porch.

MASTER (to M. and the others): "He [meaning Hazra] only argues. This moment perhaps he understands, but the next moment he is his old self again.

"When the angler hooks a big fish and finds it pulling hard, he releases the line; otherwise it will snap and the angler himself will be thrown into the water. Therefore I do not say much to him.

(To M.) "Hazra said that a man could not be liberated unless he was born in a brāhmin body. 'How is that?' I said. 'One attains liberation through bhakti alone. Savari was the daughter of a hunter. She, Ruhidās, and others belonged to the śudra caste. They were liberated through bhakti alone.' 'But still—' Hazra insisted.

"He recognized Dhruva's spiritual greatness, but not as much as he recognized Prahlāda's. When Latu said, 'Dhruva had great yearning for God from his boyhood', he kept still.

"I said that there was nothing greater than the bhakti that sought no end and had no selfish motive. Hazra contradicted me. I said to him, 'A wealthy man is annoyed when a petitioner comes to him. "There he comes", he says angrily. "Sit down", he says to him in an indifferent voice, and shows that he is much annoyed. He doesn't allow such a beggar to ride with him in his carriage.'

"But Hazra said that God was not like such wealthy people of the world; did He lack wealth, that He should feel pinched to give it away? Hazra said further: 'When rain falls from the sky, the Ganges and all the big rivers and lakes overflow with water. Small tanks, too, are filled. Likewise, God out of His grace grants wealth and riches as well as knowledge and devotion.'

(To the devotees) "But I call this impure devotion to God. Pure devotion has no desire behind it. You don't want anything from me, but you love to see me and hear my words. My mind also dwells on you. I wonder how you are and why you don't come.

"You don't want anything of God but still you love Him. That is pure bhakti, love of God with no motive behind it. Prahlāda had it. He sought neither kingdom nor riches; he sought Hari alone."

M: "Hazra is a chatterbox. He won't achieve anything unless he becomes silent."

MASTER: "Now and then he comes to me and becomes mellowed. But he is a pest; again he argues. It is very hard to get rid of egotism. You may cut down an aśwattha tree, but the next day a sprout will spring up. As long as the roots remain, the tree will grow again.

"I said to Hazra, 'Don't speak ill of anyone.' It is Nārāyana Himself who has assumed all these forms. One can worship even a wicked person. Haven't you observed the Kumāri Pujā? Why should you worship a girl who has all the physical limitations of a human being? It is because she is a form of the Divine Mother. But God dwells in a special way in His devotee. The devotee is His parlour. If the gourd has a large body then it makes a good tānpurā. It gives a nice sound."

Two monks had arrived at the temple garden in the morning. They were devoted to the study of the *Bhagavad Gītā*, the Vedānta, and other scriptures. They entered the Master's room, saluted him, and sat on the mat on the floor. Sri Ramakrishna was seated on the small couch. The Master spoke to the sādhus in Hindusthāni.

MASTER: "Have you had your meal?"

SĀDHU: "Yes, sir."

MASTER: "What did you eat?"

SĀDHU: "Dāl and bread. Will you take some?"

MASTER: "No, I take only a few morsels of rice. Well, your japa and meditation must be without any desire for results. Isn't that so?"

SĀDHU: "Yes, sir."

MASTER: "That is good. One must surrender the result to God. What do you say? That is the view of the *Gītā*."

One sādhu said to the other, quoting from the *Gītā*: "O Arjuna, whatever action you perform, whatever you eat, whatever you offer in sacrifice, whatever you give in charity, and whatever austerities you practise, offer everything to Me."

MASTER: "If you give God something, you receive it back a thousand times over. That is why after doing meritorious deeds one offers a handful of water to God. It is the symbol of offering the fruit to God. When Yudhisthira was about to offer all his sins to Krishna, Bhima warned him: 'Never do such a thing. Whatever you offer to Krishna you will receive back a thousandfold.'

(*To one of the sādhus*) "Well, sir, one should be desireless; one should renounce all desires. Isn't that so?"

SĀDHU: "Yes, sir."

MASTER: "But I have the desire for bhakti. That is not bad. Rather, it is good. Sweets are bad, for they produce acidity. But sugar candy is an exception. Isn't that so?"

SĀDHU: "Yes, sir."

MASTER: "Well, sir, what do you think of the Vedānta?"

SĀDHU: "It includes all the six systems of philosophy."

MASTER: "But the essence of Vedānta is: 'Brahman alone is real, and the world illusory; I have no separate existence; I am that Brahman alone.' Isn't that so?"

SĀDHU: "That is true, sir."

MASTER: "But for those who lead a householder's life, and those who identify themselves with the body, this attitude of 'I am He' is not good. It is not good for householders to read Vedānta or the *Yogavāśishtha*. It is very harmful for them to read these books. Householders should look on God as their Master and on themselves as His servants. They should think, 'O God, You are the Master and the Lord, and I am Your servant.' People who identify themselves with the body should not have the attitude of 'I am He'."

The devotees in the room remained silent. Sri Ramakrishna was smiling a little, a picture of self-contentment. He appeared happy in his own Self.

One of the sādhus whispered in the other's ear: "Look! This is the state of the paramàhamsa."

MASTER (*to M.*): "I feel like laughing."

Sri Ramakrishna smiled like a child. The monks left the room. The devotees were moving about in the room and on the porch.

MASTER (*to M.*): "Did you go to Nabin Sen's house?"

M: "Yes, sir. I listened to the songs from downstairs."

MASTER: "That was well done. Your wife was there. She is a cousin of Keshab Sen, isn't she?"

M: "A distant cousin."

Sri Ramakrishna strolled up and down with M. No one else was with them.

MASTER: "A man visits his father-in-law's house. I, too, often used to think that I should marry, go to my father-in-law's house, and have great fun. But see what has come of it!"

M: "Sir, you say, 'If the boy holds his father's hand, he may slip; but he doesn't if the father holds his hand.' That is exactly your condition. The Mother has taken hold of your hand."

MASTER: "I met Bamandas at the Viswases' house. I said to him, 'I have come to see you.' As I was leaving the place I heard him say: 'Goodness gracious! The Divine Mother has caught hold of him, like a tiger seizing a man.' At that time I was a young man, very stout, and always in ecstasy.

"I am very much afraid of women. When I look at one I feel as if a tigress were coming to devour me. Besides, I find that their bodies, their limbs, and even their pores are very large. This makes me look upon them as she-monsters. I used to be much more afraid of women than I am at present. I wouldn't allow one to come near me. Now I persuade my mind in various ways to look upon women as forms of the Blissful Mother.

"A woman is, no doubt, a part of the Divine Mother. But as far as a man is concerned, especially a sannyāsi or a devotee of God, she is to be shunned. I don't allow a woman to sit near me very long, no matter how great her devotion may be. After a little while I say to her, 'Go and see the temples.'

If that doesn't make her move, I myself leave the room on the pretext of smoking.

"I find that some men are not at all interested in women. Niranjan says, 'A woman never enters my thought.' I asked Hari[4] about it. He too says that his mind does not dwell on woman.

"Woman monopolizes three quarters of the mind, which should be given to God. And then, after the birth of a child, almost the whole mind is frittered away on the family. Then what is left to give to God?

"Again, there are some men who shed their last drop of blood, as it were, to keep their wives out of mischief. There is the gate-keeper, an old man, whose wife is only fourteen years old. She had to live with him. They lived in a thatched hut with walls made of dry leaves. People made holes in the wall to peep in. Now she has left him and run away.

"I know another man. He doesn't know where to keep his wife. There was some trouble at home, and now he is greatly worried. Let's not talk about these things any more.

"If a man lives with a woman, he cannot help coming under her control. Worldly men get up and sit down at the bidding of women. They all speak highly of their wives.

"Once I wanted to go to a certain place. I asked Ramlal's aunt[5] about it. She forbade me to go; so I could not. A little while later I said to myself: 'I am not a householder. I have renounced "woman and gold". If, in spite of that, this is my plight, one can well imagine how much worldly people are controlled by their wives.'"

M: "One who lives in the midst of 'woman and gold' can't help being stained by it, even if only slightly. You told us about Jaynarayan. He was such a great scholar. When you visited him he was an old man. You found him warming pillows and blankets in the sun."

MASTER: "But he had no vanity of scholarship. Further, what he said about the last days of his life came to pass. He spent them in Benares, following the injunctions of the scriptures. I saw his children. They were wearing high boots and had been educated in English schools."

By means of questions and answers Sri Ramakrishna now explained to M. his own exalted state.

MASTER: "At first I went stark mad. Why am I less so now? But I get into that state now and then."

M: "You don't have just one mood. As you said, you experience various moods. Sometimes you are like a child, sometimes like a madman, sometimes like an inert thing, and sometimes like a ghoul. And now and then you are a natural person."

MASTER: "Yes, like a child. But I also experience the moods of a boy and a young man. When I give instruction I feel like a young man. Then there is my boyishness: like a boy twelve or thirteen years old, I want to be frivolous. That is why I joke and make merry with the youngsters.

"What do you think of Naran?"

[4] Later Swami Turiyananda.
[5] His own wife.

M: "He has good traits, sir."

MASTER: "Yes, the shell of the gourd is good. The tānpurā made out of it will give good music. He says to me, 'You are everything.' Everyone speaks of me according to his comprehension. Some say that I am simply a sādhu, a devotee of God.

"If I forbid Naran to do something, he understands it very well. The other day I asked him to pull up the curtain, but he didn't do it. I had forbidden him to tie a knot, to sew his clothes, to lock a box, to pull up a curtain, and similar things. He understood it all. He who would renounce the world must practise all these disciplines. They are meant for sannyāsis.

"While practising sādhanā a man should regard a woman as a raging forest fire or a black cobra. But in the state of perfection, after the realization of God, she appears as the Blissful Mother. Then you will look on her as a form of the Divine Mother."

A few days earlier Sri Ramakrishna had spoken many words of warning to Narayan about women. He had said: "Don't let yourself touch the air near a woman's body. Cover yourself with a heavy sheet lest the air should touch your body. And keep yourself eight cubits, two cubits, or at least one cubit away from all women except your mother."

MASTER (to M.): "Naran's mother said to him about me, 'Even we are enchanted by the sight of him, not to speak of you, a mere child.' None but the guileless can realize God. How guileless Niranjan is!"

M: "True, sir."

MASTER: "Didn't you notice him that day in the carriage on the way to Calcutta? He is always the same—without guile. A man shows one side of his nature inside his house and another to the outside world. Since his father's death Narendra has been worried about his worldly affairs. He has a slightly calculating mind. How I wish that other youngsters were like Niranjan and Narendra!

"Today I went to the village to see Nilkantha's theatrical performance. It was given at Nabin Niyogi's house. The children there are very bad; they have nothing to do but find fault. In such a place a person's spiritual feeling is restrained. During a performance the other day I saw Doctor Madhu shedding tears. I looked at him alone.

(To M.) "Can you tell me why people feel so much attracted to this place [meaning himself]? What does it mean?"

M: "It reminds me of an episode in Krishna's life at Vrindāvan. Krishna transformed Himself into the cowherd boys and the calves, whereupon the cows began to feel more strongly attracted to the cowherd boys, the gopis, and the calves."

MASTER: "That is the attraction of God. The truth is, the Divine Mother creates the spell and it is that which attracts people.

"Well, not as many people come here as used to go to Keshab Sen. And how many people respect and honour Keshab! He is known even in England. Queen Victoria spoke with him. It is said in the Gītā that God's power is manifest in him who is honoured and respected by many. But so many people do not come here."

M: "It was the householders who went to Keshab Sen."

MASTER: "Yes, that is true. The worldly-minded."

M: "Will what Keshab has founded remain a long time?"

MASTER: "Why, he has written a samhitā, a book of rules for the guidance of the members of his Brāhmo Samāj."

M: "But it is quite different with the work done by a Divine Incarnation Himself—Chaitanya's work, for instance."

MASTER: "Yes, yes. That is true."

M: "You yourself tell us that Chaitanyadeva said, 'The seeds I have sown will certainly bear fruit some time or other.' A man left some seeds on the cornice of a house. Later on the house fell down and trees grew from those seeds."

MASTER: "Many people go to the Samāj founded by Shivanath and his friends. Isn't that so?"

M: "Yes, sir. People of that sort."

MASTER (smiling): "Yes, yes. The worldly-minded go there, but not many of those who long for God and are trying to renounce 'woman and gold'."

M: "It will be fine if a current flows from this place. Everything will be carried away by its force. Nothing that comes out of this place will be monotonous."

MASTER (smiling): "I keep men's own ideals intact. I ask a Vaishnava to hold to his Vaishnava attitude and a Śākta to his. But this also I say to them: 'Never feel that your path alone is right and that the paths of others are wrong and full of errors.' Hindus, Mussalmāns, and Christians are going to the same destination by different paths. A man can realize God by following his own path if his prayer is sincere.

"Vijay's mother-in-law said to me, 'Why don't you tell Balaram that it is unnecessary to worship God with form; that it will be enough if he prays to the formless Satchidānanda?' I replied, 'Why should I say such a thing, and why should he listen to me even if I should say it?'"

M: "That is true, sir. There are different paths to suit time, place, and the fitness of the candidate. Whatever path a man may follow, he will ultimately reach God if he is pure of heart and has sincere longing. That is what you say."

Sri Ramakrishna was sitting in his room. Hari, the relative of the Mukherjis, M., and other devotees were on the floor. An unknown person saluted the Master and took a seat. The Master remarked later that his eyes were not good. They were yellow, like a cat's.

Hari prepared a smoke for Sri Ramakrishna.

MASTER (to Hari): "Let me see the palm of your hand. This mark is a good sign. Relax your hand."

He took Hari's hand into his as if to feel its weight.

MASTER: "He is still childlike. As yet there is no blemish in him. (To the devotees) From the hand I can tell whether a person is deceitful or guileless. (To Hari) Why, you should go to your father-in-law's house. You should talk to your wife and have a little fun with her if you like. (*To M.*) What do you say?" (*M. and the others laugh.*)

M: "If a new pot becomes bad, one can no longer keep milk in it."

MASTER (*smiling*): "How do you know that it is not already bad?"

The two Mukherjis, Mahendra and Priyanath, were brothers. They did not work in an office, but had their own flour-mill. Priyanath had been an engineer. Sri Ramakrishna talked to Hari about the Mukherji brothers.

MASTER: "The elder brother is nice, isn't he? He is artless."

HARI: "Yes, sir."

MASTER: "Isn't the younger brother very miserly? I understand that since coming here he has improved a great deal. He once said to me, 'I didn't know anything before.' (*To Hari*) Do they give anything in charity?"

HARI: "Not much, as far as I can see. Their elder brother, now dead, was a very good man. He was very charitable."

MASTER (*to M. and the others*): "Whether a person will make spiritual progress or not can be known to a great extent by his physical marks. The hand of a deceitful person is heavy. A snub nose is not a good sign. Sambhu had that kind of nose; hence he was not quite sincere in spite of all his wisdom. Pigeon-breast is not a good sign either. Hard bones and heavy elbow-joints are bad signs too; and yellow eyes, like a cat's.

"A man becomes very mean if he has lips that are thick, like a dome's.[6] A brāhmin was here for a few months acting as priest of the Vishnu temple. I couldn't eat the food he touched. One day I suddenly exclaimed, 'He is a dome!' Afterwards he said to me: 'Yes, sir. We live in the dome quarters. I know how to make wicker baskets and such things, just like a dome.'

"There are other bad physical signs: one eye and squint eyes. It is rather better to have one eye, but never squint eyes. Squint-eyed people are wicked and deceitful.

"A student of Mahesh Nyayaratna's came here. He described himself as an atheist. He said to Hriday: 'I am an atheist. You may take up the position of a believer in God and argue with me.' Thereupon I watched him closely and noticed that his eyes were yellow, like a cat's.

"Whether a person is good or bad can also be known from the way he walks."

Sri Ramakrishna paced the verandah. M. and Baburam walked with him.

MASTER (*to Hazra*): "A man came here. I saw that his eyes were like a cat's. He asked me: 'Do you know astrology? I am in some difficulty.' I said: 'No, I don't. Go to Barānagore. There you will find astrologers.'"

Baburam and M. talked about Nilkantha's theatrical performance. Baburam had spent the previous night at the temple garden after his return from Nabin Sen's house. In the morning he had attended Nilkantha's performance with the Master.

MASTER (*to M. and Baburam*): "What are you talking about?"

M. AND BABURAM: "About Nilkantha's performance."

While pacing the verandah Sri Ramakrishna suddenly took M. aside and said, "The less people know about your thoughts of God, the better for

[6] One of the lowest castes among the Hindus.

you." Saying these words the Master abruptly went away. A short time afterwards he began to talk with Hazra.

HAZRA: "Nilkantha told you he would pay you a visit. It would be good to send for him."

MASTER: "No, he didn't sleep at all last night. It will be different if he comes here through the will of God."

Sri Ramakrishna asked Baburam to visit Narayan at his house. He looked on Narayan as God Himself, and so he longed to see him. The Master said to Baburam, "You may go to him with one of your English text-books."

About three o'clock in the afternoon Sri Ramakrishna was sitting in his room. Nilkantha arrived with five or six of his companions. The Master went toward the east door as if to welcome him. The musicians bowed before the Master, touching the ground with their foreheads.

Sri Ramakrishna went into samādhi. Baburam stood behind him. M., Nilkantha, and the musicians were in front of him, watching him in great amazement. Dinanath, an officer of the temple, looked on from the north side of the bed. Soon the room was filled with officers of the temple garden. Sri Ramakrishna's ecstasy abated a little. He seated himself on a mat on the floor, surrounded by Nilkantha and other devotees.

MASTER (still in an ecstatic mood): "I am all right."

NILKANTHA (with folded hands): "Make me all right too."

MASTER (smiling): "Why, you are already all right. Adding the letter 'a' to 'ka', one gets 'kā'. By adding another 'ā' to 'kā', one still gets the same 'kā'." (All laugh.)

NILKANTHA: "Revered sir, I am entangled in worldliness."

MASTER (smiling): "God has kept you in the world for the sake of others. There are eight fetters. One cannot get rid of them all. God keeps one or two so that a man may live in the world and teach others. You have organized this theatrical company. How many people are being benefited by seeing your bhakti! If you give up everything, then where will these musicians go?

"God is now doing all these works through you. When they are finished, you will not return to them. The housewife finishes her household duties, feeds everyone, including the menservants and maidservants, and then goes to take her bath. She doesn't come back then even if people shout for her."

NILKANTHA: "Please bless me."

MASTER: "Yaśodā went mad with grief because she was separated from Krishna. She went to Rādhikā, who was meditating. Rādhikā said to her in an ecstatic state: 'I am the Ultimate Prakriti, the Primal Power. Ask a boon of Me.' Yaśodā said to her: 'What shall I ask of You? Please bless me, that with all my body, mind, and speech I may think of God and serve Him; that with my ears I may hear the singing of God's name and glories; that with my hands I may serve Hari and His devotees; that with my eyes I may behold His form and His devotees.'

"Your eyes fill with tears when you utter the name of God. Why then should you worry about anything? Divine love has grown in you.

"To know many things is ajnāna, ignorance. To know only one thing is jnāna, Knowledge—the realization that God alone is real and that He dwells in all. And to talk to Him is vijnāna, a fuller Knowledge. To love God in different ways, after realizing Him, is vijnāna.

"It is also said that God is beyond one and two. He is beyond speech and mind. To go up from the Līlā to the Nitya and come down again from the Nitya to the Līlā is mature bhakti.

"I love that song of yours about aspiring to reach the Lotus Feet of the Divine Mother. It is enough to know that everything depends on the grace of God. But one must pray to God; it will not do to remain inactive. The lawyer gives all the arguments and finishes his pleading by saying to the judge: 'I have said all I have to say. Now the decision rests with Your Honour.'"

After a few minutes Sri Ramakrishna said to Nilkantha: "You sang so much in the morning, and now you have taken the trouble to come here. But here everything is 'honorary'."

NILKANTHA: "Why so?"

MASTER (smiling): "I know what you will say."

NILKANTHA: "I shall get a precious gem from here."

MASTER: "You already have that precious gem. What will you gain by adding again the letter 'ā' to 'kā'? If you didn't have the gem, should I like your songs so much? Rāmprasād had attained divine realization; that is why his songs appeal so much.

"I had already planned to hear your music. Later on Niyogi, too, came here to invite me."

The Master was sitting on the small couch. He told Nilkantha that he would like to hear a song or two about the Divine Mother.

Nilkantha sang two songs with his companions. When the Master heard the second song he stood up and went into samādhi. Presently he began to dance in an ecstasy of divine love. Nilkantha and the devotees sang and danced around him. Then Nilkantha sang a song about Śiva, and the Master danced with the devotees.

When the singing was over, Sri Ramakrishna said to Nilkantha, "I should like to hear that song of yours I heard in Calcutta."

M: "About Sri Gaurānga?"

MASTER: "Yes, yes!"

Nilkantha sang the song, "The beautiful Gaurānga, the youthful dancer, fair as molten gold".

Sri Ramakrishna sang again and again the line, "Everything is swept away by the onrush of love", and danced with Nilkantha and the other devotees. Those who saw that indescribable dancing were never to forget it. The room was filled with people, all intoxicated with divine joy. It seemed as if Chaitanya himself were dancing with his companions.

Manomohan was in an ecstatic mood. He was a devotee of Sri Ramakrishna and a brother-in-law of Rakhal. Several ladies of his family had come with him. They were witnessing this divine music and dancing from the north verandah.

Sri Ramakrishna sang again, this time about Gaurānga and Nityānanda:

> Behold, the two brothers have come, who weep while chanting
> Hari's name. . . .

He danced with Nilkantha and the other devotees, improvising the line:

> Behold, the two brothers have come, they who are mad with love
> of Rādhā.

Hearing the loud music, many people gathered about the room. The verandahs to the south and north, and the semicircular porch to the west of the room, were crowded with people. Even passengers in the boats going along the Ganges were attracted by the kirtan.

The music was over. Sri Ramakrishna bowed to the Divine Mother and said, "Bhāgavata—Bhakta—Bhagavān. My salutations to the jnānis, my salutations to the yogis, my salutations to the bhaktas."

The Master was seated on the semicircular porch with Nilkantha and the other devotees. The autumn moon flooded all the quarters with light. Sri Ramakrishna and Nilkantha talked.

NILKANTHA: "You are none other than Gaurānga."

MASTER: "Why should you say such a thing? I am the servant of the servant of all. The waves belong to the Ganges; but does the Ganges belong to the waves?"

NILKANTHA: "You may say whatever you like, but we regard you as Gaurānga himself."

MASTER (tenderly, in an ecstatic mood): "My dear sir, I try to seek my 'I', but I do not find it. Hanumān said: 'O Rāma, sometimes I think that You are the whole and I am a part, and sometimes that You are the Master and I am Your servant. But when I have the Knowledge of Reality, I see that You are I and I am You.' "

NILKANTHA: "What shall I say, sir? Please be gracious to us."

MASTER (smiling): "You are ferrying many people across the ocean of the world. How many hearts are illumined by hearing your music!"

NILKANTHA: "You talk of ferrying. But bless me that I may not be drowned in the ocean myself."

MASTER (smiling): "If you get drowned, it will be in the Sea of Immortality."

Sri Ramakrishna was delighted with Nilkantha's company. He said to the musician: "For you to have come here! You whom people see as a result of many austerities and prayers! Listen to a song."

The Master sang a song, two lines of which ran:

> When the Blissful Mother comes to my house, how much of the
> Chandi I shall hear!
> How many monks will come here, and how many yogis with
> matted locks!

He said, continuing, "As long as the Divine Mother has come here, many yogis with matted locks will come too."

Sri Ramakrishna laughed. To M., Baburam, and the other devotees he said: "I feel very much like laughing. Just fancy, I am singing for these musicians!"

NILKANTHA: "We go about singing; but today we have had our true reward."

MASTER (*smiling*): "When a shopkeeper sells an article, he sometimes gives a little extra something to the buyer. You sang at Nabin's house and have given the extra something here."

All laughed.

ADVICE TO ISHAN

Saturday, October 11, 1884

SRI RAMAKRISHNA lay on the small couch in his room at the Dakshineswar temple garden. It was about two in the afternoon. M. and Priya Mukherji were sitting on the floor. M. had left his school at one o'clock and had just arrived at Dakshineswar. The Master was telling anecdotes about the calculating nature of the wealthy Jadu Mallick.

MASTER: "Once I went to Jadu Mallick's house. He asked right away, 'How much is the carriage hire?' Someone told him it was three rupees and two ānnās. Then he questioned me about it. Next one of his people secretly asked the coachman, who said it was three rupees and four ānnās. (*All laugh.*) At that he ran to us and said, 'How much did you say the carriage hire was?'

"A broker was present. He said to Jadu: 'There is a plot of land at Burrabāzār for sale. Will you buy it?' Jadu asked the price and the broker told him. Jadu said, 'Won't he give it for less?' I said to Jadu: 'Come, come. You aren't going to buy the land. You're only bargaining. Isn't that so?' He turned to me and laughed.

"That is the nature of the worldly man. He wants people to come to him. That spreads his name in the market.

"Jadu went to Adhar's house. I told him it had made Adhar very happy. He said: 'What? What? Was he really happy?' A certain Mallick came to Jadu's house. He was very clever and deceitful. I saw it in his eyes. I looked at him and said: 'It isn't good to be clever. The crow is very clever, but it eats others' filth.' I could tell he was badly off. Jadu's mother was amazed and said to me, 'How did you know he hadn't a penny?' I saw it from his appearance."

Narayan entered the room and sat on the floor.

MASTER (*to Priyanath*): "Well, your Hari is a fine young man."

PRIYANATH: "What is so fine about him? Of course, he has a childlike nature."

NARAYAN: "He addressed his wife as mother."

MASTER: "What! Even I can't do that. And he calls her mother! (*To Priyanath*) You see, the boy is very quiet. His mind is directed to God."

Sri Ramakrishna changed the subject of conversation.

MASTER: "Do you know what Hem said? He said to Baburam, 'God alone is real; all else is illusory.' (*All laugh.*) Oh, no! He said it sincerely. Again, he told me he would take me to his house and sing kirtan. But he didn't do it. I understand that he said later on, 'What will people say if I sing with drums and cymbals?' He was afraid that people might think he was crazy.

"Haripada has fallen into the clutches of a woman of the Ghoshpāra sect. He can't get rid of her. He says that she takes him on her lap and feeds him. She claims that she looks on him as the Baby Krishna. I have warned him a great many times. She says that she thinks of him as a child. But this maternal affection soon degenerates into something dangerous.

"You see, you should keep far away from woman; then you may realize God. It is extremely harmful to have much to do with women who have bad motives, or to eat food from their hands. They rob a man of his spirituality. Only by being extremely careful about woman can one preserve one's love of God. One day Bhavanath, Rakhal, and some other youngsters had cooked their own meal in the temple garden. They were sitting at their meal when a Bāul arrived, sat down with them, and said he wanted to eat with them. I said that there was not enough food; if anything was left it would be kept for him. He became angry and left. On the Vijayā day a man allows anyone and everyone to feed him with his own hand. It is not good. But one can eat food from the hand of a devotee who is pure in heart.

"You must be extremely careful about women. Women speak of the attitude of Gopāla! Pay no attention to such things. The proverb says: 'A woman devours the three worlds.' Many women, when they see handsome and healthy young men, lay snares for them. That is what they call the 'attitude of Gopāla'.

"Those who develop dispassion from early youth, those who roam about yearning for God from boyhood, those who refuse all worldly life, belong to a different class. They belong to an unsullied aristocracy. If they develop true renunciation, they keep themselves at least fifty cubits away from women lest their spiritual mood should be destroyed. Once falling into the clutches of women, they no longer remain on the level of unsullied aristocracy. They fall from it and come to a lower level. People who practise renunciation from early youth belong to a very high level. Their ideal is very pure. They are stainless.

"How can a man conquer passion? He should assume the attitude of a woman. I spent many days as the handmaid of God. I dressed myself in women's clothes, put on ornaments, and covered the upper part of my body with a scarf, just like a woman. With the scarf on I used to perform the evening worship before the image. Otherwise, how could I have kept my wife with me for eight months? Both of us behaved as if we were the handmaids of the Divine Mother. I cannot speak of myself as a man. One day I was in an ecstatic mood. My wife asked me, 'How do you regard me?' 'As the Blissful Mother', I said.

"Do you know the significance of the Śiva emblem? It is the worship of the symbols of fatherhood and motherhood. The devotee worshipping the image prays, 'O Lord, please grant that I may not be born into this world again; that I may not have to pass again through a mother's womb.'"

A tutor of the Tagores entered the room with some boys of the family. Sri Ramakrishna continued talking.

MASTER (to the devotees): "Sri Krishna has a peacock feather on His crest. The feather bears the sign of the female sex. The significance of this is that Krishna carries Prakriti, the female principle, on His head. When Krishna joined the circle of the gopis to dance with them, He appeared there as a woman. That is why you see Him wearing women's apparel in the company of the gopis. Unless a man assumes the nature of a woman, he is not entitled to her company. Assuming the attitude of a woman, he can sport with her and enjoy her company. But a man must be extremely careful during the early stages of spiritual discipline. Then he must live far away from any woman. He must not go too close to one even if she is a great devotee of God. You see, a man must not sway his body while climbing to the roof; he may fall. Weak people should hold on to a support while going up the stairs.

"But it is quite different when one reaches perfection. After the realization of God there is not much for a man to fear; he has become to a great extent secure. The important thing is for a man somehow to climb to the roof. After that he can even dance there. But he cannot dance on the steps. Again, after climbing to the roof, you need no longer discard what you discarded before. You find that the stairs are made of the same materials— bricks, lime, and brick-dust—as the roof. The woman you have to be so careful about at the beginning will appear to you, after the realization of God, as the Divine Mother Herself. Then you will worship her as the Divine Mother. You won't fear her so much.

"The thing is to touch the 'granny', as children do in the game of hide-and-seek. Then you can do whatever you like.

"Man, looking outward, sees the gross; at that time his mind dwells in the annamayakosha, the gross body. Next is the subtle body. Functioning through the subtle body, the mind dwells in the manomayakosha and the vijnānamayakosha. Next is the causal body. Functioning through the causal body the mind enjoys bliss; it dwells in the ānandamayakosha. This corresponds to the semi-conscious state experienced by Chaitanya. Last of all, the mind loses itself in the Great Cause. It disappears. It merges in the Great Cause. What one experiences after that cannot be described in words. In his inmost state of consciousness, Chaitanya enjoyed this experience. Do you know what this state is like? Dayananda described it by saying, 'Come into the inner apartments and shut the door.' Anyone and everyone cannot enter that part of the house.

"I used to meditate on the flame of a light. I thought of the red part as gross, the white part inside the red as subtle, and the stick-like black part, which is the innermost of all, as the causal.

"By certain signs you can tell when meditation is being rightly practised. One of them is that a bird will sit on your head, thinking you are an inert thing.

"I first met Keshab at a meeting of the Ādi Samāj. Several members of the Samāj were sitting on the platform. Keshab was in the middle. I saw him motionless as a log. Pointing to Keshab, I said to Mathur Babu: 'Look there! That bait has been swallowed by a fish.' Because of that power of meditation he achieved what he wanted—name, fame, and so forth—, through the grace of God.

"One can meditate even with eyes open. One can meditate even while talking. Take the case of a man with toothache—"

TUTOR OF THE TAGORES: "Yes, sir. I know that very well." (All laugh.)

MASTER (smiling): "Yes, even when his teeth ache he does all his duties, but his mind is on the pain. Likewise one can meditate with eyes open and while talking to others as well."

TUTOR: "One of the epithets of God is the 'Redeemer of the sinner'. That is our hope. God is compassionate."

MASTER: "The Śikhs, too, said that God was compassionate. I asked, 'How is He compassionate?' 'Why,' they answered, 'He has begotten us; He has created so many things for us; He has brought us up to be men; and He protects us from danger at every step.' Thereupon I said: 'After begetting us, God looks after us and feeds us. Is there much credit in that? Suppose a son is born to you. Do you expect a man from another part of the city to bring him up?'"

TUTOR: "Revered sir, one man quickly succeeds in spiritual life, and another doesn't succeed at all. How do you explain that?"

MASTER: "The truth is that a man succeeds to a great extent because of tendencies inherited from his previous births. People think he has attained the goal all of a sudden. A man drank a glass of wine in the morning. It made him completely drunk. He began to behave improperly. People were amazed to see that he could be so drunk after one glass. But another man said, 'Why, he has been drinking all night.'

"Hanumān burnt down the golden city of Lankā. People were amazed that a mere monkey could burn the whole city. But then they said, 'The truth is that the city was burnt by the sighs of Sītā and the wrath of Rāma.'

"Look at Lālā Babu.[1] He had so much wealth. Could he have renounced it all so suddenly without the good tendencies of his previous births? And Rāni Bhavani. So much knowledge and devotion in a woman!

"In his last birth a man is endowed with sattva. His mind is directed to God. He longs for God. He withdraws his mind from worldly things.

"Krishnadas Pal came here. I found him full of rajas. But it must be said that he observed the Hindu customs. He left his shoes outside before entering the room. After a little conversation I discovered that he had no stuff inside. I asked him about man's duty. He said, 'To do good to the world.' I said: 'My dear sir, who are you? What good will you do to the world? Is the world such a small thing that you think you can help it?'"

Narayan arrived. Sri Ramakrishna was very happy to see him. He seated

[1] A well-known landholder of Bengal who renounced the world at an early age and lived at Mathurā as a Vaishnava monk.

Narayan by his side on the small couch. He showed him his love by stroking his body and giving him sweets to eat. Then he asked Narayan tenderly, "Will you have some water?" Narayan was a student at M.'s school. At home his people beat him for visiting Sri Ramakrishna. The Master said to Narayan with an affectionate smile, "You had better get a leather jacket; then the beating won't hurt." Turning to Harish, the Master said that he would like to have a smoke.

Again addressing Narayan, Sri Ramakrishna said: "That woman who has established an artificial relationship of mother and son with Haripada came here the other day. I have warned Haripada very often. She belongs to the Ghoshpārā sect. I asked her if she had found her 'man'. She said yes, and mentioned a man's name.

(To M.) "Ah! Nilkantha came here the other day. What spiritual fervour he has! He said he would come here another day and sing for us. They are dancing over there. Why don't you go and see it? (To Ramlal) There is no oil in the room. (Looking at the oil-jar) The servant hasn't filled it."

Sri Ramakrishna was walking up and down, now in his room, now on the south verandah. Occasionally pausing on the semicircular porch west of his room, he would look at the Ganges.

After a little while he returned to his room and sat on the small couch. It was past three in the afternoon. The devotees took their seats on the floor. The Master sat in silence before them, now and then casting a glance at the walls, where many pictures were hanging. To Sri Ramakrishna's left was a picture of Sarasvati, and beyond it, a picture of Gaur and Nitāi singing kirtan with their devotees. In front of the Master hung pictures of Dhruva, Prahlāda, and Mother Kāli. On the wall to his right was another picture of the Divine Mother, Rājarājeśvari. Behind him was a picture of Jesus Christ raising the drowning Peter. Suddenly Sri Ramakrishna turned to M. and said: "You see, it is good to keep pictures of sannyāsis and holy men in one's room. When you get up in the morning you should see the faces of holy persons rather than the faces of other men. People with rājasic qualities keep 'English' pictures on their walls—pictures of rich men, the King, the Queen, the Prince of Wales, and white men and women walking together. That shows their rājasic temperament.

"You acquire the nature of the people whose company you keep. Therefore even pictures may prove harmful. Again, a man seeks the company that agrees with his own nature. The paramahamsas keep near them a few young boys five or six years old. They allow such boys to be near them. Attaining the state of a paramahamsa, a man loves the company of boys. Like the paramahamsas, the boys are not under the control of the gunas—sattva, rajas, or tamas.

"By looking at trees a man awakens in his heart the picture of a hermitage in which a rishi is practising austerity."

A brāhmin from Sinthi entered the room and saluted Sri Ramakrishna. He had studied Vedānta in Benares. He was stout and had a smiling face.

MASTER: "Hello! How are you? You haven't been here in a long time."

PUNDIT (*smiling*): "Worldly duties, sir. You know I have very little leisure."

The pundit sat down, and the Master began to talk with him.

MASTER: "You spent a long time in Benares. Tell us what you saw there. Tell us something about Dayananda."

PUNDIT: "Yes, I met him. You also met him, didn't you?"

MASTER: "Yes, I visited him. He was living then in a garden house on the other side of the Ganges. Keshab was expected there that day. He longed for Keshab as the chātak bird longs for rain. He was a great scholar and made fun of the Bengali language. He admitted the existence of the deities, but Keshab did not. Dayananda used to say: 'God has created so many things. Couldn't He have created the deities?' Dayananda believed the Ultimate Reality to be without form. Captain was repeating the name of Rāma. Dayananda said to him sarcastically, 'Better repeat "sandesh"!' "

PUNDIT: "In Benares the pundits had great discussions with Dayananda. Finally he was left alone with all the others against him. They made it so hot for him that he thought the only way to save himself was by running away. All the pundits shouted with one voice, 'Whatever Dayananda has said is to be despised!'

"I saw Colonel Olcott too. The Theosophists believe in the existence of mahātmās. They also speak of the 'lunar', 'solar', 'stellar', and other planes. A Theosophist can go in his 'astral body' to all these planes. Oh, Olcott said many such things. Well, sir, what do you think of Theosophy?"

MASTER: "The one essential thing is bhakti, loving devotion to God. Do the Theosophists seek bhakti? They are good if they do. If Theosophy makes the realization of God the goal of life, then it is good. One cannot seek God if one constantly busies oneself with the mahātmās and the lunar, solar, and stellar planes. A man should practise sādhana and pray to God with a longing heart for love of His Lotus Feet. He should direct his mind to God alone, withdrawing it from the various objects of the world."

The Master sang:

> How are you trying, O my mind, to know the nature of God?
> You are groping like a madman locked in a dark room.
> He is grasped through ecstatic love; how can you fathom Him
>   without it? . . .
>
> And, for that love, the mighty yogis practise yoga from age to age;
> When love awakes, the Lord, like a magnet, draws to Him the
>   soul.

Continuing, the Master said: "You may speak of the scriptures, of philosophy, of Vedānta; but you will not find God in any of these. You will never succeed in realizing God unless your soul becomes restless for Him.

> Only through affirmation, never negation, can you know Him,
> Neither through Veda nor through Tantra nor the six darśanas.
> It is in love's elixir only that He delights, O mind;
> He dwells in the body's inmost depths, in Everlasting Joy.

"One must be very earnest about God. Listen to another song:

> Can everyone have the vision of Rādhā? Can everyone taste her love?
> This, the rarest treasure of all, no earthly wealth can buy;
> Without devotions and sādhanā none can ever obtain it.
>
> The raindrop falling upon the deep when Svāti shines on high
> Is formed within the oyster's shell into a priceless pearl.
> Can such a pearl be formed from rain that falls at other times?
>
> Mothers with their babes in arms may beckon to the moon
> To leave the sky and come to them; but only the babes are fooled.
> Does the moon ever leave the sky and dwell upon the earth?

"One must practise intense spiritual discipline. Can one obtain the vision of God all of a sudden, without any preparation?

"A man asked me, 'Why don't I see God?' I said to him, as the idea came to my mind: 'You want to catch a big fish. First make arrangements for it. Throw spiced bait into the water. Get a line and a rod. At the smell of the bait the fish will come from the deep water. By the movement of the water you will know that a big fish has come.'

"You want to eat butter. But what will you achieve by simply repeating that there is butter in milk? You have to work hard for it. Only thus can you separate butter from milk. Can one see God by merely repeating, 'God exists'? One needs sādhanā.

"The Divine Mother Herself practised austere sādhanā to set an example for mankind. Sri Krishna, who is none other than the Ultimate Brahman, also practised sādhanā to set an example to others.

"Sri Krishna is the Purusha and Rādhā the Prakriti, the Chitśakti, the Ādyāśakti. Rādhā is the Prakriti, the embodiment of the three gunas. Sattva, rajas, and tamas are in her. As you remove the layers of an onion, you will first see tints of both black and red, then only red, and last of all only white. The Vaishnava scriptures speak of 'Kām-Rādhā', 'Prem-Rādhā', and 'Nitya-Rādhā'. Chandrāvali is Kām-Rādhā, and Srimati is Prem-Rādhā; Nanda saw Nitya-Rādhā holding Gopāla in Her arms.[2]

"The Brahman of Vedānta and the Chitśakti are identical, like water and its wetness. The moment you think of water you must also think of its wetness, and the moment you think of water's wetness you must also think of water. Or it is like the snake and its wriggling motion. The moment you think of the snake you must also think of its wriggling motion, and the moment you think of the snake's wriggling motion you must also think of the snake. When do I call the Ultimate Reality by the name of Brahman? When It is actionless or unattached to action. When a man puts on a cloth he remains the same man as when he was naked. He was naked; now he is clothed. He may be naked again. There is poison in the snake, but it doesn't

---

[2] Kām-Rādhā, full of seductive power, is the first aspect of Rādhā; Prem-Rādhā, full of ecstatic love, is her second aspect; Nitya-Rādhā is her third aspect, as the eternal Primordial Power. Chandrāvali, one of the gopis, had a lustful attitude toward Sri Krishna. Srimati is another name of Rādhikā, the foremost of the gopis. Nanda was Sri Krishna's foster-father.

harm the snake. It is poison to him who is bitten by the snake. Brahman Itself is unattached.

"Names and forms are nothing but the manifestations of the power of Prakriti. Sītā said to Hanumān: 'My child, in one form I am Sītā, in another form I am Rāma. In one form I am Indra, in another I am Indrāni. In one form I am Brahmā, in another, Brahmāni. In one form I am Rudra, in another, Rudrāni.'[3] Whatever names and forms you see are nothing but the manifestations of the power of Chitśakti. Everything is the power of Chitśakti—even meditation and he who meditates. As long as I feel that I am meditating, I am within the jurisdiction of Prakriti. (To M.) Try to assimilate what I have said. One should hear what the Vedas and the Purānas say, and carry it out in life.

(To the pundit) "It is good to live in the company of holy men now and then. The disease of worldliness has become chronic in man. It is mitigated, to a great extent, in holy company.

"'I' and 'mine'—that is ignorance. True knowledge makes one feel: 'O God, You alone do everything. You alone are my own. And to You alone belong houses, buildings, family, relatives, friends, the whole world. All is Yours.' But ignorance makes one feel: 'I am doing everything. I am the doer. House, buildings, family, children, friends, and property are all mine.'

"Once a teacher was explaining all this to a disciple. He said, 'God alone, and no one else, is your own.' The disciple said: 'But, revered sir, my mother, my wife, and my other relatives take very good care of me. They see nothing but darkness when I am not present. How much they love me!' The teacher said: 'There you are mistaken. I shall show you presently that nobody is your own. Take these few pills with you. When you go home, swallow them and lie down in bed. People will think you are dead, but you will remain conscious of the outside world and will see and hear everything. Then I shall visit your home.

"The disciple followed the instructions. He swallowed the pills and lay as if unconscious in his bed. His mother, wife, and other relatives began to cry. Just then the teacher came in, in the guise of a physician, and asked the cause of their grief. When they had told him everything, he said to them: 'Here is a medicine for him. It will bring him back to life. But I must tell you one thing. This medicine must first be taken by one of his relatives and then given to him. But the relative who takes it first will die. I see his mother, his wife, and others here. Certainly one of you will volunteer to take the medicine. Then the young man will come back to life.'

"The disciple heard all this. First the physician called his mother, who was weeping and rolling on the ground in grief. He said to her: 'Mother, you don't need to weep any more. Take this medicine and your son will come to life. But you will die.' The mother took the medicine in her hand and began to think. After much reflection she said to the physician, with tears in her eyes: 'My child, I have a few more children. I have to think about them too. I am wondering what will happen to them if I die. Who

_____
[3] Indrāni, Brahmāni, and Rudrāni are the Consorts, or Powers, of Indra, Brahmā, and Rudra.

will feed them and look after them?' The physician next called the wife and handed the medicine to her. She had been weeping bitterly too. With the medicine in her hand she also began to reflect. She had heard that she would die from the effect of the medicine. At last, with tears in her eyes, she said: 'He has met his fate. If I die, what will happen to my young children? Who will keep them alive? How can I take the medicine?' In the mean time the disciple had got over the effect of the pills. He was now convinced that nobody was really his own. He jumped out of bed and left the place with his teacher. The guru said to him, 'There is only one whom you may call your own, and that is God.'

"Therefore a man should act in such a way that he may have bhakti for the Lotus Feet of God and love God as his very own. You see this world around you. It exists for you only for a couple of days. There is nothing to it."

PUNDIT (smiling): "Revered sir, I feel a spirit of total renunciation when I am here. I feel like going away, giving up the world."

MASTER: "No, no! Why should you give up? Give up mentally. Live unattached in the world.

"Surendra wanted to spend the night here occasionally. He brought a bed and even spent a day or two here. Then his wife said to him, 'You may go anywhere you like during the day-time, but at night you must not leave home.' What could poor Surendra do? Now he has no way of spending the night away from home.

"What will you achieve by mere reasoning? Be restless for God and learn to love Him. Reason, mere intellectual knowledge, is like a man who can go only as far as the outer court of the house. But bhakti is like a woman who goes into the inner court.

"One must take up a definite attitude toward God. Then alone can one realize Him. Rishis like Sanaka cherished the attitude of śānta; Hanumān the attitude of a servant; the cowherd boys of Vrindāvan, like Śridāma and Sudāma, the attitude of a friend; Yaśodā the attitude of a mother; and Rādhā the attitude of a sweetheart.

" 'O God, Thou art the Lord and I am Thy servant'—that is the servant's attitude, a very good one for aspirants."

PUNDIT: "Yes, sir."

The pundit from Sinthi left. It was dusk. Twilight hung over the Panchavati, the temples, and the river. Evening worship began in the different temples, accompanied by the sound of bells, gongs, and conch-shells. Sri Ramakrishna bowed before the pictures of the deities in his room. He was sitting on the small couch in an abstracted mood. A few devotees were on the floor. There was silence in the room.

An hour passed. Ishan and Kishori entered and sat down on the floor after saluting Sri Ramakrishna. Ishan was a great ritualist. He was devoted to the performance of the various rites and ceremonies prescribed by the scriptures. The Master opened the conversation.

MASTER: "Can one attain knowledge of God by merely repeating the word 'God'? There are two indications of such knowledge. First, longing, that is to say, love for God. You may indulge in reasoning or discussion, but if you feel no longing or love, it is all futile. Second, the awakening of the Kundalini. As long as the Kundalini remains asleep, you have not attained knowledge of God. You may be spending hours poring over books or discussing philosophy, but if you have no inner restlessness for God, you have no knowledge of Him.

"When the Kundalini is awakened, one attains bhāva, bhakti, prema, and so on. This is the path of devotion.

"The path of karma[4] is very difficult. Through it one obtains some powers —I mean occult powers."

ISHAN: "Let me go and see Hazra."

Sri Ramakrishna sat in silence. After a while Ishan returned to the room accompanied by Hazra. The Master was still silent. A few moments later Hazra whispered to Ishan: "Let's leave him alone. Perhaps he will meditate now." Both left the room.

Sri Ramakrishna was still silent. In a few moments the devotees noticed that he was really meditating. Then he performed japa. He placed his right hand on his head, then on his forehead, then on his throat, then on his heart, and last of all on his navel. Was it meditation on the Primordial Energy in the six centres of the body?

Ishan and Hazra had gone to the Kāli temple. Sri Ramakrishna was absorbed in meditation. Meanwhile Adhar had arrived. It was about half past seven.

A little later the Master went to the Kāli temple. He looked at the image, took some sacred flowers from the feet of the Mother, and placed them on his head. He prostrated himself before the Mother and went round the image. He waved the chāmara. He appeared ecstatic with divine fervour. Coming out, he found Ishan performing the sandhyā with the kośākuśi.

MASTER (to Ishan): "What? You are still here? Are you still performing the sandhyā? Listen to a song:

Why should I go to Gangā or Gayā, to Kāśi, Kānchi, or Prabhās,
So long as I can breathe my last with Kāli's name upon my lips?
What need of rituals has a man, what need of devotions any more,
If he repeats the Mother's name at the three holy hours?
Rituals may pursue him close, but never can they overtake him.
Charity, vows, and giving of gifts do not appeal to Madan's mind;
The Blissful Mother's Lotus Feet are his whole prayer and sacrifice. . . .

"How long must a man continue the sandhyā? As long as he has not developed love for the Lotus Feet of God, as long as he does not shed tears and his hair does not stand on end when he repeats God's name.

I bow my head, says Prasād, before desire and liberation;
Knowing the secret that Kāli is one with the highest Brahman,
I have discarded, once for all, both dharma and adharma.

[4] Here signifying religious rites and rituals.

"When the fruit grows, the flower drops off. When one has developed love of God and has beheld Him, then one gives up the sandhyā and other rites. When the young daughter-in-law is with child, the mother-in-law reduces her activities. When she has been pregnant for nine months, she is not allowed to perform any household duty. After the birth of the child, she only carries the child on her arm and nurses it. She has no other duty. After the attainment of God, the sandhyā and other rites are given up.

"You cannot achieve anything by moving at such a slow pace. You need stern renunciation. Can you achieve anything by counting fifteen months as a year? You seem to have no strength, no grit. You are as mushy as flattened rice soaked in milk. Be up and doing! Gird your loins!

"I don't like that song:

> Brother, joyfully cling to God;
> Thus striving, some day you may attain Him.

I don't care for the line, 'Thus striving, some day you may attain Him.' You need stern renunciation. I say the same thing to Hazra.

"You ask me why you don't feel stern renunciation. There is a reason for it. You have desires and tendencies within you. The same is true of Hazra. In our part of the country I have seen peasants bringing water into their paddy-fields. The fields have low ridges on all sides to prevent the water from leaking out; but these are made of mud and often have holes here and there. The peasants work themselves to death to bring the water, which, however, leaks out through the holes. Desires are the holes. You practise japa and austerities, no doubt, but they all leak out through the holes of your desires.

"They catch fish with a bamboo trap. The bamboo is naturally straight. But why is it bent in the trap? In order to catch the fish. Desires are the fish. Therefore the mind is bent down toward the world. If there are no desires, the mind naturally looks up toward God.

"Do you know what it is like? It is like the needles of a balance. On account of the weight of 'woman and gold' the two needles are not in line. It is 'woman and gold' that makes a man stray from the path of yoga. Haven't you noticed the flame of a candle? The slightest wind makes it waver. The state of yoga is like the candle-flame in a windless place.

"The mind is dispersed. Part of it has gone to Dacca, part to Delhi, and another part to Coochbehar. That mind is to be gathered in; it must be concentrated on one object. If you want sixteen ānnās' worth of cloth, then you have to pay the merchant the full sixteen ānnās. Yoga is not possible if there is the slightest obstacle. If there is a tiny break in the telegraph-wire, then the news cannot be transmitted.

"You are no doubt in the world. What if you are? You must surrender the fruit of your action to God. You must not seek any result for yourself. But mark one thing. The desire for bhakti cannot be called a desire. You may desire bhakti and pray for it. Practise the tamas of bhakti and force your demand upon the Divine Mother.

This bitterly contested suit between the Mother and Her son—
What sport it is! says Rāmprasād. I shall not cease tormenting
  Thee
Till Thou Thyself shalt yield the fight and take me in Thine arms
  at last.

"Trailokya once remarked, 'As I was born into the family, I have a share in the estate.'

"God is your own Mother. Is She a stepmother? Is it an artificial relationship? If you cannot force your demand on Her, then on whom can you force it? Say to Her:

Mother, am I Thine eight-months child?[5] Thy red eyes cannot
  frighten me!
A deed of gift I hold in my heart, attested by Thy Husband Śiva;
I shall sue Thee, if I must, and with a single point shall win.

"God is your own Mother. Enforce your demand. If you are part of a thing, you feel its attraction. Because of the element of the Divine Mother in me I feel attracted to Her. A true Śaiva has some of the characteristics of Śiva; he has in him some of the elements of Śiva. He who is a true Vaishnava is endowed with some of the elements of Nārāyana.

"Nowadays you don't have to attend to worldly duties. Spend a few days thinking of God. You have seen that there is nothing to the world."

The Master sang:

Remember this, O mind! Nobody is your own:
Vain is your wandering in this world.
Trapped in the subtle snare of māyā as you are,
Do not forget the Mother's name.

Only a day or two men honour you on earth
As lord and master; all too soon
That form, so honoured now, must needs be cast away,
When Death, the Master, seizes you.

Even your beloved wife, for whom, while yet you live,
You fret yourself almost to death,
Will not go with you then; she too will say farewell,
And shun your corpse as an evil thing.

Continuing, the Master said: "What are these things you busy yourself with—this arbitration and leadership? I hear that you settle people's quarrels and that they make you the arbiter. You have been doing this kind of work a long time. Let those who care for such things do them. Now devote your mind more and more to the Lotus Feet of God. The saying goes: 'Rāvana died in Lankā and Behulā[6] wept bitterly for him!'

"Sambhu, too, said, 'I shall build hospitals and dispensaries.' He was a devotee of God; so I said to him, 'Will you ask God for hospitals and dispensaries when you see Him?'

[5] A premature child is generally weak and fearful.

[6] Rāvana and Behulā were two persons totally unrelated to each other, having lived far apart in time and place.

"Keshab Sen asked me, 'Why do I not see God?' I said, 'You do not see God because you busy yourself with such things as name and fame and scholarship.' The mother does not come to the child as long as it sucks its toy—a red toy. But when, after a few minutes, it throws the toy away and cries, then the mother takes down the rice-pot from the hearth and comes running to the child.

"You are engaged in arbitration. The Divine Mother says to Herself: 'My child over there is now busy arbitrating and is very happy. Let him be.'"

In the mean time Ishan had been holding Sri Ramakrishna's feet. He said humbly, "It is not my will that I should do those things."

MASTER: "I know it. This is the Divine Mother's play—Her līlā. It is the will of the Great Enchantress that many should remain entangled in the world. Do you know what it is like?

> How many are the boats, O mind,
> That float on the ocean of this world!
> How many are those that sink!

Again,

> Out of a hundred thousand kites, at best but one or two break free;
> And Thou dost laugh and clap Thy hands, O Mother, watching them!

Only one or two in a hundred thousand get liberation. The rest are entangled through the will of the Divine Mother.

"Haven't you seen the game of hide-and-seek? It is the 'granny's' will that the game should continue. If all touch her and are released, then the playing comes to a stop. Therefore it is not her will that all should touch her.

"You see, in big grain stores the merchants keep rice in great heaps that touch the ceiling. Beside them there are heaps of lentils. To protect the grain from the mice, the merchants leave trays of puffed rice and sweetened rice near it. The mice like the smell and the sweet taste of these and so stay around the trays. They don't find the big heaps of grain. Similarly, men are deluded by 'woman and gold'; they do not know where God is.

"Rama said to Nārada, 'Ask a boon of Me.' Nārada said: 'O Rāma, is there anything I lack? What shall I ask of Thee? But if Thou must give me a boon, grant that I may have selfless love for Thy Lotus Feet and that I may not be deluded by Thy world-bewitching māyā.' Rāma said, 'Nārada, ask something else.' Nārada again replied: 'O Rāma, I don't want anything else. Be gracious to me and see that I have pure love for Thy Lotus Feet.'

"I prayed to the Divine Mother: 'O Mother, I don't want name and fame. I don't want the eight occult powers. I don't want a hundred occult powers. O Mother, I have no desire for creature comforts. Please, Mother, grant me the boon that I may have pure love for Thy Lotus Feet.'

"It is written in the Adhyātma Rāmāyana that Lakshmana asked Rāma: 'Rāma, in how many forms and moods do You exist? How shall I be able to recognize You?' Rāma said: 'Brother, remember this. You may be certain that I exist wherever you find the manifestation of ecstatic love.' That love makes one laugh and weep and dance and sing. If anyone has developed such love, you may know for certain that God Himself is manifest there. Chaitanyadeva reached that state."

The devotees listened spellbound to Sri Ramakrishna. His burning words entered their souls, spurring them along the path of renunciation.

Now he spoke to Ishan in a serious voice.

MASTER: "Don't forget yourself because of what you hear from your flatterers. Flatterers gather around a worldly man. Vultures gather around the carcass of a cow.

"Worldly people have no stuff in them. They are like a heap of cow-dung. Flatterers come to them and say: 'You are so charitable and wise! You are so pious!' These are not mere words but pointed bamboos thrust at them. How foolish it is! To be surrounded day and night by a bunch of worldly brāhmin pundits and hear their flattery!

"Worldly men are slaves of three things: they are slaves of their wives, slaves of their money, slaves of their masters. Can they have any inner stuff? There is a certain person whom I shall not name; he earns eight hundred rupees a month but is the slave of his wife. He stands up or sits down at her bidding.

"Arbitration and leadership? How trifling these are! Charity and doing good to others? You have had enough of these. Those who are to devote themselves to such things belong to a different class. Now the time is ripe for you to devote your mind to the Lotus Feet of God. If you realize God, you will get everything else. First God, then charity, doing good to others, doing good to the world, and redeeming people. Why need you worry about these things. 'Rāvana died in Lankā and Behulā wept for him bitterly!'

"That's the trouble with you. It will be very good if a world-renouncing sannyāsi gives you some spiritual instruction. The advice of the worldly man will not be right, be he a brāhmin pundit or anyone else.

"Be mad! Be mad with love of God! Let people know that Ishan has gone mad and cannot perform worldly duties any more. Then people will no longer come to you for leadership and arbitration. Throw aside the kośākuśi and justify your name of Ishan."[7]

Ishan quoted:

> O Mother, make me mad with Thy love!
> What need have I of knowledge or reason?

MASTER: "Mad! That's the thing! Shivanath once said that one 'loses one's head' by thinking too much of God. 'What?' said I. 'Can anyone ever become unconscious by thinking of Consciousness? God is of the nature of Eternity, Purity, and Consciousness. Through His Consciousness one becomes conscious of everything; through His Intelligence the whole world appears intelligent.' Shivanath said that some Europeans had gone insane, that they had 'lost their heads', by thinking too much about God. In their case it may be true; for they think of worldly things. There is a line in a song: 'Divine fervour fills my body and robs me of consciousness.' The consciousness referred to here is the consciousness of the outer world."

[7] An epithet of the all-renouncing Śiva.

Ishan was seated touching Sri Ramakrishna's feet and listening to his words. Now and then he cast a glance at the basalt image of Kāli in the shrine. In the light of the lamp She appeared to be smiling. It was as if the living Deity, manifesting Herself through the image, was delighted to hear the Master's words, holy as the words of the Vedas.

ISHAN (*pointing to the image*): "Those words from your sacred lips have really come from there."

MASTER: "I am the machine and She is the Operator. I am the house and She is the Indweller. I am the chariot and She is the Charioteer. I move as She moves me; I speak as She speaks through me. In the Kaliyuga one does not hear the voice of God, it is said, except through the mouth of a child or a madman or some such person.

"A man cannot be a guru. Everything happens by the will of God. Heinous sins—the sins of many births—and accumulated ignorance all disappear in the twinkling of an eye, through the grace of God. When light enters a room that has been kept dark a thousand years, does it remove the thousand years' darkness little by little, or instantly? Of course, at the mere touch of light all the darkness disappears.

"What can a man do? He may speak many words, but after all is said and done everything rests with God. The lawyer says: 'I have said all that can be said. Now the verdict rests with the judge.'

"Brahman is actionless. When It is engaged in creation, preservation, and dissolution, It is called the Primal Power, Ādyāśakti. This Power must be propitiated. Don't you know that it is so written in the *Chandi*? The gods first sang a hymn to the Ādyāśakti in order to propitiate Her. Only then did Hari wake up from His yoga sleep."

ISHAN: "Yes, sir. Brahmā and the other gods sang this hymn at the time of the death of the demons Madhu and Kaitabha:

> Svāhā, Vashat, and Svadhā art Thou;[8] Thou the inner Self of the
> mantra;
> Thou the Nectar of Immortality, O Everlasting One!
> Eternal and unutterable art Thou, and yet Thou art manifest
> In the three mātrās[9] and the half mātrā.[10]
>
> O Goddess, Thou art Sāvitri;[11] Thou art the Ultimate Mother;
> All things have their support in Thee, by whom this universe was
> made.
> O Goddess, Thou sustainest all, and all by Thee is devoured!
>
> Thou it is that we call the Creator, when Thou createst the world,
> O Embodiment of creation!
> Thou it is that we call the Preserver, when Thou preservest it;
> Thou it is that we call the Destroyer, when Thou destroyest it."

[8] Svāhā, Vashat, and Svadhā are mystic syllables. The first two are uttered while oblations are being offered to the gods, and the third while they are being offered to the ancestors.

[9] The length of time for pronouncing a vowel sound. The "three mātrās" denote the three durations—short, long, or protracted—required for pronouncing vowels.

[10] A consonant sound.

[11] The presiding deity of Om, the essence of the Vedas.

MASTER: "Yes, but you must assimilate that."

The Master rose. He mounted the platform in front of the shrine and saluted the Mother, touching the ground with his forehead. The devotees quickly gathered around him and fell at his feet. They all begged his grace. He descended from the platform and started toward his room, conversing with M. First he sang:

> I bow my head, says Prasād, before desire and liberation;
> Knowing the secret that Kāli is one with the highest Brahman,
> I have discarded, once for all, both dharma and adharma.

The Master continued: "Do you know the meaning of dharma and adharma? Here dharma means religious acts enjoined by the scriptures, such as charity, śrāddha, feeding the poor, and the like.

"The performance of this dharma is called the path of karma. It is an extremely difficult path: it is very hard to act without motive. Therefore one is asked to pursue the path of devotion.

"A man was performing the śrāddha ceremony at his house. He was feeding many people. Just then a butcher passed, leading a cow to slaughter. He could not control the animal and became exhausted. He said to himself: 'Let me go into that house and enjoy the feast of the śrāddha ceremony and strengthen my body. Then I shall be able to drag the cow along.' So he carried out his intention. But when he killed the cow, the sin of the slaughter fell also on the performer of the śrāddha. That is why I say the path of devotion is better than the path of action."

The Master entered his room accompanied by M. He was humming a song. The forceful words of renunciation that he had just spoken to Ishan found expression through its words. He sang the lines:

> Mother, take everything else away from me,
> But leave me my necklace of bones and my pot of hemp![12]

Sri Ramakrishna sat down on the small couch, and Adhar, Kishori, and the other devotees sat on the floor.

MASTER (*to the devotees*): "I was noticing Ishan. Why, he hasn't achieved anything! What can be the reason? He practised the puraścharana for five months. That would have caused a revolution in any other person."

ADHAR: "It wasn't wise of you to say those things to him in front of us."

MASTER: "How is that? He is so much given to japa! How can words affect him?"

After a while Sri Ramakrishna said to Adhar, "Ishan is very charitable, and he practises japa and austerity a great deal." The Master remained quiet a few moments. The eyes of the devotees were fixed on him. Suddenly Sri Ramakrishna said to Adhar, "You have both—yoga and bhoga."

Saturday, October 18, 1884

It was the day of the worship of Kāli, the Divine Mother. The worship was to begin at eleven o'clock at night. Several devotees arrived at the temple

[12] Siddhi, or hemp, and the necklace of bones are associated with Śiva, the model of renunciation.

garden early in the evening. They wanted to visit Sri Ramakrishna during the holy hours of the night of the new moon.

M. came alone to the garden about eight o'clock in the evening. The great religious festival had already begun. Lamps had been lighted here and there in the garden, and the temples were brightly illuminated. Music could be heard in the nahabat. The temple officers were moving about hurriedly. There was to be a theatrical performance in the early hours of the morning. The villagers had heard of the festive occasion, and a large crowd of men and women, young and old, was streaming in.

In the afternoon there had been a musical recital of the *Chandi* by Rajnarayan. Sri Ramakrishna had been present with the devotees and had enjoyed the recital immensely. As the time for the worship approached, he was overwhelmed with ecstasy.

M. found Sri Ramakrishna seated on the small couch in his room. Baburam, the younger Gopal, Haripada, Kishori, a relative of Niranjan, a young man from Āriādaha, and other devotees were seated on the floor facing him. Ramlal and Hazra were in the room part of the time. Niranjan's young relative was meditating in front of Sri Ramakrishna, as the Master had bidden.

M. saluted the Master and took a seat. After a while Niranjan's relative bowed low before Sri Ramakrishna and was about to depart. The young man from Āriādaha also wished to leave. The Master said to Niranjan's relative, "When will you come again?"

DEVOTEE: "Perhaps next Monday."

MASTER (*eagerly*): "Do you want a lantern to take with you?"

DEVOTEE: "No, sir, I live next to this garden. I don't need a lantern."

MASTER (*to the young man from Āriādaha*): "Are you going too?"

YOUNG MAN: "Yes, sir, I have a slight cold."

MASTER: "All right. Cover your head."

They again saluted the Master and took their leave.

It was the awe-inspiring night of the new moon. The worship of the Divine Mother added to its solemnity. Sri Ramakrishna was seated on the couch, leaning against a pillow. His mind was indrawn. Now and then he exchanged a word or two with the devotees. Suddenly he looked at M. and the other devotees and said: "Ah, how deep the young man's meditation was! (*To Haripada*) Wasn't it deep?"

HARIPADA: "Yes, sir, he was motionless as a log."

MASTER (*to Kishori*): "Do you know that boy? He is a cousin of Niranjan."

Again there was silence in the room. Haripada was gently stroking the Master's feet. The Master was humming some of the songs he had heard that evening during the recital of the *Chandi*. He sang softly:

> Who is there that can understand what Mother Kāli is?
> Even the six darśanas are powerless to reveal Her. . . .

Sri Ramakrishna sat up. With intense fervour he began to sing about the Divine Mother:

All creation is the sport of my mad Mother Kāli;
By Her māyā the three worlds are bewitched.
Mad is She and mad is Her Husband; mad are Her two disciples!
None can describe Her loveliness, Her glories, gestures, moods;
Śiva, with the agony of the poison in His throat,
Chants Her name again and again.

The Personal does She oppose to the Impersonal,
Breaking one stone with another;
Though to all else She is agreeable,
Where duties are concerned She will not yield.
Keep your raft, says Rāmprasād, afloat on the sea of life,
Drifting up with the flood-tide, drifting down with the ebb.

The Master was quite overwhelmed with the song. He said that songs like
these denoted a state of divine inebriation. He sang one after another:

This time I shall devour Thee utterly, Mother Kāli!
For I was born under an evil star,
And one so born becomes, they say, the eater of his mother. . . .

Then:

O Kāli, my Mother full of Bliss! Enchantress of the almighty Śiva!
In Thy delirious joy Thou dancest, clapping Thy hands
together! . . .

And then:

If at the last my life-breath leaves me as I repeat the name of Kāli,
I shall attain the realm of Śiva. What does Benares mean to me?
Infinite are my Mother's glories; who can find the end of Her
virtues?
Śiva, beholding their smallest part, lies prostrate at Her Lotus
Feet.

The singing was over. Two sons of Rajnarayan entered the room and
bowed low before the Master. In the afternoon they had sung with their
father the glories of the Divine Mother. The Master sang again with them:

All creation is the sport of my mad Mother Kāli . . .

The younger brother requested Sri Ramakrishna to sing a certain song
about Sri Gaurānga. The Master sang:

Gaur and Nitāi, ye blessed brothers!
I have heard how kind you are,
And therefore I have come to you. . . .

Ramlal entered the room. The Master said to him: "Please sing something
about the Divine Mother. It is the day of Her worship."
Ramlal sang:

Who is the Woman yonder who lights the field of battle?
Darker Her body gleams even than the darkest storm-cloud,
And from Her teeth there flash the lightning's blinding flames!

Dishevelled Her hair is flying behind as She rushes about,
Undaunted in this war between the gods and the demons.
Laughing Her terrible laugh, She slays the fleeing asuras,
And with Her dazzling flashes She bares the horror of war. . . .

Again Ramlal sang:

Who is this terrible Woman, dark as the sky at midnight?
Who is this Woman dancing over the field of battle? . . .

Sri Ramakrishna began to dance to the song. Then he himself sang:

The black bee of my mind is drawn in sheer delight
To the blue lotus flower of Mother Śyāmā's feet,
The blue flower of the feet of Kāli, Siva's Consort.
Tasteless, to the bee, are the blossoms of desire.
My Mother's feet are black, and black, too, is the bee;
Black is made one with black! This much of the mystery
These mortal eyes behold, then hastily retreat.
But Kamalākānta's hopes are answered in the end;
He swims in the Sea of Bliss, unmoved by joy or pain.

After the music and dancing Sri Ramakrishna sat on the couch and the
devotees sat on the floor. He said to M.: "It is a pity you weren't here in
the afternoon. The musical recital of the *Chandi* was very fine."

Some of the devotees went to the temple to salute the image of the Divine
Mother. Others sat quietly performing japa on the steps leading to the
Ganges. It was about eleven o'clock, the most auspicious time for contemplation of the Divine Mother. The flood-tide was rising in the Ganges, and the
lights on its banks were reflected here and there in its dark waters.

From outside the shrine M. was looking wistfully at the image. Ramlal
came to the temple with a book in his hand containing the rules of the
worship. He asked M. if he wanted to come in. M. felt highly favoured and
entered the shrine. He saw that the Divine Mother was profusely decorated.
The room was brilliantly illuminated by a large chandelier that hung from
the ceiling. Two candles were burning in front of the image. On the floor
were trays full of offerings. Red hibiscus flowers and bel-leaves adorned Her
feet. She wore garlands round Her neck M.'s eyes fell on the chāmara.
Suddenly he remembered that Sri Ramakrishna often fanned the Divine
Mother with it. With some hesitation he asked Ramlal if he might fan the
image. The priest gave his permission. M. joyously fanned the image. The
regular worship had not yet begun.

The devotees again entered the Master's room. Beni Pal had invited Sri
Ramakrishna to visit the Sinthi Brāhmo Samāj the next day, but had made
a mistake in his letter with regard to the date.

MASTER (*to M.*): "Beni Pal has sent me an invitation. But why has he put
the wrong date?"

M: "The date was not written correctly. He wrote the letter carelessly."

As Sri Ramakrishna spoke, he was standing in the middle of the room
with Baburam by his side. He leaned toward the disciple, touching his body.

Suddenly he went into samādhi. The devotees stood around with their eyes fixed on him. The Master's left foot was advanced a little; the shoulder was slightly inclined to one side; his arm rested on Baburam's neck near the ear. After a while he came down from the ecstatic state. As he stood there he put one hand to his cheek and appeared to be brooding over something. Then, smiling, he addressed the devotees.

MASTER: "I saw everything—how far the devotees had advanced. I saw Rakhal, him (*pointing to M.*), Surendra, Baburam, and many others."

HAZRA: "Me?"

MASTER: "Yes."

HAZRA: "Many more obstacles?"

MASTER: "No."

HAZRA: "What about Narendra?"

MASTER: "I didn't see him. But I can tell about him. He is a little entangled. But I saw that everyone will succeed. (*To M.*) I saw that all are in hiding."

The devotees listened to these words with great wonder. It seemed to them that they were hearing an oracle.

MASTER: "But I got into that mood by touching Baburam."

HAZRA: "Who is first?"

Sri Ramakrishna was quiet for a time. Then he said, "I wish I had a few like Nityagopal." Again he appeared thoughtful. He remained standing. He said: "I wish Adhar Sen's duties would become fewer. But I am afraid the English officer will scold him. He may say, 'What is all this nonsense?'" (*All smile.*)

Sri Ramakrishna sat on the small couch, and the devotees on the floor. Baburam and Kishori came quickly to the Master and began to stroke his feet gently.

MASTER (*to Kishori*): "What's the matter? Why so much service today?"

Ramlal entered the room and saluted Sri Ramakrishna, touching the ground with his forehead. Then with great respect he touched the Master's feet. He was ready to worship the Divine Mother in the temple.

RAMLAL: "Please permit me to go to the shrine."

The Master twice uttered the words "Om Kāli" and said: "Perform the worship carefully. There is also a sheep to be slaughtered."

It was midnight. The worship began in the Kāli temple. The Master went to watch the ceremony. During the worship he stood near the image. Now the sheep was going to be slaughtered. The animal was consecrated before the Deity. People stood in lines watching the ceremony. While the sheep was being taken to the block Sri Ramakrishna returned to his room. He could not bear the sight.

Several devotees remained in the temple till two o'clock in the morning. Haripada came and asked them to take the prasād to the Master's room. After finishing their meal they lay down wherever they could for the remainder of the night.

It was morning. The dawn service in the temples was over and the theatrical performance was going on in the open hall in front of the shrine. M. was coming through the courtyard with Sri Ramakrishna. He wanted to take leave of the Master.

MASTER: "Why should you go now?"

M: "You are going to Sinthi in the afternoon. I too intend to be there. So I should like to go home for a few hours."

They came to the Kāli temple. At the foot of the steps M. saluted the Master.

MASTER: "You are going? All right. Please bring two pieces of cheap cloth for me. I shall use them while taking my bath."

VISIT TO THE SINTHI BRĀHMO SAMĀJ

ON THIS DAY Sri Ramakrishna again visited the Sinthi Brāhmo Samāj. It was the occasion of the autumn festival of the Samāj, which was being celebrated at Benimadhav Pal's garden house. The hall was decorated with flowers and greens, flags and festoons, of various colours. Outside, the blue autumn sky with its fleecy clouds was reflected in the water of the lake.

Sri Ramakrishna arrived at half past four in the afternoon. Entering the hall, he bowed down before the altar. The Brāhmo devotees, among whom could be noticed Vijay and Trailokya, sat around him. A sub-judge, who was a member of the Brāhmo Samāj, was with them.

Trailokya was entertaining the devotees with his melodious music.

MASTER (to Trailokya): "That song of yours, 'O Mother, make me mad with Thy love', I enjoy very much. Won't you sing it?"

Trailokya sang:

> O Mother, make me mad with Thy love!
> What need have I of knowledge or reason?
> Make me drunk with Thy love's Wine;
> O Thou who stealest Thy bhaktas' hearts,
> Drown me deep in the Sea of Thy love!
> Here in this world, this madhouse of Thine,
> Some laugh, some weep, some dance for joy:
> Jesus, Buddha, Moses, Gaurānga,
> All are drunk with the Wine of Thy love.
> O Mother, when shall I be blessed
> By joining their blissful company?

As he listened to the song, the Master's mind underwent a transformation, and presently he went into deep samādhi. Coming down a little to the plane of the sense world, he gave instruction to the devotees. His mind was still charged with the divine experience. His words were spoken as if in a state of intoxication. Gradually he became again fully conscious of the world.

MASTER: "O Mother! I don't want the bliss of divine inebriation. I shall eat siddhi.

(*To the devotees*) "By 'siddhi' I mean the attainment of the spiritual goal and not one of the eight occult powers. About the occult powers, Sri Krishna said to Arjuna, 'Friend, if you find anyone who has acquired even one of the eight powers, then know for certain he will not realize Me.' For powers surely beget pride, and God cannot be realized if there is the slightest trace of pride.

"According to a certain school of thought there are four classes of devotees: the pravartaka, the sādhaka, the siddha, and the siddha of the siddha. He who has just begun religious life is a pravartaka. Such a man puts his denominational marks on his body and forehead, wears a rosary around his neck, and scrupulously follows other outer conventions. The sādhaka has advanced farther. His desire for outer show has become less. He longs for the realization of God and prays to Him sincerely. He repeats the name of God and calls on Him with a guileless heart. Now, whom should we call the siddha? He who has the absolute conviction that God exists and is the sole Doer; he who has seen God. And who is the siddha of the siddha? He who has not merely seen God, but has intimately talked with Him as Father, Son, or Beloved.

"It is one thing to believe beyond a doubt that fire exists in wood, but it is quite another to get the fire from the wood, cook rice with its help, appease one's hunger, and so be satisfied. These are two entirely different things.

"No one can put a limit to spiritual experience. If you refer to one experience, there is another beyond that, and still another, and so on.

(*In an ecstatic mood, referring to the Brāhmos*) "They are Brahma-jnānis. They believe in the formless Deity. That is good.

(*To the Brāhmo devotees*) "Be firm in one ideal—either in God with form or in the formless God. Then alone will you realize God; otherwise not. With firm and unwavering belief the followers of God with form will realize Him, as will those who speak of Him as formless. You may eat a cake with icing either straight or sidewise; it will taste sweet either way. (*All laugh.*)

"But you must have firm conviction, you must pray to Him wholeheartedly. Do you know what the God of worldly people is like? It is like children's saying to one another while at play, 'I swear by God.' They have learnt the word from the quarrels of their aunts or grandmothers. Or it is like God to a dandy. The dandy, all spick and span, his lips red from chewing betel-leaf, walks in the garden, cane in hand, and, plucking a flower, exclaims to his friend, 'Ah! What a beautiful flower God has made!' But this feeling of a worldly person is momentary. It lasts as long as a drop of water on a red-hot frying-pan.

"You must be firm in one ideal. Dive deep. Otherwise you cannot get the gems at the bottom of the ocean. You cannot pick up the gems if you only float on the surface."

With these words the Master sang in the sweet voice that had bewitched the hearts of devotees like Keshab:

Dive deep, O mind, dive deep in the Ocean of God's Beauty;
If you descend to the uttermost depths,
There you will find the gem of Love. . . .

The devotees felt as if they were in paradise itself.

MASTER (*to the Brāhmos*): "Dive deep. Learn to love God. Plunge into divine love. You see, I have heard how you pray. Why do you Brāhmos dwell so much on the glories of God? Is there such great need of your saying over and over again, 'O God, You have created the sky, the great oceans, the lunar world, the solar world, and the stellar world'?

"Everybody is wonder-struck at the mere sight of a rich man's garden house. People become speechless at the sight of the trees, the flowers, the ponds, the drawing-room, the pictures. But alas, how few are they who seek the owner of all these! Only one or two inquire after him. He who seeks God with a longing heart can see Him, talk to Him as I am talking to you. Believe my words when I say that God can be seen. But ah! To whom am I saying these words? Who will believe me?

"Can one find God in the sacred books? By reading the scriptures one may feel at the most that God exists. But God does not reveal Himself to a man unless he himself dives deep. Only after such a plunge, after the revelation of God through His grace, is one's doubt destroyed. You may read scriptures by the thousands and recite thousands of texts; but unless you plunge into God with yearning of heart, you will not comprehend Him. By mere scholarship you may fool man, but not God.

"Scriptures and books—what can one achieve with these alone? Nothing can be realized without His grace. Strive with a longing heart for His grace. Through His grace you will see Him and He will talk to you."

SUB-JUDGE: "Sir, does God show more grace to one than to another? If so, He can be accused of the fault of partiality."

MASTER: "What are you saying? Do you mean to say that the moon and a glow-worm are the same, though both give light? Iswar Vidyāsāgar asked me the same question. He said, 'Is it a fact, sir, that God gives more power to one and less to another?' 'God', I said, 'exists in every being as the All-pervading Spirit. He is in the ant as well as in me. But there are different manifestations of His Power in different beings. If all are the same, then why have we come here to see you, attracted by your renown? Have you grown a pair of horns? Oh, no! It is not that. You have compassion; you have scholarship; there is a greater degree of these virtues in you than in others. That is the reason you are so well known.' Don't you see that there are men who, single-handed, can defeat a hundred persons? Again, one man takes to his heels in fear of another; you see such a person, too. If there are not different manifestations of power in different beings, then why did people respect Keshab Sen so much?

"It is said in the *Gītā* that if a man is respected and honoured by many, whether it be for his scholarship or his music or his oratory or anything else, then you may know for certain that he is endowed with a special divine power."

A BRĀHMO (*to the sub-judge*): "Why don't you accept what he says?"

MASTER (*sharply, to the Brāhmo*): "What sort of man are you? To accept words without conviction! Why, that is hypocrisy! I see you are only a counterfeit."

The Brāhmo was much embarrassed.

SUB-JUDGE: "Sir, must we renounce the world?"

MASTER: "No. Why should you? A man can realize God even in the world. But at the beginning he must spend a few days in solitude. He must practise spiritual discipline in a solitary place. He should take a room near his house, so that he may come home only for his meals. Keshab, Pratap, and others said to me, 'Sir, we follow the ideal of King Janaka.' 'Mere words don't make a King Janaka', I replied. 'How many austerities King Janaka first had to perform in solitude—standing on his head,[1] and so on! Do something first; then you may become a King Janaka.' You see a man writing English fluently; but could he do that at the very start? Perhaps he was the son of poor parents; he was cook in a family and earned his meals by his service. Perhaps he had to struggle hard to go on with his studies. It is after all these efforts that he can now write such fluent English.

"I said to Keshab Sen further, 'How can the worldly man be cured of his serious disease unless he goes into solitude?' A worldly man is suffering from delirious fever, as it were. Suppose there are pickled tamarind and jars of water in the room of such a patient. Now, how can you expect him to get rid of the disease? Just see, the very mention of pickled tamarind is making my mouth water! (*All laugh.*) You can very well imagine what will happen if the tamarind is actually put in front of me. To a man, a woman is the pickled tamarind, and his desire for enjoyment, the jars of water. There is neither end nor limit to this desire for worldly enjoyment. And the things are in the patient's very room. Can you expect the patient to get rid of the delirious fever in this fashion? He must be removed for a few days to another place where there are neither pickled tamarind nor water-jars. Then he will be cured. After that if he returns to his old room he will have nothing to fear. 'Woman and gold' cannot do any harm to the man who lives in the world after attaining God. Only then can he lead a detached life in the world as King Janaka did. But he must be careful at the beginning. He must practise spiritual discipline in strict solitude. The peepal-tree, when young, is fenced around to protect it from cattle. But there is no need for the fence when the trunk grows thick and strong. Then no harm will be done to the tree even if an elephant is tied to it. 'Woman and gold' will not be able to harm you in the least, if you go home and lead a householder's life after increasing your spiritual strength and developing love for the Lotus Feet of God through the practice of spiritual discipline in solitude.

"A man sets milk in a quiet place to curdle, and then he extracts butter from the curd. After once extracting the butter of Devotion and Knowledge from the milk of the mind, if you keep that transformed mind in the water of the world, it will float in the world unattached. But if the mind in its 'unripe' state—that is to say, when it is just like liquid milk—is kept in the

[1] One of the exercises sometimes practised by hathayogis; also an expression to describe the austerities of yoga in general.

water of the world, then the milk and water will get mixed. In that case it will be impossible for the mind to float unattached in the world.

"Live in the world but, in order to realize God, hold fast to His Lotus Feet with one hand and with the other do your duties. When you get a respite from your duties, cling to God's Lotus Feet with both hands—live in solitude and meditate on Him and serve Him ceaselessly."

SUB-JUDGE (*joyously*): "Sir, these are very beautiful words indeed. Of course one must practise spiritual discipline in solitude. But we forget all about it. We think we have become King Janaka outright! (*The Master and the devotees laugh.*) I feel very happy and peaceful even to hear that there is no need to give up the world and that God can be realized from home as well."

MASTER: "Why should you give up the world? Since you must fight, it is wise for you to fight from a fort. You must fight against your sense-organs, against your hunger and thirst. Therefore you will be wise to face the battle from the world. Further, in the Kaliyuga the life of a man depends on his food. If one day you have nothing to eat, then you will forget all about God. A man once said to his wife, 'I am going to leave the world.' She was a sensible woman. She said: 'Why should you wander about? If you don't have to knock at ten doors for your stomach's sake, go. But if that is the case, then better live in this one place.'

"Again I say, why should you give up the world? You will find it more convenient at home. You won't have to worry about food. You may even live with your wife. It isn't harmful. You will find near at hand all that the body needs at different times. When you are ill, you will have someone near you to nurse you.

"Sages like Janaka, Vyāsa, and Vaśishtha lived in the world after attaining Knowledge. They fenced with two swords, the one of Knowledge and the other of action."

SUB-JUDGE: "How can we know that we have Knowledge?"

MASTER: "When one has Knowledge one does not see God any more at a distance. One does not think of Him any more as 'He'. He becomes 'This'. Then He is seen in one's own heart. God dwells in every man. He who seeks God realizes Him."

SUB-JUDGE: "Sir, I am a sinner. How can I say that God dwells in me?"

MASTER: "That's the one trouble with you Brāhmos. With you it is always sin and sin! That's the Christian view, isn't it? Once a man gave me a Bible. A part of it was read to me, and it was full of that one thing—sin and sin! One must have such faith that one can say: 'I have uttered the name of God; I have repeated the name of Rāma or Hari. How can I be a sinner?' One must have faith in the glory of God's name."

SUB-JUDGE: "Sir, how can one have such faith?"

MASTER: "Have passionate love for God. One of your Brāhmo songs says:

> O Lord, is it ever possible to know Thee without love,
> However much one may perform worship and sacrifice?

Pray to God in secret and with yearning, that you may have that passionate attachment and devotion to Him. Shed tears for Him. A man sheds a jugful of tears because his wife is sick or because he is losing money or because he is worrying about getting a job. But tell me, who ever weeps for God?"

TRAILOKYA: "Sir, where is people's leisure? They must serve their English masters."

MASTER: "Well, then give God the power of attorney. If a man entrusts his affairs to a good person, will the latter do him any harm? With all the sincerity of your heart resign yourself to God and drive all your worries out of your mind. Do whatever duties He has assigned to you. The kitten does not have a calculating mind. It only cries, 'Mew, mew!' It lies in the kitchen contentedly if the mother cat leaves it there, and only calls the mother, crying, 'Mew, mew!' It has the same feeling of contentment when the mother cat puts it on the soft bed of the master of the house. It only cries for its mother."

SUB-JUDGE: "Sir, we are householders. How long should we perform our worldly duties?"

MASTER: "Surely you have duties to perform. You must bring up your children, support your wife, and provide for her in case of your death. If you don't, then I shall call you unkind. Sages like Śukadeva had compassion. He who has no compassion is no man."

SUB-JUDGE: "How long should one support one's children?"

MASTER: "As long as they have not reached their majority. When the chick becomes a full-grown bird and can look after itself, then the mother bird pecks it and doesn't allow it to come near her." (All laugh.)

SUB-JUDGE: "What is a householder's duty to his wife?"

MASTER: "You should give her spiritual advice and support her during your lifetime and provide for her livelihood after your death, if she is a chaste wife.

"But if you are intoxicated with the Knowledge of God, then you have no more duties to perform. Then God Himself will think about your morrow if you yourself cannot do so. God Himself will think about your family if you are intoxicated with Him. If a landlord dies leaving behind a minor son, then a guardian appointed by the court takes charge of the son. These are all points of law; you know them."

SUB-JUDGE: "Yes, sir."

VIJAY: "Ah! Priceless words! God Himself carries on His shoulders all the responsibilities of a person who thinks of Him with single-minded devotion and is mad with divine love. A minor gets his guardian without seeking him. Alas, when shall I have that state of mind? How lucky they are who feel that way!"

TRAILOKYA: "Is it ever possible, sir, to have true knowledge of God while living in the world? Can one realize God here?"

MASTER (with a smile): "Why do you worry? You are enjoying both treacle and refined sugar. (All laugh.) You are living in the world with your mind in God. Isn't that true? Why shouldn't a man realize God in the world? Certainly he can."

TRAILOKYA: "What are the signs of a householder's having attained Knowledge?"

MASTER: "His tears will flow, and the hair on his body will stand on end. No sooner does he hear the sweet name of God than the hair on his body stands on end from sheer delight, and tears roll down his cheeks.

"A man cannot get rid of body-consciousness as long as he is attached to worldly things and loves 'woman and gold'. As he becomes less and less attached to worldly things, he approaches nearer and nearer to the Knowledge of Self. He also becomes less and less conscious of his body. He attains Self-Knowledge when his worldly attachment totally disappears. Then he realizes that body and soul are two separate things. It is very difficult to separate with a knife the kernel of a coconut from the shell before the milk inside has dried up. When the milk dries up, the kernel rattles inside the shell. At that time it loosens itself from the shell. Then the fruit is called a dry coconut.

"The sign of a man's having realized God is that he has become like a dry coconut. He has become utterly free from the consciousness that he is the body. He does not feel happy or unhappy with the happiness or unhappiness of the body. He does not seek the comforts of the body. He roams about in the world as a jīvanmukta, one liberated in life. 'The devotee of Kāli is a jīvanmukta, full of Eternal Bliss.'

"When you find that the very mention of God's name brings tears to your eyes and makes your hair stand on end, then you will know that you have freed yourself from attachment to 'woman and gold' and attained God. If the matches are dry, you get a spark by striking only one of them. But if they are damp, you don't get a spark even if you strike fifty. You only waste matches. Similarly, if your mind is soaked in the pleasure of worldly things, in 'woman and gold', then God-Consciousness will not be kindled in you. You may try a thousand times, but all your efforts will be futile. But no sooner does attachment to worldly pleasure dry up than the spark of God flashes forth."

TRAILOKYA: "What is the way to dry up the craving for worldly pleasure?"

MASTER: "Pray to the Divine Mother with a longing heart. Her vision dries up all craving for the world and completely destroys all attachment to 'woman and gold'. It happens instantly if you think of Her as your own mother. She is by no means a godmother. She is your own mother. With a yearning heart persist in your demands on Her. The child holds to the skirt of its mother and begs a penny of her to buy a kite. Perhaps the mother is gossiping with her friends. At first she refuses to give the penny and says to the child: 'No, you can't have it. Your daddy has asked me not to give you money. When he comes home I'll ask him about it. You will get into trouble if you play with a kite now.' The child begins to cry and will not give up his demand. Then the mother says to her friends: 'Excuse me a moment. Let me pacify this child.' Immediately she unlocks the cash-box with a click and throws the child a penny.

"You too must force your demand on the Divine Mother. She will come to you without fail. I once said the same thing to some Śikhs when they visited the temple at Dakshineswar. We were conversing in front of the Kāli temple. They said, 'God is compassionate.' 'Why compassionate?' I asked. They said, 'Why, revered sir, He constantly looks after us, gives us righteousness and wealth, and provides us with our food.' 'Suppose', I said, 'a man has children. Who will look after them and provide them with food —their own father, or a man from another village?' "

SUB-JUDGE: "Is not God, then, compassionate, sir?"

MASTER: "Why should you think that? I just made a remark. What I mean to say is that God is our very own. We can exert force on Him. With one's own people one can even go so far as to say, 'You rascal! Won't you give it to me?'

(To the sub-judge) "Let me ask you one thing. Are vanity and egotism the result of knowledge or of ignorance? Egotism is of the nature of tamas; it is begotten by ignorance. On account of the barrier of ego one does not see God. 'All troubles come to an end when the ego dies.' It is futile to be egotistic. Neither body nor wealth will last. Once a drunkard was looking at the image of Durgā. At the sight of Her decorations, he said, 'Well, Mother! However You may fix Yourself up, after two or three days they will drag You out and throw You into the Ganges.'[2] (All laugh.)

"So I say to you all, you may be a judge or anybody else, but it is all for two days only. Therefore you should give up vanity and pride.

"The characteristics of sattva, rajas, and tamas are very different. Egotism, sleep, gluttony, lust, anger, and the like, are the traits of people with tamas. Men with rajas entangle themselves in many activities. Such a man has clothes all spick and span. His house is immaculately clean. A portrait of the Queen[3] hangs on a wall in his drawing-room. When he worships God he wears a silk cloth. He has a string of rudrāksha beads around his neck, and in between the beads he puts a few gold ones. When someone comes to visit the worship hall in his house, he himself acts as guide. After showing the hall, he says to the visitor: 'Please come this way, sir. There are other things too—the floor of white marble and the nātmandir with its exquisite carvings.' When he gives in charity he makes a show of it. But a man endowed with sattva is quiet and peaceful. So far as dress is concerned, anything will do. He earns only enough money to give his stomach the simplest of food; he never flatters men to get money. His house is out of repair. He never worries about his children's clothing. He does not hanker for name and fame. His worship, charity, and meditation are all done in secret; people do not know about them at all. He meditates inside his mosquito curtain. People think he doesn't sleep well at night and for that reason sleeps late in the morning. Sattva is the last step of the stairs; next is the roof. As soon as sattva is acquired there is no further delay in attaining God. One step forward and God is realized. (To the sub-judge) Didn't you say that all men were equal? Now you see that there are so many varieties of human nature.

"There are still other classes and kinds of people. For instance, there are

[2] An allusion to the immersion of the image after the worship.
[3] Queen Victoria.

those who are eternally free, those who have attained liberation, those struggling for liberation, and those entangled in the world. So many varieties of men! Sages like Nārada and Śukadeva are eternally free. They are like a steamship, which not only crosses the ocean but can carry big animals, even an elephant. Further, the soul that is eternally free is like the superintendent of an estate. After bringing one part of the estate under control, he goes to another. Those struggling for liberation strive heart and soul to free themselves from the net of the world. One or two of them may get out of the net. They are called the liberated. The souls that are eternally free are like clever fish; they are never caught in the net.

"But the souls that are entangled, involved in worldliness, never come to their senses. They lie in the net but are not even conscious that they are entangled. If you speak of God before them, they at once leave the place. They say: 'Why God now? We shall think of Him in the hour of death.' But when they lie on their death-beds, they say to their wives or children: 'Why have you put so many wicks in the lamp? Use only one wick. Otherwise too much oil will be burnt.' While dying they think of their wives and children, and weep, 'Alas! What will happen to them after my death?'

"The entangled souls repeat those very actions that make them suffer so much. They are like the camel, which eats thorny bushes till the blood streams from its mouth, but still will not give them up. Such a man may have lost his son and be stricken with grief, but still he will have children year after year. He may ruin himself by his daughter's marriage, but still he will go on having daughters every year. And he says: 'What can I do? It's just my luck!' When he goes to a holy place he doesn't have any time to think of God. He almost kills himself carrying bundles for his wife. Entering the temple, he is very eager to give his child the holy water to drink or make him roll on the floor; but he has no time for his own devotions. These bound creatures slave for their masters to earn food for themselves and their families; and they earn money by lying, cheating, flattery. They laugh at those who think of God and meditate on Him, and call them lunatics.

"So you see how many different kinds of men there are. You said that all men were equal. But how many varieties of men there are! Some have more power and some less.

"The entangled creatures, attached to worldliness, talk only of worldly things in the hour of death. What will it avail such men if they outwardly repeat the name of God, take a bath in the Ganges, or visit sacred places? If they cherish within themselves attachment to the world, it must show up at the hour of death. While dying they rave nonsense. Perhaps they cry out in a delirium, 'Turmeric powder! Seasoning! Bay-leaf!' The singing parrot, when at ease, repeats the holy names of Rādhā and Krishna, but when it is seized by a cat it utters its own natural sound; it squawks, 'Kaa! Kaa!' It is said in the *Gītā* that whatever one thinks in the hour of death, one becomes in the after-life. King Bharata gave up his body exclaiming, 'Deer! Deer!' and was born as a deer in his next life. But if a man dies thinking of God, then he attains God, and he does not have to come back to the life of this world."

A BRĀHMO DEVOTEE: "Sir, suppose a man has thought of God at other times during his life, but at the time of his death forgets Him. Would he, on that account, come back to this world of sorrow and suffering? Why should it be so? He certainly thought of God some time during his life."

MASTER: "A man thinks of God, no doubt, but he has no faith in Him. Again and again he forgets God and becomes attached to the world. It is like giving the elephant a bath; afterwards he covers his body with mud and dirt again. 'The mind is a mad elephant.' But if you can make the elephant go into the stable immediately after bathing him, then he stays clean. Just so, if a man thinks of God in the hour of death, then his mind becomes pure and it gets no more opportunity to become attached to 'woman and gold'.

"Man has no faith in God. That is the reason he suffers so much. They say that when you plunge into the holy waters of the Ganges your sins perch on a tree on the bank. No sooner do you come out of the water after the bath than the sins jump back on your shoulders. (All laugh.) A man must prepare the way beforehand, so that he may think of God in the hour of death. The way lies through constant practice. If a man practises meditation on God, he will remember God even on the last day of his life."

BRĀHMO DEVOTEE: "You have spoken very beautifully, sir. Beautiful words, indeed."

MASTER: "Oh, this is just idle talk. But do you know my inner feeling? I am the machine and God is the Operator. I am the house and He is the Indweller. I am the engine and He is the Engineer. I am the chariot and He is the Charioteer. I move as He moves me; I do as He makes me do."

Presently Trailokya began to sing to the accompaniment of drums and cymbals. Sri Ramakrishna danced, intoxicated with divine love. Many times he went into samādhi. He stood still, his eyes fixed, his face beaming, with one hand on the shoulder of a beloved disciple. Coming down a little from the state of ecstasy, he danced again like a mad elephant. Regaining consciousness of the outer world, he improvised lines to the music:

> O Mother, dance about Thy devotees!
> Dance Thyself and make them dance as well.
> O Mother, dance in the lotus of my heart;
> Dance, O Thou the ever blessed Brahman!
> Dance in all Thy world-bewitching beauty.

An indescribable scene. The exquisite and celestial dance of a child completely filled with ecstatic love of God and identified heart and soul with the Divine Mother! The Brāhmo devotees danced around the Master again and again, attracted like iron to a magnet. In ecstatic voices they chanted the name of Brahman. Again, they chanted the name of the Divine Mother. Many of them wept like children, crying, "Mother! Mother!"

When the music was over, the devotees and the Master sat down. Although it was about eight o'clock, the evening worship of the Brāhmo Samāj had not yet begun. In the joy of this divine music they had forgotten all about their formal worship. Vijay, who was to conduct the evening service, sat facing the Master. His mother-in-law and the other Brāhmo ladies wanted to see Sri Ramakrishna; so the Master went to meet them in another room.

After a time the Master came back and said to Vijay: "What devotion to God your mother-in-law has! About the worldly life she said to me: 'Oh, you needn't tell me about the world. No sooner does one wave disappear than another rises up.' 'But', I said, 'what is that to you? You have knowledge.' She replied: 'Where is my knowledge? I haven't yet been able to go beyond vidyāmāyā and avidyāmāyā. It won't help me much to go beyond just the illusion of ignorance; I shall have to transcend the illusion of knowledge as well. Only then shall I have true knowledge of God. I am quoting your own words.'"

While they were talking, Beni Pal, their host, entered the room.

BENI (to Vijay): "Sir, please get up. It is already late. Please begin the worship."

VIJAY: "What further need is there of worship? I find that according to your arrangement the rice pudding is served first, and then the soup and other dishes."

MASTER (with a smile): "The devotees provide offerings according to their temperaments. The sāttvic devotee offers the Deity simple rice pudding, and the rājasic devotee, fifty different dishes. The tāmasic devotee slaughters goats and other animals."

Vijay began to hesitate about going to the platform to conduct the worship. He said to the Master, "I shall conduct the worship from the platform only if you give me your blessing."

MASTER: "It will be all right if you don't feel any egotism, if you don't have the vain feeling: 'I am giving a lecture. Listen to me.' What begets egotism? Knowledge or ignorance? It is only the humble man who attains Knowledge. In a low place rain-water collects. It runs down from a mound.

"A man achieves neither Knowledge nor liberation as long as he has egotism. He comes back again and again to the world. The calf bellows, 'Hāmbā! Hāmbā!', that is, 'I! I!' That is why it suffers such agony. The butcher slaughters it and the shoe-maker makes shoes from its hide. Besides, its hide is used for the drum, which is beaten mercilessly. Still no end to its misery! At long last a carding-machine is made from its entrails. While carding the cotton the machine makes the sound 'Tuhu! Tuhu!', that is, 'Thou! Thou!' Then the poor calf is released from all suffering. It no longer says, 'Hāmbā! Hāmbā!' but repeats, 'Tuhu! Tuhu!' The calf says, as it were, 'O God, Thou art the Doer and I am nothing. Thou art the Operator and I am the machine. Thou art everything.'

"Three words—'master', 'teacher', and 'father'—prick me like thorns. I am the son of God, His eternal child. How can I be a 'father'? God alone is the Master and I am His instrument. He is the Operator and I am the machine.

"If somebody addresses me as guru, I say to him: 'Go away, you fool! How can I be a teacher?' There is no teacher except Satchidānanda. There is no refuge except Him. He alone is the Ferryman to take one across the ocean of the world. (To Vijay) It is very difficult to act as an āchārya. It harms the āchārya himself. Finding a number of men doing him reverence, he sits erect, crossing his legs, and says proudly: 'I am preaching. Hear ye all!' This is a very bad attitude. He gets a little prestige and it ends there. People will say at most: 'Ah! Vijay Babu has spoken very well. He knows a great deal.' Never cherish the attitude, 'I am preaching.' I always say to the Divine Mother: 'O Mother! Thou art the Operator and I am the machine. I do as Thou makest me do, I speak as Thou makest me speak.' "

VIJAY (humbly): "Please give me your permission. Only then will I sit on the platform."

MASTER (with a smile): "What shall I say? Pray to God yourself. He belongs to all, even as 'Uncle Moon'[4] is the uncle of all children. You have nothing to fear if you are sincere."

On being further requested by Vijay, the Master said: "Yes, go. Follow the rules. Everything is all right if one has sincere love for God."

Vijay sat on the platform and conducted the worship according to the rules of the Brāhmo Samāj. At the time for prayer he repeatedly called on the Mother, touching the hearts of all. After the worship their host entertained the Master and the devotees with a sumptuous feast.

Soon they were ready to return home. Sri Ramakrishna became engaged in conversation with Vijay, no one else but M. being present.

MASTER: "You prayed to God, addressing Him as Mother. That is very good. People say that the mother's attachment to the child is stronger than the father's. A son can force his demand on his mother but not on his father. Once cartloads of money were coming from the estate of Trailokya's mother. They were guarded by many red-turbaned stalwarts armed with big sticks. Trailokya, who had been waiting on the road with his men, pounced upon the money and took it away by force. A son has a very strong claim on his mother's wealth. People say that a mother cannot very well sue her son in a court of law."

VIJAY: "If Brahman is our Mother, then has It any form or is It formless?"

MASTER: "That which is Brahman is also Kāli, the Mother, the Primal Energy. When inactive It is called Brahman. Again, when creating, preserving, and destroying, It is called Śakti. Still water is an illustration of Brahman. The same water, moving in waves, may be compared to Śakti, Kāli. What is the meaning of Kāli? She who communes with Mahā-Kāla, the Absolute, is Kāli. She is formless and, again, She has forms. If you believe in the formless aspect, then meditate on Kāli as that. If you meditate on any aspect of Her with firm conviction, She will let you know Her true nature. Then you will realize that not merely does God exist, but He will come near you and talk to you as I am talking to you. Have faith and you will achieve everything. Remember this, too. If you believe that God is formless, then stick to that belief with firm conviction. But don't be dogmatic: never say emphatically about God that He can be only this and not that. You may say: 'I believe that God is formless. But He can be many things more. He alone knows what else He can be. I do not know; I do not understand.' How can man with his one ounce of intelligence know the real nature of God? Can

[4] In the folk-lore of Bengal the moon is often pointed out to the children as their maternal uncle.

you put four seers of milk in a one-seer jar? If God, through His grace, ever reveals Himself to His devotee and makes him understand, then he will know; but not otherwise.

"That which is Brahman is Śakti, and That, again, is the Mother.

> He it is, says Rāmprasād, that I approach as Mother;
> But must I give away the secret, here in the market-place?
> From the hints I have given, O mind, guess what that Being is!

Rāmprasād implies that he has known the truth of Brahman. He addresses Brahman as Mother.

"In another song Rāmprasād expresses the same idea thus:

> Knowing the secret that Kāli is one with the highest Brahman,
> I have discarded, once for all, both dharma and adharma.

Adharma means unrighteous actions, actions forbidden by religion. Dharma means the pious actions prescribed by religion, as, for instance, charity to the poor, feeding the brāhmins, and so on."

VIJAY: "What remains if one renounces both dharma and adharma?"

MASTER: "Pure love of God. I prayed to the Divine Mother: 'O Mother, here, take Thy dharma; here, take Thy adharma; and give me pure love for Thee. Here, take Thy virtue; here, take Thy vice; and give me pure love for Thee. Here, take Thy knowledge; here, take Thy ignorance; and give me pure love for Thee.' You see, I didn't ask even for knowledge or public recognition. When one renounces both dharma and adharma, there remains only pure love of God—love that is stainless, motiveless, and that one feels only for the sake of love."

A BRĀHMO DEVOTEE: "Is God different from His Śakti?"

MASTER: "After attaining Perfect Knowledge one realizes that they are not different. They are the same, like the gem and its brilliance. Thinking of the gem, one cannot but think of its brilliance. Again, they are like milk and its whiteness. Thinking of the one, you must also think of the other. But you cannot realize this non-duality before the attainment of Perfect Knowledge. Attaining Perfect Knowledge, one goes into samādhi, beyond the twenty-four cosmic principles. Therefore the principle of 'I' does not exist in that stage. A man cannot describe in words what he feels in samādhi. Coming down, he can give just a hint about it. I come down a hundred cubits, as it were, when I say 'Om' after samādhi. Brahman is beyond the injunctions of the Vedas and cannot be described. There neither 'I' nor 'you' exists.

"As long as a man is conscious of 'I' and 'you', and as long as he feels that it is he who prays or meditates, so long will he feel that God is listening to his prayer and that God is a Person. Then he must say: 'O God, Thou art the Master and I am Thy servant. Thou art the whole and I am a part of Thee. Thou art the Mother and I am Thy child.' At that time there exists a feeling of difference: 'I am one and Thou art another.' It is God Himself who makes us feel this difference; and on account of this difference one sees man and woman, light and darkness, and so on. As long as one is aware of this difference, one must accept Śakti, the Personal God. It is God who has put 'I-consciousness' in us. You may reason a thousand times; still this 'I' does not disappear. As long as 'I-consciousness' exists, God reveals Himself to us as a Person.

"Therefore, as long as a man is conscious of 'I' and of differentiation, he cannot speak of the attributeless Brahman and must accept Brahman with attributes. This Brahman with attributes has been declared in the Vedas, the Purānas, and the Tantra, to be Kāli, the Primal Energy."

VIJAY: "How, sir, can one have the vision of the Primal Energy and attain Brahmajnāna, the Knowledge of the attributeless Brahman?"

MASTER: "Pray to Him with a yearning heart, and weep. That will purify your heart. You see the reflection of the sun in clear water. In the mirror of his 'I-consciousness' the devotee sees the form of the Primal Energy, Brahman with attributes. But the mirror must be wiped clean. One does not see the right reflection if there is any dirt on the mirror.

"As long as a man must see the Sun in the water of his 'I-consciousness' and has no other means of seeing It, as long as he has no means of seeing the real Sun except through Its reflection, so long is the reflected sun alone one hundred per cent real to him. As long as the 'I' is real, so long is the reflected sun real—one hundred per cent real. That reflected sun is nothing but the Primal Energy.

"But if you seek Brahmajnāna, the Knowledge of the attributeless Brahman, then proceed to the real Sun through Its reflection. Pray to Brahman with attributes, who listens to your prayers, and He Himself will give you full Knowledge of Brahman; for that which is Brahman with attributes is verily Brahman without attributes, that which is Brahman is verily Śakti. One realizes this non-duality after the attainment of Perfect Knowledge.

"The Divine Mother gives Her devotee Brahmajnāna too. But a true lover of God generally does not seek the Knowledge of Brahman.

"There is another path, the path of knowledge, which is very difficult. You members of the Brāhmo Samāj are not jnānis. You are bhaktas. The jnāni believes that Brahman alone is real and the world illusory as a dream. To him, 'I' and 'you' are illusory as a dream.

"God is our Inner Controller. Pray to Him with a pure and guileless heart. He will explain everything to you. Give up egotism and take refuge in Him. You will realize everything."

The Master sang:

> Dwell, O mind, within yourself;
> Enter no other's home.
> If you but seek there, you will find
> All you are searching for.
>
> God, the true Philosopher's Stone,
> Who answers every prayer,
> Lies hidden deep within your heart,
> The richest gem of all.

> How many pearls and precious stones
> Are scattered all about
> The outer court that lies before
> The chamber of your heart!

He continued: "When you mix with people outside your Samāj, love them all. When in their company be one of them. Don't harbour malice toward them. Don't turn up your nose in hatred and say: 'Oh, this man believes in God with form and not in the formless God. That man believes in the formless God and not in God with form. This man is a Christian. This man is a Hindu. And this man is a Mussalmān.' It is God alone who makes people see things in different ways. Know that people have different natures. Realize this and mix with them as much as you can. And love all. But enter your own inner chamber to enjoy peace and bliss.

> Lighting the lamp of Knowledge in the chamber of your heart,
> Behold the face of the Mother, Brahman's Embodiment.

You can see your true Self only within your own chamber. The cowherds take the cows to graze in the pasture. There the cattle mix. They all form one herd. But on returning to their sheds in the evening they are separated. Then each stays by itself in its own stall. Therefore I say, dwell by yourself in your own chamber."

It was ten o'clock in the evening. The Master got into a carriage to return to Dakshineswar. One or two attending devotees got in with him. The carriage stood under a tree, in deep darkness. Beni Pal wanted to send some sweets and other food with Sri Ramakrishna for Ramlal, the Master's nephew.

BENI PAL: "Sir, Ramlal was not here this evening. With your permission I should like to send some sweets for him by your attendants."

MASTER (*with great anxiety*): "Oh, Beni Pal! Oh, sir! Please don't send these things with me. That will do me harm. It is never possible for me to lay up anything. I hope you won't mind."

BENI PAL: "As you please, sir. Please give me your blessing."

MASTER: "Oh, we have been very happy today! You see, he alone is a true man who has made money his servant. But those who do not know the use of money are not men even though they have human forms. They may have human bodies, but they behave like animals. You are blessed indeed. You have made so many devotees happy today."

Monday, October 20, 1884

Two days after the worship of Kāli, the Mārwāris of the Burrabāzar section of Calcutta were celebrating the Annakuta[5] festival. Sri Ramakrishna had been invited by the Mārwāri devotees to the ceremony at 12 Mallick Street. It was the second day of the bright fortnight of the moon. The festival connected with the worship of Kāli, known as the "Festival of Light", was still going on at Burrabāzar.

---

[5] Literally, "hill of food". During this festival a vast quantity of cooked food is offered to the Deity and later distributed among the devotees and the poor.

About three o'clock in the afternoon M. and the younger Gopal came to Burrabāzār. M. had in his hand a bundle of cloths he had purchased for Sri Ramakrishna. Mallick Street was jammed with people, bullock-carts, and carriages. As M. and Gopal approached 12 Mallick Street they noticed Sri Ramakrishna in a carriage, which could hardly move because of the jam. Baburam and Ram Chakravarty were with the Master. He smiled at M. and Gopal.

Sri Ramakrishna alighted from the carriage. With Baburam he proceeded on foot to the house of his host, M. leading the way. They saw the courtyard of the house filled with big bales of clothes which were being loaded into bullock-carts for shipment. The Mārwāri host greeted the Master and led him to the third floor of the house. A painting of Kāli hung on the wall. Sri Ramakrishna bowed before it. He sat down and became engaged in conversation with the devotees. One of the Mārwāris began to stroke his feet. The Master asked him to stop. After reflecting a minute he said, "All right, you can stroke them a little." His words were full of compassion.

MASTER (to M.): "What about your school?"

M: "Today is a holiday, sir."

MASTER (smiling): "Tomorrow there will be a musical recital of the Chandi at Adhar's house."

The host sent a pundit to Sri Ramakrishna. He saluted the Master and took a seat. Soon they were engaged in conversation. They talked about spiritual things.

MASTER: "God incarnates Himself for the bhakta and not for the jnāni."

PUNDIT: " 'I incarnate Myself in every age for the protection of the good, for the destruction of the wicked, and for the establishment of dharma.'[6] God becomes man, first, for the joy of the bhakta, and secondly, for the destruction of the wicked. The jnāni has no desire."

MASTER (smiling): "But I have not got rid of all desires. I have the desire for love of God."

The pundit's son entered the room. He saluted the Master and took a seat.

MASTER (to the pundit): "Well, what is bhāva and what is bhakti?"

PUNDIT: "Meditation on God mellows the mind. This mellowness is called bhāva. It is like the thawing of ice when the sun rises."

MASTER: "Well, what is prema?"

The pundit and Sri Ramakrishna were talking in Hindusthāni. The former gave some sort of explanation of prema.

MASTER (to the pundit): "No! No! That is not the meaning. Prema means such love for God that it makes a man forget the world and also his body, which is so dear to him. Chaitanyadeva had prema."

PUNDIT: "Yes, sir. One behaves like a drunkard."

MASTER: "Some people develop bhakti and others do not; how do you explain that, sir?"

PUNDIT: "There is no partiality in God. He is the Wish-fulfilling Tree. Whatever a man asks of God he gets. But he must go near the Tree to ask the boon."

[6] Bhagavad Gītā, IV, 8.

The pundit said all this in Hindusthāni. The Master explained it to M. in Bengali.

MASTER: "Sir, please describe samādhi to us."

PUNDIT: "There are two kinds of samādhi: savikalpa and nirvikalpa. In nirvikalpa samādhi the functioning of the mind stops altogether."

MASTER: "Yes. 'The mind completely takes the form of Reality.' The distinction between the meditator and the object of meditation does not exist. There are two other kinds of samādhi: chetana and jada. Nārada and Śukadeva attained chetana samādhi. Isn't that true, sir?"

PUNDIT: "Yes, sir, that is so."

MASTER: "Further, there are the unmanā samādhi and the sthita samādhi. Isn't that true, sir?"

The pundit remained silent. He did not venture an opinion.

MASTER: "Well, sir, through the practice of japa and austerity one can get occult powers, such as walking on the water of the Ganges. Isn't that true?"

PUNDIT: "Yes, one can. But a devotee doesn't want them."

The conversation continued for some time. The pundit said he would visit the Master at Dakshineswar the next ekādasi day.

MASTER: "Ah! Your boy is very nice."

PUNDIT: "Well, revered sir, all this is transitory. It is like the waves in a river—one goes down and another comes up."

MASTER: "You have substance in you."

After a few minutes the pundit saluted Sri Ramakrishna. He said: "I shall have to perform my daily devotions. Please let me go."

MASTER: "Oh, sit down! Sit down!"

The pundit sat down again. The conversation turned to hathayoga. The pundit discussed the subject with the Master in Hindusthāni. Sri Ramakrishna said: "Yes, that is also a form of austerity. But the hathayogi identifies himself with his body. His mind dwells on his body alone." The pundit took leave of the Master. Sri Ramakrishna conversed with the pundit's son.

MASTER: "One can understand the *Bhāgavata* well if one has already studied the Nyāya, the Vedānta, and the other systems of philosophy. Isn't that so?"

PUNDIT'S SON: "Yes, sir. It is very necessary to study the Sāmkhya philosophy."

The conversation went on. Sri Ramakrishna was leaning against a big pillow; the devotees were sitting on the floor. Lying in that position, the Master began to sing:

> Brother, joyfully cling to God;
> Thus striving, some day you may attain Him.

Their host entered the room and saluted Sri Ramakrishna. He was a pious man and devoted to the Master. The pundit's son was still there. The Master asked if the *Pānini*, the Sanskrit grammar, was taught in the schools. He further asked about the Nyāya and the Vedānta philosophies. The host did not show much interest in the discussion and changed the subject.

HOST: "Revered sir, what is the way for us?"

MASTER: "Chanting the name and glories of God, living in the company of holy men, and earnestly praying to God."

HOST: "Please bless me, sir, that I may pay less and less attention to worldly things."

MASTER (smiling): "How much attention do you give to the world? Fifty per cent?" (Laughter.)

HOST: "You know that, sir. We cannot achieve anything without the grace of a holy person like yourself."

MASTER: "If you please God, everyone will be pleased. It is God alone that exists in the heart of the holy man."

HOST: "Nothing, of course, remains unrealized when one attains God. If a man attains God, he can give up everything else. If a man gets a rupee, he gives up the joy of a penny."

MASTER: "A little spiritual discipline is necessary. Through the practice of discipline one gradually obtains divine joy. Suppose a jar with money inside is hidden deep under the earth and someone wants to possess it. In that case he must take the trouble of digging for it. As he digs, he perspires. After much digging the spade strikes the metal jar. He feels a thrill at the sound. The more sound the spade makes, striking against the jar, the more joy he feels.

"Pray to Rāma. Meditate on Him. He will certainly provide you with everything."

HOST: "Revered sir, you are Rāma Himself."

MASTER: "How is that? The waves belong to the river; does the river belong to the waves?"

HOST: "Rāma dwells only in the hearts of holy men. He cannot be seen in any other way. There is no Incarnation of God at the present time."

MASTER (smiling): "How do you know there is no Divine Incarnation?" The host remained silent.

MASTER: "All cannot recognize an Incarnation. When Nārada visited Rāma, Rāma prostrated Himself before Nārada and said: 'We are worldly creatures. How can we be sanctified unless holy men like you visit us?' Further, Rāma went into exile in the forest to redeem His father's pledges. He saw that, since hearing of His exile, the rishis of the forest had been fasting. Many of them did not know that Rāma was none other than the Supreme Brahman."

HOST: "You too are that same Rāma."

MASTER: "For heaven's sake! Never say that."

As Sri Ramakrishna spoke these words, he bowed down to the host and said, with folded hands: " 'That Rāma dwells in all beings; He exists everywhere in the universe.' I am your servant. It is Rāma Himself who has become all men, animals, and other living beings."

HOST: "But sir, we do not know that."

MASTER: "Whether you know it or not, you are Rāma."

HOST: "You are free from love and hatred."

MASTER: "How so? I engaged a carriage to bring me to Calcutta and advanced the coachman three ānnās. But he didn't turn up. I became very angry with him. He is a very wicked man. He made me suffer a lot."

Sri Ramakrishna was resting. The Mārwāri devotees had been singing bhajan on the roof. They were celebrating the Krishna festival. Arrangements had been made for worship and food offering. At the host's request the Master went to see the image. He bowed down before the Deity.

Sri Ramakrishna was profoundly moved as he stood before the image. With folded hands he said: "O Govinda, Thou art my soul! Thou art my life! Victory to Govinda! Hallowed be the name of Govinda! Thou art the Embodiment of Satchidānanda! Oh, Krishna! Ah, Krishna! Krishna is knowledge. Krishna is mind. Krishna is life. Krishna is soul. Krishna is body. Krishna is caste. Krishna is family. O Govinda, my life and soul!" Uttering these words, Sri Ramakrishna went into samādhi. He remained standing. Ram Chatterji supported him.

After a long time the Master regained consciousness of the world. The Mārwāri devotees were about to take out the image. The offering of food was to take place outside the room. The Master joined the procession of devotees. The food was offered with ārati and music. Sri Ramakrishna fanned the image.

Then began the ceremony of feeding the brāhmins. They were seated on the roof. The Master and his devotees also partook of the prasād.

Sri Ramakrishna took leave of the host. It was evening and the street was jammed as before with people and vehicles. He said: "Let us get out of the carriage. It can go by a back street." Proceeding on foot, he found that a betel-leaf seller had opened his stall in front of a small room that looked like a hole. One could not possibly enter it without bending one's head. The Master said: "How painful it is to be shut in such a small space! That is the way of worldly people. And they are happy in such a life."

The carriage came up after making the detour. The Master entered it with Baburam, M., and Ram Chatterji. The younger Gopal sat on the roof of the carriage.

A beggar woman with a baby on her arm stood in front of the carriage waiting for alms. The Master said to M., "Have you any money?" Gopal gave her something.

The carriage rolled along Burrabāzār. Everywhere there were signs of great festivity. The night was dark but illuminated with myriads of lights. The carriage came to the Chitpur road, which was also brightly lighted. The people moved in lines like ants. The crowd looked at the gaily decorated stores and stalls on both sides of the road. There were sweetmeat stores and perfume stalls. Pictures, beautiful and gaudy, hung from the walls. Well-dressed shopkeepers sprayed the visitors with rose-water. The carriage stopped in front of a perfume stall. The Master looked at the pictures and lights and felt happy as a child. People were talking loudly. He cried out: "Go forward! Move on!" He laughed. He said to Baburam with a loud laugh: "Move on!

What are you doing?" The devotees laughed too. They understood that the Master wanted them to move forward to God and not to be satisfied with their present state.

The carriage drove on. The Master noticed that M. had brought some cloths for him. M. had with him two pieces of unbleached and two pieces of washed cloth. But the Master had asked him only for the unbleached ones. He said to M.: "Give me the unbleached ones. You may keep the others. All right. You may give me one of them."

M: "Then shall I take back one piece?"

MASTER: "Then take both."

M: "As you please, sir."

MASTER: "You can give me those when I need them. You see, yesterday Beni Pal wanted me to carry away some food for Ramlal. I told him I couldn't. It is impossible for me to lay up for the future."

M: "That's all right, sir. I shall take back the two pieces of washed cloth."

MASTER (tenderly): "Don't you see, if any desire arises in my mind, it is for the good of you all? You are my own. I shall tell you if I need anything."

M. (humbly): "Yes, sir."

Referring to a devotee, Sri Ramakrishna said: "I said to him yesterday, 'Tomorrow I shall go to Burrabāzār; please meet me there.' Do you know what he said? He said: 'The tram fare will be one ānnā. Where shall I get it?' He had been to Beni Pal's garden yesterday and had officiated there as priest. No one had asked him to do it. He had put on the show himself. He wanted people to know that he was a member of the Brāhmo Samāj. (To M.) Can you tell me what he meant when he said that the tram would cost him one ānnā?"

The conversation turned to the Annakuta festival of the Mārwāris.

MASTER (to the devotees): "What you have seen here one sees at Vrindāvan too. Rakhal has been seeing the same thing there. But the mound of food at Vrindāvan is higher, and more people gather there. There you also see the Govardhan hill. That's the only difference.

"Did you notice the Mārwāris' devotion? That is the real Hindu ideal. That is the Sanātana Dharma. Did you notice their joy when they carried the image in procession? They were happy to think that they bore the throne of God on their shoulders.

"The Hindu religion alone is the Sanātana Dharma. The various creeds you hear of nowadays have come into existence through the will of God and will disappear again through His will. They will not last forever. Therefore I say, 'I bow down at the feet of even the modern devotees.' The Hindu religion has always existed and will always exist."

M. was going home. He saluted the Master and got out of the carriage near Sobhābāzār. Sri Ramakrishna proceeded to Dakshineswar in a happy mood.

33

WITH VARIOUS DEVOTEES

IT WAS AFTERNOON, and many devotees were present in the Master's room. Among them were Manomohan, Mahimacharan, and M. They were joined later by Ishan and Hazra. Balaram and Rakhal were still staying at Vrindāvan. The many young boys who at this time began to seek the Master's company later became his intimate disciples. Latu lived with the Master, and Jogin,[1] who lived in the village, was a frequent visitor.

Sri Ramakrishna, happy child of the Divine Mother that he was, radiated a joy and peace that were reflected in the hearts of his devotees and found expression in their happy faces. They were seated on the floor and had their eyes fixed on the Master, who was standing in a pensive mood, like a boy.

MASTER (*to Manomohan*): "I see Rāma in all things. You are all sitting here, but I see only Rāma in every one of you."

MANOMOHAN: "Yes, sir. It is Rāma who has become everything. But, as you say, though all water is Nārāyana, yet some water is fit for drinking, some for washing the hands and face, and some only for cleaning pots and pans."

MASTER: "It is true. But I see that it is God Himself who has become everything—the universe and its living beings."

Presently the Master sat down on the small couch near his bed.

MASTER (*to Mahimacharan*): "There is no question of my being truthful; but must I develop a mania for it? If I once say that I shall not eat, then it is impossible for me to eat, even if I am hungry. Again, if I ask a particular man to take my water-jug to the pine-grove, he alone must carry it. If another man carries it, he will have to take it back. What a fix I am in! Is there no way out of it?

"Besides, I can't carry anything with me, neither food nor betel-leaf; for that means laying up for the future. I can't carry a little clay in my hand."

Just then a man entered the room and told the Master that Hriday was waiting to see him in Jadu Mallick's garden, near the gate.

The Master said to the devotees: "I shall have to see Hriday. Please don't leave the room." He put on his slippers and went toward the east gate of

---

[1] A monastic disciple of Sri Ramakrishna, later known as Swami Jogananda.

the temple garden, M. accompanying him. The road through the garden was covered with red brick-dust. The manager of the temple, who was standing on the road, saluted Sri Ramakrishna. The Master passed the north entrance of the temple compound, where the bearded sentries sat. On his left he passed the kuthi, the building used by the proprietors of the temple. Then he walked on down the road which was lined on both sides with flowering trees, passing the reservoir on his right, and went outside the temple garden. He found Hriday waiting for him near the gate of Jadu Mallick's garden.

At the sight of the Master, Hriday, who had been standing there with folded hands, prostrated himself before him. When the Master told him to get up, he rose and began to cry like a child. How strange! Tears also appeared in the Master's eyes. He wiped them away with his hands. Hriday had made him suffer endless agonies, yet the Master wept for him.

MASTER: "Why are you here now?"

HRIDAY (weeping): "I have come to see you. To whom else shall I tell my sorrows?"

Sri Ramakrishna smiled and said to him by way of consolation: "One cannot avoid such sorrows in the world. Pleasure and pain are inevitable in worldly life. (Pointing to M.) That is why they come here now and then. They get peace of mind by hearing about God. What is your trouble?"

HRIDAY (weeping): "I am deprived of your company and so I suffer."

MASTER: "Why, was it not you who said to me, 'You follow your ideal and let me follow mine'?"

HRIDAY: "Yes, I did say that. But what did I know?"

MASTER: "I shall say good-bye to you now. Come another day and we shall talk together. Today is Sunday and many people have come to see me. They are waiting in my room. Have you had a good crop in the country?"

HRIDAY: "It isn't bad."

MASTER: "Let me say good-bye. Come another day."

Hriday again prostrated himself before the Master, who started back to his room with M.

MASTER (to M.): "He tormented me as much as he served me. When my stomach trouble had reduced my body to a couple of bones and I couldn't eat anything, he said to me one day: 'Look at me—how well I eat! You've just taken a fancy that you can't eat.' Again he said: 'You are a fool! If I weren't living with you, where would your profession of holiness be?' One day he tormented me so much that I stood on the embankment ready to give up my body by jumping into the Ganges, which was then at flood-tide."

M. became speechless at these words of the Master. For such a man he had shed tears a few minutes before!

MASTER (to M.): "Well, he served me a great deal; then why should he have fallen on such evil days? He took care of me like a parent bringing up a child. As for me, I would remain unconscious of the world day and night. Besides, I was ill for a long time. I was completely at his mercy."

M. did not know how to answer Sri Ramakrishna; so he kept silent.

Sri Ramakrishna returned to his room and sat on the small couch. The devotees had been waiting for him eagerly. Several devotees from Konnagar had arrived. One of them came forward to question the Master.

DEVOTEE: "Sir, we hear that you go into samādhi and experience ecstasy. Please explain why and how you get into that mood."

MASTER: "Sri Rādhā used to experience mahābhāva. If any of her companions wanted to touch her while she was in that state, another of them would say: 'Please do not touch that body, the playground of Sri Krishna. Krishna is now sporting in her body.' It is not possible to experience bhāva or mahābhāva without the realization of God. When a fish comes up from a great depth, you see a movement on the surface of the water; and if it is a big one there is much splashing about. That is why a devotee 'laughs and weeps and dances and sings in the ecstasy of God'.

"One cannot remain in bhāva very long. People take a man to be crazy if he sits before a mirror and looks at his face all the time."

DEVOTEE: "Sir, we hear that you see God. If you do, please show Him to us."

MASTER: "Everything depends on God's will. What can a man do? While chanting God's name, sometimes tears flow and at other times the eyes remain dry. While meditating on God, some days I feel a great deal of inner awakening, and some days I feel nothing.

"A man must work. Only then can he see God. One day, in an exalted mood, I had a vision of the Hāldārpukur. I saw a low-caste villager drawing water after pushing aside the green scum. Now and then he took up the water in the palm of his hand and examined it. In that vision it was revealed to me that the water cannot be seen without pushing aside the green scum that covers it; that is to say, one cannot develop love of God or obtain His vision without work. Work means meditation, japa, and the like. The chanting of God's name and glories is work too. You may also include charity, sacrifice, and so on.

"If you want butter, you must let the milk turn to curd. It must be left in a quiet place. When the milk becomes curd, you must work hard to churn it. Only then can you get butter from the milk."

MAHIMACHARAN: "That is true, sir. Work is certainly necessary. One must labour hard. Only then does one succeed. There is so much to read! The scriptures are endless."

MASTER (to Mahimacharan): "How much of the scriptures can you read? What will you gain by mere reasoning? Try to realize God before anything else. Have faith in the guru's words, and work. If you have no guru, then pray to God with a longing heart. He will let you know what He is like.

"What will you learn of God from books? As long as you are at a distance from the market-place you hear only an indistinct roar. But it is quite different when you are actually there. Then you hear and see everything distinctly. You hear people saying: 'Here are your potatoes. Take them and give me the money.'

"From a distance you hear only the rumbling noise of the ocean. Go near it and you will see many boats sailing about, birds flying, and waves rolling.

"One cannot get true feeling about God from the study of books. This feeling is something very different from book-learning. Books, scriptures, and science appear as mere dirt and straw after the realization of God.

"The one thing needful is to be introduced to the master of the house. Why are you so anxious to know beforehand how many houses and gardens, and how many government securities, the master possesses? The servants of the house would not allow you even to approach these, and they would certainly not tell you about their master's investments. Therefore, somehow or other become acquainted with the master, even if you have to jump over the fence or take a few pushes from the servants. Then the master himself will tell you all about his houses and gardens and his government securities. And what is more, the servants and the door-keeper will salute you when you are known to the master." (All laugh.)

DEVOTEE: "Now the question is how to become acquainted with the master." (Laughter.)

MASTER: "That is why I say that work is necessary. It will not do to say that God exists and then idle away your time. You must reach God somehow or other. Call on Him in solitude and pray to Him, 'O Lord! reveal Thyself to me.' Weep for Him with a longing heart. You roam about in search of 'woman and gold' like a madman; now be a little mad for God. Let people say, 'This man has lost his head for God.' Why not renounce everything for a few days and call on God in solitude?

"What will you achieve by simply saying that God exists and doing nothing about it? There are big fish in the Hāldārpukur; but can you catch them by merely sitting idly on the bank? Prepare some spiced bait and throw it into the lake. Then the fish will come from the deep water and you will see ripples. That will make you happy. Perhaps a fish will jump with a splash and you will get a glimpse of it. Then you will be so glad!

"Milk must be turned to curd and the curd must be churned. Only then will you get butter. (To Mahima) What a nuisance! Someone must show God to a man, while he himself sits idly by all the while! Someone must extract the butter and hold it in front of his mouth! (All laugh.) What a bother! Someone else must catch the fish and give it to him!

"A man wanted to see the king. The king lived in the inner court of the palace, beyond seven gates. No sooner did the man pass the first gate than he exclaimed, 'Oh, where is the king?' But there were seven gates, and he must pass them one after another before he could see the king."

MAHIMACHARAN: "By what kind of work can one realize God?"

MASTER: "It is not that God can be realized by this work and not by that. The vision of God depends on His grace. Still a man must work a little with longing for God in his heart. If he has longing he will receive the grace of God.

"To attain God a man must have certain favourable conditions: the company of holy men, discrimination, and the blessings of a real teacher. Perhaps his elder brother takes the responsibility for the family; perhaps his wife has spiritual qualities and is very virtuous; perhaps he is not married at all or entangled in worldly life. He succeeds when conditions like these are fulfilled.

"In a certain family a man lay seriously ill. He was at the point of death. Someone said: 'Here is a remedy: First it must rain when the star Svāti is in the ascendant; then some of that rain-water must collect in a human skull; then a frog must come there and a snake must chase it; and as the frog is about to be bitten by the snake, it must jump away and the poison of the snake must drop into the skull. You must prepare a medicine from this poison and give it to the patient. Then he will live.' The head of the family consulted the almanac about the star and set out at the right moment. With great longing of heart he began to search for the different ingredients. He prayed to God, 'O Lord, I shall succeed only if You bring together all the ingredients.' As he was roaming about he actually saw a skull lying on the ground. Presently there came a shower of rain. Then the man exclaimed: 'O gracious Lord, I have got the rain-water under Svāti, and the skull too. What is more, some of the rain has fallen into the skull. Now be kind enough to bring together the other ingredients.' He was reflecting with a yearning heart when he saw a poisonous snake approaching. His joy knew no bounds. He became so excited that he could feel the thumping of his own heart. 'O God,' he prayed, 'now the snake has come too. I have procured most of the ingredients. Please be gracious and give me the remaining ones.' No sooner did he pray thus than a frog hopped up. The snake pursued it. As they came near the skull and the snake was about to bite the frog, the frog jumped over the skull and the snake's poison fell into it. The man began to dance, clapping his hands for joy.—So I say that one gets everything through yearning.

"A man cannot realize God unless he renounces everything mentally. A sādhu cannot lay things up. 'Birds and wandering monks do not make provision for the morrow.' Such is the state of my mind that I cannot carry even clay in my hand. Once, when Hriday tormented me, I thought of leaving this place and going to Benares. I thought of taking some clothes with me. But how could I take money? So I could not go to Benares. (*All laugh.*)

(*To Mahima*) "You are a householder. Therefore you should hold both to 'this' and to 'that'—both to the world and to God."

MAHIMA: "Sir, can one who holds to 'that' also hold to 'this'?"

MASTER: "Once, sitting on the bank of the Ganges near the Panchavati, holding a rupee in one hand and clay in the other, I discriminated, 'The rupee is the clay—the clay is verily the rupee, and the rupee is verily the clay', and then threw the rupee into the river. But I was a little frightened. 'How foolish of me to offend the goddess of fortune!' I thought. 'What shall I do if she doesn't provide me with food any more?' Then, like Hazra, I sought help in a ruse. I said to the goddess, 'Mother, may you dwell in my heart.' Once the Divine Mother was pleased with a man's austerities and said to him, 'You may ask a favour of Me.' 'O Mother,' said he, 'if You are so pleased with me, then grant that I may eat from a gold plate with my grandchildren.' Now, in one boon the man got everything: grandchildren, wealth, and gold plate. (*All laugh.*)

"When the mind is freed from 'woman and gold', it can be directed to God and become absorbed in Him. It is the bound alone who can be freed.

The moment the mind turns away from God, it is bound. When does the lower needle of a pair of scales move away from the upper one? When one pan is pressed down by a weight. 'Woman and gold' is the weight.

"Why does a child cry on coming out of its mother's womb? With its cry it says, as it were: 'Just see where I am now! In my mother's womb I was meditating on the Lotus Feet of God; but see where I am now!'

(To Mahima) "You should renounce mentally. Live the life of a house-holder in a spirit of detachment."

MAHIMA: "Can a man live in the world if his mind is once directed to God?"

MASTER: "Why not? Where will he go away from the world? I realize that wherever I live I am always in the Ayodhyā of Rāma. This whole world is Rāma's Ayodhyā. After receiving instruction from His teacher, Rāma said that He would renounce the world. Daśaratha ṣent the sage Vaśishtha to Rāma to dissuade Him. Vaśishtha found Him filled with intense renuncia-tion. He said to Rāma: 'First of all, reason with me, Rāma; then You may leave the world. May I ask You if this world is outside God? If that is so, then You may give it up.' Rāma found that it is God alone who has become the universe and all its living beings. Everything in the world appears real on account of God's reality behind it. Thereupon Rāma became silent.

"In the world a man must fight against passions like lust and anger, against many desires, against attachment. It is convenient to fight from inside a fort—from his own home. At home he gets his food and other help from his wife. In the Kaliyuga the life of a man depends entirely on food. It is better to get food at one place than to knock at seven doors for it.[2] Living at home is like facing the battle from a fort.

"Live in the world like a cast-off leaf in a gale. Such a leaf is sometimes blown inside a house and sometimes to a rubbish heap. The leaf goes wherever the wind blows—sometimes to a good place and sometimes to a bad. Now God has put you in the world. That is good. Stay here. Again, when He lifts you from here and puts you in a better place, that will be time enough to think about what to do then.

"God has put you in the world. What can you do about it? Resign every-thing to Him. Surrender yourself at His feet. Then there will be no more confusion. Then you will realize that it is God who does everything. All depends on 'the will of Rāma'."

A DEVOTEE: "What is that story about 'the will of Rāma'?"

MASTER: "In a certain village there lived a weaver. He was a very pious soul. Everyone trusted him and loved him. He used to sell his goods in the market-place. When a customer asked him the price of a piece of cloth, the weaver would say: 'By the will of Rāma the price of the yarn is one rupee and the labour four ānnās; by the will of Rāma the profit is two ānnās. The price of the cloth, by the will of Rāma, is one rupee and six ānnās.' Such was the people's faith in the weaver that the customer would at once pay the price and take the cloth. The weaver was a real devotee of God. After finishing his supper in the evening, he would spend long hours in the

[2] It is the custom of monks in India to beg their food from householders.

worship hall meditating on God and chanting His name and glories. Now, late one night the weaver couldn't get to sleep. He was sitting in the worship hall, smoking now and then, when a band of robbers happened to pass that way. They wanted a man to carry their goods and said to the weaver, 'Come with us.' So saying, they led him off by the hand. After committing a robbery in a house, they put a load of things on the weaver's head, commanding him to carry them. Suddenly the police arrived and the robbers ran away. But the weaver, with his load, was arrested. He was kept in the lock-up for the night. Next day he was brought before the magistrate for trial. The villagers learnt what had happened and came to court. They said to the magistrate, 'Your Honour, this man could never commit a robbery.' Thereupon the magistrate asked the weaver to make his statement.

"The weaver said: 'Your Honour, by the will of Rāma I finished my meal at night. Then by the will of Rāma I was sitting in the worship hall. It was quite late at night by the will of Rāma. By the will of Rāma I had been thinking of God and chanting His name and glories, when by the will of Rāma a band of robbers passed that way. By the will of Rāma they dragged me with them; by the will of Rāma they committed a robbery in a house; and by the will of Rāma they put a load on my head. Just then, by the will of Rāma the police arrived, and by the will of Rāma I was arrested. Then by the will of Rāma the police kept me in the lock-up for the night, and this morning by the will of Rāma I have been brought before Your Honour.' The magistrate realized that the weaver was a pious man and ordered his release. On his way home the weaver said to his friends, 'By the will of Rāma I have been released.'

"Whether a man should be a householder or a monk depends on the will of Rāma. Surrender everything to God and do your duties in the world. What else can you do? A clerk was once sent to prison. After the prison term was over he was released. Now, what do you think he did? Cut capers or do his old clerical work?

"If the householder becomes a jīvanmukta, then he can easily live in the world if he likes. A man who has attained Knowledge does not differentiate between 'this place' and 'that place'. All places are the same to him. He who thinks of 'that place' also thinks of 'this place'.

"When I first met Keshab at Jaygopal's garden house, I remarked, 'He is the only one who has dropped his tail.' At this people laughed. Keshab said to them: 'Don't laugh. There must be some meaning in his words. Let us ask him.' Thereupon I said to Keshab: 'The tadpole, so long as it has not dropped its tail, lives only in the water. It cannot move about on dry land. But as soon as it drops its tail it hops out on the bank; then it can live both on land and in water. Likewise, as long as a man has not dropped his tail of ignorance, he can live only in the water of the world. But when he drops his tail, that is to say, when he attains the Knowledge of God, then he can roam about as a free soul, or live as a householder if he likes.' "

Mahimacharan and the other devotees remained spellbound, listening to the Master's words.

MASTER: "Once I visited Devendranath Tagore[3] with Mathur Babu. I said to Mathur: 'I have heard that Devendra Tagore thinks of God. I should like to see him.' 'All right,' said Mathur, 'I will take you to him. We were fellow students in the Hindu College and I am very friendly with him.' We went to Devendra's house. Mathur and Devendra had not seen each other for a long time. Devendra said to Mathur: 'You have changed a little. You have grown fat around the stomach.' Mathur said, referring to me: 'He has come to see you. He is always mad about God.' I wanted to see Devendra's physical marks and said to him, 'Let me see your body.' He pulled up his shirt, and I found that he had very fair skin tinted red. His hair had not yet turned grey.

"At the outset I noticed a little vanity in Devendra. And isn't that natural? He had such wealth, such scholarship, such name and fame! Noticing that streak of vanity, I asked Mathur: 'Well, is vanity the outcome of knowledge or ignorance? Can a knower of Brahman have such a feeling as, "I am a scholar; I am a jnāni; I am rich"?'

"While I was talking to Devendra, I suddenly got into that state of mind in which I can see a man as he really is. I was convulsed with laughter inside. In that state I regard scholars and the book-learned as mere straw. If I see that a scholar has no discrimination and renunciation, I regard him as worthless straw. I see that he is like a vulture, which soars high but fixes its look on a charnel-pit down below.

"I found that Devendra had combined both yoga and bhoga in his life. He had a number of children, all young. The family physician was there. Thus, you see, though he was a jnāni, yet he was preoccupied with worldly life. I said to him: 'You are the King Janaka of this Kaliyuga.

> Holding to one as well as the other,
> He drank his milk from a brimming cup!

I have heard that you live in the world and think of God; so I have come to see you. Please tell me something about God.'

"He recited some texts from the Vedas. He said, 'This universe is like a chandelier and each living being is a light in it.' Once, meditating in the Panchavati, I too had had a vision like that. I found his words agreed with my vision, and I thought he must be a very great man. I asked him to explain his words. He said: 'God has created men to manifest His own glory; otherwise, who could know this universe? Everything becomes dark without the lights in the chandelier. One cannot even see the chandelier itself.'

"We talked a long time. Devendra was pleased and said to me, 'You must come to our Brāhmo Samāj festival.' 'That', I said, 'depends on the will of God. You can see the state of my mind. There's no knowing when God will put me into a particular state.' Devendra insisted: 'No, you must come. But put on your cloth and wear a shawl over your body. Someone might say something unkind about your untidiness, and that would hurt me.' 'No,' I replied, 'I cannot promise that. I cannot be a babu.' Devendra and Mathur laughed.

[3] The father of Rabindranath Tagore.

"The very next day Mathur received a letter from Devendra forbidding me to go to the festival. He wrote that it would be ungentlemanly of me not to cover my body with a shawl. (*All laugh.*)

"There is another big man: Captain. Though a man of the world, he is a great lover of God. (*To Mahima*) Talk to him some time. He knows the Vedas, the Vedānta, the *Bhāgavata*, the *Gītā*, the *Adhyātma Rāmāyana*, and other scriptures by heart. You will find that out when you talk to him.

"He has great piety. Once I was going along a street in Barānagore and he held an umbrella over my head. He invites me to his house and shows me great attention. He fans me, massages my feet, and feeds me with various dishes. Once at his house I went into samādhi in the toilet; and he took care of me there though he is so particular about his orthodox habits. He didn't show any abhorrence for the place.

"He has many expenses. He supports his brothers who live in Benares. His wife was a miserly woman at first. Now she is so burdened by the expenses of the family that she cannot spend all the money she would like to.

"Captain's wife said to me: 'He doesn't enjoy worldly life. That is why he once said he would renounce the world.' True, every now and then he expressed that desire.

"Captain was born in a family of devotees. His father was a soldier. I have heard that on the battle-field he would worship Śiva with one hand and hold a naked sword in the other.

"Captain is a strong upholder of orthodox conventions. Because of my visiting Keshab Chandra Sen, he stopped coming here for a month. He said to me that Keshab had violated the social conventions: he dined with the English, had married his daughter into another caste, and had lost his own caste. I said to Captain: 'What do I care for such things? Keshab chants the name of God; so I go to him to hear about God. I eat only the plum; what do I care about the thorns?' But Captain remained stubborn. He said to me, 'Why do you see Keshab?' I answered him rather sharply: 'But I don't go to him for money; I go there to hear the name of God. And how is it that you visit the Viceroy's house? He is a mlechchha. How can you be in his company?' That silenced him a little.

"But he is a great devotee. When he worships he performs ārati with camphor. When he recites hymns he becomes a totally different person. He becomes absorbed.

(*To Mahimacharan*) "In the light of Vedāntic reasoning the world is illusory, unreal as a dream. The Supreme Soul is the Witness—the witness of the three states of waking, dream, and deep sleep. These things are in your line of thought. The waking state is only as real as the dream. Let me tell you a story that agrees with your attitude.

"There was a farmer who lived in the countryside. He was a real jnāni. He earned his living by farming. He was married, and after many years a son was born to him, whom he named Haru. The parents loved the boy dearly. This was natural, since he was the one precious gem in the family. On account of his religious nature the farmer was loved by the villagers. One day he was working in the field when a neighbour came and told him that

Haru had had an attack of cholera. The farmer at once returned home and arranged for treatment for the boy. But Haru died. The other members of the family were grief-stricken, but the farmer acted as if nothing had happened. He consoled his family and told them that grieving was futile. Then he went back to his field. On returning home he found his wife weeping even more bitterly. She said to him: 'How heartless you are! You haven't shed one tear for the child.' The farmer replied quietly: 'Shall I tell you why I haven't wept? I had a very vivid dream last night. I dreamt I had become a king; I was the father of eight sons and was very happy with them. Then I woke up. Now I am greatly perplexed. Should I weep for those eight sons or for this one Haru?'

"The farmer was a jnani; therefore he realized that the waking state is as unreal as the dream state. There is only one eternal Substance, and that is the Ātman.

"But for my part I accept everything: Turiya and also the three states of waking, dream, and deep sleep. I accept all three states. I accept all—Brahman and also māyā, the universe, and its living beings. If I accepted less I should not get the full weight."

A DEVOTEE: "The full weight? How is that?" (All laugh.)

MASTER: "Brahman is qualified by the universe and its living beings. At the beginning, while following the method of 'Not this, not this', one has to eliminate the universe and its living beings. But as long as 'I-consciousness' remains, one cannot but feel that it is God Himself who has become everything. He alone has become the twenty-four cosmic principles.

"When a man speaks of the essential part of the bel-fruit, he means its flesh only, and not the seeds and shell. But if he wants to speak of the total weight of the fruit, it will not do for him to weigh only the flesh. He must accept the whole thing: seeds and shell and flesh. Seeds and shell and flesh belong to one and the same fruit.

"The Nitya and the Līlā belong to the same Reality. Therefore I accept everything, the Relative as well as the Absolute. I don't explain away the world as māyā. Were I to do that I should get short weight."

MAHIMACHARAN: "It is a good synthesis: from the Absolute to the Relative, and from the Relative to the Absolute."

MASTER: "The jnānis regard everything as illusory, like a dream; but the bhaktas accept all the states. The milk flows only in dribblets from the jnāni. (All laugh.) There are some cows that pick and choose their fodder; hence their milk flows only in dribblets. But cows that don't discriminate so much, and eat whatever they get, give milk in torrents. A superior devotee of God accepts both the Absolute and the Relative; therefore he is able to enjoy the Divine even when his mind comes down from the Absolute. Such a devotee is like the cows that give milk in torrents." (All laugh.)

MAHIMA: "But the milk of a cow that eats without discrimination smells a little." (Laughter.)

MASTER (with a smile): "That's true, no doubt. Therefore that milk should be boiled. One should boil such milk over the fire a little while;

there will be no smell whatever if you boil the milk over the fire of Knowledge. (*All laugh.*)

(*To Mahima*) "You explain 'Aum' with reference to 'a', 'u', and 'm' only."

MAHIMA: " 'A', 'u', and 'm' mean creation, preservation, and destruction."

MASTER: "But I give the illustration of the sound of a gong: 'tom',[4] t—o—m. It is the merging of the Līlā in the Nitya: the gross, the subtle, and the causal merge in the Great Cause; waking, dream, and deep sleep merge in Turiya. The striking of the gong is like the falling of a heavy weight into a big ocean. Waves begin to rise: the Relative rises from the Absolute; the causal, subtle, and gross bodies appear out of the Great Cause; from Turiya emerge the states of deep sleep, dream, and waking. These waves arising from the Great Ocean merge again in the Great Ocean. From the Absolute to the Relative, and from the Relative to the Absolute. Therefore I give the illustration of the gong's sound, 'tom'. I have clearly perceived all these things. It has been revealed to me that there exists an Ocean of Consciousness without limit. From It come all things of the relative plane, and in It they merge again. Millions of Brahmāndas rise in that Chidākāśa and merge in It again. All this has been revealed to me; I don't know much about what your books say."

MAHIMA: "Those to whom such things were revealed did not write the scriptures. They were rapt in their own experiences; when would they write? One needs a somewhat calculating mind to write. Others learnt these things from the seers and wrote the books."

MASTER: "Worldly people ask why one does not get rid of attachment to 'woman and gold'. That attachment disappears after the realization of God. If a man once tastes the Bliss of Brahman, then his mind no longer runs after the enjoyment of sense pleasures or wealth or name and fame. If the moth once sees the light, it no longer goes into the darkness.

"Some friends said to Rāvana: 'You have been assuming different forms[5] for Sītā. Why don't you go to her in the form of Rāma?' Rāvana replied: 'When I contemplate Rāma, even the position of Brahmā appears insignificant to me, not to speak of the company of another man's wife! How could I take the form of Rāma for such a purpose?'

"All worship and spiritual discipline are directed to one end alone, namely, to get rid of worldly attachment. The more you meditate on God, the less you will be attached to the trifling things of the world. The more you love the Lotus Feet of God, the less you will crave the things of the world or pay heed to creature comforts. You will look on another man's wife as your mother and regard your own wife as your companion in spiritual life. You will get rid of your bestial desires and acquire godly qualities. You will be totally unattached to the world. Though you may still have to live in the world, you will live as a jīvanmukta. The disciples of Sri Chaitanya lived as householders in a spirit of detachment.

"You may quote thousands of arguments from Vedānta philosophy to a

[4] The "o" is to be pronounced as "aw" in dawn.

[5] During the period when Sītā was kept in prison in his capital, Rāvana used to visit her in various forms in order to court her favour.

true lover of God, and try to explain the world as a dream, but you cannot shake his devotion to God.[6] In spite of all your efforts he will come back to his devotion.

"A man born with an element of Śiva becomes a jñāni; his mind is always inclined to the feeling that the world is unreal and Brahman alone is real. But when a man is born with an element of Vishnu he develops ecstatic love of God. That love can never be destroyed. It may wane a little now and then, when he indulges in philosophical reasoning, but it ultimately returns to him increased a thousandfold."

After the devotees had left the Master, Mahimacharan brought Hazra to the room. M. was present. Mahima said to Sri Ramakrishna: "Sir, I have a complaint against you. Why have you asked Hazra to go home? He has no desire to return to his family."

MASTER: "His mother has told Ramlal how much she is suffering on account of his being away from home; so I have asked Hazra to go home, at least for three days, and see her. Can anyone succeed in spiritual discipline if it causes suffering to his mother? While visiting Vrindāvan I had almost made up my mind to live there, when I remembered my mother. I said to myself, 'My mother will weep if I stay away from her.' So I returned here with Mathur Babu. Besides, why should a jñāni like Hazra be afraid of going back to the world?"

MAHIMA (with a smile): "Sir, that would be a pertinent question if Hazra were a jñāni."

MASTER (smiling): "Oh, Hazra has attained everything. He has just a little attachment to the world because of his children and a small debt. As people say, my aunt is now in perfect health, only she is slightly ill!"

MAHIMA: "Where, sir, is Hazra's knowledge?"

MASTER (smiling): "Oh, you don't know! Everybody says Hazra is quite a man. Everybody knows that he lives in the Dakshineswar temple garden. People talk of nothing but Hazra. Who would bother to mention my name?" (All laugh.)

HAZRA: "You, sir, are incomparable. You have no peer in the world. Therefore nobody understands you."

MASTER: "There you are! To be sure, no one can have dealings with the incomparable. So why should people mention me at all?"

MAHIMA: "What does he know, sir? He will do your bidding."

MASTER: "That is not so. You had better ask him about it. He said to me, 'You and I are on even terms.'"

MAHIMA: "He argues a great deal."

MASTER: "Now and then he teaches me a lesson. (All laugh.) Sometimes I scold him when he argues too much. Later, when I am lying in bed inside the mosquito curtain, I feel unhappy at the idea of having offended him. So I leave the bed, go to Hazra, and salute him. Then I feel peace of mind.

(To Hazra) "Why do you address the Pure Ātman as 'Īśvara'? The Pure

---

[6] According to the non-dualistic Vedānta the Personal God is as illusory as the relative universe; but to a bhakta, a devotee, He is real.

Ātman is inactive and is the Witness of the three states. When I think of the acts of creation, preservation, and destruction, then I call the Pure Ātman 'Īśvara'. What is the Pure Ātman like? It is like a magnet lying at a great distance from a needle. The needle moves, but the magnet lies motionless, inactive."

Toward evening Sri Ramakrishna was pacing the room. M. was sitting alone, thinking. Suddenly the Master said to him tenderly: "Please give me a couple of linen shirts. As you know, I cannot use everybody's things. I thought of asking Captain for the shirts, but you had better give them to me." M. felt highly gratified and said, "As you please, sir."

At dusk incense was burnt in Sri Ramakrishna's room, and, as usual, he bowed before the pictures of gods and goddesses on the walls and chanted their names softly. From outside one could hear the murmuring of the Ganges and the music of the evening worship in the temples of Kāli, Vishnu, and Śiva. Through the door one could see the priest at a distance moving from one temple to another, a bell in his left hand and a light in his right, an attendant carrying the gong. The evening melody was in harmony with the spirit of the hour and place and with the innermost thoughts of the worshippers. For the time being the sordid things of daily life were forgotten.

Later Sri Ramakrishna was seated in his room in his usual blissful mood. Ishan had come from Calcutta. He had burning faith in God. He used to say, "If a man leaves the house with the hallowed name of Durgā on his lips, then Śiva Himself protects him with His celestial weapons."

MASTER (to Ishan): "You have great faith. But I haven't so much. (All laugh.) God can be realized only through faith."

ISHAN: "Yes, sir."

MASTER: "You practise religious rites—japa, fasting, and the like. That is very good. If a man feels sincerely drawn to God, then God makes him practise all these disciplines. The devotee will certainly realize God if he practises them without desiring their results. A devotee observes many rites because of the injunctions of the scriptures. Such devotion is called vaidhi-bhakti. But there is a higher form of devotion known as rāga-bhakti, which springs from yearning and love for God. Prahlāda had such devotion. When the devotee develops that love, he no longer needs to perform prescribed rites."

November 9, 1884

Sri Ramakrishna was in his room, seated on the small couch and facing the east. The devotees were sitting on the floor. It was about midday when M. arrived and took a seat after saluting the Master. Gradually other devotees began to gather. Vijaykrishna Goswami was there with several Brāhmo devotees. The priest Ram Chakravarty was present also. Mahimacharan, Narayan, and Kishori arrived a few minutes later.

It was the beginning of winter. Sri Ramakrishna had felt the need of some shirts and had asked M. to bring them. Besides two broadcloth shirts, M.

had brought another of a heavy material, for which Sri Ramakrishna had not asked.

MASTER (to M.): "You had better take that one back with you. You can use it yourself. There is nothing wrong in that. Tell me, what kind of shirt did I ask you to bring?"

M: "Sir, you told me to get you plain ones. You didn't ask me to buy the heavier one."

MASTER: "Then please take that one back. (To Vijay and the others) You see, Dwarika Babu gave me a shawl. The Mārwāri devotees also brought one for me. I couldn't accept —"

Vijay interrupted the Master, saying: "That is right, sir. If a man needs a thing, he must accept it. And there must be a man to give it. Who but a man will give?"

MASTER: "The giver is the Lord Himself. The mother-in-law said to her daughter-in-law: 'My child, I see that everybody has someone to render him a little personal service. It would be so nice if you could find someone to massage your feet.' The daughter-in-law said: 'Mother, God Himself will massage my feet. I don't need anyone else.' She spoke thus because she was a sincere lover of God.

"Once a fakir went to the Emperor Ākbar to ask for money. The Emperor was saying his prayers. He prayed, 'O Lord, give me money; give me wealth.' The fakir started to leave the palace, but the Emperor motioned to him to wait. After finishing his prayers, Ākbar came to the holy man and said, 'Why were you going away?' The fakir replied, 'You yourself were begging for money and wealth; so I thought that if I must beg, I would beg of God and not of a beggar.'"

VIJAY: "I saw a sādhu at Gayā. He did not take the initiative in anything. One day he wanted to feed some devotees. Suddenly we found that butter, flour, fruits, and other food-stuff had arrived from no one knew where."

MASTER (to Vijay and the others): "There are three classes of sādhus: good, mediocre, and bad. The good sādhu makes no effort to get his food. The dandis, among others, belong to the mediocre and bad classes. To get food the mediocre sādhu will knock at the door of a house and say, 'Namo Nārāyana'.[7] The bad sādhu starts a quarrel if he doesn't get his alms.

"The good sādhu behaves like a python. He sits in one place and the food comes to him. The python doesn't move from where it is. A young sādhu, who had been a brahmachāri from his boyhood, went out to beg. A young girl offered him alms. The sādhu saw her breasts and thought she had abscesses. He asked about them. The elderly women of the family explained that she would some day be a mother and that God had given her breasts to give milk to her children; God had provided for all this beforehand. At these words the sādhu was struck with wonder. He said: 'Then I don't need to beg. God must have provided for me too.'"

Some of the devotees thought that in that case they should not take any initiative either.

---

[7] "Salutations to God." With these words a sādhu greets another person.

MASTER: "But those who think that an effort is needed must make the effort."

VIJAY: "There is a nice story about that in the *Bhaktamāla*."

MASTER: "Tell it to us."

VIJAY: "Please tell us yourself."

MASTER: "No, you tell it. I don't remember it very well.

"One should hear these things at the beginning. That is why I listened to them years ago. But now I am no longer in that mood. Hanumān said: 'I don't know the position of the stars or the phase of the moon. I only think of Rāma.'

"The chātak bird craves only rain-water. Even when it is dying of thirst, it turns its beak upward and wants only water from the sky. The Ganges, the Jamunā, and the seven oceans are filled to the brim, but still it will not touch the water of the earth.

"Rāma and Lakshmana visited Pampā Lake. Lakshmana saw a crow very eager for water. Again and again it went to the edge of the water but would not drink. Lakshmana asked Rāma about it. Rāma said: 'Brother, this crow is a great devotee of God. Day and night it repeats the name of Rāma. Its throat is parched with thirst, but still it won't drink for fear of missing a repetition of Rāma's name.'

"On a full-moon night I said to Haladhari, 'Brother, is it the night of the new moon?' (*All laugh.*)

(*Smiling*) "Yes, it is true. Once I was told that a characteristic of a man of Perfect Knowledge is that he cannot distinguish between the full moon and the new moon. But how could one convince Haladhari of that? He said: 'This is certainly the dark Kaliyuga. He cannot distinguish the full moon from the new moon! And people respect him!' "

Mahimacharan entered the room.

MASTER (*respectfully*): "Come in. Come in, sir. Please take a seat.

(*To Vijay and the other devotees*) "In the ecstatic state of mind I cannot remember a date. The other day there was a religious festival at Beni Pal's garden. I forgot the date. I can no longer remember the last day of the month, when it is very auspicious to repeat the name of God."

Sri Ramakrishna remained thoughtful a few minutes.

MASTER: "But I remember if a man makes an engagement to visit me.

"A man attains this state when his mind is one hundred per cent absorbed in God. When Hanumān returned from Ceylon, Rāma said to him: 'You have seen Sītā. Tell me, how did you find her?' Hanumān said: 'O Rāma, I saw that only the body of Sītā lay there; it held neither her mind nor her soul. She has indeed consecrated her mind and soul to Your Lotus Feet. Therefore I saw only her body in Ceylon. Further, I saw the King of Death prowling about. But what could he do? It was only a body; it had neither mind nor soul.'

"If you meditate on an ideal you will acquire its nature. If you think of God day and night, you will acquire the nature of God. A salt doll went into the ocean to measure its depth. It became one with the ocean. What is the goal of books or scriptures? The attainment of God. A man opened a book belonging to a sādhu. He saw the word 'Rāma' written on every page. There was nothing else.

"If a man loves God, even the slightest thing kindles spiritual feeling in him. Then, repeating the name of Rāma but once, he gets the fruit of ten million sandhyās. At the sight of a cloud the peacock's emotion is awakened: he dances, spreading his tail. Rādhā had the same experience. Just the sight of a cloud recalled Krishna to her mind.

"Chaitanyadeva was passing a village. He heard that drums were made from the earth of that place. At once he was overwhelmed with ecstasy because drums are used in kirtan.

"But who can have this spiritual awakening? Only he who has renounced his attachment to worldly things. If the sap of attachment is totally dried up in a man, the slightest suggestion kindles his spiritual emotion. Though you strike a wet match a thousand times, it will not produce a spark. But if it is dried, the slightest rubbing will set it aflame.

"Pain and pleasure are inevitable in a body. He who has realized God dedicates his mind and life, his body and soul, to God. When Rāma and Lakshmana went to take their bath in Pampā Lake, they thrust their bows into the ground. Coming out of the water, Lakshmana took out his bow and found its tip stained with blood. Rāma said to him: 'Look, brother! Look. Perhaps we have hurt some creature.' Lakshmana dug in the earth and found a big bullfrog. It was dying. Rāma said to the frog in a sorrowful voice: 'Why didn't you croak? We should have tried to save you. You croak lustily enough when you are in the jaws of a snake.' The frog said: 'O Lord, when I am attacked by a snake I croak, saying: "O Rāma, save me! O Rāma, save me!" This time I found that it was Rāma who was killing me; so I kept still.' "

Sri Ramakrishna remained silent a few moments watching the devotees. He had heard that Mahimacharan did not believe in following a guru. He began the conversation again.

MASTER: "A man should have faith in the words of his guru. He doesn't have to look into his guru's character. 'Though my guru visits the grog-shop, still he is the Embodiment of Eternal Bliss.'

"A man who used to give recitals of the *Chandi* and the *Bhāgavata* once said, 'A broomstick is itself unclean, but it cleans dirty places.'"

Mahimacharan studied the Vedānta. His aim was to attain Brahmajnāna. He followed the path of knowledge and was always reasoning.

MASTER (*to Mahima*): "The aim of the jnāni is to know the nature of his own Self. This is Knowledge; this is liberation. The true nature of the Self is that It is the Supreme Brahman: I and the Supreme Brahman are one. But this Knowledge is hidden on account of māyā.

"I said to Harish, 'This is the whole thing: the gold is hidden under a few basketfuls of earth, and you must remove the earth.'

"The bhaktas retain 'I-consciousness'; the jnānis do not. Nangtā used to teach how to establish oneself in the true Self, saying, 'Merge the mind in the buddhi and the buddhi in the Ātman; then you will be established in your true Self.'

"But the 'I' persists. It cannot be got rid of. Imagine a limitless expanse of water: above and below, before and behind, right and left, everywhere there is water. In that water is placed a jar filled with water. There is water inside the jar and water outside, but the jar is still there. The 'I' is the jar.

"Even after attaining Knowledge, the jnāni keeps his body as before. But the fire of Knowledge burns away his lust and other passions. Many days ago, during an electric storm, a thunderbolt struck the Kāli temple. We saw that no injury had been done to the doors; only the points of the screws were broken. The doors are the body, and the passions—lust and so forth—are the screws.

"A jnāni loves to talk only about God. He feels pained if one talks about worldly things. But a worldly man belongs to a different class. He always has the turban of ignorance on his head. He always comes back to worldly topics.

"The Vedas speak of the 'seven planes' of mind. When the jnāni's mind ascends to the fifth plane, he cannot listen to anything or talk of anything but God. At that stage only words of wisdom come from his lips.

"The Vedas speak of Satchidānanda Brahman. Brahman is neither one nor two; It is between one and two. It cannot be described either as existence or as non-existence; It is between existence and non-existence.

"When the devotee develops rāga-bhakti, passionate love of God, he realizes Him. But one loses vaidhi-bhakti, formal devotion, as easily as one gains it. This is formal devotion: so much japa, so much meditation, so much sacrifice and homa, so many articles of worship, and the recitation of so many mantras before the Deity. Such devotion comes in a moment and goes in a moment. Many people say: 'Well, friend, we have lived on havishya for so many days! How many times we have worshipped the Deity at our home! And what have we achieved?' But there is no falling away from rāga-bhakti. And who gets this passionate love for God? Those who have performed many meritorious deeds in their past births, or those who are eternally perfect. Think of a dilapidated house, for instance: while clearing away the undergrowth and rubbish one suddenly discovers a fountain fitted with a pipe. It has been covered with earth and bricks, but as soon as they are removed the water shoots up.

"Those who have passionate love for God do not say any such thing as: 'O brother, how strict I have been about food! But what have I achieved?' New farmers give up cultivating if their fields do not yield any crops. But hereditary farmers will continue to cultivate their fields whether they get a crop or not. Their fathers and grandfathers were farmers; they know that they too must accept farming as their means of livelihood.

"Only those who have developed rāga-bhakti for God may be called His sincere devotees. God becomes responsible for them. If you enter your name in a hospital register, the doctor will not discharge you until you are cured. Those who are held by God have nothing to fear. The son who holds to his father, while walking along the narrow ridge of a paddy-field, may slip if he absent-mindedly lets go his father's hand; but if the father holds the son by the hand, there is no such danger.

"Is there anything that is impossible for faith? And a true devotee has faith in everything: the formless Reality, God with form, Rāma, Krishna, and the Divine Mother.

"Once, while going to Kāmārpukur, I was overtaken by a storm. I was in the middle of a big meadow. The place was haunted by robbers. I began to repeat the names of all the deities: Rāma, Krishna, and Bhagavati. I also repeated the name of Hanumān. I chanted the names of them all. What does that mean? Let me tell you. While the servant is counting out the money to purchase supplies, he says, 'These pennies are for potatoes, these for egg-plants, these for fish.' He counts the money separately, but after the list is completed, he puts the coins together.

"When one develops love of God, one likes to talk only of God. If you love a person, you love to talk and hear about him. A worldly person's mouth waters while he talks about his son. If someone praises his son, he will at once say to the boy, 'Go and get some water for your uncle to wash his feet.'

"Those who love pigeons are highly pleased if you praise pigeons before them. But if you speak ill of pigeons, they will at once exclaim, 'Has anyone in your line for fourteen generations ever raised pigeons?' "

Sri Ramakrishna now addressed Mahimacharan, who was a householder.

MASTER: "What need is there of renouncing the world altogether? It is enough if you can rid yourself of attachment. But you must have sādhanā; you have to fight the sense-organs.

"It is a great advantage to fight from inside a fort. You get much help from the fort. The world is the place for enjoyment. After enjoying different things, you should give them up one by one. Once I had a desire to put a gold chain around my waist. I obtained one at last and put it on, but I had to take it off immediately.

"Once I ate some onion.[8] While eating it I discriminated, 'O mind, this is onion.' Then I moved it to different places in my mouth and at last spat it out."

A musician was expected. He was to sing with his party. Sri Ramakrishna asked the devotees every now and then, "Where is the musician?"

MAHIMA: "We are quite all right as we are."

MASTER: "No, sir. You get this all through the year."

A devotee outside the room said, "The musician has come."

Sri Ramakrishna was filled with joy and said, "Ah! Has he?"

Mats were spread on the floor of the long verandah northeast of the Master's room. Sri Ramakrishna said: "Sprinkle a little Ganges water on the mats. Many worldly people have sat on them."

The ladies of Pyari Babu's family, from Bali, had come to visit the temples. They wanted to listen to the kirtan. A devotee said to Sri Ramakrishna: "These ladies have been inquiring whether there would be any place in the room for them. Can they have seats?" The kirtan had already begun. The Master said, "No, no! Where is any room here?"

Narayan arrived and saluted Sri Ramakrishna. The latter said tenderly: "Why have you come? Your people at home have beaten you so much!" He

---

[8] The onion is considered a rājasic food and not conducive to spiritual life.

signed to Baburam to give Narayan something to eat. Narayan entered the Master's room. Suddenly Sri Ramakrishna followed him. He wanted to feed Narayan with his own hands. Afterwards he returned to the verandah.

Many devotees were present, including Vijay, Mahimacharan, Narayan, M., and the younger Gopal. Soon Narayan came back to the verandah and took his seat by the Master.

About three o'clock Adhar arrived. At the sight of him Sri Ramakrishna appeared excited. The devotee saluted the Master and sat on the floor. Sri Ramakrishna beckoned to him to come nearer.

When the music was over the gathering of devotees broke up. Some began to stroll in the garden and some went to the temples to watch the evening service.

In the evening arrangements were made for kirtan inside the Master's room. Sri Ramakrishna eagerly asked a devotee to have an extra lamp. The two lamps lit the room brightly.

Sri Ramakrishna said to Vijay: "Why are you sitting there? Come nearer to me." This time the kirtan created an intense atmosphere. The Master danced in an ecstasy of joy; the devotees also danced encircling him. While Vijay was dancing his cloth dropped. He was unconscious.

When the music was over, Vijay began to look for his key, which had fallen somewhere. The Master said to him with a laugh, "Why bother about it any more?" He meant that Vijay should have nothing more to do with boxes and keys.

Kishori saluted Sri Ramakrishna and was about to take his leave. The Master blessed him, touching his chest tenderly, and bade him good-bye. His words were full of love. M. and Gopal saluted the Master. They too were about to take their leave. He said to them with the same affection: "Couldn't you go tomorrow morning? You may catch cold at night."

M. and Gopal decided to spend the night with Sri Ramakrishna. They sat on the floor with a few other devotees.

Sri Ramakrishna had had no rest the whole day: the devotees had been with him all the time. He went out for a few minutes. Returning to the room he saw M. taking down a song from Ramlal.

MASTER: "What are you doing?"

M. said that he was writing down a song. On being told what the song was, the Master remarked that it was a rather long song. M. wrote a line or two and then stopped writing.

A little later Sri Ramakrishna took his supper of farina pudding and one or two luchis. A lighted lamp stood on a stand by his side. M. sat near him. The Master asked if there were any sweets in the room. M. had brought some sandesh which he had put on the shelf. Sri Ramakrishna asked M. to give him a sweet. M. searched for the sweets but could not find them. He was embarrassed. They had been given to the devotees.

After finishing his supper, Sri Ramakrishna sat on the small couch and M. seated himself on the foot-rug. The Master, talking about Narayan, was overcome with emotion.

MASTER: "I saw Naran today."

M: "Yes, sir. His eyes were moist. When I looked at his face I felt like weeping."

MASTER: "The sight of him arouses a mother's love in me, as it were. His relatives beat him at home because he comes here. There is none to defend him."

M: "The other day he left his books at Haripada's house and fled to you."

MASTER: "It was not good for him to do that."

Sri Ramakrishna was silent. After a few minutes he continued.

MASTER: "You see, he has much substance in him. Otherwise, how could I be attracted to him even though I was listening to the kirtan at the time? I had to leave the music and go into the room. That never happened before."

Again Sri Ramakrishna fell silent. A few minutes later he began to talk.

MASTER: "In an ecstatic state I asked him how he was feeling. He just said he was happy. (To M.) Feed him now and then—as parents do their child."

Sri Ramakrishna then spoke about Tejchandra.

MASTER (to M.): "Please ask him what he thinks of me. Does he think of me as a jnāni? Or what does he say about me? I understand that he is very reticent. (To Gopal) Ask Tejchandra to come here Saturdays and Tuesdays. (To M.) Suppose I go to your school and look for—"

M. thought that Sri Ramakrishna wanted to go to his school to see Narayan. He said to the Master, "You might as well wait at our house."

MASTER: "No, I have something else in mind. I should like to see whether there are other worth-while boys in the school."

M: "Of course you can go. Other visitors come to the school. You can come too."

Sri Ramakrishna was smoking. M. and Gopal finished their supper. They decided to sleep in the nahabat. M. again sat on the floor near Sri Ramakrishna.

MASTER (to M.): "There may be some pots and pans in the nahabat. Why not sleep here in this room?"

M: "Very well, sir."

It was ten or eleven o'clock at night. Sri Ramakrishna was sitting on the small couch, resting against a pillow. M. sat on the floor. The Master was conversing with him. A lamp burnt on a stand near the wall.

The Master felt great compassion for his devotees. He wanted to bless M. by accepting his personal service.

MASTER: "My feet ache. Please rub them gently."

M. seated himself on the small couch and took the Master's feet on his lap. He stroked them. Now and then Sri Ramakrishna would ask his disciple a question.

MASTER (smiling): "How did you like today's conversation?"

M: "Very much indeed."

MASTER (smiling): "How I spoke about the Emperor Ākbar!"

M: "It was very good."

MASTER: "Repeat it to me."

M: "A fakir came to visit Ākbar. The Emperor was saying his prayers. In his prayers he was asking God to give him wealth and riches. Thereupon the fakir was about to leave the room quietly. Later, when the Emperor asked him about it, the fakir said, 'If I must beg, why should I beg of a beggar?' "

MASTER: "What else did we talk about?"

M: "You told us a great deal about saving up for the future."

MASTER (*smiling*): "What did I say?"

M: "As long as a man feels that he must try, he should make an effort. How well you told us about it at Sinthi!"

MASTER: "What did I say?"

M: "God takes upon Himself complete responsibility for one who totally depends upon Him. It is like a guardian taking charge of a minor. You also told us that at a feast a child cannot by himself find a place to eat his meal; someone finds a place for him."

MASTER: "No, that is not quite to the point. I said that the child doesn't fall if the father leads him and holds his hand."

M: "You also described the three classes of sādhus. The best sādhu does not move about to get his food; he lives in one place and gets his food there. You told us about that young sādhu who said, when he saw the breasts of a young girl, 'Why has she those abscesses?' You told us many other things."

MASTER (*smiling*): "What else?"

M: "About the crow of Pampā Lake. He repeated the name of Rāma day and night. That is why he couldn't drink the water though he went to its edge. And about the holy man in whose book was written only 'Om Rāma'. And what Hanumān said to Rāma."

MASTER: "What did he say?"

M: "Hanumān said to Rāma: 'I saw Sītā in Ceylon; but it was only her body. Her mind and soul were lying at Your feet.'

"And about the chātak bird. He will not drink anything but rain-water. And about jnānayoga and bhaktiyoga."

MASTER: "What did I say about them?"

M: "As long as one is conscious of the 'jar', the ego will certainly remain. As long as one is conscious of 'I', one cannot get rid of the idea, 'I am the devotee and Thou art God'."

MASTER: "No, it is not that; the 'jar' doesn't disappear whether one is conscious of it or not. One cannot get rid of the 'I'. You may reason a thousand times; still it will not go."

M. remained silent a few moments.

M: "You had that talk with Ishan Mukherji in the Kāli temple. We were very lucky to be there."

MASTER (*smiling*): "Yes, yes. Tell me, what did I say?"

M: "You said that work is only the first step. You told us that you said to Sambhu Mallick, 'If God appears before you, will you ask Him for a number of hospitals and dispensaries?'

"You said another thing: God does not reveal Himself to a person as long as he is attached to work. You said that to Keshab Sen."

MASTER: "What did I say?"

M: "As long as the baby plays with the toy and forgets everything else, its mother looks after her cooking and other household duties; but when the baby throws away the toy and cries, then the mother puts down the rice-pot and comes to the baby.

"You said another thing that day: Lakshmana asked Rāma where one could find God; after a great deal of explanation, Rāma said to him, 'Brother, I dwell in the man in whom you find ecstatic love—a love which makes him laugh and weep and dance and sing.' "

MASTER: "Ah me! Ah me!"

Sri Ramakrishna sat in silence a few minutes.

M: "That day you spoke only words of renunciation to Ishan. Since then many of us have come to our senses. Now we are eager to reduce our duties. You said that day, 'Rāvana died in Ceylon and Behulā wept bitterly for him.' "

Sri Ramakrishna laughed aloud.

M. (humbly): "Sir, isn't it desirable to reduce the number of one's duties and entanglements?"

MASTER: "Yes. But it is a different thing if you happen to come across a sādhu or a poor man. Then you should serve him."

M: "And that day you spoke very rightly to Ishan about flatterers. They are like vultures on a carcass. You once said that to Padmalochan also."

MASTER: "No, to Vamandas of Ulo."

After a while M. sat on the floor near the small couch. Sri Ramakrishna felt sleepy; he said to M.: "Go to sleep. Where is Gopal? Please shut the door."

Next morning Sri Ramakrishna left his bed very early. As usual, he chanted the holy names of the different gods and goddesses. Now and then he looked at the sacred river. The morning worship began in the temples of Rādhākānta and Mother Kāli. M. had spent the night on the floor of the Master's room. He left his bed and watched the worship in the different temples.

Sri Ramakrishna finished his bath and went with M. to the Kāli temple. He asked the disciple to lock the door of his room.

In the temple he took the seat in front of the image of Kāli and offered flowers, sometimes at Her feet and sometimes on his own head. He fanned the Deity. Then he returned to his room and asked M. to unlock the door. Entering the room, he sat on the small couch. He was completely overwhelmed with divine fervour and began to chant the name of God. M. sat alone on the floor. Sri Ramakrishna began to sing about the Divine Mother:

> Who is there that can understand what Mother Kāli is?
> Even the six darśanas are powerless to reveal Her.
> It is She, the scriptures say, that is the Inner Self
> Of the yogi, who in Self discovers all his joy;
> She that, of Her own sweet will, inhabits every living thing. . . .

Then he sang:

> All creation is the sport of my mad Mother Kāli;
> By Her māyā the three worlds are bewitched. . . .

He continued:

> O Kāli, who can know Thee? Numberless are Thy forms. . . .

Again he sang:

> O Mother, redeem me speedily!
> From terror of the King of Death I am about to die. . . .

M. said to himself, "I wish he would sing:

> Mother, Thou canst not trick me any more,
> For I have seen Thy crimson Lotus Feet."

Strangely enough, no sooner had the thought passed through M.'s mind than Sri Ramakrishna sang the song. A few minutes later he said to M., "What do you think of the present state of my mind?"

M. (*smiling*): "It is your simple and natural state."

Sri Ramakrishna sang to himself the following refrain of a song:

> Unless a man is simple, he cannot recognize God, the Simple One.

BANKIM CHANDRA

Saturday, December 6, 1884

ADHAR, A GREAT DEVOTEE of Sri Ramakrishna, lived in Sobhābāzār in the northern section of Calcutta. Almost every day, after finishing his hard work at the office and returning home in the late afternoon, he paid Sri Ramakrishna a visit. From his home in Calcutta he would go to Dakshineswar in a hired carriage. His sole delight was to visit the Master. But he would hear very little of what Sri Ramakrishna said; for, after saluting the Master and visiting the temples, he would lie down, at the Master's request, on a mat spread on the floor and would soon fall asleep. At nine or ten o'clock he would be awakened to return home. However, he considered himself blessed to be able to visit the God-man of Dakshineswar. At Adhar's request Sri Ramakrishna often visited his home. His visits were occasions for religious festivals. Devotees in large numbers would assemble, and Adhar would feed them sumptuously. One day, while Sri Ramakrishna was visiting his home, Adhar said to him: "Sir, you haven't come to our house for a long time. The rooms seemed gloomy; they had a musty smell. But today the whole house is cheerful; the sweetness of your presence fills the atmosphere. Today I called on God earnestly. I even shed tears while praying." "Is that so?" the Master said tenderly, casting a kindly glance on his disciple.

Sri Ramakrishna arrived at Adhar's house with his attendants. Everyone was in a joyous mood. Adhar had arranged a rich feast. Many strangers were present. At Adhar's invitation, several other deputy magistrates had come; they wanted to watch the Master and judge his holiness. Among them was Bankim Chandra Chatterji, perhaps the greatest literary figure of Bengal during the later part of the nineteenth century. He was one of the creators of modern Bengali literature and wrote on social and religious subjects. Bankim was a product of the contact of India with England. He gave modern interpretations of the Hindu scriptures and advocated drastic social reforms.

Sri Ramakrishna had been talking happily with the devotees when Adhar introduced several of his personal friends to him.

ADHAR (*introducing Bankim*): "Sir, he is a great scholar and has written many books. He has come here to see you. His name is Bankim Babu."

MASTER (*smiling*): "Bankim![1] Well, what has made you bent?"

[1] Literally the word means "bent" or "curved".

666

BANKIM (*smiling*): "Why, sir, boots are responsible for it. The kicks of our white masters have bent my body."

MASTER: "No, my dear sir! Sri Krishna was bent on account of His ecstatic love. His body was bent in three places owing to His love for Rādhā. That is how some people explain Sri Krishna's form. Do you know why He has a deep-blue complexion? And why He is of such small stature—only three and a half cubits measured by His own hand? God looks so as long as He is seen from a distance. So the water of the ocean looks blue from afar. But if you go near the ocean and take the water in your hand, you will no longer find it blue; it will be very clear, transparent. So the sun appears small because it is very far away; if you go near it, you will no longer find it small. When one knows the true nature of God, He appears neither blue nor small. But that is a far-off vision: one does not see it except in samādhi. As long as 'I' and 'you' exist, name and form will also exist. Everything is God's līlā, His sportive pleasure. As long as a man is conscious of 'I' and 'you', he will experience the manifestations of God through diverse forms.

"Sri Krishna is the Purusha; Śrimati[2] is His Śakti, the Primal Power. The two are Purusha and Prakriti. What is the meaning of the Yugala Murti, the conjoined images of Rādhā and Krishna? It is that Purusha and Prakriti are not different; there is no difference between them. Purusha cannot exist without Prakriti, and Prakriti cannot exist without Purusha. If you mention the one, the other is understood. It is like fire and its power to burn: one cannot think of fire without its power to burn; again, one cannot think of fire's power to burn without fire. Therefore in the conjoined images of Rādhā and Krishna, Krishna's eyes are fixed on Rādhā and Rādhā's on Krishna. Rādhā's complexion is golden, like lightning; so Krishna wears yellow apparel. Krishna's complexion is blue, like a dark cloud; so Rādhā wears a blue dress; she has also decked herself with blue sapphires. Rādhā has tinkling anklets; so Krishna has them too. In other words, there is inner and outer harmony between Purusha and Prakriti."

As Sri Ramakrishna finished these words, Bankim and his friends began to whisper in English.

MASTER (*smiling, to Bankim and the others*): "Well, gentlemen! What are you talking about in English?"

ADHAR: "We are discussing what you have just said, your explanation of Krishna's form."

MASTER (*smiling*): "That reminds me of a funny story. It makes me want to laugh. Once a barber was shaving a gentleman. The latter was cut slightly by the razor. At once he cried out, 'Damn!' But the barber didn't know the meaning of the word. He put his razor and other shaving articles aside, tucked up his shirt-sleeves—it was winter—, and said: 'You said "damn" to me. Now you must tell me its meaning.' The gentleman said: 'Don't be silly. Go on with your shaving. The word doesn't mean anything in particular; but shave a little more carefully.' But the barber wouldn't let him off so easily. He said, 'If "damn" means something good, then I am a "damn", my father

[2] Rādhikā, the Divine Consort of Krishna.

is a "damn", and all my ancestors are "damns". (*All laugh.*) But if it means something bad, then you are a "damn", your father is a "damn", and all your ancestors are "damns". (*All laugh.*) They are not only "damns", but "damn —damn—damn—dā-damn—damn".' " (*Loud laughter.*)

As the laughter stopped, Bankim began the conversation.

BANKIM: "Sir, why don't you preach?"

MASTER (*smiling*): "Preaching? It is only a man's vanity that makes him think of preaching. A man is but an insignificant creature. It is God alone who will preach—God who has created the sun and moon and so illumined the universe. Is preaching such a trifling affair? You cannot preach unless God reveals Himself to you and gives you the command to preach. Of course, no one can stop you from preaching. You haven't received the command, but still you cry yourself hoarse. People will listen to you a couple of days and then forget all about it. It is like any other sensation: as long as you speak, people will say, 'Ah! He speaks well'; and the moment you stop, everything will disappear.

"The milk in the pot hisses and swells as long as there is heat under it. Take away the heat, and the milk will quiet down as before.

"One must increase one's strength by sādhanā; otherwise one cannot preach. As the proverb goes: 'You have no room to sleep yourself and you invite a friend to sleep with you.' There is no place for you to lie down and you say: 'Come, friend! Come and lie down with me.' (*Laughter.*)

"Some people used to befoul the bank of the Hāldārpukur at Kāmārpukur every morning. The villagers would notice it and abuse the offenders. But that didn't stop it. At last the villagers filed a petition with the Government. An officer visited the place and put up a sign: 'Commit no nuisance. Offenders will be punished.' That stopped it completely. Afterwards there was no more trouble. It was a government order, and everyone had to obey it.

"Likewise, if God reveals Himself to you and gives you the command, then you can preach and teach people. Otherwise, who will listen to you?"

The visitors were listening seriously.

MASTER (*to Bankim*): "I understand you are a great pundit and have written many books. Please tell me what you think about man's duties? What will accompany him after death? You believe in the hereafter, don't you?"

BANKIM: "The hereafter? What is that?"

MASTER: "True. When a man dies after attaining Knowledge, he doesn't have to go to another plane of existence; he isn't born again. But as long as he has not attained Knowledge, as long as he has not realized God, he must come back to the life of this earth; he can never escape it. For such a person there is a hereafter. A man is liberated after attaining Knowledge, after realizing God. For him there is no further coming back to earth. If a boiled paddy-grain is sown, it doesn't sprout. Just so, if a man is boiled by the fire of Knowledge, he cannot take part any more in the play of creation; he cannot lead a worldly life, for he has no attachment to 'woman and gold'. What will you gain by sowing boiled paddy?"

BANKIM (*smiling*): "Sir, neither does a weed serve the purpose of a tree."

MASTER: "But you cannot call a jnāni a weed. He who has realized God has obtained the fruit of Immortality—not a common fruit like a gourd or a pumpkin. He is free from rebirth. He is not born anywhere—on earth, in the solar world, or in the lunar world.

"Analogy is one-sided. You are a pundit; haven't you read logic? Suppose you say that a man is as terrible as a tiger. That doesn't mean that he has a fearful tail or a tiger's pot-face! (*All laugh.*)

"I said the same thing to Keshab. He asked me, 'Sir, is there an after-life?' I didn't commit myself either way. I said that the potters put their pots in the sun to bake. Among them you see both baked and soft pots. Sometimes cattle trample over them. When the baked pots are broken, the potters throw them away; but when the soft ones are broken they keep them. They mix them with water and put the clay on the wheel and make new pots. They don't throw away the unbaked pots. So I said to Keshab: 'The Potter won't let you go as long as you are unbaked. He will put you on the wheel of the world as long as you have not attained Knowledge, as long as you have not realized Him. He won't let you go. You will have to return to the earth again and again: there is no escape. You will be liberated only when you realize God. Then alone will the Potter let you go. It is because then you won't serve any purpose in this world of māyā.' The jnāni has gone beyond māyā. What will he do in this world of māyā?

"But God keeps some jnānis in the world of māyā to be teachers of men. In order to teach others the jnāni lives in the world with the help of vidyāmāyā. It is God Himself who keeps the jnāni in the world for His work. Such was the case with Śukadeva and Śankarāchārya.

(*To Bankim, smiling*) "Well, what do you say about man's duties?"

BANKIM (*smiling*): "If you ask me about them, I should say they are eating, sleeping, and sex-life."

MASTER (*sharply*): "Eh? You are very saucy! What you do day and night comes out through your mouth. A man belches what he eats. If he eats radish, he belches radish; if he eats green coconut, he belches green coconut. Day and night you live in the midst of 'woman and gold'; so your mouth utters words about that alone. By constantly thinking of worldly things a man becomes calculating and deceitful. On the other hand, he becomes guileless by thinking of God. A man who has seen God will never say what you have just said. What will a pundit's scholarship profit him if he does not think of God and has no discrimination and renunciation? Of what use is erudition if the mind dwells on 'woman and gold'?

"Kites and vultures soar very high indeed, but their gaze is fixed only on the charnel-pit. The pundit has no doubt studied many books and scriptures; he may rattle off their texts, or he may have written books. But if he is attached to women, if he thinks of money and honour as the essential things, will you call him a pundit? How can a man be a pundit if his mind does not dwell on God?

"Some may say about the devotees: 'Day and night these people speak about God. They are crazy; they have lost their heads. But how clever we are! How we enjoy pleasure—money, honour, the senses!' The crow, too.

thinks he is a clever bird; but the first thing he does when he wakes up in the early morning is to fill his stomach with nothing but others' filth. Haven't you noticed how he struts about? Very clever indeed!"

There was dead silence.

Sri Ramakrishna continued: "But like the swan are those who think of God, who pray day and night to get rid of their attachment to worldly things and their love for 'woman and gold', who do not enjoy anything except the nectar of the Lotus Feet of the Lord, and to whom worldly pleasures taste bitter. If you put a mixture of milk and water before the swan, it will leave the water and drink only the milk. And haven't you noticed the gait of a swan? It goes straight ahead in one direction. So it is with genuine devotees: they go toward God alone. They seek nothing else; they enjoy nothing else.

(*Tenderly, to Bankim*) "Please don't take offence at my words."

BANKIM: "Sir, I haven't come here to hear sweet things."

MASTER (*to Bankim*): "'Woman and gold' alone is the world; that alone is māyā. Because of it you cannot see or think of God. After the birth of one or two children, husband and wife should live as brother and sister and talk only of God. Then both their minds will be drawn to God, and the wife will be a help to the husband on the path of spirituality. None can taste divine bliss without giving up his animal feeling. A devotee should pray to God to help him get rid of this feeling. It must be a sincere prayer. God is our Inner Controller; He will certainly listen to our prayer if it is sincere.

"And 'gold'. Sitting on the bank of the Ganges below the Panchavati, I used to say, 'Rupee is clay and clay is rupee.' Then I threw both into the Ganges."

BANKIM: "Indeed! Money is clay! Sir, if you have a few pennies you can help the poor. If money is clay, then a man cannot give in charity or do good to others."

MASTER (*to Bankim*): "Charity! Doing good! How dare you say you can do good to others? Man struts about so much; but if one pours foul water into his mouth when he is asleep, he doesn't even know it; his mouth overflows with it. Where are his boasting, his vanity, his pride, then?

"A sannyāsi must give up 'woman and gold'; he cannot accept it any more. One must not swallow one's own spittle. When a sannyāsi gives something to another, he knows that it is not himself who gives. Kindness belongs to God alone. How can a man lay claim to it? Charity depends on the will of Rāma. A true sannyāsi renounces 'woman and gold' both mentally and outwardly. He who eats no molasses must not even keep molasses about. If he does, and yet tells others not to eat it, they won't listen to him.

"A householder, of course, needs money, for he has a wife and children. He should save up to feed them. They say that the bird and the sannyāsi should not provide for the future. But the mother bird brings food in her mouth for her chicks; so she too provides. A householder needs money. He has to support his family.

"If a householder is a genuine devotee he performs his duties without attachment; he surrenders the fruit of his work to God—his gain or loss, his pleasure or pain—and day and night he prays for devotion and for nothing else. This is called motiveless work, the performance of duty without attachment. A sannyāsi, too, must do all his work in that spirit of detachment; but he has no worldly duties to attend to, like a householder.

"If a householder gives in charity in a spirit of detachment, he is really doing good to himself and not to others. It is God alone that he serves—God, who dwells in all beings; and when he serves God, he is really doing good to himself and not to others. If a man thus serves God through all beings, not through men alone but through animals and other living beings as well; if he doesn't seek name and fame, or heaven after death; if he doesn't seek any return from those he serves; if he can carry on his work of service in this spirit—then he performs truly selfless work, work without attachment. Through such selfless work he does good to himself. This is called karmayoga. This too is a way to realize God. But it is very difficult, and not suited to the Kaliyuga.

"Therefore I say, he who works in such a detached spirit—who is kind and charitable—benefits only himself. Helping others, doing good to others —this is the work of God alone, who for men has created the sun and moon, father and mother, fruits, flowers, and corn. The love that you see in parents is God's love: He has given it to them to preserve His creation. The compassion that you see in the kind-hearted is God's compassion: He has given it to them to protect the helpless. Whether you are charitable or not, He will have His work done somehow or other. Nothing can stop His work.

"What then is man's duty? What else can it be? It is just to take refuge in God and to pray to Him with a yearning heart for His vision.

"Sambhu said to me: 'It is my desire to build a large number of hospitals and dispensaries. Thus I can do much good to the poor.' I said to him: 'Yes, that is not bad if you can do it in a detached spirit. But to be detached is very difficult unless you sincerely love God. And further, if you entangle yourself in many activities, you will be attached to them in a way unknown to yourself. You may think you have no motive behind your work, but perhaps there has already grown a desire for fame and the advertising of your name. Then again, if you are entangled in too many activities, the pressure of them will make you forget God.' I also said to him: 'Sambhu, let me ask you one thing. If God appears before you, will you want Him or a number of hospitals and dispensaries?' If one realizes God, one doesn't enjoy anything else. One who has tasted syrup of sugar candy cannot enjoy a drink made from common treacle.

"Those who build hospitals and dispensaries, and get pleasure from that, are no doubt good people; but they are of a different type. He who is a real devotee of God seeks nothing but God. If he finds himself entangled in too much work, he earnestly prays, 'Lord, be gracious and reduce my work; my mind, which should think of Thee day and night, has been wasting its power; it thinks of worldly things alone.' Pure-souled devotees are in a class by themselves. You cannot have real love of God unless you know that God alone is real and all else illusory. You cannot have real love of God unless you know that the world is impermanent, only of two days' existence, while its Creator alone is real and eternal.

"Janaka and sages like him worked in the world at the command of God.

(*To Bankim*) "Some people think that God cannot be realized without the study of books and scriptures. They think that first of all one should learn of this world and its creatures; that first of all one should study 'science'. (*All laugh.*) They think that one cannot realize God without first understanding His creation. Which comes first, 'science' or God? What do you say?"

BANKIM: "I too think that we should first of all know about the different things of the world. How can we know of God without knowing something of this world? We should first learn from books."

MASTER: "That's the one cry from all of you. But God comes first and then the creation. After attaining God you can know everything else, if it is necessary.

"If you can somehow get yourself introduced to Jadu Mallick, then you will be able to learn, if you want to, the number of his houses and gardens and the amount of his money invested in government securities. Jadu Mallick himself will tell you all about them. But if you haven't met him and if you are stopped by his door-keepers when you try to enter his house, then how will you get the correct information about his houses, gardens, and government securities? When you know God you know all else; but then you don't care to know small things. The same thing is stated in the Vedas. You talk about the virtues of a person as long as you haven't seen him, but no sooner does he appear before you than all such talk stops. You are beside yourself with joy simply to be with him. You feel overwhelmed by simply conversing with him. You don't talk about his virtues any more.

"First realize God, then think of the creation and other things. Vālmiki was given the name of Rāma to repeat as his mantra, but was told at first to repeat 'marā'. 'Ma' means God and 'rā' the world. First God and then the world. If you know one you know all. If you put fifty zeros after a one, you have a large sum; but erase the one and nothing remains. It is the one that makes the many. First one, then many. First God, then His creatures and the world.

"The one thing you need is to realize God. Why do you bother so much about the world, creation, 'science', and all that? Your business is to eat mangoes. What need have you to know how many hundreds of trees there are in the orchard, how many thousands of branches, and how many millions of leaves? You have come to the garden to eat mangoes. Go and eat them. Man is born in this world to realize God; it is not good to forget that and divert the mind to other things. You have come to eat mangoes. Eat the mangoes and be happy."

BANKIM: "Where do we get the mangoes?"

MASTER: "Pray to God with a longing heart. He will surely listen to your prayer if it is sincere. Perhaps He will direct you to holy men with whom you can keep company; and that will help you on your spiritual path. Perhaps someone will tell you, 'Do this and you will attain God.'"

BANKIM: "Who? The guru? He enjoys all the good mangoes himself and gives us the bad ones!" (*Laughter.*)

MASTER: "Why should that be so? The mother knows what food suits the stomachs of her different children. Can all of them digest pilau and kālia? Suppose a fish has been procured. The mother doesn't give pilau and kālia to all the children. For the weak child with a poor stomach she prepares simple soup. But does that mean she loves him the less?

"One must have faith in the guru's words. The guru is none other than Satchidānanda. God Himself is the Guru. If you only believe his words like a child, you will realize God. What faith a child has! When a child's mother says to him about a certain man, 'He is your brother', the child believes he really is his brother. The child believes it one hundred and twenty-five per cent, though he may be the son of a brāhmin, and the man the son of a blacksmith. The mother says to the child, 'There is a bugaboo in that room', and the child really believes there is a bugaboo in the room. Such is the faith of a child! One must have this childlike faith in the guru's words. God cannot be realized by a mind that is hypocritical, calculating, or argumentative. One must have faith and sincerity. Hypocrisy will not do. To the sincere, God is very near; but He is far, far away from the hypocrite.

"One must have for God the yearning of a child. The child sees nothing but confusion when his mother is away. You may try to cajole him by putting a sweetmeat in his hand; but he will not be fooled. He only says, 'No, I want to go to my mother.' One must feel such yearning for God. Ah, what yearning! How restless a child feels for his mother! Nothing can make him forget his mother. He to whom the enjoyment of worldly happiness appears tasteless, he who takes no delight in anything of the world—money, name, creature comforts, sense pleasure—, becomes sincerely grief-stricken for the vision of the Mother. And to him alone the Mother comes running, leaving all Her other duties.

"Ah, that restlessness is the whole thing. Whatever path you follow—whether you are a Hindu, a Mussalmān, a Christian, a Śākta, a Vaishnava, or a Brāhmo—the vital point is restlessness. God is our Inner Guide. It doesn't matter if you take a wrong path—only you must be restless for Him. He Himself will put you on the right path.

"Besides, there are errors in all paths. Everyone thinks his watch is right; but as a matter of fact no watch is absolutely right. But that doesn't hamper one's work. If a man is restless for God he gains the company of sādhus and as far as possible corrects his own watch with the sādhus' help."

Trailokya of the Brāhmo Samāj began to sing. Presently Sri Ramakrishna stood up and lost consciousness of the outer world. He became completely indrawn, absorbed in samādhi. The devotees stood around him in a circle. Pushing aside the crowd, Bankim came near the Master and began to watch him attentively. He had never seen anyone in samādhi.

After a few minutes Sri Ramakrishna regained partial consciousness and began to dance in an ecstatic mood. It was a never-to-be-forgotten scene. Bankim and his Anglicized friends looked at him in amazement. Was this the God-intoxicated state? The devotees also watched him with wondering eyes.

The singing and dancing over, the Master touched the ground with his forehead, saying, "Bhāgavata—Bhakta—Bhagavān! Salutations to the jnānis, yogis, and bhaktas! Salutations to all!" He sat down again and all sat around him.

BANKIM (to the Master): "Sir, how can one develop divine love?"

MASTER: "Through restlessness—the restlessness a child feels for his mother. The child feels bewildered when he is separated from his mother, and weeps longingly for her. If a man can weep like that for God he can even see Him.

"At the approach of dawn the eastern horizon becomes red. Then one knows it will soon be sunrise. Likewise, if you see a person restless for God, you can be pretty certain that he hasn't long to wait for His vision.

"A disciple asked his teacher, 'Sir, please tell me how I can see God.' 'Come with me,' said the guru, 'and I shall show you.' He took the disciple to a lake, and both of them got into the water. Suddenly the teacher pressed the disciple's head under the water. After a few moments he released him and the disciple raised his head and stood up. The guru asked him, 'How did you feel?' The disciple said, 'Oh! I thought I should die; I was panting for breath.' The teacher said, 'When you feel like that for God, then you will know you haven't long to wait for His vision.'

(To Bankim) "Let me tell you something. What will you gain by floating on the surface? Dive a little under the water. The gems lie deep under the water; so what is the good of throwing your arms and legs about on the surface? A real gem is heavy. It doesn't float; it sinks to the bottom. To get the real gem you must dive deep."

BANKIM: "Sir, what can we do? We are tied to a cork. It prevents us from diving." (All laugh.)

MASTER: "All sins vanish if one only remembers God. His name breaks the fetters of death. You must dive; otherwise you can't get the gem. Listen to a song."

The Master sang in his sweet voice:

> Dive deep, O mind, dive deep in the Ocean of God's Beauty;
> If you descend to the uttermost depths,
> There you will find the gem of Love.
>
> Go seek, O mind, go seek Vrindāvan in your heart,
> Where with His loving devotees
> Sri Krishna sports eternally.
>
> Light up, O mind, light up true wisdom's shining lamp,
> And let it burn with steady flame
> Unceasingly within your heart.
>
> Who is it that steers your boat across the solid earth?
> It is your guru, says Kubir;
> Meditate on his holy feet.

All listened spellbound. Again Sri Ramakrishna began to talk.

MASTER (to Bankim): "There are some who do not want to dive. They say, 'Won't we become deranged if we go to excess about God?' Referring to those who are intoxicated with divine love, they say, 'These people have lost their heads.' But they don't understand this simple thing: God is the Ocean of Amrita, Immortality. Once I said to Narendra: 'Suppose there were a cup of syrup and you were a fly. Where would you sit to drink the syrup?' Narendra said, 'I would sit on the edge of the cup and stretch out my neck to drink it.' 'Why?' I asked. 'What's the harm of plunging into the middle of the cup and drinking the syrup?' Narendra answered, 'Then I should stick in the syrup and die.' 'My child,' I said to him, 'that isn't the nature of the Nectar of Satchidānanda. It is the Nectar of Immortality. Man does not die from diving into It. On the contrary he becomes immortal.'

"Therefore I say, dive deep. Don't be afraid. By diving deep in God one becomes immortal."

Bankim bowed low before the Master. He was about to take his leave.

BANKIM: "Sir, I am not such an idiot as you may think. I have a prayer to make. Please be kind enough to grace my house with the dust of your holy feet."

MASTER: "That's nice. I shall go if God wills."

BANKIM: "There too you will see devotees of God."

MASTER (smiling): "How so? What kind of devotees are they? Are they like those who said, 'Gopāl! Gopāl! Keśava! Keśava!'?" (All laugh.)

A DEVOTEE: "What is the story of 'Gopāl', sir?"

MASTER (smiling): "Let me tell you. At a certain place there is a goldsmith's shop. The workers there are known as pious Vaishnavas: they have strings of beads around their necks, religious marks on their foreheads, and bags containing rosaries in their hands. They repeat the names of God aloud. One can almost call them sādhus; only they have to work as goldsmiths to earn their bread and support their wives and children. Many customers, hearing of their piety, come to the shop because they believe that in that shop there will be no trickery with their gold or silver. When the customers enter the shop, they see the workers repeating the name of Hari with their tongues and doing their work with their hands. No sooner do the customers take seats in the shop than one of the workers cries out, 'Keśava! Keśava! Keśava!' A few minutes later another says, 'Gopāl! Gopāl! Gopāl!' After they talk a little while, the third man cries out, 'Hari! Hari! Hari!' In the mean time the customers have almost finished their transactions. Then the fourth exclaims, 'Hara! Hara! Hara!' The customers are very much impressed with the devotion and fervour of the owners and feel themselves quite secure in handing them the money. They are sure they won't be cheated.

"But do you know what lies behind all this? The man who says 'Keśava! Keśava!'[3] after the arrival of the customers means, 'Who are they?' In other words, he wants to know how intelligent they are. The man who says 'Gopāl! Gopāl!' means to say he finds them no better than a *herd of cows*. The man saying 'Hari! Hari!' means, '*May I rob them?*'; he suggests that since they are like a herd of cows they can be robbed. And the last man, who says 'Hara! Hara!', replies, '*Yes, rob them.*' He means that since the

[3] These four names of God have a double meaning in Bengali. The second meaning of each word is given in italics.

customers are like a herd of cows, they can certainly be robbed. Here, too, you see a group of pious men, very much devoted to God!" (*All laugh.*)

Bankim took his leave; but he was absent-minded. When he reached the door he discovered that he had dropped his shawl in the room; he was in his shirt-sleeves. A gentleman handed him his shawl.

Of the devotees at Adhar's house, Sarat[4] and Sannyal were brāhmins. But Adhar belonged to the lower caste of the goldsmiths, and so the two brāhmins quickly left, lest they should be pressed by their host to take their meal there. Sarat and Sannyal had been coming to the Master only a short time and did not know how fond the Master was of Adhar. The Master used to say that the devotees formed a separate caste by themselves; among them there could be no caste distinction.

Adhar entertained the Master and the devotees with a feast. It was quite late in the evening when the devotees returned home, cherishing in their hearts the image of the Master in his spiritual ecstasy and remembering his words of great wisdom.

Since Bankim had invited Sri Ramakrishna to visit his home, the Master a few days later sent Girish and M. to his Calcutta residence. At that time Bankim had a long discussion with these two devotees about the Master. He told them that he wanted to visit Sri Ramakrishna again. But his desire was not fulfilled.

[4] Sarat became a monastic disciple of Sri Ramakrishna under the name of Swami Saradananda.

Sri Ramakrishna in samādhi

Sri Ramakrishna

Sarada Devi, afterwards known as the Holy Mother

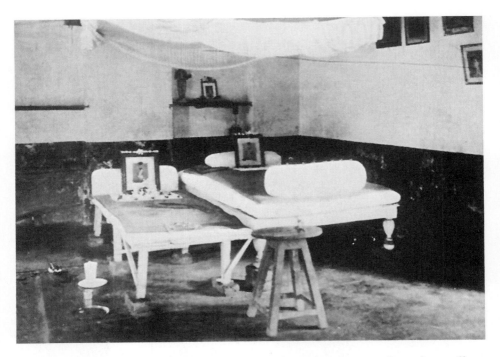

Sri Ramakrishna's room (The Master talked to the devotees from the smaller couch and slept on the larger couch.)

The Panchavati (The place of the Master's sādhanā)

The temple garden at Dakshineswar (Facing the Ganges are the twelve Śiva temples, with the chāndni, or portico, in the middle and Sri Ramakrishna's room at the left. Behind them is the Kāli temple, and to the extreme left and right are the two nahabats.)

Sri Ramakrishna's birth-place at Kāmārpukur

At left: The room where Sri Ramakrishna was born

Below: The Holy Mother's residence at Jayrāmbāti

Sri Ramakrishna
(*This picture was taken on December 9, 1881.*)

Mahendranath Gupta, or M. (The recorder of The Gospel of Sri Ramakrishna *in Bengali)*

Keshab Chandra Sen

Girish Chandra Ghosh

Mathurnath Biswas

Kāli, the Divine Mother, also known as Bhavatārini, the Saviour of the Universe (Sri Ramakrishna worshipped this image in the Dakshineswar temple.)

The Dakshineswar temples: view from the Ganges

The semicircular porch outside the Master's room (next to the Śiva temples)

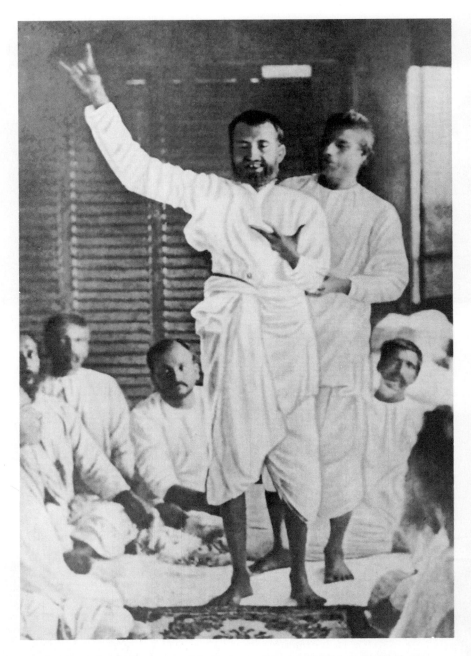

Sri Ramakrishna in samādhi during a kirtan at Keshab Sen's house
(The Master is supported by Hriday.)

Swami Brahmananda (Rakhal)

Swami Turiyananda (Hari)

Swami Premananda (Baburam)

Swami Saradananda (Sarat)

Swami Vivekananda (Narendranath) as a wandering monk after Sri Ramakrishna's passing away

A group of devotees, standing by the Master's body after his passing away

(1) Mahendra, or M.	(15) Vaikuntha	(25) Niranjan
(3) Kali	(17) Manomohan	(26) Narendra
(5) Sarat	(18) Harish	(27) Ramchandra Dutta
(6) Mani Mallick	(19) Narayan	(28) Balaram Bose
(7) Gangadhar	(21) Sashi	(29) Rakhal
(8) Navagopal	(22) Latu	(30) Nityagopal
(11) Tarak	(23) Bhavanath	(31) Jogin
(13) The elder Gopal	(24) Baburam	(32) Devendra

The Cossipore Garden House

AT THE STAR THEATRE (II)

SRI RAMAKRISHNA arrived at the Star Theatre on Beadon Street in Calcutta to see a play about the life of Prahlāda. M., Baburam, Narayan, and other devotees were with him. The hall was brightly lighted. The play had not yet begun. The Master was seated in a box, talking with Girish.

MASTER (*smiling*): "Ah! You have written nice plays."

GIRISH: "But, sir, how little I assimilate! I just write."

MASTER: "No, you assimilate a great deal. The other day I said to you that no one could sketch a divine character unless he had love of God in his heart.

"Yes, one needs to assimilate spiritual ideas. I went to Keshab's house to see the play, *Nava-Vrindāvan*. I saw a deputy magistrate there who earned eight hundred rupees a month. Everyone said that he was a very learned man; but I found him restless because of a boy, his son. He was very anxious to find a good seat for the boy; he paid no attention to the spiritual conversation of the players. The boy was pestering him with questions: 'Father! What is this? What is that?' He was extremely busy with the boy. You see, he merely read books; but he didn't assimilate their ideas."

GIRISH: "I often ask myself, 'Why bother about the theatre any more?' "

MASTER: "No, no! Let things be as they are. People will learn much from your plays."

The performance began. Prahlāda was seen entering the schoolroom as a student. At the sight of him Sri Ramakrishna uttered once or twice the word "Prahlāda" and went into samādhi.

During another scene Sri Ramakrishna wept to see Prahlāda under an elephant's feet. He cried when the boy was thrown into the fire.

The scene changed. Lakshmi and Nārāyana were seen seated in Goloka. Nārāyana was worried about Prahlāda. This scene, too, threw Sri Ramakrishna into an ecstatic mood.

After the performance Girish conducted Sri Ramakrishna to his private room in the theatre. He said to the Master, "Would you care to see the farce, *Vivāha Vibhrāta* ['The Confusion of Marriage']?"

MASTER: "Oh, no! Why something like that after the life of Prahlāda? I once said to the leader of a theatrical troupe, 'End your performance with some religious talk.' We have been listening to such wonderful spiritual conversation; and now to see 'The Confusion of Marriage'! A worldly topic! We should become our old selves again. We should return to our old mood."

GIRISH: "How did you like the performance?"

MASTER: "I found that it was God Himself who was acting the different parts. Those who played the female parts seemed to me the direct embodiments of the Blissful Mother, and the cowherd boys of Goloka the embodiments of Nārāyana Himself. It was God alone who had become all these.

"There are signs by which you can know whether a man has truly seen God. One of these is joy; there is no hesitancy in him. He is like the ocean: the waves and sounds are on the surface; below are profound depths. The man who has seen God behaves sometimes like a madman; sometimes like a ghoul, without any feeling of purity or impurity; sometimes like an inert thing, remaining speechless because he sees God within and without; sometimes like a child, without any attachment, wandering about unconcernedly with his cloth under his arm. Again, in the mood of a child, he acts in different ways: sometimes like a boy, indulging in frivolity; sometimes like a young man, working and teaching with the strength of a lion.

"Man cannot see God on account of his ego. You cannot see the sun when a cloud rises in the sky. But that doesn't mean there is no sun; the sun is there just the same.

"But there is no harm in the 'ego of a child'. On the contrary, this ego is helpful. Greens are bad for the stomach; but hinchē is good. So hinchē cannot properly be called greens. Sugar candy, likewise, cannot be classed with other sweets. Other sweets are injurious to the health, but not sugar candy.

"So I said to Keshab, 'If I tell you more than I have already said, you won't be able to keep your organization together.' That frightened him. Then I said to him, 'There is no harm in the "ego of a child" or the "ego of a servant".'

"He who has seen God finds that God alone has become the world and all its living beings; it is He who has become all. Such a person is called a superior devotee."

GIRISH (smiling): "Yes, God is everything. But the devotee keeps a trace of ego; that is not harmful."

MASTER (smiling): "Yes, there is no harm in that. That trace of ego is kept in order to enjoy God. You can enjoy divine bliss only when you make a distinction between yourself and God—the distinction between the servant and the Master.

"There is also the devotee of the mediocre class: he sees that God dwells in all beings as their Inner Guide. But the inferior devotee says, 'God exists; He is up there', that is to say, beyond the sky. (All laugh.)

"When I saw the cowherd boys of Goloka in your performance I felt that God has become all. He who has seen God knows truly that God alone is the Doer, that it is He who does everything."

GIRISH: "Sir, I know truly that it is God who does everything."

MASTER: "I say, 'O Mother, I am the machine and You are the Operator;

I am inert and You make me conscious; I do as You make me do; I speak as You make me speak.' But the ignorant say, 'I am partly responsible, and God is partly responsible.' "

GIRISH: "Sir, I am not really doing anything. Why should I bother about work at all?"

MASTER: "No, work is good. When the ground is well cultivated and cleared of stones and pebbles, whatever you plant will grow. But one should work without any personal motive.

"There are two types of paramahamsas: the jnāni and the premi.[1] The jnāni is self-centred; he feels that it is enough to have Knowledge for his own self. The premi, like Śukadeva, after attaining his own realization, teaches men. Some eat mangoes and wipe off the traces from their mouths; but some share their mangoes with others. Spades and baskets are needed to dig a well. After the digging is over, some throw the spades and baskets into the well. But others put them away; for a neighbour may use them. Śukadeva and a few others kept the spades and baskets for the benefit of others. (*To Girish*) You should do the same."

GIRISH: "Please bless me, sir."

MASTER: "Have faith in the Divine Mother and you will attain everything."

GIRISH: "But I am a sinner."

MASTER: "The wretch who constantly harps on sin becomes a sinner."

GIRISH: "Sir, the very ground where I used to sit would become unholy."

MASTER: "How can you say that? Suppose a light is brought into a room that has been dark a thousand years; does it illumine the room little by little, or all in a flash?"

GIRISH: "Then you have blessed me."

MASTER: "If you sincerely believe it. What more shall I say? I eat and drink and chant the name of God."

GIRISH: "I have no sincerity. Please give it to me."

MASTER: "I? Sages like Nārada and Śukadeva could have done that."

GIRISH: "I don't see Nārada and Śukadeva. But you are here before me."

MASTER (*smiling*): "All right. You have faith."

All remained silent. The conversation began again.

GIRISH: "I have one desire: love of God for its own sake."

MASTER: "Only the Iśvarakotis have such love. It is not for ordinary men."

All sat in silence. The Master began to sing in an absent-minded mood, his gaze turned upward:

> Can everyone have the vision of Śyāmā? Is Kāli's treasure for
>   everyone?
> Oh, what a pity my foolish mind will not see what is true!
> Even with all His penances, rarely does Śiva Himself behold
> The mind-bewitching sight of Mother Śyāmā's crimson feet.
>
> To him who meditates on Her the riches of heaven are poor indeed;
> If Śyāmā casts Her glance on him, he swims in Eternal Bliss.

[1] Lover of God.

The Prince of yogis, the King of the gods, meditate on Her feet in
vain;
Yet worthless Kamalākānta yearns for the Mother's blessed feet!

Girish repeated:

Yet worthless Kamalākānta yearns for the Mother's blessed feet!

MASTER (to Girish): "One can realize God through intense renunciation.
But the soul must be restless for Him, as restless as one feels for a breath of
air when one's head is pressed under water.

"A man can see God if he unites in himself the force of these three attractions: the attraction of worldly possessions for the worldly man, the husband's attraction for the chaste wife, and the child's attraction for its mother.
If you can unite these three forms of love and give it all to God, then you
can see Him at once.

Cry to your Mother Śyāmā with a real cry, O mind!
And how can She hold Herself from you?

"If a devotee prays to God with real longing, God cannot help revealing
Himself to him.

"The other day I told you the meaning of bhakti. It is to adore God with
body, mind, and words. 'With body' means to serve and worship God with
one's hands, go to holy places with one's feet, hear the chanting of the name
and glories of God with one's ears, and behold the divine image with one's
eyes. 'With mind' means to contemplate and meditate on God constantly
and to remember and think of His līlā. 'With words' means to sing hymns to
Him and chant His name and glories.

"Devotion as described by Nārada is suited to the Kaliyuga. It means to
chant constantly the name and glories of God. Let those who have no leisure
worship God at least morning and evening by whole-heartedly chanting
His name and clapping their hands.

"The 'ego of a devotee' begets no pride; it does not create ignorance. On
the contrary it helps one realize God. This ego is no more like the ordinary
ego than hinchē is like ordinary greens. One generally becomes indisposed
by eating greens; but hinchē removes excessive bile; it does one good. Sugar
candy is not like ordinary sweets. Sweets are generally harmful, but sugar
candy removes acidity.

"Nishthā leads to bhakti; bhakti, when mature, becomes bhāva; bhāva,
when concentrated, becomes mahābhāva; and last of all is prema. Prema is
like a cord: by prema God is bound to the devotee; He can no longer run
away. An ordinary man can at best achieve bhāva. None but an Iśvarakoti
attains mahābhāva and prema. Chaitanyadeva attained them.

"What is the meaning of jnānayoga? It is the path by which a man can
realize the true nature of his own Self; it is the awareness that Brahman
alone is his true nature. Prahlāda sometimes was aware of his identity with
Brahman. And sometimes he would see that God was one and he another;
at such times he would remain in the mood of bhakti.

"Hanumān said, 'O Rāma, sometimes I find that You are the whole and I a part, sometimes that You are the Master and I Your servant; but, O Rāma, when I have the Knowledge of Reality, I see that You are I and I am You.' "

GIRISH: "Ah!"

MASTER: "Why shouldn't a man be able to realize God in the world? But he must have discrimination and dispassion; he must have the unshakable awareness that God alone is real and all else is unreal and has but a two-days' existence. It will not do to float on the surface. You must dive deep."

With these words, the Master sang:

> Dive deep, O mind, dive deep in the Ocean of God's Beauty;
> If you descend to the uttermost depths,
> There you will find the gem of Love. . . .

MASTER: "You must remember another thing: in the ocean there is danger of alligators, that is to say, of lust and the like."

GIRISH: "I am not afraid of the King of Death."

MASTER: "But I am speaking of the danger of the alligators of lust and the like. Because of them one should smear one's body with turmeric before diving in—the turmeric of discrimination and dispassion.

"Some attain knowledge of God in the world. Mention is made of two classes of yogis: the hidden and the known. Those who have renounced the world are 'known' yogis: all recognize them. But the 'hidden' yogis live in the world. They are not known. They are like the maidservant who performs her duties in the house but whose mind is fixed on her children in the country. They are also, as I have told you, like the loose woman who performs her household duties zealously but whose mind constantly dwells on her lover. It is very hard to cultivate discrimination and dispassion. It is not easy to get rid of the idea, 'I am the master and all these are mine.' I saw a deputy magistrate, who earns a salary of eight hundred rupees, paying no attention to a religious discourse. He had brought one of his children with him and was busy finding a good place for him to sit. I know another man, whom I shall not name, who used to devote a great deal of time to japa; but he bore false witness in court for the sake of ten thousand rupees. Therefore I say that a man can realize God in the world, too, but only if he has discrimination and dispassion."

GIRISH: "What will happen to this sinner?"

Sri Ramakrishna sang in a tender voice, turning his eyes upward:

> Meditate on the Lord, the Slayer of hell's dire woes,
> He who removes the fear of death;
> Thinking of Him, the soul is freed from worldly grief
> And sails across the sea of life in the twinkling of an eye.
>
> Consider, O my mind, why you have come to earth;
> What gain is there in evil thoughts and deeds?
> Your way lies not through these: perform your penance here
> By meditating long and deep on the everlasting Lord.

MASTER: " 'Sails across the sea of life in the twinkling of an eye.' One attains the vision of God if Mahāmāyā steps aside from the door. Mahāmāyā's grace is necessary: hence the worship of Śakti. You see, God is near us, but it is not possible to know Him because Mahāmāyā stands between. Rāma, Lakshmana, and Sītā were walking along. Rāma walked ahead, Sītā in the middle, and Lakshmana last. Lakshmana was only two and a half cubits away from Rāma, but he couldn't see Rāma because Sītā—Mahāmāyā— was in the way.

"While worshipping God, one should assume a definite attitude. I have three attitudes: the attitude of a child, the attitude of a maidservant, and the attitude of a friend. For a long time I regarded myself as a maidservant and a woman companion of God; at that time I used to wear skirts and ornaments, like a woman. The attitude of a child is very good.

"The attitude of a 'hero' is not good. Some people cherish it. They regard themselves as Purusha and woman as Prakriti; they want to propitiate woman through intercourse with her. But this method often causes disaster."

GIRISH: "At one time I too cherished that idea."

Sri Ramakrishna looked at Girish pensively.

GIRISH: "I still have that twist in my mind. Tell me what I should do."

Sri Ramakrishna reflected a minute and said, "Give God your power of attorney. Let Him do whatever He likes."

The conversation then turned to Sri Ramakrishna's young devotees.

MASTER (to Girish and the others): "In meditation I see the inner traits of these youngsters. They have no thought of acquiring house and property. They do not crave sex pleasure. Those of the youngsters who are married do not sleep with their wives. The truth is that unless a man has got rid of rajas and has acquired sattva, he cannot steadily dwell in God; he cannot love God and realize Him."

GIRISH: "You have blessed me."

MASTER: "How is that? I said that you would succeed if you were sincere."

Saying this, the Master exclaimed, "Ānandamayi!" and went into samādhi. He remained in that state a long time. Regaining partial consciousness, he said, "Where are those rascals?" M. brought Baburam to him. Sri Ramakrishna looked at Baburam and the other devotees and said, still in ecstasy, "The bliss of Satchidānanda is indeed good; but what about the bliss of divine inebriation?"

He began to sing:

> Once for all, this time, I have thoroughly understood;
> From One who knows it well, I have learnt the secret of bhāva. . . .

Again he sang:

> Why should I go to Gangā or Gayā, to Kāśi, Kānchi, or Prabhās,
> So long as I can breathe my last with Kāli's name upon my
>   lips? . . .

The Master continued, saying, "While praying to the Divine Mother, I said, 'O Mother, I don't seek anything else: give me only pure love for Thee.'"

Sri Ramakrishna was pleased with Girish's calm mood. He said to him, "This mood of yours is good; the calm mood is the best."

The Master was seated in the manager's room. A man entered and said, "Will you see the farce. 'The Confusion of Marriage'? It is being played now."

Sri Ramakrishna said to Girish: "What have you done? This farce after the life of Prahlāda! First sweets and rice pudding and then a dish of bitter herbs!"

After the theatre, the actresses, following Girish's instructions, came to the room to salute Sri Ramakrishna. They bowed before him, touching the ground with their foreheads. The devotees noticed that some of the actresses, in saluting the Master, touched his feet. He said to them very tenderly, "Please don't do that, mother!"

After the actresses had left the room, Sri Ramakrishna said to the devotees, "It is all He, only in different forms."

The carriage was ready at the door. Girish and the others came to the street to see the Master off. As soon as Sri Ramakrishna stepped into the carriage, he went into deep samādhi. Narayan and several other devotees were with him. The carriage started for Dakshineswar.

Saturday, December 27, 1884

It was the Christmas season. Taking advantage of the holiday, many devotees came to the temple garden to visit the Master, some of them arriving in the morning. Among these were Kedar, Ram, Nityagopal, Tarak, Surendra, M., Sarada Prasanna, and a number of young devotees. This was Sarada Prasanna's first visit.

MASTER (to M.): "Where is Bankim? Haven't you brought him with you?"

Bankim was a schoolboy whom Sri Ramakrishna had met in Bāghbāzār. Noticing him even from a distance, the Master had said that he was a fine boy.

After a while Sri Ramakrishna went to the Panchavati with the devotees. They surrounded him, some sitting and some standing. He was seated on the cement platform around the tree, facing the southwest. He asked M. with a smile, "Have you brought the book?"

M: "Yes, sir."

MASTER: "Read a little to me."

The devotees were eager to know the name of the book. It was called *Devi Choudhurāni*. The Master had heard that the book dealt with motiveless action. He had also heard of the great renown of its author, Bankim Chandra Chatterji, whom he had met some days before, and he wanted to gauge the author's mind from the book.

M. said: "A young girl—the heroine—fell into the hands of a robber named Bhavani Pathak. Her name had been Prafulla, but the robber changed it to 'Devi Choudhurāni'. At heart Bhavani was a good man. He made Prafulla go through many spiritual disciplines; he also taught her how to perform selfless action. He robbed wicked people and with that money fed the poor and helpless. He said to Prafulla, 'I chastise the wicked and protect the virtuous.' "

MASTER: "But that is a king's duty."

M: "In one place the author writes of bhakti. Bhavani Pathak sent a girl named Nishi to keep Prafulla company. Nishi was full of piety and looked on Krishna as her husband. Prafulla was already married; she had lost her father and lived with her mother. The neighbours had created a scandal about her character and avoided her, and so her father-in-law had not allowed her to live with his son. Later her husband had married again; but Prafulla was extremely devoted to her husband.

(*To Sri Ramakrishna*) "Now, sir, you can follow the story."

M. read:

> NISHI: "I am a daughter of Bhavani Pathak. He is my father. He has also, in a way, given me in marriage."
>
> PRAFULLA: "What do you mean?"
>
> NISHI: "I have surrendered my all to Krishna."
>
> PRAFULLA: "How is that?"
>
> NISHI: "My beauty, youth, and soul."
>
> PRAFULLA: "Then He is your husband."
>
> NISHI: "Yes, because he alone is my husband who completely possesses me."
>
> PRAFULLA (*with a sigh*): "I do not know. You talk that way because you do not know what a husband is. If you had a real husband, you could never have liked Sri Krishna."
>
> The foolish Brajeswar—Prafulla's husband—was unaware that his wife loved him so much.
>
> NISHI: "All can love Sri Krishna, because He has infinite beauty, infinite youth, and infinite splendour."
>
> This young lady was a disciple of Bhavani and well-versed in logic. But Prafulla was illiterate; she could not answer Nishi's arguments. But the writers of the Hindu social laws knew the reply. God is infinite, no doubt; but one cannot keep the infinite in the small cage of the heart. One can do so only with the finite. Therefore the infinite Creator of the universe is worshipped by the Hindu in the cage of his heart as Sri Krishna, the finite Personal God. The husband of a woman has a still more definite form. Therefore if the wife cherishes pure conjugal love, the husband becomes the first step toward God. Hence the husband is the only Deity to the Hindu woman. Other societies are inferior to Hindu society in this respect.
>
> Prafulla was an ignorant girl; she could not understand Nishi's arguments. She said, "Friend, I do not understand all these arguments; but you haven't yet told me your name."
>
> NISHI: "Bhavani Pathak has given me the name of Nishi, Night. I am the sister of Divā, Day. One day I shall introduce my sister to you. Let me continue what I was saying. God alone is the real Husband; and to a woman the husband is her only God. Sri Krishna is the God of all. Why should we cherish two Deities, two Gods? If you divide the little bhakti of this small heart, how little there will be!"
>
> PRAFULLA: "Don't be silly. Is there any limit to a woman's bhakti?"

NISHI: "There is no end to a woman's *love*. But bhakti is one thing, and love another."

Summarizing part of the book, M. said that Bhavani initiated Prafulla into spiritual life.

He continued reading:

> During the first year Bhavani did not allow any man to enter Prafulla's house nor did he allow her to speak to any man outside the house. During the second year the rule about speaking was withdrawn, but no man was allowed inside her house. In the third year Prafulla shaved her head. Now Bhavani allowed his select disciples to see her. The shaven-headed disciple would converse with them on scriptural topics, keeping her eyes cast on the ground.

M. then read that Prafulla began the study of the scriptures; that she finished grammar and read *Raghuvamsa, Kumāra Sambhava, Śakuntalā,* and *Naishādha*; and that she studied a little of the Sāmkhya, Vedānta, and Nyāya philosophies.

MASTER: "Do you know what that means? People like the author of this book believe that knowledge is impossible without the study of books. They think that first comes the knowledge of books and then comes the knowledge of God. In order to know God one must read books! But if I want to know Jadu Mallick, must I first know the number of his houses and the amount of money he has in government securities? Do I really need all this information? Rather I should somehow enter his house, be it by flattering his gate-keepers or by disregarding their rough treatment, and talk to Jadu Mallick himself. Then, if I want to know about his wealth or possessions, I shall only have to ask him about them. Then it will be a very easy matter for me. First comes Rāma, then His riches, that is, the universe. This is why Vālmiki repeated the mantra, 'marā'. 'Ma' means God, and 'rā' the world, that is to say, His riches."

The devotees listened to the Master's words with rapt attention.

M. continued with the story of Prafulla:

> Prafulla finished her studies and then practised spiritual austerity for many days. Then one day Bhavani visited her; he wanted to instruct her about selfless work. He quoted to her from the *Gītā*: "Therefore do thou always perform obligatory actions without attachment; by performing action without attachment one attains to the highest."
>
> He told her the three characteristics of disinterested action: first, control of the sense-organs; second, absence of egotism; and third, surrendering the fruit of action to Sri Krishna. He further told her that no dharma is possible for the egotistic person. Quoting from the *Gītā*, he said: "The gunas of Prakriti perform all action. With the understanding deluded by egotism, man thinks, I am the doer."
>
> Bhavani next spoke to her about surrendering the fruit of action to Sri Krishna. Again he quoted from the *Gītā*: "Whatever thou doest, whatever thou eatest, whatever thou givest away, whatever austerity thou practisest, O son of Kunti, do that as an offering unto Me."

MASTER: "This is fine. These are the words of the *Gītā*; one cannot refute them. But something else must be noted. The author speaks about surrendering the fruit of action to Sri Krishna, but not about cultivating bhakti for Him."

M: "No, that is not especially mentioned here.

"Next Prafulla and Bhavani talked about the use of money. Prafulla said that she offered all her wealth to Krishna."

M. read from the book again.

> PRAFULLA: "Like my actions, I offer all my wealth to Sri Krishna."
> BHAVANI: "All?"
> PRAFULLA: "Yes, all."
> BHAVANI: "In that case you won't be able to perform action in a detached spirit. If you have to work to earn your food, you will be attached to that work. Hence there are two alternatives before you: either you will have to get your food by begging, or you will have to live on your money. Even a beggar becomes attached to the alms he receives; therefore you must use your own money to maintain your body."

M. (*to the Master, smiling*): "That is the nature of the calculating mind."

MASTER: "Yes, that is the nature of the calculating mind; that is the way the worldly man thinks. But he who seeks God plunges headlong; he doesn't calculate about how much or how little he needs for the protection of his body."

M: "Next Bhavani asked Prafulla, 'How will you offer all this money to Sri Krishna?' Prafulla said: 'Why, Sri Krishna dwells in all beings. I shall distribute the money among them.' Bhavani answered, 'Good! Good!'

"Quoting from the *Gītā*, Bhavani said: 'He who sees Me in all things and all things in Me, never becomes separated from Me, nor do I become separated from him. That yogi who, established in unity, worships Me dwelling in all beings, abides in Me, whatever his mode of life. O Arjuna, that yogi is regarded as the highest who judges the pleasure and pain of all beings by the same standard that he applies to himself.'"

MASTER: "These are the characteristics of the highest bhakta."

M. again read from the book:

> A man must work hard if he wants to help all beings with charity. Hence it is necessary for him to make a little display of clothes, of pomp and luxury. Therefore Bhavani said, "A little shopkeeping is necessary."

MASTER (*sharply*): " 'A little shopkeeping is necessary'! One speaks as one thinks. If a man thinks of worldly things day and night, and deals with people hypocritically, then his words are coloured by his thoughts. If one eats radish, one belches radish. Instead of talking about 'shopkeeping', he should rather have said, 'A man should act as if he were the doer, knowing very well that he is really not the doer.' The other day a man was singing here. The song contained words like 'profit' and 'loss'. I stopped him. If one contemplates a particular subject day and night, one cannot talk of anything else."

The reading continued. The author was describing the realization of God. Prafulla had become Devi Choudhurāni. It was the month of Vaiśākh. Devi was seated on the roof of her house-boat talking with Divā and another woman companion. The moon was up. The boat had cast anchor in the Ganges. The conversation turned to the question of whether one could see God. Devi said, "As the aroma of a flower is directly perceived by the nose, so God is directly perceived by the mind."

At this point the Master interrupted and said: "Yes, God is directly perceived by the mind, but not by this ordinary mind. It is the pure mind that perceives God, and at that time this ordinary mind does not function. A mind that has the slightest trace of attachment to the world cannot be called pure. When all the impurities of the mind are removed, you may call that mind Pure Mind or Pure Ātman."

M: "The author says a little later that God cannot easily be perceived by the mind. He says that one needs a telescope to have that direct vision. Yoga is the telescope. Yoga, as it is described in the *Gītā*, is of three kinds: jnāna, bhakti, and karma. One is able to see God through this telescope of yoga."

MASTER: "That is very good. These are the words of the *Gītā*."

M: "At last Devi Choudhurāni met her husband. She showed him great devotion and said to him: 'You are my God. I wanted to learn the worship of another God but I did not succeed. You have taken the place of all gods.'"

MASTER (*smiling*): "'I did not succeed.' This is the dharma of a woman totally devoted to her husband. This also is a path."

The reading was over. The Master was smiling. The devotees looked at him, eagerly waiting to hear what he would say.

MASTER (*to the devotees, smiling*): "This is not so bad; it is called the dharma of chastity, the single-minded devotion of a wife to her husband. If God can be worshipped through an image, why shouldn't it be possible to worship Him through a living person? It is God Himself who sports in the world as men.

"Oh, what a state I passed through! I passed some days absorbed in Śiva and Durgā, some days absorbed in Rādhā and Krishna, and some days absorbed in Sītā and Rāma. Assuming Rādhā's attitude, I would cry for Krishna, and assuming Sītā's attitude, I would cry for Rāma.

"But līlā is by no means the last word. Passing through all these states, I said to the Divine Mother: 'Mother, in these states there is separation. Give me a state where there is no separation.' Then I remained for some time absorbed in the Indivisible Satchidānanda. I removed the pictures of the gods and goddesses from my room. I began to perceive God in all beings. Formal worship dropped away. You see that bel-tree. I used to go there to pluck its leaves. One day, as I plucked a leaf, a bit of the bark came off. I found the tree full of Consciousness. I felt grieved because I had hurt the tree. One day I tried to pluck some durvā grass, but I found I couldn't do it very well. Then I forced myself to pluck it.

"I cannot cut a lemon. The other day I managed to cut one only with great difficulty; I chanted the name of Kāli and cut the fruit as they slaughter an animal before the Goddess. One day I was about to gather some flowers.

They were everywhere on the trees. At once I had a vision of Virāt; it appeared that His worship was just over. The flowers looked like a bouquet placed on the head of the Deity. I could not pluck them.

"God sports through man as well. I see man as the embodiment of Nārāyana. As fire is kindled when you rub two pieces of wood together, so God can be seen in man if you have intense devotion. If there is suitable bait, big fish like carp gulp it down at once. When one is intoxicated with prema, one sees God in all beings. The gopis saw Krishna in everything; to them the whole world was filled with Krishna. They said that they themselves were Krishna. They were then in a God-intoxicated state. Looking at the trees, they said, 'These are hermits absorbed in meditation on Krishna.' Looking at the grass they said, 'The hair of the earth is standing on end at the touch of Krishna.'

"Devotion to the husband is also a dharma. The husband is God. Why shouldn't it be so? If God can be worshipped through an image, why not also through a living man? But three things are necessary in order to feel the presence of God in an image: first, the devotion of the priest; second, a beautiful image; and third, the devotion of the householder. Vaishnavcharan once said that in the end the mind of the devotee is absorbed in the human manifestation of God.

"But you must remember one thing. One cannot see God sporting as man unless one has had the vision of Him. Do you know the sign of one who has God-vision? Such a man acquires the nature of a child. Why a child? Because God is like a child. So he who sees God becomes like a child.

"God-vision is necessary. Now the question is, how can one get it? Intense renunciation is the means. A man should have such intense yearning for God that he can say, 'O Father of the universe, am I outside Your universe? Won't You be kind to me, You wretch?'

"You partake of the nature of him on whom you meditate. By worshipping Siva you acquire the nature of Siva. A devotee of Rāma meditated on Hanumān day and night. He used to think he had become Hanumān. In the end he was firmly convinced that he had even grown a little tail. Jnāna is the characteristic of Siva, and bhakti of Vishnu. One who partakes of Siva's nature becomes a jnāni, and one who partakes of Vishnu's nature becomes a bhakta."

M: "But what about Chaitanyadeva? You said he had both knowledge and devotion."

MASTER (sharply): "His case was different. He was an Incarnation of God. There is a great difference between him and an ordinary man. The fire of Chaitanya's renunciation was so great that when Sārvabhauma poured sugar on his tongue, instead of melting, it evaporated into air. He was always absorbed in samādhi. How great was his conquest of lust! To compare him with a man! A lion eats meat and yet it mates only once in twelve years; but a sparrow eats grain and it indulges in sex-life day and night. Such is the difference between a Divine Incarnation and an ordinary human being. An ordinary man renounces lust; but once in a while he forgets his vow. He cannot control himself.

(*To M.*) "He who has realized God looks on man as a mere worm. 'One cannot succeed in religious life if one has shame, hatred, or fear.' These are fetters. Haven't you heard of the eight fetters?

"How can one who is eternally perfect be afraid of the world? He knows how to play his game. An eternally perfect soul can even lead a worldly life if he desires. There are people who can fence with two swords at the same time; they are such expert fencers that, if stones are thrown at them, the stones hit the swords and come back."

A DEVOTEE: "Sir, how can one see God?"

MASTER: "Can you ever see God if you do not direct your whole mind toward Him? The *Bhāgavata* speaks about Śukadeva. When he walked about he looked like a soldier with fixed bayonet. His gaze did not wander; it had only one goal and that was God. This is the meaning of yoga.

"The chātak bird drinks only rain-water. Though the Ganges, the Jamunā, the Godāvari, and all other rivers are full of water, and though the seven oceans are full to the brim, still the chātak will not touch them. It will drink only the water that falls from the clouds.

"He who has developed such yoga can see God. In the theatre the audience remains engaged in all kinds of conversation, about home, office, and school, till the curtain goes up; but no sooner does it go up than all conversation comes to a stop, and the people watch the play with fixed attention. If after a long while someone utters a word or two, it is about the play.

"After a drunkard has drunk his liquor he talks only about the joy of drunkenness."

Nityagopal was seated in front of Sri Ramakrishna. He was always in ecstasy. He sat there in silence.

MASTER (*to Nityagopal, smiling*): "Gopal! Why are you always silent?"

Nityagopal answered like a child, "I—do—not—know."

MASTER: "I understand why you don't say anything; perhaps you are afraid of committing a transgression. You are right. Jaya and Vijaya were gate-keepers for Nārāyana. They refused Sanaka, Sanātana, and other rishis admission into His palace. For this transgression Jaya and Vijaya had to be born three times on earth.

"Again, there is the instance of Śridāma; he was Virajā's[2] gate-keeper in Goloka. Sri Krishna was in Virajā's house. Rādhikā went there to surprise Krishna and wanted to enter the house. Śridāma would not admit her, and so Rādhikā cursed him to be born as a demon on earth. But Śridāma, too, cursed her.

"But there is one thing you should remember. When a boy walks holding his father's hand, he may fall into the gutter; but what has he to fear if the father holds him by the hand?"

The story of Śridāma is narrated in the *Brahmavaivarta Purāna*.

Kedar, who was a government official, had been living at Dacca for some time. He had been transferred there from Calcutta. He was a devotee of Sri Ramakrishna and had gathered together at Dacca many devotees, who came to him regularly for spiritual instruction. As one should not come empty-

[2] A woman companion of Krishna.

handed to a religious man, the devotees would bring Kedar sweets and other offerings.

KEDAR (to the Master, humbly): "Should I eat those offerings?"

MASTER: "It won't injure you if the offerings are given out of love for God. But they are harmful if they are given with any selfish motive."

KEDAR: "I have explained everything to the devotees and now I feel relieved. I have told them that he[3] who has given me his blessing knows all."

MASTER (smiling): "That is true. You see, people of all sorts come here. So they find here different things."

KEDAR: "I do not need to know different things."

MASTER (smiling): "Why not? One should know a little of everything. If a man starts a grocery-shop, he keeps all kinds of articles there, including a little lentil and tamarind. An expert musician knows how to play a little on all instruments."

Sri Ramakrishna left the room and went toward the pine-grove. The devotees began to walk about in the garden. Several went to the Panchavati. Sri Ramakrishna met them there and said: "I have indigestion. I took a meal at the Mallicks'. They are very worldly people."

A few of the Master's personal things lay scattered on the cement platform of the Panchavati, and he asked M. to bring them. He proceeded to his room and the devotees followed.

In the afternoon the Master rested awhile. Afterwards a few devotees arrived. The Master sat on the small couch reclining against a pillow.

A DEVOTEE: "Sir, can one know God's attributes through the intellect?"

MASTER: "Certainly not by this ordinary intellect. Can one know God so easily? One must practise sādhana. One must also adopt a particular attitude toward God, for instance, the attitude of a servant toward his master. The rishis of old had the attitude of śānta. Do you know the attitude of the jnānis? It is to meditate on one's own Self. (To a devotee, with a smile) What is your attitude?"

The devotee gave no answer.

MASTER (smiling): "You have two attitudes: you meditate on your own Self and also cherish toward God the attitude of a servant. Am I not right?"

DEVOTEE (hesitating and smiling): "Yes, sir."

MASTER (smiling): "You see, as Hazra says, I can read people's thoughts.

"One can maintain those two attitudes only at a very advanced stage. Prahlāda maintained them. But one must work hard in order to practise this ideal.

"Let me give an illustration. Suppose a man is grasping the thorny branch of a plum-tree. His hand bleeds profusely; but he says, 'There is nothing the matter with me; I am not hurt.' If you ask him about his wound, he will say, 'It's all right; I am quite well.' Now is there any meaning in the mere utterance of these words? One must practise discipline in keeping with this ideal."

The devotees were giving their whole attention to what the Master was saying.

[3] Sri Ramakrishna.

THE MASTER'S BIRTHDAY

SRI RAMAKRISHNA was sitting on the northeast verandah outside his room at Dakshineswar. It was about eight o'clock in the morning. Many devotees, including Narendra, Rakhal, Girish, Baburam, and Surendra, were present. They were celebrating the Master's birthday, which had fallen on the previous Monday. M. arrived and saluted him. The Master signed to him to take a seat near him.

Narottam was singing kirtan. Sri Ramakrishna was in partial ecstasy. The subject was Krishna's meeting with His cowherd friends in the meadow. Krishna had not yet arrived. The cowherd boys were restless for Him. One of them said that Mother Yaśodā was preventing Krishna from coming. Balāi said in a determined voice that he would bring Krishna with the sound of his horn. Balāi's love for Krishna knew no bounds. The music went on. The cowherd boys and girls heard Krishna's flute and were filled with spiritual emotion.

Suddenly Sri Ramakrishna's eyes fell on Narendra, who was sitting very near him. He stood up and went into samādhi; he stood there touching Narendra's knee with his foot. Regaining consciousness he took his seat again. Narendra left the room. The music went on.

Sri Ramakrishna whispered to Baburam: "There is kshir in the room. Give Narendra some."

Did the Master see Narendra as the embodiment of God?

After the kirtan Sri Ramakrishna returned to his room. Tenderly he began to feed Narendra with sweets.

It was Girish's belief that God Himself had been born in the person of Sri Ramakrishna.

GIRISH (*to the Master*): "Your ways are like Krishna's. He too pretended many things to His mother Yaśodā."

MASTER: "True. It was because Krishna was an Incarnation of God. When God is born as a man He acts that way. You see, Krishna easily lifted the hill of Govardhan with His hand, but He made Nanda believe that He found it very hard to carry a footstool."

GIRISH: "Yes, sir, I have understood you now."

Sri Ramakrishna was sitting on the small couch. It was about eleven o'clock. Ram and the other devotees wanted to dress him in a new cloth. The Master said, "No, no." Pointing to an English-educated man, he said, "What will he say about it?" At the earnest request of the devotees he said, "Well, since you insist, I shall have to agree."

The devotees were arranging the Master's meal in the room. He asked Narendra to sing.

Narendra sang:

> In dense darkness, O Mother, Thy formless beauty sparkles;
> Therefore the yogis meditate in a dark mountain cave.
> In the lap of boundless dark, on Mahānirvāna's waves upborne,
> Peace flows serene and inexhaustible.
> Taking the form of the Void, in the robe of darkness wrapped,
> Who art Thou, Mother, seated alone in the shrine of samādhi?
> From the Lotus of Thy fear-scattering Feet flash Thy love's
> 　　lightnings;
> Thy Spirit-Face shines forth with laughter terrible and loud!

As Narendra sang the line, "Who art Thou, Mother, seated alone in the shrine of samādhi?", Sri Ramakrishna went into deep samādhi and lost all outer consciousness. After a long time, when he was regaining partial consciousness, the devotees seated him on the carpet and placed a plate of food before him. Still overcome with divine emotion, he began to eat the rice with both hands. He said to Bhavanath, "Feed me." Because of his ecstatic mood he could not use his own right hand. Bhavanath began to feed him. Sri Ramakrishna could eat very little. Ram said to him, "Nityagopal will eat from your plate."

MASTER: "Why from my plate? Why?"

RAM: "Why not?"

Nityagopal was also in an ecstatic mood. The Master put a morsel or two into his mouth with his own hand.

Some devotees from Konnagar arrived by boat. They entered Sri Ramakrishna's room singing kirtan; afterwards they went out to take some refreshments. Narottam was in the room. The Master said to him and the other devotees: "The music of the Konnagar devotees was dull. Music should be so lively as to make everyone dance. One should sing a song like this:

> See how all Nadiā is shaking
> Under the waves of Gaurānga's love!

And along with it these lines:

> Behold, the two brothers[1] have come, who weep while chanting
> 　　Hari's name,
> The brothers who, in return for blows, offer to sinners Hari's
> 　　love. . . .

And these too:

> Gaur and Nitāi, ye blessed brothers!
> I have heard how kind you are,
> And therefore I have come to you. . . ."

---

[1] Gaurānga and Nityānanda.

The devotees were taking the prasād. It was a sumptuous feast. Sri Rama-krishna said to M.: "Haven't you invited the Mukherjis? Ask Surendra to feed the musicians."

Bepin Sarkar arrived. The devotees introduced him to the Master. Sri Ramakrishna sat up and said to the devotees, "Give him a seat and some betel-leaf." He said to Bepin humbly: "I am sorry not to be able to talk to you. There is a great crowd today."

Pointing to Girindra, Sri Ramakrishna said to Baburam, "Give him a car-pet." Nityagopal was sitting on the floor. The Master asked a devotee to give him a carpet too.

Physician Mahendra of Sinthi arrived. The Master, smiling, asked Rakhal by a sign to have the physician examine his pulse.

Turning to Ramlal, the Master said, "Be friendly with Girish Ghosh; then you will get a free ticket to the theatre."

Narendra had been talking a long time with Hazra on the porch. Since his father's death Narendra had been having financial worries. He entered the room and took a seat.

MASTER (to Narendra): "Were you with Hazra? Both of you are in the same boat. You know the saying about the two friends: 'You are away from your country and he is away from his beloved.' Hazra, too, needs fifteen hundred rupees. (Laughter.)

"Hazra says: 'Narendra has acquired one hundred per cent sattva, though still there is in him a pink glow of rajas. But I have one hundred and twenty-five per cent pure sattva.' (All laugh.)

"I say to Hazra, 'You indulge in reasoning only: that is why you are so dry.' He retorts, 'No, I am dry because I drink the nectar of the sun.'

"Speaking of pure bhakti, I say to Hazra, 'A real devotee does not pray to God for money or riches.' Hazra replies: 'When the flood of divine grace descends, the rivers overflow; and further, the pools and canals are filled. By the grace of God one gets not only pure devotion but also the six super-natural powers, and money too.'"

Narendra and many other devotees were seated on the floor. Girish entered the room and joined them.

MASTER (to Girish): "I look on Narendra as Ātman. I obey him."

GIRISH: "Is there anyone you don't obey?"

MASTER (smiling): "He has a manly nature and I have the nature of a woman. He is a noble soul and belongs to the realm of the Indivisible Brahman."

Girish went out to have a smoke.

NARENDRA (to the Master): "I had a talk with Girish Ghosh. He is indeed a great man. We talked about you."

MASTER: "What did you say about me?"

NARENDRA: "That you are illiterate and we are scholars. Oh, we talked in that vein!" (Laughter.)

MANI MALLICK (to the Master): "You have become a pundit without reading a book."

MASTER (*to Narendra and the others*): "Let me tell you this: really and truly I don't feel sorry in the least that I haven't read the Vedānta or the other scriptures. I know that the essence of the Vedānta is that Brahman alone is real and the world illusory. And what is the essence of the *Gītā*? It is what you get by repeating the word ten times. Then it is reversed into 'tāgi', which refers to renunciation. The pupil should hear the essence of the scriptures from the guru; then he should practise austerity and devotions. A man needs the letter he has received from home as long as he has not learnt its contents. After reading it, however, he sets out to get the things he has been asked to send. Likewise, what need is there of the scriptures if you know their essence? The next thing is the practice of spiritual discipline."

Girish entered the room.

MASTER (*to Girish*): "Hello! What were you saying about me? I eat, drink, and make merry."

GIRISH: "What should we have been saying about you? Are you a holy man?"

MASTER: "No, nothing of the sort. Truly I do not feel I am a holy man."

GIRISH: "I am not your equal even in joking."

MASTER: "I once went to Jaygopal Sen's garden house wearing a red-bordered cloth. Keshab was there. Looking at the red borders Keshab said: 'What's this? Such a flash of colour today! Such a display of red borders!' I said, 'I have to cast a spell on Keshab; hence this display.'"

Narendra was going to sing again. Sri Ramakrishna asked M. to take down the tānpurā from the wall. Narendra was a long time tuning it. The Master and the devotees became impatient. Binode said, "He will tune it today and sing another day." (*Laughter.*)

Sri Ramakrishna laughed. He said: "I feel like breaking the tānpurā to pieces! What is this? Only 'Tong—tong'! Then he will practise: 'Tānā-nānā-nērē-num'!"[2]

BHAVANATH: "Everybody feels annoyed like this before a musical performance begins."

NARENDRA (*still tuning*): "If you don't understand it."

MASTER (*smiling*): "There! He explains away our complaints!"

Narendra began to sing. Sri Ramakrishna was seated on the small couch. Nityagopal and the other devotees were on the floor.

Narendra sang:

> O Mother, Thou my Inner Guide, ever awake within my heart!
> Day and night Thou holdest me in Thy lap.
> Why dost Thou show such tenderness to this unworthy child of
> Thine? . . .

Then he sang:

> O my lute of a single string!
> Sing the blessed Mother's name,
> For She is the solace of my soul. . . .

[2] The sound of a stringed instrument.

And again:

> In dense darkness, O Mother, Thy formless beauty sparkles;
> Therefore the yogis meditate in a dark mountain cave. . . .

In an ecstatic mood Sri Ramakrishna came down and sat by Narendra's side. He began to talk, still in ecstasy.

MASTER: "Shall I sing? Fie! (*To Nityagopal*) What do you say? One should listen to singing to awaken the inner spirit. Nothing matters afterwards.

"He has kindled the fire. That is nice. Now all is silence. That's nice too. I am silent; you be silent too. The thing is to dive into the Elixir of Bliss.

"Shall I sing? Well, I may. Water is water whether it is still or in waves."

Narendra was seated near the Master. He was constantly worried about his financial difficulties at home. He was now twenty-three years old. Sri Ramakrishna looked at him intently.

MASTER (*to Narendra, smiling*): "Undoubtedly you are 'Kha'. But you have to worry about 'taxes'; that's the trouble."

By "taxes" the Master meant Narendra's financial difficulties at home.

MASTER: "Krishnakishore used to say that he was 'Kha'. One day I visited him at his home and found him worried. He wouldn't talk to me freely. I asked him: 'What's the matter? Why are you brooding like this?' Krishnakishore said: 'The tax-collector came today. He said my pots and pans would be sold at auction if I didn't pay my taxes. That's what I am worrying about.' I laughed and said: 'How is that? You are surely 'Kha', the ākāśa. Let the rascals take away your pots and pans. What is that to you?'

(*To Narendra*) "So I am saying that you are 'Kha'. Why are you so worried? Don't you know that Sri Krishna said to Arjuna, 'If you have one of the eight siddhis, you may get a little power, but you will not realize Me.' By siddhis one may acquire powers, strength, money, and such things, but not God.

"Let me tell you something else. Go beyond knowledge and ignorance. People say that such and such a one is a jnāni; but in reality it is not so. Vasishtha was a great jnāni, but even he was stricken with grief on account of the death of his sons. At this Lakshmana said to Rāma: 'This is amazing, Rāma. Even Vasishtha is so grief-stricken!' Rāma said: 'Brother, he who has knowledge has ignorance as well. He who is aware of light is also aware of darkness. He who knows good also knows bad. He who knows happiness also knows misery. Brother, go beyond duality, beyond pleasure and pain, beyond knowledge and ignorance.' (*To Narendra*) So I am asking you to go beyond both knowledge and ignorance."

Sri Ramakrishna went back to his small couch. The devotees were seated on the floor. Surendra sat by his side. The Master cast an affectionate look on him and began to give him advice.

MASTER (*to Surendra*): "Come here every now and then. Nangtā used to say that a brass pot must be polished every day; otherwise it gets stained. One should constantly live in the company of holy men.

"The renunciation of 'woman and gold' is for sannyāsis. It is not for you.

Now and then you should go into solitude and call on God with a yearning heart. Your renunciation should be mental.

"Unless a devotee is of the heroic type he cannot pay attention to both God and the world. King Janaka lived a householder's life only after attaining perfection through austerity and prayer. He fenced with two swords, the one of Knowledge and the other of action."

The Master sang:

> This very world is a mansion of mirth;
> Here I can eat, here drink and make merry.
> Janaka's might was unsurpassed;
> What did he lack of the world or the Spirit?
> Holding to one as well as the other,
> He drank his milk from a brimming cup!

MASTER: "For you, as Chaitanya said, the disciplines to be practised are kindness to living beings, service to the devotees, and chanting the name of God.

(To Surendra) "Why do I say all this to you? You work in a merchant's office. I say this to you because you have many duties to perform there.

"You tell lies at the office. Then why do I eat the food you offer me? Because you give your money in charity; you give away more than you earn. 'The seed of the melon is bigger than the fruit', as the saying goes.

"I cannot eat anything offered by miserly people. Their wealth is squandered in these ways: first, litigation; second, thieves and robbers; third, physicians; fourth, their wicked children's extravagance. It is like that.

"Your giving money away in charity is very good. Those who have money should give in charity. The miser's wealth is spirited away, but the money of the charitable person is saved. He spends it for a righteous purpose. At Kāmārpukur I have seen the farmers cutting channels to irrigate their fields. Sometimes the water rushes in with such force that the ridges around the fields are washed away and the crops destroyed. For this reason the farmers make holes here and there in the ridges. Since the water escapes through the holes, the ridges are not destroyed by the rush of the water. Furthermore, the escaping water deposits soft clay in the fields, which increases their fertility and gives a richer crop. He who gives away in charity achieves great results. He achieves the four fruits: dharma, artha, kāma, and moksha."

The devotees listened with great attention to Sri Ramakrishna's words.

SURENDRA: "I cannot meditate well. I repeat the Divine Mother's name now and then. Lying in bed, I repeat Her name and fall asleep."

MASTER: "That is enough. You remember Her, don't you?

"There are two kinds of yoga: manoyoga and karmayoga. To perform, following the guru's instructions, such pious acts as worship, pilgrimage, and service to living beings is called karmayoga. The duties that Janaka performed are also called karmayoga. The meditation and contemplation of the yogis is called manoyoga.

"Sometimes I say to myself in the Kāli temple, 'O Mother, the mind is nothing but Yourself.' Therefore Pure Mind, Pure Buddhi, and Pure Ātman are one and the same thing."

It was about dusk. Many of the devotees saluted Sri Ramakrishna and started to go home. The Master went to the west porch. Bhavanath and M. were with him.

MASTER (*to Bhavanath*): "Why do you come here so seldom?"

BHAVANATH (*smiling*): "Sir, I visit you once in a fortnight. I saw you in the street the other day, so I didn't come here."

MASTER: "What do you mean? What can you gain by mere seeing? Touch and talk are also necessary."

The evening worship had begun in the temples. It was the eighth day of the bright fortnight of the moon; the temple domes, the courtyard, the gardens, and the trees were shining in the moonlight. The Ganges was flowing north with a murmuring sound. Sri Ramakrishna sat on the small couch in his room absorbed in contemplation of the Divine Mother.

The evening worship was over. One or two devotees were still in the temple garden. Narendra had left. Sri Ramakrishna was pacing the verandah northeast of his room. M. stood there looking at him. Suddenly he said to M., "Ah, how sweet Narendra's music is!"

M: "Yes, sir. That song beginning with 'In dense darkness' is particularly beautiful."

MASTER: "You are right. That song has a deep meaning. A part of my mind is still drawn to it."

M: "Yes, sir."

MASTER: "Meditation in darkness is prescribed in the Tantra."

Girish Ghosh came and stood by Sri Ramakrishna, who had started to sing:

> Is Kāli, my Mother, really black?
> The Naked One, of blackest hue,
> Lights the Lotus of the Heart. . . .

Sri Ramakrishna was filled with divine fervour. Standing with one arm resting on Girish's body he sang:

> Why should I go to Gangā or Gayā, to Kāśi, Kānchi, or Prabhās,
> So long as I can breathe my last with Kāli's name upon my lips?
> What need of rituals has a man, what need of devotions any more,
> If he repeats the Mother's name at the three holy hours?
> Rituals may pursue him close, but never can they overtake
>   him. . . .

Then he sang:

> Once for all, this time, I have thoroughly understood;
> From One[3] who knows it well, I have learnt the secret of bhāva.
> A man has come to me from a country where there is no night,
> And now I cannot distinguish day from night any longer;
> Rituals and devotions have all grown profitless for me.

[3] God, whom the poet worshipped as the Divine Mother.

My sleep is broken; how can I slumber any more?
For now I am wide awake in the sleeplessness of yoga.
O Divine Mother, made one with Thee in yoga-sleep[4] at last,
My slumber I have lulled asleep for evermore.

I bow my head, says Prasād, before desire and liberation;
Knowing the secret that Kāli is one with the highest Brahman,
I have discarded, once for all, both righteousness and sin.

As Sri Ramakrishna looked at Girish, his ecstatic fervour became more intense.

He sang:

I have surrendered my soul at the fearless feet of the Mother;
Am I afraid of Death any more?
Unto the tuft of hair on my head
Is tied the almighty mantra, Mother Kāli's name.
My body I have sold in the market-place of the world
And with it have bought Sri Durgā's name. . . .

Intoxicated with God, Sri Ramakrishna repeated the lines:

My body I have sold in the market-place of the world
And with it have bought Sri Durgā's name.

Looking at Girish and M. he said, " 'Divine fervour fills my body and robs me of consciousness.'

"Here 'consciousness' means consciousness of the outer world. One needs the Knowledge of Reality and Brahman.

"Bhakti, love of God, is the only essential thing. One kind of bhakti has a motive behind it. Again, there is a motiveless love, pure devotion, a love of God that seeks no return. Keshab Sen and the members of the Brāhmo Samāj didn't know about motiveless love. In this love there is no desire; it is nothing but pure love of the Lotus Feet of God.

"There is another kind of love, known as urjhitā bhakti, an ecstatic love of God that overflows, as it were. When it is awakened, the devotee 'laughs and weeps and dances and sings'. Chaitanyadeva is an example of this love. Rāma said to Lakshmana, 'Brother, if anywhere you see the manifestation of urjhitā bhakti, know for certain that I am there.' "

GIRISH: "Everything is possible through your grace. What was I before? And see what I am now."

MASTER: "You had latent tendencies; so they are manifesting themselves now. Nothing happens except at the proper time. Take the case of a patient. Nature has almost cured him, when the physician prescribes a herb and asks him to drink its juice. After taking the medicine he is completely cured. Now, is the patient cured by the medicine, or does he get well by himself? Who can tell?

"Lakshmana said to Lava and Kuśa:[5] 'You are mere children; you don't

---

[4] Samādhi, which makes one appear asleep.
[5] Rāma's two sons.

know Rāma's power. At the touch of His feet, Ahalyā,[6] who had been turned into a stone, got back her human form.' Lava and Kuśa said: 'Revered sir, we know that. We have heard the story. The stone became Ahalyā because of the power of the holy man's words. The sage Gautama said to her: "In the Tretāyuga, Rāma will pass this hermitage. You will become a human being again at the touch of His feet." ' Now, who can tell whether the miracle happened in order that the sage's words should be fulfilled or on account of Rāma's holiness?

"Everything happens by the will of God. If your spiritual consciousness has been awakened at this place, know that I am only an instrument. 'Uncle Moon is everybody's uncle.' All happens by the will of God."

GIRISH (smiling): "Did you say 'by the will of God'? What I am saying is the very same thing." (All laugh.)

MASTER (to Girish): "By being guileless one can speedily realize God. There are several kinds of people who do not attain divine knowledge. First, a man with a perverse mind; he is not guileless. Second, one who is very fastidious about outer purity. Third, a doubting person."

Sri Ramakrishna spoke highly of Nityagopal's ecstasy.

Three or four devotees stood near Sri Ramakrishna on the verandah and listened to his words about the exalted state of the paramahamsa. The Master said: "A paramahamsa is always conscious that God alone is real and all else illusory. Only the swan has the power to separate milk from a mixture of milk and water. The swan's tongue secretes an acid that separates the milk from the mixture. The paramahamsa also possesses such a juice; it is his ecstatic love for God. That separates the Real from the mixture of the Real and the unreal. Through it one becomes aware of God and sees Him."

Wednesday, February 25, 1885

Sri Ramakrishna was at the house of Girish Ghosh in Bosepārā Lane, Calcutta. It was about three o'clock when M. arrived and prostrated himself before him. The Master was going to see a play at the Star Theatre. He was talking with the devotees about the Knowledge of Brahman.

MASTER: "Man experiences three states of consciousness: waking, dream, and deep sleep. Those who follow the path of knowledge explain away the three states. According to them, Brahman is beyond the three states. It is also beyond the gross, the subtle, and the causal bodies, and beyond the three gunas—sattva, rajas, and tamas. All these are māyā, like a reflection in a mirror. The reflection is by no means the real substance. Brahman alone is the Substance and all else is illusory.

"The knowers of Brahman say, further, that it is the identification of the soul with the body that creates the notion of duality. In that state of

---

[6] The beautiful and devoted wife of a great sage named Gautama. Indra, the king of heaven, infatuated with her beauty, seduced her, impersonating her husband. The sage, coming to know of this, cursed her and turned her into a stone; but he said that the touch of Rāma's feet would restore her human form. Indra, too, received his share of the curse, as a result of which he had a thousand eruptions on his body. Hence he is known as the "thousand-eyed god".

identification the reflection appears real. When this identification disappears, a man realizes, 'I am He; I am Brahman.'

A DEVOTEE: "Then shall we all follow the path of reasoning?"

MASTER: "Reasoning is one of the paths; it is the path of the Vedāntists. But there is another path, the path of bhakti. If a bhakta weeps longingly for the Knowledge of Brahman, he receives that as well.[7] These are the two paths: jnāna and bhakti.

"One may attain the Knowledge of Brahman by either path. Some retain bhakti even after realizing Brahman, in order to teach humanity. An Incarnation of God is one of these.

"A man cannot easily get rid of the ego and the consciousness that the body is the soul. It becomes possible only when, through the grace of God, he attains samādhi—nirvikalpa samādhi, jada samādhi.

"The ego of the Incarnations returns to them when they come down from the plane of samādhi; but then it is the 'ego of Knowledge' or the 'ego of Devotion'. Through the 'ego of Knowledge' they teach men. Śankarāchārya kept the 'ego of Knowledge'.

"Through the 'ego of Devotion' Chaitanyadeva tasted divine love and enjoyed the company of the devotees. He talked about God and chanted His name.

"Since one cannot easily get rid of the ego, a bhakta does not explain away the states of waking, dream, and deep sleep. He accepts all the states. Further, he accepts the three gunas—sattva, rajas, and tamas. A bhakta sees that God alone has become the twenty-four cosmic principles, the universe, and all living beings. He also sees that God reveals Himself to His devotees in a tangible form, which is the embodiment of Spirit.

"The bhakta takes shelter under vidyāmāyā. He seeks holy company, goes on pilgrimage, and practises discrimination, devotion, and renunciation. He says that, since a man cannot easily get rid of his ego, he should let the rascal remain as the servant of God, the devotee of God.

"But a bhakta also attains the Knowledge of Oneness; he sees that nothing exists but God. He does not regard the world as a dream, but says that it is God Himself who has become everything. In a wax garden you may see various objects, but everything is made of wax.

"But a man realizes this only when his devotion to God has matured. One gets jaundice when too much bile accumulates. Then one sees everything as yellow. From constantly meditating on Krishna, Rādhikā saw everything as Krishna; moreover, she even felt that she herself had become Krishna. If a piece of lead is kept in a lake of mercury a long time, it turns into mercury. The cockroach becomes motionless by constantly meditating on the kumira worm; it loses the power to move. At last it is transformed into a kumira. Similarly, by constantly meditating on God the bhakta loses his ego; he realizes that God is he and he is God. When the cockroach becomes the kumira everything is achieved. Instantly one obtains liberation.

"As long as God retains the ego in a man, he should establish a definite relationship with God, calling on Him as Master, Mother, Friend, or the

[7] Usually the ideal of a bhakta is the vision of the Personal God.

like. I spent one year as a handmaid—the handmaid of the Divine Mother, the Embodiment of Brahman. I used to dress myself as a woman. I put on a nose-ring. One can conquer lust by assuming the attitude of a woman.

"One must worship the Ādyāśakti. She must be propitiated. She alone has assumed all female forms. Therefore I look on all women as mother. The attitude of looking on woman as mother is very pure. The Tantra mentions the vāmāchāra[8] method also. But that is not a good method; it causes the aspirant's downfall. A devotee keeping an object of enjoyment near him has reason to be afraid.

"Looking on woman as mother is like fasting on the ekādaśi day without touching even a drop of water; in this attitude there is not the slightest trace of sensual enjoyment. Another way of observing the ekādaśi allows the taking of fruit and the like. One can also observe the day by eating luchi and curries! But my attitude is not to touch even a drop of water while I observe the fast. I worshipped the Shorāśi[9] as my mother; I looked on all parts of her body as those of my mother. This attitude of regarding God as Mother is the last word in sādhanā. 'O God, Thou art my Mother and I am Thy child'—this is the last word in spirituality.

"The sannyāsi's way of living is like observing the ekādaśi fast without taking even a drop of water. If he clings to enjoyment, then he has reason to be afraid. 'Woman and gold' is enjoyment. If a monk enjoys it, he is swallowing his own spittle, as it were. There are different kinds of enjoyment: money, wealth, name, fame, and sense pleasures. It is not good for a sannyāsi to sit in the company of a woman devotee, or even to talk to her. This injures him and others as well. Then others cannot learn from him; he cannot set an example to humanity. A sannyāsi keeps his body in order to teach mankind.

"To sit with a woman or talk to her a long time has also been described as a kind of sexual intercourse. There are eight kinds. To listen to a woman and enjoy her conversation is one kind; to speak about a woman is another kind; to whisper to her privately is a third kind; to keep something belonging to a woman and enjoy it is a fourth kind; to touch her is a fifth. Therefore a sannyāsi should not salute his guru's young wife, touching her feet. These are the rules for sannyāsis.

"But the case is quite different with householders. After the birth of one or two children, the husband and wife should live as brother and sister. The other seven kinds of sexual intercourse do not injure them much.

"A householder has various debts: debts to the gods, to the fathers, and to the rishis. He also owes a debt to his wife. He should make her the mother of one or two children and support her if she is a chaste woman.

"Householders do not know who is a good wife and who is a bad wife, who is a vidyāśakti and who is an avidyāśakti. A vidyāśakti, a good wife, has very little lust and anger. She sleeps little. She pushes her husband's head

[8] Literally, "left-hand path". According to this attitude the aspirant seeks to conquer lust by fulfilling its urge.

[9] Literally, "maiden sixteen years old". The worship of a maiden is a discipline prescribed in the Tantra.

away from her. She is full of affection, kindness, devotion, modesty, and other noble qualities. Such a wife serves all, looking on all men as her children. Further, she helps increase her husband's love of God. She doesn't spend much money lest her husband should have to work hard and thus not get leisure to think of God.

"Mannish women have different traits. These are bad traits: squint eyes and hollow eyes, catlike eyes, lantern jaws like a calf's, and pigeon-breast."

GIRISH: "What is the way for people like us?"

MASTER: "Bhakti is the only essential thing. Bhakti has different aspects: the sāttvic, the rājasic, and the tāmasic. One who has sāttvic bhakti is very modest and humble. But a man with tāmasic bhakti is like a highwayman in his attitude toward God. He says: 'O God, I am chanting Your name; how can I be a sinner? O God, You are my own Mother; You must reveal Yourself to me.'"

GIRISH (smiling): "It is you, sir, who teach us tāmasic bhakti."

MASTER (smiling): "There are certain signs of God-vision. When a man sees God he goes into samādhi. There are five kinds of samādhi. First, he feels the Mahāvāyu[10] rise like an ant crawling up. Second, he feels It rise like a fish swimming in the water. Third, he feels It rise like a snake wriggling along. Fourth, he feels It rise like a bird flying—flying from one branch to another. Fifth, he feels It rise like a monkey making a big jump; the Mahāvāyu reaches the head with one jump, as it were, and samādhi follows.

"There are two other kinds of samādhi. First, the sthita samādhi, when the aspirant totally loses outer consciousness: he remains in that state a long time, it may be for many days. Second, the unmana samādhi: it is to withdraw the mind suddenly from all sense-objects and unite it with God.

(To M.) "Do you understand this?"

M: "Yes, sir."

GIRISH: "Can one realize God by sādhanā?"

MASTER: "People have realized God in various ways. Some through much austerity, worship, and devotion; they have attained perfection through their own efforts. Some are born perfect, as for example Nārada and Śukadeva; they are called nityasiddha, eternally perfect. There are also those who have attained perfection all of a sudden; it is like a man's unexpectedly coming into a great fortune. Again, there are instances of people's realizing God in a dream and by divine grace."

Saying this, Sri Ramakrishna sang, intoxicated with divine fervour:

Can everyone have the vision of Śyāmā? Is Kāli's treasure for everyone?
Oh, what a pity my foolish mind will not see what is true! . . .

Sri Ramakrishna remained in ecstasy a few moments. Girish and the other devotees were seated before him. A few days earlier Girish had been very rude to the Master at the Star Theatre; but now he was in a calm state of mind.

MASTER (to Girish): "This mood of yours is very good; it is peaceful. I

10 The great nerve current whose rising is felt in the spinal column.

prayed about you to the Divine Mother, 'O Mother, make him peaceful so that he won't abuse me.'"

GIRISH (to M.): "I feel as if someone were pressing my tongue. I can't talk."

Sri Ramakrishna was still in an indrawn mood; he seemed to be gradually forgetting the men and the objects around him. He tried to bring his mind down to the relative world. He looked at the devotees.

Looking at M., he said: "They all come to Dakshineswar. Let them. Mother knows everything." To a young man of the neighbourhood he said: "Hello! What do you think? What is the duty of man?" All sat in silence. To Narayan he said: "Don't you want to pass the examinations? But, my dear child, a man freed from bondage is Śiva; entangled in bondage, he is jīva."

Sri Ramakrishna was still in the God-intoxicated mood. There was a glass of water near him. He drank the water. He said to himself, "Why, I have drunk water in this mood!"

It was not yet dusk. Sri Ramakrishna was talking to Atul, who was seated in front of him. Atul was Girish's brother and a lawyer of the High Court of Calcutta. A brāhmin neighbour was also seated near him.

MASTER (to Atul): "All I want to tell you is this. Follow both; perform your duties in the world and also cultivate love of God."

BRĀHMIN: "Can anyone but a brāhmin achieve perfection?"

MASTER: "Why should you ask that? It is said that in the Kaliyuga the śudras achieve love of God. There are the instances of Śavari, Ruhidās, the untouchable Guhaka, and others."

NARAYAN (smiling): "Brāhmins and śudras—all are one."

BRĀHMIN: "Can a man realize God in one birth?"

MASTER: "Is anything impossible for the grace of God? Suppose you bring a light into a room that has been dark a thousand years; does it remove the darkness little by little? The room is lighted all at once. (To Atul) Intense renunciation is what is needed. One should be like an unsheathed sword. When a man has that renunciation, he looks on his relatives as black cobras and his home as a deep well.

"One should pray to God with sincere longing. God cannot but listen to prayer if it is sincere."

All sat in silence, pondering Sri Ramakrishna's words.

MASTER (to Atul): "What is worrying you? Is it that you haven't that grit, that intense restlessness for God?"

ATUL: "How can we keep our minds on God?"

MASTER: "Abhyāsayoga, the yoga of practice. You should practise calling on God every day. It is not possible to succeed in one day; through daily prayer you will come to long for God.

"How can you feel that restlessness if you are immersed in worldliness day and night? Formerly Jadu Mallick enjoyed spiritual talk; he liked to engage in it himself. But nowadays he doesn't show that much interest. He surrounds himself with flatterers day and night and indulges in worldly talk."

It was dusk. The lamp was lighted in the room. Sri Ramakrishna chanted the divine names. He was singing and praying. He said, "Chant the name of

Hari, repeat the name of Hari, sing the name of Hari." Again he said, "Rāma! Rāma! Rāma!" Then: "O Mother! Thou dost ever enjoy Thine eternal sports. Tell us, O Mother, what is the way? We have taken refuge in Thee; we have taken shelter at Thy feet."

Finding Girish restless, Sri Ramakrishna remained silent a moment. He asked Tejchandra to sit near him. The boy sat near the Master. He whispered to M. that he would have to leave soon.

MASTER (to M.): "What did he say?"

M: "He said he would have to go home."

MASTER: "Why do I attract these boys to me so much? They are pure vessels untouched by worldliness. A man cannot assimilate instruction if his mind is stained with worldliness. Milk can be safely kept in a new pot; but it turns sour if kept in a pot in which curd has been made. You may wash a thousand times a cup that has held a solution of garlic, but still you cannot remove the smell."

Sri Ramakrishna arrived at the Star Theatre, on Beadon Street, to see a performance of *Vrishaketu*.[11] He sat in a box, facing the south. M. and other devotees were near him.

MASTER (to M.): "Has Narendra come?"

M: "Yes, sir."

The performance began. Karna and his wife Padmāvati sacrificed their son to please God, who had come to them in the guise of a brāhmin to test Karna's charity. During this scene one of the devotees gave a suppressed sigh. Sri Ramakrishna also expressed his sorrow.

After the play Sri Ramakrishna went to the recreation room of the theatre. Girish and Narendra were already there. The Master stood near Narendra and said, "I have come."

Sri Ramakrishna took a seat. The orchestra was playing in the auditorium.

MASTER (to the devotees): "I feel happy listening to the concert. The musicians used to play on the sānāi at Dakshineswar and I would go into ecstasy. Noticing this, a certain sādhu said, 'This is a sign of the Knowledge of Brahman.' "

The orchestra stopped playing and Sri Ramakrishna began the conversation.

MASTER (to Girish): "Does this theatre belong to you?"

GIRISH: "It is *ours*, sir."

MASTER: " 'Ours' is good; it is not good to say 'mine'. People say 'I' and 'mine'; they are egotistic, small-minded people."

NARENDRA: "The whole world is a theatre."

MASTER: "Yes, yes, that's right. In some places you see the play of vidyā and in some, the play of avidyā."

NARENDRA: "Everything is the play of vidyā."

MASTER: "True, true. But a man realizes that when he has the Knowledge

[11] Vrishaketu was the son of Karna, a hero of the *Mahābhārata*, who was celebrated alike for charity and heroism. Karna sacrificed his son to fulfil a promise.

of Brahman. But for a bhakta, who follows the path of divine love, both exist—vidyāmāyā and avidyāmāyā.

"Please sing a little."

Narendra sang:

> Upon the Sea of Blissful Awareness waves of ecstatic love arise:
> Rapture divine! Play of God's Bliss!
> Oh, how enthralling!
> Wondrous waves of the sweetness of God, ever new and ever enchanting,
> Rise on the surface, ever assuming
> Forms ever fresh.
> Then once more in the Great Communion all are merged, as the barrier walls
> Of time and space dissolve and vanish:
> Dance then, O mind!
> Dance in delight with hands upraised, chanting Lord Hari's holy name.

As Narendra sang the words, "Then once more in the Great Communion all are merged", Sri Ramakrishna said to him, "One realizes this after attaining the Knowledge of Brahman; then all is vidyā, Brahman, as you said."

As Narendra sang the line, "Dance in delight with hands upraised, chanting Lord Hari's holy name", the Master said to him, "Sing that line twice."

After the song Sri Ramakrishna resumed the conversation.

GIRISH: "Devendra Babu hasn't come. He says in a mood of wounded pride: 'We haven't any stuff inside us, no filling of thickened milk. We are filled only with worthless lentil-paste. Why should we go there?'"

MASTER (surprised): "Does he say that? He never said so before."

Sri Ramakrishna took some refreshments and handed some to Narendra.

JATIN DEVA (to the Master): "You always say: 'Narendra, eat this! Eat that!' Are the rest of us fools? Are we like straw washed ashore by the flood-tide?"

Sri Ramakrishna loved Jatin dearly. Jatin visited the Master now and then at Dakshineswar and occasionally spent the night there. He belonged to an aristocratic family of Sobhābāzār. The Master said laughingly to Narendra, "He is talking about you."

Sri Ramakrishna laughed and showed his affection to Jatin by touching his chin. He said to Jatin, "Come to Dakshineswar; I'll give you plenty to eat."

The Master went into the auditorium to see a farce. He sat in a box. He laughed at the conversation of the maidservant. After a while he became absent-minded and whispered a few words to M.

MASTER (to M.): "Well, is what Girish Ghosh says true?"

Girish had lately been speaking of Sri Ramakrishna as an Incarnation of God.

M: "Yes, sir, it must be true. Otherwise why should it appeal to our minds?"

MASTER: "You see, a change is coming over me. The old mood has changed. I am not able to touch any metal now."

M. listened to these words in wonder.

MASTER: "There is a very deep meaning in this new mood."

Was the Master hinting that a God-man cannot bear any association with worldly treasure?

MASTER (to M.): "Well, do you notice any change in me?"

M: "In what respect, sir?"

MASTER: "In my activities."

M: "Your activities are increasing as more people come to know about you."

MASTER: "Do you see? What I said before is now coming true."

After a few moments he said, "Can you tell me why Paltu can't meditate well?"

Sri Ramakrishna was ready to leave for Dakshineswar. He had remarked to a devotee about Girish, "You may wash a thousand times a cup that has held a solution of garlic; but is it ever possible to get rid of the smell altogether?" Girish was offended by this remark. When the Master was about to leave, Girish spoke.

GIRISH: "Will this smell of garlic go?"

MASTER: "Yes, it will."

GIRISH: "So you say it will."

MASTER: "All smell disappears when a blazing fire is lighted. If you heat the cup smelling of garlic, you get rid of the smell; it becomes a new cup.

"The man who says he will not succeed will never succeed. He who feels he is liberated is indeed liberated; and he who feels he is bound verily remains bound. He who forcefully says, 'I am free' is certainly free; and he who says day and night, 'I am bound' is certainly bound."

THE MASTER AND NARENDRA

SRI RAMAKRISHNA was seated on the small couch in his room, absorbed in deep samādhi. Mahimacharan, Ram, Manomohan, Nabai Chaitanya, M., and other devotees were sitting on a mat spread on the floor. They were watching the Master intently.

It was the day of the Dolayātrā, a Hindu religious festival. Sri Krishna and Rādhā are the central figures of this celebration, their images being placed on a swing which is rocked now and then. A red powder is showered on the images. Later, friends and relatives throw the powder at one another. This festival is celebrated when winter passes into spring, on a full-moon day rendered doubly sacred by its association with the birth of Sri Chaitanya.

The devotees saw that the Master was returning to consciousness of the world, though his mind still lingered in the realm of God-vision.

The Master said to Mahimacharan, "My dear sir, please tell us something about love of God."

Mahimacharan chanted the following lines from the *Nārada Pancharātra*:

> What need is there of penance if God is worshipped with love?
> What is the use of penance if God is not worshipped with love?
> What need is there of penance if God is seen within and without?
> What is the use of penance if God is not seen within and without?
>
> O Brahman! O my child! Cease from practising further penances.
> Hasten to Śankara, the Ocean of Heavenly Wisdom;
> Obtain from Him the love of God, the pure love praised by devotees,
> Which snaps in twain the shackles that bind you to the world.

Mahima said, "Once while the great sage Nārada was practising austerity, he suddenly heard a heavenly voice repeating those lines."

MASTER: "There are two classes of devotees: jīvakotis, or ordinary men, and Iśvarakotis, or Divine Messengers. The jīvakoti's devotion to God is called vaidhi, formal; that is, it conforms to scriptural laws. He worships God with a fixed number of articles, repeats God's holy name a specified number of times, and so on and so forth. This kind of devotion, like the path of knowledge, leads to the Knowledge of God and to samādhi. The jīvakoti does not return from samādhi to the relative plane.

"But the case of the Iśvarakoti is different. He follows the process of 'negation' and 'affirmation'. First he negates the world, realizing that it is not Brahman; but then he affirms the same world, seeing it as the manifestation of Brahman. To give an illustration: a man wanting to climb to the roof first negates the stairs as not being the roof, but on reaching the roof he finds that the stairs are made of the same materials as the roof: brick, lime, and brick-dust. Then he can either move up and down the stairs or remain on the roof, as he pleases.

"Śukadeva was absorbed in samādhi—nirvikalpa samādhi, jaḍa samādhi. Since Śuka was to recite the *Bhāgavata* to King Parikshit, the Lord sent the sage Nārada to him. Nārada saw him seated like an inert thing, absolutely unconscious of the world around him. Thereupon Nārada sang four couplets on the beauty of Hari, to the accompaniment of the vīnā. While the first couplet was being sung the hair on Śuka's body stood on end. Next he shed tears; for he saw the form of God, the Embodiment of Spirit, within himself, in his heart. Thus Śukadeva saw the form of God even after jaḍa samādhi. He was an Iśvarakoti.

"Hanumān, after having the vision of God both with form and without, remained firmly devoted to the form of Rāma, the Embodiment of Consciousness and Bliss.

"Prahlāda sometimes realized, 'I am He'; sometimes he felt that he was the servant of God. How can such a person live without love of God? That is why he must accept the relationship of master and servant, feeling that God is the Master and himself the servant. This enables him to enjoy the Bliss of Hari. In this attitude he feels that God is the Bliss and he himself is the enjoyer.

"The 'ego of Devotion', the 'ego of Knowledge', and the 'ego of a child' do not harm the devotee. Śankarāchārya kept the 'ego of Knowledge'. The 'ego of a child' is not attached to anything. The child is beyond the three gunas; he is not under the control of any of them. One moment you find him angry; the next moment it is all over. One moment you see him building his play house; the next moment he forgets all about it. Now you see him love his playmates; but if they are out of his sight a few days he forgets all about them. A child is not under the control of any of the gunas—sattva, rajas, or tamas.

"The bhakta feels, 'O God, Thou art the Lord and I am Thy devotee.' This 'I' is the 'ego of bhakti'. Why does such a lover of God retain the 'ego of Devotion'? There is a reason. The ego cannot be got rid of; so let the rascal remain as the servant of God, the devotee of God.

"You may reason a thousand times, but you cannot get rid of the ego. The ego is like a pitcher, and Brahman like the ocean—an infinite expanse of water on all sides. The pitcher is set in this ocean. The water is both inside and out; the water is everywhere; yet the pitcher remains. Now, this pitcher is the 'ego of the devotee'. As long as the ego remains, 'you' and 'I' remain, and there also remains the feeling, 'O God, Thou art the Lord and I am Thy devotee; Thou art the Master and I am Thy servant.' You may reason a million times, but you cannot get rid of it. But it is different if there is no pitcher."

Narendra entered the room and saluted the Master. They began to talk together. Presently the Master came down from the couch and sat on the floor, on which a mat had been spread. In the mean time the room had become filled with people, both devotees and visitors.

MASTER (to Narendra): "Are you well? I hear that you often visit Girish Ghosh at his house. Is it true?"

NARENDRA: "Yes, sir, I go there now and then."

Girish had been visiting Sri Ramakrishna for some months. The Master said that none could fathom the depth of Girish's faith. And his longing for God was as intense as his faith was deep. At home, he was always absorbed in the thought of Sri Ramakrishna. Many of the Master's devotees visited him; they talked only about Sri Ramakrishna. But Girish was a householder who had had varied experiences of worldly life, and the Master knew that Narendra would renounce the world, that he would shun "woman and gold" both mentally and outwardly.

MASTER: "Do you visit Girish frequently? No matter how much one washes a cup that has contained a solution of garlic, still a trace of the smell will certainly linger. The youngsters who come here are pure souls—untouched by 'woman and gold'. Men who have associated a long time with 'woman and gold' smell of the garlic, as it were. They are like a mango pecked by crows. Such a fruit cannot be offered to the Deity in the temple, and you would hesitate to eat it yourself. Again, take the case of a new pot and another in which curd has been made. One is afraid to keep milk in the second pot, for the milk very often turns sour.

"Householder devotees like Girish form a class by themselves. They desire yoga and also bhoga. Their attitude is that of Rāvana, who wanted to enjoy the maidens of heaven and at the same time realize Rāma. They are like the asuras, the demons, who enjoy various pleasures and also realize Nārāyana."

NARENDRA: "But Girish has given up his old associates."

MASTER: "Yes, yes. He is like a bull castrated in old age. In Burdwān I once saw an ox moving about the cows. I asked a bullock-cart driver: 'What is this? An ox? How strange!' He said to me: 'True, sir. But it was castrated in old age, and so it hasn't altogether shaken off the old tendencies.'

"In a certain place there sat some sannyāsis. A young woman happened to pass by. All continued as before to meditate on God, except one of them, who cast sidelong glances at her. Before becoming a monk he had been the father of three children.

"If you make a solution of garlic in a cup, won't it be hard to remove the smell from it? Can a worthless tree like the babui produce mangoes? Of course such a thing may become possible through the occult powers of a yogi; but can everyone acquire such powers?

"When have worldly people time to think of God? A man wanted to engage a pundit who could explain the *Bhāgavata* to him. His friend said: 'I know of an excellent pundit. But there is one difficulty: he does a great deal of farming. He has four ploughs and eight bullocks and is always busy with them; he has no leisure.' Thereupon the man said: 'I don't care for a pundit who has no leisure. I am not looking for a *Bhāgavata* scholar burdened with ploughs and bullocks. I want a pundit who can really expound the sacred book to me.'

"There was a king who used to listen daily to a pundit's exposition of the *Bhāgavata*. Every day at the end of their study the pundit would ask the king, 'O King, have you understood what I have read?' To this question the king would daily give the same reply: 'Sir, you had better understand it first yourself.' Each day, when the pundit returned home, he would ponder the meaning of the king's words. He was a pious man, devoted to prayer and meditation. Gradually he came to his senses and realized that the only real thing in the world is the Lotus Feet of God, and that all else is illusory. He felt dispassion for the world and took up the life of a monk. As he was leaving the world he sent a man to the king with the message: 'Yes, O King! Now I have understood.'

"But do I look down on worldly people? Of course not. When I see them, I apply the Knowledge of Brahman, the Oneness of Existence. Brahman Itself has become everything; all are Nārāyana Himself. Regarding all women as so many forms of the Divine Mother, I see no difference between a chaste woman and a streetwalker.

"Alas! I find no customers who want anything better than kalāi pulse. No one wants to give up 'woman and gold'. Man, deluded by the beauty of woman and the power of money, forgets God. But to one who has seen the beauty of God, even the position of Brahmā, the Creator, seems insignificant.

"A man said to Rāvana, 'You have been going to Sītā in different disguises; why don't you go to her in the form of Rāma?' 'But', Rāvana replied, 'when I meditate on Rāma in my heart, the most beautiful women—celestial maidens like Rambhā and Tilottamā—appear no better than ashes of the funeral pyre. Then even the position of Brahmā appears trivial to me, not to speak of the beauty of another man's wife.'

"Alas! I find that all the customers here seek worthless kalāi pulse. Unless the soul is pure, it cannot have genuine love of God and single-minded devotion to the ideal. The mind wanders away to various objects.

(*To Manomohan*[1]) "You may take offence at my words, but I said to Rakhal, 'I would rather hear that you had drowned yourself in the Ganges than learn that you had accepted a job under another person and become his servant.'

"One day a Nepalese girl came here. She sang devotional songs to the accompaniment of the esrāj. When someone asked her if she was married, she said sharply: 'What? I am the handmaid of God! Whom else could I serve?'

"How can a man living in the midst of 'woman and gold' realize God? It is very hard for him to lead an unattached life. First, he is the slave of his wife, second, of money, and third, of the master whom he serves.

"When Ākbar was Emperor of Delhi there lived a hermit in a hut in the

[1] A householder disciple of the Master, whose sister was married to Rakhal.

forest. Many people visited the holy man. At one time he felt a great desire to entertain his visitors. But how could he do so without money? So he decided to go to the Emperor for help, for the gate of Ākbar's palace was always open to holy men. The hermit entered the palace while the Emperor was at his daily devotions and took a seat in a corner of the room. He heard the Emperor conclude his worship with the prayer, 'O God, give me money; give me riches', and so on and so forth. When the hermit heard this he was about to leave the prayer hall; but the Emperor signed to him to wait. When the prayer was over, Ākbar said to him, 'You came to see me; how is it that you were about to leave without saying anything to me?' 'Your Majesty need not trouble yourself about it', answered the hermit. 'I must leave now.' When the Emperor insisted, the hermit said, 'Many people visit my hut, and so I came here to ask you for some money.' 'Then', said Ākbar, 'why were you going away without speaking to me?' The hermit replied: 'I found that you too were a beggar; you too prayed to God for money and riches. Thereupon I said to myself, "Why should I beg of a beggar? If I must beg, let me beg of God." ' "

NARENDRA: "Nowadays Girish Ghosh thinks of nothing but spiritual things."

MASTER: "That is very good. But why is he so abusive? Why does he use such vulgar language to me? In my present state of mind I cannot bear such rudeness. When a thunderbolt strikes near a house, the heavy things inside the house are not much affected; but the window-panes rattle. Nowadays I cannot bear such roughness. A man living on the plane of sattva cannot bear noise and uproar. That is why Hriday was sent away. It was the Divine Mother who sent him away. During the later part of his stay he went to extremes; he became very rough and abusive. (*To Narendra*) Do you agree with Girish about me?"

NARENDRA: "He said he believed you to be an Incarnation of God. I didn't say anything in answer to his remarks."

MASTER: "But how great his faith is! Don't you think so?"

The devotees listened intently to the Master's words. He was still seated on the mat spread on the floor, with M. by his side and Narendra in front of him. The devotees were sitting around.

After a few minutes' silence he said to Narendra tenderly, "My child, you will not attain God without renouncing 'woman and gold'." As he said this, great emotion welled up in his heart. Fixing on Narendra an earnest and tender look, he sang:[2]

[2] This was a very critical period in Narendranath's life. After his father's death he had been faced with extreme poverty; friends and relatives had proved indifferent or treacherous. His rational mind could not reconcile the existence of human misery with the mercy of God. A few days before this meeting with the Master, on his way home, almost exhausted after a futile search for a job, he had sat down on the open porch of a house by the street, waiting for a shower of rain to pass. There he had received a revelation in which he had found the solution of all his conflicting problems. He had felt refreshed, realizing the unreality of the world, and had determined to become a monk at once. So he had come to the Master to take leave of him, but had not told him of his intention. Yet nothing could be hidden from Sri Ramakrishna; hence the song.

We are afraid to speak, and yet we are afraid to keep still;
Our minds, O Rādhā, half believe that we are about to lose you!
We tell you the secret that we know—
The secret whereby we ourselves, and others, with our help,
Have passed through many a time of peril;
Now it all depends on you.

Sri Ramakrishna seemed to be afraid lest Narendra should leave him. Narendra looked at the Master with tears in his eyes.

A visitor who was there for the first time heard and saw all this. He said to the Master, "Sir, if one must renounce 'woman and gold', then what shall a householder do?"

MASTER: "You may enjoy 'woman and gold'. What has passed between us is no concern of yours."

Mahimacharan, a householder devotee, heard everything and sat speechless.

MASTER (to Mahima): "Go forward. Push on. You will discover the forest of sandal-wood. Go farther and you will find the silver-mine. Go farther still and you will see the gold-mine. Do not stop there. Go forward, and you will reach the mines of rubies and diamonds. Therefore I say, go forward."

MAHIMA: "But, sir, something holds us back. We can't move."

MASTER (with a smile): "Why? Cut the reins. Cut them with the sword of God's name. 'The shackles of Kāla, Time, are cut by Kāli's name.'"

Every now and then the Master cast his gracious look on Narendra. He said, "Have you now become an experienced physician?" Quoting a Sanskrit verse he said, "He who has killed only a hundred patients is a novice in medicine; but he becomes an expert after killing a thousand!"

Was the Master hinting that Narendra, even though still young, had had many painful experiences of life?

Narendra smiled and kept silent.

It was afternoon. The devotees were seated around the Master, listening to Nabai Chaitanya's singing. Suddenly the Master left the room, but the music continued. M. accompanied the Master.

Sri Ramakrishna walked across the courtyard and entered the temple of Rādhākānta. He bowed down before the images, M. following him. There was some red powder in a tray. The Master offered a little powder to the images and bowed down again.

Next he proceeded to the Kāli temple. Passing up the seven steps, he stood on the open porch and looked at the image. Then he entered the shrine, offered red powder to the Divine Mother, and saluted Her. As he left the temple he asked M., "Why didn't you bring Baburam with you?"

Sri Ramakrishna returned to his room accompanied by M. and another devotee carrying the tray of red powder. He offered a little of it to all the pictures of gods and goddesses in his room, but not to those of Jesus Christ and himself. Then he threw the powder on the bodies of Narendra and the other devotees. They all took the dust of his feet.

In the cool shade of the late afternoon the devotees walked about in the temple garden, leaving the Master and M. in the room. The Master whispered to M.: "All say that they meditate well. But why is it different with Paltu? What do you think of Narendra? He is utterly guileless. Just now he is faced with many difficult family problems and so his spiritual progress is a little checked; but it will not be so for long."

Narendra was arguing on the verandah with a Vedāntist. Now and then the Master went out to look at them. As the devotees gathered in the room he asked Mahima to recite a hymn. Mahima chanted a verse from the *Mahānirvāna Tantra*:

> We worship the Brahman-Consciousness in the Lotus of the Heart,
> The Undifferentiated, who is adored by Hari, Hara, and Brahmā. . . .

Mahima recited a few more hymns and at last one to Śiva, by Śankarāchārya, that compared the world to a deep well and a wilderness. Mahima was a householder.

The hymn ran thus:

> O Great God! O Thou Auspicious One, with the moon shining in Thy crest!
> Slayer of Madana![3] Wielder of the trident! Unmoving One! Lord of the Himālayas!
> O Consort of Durgā, Lord of all creatures! Thou who scatterest the distress of the fearful!
> Rescue me, helpless as I am, from the trackless forest of this miserable world.
>
> O Beloved of Pārvati's heart! O Thou moon-crested Deity!
> Master of every being! Lord of hosts! O Thou, the Lord of Pārvati!
> O Vāmadeva, Self-existent One! O Rudra, Wielder of the bow!
> Rescue me, helpless as I am, from the trackless forest of this miserable world.
>
> O blue-throated God! Śiva, whose ensign is the bull! O Five-faced One!
> Lord of the worlds, who wearest snakes upon Thy wrists! O Thou Auspicious One!
> O Śiva! O Paśupati![4] O Thou, the Lord of Pārvati!
> Rescue me, helpless as I am, from the trackless forest of this miserable world.
>
> O Lord of the Universe! O Śiva Śankara! O God of Gods!
> Thou who dost bear the river Ganges in Thy matted locks!
> Thou, the Master of Pramatha and Nandika![5] O Hara, Lord of the world!
> Rescue me, helpless as I am, from the trackless forest of this miserable world.

[3] The god of love.
[4] Lord of beings.
[5] Attendants of Śiva.

O King of Kāśi, Lord of the cremation ground of Manikarnikā!
O mighty Hero, Thou the Destroyer of Daksha's[6] sacrifice! O All-
    pervasive One!
O Lord of hosts! Omniscient One, who art the sole Indweller in
    every heart! O Lord!
Rescue me, helpless as I am, from the trackless forest of this miser-
    able world.

O Great God! Compassionate One! O Benign Deity!
O Byomakeśa![7] Blue-throated One! O Lord of hosts!
Thy body is smeared with ashes! Thou art garlanded with human
    skulls!
Rescue me, helpless as I am, from the trackless forest of this miser-
    able world.

O Thou who dwellest on Mount Kailās! Thou whose carrier is the
    bull!
O Conqueror of death! O Three-eyed One! Lord of the three
    worlds!
Beloved of Nārāyana! Conqueror of lust! Thou, Śakti's Lord!
Rescue me, helpless as I am, from the trackless forest of this miser-
    able world.

Lord of the Universe! Refuge of the whole world! O Thou of
    infinite forms!
Soul of the Universe! O Thou in whom repose the infinite virtues
    of the world!
O Thou adored by all! Compassionate One! O Friend of the poor!
Rescue me, helpless as I am, from the trackless forest of this miser-
    able world.

MASTER (*to Mahima*): "Why do you call the world a deep well or a trackless forest? An aspirant may think so in the beginning; but how can he be
frightened by the world if he holds fast to God? Then he finds that—

> This very world is a mansion of mirth;
> Here I can eat, here drink and make merry.

"Why should you be frightened? Hold fast to God. What if the world is
like a forest of thorns? Put on shoes and walk on the thorns. Whom should
you fear? You won't have to play again the part of the 'thief' in the game of
hide-and-seek, once you touch the 'granny'.[8]

"King Janaka used to fence with two swords—the one of Knowledge and
the other of action. Nothing can frighten an expert player."

(*To M.*) "My mind is still drawn to what he just recited."

Sri Ramakrishna referred to the hymns chanted by Mahima.

Nabai Chaitanya and the other devotees began to sing. They were joined
by the Master, who danced, drunk with divine love. Afterwards he said:
"This is the one thing needful, the chanting of God's name. All else is

[6] Śiva's father-in-law.
[7] A name of Śiva.
[8] See foot-note 6, p. 136.

unreal. Love and devotion alone are real, and other things are of no consequence."

Later Sri Ramakrishna went out in the direction of the Panchavati. He asked M. about Binode, a student in M.'s school, who now and then experienced ecstasy while thinking of God. The Master loved him dearly.

As he was returning to his room with M., he asked: "Well, some speak of me as an Incarnation of God. What do you think about it?" The Master came back to his room and sat on the small couch. He repeated the question to M. The other devotees were seated at a distance and could not follow the conversation.

MASTER: "What do you say?"

M: "I think so too. You are like Sri Chaitanya."

MASTER: "Is it a full manifestation of God, or a part? Tell me how much."

M: "I don't know, sir. But it is true that there is in you an Incarnation of the Divine Power. There is no doubt that God alone dwells in you."

MASTER: "That is true. Chaitanya also wanted to realize Śakti, the Divine Power."

Narendra was engaged in a heated discussion. Ram, who had recently recovered from an illness, joined him.

MASTER (to M.): "I don't like such discussions. (To Ram) Will you stop that? You haven't been well. All right, go on softly; don't get so excited. (To M.) I don't like these discussions. I used to weep and pray to the Divine Mother saying: 'O Mother, one man says it is this, while another says it is that. Do Thou tell me, O Mother, what is the truth.'"

Saturday, March 7, 1885

At three o'clock in the afternoon Sri Ramakrishna was in his room at Dakshineswar conversing happily with his devotees. Baburam, the younger Naren, Paltu, Haripada, Mohinimohan, and others were present. A young brāhmin who had been staying with the Master a few days was also there.

The Holy Mother, Sri Ramakrishna's wife, was living in the nahabat. Occasionally she would come to Sri Ramakrishna's room to attend to his needs. Mohinimohan had brought his wife and Nabin's mother with him to the temple garden from Calcutta. The ladies were with the Holy Mother; they were waiting for an opportunity to visit the Master when the men devotees would leave the room.

Sri Ramakrishna was sitting on the small couch. As he looked at the young devotees his face beamed with joy.

Rakhal was not then living at Dakshineswar with the Master. Since his return from Vrindāvan he had been living at home.

MASTER (smiling): "Rakhal is now enjoying his 'pension'. Since his return from Vrindāvan he has been staying at home. His wife is there. But he said to me that he would not accept any work even if he were offered a salary of a thousand rupees.

"Rakhal would lie down here and say to me that he didn't care even for my company. He was then passing through such an exalted state.

"Bhavanath is married; but he spends the whole night in spiritual conversation with his wife. The couple pass their time talking of God alone. I said to him, 'Have a little fun with your wife now and then.' 'What?' he retorted angrily. 'Shall we too indulge in frivolity?'"

Sri Ramakrishna began to talk about Narendra.

MASTER (to the devotees): "I haven't felt the same strong longing for the younger Naren that I felt for Narendra.

(To Haripada) "Do you go to Girish Ghosh's house?"

HARIPADA: "Yes, I go there very often. He is our neighbour."

MASTER: "Does Narendra, too, go there?"

HARIPADA: "Yes, I see him there occasionally."

MASTER: "What does he say in reply to Girish?" [Girish Ghosh spoke of Sri Ramakrishna as an Incarnation of God.]

HARIPADA: "Narendra has been defeated in the argument."

MASTER: "No, Narendra says, 'Girish Ghosh has such strong faith; why should I contradict him?'"

The brother of Judge Anukal Mukhopadhyaya's son-in-law was in the room. The Master asked him, "Do you know Narendra?"

BROTHER: "Yes, sir. He is a very intelligent young man."

MASTER (to the devotees): "He must be a good man because he speaks highly of Narendra. Narendra was here the other day and sang with Trailokya Sannyal. But that day his singing seemed flat to me."

Baburam was a student in the Entrance Class in the school where M. taught.

MASTER (to Baburam): "Where are your books? Aren't you attending to your studies? (To M.) He wants to stick to both.[9]

"That is very difficult. What will you gain by knowing God partially? Vaśishthadeva, great sage that he was, was overcome at the death of his sons. That amazed Lakshmana and he asked Rāma the reason. Rāma said: 'Brother, what is there to wonder at? He who has knowledge has ignorance also. Brother, go beyond both knowledge and ignorance.' If a thorn enters the sole of your foot, you get another thorn to take out the first one. Afterwards you throw both away. Likewise, one procures the thorn of knowledge to remove the thorn of ignorance; then one goes beyond both knowledge and ignorance."

BABURAM (smiling): "That's what I want."

MASTER (smiling): "But, my child, can you attain it by holding to both? If you want that, then come away."

BABURAM (smiling): "Take me away from the world."

MASTER (to M.): "Rakhal lived with me, but that was different; his father agreed to it. If these boys stay here there will be trouble.

(To Baburam) "You have no strength of mind; you haven't much courage. Just see how the younger Naren says, 'I will come away for good.'"

Sri Ramakrishna came down from the small couch and sat among the youngsters on the floor. M. sat by his side.

MASTER (to M.): "I have been seeking one who has totally renounced

[9] God and the world.

'woman and gold. When I find a young man, I think that perhaps he will live with me; but everyone raises some objection or other.

"A ghost sought a companion. It is said that a man who dies on a Saturday or Tuesday becomes a ghost. Therefore, whenever the ghost saw anybody fall from a roof or stumble and faint on the road on either of those days, he would run to him, hoping that the man, through an accidental death, would become a ghost and be his companion. But such was his ill luck that everyone revived. The poor thing could not get a companion.

"Just see, Rakhal always gives his wife as an excuse. He says, 'What will become of her?' When I touched Narendra on the chest, he became unconscious; then he cried out: 'Oh, what have you done to me? Don't you know that I have a father and mother?'

"Why has God made me lead this kind of life?[10] Chaitanyadeva became a sannyāsi so that all would salute him. Whoever salutes an Incarnation, even once, obtains liberation."

Mohinimohan had brought a basket of sweetmeats for Sri Ramakrishna.

MASTER: "Who has brought these sweets?"

Baburam pointed to Mohinimohan.

Sri Ramakrishna touched the sweets, uttering the word "Om", and ate a little. Then he distributed them among the devotees. To the surprise of the others, he fed the younger Naren and a few of the boys with his own hand.

MASTER (to M.): "This has a meaning. There is a greater manifestation of God in men of pure heart. In former years, when I used to go to Kāmārpukur, I would feed some of the young boys with my own hand. Chiné Sankhari would say, 'Why doesn't he feed us that way?' But how could I? They led an immoral life. Who would feed them?"

Sri Ramakrishna was in the happiest mood with his young and pure-souled devotees. He was seated on the small couch and was doing funny imitations of a kirtani. The devotees laughed heartily. The kirtani·is dressed lavishly and covered with ornaments. She sings, standing on the floor, a coloured kerchief in her hand. Now and then she coughs to draw people's attention and blows her nose, raising her nose-ring. When a respectable gentleman enters the room, she welcomes him with appropriate words, still continuing her song. Now and then she pulls her sāri from her arms to show off her jewels.

The devotees were convulsed with laughter at this mimicry by Sri Ramakrishna. Paltu rolled on the ground. Pointing to him, the Master said to M.: "Look at that child! He is rolling with laughter." He said to Paltu with a smile: "Don't report this to your father, or he will lose the little respect he has for me. You see, he is an 'Englishman'."

MASTER (to the devotees): "There are people who indulge in all kinds of gossip at the time of their daily devotions. As you know, one is not permitted to talk then; so they make all kinds of signs, keeping their lips closed. In order to say, 'Bring this', 'Bring that', they make sounds like 'Huh', 'Uhuh'. All such things they do! (Laughter.)

"Again, there are some who bargain for fish while telling their beads.

[10] Evidently Sri Ramakrishna was referring to his monastic life.

As they count the rosary, with a finger they point out the fish, indicating, 'That one, please.' They reserve all their business for that time! (*Laughter.*)

"There are women who come to the Ganges for their bath and, instead of thinking of God, gossip about no end of things. 'What jewels did you offer at the time of your son's marriage?'—'Has so-and-so returned from her father-in-law's house?'—'So-and-so is seriously ill.'—'So-and-so went to see the bride; we hope that they will offer a magnificent dowry and that there will be a great feast.'—'Harish always nags at me; he can't stay away from me even an hour.'—'My child, I couldn't come to see you all these days; I was so busy with the betrothal of so-and-so's daughter.'

"You see, they have come to bathe in the holy river, and yet they indulge in all sorts of worldly talk."

The Master began to look intently at the younger Naren and went into samādhi. Did he see God Himself in the pure-souled devotee?

The devotees silently watched the figure of Sri Ramakrishna motionless in samādhi. A few minutes before there had been so much laughter in the room; now there was deep silence, as if no one were there. The Master sat with folded hands as in his photograph.

After a short while his mind began to come down to the relative plane. He heaved a long sigh and became aware of the outer world. He looked at the devotees and began to talk with them of their spiritual progress.

MASTER (*to the younger Naren*): "I have been eager to see you. You will succeed. Come here once in a while. Well, which do you prefer—jnana or bhakti?"

THE YOUNGER NAREN: "Pure bhakti."

MASTER: "But how can you *love* someone unless you *know* him? (*Pointing to M., with a smile*) How can you love him unless you know him? (*To M.*) Since a pure-souled person has asked for pure bhakti, it must have some meaning.

"One does not seek bhakti of one's own accord without inborn tendencies. This is the characteristic of premā-bhakti. There is another kind of bhakti, called jnāna-bhakti, which is love of God based on reasoning.

(*To the younger Naren*) "Let me look at your body; take off your shirt. Fairly broad chest. You will succeed. Come here now and then."

Sri Ramakrishna was still in the ecstatic mood. He spoke tenderly to the other devotees about their future.

MASTER (*to Paltu*): "You will succeed, too, but it will take a little time.

(*To Baburam*) "Why don't I attract you to me? It is just to avoid trouble.

(*To Mohinimohan*) "As for you, you are all right. There is a little yet to be done. When that is achieved, nothing will remain—neither duty nor work nor the world itself. Is it good to get rid of everything?"

As Sri Ramakrishna spoke these words he looked at Mohini affectionately, as if scanning his inmost feelings. Was Mohini really wondering whether it would be wise to renounce all for God? After a while Sri Ramakrishna said, "God binds the *Bhāgavata* pundit to the world with one tie; otherwise, who would remain to explain the sacred book? He keeps the pundit bound for the good of men. That is why the Divine Mother has kept you in the world."

Now Sri Ramakrishna spoke to the young brāhmin.

MASTER: "Give up knowledge and reasoning; accept bhakti. Bhakti alone is the essence. Is this the third day of your stay here?"

BRĀHMIN (with folded hands): "Yes, sir."

MASTER: "Have faith. Depend on God. Then you will not have to do anything yourself. Mother Kāli will do everything for you.

"Jnāna goes as far as the outer court, but bhakti can enter the inner court. The Pure Self is unattached. Both vidyā and avidyā are in It, but It is unattached. Sometimes there is a good and sometimes a bad smell in the air, but the air itself is unaffected.

"Once Vyāsadeva was about to cross the Jamunā. The gopis also were there. They wanted to go to the other side of the river to sell curd, milk, and cream. But there was no ferry at that time. They were all worried about how to cross the river, when Vyāsa said to them, 'I am very hungry.' The milkmaids fed him with milk and cream. He finished almost all their food. Then Vyāsa said to the river, 'O Jamunā, if I have not eaten anything, then your waters will part and we shall walk through.' It so happened. The river parted and a pathway was formed between the waters. Following that path, the gopis and Vyāsa crossed the river. Vyāsa had said, 'If I have not eaten anything'. That means, the real man is Pure Ātman. Ātman is unattached and beyond Prakriti. It has neither hunger nor thirst; It knows neither birth nor death; It does not age, nor does It die. It is immutable as Mount Sumeru.

"He who has attained this Knowledge of Brahman is a jīvanmukta, liberated while living in the body. He rightly understands that the Ātman and the body are two separate things. After realizing God one does not identify the Ātman with the body. These two are separate, like the kernel and the shell of the coconut when its milk dries up. The Ātman moves, as it were, within the body. When the 'milk' of worldly-mindedness has dried up, one gets Self-Knowledge. Then one feels that Ātman and body are two separate things. The kernel of a green almond or betel-nut cannot be separated from the shell; but when they are ripe the juice dries up and the kernel separates from the shell. After the attainment of the Knowledge of Brahman, the 'milk' of worldly-mindedness dries up.

"But it is extremely difficult to attain the Knowledge of Brahman. One doesn't get it by merely talking about it. Some people feign it. (Smiling) There was a man who was a great liar; but, on the other hand, he used to say he had the Knowledge of Brahman. When someone took him to task for telling lies, he said: 'Why, this world is truly like a dream. If everything is unreal, then can truth itself be real? Truth is as unreal as falsehood.'" (All laugh.)

Sri Ramakrishna sat with the devotees on the mat on the floor. He was smiling. He said to the devotees, "Please stroke my feet gently." They carried out his request. He said to M., "There is great significance in this."[11] Placing

---

[11] The stroking of his feet.

his hand on his heart, the Master said, "If there is anything here, then through this service the ignorance and illusion of the devotees will be completely destroyed."

Suddenly Sri Ramakrishna became serious, as if about to reveal a secret.

MASTER (to M.): "There is no outsider here. The other day, when Harish was with me, I saw Satchidānanda come out of this sheath.[12] It said, 'I incarnate Myself in every age.' I thought that I myself was saying these words out of mere fancy. I kept quiet and watched. Again Satchidānanda Itself spoke, saying, 'Chaitanya, too, worshipped Śakti.' "

The devotees listened to these words in amazement. Some wondered whether God Himself was seated before them in the form of Sri Ramakrishna. The Master paused a moment. Then he said, addressing M., "I saw that it is the fullest manifestation of Satchidānanda; but this time the Divine Power is manifested through the glory of sattva."

The devotees sat spellbound.

MASTER (to M.): "Just now I was saying to the Mother, 'I cannot talk much.' I also said to Her, 'May people's inner consciousness be awakened by only one touch!' You see, such is the power of Yogamāyā that She can cast a spell. She did so at Vrindāvan. That is why Subol[13] was able to unite Sri Krishna and Rādhikā. Yogamāyā, the Primal Power, has a power of attraction. I applied that power myself.

(To M.) "Well, do you think that those who come here are realizing anything?"

M: "Yes, sir, it must be so."

MASTER: "How do you know?"

M. (smiling): "Everyone says, 'Whoever goes to him doesn't return to the world.' "

MASTER (smiling): "A bullfrog was caught by a water-snake. The snake could neither swallow the frog nor let it go. As a result the frog suffered very much; he croaked continuously. And the snake suffered too. But if the frog had been seized by a cobra, he would have been quiet after one or two croaks. (All laugh.)

(To the young devotees) "Read the Bhaktichaitanyachandrikā by Trailokya. Ask Trailokya for a copy. He has written well about Chaitanyadeva."

A DEVOTEE: "Will he give it to us?"

MASTER (smiling): "Why not? If a farmer has a good crop of melons he can easily give away two or three. (All laugh.) Won't Trailokya give you the book free?

(To Paltu) "Come here now and then."

PALTU: "I shall come whenever I can."

MASTER: "Will you see me in Calcutta when I go there?"

PALTU: "Yes, I shall try."

MASTER: "That's the answer of a calculating mind."

PALTU: "If I don't say, 'I shall try', I may be a liar."

[12] Sri Ramakrishna's body.
[13] One of the companions of Sri Krishna.

MASTER (*to M.*): "I don't mind the lies of these boys. They are not free. (*To Haripada*) "Why hasn't Mahendra Mukherji come here lately?"
HARIPADA: "I'm not quite sure why."
M. (*smiling*): "He's practising jnanayoga!"
MASTER: "No, it's not that. The other day he promised to send me in his carriage to the theatre to see a play about the life of Prahlāda; but he didn't send the carriage. Perhaps that is why he doesn't come."
M: "One day I saw Mahima Chakravarty and had a talk with him. It seems that Mahendra visits him."
MASTER: "But Mahima talks about bhakti also. He loves to recite the hymn: 'What need is there of penance if God is worshipped with love?'"
M. (*smiling*): "He says that because you make him say it."
Girish Chandra Ghosh was always talking to the devotees about the Master.
HARIPADA: "Girish Ghosh sees many visions nowadays. After going home from here he remains absorbed in spiritual moods and sees many things."
MASTER: "That may be true. Coming to the Ganges, one sees many things —boats, ships, and what not."
HARIPADA: "Girish Ghosh says: 'From now on I shall occupy myself only with my work. In the morning, on the stroke of the clock, I shall sit down with my pen and ink-pot and write for the whole day.' He makes the resolve, no doubt, but cannot carry it out. No sooner do we visit him than he begins to talk about you. You asked him to send Narendra here in a carriage. He said, 'I shall hire a carriage for Narendra.'"
At five o'clock the younger Naren was ready to go home. Sri Ramakrishna stood by his side on the northeast verandah and gave him various instructions. Then the boy saluted the Master and departed. Many of the devotees also took their leave.
Sri Ramakrishna was sitting on the small couch talking to Mohini. Mohini's wife was almost mad with grief on account of her son's death. Sometimes she laughed and sometimes she wept. But she felt peaceful in Sri Ramakrishna's presence.
MASTER: "How is your wife now?"
MOHINI: "She becomes quiet whenever she is here; but sometimes at home she becomes very wild. The other day she was going to kill herself."
When Sri Ramakrishna heard this he appeared worried. Mohini said to him humbly, "Please give her a few words of advice."
MASTER: "Don't allow her to cook. That will heat her brain all the more. And keep her in the company of others so that they may watch her."
It was dusk. Preparations were going on in the temples for the evening worship. The lamp was lighted in the Master's room and incense was burnt. Seated on the small couch, Sri Ramakrishna saluted the Divine Mother and chanted Her name in a tender voice. There was nobody in the room except M., who was sitting on the floor.
Sri Ramakrishna rose from the couch. M. also stood up. The Master asked him to shut the west and north doors of the room. M. obeyed and stood by Sri Ramakrishna on the porch. The Master said that he wanted to go to

the Kāli temple. Leaning on M.'s arm, he came down to the terrace of the temple. He asked M. to call Baburam and sat down.

After visiting the Divine Mother, the Master returned to his room across the court, chanting, "O Mother! Mother! Rājarājesvari!"

Sri Ramakrishna entered his room and sat on the small couch. He had been passing through an extraordinary state of mind: he could not touch any metal. He had said a few days before, "It seems that the Divine Mother has been removing from my mind all ideas of possession." He had been eating from plantain-leaves and drinking water from an earthen tumbler. He could not touch a metal jar; so he had asked the devotees to get a few earthen jars for him. If he touched metal plates or pots, his hand ached as if stung by a horned fish.

Prasanna had brought a few earthen pots, but they were very small. The Master said with a smile: "These pots are too small. But he is a nice boy. Once I asked him to take off his clothes, and he stood naked in front of me. What a child he is!"

Tarak of Belgharia arrived with a friend and bowed low before Sri Ramakrishna, who was sitting on the small couch. The room was lighted by an oil lamp. A few devotees were sitting on the floor.

Tarak was about twenty years old, and married. His parents did not allow him to come to Sri Ramakrishna. He lived mostly at his home near Bowbāzār. The Master was very fond of him. Tarak's friend had a tāmasic nature; he rather scoffed at the Master and religious ideas in general.

MASTER (to Tarak's friend): "Why don't you go and visit the temples?"

FRIEND: "Oh, I've seen them before."

MASTER: "Is it wrong for Tarak to come here?"

FRIEND: "You know best."

MASTER (pointing to M.): "He is a headmaster."

FRIEND: "Oh!"

Sri Ramakrishna asked about Tarak's health and talked with him at length. Tarak was ready to leave. Sri Ramakrishna asked him to be careful about many things.

MASTER: "My good man, beware. Beware of 'woman and gold'. Once you sink in the māyā of a woman, you will not be able to rise. It is the whirlpool of the Visālākshi.[14] He who has fallen into it cannot pull himself out again. Come here now and then."

TARAK: "My people at home don't let me."

A DEVOTEE: "Suppose someone's mother says to him, 'Don't go to Dakshineswar.' Suppose she curses him, saying, 'If you go there you will be drinking my blood!' "

MASTER: "A mother who says that is no mother; she is the embodiment of avidyā. There is no sin in disobeying such a mother. She obstructs her son's path to God. There is no harm in disobeying your elders for the sake of God. For Rāma's sake Bharat did not obey his mother Kaikeyi.[15] The gopis did

_____

[14] A stream near Kāmārpukur.

[15] Through Kaikeyi's machinations, her stepson, Rāma, was exiled to the forest so that Bharat might become king; but Bharat refused to ascend the throne.

not obey their husbands when they were forbidden to visit Krishna. Prahlāda disobeyed his father for God. Vali disregarded the words of Śukrāchārya, his teacher, in order to please God. Bibhishana went against the wishes of Rāvana, his elder brother, to please Rāma. But you must obey your elders in all other things. Let me see your hand."

Sri Ramakrishna took Tarak's hand into his own and seemed to feel its weight. A few moments later he said: "There is a little crookedness in your mind; but that will go. Pray to God a little and come here now and then. Yes, that twist will go. Is it you that have hired the house at Bowbāzār?"

TARAK: "Not I, sir, but my parents."

MASTER (smiling): "They or you? Is it because you are afraid of the 'tiger'?"

Tarak had a young wife. Did the Master mean that a woman is like a tiger to a man?

Tarak saluted Sri Ramakrishna and took his leave. The Master lay down on the small couch. He seemed worried about Tarak. Suddenly he said to M., "Why do I worry so much about these young boys?" M. kept still. He was thinking over a reply. The Master asked him, "Why don't you speak?"

Mohini's wife entered the room and sat at one side. Sri Ramakrishna spoke to M. about Tarak's friend.

MASTER: "Why did Tarak bring that fellow with him?"

M: "Perhaps he wanted a companion for the road. It is a long way from Calcutta; so he brought a friend with him."

The Master suddenly addressed Mohini's wife and said: "By unnatural death one becomes an evil spirit. Beware. Make it clear to your mind. Is this what you have come to after hearing and seeing so much?"

Mohini was about to take his leave. He saluted Sri Ramakrishna. His wife also saluted the Master, who stood near the north door of the room. Mohini's wife spoke to him in a whisper.

MASTER: "Do you want to stay here?"

MOHINI'S WIFE: "Yes, I want to spend a few days with the Holy Mother at the nahabat. May I?"

MASTER: "That will be all right. But you talk of dying. That frightens me. And the Ganges is so near!"

38

WITH THE DEVOTEES IN CALCUTTA

ON THE MORNING of Wednesday, March 11, Sri Ramakrishna and some of his disciples visited Balaram Bose's house. Balaram was indeed blessed among the householder disciples of the Master. Sri Ramakrishna often described him as a rasaddār, or supplier of stores, appointed by the Divine Mother to take care of his physical needs. Balaram's house in Calcutta had been sanctified many times by the Master's presence. There he frequently lost himself in samādhi, dancing, singing, or talking about God. Those of the Master's disciples and devotees who could not go to Dakshineswar visited him there and received his instruction. He often asked Balaram to invite young disciples such as Rakhal, Bhavanath, and Narendra to his house, saying: "These pure souls are the veritable manifestations of God. To feed them is to feed God Himself. They are born with special divine attributes. By serving them you will be serving God." And so it happened that whenever the Master was at Balaram's house the devotees would gather there. It was the Master's chief vineyard in Calcutta. It was here that the devotees came to know each other intimately.

M. taught in a school in the neighbourhood. He often brought his young students to visit the Master at Balaram's house. On this day, having learnt of Sri Ramakrishna's arrival, M. went there at noon during the recess hour of the school. He found the Master resting in the drawing-room after his midday meal. Several young boys were in the room. M. prostrated himself before the Master and sat by his side.

MASTER (tenderly): "How could you come now? Have you no school work?"

M: "I have come directly from school. Just now I have no important work to do."

A DEVOTEE: "No, sir; he is playing truant today." (All laugh.)

M. said to himself, "Alas! It is indeed as if some invisible power had drawn me here."

The Master, looking a little thoughtful, asked M. to come nearer. He said, "Please wring out my wet towel and put my coat in the sun." Then he continued: "My legs and feet ache. Please rub them gently."

M. felt very happy to be given the privilege of rendering these services to the Master.

Sri Ramakrishna said to M.: "Can you tell me why I have been feeling like this the past few days? It is impossible for me to touch any metal. When I touched a metal cup I felt as if I had been stung by a horned fish. There was an excruciating pain all over my arm. But I must use a brass water-jar, and so I tried to carry it after covering it with my towel. But the moment I touched the jar I felt the same acute pain in my arm. It was an unbearable pain! At last I prayed to the Divine Mother: 'O Mother, I shall never do it again. Please forgive me this time.'

"The younger Naren often visits me. Do you think his people at home will object? He is very pure and doesn't know what carnal pleasure is."

M: "He is a 'large receptacle'."

MASTER: "That is true. Further, he says he remembers spiritual things after hearing them once only. He told me, 'I used to weep in my boyhood because I couldn't see God.'"

The Master and M. were thus talking about the young devotee when someone reminded M. of his school.

MASTER: "What is the time now?"

A DEVOTEE: "It is ten minutes to one."

MASTER (to M.): "You had better go now. It is getting late for you. You have left your duties. (To Latu) Where is Rakhal?"

LATU: "He has gone home."

MASTER: "What? Has he gone away without seeing me?"

After school-hours M. returned to Balaram's house and found the Master sitting in the drawing-room, surrounded by his devotees and disciples. Among them were Girish, Suresh, Balaram, Latu, and Chunilal. The Master's face was beaming with a sweet smile, which was reflected in the happy faces of those in the room. M. was asked to take a seat by the Master's side.

MASTER (to Girish): "You had better argue this point with Narendra and see what he has to say."

GIRISH: "Narendra says that God is infinite; we cannot even so much as say that the things or persons we perceive are parts of God. How can Infinity have parts? It cannot."

MASTER: "However great and infinite God may be, His Essence can and does manifest itself through man by His mere will. God's Incarnation as a man cannot be explained by analogy. One must feel it for oneself and realize it by direct perception. An analogy can give us only a little glimpse. By touching the horns, legs, or tail of a cow, we in fact touch the cow herself; but for us the essential thing about a cow is her milk, which comes through the udder. The Divine Incarnation is like the udder. God incarnates Himself as man from time to time in order to teach people devotion and divine love."

GIRISH: "Narendra says: 'Is it ever possible to know all of God? He is infinite.'"

MASTER (to Girish): "Who can comprehend everything about God? It is not given to man to know any aspect of God, great or small. And what need is there to know everything about God? It is enough if we only realize Him. And we see God Himself if we but see His Incarnation. Suppose a person goes to the Ganges and touches its water. He will then say, 'Yes, I have seen and touched the Ganges.' To say this it is not necessary for him to touch the whole length of the river from Hārdwār to Gangāsāgar. (*Laughter.*)

"If I touch your feet, surely that is the same as touching you. (*Laughter.*) If a person goes to the ocean and touches but a little of its water, he has surely touched the ocean itself. Fire, as an element, exists in all things, but in wood it is present to a greater degree."

GIRISH (*smiling*): "I am looking for fire. Naturally I want to go to a place where I can get it."

MASTER (*smiling*): "Yes, fire, as an element, is present more in wood than in any other object. If you seek God, then seek Him in man; He manifests Himself more in man than in any other thing. If you see a man endowed with ecstatic love, overflowing with prema, mad after God, intoxicated with His love, then know for certain that God has incarnated Himself through that man.

(*To M.*) "There is no doubt that God exists in all things; but the manifestations of His Power are different in different beings. The greatest manifestation of His Power is through an Incarnation. Again, in some Incarnations there is a complete manifestation of God's Power. It is the Śakti, the Power of God, that is born as an Incarnation."

GIRISH: "Narendra says that God is beyond our words and thought."

MASTER: "That is not altogether true. He is, no doubt, unknowable by this ordinary mind, but He can indeed be known by the pure mind. The mind and intellect become pure the moment they are free from attachment to 'woman and gold'. The pure mind and pure intellect are one and the same. God is known by the pure mind. Didn't the sages and seers of olden times see God? They realized the All-pervading Consciousness by means of their inner consciousness."

GIRISH (*with a smile*): "I defeated Narendra in the argument."

MASTER: "Oh, no! He said to me: 'When Girish Ghosh has so much faith in God's Incarnation as man, what can I say to him? It is not proper to meddle with such faith.'"

GIRISH (*with a smile*): "Sir, we are very free and easy with our words. But M. is sitting there with his lips shut tight. What in the world is passing through his mind? What do you say about it, sir?"

MASTER (*with a laugh*): "There is a common adage that tells people to beware of the following: a man with a loose tongue, a man whose mind cannot be fathomed even by an expert diver, a man who sticks the sacred tulsi-leaf in his ears as a sign of holiness, a woman wearing a long veil to proclaim her chastity, and the cold water of a reservoir covered with green scum, by bathing in which one gets typhoid fever. These are all dangerous things. (*With a smile*) But it is different with M. He is a serious man." (*All laugh.*)

CHUNILAL: "People have begun to whisper about M.'s conduct. The younger Naren and Baburam are his students, as are Naran, Paltu, Purna, and Tejchandra. The rumour is that he brings these boys to you and so they neglect their studies. The boys' guardians hold M. responsible."

MASTER: "But who would believe their words?"

They were thus talking when Naran entered the room and bowed low before the Master. He was a student seventeen or eighteen years old and of fair complexion. He was dearly loved by the Master, who was very eager to see the boy and feed him. Many a time at the temple garden at Dakshineswar the Master wept silently for Naran. He looked on him as the manifestation of Nārāyana Himself.

GIRISH (at the sight of Naran): "There! Who told him about this? Now we realize that M. is at the root of all the mischief." (All laugh.)

MASTER (smiling): "Stop! Hold your tongue. There is already an evil rumour about him."

The conversation next turned to Narendra.

A DEVOTEE: "Why doesn't he come to you so frequently nowadays?"

MASTER (quoting a proverb): "Man's worries over bread and butter are simply amazing; they make even Kālidāsa lose his wits."

BALARAM: "Narendra frequently visits his friend Annada Guha of the family of Shiva Guha."

MASTER: "Yes, I have heard that too. Narendra and his friends meet at the house of a government officer and conduct meetings of the Brāhmo Samāj there."

A DEVOTEE: "The officer's name is Tarapada."

BALARAM (smiling): "The brāhmins say that Annada Guha is a very egotistic man."

MASTER: "Never listen to what the brāhmins say. You know their nature very well. If a man doesn't give them money, they will call him bad; on the other hand, if a man is generous to them, they will call him good. (All laugh.) I know Annada. He is a good man."

The drawing-room was full of devotees. The Master wanted to hear some songs. At his request Tarapada sang about Krishna:

> O Keśava, bestow Thy grace
> Upon Thy luckless servants here!
> O Keśava, who dost delight
> To roam Vrindāvan's glades and groves!
>
> O Mādhava, our mind's Bewitcher!
> Sweet One, who dost steal our hearts,
> Sweetly playing on Thy flute!
>
> (Chant, O Mind, the name of Hari,
> Sing aloud the name of Hari,
> Praise Lord Hari's name!)
>
> O Thou Eternal Youth of Braja,
> Tamer of fierce Kāliya,
> Slayer of the afflicted's fear!

Beloved, with the arching eyes
And crest with arching peacock feather,
Charmer of Sri Rādhā's heart!

Govardhan's mighty Lifter, Thou,
All garlanded with sylvan flowers!
O Dāmodara, Kamśa's Scourge!

O Dark One, who dost sport in bliss
With sweet Vrindāvan's gopi maids.

(Chant, O mind, the name of Hari,
Sing aloud the name of Hari,
Praise Lord Hari's name!)

MASTER (to Girish): "Ah! It is a beautiful song. Did you write it?"
A DEVOTEE: "Yes, sir, he wrote all the songs for his play, the *Chaitanyalīlā*."
MASTER: "This one has really hit the mark."

At Sri Ramakrishna's request Tarapada sang two more songs. In the first,
Nitāi exhorts people to share Rādhā's love for Sri Krishna:

Come one and all! Take Rādhā's love!
The high tide of her love flows by;
It will not last for very long.
Oh, come then! Come ye, one and all!
In countless streams it flows from her;
As much as you desire is yours.

Made all of love, she pours out love
Unstintingly for everyone;
Her love intoxicates the heart
With heavenly bliss, and thrills the soul.
Oh, come and sing Lord Hari's name,
Drawn by her love. Oh, come ye all!

Next he sang about Gaurānga:

Who art Thou, Gaur of the golden hue,
That quenchest the thirst of my soul?
Thou raisest a storm in the sea of Love,
And scarcely can I steady my boat.

Once as a cowherd boy in Vrindāvan
Thou didst tend the cows;
In Thy hands Thou heldest the flute
That so bewitched the gopi maids.

Lifting Govardhan's mount in Thine arms,
Thou shieldedst Vrindāvan from ill;
And at the wounded gopis' feet
Humbledst Thyself in repentant love.

The devotees pressed M. to sing; but M. was shy and asked them in a
whisper to excuse him.

GIRISH (to the Master): "Sir, we can't find a way to persuade M. to sing.'

MASTER (*annoyed*): "Yes, he can bare his teeth at school, but shyness overpowers him when he is asked to sing!"

M., feeling greatly distressed, remained speechless.

Suresh Mitra, a beloved householder disciple of the Master, was seated at a distance. The Master cast an affectionate glance at him and said to him, pointing to Girish, "You talk of having lived a wild life, but here is one you could not surpass."

SURESH (*with a smile*): "Yes, sir, he is my elder brother in that respect." (*All laugh.*)

GIRISH (*to the Master*): "Well, sir, I didn't have any education during my boyhood, but still people say I am a learned man."

MASTER: "Mahimacharan has studied many scriptures. A big man. (*To M.*) Isn't that so?"

M: "Yes, sir."

GIRISH: "What? Book-learning? I have seen enough of it. It can't fool me any more."

MASTER (*with a smile*): "Do you know my attitude? Books, scriptures, and things like that only point out the way to reach God. After finding the way, what more need is there of books and scriptures? Then comes the time for action.

"A man received a letter from home informing him that certain presents were to be sent to his relatives. The names of the articles were given in the letter. As he was about to go shopping for them, he found that the letter was missing. He began anxiously to search for it, several others joining in the search. For a long time they continued to search. When at last the letter was discovered, his joy knew no bounds. With great eagerness he opened the letter and read it. It said that he was to buy five seers of sweets, a piece of cloth, and a few other things. Then he did not need the letter any more, for it had served its purpose. Putting it aside, he went out to buy the things. How long is such a letter necessary? As long as its contents are not known. When the contents are known one proceeds to carry out the directions.

"In the scriptures you will find the way to realize God. But after getting all the information about the path, you must begin to work. Only then can you attain your goal.

"What will it avail a man to have mere scholarship? A pundit may have studied many scriptures, he may recite many sacred texts, but if he is still attached to the world and if inwardly he loves 'woman and gold', then he has not assimilated the contents of the scriptures. For such a man the study of scriptures is futile.

"The almanac forecasts the rainfall for the year. You may squeeze the book, but you won't get a drop of water—not even a single drop." (*Laughter.*)

GIRISH (*smiling*): "What did you say, sir, about squeezing the almanac? Won't a single drop of water come out of it?" (*All laugh.*)

MASTER (*with a smile*): "The pundits talk big, but where is their mind fixed? On 'woman and gold', on creature comforts and money. The vulture soars very high in the sky, but its eyes are fixed on the charnel-pit. It is continually looking for charnel-pits, carcasses, and dead bodies.

(*To Girish*) "Narendra is a boy of a very high order. He excels in everything: vocal and instrumental music and studies. Again, he has control over his sense-organs. He is truthful and has discrimination and dispassion. So many virtues in one person! (*To M.*) What do you say? Isn't he unusually good?"

M: "Yes, sir, he is."

MASTER (*aside to M.*): "He [meaning Girish] has great earnestness and faith."

M. looked at Girish, and marvelled at his tremendous faith. Girish had been coming to Sri Ramakrishna only a short time and had already recognized his spiritual power. To M. he seemed a familiar friend and kinsman, related to him by the strong bond of spirituality. Girish was one of the gems in the necklace of the Master's devotees.

Narayan asked the Master whether he would sing. Sri Ramakrishna sang of the Divine Mother:

> Cherish my precious Mother Śyāmā
> Tenderly within, O mind;
> May you and I alone behold Her,
> Letting no one else intrude.
>
> O mind, in solitude enjoy Her,
> Keeping the passions all outside;
> Take but the tongue, that now and again
> It may cry out, "O Mother! Mother!"
>
> Suffer no breath of base desire
> To enter and approach us there,
> But bid true knowledge stand on guard,
> Alert and watchful evermore.

Then he sang, as if he were one of the afflicted souls of the world:

> O Mother, ever blissful as Thou art,
> Do not deprive Thy worthless child of bliss!
> My mind knows nothing but Thy Lotus Feet.
> The King of Death scowls at me terribly;
> Tell me, Mother, what shall I say to him? . . .

Again he sang about the bliss of the Divine Mother:

> Behold my Mother playing with Śiva, lost in an ecstasy of joy!
> Drunk with a draught of celestial wine, She reels and yet She
>   does not fall. . . .

The devotees listened to the songs in deep silence. After a few moments Sri Ramakrishna said, "I have a slight cold; so I couldn't sing well."

Gradually it became dusk. The shadow of evening fell on Calcutta. For the moment the noise of the busy metropolis was stilled. Gongs and conch-shells proclaimed the evening worship in many Hindu homes. Devotees of God set aside their worldly duties and turned their minds to prayer and meditation. This joining of day and night, this mystic twilight, always created an ecstatic mood in the Master.

The devotees seated in the room looked at Sri Ramakrishna as he began to chant the sweet name of the Divine Mother. After the chanting he began to pray. What was the need of prayer to a soul in constant communion with God? Did he not rather want to teach erring mortals how to pray? Addressing the Divine Mother, he said, "O Mother, I throw myself on Thy mercy; I take shelter at Thy Hallowed Feet. I do not want bodily comforts; I do not crave name and fame; I do not seek the eight occult powers. Be gracious and grant that I may have pure love for Thee, a love unsmitten by desire, untainted by any selfish ends—a love craved by the devotee for the sake of love alone. And grant me the favour, O Mother, that I may not be deluded by Thy world-bewitching māyā, that I may never be attached to the world, to 'woman and gold', conjured up by Thy inscrutable māyā! O Mother, there is no one but Thee whom I may call my own. Mother, I do not know how to worship; I am without austerity; I have neither devotion nor knowledge. Be gracious, Mother, and out of Thy infinite mercy grant me love for Thy Lotus Feet."

Every word of this prayer, uttered from the depths of his soul, stirred the minds of the devotees. The melody of his voice and the childlike simplicity of his face touched their hearts very deeply.

Girish invited the Master to his house, saying that he must go there that very night.

MASTER: "Don't you think it will be late?"

GIRISH: "No, sir. You may return any time you like. I shall have to go to the theatre tonight to settle a quarrel there."

It was nine o'clock in the evening when the Master was ready to start for Girish's house. Since Balaram had prepared supper for him, Sri Ramakrishna said to Balaram: "Please send the food you have prepared for me to Girish's. I shall enjoy it there." He did not want to hurt Balaram's feelings.

As the Master was coming down from the second floor of Balaram's house, he became filled with divine ecstasy. He looked as if he were drunk. Narayan and M. were by his side; a little behind came Ram, Chuni, and the other devotees. No sooner did he reach the ground floor than he became totally overwhelmed. Narayan came forward to hold him by the hand lest he should miss his footing and fall. The Master expressed annoyance at this. A few minutes later he said to Narayan affectionately: "If you hold me by the hand people may think I am drunk. I shall walk by myself."

Girish's house was not far away. The Master passed the crossing at Bosepārā Lane. Suddenly he began to walk faster. The devotees were left behind. Presently Narendra was seen coming from a distance. At other times the Master's joy would have been unbounded at the thought of Narendra or at the mere mention of his name; but now he did not even exchange a word with his beloved disciple.

As the Master and the devotees entered the lane where Girish lived, he was able to utter words. He said to Narendra: "Are you quite well, my child? I could not talk to you then." Every word the Master spoke was full of infinite tenderness. He had not yet reached the door of Girish's house, when suddenly he stopped and said, looking at Narendra: "I want to tell you something. 'This' is one and 'that' is another." Who could know what was passing through his innermost soul at that moment?

Girish stood at the door to welcome the Master. As Sri Ramakrishna entered the house, Girish fell at his feet and lay there on the floor like a rod. At the Master's bidding he stood up, touching the Master's feet with his forehead. Sri Ramakrishna was taken to the drawing-room on the second floor. The devotees followed him and sat down, eager to get a view of the Master and listen to every word that fell from his lips.

As Sri Ramakrishna was about to take the seat reserved for him, he saw a newspaper lying near it. He signed to someone to remove the paper. Since a newspaper contains worldly matters—gossip and scandal—, he regarded it as unholy. After the paper was removed he took his seat. Nityagopal came forward and bowed low before the Master.

MASTER: "Well! You haven't been to Dakshineswar for a long time."

NITYAGOPAL: "True, sir. I haven't been able to go there. I haven't been well. I have had pains all over my body."

MASTER: "How are you now?"

NITYAGOPAL: "Not so well, sir."

MASTER: "Bring your mind down one or two notes."

NITYAGOPAL: "I don't like people's company. They say all kinds of things about me. That sometimes frightens me, but again I feel great strength within."

MASTER: "That's only natural. Who lives with you?"

NITYAGOPAL: "Tarak.[1] He is always with me. But sometimes he too gets on my nerves."

MASTER: "Nangtā told me that there lived at his monastery an ascetic who had acquired occult powers. He used to go about with his eyes fixed on the sky. But when one of his companions left him, he became disconsolate."

Again the Master went into an ecstatic mood. Strange thoughts seemed to stir his mind and he remained speechless. After a while he said: "Art Thou come? I too am here." Who could pretend to understand these words?

Many of his devotees were in the room: Narendra, Girish, Ram, Haripada, Chuni, Balaram, and M. Narendra did not believe that God could incarnate Himself in a human body. But Girish differed with him; he had the burning faith that from time to time the Almighty Lord, through His inscrutable Power, assumes a human body and descends to earth to serve a divine purpose.

The Master said to Girish, "I should like to hear you and Narendra argue in English."

The discussion began; but they talked in Bengali. Narendra said: "God is Infinity. How is it possible for us to comprehend Him? He dwells in every human being. It is not the case that He manifests Himself through one person only."

SRI RAMAKRISHNA (tenderly): "I quite agree with Narendra. God is

[1] A disciple of Sri Ramakrishna later known as Swami Shivananda.

everywhere. But then you must remember that there are different manifestations of His Power in different beings. At some places there is a manifestation of His avidyāśakti, at others a manifestation of His vidyāśakti. Through different instruments God's Power is manifest in different degrees, greater and smaller. Therefore all men are not equal."

RAM: "What is the use of these futile arguments?"

MASTER (*sharply*): "No! No! There is a meaning in all this."

GIRISH (*to Narendra*): "How do you know that God does not assume a human body?"

NARENDRA: "God is 'beyond words or thought'."

MASTER: "No, that is not true. He can be known by the pure buddhi, which is the same as the Pure Self. The seers of old directly perceived the Pure Self through their pure buddhi."

GIRISH (*to Narendra*): "Unless God Himself teaches men through His human Incarnation, who else will teach them spiritual mysteries? God takes a human body to teach men divine knowledge and divine love. Otherwise, who will teach?"

NARENDRA: "Why, God dwells in our own heart; He will certainly teach us from within the heart."

MASTER (*tenderly*): "Yes, yes. He will teach us as our Inner Guide."

Gradually Narendra and Girish became involved in a heated discussion. If God is Infinity, how can He have parts? What did Hamilton say? What were the views of Herbert Spencer, of Tyndall, of Huxley? And so forth and so on.

MASTER (*to M.*): "I don't enjoy these discussions. Why should I argue at all? I clearly see that God is everything; He Himself has become all. I see that whatever is, is God. He is everything; again, He is beyond everything. I come to a state in which my mind and intellect merge in the Indivisible. At the sight of Narendra my mind loses itself in the consciousness of the Absolute. (*To Girish*) What do you say to that?"

GIRISH (*with a smile*): "Why ask me? As if I understood everything except that one point!" (*All laugh.*)

MASTER: "Again, I cannot utter a word unless I come down at least two steps from the plane of samādhi. Śankara's Non-dualistic explanation of Vedānta is true, and so is the Qualified Non-dualistic interpretation of Rāmānuja."

NARENDRA: "What is Qualified Non-dualism?"

MASTER: "It is the theory of Rāmānuja. According to this theory, Brahman, or the Absolute, is qualified by the universe and its living beings. These three—Brahman, the world, and living beings—together constitute One. Take the instance of a bel-fruit. A man wanted to know the weight of the fruit. He separated the shell, the flesh, and the seeds. But can a man get the weight by weighing only the flesh? He must weigh flesh, shell, and seeds together. At first it appears that the real thing in the fruit is the flesh, and not its seeds or shell. Then by reasoning you find that the shell, seeds, and flesh all belong to the fruit; the shell and seeds belong to the same thing that the flesh belongs to. Likewise, in spiritual discrimination one must first reason, following the method of 'Not this, not this': God is not the universe; God is not the living beings; Brahman alone is real and all else is unreal. Then one realizes, as with the bel-fruit, that the Reality from which we derive the notion of Brahman is the very Reality that evolves the idea of living beings and the universe. The Nitya and the Līlā are the two aspects of one and the same Reality; therefore, according to Rāmānuja, Brahman is qualified by the universe and the living beings. This is the theory of Qualified Non-dualism.

(To M.) "I do see God directly. What shall I reason about? I clearly see that He Himself has become everything; that He Himself has become the universe and all living beings.

"But without awakening one's own inner consciousness one cannot realize the All-pervading Consciousness. How long does a man reason? So long as he has not realized God. But mere words will not do. As for myself, I clearly see that He Himself has become everything. The inner consciousness must be awakened through the grace of God. Through this awakening a man goes into samādhi. He often forgets that he has a body. He gets rid of his attachment to 'woman and gold' and does not enjoy any talk unless it is about God. Worldly talk gives him pain. Through the awakening of the inner consciousness one realizes the All-pervading Consciousness."

The discussion came to a close. Sri Ramakrishna said to M.: "I have observed that a man acquires one kind of knowledge about God through reasoning and another kind through meditation; but he acquires a third kind of Knowledge about God when God reveals Himself to him, His devotee. If God Himself reveals to His devotee the nature of Divine Incarnation—how He plays in human form—, then the devotee doesn't have to reason about the problem or need an explanation. Do you know what it is like? Suppose a man is in a dark room. He goes on rubbing a match against a match-box and all of a sudden light comes. Likewise, if God gives us this flash of divine light, all our doubts are destroyed. Can one ever know God by mere reasoning?"

Sri Ramakrishna asked Narendra to sit by his side. He tenderly inquired about his health and showed him much affection.

NARENDRA (to the Master): "Why, I have meditated on Kāli for three or four days, but nothing has come of it."

MASTER: "All in good time, my child. Kāli is none other than Brahman. That which is called Brahman is really Kāli. She is the Primal Energy. When that Energy remains inactive, I call It Brahman, and when It creates, preserves, or destroys, I call It Śakti or Kāli. What you call Brahman I call Kāli.

"Brahman and Kāli are not different. They are like fire and its power to burn: if one thinks of fire one must think of its power to burn. If one recognizes Kāli one must also recognize Brahman; again, if one recognizes Brahman one must recognize Kāli. Brahman and Its Power are identical. It is Brahman whom I address as Śakti or Kāli."

It was late at night. Girish asked Haripada to call a cab, for he had to go to the theatre. As Haripada was about to leave the room the Master said with a smile: "Mind, a cab. Don't forget to bring one." (*All laugh.*)

HARIPADA (*smiling*): "Yes, sir. I am going out just for that. How can I forget it?"

GIRISH: "That I should have to go to the theatre and leave you here!"

MASTER: "No, no. You must hold to both. King Janaka paid attention to both religious and worldly duties and 'drank his milk from a brimming cup'." (*All laugh.*)

GIRISH: "I have been thinking of leaving the theatre to the youngsters."

MASTER: "No, no. It is all right. You are doing good to many."

Narendra said in a whisper, "Just a moment ago he [meaning Girish] was calling him [meaning Sri Ramakrishna] God, an Incarnation, and now he is attracted to the theatre!"

Narendra was sitting beside the Master. The latter looked at him intently and suddenly moved closer to his beloved disciple. Narendra did not believe in God's assuming a human body; but what did that matter? Sri Ramakrishna's heart overflowed with more and more love for his disciple. He touched Narendra's body and said, quoting from a song:

> Do you[2] feel that your pride is wounded?
> So be it, then; we too have our pride.

Then the Master said to Narendra: "As long as a man argues about God, he has not realized Him. You two were arguing. I didn't like it.

"How long does one hear noise and uproar in a house where a big feast is being given? So long as the guests are not seated for the meal. As soon as food is served and people begin to eat, three quarters of the noise disappears. (*All laugh.*) When the dessert is served there is still less noise. But when the guests eat the last course, buttermilk, then one hears nothing but the sound 'soop, sup'. When the meal is over, the guests retire to sleep and all is quiet.

"The nearer you approach to God, the less you reason and argue. When you attain Him, then all sounds—all reasoning and disputing—come to an end. Then you go into samādhi—sleep—, into communion with God in silence."

The Master gently stroked Narendra's body and affectionately touched his chin, uttering sweetly the holy words, "Hari Om! Hari Om! Hari Om!" He was fast becoming unconscious of the outer world. His hand was on Narendra's foot. Still in that mood he gently stroked Narendra's body. Slowly a change came over his mind. With folded hands he said to Narendra: "Sing a song, please; then I shall be all right. How else shall I be able to stand on my own legs?" Again he became speechless. He sat motionless as a statue. Presently he became intoxicated with divine love and said: "O Rādhā, watch your step! Otherwise you may fall into the Jamunā. Ah! How mad she is with love of Krishna!"

[2] These words are addressed to Rādhā, the beloved of Krishna, by her companions, the gopis.

The Master was in a rapturous mood. Quoting from a song, he said:

> Tell me, friend, how far is the grove
> Where Krishna, my Beloved, dwells?
> His fragrance reaches me even here,
> But I am tired and can walk no farther.

Then the Master completely forgot the outer world. He did not notice anyone in the room, not even his beloved Narendra seated by his side. He did not know where he himself was seated. He was totally merged in God. Suddenly he stood up, shouting, "Deep drunk with the Wine of Divine Love!" As he took his seat again, he muttered, "I see a light coming, but I know not whence it comes."

Now Narendra sang:

> Lord, Thou hast lifted all my sorrow with the vision of Thy face,
> And the magic of Thy beauty has bewitched my mind;
> Beholding Thee, the seven worlds forget their never-ending woe;
> What shall I say, then, of myself, a poor and lowly soul? . . .

Listening to the song, Sri Ramakrishna again went into deep samādhi. His eyes were closed and his body was transfixed.

Coming down from the ecstatic mood he looked around and said, "Who will take me to the temple garden?" He appeared like a child who felt confused in the absence of his companion.

It was late in the evening. The night was dark. The devotees stood by the carriage that had been brought to take the Master to Dakshineswar. They helped him in gently, for he was still in deep ecstasy. The carriage moved down the street and they looked after it with wistful eyes.

Soon the devotees turned homeward, a gentle south wind blowing in their faces. Some were humming the lines of the song:

> Lord, Thou hast lifted all my sorrow with the vision of Thy face,
> And the magic of Thy beauty has bewitched my mind.

April 6, 1885

Sri Ramakrishna sat in the drawing-room of Balaram's house talking to M. It was a very hot day and long past three o'clock. He had come to Calcutta to see some of his young disciples and also to visit Devendra's house.

MASTER (*to M.*): "I gave my word that I would be here at three o'clock; so I have come. But it is very hot."

M: "Yes, sir, you must have suffered very much."

The devotees were fanning Sri Ramakrishna.

MASTER: "I have come here for Baburam and the younger Naren. Why haven't you brought Purna?"

M: "He doesn't like to come to a gathering of people. He is afraid you might praise him before others and his relatives might then hear about it."

MASTER: "Yes, that's true. I won't do it in the future. Well, I understand that you are giving Purna religious instruction. That is fine."

M: "As a matter of fact, the same thing is written in one of the text-books of the school. It says:

> With all thy soul love God above;
> And as thyself thy neighbour love.

If their guardians are displeased with such teachings, it can't be helped."

MASTER: "No doubt many things like that are written in those books; but the authors themselves do not assimilate what they write. This power of assimilation comes from associating with holy men. People listen to instruction only when it is given by a sādhu who has truly renounced the world; they are not much impressed by the writings or the words of a mere scholar. Suppose a physician has a big jar of molasses by his side, and he asks his patients not to eat molasses; the patients won't pay much attention to his advice.

"Well, how do you find Purna? Does he go into ecstatic moods?"

M: "No, I haven't noticed in him any outer sign of such emotion. One day I told him those words of yours."

MASTER: "What words?"

M: "You told us that if a man is a 'small receptacle' he cannot control spiritual emotion; but if he is a 'large receptacle' he experiences intense emotion without showing it outwardly. You said that a big lake does not become disturbed when an elephant enters it; but when the elephant enters a pool, one sees tremendous confusion and the water splashes on the banks."

MASTER: "Purna will not show his emotion outwardly; he hasn't that kind of temperament. His other signs are good. What do you say?"

M: "His eyes are very bright and prominent."

MASTER: "Mere bright eyes are not enough. The eyes of a godly person are different. Did you ask him what he felt after meeting me?"

M: "Yes, sir, we talked about that. He has been telling me for the last four or five days that whenever he thinks of God or repeats His name, tears flow from his eyes and the hair on his body stands on end—such is his joy."

MASTER: "Indeed! That's all he needs."

The Master and M. were silent a few moments. Then M. said, "He is waiting—"

MASTER: "Who?"

M: "Purna. Perhaps he has been standing at the door of his house. When any of us passes that way he will come running and salute us."

MASTER: "Ah! Ah!"

Sri Ramakrishna was resting, reclining against a bolster. M. had brought with him a twelve-year-old boy who was a student in his school. His name was Kshirode.

M: "He is a nice boy. He finds great joy in spiritual talk."

MASTER (smiling): "He has eyes like a deer's."

The boy saluted Sri Ramakrishna, touching his feet. Then he gently stroked the Master's feet.

MASTER (to M.): "Rakhal is staying at home now; he has an abscess and is not well. I understand that his wife expects a baby."

Paltu and Binode were seated in front of Sri Ramakrishna.

MASTER (to Paltu, smiling): "What did you say to your father? (To M.) He answered back when his father told him not to come here. (To Paltu) What did you say?"

PALTU: "I said to him: 'Yes, I go to him. Is that wrong?' (The Master and M. laugh.) I shall say more if necessary."

MASTER (to M., smiling): "No, no! Should he go so far?"

M: "No, sir, he should not go too far." (Sri Ramakrishna laughs.)

MASTER (to Binode): "How are you? Why haven't you come to Dakshineswar?"

BINODE: "I almost came, but then I was afraid of falling ill again. I have been ill and am not doing well."

MASTER: "Come to Dakshineswar with me. The air is very good there. You will recover."

The younger Naren entered the room. Sri Ramakrishna was going out to wash his hands and face. The younger Naren followed him with a towel; he wanted to pour water for the Master. M. was with them.

MASTER: "It's very hot today."

M: "Yes, sir."

MASTER: "How do you live in that small room of yours? Doesn't it get very hot on the upper floor?"

M: "Yes, sir, it gets very hot."

MASTER: "Besides, your wife has been suffering from brain trouble. You should keep her in a cool room."

M: "Yes, sir. I have asked her to sleep downstairs."

Sri Ramakrishna returned to the drawing-room and took his seat.

MASTER (to M.): "Why didn't you come to Dakshineswar last Sunday?"

M: "Sir, there was no one else at home. My wife was not well and no one was there to look after her."

Sri Ramakrishna was on his way in a carriage to Devendra's house in Nimu Goswami's Lane. The younger Naren, M., and one or two other devotees were with him. The Master felt great yearning for Purna. He began to talk of the young disciple.

MASTER (to M.): "A great soul! Or how could he make me do japa for his welfare? But Purna doesn't know anything about it."

M. and the other devotees were amazed at these words.

MASTER: "It would have been nice if you had brought him here with you today. Why didn't you?"

Seeing the younger Naren laugh, the Master and the other devotees laughed too. The Master said to M., laughing and pointing to Naren: "Look at him! Look! How naïve he looks when he laughs, as if he knew nothing. He never thinks of these three things: land, wife, and money. God cannot be realized unless the mind is totally free from 'woman and gold'."

The carriage proceeded to Devendra's house. Once Sri Ramakrishna had said to Devendra at Dakshineswar, "I have been thinking of visiting your house one day." Devendra had replied: "The same idea came to my mind today, and I have come here to ask that favour of you. You must grace my house this Sunday." "But", the Master had said, "you have a small income. Don't invite many people. The carriage hire will also run to a big amount." Devendra had answered, laughing: "What if my income is small? 'One can run into debt to eat butter!' " At these words Sri Ramakrishna had laughed a long time.

Soon the carriage reached Devendra's house. Sri Ramakrishna said to him: "Devendra, don't make elaborate arrangements for my meal. Something very simple will do. I am not very well today."

Sri Ramakrishna seated himself in the drawing-room on the ground floor of Devendra's house. The devotees sat around him. It was evening. The room was well lighted. The younger Naren, Ram, M., Girish, Devendra, Akshay, Upendra, and some other devotees were present. As the Master cast his glance on a young devotee, his face beamed with joy. Pointing to the devotee, Sri Ramakrishna said to the others: "He is totally free from attachment to land, wife, and money, the three things that entangle one in worldliness. The mind that dwells on these three cannot be fixed on God. He saw a vision, too. (To the devotee) Tell us, what did you see?"

DEVOTEE (laughing): "I saw a heap of dung. Some were seated on it, and some sat at a distance."

MASTER: "It was a vision of the plight of the worldly people who are forgetful of God. It shows that all these desires are disappearing from his mind. Need one worry about anything if one's mind is detached from 'woman and gold'? How strange! Only after much meditation and japa could I get rid of these desires; and how quickly he could banish them from his mind! Is it an easy matter to get rid of lust? I myself felt a queer sensation in my heart six months after I had begun my spiritual practice. Then I threw myself on the ground under a tree and wept bitterly. I said to the Divine Mother, 'Mother, if it comes to that, I shall certainly cut my throat with a knife!'

(To the devotees) "If the mind is free from 'woman and gold', then what else can obstruct a man? He enjoys then only the Bliss of Brahman."

Sashi[3] had recently been visiting Sri Ramakrishna. He was studying at the Vidyāsāgar College for his Bachelor's degree. The Master began to talk about him.

MASTER (to the devotees): "That boy will think of money for some time. But there are some who will never do so. Some of the youngsters will not marry."

The devotees listened silently to the Master.

MASTER: "It is hard to recognize an Incarnation of God unless the mind is totally free from 'woman and gold'. A man asked a seller of egg-plants the value of a diamond. He said, 'I can give nine seers of egg-plants in exchange, and not one more.' "[4]

At these words all the devotees laughed. The younger Naren laughed

---

[3] Sashi later became a monastic disciple of the Master and assumed the name of Swami Ramakrishnananda.

[4] The story is given on p. 759.

very loudly. Sri Ramakrishna noticed that he had quickly understood the implication of these words.

MASTER: "What a subtle mind he has! Nangtā also could understand things that way, in a flash—the meaning of the *Gītā*, the *Bhāgavata*, and other scriptures.

"Renunciation of 'woman and gold' from boyhood! Amazing indeed! It falls to the lot of a very few. A person without such renunciation is like a mango struck by a hail-stone. The fruit cannot be offered to the Deity, and even a man hesitates to eat it.

"There are people who during their youth committed many sins, but in old age chant the name of God. Well, that is better than nothing.

"The mother of a certain Mallick, who belonged to a very noble family, asked me if prostitutes would ever be saved. She herself had led that kind of life; that is why she asked the question. I said: 'Yes, they too will be saved, if only they cry to God with a yearning heart and promise not to repeat their sins.' What will the mere chanting of Hari's name accomplish? One must weep sincerely."

The kirtan began to the accompaniment of drums and cymbals. The singer was a professional. He sang about Sri Gaurānga's initiation as a monk by Keshab Bhārati:

> Oh, what a vision I have beheld in Keshab Bhārati's hut!
> Gorā, in all his matchless grace,
> Shedding tears in a thousand streams! . . .

Sri Ramakrishna went into ecstasy when he heard the song. The musician sang again, describing the suffering of a milkmaid of Vrindāvan at her separation from Sri Krishna. She was seeking her Krishna in the mādhavi[5] bower:

> O mādhavi, give me back my Sweet One!
> Give me, give me back my Sweet One!
> Give Him back, for He is mine,
> And make me your slave for ever.
> He is my life, as water is to the fish;
> O mādhavi, you have hidden Him in your bosom!
> I am a simple, guileless girl,
> And you have stolen my Beloved.
> O mādhavi, I die for my Sweet One;
> I cannot bear to live without Him.
> Without my Mādhava[6] I shall die;
> Oh, give Him, give Him back to me!

Now and then Sri Ramakrishna sang with the musicians, improvising lines:

> How far from here is Mathurā,
> Where dwells the Beloved of my soul?

---

[5] A spring creeper with fragrant flowers.
[6] A name of Krishna.

Sri Ramakrishna went into samādhi. His body was motionless. He remained in that state a long time.

Gradually he came down to the consciousness of the outer world. Still in a spiritual mood, he began to talk, sometimes addressing the devotees, sometimes the Divine Mother.

MASTER: "Mother, please attract him to Thee. I can't worry about him any more. (*To M.*) My mind is inclined a little to your brother-in-law.

(*To Girish*) "You utter many abusive and vulgar words; but that doesn't matter. It is better for these things to come out. There are some people who fall ill on account of blood-poisoning; the more the poisoned blood finds an outlet, the better it is for them. At the time when the upādhi of a man is being destroyed, it makes a loud noise, as it were. Wood crackles when it burns; there is no more noise when the burning is over.

"You will be purer day by day. You will improve very much day by day. People will marvel at you.

"I may not come many more times; but that doesn't matter. You will succeed by yourself."

The Master's spiritual mood became very intense. Again he talked to the Divine Mother.

MASTER: "Mother, what credit is there in making a man good who is already good? O Mother, what wilt Thou accomplish by killing one who is already dead? Only if Thou canst kill a person who is still standing erect wilt Thou show Thy glory."

Sri Ramakrishna remained silent a few moments. Suddenly he said in a slightly raised voice: "I have come from Dakshineswar. I am going, Mother!" It was as if a child had heard the call of its mother from a distance and was responding to it. He again became motionless, absorbed in samādhi. The devotees looked at him with unwinking eyes. Still in an ecstatic mood he said, "I shall not eat any more luchi." At this point a few Vaishnava priests, who had come from the neighbourhood, left the place.

Sri Ramakrishna began to talk with his devotees in a very joyous spirit. It was the month of April and the day was very sultry. Devendra had made ice-cream. He offered it to the Master and the devotees. M. said in a low voice, "Encore! Encore!" The devotees laughed. At the sight of the ice-cream Sri Ramakrishna was happy as a child.

MASTER: "The kirtan was very nice. The song described beautifully the gopis' state of mind: 'O mādhavi, give me back my Sweet One!' The milk-maids of Vrindāvan were drunk with ecstatic love for Krishna. How wonderful! Mad for Krishna!"

A devotee, pointing to another devotee, said, "He has the attitude of the gopis."

RAM: "No, he has both—the attitude of tender love and the attitude of austere knowledge."

MASTER: "What is it you are talking about?"

Sri Ramakrishna inquired about Surendra.

RAM: "I sent him word, but he hasn't come."

MASTER: "He gets very tired from his heavy office-work."

A DEVOTEE: "Ram Babu has been writing about you."

MASTER (*smiling*): "What is he writing?"

DEVOTEE: "He is writing an article on 'The Bhakti of the Paramahamsa'."

MASTER: "Good! That will make Ram famous."

GIRISH (*smiling*): "He says he is your disciple."

MASTER: "I have no disciple. I am the servant of the servant of Rāma."

Some people of the neighbourhood had dropped in; but they did not please the Master. He said: "What sort of place is this? I don't find a single pious soul here."

Devendra took Sri Ramakrishna into the inner apartments and offered him refreshments. Afterwards the Master returned to the drawing-room with a happy face and took his seat. The devotees sat around him. Upendra[7] and Akshay[8] sat on either side of him and stroked his feet. The Master spoke highly of the women of Devendra's family, saying: "They are very nice. They come from the country; so they are very pious."

The Master was absorbed in his own joy. In a happy mood he began to sing:

> Unless a man is simple, he cannot recognize God, the Simple
> One. . . .

Again he sang:

> Stay your steps, O wandering monk!
> Stand there with begging-bowl in hand,
> And let me behold your radiant face. . . .

Once more:

> A mendicant has come to us, ever absorbed in divine moods;
> Holy alike is he to Hindu and Mussalmān. . . .

Girish saluted the Master and took his leave. Devendra and the other devotees took the Master to his carriage. Seeing that one of his neighbours was sound asleep on a bench in the courtyard, Devendra woke him up. The neighbour rubbed his eyes and said, "Has the Paramahamsa come?" All burst into laughter. The man had come a long time before Sri Ramakrishna's arrival, and because of the heat had spread a mat on the bench, lain down, and gone sound asleep.

Sri Ramakrishna's carriage proceeded to Dakshineswar. He said to M. happily, "I have eaten a good deal of ice-cream; bring four or five cones for me when you come to Dakshineswar." Continuing, he said, "Now my mind is drawn to these few youngsters: the younger Naren, Purna, and your brother-in-law."

M: "Do you mean Dwija?"

MASTER: "No, he is all right; I mean his elder brother."

The carriage rolled on to the Kāli temple at Dakshineswar.

---

[7] Later a famous publisher in Calcutta.

[8] The author of a life of Sri Ramakrishna in Bengali verse.

THE MASTER'S REMINISCENCES

SRI RAMAKRISHNA was sitting with the devotees in Balaram's drawing-room in Calcutta. M. arrived at three o'clock. Girish, Balaram, the younger Naren, Paltu, Dwija, Purna, Mahendra Mukherji, and many other devotees were there. Shortly Trailokya Sannyal, Jaygopal Sen, and other members of the Brāhmo Samāj arrived. Many woman devotees were present also, seated behind a screen. Among them was Mohini's wife, who had almost gone insane on account of her son's death. There were a few other afflicted souls like her who used to visit the Master to obtain peace of mind.

Sri Ramakrishna was describing to the devotees the various incidents of his sādhanā and the phases of his spiritual realization.

MASTER: "During my sādhanā, when I meditated, I would actually see a person sitting near me with a trident in his hand. He would threaten to strike me with the weapon unless I fixed my mind on the Lotus Feet of God, warning me that it would pierce my breast if my mind strayed from God.

"The Divine Mother would put me in such a state that sometimes my mind would come down from the Nitya to the Līlā, and sometimes go up from the Līlā to the Nitya.

"Sometimes, when the mind descended to the Līlā, I would meditate day and night on Sītā and Rāma. At those times I would constantly behold the forms of Sītā and Rāma. Rāmlālā[1] was my constant companion. Sometimes I would bathe Him and sometimes feed Him.

"Again, I used to be absorbed in the ideal of Rādhā and Krishna and would constantly see their forms. Or again, I would be absorbed in Gaurānga. He is the harmonization of two ideals: the Purusha and the Prakriti. At such times I would always see the form of Gaurānga.

"Then a change came over me. The mind left the plane of the Līlā and ascended to the Nitya. I found no distinction between the sacred tulsi and the ordinary sajinā plant. I no longer enjoyed seeing the forms of God; I said to myself, 'They come and go.' I lifted my mind above them. I removed all the pictures of gods and goddesses from my room and began to meditate

[1] A metal image of the Boy Rāma given to Sri Ramakrishna during his sādhanā period by a Vaishnava saint.

on the Primal Purusha, the Indivisible Satchidānanda, regarding myself as His handmaid.

"I practised all sorts of sādhanā. There are three classes of sādhanā: sāttvic, rājasic, and tāmasic. In the sāttvic sādhanā the devotee calls on the Lord with great longing or simply repeats His name; he doesn't seek any result in return. The rājasic sādhanā prescribes many rituals: puraścharana, pilgrimage, panchatapā, worship with sixteen articles, and so forth. The tāmasic sādhanā is a worship of God with the help of tamas. The attitude of a tāmasic devotee is this: 'Hail, Kāli! What? Wilt Thou not reveal Thyself to me? If not, I will cut my throat with a knife!' In this discipline one does not observe conventional purity; it is like some of the disciplines prescribed by the Tantra.

"During my sādhanā period I had all kinds of amazing visions. I distinctly perceived the communion of Ātman. A person exactly resembling me entered my body and began to commune with each one of the six lotuses.[2] The petals of these lotuses had been closed; but as each of them experienced the communion, the drooping flower bloomed and turned itself upward. Thus blossomed forth the lotuses at the centres of Mulādhāra, Svādhisthāna, Anāhata, Viśuddha, Ājnā, and Sahasrāra. The drooping flowers turned upward. I perceived all these things directly.

"When I meditated during my sādhanā, I used to think of the unflickering flame of a lamp set in a windless place.

"In deep meditation a man is not at all conscious of the outer world. A hunter was aiming at a bird. A bridal procession passed along beside him, with the groom's relatives and friends, music, carriages, and horses. It took a long time for the procession to pass the hunter, but he was not at all conscious of it. He did not know that the bridegroom had gone by.

"A man was angling in a lake all by himself. After a long while the float began to move. Now and then its tip touched the water. The angler was holding the rod tight in his hands, ready to pull it up, when a passer-by stopped and said, 'Sir, can you tell me where Mr. Bannerji lives?' There was no reply from the angler, who was just on the point of pulling up the rod. Again and again the stranger said to him in a loud voice, 'Sir, can you tell me where Mr. Bannerji lives?' But the angler was unconscious of everything around him. His hands were trembling, his eyes fixed on the float. The stranger was annoyed and went on. When he had gone quite a way, the angler's float sank under water and with one pull of the rod he landed the fish. He wiped the sweat from his face with his towel and shouted after the stranger. 'Hey!' he said. 'Come here! Listen!' But the man would not turn his face. After much shouting, however, he came back and said to the angler, 'Why are you shouting at me?' 'What did you ask me about?' said the angler. The stranger said, 'I repeated the question so many times, and now you are asking me to repeat it once more!' The angler replied, 'At that time my float was about to sink; so I didn't hear a word of what you said.'

[2] A reference to the lotuses at the six centres, through which the Kundalini rises. See Glossary under Kundalini.

"A person can achieve such single-mindedness in meditation that he will see nothing, hear nothing. He will not be conscious even of touch. A snake may crawl over his body, but he will not know it. Neither of them will be aware of the other.

"In deep meditation the sense-organs stop functioning; the mind does not look outward. It is like closing the gate of the outer court in a house. There are five objects of the senses: form, taste, smell, touch, and sound. They are all left outside.

"At the beginning of meditation the objects of the senses appear before the aspirant. But when the meditation becomes deep, they no longer bother him. They are left outside. How many things I saw during meditation! I vividly perceived before me a heap of rupees, a shawl, a plate of sweets, and two women with rings in their noses. 'What do you want?' I asked my mind. 'Do you want to enjoy any of these things?' 'No,' replied the mind, 'I don't want any of them. I don't want anything but the Lotus Feet of God.' I saw the inside and the outside of the women, as one sees from outside the articles in a glass room. I saw what is in them: entrails, blood, filth, worms, phlegm, and such things."

Girish Chandra Ghosh used to say now and then that he could cure illness by the strength of the Master's name.

MASTER (to Girish and the other devotees): "People of small intellect seek occult powers—powers to cure disease, win a lawsuit, walk on water, and such things. But the genuine devotees of God don't want anything except His Lotus Feet. One day Hriday said to me, 'Uncle, please ask the Mother for some powers, some occult powers.' I have the nature of a child. While I was practising japa in the Kāli temple, I said to Kāli, 'Mother, Hriday asked me to pray to You for some occult powers.' The Divine Mother at once showed me a vision. A middle-aged prostitute, about forty years old, appeared and sat with her back to me. She had large hips and wore a black-bordered sāri. Soon she was covered with filth. The Mother showed me that occult powers are as abominable as the filth of that prostitute. Thereupon I went to Hriday and scolded him, saying: 'Why did you teach me such a prayer? It is because of you that I had such an experience.'

"People with a little occult power gain such things as name and fame. Many of them want to follow the profession of guru, gain people's recognition, and make disciples and devotees. Men say of such a guru: 'Ah! He is having a wonderful time. How many people visit him! He has many disciples and followers. His house is overflowing with furniture and other things. People give him presents. He has such power that he can feed many people if he so desires.'

"The profession of a teacher is like that of a prostitute. It is the selling of oneself for the trifle of money, honour, and creature comforts. For such insignificant things it is not good to prostitute the body, mind, and soul, the means by which one can attain God. A man once said about a certain woman: 'Ah! She is having a grand time now. She is so well off! She has rented a room and furnished it with a couch, a mat, pillows, and many other things. And how many people she controls! They are always visiting her.' In other words, the woman has now become a prostitute. Therefore her happiness is unbounded. Formerly she was a maidservant in a gentleman's house; now she is a prostitute. She has ruined herself for a mere trifle.

"How many other visions I saw while meditating during my sādhanā! Once I was meditating under the bel-tree when 'Sin' appeared before me and tempted me in various ways. He came to me in the form of an English soldier. He wanted to give me wealth, honour, sex pleasure, various occult powers, and such things. I began to pray to the Divine Mother. Now I am telling you something very secret. The Mother appeared. I said to Her, 'Kill him, Mother!' I still remember that form of the Mother, Her world-bewitching beauty. She came to me taking the form of Krishnamayi.[3] But it was as if her glance moved the world."

Sri Ramakrishna became silent. Resuming his reminiscences, he said: "How many other visions I saw! But I am not permitted to tell them. Some-one is shutting my mouth, as it were. I used to find no distinction between the sacred tulsi and the insignificant sajinā leaf. The feeling of distinction was entirely destroyed. Once I was meditating under the banyan when I was shown a Mussalmān[4] with a long beard. He came to me with rice in an earthen plate. He fed some other Mussalmāns with the rice and also gave me a few grains to eat. The Mother showed me that there exists only One, and not two. It is Satchidānanda alone that has taken all these various forms; He alone has become the world and its living beings. Again, it is He who has become food.

(To Girish, M., and the others) "I have the nature of a child. Hriday said to me, 'Uncle, ask the Mother for some occult powers.' At once I went to the temple to ask Her about them. At that time God had put me in such a state that I had to listen to those who lived with me. I felt like a child who sees darkness all around unless someone is with him. I felt as if I should die unless Hriday was near me. You see I am in that state of mind just now. While I am speaking to you my inner spirit is being awakened."

As Sri Ramakrishna uttered these words, he was on the point of plunging into samādhi and losing consciousness of time and space. But he was trying with the utmost difficulty to control himself. He said to the devotees in an ecstatic mood: "I still see you. But I feel as if you had been sitting here for ever. I don't recall when you came or where you are."

Sri Ramakrishna was silent a few minutes. Then, regaining partial con-sciousness, he said, "I shall have a drink of water." He often said things like this after samādhi, in order to bring down his mind to the ordinary plane of consciousness. Girish was a new-comer and did not know this; so he started to bring some water. Sri Ramakrishna asked him not to, saying, "No, my dear sir, I cannot drink now."

The Master and the devotees were silent awhile. Sri Ramakrishna re-sumed the conversation.

MASTER (to M.): "Well, have I done any wrong in telling these secret experiences?"

---

[3] The young daughter of Balaram Bose.
[4] It was perhaps a vision of Mohammed, the founder of Islam.

M. did not know what to say and kept quiet.

MASTER: "Why should there be any harm in it? I have told these things to create faith in you all."

After a while he said to M. very humbly, "Will you kindly bring him here?" He referred to Purna.

M. (*hesitating*): "Yes, sir. I shall send for him this very moment."

MASTER (*eagerly*): "In Purna I have reached the 'post'."

Was Sri Ramakrishna hinting that Purna was perhaps the last devotee of his inner circle?

Sri Ramakrishna then described to Girish, M., and the other devotees his own experience of mahābhāva.

MASTER (*to the devotees*): "My joy after that experience was equal to the pain I suffered before it. Mahābhāva is a divine ecstasy; it shakes the body and mind to their very foundation. It is like a huge elephant entering a small hut. The house shakes to its foundation. Perhaps it falls to pieces.

"The burning pain that one feels when one is separated from God is not an ordinary feeling. It is said that the fire of this anguish in Rupa and Sanātana[5] scorched the leaves of the tree under which they sat. I was unconscious three days in that state. I couldn't move. I lay in one place. When I regained consciousness, the Brāhmani[6] took me out for a bath. But my skin couldn't bear the touch of her hand; so my body had to be covered with a heavy sheet. Only then could she hold me with her hand and lead me to the bathing-place. The earth that had stuck to my body while I was lying on the ground had become baked.

"In that state I felt as if a ploughshare were passing through my backbone. I cried out: 'Oh, I am dying! I am dying!' But afterwards I was filled with great joy."

The devotees listened breathlessly to these experiences of the Master.

MASTER (*to Girish*): "But it isn't necessary for you to go so far. My experiences are for others to refer to. You busy yourself with five different things, but I have one ideal only. I do not enjoy anything but God. This is what God has ordained for me. (*Smiling*) There are different trees in the forest, some shooting up with one trunk and others spreading out with five branches. (*All smile.*)

"Yes, my experiences are for others to refer to. But you should live in the world in a spirit of detachment. You will no doubt have dirt on your body, but you must shake it off as the mudfish shakes off the mud. You may swim in the black ocean of the world, but your body should not be stained."

GIRISH (*smiling*): "But you too had to marry." (*Laughter.*)

MASTER (*smiling*): "Marriage is necessary for the sake of samskāra.[7] But how could I lead a worldly life? So uncontrollable was my divine fervour that every time the sacred thread was put around my neck it dropped off.

[5] Two great disciples of Sri Chaitanya.

[6] A brāhmin woman who was one of Sri Ramakrishna's spiritual teachers.

[7] According to Hindu religious law, marriage is one of the ten samskāras, or purificatory rites, prescribed for the three higher castes, namely, the brāhmin, kshatriya, and vaiśya.

Some believe that Śukadeva also had to marry—for the sake of samskāra. They say he even had a daughter. (*All laugh.*)

" 'Woman and gold' alone is the world. It makes one forget God."

GIRISH: "But how can we get rid of 'woman and gold'?"

MASTER: "Pray to God with a yearning heart. Pray to Him for discrimination. 'God alone is real and all else illusory'—this is discrimination. One strains water through a fine sieve in order to separate the dirt from it. The clear water goes through the sieve leaving the dirt behind. Apply the sieve of discrimination to the world. Live in the world after knowing God. Then it will be the world of vidyā.

"Just see the bewitching power of women! I mean the women who are the embodiment of avidyā, the power of delusion. They fool men, as it were. They take away their inner substance. When I see a man and woman sitting together, I say to myself, 'Alas, they are done for!' (*Looking at M.*) Haru, such a nice boy, is possessed by a witch. People ask: 'Where is Haru? Where is he?' But where do you expect him to be? They all go to the banyan and find him sitting quietly under it. He no longer has his beauty, power, or joy. Ah! He is possessed by the witch that lives in the banyan.

"If a woman says to her husband, 'Go there', he at once stands up, ready to go. If she says, 'Sit down here', immediately he sits down.

"A job-seeker got tired of visiting the manager in an office. He couldn't get the job. The manager said to him, 'There is no vacancy now; but come and see me now and then.' This went on for a long time, and the candidate lost all hope. One day he told his tale of woe to a friend. The friend said: 'How stupid you are! Why are you wearing away the soles of your feet going to that fellow? You had better go to Golap. You will get the job tomorrow.' 'Is that so?' said the candidate. 'I am going right away.' Golap was the manager's mistress. The candidate called on her and said: 'Mother, I am in great distress. You must help me out of it. I am the son of a poor brāhmin. Where else shall I go for help? Mother, I have been out of work many days. My children are about to starve to death. I can get a job if you but say the word.' Golap said to him, 'Child, whom should I speak to?' She said to herself: 'Ah, the poor brāhmin! He has been suffering too much.' The candidate said to her, 'I am sure to get the job if you just put in a word about it to the manager.' Golap said, 'I shall speak to him today and settle the matter.' The very next morning a man called on the candidate and said, 'You are to work in the manager's office, beginning today.' The manager said to his English boss: 'This man is very competent. I have appointed him. He will do credit to the firm.'

"All are deluded by 'woman and gold'. But I do not care for it at all. And I swear to you that I do not know anything but God."

A DEVOTEE: "Sir, a new sect, named 'Nava Hullol', has been started. Lalit Chatterji is one of the members."

MASTER: "There are different views. All these views are but so many paths to reach the same goal. But everyone believes that his view alone is right, that his watch alone keeps correct time."

GIRISH (*to M.*): "Do you remember what Pope says about it?

'Tis with our judgments as our watches, none
Go just alike, yet each believes his own."

MASTER (*to M.*): "What does it mean?"

M: "Everyone thinks that his own watch keeps the correct time. But different watches do not give the same time."

MASTER: "But however wrong the watches may be, the sun never makes a mistake. One should check one's watch with the sun."

A DEVOTEE: "Mr. X— tells lies."

MASTER: "Truthfulness in speech is the tapasyā of the Kaliyuga. It is difficult to practise other austerities in this cycle. By adhering to truth one attains God. Tulsidās said: 'Truthfulness, obedience to God, and the regarding of others' wives as one's mother, are the greatest virtues. If one does not realize God by practising them, then Tulsi is a liar.'

"Keshab Sen assumed his father's debts. Others would have repudiated them. I visited Devendra's Samāj at Jorāshanko and found Keshab meditating on the dais. He was then a young man. I said to Mathur Babu, 'Of all who are meditating here, this young man's "float" alone has sunk under water. The "fish" is biting at the hook.'

"There was a man—whom I shall not name—who for ten thousand rupees told a lie in court. In order to win the lawsuit he made me give an offering to the Divine Mother. He said to me, 'Father, please give this offering to the Mother.' Trusting him like a child, I gave the offering."

DEVOTEE: "A nice man indeed!"

MASTER: "But he had such faith in me that he believed the Mother would grant his prayer if I but made the offering."

Referring to Lalit Babu, Sri Ramakrishna said: "Is it an easy matter to get rid of pride? There are very few who are without pride. Balaram is one of them. (*Pointing to a devotee*) And here is another. Other people in their position would have swelled with pride. They would have parted their hair and showed other traits of tamas. They would have been proud of their learning. The 'fat brāhmin' [referring to Prankrishna] still has a little of it. (*To M.*) Mahima Chakravarty has read many books, hasn't he?"

M: "Yes, sir, he has read a great deal."

MASTER (*smiling*): "I wish he and Girish could meet. Then we could enjoy a little discussion."

GIRISH (*smiling*): "Doesn't he say that by means of sādhanā all people can be like Sri Krishna?"

MASTER: "Not exactly that, but something like it."

DEVOTEE: "Sir, can all be like Sri Krishna?"

MASTER: "An Incarnation of God or one born with some of the characteristics of an Incarnation is called an Iśvarakoti. An ordinary man is called a jīva or jīvakoti. By dint of sādhanā a jīvakoti can realize God; but after samādhi he cannot come back to the plane of relative consciousness.

"The Iśvarakoti is like the king's son. He has the keys to all the rooms of the seven-storey palace; he can climb to all the seven floors and come down at will. A jīvakoti is like a petty officer. He can enter some of the rooms of the palace; that is his limit.

"Janaka was a jnāni. He attained Knowledge by means of his sādhanā. But Śukadeva was Knowledge itself."

GIRISH: "Ah!"

MASTER: "Śukadeva did not attain Knowledge through sādhanā. Like Śukadeva, Nārada also had the Knowledge of Brahman. But he retained bhakti in order to teach people. Prahlāda sometimes assumed the attitude of 'I am He', sometimes that of a servant of God, and sometimes that of His child. Hanumān also was like that.

"All may wish for such a lofty state, but all cannot attain it. Some bamboos are hollower than others; some are more solid inside."

A DEVOTEE: "You say that your spiritual experiences are for others to refer to. Tell us what we should do."

MASTER: "If you want to realize God, then you must cultivate intense dispassion. You must renounce immediately what you feel to be standing in your way. You should not put it off till the future. 'Woman and gold' is the obstruction. The mind must be withdrawn from it.

"One must not be slow and lazy. A man was going to bathe; he had his towel on his shoulder. His wife said to him: 'You are worthless. You are getting old and still you cannot give up some of your habits. You cannot live a single day without me. But look at that man! What a renouncer he is!'

"HUSBAND: 'Why? What has he done?'

"WIFE: 'He has sixteen wives and he is renouncing them one by one. You will never be able to renounce.'

"HUSBAND: 'Renouncing his wives one by one! You are crazy. He won't be able to renounce. If a man wants to renounce, does he do it little by little?'

"WIFE (smiling): 'Still he is better than you.'

"HUSBAND: 'You are silly; you don't understand. He cannot renounce. But I can. See! Here I go!'"

The Master continued: "That is called intense renunciation. No sooner did the man discriminate than he renounced. He went away with the towel on his shoulder. He didn't turn back to settle his worldly affairs. He didn't even look back at his home.

"He who wants to renounce needs great strength of mind. He must have a dare-devil attitude like a dacoit's. Before looting a house, the dacoits shout: 'Kill! Murder! Loot!'

"Cultivate devotion and love of God and so pass your days. What else can you do? When Krishna went away, Yaśodā became insane with grief and visited Rādhā. Rādhā was moved by her sorrow and appeared before her as Ādyāśakti. She said, 'My child, ask a boon of Me.' Yaśodā replied: 'Mother, what else shall I ask of You? Bless me that I may serve Krishna alone with my body, mind, and speech; that I may behold His devotees with these eyes; that I may go with these feet to the place where His divine sport is manifested; that I may serve Him and His devotees with these hands; and that I may devote all my sense-organs to His service alone.'"

As Sri Ramakrishna uttered these words, he was about to go into ecstasy.

Suddenly he exclaimed: "Kāli, the Embodiment of Destruction! No, Nitya-Kāli, my eternal Divine Mother!" With great difficulty he restrained himself. He was starting to say more about Yaśodā, when Mahendra Mukherji arrived. Mahendra and his younger brother, Priya, had been visiting the Master for some time. Mahendra owned a flour-mill and other businesses. His brother was an engineer. Both the brothers engaged people to manage their affairs and therefore had considerable leisure. Mahendra was thirty-six or thirty-seven and his brother two years younger. Besides their country home at Kedeti, they had a house at Bāghbāzār, Calcutta. A young devotee named Hari accompanied them on their visits to Sri Ramakrishna. Hari was married but greatly devoted to the Master. Mahendra and Hari had not visited Dakshineswar for a long time. They saluted Sri Ramakrishna.

MASTER: "Hello! Why haven't you visited Dakshineswar for so long?"

MAHENDRA: "Sir, I have been away from Calcutta. I was at Kedeti."

MASTER: "You have no children. You don't serve anybody. And still you have no leisure! Goodness gracious!"

The devotees remained silent. Mahendra was a little embarrassed.

MASTER (to Mahendra): "Why am I saying all this to you? You are sincere and generous. You have love for God."

MAHENDRA: "You are saying these words for my good."

MASTER (smiling): "You see, we don't take any collection during the performance at our place. Jadu's mother says to me, 'Other sādhus always ask for money, but you do not.' Worldly people feel annoyed if they have to spend money.

"A theatrical performance was being given at a certain place. A man felt a great desire to take a seat and see it. He peeped in and saw that a collection was being taken from the audience. Quietly he slipped away. Another performance was being given at some other place. He went there and, inquiring, found that no collection would be taken. There was a great rush of people. He elbowed his way through the crowd and reached the centre of the hall. There he picked out a nice seat for himself, twirled his moustaches, and sat through the performance. (All laugh.)

"You have no children to divert your mind. I know a deputy magistrate who draws a salary of eight hundred rupees a month. He went to Keshab's house to see a performance. I was there too. Rakhal and a few other devotees were with me and sat beside me. After a while Rakhal went out for a few minutes. The deputy magistrate came over and made his young son take Rakhal's seat. I said, 'He can't sit there.' At that time I was in such a state of mind that I had to do whatever the person next to me would ask me to do; so I had seated Rakhal beside me. As long as the performance lasted the deputy did nothing but gibber with his son. The rascal didn't look at the performance even once. I heard, too, that he is a slave to his wife; he gets up and sits down as she tells him to. And he didn't see the performance for that snub-nosed monkey of a boy. . . .

(To Mahendra) "Do you practise meditation?"

MAHENDRA: "Yes, sir. A little."

MASTER: "Come to Dakshineswar now and then."

MAHENDRA (*smiling*): "Yes, sir. I will. You know where my knots and twists are. You will straighten them out."

MASTER (*smiling*): "First come to Dakshineswar; then I shall press your limbs to see where your twists are. Why don't you come?"

MAHENDRA: "Because of the pressure of my duties. Besides, I have to go to my country home now and then."

MASTER (*to Mahendra, pointing his finger at the devotees*): "Have they no homes or dwelling-places? Have they no duties? How is it that they come?

(*To Hari*) "Why haven't you come to Dakshineswar? Is your wife living with you?"

HARI: "No, sir."

MASTER: "Then why did you forget me?"

HARI: "I haven't been well, sir."

MASTER (*to the devotees*): "He looks thin. He has no small measure of bhakti. He is overflowing with it, but it is of a rather troublesome nature." (*Laughter.*)

Sri Ramakrishna used to address a certain devotee's wife by the name of "Habi's mother". Her brother, a college student aged about twenty, was there. He stood up, ready to go and play cricket. His younger brother, named Dwija, was also a devotee of the Master. Both brothers left the room. A few minutes later Dwija returned. The Master said, "Why didn't you go?" A devotee answered: "He wants to hear the music. Perhaps that is why he has come back."

Trailokya, the Brāhmo devotee, was to sing for the Master. Paltu arrived. The Master said: "Who is this? Ah! It is Paltu."

Purna, another young devotee, also arrived. It was with great difficulty that Sri Ramakrishna had managed to have him come. His relatives strongly objected to his visiting the Master. Purna was a student in the fifth grade of the school where M. taught. The boy prostrated himself before Sri Ramakrishna. The Master seated him by his side and was talking to him in a low voice. M. alone was sitting near them. The other devotees were talking about various things. Girish, sitting on the other side of the room, was reading a life of Keshab.

MASTER (*to Purna*): "Come nearer."

GIRISH (*to M.*): "Who is this boy?"

M. was afraid that others might notice the boy. This would make trouble for him at home and M. would be responsible for it.

M. (*sharply*): "Don't you see he is a boy?"

GIRISH (*smiling*): "I need no ghost to tell me that."

The Master and the boy were talking in low tones.

MASTER: "Do you practise what I asked you to?"

PURNA: "Yes, sir."

MASTER: "Do you dream? Do you dream of a flame? A lighted torch? A married woman? A cremation ground? It is good to dream of these things."

PURNA: "I dreamt of you. You were seated and were telling me something."

MASTER: "What? Some instructions? Tell me some of it."

PURNA: "I don't remember now."

MASTER: "Never mind. But it is very good. You will make progress. You feel attracted to me, don't you?"

A few minutes later Sri Ramakrishna said to the boy, "Won't you come there?" He meant Dakshineswar. "I can't promise", answered the boy.

MASTER: "Why? Doesn't one of your relatives live there?"

PURNA: "Yes, sir. But it won't be very convenient for me to go."

Girish was reading a life of Keshab written by Trailokya of the Brāhmo Samāj. In it Trailokya said that at first Sri Ramakrishna had been very much opposed to the world but that after meeting Keshab he had changed his mind and had come to believe that one could lead a spiritual life in the world as well. Several devotees had told the Master about this. They wanted to discuss it with Trailokya. Those passages in the book had been read to the Master.

Noticing the book in Girish's hand, Sri Ramakrishna said to Girish, M., Ram, and the other devotees: "Those people are busy with the world. That is why they set such a high value on worldly life. They are drowned in 'woman and gold'. One doesn't talk that way after realizing God. After enjoying divine bliss, one looks on the world as crow-droppings. At the very outset I utterly renounced everything. Not only did I renounce the company of worldly people, but now and then the company of devotees as well. I noticed that the devotees were dropping dead one by one, and that made my heart writhe with pain. But now I keep one or two of them with me."

Girish left for home, saying he would come back.

Trailokya arrived with Jaygopal Sen. They bowed before the Master and sat down. He inquired about their health. The younger Naren entered the room and saluted Sri Ramakrishna. The Master said to him, "Why didn't you see me last Saturday?"

Trailokya was ready to sing.

MASTER: "Ah! You sang that day about the Blissful Mother. How sweetly you sang! Others' songs seem insipid to me. That day I didn't enjoy even Narendra's singing. Why don't you sing those same songs again?"

Trailokya sang:

> Victory to Gorā, Sachi's son!
> Hail, Abode of every virtue,
> Touchstone of Love, Ocean of Bliss,
> Man's bewitcher, beauteous of form,
> Enchanting the eye like shining gold!
> His tender arms that reach to the knee,
> Graceful and long as lotus stalks,
> Are lovingly stretched to all mankind;
> His lotus face of matchless beauty
> Overflows with the nectar of Love;
> His cheeks are covered with curling hair!
>
> Alight with heavenly love, his beauty
> Charms the eye! Beaming with fervour,

Radiant with Bliss, his body trembling
With Hari's joy, Gaurānga the golden
Dances like a mad elephant, shaking
In all his limbs with the frenzy of love!
Gaurānga, singer of Hari's glories,
Prize of every sādhu's heart,
Rarest of men, the Ocean of Love,
Embraces the outcaste, calls him brother,
Takes him in his arms in fervent love!

He dances with both his arms upraised,
And sings Hari's name; the tears are streaming
Down his cheeks; he weeps, he cries,
He trembles, roars, and rages, saying,
"Where is Hari, the Jewel of my heart?"
The hair on his limbs is standing on end;
Like a kadamba flower is his body;
Covered with dust he rolls on the ground.
O Thou, the Abode of Hari's līlā,
Fountain-head of Love's elixir,
Friend of the helpless, Glory of Banga,
Hail Chaitanya, Thou who shinest
Bright as the moon, in the bhakta's heart!

Sri Ramakrishna left the room for a minute. The women devotees were seated near the screen. They were eager to see Sri Ramakrishna. Trailokya went on with his music.

Sri Ramakrishna entered the room again and said to Trailokya, "Please sing a little about the Blissful Mother."

Trailokya sang:

O Mother, how deep is Thy love for men!
Mindful of it, I weep for joy. . . .

Listening to the song, the younger Naren went into deep meditation. He remained as still as a log. Sri Ramakrishna said to M.; "Look at him. He is totally unaware of the outer world."

The song was over. At Sri Ramakrishna's request, Trailokya sang:

O Mother, make me mad with Thy love!
What need have I of knowledge or reason? . . .

Ram asked him to sing about Hari.

Trailokya sang:

Chant, O mind, the name of Hari,
Sing aloud the name of Hari,
Praise Lord Hari's name!
And praising Hari's name, O mind,
Cross the ocean of this world.

Hari dwells in earth, in water,
Hari dwells in fire and air;

In sun and moon He dwells.
Hari's ever living presence
Fills the boundless universe.

M. said in a low voice to Trailokya, "Please—'Gaur and Nitāi, ye blessed brothers'."

Sri Ramakrishna, too, asked him to sing the song. Trailokya and the devotees sang it in chorus, the Master joining them. When it was over, the Master sang:

> Behold, the two brothers[8] have come, who weep while chanting
> Hari's name,
> The brothers who, in return for blows, offer to sinners Hari's love,
> Embracing everyone as brother, even the outcaste shunned by men.
> Behold, the two brothers have come, who once were Kānāi and
> Balāi of Braja. . . .

Sri Ramakrishna sang again:

> See how all Nadiā is shaking
> Under the waves of Gaurānga's love! . . .

Then:

> Who are they that walk along, chanting Hari's name?
> O Mādhāi, go out and see!
> They seem to be Gaur and Nitāi,
> With golden anklets on their lovely feet;
> Shaven of head and clad in rags,
> They reel like madmen as they go. . . .

The younger Naren was about to leave.

MASTER: "Show great devotion to your parents; but don't obey them if they stand in your way to God. You must gird your loins with great determination and say, 'This rogue of a father!' "

NAREN: "Truly, I have no fear."

Girish arrived. Sri Ramakrishna introduced him to Trailokya. He asked them to talk to each other. A few minutes later the Master said, "That song again, please."

Trailokya sang:

> Victory to Gorā, Sachi's son!
> Hail, Abode of every virtue,
> Touchstone of Love, Ocean of Bliss,
> Man's bewitcher, beauteous of form,
> Enchanting the eye like shining gold! . . .

Sri Ramakrishna went into samādhi. He stood up, totally unconscious of the world.

Regaining partial consciousness, he begged Trailokya to sing "Oh, what a vision I have beheld".

[8] Gaurānga and Nityānanda.

Trailokya sang:

> Oh, what a vision I have beheld in Keshab Bhārati's[9] hut!
> Gorā, in all his matchless grace
> Shedding tears in a thousand streams!
> Like a mad elephant
> He dances in ecstasy and sings,
> Drunk with an overwhelming love.
>
> Rolling flat upon the ground and swimming in his tears,
> He weeps and shouts Lord Hari's name,
> Piercing the very heavens with his cries,
> Loud as a lion's roar;
> Then most humbly he begs men's love,
> To feel himself the servant of God.
>
> Shorn of his locks, he has put on the yogi's ochre robe;
> Even the hardest heart must melt
> To see his pure and heavenly love.
> Smitten with man's deep woe,
> He has abandoned everything
> And pours out love unstintingly.
>
> Oh, would that Premdās were his slave and, passing from
>   door to door,
> Might sing Gaurānga's endless praise!

The music was over. It was about dusk. Sri Ramakrishna was surrounded by the devotees.

MASTER (to Ram): "There were no instruments to accompany the songs. The singing creates an atmosphere when there is proper accompaniment. (Smiling) Do you know how Balaram manages a festival? He is like a miserly brāhmin raising a cow. The cow must eat very little but give milk in torrents. (All laugh.) Sing your own songs and beat your own drums: that's Balaram's idea!" (All laugh.)

As evening came on, lamps were lighted in the drawing-room and on the verandah. Sri Ramakrishna bowed to the Divine Mother and began to chant the name of God. The devotees sat around and listened to his sweet chanting. They wanted to discuss with Trailokya his remarks about the Master's change of opinion on worldly life. Girish started the discussion.

GIRISH (to Trailokya): "You have written that, after coming in contact with Keshab, Sri Ramakrishna changed his views about worldly life; but it isn't true."

MASTER (to Trailokya and the other devotees): "If a man enjoys the Bliss of God, he doesn't enjoy the world. Having tasted divine bliss, he finds the world insipid. If a man gets a shawl, he doesn't care for broadcloth."

TRAILOKYA: "I referred to those who wanted to lead a worldly life. I didn't mean renouncers."

MASTER: "What are you talking about? People talk about leading a religious life in the world. But if they once taste the bliss of God they will not enjoy anything else. Their attachment to worldly duties declines. As their

[9] The monastic teacher of Sri Chaitanya.

spiritual joy becomes deeper, they simply cannot perform their worldly duties. More and more they seek that joy. Can worldly pleasures and sex pleasures be compared to the bliss of God? If a man once tastes that bliss, he runs after it ever afterwards. It matters very little to him then whether the world remains or disappears.

"Though the chātak bird is about to die of a parched throat, and around it there are seven oceans, rivers, and lakes overflowing with water, still it will not touch that water. Its throat is cracking with thirst, and still it will not drink that water. It looks up, mouth agape, for the rain to fall when the star Svāti is in the ascendant. 'To the chātak bird all waters are mere dryness beside Svāti water.'

"People say they will hold to both God and the world. After drinking an ounce of wine, a man may be pleasantly intoxicated and also conscious of the world; but can he be both when he has drunk a great deal more?

"After the bliss of God nothing else tastes good. Then talk about 'woman and gold' stabs the heart, as it were. (*Intoning*) 'I cannot enjoy the talk of worldly people.' When a man becomes mad for God, he doesn't enjoy money or such things."

TRAILOKYA: "But, sir, if a man is to remain in the world, he needs money and he must also save. He has to give in charity and—"

MASTER: "What? Do you mean that one must first save money and then seek God? And you talk about charity and kindness! A worldly man spends thousands of rupees for his daughter's marriage. Yet, all the while, his neighbours are dying of starvation; and he finds it hard to give them two morsels of rice; he calculates a thousand times before giving them even that much. The people around him have nothing to eat; but what does he care about that? He says to himself: 'What can I do? Let the rascals live or die. All I care about is that the members of my family should live well.' And they talk about doing good to others!"

TRAILOKYA: "But, sir, there are good people in the world as well. Take the case of Pundarika Vidyānidhi, the devotee of Chaitanya. He lived in the world."

MASTER: "He had drunk wine up to his neck. If he had drunk a little more, he couldn't have led a worldly life."

Trailokya remained silent. M. said aside to Girish, "Then what he has written is not true."

GIRISH (*to Trailokya*): "Then what you have written is not true."

TRAILOKYA: "Why so? Doesn't he [meaning Sri Ramakrishna] admit that a man can lead a spiritual life in the world?"

MASTER: "Yes, he can. But such a man should first of all attain Knowledge and then live in the world. First he should realize God. Then 'he can swim in a sea of slander and not be stained.' After realizing God, a man can live in the world like a mudfish. The world he lives in after attaining God is the world of vidyā. In it he sees neither woman nor gold. He finds there only devotion, devotee, and God. You see, I too have a wife, and a few pots and pans in my room; I too feed a few vagabonds; I too worry about the devotees—Habi's mother for instance—when they come here."

A DEVOTEE (to Trailokya): "I have read in your book that you do not believe in the Incarnation of God. You said so in connection with Chaitanya."

TRAILOKYA: "Why, Chaitanya himself protested against the idea of Divine Incarnation. Once, in Puri, Advaita and the other devotees sang a song to the effect that Chaitanya was God. At this Chaitanya shut the door of his room. Infinite are the glories of God. As he [meaning Sri Ramakrishna] says, the devotee is the parlour of God. Suppose a parlour is very well furnished; does that mean that the master of the house has exhausted all his power and splendour in that one parlour?"

GIRISH: "He [meaning Sri Ramakrishna] says that prema alone is the essence of God; we need the man through whom this ecstatic love of God flows. He says that the milk of the cow flows through the udder; we need the udder; we do not care for the other parts of the cow—the legs, tail, or horns."

TRAILOKYA: "The milk of God's prema flows through an infinite number of channels. God has infinite powers."

GIRISH: "But what other power can stand before prema?"

TRAILOKYA: "It is possible if He who has the power wants it. Everything is in God's power."

GIRISH: "Yes, I admit that. But there is also a thing called the power of avidyā."

TRAILOKYA: "Is avidyā a thing? Does there exist a substance called avidyā? It is only a negation, as darkness is the negation of light. There is no doubt that we prize prema most: what is a drop to God is an ocean to us. But if you say that prema is the last word about God, then you limit God Himself."

MASTER (to Trailokya and the other devotees): "Yes, yes, that is true. But an ounce of wine makes me drunk. What need have I to count the gallons of wine in the tavern? What need have we to know about the infinite powers of God?"

GIRISH (to Trailokya): "Do you believe in the Incarnation of God?"

TRAILOKYA: "God incarnates Himself through His devotees alone. There cannot be a manifestation of infinite powers. It simply isn't possible. It is impossible for any man to manifest infinite powers."

GIRISH: "You can serve your children as 'Brahma Gopāla'.[10] Then why isn't it possible to worship a great soul as God?"

MASTER (to Trailokya): "Why all this bother about infinity? If I want to touch you, must I touch your entire body? If you want to bathe in the Ganges, must you touch the whole river from Hardwār down to the ocean?

" 'All troubles come to an end when the ego dies.' As long as a trace of 'I-consciousness' remains, one is conscious of difference. Nobody knows what remains after the 'I' disappears. Nobody can express it in words. That which is remains. After the 'I' disappears one cannot say that a part manifests through this man and the rest through another. Satchidānanda is the ocean. The pot of 'I' is immersed in it. As long as the pot exists, the water seems to be divided into two parts: one part inside the pot and the other part

10 A name of God.

outside it. But when the pot is broken there is only one stretch of water. One cannot even say that. Who would say that?"

After the discussion Sri Ramakrishna became engaged in pleasant conversation with Trailokya.

MASTER: "You are happy. Isn't that so?"

TRAILOKYA: "But I shall become my old self again as soon as I leave this place. Here I feel very much the awakening of spiritual consciousness."

MASTER: "You don't have to be afraid of walking on thorns if you are wearing shoes. You needn't be afraid of 'woman and gold' if you know that God alone is real and all else illusory."

It was about nine o'clock in the evening. Balaram took Trailokya to another room and gave him refreshments. Sri Ramakrishna began to tell the devotees about Trailokya and people of his views.

MASTER (to Girish, M., and the other devotees): "Do you know what these people are like? They are like a frog living in a well, who has never seen the outside world. He knows only his well; so he will not believe that there is such a thing as the world. Likewise, people talk so much about the world because they have not known the joy of God.

(To Girish) "Why do you argue with them so much? They busy themselves with both—the world and God. One cannot understand the joy of God unless one has tasted it. Can anybody explain sex pleasure to a five-year-old boy? Worldly people talk about God only from hearsay. Children, hearing their old aunts quarrelling among themselves, learn to say, 'There is my God', 'I swear by God.'

"But that doesn't matter. I don't blame such people. Can all comprehend the Indivisible Satchidānanda? Only twelve rishis could recognize Rāmachandra. All cannot recognize an Incarnation of God. Some take him for an ordinary man, some for a holy person, and only a few recognize him as an Incarnation.

"One offers a price for an article according to one's capital. A rich man said to his servant: 'Take this diamond to the market and let me know how different people price it. Take it, first of all, to the egg-plant seller.' The servant took the diamond to the egg-plant seller. He examined it, turning it over in the palm of his hand, and said, 'Brother, I can give nine seers of egg-plants for it.' 'Friend,' said the servant, 'a little more—say, ten seers.' The egg-plant seller replied: 'No, I have already quoted above the market price. You may give it to me if that price suits you.' The servant laughed. He went back to his master and said: 'Sir, he would give me only nine seers of egg-plants and not one more. He said he had offered more than the market price.' The master smiled and said: 'Now take it to the cloth-dealer. The other man deals only in egg-plants. What does he know about a diamond? The cloth-dealer has a little more capital. Let us see how much he offers for it.' The servant went to the cloth-dealer and said: 'Will you buy this? How much will you pay for it?' The merchant said: 'Yes, it is a good thing. I can make a nice ornament out of it. I will give you nine hundred rupees for it.' 'Brother,' said the servant, 'offer a little more and I will sell it to you. Give me at least a thousand rupees.' The cloth-dealer said: 'Friend, don't

759 The Gospel of Sri Ramakrishna

press me for more. I have offered more than the market price. I cannot give a rupee more. Suit yourself.' Laughing the servant returned to his master and said: 'He won't give a rupee more than nine hundred. He too said he had quoted above the market price.' The master said with a laugh: 'Now take it to a jeweller. Let us see what he has to say.' The servant went to a jeweller. The jeweller glanced at the diamond and said at once, 'I will give you one hundred thousand rupees for it.'

"They talk of practising religion in the world. Suppose a man is shut up in a room. All the doors and windows are closed. Only a little light comes through a hole in the ceiling. Can he see the sun with that roof over his head? And what will he do with only one ray of light? 'Woman and gold' is the roof. Can he see the sun unless he removes the roof? Worldly people are shut up in a room, as it were.

"The Incarnations of God belong to the class of the Iśvarakotis. They roam about in the open spaces. They are never imprisoned in the world, never entangled by it. Their ego is not the 'thick ego' of worldly people. The ego, the 'I-consciousness', of worldly people is like four walls and a roof: the man inside them cannot see anything outside. The ego of the Incarnations and other Iśvarakotis is a 'thin ego': through it they have an uninterrupted vision of God. Take the case of a man who stands by a wall on both sides of which there are meadows stretching to infinity. If there is a hole in the wall, through it he can see everything on the other side. If the hole is a big one, he can even pass through it. The ego of the Incarnations and other Iśvarakotis is like the wall with a hole. Though they remain on this side of the wall, still they can see the endless meadow on the other side. That is to say, though they have a human body, they are always united with God. Again, if they will, they can pass through the big hole to the other side and remain in samādhi. And if the hole is big enough, they can go through it and come back again. That is to say, though established in samādhi, they can again descend to the worldly plane."

The devotees listened breathlessly to these words about the mystery of Divine Incarnation.

THE MASTER AT THE HOUSES OF
BALARAM AND GIRISH

Friday, April 24, 1885

ABOUT ONE O'CLOCK in the afternoon M. arrived at Balaram's house in Calcutta and found the Master asleep in the drawing-room, one or two devotees resting near him. M. began to fan the Master gently. A few minutes later Sri Ramakrishna woke up and sat on the bed with his clothes in a rather untidy condition. M. saluted him and took the dust of his feet.

MASTER (*tenderly to M.*): "Are you well? I'm feeling rather uneasy. I have a sore[1] in my throat. I suffer very much during the early hours of the morning. Can you tell me how I may be cured? (*In a worried tone*) They served pickled mango with the meal. I ate a little of it.

"How is your wife? I noticed the other day that she was looking rather sickly. Give her soothing drinks to keep her nerves cool."

M: "Green coconut milk, sir?"

MASTER: "Yes. A drink made of sugar candy is also good."

M: "Since last Sunday I have been living at our house with my parents."

MASTER: "You have done well. It will be convenient for you to live at home. Since your parents live there, you won't have to worry so much about the family."

While Sri Ramakrishna was talking, his mouth became dry. He said to M., like a child: "I feel a dryness in my mouth. Do you all feel that way?"

M. (*to Jogin*): "Is your mouth also drying up?"

JOGIN: "No. Perhaps it is due to the heat."

Jogindra of Āriādaha was an intimate disciple of Sri Ramakrishna, and later, after the passing away of the Master, renounced the world.

Sri Ramakrishna's clothes were still untidy. Some of the devotees smiled.

MASTER: "I look like a mother nursing her babies. (*All laugh.*) Well, my tongue is drying up. Shall I eat a pear or a jāmrul?"[2]

BABURAM: "Let me get a jāmrul for you."

MASTER: "You don't have to go out in this sun."

[1] The beginning of his cancer of the throat.
[2] A kind of juicy fruit.

M. was still fanning the Master.

MASTER: "You may stop now. You have been fanning a long time."

M: "I am not tired, sir."

MASTER (*tenderly*): "No?"

M. taught in a school in the neighbourhood. He had a little recess at one o'clock, during which he visited Sri Ramakrishna. It was time for him to go back to the school. He saluted the Master.

MASTER (*to M.*): "Must you go now?"

A DEVOTEE: "School is not over yet. He came here during recess."

MASTER (*smiling*): "He is like a mother with seven or eight children. Day and night she is busy with her worldly duties. But now and then she makes time to serve her husband."

M.'s school closed at four o'clock. He came back to Balaram's house and found the Master sitting in the drawing-room. The devotees were arriving one by one. The younger Naren and Ram came. Narendra, too, was there. M. saluted the Master and took a seat. The ladies sent a plate of hāluā for Sri Ramakrishna. Because of the sore in his throat he could not eat any hard food.

MASTER (*to Narendra*): "Ah! This is nice stuff! Eat some! It is good! Eat some!" (*All laugh.*)

Dusk was coming on. Sri Ramakrishna was about to go to the house of Girish, who had arranged a festival to celebrate the Master's coming. The Master came down from the second floor of Balaram's house with M. and a few other devotees. Near the gate he saw a beggar chanting the name of Rāma, and he stood still. He fell into a meditative mood and remained standing a few minutes. He said to M., "He sings well." A devotee gave the beggar four pice.

Sri Ramakrishna entered Bosepārā Lane. Laughing, he said to M.: "What are these people saying? 'There comes Paramahamsa's battalion!' What these fools say!" (*All laugh.*)

Sri Ramakrishna entered Girish's house. The latter had invited a large number of devotees to join the festival. Many of them were present. They all stood up to receive the Master, who, smiling, took his seat. The devotees sat around him. Among them were Girish, Mahimacharan, Ram, and Bhavanath, and also Baburam, Narendra, Jogin, the younger Naren, Chuni, Balaram, M., and the other devotees who had accompanied the Master from Balaram's house.

MASTER (*to Mahimacharan*): "I said to Girish about you, 'There is one—very deep. You are only knee-deep.' Now you must help me check up on what I said. I want to see you two argue. But don't compromise." (*All laugh.*)

Girish and Mahimacharan started their discussion. Soon Ram said: "Let them stop. Let us have some kirtan."

MASTER (*to Ram*): "No, no! This has a great deal of meaning. They are 'Englishmen'. I want to hear what they say."

Mahimacharan contended that all could become Krishna by means of sādhanā. Girish said that Sri Krishna was an Incarnation of God. However much a man practised sādhanā, he could never be an Incarnation.

MAHIMA: "Do you know what I mean? Let me give an illustration. The bel-tree can become a mango-tree if only the obstructions are removed. It can be done by the practice of yoga."

GIRISH: "You may say whatever you like, but it cannot be done either by the practice of yoga or by anything else. Only a Krishna can become Krishna. If anybody has all the attributes of another person, Rādhā for instance, then he is none other than that person—Rādhā herself. If I see in a person all the attributes of Krishna, then I shall conclude that I am seeing Krishna Himself."

Mahimacharan could not argue well. At last he had to accept Girish's views.

MAHIMA (to Girish): "Yes, sir, both views are right. God has willed the path of knowledge; He has also willed the path of bhakti. (Pointing to Sri Ramakrishna) As he says, by different paths people ultimately reach one and the same goal."

MASTER (aside to Mahima): "You see, what I said was right, wasn't it?"

MAHIMA: "Yes, sir. As you say, both paths are right."

MASTER (pointing to Girish): "Haven't you noticed how deep his faith is? He forgot to eat his refreshments. Like a dog, he would have torn your throat if you hadn't accepted his view. But we have enjoyed the discussion. You two have known each other and I myself have learnt many things."

The musician arrived with his party and sat in the middle of the room. He was waiting for a sign from Sri Ramakrishna to begin the kirtan. The Master gave his permission.

RAM (to the Master): "Please tell them what to sing."

MASTER: "What shall I suggest? (After a little reflection) Well, let them sing the prelude to the union of Rādhā and Krishna."

The musician sang:

> My Gorā, my treasure, the jewel among men,
> Weeps as he chants Sri Rādhā's name
> And rolls on the ground; with fervent love
> He chants her name again and again.
> The tears stream from his love-filled eyes;
> Once more he rolls upon the ground,
> As chanting her name he faints away.
> The hair on his body stands on end;
> His tongue can lisp but a single word.
> Says Bāsu:[3] Why is Gorā so restless?

The kirtan continued.

Rādhā had met Krishna on the bank of the Jamunā under the kadamba tree. Her companions describe her physical and mental condition:

> A hundred times each hour, in and out of the room she goes;
> Restless, breathing hard, she looks toward the kadamba grove.
> Is she afraid of the elders? Has she been possessed by a ghost?
> Filled with restlessness, she cannot keep her dress arranged;

[3] The author of the song.

Her jewels have fallen off; she trembles every now and then.
Alas, she is so young! A princess born, and a wife besides!
What is it that she craves? We do not understand her mind;
But we can guess her hand is reaching out to catch the moon.
Humbly says Chandidās:[4] Rādhā has fallen in Krishna's trap.

The kirtan went on.
Rādhā's friends say to her.

Tell us, O Rādhā of comely face! Tell us what it is that ails you.
Why has your mind wandered away? Why do you claw the earth
    in frenzy?
Tell us why your golden skin has taken the ashy hue of cinders.
From your body the scarlet cloth has dropped unheeded to the
    ground;
Ah! Your eyes are red with tears; your lovely lotus face has
    withered.
Tell us what it is that ails you, lest our hearts should break with
    grief.

Rādhā says to her friends:

I long for the sight of Krishna's face.

The musician sang again.
Hearing Krishna's flute, Rādhā has gone mad. She says to her friends:

Who is the Sorcerer that dwells in the kadamba grove?
His flute-notes suddenly enter my ears and strike a chord in my
    heart;
Piercing my very soul, they slay my dharma and drive me mad.
With restless mind and streaming eyes, alas! I can scarcely breathe:
How He plays His magic flute, whose music thrills my soul!
Because He is out of my sight, my heart expires; I cannot stay
    home.
My soul yearns for Him; racked with pain, it longs to see Him once
    more.
Says Uddhava Dās: But you will die, O Rādhā, when you behold
    Him!

The music continued.
Rādhā's heart yearns for the vision of Krishna. She says to her friends:

First I heard His magic flute from the kadamba grove,
And the next day the minstrel told me of Him and thrilled my
    soul;
Another day, O friend of my heart, you chanted His blessed name.
(Ah, the blessed name of Krishna, full of honeyed sweetness!)
The wise men, too, described to me His virtues without number.
I am a weak and simple girl, and stern, alas! are my elders;
My love for my Beloved grows; how can I live any longer?
After reflecting long, I find that I must die at last:
Can you not tell me a way, O friend, by which I may meet my
    Krishna?

[4] The author of the song.

As Sri Ramakrishna heard the line, "Ah, the blessed name of Krishna, full of honeyed sweetness!", he could not remain seated any longer. He stood up in a state of unconsciousness and went into deep samādhi. The younger Naren stood at his right. Regaining partial consciousness, the Master repeated the name of Krishna in his melodious voice. Tears flowed down his cheeks. He sat down again. The musician continued his singing.

Viśākhā, a friend of Rādhā, runs out and brings a portrait of Krishna. She holds it before Rādhā's eyes. Rādhā says: "I see the picture of Him whom I beheld on the Jamunā's bank. Ever since then I have been in this plight.

> I see the picture of Him whom I beheld on the Jamunā's bank;
> The name Viśākhā spoke is the name of Him who is painted here.
> He who played on the flute is the Beloved of my soul;
> His virtues the minstrel sang to me; He has bewitched my heart.
> It is none other than He!" So saying, Rādhā falls in a swoon.
> Restored to her senses by her friends, at once she says to them,
> "Show me Him, O friends, whom I saw reflected in my soul."
> And they promise her that they will.

Now Sri Ramakrishna with Narendra and the other devotees began to sing the kirtan in a loud voice. They sang:

> Behold, the two brothers have come, who weep while chanting
>   Hari's name. . . .

They continued:

> See how all Nadiā is shaking
> Under the waves of Gaurānga's love. . . .

Again Sri Ramakrishna went into samādhi. After regaining consciousness of the outer world, he returned to his seat. Turning to M., he said, "I don't remember which way I was facing before." Then he began to talk to the devotees.

NARENDRA (to the Master): "Hazra has now become a good man."

MASTER: "You don't know. There are people who repeat Rāma's name with their tongues but hide stones under their arms to throw at others."

NARENDRA: "I don't agree with you, sir. I asked him about the things people complain of. He denied them."

MASTER: "He is steadfast in his devotions. He practises japa a little. But he also behaves in a queer way. He doesn't pay the coachman his fare."

NARENDRA: "That isn't true, sir. He said he had paid it."

MASTER: "Where did he get the money?"

NARENDRA: "From Ramlal or someone else."

MASTER: "Did you ask him all these things in detail? Once I prayed to the Divine Mother, 'O Mother, if Hazra is a hypocrite then please remove him from here.' Later on I told him of my prayer. After a few days he came to me and said, 'You see, I am still here.' (The Master and the others laugh.) But soon afterwards he left.

"Hazra's mother begged me through Ramlal to ask Hazra to come home. She was almost blind with weeping. I tried in various ways to persuade him to visit her. I said: 'Your mother is old. Go and see her once.' I couldn't make him go. Afterwards the poor mother died weeping for him."

NARENDRA: "This time he will go home."

MASTER: "Yes, yes! He will go home! He is a rogue. He is a rascal. You don't understand him. You are a fool. Gopal said that Hazra stayed at Sinthi a few days. People used to supply him with butter, rice, and other food. He had the impudence to tell them he couldn't swallow such coarse rice and bad butter. Ishan of Bhātpārā accompanied him there. He ordered Ishan to carry water for him. That made the other brāhmins very angry."

NARENDRA: "I asked him about that too. He said that Ishan Babu had himself come forward with the water. Besides, many brāhmins of Bhātpārā showed him respect."

MASTER (smiling): "That was the result of his japa and austerity. You see, physical traits to a great extent influence character. Short stature and a body with dents here and there are not good traits. People with such traits take a long time to acquire spiritual knowledge."

BHAVANATH: "Let us stop talking about these things."

MASTER: "Don't misunderstand me. (To Narendra) You say you understand people; that is why I am telling you all this. Do you know how I look on people like Hazra? I know that just as God takes the form of holy men, so He also takes the form of cheats and rogues. (To Mahimacharan) What do you say? All are God."

MAHIMA: "Yes, sir. All are God."

GIRISH (to the Master): "Sir, what is ekāngi prema?"

MASTER: "It means one-sided love. For instance, the water does not seek the duck, but the duck loves water. There are other kinds of love: sādhārani, samanjasā, and samarthā. In the first, which is ordinary love, the lover seeks his own happiness; he doesn't care whether the other person is happy or not. That was Chandrāvali's attitude toward Krishna. In the second, which is a compromise, both seek each other's happiness. This is a noble kind of love. But the third is the highest of all. Such a lover says to his beloved, 'Be happy yourself, whatever may happen to me.' Rādhā had this highest love. She was happy in Krishna's happiness. The gopis, too, had attained this exalted state.

"Do you know who the gopis were? Rāmachandra was wandering in the forest where sixty thousand rishis dwelt. They were very eager to see Him. He cast a tender glance at them. According to a certain Purāna, they were born later on as the gopis of Vrindāvan."

A DEVOTEE: "Sir, who may be called an antaranga?"

MASTER: "Let me give an illustration. A nātmandir has pillars inside and outside. An antaranga is like the inside pillars. Those who always live near the guru are the antarangas.

(To Mahimacharan) "The jnāni wants neither a form of God nor His Incarnation. While wandering in the forest, Rāmachandra saw a number of rishis. They welcomed Him to their āsrama with great love and said to Him: 'O Rāma, today our life is blessed because we have seen You. But we know You as the son of Daśaratha. Bharadvāja and other sages call You a Divine

Incarnation; but that is not our view. We meditate on the Indivisible Satchidānanda.' Rāma was pleased with them and smiled.

"Ah, what a state of mind I passed through! My mind would lose itself in the Indivisible Absolute. How many days I spent that way! I renounced bhakti and bhakta, devotion and devotee. I became inert. I could not feel the form of my own head. I was about to die. I thought of keeping Ramlal's aunt[5] near me.

"I ordered the removal of all pictures and portraits from my room. When I regained outer consciousness, when the mind climbed down to the ordinary level, I felt as if I were being suffocated like a drowning person. At last I said to myself, 'If I can't bear people, then how shall I live?' Then my mind was again directed to bhakti and bhakta. 'What has happened to me?' I kept asking people. Bholanath[6] said to me, 'This state of mind has been described in the *Mahābhārata*.' How can a man live, on coming down from the plane of samādhi? Surely he requires devotion to God and the company of devotees. Otherwise, how will he keep his mind occupied?"

MAHIMACHARAN (*to the Master*): "Sir, can a man return from the plane of samādhi to the plane of the ordinary world?"

MASTER (*in a low voice, to Mahima*): "I shall tell you privately. You are the only one fit to hear it.

"Koar Singh also asked me that question. You see, there is a vast difference between the jīva and Iśvara. Through worship and austerity, a jīva can at the utmost attain samādhi; but he cannot come down from that state. On the other hand, an Incarnation of God can come down from samādhi. A jīva is like an officer of the king; he can go as far as the outer court of the seven-storey palace. But the king's son has access to all the seven floors; he can also go outside. Everybody says that no one can return from the plane of samādhi. In that case, how do you account for sages like Śankara and Rāmānuja? They retained the 'ego of Knowledge'."

MAHIMA: "That is true, indeed. Otherwise, how could they write books?"

MASTER: "Again, there are the instances of sages like Prahlāda, Nārada, and Hanumān. They too retained bhakti after attaining samādhi."

MAHIMA: "That is true, sir."

MASTER: "Some people indulge in philosophical speculation and think much of themselves. Perhaps they have studied a little Vedānta. But a man cannot be egotistic if he has true knowledge. In other words, in samādhi man becomes one with God and gets rid of his egotism. True knowledge is impossible without samādhi. In samādhi man becomes one with God. Then he can have no egotism.

"Do you know what it is like? Just at noon the sun is directly overhead. If you look around then, you do not see your shadow. Likewise, you will not find the 'shadow' of ego after attaining Knowledge, samādhi.

"But if you see in anyone a trace of 'I-consciousness' after the attainment of true Knowledge, then know that it is either the 'ego of Knowledge' or the 'ego of Devotion' or the 'servant ego'. It is not the 'ego of ignorance'.

[5] Referring to his own wife.
[6] A clerk at the Dakshineswar temple garden.

"Again, jnāna and bhakti are twin paths. Whichever you follow, it is God that you will ultimately reach. The jnāni looks on God in one way and the bhakta looks on Him in another way. The God of the jnāni is full of brilliance, and the God of the bhakta full of sweetness."

Bhavanath was seated near the Master, listening to these words.

BHAVANATH (to the Master): "Sir, I have a question to ask. I don't quite understand the Chandi. It is written there that the Divine Mother kills all beings. What does that mean?"

MASTER: "This is all Her līlā, Her sportive pleasure. That question used to bother me too. Later I found out that all is māyā. Both creation and destruction are God's māyā."

Girish conducted Sri Ramakrishna and the devotees to the roof, where the meal was served. There was a bright moon in the sky. The devotees took their seats. The Master occupied a seat in front of them. All were in a joyous mood.

Sri Ramakrishna was beside himself with joy at the sight of Narendra. The beloved disciple sat in the front row. Every now and then the Master asked how he was getting along. He had hardly finished half his meal when he came to Narendra with some water-melon sherbet and curd from his own plate. Tenderly he said to the disciple, "Please eat this." Then he went back to his own place.

Saturday, May 9, 1885

It was about three o'clock in the afternoon. Sri Ramakrishna sat in Balaram's drawing-room in a happy mood. Many devotees were present. Narendra, M., Bhavanath, Purna, Paltu, the younger Naren, Girish, Ram, Binode, Dwija, and others sat around him.

Balaram was not there. He had gone to Monghyr for a change of air. His eldest daughter had invited Sri Ramakrishna and the devotees and celebrated the occasion with a feast. The Master was resting after the meal.

Again and again the Master asked M.: "Am I liberal-minded? Tell me."

BHAVANATH (smiling): "Why do you ask him? He will only keep quiet."

A beggar entered the room. He wanted to sing. The devotees listened to a song or two. Narendra liked his singing and asked him to sing more.

MASTER: "Stop! Stop! We don't want any more songs. Where is the money? (To Narendra) You may order the music, but who will pay?"

A DEVOTEE (smiling): "Sir, the beggar may think you are an āmir, a wealthy aristocrat, the way you are leaning against that big pillow." (All laugh.)

MASTER (smiling): "He may also think I am ill."

The conversation drifted to Hazra and his egotism. For some reason he had had to go away from Dakshineswar.

NARENDRA: "Hazra now admits he was egotistic."

MASTER: "Don't believe him. He says so in order to come back to Dakshineswar. (To the devotees) Narendra always insists that Hazra is a grand person."

NARENDRA: "Even now I say so."

MASTER: "Why? You have heard so much about him, and still you think so?"

NARENDRA: "He has slight defects but many virtues."

MASTER: "I admit that he has devotion to his ideal. He said to me, 'You don't care for me now, but later you will be seeking my company.' A goswāmi came from Srerāmpore. He was a descendant of Advaita Goswāmi. He intended to spend a night or two at the temple garden. I asked him very cordially to stay. Do you know what Hazra said to me? He said, 'Send him to the temple officer.' What was in his mind was that the goswāmi might ask for milk or food, and that he might have to give him some from his own share. I said to Hazra: 'Now, you rogue! Even I prostrate myself before him because he is a goswāmi. And you, after leading a worldly life and indulging a great deal in "woman and gold", have so much pride because of a little japa! Aren't you ashamed of yourself?'

"One realizes God through sattva. Rajas and tamas take one away from Him. The scriptures describe sattva as white, rajas as red, and tamas as black. Once I asked Hazra: 'Tell me what you think of the people that come here. How much sattva does each one possess?' He said, 'Narendra has one hundred per cent and I have one hundred and ten per cent.' 'What about me?' I asked. And he said: 'You still have a trace of pink. You have only seventy-five per cent, I should say.' (All laugh.)

"Hazra used to practise japa at Dakshineswar. While telling his beads, he would also try to do a little brokerage business. He has a debt of a few thousand rupees which he must clear up. About the brāhmin cooks of the temple he remarked, 'Do you think I talk with people of that sort?'

"The truth is that you cannot attain God if you have even a trace of desire. Subtle is the way of dharma. If you are trying to thread a needle, you will not succeed if the thread has even a slight fibre sticking out.

"There are people who perform japa for thirty years and still do not attain any result. Why? A gangrenous sore requires very drastic treatment. Ordinary medicine won't cure it.

"No matter how much sādhanā you practise, you will not realize the goal as long as you have desire. But this also is true, that one can realize the goal in a moment through the grace of God, through His kindness. Take the case of a room that has been dark a thousand years. If somebody suddenly brings a lamp into it, the room is lighted in an instant.

"Suppose a poor man's son has fallen into the good graces of a rich person. He marries his daughter. Immediately he gets an equipage, clothes, furniture, a house, and other things."

A DEVOTEE: "Sir, how does one receive God's grace?"

MASTER: "God has the nature of a child. A child is sitting with gems in the skirt of his cloth. Many a person passes by him along the road. Many of them pray to him for gems. But he hides the gems with his hands and says, turning away his face, 'No, I will not give any away.' But another man comes along. He doesn't ask for the gems, and yet the child runs after him and offers him the gems, begging him to accept them.

"One cannot realize God without renunciation. Who will accept my words? I have been seeking a companion, a sympathetic soul who will understand my feelings. When I see a great devotee, I say to myself, 'Perhaps he will accept my ideal.' But later on I find that he behaves in a different way.

"A ghost sought a companion. One becomes a ghost if one dies from an accident on a Saturday or a Tuesday. So whenever the ghost found someone who seemed to be dying from an accident on either of these days, he would run to him. He would say to himself that at last he had found his companion. But no sooner would he run to the man than he would see the man getting up. The man, perhaps, had fallen from a roof and after a few moments regained consciousness.

"Once Mathur Babu was in an ecstatic mood. He behaved like a drunkard and could not look after his work. At this all said: 'Who will look after his estate if he behaves like that? Certainly the young priest[7] has cast a spell upon him.'

"During one of Narendra's early visits I touched his chest and he became unconscious. Regaining consciousness, he wept and said: 'Oh, why did you do that to me? I have a father! I have a mother!' This 'I' and 'mine' spring from ignorance.

"A guru said to his disciple: 'The world is illusory. Come away with me.' 'But, revered sir,' said the disciple, 'my people at home—my father, my mother, my wife—love me so much. How can I give them up?' The guru said: 'No doubt you now have this feeling of "I" and "mine" and say that they love you; but this is all an illusion of your mind. I shall teach you a trick, and you will know whether they love you truly or not.' Saying this, the teacher gave the disciple a pill and said to him: 'Swallow this at home. You will appear to be a corpse, but you will not lose consciousness. You will see everything and hear everything. Then I shall come to your house and gradually you will regain your normal state.'

"The disciple followed the teacher's instructions and lay on his bed like a dead person. The house was filled with loud wailing. His mother, his wife, and the others lay on the ground weeping bitterly. Just then a brāhmin entered the house and said to them, 'What is the matter with you?' 'This boy is dead', they replied. The brāhmin felt his pulse and said: 'How is that? No, he is not dead. I have a medicine for him that will cure him completely.' The joy of the relatives was unbounded; it seemed to them that heaven itself had come down into their house. 'But', said the brāhmin, 'I must tell you something else. Another person must take some of this medicine first, and then the boy must swallow the rest. But the other person will die. I see he has so many dear relatives here; one of them will certainly agree to take the medicine. I see his wife and mother crying bitterly. Surely they will not hesitate to take it.'

"At once the weeping stopped and all sat quiet. The mother said: 'Well, this is a big family. Suppose I die; then who will look after the family?' She fell into a reflective mood. The wife, who had been crying a minute before and bemoaning her ill luck, said: 'Well, he has gone the way of mortals. I have these two or three young children. Who will look after them if I die?'

[7] Sri Ramakrishna, who was at that time a priest in the Kāli temple.

"The disciple saw everything and heard everything. He stood up at once and said to the teacher: 'Let us go, revered sir. I will follow you.' (*All laugh.*)

"Another disciple said to his teacher: 'Revered sir, my wife takes great care of me. It is for her sake that I cannot give up the world.' The disciple practised hathayoga. The teacher taught him, too, a trick to test his wife's love. One day there was a great wailing in his house. The neighbours came running and saw the hathayogi seated in a posture, his limbs paralysed and distorted. They thought he was dead. His wife fell on the ground, weeping piteously: 'Oh, what has befallen me? How have you provided for our future? Oh, friends, I never dreamt I should meet such a fate!'

"In the mean time the relatives and friends had brought a cot to take the corpse out. But suddenly a difficulty arose as they started to move it. Since the body was twisted and stiff, it could not be taken out through the door. A neighbour quickly brought an axe and began to chop away the door-frame. The wife was crying bitterly, when she heard the sound of the axe. She ran to the door. 'What are you doing, friends?' she asked, still weeping. The neighbour said, 'We can't take the body out; so we are chopping away the door-frame.'

" 'Please', said the wife, 'don't do any such thing. I am a widow now; I have no one to look after me. I have to bring up these young children. If you destroy this door, I shall not be able to replace it. Friends, death is inevitable for all, and my husband cannot be called back to life. You had better cut his limbs.' The hathayogi at once stood up. The effect of the medicine had worn off. He said to his wife: 'You evil one! You want to cut off my hands and feet, do you?' So saying, he renounced home and followed his teacher. (*All laugh.*)

"Many women make a show of grief. Knowing beforehand that they will have to weep, they first take off their nose-rings and other ornaments, put them securely in a box, and lock it. Then they fall on the ground and weep, 'O friends, what has befallen us?' "

NARENDRA: "How can I believe, without proof, that God incarnates Himself as a man?"

GIRISH: "Faith alone is sufficient. What is the proof that these objects exist here? Faith alone is the proof."

A DEVOTEE: "Have philosophers been able to prove that the external world exists outside us? But they say we have an irresistible belief in it."

GIRISH (*to Narendra*): "You wouldn't believe, even if God appeared before you. God Himself might say that He was God born as a man, but perhaps you would say that He was a liar and a cheat."

The conversation turned to the immortality of the gods.

NARENDRA: "What is the proof of their immortality?"

GIRISH: "You wouldn't believe it even if the gods appeared before you."

NARENDRA: "That the immortals existed in the past requires proof."

M. whispered something to Paltu.

PALTU (*smiling, to Narendra*): "What need is there for the immortals to be without beginning? To be immortal one need only be without end."

MASTER (*smiling*): "Narendra is the son of a lawyer, but Paltu of a deputy magistrate." (*All laugh.*)

All kept silent awhile.

JOGIN (*smiling*): "He [meaning the Master] doesn't accept Narendra's words any more."

MASTER (*smiling*): "One day I remarked that the chātak bird doesn't drink any water except that which falls from the sky. Narendra said, 'The chātak drinks ordinary water as well.' Then I said to the Divine Mother, 'Mother, then are my words untrue?' I was greatly worried about it. Another day, later on, Narendra was here. Several birds were flying about in the room. He exclaimed, 'There! There!' 'What is there?' I asked. He said, 'There is your chātak!' I found they were only bats. Since that day I don't accept what he says. (*All laugh.*)

"At Jadu Mallick's garden house Narendra said to me, 'The forms of God that you see are the fiction of your mind.' I was amazed and said to him, 'But they speak too!' Narendra answered, 'Yes, one may think so.' I went to the temple and wept before the Mother. 'O Mother,' I said, 'what is this? Then is this all false? How could Narendra say that?' Instantly I had a revelation. I saw Consciousness—Indivisible Consciousness—and a divine being formed of that Consciousness. The divine form said to me, 'If your words are untrue, how is it that they tally with the facts?' Thereupon I said to Narendra: 'You rogue! You created unbelief in my mind. Don't come here any more.'"

The discussion continued. Narendra was arguing. He was then slightly over twenty-two years of age.

NARENDRA (*to Girish, M., and the others*): "How am I to believe in the words of scripture? The *Mahānirvāna Tantra* says, in one place, that unless a man attains the Knowledge of Brahman he goes to hell; and the same book says, in another place, that there is no salvation without the worship of Pārvati, the Divine Mother. Manu writes about himself in the *Manusamhitā*; Moses describes his own death in the Pentateuch.

"The Sāmkhya philosophy says that God does not exist, because there is no proof of His existence. Again, the same philosophy says that one must accept the Vedas and that they are eternal.

"But I don't say that these are not true. I simply don't understand them. Please explain them to me. People have explained the scriptures according to their fancy. Which explanation shall we accept? White light coming through a red medium appears red, through a green medium, green."

A DEVOTEE: "The *Gītā* contains the words of God."

MASTER: "Yes, the *Gītā* is the essence of all scriptures. A sannyāsi may or may not keep with him another book, but he always carries a pocket *Gītā*."

A DEVOTEE: "The *Gītā* contains the words of Krishna."

NARENDRA: "Yes, Krishna or any fellow for that matter!"

Sri Ramakrishna was amazed at these words of Narendra.

MASTER: "This is a fine discussion. There are two interpretations of the scriptures: the literal and the real. One should accept the real meaning alone—what agrees with the words of God. There is a vast difference between the words written in a letter and the direct words of its writer. The scriptures are like the words of the letter; the words of God are direct words. I do not accept anything unless it agrees with the direct words of the Divine Mother."

The conversation again turned to Divine Incarnation.

NARENDRA: "It is enough to have faith in God. I don't care about what He is doing or what He hangs from. Infinite is the universe; infinite are the Incarnations."

As Sri Ramakrishna heard the words, "Infinite is the universe; infinite are the Incarnations", he said with folded hands, "Ah!"

M. whispered something to Bhavanath.

BHAVANATH: "M. says: 'As long as I have not seen the elephant, how can I know whether it can pass through the eye of a needle? I do not know God; how can I understand through reason whether or not He can incarnate Himself as man?"

MASTER: "Everything is possible for God. It is He who casts the spell. The magician swallows the knife and takes it out again; he swallows stones and bricks."

A DEVOTEE: "The Brāhmos say that a man should perform his worldly duties. He must not renounce them."

GIRISH: "Yes, I saw something like that in their paper, the *Sulabha Samāchār*. But a man cannot even finish all the works that are necessary for him in order to know God, and still he speaks of worldly duties."

Sri Ramakrishna smiled a little, looked at M., and made a sign with his eye, as if to say, "What he says is right."

M. understood that this question of performing duties was an extremely difficult one.

Purna arrived.

MASTER: "Who told you about our being here?"

PURNA: "Sarada."

MASTER (*to the woman devotees*): "Give him some refreshments."

Narendra was preparing to sing. The Master and the devotees were eager to hear his music. Narendra sang:

> Śiva, Thy ready thunderbolt rules over meadows, hills, and sky!
> O God of Gods! O Slayer of Time! Thou the Great Void, the King
>   of Dharma!
> Śiva, Thou Blessed One, redeem me; take away my grievous sin.

He sang again:

> Sweet is Thy name, O Refuge of the humble!
> It falls like sweetest nectar on our ears
> And comforts us, Beloved of our souls! . . .

Again:

> Why, O mind, do you never call on Him
> Who takes away all fear of danger?
> Tricked by delusion you forget yourself,
> Enamoured of the world's bleak wilderness.
> Alas, what mockery is here!

Comrades and wealth you cannot always keep;
Take care lest you forget Him quite.
Give up the false, O mind! Adore the Real;
And all the grief will vanish from your life.
Keep my good counsel in your heart.

With sounding voice proclaim Lord Hari's name
And cast away your false desires,
If you would cross the ocean of this life;
Surrender to Him body, mind, and soul,
And worship Him with trusting love.

PALTU: "Won't you sing that one?"
NARENDRA: "Which one?"
PALTU: " 'When I behold Thy peerless face.' "
Narendra sang:

When I behold Thy peerless face, beaming with love, O Lord,
What fear have I of earthly woe or of the frown of sorrow?
As the first ray of the dawning sun dispels the dark,
So too, Lord, when Thy blessed light bursts forth within the heart,
It scatters all our grief and pain with sweetest balm.
When on Thy love and grace I ponder, in my heart's deepest
    depths,
Tears of joy stream down my cheeks beyond restraining.
Hail, Gracious Lord! Hail, Gracious One! I shall proclaim Thy
    love.
May my life-breath depart from me as I perform Thy works!

At M.'s request Narendra sang again, M. and many of the devotees
listening with folded hands:

Be drunk, O mind, be drunk with the Wine of Heavenly Bliss!
Roll on the ground and weep, chanting Hari's sweet name! . . .

Narendra sang again:

Meditate, O my mind, on the Lord Hari,
The Stainless One, Pure Spirit through and through.
How peerless is the light that in Him shines!
How soul-bewitching is His wondrous form!
How dear is He to all His devotees! . . .

He sang another song:

This universe, wondrous and infinite,
O Lord, is Thy handiwork;
And the whole world is a treasure-house
Full of Thy beauty and grace.
The stars glisten innumerable,
Like gems on a necklace of gold;
How can the myriad suns and moons
Ever be numbered above?
The earth is glowing with grain and gold,
Thine ever brimming store;

Uncounted stars, O God, sing forth:
Blessed, blessed art Thou!

Then he sang:

Upon the tray of the sky blaze bright
The lamps of sun and moon;
Like diamonds shine the glittering stars
To deck Thy wondrous form. . . .

He continued:

Fasten your mind, O man, on the Primal Purusha,
Who is the Cause of all causes,
The Stainless One, the Beginningless Truth.
As Prāna He pervades the infinite universe;
The man of faith beholds Him,
Living, resplendent, the Root of all. . . .

At Narayan's request Narendra sang:

Come! Come, Mother! Doll of my soul! My heart's Delight!
In my heart's lotus come and sit, that I may see Thy face.
Alas! sweet Mother, even from birth I have suffered much;
But I have borne it all, Thou knowest, gazing at Thee.
Open the lotus of my heart, dear Mother! Reveal Thyself there.

Then Narendra sang a song of his own choice:

In dense darkness, O Mother, Thy formless beauty sparkles;
Therefore the yogis meditate in a dark mountain cave. . . .

As Sri Ramakrishna heard this soul-enthralling song, he went into samādhi. Narendra again sang:

Be drunk, O mind, be drunk with the Wine of Heavenly Bliss! . . .

The Master was in samādhi. He was sitting on a pillow, dangling his feet, facing the north and leaning against the wall. The devotees were seated around him.

In an ecstatic mood Sri Ramakrishna talked to the Divine Mother. He said: "I shall take my meal now. Art Thou come? Hast Thou found Thy lodging and left Thy baggage there and then come out?" He continued: "I don't enjoy anybody's company now. Why should I listen to the music, Mother? That diverts part of my mind to the outside world."

The Master was gradually regaining consciousness of the outer world. Looking at the devotees he said: "Years ago I used to be amazed to see people keeping kai fish alive in a pot of water. I would say: 'How cruel these people are! They will finally kill the fish.' But later, as changes came over my mind, I realized that bodies are like pillow-cases. It doesn't matter whether they remain or drop off."

BHAVANATH: "Then may one injure a man without incurring sin? Kill him?"

MASTER: "Yes, it is permissible if one has achieved that state of mind. But not everyone has it. It is the state of Brahmajnāna.

"By coming down a step or two from samādhi I enjoy bhakti and bhakta.

"There exist in God both vidyā and avidyā. Vidyāmāyā leads one to God, and avidyāmāyā away from Him. Knowledge, devotion, compassion, and renunciation belong to the realm of vidyā. With the help of these a man comes near God. One step more and he attains God, Knowledge of Brahman. In that state he clearly feels and sees that it is God who has become everything. He has nothing to give up and nothing to accept. It is impossible for him to be angry with anyone.

"One day I was riding in a carriage. I saw two prostitutes standing on a verandah. They appeared to me to be embodiments of the Divine Mother Herself. I saluted them.

"When I first attained this exalted state I could not worship Mother Kāli or give Her the food offering. Haladhari and Hriday told me that on account of this the temple officer had slandered me. But I only laughed; I wasn't in the least angry. Attain Brahmajnāna and then roam about enjoying God's lilā. A holy man came to a town and went about seeing the sights. He met another sādhu, an acquaintance. The latter said: 'I see you are gadding about. Where is your baggage? I hope no thief has stolen it.' The first sādhu said: 'Not at all. First I found a lodging, put my things in the room in proper order, and locked the door. Now I am enjoying the fun of the city.' " (All laugh.)

BHAVANATH: "These are very lofty words."

M. (to himself): "Tasting God's lilā after Brahmajnāna! Climbing down to the ordinary plane of consciousness after the attainment of samādhi!"

MASTER (to M. and the others): "Is it an easy thing to obtain the Knowledge of Brahman? It is not possible unless the mind is annihilated. The guru said to the disciple, 'Give me your mind and I shall give you Knowledge.' In this state one enjoys only spiritual talk and the company of devotees.

(To Ram) "You are a physician. You know that medicine works only when it mixes with the patient's blood and becomes one with it. Likewise, in the state of Brahmajnāna one sees God both within and without. One sees that it is God Himself who has become the body, mind, life, and soul."

M. (to himself): "Assimilation!"

MASTER: "A man attains Brahmajnāna as soon as his mind is annihilated. With the annihilation of the mind dies the ego, which says 'I', 'I'. One also attains the Knowledge of Brahman by following the path of devotion. One also attains It by following the path of knowledge, that is to say, discrimination. The jnānis discriminate, saying, 'Neti, neti', that is, 'All this is illusory, like a dream.' They analyse the world through the process of 'Not this, not this'; it is māyā. When the world vanishes, only the jīvas, that is to say, so many egos, remain.

"Each ego may be likened to a pot. Suppose there are ten pots filled with water, and the sun is reflected in them. How many suns do you see?"

A DEVOTEE: "Ten reflections. Besides, there certainly exists the real sun."

MASTER: "Suppose you break one pot. How many suns do you see now?"

DEVOTEE: "Nine reflected suns. But there certainly exists the real sun."

MASTER: "All right. Suppose you break nine pots. How many suns do you see now?"

DEVOTEE: "One reflected sun. But there certainly exists the real sun."

MASTER (to Girish): "What remains when the last pot is broken?"

GIRISH: "That real sun, sir."

MASTER: "No. What remains cannot be described. What *is* remains. How will you know there is a real sun unless there is a reflected sun? 'I-consciousness' is destroyed in samādhi. A man climbing down from samādhi to the lower plane cannot describe what he has seen there."

It was late in the evening. Lamps were burning in the drawing-room. Sri Ramakrishna was in a spiritual mood. The devotees sat around him.

MASTER (in the ecstatic mood): "There is no one else here; so I am telling you this. He who from the depth of his soul seeks to know God will certainly realize Him. He must. He alone who is restless for God and seeks nothing but Him will certainly realize Him.

"Those who belong to this place[8] have already come. Those who will come from now on are outsiders. Such people will come now and then. The Divine Mother will tell them: 'Do this. Call on God in this way.'

"Why doesn't man's mind dwell on God? You see, more powerful than God is His Mahāmāyā, His Power of Illusion. More powerful than the judge is his orderly. (All laugh.)

"Rāma said to Nārada: 'I am very much pleased with your prayer. Ask a boon of Me.' Nārada replied, 'O Rāma, may I have pure devotion to Your Lotus Feet, and may I not be deluded by Your world-bewitching māyā!' Rāma said, 'Be it so: ask for something else.' Nārada replied, 'No, Rāma, I do not want any other boon.'

"Everyone is under the spell of this world-bewitching māyā. When God assumes a human body, He too comes under the spell. Rāma wandered about weeping for Sītā. 'Brahman weeps entangled in the snare of the five elements.' But you must remember this: God, by His mere will, can liberate Himself from this snare."

BHAVANATH: "The guard of a railway train shuts himself of his own will in a carriage; but he can get out whenever he wants to."

MASTER: "The Iśvarakotis—Divine Incarnations, for instance—can liberate themselves whenever they want to; but the jīvakotis cannot. Jīvas are imprisoned by 'woman and gold'. When the doors and windows of a room are fastened with screws, how can a man get out?"

BHAVANATH (smiling): "Ordinary men are like the third-class passengers on a railway train. When the doors of their compartments are locked, they have no way to get out."

GIRISH: "If a man is so strongly tied hand and foot, then what is his way?"

MASTER: "He has nothing to fear if God Himself, as the guru, cuts the chain of māyā."

[8] The inner circle of the Master's devotees.

41

AT RAM'S HOUSE

SRI RAMAKRISHNA was sitting in the drawing-room on the ground floor of Ram's house. He was surrounded by devotees and was conversing with them. Mahima sat in front of him, M. to his left. Paltu, Bhavanath, Nityagopal, Haramohan, and a few others sat around him. It was about five o'clock in the afternoon. The Master inquired after several devotees.

MASTER (to M.): "Hasn't the younger Naren arrived yet?"

Presently the younger Naren entered the room.

MASTER: "What about him?"

M: "Who, sir?"

MASTER: "Kishori. Isn't Girish Ghosh coming? What about Narendra?"

A few minutes later Narendra arrived and saluted Sri Ramakrishna.

MASTER (to the devotees): "It would be fine if Kedar were here. He agrees with Girish. (To Mahima, smiling) He says the same thing."[1]

Ram had arranged the kirtan. With folded hands the musician said to Sri Ramakrishna, "Sir, I can begin if you give the order."

The Master drank some water and chewed spices from a small bag. He asked M. to close the bag.

The musician started the kirtan. As Sri Ramakrishna heard the sound of the drum he went into an ecstatic mood. While listening to the prelude of the kirtan he plunged into deep samādhi. He placed his legs on the lap of Nityagopal, who was sitting near him. The devotee, too, was in an ecstatic mood. He was weeping. The other devotees looked on intently.

Regaining partial consciousness, Sri Ramakrishna said: "From the Nitya to the Līlā and from the Līlā to the Nitya. (To Nityagopal) What is your ideal?"

NITYAGOPAL: "Both are good."

Sri Ramakrishna closed his eyes and said: "Is it only this? Does God exist only when the eyes are closed, and cease to exist when the eyes are opened? The Līlā belongs to Him to whom the Nitya belongs, and the Nitya belongs to Him to whom the Līlā belongs. (To Mahima) My dear sir, let me tell you—"

MAHIMA: "Revered sir, both are according to the will of God."

---

[1] Kedar spoke of Sri Ramakrishna as an Incarnation of God.

778

MASTER: "Some people climb the seven floors of a building and cannot get down; but some climb up and then, at will, visit the lower floors.

"Uddhava said to the gopis: 'He whom you address as your Krishna dwells in all beings. It is He alone who has become the universe and its living beings.'

"Therefore I say, does a man meditate on God only when his eyes are closed? Doesn't he see anything of God when his eyes are open?"

MAHIMA: "I have a question to ask, sir. A lover of God needs Nirvāna[2] some time or other, doesn't he?"

MASTER: "It can't be said that bhaktas need Nirvāna. According to some schools there is an eternal Krishna and there are also His eternal devotees. Krishna is Spirit embodied, and His Abode also is Spirit embodied. Krishna is eternal and the devotees also are eternal. Krishna and the devotees are like the moon and the stars—always near each other. You yourself repeat: 'What need is there of penance if God is seen within and without?' Further, I have told you that the devotee who is born with an element of Vishnu cannot altogether get rid of bhakti. Once I fell into the clutches of a jñāni,[3] who made me listen to Vedānta for eleven months. But he couldn't altogether destroy the seed of bhakti in me. No matter where my mind wandered, it would come back to the Divine Mother. Whenever I sang of Her, Nangtā would weep and say, 'Ah! What is this?' You see, he was such a great jñāni and still he wept. (To the younger Naren and the others) Remember the popular saying that if a man drinks the juice of the ālekh creeper, a plant grows inside his stomach. Once the seed of bhakti is sown, the effect is inevitable: it will gradually grow into a tree with flowers and fruits.

"You may reason and argue a thousand times, but if you have the seed of bhakti within you, you will surely come back to Hari."

The devotees listened silently to the Master. Sri Ramakrishna asked Mahima, laughing, "What is the thing you enjoy most?"

MAHIMA (smiling): "Nothing, sir. I like mangoes."

MASTER (smiling): "All by yourself? Or do you want to share them with others?"

MAHIMA (smiling): "I am not so anxious to give others a share. I may as well eat them all by myself."

MASTER: "But do you know my attitude? I accept both, the Nitya and the Līlā. Doesn't God exist if one looks around with eyes open? After realizing Him, one knows that He is both the Absolute and the universe. It is He who is the Indivisible Satchidānanda. Again, it is He who has become the universe and its living beings.

"One needs sādhanā. Mere study of the scriptures will not do. I noticed that though Vidyāsāgar had no doubt read a great deal, he had not realized what was inside him; he was satisfied with helping boys get their education, but had not tasted the Bliss of God. What will mere study accomplish? How

---

[2] Nirvāna, or total annihilation of the ego, is the ideal of the jñānis, the non-dualists.

[3] The Master was speaking of Totapuri, whom he always referred to as "Nangtā", the "naked one".

little one assimilates! The almanac may forecast twenty measures of rain; but you don't get a drop by squeezing its pages."

MAHIMA: "We have so many duties in the world. Where is the time for sādhanā?"

MASTER: "Why should you say such a thing? It is you who describe the world as illusory, like a dream.

"Rāma and Lakshmana wanted to go to Ceylon. But the ocean was before them. Lakshmana was angry. Taking his bow and arrow, he said: 'I shall kill Varuna. This ocean prevents our going to Ceylon.' Rāma explained the matter to him, saying: 'Lakshmana, all that you are seeing is unreal, like a dream. The ocean is unreal. Your anger is also unreal. It is equally unreal to think of destroying one unreal thing by means of another.'"

Mahimacharan kept quiet. He had many duties in the world. He had lately started a school to help others.

MASTER (to Mahima): "Sambhu once said to me: 'I have some money. It is my desire to spend it for good works—for schools and dispensaries, roads, and so forth.' I said to him: 'It will be good if you can do these works in a selfless spirit. But it is extremely difficult to perform unselfish action. Desire for fruit comes from nobody knows where. Let me ask you something. Suppose God appears before you; will you pray to Him, then, for such things as schools and dispensaries and hospitals?'"

A DEVOTEE: "Sir, what is the way for worldly people?"

MASTER: "The company of holy men. Worldly people should listen to spiritual talk. They are in a state of madness, intoxicated with 'woman and gold'. A drunkard should be given rice-water as an antidote. Drinking it slowly, he gradually recovers his normal consciousness.

"A worldly person should also receive instructions from a sadguru, a real teacher. Such a teacher has certain signs. You should hear about Benares only from a man who has been to Benares and seen it. Mere book-learning will not do. One should not receive instruction from a pundit who has not realized the world to be unreal. Only if a pundit has discrimination and renunciation is he entitled to instruct.

"Samadhyayi remarked that God was dry. Think of his speaking like that of Him who is the embodiment of sweetness! It sounds like the remark, 'My uncle's cow-shed is full of horses.' (All laugh.)

"Yes, a worldly person is in a state of intoxication. He always says to himself: 'It is I who am doing everything. All these—the house and family —are mine.' Baring his teeth, he says: 'What will happen to my wife and children without me? How will they get along? Who will look after my wife and children?' Rakhal said one day, 'What will happen to my wife?'"

HARAMOHAN: "Did Rakhal say that?"

MASTER: "What else could he do? He who has knowledge has ignorance also. 'How amazing!' Lakshmana said to Rāma. 'Even a sage like Vaśishtha is stricken with grief because of the death of his sons!' 'Brother,' replied Rāma, 'he who has knowledge has ignorance also. Therefore go beyond both knowledge and ignorance.'

"Suppose a thorn has pierced a man's foot. He picks another thorn to pull out the first one. After extracting the first thorn with the help of the second, he throws both away. One should use the thorn of knowledge to pull out the thorn of ignorance. Then one throws away both the thorns, knowledge and ignorance, and attains vijnāna. What is vijnāna? It is to know God distinctly by realizing His existence through an intuitive experience and to speak to Him intimately. That is why Sri Krishna said to Arjuna, 'Go beyond the three gunas.'

"In order to attain vijnāna one has to accept the help of vidyāmāyā. Vidyāmāyā includes discrimination—that is to say, God is real and the world illusory—and dispassion, and also chanting God's name and glories, meditation, the company of holy persons, prayer, and so forth. Vidyāmāyā may be likened to the last few steps before the roof. Next is the roof, the realization of God.

"Worldly people are in a state of chronic intoxication—mad with 'woman and gold'; they are insensible to spiritual ideas. That is why I love the youngsters not yet stained by 'woman and gold'. They are 'good receptacles' and may become useful in God's work. But as for worldly people, you lose almost everything while trying to eliminate the worthless stuff in them. They are like bony fish—almost all bones and very little meat.

"Worldly people are like mangoes struck by hail. If you want to offer them to God, you have to purify them by sprinkling them with Ganges water. Even then they are seldom used in the temple worship. If you are to use them at all, you have to apply Brahmajnāna, that is to say, you have to persuade yourself that it is God alone who has become everything."

A Theosophist gentleman arrived with Aswini Kumar Dutta and the son of Behari Bhaduri. The Mukherji brothers entered the room and saluted Sri Ramakrishna. Arrangements were being made for devotional music in the courtyard. At the first beat of the drum the Master left the room and went there. The devotees followed him.

Bhavanath introduced Aswini to the Master. The Master introduced him to M. Aswini and M. were talking together when Narendra arrived. Sri Ramakrishna said to Aswini, "This is Narendra."

Saturday, June 13, 1885

About three o'clock in the afternoon Sri Ramakrishna was resting in his room after the midday meal. A pundit was sitting on a mat on the floor. Near the north door of the room stood a brāhmin woman who had recently lost her only daughter and was stricken with grief. Kishori, too, was in the room. M. arrived and saluted the Master. He was accompanied by Dwija and a few other devotees.

Sri Ramakrishna was not well. He had been suffering from an inflamed throat. These were the hot days of summer. M. was not keeping well either, and of late he had not been able to visit Sri Ramakrishna frequently.

MASTER (*to M.*): "How are you? It is nice to see you. The bel-fruit you sent me was very good."

M: "I am slightly better now, sir."

MASTER: "It is very hot. Take a little ice now and then. I have been feeling the heat very much myself; so I ate a great deal of ice-cream. That is why I have this sore throat. The saliva smells very bad.

"I have said to the Divine Mother: 'Mother, make me well. I shall not eat ice-cream any more.' Next I said to Her that I wouldn't eat ice either. Since I have given my word to the Mother, I shall certainly not eat these things. But sometimes I become forgetful. Once I said that I wouldn't eat fish on Sundays; but one Sunday I forgot and ate fish. But I cannot consciously go back on my word. The other day I asked a devotee to bring my water-jug to the pine-grove. As he had to go elsewhere, another man brought the jug. But I couldn't use that water. I was helpless. I waited there until the first man brought water for me.

"When I renounced everything with an offering of flowers at the Lotus Feet of the Mother, I said: 'Here, Mother, take Thy holiness, take Thy unholiness. Here, Mother, take Thy dharma, take Thy adharma. Here, Mother, take Thy sin, take Thy virtue. Here, Mother, take Thy good, take Thy evil. And give me only pure bhakti.' But I could not say, 'Here, Mother, take Thy truth, take Thy falsehood.' "

A devotee had brought some ice. Again and again the Master asked M., "Shall I eat it?"

M. said humbly, "Please don't eat it without consulting the Mother." Sri Ramakrishna could not take the ice.

MASTER: "It is the bhakta, and not the jnāni, who discriminates between holiness and unholiness. Vijay's mother-in-law said to me: 'How little I have achieved of my spiritual ideal! I cannot take food from everybody.' I said to her: 'Is eating everybody's food a sign of jnāna? A dog eats anything and everything. Does that make it a jnāni?'

(To M.) "Why do I eat a variety of dishes? In order not to become monotonous. Otherwise I should have to renounce the devotees.

"I said to Keshab: 'If I instruct you from a still higher standpoint, then you won't be able to preserve your organization. In the state of jnāna organizations and things like that become unreal, like a dream.'

"One time I gave up fish. At first I suffered from it; afterwards it didn't bother me much. If someone burns up a bird's nest, the bird flies about; it takes shelter in the sky. If a man truly realizes that the body and the world are unreal, then his soul attains samādhi.

"Formerly I had the state of mind of a jnāni: I couldn't enjoy the company of men. I would hear that a jnāni or a bhakta lived at a certain place; then, a few days later, I would learn that he was dead. Everything seemed to me impermanent; so I couldn't enjoy people's company. Later the Mother brought my mind down to a lower plane; She so changed my mind that I could enjoy love of God and His devotees."

Next the Master began to talk about Divine Incarnation.

MASTER (to M.): "Do you know why God incarnates Himself as a man? It is because through a human body one can hear His words. He sports through it. He tastes divine bliss through a human body. But through His other devotees God manifests only a small part of Himself. A devotee is like something you get a little juice from after much sucking—like a flower you get a drop of honey from after much sucking. (*To M.*) Do you understand this?"

M: "Yes, sir. Very well."

Sri Ramakrishna began to talk to Dwija, who was about sixteen years old. His father had married a second time. Dwija often accompanied M. to Dakshineswar, and Sri Ramakrishna was fond of him. The boy said that his father opposed his coming to Dakshineswar.

MASTER: "And your brothers too? Do they speak slightingly of me?"

Dwija did not answer.

M. (*to the Master*): "Those who speak slightingly of you will be cured of it after getting a few more blows from the world."

MASTER (*referring to Dwija's brothers*): "They live with their step-mother. So they are getting blows."

All were silent a moment.

MASTER (*to M.*): "Introduce Dwija to Purna some time."

M: "Yes, I shall. (*To Dwija*) Go to Pānihāti."

MASTER: "I am asking everyone to send people to Pānihāti. (*To M.*) Won't you go?"

Sri Ramakrishna intended to visit the religious festival at Pānihāti; so he was asking the devotees to go too.

M: "Yes, sir, I want to go."

MASTER: "We shall engage a big boat; then it won't toss about. Will Girish Ghosh be there?"

Sri Ramakrishna looked steadily at Dwija.

Master: "Well, there are so many youngsters in the city; why does this boy come here? (*To M.*) Tell me what you think. Certainly he has inherited some good tendencies from his previous birth."

M: "Undoubtedly, sir."

MASTER: "There is such a thing as inborn tendencies. When a man has performed many good actions in his previous births, in the final birth he becomes guileless. In the final birth he acts somewhat like a madcap.

"To tell you the truth, everything happens by God's will. When He says 'Yea', everything comes to pass, and when He says 'Nay', everything comes to a standstill.

"Why is it that one man should not bless another? Because nothing can happen by man's will: things come to pass or disappear by God's will.

"The other day I went to Captain's house. I saw some young boys going along the road. They belong to a different class. I saw one of them, about nineteen or twenty years old, with his hair parted on the side. He was whistling as he walked along.

"I see some immersed in the thickest tamas. They play the flute and are proud of it.

(*To Dwija*) "Why should a man of Knowledge be afraid of criticism? His understanding is as immovable as the anvil in a blacksmith's shop. Blows from the hammer fall continually on the anvil but cannot affect it in the least.

"I saw X—'s father going along the street."

M: "He is a very artless man."

MASTER: "But he has red eyes."

Sri Ramakrishna told the devotees about his visit to Captain's house. Captain had criticized the young men who visited the Master. Perhaps Hazra had poisoned his mind.

MASTER: "I was talking to Captain. I said: 'Nothing exists except Purusha and Prakriti. Nārada said to Rāma, "O Rāma, all the men You see are parts of Yourself, and all the women are parts of Sītā."'

"Captain was highly pleased. He said: 'You alone have the right perception. All men are really Rāma, being parts of Rāma; all women are really Sītā, being parts of Sītā.'

"Immediately after saying this he began to criticize the young devotees. He said: 'They study English books and don't discriminate about their food. It is not good that they should visit you frequently. It may do you harm. Hazra is a real man, a grand fellow. Don't allow those young people to visit you so much.' At first I said, 'What can I do if they come?' Then I gave him some mortal blows. His daughter laughed. I said to him: 'God is far, far away from the worldly-minded. But God is very near the man—nay, within a distance of three cubits—whose mind is free from worldliness.' Speaking of Rakhal, Captain said, 'He eats with all sorts of people.' Perhaps he had heard it from Hazra. Thereupon I said to him: 'A man may practise intense austerity and japa, but he won't achieve anything if his mind dwells on the world. But blessed is the man who keeps his mind on God even though he eats pork. He will certainly realize God in due time. Hazra, with all his austerity and japa, doesn't allow an opportunity to slip by for earning money as a broker.'

"'Yes, yes!' said Captain. 'You are right.' I said to him further, 'A few minutes ago you said that all men were parts of Rāma and all women parts of Sītā, and now you are talking like this!'

"Captain said: 'Yes, that's true. But you don't love everybody.'

"I said: 'According to the scriptures, water is God. We see water everywhere. But some water we drink, some we bathe in, and some we use for washing dirty things. Here sit your wife and daughter. I see them as embodiments of the Blessed Mother.'

"Thereupon Captain said, 'Yes, yes! That's true.' He wanted to apologize by touching my feet."

After speaking thus, Sri Ramakrishna laughed. Then he began to tell of Captain's many virtues.

MASTER: "Captain has many virtues. Every day he attends to his devotions. He himself performs the worship of the Family Deity. How many mantras he recites while bathing the image! He is a great ritualist. He performs his daily devotions, such as worship, japa, ārati, recital of the scriptures, and chanting of hymns.

"I scolded Captain and said: 'Too much reading has spoiled you. Don't read any more.'

"About my own spiritual state Captain said, 'Your soul, like a bird, is ready to fly.' There are two entities: jīvātmā, the embodied soul, and Paramātmā,

the Supreme Soul. The embodied soul is the bird. The Supreme Soul is like
the ākāśa; it is the Chidākāśa, the ākāśa of Consciousness. Captain said:
'Your embodied soul flies into the ākāśa of Consciousness. Thus you go into
samādhi.'

(*Smiling*) "He criticized the Bengalis. He said: 'The Bengalis are fools.
They have a gem[4] near them, but they cannot recognize it.'

"Captain's father was a great devotee. He was a subādār in the English
army. Even on the battle-field he would perform his worship at the proper
time. With one hand he would worship Śiva and with the other he
would wield his gun and sword.

(*To M.*) "But Captain is engaged in worldly duties day and night. Whenever I go to his house I see him surrounded by his wife and children. Besides, his men bring him their account books now and then. But at times his
mind dwells on God also. It is like the case of a typhoid patient who is
always in a delirium. Now and then he gets a flash of consciousness and
cries out: 'I want a drink of water! I want a drink of water!' But while you
are giving him the water, he becomes unconscious again and is not aware of
anything. I said to Captain, 'You are a ritualist.' He said: 'Yes, I feel very
happy while performing worship and things like that. Worldly people have
no other way.'

"I said to him: 'But must one perform formal worship for ever? How long
does a bee buzz about? As long as it hasn't lighted on a flower. While sipping honey it doesn't buzz.' 'But', he said, 'can we, like you, give up worship
and other rituals?' Yet he doesn't always say the same thing. Sometimes he
says that all this is inert, sometimes that all this is conscious. I say: 'What do
you mean by inert? Everything is Chaitanya, Consciousness.' "

Sri Ramakrishna asked M. about Purna.

MASTER: "If I see Purna once more, then my longing for him will dimin-
ish. How intelligent he is! His mind is much drawn to me. He says, 'I too
feel a strange sensation in my heart for you.' (*To M.*) They have taken him
away from your school. Will that harm you?"

M: "If Vidyāsāgar[5] tells me that Purna's relatives have taken him away
from the school on my account, I have an explanation to give him."

MASTER: "What will you say?"

M: "I shall say that one thinks of God in holy company. That is by no
means bad. Further, I shall tell him that the text-books prescribed by the
school authorities say that one should love God with all one's soul." (*The
Master laughs.*)

MASTER: "At Captain's house I sent for the younger Naren. I said to him:
'Where is your house? I want to see it.' 'Please do come', he said. But he
became nervous as we were going there, lest his father should know about
it. (*All laugh.*)

(*To a visitor*) "You haven't been here for a long time—about seven or
eight months."

VISITOR: "About a year, sir."

[4] Sri Ramakrishna.
[5] The founder of the school.

MASTER: "Another gentleman used to come with you."

VISITOR: "Yes, sir. Nilmani Babu."

MASTÈR: "Why doesn't he come any more? Ask him to come some time. I want to see him. Who is this boy with you?"

VISITOR: "He comes from Assam."

MASTER: "Where is Assam? In which direction?"

Dwija spoke to the Master about Ashu. Ashu's father was arranging for his marriage, but Ashu had no wish to marry.

MASTER: "See, he doesn't want to marry. They are forcing him."

Sri Ramakrishna said to a devotee that he should show respect to his elder brother. He said: "The elder brother is like one's father. Respect him."

A pundit was sitting with the devotees. He came from upper India.

MASTER (smiling, to M.): "The pundit is a great student of the *Bhāgavata.*"

M. and the devotees looked at the pundit.

MASTER (to the pundit): "Well, sir, what is Yogamāyā?"

The pundit gave some sort of explanation.

MASTER: "Why isn't Rādhikā called Yogamāyā?"

The pundit also answered this question after a fashion.

MASTER: "Rādhikā is full of unmixed sattva, the embodiment of prema. Yogamāyā contains all the three gunas—sattva, rajas, and tamas; but Rādhikā has nothing but pure sattva.

(To M.) "Narendra now respects Rādhikā very much. He says that if anyone wants to know how to love Satchidānanda, he can learn it from her.

"Satchidānanda wanted to taste divine bliss for Itself. That is why It created Rādhikā. She was created from the person of Satchidānanda Krishna. Satchidānanda Krishna is the 'container', and He Himself, in the form of Rādhikā, is the 'contained'. He manifested Himself in that way in order to taste His own bliss, that is to say, in order to experience divine bliss by loving Satchidānanda.

"Therefore it is written in the Vaishnava books that after her birth Rādhikā did not open her eyes. The idea is that she did not wish to see any human being. Yaśodā came with Krishna in her arms to see Rādhikā. Only then did she open her eyes, to behold Krishna. In a playful mood Krishna touched her eyes. (To the Assamese boy) Haven't you seen this? Small children touch others' eyes with their hands."

The pundit was about to take leave of Sri Ramakrishna.

PUNDIT: "I must go home."

MASTER (tenderly): "Have you earned anything?"

PUNDIT: "The market is very dull. I've earned nothing."

A few minutes later he saluted the Master and departed.

MASTER (to M.): "You see how great the difference is between worldly people and the youngsters? This pundit has been worrying about money day and night. He has come to Calcutta to earn money; otherwise his people at home will have nothing to eat. So he has to knock at different doors. When will he concentrate his mind on God? But the youngsters are untouched by 'woman and gold'; hence they can direct their mind to God whenever they desire.

"The youngsters do not enjoy worldly people's company. Rakhal used to say, 'I feel nervous at the sight of the worldly-minded.' When I was first beginning to have spiritual experiences, I used to shut the doors of my room when I saw worldly people coming.

"As a boy, at Kāmārpukur, I loved Ram Mallick dearly. But afterwards, when he came here, I couldn't even touch him. Ram Mallick and I were great friends during our boyhood. We were together day and night; we slept together. At that time I was sixteen or seventeen years old. People used to say, 'If one of them were a woman they would marry each other.' Both of us used to play at his house. I remember those days very well. His relatives used to come riding in palanquins. Now he has a shop at Chānak. I sent for him many a time; he came here the other day and spent two days. Ram said he had no children; he brought up his nephew, but the boy died. He told me this with a sigh; his eyes were filled with tears; he was grief-stricken for his nephew. He said further that since they had no children of their own, all his wife's affection had been turned to the nephew. She was completely overwhelmed with grief. Ram said to her: 'You are crazy. What will you gain by grieving? Do you want to go to Benares?' You see, he called his wife crazy. Grief for the boy totally 'diluted' him. I found he had no stuff in him. I couldn't touch him."

The brāhmin lady still stood near the north door. She was a widow. Her only daughter had been married to a very aristocratic man, a landlord in Calcutta with the title of Rāja. Whenever the daughter visited her she was escorted by liveried footmen. Then the mother's heart swelled with pride. Just a few days ago the daughter had died, and now she was beside herself with sorrow.

The brāhmin lady listened to the account of Ram Mallick's grief for his nephew. For the last few days she had been running to the Master from her home at Bāghbāzar like an insane person. She was eager to know whether Sri Ramakrishna could suggest any remedy for her unquenchable grief. Sri Ramakrishna resumed the conversation.

MASTER: "A man came here the other day. He sat a few minutes and then said, 'Let me go and see the "moon-face" of my child.' I couldn't control myself and said: 'So you prefer your son's "moon-face" to God's "moon-face"! Get out, you fool!'

(To M.) "The truth is that God alone is real and all else unreal. Men, universe, house, children—all these are like the magic of the magician. The magician strikes his wand and says: 'Come delusion! Come confusion!' Then he says to the audience, 'Open the lid of the pot; see the birds fly into the sky.' But the magician alone is real and his magic unreal. The unreal exists for a second and then vanishes.

"Śiva was seated in Kailās. His companion Nandi was near Him. Suddenly a terrific noise arose. 'Revered Sir,' asked Nandi, 'what does that mean?' Śiva said: 'Rāvana is born. That is its meaning.' A few moments later another terrific noise was heard. 'Now what is this noise?' Nandi asked. Śiva said with a smile, 'Now Rāvana is dead.' Birth and death are like magic: you see the magic for a second and then it disappears. God alone is real and all else unreal. Water alone is real; its bubbles appear and disappear. They disappear into the very water from which they rise.

"God is like an ocean, and living beings are its bubbles. They are born there and they die there. Children are like the few small bubbles around a big one.

"God alone is real. Make an effort to cultivate love for Him and find out the means to realize Him. What will you gain by grieving?"

All sat in silence. The brāhmin lady said, "May I go home now?" The Master said to her tenderly: "Do you want to go now? It is very hot. Why now? You can go later in a carriage with the devotees."

Because the day was so hot, a devotee gave the Master a new fan made of sandal-wood. He was very much pleased and said: "Good! Good! Om Tat Sat! Kālī!" First he fanned the pictures of the gods and goddesses, and then he fanned himself. He said to M.: "See! Feel the breeze!" M. was highly pleased.

Captain arrived with his children.

Sri Ramakrishna said to Kishori, "Please show the temples to the children." He began to talk to Captain. M., Dwija, and the other devotees were sitting on the floor. Sri Ramakrishna was sitting on the small couch, facing the north. He asked Captain to sit in front of him on the same couch.

MASTER: "I was telling the devotees about you—your devotion, worship, and ārati."

CAPTAIN (bashfully): "What do I know of worship and ārati? How insignificant I am!"

MASTER: "Only the ego that is attached to 'woman and gold' is harmful. But the ego that feels it is the servant of God does no harm to anybody. Neither does the ego of a child, which is not under the control of any guna. One moment children quarrel, and the next moment they are on friendly terms. One moment they build their toy houses with great care, and immediately afterwards they knock them down. There is no harm in the 'I-consciousness' that makes one feel oneself to be a child of God or His servant. This ego is really no ego at all. It is like sugar candy, which is not like other sweets. Other sweets make one ill; but sugar candy relieves acidity. Or take the case of Om. It is unlike other sounds.

"With this kind of ego one is able to love Satchidānanda. It is impossible to get rid of the ego. Therefore it should be made to feel that it is the devotee of God, His servant. Otherwise, how can one live? How intense was the love of the gopis for Sri Krishna! (To Captain) Please tell us something about the gopis. You read the Bhāgavata so much."

CAPTAIN: "When Sri Krishna lived at Vrindāvan, without any of His royal splendour, even then the gopis loved Him more than their own souls. Therefore Sri Krishna said, 'How shall I be able to pay off my debt to the gopis, who surrendered to me their all—their bodies, minds, and souls?' "

Captain's words awakened intense love for Krishna in the Master's mind.

He exclaimed, "Govinda! Govinda! Govinda!" and was about to go into an ecstatic mood. Captain was amazed and said: "How blessed he is! How blessed he is!"

Captain and the devotees watched this love-ecstasy of Sri Ramakrishna. They sat quietly gazing at him, awaiting his return to the consciousness of the world.

MASTER: "Tell us more."

CAPTAIN: "Sri Krishna is unattainable by the yogis, by yogis like you; but He can be attained by lovers like the gopis. How many years did the yogis practise yoga for His vision! Yet they did not succeed. But the gopis realized Him with such ease!"

MASTER (*smiling*): "Yes, He ate from the hands of the gopis, wept for them, played with them, and made many demands on them."

A DEVOTEE: "Bankim has written a life of Krishna."

MASTER: "He accepts Krishna but not Rādhikā."

CAPTAIN: "I see he doesn't accept Krishna's līlā with the gopis."

MASTER: "I also hear that Bankim says that one needs passions such as lust."

A DEVOTEE: "He has written in his magazine that the purpose of religion is to give expression to our various faculties: physical, mental, and spiritual."

CAPTAIN: "I see. He believes that lust and so forth are necessary. But he doesn't believe that Sri Krishna could enjoy His sportive pleasure in the world, that God could incarnate Himself in a human form and sport in Vrindāvan with Rādhā and the gopis."

MASTER (*smiling*): "But these things are not written in the newspaper. How could he believe them?

"A man said to his friend, 'Yesterday, as I was passing through a certain part of the city, I saw a house fall with a crash.' 'Wait', said the friend. 'Let me look it up in the newspaper.' But this incident wasn't mentioned in the paper. Thereupon the man said, 'But the paper doesn't mention it.' His friend replied, 'I saw it with my own eyes.' 'Be that as it may,' said the man, 'I can't believe it as long as it isn't in the paper.'

"How can Bankim believe that God sports about as a man? He doesn't get it from his English education. It is very hard to explain how God fully incarnates Himself as man. Isn't that so? The manifestation of Infinity in this human body only three and a half cubits tall!"

CAPTAIN: "Krishna is God Himself. In describing Him we have to use such terms as 'whole' and 'part'."

MASTER: "Whole and part are like fire and its sparks. An Incarnation of God is for the sake of the bhaktas and not of the jnānis. It is said in the *Adhyātma Rāmāyana* that Rāma alone is both the Pervading Spirit and everything pervaded. 'You are the Supreme Lord distinguished as the vāchaka, the signifying symbol, and the vāchya, the object signified.' "

CAPTAIN: "The 'signifying symbol' means the pervader, and the 'object signified' means the thing pervaded."

MASTER: "The pervader in this case is a finite form. It is God incarnating Himself as a human being."

Sri Ramakrishna was talking thus to Captain and the devotees when Jaygopal Sen and Trailokya of the Brāhmo Samāj arrived. They saluted the Master and sat down. Sri Ramakrishna looked at Trailokya with a smile and continued the conversation.

MASTER: "It is on account of the ego that one is not able to see God. In front of the door of God's mansion lies the stump of ego. One cannot enter the mansion without jumping over the stump.

"There was once a man who had acquired the power to tame ghosts. One day, at his summons, a ghost appeared. The ghost said: 'Now tell me what you want me to do. The moment you cannot give me any work I shall break your neck.' The man had many things to accomplish, and he had the ghost do them all, one by one. At last he could find nothing more for the ghost to do. 'Now', said the ghost, 'I am going to break your neck.' 'Wait a minute', said the man. 'I shall return presently.' He ran to his teacher and said: 'Revered sir, I am in great danger. This is my trouble.' And he told his teacher his trouble and asked, 'What shall I do now?' The teacher said: 'Do this. Tell the ghost to straighten this kinky hair.' The ghost devoted itself day and night to straightening the hair. But how could it make a kinky hair straight? The hair remained kinky.

"Likewise, the ego seems to vanish this moment, but it reappears the next. Unless one renounces the ego, one does not receive the grace of God.

"Suppose there is a feast in a house and the master of the house puts a man in charge of the stores. As long as the man remains in the store-room, the master doesn't go there; but when of his own will he renounces the store-room and goes away, then the master locks it and takes charge of it himself.

"A guardian is appointed only for a minor. A boy cannot safeguard his property; therefore the king assumes responsibility for him. God does not take over our responsibilities unless we renounce our ego.

"Once Lakshmi and Nārāyana were seated in Vaikuntha, when Nārāyana suddenly stood up. Lakshmi had been stroking His feet. She said, 'Lord, where are You going?' Nārāyana answered: 'One of My devotees is in great danger. I must save him.' With these words He went out. But He came back immediately. Lakshmi said, 'Lord, why have You returned so soon?' Nārāyana smiled and said: 'The devotee was going along the road overwhelmed with love for Me. Some washermen were drying clothes on the grass, and the devotee walked over the clothes. At this the washermen chased him and were going to beat him with their sticks. So I ran out to protect him.' 'But why have You come back?' asked Lakshmi. Nārāyana laughed and said: 'I saw the devotee himself picking up a brick to throw at them. (All laugh.) So I came back.'

"I said to Keshab, 'You must renounce your ego.' Keshab replied, 'If I do, how can I keep my organization together?'

"I said to him: 'How slow you are to understand! I am not asking you to renounce the "ripe ego", the ego that makes a man feel he is a servant of God or His devotee. Give up the "unripe ego", the ego that creates attachment to "woman and gold". The ego that makes a man feel he is God's servant, His child, is the "ripe ego". It doesn't harm one.'"

TRAILOKYA: "It is very difficult to get rid of the ego. People only think they are free from it."

MASTER: "Gauri would not refer to himself as 'I' lest he should feel egotistic. He would say 'this' instead. I followed his example and would refer to myself as 'this' instead of 'I'. Instead of saying, 'I have eaten,' I would say, 'This has eaten.' Mathur noticed it and said one day: 'What is this, revered father? Why should you talk that way? Let them talk that way. They have their egotism. You are free from it; you don't have to talk like them.'

"I said to Keshab, 'Since the ego cannot be given up, let it remain as the servant, the servant of God.' Prahlāda had two moods. Sometimes he would feel that he was God. In that mood he would say, 'Thou art verily I, and I am verily Thou.' But when he was conscious of his ego, he felt that God was the Master and he was His servant. After a man is firmly established in the ideal of 'I am He', he can live as God's servant. He may then think of himself as the servant of God.

(To Captain) "When a man attains the Knowledge of Brahman he shows certain characteristics. The Bhāgavata describes four of them: the state of a child, of an inert thing, of a madman, and of a ghoul. Sometimes the knower of Brahman acts like a five-year-old child. Sometimes he acts like a madman. Sometimes he remains like an inert thing. In this state he cannot work; he renounces all action. You may say that jnānis like Janaka were active. The truth is that people in olden times gave responsibility to their subordinate officers and thus freed themselves from worry. Further, at that time men possessed intense faith."

Sri Ramakrishna began to speak about the renunciation of action. But he also said that those who felt they must do their duties should do them in a detached spirit.

MASTER: "After attaining Knowledge one cannot do much work."

TRAILOKYA: "Why so, sir? Pāvhāri Bābā was a great yogi and yet he reconciled people's quarrels, even lawsuits."

MASTER: "Yes, yes. That's true. Dr. Durgacharan was a great drunkard. He used to drink twenty-four hours a day. But he was precise in his actions; he did not make any mistake in treating his patients. There is no harm in doing work after the attainment of bhakti. But it is very hard. One needs intense tapasyā.

"It is God who does everything. We are His instruments. Some Sikhs said to me in front of the Kāli temple, 'God is compassionate.' I said, 'To whom is He compassionate?' 'Why, revered sir, to all of us', said the Sikhs. I said: 'We are His children. Does compassion to one's own children mean much? A father must look after his children; or do you expect the people of the neighbourhood to bring them up?' Well, won't those who say that God is compassionate ever understand that we are God's children and not someone else's?"

CAPTAIN: "You are right. They don't regard God as their own."

MASTER: "Should we not, then, address God as compassionate? Of course we should, as long as we practise sādhanā. After realizing God, one rightly feels that God is our Father or Mother. As long as we have not realized God, we feel that we are far away from Him, children of someone else.

"During the stage of sādhanā one should describe God by all His attributes. One day Hazra said to Narendra: 'God is Infinity. Infinite is His splendour. Do you think He will accept your offerings of sweets and bananas or listen to your music? This is a mistaken notion of yours.' Narendra at once sank ten fathoms. So I said to Hazra, 'You villain! Where will these youngsters be if you talk to them like that?' How can a man live if he gives up devotion? No doubt God has infinite splendour; yet He is under the control of His devotees. A rich man's gate-keeper comes to the parlour where his master is seated with his friends. He stands on one side of the room. In his hand he has something covered with a cloth. He is very hesitant. The master asks him, 'Well, gate-keeper, what have you in your hand?' Very hesitantly the servant takes out a custard-apple from under the cover, places it in front of his master, and says, 'Sir, it is my desire that you should eat this.' The Master is impressed by his servant's devotion. With great love he takes the fruit in his hand and says: 'Ah! This is a very nice custard-apple. Where did you pick it? You must have taken a great deal of trouble to get it.'

"God is under the control of His devotees. King Duryodhana was very attentive to Krishna and said to Him, 'Please have your meal here.' But the Lord went to Vidura's hut. He is very fond of His devotees. He ate Vidura's simple rice and greens as if they were celestial food.

"Sometimes a perfect jnāni behaves like a ghoul. He does not discriminate about food and drink, holiness and unholiness. A perfect knower of God and a perfect idiot have the same outer signs. A perfect jnāni perhaps does not utter the mantras while bathing in the Ganges. While worshipping God, perhaps he offers all the flowers together at His feet. He doesn't utter the mantras, nor does he observe the rituals.

"A man cannot renounce action as long as he desires worldly enjoyment. As long as one cherishes a desire for enjoyment, one performs action.

"A bird sat absent-mindedly on the mast of a ship anchored in the Ganges. Slowly the ship sailed out into the ocean. When the bird came to its senses, it could find no shore in any direction. It flew toward the north hoping to reach land; it went very far and grew very tired but could find no shore. What could it do? It returned to the ship and sat on the mast. After a long while the bird flew away again, this time toward the east. It couldn't find land in that direction either; everywhere it saw nothing but limitless ocean. Very tired, it again returned to the ship and sat on the mast. After resting a long while, the bird went toward the south, and then toward the west. When it found no sign of land in any direction, it came back and settled down on the mast. It did not leave the mast again, but sat there without making any further effort. It no longer felt restless or worried. Because it was free from worry, it made no further effort."

CAPTAIN: "Ah, what an illustration!"

MASTER: "Worldly people wander about to the four quarters of the earth for the sake of happiness. They don't find it anywhere; they only become tired and weary. When through their attachment to 'woman and gold' they only suffer misery, they feel an urge toward dispassion and renunciation. Most people cannot renounce 'woman and gold' without first enjoying it.

There are two sorts of people: those who stay in one place and those who go about to many places. There are some sādhakas who visit many sacred places. They cannot settle down in one spot; they must drink the water of many holy places. Thus roaming about, they satisfy their unfulfilled desires. And at last they build a hut in one place and settle down there. Then, free from worry and effort, they meditate on God.

"But what is there to enjoy in the world? 'Woman and gold'? That is only a momentary pleasure. One moment it exists and the next moment it disappears.

"The world is like an overcast sky that steadily pours down rain: the face of the sun is seldom seen. There is mostly suffering in the world. On account of the cloud of 'woman and gold' one cannot see the sun. Some people ask me: 'Sir, why has God created such a world? Is there no way out for us?' I say to them: 'Why shouldn't there be a way out? Take shelter with God and pray to Him with a yearning heart for a favourable wind, that you may have things in your favour. If you call on Him with yearning, He will surely listen to you.'

"A man had a son who was on the point of death. In a frenzy he asked remedies of different people. One of them said: 'Here is a remedy: First it must rain when the star Svāti is in the ascendant; then some of the rain must fall into a skull; then a frog must come there to drink the water, and a snake must chase it; and when the snake is about to bite the frog, the frog must hop away and the poison must fall into the skull. You should give the patient a little of the poison and rain-water from the skull.' The father set out eagerly to find the medicine when the star Svāti was in the sky. It started raining. Fervently he said to God, 'O Lord, please get a skull for me.' Searching here and there, he at last found a skull with rain-water in it. Again he prayed to God, saying, 'O Lord, I beseech Thee, please help me find the frog and the snake.' Since he had great longing, he got the frog and the snake also. In the twinkling of an eye he saw a snake chasing a frog, and as it was about to bite the frog, its poison fell into the skull.

"If one takes shelter with God and prays to Him with great longing, God will surely listen; He will certainly make everything favourable."

CAPTAIN: "What an apt illustration!"

MASTER: "Yes, God makes everything favourable. Perhaps the aspirant doesn't marry. Thus he is able to devote his whole attention to God. Or perhaps his brothers earn the family's livelihood. Or perhaps a son takes on the responsibilities of the family. Then the aspirant will not have to bother about the world; he can give one hundred per cent of his mind to God.

"But one cannot succeed unless one renounces 'woman and gold'. Only by renunciation is ignorance destroyed. The sun's rays, falling on a lens, burn many objects. But if a room is dark inside, you cannot get that result. You must come out of the room to use the lens.

"But some people live in the world even after attaining jnāna. They see both what is inside and what is outside the room. The light of God illumines the world. Therefore with that light they can discriminate between good and bad, permanent and impermanent. The ignorant, who lead a worldly life without knowing God, are like people living in a house with mud walls.

With the help of a dim light they can see the inside of the house but nothing more. But those who live in the world after having attained Knowledge and realized God, are like people living in a glass house. They see the inside of the room and also all that is outside. The light from the sun of Knowledge enters strongly into the room. They perceive everything inside the room very clearly. They know what is good and what is bad, what is permanent and what is impermanent.

"God alone is the Doer, and we are all His instruments. Therefore it is impossible even for a jnāni to be egotistic. The writer of a hymn to Śiva felt proud of his achievement; but his pride was dashed to pieces when Śiva's bull bared his teeth. He saw that each tooth was a word of the hymn. Do you understand the meaning of this? These words had existed from the beginningless past. The writer had only discovered them.

"It is not good to be a guru by profession. One cannot be a teacher without a command from God. He who says he is a guru[6] is a man of mean intelligence. Haven't you seen a balance? The lighter side goes higher. He who is spiritually higher than others does not consider himself a guru.[7] Everyone wants to be a teacher, but a disciple is hard to find."

Trailokya was seated on the floor, to the north of the small couch. He was going to sing. Sri Ramakrishna said to him, "Ah, how sweetly you sing!"

Trailokya sang to the accompaniment of a tānpurā:

> I have joined my heart to Thee: all that exists art Thou;
> Thee only have I found, for Thou art all that exists.
> O Lord, Beloved of my heart! Thou art the Home of all;
> Where indeed is the heart in which Thou dost not dwell?
> Thou hast entered every heart: all that exists art Thou.
> Whether sage or fool, whether Hindu or Mussalmān,
> Thou makest them as Thou wilt: all that exists art Thou.
>
> Thy presence is everywhere, whether in heaven or in Kaabā;
> Before Thee all must bow, for Thou art all that exists.
> From earth below to the highest heaven, from heaven to deepest
>   earth,
> I see Thee wherever I look: all that exists art Thou.
> Pondering, I have understood; I have seen it beyond a doubt;
> I find not a single thing that may be compared to Thee.
> To Jāfar[8] it has been revealed that Thou art all that exists.

He sang again:

> Thou art my All in All, O Lord!—the Life of my life, the Essence
>   of essence;
> In the three worlds I have none else but Thee to call my own.

[6] The word means both "spiritual teacher" and "heaviness".

[7] The meaning is that if a man thinks of himself as "guru" he is "heavy" and goes down, like the heavier pan of a balance.

[8] The author of the song.

Thou art my peace, my joy, my hope; Thou my support, my
wealth, my glory;
Thou art my wisdom and my strength.

Thou art my home, my place of rest; my dearest friend, my next
of kin;
My present and my future, Thou; my heaven and my salvation.
Thou art my scriptures, my commandments; Thou art my ever
gracious Guru;
Thou the Spring of my boundless bliss.

Thou art the Way, and Thou the Goal; Thou the Adorable One,
O Lord!
Thou art the Mother tender-hearted; Thou the chastising Father;
Thou the Creator and Protector; Thou the Helmsman who dost
steer
My craft across the sea of life.

While Sri Ramakrishna listened to the songs he was overwhelmed with
emotion. Again and again he said: "Ah, Thou art all! Ah me! Ah me!"

The music was over. It was six o'clock in the evening. Sri Ramakrishna
went to the pine-grove, M. accompanying him. Sri Ramakrishna was laughing and talking. Suddenly he said to M.: "Why haven't you eaten any
refreshments? Why haven't the others eaten either?" He was eager for the
devotees to take some refreshments.

Sri Ramakrishna was to go to Calcutta in the evening. While returning
from the pine-grove he said to M., "I don't know who will take me to
Calcutta in his carriage."

It was evening. A lamp was lighted in Sri Ramakrishna's room and
incense was burnt. Lamps also were lighted in the different temples and
buildings. The orchestra was playing in the nahabat. Soon the evening
service would begin in the temples.

Sri Ramakrishna sat on the small couch. After chanting the names of the
different deities, he meditated on the Divine Mother. The evening service
was over. Sri Ramakrishna paced the room, now and then talking to the
devotees. He also consulted M. about his going to Calcutta.

Presently Narendra arrived. He was accompanied by Sarat and one or
two other young devotees. They all saluted the Master.

At the sight of Narendra Sri Ramakrishna's love overflowed. He tenderly
touched Narendra's chin as one touches a baby's to show one's love. He
said in a loving voice, "Ah, you have come!"

The Master was standing in his room, facing the Ganges. Narendra and
his young friends were talking to him, facing the east. The Master turned
toward M. and said: "Narendra has come. How can I go to Calcutta now?
I sent for Narendra. How can I go now? What do you think?"

M: "As you wish, sir. Let us put it off today."

MASTER: "All right. We shall go tomorrow, either by boat or by carriage.
(To the other devotees) It is late. Go home now."

One by one the devotees saluted him and departed.

CAR FESTIVAL AT BALARAM'S HOUSE

SRI RAMAKRISHNA was sitting in Balaram's drawing-room with the devotees. It was nine o'clock in the morning. Balaram was going to celebrate the Car Festival the following day. The Deity Jagannāth[1] was worshipped daily at his house. He had a small car which would be drawn along the verandah to celebrate the festival. The Master had been specially invited for the occasion.

Sri Ramakrishna and M. were talking together. Narayan, Tejchandra, Balaram, and other devotees were in the room. The Master was talking about Purna, a lad of fifteen. He was very eager to see the boy.

MASTER (to M.): "Well, by which road will he come to see me? Please have Purna and Dwija meet each other.

"When two people are of the same age and have the same inner nature, I bring them together. There is a meaning in this. In this way both make progress. Have you noticed Purna's longing for God?"

M: "Yes, sir. One day I was riding on a tram. He saw me from the roof of his house and ran down to the street. With great fervour he saluted me from the street."

MASTER (with tears in his eyes): "Ah! Ah! It is because you have helped him make the contact through which he will find out the supreme ideal of his life. One doesn't act like that unless one longs for God.

"Narendra, the younger Naren, and Purna—these three have a manly nature. It is not so with Bhavanath. He has a womanly nature.

"Purna is in such an exalted state that either he will very soon give up his body—the body is useless after the realization of God—or his inner nature will within a few days burst forth.

"He has a divine nature—the traits of a god. It makes a person less fearful of men. If you put a garland of flowers round his neck or smear his body with sandal-paste or burn incense before him, he will go into samādhi; for

[1] The name of Krishna as He is worshipped in Puri; literally, "Lord of the Universe".

796

then he will know beyond the shadow of a doubt that Nārāyana Himself dwells in his body, that it is Nārāyana who has assumed the body. I have come to know about it.

"A few days after my first experience of the God-intoxicated state at Dakshineswar, a lady of a brāhmin family arrived there. She had many good traits. No sooner was a garland put round her neck and incense burnt before her than she went into samādhi. A few moments later she experienced great bliss; tears streamed from her eyes. I saluted her and said, 'Mother, shall I succeed?' 'Yes', she replied.

"I want to see Purna once more. But how will it be possible for me? It seems he is a part.[2] How amazing! Not a mere particle, but a part. Very intelligent, too. I understand that he is very clever in his studies. Therefore I have hit it right.

"By dint of austerity, a man may obtain God as his son. By the roadside on the way to Kāmārpukur is Ranjit Raya's lake. Bhagavati, the Divine Mother, was born as his daughter. Even now people hold an annual festival there in the month of Chaitra, in honour of this divine daughter. I feel very much like going there.

"Ranjit Raya was the landlord of that part of the country. Through the power of his tapasyā he obtained the Divine Mother as his daughter. He was very fond of her, and she too was much attached to him; she hardly left his presence. One day Ranjit Raya was engaged in the duties of his estate. He was very busy. The girl, with her childlike nature, was constantly interrupting him, saying: 'Father, what is this? What is that?' Ranjit Raya tried, with sweet words, to persuade her not to disturb him, and said: 'My child, please leave me alone. I have much work to do.' But the girl would not go away. At last, absent-mindedly, the father said, 'Get out of here!' On this pretext she left home. A pedlar of conch-shell articles was going along the road. From him she took a pair of bracelets for her wrists. When he asked for the price, she said that he could get the money from a certain box in her home. Then she disappeared. Nobody saw her again. In the mean time the pedlar came to the house and asked for the price of his bracelets. When she was not to be found at home, her relatives began to run about looking for her. Ranjit Raya sent people in all directions to search for her. The money owed to the pedlar was found in the box, as she had indicated. Ranjit Raya was weeping bitterly, when people came running to him and said that they had noticed something in the lake. They all ran there and saw an arm, with conch-shell bracelets on the wrist, being waved above the water. A moment afterwards it disappeared. Even now people worship her as the Divine Mother at the time of the annual festival. (*To M.*) All this is true."

M: "Yes, sir."

MASTER: "Narendra now believes these things.

"Purna was born with an element of Vishnu. I worshipped him mentally with bel-leaves; but the offering was not accepted. Then I worshipped him

[2] A part of the Divine Incarnation.

with tulsi-leaves and sandal-paste.[3] That proved to be all right. God reveals Himself in many ways: sometimes as man, sometimes in other divine forms made of Spirit. One must believe in divine forms. What do you say?"

M: "It is true, sir."

MASTER: "The brāhmani of Kāmārhāti[4] sees many visions. She lives all by herself in a lonely room in a garden on the bank of the Ganges. She spends her time in japa. Gopāla[5] sleeps with her. (*The Master gives a start.*) It is not imagination, but fact. She saw that Gopāla's palms were red. He walks with her. She suckles Him at her breast. They talk to each other. When Narendra heard the story he wept. Formerly I too used to see many visions, but now in my ecstatic state I don't see so many. I am gradually getting over my feminine nature; I feel nowadays more like a man. Therefore I control my emotion; I don't manifest it outwardly so much.

"The younger Naren has the nature of a man. Therefore in meditation his mind completely merges in the Ideal. He does not show emotion. Nitya-gopal has a feminine nature. Therefore while he is in a spiritual mood his body becomes distorted and twisted; it becomes flushed.

(*To M.*) "Well, people renounce grain by grain, but what a mood these youngsters are in!

"Binode said: 'I have to sleep with my wife. That makes me feel very bad.' It is bad for an aspirant to sleep with his wife, whether he has intercourse with her or not. There is the friction of the body and also the physical warmth.

"What a state Dwija is passing through! In my presence he only sways his body and fixes his glance on me. Is that a trifling thing? If a man gathers his whole mind and fixes it on me, then, indeed, he achieves everything.

"But what am I? It is all He. I am the machine and He is its Operator. It is God alone who exists in this [meaning his body]. That is why so many people are feeling more and more attracted to it. A mere touch is enough to awaken their spirituality. This attraction, this pull, is the attraction of God and of none else.

"Tarak of Belgharia was going home from Dakshineswar. I clearly noticed that a flame-like thing came out of this [meaning his body] and followed him. A few days later Tarak came back to Dakshineswar. In a state of samādhi He who dwells in this body placed His foot on Tarak's chest.

"Well, are there more youngsters like these?"

M: "Mohit is very nice. He came to you once or twice. He is studying enough books to pass two university examinations. He has great longing for God."

MASTER: "That may be. But he doesn't belong to a high plane. His physical traits are not so good; he has a puggish face. But these other young-sters belong to a high plane.

"Many troubles and worries follow in the wake of a birth in a physical

---

[3] The leaves of the bel-tree are offered to Śiva, whereas tulsi-leaves and sandal-paste are offered to Vishnu.

[4] Referring to one of the Master's woman devotees known as Gopāl Mā.

[5] The Baby Krishna.

body. Further, if a person is cursed, he may have to be born seven times. One must be very careful. One has to assume a human body if one cherishes the slightest desire."

A DEVOTEE: "What are the desires of those who are Incarnations of God?"

MASTER (*smiling*): "I find that I have not got rid of all my desires. Once I saw a holy man with a shawl, and I too wanted to put on one like it. Even now I have that desire. I don't know whether I shall have to be born again for it."

BALARAM (*smiling*): "Then will you be born again just for a shawl?" (*All laugh.*)

MASTER (*smiling*): "One has to keep a good desire so that one may give up the body meditating on it. There are four holy places for the sādhus to visit. They visit three and leave out one. Many of them leave out Puri, the place of Jagannāth, so that they can give up their bodies meditating on Jagannāth."

A man dressed in an ochre robe entered the room and greeted the Master. Privately he was in the habit of criticizing Sri Ramakrishna; so at the sight of him Balaram laughed. Sri Ramakrishna could read a man's mind. He said to Balaram: "Never mind. Let him say I am a cheat."

Sri Ramakrishna was talking to Tejchandra.

MASTER: "I send for you so often. Why don't you come? If you practise meditation and prayer it will make me happy. I look on you as my own; that is why I send for you."

TEJCHANDRA: "Sir, I have to go to the office. I am very busy with my duties."

M. (*smiling*): "There was a marriage ceremony at his home and he got leave from his office for ten days."

MASTER: "Well, well! You say you have no leisure. You told me just now that you were going to renounce the world."

NARAYAN: "M. said to us one day that this world is a wilderness."

MASTER (*to M.*): "Please tell them that story of the disciple who became unconscious after taking the medicine. His teacher arrived at the house and said he would revive if someone else swallowed a pill that he would prescribe. The disciple would get back his life, but the man who swallowed the pill would die.

"Please tell the other one, too, of the hathayogi who thought that his wife and children were his very own, and who feigned death with his limbs stretched out. It will do them good to hear those stories."

It was noon. Sri Ramakrishna partook of the food that had been offered to the Family Deity, Jagannāth. The Master often used to say that the food at Balaram's house was very pure. Afterwards he rested awhile.

Late in the afternoon Sri Ramakrishna sat with the devotees in the drawing-room of Balaram's house. Chandra Babu, of the Kartābhajā sect, and a witty brāhmin were there. The brāhmin was something of a buffoon; his words made everybody laugh.

About six o'clock Girish's brother Atul and Tejchandra's brother arrived. Sri Ramakrishna was in samādhi. A few minutes later he said, still in the ecstatic mood: "Can one become unconscious by meditating on Consciousness? Can one lose one's mind by thinking of God? God is of the very nature of Knowledge; He is of the very nature of Eternity, Purity, and Consciousness."

Sri Ramakrishna said to the witty brāhmin: "Why do you waste your time with these frivolous jokes about insignificant worldly things? Direct your mind to God. If a man can calculate about salt, he can also calculate about sugar candy."

BRĀHMIN (smiling): "Please attract me."

MASTER: "What can I do? Everything depends on your effort. Your mind is your own. Give up this trifling buffoonery and go forward toward God. You can go farther and farther along that way. The brahmachāri asked the wood-cutter to go forward. At first the wood-cutter found a sandal-wood forest; next, a silver-mine; next, a gold-mine; and then gems and diamonds."

BRĀHMIN: "There is no end to this path."

MASTER: "Where you find peace, there is the end."

About a new visitor Sri Ramakrishna said: "I didn't find any substance in him. He seemed worthless."

It was dusk. Lamps were lighted in the room. Sri Ramakrishna was meditating on the Divine Mother and chanting Her name in his melodious voice. The devotees sat around him. Since Balaram was going to celebrate the Car Festival at his house the following day, Sri Ramakrishna intended to spend the night there.

After taking some refreshments in the inner apartments, Sri Ramakrishna returned to the parlour. It was about ten o'clock. The Master said to M., "Please bring my towel from the other room."

A bed was made for Sri Ramakrishna in the adjoining small room. About half past ten Sri Ramakrishna lay down to sleep. It was summertime. He said to M., "You had better bring a fan." He asked the disciple to fan him. At midnight Sri Ramakrishna woke up. He said to M., "Don't fan me any more; I feel chilly."

Tuesday, July 14, 1885

It was the day of the Car Festival. Sri Ramakrishna left his bed very early in the morning. He was alone in the room, dancing and chanting the name of God. M. entered and saluted the Master. Other devotees arrived one by one. They saluted the Master and took seats near him. Sri Ramakrishna was longing intensely for Purna. He was talking to M. about him.

MASTER: "Did you give Purna any instruction?"

M: "I asked him to read the life of Chaitanya. He is familiar with the incidents of his life. I told him further that you ask people to stick to the truth."

MASTER: "How did he take it when you said about me, 'He is an Incarnation of God'?"

M: "I said to him, 'Come with me if you want to see a person like Chaitanya.'"

MASTER: "Anything else?"

M: "Also that remark of yours that when an elephant enters a small pool there is a great splashing of water all around; likewise, in the case of a 'small receptacle', emotion overflows.

"About his giving up of fish, I said to him: 'Why have you done that? Your family will make a great fuss about it.' "

MASTER: "That's good. One should keep one's feelings and emotions to oneself."

It was about half past six in the morning. M. was going to bathe in the Ganges, when suddenly tremors of an earthquake were felt. At once he returned to Sri Ramakrishna's room. The Master stood in the drawing-room. The devotees stood around him. They were talking about the earthquake. The shaking had been rather violent, and many of the devotees were frightened.

M: "You should all have gone downstairs."

MASTER: "Such is the fate of the house under whose roof one lives; and still people are so egotistic. (To M.) Do you remember the great storm of the month of Āswin?"

M: "Yes, sir. I was very young at that time—nine or ten years old. I was alone in a room while the storm was raging, and I prayed to God."

M. was surprised and said to himself: "Why did the Master suddenly ask me about the great storm of Āswin? Does he know that I was alone at that time earnestly praying to God with tears in my eyes? Does he know all this? Has he been protecting me as my guru since my very birth?"

MASTER: "It was quite late in the day at Dakshineswar when the storm broke, but somehow they managed to cook the meals. The trees were uprooted. You see, this is the fate of the house one lives in.

"But when one attains Perfect Knowledge, then one finds that dying and killing are one and the same thing; that is to say, both are unreal. When one is dead, one has not really died; and when one has killed another, the man is not really dead. Both the Līlā and the Nitya belong to the same Reality. In one form It is the Absolute, and in another, the Līlā. Even though the Līlā is destroyed, the Nitya always exists. Water is water, whether it is still or in waves; it is the same water when the waves quiet down."

Sri Ramakrishna sat in the drawing-room with the devotees. Mahendra Mukherji, Hari, the younger Naren, and many other devotees were there. Hari lived alone and studied Vedānta. He was about twenty-three years old, and unmarried. Sri Ramakrishna was very fond of him. He wanted Hari to visit him frequently. But since Hari loved solitude he did not often come to the Master.

MASTER (to Hari): "Well, I haven't seen you for a long time.

"You see, in one form He is the Absolute and in another He is the Relative. What does Vedānta teach? Brahman alone is real and the world illusory. Isn't that so? But as long as God keeps the 'ego of a devotee' in a man, the Relative is also real. When He completely effaces the ego, then what is remains. That cannot be described by the tongue. But as long as God keeps the ego, one must accept all. By removing the outer sheaths of the plantain-tree, you reach the inner pith. As long as the tree contains sheaths, it also contains pith. So too, as long as it contains pith, it also contains sheaths. The pith goes with the sheaths and the sheaths go with the pith. In the same way, when you speak of the Nitya, it is understood that the Līlā also exists; and when you speak of the Līlā, it is understood that the Nitya also exists.

"It is He alone who has become the universe, living beings, and the twenty-four cosmic principles. When He is actionless, I call Him Brahman; when He creates, preserves, and destroys, I call Him Śakti. Brahman and Śakti are not different from each other. Water is water, whether it is still or moving.

"It is not possible to rid oneself of 'I-consciousness'. And as long as one is aware of this 'I-consciousness', one cannot speak of the universe and its living beings as unreal. You cannot get the correct weight of the bel-fruit if you leave out its shell and pits.

"The brick, lime, and brick-dust of which the stairs are made are the same brick, lime, and brick-dust of which the roof is made. The universe and its living beings exist on account of the Reality of Him who is known as Brahman.

"The devotees—I mean the vijnānis—accept both God with form and the Formless, both the Personal God and the Impersonal. In a shoreless ocean —an infinite expanse of water—visible blocks of ice are formed here and there by intense cold. Similarly, under the cooling influence, so to say, of the deep love of Its worshipper, the Infinite reduces Itself to the finite and appears before the worshipper as God with form. Again, as, on the rising of the sun, the ice melts away, so, on the awakening of Knowledge, God with form melts away into the same Infinite and Formless.

"As long as a man analyses with the mind, he cannot reach the Absolute. As long as you reason with your mind, you have no way of getting rid of the universe and the objects of the senses—form, taste, smell, touch, and sound. When reasoning stops, you attain the Knowledge of Brahman. Ātman cannot be realized through this mind; Ātman is realized through Ātman alone. Pure Mind, Pure Buddhi, Pure Ātman—all these are one and the same.

"Just think how many things you need to perceive an object. You need eyes; you need light; you need mind. You cannot perceive the object if you leave out any one of these three. As long as the mind functions, how can you say that the universe and the 'I' do not exist?

"When the mind is annihilated, when it stops deliberating pro and con, then one goes into samādhi, one attains the Knowledge of Brahman. You know the seven notes of the scale: sā, re, gā, mā, pā, dhā, ni. One cannot keep one's voice on 'ni' very long."

Looking at the younger Naren, Sri Ramakrishna said: "What will you gain by merely being intuitively aware of God's existence? A mere vision of God is by no means everything. You have to bring Him into your room. You have to talk to Him.

"Some have heard of milk, some have seen milk, and some have drunk milk. Some have seen the king, but only one or two can bring the king home and entertain him."

M. went to the Ganges to take his bath. It was ten o'clock. Sri Ramakrishna was still talking with the devotees. After finishing his bath, M. returned to Balaram's house. He saluted the Master and sat down near him.

Sri Ramakrishna was filled with intense spiritual fervour. Words of wisdom flowed from him. Now and then he narrated his profound mystical experiences to the devotees.

MASTER: "I went to Benares with Mathur Babu. Our boat was passing the Manikarnikā Ghāt on the Ganges, when suddenly I had a vision of Śiva. I stood near the edge of the boat and went into samādhi. The boatman, fearing that I might fall into the water, cried to Hriday: 'Catch hold of him! Catch hold of him!' I saw Śiva standing on that ghāt, embodying in Himself all the seriousness of the world. At first I saw Him standing at a distance; then I saw Him approaching me. At last He merged in me.

"Another time, in an ecstatic mood, I saw that a sannyāsi was leading me by the hand. We entered a temple and I had a vision of Annapurnā made of gold.

"God alone has become all this; but He manifests Himself more in certain things than in others.

(*To M.*) "Perhaps you do not believe in the śalagrām. 'Englishmen' do not believe in it. It doesn't matter whether you believe in it or not. A śalagrām should contain the mark of a disc and other signs; only then can it be worshipped as an emblem of God."

M: "Yes, sir. It is like the fuller manifestation of God in a man with good physical traits."

MASTER: "At first Narendra used to say that these were figments of my imagination; but now he accepts everything."

Sri Ramakrishna was describing the vision of God, when he went into samādhi. The devotees looked at him with fixed gaze. After a long time he regained consciousness of the world and talked to the devotees.

MASTER (*to M.*): "What do you think I saw? I saw the whole universe as a śalagrām, and in it I saw your two eyes."

In silent wonder M. and the devotees listened to these words about his inner experience. At this moment Sarada, another young disciple of the Master, entered the room and saluted him.

MASTER (*to Sarada*): "Why don't you come to Dakshineswar? Why don't you see me when I come to Calcutta?"

SARADA: "Nobody tells me about it."

MASTER: "Next time I shall let you know. (*To M., smiling*) Make a list of these youngsters." (*M. and the devotees laugh.*)

SARADA: "My relatives at home want me to marry. (*Pointing to M.*) How many times he has scolded me about marriage!"

MASTER: "Why should you marry just now? (*To M.*) Sarada is now in a very good state of mind. Formerly he had a hesitant look; now his face beams with joy."

Sri Ramakrishna said to a devotee, "Will you kindly fetch Purna?"

Narendra arrived. Sri Ramakrishna asked a devotee to give him some refreshments. He was greatly pleased at the sight of Narendra. When he fed Narendra, he felt that he was feeding Nārāyana Himself. He stroked Narendra's body affectionately.

Gopāl Mā entered the room. She was a great devotee of Gopāla and was blessed with many lofty spiritual visions. Sri Ramakrishna had asked Balaram to send a man to bring her from Kāmārhāti. As soon as she entered the room she said, "I am shedding tears of joy." With these words she bowed before the Master, touching the ground with her forehead.

MASTER: "What is this? You address me as 'Gopāla' and still you salute me! Now go into the inner apartments and cook some curry for me. Put some spicy seasoning in it so that I may get the smell from here." (All laugh.)

GOPĀL MĀ: "What will they [meaning the members of the household] think of me?"

Before she left the room she said to Narendra in a very fervent voice, "My child, have I reached the goal, or have I farther to go?"

It was the day of the Çar Festival; so there was some delay in the worship of the Family Deity. When the worship was finished Sri Ramakrishna was asked to have his meal. He went to the inner apartments. The woman devotees were anxious to see him.

Sri Ramakrishna had many woman devotees, but he did not talk much about them to his man devotees. He would warn the men against visiting woman devotees. He would say: "Don't overdo it. Otherwise you will slip." To some of his man devotees he would say, "Don't go near a woman even if she rolls on the ground with devotion." The Master wanted the men to live apart from woman devotees; only thus would the two groups make progress. He did not like the woman devotees to caress the men as "Gopāla"; for too much of this motherly affection was not good; it degenerated in time into a harmful relationship.

After his midday meal Sri Ramakrishna sat in the drawing-room with the devotees. It was one o'clock. A devotee brought Purna from his home. With great joy the Master exclaimed to M.: "Here he is! Purna has come." Narendra, the younger Naren, Narayan, Haripada, and other devotees were talking with the Master.

THE YOUNGER NAREN: "Sir, have we any free will?"

MASTER: "Just try to find out who this 'I' is. While you are searching for 'I', 'He' comes out. 'I am the machine and He is the Operator.' You have heard of a mechanical toy that goes into a store with a letter in its hand. You are like that toy. God alone is the Doer. Do your duties in the world as if you were the doer, but knowing all the time that God alone is the Doer and you are the instrument.

"As long as the upādhi exists there is ignorance. 'I am a scholar', 'I am a jnāni', 'I am wealthy', 'I am honourable', 'I am the master, father, and teacher'—all these ideas are begotten of ignorance. 'I am the machine and You are the Operator'—that is Knowledge. In the state of Knowledge all upādhis are destroyed. When the log is burnt up entirely, there is no more sound; no heat either. Everything cools down. Peace! Peace! Peace! (*To Narendra*) Sing a little."

NARENDRA: "I must go home. I have many things to do."

MASTER: "Yes, yes, my child! Why should you listen to us? 'The words of those who have gold in their ears are valuable; no one listens to him who hasn't even a rag round his waist.' (*All laugh.*) You frequent the garden house of the Guhas. I always hear about it. Whenever I ask, 'Where is Narendra today?' I am told, 'Oh, he has gone to the Guhas.' I should not have said all these things, but you have wrung them out of me."

Narendra kept quiet a few moments. Then he said: "There are no instruments to accompany me. Shall I just sing?"

MASTER: "My child, this is all we have. Please sing if it suits you. You must know how Balaram arranges things.

"Balaram says to me, 'Please come to Calcutta by boat; take a carriage only if you must.' (*All laugh.*) You see, he has given us a feast today; so this afternoon he will make us all dance! (*All laugh.*) One day he hired a carriage for me from here to Dakshineswar. He said that the carriage hire was twelve ānnās. I said to him, 'Will the coachman take me to Dakshineswar for twelve ānnās?' 'Oh, that will be plenty', he replied. One side of the carriage broke down before we reached Dakshineswar. (*All laugh.*) Besides, the horse stopped every now and then; it simply would not go. Once in a while the coachman whipped the horse, and then it ran a short distance. (*All laugh.*) The program for the evening is that Ram will play on the drum and we shall all dance. Ram has no sense of rhythm. (*All laugh.*) Anyhow, that is Balaram's attitude—sing yourselves, dance yourselves, and make yourselves happy!" (*All laugh.*)

Other devotees were arriving. Mahendra Mukherji saluted the Master from a distance. The Master returned the salute. Then he salaamed to Mahendra like a Mussalmān. The Master said to a young devotee who sat next to him: "Why don't you tell him I have salaamed to him? He will appreciate it." (*All laugh.*)

Many of the householder devotees were accompanied by their wives and other woman relatives. They wanted to salute the Master and watch his dancing before the car. Ram, Girish, and other devotees gradually assembled. Many young devotees were present.

Narendra sang:

> Oh, when will dawn the blessed day
> When Love will waken in my heart?
> When will my tears flow uncontrolled
> As I repeat Lord Hari's name,
> And all my longing be fulfilled?
> When will my mind and soul be pure?
> Oh, when shall I at last repair
> Unto Vrindāvan's sacred groves?
> When will my worldly bonds fall off
> And my imperfect sight be healed
> By Wisdom's cool collyrium?

When shall I learn true alchemy
And, touching the Philosopher's Stone,
Transmute my body's worthless iron
Into the Spirit's purest gold?
When shall I see this very world
As God, and roll on Love's highway?
When shall I give up piety
And duty and the thought of caste?
When shall I leave behind all fear,
All shame, convention, worry, pride?

Oh, I shall smear my body then
With dust from the feet of devotees;
Across my shoulders I shall sling
Renunciation's pack, and drink
From my two hands a cooling draught
Of Jamunā's life-renewing stream.
Oh, then I shall be mad with love;
I shall both laugh and weep for joy!
Then I shall swim upon the Sea
Of blessed Satchidānanda;
Drunk with His love, I shall make all
As drunk as I! Oh, I shall sport
At Hari's feet for evermore!

He sang again:

In dense darkness, O Mother, Thy formless beauty sparkles;
Therefore the yogis meditate in a dark mountain cave. . . .

Balaram had arranged for kirtan with Vaishnavcharan, the musician
Vaishnavcharan sang:

O tongue, always repeat the name of Mother Durgā;
Who but your Mother Durgā will save you in distress? . . .

When Sri Ramakrishna had heard a line or two of the song he went into
samādhi. He stood up in that ecstatic mood. The younger Naren supported
him. The Master's face was lighted with a smile. Gradually his body became
motionless; his mind appeared to have gone to another realm. All the devotees
in the room looked at him in amazement. The woman devotees watched the
scene from behind the screen. After a long time he came down from
samādhi, chanting the holy name of God.

As the Master sat down, Vaishnavcharan sang again:

O vīnā, sing Lord Hari's name!
Without the blessing of His feet
You cannot know the final Truth.
The name of Hari slays all grief:
Sing Hari's name! Sing Krishna's name! . . .

Then he sang:

O vīnā, forgetting to worship Hari,
I pass the days of my life in vain. . . .

It was afternoon. In the mean time the small car of Jagannāth, decorated with flowers, flags, and bunting, had been brought to the inner verandah. The images of Jagannāth, Subhadrā, and Balarāma, were adorned with sandal-paste, flower garlands, robes, and jewelry. Sri Ramakrishna left the room where the professional musicians were singing and came to the verandah, accompanied by the devotees. He stood in front of the car and pulled it by the rope. He began to sing and dance with the devotees in front of the car.

The Master sang:

> Behold, the two brothers[6] have come, who weep
> while chanting Hari's name. . . .

He sang again:

> See how all Nadiā is shaking
> Under the waves of Gaurānga's love! . . .

The music and dancing went on in the verandah as the car was pulled to and fro. A large crowd entered the house on hearing the loud music and the beating of the drums. Sri Ramakrishna was completely intoxicated with divine love. The devotees felt its contagion and danced with the Master in an ecstasy of love.

Afterwards Sri Ramakrishna returned to the drawing-room. M. and other devotees stroked his feet.

Filled with divine fervour, Narendra sang to the accompaniment of the tānpurā:

> Come! Come, Mother! Doll of my soul! My heart's Delight!
> In my heart's lotus come and sit, that I may see Thy face. . . .

Then he sang:

> Mother, Thou art our sole Redeemer,
> Thou the Support of the three gunas,
> Higher than the most high.
> Thou art compassionate, I know,
> Who takest away our bitter grief.
>
> Sandhyā art Thou, and Gāyatri;
> Thou dost sustain this universe.
> Mother, the Help art Thou
> Of those that have no help but Thee,
> O Eternal Beloved of Śiva!
>
> Thou art in earth, in water Thou;
> Thou liest at the root of all.
> In me, in every creature,
> Thou hast Thy home; though clothed with form,
> Yet art Thou formless Reality.

[6] Gaurānga and Nityānanda.

He sang another song:

> I have made Thee, O Lord, the Pole-star of my life;
> No more shall I lose my way on the world's trackless sea.
> Wherever I wander here, Thy brilliance shines undimmed;
> With Thy serene and gracious light
> Thou drivest all the tears out of my troubled soul.
>
> In my heart's inmost shrine Thy face for ever beams;
> If, for a moment even, I cannot find it there,
> My soul is overwhelmed with woe;
> And when my witless mind strays from the thought of Thee,
> The vision of Thy face strikes me with deepest shame.

A devotee said to Narendra, "Will you sing that one—'O Mother, Thou my Inner Guide, ever awake within my heart'?"

MASTER: "Oh, no! Why that song now? The proper thing now is to sing of divine bliss—a song like 'O Mother Śyāmā, full of the waves of drunkenness divine'."

Narendra sang:

> O Mother Śyāmā, full of the waves of drunkenness divine!
> Who knows how Thou dost sport in the world?
> Thy fun and frolic and Thy glances put to shame the god of love.
> O Wielder of the sword! O Thou of terrifying face!
> The earth itself is shaken under Thy leaps and strides!
>
> O Thou Abode of the three gunas! O Redeemer! Fearsome One!
> Thou who art the Consort of Śiva!
> Many the forms Thou dost assume, fulfilling Thy bhaktas' prayers.
> Thou dancest in the Lotus of the Heart,
> O Mother, Eternal Consort of Brahman!

Full of divine ecstasy, Narendra sang again and again the lines:

> Thou dancest in the Lotus of the Heart,
> O Mother, Eternal Consort of Brahman!

Sri Ramakrishna was dancing, drunk with divine love, and he sang again and again, "O Mother, Eternal Consort of Brahman!"

After dancing a long time Sri Ramakrishna resumed his seat. He was very much pleased to see Narendra in a spiritual mood, singing with tears in his eyes.

It was about nine o'clock in the evening. The devotees still sat around the Master. Vaishnavcharan sang about Gaurānga:

> The beautiful Gaurānga, the youthful dancer, fair as molten
> gold. . . .

Next he sang about Sri Krishna. Krishna had left His pastoral life in Vrindāvan and become the king of Mathurā. A gopi met Him there and said:

> O Hari, how shall we know You now?
> In Mathurā's royal splendour You have forgotten us.

Now, in Your kingly robes, You ride an elephant;
Have You utterly forgotten how in Vrindāvan You tended cows?
O Hari, have You forgotten how You would steal the butter
From Braja's innocent gopi maids?

About eleven o'clock the devotees saluted the Master and were departing one by one.

MASTER: "You may all go. (*Pointing to Narendra and the younger Naren*) It will be enough if these two stay. (*To Girish*) Will you eat your supper at home? You may stay a few minutes if you want to. You want a smoke! But Balaram's servant is just like his master. Ask him for a smoke; he won't give it! (*All laugh.*) But don't go away without having your smoke."

Girish had brought with him a bespectacled friend. The latter observed all these things and left the place. Sri Ramakrishna said to Girish: "I say this to you and to everyone: Please do not force anybody to come here. Nothing happens except at the right time."

Before leaving, a devotee saluted the Master. He had a young boy with him. Sri Ramakrishna said to him affectionately, "It is getting late, and you have this boy with you." Narendra, the younger Naren, and a few other devotees stayed awhile and then took their leave.

Wednesday, July 15, 1885

It was four o'clock in the morning. Sri Ramakrishna was in bed in the small room next to the drawing-room. M. was sitting on a bench on the outer verandah to the south of the room. A few minutes later Sri Ramakrishna came out to the verandah. M. saluted him.

MASTER: "I have already been up once. Well, shall we go to Dakshineswar this morning?"

M: "The Ganges is less choppy in the morning."

Day was gradually breaking. The devotees had not yet arrived. Sri Ramakrishna had washed his mouth and was chanting the names of God in his sweet voice. He stood near the north door of the room. M. was by his side. A few minutes later Gopāl Mā arrived and stood near him. One or two woman devotees were looking at the Master from behind the doors of the inner apartments. They were like the gopis of Vrindāvan looking at Sri Krishna, or the woman devotees of Nadiā looking at Gaurānga from behind the screen.

After chanting the name of Rāma, Sri Ramakrishna chanted the name of Krishna: "Krishna! Krishna! Krishna of the gopis! Gopi! Gopi! Krishna, the Life of the cowherd boys of Vrindāvan! Krishna, the son of Nanda! Govinda! Govinda!"

Next he chanted the name of Gaurānga. Then he repeated, "Ālekh Niranjana", which is a name of God. Saying, "Niranjana", he wept. The devotees wept too. With tears in his eyes the Master said: "O Niranjan! O my child! Come! Eat this! Take this! When shall I make my life blessed by feeding you? You have assumed this human form for my sake."

He prayed to Jagannāth in a very touching voice: "O Jagannāth, Lord

of the Universe! O Friend of the world! O Friend of the poor! I am not,
O Lord, outside Thy universe. Be gracious to me!"

While he sang in praise of Jagannāth he was beside himself with divine
love.

Now he chanted the name of Nārāyana. He danced and sang: "O
Nārāyana! O Nārāyana! Nārāyana! Nārāyana!"

He danced and sang again:

> Ah, friend! I have not found Him yet, whose love has driven me
> mad. . . .

Afterwards the Master sat in the small room with the devotees. He was
completely stripped of his clothes, like a five-year-old child. M., Balaram,
and a few other devotees were in the room.

MASTER: "One can see God's form. One sees God when all upādhis disappear and reasoning stops. Then a man becomes speechless and goes into
samādhi. Coming to the theatre, people indulge in all kinds of gossip. But
the moment the curtain goes up, all conversation stops; the spectators become fully absorbed in what they see on the stage.

"I want to tell you something very secret. Why do I love boys like Purna
and Narendra so much? Once, in a spiritual mood, I felt intense love for
Jagannāth, love such as a woman feels for her sweetheart. In that mood I
was about to embrace Him, when I broke my arm. It was then revealed to
me: 'You have assumed this human body. Therefore establish with human
beings the relationship of friend, father, mother, or son.'

"I now feel for Purna and the other young boys as I once felt for
Rāmlālā.[7] I used to bathe Rāmlālā, feed Him, put Him to bed, and take
Him wherever I went. I used to weep for Rāmlālā. Now I have the same
feeling for these young boys. Look at Niranjan. He is not attached to anything. He spends money from his own pocket to take poor patients to the
hospital. At the proposal of marriage he says, 'Goodness! That is the whirlpool of the Viśālākshi!'[8] I see him seated on a light.

"Purna belongs to the realm of the Personal God. He was born with an
element of Vishnu. Ah, what yearning he has!

(To M.) "Didn't you notice that he looked at you as if you were his
spiritual brother, his very own? He said he would visit me again, at Captain's house.

"Narendra belongs to a very high plane—the realm of the Absolute. He
has a manly nature. So many devotees come here, but there is not one like
him.

"Every now and then I take stock of the devotees. I find that some are
like lotuses with ten petals, some like lotuses with sixteen petals, some like
lotuses with a hundred petals. But among lotuses Narendra is a thousand-
petalled one.

"Other devotees may be like pots or pitchers; but Narendra is a huge
water-barrel.

[7] A name of the Boy Rāma. See foot-note, p. 743.
[8] A stream near Kāmārpukur.

"Others may be like pools or tanks; but Narendra is a huge reservoir like the Hāldārpukur.

"Among fish, Narendra is a huge red-eyed carp; others are like minnows or smelts or sardines. Tarak of Belgharia may be called a bass.

"Narendra is a 'very big receptacle', one that can hold many things. He is like a bamboo with a big hollow space inside.

"Narendra is not under the control of anything. He is not under the control of attachment or sense pleasures. He is like a male pigeon. If you hold a male pigeon by its beak, it breaks away from you; but the female pigeon keeps still. Narendra has the nature of a man; so he sits on the right side in a carriage. Bhavanath has a woman's nature; so I make him sit on the other side. I feel great strength when Narendra is with me in a gathering."

About eight o'clock in the morning Mahendra Mukherji arrived and saluted the Master. Haripada, Tulsiram, and other devotees arrived one by one and saluted him. Baburam was laid up with fever and could not come.

MASTER (to M. and the others): "Hasn't the younger Naren come? Perhaps he thought I had left. (To Mukherji) How amazing! Even during his boyhood, on returning from school, he cried for God. Is it a small thing to cry for God? He is very intelligent, too. He is like a bamboo with a big hollow space inside. All of his mind is fixed on me. Girish Ghosh said to me: 'The younger Naren went to Navagopal's house when a kirtan was going on. On entering the house he inquired about you and exclaimed, "Where is he?" He was totally unconscious of his surroundings and practically walked over the people.' He has no fear of his relatives' threats. Sometimes he spends three nights at a stretch at Dakshineswar."

MUKHERJI: "Hari[9] became simply speechless at what you said yesterday. He said to me: 'Such wisdom can be found only in the philosophical systems of Sāmkhya, Yoga, and Vedānta. He is no ordinary person.'"

MASTER: "But I have never studied Sāmkhya or Vedānta.

"Perfect jnāna and perfect bhakti are one and the same thing. A man reasons, saying, 'Not this, not this'; he rejects the unreal. When his reasoning comes to an end, he attains the Knowledge of Brahman. Then he accepts what he rejected before. A man carefully climbs to the roof, rejecting the steps one by one. After reaching the roof he realizes that the steps are made of the same materials as the roof, namely, brick, lime, and brick-dust.

"He who is aware of the high is also aware of the low. After the attainment of Knowledge one looks alike on high and low.

"While Prahlāda dwelt on the plane of the Supreme Reality, he maintained the attitude of 'I am He'; but when he climbed down to the physical plane, he would look on himself as the servant of God.

"Hanumān also sometimes said, 'I am He', sometimes, 'I am the servant of God', sometimes, 'I am a part of God.'

"Why should a man cherish love of God in his heart? How else will he live? How else will he spend his days?

"To be sure, the ego does not disappear altogether. As long as the pot of

[9] Later Hari embraced the monastic life and became known as Swami Turiyananda.

'I'[10] persists, one cannot realize 'I am He.' In samādhi the ego totally disappears; then what *is* remains. Rāmprasād says: 'O Mother, when I shall attain Knowledge, then You alone will know whether I am good or You are good.'

"As long as 'I-consciousness' exists, one should have the attitude of a bhakta; one should not say, 'I am God.' A man aware of his body should feel that he is not Krishna Himself, but His devotee. But if God draws the devotee to Himself, then it is different. It is like the master saying to his beloved servant: 'Come, take your seat near me. You are the same as I.'

"The waves are part of the Ganges, but the Ganges is not part of the waves.

"Śiva experiences two states of mind. When He is completely absorbed in His own Self, He feels, 'I am He.' In that union neither body nor mind functions. But when He is conscious of His separate ego, He dances, exclaiming, 'Rāma! Rāma!'

"That which is unmoving also moves. Just now you are still, but a few moments later the same you will be engaged in action.

"Jnāna and bhakti are one and the same thing. The difference is like this: one man says 'water', and another, 'a block of ice'.

"Generally speaking there are two kinds of samādhi. First, sthita or jaḍa samādhi: one attains it by following the path of knowledge—as a result of the destruction of the ego through reasoning. Second, bhāva samādhi: one attains this by following the path of bhakti. In this second samādhi a trace of ego remains, like a line, in order to enable the devotee to enjoy God, to taste His līlā. But one cannot understand all this if one is attached to 'woman and gold'.

"I said to Kedar, 'You will never succeed if your mind dwells on "woman and gold".' I wanted to pass my hand over his chest, but I could not. He has knots and twists inside. It was like a room smelling of filth, which I could not enter. His attachment to the world is very deep; it is like a natural emblem of Śiva, whose root spreads as far as Benares. One will never succeed if one is attached to the world—to 'woman and gold'.

"The youngsters are yet untouched by 'woman and gold'. That is why I love them so dearly. Hazra says to me, 'You love a boy if he comes from a wealthy family or if he is handsome.' If that is so, then why do I love Harish, Latu, and Narendra? Narendra hasn't a penny to buy salt to season his rice.

"The youngsters' minds are not yet coloured by worldliness. That is why they are so pure in heart. Besides, many of them are eternally perfect; they have been drawn to God from their very birth. It is like a garden in which, while cleaning it, you suddenly discover water-pipes. The water gushes forth without any effort on your part."

BALARAM: "Sir, how was it possible for Purna to know all of a sudden that the world is illusory?"

MASTER: "He has inherited that knowledge from his previous births. In

10 Body-consciousness.

his past lives he practised many disciplines. It is the body alone that is small or grows big, and not the Ātman.

"Do you know what these youngsters are like? They are like certain plants that grow fruit first and then flowers. These devotees first of all have the vision of God; next they hear about His glories and attributes; and at last they are united with Him. Look at Niranjan. He always keeps his accounts clear. He will be able to go whenever he hears the call. But one should look after one's mother as long as she is alive. I used to worship my mother with flowers and sandal-paste. It is the Mother of the Universe who is embodied as our earthly mother.

"As long as you look after your own body, you must look after your mother too. Therefore I said to Hazra: 'When you have a cold, you procure black pepper, sugar candy, and salt. As long as you feel you must look after your body, you must look after your mother too.'

"But it is quite different when you completely forget your body. Then God Himself assumes your responsibilities. A minor cannot look after himself; therefore a guardian is appointed for him. Chaitanyadeva, like a minor, could not look after himself."

M. went to the Ganges to bathe.

Sri Ramakrishna was talking with the devotees in the small room in Balaram's house. Mahendra, Balaram, Tulasi, Haripada, Girish, and other devotees were sitting on the floor. M. returned from the Ganges. After saluting the Master he took a seat near him. Sri Ramakrishna was recounting to the devotees some of his spiritual experiences.

MASTER: "One day in the Kāli temple Haladhari and Nangtā were reading the *Adhyātma Rāmāyana*. Suddenly I had a vision of a river with woods on both sides. The trees and plants were green. Rāma and Lakshmana were walking along wearing their shorts. One day, in front of the kuthi, I saw Arjuna's chariot. Sri Krishna was seated in it as the charioteer. I still remember it. Another day, while listening to kirtan at Kāmārpukur, I saw Gaurānga in front of me.

"At that time a naked person, emerging from my body, used to go about with me. I used to joke with him. He looked like a boy and was a paramahamsa. I can't describe to you all the divine forms I saw at that time. I was suffering then from indigestion, which would become worse when I saw visions; so I would try to shun these divine forms and would spit on the ground when I saw them. But they would follow me and obsess me like ghosts. I was always overwhelmed with divine ecstasy and couldn't tell the passing of day and night. On the day after such a vision I would have a severe attack of diarrhoea, and all these ecstasies would pass out through my bowels."

GIRISH (*smiling*): "I am examining your horoscope."

MASTER (*smiling*): "I was born on the second day of the bright fortnight of the moon. My horoscope shows the positions of the sun, the moon, and Mercury at the time of my birth. There are not many more details."

GIRISH: "You were born under Kumbha. Rāma and Krishna were born under Karkat and Brisha, and Chaitanya under Simha."[11]

MASTER: "I had two desires: first, that I should be the king of the devotees, and second, that I should not be a dry sādhu."

GIRISH (smiling): "Why did you have to practise spiritual discipline?"

MASTER (smiling): "Even the Divine Mother had to practise austere sādhanā to obtain Śiva as Her husband. She practised the panchatapā. She would also immerse Her body in water in wintertime, and look fixedly at the sun. Krishna Himself had to practise much sādhanā. I had many mystic experiences, but I cannot reveal their contents. Under the bel-tree I had many flaming visions. There I practised the various sādhanās prescribed in the Tantra. I needed many articles—human skulls, and so forth and so on. The Brāhmani used to collect these things for me. I practised a number of mystic postures.

"I had another strange experience: if I felt egotistic on a particular day, I would be sick the following day."

M. sat motionless as a picture on canvas, hearing about these unique visions of the Master. The other devotees also were spellbound. There was a dead silence in the room.

TULASI (pointing to M.): "He never laughs."

MASTER: "But he laughs inside. The surface of the river Phalgu is covered with sand; but if you dig into the sand, water comes up.

(To M.) "Don't you scrape your tongue? Scrape it every day."

BALARAM: "Well, Purna has heard much about you from M."

MASTER: "Perhaps the account of my early spiritual experiences."

BALARAM: "If Purna is perfect by nature, then what is M.'s function?"

MASTER: "A mere instrument."

It was nine o'clock. Sri Ramakrishna was about to leave for Dakshineswar. Arrangements were being made for his departure. A boat had been hired at Bāghbāzār. The devotees saluted the Master.

Sri Ramakrishna went to the boat with one or two devotees. Gopāl Mā accompanied them. She intended to spend the morning at Dakshineswar and go to Kāmārhāti in the afternoon. The camp cot generally used by Rakhal at Dakshineswar had been sent to Calcutta for repair. It was put in the boat, and the boat left for Dakshineswar.

According to the Hindu almanac the day was not auspicious. So Sri Ramakrishna decided to return to Balaram's house the next Saturday and start again for Dakshineswar on an auspicious day.

[11] Kumbha, Karkat, Brisha, and Simha are signs of the Hindu zodiac corresponding to Aquarius, Scorpio, Taurus, and Leo.

43

VISIT TO NANDA BOSE'S HOUSE

IT WAS ABOUT THREE O'CLOCK in the afternoon. Sri Ramakrishna was sitting in Balaram's drawing-room with the devotees. Among others, Binode, Rakhal, the younger Naren, and M. were present. The Master had come to Balaram's house in the morning and had taken his midday meal there. At Balaram's house the Deity was worshipped as Jagannāth, and the members of the family partook of the food offered to the Deity. Sri Ramakrishna used to say that the food at Balaram's house was very pure.

Narayan and certain other devotees had remarked to the Master that Nanda Bose, an aristocrat of Bāghbāzār, had many pictures of gods and goddesses in his house. Hence Sri Ramakrishna intended to pay a visit to Nanda's house in the afternoon. A brāhmin woman devoted to the Master lived near by. She often came to see him at Dakshineswar. She was extremely sorrowful over the death of her only daughter, and the Master had agreed to go to her house. She had invited him with great earnestness. From her house the Master was to go to the house of Ganu's mother, another devotee.

The younger Naren had said to Sri Ramakrishna that he would not be able to visit him often on account of his having to prepare for his examinations.

MASTER (*to the younger Naren*): "I didn't send for you today."

THE YOUNGER NAREN (*smiling*): "What can be done about it now?"

MASTER: "Well, my child, I don't want to interfere with your studies. You may visit me when you have leisure."

The Master said these words as if he were piqued.

He was ready to go to Nanda Bose's house. A palanquin was brought for him, and he got into it repeating the name of God. He had put on a pair of black varnished slippers and a red-bordered cloth. As Sri Ramakrishna sat down in the palanquin, M. put the slippers by his side. He accompanied the palanquin on foot. Paresh joined them.

They entered the gate of Nanda's house, crossed the spacious square, and stopped in front of the building. The members of the family greeted the Master. He asked M. to hand him the slippers and then got out of the palanquin and entered the large hall. It was a very spacious room. Pictures of gods and goddesses were hanging on all sides.

Nanda Bose and his brother Pasupati saluted Sri Ramakrishna. The devotees of the Master also arrived. Girish's brother Atul came, and Prasanna's father, who was a frequent visitor at Nanda's house, was there. Prasanna was a devotee of the Master.

The Master looked at the pictures. M. and a few other devotees stood around him. Pasupati was explaining the pictures to them.

The first picture was of Vishnu with four arms. At the very sight of it Sri Ramakrishna was overwhelmed with ecstasy; he sat down on the floor and remained a few minutes in that spiritual mood.

In the second picture Rāma was blessing Hanumān, with His hand on the devotee's head. Hanumān's gaze was fixed on Rāma's Lotus Feet. The Master looked at the picture a long time and exclaimed with great fervour, "Ah me! Ah me!"

The third picture was of Krishna standing with flute to His lips under the kadamba tree.

The fourth was of Vāmana, the Dwarf, who was an Incarnation of Vishnu. The Master looked intently at this picture.

Next the Master looked at a picture of Nrisimha,[1] and then at one of Krishna with a herd of cows. Krishna was tending the cows with His cowherd friends on the bank of the Jamunā at Vrindāvan. M. said, "A lovely picture!"

Sri Ramakrishna then saw pictures of Dhumāvati, Shorasi, Bhuvaneśvari, Tārā, and Kāli. He said: "All these portray the terrible aspects of the Divine Mother. If one keeps these pictures, one should worship them. But you must be lucky, to be able to hang them like that on the wall."

At the sight of Annapurnā's picture, Sri Ramakrishna exclaimed with great fervour, "Grand! Grand!"

The next picture was one of Rādhikā as monarch. She was seated on a throne in the nikunja grove, surrounded by her woman attendants. Sri Krishna guarded the entrance of the grove as her officer.

Next was Sri Krishna's picture. Then came a picture of Sarasvati, the goddess of learning and music. It was in a glass case. She was in an ecstatic mood, playing melodies on the vīnā.

After seeing the pictures, Sri Ramakrishna went to the master of the house and said: "I am very happy today. It is grand! You are a real Hindu. You have these pictures instead of English ones. I am surprised!"

Nanda Bose was seated. He said to the Master: "Please take a seat. Why are you standing?"

Sri Ramakrishna sat down. He said: "These are very large pictures. You are a real Hindu."

NANDA: "I have European pictures also."

MASTER (smiling): "They are not like these. I am sure you don't pay much attention to them."

---

[1] God incarnated as half lion and half man to protect Prahlāda and destroy the demon Hiranyakaśipu, his father.

A picture of Keshab's Navavidhān hung on the wall. Suresh Mitra, a beloved householder disciple of the Master, had had it painted. In this picture Sri Ramakrishna was pointing out to Keshab that people of different religions proceed to the same goal by different paths.

MASTER: "That was painted for Surendra."

PRASANNA'S FATHER (smiling): "You too are in that picture."

MASTER (smiling): "Yes, it contains everything. This is the ideal of modern times."

As he spoke Sri Ramakrishna manifested great spiritual fervour. He was in an ecstatic mood, talking to the Divine Mother. A few minutes later he said, like a drunkard, "I am not unconscious." Looking at the house, he said: "It is a huge mansion. But what does it consist of? Bricks, timber, and clay."

A little later he said, "I am very happy to see these pictures of gods and goddesses." He added: "It is not good to keep pictures of the terrible aspects of the Divine Mother. If one does, one should worship them."

PASUPATI (smiling): "Well, things will go on as long as She keeps them going."

MASTER: "That is true. But one should think of God. It is not good to forget Him."

NANDA: "But how little we think of God!"

MASTER: "One thinks of God through His grace."

NANDA: "But how can we obtain God's grace? Has He really the power to bestow grace?"

MASTER (smiling): "I see. You think as the intellectuals do: one reaps the results of one's actions. Give up these ideas. The effect of karma wears away if one takes refuge in God. I prayed to the Divine Mother with flowers in my hand: 'Here, Mother, take Thy sin; here, take Thy virtue. I don't want either of these; give me only real bhakti. Here, Mother, take Thy good; here, take Thy bad. I don't want any of Thy good or bad; give me only real bhakti. Here, Mother, take Thy dharma; here, take Thy adharma. I don't want any of Thy dharma or adharma; give me only real bhakti. Here, Mother, take Thy knowledge; here, take Thy ignorance. I don't want any of Thy knowledge or ignorance; give me only real bhakti. Here, Mother, take Thy purity; here, take Thy impurity. Give me only real bhakti.'"

NANDA: "Can God violate law?"

MASTER: "What do you mean? He is the Lord of all. He can do everything. He who has made the law can also change it.

"But you may very well talk that way. Perhaps you want to enjoy the world, and that is why you talk that way. There is a view that a man's inner spirit is not awakened unless he is through with enjoyment. But what is there to enjoy? The pleasures of 'woman and gold'? This moment they exist and the next moment they disappear. It is all momentary. And what is there in 'woman and gold'? It is like the hog plum—all stone and skin. If one eats it, one suffers from colic. Or like a sweetmeat. Once you swallow it, it is gone."

Nanda remained silent a few minutes. Then he said: "Oh, yes. People no doubt talk that way. But is God partial? If things happen through God's grace, then I must say God is partial."

MASTER: "But God Himself has become everything—the universe and its living beings. You will realize it when you have Perfect Knowledge. God Himself has become the twenty-four cosmic principles: the mind, intellect, body, and so forth. Is there anyone but Himself to whom He can show partiality?"

NANDA: "Why has He assumed all these different forms? Why are some wise and some ignorant?"

MASTER: "It is His sweet will."

ATUL: "Kedar Babu puts it nicely. Once a man asked him, 'Why has God created the world?' He replied, 'I was not present at the conference where God made the plans of His creation.'"

MASTER: "Oh! It is His sweet will."

So saying, the Master sang:

> O Mother, all is done after Thine own sweet will;
> Thou art in truth self-willed, Redeemer of mankind!
> Thou workest Thine own work; men only call it theirs.
> Thou it is that holdest the elephant in the mire;
> Thou, that helpest the lame man scale the loftiest hill.
> On some Thou dost bestow the bliss of Brahmanhood;
> Yet others Thou dost hurl into this world below.
> Thou art the Moving Force, and I the mere machine;
> The house am I, and Thou the Spirit dwelling there;
> I am the chariot, and Thou the Charioteer:
> I move alone as Thou, O Mother, movest me.

He continued: "The Divine Mother is full of bliss. Creation, preservation, and destruction are the waves of Her sportive pleasure. Innumerable are the living beings. Only one or two among them obtain liberation. And that makes Her happy.

> Out of a hundred thousand kites, at best but one or two break free;
> And Thou dost laugh and clap Thy hands, O Mother, watching
> them!

Some are being entangled in the world and some are being liberated from it.

> How many are the boats, O mind,
> That float on the ocean of this world!
> How many are those that sink!"

NANDA: "It may be Her sweet will; but it is death to us."

MASTER: "But who are you? It is the Divine Mother who has become all this. It is only as long as you do not know Her that you say, 'I', 'I'.

"All will surely realize God. All will be liberated. It may be that some get their meal in the morning, some at noon, and some in the evening; but none will go without food. All, without any exception, will certainly know their real Self."

PASUPATI: "True, sir. It seems that it is God alone who has become everything."

MASTER: "Try to find out what this 'I' is. Is this 'I' the bones or flesh or blood or intestines? Seeking the 'I', you discover 'Thou'. In other words, nothing exists inside you but the power of God. There is no 'I', but only 'He'. (*To Pasupati*) You have so much wealth, but you have no egotism. It is not possible to rid oneself altogether of the ego; so, as long as it is there, let the rascal remain as the servant of God. (*All laugh.*) The ego that makes a man feel he is a devotee of God or a son of God or a servant of God is good. But the ego that makes a man attached to 'woman and gold' is the 'unripe ego'. That ego is to be renounced."

The head of the household and the others were very much pleased to hear this interpretation of the ego.

MASTER (*to Pasupati*): "There are two signs of knowledge: first, absence of pride, and second, a peaceful nature. You have both. Therefore you must have received the grace of God.

"Too much wealth makes one forget God. That is the very nature of wealth. Jadu Mallick has become very rich. Nowadays he doesn't talk of God. Formerly he used to enjoy spiritual talk a great deal.

"'Woman and gold' is a kind of wine. If a man drinks too much wine, he does not show his father and uncle the respect that is due to them. Very often he abuses them. A drunkard cannot distinguish between his superior and his inferior."

NANDA: "That is true, sir."

PASUPATI: "Sir, what do you think of Theosophy and Spiritualism? Are these true? What do you think of the solar plane, the lunar plane, the stellar plane?"

MASTER: "My dear sir, I don't know about these things. Why bother about them so much? You have come to the orchard to eat mangoes. Enjoy them. What is the use of your calculating how many mango-trees there are, how many millions of branches, how many billions of leaves? I have come to the orchard to eat mangoes. Let me enjoy them.

"Once a man's inner spirit is awakened, once he succeeds in knowing God, he doesn't feel the desire even to know about all this rubbish. How incoherently a delirious patient talks: 'I shall eat five seers of rice! I shall drink a whole tank of water!' 'Will you?' says the physician. 'All right! You will have them.' Saying this, the physician goes on with his smoke. But he pays attention to what the patient says when the patient is no longer delirious."

PASUPATI: "Will our delirium last for ever?"

MASTER: "Why should you think so? Fix your mind on God, and spiritual consciousness will be awakened in you."

PASUPATI (*smiling*): "Our union with God is only momentary. It doesn't last any longer than a pipeful of tobacco." (*All laugh.*)

MASTER: "What if that is so? Union with God even for one moment surely gives a man liberation.

"Ahalyā said to Rāma, 'O Rāma, it doesn't matter if I am born as a pig or any other being; only bless me that my mind may dwell on Thy Lotus Feet and be filled with real devotion to Thee.'

"Nārada said to Rāma: 'O Rāma, I want from Thee no other favour. Please give me real love for Thee; and please bless me, that I may not come under the spell of Thy world-bewitching māyā.'

"When a man sincerely prays to God, he is able to fix his mind on God and develop real love for His Lotus Feet.

"Give up all such notions as: 'Shall we be cured of our delirium?', 'What will happen to us?', 'We are sinners!' (*To Nanda*) One must have this kind of faith: 'What? Once I have uttered the name of Rāma, can I be a sinner any more?'"

NANDA: "Is there no after-life? What about punishment for our sins?"

MASTER: "Why not enjoy your mangoes? What need have you to calculate about the after-life and what happens then, and things like that? Eat your mangoes. You need mangoes. You need devotion to God—"

NANDA: "But where is the mango-tree? Where do I get mangoes?"

MASTER: "Tree? God is the eternal and infinite Brahman. He *does* exist; there is no doubt about it. He is eternal. But you must remember this, that He is the Kalpataru.

> Come, let us go for a walk, O mind, to Kāli, the Wish-fulfilling
> Tree,
> And there beneath It gather the four fruits of life.

"You must go to the Kalpataru and pray. Only then will you obtain the fruits. Only then will the fruits fall from the tree. Only then will you be able to gather them. There are four fruits: dharma, artha, kāma, and moksha. The jnānis seek the fruit of liberation; and the bhaktas, love of God, love without any motive behind it. They seek neither dharma nor artha nor kāma.

"You ask about the after-life. According to the *Gītā* you will become in the next life what you think of in the hour of death. King Bharata was very much grieved over his pet deer; he died repeating the word 'deer'; therefore he was reborn as a deer. That is why day and night a man should practise worship, japa, meditation, and other spiritual exercises. Only then, by virtue of practice, will he be able to think of God in the hour of death. If one dies thus, thinking of God, one will acquire God's nature.

"Keshab Sen, too, asked me about the after-life. I said to him also, 'What need have you of all these calculations?' Then I said: 'As long as a man does not realize God, he will return to the world. The potter puts his clay jars and lids out in the sun to bake. If cattle trample them underfoot, he throws away the baked ones. But he collects the soft ones, mixes them with more clay, puts them on the wheel, and makes new vessels from them.'"

The master of the house had not yet shown any sign of serving Sri Ramakrishna with refreshments. Sri Ramakrishna himself said to Nanda: "You see, you should offer me something to eat. That is why the other day I said to Jadu's mother: 'Look here. Give me something to eat.' Otherwise it brings harm to the householder."

Nanda Bose ordered some sweets. Sri Ramakrishna began to eat them. Nanda and the others were watching the Master and his actions. After eating the sweets, Sri Ramakrishna wanted to wash his hands. The plate on which the sweets were served had been placed on the sheet covering the carpet; so the Master could not wash his hands in the plate. A servant brought a brass bowl for him to use. But Sri Ramakrishna would not use it, since only rājasic people used such things. He asked the servant to take it away. The master of the house said to him, "Please wash your hands." Absent-mindedly Sri Ramakrishna said: "What? Shall I wash my hands?"

The Master walked to the south verandah. He asked M. to pour water into his hands. M. poured water from a jug. The Master dried his hands with his cloth and returned to the room. Then he was offered betel-leaf on a tray. But the other guests had already taken some from the same tray; the Master did not accept any.

NANDA (to the Master): "May I say something?"

MASTER (smiling): "What?"

NANDA: "Why didn't you eat any betel-leaf? Everything else you did was proper; this alone seems to be otherwise."

MASTER: "Before I eat anything I offer it to God.[2] It is a notion of mine."

NANDA: "But the betel-leaf would have gone to God all the same."

MASTER: "There is the path of jnāna, and there is also the path of bhakti. According to the jnāni everything can be eaten by applying the Knowledge of Brahman;[3] but the follower of bhakti keeps a little distinction."[4]

NANDA: "But I still maintain that you did not act rightly."

MASTER (smiling): "It is just a notion of mine. What you say is also right. That too is supported by the scriptures."

Sri Ramakrishna was warning Nanda of flatterers.

MASTER: "Beware of flatterers. They are after their own selfish purpose. (To Prasanna's father) Do you live in this house?"

PRASANNA'S FATHER: "No, sir, I am a neighbour. Won't you have a smoke?"

MASTER (very humbly): "No, please enjoy yourself. I don't feel like smoking now."

Nanda's house was like a palace. Sri Ramakrishna said to him: "Jadu hasn't such a big house. I told him so the other day."

NANDA: "He has built a new house at Jorāshānko."

Sri Ramakrishna was encouraging Nanda.

MASTER (to Nanda): "Though you are a householder, still you have kept your mind on God. Is that a small thing? The man who has renounced the world will pray to Him as a matter of course. Is there any credit in that? But blessed indeed is he who, while leading a householder's life, prays to

---

[2] According to Hindu religious custom a thing can be offered to God only if no part of it has been eaten by anyone else beforehand.

[3] The jnāni sees everything as Brahman; therefore he does not distinguish between holy and unholy.

[4] Between holy and unholy.

God. He is like a man who finds an object after removing a stone weighing twenty maunds.

"One should pray to God, establishing with Him an appropriate relationship. Hanumān's love for God was mixed with knowledge; but Nārada's love for God was pure and unadulterated.

"Rāma asked Hanumān, 'Hanumān, what attitude do you cherish toward Me when you worship Me?' Hanumān answered: 'Sometimes I see that You are the whole and I am a part; sometimes I see that You are the Master and I am Your servant. But Rāma, when I have the Knowledge of Reality, then I find that You are I and I am You.'

"Rāma said to Nārada, 'Ask a favour of Me.' Nārada said, 'O Rāma, grant me the boon that I may have genuine love for Thy Lotus Feet and that I may not come under the spell of Thy world-bewitching māyā!' "

Sri Ramakrishna was about to take his leave.

MASTER (to Nanda): "According to the Gītā a man who is honoured and respected by many people possesses a special power of God. You have divine power."

NANDA: "All men have the same power."

MASTER (sharply): "You all say the same thing. Can all men ever possess power to the same degree? God no doubt dwells in all beings as the all-pervading Spirit, but the manifestations of His Power are different in different beings.

"Vidyāsāgar, too, said the same thing. He said, 'Has God given some more power and some less?' Thereupon I said to him: 'If there are not different manifestations of His Power, then why have we come to see you? Have you grown two horns on your head?' "

Sri Ramakrishna rose. The devotees followed him. Pasupati accompanied them to the door.

The Master arrived at the house of the brāhmin lady who was grief-stricken on account of her daughter's death. It was an old brick house. Entering the house, the Master passed the cow-shed on his left. He and the devotees went to the roof, where they took seats. People were standing there in rows. Others were seated. They were all eager to get a glimpse of Sri Ramakrishna.

The brāhmani had a sister; both of them were widows. Their brothers also lived in the house with their families. The brāhmani had been busy all day making arrangements to receive Sri Ramakrishna. While the Master was at Nanda Bose's house she had been extremely restless, going out of the house every few minutes to see if he was coming. He had promised to come to her place from Nanda's. Because of his delay she had thought perhaps he would not come at all.

Sri Ramakrishna was seated on a carpet. M., Narayan, Jogin, Devendra, and others were seated on a mat. A few minutes later the younger Naren and some other devotees arrived. The brāhmani's sister came to the Master and saluted him. She said, "Sister has just gone to Nanda Bose's house to inquire the reason for your delay in coming here. She will return presently."

A sound was heard downstairs and she exclaimed, "There she comes!" She went down. But it was not the brāhmani.

Sri Ramakrishna sat there smiling, surrounded by devotees.

M. (to Devendra): "What a grand sight! All these people—young and old, men and women—standing in lines, eager to have a glimpse of him and hear his words."

DEVENDRA (to the Master): "M. says that this place is better than Nanda's. The devotion of these people is amazing."

Sri Ramakrishna laughed.

The brāhmani's sister exclaimed, "Here comes sister!"

The brāhmani came and saluted the Master. She was beside herself with joy. She did not know what to say. In a half-choked voice she said: "This joy is too much for me. Perhaps I shall die of it. Tell me, friends, how shall I be able to live? I did not feel such a thrill even when Chandi, my daughter, used to visit the house accompanied by liveried footmen, with armed guards lining both sides of the street. Oh! Now I have no trace of my grief at her death. I was afraid he[5] would not come. Then I thought that, if that happened, I should throw into the Ganges all the things I had arranged for his reception and entertainment. I should not speak to him any more. If he visited a place, I should go there, look at him from a distance, and then come away.

"Let me go and tell everybody how happy I am. Let me go and tell Yogin of my good luck."

Still overwhelmed with joy she said: "A labourer won a hundred thousand rupees in a lottery. The moment he heard the news he died of joy. Yes, he really and truly died. I am afraid the same thing is going to happen to me. Please bless me, friends, or else I shall certainly die."

M. was amazed to see the brāhmani's sincere joy and her ecstatic mood. He was about to take the dust of her feet. "What are you doing?" she exclaimed and saluted M.

The brāhmani was extremely happy at the sight of the devotees. She said: "I am so happy to see you all here. I have brought the younger Naren; without him, who would there be to make us laugh?"

She was talking like this when her sister came up and said: "Come down, sister! How can I manage things if you stay here? Can I do it all by myself?"

But the brāhmani was overwhelmed with joy. She could not take her eyes from the Master and the devotees.

After a while she very respectfully took Sri Ramakrishna to another room and offered him sweets and other refreshments. The devotees were entertained on the roof.

It was about eight o'clock in the evening. Sri Ramakrishna was ready to leave. When he came to the door, the brāhmani asked her sister-in-law to salute the Master. Next, one of her brothers took the dust of the Master's feet. Referring to him, she said: "He is one of my brothers. He is a fool." "No, no!" said the Master. "They are all good."

A man showed the way with a light. At places it was dark. Sri Rama-

[5] Meaning Sri Ramakrishna.

krishna stood in front of the cow-shed. The devotees gathered around him. M. saluted the Master, who was about to go to the house of Ganu's mother.

Sri Ramakrishna was seated in the drawing-room of Ganu's mother's house. It was on the street floor. The room was used by a concert party. Several young men played on their instruments now and then for the pleasure of the Master.

It was eight-thirty in the evening. Moonlight flooded the streets, the houses, and the sky. It was the first day after the full moon.

The brāhmani, who had also come, was visiting the drawing-room and the inner apartments alternately. Every few minutes she would come to the door of the drawing-room and look at the Master. Some youngsters from the neighbourhood also looked at him through the windows. The people of the locality, young and old, came thronging to see the saint.

The younger Naren saw the boys in the street climbing the windows. He said to them: "Why are you here? Get away! Go home!" The Master said tenderly, "Let them stay." Every now and then he chanted: "Hari Om! Hari Om!"

The floor of the drawing-room was covered with a carpet. The young musicians sat on it and sang:

> O Keśava, bestow Thy grace
> Upon Thy luckless servants here!
> O Keśava, who dost delight
> To roam Vrindāvan's glades and groves! . . .

MASTER: "Ah, how sweet the music is! How melodious the violin is! How good the accompaniments are! (*Pointing to a boy*) He and the flutist seem to be a nice pair."

The orchestra went on playing. After it was over, Sri Ramakrishna said joyfully, "It is very fine indeed." Pointing to a young man, he said, "He seems to know how to play every instrument." He said to M., "They are all good people."

After the concert the young musician said to the devotees, "We should like to hear some of you sing." The brāhmani stood near the door. She said: "None of them knows how to sing. Perhaps Mohin Babu can sing. But he will not sing before the Master."

A YOUNG MAN: "Why? I can sing even before my father."

THE YOUNGER NAREN (*laughing*): "But he has not yet advanced that far."

All laughed. A few minutes later the brāhmani said to Sri Ramakrishna, "Please come inside."

MASTER: "Why?"

BRĀHMANI: "The refreshments are served there. Please come."

MASTER: "Why not bring them here?"

BRĀHMANI: "Ganu's mother requests you to bless the room with the dust of your feet. Then the room will be turned into Benares, and anyone dying in it will have no trouble hereafter."

Sri Ramakrishna went inside accompanied by the brāhmani and the young men of the family. The devotees were strolling outside in the moonlight. M. and Binode were pacing the street south of the house and recalling the various incidents in the life of their beloved Master.

Sri Ramakrishna had returned to Balaram's house. He was resting in the small room to the west of the drawing-room. It was quite late, almost a quarter to eleven.

Sri Ramakrishna said to Jogin, "Please rub my feet gently." M. was sitting near by. While Jogin was rubbing his feet the Master said suddenly: "I feel hungry. I shall eat some farina pudding."

The brāhmani had accompanied the Master and the devotees to Balaram's house. Her brother knew how to play the drums. Sri Ramakrishna said, "It will serve our purpose to send for her brother when Narendra or some other singer wants to sing."

Sri Ramakrishna ate a little pudding. Jogin and the other devotees left the room. M. was stroking the Master's feet. They talked together.

MASTER (referring to the brāhmani and her relatives): "Ah! How happy they were!"

M: "How amazing! A similar thing happened with two women at the time of Jesus. They too were sisters, and devoted to Christ. Martha and Mary."

MASTER (eagerly): "Tell me the story."

M: "Jesus Christ, like you, went to their house with His devotees. At the sight of Him one of the sisters was filled with ecstatic happiness. It reminds me of a song about Gaurānga:

> My two eyes sank in the sea of Gorā's heavenly beauty
> And did not come back to me again;
> Down went my mind, as well, forgetting how to swim.

"The other sister, all by herself, was arranging the food to entertain Jesus. She complained to the Master, saying: 'Lord, please judge for Yourself—how wrong my sister is! She is sitting in Your room and I am doing all these things by myself.' Jesus said: 'Your sister indeed is blessed. She has developed the only thing needful in human life: love of God.' "

MASTER: "Well, after seeing all this, what do you feel?"

M: "I feel that Christ, Chaitanyadeva, and yourself—all three are one and the same. It is the same Person that has become all these three."

MASTER: "Yes, yes! One! One! It is indeed one. Don't you see that it is He alone who dwells here in this way."

As he said this, Sri Ramakrishna pointed with his finger to his own body.

M: "You explained clearly, the other day, how God incarnates Himself on earth."

MASTER: "Tell me what I said."

M: "You told us to imagine a field extending to the horizon and beyond. It extends without any obstruction; but we cannot see it on account of a wall in front of us. In that wall there is a round hole. Through the hole we see a part of that infinite field."

MASTER: "Tell me what that hole is."

M: "You are that hole. Through you can be seen everything—that Infinite Meadow without any end."

Sri Ramakrishna was very much pleased. Patting M.'s back, he said: "I see you have understood that. That's fine!"

M: "It is indeed difficult to understand that. One cannot quite grasp how God, Perfect Brahman that He is, can dwell in that small body."

The Master quoted from a song:

> Oh, no one at all has found out who He is;
> Like a madman from door to door He roams,
> Like a poor beggar He roams from door to door.

M: "You also told us about Jesus."

MASTER: "What did I say?"

M: "You went into samādhi at the sight of Jesus Christ's picture in Jadu Mallick's garden house. You saw Jesus come down from the picture and merge in your body."

Sri Ramakrishna was silent a few moments. Then he said to M.: "Perhaps there is a meaning in what has happened to my throat [referring to the sore in his throat]. This has happened lest I should make myself light before all; lest I should go to all sorts of places and sing and dance."

Sri Ramakrishna began to talk about Dwija.

MASTER: "He didn't come today. Why?"

M: "I asked him to come. He said he would. I don't know why he didn't."

MASTER: "He has great yearning. Well, he must be someone belonging to this.[6] Isn't that so?"

M: "Yes, sir, it must be so. Otherwise, how could he have such yearning?"

Sri Ramakrishna lay down inside the mosquito curtain. M. fanned him. The Master turned on his side. He told M. how God incarnates Himself in a human body. He told him, further, about his, M.'s, spiritual ideal.

MASTER: "At the beginning I too passed through such states that I did not see divine forms. Even now I don't see them often."

M: "Among all the forms God chooses for His līlā, I like best His play as a human being."

MASTER: "That is enough. And you are seeing me."

[6] Meaning the circle of the Master's devotees.

THE MASTER ON HIMSELF AND
HIS EXPERIENCES

August 9, 1885

SRI RAMAKRISHNA was sitting in his room at Dakshineswar. Rakhal, M., Dwija and his father, and other devotees were present. It was about four o'clock in the afternoon.

After returning from Vrindāvan Rakhal had spent a few days at home. Now he was staying with the Master. Latu, Harish, and Ramlal were also staying at the temple garden.

Sri Ramakrishna was not well. It was the beginning of the illness subsequently diagnosed as the fatal cancer. But this did not disturb the serenity of his mind. Day and night he had only one thought, and that was the spiritual welfare of his disciples. He was guiding them toward the attainment of God. He encouraged them constantly to cultivate knowledge and devotion and warned them of the snares of "woman and gold". He was completely indifferent to his own illness and devoted himself whole-heartedly to the fulfilment of his earthly mission.

Dwija was about sixteen years old. After the death of his mother, his father had married a second time. Dwija often accompanied M. to Dakshineswar; but his father did not approve of it.

Dwija's father had for a long time been speaking of visiting Sri Ramakrishna. Today he had come to Dakshineswar. He was the manager of a business firm in Calcutta and had passed his examination in law.

MASTER (*to Dwija's father*): "Please don't mind your children's coming here.

"I ask people to live in the world after the awakening of their spiritual consciousness. After extracting gold through hard labour, a man may keep it under earth or in a box or under water. The gold is not affected.

"I ask people to live in the world in a spirit of detachment. If you break the jack-fruit after rubbing oil on your hands, its sticky juice will not smear them.

"If the 'unripe' mind dwells in the world, the mind gets soiled. One should first attain knowledge and then live in the world.

"If you put milk in water the milk is spoiled. But this will not happen if butter, churned from the milk, is put in water."

DWIJA'S FATHER: "That is true, sir."

MASTER (smiling): "I know why you scold your children. You only threaten them. The brahmachāri said to the snake: 'You are a fool indeed! I forbade you to bite but not to hiss. Your enemies would not have beaten you, if only you had hissed at them.' Your scolding of the children is really a hissing. (Dwija's father smiles.)

"A good son is an indication of his father's spiritual nature. If good water comes out when a reservoir is dug, it only indicates the virtue of the owner.

"A son is called Ātmaja, 'the self reborn'. There is no difference between you and your son. In one way you yourself are reborn as your son. In one sense you are a worldly person, working in a business office and enjoying worldly life; in another sense you are a devotee of God, in the form of your son. I heard that you were a very worldly person; but now I find it isn't so. (Smiling) You know all this. I understand that you are very circumspect. Perhaps that is why you are nodding your assent to what I am saying. (Dwija's father smiles.)

"If your children visit this place, they will be able to know what you really are. How precious one's father is! If a person deceives his father and mother in order to seek religion, he gets only worthless trash.

"A man is born with several debts: debts to his father, the devas, and the rishis. Besides, there is his debt to his mother. He also has a debt to his wife. She must be supported. If the wife is chaste, the husband must provide for her after his death.

"I could not live at Vrindāvan on account of my mother. When I remembered that my mother was living in the temple garden here at Dakshineswar, I could not feel peaceful at Vrindāvan.

"I ask people to live in the world and at the same time fix their minds on God. I don't ask them to give up the world. I say, 'Fulfil your worldly duties and also think of God.'"

DWIJA'S FATHER: "I tell my children that they should attend to their studies. I don't forbid them to come to you, but I don't want them to waste time in frivolities with the youngsters."

MASTER (referring to Dwija): "This boy must have been born with some good tendencies. Why are the two other brothers different from him? Why is he alone spiritually minded? Will you be able to compel him not to visit this place? Sooner or later everyone unfolds his inborn tendencies."

DWIJA'S FATHER: "Yes, that is true."

Sri Ramakrishna came down from the couch and sat on the floor beside Dwija's father. While talking with him he touched him now and then.

It was nearly evening. Sri Ramakrishna asked M. and the others to show Dwija's father the temples. He said to them, "I should have accompanied him myself if I were well." He asked someone to give sweets to the young men and said to Dwija's father: "Let the children have a little refreshment. It is customary." Dwija's father visited the temples and the images and took a stroll in the garden.

Sri Ramakrishna engaged happily in conversation with Bhupen, Dwija, M., and others on the southeast porch of his room. He playfully slapped Bhupen and M. on the back. He said to Dwija with a laugh, "How I talked to your father!"

Dwija's father returned to Sri Ramakrishna's room after dusk. He intended to leave shortly. He was feeling hot. Sri Ramakrishna fanned him himself. In a few minutes the father took leave of the Master. Sri Ramakrishna stood up to bid him farewell.

It was eight o'clock. Sri Ramakrishna was talking to Mahimacharan. Rakhal, M., and one or two companions of Mahimacharan were in the room. Mahimacharan was going to spend the night at the temple garden.

MASTER (to Mahima): "Well, how do you find Kedar? Has he only seen milk, or has he drunk it too?"

MAHIMA: "Yes, he is enjoying bliss."

MASTER: "Nityagopal?"

MAHIMA: "Very good. He is in a lofty state of mind."

MASTER: "Yes. Well, what about Girish Ghosh?"

MAHIMA: "He too has developed nicely. But he belongs to another class."

MASTER: "And Narendra?"

MAHIMA: "He is now in the state I was in fifteen years ago."

MASTER: "The younger Naren? How guileless he is!"

MAHIMA: "Yes, quite guileless."

MASTER: "You are right. (Reflecting a little) Let me see who else. It will be sufficient for the youngsters who come here if they know only two things. If they know these, they will not have to practise much discipline and austerity. First, who I am, and second, who they are. Many of the youngsters belong to the inner circle.

"Those belonging to the inner circle will not attain liberation. I shall have to assume a human body again, in a northwesterly direction.

"I feel peace of mind when I see the youngsters. How can I feel joy at the sight of those who have begotten children and are engaged in lawsuits and are involved in 'woman and gold'? How could I live without seeing pure-souled persons?"

Mahimacharan recited some texts from the scriptures. He also described various mystic rites of the Tantra.

MASTER: "Well, some say that my soul, going into samādhi, flies about like a bird in the Mahākāśa, the Infinite Space.

"Once a sādhu of Hrishikesh came here. He said to me: 'There are five kinds of samādhi. I find you have experienced them all. In these samādhis one feels the sensation of the Spiritual Current to be like the movement of an ant, a fish, a monkey, a bird, or a serpent.'

"Sometimes the Spiritual Current rises through the spine, crawling like an ant.

"Sometimes, in samādhi, the soul swims joyfully in the ocean of divine ecstasy, like a fish.

"Sometimes, when I lie down on my side, I feel the Spiritual Current pushing me like a monkey and playing with me joyfully. I remain still.

That Current, like a monkey, suddenly with one jump reaches the Sahasrāra. That is why you see me jump up with a start.

"Sometimes, again, the Spiritual Current rises like a bird hopping from one branch to another. The place where it rests feels like fire. It may hop from Mulādhāra to Svādhisthāna, from Svādhisthāna to the heart, and thus gradually to the head.

"Sometimes the Spiritual Current moves up like a snake. Going in a zigzag way, at last it reaches the head and I go into samādhi.

"A man's spiritual consciousness is not awakened unless his Kundalini is aroused.

"The Kundalini dwells in the Mulādhāra. When it is aroused, it passes along the Sushumnā nerve, goes through the centres of Svādhisthāna, Manipura, and so on, and at last reaches the head. This is called the movement of the Mahāvāyu, the Spiritual Current. It culminates in samādhi.

"One's spiritual consciousness is not awakened by the mere reading of books. One should also pray to God. The Kundalini is aroused if the aspirant feels restless for God. To talk of Knowledge from mere study and hearsay! What will that accomplish?

"Just before my attaining this state of mind, it had been revealed to me how the Kundalini is aroused, how the lotuses of the different centres blossom forth, and how all this culminates in samādhi. This is a very secret experience. I saw a boy twenty-two or twenty-three years old, exactly resembling me, enter the Sushumnā nerve and commune with the lotuses, touching them with his tongue. He began with the centre at the anus and passed through the centres at the sexual organ, navel, and so on. The different lotuses of those centres—four-petalled, six-petalled, ten-petalled, and so forth —had been drooping. At his touch they stood erect.

"When he reached the heart—I distinctly remember it—and communed with the lotus there, touching it with his tongue, the twelve-petalled lotus, which was hanging head down, stood erect and opened its petals. Then he came to the sixteen-petalled lotus in the throat and the two-petalled lotus in the forehead. And last of all, the thousand-petalled lotus in the head blossomed. Since then I have been in this state."

Sri Ramakrishna came down to the floor and sat near Mahimacharan. M. and a few other devotees were near him. Rakhal also was in the room.

MASTER (to Mahima): "For a long time I have wanted to tell you my spiritual experiences, but I could not. I feel like telling you today.

"You say that by mere sādhana one can attain a state of mind like mine. But it is not so. There is something special here [referring to himself]."

Rakhal, M., and the others became eager to hear what the Master was going to say.

MASTER: "God talked to me. It was not merely His vision. Yes, He talked to me. Under the banyan-tree I saw Him coming from the Ganges. Then we laughed so much! By way of playing with me He cracked my fingers. Then He talked. Yes, He talked to me.

"For three days I wept continuously. And He revealed to me what is in the Vedas, the Purānas, the Tantras, and the other scriptures.

"One day He showed me the māyā of Mahāmāyā. A small light inside a room began to grow, and at last it enveloped the whole universe.

"Further, He revealed to me a huge reservoir of water covered with green scum. The wind moved a little of the scum and immediately the water became visible; but in the twinkling of an eye, scum from all sides came dancing in and again covered the water. He revealed to me that the water was like Satchidānanda, and the scum like māyā. On account of māyā, Satchidānanda is not seen. Though now and then one may get a glimpse of It, again māyā covers It.

"God reveals the nature of the devotees to me before they arrive. I saw Chaitanya's party singing and dancing near the Panchavati, between the banyan-tree and the bakul-tree. I noticed Balaram there. If it weren't for him, who would there be to supply me with sugar candy and such things? (Pointing to M.) And I saw him too.

"I had seen Keshab before I actually met him—I had seen him and his party in my samādhi. In front of me sat a roomful of men. Keshab looked like a peacock sitting with its tail spread out. The tail meant his followers. I saw a red gem on Keshab's head. That indicated his rajas. He said to his disciples, 'Please listen to what he [meaning the Master] is saying.' I said to the Divine Mother: 'Mother, these people hold the views of "Englishmen". Why should I talk to them?' Then the Mother explained to me that it would be like this in the Kaliyuga.

"Keshab and his followers got from here [meaning himself] the names of Hari and the Divine Mother. That is why the Divine Mother took Vijay away from Keshab's party. But Vijay did not join the Ādi Samāj.[1]

(Pointing to himself) "There must be something special here. Long ago a young man named Gopal Sen used to visit me. He who dwells in me placed His foot on Gopal's chest. Gopal said in an ecstatic mood: 'You will have to wait here a long time. I cannot live any more with worldly people.' He took leave of me. Afterwards I heard that he was dead. Perhaps he was born as Nityagopal.

"I have had many amazing visions. I had a vision of the Indivisible Satchidānanda. Inside It I saw two groups with a fence between them. On one side were Kedar, Chuni, and other devotees who believe in the Personal God. On the other side was a luminous space like a heap of red brick-dust. Inside it was seated Narendra immersed in samādhi. Seeing him absorbed in meditation, I called aloud, 'Oh, Narendra!' He opened his eyes a little. I came to realize that he had been born, in another form, in Simlā[2] in a kāyastha family. At once I said to the Divine Mother, 'Mother, entangle him in māyā; otherwise he will give up his body in samādhi.' Kedar, a believer in the Personal God, peeped in and ran away with a shudder.

"Therefore I feel that it is the Divine Mother Herself who dwells in this body and plays with the devotees. When I first had my exalted state of mind, my body would radiate light. My chest was always flushed. Then I said to the Divine Mother: 'Mother, do not reveal Thyself outwardly. Please go

---

[1] A sect of the Brāhmo Samāj.
[2] The section of Calcutta in which Narendra was born.

inside.' That is why my complexion is so dull now. If my body were still luminous, people would have tormented me; a crowd would always have thronged here. Now there is no outer manifestation. That keeps weeds away. Only genuine devotees will remain with me now. Do you know why I have this illness? It has the same significance. Those whose devotion to me has a selfish motive behind it will run away at the sight of my illness.

"I cherished a desire. I said to the Mother, 'O Mother, I shall be the king of the devotees.'

"Again, this thought arose in my mind: 'He who sincerely prays to God will certainly come here. He must.' You see, that is what is happening now. Only people of that kind come.

"My parents knew who dwells inside this body. Father had a dream at Gayā. In that dream Raghuvir said to him, 'I shall be born as your son.'

"God alone dwells inside this body. Such renunciation of 'woman and gold'! Could I have accomplished that myself? I have never enjoyed a woman, even in a dream.

"Nangtā instructed me in Vedānta. In three days I went into samādhi. At the sight of my samādhi under the mādhavi vine, he was quite taken aback and exclaimed, 'Ah! What is this?' Then he came to know who resides in this body. He said to me, 'Please let me go.' At these words of Totapuri, I went into an ecstatic mood and said, 'You cannot go till I realize the Truth of Vedānta.'

"Day and night I lived with him. We talked only Vedānta. The Brāhmani used to say to me: 'Don't listen to Vedānta. It will injure your devotion to God.'

"I said to the Divine Mother: 'Mother, please get me a rich man. If You don't, how shall I be able to protect this body? How shall I be able to keep the sādhus and devotees near me?' That is why Mathur Babu provided for my needs for fourteen years.

"He who dwells in me tells me beforehand what particular class of devotees will come to me. When I have a vision of Gaurānga, I know that devotees of Gaurānga are coming. When I have a vision of Kāli, the Śāktas come.

"At the time of the evening service I used to cry out from the roof of the kuthi, weeping: 'Oh, where are you all? Come to me!' You see, they are all gathering here, one by one.

"God Himself dwells in this body. It is He who, of His own accord, is working with these devotees.

"What a wonderful state of mind some of the devotees have! The younger Naren gets kumbhaka without any effort, and samādhi too. Sometimes he stays in an ecstatic mood for two and a half hours; sometimes even more. How wonderful!

"I have practised all kinds of sādhanā: jnānayoga, karmayoga, and bhakti-yoga. I have even gone through the exercises of hathayoga to increase longevity. There is another Person dwelling in this body. Otherwise, after attaining samādhi, how could I live with the devotees and enjoy the love of

God? Koar Singh used to say to me: 'I have never before seen a person who has returned from the plane of samādhi. You are none other than Nānak.'

"I live in the midst of worldly people; on all sides I see 'woman and gold'. Nevertheless, this is the state of my mind: unceasing samādhi and bhāva. That is the reason Pratap[3] said, at the sight of my ecstatic mood: 'Good heavens! It is as if he were possessed by a ghost!'"

Rakhal, M., and the others were speechless as they drank in this account of Sri Ramakrishna's unique experiences.

But did Mahimacharan understand the import of these words? Even after hearing them, he said to the Master, "These things have happened to you on account of your meritorious actions in your past births." Mahima still thought that Sri Ramakrishna was a sādhu or a devotee of God. The Master nodded assent to Mahima's words and said: "Yes, the result of past actions. God is like an aristocrat who has many mansions. Here [referring to himself] is one of His drawing-rooms. The bhakta is God's drawing-room."

It was nine o'clock in the evening. Sri Ramakrishna was sitting on the small couch. It was Mahimacharan's desire to form a brahmachakra[4] in the presence of the Master. Mahima formed a circle, on the floor, with Rakhal, M., Kishori, and one or two other devotees. He asked them all to meditate. Rakhal went into an ecstatic state. The Master came down from the couch and placed his hand on Rakhal's chest, repeating the name of the Divine Mother. Rakhal regained consciousness of the outer world.

It was one o'clock in the morning, the fourteenth day of the dark fortnight of the moon. There was intense darkness everywhere. One or two devotees were pacing the concrete embankment of the Ganges. Sri Ramakrishna was up. He came out and said to the devotees, "Nangtā told me that at this time, about midnight, one hears the Anāhata sound."

In the early hours of the morning Mahimacharan and M. lay down on the floor of the Master's room. Rakhal slept on a camp cot. Now and then Sri Ramakrishna paced up and down the room with his clothes off, like a five-year-old child.

Monday, August 10

It was dawn. The Master was chanting the name of the Divine Mother. He went to the porch west of his room and looked at the Ganges; then he stopped in front of the pictures of different gods and goddesses in the room and bowed to them. The devotees left their beds, saluted Sri Ramakrishna, and went out.

The Master was talking to a devotee in the Panchavati. The latter had dreamt of Chaitanyadeva.

MASTER (*in an ecstatic mood*): "Ah me! Ah me!"

DEVOTEE: "But, sir, it was only a dream."

MASTER: "Is a dream a small thing?"

The Master's voice was choked. His eyes were filled with tears.

[3] Pratap Chandra Mazumdar, a distinguished member of the Brāhmo Samāj.
[4] A mystic circle prescribed in Tantra.

Sri Ramakrishna was told of a devotee who had divine visions even while he was awake. The Master said: "I am not surprised. Narendra, too, sees forms of God nowadays."

Mahimacharan went to one of the Śiva temples to the west of the courtyard and chanted hymns from the Vedas. He was alone.

It was eight o'clock in the morning. M. bathed in the Ganges and came to Sri Ramakrishna. The brāhmani who was grief-stricken on account of her daughter's death also entered the room.

The Master asked the brāhmani to give M. some prasād to eat.

BRĀHMANI: "Please eat something yourself first; then he will eat."

MASTER (to M.): "Take some prasād of Jagannāth first and then eat."

After eating the prasād, M. went to the Śiva temples and saluted the Deity. Then he returned to the Master's room and saluted him. He was ready to go to Calcutta.

MASTER (tenderly): "Go home safely. You have to attend to your duties."

Tuesday, August 11

Sri Ramakrishna was in his room at the temple garden. He had been observing silence since eight o'clock in the morning. Did he know the fatal nature of his illness? At his silence the Holy Mother wept. Rakhal and Latu also wept. The brāhmani widow from Bāghbāzār arrived. She too was weeping at this strange mood of the Master. Now and then the devotees asked him whether he would remain silent for good. The Master answered them in the negative, by a sign.

At three o'clock in the afternoon Narayan arrived. Sri Ramakrishna said to him, "The Divine Mother will bless you." Narayan told the other devotees that the Master had spoken to him. A heavy weight was lifted from their breasts. They all came into the Master's room and sat on the floor.

MASTER (to the devotees): "The Mother showed me that all this is verily māyā. She alone is real, and all else is the splendour of Her māyā.

"Another thing was revealed to me. I found out how far the different devotees have progressed."

DEVOTEES: "Please tell us about it."

MASTER: "I came to know about all these devotees: Nityagopal, Rakhal, Narayan, Purna, Mahima Chakravarty, and the others."

Sunday, August 16, 1885

The news of Sri Ramakrishna's illness had been reported to the devotees in Calcutta. They thought it was just a sore in his throat. Many devotees arrived at Dakshineswar to visit him. Among them were Girish, Ram, Nityagopal, Mahima, Kishori, and Pundit Shashadhar.

Sri Ramakrishna was in his usual happy mood. He was talking to the devotees.

MASTER: "I cannot tell the Mother about my illness. I feel ashamed to talk of it."

GIRISH: "God will cure you."

RAM: "Yes, you will be all right."

MASTER (*smiling*): "Yes, give me your blessing." (*All laugh.*)

Girish was a recent visitor to Dakshineswar. The Master said to him: "You have so many duties to perform. You have to face so many troubles. Come here only three times more.

(*To Shashadhar*) "Please tell us something about the Ādyāśakti."

SHASHADHAR: "What do I know, sir?"

MASTER (*smiling*): "A certain man had great respect for another man. The second man asked him to bring him a little fire for his tobacco. He answered humbly, 'Sir, am I fit to carry your fire?' He didn't bring the fire." (*All laugh.*)

SHASHADHAR: "The Primal Power alone is both the instrumental and the material cause of the universe. It is She who has created the universe and its living beings; further, She Herself has become all these. To give an example: the spider, as the instrumental cause, makes the web and, as the material cause, brings the web out of its own body."

MASTER: "It is also stated that He who is Purusha is also Prakriti; He who is Brahman is also Śakti. He is called Purusha or Brahman when He is inactive, that is to say, when He ceases to create, preserve, or destroy; and He is called Śakti or Prakriti when He engages in those activities. But He who is Brahman is none other than Śakti; He who is Purusha has verily become Prakriti. Water is water whether it moves or is still. A snake is a snake whether it wriggles along or stays still and coiled up.

"What Brahman is cannot be described. Speech stops there. In the kirtan the singers at first sing: 'My Nitāi dances like a mātā hāti.'[5] As they become more and more ecstatic, they can hardly utter the whole sentence. They sing only: 'Hāti! Hāti!' As their mood deepens they sing only: 'Hā! Hā!' At last they cannot sing even that; they become completely unconscious."

As the Master spoke these words, he himself became transfixed in samādhi. He was standing.

Regaining consciousness of the world, he said, "That which is beyond both kshara and akshara cannot be described."

The devotees sat in silence.

MASTER: "You cannot go into samādhi as long as your worldly experiences are not finished, or as long as you have duties to perform.

(*To Shashadhar*) "God is now making you perform such duties as delivering lectures. You must do these things now. You will have peace when your duties are finished. After completing her household duties, the mistress of the family goes for her bath. She will not come back then even if you shout after her."

Thursday, August 27, 1885

Sri Ramakrishna was sitting in his room at Dakshineswar. It was five o'clock in the afternoon. There were two or three devotees with him. While

---

[5] Mad elephant.

with the devotees he never gave a thought to his physical illness, often spending the whole day with them talking and singing.

Doctor Madhu was treating Sri Ramakrishna. He frequently visited the Master at Dakshineswar, coming by country boat from Calcutta. The devotees were very much worried about the Master; it was their secret desire that the physician should see him daily. M. said to the Master, "Doctor Madhu is an experienced physician. It will be nice if he sees you every day."

Pundit Shyamapada of Antpur arrived. It was dusk. The pundit went to the bank of the Ganges to perform his evening worship; he had some amazing visions during the worship. He returned to the Master's room and sat on the floor. Sri Ramakrishna had just finished meditation and the chanting of the holy names. He was sitting on the small couch and M. on the foot-rug. Rakhal, Latu, and the others were in and out of the room.

MASTER (to M., pointing to the pundit): "He is very nice. (To the pundit) Where the mind attains peace by practising the discipline of 'Neti, neti', there Brahman is.

"The king dwells in the inmost room of the palace, which has seven gates. The visitor comes to the first gate. There he sees a lordly person with a large retinue, surrounded on all sides by pomp and grandeur. The visitor asks his companion, 'Is he the king?' 'No', says his friend with a smile.

"At the second and the other gates he repeats the same question to his friend. He finds that the nearer he comes to the inmost part of the palace, the greater is the glory, pomp, and grandeur. When he passes the seventh gate he does not ask his companion whether it is the king; he stands speechless at the king's immeasurable glory. He realizes that he is face to face with the king. He hasn't the slightest doubt about it."

PUNDIT: "One sees God beyond the realm of māyā."

MASTER: "But after realizing God one finds that He alone has become māyā, the universe, and all living beings. This world is no doubt a 'framework of illusion', unreal as a dream. One feels that way when one discriminates following the process of 'Not this, not this'. But after the vision of God this very world becomes 'a mansion of mirth'.

"What will you gain by the mere study of scriptures? The pundits merely indulge in reasoning."

PUNDIT: "I hate the idea of being called a pundit."

MASTER: "That is due to the grace of God. The pundits merely indulge in reasoning. Some have heard of milk and some have drunk milk. After you have the vision of God you will find that everything is Nārāyana. It is Nārāyana Himself who has become everything."

The pundit recited a hymn to Nārāyana. Sri Ramakrishna was overwhelmed with joy.

PUNDIT (quoting from the Gītā): "'With the heart concentrated by yoga, with the eye of evenness for all things, he beholds the Self in all beings and all beings in the Self.'"

MASTER: "Have you read the Adhyātma Rāmāyana?"

PUNDIT: "Yes, sir, a little."

MASTER: "The book is filled with ideas of knowledge and devotion. The life of Śavari and the hymn by Ahalyā are filled with bhakti.

"But you must remember one thing: God is very far away from the mind tainted with worldliness."

PUNDIT: "Yes, sir. God is far, far away from worldly intelligence. And God is very near, where that does not exist. I visited a certain zemindar, one Mukherji of Uttarpārā. He is now an elderly man; but he listens only to stories and novels."

MASTER: "It is further said in the *Adhyātma Rāmāyana* that God alone has become the universe and its living beings."

The pundit was delighted. He recited a hymn to that effect from the tenth chapter of the *Bhāgavata*:

> O Krishna! Krishna! Mighty Yogi! Thou art the Primal Supreme
>   Purusha:
> This universe, manifest and unmanifest, is Thy form, as the sages
>   declare.
> Thou alone art the soul, the sense-organs, the Lord dwelling in the
>   bodies of all;
> Thou art the subtle Great Prakriti, made of sattva, rajas, and tamas;
> Thou alone art the Purusha, the Lord dwelling in the bodies of all.

As Sri Ramakrishna listened to the hymn he went into samādhi. He remained standing. The pundit was seated. The Master placed his foot on the pundit's lap and chest, and smiled.

The pundit clung to his feet and said, "O Guru! Please give me God-Consciousness."

After the pundit had left the room Sri Ramakrishna said to M.: "Don't you see that what I have said is coming to pass? Those who have sincerely practised meditation and japa must come here."

It was ten o'clock. Sri Ramakrishna ate a little farina pudding and lay down. He asked M. to stroke his feet. A few minutes later he asked the disciple to massage his body and chest gently. He enjoyed a short nap. Then he said to M.: "Now go to sleep. Let me see if I can sleep better when I am alone." He said to Ramlal, "He [meaning M.] and Rakhal may sleep in the room."

Friday, August 28

It was dawn. Sri Ramakrishna was awake and meditating on the Divine Mother. On account of his illness the devotees were deprived of his sweet chanting of the Mother's name.

Sri Ramakrishna was seated on the small couch. He asked M., "Well, why have I this illness?"

M: "People will not have the courage to approach you unless you resemble them in all respects. But they are amazed to find that in spite of such illness you don't know anything but God."

MASTER (*smiling*): "Balaram also said, 'If even you can be ill, then why should we wonder about our illnesses?' Lakshmana was amazed to see that

Rāma could not lift His bow on account of His grief for Sītā. 'Even Brahman weeps, entangled in the snare of the five elements.'"

M: "Jesus Christ, too, wept like an ordinary man at the suffering of His devotees."

MASTER: "How was that?"

M: "There were two sisters, Mary and Martha. Lazarus was their brother. All three were devoted to Jesus. Lazarus died. Jesus was on His way to their house. One of the sisters, Mary, ran out to meet Him. She fell at His feet and said weeping, 'Lord, if You had been here, my brother would not have died!' Jesus wept to see her cry.

"Then Jesus went to the tomb of Lazarus and called him by name. Immediately Lazarus came back to life and walked out of the tomb."

MASTER: "But I cannot do those things."

M: "That is because you don't want to. These are miracles; therefore you aren't interested in them. These things draw people's attention to their bodies. Then they do not think of genuine devotion. That is why you don't perform miracles. But there are many similarities between you and Jesus Christ."

MASTER (smiling): "What else?"

M: "You don't ask your devotees to fast or practise other austerities. You don't prescribe hard and fast rules about food. Christ's disciples did not observe the sabbath; so the Pharisees took them to task. Thereupon Jesus said: 'They have done well to eat. As long as they are with the bridegroom, they must make merry.'"

MASTER: "What does that mean?"

M: "Christ meant that as long as the disciples live with the Incarnation of God, they should only make merry. Why should they be sorrowful? But when He returns to His own abode in heaven, then will come the days of their sorrow and suffering."

MASTER (smiling): "Do you find anything else in me that is similar to Christ?"

M: "Yes, sir. You say: 'The youngsters are not yet touched by "woman and gold"; they will be able to assimilate instruction. It is like keeping milk in a new pot: the milk may turn sour if it is kept in a pot in which curd has been made.' Christ also spoke like that."

MASTER: "What did He say?"

M: "'If new wine is kept in an old bottle, the bottle may crack. If an old cloth is patched with new cloth, the old cloth tears away.'

"Further, you tell us that you and the Mother are one. Likewise, Christ said, 'I and My Father are one.'"

MASTER (smiling): "Anything else?"

M: "You say to us, 'God will surely listen to you if you call on Him earnestly.' So also Christ said, 'Knock and it shall be opened unto you.'"

MASTER: "Well, if God has incarnated Himself again, is it a fractional or a partial or a complete manifestation of God? Some say it is a complete manifestation."

M: "Sir, I don't quite understand the meaning of complete or partial or fractional Incarnation. But I have understood, as you explained it, the idea of a round hole in a wall."

MASTER: "Tell me about it."

M: "There is a round hole in the wall. Through it one is able to see part of the meadow on the other side of the wall. Likewise, through you one sees part of the Infinite God."

MASTER: "True. You can see five or six miles of the meadow at a stretch."

M. finished his bath in the Ganges and went to the Master's room. It was eight o'clock in the morning. He asked Latu to give him the rice prasād of Jagannāth. The Master stood near him and said: "Take this prasād regularly. Those who are devotees of God do not eat anything before taking the prasād."

M: "Yesterday I got some prasād of Jagannāth from Balaram Babu's house. I take one or two grains daily."

M. saluted the Master and took his leave. Sri Ramakrishna said to him tenderly: "Come early in the morning tomorrow. The hot sun of the rainy season is bad for the health."

Monday, August 31, 1885

Sri Ramakrishna was resting in his room. It was about eight o'clock in the evening. Though ill and suffering, he constantly devoted himself to the welfare of the devotees. Sometimes he felt restless, like a child; but the next moment he forgot all about his illness and became filled with ecstatic love of God. His love for the devotees was like that of a mother for her children.

Two days earlier, on Saturday night, he had received a letter from Purna. Purna had written: "I am feeling extremely happy. Now and then I cannot sleep at night for joy." After hearing the letter the Master had remarked: "I feel thrilled to hear this. Even later on he will be able to keep this bliss. Let me see the letter." He had pressed the letter in the palm of his hand and said: "Generally I cannot touch letters. But this is a good letter." That same night, while the Master was in bed, he had suddenly become covered with perspiration. He had sat up in bed, saying, "It seems to me that I shall not recover from this illness." It had worried the devotees very much to hear this. The Holy Mother had come to the temple garden to wait on Sri Ramakrishna and was living in a room in the nahabat. The devotees, with the exception of one or two, were not aware of her presence. A woman devotee staying with the Holy Mother had begun to pay frequent visits to Sri Ramakrishna in his room. After a few days Sri Ramakrishna had said to her: "You have been here some time. What will people think about it? You had better go home for a week or so."

Sri Ramakrishna lay in bed, on his side, with his back to the room. After dusk Gangadhar and M. arrived from Calcutta. Gangadhar sat at the feet of the Master, who was talking to M.

MASTER: "Two boys came here the other day. One of them was Subodh. He is Sankar Ghosh's great-grandson. The other, Kshirode, is his neighbour. They are nice boys. I told them I was ill and asked them to go to you for instruction. Please look after them a little."

M: "Yes, sir. They are our neighbours."

MASTER: "The other day, again, I woke up covered with perspiration. I don't understand this illness."

M: "We have decided to ask Bhagavan Rudra to see you once. He is an M.D. and an expert physician."

MASTER: "How much will he charge?"

M: "His regular fee is twenty or twenty-five rupees."

MASTER: "Then don't bother about him."

M: "But we shall pay him four or five rupees at the most."

MASTER: "Listen. Suppose you say this to him, 'Sir, please be kind enough to come and see him.' Hasn't he heard anything about this place?"[6]

M: "Perhaps he has. He has almost agreed not to charge any fee. But we shall pay him a little. If we do that, he will come again."

MASTER: "Ask Dr. Nitai to come. He is a good physician. But what will the doctors do, I wonder? They press my throat and make my illness worse."

It was nine o'clock in the evening. Sri Ramakrishna ate a little farina pudding and had no difficulty in swallowing it. He said to M. cheerfully: "I was able to eat a little. I feel very happy."

Tuesday, September 1

Sri Ramakrishna was about to take his bath. A devotee was rubbing his body with oil on the verandah south of his room. M. came there after finishing his bath in the Ganges and saluted the Master.

After bathing, Sri Ramakrishna wrapped himself in a towel and with folded hands saluted the deities in the temples from afar. He could not go to the temples because of his illness.

It was the sacred Janmāsthami day, the birthday of Krishna. Ram and other devotees had brought new clothes for Sri Ramakrishna. He put them on and looked charming. Again he saluted the deities.

Gopāl Mā brought her Gopāla[7] some food that she had prepared at her home at Kāmārhāti. She said to the Master sorrowfully, "But you won't eat any of it."

MASTER: "You see, I am ill."

GOPĀL MĀ: "That is my bad luck. Please take a little in your hand."

MASTER: "Please give me your blessing."

A devotee brought some sugar candy. Gopāl Mā said, "Let me take it to the Holy Mother in the nahabat." The Master said: "No, keep it here. I give sweets to the devotees. Who wants to send a messenger a hundred times to the nahabat for sugar candy? Let it be kept here."

It was eleven o'clock in the morning. The devotees were gradually arriving from Calcutta. Balaram, Narendra, the younger Naren, Navagopal, and a Vaishnava from Kātoā arrived. Rakhal and Latu were staying with Sri Ramakrishna. A Punjabi sādhu had been staying in the Panchavati for some days.

[6] Referring to himself.

[7] The Baby Krishna. Gopāl Mā regarded Sri Ramakrishna as Gopāla and addressed him by that name.

The younger Naren had a tumour on his forehead. Sri Ramakrishna was strolling in the Panchavati with the devotees. He said to the younger Naren: "Why don't you have your tumour operated on? It is not in the *throat* but only on the forehead. That is a simple thing. People have their orchitis operated on."

The Punjabi sādhu was going along the foot-path in the garden. The Master said: "I don't attract him. He has the attitude of a jnāni. I find him to be dry as wood."

Sri Ramakrishna and the devotees returned to the Master's room. The conversation turned to Shyamapada Bhattacharya.

BALARAM: "Shyamapada said, 'When he, the Master, placed his foot on Narendra's chest, Narendra went into bhāva; but I didn't have that experience.'"

MASTER: "Shall I tell you the truth about it? It is very difficult to gather the dispersed mind when it is attached to 'woman and gold'. The pundit told me he was called upon to act as arbiter to settle people's quarrels. Besides, he has to worry about his children. But the minds of Narendra and other youngsters are not scattered like that; they are not yet touched by 'woman and gold'.

"But Shyamapada is a grand person."

The Vaishnava from Kātoā began to ask Sri Ramakrishna questions. He was squint-eyed.

VAISHNAVA: "Sir, is a man born again?"

MASTER: "It is said in the *Gītā* that a man is reborn with those tendencies that are in his mind at the time of his death. King Bharata thought of his deer at the time of death and was reborn as a deer."

VAISHNAVA: "I could believe in rebirth only if an eye-witness told me about it."

MASTER: "I don't know about that, my dear sir. I cannot cure my own illness, and you ask me to tell you what happens after death!

"What you are talking about only shows your petty mind. Try to cultivate love of God. You are born as a human being only to attain divine love. You have come to the orchard to eat mangoes; what need is there of knowing how many thousands of branches and millions of leaves there are in the orchard? To bother about what happens after death! How silly!"

Girish Ghosh arrived in a carriage with one or two friends. He was drunk. He was weeping as he entered the room. He wept as he placed his head on Sri Ramakrishna's feet.

Sri Ramakrishna affectionately patted him on the back. He said to a devotee, "Prepare a smoke for him."

Girish raised his head and said with folded hands: "You alone are the Perfect Brahman! If that is not so then everything is false.

"It is such a pity that I could not be of any service to you." He uttered these words with a tenderness that made several devotees weep.

Girish continued: "O Lord! please grant me the boon that I may serve you for a year. Who cares for salvation? One finds it everywhere. I spit on it. Please tell me that you will accept my service for one year."

MASTER: "People around here are not good. Some may criticize you."

GIRISH: "I don't care. Please tell—"

MASTER: "All right. You may serve me when I go to your house—"

GIRISH: "No, it is not that. I want to serve you here."

Girish was insistent. The Master said, "Well, that depends on God's will."

Referring to the Master's throat trouble, Girish said: "Please say, 'Let it be cured.' All right, I shall thrash it out. Kāli! Kāli!"

MASTER: "You will hurt me."

GIRISH: "O throat, be cured! (*He blows at the throat like an exorciser.*) Are you not all right? If you aren't cured by this time, you certainly will be if I have any devotion to your feet. Say that you are cured."

MASTER (*sharply*): "Leave me alone. I can't say those things. I can't ask the Divine Mother to cure my illness.

"All right. I shall be cured if it is the will of God."

GIRISH: "You are trying to fool me. All depends on your will."

MASTER: "Shame! Never say that again. I look on myself as a devotee of Krishna, not as Krishna Himself. You may think as you like. You may look on your guru as God. Nevertheless, it is wrong to talk as you are talking. You must not talk that way again."

GIRISH: "Please say you will be cured."

MASTER: "Very well, if that pleases you."

Girish was still under the influence of drink. Now and then he said to Sri Ramakrishna, "Well, sir, how is it that you were not·born this time with your celestial beauty?"

A few moments later he said, "I see, this time it will be the salvation of Bengal."

A devotee said to himself: "Why Bengal alone? It will be the salvation of the whole world."

Girish said, addressing the devotees: "Does any of you understand why he is here? It is for the liberation of men. Their suffering has moved him to assume a human body."

The coachman was calling Girish. He got up and was going toward the man. The Master said to M.: "Watch him. Where is he going? I hope he won't beat the coachman!" M. accompanied Girish.

Presently Girish returned. He prayed to Sri Ramakrishna and said, "O God, give me purity that I may not have even a trace of sinful thought."

MASTER: "You are already pure. You have such faith and devotion! You are in a state of joy, aren't you?"

GIRISH: "No, sir. I feel bad. I have worries. That is why I have drunk so much liquor."

A few minutes afterwards Girish said: "Lord, I am amazed to find that I, even I, have been given the privilege of serving the Perfect Brahman. What austerities have I practised to deserve this privilege?"

Sri Ramakrishna took his midday meal. On account of his illness he ate very little.

The Master's natural tendency of mind was to soar into the plane of God-Consciousness. He would force his mind to be conscious of the body. But, like a child, he was incapable of looking after his body. Like a child he said to the devotees: "I have eaten a little. I shall rest now. You may go out for a little while." Sri Ramakrishna rested a few minutes. The devotees returned to the room.

GIRISH: "The guru and the Ishta. I like very much the form of the guru. I am not afraid of him. Why should it be so? I am afraid of ecstasy. At the sight of ecstasy I run away."

MASTER: "He who is the Ishta appears in the form of the guru. The aspirant practises meditation on a corpse.[8] When he obtains the vision of his Chosen Ideal, it is really the guru who appears to him and says, 'This is that', that is to say, he points out to the disciple his Ishta. Uttering these words, the guru disappears into the form of the Ishta. The disciple no longer sees the guru. In the state of perfect jnāna, who is the guru and who is the śishya? That creates a very difficult situation; there the teacher and the disciple do not see each other.' "

A DEVOTEE: "Guru's head and disciple's feet."

GIRISH (joyously): "Yes! Yes! It is true."

NAVAGOPAL: "But listen to its meaning. The disciple's head belongs to the guru; and the guru's feet belong to the disciple. Do you understand?"

GIRISH: "No, that is not the meaning. Haven't you seen the child climbing on the head of the father? That is why the disciple's feet are mentioned."

NAVAGOPAL: "But then the disciple must feel like a young baby."

MASTER: "There are two classes of devotees. One class has the nature of the kitten. The kitten depends completely on its mother. It accepts whatever its mother does for it. The kitten only cries, 'Mew, mew!' It doesn't know what to do or where to go. Sometimes the mother puts the kitten near the hearth, sometimes on the bed. Devotees of this class give God the power of attorney and thus become free of all worry. The Sikhs said to me that God was kind. I said to them: 'How is that? He is our Father and our Mother. Shouldn't parents bring up their children after begetting them? Do you mean to say that the neighbours will look after them?' Devotees of this class have an unwavering conviction that God is our Mother and our Father.

"There is another class of devotees. They have the nature of the young monkey. The young monkey clings to its mother with might and main. The devotees who behave like the young monkey have a slight idea of being the doer. They feel: 'We must go to the sacred places; we must practise japa and austerity; we must perform worship with sixteen articles as prescribed by the śāstras. Only then shall we be able to realize God.' Such is their attitude.

"The aspirants of both classes are devotees of God. The farther you advance, the more you will realize that God alone has become everything. He alone does everything. He alone is the Guru and He alone is the Ishta. He alone gives us knowledge and devotion.

"The farther you advance, the more you will see that there are other
_____
[8] One of the forms of meditation prescribed in the Tantra.

things even beyond the sandal-wood forest—mines of silver and gold and precious gems. Therefore go forward.

"But how can I ask people to go forward? If worldly people go too far, then the bottom will drop out of their world. One day Keshab was conducting a religious service. He said, 'O God, may we all sink and disappear in the river of bhakti!' When the worship was over I said to him: 'Look here. How can you disappear altogether in the river of bhakti? If you do, what will happen to those seated behind the screen?[9] But do one thing: sink now and then, and come back again to dry land.' " (All laugh.)

The Vaishnava from Kātoā was arguing.

MASTER (to the Vaishnava): "Stop that sizzling noise! When butter containing water is heated over a fire, it makes that sound.

"If a man but once tastes the joy of God, his desire to argue takes wing. The bee, realizing the joy of sipping honey, doesn't buzz about any more. What will you achieve by quoting from books? The pundits recite verses and do nothing else.

"What will you gain by merely repeating 'siddhi'? You will not be intoxicated even by gargling with a solution of siddhi. It must go into your stomach; not until then will you be intoxicated. One cannot comprehend what I am saying unless one prays to God in solitude, all by oneself, with a longing heart."

Dr. Rakhal arrived to examine Sri Ramakrishna. The Master said to him eagerly, "Come in and sit down."

The conversation with the Vaishnava continued.

MASTER: "Man should possess dignity and alertness. Only he whose spiritual consciousness is awakened possesses this dignity and alertness and can be called a man. Futile is the human birth without the awakening of spiritual consciousness.

"There are many men at Kāmārpukur with big bellies and imposing moustaches. Yet the villagers go with palanquins and bring righteous and truthful persons from twenty miles away to arbitrate their quarrels. They do not bring mere pundits.

"Truthfulness is the tapasyā of the Kaliyuga. 'Truthfulness, submission to God, and looking on the wives of other men as one's own mother'—these are the means to realize God."

Like a child Sri Ramakrishna said to the physician, "Sir, please cure my throat."

DOCTOR: "Do you ask me to cure you?"

MASTER: "The physician is Nārāyana Himself. I honour everybody. You may say that if I look on all as Nārāyana then I should keep quiet. But I also accept the words of the 'māhut Nārāyana'.

"The Pure Mind and the Pure Ātman are one and the same thing. Whatever comes up in the Pure Mind is the voice of God. God alone is the 'māhut Nārāyana'.

"Why should I not listen to God? He alone is the Master. As long as He keeps 'I-consciousness' in me, I shall obey His orders."

[9] The Master referred to the ladies.

The doctor was going to examine Sri Ramakrishna's throat. The Master said, "Dr. Mahendra Sarkar pressed my tongue the way they press a cow's."

Like a child Sri Ramakrishna said to the physician, pulling at his shirt-sleeves again and again, "Sir! My dear sir! Please cure my throat." Looking at the laryngoscope, he said with a smile: "I know it. You will see the reflection in it."

Narendra sang. But on account of the Master's illness there was not much music.

September 2

After finishing his midday meal Sri Ramakrishna sat on the small couch and talked to Dr. Bhagavan Rudra and M. Rakhal, Latu, and other devotees were in the room. The physician heard all about the Master's illness. Sri Ramakrishna came down to the floor and sat near the doctor.

MASTER: "You see, medicine does not agree with me. My system is different.

"Well, what do you think of this? When I touch a coin my hand gets twisted; my breathing stops. Further, if I tie a knot[10] in the corner of my cloth, I cannot breathe. My breathing stops until the knot is untied."

The Master asked a devotee to bring a rupee. When Sri Ramakrishna held it in his hand, the hand began to writhe with pain. The Master's breathing also stopped. After the coin had been taken away, he breathed deeply three times and his hand relaxed. The doctor became speechless with wonder to see this strange phenomenon.

The doctor said to M., "Action on the nerves."

MASTER (*to the doctor*): "I get into another state of mind. It is impossible for me to lay up anything. One day I visited Sambhu Mallick's garden house. At that time I had been suffering badly from stomach trouble. Sambhu said to me: 'Take a grain of opium now and then. It will help you.' He tied a little opium in a corner of my cloth. As I was returning to the Kāli temple, I began to wander about near the gate as if unable to find the way. Then I threw the opium away and at once regained my normal state. I returned to the temple garden.

"One day at Kāmārpukur I picked some mangoes. I was carrying them home. But I could not walk; I had to stay standing in one place. Then I left the mangoes in a hollow. Only after that could I return home. Well, how do you explain that?"

DOCTOR: "There is a force behind it. Will-force."

M: "He [meaning the Master] says that it is God-force. You say that it is will-force."

MASTER (*to the doctor*): "Again, I get into such a state of mind that if someone says I am better, I at once feel much better. The other day the brāhmani said, 'You are fifty per cent better.' At once I began to dance."

Sri Ramakrishna was much pleased with the physician. He said to him:

[10] The common people in India tie their money or other small articles in a corner of their cloths.

"You have a very fine nature. There are two characteristics of knowledge: a peaceful nature and absence of pride."

M: "The doctor has lost his wife."

MASTER (*to the doctor*): "I say that God can be realized if one feels drawn to Him by the intensity of these three attractions: the child's attraction for the mother, the husband's attraction for the chaste wife, and the attraction of worldly possessions for the worldly man.

"Please cure me of my illness."

The doctor was going to examine the Master's throat. Sri Ramakrishna was seated in a chair on the semicircular porch. Referring to Dr. Sarkar, the Master said: "He is a villain. He pressed my tongue as if I were a cow."

DOCTOR: "He didn't hurt you purposely."

MASTER: "No, he pressed the tongue to make a thorough examination."

Sunday, September 20, 1885

Sri Ramakrishna was sitting in his room, surrounded by devotees. Navagopal, Haralal, Rakhal, Latu, and others were present. A goswāmi who was a musician was also there.

M. arrived with Dr. Rakhal of Bowbāzār. The physician began to examine the Master. He was a stout person and had rather thick fingers.

MASTER (*smiling, to the physician*): "Your fingers are like a wrestler's. Mahendra Sarkar also examined me. He pressed my tongue so hard that it hurt me. He pressed my tongue the way they press a cow's."

DOCTOR: "I shall not hurt you, sir."

The physician made out his prescription. Sri Ramakrishna was talking.

MASTER (*to the devotees*): "Well, people ask why, if I am such a holy person, I should be ill."

TARAK: "Bhagavan Das Bābāji, too, was ill and bed-ridden a long time."

MASTER: "But look at Dr. Madhu. At the age of sixty he carries food to the house of his mistress; and he has no illness."

GOSWĀMI: "Sir, your illness is for the sake of others. You take upon yourself the sins of those who come to you. You fall ill because you accept their sins."

A DEVOTEE: "You will soon be cured if only you say to the Divine Mother, 'Mother, please make me well.'"

MASTER: "I cannot ask God to cure my disease. The attitude of the servant-master relationship is nowadays less strong in me. Once in a while I say, 'O Mother, please mend the sheath[11] of the sword a little.' But such prayers are also becoming less frequent. Nowadays I do not find my 'I'; I see that it is God alone who resides in this sheath."

The goswāmi had been invited to sing kirtan. A devotee asked, "Will there be any kirtan?" Sri Ramakrishna was ill, and all were afraid that the kirtan might throw his mind into ecstasy and thus aggravate the illness.

Sri Ramakrishna said: "Let there be a little singing. All are afraid of my going into ecstasy. Spiritual emotion hurts the throat."

The goswāmi began the kirtan. Sri Ramakrishna could not control himself.

11 The Master referred to his body.

He stood up and began to dance with the devotees. The physician watched the whole scene.

A hired carriage was waiting for Dr. Rakhal. He and M. were ready to leave for Calcutta. They saluted the Master. Sri Ramakrishna said to M. affectionately, "Have you had your meal?"

Thursday, September 24, 1885

It was the night of the full moon. Sri Ramakrishna was sitting on the small couch. He was very ill. M. and some other devotees were sitting on the floor.

MASTER (*to M.*): "Every now and then I think that the body is a mere pillow-case. The only real substance is the Indivisible Satchidānanda.

"When I go into divine ecstasy this illness of the throat remains away from me. I am now somewhat in that mood and so I feel like laughing."

Some ladies of Dwija's family arrived. They saluted the Master and sat on one side. Pointing to one of the ladies, Sri Ramakrishna asked: "Who is this lady? Is it she who brought up Dwija? Why has Dwija bought an ektārā?"

M: "It has two strings, sir."

MASTER: "Dwija's father is opposed to his views. Won't other people criticize him? It is wise for him to pray to God secretly."

A picture of Gaurānga and Nitāi hung on the wall of the Master's room. It was a picture of the two brothers singing devotional songs with their companions at Navadvip.

RAMLAL (*to the Master*): "Then may I give him [meaning M.] the picture?"

MASTER: "Yes."

Sri Ramakrishna was then under Dr. Pratap's treatment. He awoke at midnight and felt extremely restless. Harish, his attendant, was in the room. Rakhal also was there. Ramlal was asleep on the verandah. The Master remarked later on: "I was feeling extremely restless. I felt like embracing Harish. They rubbed a little medicinal oil on my head. Then I began to dance."

45

SRI RAMAKRISHNA AT
ŚYĀMPUKUR

October 18, 1885

THE DOCTORS HAD DEFINITELY diagnosed Sri Ramakrishna's illness as cancer. No proper arrangement for his treatment and nursing could be made
at Dakshineswar. He needed the constant attention of a physician,
which could not be given at the temple garden. Furthermore, the devotees
who lived in Calcutta found it very inconvenient to attend on him daily at
Dakshineswar. Therefore the older devotees had rented a small two-storey
house in Bāghbāzār, Calcutta, and had brought the Master there. Sri Ramakrishna, however, had not liked the place and had gone to Balaram's house.
In a few days a new house had been engaged in Śyāmpukur, in the northern
section of Calcutta, and the Master had been taken there. He had been placed
under the treatment of Dr. Mahendra Lal Sarkar. The new building had
two large rooms and two smaller ones on the second floor. One of the larger
rooms was used as the parlour, and in the other the Master lived. Of the
two smaller rooms, one was used as a sleeping-room by the devotees, and the
other by the Holy Mother when she came there. Near the exit to the roof
was a small, covered, square space, where the Holy Mother stayed during
the day and prepared the Master's food.

It was Vijayā day, the fourth day of the worship of Durgā, when the
image is immersed in water. On that day the Divine Mother returns to Her
heavenly abode at Mount Kailāś, leaving gloom in the hearts of Her devotees.

It was eight o'clock in the morning. The air was chilly. Though ill, Sri
Ramakrishna was sitting on his bed. He was like a five-year-old child who
knows nothing but its mother. Navagopal, M., and a few other devotees were
present. Surendra arrived and sat down. The Divine Mother had been worshipped at his house for the past three days. Sri Ramakrishna had not been
able to go there on account of his illness, but he had sent some of his disciples. Surendra was in a very unhappy mood because on this day the image
of the Mother was to be immersed in the water.

SURENDRA: "I had to run away from home."

MASTER (to M.): "What if the image is thrown into the water? May
Mother dwell in the heart!"

Surendra was disconsolate. He was crying to the Divine Mother and talking to Her. At this yearning of his beloved disciple Sri Ramakrishna could not control his tears. He looked at M. and said in a choked voice: "What bhakti! Ah, what great love he feels for God!"

MASTER (*to Surendra*): "Yesterday evening at seven or seven-thirty I saw your worship hall in a vision. I saw the divine image full of effulgence. This place and your hall were joined by a stream of light flowing between them."

SURENDRA: "At that time I was crying to the Mother in the worship hall. My elder brothers had gone upstairs. I thought the Mother said, 'I will come again.'"

It was about eleven o'clock in the morning. Sri Ramakrishna finished his meal. M. poured water into his hand for him to rinse his mouth.

MASTER (*to M.*): "Rakhal has indigestion. It is best to take only sāttvic food. Haven't you read about it in the *Gītā*? Don't you read the *Gītā*?"

M: "Yes, sir. The *Gītā* speaks of temperance in eating. Sāttvic food, rājasic food, tāmasic food; sāttvic kindness, sāttvic ego, and so on—all these are described in the *Gītā*."

MASTER: "Have you a copy of the book?"

M: "Yes, sir."

MASTER: "It contains the essence of all the scriptures."

M: "The *Gītā* describes various ways of realizing God. You too say that God can be reached by various paths: knowledge, devotion, work, and meditation."

MASTER: "Do you know the meaning of karmayoga? It is to surrender to God the fruit of all action."

M: "Yes, sir, I have read that in the *Gītā*. It also says that there are three ways of performing action."

MASTER: "What are they?"

M: "First, one may perform karma to attain jnāna; second, to teach others; third, under the impulse of one's nature."

After rinsing his mouth the Master chewed betel-leaf.

Sri Ramakrishna was talking with M. about Dr. Sarkar. M. had been at the doctor's house the previous day to report the Master's condition.

MASTER: "What did you talk about?"

M: "There are many books in the doctor's room. I took out one to read, and now and then read a passage aloud to Dr. Sarkar. It was a book by Sir Humphry Davy. He wrote about the necessity of Divine Incarnation."

MASTER: "Indeed! What did you say to the doctor?"

M: "There was one passage that stated that Divine Truth must be made human truth to be appreciated by us; therefore Divine Incarnation is necessary."

MASTER: "Splendid! That's very good."

M: "The author gave the illustration of the sun: one cannot look at the sun, but one can look at its reflected rays."

MASTER: "Very fine. Anything else?"

M: "Another passage stated that real knowledge is faith."

MASTER: "That too is very good. If one has faith one has everything."

M: "The author dreamt of the Roman gods and goddesses."

MASTER: "Do such books really exist? Surely the author was inspired by God. Did you talk of anything else?"

M: "People like Dr. Sarkar speak of doing good to the world. So I told him what you had said about it."

MASTER (*smiling*): "What did I say?"

M: "About Sambhu Mallick. He had said to you: 'It is my desire to devote my money to the building of schools, hospitals, dispensaries, and the like. That will do good to many.' Thereupon you had said to him, 'Suppose God appears before you; will you then ask Him to build schools, hospitals, and dispensaries?' I told the doctor another thing."

MASTER: "Those who are born to do work belong to a different class. What else did you say?"

M: "I said to the doctor: 'If your aim is to visit the image of Mother Kāli, what will you gain by spending all your time in giving alms to the poor by the roadside? First you had better somehow visit the image. Afterwards you may give alms to your heart's content."

MASTER: "Did you talk about anything else?"

M: "Yes. I told him that many of those who come to you have conquered lust. Thereupon the doctor replied, 'I too have conquered lust.' I said: 'You are a great man. It is no wonder that you have conquered lust. But the amazing thing is that under his influence even insignificant creatures have conquered it.' Afterwards I told him what you had said to Girish."

MASTER (*smiling*): "What did I say?"

M: "You said to Girish, 'The doctor has not been able to surpass you.' You said that with reference to his calling you a Divine Incarnation."

MASTER: "Discuss the doctrine of Divine Incarnation with Dr. Sarkar. He who liberates others is an Incarnation of God. The scriptures speak of ten, of twenty-four, and also of innumerable Incarnations."

M: "Dr. Sarkar is keenly interested in Girish Ghosh. He always asks me whether Girish has given up drinking. He keeps a sharp eye on him."

MASTER: "Did you tell Girish about that?"

M: "Yes, sir, I did. And I also told him about giving up drinking."

MASTER: "What did he say?"

M: "He said: 'Since you all say so, I take your words as the words of the Master himself. But I won't promise anything.'"

MASTER (*joyously*): "Kalipada told me that he had altogether given up drinking."

It was afternoon. Dr. Sarkar arrived accompanied by his son Amrita and Hem. Narendra and other devotees were present.

Sri Ramakrishna was talking aside to Amrita. He asked him, "Do you meditate?" He further said to him: "Do you know what one feels in meditation? The mind becomes like a continuous flow of oil—it thinks of one object only, and that is God. It does not think of anything else."

Sri Ramakrishna was talking to the devotees.

MASTER (*to the doctor*): "Your son does not believe in the Incarnation of God. That's all right. It doesn't matter if he does not believe in it.

"Your son is a nice boy. Why shouldn't he be? Does a mango-tree of the fine 'Bombay' variety ever bear sour mangoes? How firm his faith in God is! That man is a true man whose mind dwells on God. He alone is a man whose spiritual consciousness has been awakened and who is firmly convinced that God alone is real and all else illusory. He does not believe in Divine Incarnation; but what does that matter? It is enough if he believes that God exists, and that all this universe and its living beings are the manifestations of His Power—like a rich man and his garden.

"Some say that there are ten Divine Incarnations, some twenty-four, while others say that there are innumerable Incarnations. If you see anywhere a special manifestation of God's Power, you may know that God has incarnated Himself there. That is my opinion.

"There is another view, according to which God has become all that you see. It is like a bel-fruit, which consists of three parts: seeds, shell, and flesh. That which is the Absolute has also its relative aspect, and that which is the Relative has also its absolute aspect. You cannot set aside the Absolute and understand just the Relative. And it is only because there is the Relative that you can transcend it step by step and reach the Absolute.

"So long as 'I-consciousness' exists, a man cannot go beyond the Relative. Through meditation he can negate the phenomena, following the process of 'Neti, neti', and reach the Absolute; but nothing can really be denied, as in the instance of the bel-fruit."

DOCTOR: "Quite true."

MASTER: "Kacha had been immersed in nirvikalpa samādhi. When his mind was coming down to the relative plane, someone asked him, 'What do you see now?' Kacha replied: 'I see that the universe is soaked, as it were, in God. Everything is filled with God. It is God alone who has become all that I see. I do not know what to accept and what to reject.'

"In my opinion one should realize both the Nitya and the Līlā and then live in the world as the servant of God. Hanumān saw both the Personal God and the formless Reality. He then lived as a devotee of God, as His servant."

M. (to himself): "So we must accept both—the Absolute and the Relative. Since the introduction of the Vedānta philosophy in Germany, some of the European philosophers, too, have been thinking along that line. But the Master says that one cannot realize both the Nitya and the Līlā without complete renunciation, that is to say, without totally giving up 'woman and gold'. Such a person must be a true renouncer; he must be totally detached from the world. Here lies the real difference between him and such European philosophers as Hegel."

In Dr. Sarkar's opinion, God created men and ordained that every soul should make infinite progress. He would not believe that one man was greater than another. That was why he did not believe in the doctrine of Divine Incarnation.

DOCTOR: "I believe in infinite progress. If that is not so, then what is the use of leading a mere five or six years' existence in the world? I would rather hang myself with a rope round my neck.

"Incarnation! What is that? To cower before a man who excretes filth! It is absurd. But if you speak of a man as the reflection of God's Light—yes, that I admit."

GIRISH (smiling): "But you have not seen God's Light."

Dr. Sarkar was hesitating before giving a reply. A friend who sat near him whispered something into his ear.

DOCTOR (to Girish): "You too have not seen anything but a reflection."

GIRISH: "I see It! I see the Light! I shall prove that Sri Krishna is an Incarnation of God or I shall cut out my tongue!"

MASTER: "All this is useless talk. It is like the ravings of a delirious patient. A delirious patient says, 'I shall drink a whole tank of water; I shall eat a whole pot of rice.' The physician says: 'Yes, yes. You will have all these. We shall give you whatever you want when you are convalescent.'

"When butter is heated it sizzles and crackles. But all sound comes to a stop when it is thoroughly boiled. As a man's mind is, so is his conception of God. I have seen in rich men's houses portraits of the Queen[1] and other aristocrats. But the devotees keep in their houses pictures of gods and goddesses.

"Lakshmana said, 'O Rāma, even a sage like Vaśishthadeva was overcome with grief on account of the death of his sons!' 'Brother,' replied Rāma, 'whoever has knowledge has ignorance also. Whoever is conscious of light is also conscious of darkness. Therefore go beyond knowledge and ignorance.' One attains that state through an intimate knowledge of God. This knowledge is called vijnāna.

"When a thorn enters the sole of your foot you have to get another thorn. You then remove the first thorn with the help of the second. Afterwards you throw away both. Likewise, after removing the thorn of ignorance' with the help of the thorn of knowledge, you should throw away the thorns of both knowledge and ignorance.

"There are signs of Perfect Knowledge. One is that reasoning comes to an end. As I have just said, the butter sizzles and crackles as long as it is not thoroughly boiled."

DOCTOR: "But can one retain Perfect Knowledge permanently? You say that all is God. Then why have you taken up this profession of a paramahamsa? And why do these people attend on you? Why don't you keep silent?"

MASTER (smiling): "Water is water whether it is still or moves or breaks into waves.

"I must tell you something else. Why should I not listen to the 'māhut Nārāyana'? The guru had taught his disciple that everything was Nārāyana. A mad elephant was coming toward the disciple, but he did not move away since he believed the guru's words. He thought that the elephant was Nārāyana. The māhut shouted to him: 'Get away! Get away!' But the disciple did not move. The elephant picked him up and threw him to the ground. The disciple was not quite dead; when his face was sprinkled with water he regained consciousness. Being asked why he had not moved away, he said: 'Why should I? The guru said, "Everything is Nārāyana."' 'But, my

[1] Queen Victoria.

child,' said the guru, 'why didn't you listen to the words of the māhut Nārāyana?'

"It is God who dwells within as the Pure Mind and Pure Intelligence. I am the machine and He is its Operator. I am the house and He is the Indweller. It is God who is the māhut Nārāyana."

DOCTOR: "Let me ask you something. Why do you ask me to cure your illness?"

MASTER: "I talk that way as long as I am conscious of the 'jar' of the 'ego'. Think of a vast ocean filled with water on all sides. A jar is immersed in it. There is water both inside and outside the jar; but the water does not become one unless the jar is broken. It is God who has kept this 'jar' of the 'ego' in me."

DOCTOR: "What is the meaning of 'ego' and all that you are talking about? You must explain it to me. Do you mean to say that God is playing tricks on us?"

GIRISH: "Sir, how do you know that He is not playing tricks?"

MASTER (smiling): "It is God who has kept this 'ego' in us. All this is His play, His līlā. A king has four sons. They are all princes; but when they play, one becomes a minister, another a police officer, and so on. Though a prince, he plays as a police officer.

(To the doctor) "Listen. If you realize Ātman you will see the truth of all I have said. All doubts disappear after the vision of God."

DOCTOR: "But is it ever possible to get rid of all doubts?"

MASTER: "Learn from me as much as I have told you. But if you want to know more, you must pray to God in solitude. Ask Him why He has so ordained.

"The son of the house can give a beggar only a small measure of rice. But if the beggar asks for his train fare, then the master of the house must be called."

The doctor remained silent.

MASTER: "Well, you love reasoning. All right. Let us reason a little. Listen. According to the jnāni there is no Incarnation of God. Krishna said to Arjuna: 'You speak of Me as an Incarnation of God. Let Me show you something. Come with Me.' Arjuna had followed Sri Krishna a short distance, when Sri Krishna asked him, 'What do you see there?' Arjuna replied, 'A big tree with black berries hanging in bunches.' Krishna said, 'Those are not black berries. Go nearer and look at them.' Arjuna went nearer and saw that they were Krishnas hanging in bunches. 'Do you see now', said Krishna, 'how many Krishnas like Me have grown there?'

"Kavirdās said of Krishna, 'He danced like a monkey to the clapping of the gopis!'

"As you go nearer to God you see less and less of His upādhis, His attributes. A devotee at first may see the Deity as the ten-armed Divine Mother; when he goes nearer he sees Her possessed of six arms; still nearer, he sees the Deity as the two-armed Gopāla. The nearer he comes to the Deity, the fewer attributes he sees. At last, when he comes into the presence of the Deity, he sees only Light without any attributes.

"Listen a little to the Vedāntic reasoning. A magician came to a king to show his magic. When the magician moved away a little, the king saw a rider on horseback approaching him. He was brilliantly arrayed and had various weapons in his hands. The king and the audience began to reason out what was real in the phenomenon before them. Evidently the horse was not real, nor the robes, nor the armour. At last they found out beyond the shadow of a doubt that the rider alone was there. The significance of this is that Brahman alone is real and the world unreal. Nothing whatsoever remains if you analyse."

DOCTOR: "I don't object to this."

MASTER: "But it is not easy to get rid of illusion. It lingers even after the attainment of Knowledge. A man dreamt of a tiger. Then he woke up and his dream vanished. But his heart continued to palpitate.

"Some thieves came to a field. A straw figure resembling a man had been put there to frighten intruders. The thieves were scared by the figure and could not persuade themselves to enter the field. One of them, however, approached and found that it was only a figure made of straw. He came back to his companions and said, 'There is nothing to be afraid of.' But still they refused to go; they said that their hearts were beating fast. Then the daring thief laid the figure on the ground and said, 'It is nothing, it is nothing.' This is the process of 'Neti, neti'."

DOCTOR: "These are fine words."

MASTER (smiling): "What kind of words?"

DOCTOR: "Fine."

MASTER: "Then give me a 'Thank you'." [The Master said the words "thank you" in English.]

DOCTOR: "Don't you know what is in my mind? I go to so much trouble to come and visit you!"

MASTER (smiling): "No, it is not that. Say something for the good of the ignorant. After the death of Rāvana, his brother Bibhishana refused to be king of Ceylon. He said: 'O Rāma, I have obtained You. What shall I do with kingship?' Rāma said: 'Bibhishana, be king for the sake of the ignorant, for those who might ask what riches you have gained by serving Me so much. Be king to give them a lesson.'"

DOCTOR: "Are there such ignorant people here?"

MASTER (smiling): "Oh, yes! Here you will find oysters and snails as well as conchs." (All laugh.)

Doctor Sarkar, who was a homeopath, gave Sri Ramakrishna two globules of medicine. He said, "I am giving you these two globules: one is Purusha and the other is Prakriti." (All laugh.)

MASTER (smiling): "Oh yes, Purusha and Prakriti are always together. Haven't you observed pigeons? The male and female cannot live separately. Wherever Purusha is, there is Prakriti, and wherever Prakriti is, there is Purusha."

It was Vijayā day. Sri Ramakrishna asked Dr. Sarkar to have some refreshments. The devotees served him with sweets.

DOCTOR (*while eating*): "Now I say 'Thank you' for the sweets; but it is not for your teachings. Why should I give that 'Thank you' in words?"

MASTER (*smiling*): "The essential thing is to fix the mind on God and to practise meditation a little. What more shall I say? (*Pointing to the younger Naren*) Look at him. His mind totally merges in God. Those things I was telling you—"

DOCTOR: "Tell the others also."

MASTER: "No, a man should be given food according to his power of digestion. Can all understand what I told you? I cannot talk to everyone as I talked to you. Suppose a mother has bought a fish for the family. All her children have not the same power of digestion. For some she makes pilau and for others she makes stew. These latter have weak stomachs." (*All laugh.*)

Dr. Sarkar took his leave. It was Vijayā day, when people show their love and respect to their friends and elders with appropriate greetings. The devotees all prostrated themselves before Sri Ramakrishna and took the dust of his feet. Then they embraced one another. Their joy knew no bounds. The Master was seriously ill, but he made them all forget about his illness. The embracing and exchange of greetings continued a long time. The devotees also took light refreshments. The younger Naren, M., and a few other devotees sat near Sri Ramakrishna. The Master talked to them joyfully. He spoke of Dr. Sarkar.

MASTER: "I shall not have to tell him very much. When the trunk of a tree is cut almost to the other side, the cutter steps aside. A little later the tree falls down of itself."

THE YOUNGER NAREN (*smiling*): "Here everything is principle!"

MASTER (*to M.*): "The doctor has already changed a great deal, hasn't he?"

M: "Yes, sir. When he comes here he loses his wits. He never talks about medicine. When we remind him of it, he says: 'Oh, yes, yes! I shall have to give the medicine.'"

Some of the devotees were singing in the parlour. They returned to the Master's room. Sri Ramakrishna said: "I heard your music; but why did you make mistakes in the rhythm? I once heard of a man who was an adept in discord. You sang like him." (*All laugh.*)

A young man, a relative of the younger Naren, arrived. He was bespectacled and foppishly dressed. Sri Ramakrishna spoke to the younger Naren.

MASTER: "You see, a young man was going along the road. He had put on a pleated shirt. And how he strutted! Now and again he would display the shirt by removing his scarf, and then look around to see if anyone was admiring him. But when he walked you could see that he was knock-kneed. (*All laugh.*) The peacock displays its feathers; but its feet are very dirty. (*All laugh.*) The camel is very ugly. Everything about it is ugly."

YOUNG MAN: "But it acts well."

MASTER: "Yes. But it browses on briars. It will continue to eat thorns though its mouth bleeds. The worldly man loses his children and still clamours for more."

October 22, 1885

It was Thursday evening, a few days after the Durgā Pujā. Sri Ramakrishna sat on his bed in his room on the second floor, with Dr. Sarkar, Ishan, and other devotees. Although Dr. Sarkar was a very busy physician, he would spend a long time—sometimes six or seven hours—in Sri Ramakrishna's company. He had great love for the Master and looked on the devotees as his own kith and kin. A lamp was burning in the room. Moonlight illumined the outside world.

Addressing Ishan, a householder devotee, the Master said: "Blessed indeed is the householder who performs his duties in the world, at the same time cherishing love for the Lotus Feet of God. He is indeed a hero. He is like a man who carries a heavy load of two maunds on his head and at the same time watches a bridal procession. One cannot lead such a life without great spiritual power. Again, such a man is like the mudfish, which lives in the mud but is not stained by it. Further, such a householder may be compared to a waterfowl. It is constantly diving under water; yet, by fluttering its wings only once, it shakes off all trace of wet.

"But a man must practise some spiritual discipline in order to be able to lead a detached life in the world. It is necessary for him to spend some time in solitude—be it a year, six months, three months, or even one month. In that solitude he should fix his mind on God and pray with a longing heart for love of God. He should also say to himself: 'There is nobody in this world who is my own. Those whom I call my own are here only for two days. God alone is my own. He alone is my all in all. Alas, how shall I realize Him?'

"One can live in the world after acquiring love of God. It is like breaking the jack-fruit after rubbing your hands with oil; the sticky juice of the fruit will not smear them. The world is like water and the mind like milk. If you put milk in water it will mix with the water. But first keep the milk in a quiet place and let it turn into curd. Then from the curd extract butter. That butter you may keep in water; it will not mix with the water, but will float on it.

"Some members of the Brāhmo Samāj said to me: 'Sir, our attitude toward the world is that of King Janaka. Like him, we want to enjoy the world in a detached spirit.' I said to them: 'To live in the world in a detached spirit is very difficult. By merely saying so you cannot be a King Janaka. How much austerity Janaka practised! How long he remained in one posture, with head down and feet up! You don't have to practise these extreme disciplines. But you need sādhanā; you should live in solitude. You may lead the life of a householder after having attained divine knowledge and love in solitude. Milk turns into curd only when it is not disturbed. The curd does not set if the milk is often moved from place to place or is too much disturbed.'

"On account of his detachment from the world Janaka was also known as the 'Videha', that is, one free from consciousness of the body. Though living in the world, he moved about as a jīvanmukta, a free soul living in a body. But for most people freedom from body-consciousness is something very far off. Intense spiritual discipline is necessary.

"Janaka was a great hero. He fenced with two swords, the one of knowledge and the other of work.

"You may ask, 'Is there any difference between the realizations of two jnānis, one a householder and the other a monk?' The reply is that the two belong to one class. Both of them are jnānis; they have the same experience. But a householder jnāni has reason to fear. He cannot altogether get rid of his fear as long as he is to live in the midst of 'woman and gold'. If you constantly live in a room full of soot, you are sure to soil your body, be it ever so little, no matter how clever you may be.

"After extracting the butter, if you keep it in a new pot, then there is no chance of its getting spoiled. But if you keep the butter in a pot where curd has been kept, well, then it is doubtful whether it will keep its flavour. (*Laughter.*)

"When they parch rice, a few grains jump out of the frying-pan to the ground. These are white, like mallikā flowers, without the slightest stain on them. But the grains that remain in the pan are also good, though not as immaculate as the fresh mallikā flower. They are a little stained. In the same way, if a monk who has renounced the world attains divine wisdom, he appears as spotless as the white flower; but one who stays in the frying-pan of the world after attaining Knowledge may get a little blemish. (*All laugh.*)

"Once a bhairavi came to King Janaka's court. At the sight of the woman, the king bent his head and cast his eyes to the ground. At this the bhairavi said, 'O Janaka, even now you are afraid of a woman!' Through Perfect Knowledge a man becomes like a child five years old; he does not know the distinction between a man and a woman.

"Although a jnāni living in the world may have a little blemish, yet this does not injure him. The moon undoubtedly has dark spots, but these do not obstruct its light.

"After realizing God, some souls perform work in order to teach men. Janaka, Nārada, and others like them, belong to this group. But one must possess power in order to be able to teach others. The sages of old were busy attaining knowledge for themselves. But teachers like Nārada went about doing good to others. They were real heroes.

"A worthless stick floating on the water sinks under the weight of a bird; but a heavy and substantial log floating on the water can support a cow, a man, or even an elephant. A steamboat not only crosses the water itself but carries many human beings with it. Teachers like Nārada may be compared to the heavy log of wood or the steamboat.

"One man, after eating a tasty morsel, removes every trace of it by wiping his face carefully with a towel, lest anyone should know. (*All laugh.*) Another, again, having got a mango, not only enjoys it himself but shares it with others.

"Even after having attained Perfect Knowledge, teachers like Nārada retained love of God in their minds for the welfare of others."

DOCTOR: "Jnāna makes a man speechless. He closes his eyes and sheds tears. Then he needs bhakti."

MASTER: "Bhakti may be likened to a woman who has access to the inner court of a house. Jnāna can go only as far as the outer rooms."

DOCTOR: "All women are not allowed to enter the inner court, for instance, prostitutes. Hence the need of jnāna."

MASTER: "A man may not know the right path, but if he has bhakti and the desire to know God, then he attains Him through the force of sheer bhakti. Once a sincere devotee set out on a pilgrimage to the temple of Jagannāth in Puri. He did not know the way; he went west instead of south. He no doubt strayed from the right path, but he always eagerly asked people the way, and they gave him the right directions, saying, 'This is not the path; follow that one.' At last the devotee was able to get to Puri and worship the Deity. So you see, even if you are ignorant, someone will tell you the way if you are earnest."

DOCTOR: "But the devotee in his ignorance did lose his way."

MASTER: "Yes, such a thing happens, no doubt. But a man reaches the goal in the end."

A DEVOTEE: "Has God a form or is He formless?"

MASTER: "God has form and, again, He is formless. Once upon a time a sannyāsi entered the temple of Jagannāth. As he looked at the holy image he debated within himself whether God had a form or was formless. He passed his staff from left to right to feel whether it touched the image. The staff touched nothing. He understood that there was no image before him; he concluded that God was formless. Next he passed the staff from right to left. It touched the image. The sannyāsi understood that God had form Thus he realized that God has form and, again, is formless.

"But it is extremely difficult to understand this. Naturally the doubt arises in the mind: if God is formless, how then can He have form? Further, if He has a form, why does He have so many forms?"

DOCTOR: "God has created all these forms in the world; therefore He Himself has a form. Again, He has created the mind; therefore He is formless. It is possible for God to be everything."

MASTER: "These things do not become clear until one has realized God. He assumes different forms and reveals Himself in different ways for the sake of His devotees. A man kept a solution of dye in a tub. Many people came to him to have their clothes dyed. He would ask a customer, 'What colour should you like to have your cloth dyed?' If the customer wanted red, then the man would dip the cloth in the tub and say, 'Here is your cloth dyed red.' If another customer wanted his cloth dyed yellow, the man would dip his cloth in the same tub and say, 'Here is your cloth dyed yellow.' If a customer wanted his cloth dyed blue, the man would dip it in the same tub and say, 'Here is your cloth dyed blue.' Thus he would dye the clothes of his customers different colours, dipping them all in the same solution. One of the customers watched all this with amazement. The man asked him, 'Well? What colour do you want for your cloth?' The customer said, 'Brother, dye my cloth the colour of the dye in your tub.' (*Laughter.*)

"Once a man went into a wood and saw a beautiful creature on a tree. Later he told a friend about it and said, 'Brother, on a certain tree in the wood I saw a red-coloured creature.' The friend answered: 'I have seen it too. Why do you call it red? It is green.' A third man said: 'Oh, no, no! Why do you call it green? It is yellow.' Then other persons began to describe the animal variously as violet, blue, or black. Soon they were quarrelling about the colour. At last they went to the tree and found a man sitting under it. In answer to their questions he said: 'I live under this tree and know the creature very well. What each of you has said about it is true. Sometimes it is red, sometimes green, sometimes yellow, sometimes blue, and so forth and so on. Again, sometimes I see that it has no colour whatsoever.'

"Only he who constantly thinks of God can know His real nature. He alone knows that God reveals Himself in different forms and different ways, that He has attributes and, again, has none. Only the man who lives under the tree knows that the chameleon can assume various colours and that sometimes it remains colourless. Others, not knowing the whole truth, quarrel among themselves and suffer.

"Yes, God has form and, again, He has none. Do you know how it is? Brahman, Existence-Knowledge-Bliss Absolute, is like a shoreless ocean. In the ocean visible blocks of ice are formed here and there by intense cold. Similarly, under the cooling influence, so to speak, of the bhakti of Its worshippers, the Infinite transforms Itself into the finite and appears before the worshipper as God with form. That is to say, God reveals Himself to His bhaktas as an embodied Person. Again, as, on the rising of the sun, the ice in the ocean melts away, so, on the awakening of jnāna, the embodied God melts back into the infinite and formless Brahman."

DOCTOR: "Yes. When the sun is up, the ice melts; and what is more, the heat of the sun turns the water into invisible vapour."

MASTER: "Yes, that is true. As a result of the discrimination that Brahman alone is real and the world illusory, the aspirant goes into samādhi. Then, for him, the forms or attributes of God disappear altogether. Then he does not feel God to be a Person. Then he cannot describe in words what God is. And who will describe it? He who is to describe does not exist at all; he no longer finds his 'I'. To such a person Brahman is attributeless. In that state God is experienced only as Consciousness, by man's inmost consciousness. He cannot be comprehended by the mind and intelligence.

"Therefore people compare bhakti, love of God, to the cooling light of the moon, and jnāna, knowledge, to the burning rays of the sun. I have heard that there are oceans in the extreme north and extreme south where the air is so cold that it freezes the water into huge blocks of ice here and there. Ships cannot move there; they are stopped by the ice."

DOCTOR: "Then in the path of bhakti the aspirant meets with obstacles."

MASTER: "Yes, that is true. But it does not cause the devotee any harm. After all, it is the water of the Ocean of Brahman, Existence-Knowledge-Bliss Absolute, that is frozen into ice. It will not injure you if you continue to reason, saying, for instance, that Brahman alone is real and the world illusory. This reasoning will awaken in you jnāna, which, like the sun, will melt the ice of divine forms back into the infinite Ocean of Brahman, Existence-Knowledge-Bliss Absolute.

"In the samādhi that comes at the end of reasoning and discrimination, no such thing as 'I' exists. But it is extremely difficult to attain it; 'I-consciousness' lingers so persistently. That is why a man is born again and again in this world.

"The cow suffers so much because she says, 'Hāmbā! Hāmbā!', that is, 'I! I!' She is yoked to the plough all day long, rain or shine. Or she is slaughtered by the butcher. But even that doesn't put an end to her misery. The cobbler tans her hide to make shoes from it. At last the carder makes a string for his bow from her entrails and uses the string in carding; then it says, 'Tuhu! Tuhu!', that is, 'Thou! Thou!' Only then does the cow's suffering come to an end.

"Likewise, only when a man says: 'Not I! Not I! I am nobody. O Lord, Thou art the Doer and I am Thy servant; Thou art the Master', is he freed from all sufferings; only then is he liberated."

DOCTOR: "But one must fall into the hands of the carder." (All laugh.)

MASTER: "If this ego cannot be got rid of, then let the rascal remain as the servant of God. (All laugh.)

"A man may keep this ego even after attaining samādhi. Such a man feels either that he is a servant of God or that he is a lover of God. Śankarāchārya retained the 'ego of Knowledge'[2] to teach men spiritual life. The 'servant ego', the 'Knowledge ego', or the 'devotee ego' may be called the 'ripe ego'. It is different from the 'unripe ego', which makes one feel: 'I am the doer. I am the son of a wealthy man. I am learned. I am rich. How dare anyone slight me?' A man with an 'unripe ego' cherishes such ideas. Suppose a thief has entered such a man's house and stolen some of his belongings. If the thief is caught, all the articles will be snatched away from him. Then he will be beaten. At last he will be handed over to the police. The owner of the stolen goods will say: 'What! This rogue doesn't know whose house he has entered!'

"After realizing God, a man becomes like a child five years old. The ego of such a man may be called the 'ego of a child', the 'ripe ego'. The child is not under the control of any of the gunas. He is beyond the three gunas. He is not under the control of any of the gunas—sattva, rajas, or tamas. Just watch a child and you will find that he is not under the influence of tamas. One moment he quarrels with his chum or even fights with him, and the next moment he hugs him, shows him much affection, and plays with him again. He is not even under the control of rajas. Now he builds his play house and makes all kinds of plans to make it beautiful, and the next moment he leaves everything behind and runs to his mother. Again, you see him wearing a beautiful piece of cloth worth five rupees. After a few moments the cloth lies on the ground; he forgets all about it. Or he may carry it under his arm. If you say to the child: 'That's a beautiful piece of

[2] The ego illumined and purified by the Knowledge of God. See foot-note 2, p. 416.

cloth. Whose is it?', he answers: 'Why, it is mine. My daddy gave it to me.'
You may say, 'My darling, won't you give it to me?' and he will reply: 'Oh
no, it is mine. My daddy gave it to me. I won't give it to you.' Some minutes
later you may coax him with a toy or a music-box worth a penny, and he
will give you the cloth. Again, a child five years old is not attached even to
sattva. You may find him today very fond of his playmates in the neighbourhood; he doesn't feel happy for a moment without seeing them; but tomorrow, when he goes to another place with his parents, he finds new playmates; all his love is now directed to his new friends, and he almost forgets
about his old ones. Further, a child has no pride of caste or family. If his
mother says to him about a certain person, 'This man is your elder brother',
he believes this to be one hundred per cent true. One of the two may have
been born in a brāhmin family and the other may belong to a low caste,
say that of the blacksmiths, but they will take their meal from the same
plate. A child is beyond all ideas of purity and impurity. He is not bound
by social conventions. He doesn't hesitate to come out naked before others.

"Then there is an 'ego of old age'. (*Dr. Sarkar laughs.*) An old man has
many shackles: caste, pride, shame, hatred, and fear. Furthermore, he is
bound by the ideas of worldly cleverness, calculating intelligence, and deceit.
If he is angry with anybody, he cannot shake it off easily; perhaps he keeps
the feeling as long as he lives. Again, there is the 'ego of scholarship' and
the 'ego of wealth'. The 'ego of old age' is an 'unripe ego'.

(*To the doctor*) "There are a few men who cannot attain knowledge of
God: men proud of their scholarship, proud of their education, or proud
of their wealth. If you speak to such people about a holy man and ask them
to visit him, they make all kinds of excuses and will not go. But in their
heart of hearts they think: 'Why, we are big people ourselves. Must we go
and visit someone else?'

"A characteristic of tamas is pride. Pride and delusion come from tamas.

"It is said in the Purāna that Rāvana had an excess of rajas, Kumbhakarna
of tamas, and Bibhishana of sattva. That is why Bibhishana was able to
receive the grace of Rāma. Another characteristic of tamas is anger. Through
anger one loses one's wits and cannot distinguish between right and wrong.
In a fit of anger Hanumān set fire to Lankā, without thinking for a moment
that the fire might also burn down the hut where Sītā lived.

"Still another feature of tamas is lust. Girindra Ghosh of Pāthuriāghāta
once remarked, 'Since you cannot get rid of your passions—your lust, your
anger, and so on—give them a new direction. Instead of desiring worldly pleasures, desire God. Have intercourse with Brahman. If you cannot get rid of
anger, then change its direction. Assume the tāmasic attitude of bhakti, and
say: 'What? I have repeated the hallowed name of Durgā, and shall I not be
liberated? How can I be a sinner any more? How can I be bound any more?'
If you cannot get rid of temptation, direct it toward God. Be infatuated with
God's beauty. If you cannot get rid of pride, then be proud to say that you
are the servant of God, you are the child of God. Thus turn the six passions
toward God."

DOCTOR: "It is very hard to control the sense-organs. They are like restive horses, whose eyes must be covered with blinkers. In the case of some horses it is necessary to prevent them from seeing at all."

MASTER: "A man need not fear anything if but once he receives the grace of God, if but once he obtains the vision of God, if but once he attains Self-Knowledge. Then the six passions cannot do him any harm.

"Eternally perfect souls like Nārada and Prahlāda did not have to take the trouble to put blinkers on their eyes. The child who holds his father's hand, while walking along the narrow balk in the paddy-field, may loosen his hold in a moment of carelessness and slip into the ditch. But it is quite different if the father holds the child's hand. Then the child never falls into the ditch."

DOCTOR: "But it is not proper for a father to hold his child by the hand."

MASTER: "It is not quite like that. Great sages have childlike natures. Before God they are always like children. They have no pride. Their strength is the strength of God, the strength of their Father. They have nothing to call their own. They are firmly convinced of that."

DOCTOR: "Can you make a horse move forward without first covering his eyes with blinkers? Can one realize God without first controlling the passions?"

MASTER: "What you say is according to the path of discrimination. It is known as jnānayoga. Through that path, too, one attains God. The jnānis say that an aspirant must first of all purify his heart. First he needs spiritual exercises; then he will attain Knowledge.

"But God can also be realized through the path of devotion. Once the devotee develops love for the Lotus Feet of God and enjoys the singing of His name and attributes, he does not have to make a special effort to restrain his senses. For such a devotee the sense-organs come under control of themselves.

"Suppose a man has just lost his son and is mourning his death. Can he be in a mood to quarrel with others that very day, or enjoy a feast in the house of a friend? Can he, that very day, show his pride before others or enjoy sense pleasures?

"If the moth discovers light, can it remain in darkness any longer?"

DOCTOR (with a smile): "Of course it cannot. It would rather fly into the flame and perish."

MASTER: "Oh no, that's not so. A lover of God does not burn himself to death, like a moth. The light to which he rushes is like the light of a gem. That light is brilliant, no doubt, but it is also cooling and soothing. That light does not scorch his body; it gives him joy and peace.

"One realizes God by following the path of discrimination and knowledge. But this is an extremely difficult path. It is easy enough to say such things as, 'I am not the body, mind, or intellect; I am beyond grief, disease, and sorrow; I am the embodiment of Existence-Knowledge-Bliss Absolute; I am beyond pain and pleasure; I am not under the control of the sense-organs', but it is very hard to assimilate these ideas and practise them. Suppose I see my hand cut by a thorn and blood gushing out; then it is not right for me to say: 'Why, my hand is not cut by the thorn! I am all right.' In order to be able to say that, I must first of all burn the thorn itself in the fire of Knowledge.

"Many people think they cannot have knowledge or understanding of God without reading books. But hearing is better than reading, and seeing is better than hearing. Hearing about Benares is different from reading about it; but seeing Benares is different from either hearing or reading.

"Those actually engaged in a game of chess do not always judge the moves on the board correctly. The onlookers often judge the moves better than the players. Worldly people often think themselves very intelligent, but they are attached to the things of the world. They are the actual players and cannot understand their own moves correctly. But holy men, who have renounced everything, are unattached to the world; they are really more intelligent than worldly people. Since they do not take any part in worldly life, their position is that of onlookers, and so they see things more clearly."

DOCTOR (to the devotees): "If he [meaning Sri Ramakrishna] had studied books he could not have acquired so much knowledge. Faraday communed with nature; that is why he was able to discover many scientific truths. He could not have known so much from the mere study of books. Mathematical formulas only throw the brain into confusion and bar the path of original inquiry."

MASTER: "There was a time when I lay on the ground in the Panchavati and prayed to the Divine Mother, 'O Mother, reveal to me what the karmis[3] have realized through their ritualistic worship, what the yogis have realized through yoga, and what the jnānis have realized through discrimination.' How much I communed with the Divine Mother! How can I describe it all?

"Ah, what a state I passed through! Sleep left me completely."

The Master sang:

> My sleep is broken; how can I slumber any more?
> For now I am wide awake in the sleeplessness of yoga.
> O Divine Mother, made one with Thee in yoga-sleep[4] at last,
> My slumber I have lulled asleep for evermore.
> A man has come to me from a country where there is no night;
> Rituals and devotions have all grown profitless for me.

He continued: "I have not read books. But people show me respect because I chant the name of the Divine Mother. Sambhu Mallick said about me, 'Here is a great hero without a sword or shield!'" (Laughter.)

The conversation turned to the performance of a drama by Girish Ghosh called The Life of Buddha. The doctor had seen the play and been much pleased with it.

DOCTOR (to Girish): "You are a very bad man. Must I go to the theatre every day?"

MASTER (to M.): "What does he say? I don't quite understand."

M: "The doctor liked the play very much."

MASTER (to Ishan): "Why don't you say something? (Pointing to the

---

[3] The ritualists.
[4] Samādhi, which makes one appear asleep.

doctor) He does not believe that God can incarnate Himself in a human form."

ISHAN: "What shall I say, sir? I don't like to argue any more."

MASTER (*sharply*): "Why? Won't you say the right thing?"

ISHAN (*to the doctor*): "Our faith is shallow on account of our pride. It is said in the *Rāmāyana* that a crow named Bhushandi did not at first accept Rāma as an Incarnation of God. Once it incurred Rāma's displeasure. It travelled through the different worlds—the lunar, solar, and so forth—and through Mount Kailās, to escape Rāma's wrath. But it found that it could not escape. Then it surrendered itself to Him and took refuge at His feet. Rāma took the crow in His hand and swallowed it. Thereupon the crow found that it was seated in its own nest in a tree. After its pride had thus been crushed, the bird came to realize that though Rāma looked like any other man, yet He contained in His stomach the entire universe—sky, moon, sun, stars, oceans, rivers, men, animals, and trees."

MASTER (*to the doctor*): "It is very difficult to understand that God can be a finite human being and at the same time the all-pervading Soul of the universe. The Absolute and the Relative are His two aspects. How can we say emphatically with our small intelligence that God cannot assume a human form? Can we ever understand all these ideas with our little intellect? Can a one-seer pot hold four seers of milk?

"Therefore one should trust in the words of holy men and great souls, those who have realized God. They constantly think of God, as a lawyer of his lawsuits. Do you believe the story of the crow Bhushandi?"

DOCTOR: "I accept as much as I want to. All difficulties come to an end if only God reveals His true nature to the seeker. Then there can be no confusion. How can I accept Rāma as an Incarnation of God? Take the example of His killing Vāli, the monkey chieftain. He hid Himself behind a tree, like a thief, and murdered Vāli. This is how a man acts, and not God."

GIRISH: "But, sir, such an action is possible only for God."

DOCTOR: "Then take the example of His sending Sītā into exile."

GIRISH: "This too, sir, is possible only for God, not for man."

ISHAN (*to the doctor*): "Why don't you believe in the Incarnation of God? Just now you said that God has form since He has created all these forms, and that God is formless since He has created the mind, which is without form. A moment ago you said that everything is possible for God."

MASTER (*laughing*): "It is not mentioned in his 'science' that God can take human form; so how can he believe it? (*All laugh.*)

"Listen to a story. A man said to his friend, 'I have just seen a house fall down with a terrific crash.' Now, the friend to whom he told this had received an English education. He said: 'Just a minute. Let me look it up in the newspaper.' He read the paper but could not find the news of a house falling down with a crash. Thereupon he said to his friend: 'Well, I don't believe you. It isn't in the paper; so it is all false.'" (*All laugh.*)

GIRISH (*to the doctor*): "You must admit that Krishna is God. I will not let you look on Him as a mere man. You must admit that He is either God or a demon."

MASTER: "Unless a man is guileless, he cannot so easily have faith in God. God is far, far away from the mind steeped in worldliness. Worldly intelligence creates many doubts and many forms of pride—pride of learning, wealth, and the rest. (*Pointing to the doctor*) But he is guileless.

"How guileless Keshab Sen was! One day he visited the Kāli temple at Dakshineswar. At about four in the afternoon he went around to the guesthouse, where the poor are fed, and asked when the beggars would be fed. He didn't know that it was too late in the day for the feeding of the poor. As a man's faith increases, so does his knowledge of God. The cow that discriminates too much about food gives milk in dribblets. But the cow that gulps down everything—herbs, leaves, grass, husks, straw—gives milk in torrents. (*All laugh.*)

"God cannot be realized without childlike faith. The mother says to her child, pointing to a boy, 'He is your elder brother.' And the child at once believes that the boy is one hundred per cent his brother. Again, the mother says that a bogy man lives in a certain room, and the child believes one hundred per cent that the bogy man lives in the room. God bestows His grace on the devotee who has this faith of a child. God cannot be realized by the mind steeped in worldliness."

DOCTOR (*to the devotees*): "It is not right, however, to make the cow yield milk by feeding her all sorts of things. One of my cows was fed that way. I drank its milk and the result was that I became seriously ill. At first I was at a loss to know the cause. After much inquiry I found out that the cow had been given the wrong things to eat. I was in a great fix. I had to go to Lucknow for a change to get rid of the illness. I spent twelve thousand rupees. (*Roars of laughter.*)

"It is very difficult always to find out the precise relationship between cause and effect. A child of seven months, in a wealthy family, had an attack of whooping-cough. I was called in for consultation. Even after much effort I could not find out the cause of the illness. At last I learnt that the child had been given the milk of an ass that had been drenched in the rain." (*All laugh.*)

MASTER (*to the devotees*): "How strange! It is like saying that a man has an acid stomach because he passed, in his coach, under a tamarind tree." (*All laugh.*)

DOCTOR (*with a smile*): "Let me tell you another. The captain of a ship had a bad headache. After consultation, the doctors on board had a blister applied to the side of the boat." (*All laugh.*)

MASTER (*to the doctor*): "For the seekers of God the constant company of holy men is necessary. The disease of worldly people has become chronic, as it were. They should carry out the instruction of holy men. What will they gain by merely listening to their advice? They must not only take the prescribed medicine, but also follow a strict diet. Diet is important."

DOCTOR: "Yes, it is the diet, more than anything else, that causes the cure."

MASTER: "There are three classes of physicians: superior, mediocre, and inferior. The inferior physician feels the patient's pulse, merely asks him to take medicine, and then goes away. He doesn't bother to find out whether the patient has followed his directions. The mediocre physician gently tries to persuade the patient to take the medicine. He says: 'Look here. How can you get well without medicine? Take the medicine, my dear. I am preparing it with my own hands.' But the superior physician follows a different method. If he finds the patient stubbornly refusing to swallow the medicine, he presses the patient's chest with his knee and forces the medicine down his throat."

Doctor: "There is a form of treatment that does not require the physician to press the patient's chest with his knee. For instance, homeopathy."

Master: "There is no fear if a good physician presses the patient's chest with his knee.

"Like the physicians, there are three classes of religious teachers. The inferior teacher is content with merely giving spiritual instruction; he doesn't bother about the student after that. The mediocre teacher explains the teaching again and again for the good of the student, that he may assimilate it; he persuades the student through love and kindness to follow it. But the superior teacher uses force, if necessary, on the stubborn student.

(To the doctor) "The renunciation of 'woman and gold' is meant for the sannyāsi. He must not look even at the picture of a woman. Do you know what a woman is to a man? She is like spiced pickle. The very thought of pickle brings water to the tongue; it doesn't have to be brought near the tongue.

"But this renunciation is not meant for householders like you. It is meant only for sannyāsis. You may live among women, as far as possible in a spirit of detachment. Now and then you must retire into solitude and think of God. Women must not be allowed there. You can lead an unattached life to a great extent if you have faith in God and love for Him. After the birth of one or two children a married couple should live as brother and sister. They should then constantly pray to God that their minds may not run after sense pleasures any more and that they may not have any more children."

Girish (to the doctor, with a smile): "You have already spent three or four hours here. What about your patients?"

Doctor: "Well, my practice and patients! I shall lose everything on account of your paramahamsa!" (All laugh.)

Master: "There is a river called the 'Karmanāsā'.[5] It is very dangerous to dive into that river. If a man plunges into its waters he cannot perform any more action. It puts an end to his duties." (All laugh.)

Doctor (to Girish, M., and the other devotees): "My friends, consider me as one of you. I am not saying this as a physician. But if you think of me as your own, then I am yours."

Master (to the doctor): "There is such a thing as love for love's sake. It is very good if one can grow such love. Prahlāda loved God for the sake of love. A devotee like Prahlāda says: 'O God, I do not want wealth, fame, creature comforts, or any such thing. Please grant me the boon that I may have genuine love for Thy Lotus Feet.'"

[5] Literally, "destroyer of duties."

DOCTOR: "You are right, sir. I have seen people bowing down before the image of Kāli. They seek worldly objects from the Goddess, such as a job, the healing of disease, and so forth.

(*To the Master*) "The illness you are suffering from does not permit the patient to talk with people. But my case is an exception. You may talk with me when I am here." (*All laugh.*)

MASTER: "Please cure my illness. I cannot chant the name and glories of God."

DOCTOR: "Meditation is enough."

MASTER: "What do you mean? Why should I lead a monotonous life? I enjoy my fish in a variety of dishes: curried fish, fried fish, pickled fish, and so forth! Sometimes I worship God with rituals, sometimes I repeat His name, sometimes I meditate on Him, sometimes I sing His name and glories, sometimes I dance in His name."

DOCTOR: "Neither am I monotonous."

MASTER: "Your son Amrita does not believe in the Incarnation of God. What is the harm in that? One realizes God even if one believes Him to be formless. One also realizes God if one believes that God has form. Two things are necessary for the realization of God: faith and self-surrender. Man is ignorant by nature. Errors are natural to him. Can a one-seer pot hold four seers of milk? Whatever path you may follow, you must pray to God with a restless heart. He is the Ruler of the soul within. He will surely listen to your prayer if it is sincere. Whether you follow the ideal of the Personal God or that of the Impersonal Truth, you will realize God alone, provided you are restless for Him. A cake with icing tastes sweet whether you eat it straight or sidewise.

"Your son Amrita is a nice boy."

DOCTOR: "He is your disciple."

MASTER (*with a smile*): "There is not a fellow under the sun who is my disciple. On the contrary, I am everybody's disciple. All are the children of God. All are His servants. I too am a child of God. I too am His servant. 'Uncle Moon' is every child's uncle!"

46

THE MASTER AND DR. SARKAR

I T WAS THE DAY of the full moon following the Durgā Pujā, the worship of the Divine Mother. At ten o'clock in the morning Sri Ramakrishna was talking to M., who was helping him with his socks.

MASTER (*smiling*): "Why can't I cut my woolen scarf into two pieces and wrap them around my legs like socks? They will be nice and warm."

M. smiled. The previous evening Sri Ramakrishna had had a long conversation with Dr. Sarkar. Referring to it, the Master said laughingly, "I told him the story of the calf, and about egotism being the cause of all suffering."

The younger Naren reminded Sri Ramakrishna that he, the Master, had told the doctor about people's suffering from the threefold misery of the world and still bragging of their well-being. The disciple said, "That was a very nice thing you said yesterday about the thorn, and also about burning it in the fire of Knowledge."

MASTER: "I had direct visions of those things. One day I was passing back of the kuthi when my whole body burst into flames, as it were, like the fire in a homa. Padmalochan once said to me, 'I shall convene an assembly of pundits and proclaim your spiritual experiences before all.' But he died shortly after."

At eleven o'clock M. went to Dr. Sarkar's house to report Sri Ramakrishna's condition. The doctor showed great eagerness to hear about him.

DOCTOR (*laughing*): "How well I told him yesterday that in order to be able to say 'Tuhu! Tuhu!', 'Thou! Thou!', one must fall into the hands of an expert carder!"

M: "It is true, sir. One cannot get rid of egotism without the help of a capable teacher. How well he spoke last night of bhakti! Bhakti, like a woman, can go into the inner court."

DOCTOR: "Yes, that is very nice. But still one cannot give up jnāna."

M: "But he does not say that. He accepts both knowledge and love, the Impersonal Truth and the Personal God. He says that through the cooling influence of bhakti a part of the Reality takes the solid form of the Personal God; and with the rise of the sun of jnāna the ice of form melts again into the formless water of the Absolute. In other words, you realize God with form through bhaktiyoga, and the formless Absolute through jñānayoga.

"You must have noticed that he sees God so near him that he always converses with Him. When suffering from illness, he says to God, like a small child, 'Oh, Mother, it is hurting me!'

"How wonderful his power of observation is! He saw a fossil in the museum. At once he gave it as an example of the effect of companionship with holy persons. Just as an object is turned into stone by remaining near stone, so does a man become holy by living with a holy man."

Doctor: "Yesterday Ishan Babu talked of the Incarnation of God. What is that? To call man God!"

M: "Everyone has his own faith. What is the use of interfering with it?"

Doctor: "Yes, what is the use?"

M: "How the Master made us laugh when he told us about a certain man who refused to believe that a house had collapsed, because it was not published in the newspaper!"

Doctor Sarkar remained silent. Sri Ramakrishna had said to him, "Your 'science' does not speak of God's Incarnation; therefore you say that God cannot incarnate Himself as man."

It was midday. Doctor Sarkar took M. with him in his carriage. He was going to visit Sri Ramakrishna after seeing his other patients.

A few days before, at Girish's invitation, Doctor Sarkar had seen his play about Buddha's life. He said to M.: "It would have been better to speak of Buddha as the Incarnation of Compassion. Why did he speak of him as an Incarnation of Vishnu?"

The doctor set M. down at the corner of Cornwallis Square.

It was three o'clock in the afternoon. One or two devotees were seated near Sri Ramakrishna. He became impatient, like a child. Repeatedly he asked the devotees, "When is the doctor coming?" "What time is it now?" Doctor Sarkar was expected in the evening.

Suddenly Sri Ramakrishna was overwhelmed with a strange mood. He placed his pillow on his lap. Filled with maternal love, he began to caress it and hold it to his breast as if it were his child. He was in an ecstatic mood. His face was lighted with a childlike smile. He put on his cloth in a strange manner. The devotees looked at him in amazement.

A little later Sri Ramakrishna was in his normal mood. It was time for his meal. He ate a little boiled farina.

He was talking to M. about his mystic experiences.

Master (to M., aside): "Do you know what I saw just now in my ecstatic state? There was a meadow covering an area of seven or eight miles, through which lay the road to Sihore. I was alone in that meadow. I saw a sixteen-year-old paramahamsa boy exactly like the one I had seen in the Panchavati.

"A mist of bliss lay all around. Out of it emerged a boy thirteen or fourteen years old. I saw his face. He looked like Purna. Both of us were naked. Then we began to run around joyfully in the meadow. Purna felt thirsty. He drank some water from a tumbler and offered me what was left. I said to him, 'Brother, I cannot take your leavings.' Thereupon he laughed, washed the glass, and brought me fresh water."

Sri Ramakrishna was again in samādhi. He regained consciousness and began to talk to M.

MASTER: "My mind is undergoing a change. I cannot take prasād any more. The Real and the Appearance are becoming one to me. Do you know what I saw just now? A divine form—a vision of the Divine Mother. She had a child in Her womb. She gave birth to it and the next instant began to swallow it; and as much of it as went into Her mouth became void. It was revealed to me that everything is void. The Divine Mother said to me, as it were: 'Come confusion! Come delusion! Come!' "

This reminded M. of Sri Ramakrishna's saying that the magician alone is real and all else unreal.

MASTER: "Well, how is it that the other time I tried to attract Purna but failed? This weakens my faith a little."

M: "But to attract a person is to work a miracle."

MASTER: "Yes, a downright miracle."

M: "You remember, one day we were returning to Dakshineswar in a carriage from Adhar's house, when a bottle broke. One of us said to you: 'Does this mean that any harm will befall us? What do you think?' You said: 'What do I care? Why should I bother about it? That would be miracle-working.' "

MASTER: "Yes, people lay ailing children down on the ground where men chant the name of God, in order that they may be cured; or people cure disease through occult powers. All this is miracle-working. Only those whose spiritual experience is extremely shallow call on God for the healing of disease."

It was evening. Sri Ramakrishna was seated on his bed, thinking of the Divine Mother and repeating Her hallowed name. The devotees sat near him in silence. Latu, Sashi, Sarat, the younger Naren, Paltu, Bhupati, Girish, and others were present. Ramtaran of the Star Theatre had come with Girish to entertain Sri Ramakrishna with his singing. A few minutes later Dr. Sarkar arrived.

DOCTOR (to the Master): "I was much worried about you last night at three o'clock. It was raining. I said to myself, 'Who knows whether or not the doors and windows of his room are shut?' "

"Really?" said Sri Ramakrishna. He was much pleased at the doctor's love and thoughtfulness for him.

MASTER: "As long as there is the body, one should take care of it. But I find that the body is quite separate from the Self. When a man rids himself entirely of his love for 'woman and gold', then he clearly perceives that the body is one thing and the Self another. When the milk inside the coconut is all dried up, then the kernel becomes separated from the shell; you feel the kernel rattling inside when you shake the coconut. Or it is just like a sword and its sheath. The sword is one thing and the sheath is another.

"Therefore I cannot speak much to the Divine Mother about the illness of the body."

GIRISH (*to the devotees*): "Pundit Shashadhar said to him [meaning the Master]: 'Please bring your mind to bear on the body during samādhi. That will cure your illness.' And he, the Master, saw in a vision that the body was nothing but a loose mass of flesh and bones."

MASTER: "Once, a long time ago, I was very ill. I was sitting in the Kāli temple. I felt like praying to the Divine Mother to cure my illness, but couldn't do so directly in my own name. I said to Her, 'Mother, Hriday asks me to tell You about my illness.' I could not proceed any farther. At once there flashed into my mind the Museum of the Asiatic Society, and a human skeleton strung together with wire. I said to Her, 'Please tighten the wire of my body like that, so that I may go about singing Your name and glories.' It is impossible for me to ask for occult powers.

"At first Hriday asked me—I was then under his control—to pray to the Mother for powers. I went to the temple. In a vision I saw a widow thirty or thirty-five years old, covered with filth. It was revealed to me that occult powers are like that filth. I became angry with Hriday because he had asked me to pray for powers."

Ramtaran began to sing:

> Behold my vīnā, my dearly beloved,
> My lute of sweetest tone;
> If tenderly you play on it,
> The strings will waken, at your touch,
> To rarest melodies.
> Tune it neither low nor high,
> And from it in a hundred streams
> The sweetest sound will flow;
> But over-slack the strings are mute,
> And over-stretched they snap in twain.

DOCTOR (*to Girish*): "Is it an original song?"
GIRISH: "No, it is an adaptation from Edwin Arnold."
Ramtaran sang from the play, *The Life of Buddha*:

> We moan for rest, alas! but rest can never find;
> We know not whence we come, nor where we float away.
> Time and again we tread this round of smiles and tears;
> In vain we pine to know whither our pathway leads,
> And why we play this empty play.

> We sleep, although awake, as if by a spell bewitched;
> Will darkness never break into the light of dawn?
> As restless as the wind, life moves unceasingly:
> We know not who we are, nor whence it is we come;
> We know not why we come, nor where it is we drift;
> Sharp woes dart forth on every side.

> How many drift about, now gay, now drowned in tears!
> One moment they exist; the next they are no more.
> We know not why we come, nor what our deeds have been,
> Nor, in our bygone lives, how well we played our parts;

Like water in a stream, we cannot stay at rest;
Onward we flow for evermore.

Burst Thou our slumber's bars, O Thou that art awake!
How long must we remain enmeshed in fruitless dreams?
Are you indeed awake? Then do not longer sleep!
Thick on you lies the gloom fraught with a million woes.
Rise, dreamer, from your dream, and slumber not again!
Shine forth, O Shining One, and with Thy shafts of light
Slay Thou the blinding dark! Our only Saviour Thou!
We seek deliverance at Thy feet.

As Sri Ramakrishna listened to the song he went into samādhi.
Ramtaran sang again:

Blow, storm! Rage and roar! . . .

When the song was over, Sri Ramakrishna said to the singer: "What is this? Why this decoction of bitter neem-leaves after the rice pudding? The moment you sang—

Shine forth, O Shining One, and with Thy shafts of light
Slay Thou the blinding dark!

I had a vision of the Sun. As He arose, the darkness vanished, and all men took refuge at His feet."

Ramtaran sang again:

O Mother, Saviour of the helpless, Thou the Slayer of sin!
In Thee do the three gunas dwell—sattva, rajas, and tamas.
Thou dost create the world; Thou dost sustain it and destroy it;
Binding Thyself with attributes, Thou yet transcendest them;
For Thou, O Mother, art the All.
Kāli Thou art, and Tārā, and Thou the Ultimate Prakriti;
Thou art the Fish, the Turtle, the Boar, and all other Avatārs;
Earth, water, air, and fire art Thou, and Thou the sky,
O Mother of the Absolute!

The Sāmkhya, Pātanjala, Mimāmsaka, and Nyāya
For ever seek to fathom Thee and know Thine inmost nature;
Vedānta and Vaiśeshika are searching after Thee;
But none of them has found Thee out.
Though free of limitations, beginningless and without end,
Yet for Thy loving bhaktas' sake Thou wearest varying forms.
The terrors of this world Thou dost remove, and Thou dost dwell
Alike in present, past, and future.

Thou dost appear with form, to him who loves Thee as a Person;
Thou art the Absolute, to him who worships formless Truth.
Some there are who speak alone of the resplendent Brahman;
Even this, O Blissful Mother, is nothing else but Thee!
Each man, according to his measure, makes his image of the Truth,
Calling it the Highest Brahman.
Beyond this does Turiya shine, the Indescribable;
O Mother of all things, who dost pervade the universe,
Every one of these art Thou!

Then he sang:

> Dear friend, my religion and piety have come to an end:
> No more can I worship Mother Śyāmā; my mind defies control.
> Oh, shame upon me! Bitter shame!
> I try to meditate on the Mother with sword in hand,
> Wearing Her garland of human heads;
> But it is always the Dark One,[1] wearing His garland of wild wood-
> flowers
> And holding the flute to His tempting lips,
> That shines before my eyes.
>
> I think of the Mother with Her three eyes, but alas! I see
> Him alone with the arching eyes, and I forget all else!
> Oh, shame upon me! Bitter shame!
> I try to offer fragrant flowers at the Mother's feet,
> But the ravishing thought of His graceful form unsettles my help-
> less mind,
> And all my meditations meant for the Naked One[2] are drawn away
> By the sight of His yellow scarf.

Sri Ramakrishna was in an ecstatic mood as he listened to the song. The musician sang again:

> O Mother, who has offered these red hibiscus flowers at Thy feet?
> I beg of Thee, O Mother, place one or two upon my head.
> Then I shall cry aloud to Thee, "Oh, Mother! Mother!"
> And I shall dance around Thee and clap my hands for joy,
> And Thou wilt look at me and laugh, and tie the flowers in my
> hair.

The singing was over. Many of the devotees were in a rapturous mood. There was a deep silence in the room. The younger Naren was absorbed in meditation. He sat like a stump. Pointing him out to the doctor, Sri Rama-krishna said, "A very pure soul, unstained by the slightest touch of worldli-ness."

MANOMOHAN (*to the doctor*): "He (*pointing to the Master*) says of your son, 'I don't care for the father if I have the son.'"

DOCTOR: "Ah, you see! That is why I say that you forget everything else when you have the 'Son'."[3]

MASTER (*smiling*): "I don't say that I do not want the Father."

DOCTOR: "Yes, I understand you. How can you save your face unless you say a few things like that?"

MASTER: "Your boy is quite guileless. One day Sambhu's face became red as he said, 'God will surely listen to a man's prayer if he prays to Him with sincerity.'

"Why am I so fond of the boys? They are like unadulterated milk: only a little boiling is needed. Moreover it can be offered to the Deity. But milk

---

[1] Krishna.

[2] Śyāmā.

[3] A man forgets God the Father, being engrossed in the Son, the Avatār or Incarnation.

adulterated with water needs much boiling. It consumes a large quantity of fuel.

"The boys are like fresh earthen pots, good vessels in which one can keep milk without any worry. Spiritual instruction arouses their inner consciousness without delay. But it is not so with the worldly-minded. One is afraid to keep milk in a pot that has been used for curd. The milk may turn sour.

"Your boy is still free from worldliness, untouched by 'woman and gold'."

DOCTOR: "That is because he is living on his father's earnings. I should love to see how free he would keep himself from worldliness if he had to earn his own livelihood."

MASTER: "Yes, yes. That is true. But God is far, far away from the worldly-minded. For those who have renounced the world He is in the palm of the hand.

(To Dr. Sarkar and Dr. Dukari) "But renunciation of 'woman and gold' is not meant for you. You may renounce these mentally. That is why I said to the goswāmis: 'Why do you speak of renunciation? That will not do for you. You have to attend the daily worship of Śyāmasundar.'

"Total renunciation is for sannyāsis. They must not look even at the picture of a woman. To them a woman is poison. They must keep themselves at least ten cubits away from her; and if that is not possible, at least one cubit. And they must not talk much with a woman, no matter how devout she may be. Further, they should choose their dwelling at a place where they will never, or scarcely ever, see the face of a woman.

"Money, too, is like poison to a sannyāsi. If he keeps money with him, he has worries, pride, anger, and the desire for physical comforts. Money inflames his rajas, which brings tamas in its train. Therefore a sannyāsi must not touch 'gold'. 'Woman and gold' makes him forget God.

"For householders money is a means of getting food, clothes, and a dwelling-place, worshipping the Deity, and serving holy men and devotees.

"It is useless to try to hoard money. With great labour the bees build a hive; but a man breaks it and takes the honey away."

DOCTOR: "Whom shall we hoard for?—For a wicked son, perhaps."

MASTER: "It is not a wicked son alone. Perhaps the wife is unchaste. She may have a secret lover. Perhaps she will give him your watch and chain!

"You should not renounce woman completely. It is not harmful for a householder to live with his wife. But after the birth of one or two children, husband and wife should live as brother and sister.

"It is attachment to 'woman and gold' that begets pride of learning, pride of money, and pride of social position.

"One cannot attain divine knowledge till one gets rid of pride. Water does not stay on the top of a mound; but into low land it flows in torrents from all sides."

DOCTOR: "But the water that flows into the low land from all sides contains good water and bad water, muddy water and ditch-water. Again, there are hollows on mountain-tops as well, as at Nainitāl and Mānasoravar. These contain only pure water from the sky."

MASTER: "Only pure water from the sky—that is good!"

DOCTOR: "Further, from an elevated place the water can be distributed on all sides."

MASTER (*smiling*): "A certain man came to possess a siddha mantra.[4] He then went to the top of a hill and cried aloud. 'Repeat this mantra and you will realize God.'"

DOCTOR: "Yes."

MASTER: "But you must remember one thing. When his soul feels restless for God, a man forgets the difference between good water and ditch-water. In order to know God, he sometimes goes to good men, sometimes to imperfect men. Dirty water cannot injure an aspirant if God's grace descends on him. When God grants him Knowledge, He reveals to the aspirant what is good and what is bad.

"There may be hollows on the top of a hill, but they cannot exist on the hill of the 'wicked ego'. Only if it is an 'ego of Knowledge' or an 'ego of bhakti', does the pure water from the sky collect there.

"It is true that the water from a hill-top may flow in all directions, but that is possible only from the hill of the 'ego of Knowledge'.

"One cannot teach men without the command of God. After attaining Knowledge, Śankarāchārya retained the 'ego of Knowledge' in order to teach mankind. But to lecture without realizing God! What good will that do?

"I went to the Nandanbāgān Brāhmo Samāj. After the worship the preacher gave a lecture from the raised platform. He had written it at home. As he read from the manuscript he looked around. While meditating he opened his eyes from time to time to look at people.

"The instruction of a man who has not seen God does not produce the right effect. He may say one thing rightly, but he becomes confused about the next.

"Samadhyayi delivered a lecture. He said: 'God is beyond words and mind; He is dry. Worship Him through the bliss of your love and devotion.' Just see, he thus described God, whose very nature is Joy and Bliss! What will such a lecture accomplish? Can it teach people anything? Such a lecturer is like the man who said, 'My uncle's cow-shed is full of horses.' Horses in the cow-shed! (*All laugh.*) From that you can understand that there were no horses at all."

DOCTOR (*smiling*): "Nor cows either!" (*All laugh.*)

In the mean time the devotees who had been in a rapturous state had regained their normal mood. The doctor was highly pleased with them and asked M. about them. M. introduced to him Paltu, the younger Naren, Bhupati, Sarat, Sashi, and the other youngsters. About Sashi, M. said, "He is going to appear for the B. A. examination."

The doctor was a little inattentive.

MASTER (*to the doctor*): "Look here! Listen to what he is saying."

The doctor heard from M. about Sashi.

MASTER (*to the doctor, pointing to M.*): "He instructs the school-boys."

DOCTOR: "So I have heard."

[4] A sacred word by repeating which one attains perfection.

MASTER: "I am unlettered and yet educated people come here. How amazing! You must admit that it is the play of God."

It was nine o'clock in the evening. The doctor had been sitting there since six o'clock, watching all these things.

GIRISH (to the doctor): "Well, sir, does it ever happen to you that, though you do not intend to come here, you are drawn as if by a subtle force? I feel that way; that is why I am asking you."

DOCTOR: "I don't know whether I feel that. But the heart alone knows the promptings of the heart. (To Sri Ramakrishna) Besides, there isn't much use in speaking about it."

October 24, 1885

It was about one o'clock in the afternoon. Sri Ramakrishna was seated on the second floor of the house at Syāmpukur. Dr. Sarkar, Narendra, Mahimacharan, M., and other devotees were in the room. Referring to the homeopathic system of medicine, the Master said to Dr. Sarkar, "This treatment of yours is very good."

DOCTOR: "According to homeopathy the physician has to check up the symptoms of the disease with the medical book. It is like Western music. The singer follows the score.

"Where is Girish Ghosh? Never mind. Don't trouble him. He didn't sleep last night."

MASTER: "Well, when I am in samādhi I feel intoxicated as if I were drunk with siddhi. What have you to say about that?"

DOCTOR (to M.): "In that state the nerve centres cease to function. Hence the limbs become numb. Again, the legs totter because all the energy rushes toward the brain. Life consists of the nervous system. There is a nerve centre in the nape of the neck called the medulla oblongata. If that is injured, one may die."

Mahima Chakravarty began to describe the Kundalini. He said: "The Sushumnā nerve runs through the spinal cord in a subtle form. None can see it. That is what Śiva says."

DOCTOR: "Śiva examined man only in his maturity. But the Europeans have examined man in all stages of his life from the embryo to maturity. It is good to know comparative history. From the history of the Sonthāls one learns that Kāli was a Sonthāl woman. She was a valiant fighter. (All laugh.)

"Don't laugh, please. Let me tell you how greatly the study of comparative anatomy has benefited men. The difference between the actions of the pancreatic juice and bile was at first unknown. But later Claude Bernard examined the stomach, liver, and other parts of the rabbit and demonstrated that the action of bile is different from the action of the pancreatic juice. Therefore it stands to reason that we should watch the lower animals as well. The study of man alone is not enough.

"Similarly, the study of comparative religion is highly beneficial.

"Why do his [meaning the Master's] words go straight to our hearts? He has experienced the truths of different religions. He himself has practised the disciplines of the Hindu, Christian, Mussalmān, Śākta, and Vaishnava religions. The bees can make good honey only if they gather nectar from different flowers."

M. (*to Dr. Sarkar*): "He (*pointing to Mahimacharan*) has studied science a great deal."

DOCTOR (*smiling*): "What science? Do you mean Max Müller's *Science of Religion?*"

MAHIMA (*to the Master*): "You are ill. But what can the doctor do about it? When I heard of your illness, I thought that you were only going to pamper the doctor's pride."

MASTER (*pointing to Dr. Sarkar*): "But he is a very good physician. He is very learned too."

MAHIMA: "Yes, sir. He is a ship and we are only small boats."

Dr. Sarkar folded his hands in humility.

MAHIMA: "But here in the Master's presence all are equal."

Sri Ramakrishna asked Narendra to sing. Narendra sang:

> I have made Thee, O Lord, the Pole-star of my life;
> No more shall I lose my way on the world's trackless sea. . . .

Then he sang:

> Ever insane with pride am I, and many the cravings of my
>   heart! . . .

He sang again:

> This universe, wondrous and infinite,
> O Lord, is Thy handiwork;
> And the whole world is a treasure-house
> Full of Thy beauty and grace. . . .

Narendra continued:

> O Father of the Universe, upon Thy lofty throne,
> Thou dost enjoy the music of the worlds,
> As Thy creation's praise they sweetly sing.
> Behold, I too, though born of earth, have come with feeble voice
> Before the portal of Thy House.
>
> I seek alone Thy vision, Lord! I crave no other boon.
> Here I have come to sing my song for Thee;
> From a far corner of the mighty throng
> Where sun and moon are hymning Thee, I too would sing Thy
>   praise:
> This is Thy lowly servant's prayer.

He sang another song:

> O King of Kings, reveal Thyself to me!
> I crave Thy mercy. Cast on me Thy glance!
> At Thy dear feet I dedicate my life,
> Seared in the fiery furnace of this world.
>
> My heart, alas, is deeply stained with sin;
> Ensnared in māyā, I am all but dead.

> Compassionate Lord! Revive my fainting soul
> With the life-giving nectar of Thy grace.

Again:

> Be drunk, O mind, be drunk with the Wine of Heavenly Bliss!
> Roll on the ground and weep, chanting Hari's sweet name! . . .

MASTER: "And sing that one—'All that exists art Thou.'"

DOCTOR: "Ah!"

Narendra sang:

> I have joined my heart to Thee: all that exists art Thou;
> Thee only have I found, for Thou art all that exists. . . .

The singing was over. Dr. Sarkar sat there almost spellbound. After a time, with folded hands, he said very humbly to Sri Ramakrishna: "Allow me to take my leave now. I shall come again tomorrow."

MASTER: "Oh, stay a little. Girish Ghosh has been sent for. (*Pointing to Mahima*) He is a scholar, yet he dances in the name of Hari. He has no pride. He went to Konnagar just because we were there. He is wealthy; he is free; he serves nobody. (*Pointing to Narendra*) What do you think of him?"

DOCTOR: "Excellent!"

MASTER (*pointing to a devotee*): "And him?"

DOCTOR: "Splendid!"

MAHIMA: "It can by no means be said that one knows philosophy unless one has read Hindu philosophy. The European philosophers do not know the twenty-four cosmic principles of the Sāmkhya philosophy. They cannot even grasp them."

MASTER (*smiling*): "What are the three paths you speak of?"

MAHIMA: "The path of Sat, which is the path of knowledge. Next, the path of Chit, of yoga, of karmayoga, which includes the duties and functions of the four stages of life. Last, the path of Ānanda, the path of devotion and ecstatic love. You are an adept in all three paths; you can speak of them all with authority."

Sri Ramakrishna laughed.

Dr. Sarkar took his leave. It was evening, the first night after the full moon. Sri Ramakrishna stood up, lost·in samādhi. Nityagopal stood beside him in a reverent attitude.

Sri Ramakrishna took his seat. Nityagopal was stroking his feet. Devendra, Kalipada, and many other devotees were seated by his side.

MASTER (*to the devotees*): "My mind tells me that Nityagopal's present state will undergo a change. His entire mind will be concentrated on me —on Him who dwells in me. Don't you see how Narendra's whole mind is being drawn toward me?"

Many of the devotees were taking their leave. Sri Ramakrishna stood up. Referring to japa, he said to a devotee: "Japa means silently repeating God's name in solitude. When you chant His name with single-minded devotion you can see God's form and realize Him. Suppose there is a piece of timber sunk in the water of the Ganges and fastened with a chain to the bank. You proceed link by link, holding to the chain, and you dive into the water and follow the chain. Finally you are able to reach the timber. In the same way, by repeating God's name you become absorbed in Him and finally realize Him."

KALIPADA (*smiling, to the devotees*): "Ours is a grand teacher! We are not asked to practise meditation, austerity, and other disciplines."

Suddenly Sri Ramakrishna said, "This is troubling me." The Master's throat was hurting him. Devendra said, "Your words cannot fool us any more." He thought that the Master feigned illness to hoodwink the devotees.

Most of the devotees departed. It was arranged that a few of the younger men should stay to nurse the Master by turns. M. also was going to spend the night there.

Sunday, October 25, 1885

It was about half past six in the morning when M. arrived at Śyāmpukur and asked Sri Ramakrishna about his health. He was on his way to Dr. Sarkar to report the Master's condition. The Master said to M.: "Tell the doctor that during the early hours of the morning my mouth becomes filled with water and I cough. Also ask him if I may take a bath."

After seven o'clock M. came to Dr. Sarkar's house and told him about the Master's condition. The physician's old teacher and one or two friends were in the room. Dr. Sarkar said to his teacher, "Sir, I have been thinking of the Paramahamsa[5] since three in the morning. I couldn't sleep at all. Even now he is in my mind."

One of the doctor's friends said to him: "Sir, I hear that some speak of the Paramahamsa as an Incarnation of God. You see him every day. How do you feel about it?"

DOCTOR: "I have the greatest regard for him as a man."

M. (*to the doctor's friend*): "It is very kind of Dr. Sarkar to treat him."

DOCTOR. "Kindness? What do you mean?"

M: "Not toward him, but toward us."

DOCTOR: "You see, you don't know my actual loss on account of the Paramahamsa. Every day I fail to see two or three patients. When the next day I go to their houses, of my own accord, I cannot accept any fee since I am seeing them without being called. How can I charge them for my visit?"

The conversation turned to Mahima Chakravarty. He had been with the Master when Dr. Sarkar had visited him the previous Saturday. Pointing to the doctor, Mahima had said to Sri Ramakrishna, "Sir, you yourself have created this disease in order to pamper the doctor's pride."

M. (*to the doctor*): "Mahima Chakravarty used to come to your place to attend your lectures on medical science."

DOCTOR: "Is that so? How full of tamas he is! Didn't you notice it? I saluted him as 'God's Lower Third'. There exist in God sattva, rajas, and tamas. Tamas is the third and an inferior quality. Didn't you hear him say

[5] Referring to Sri Ramakrishna.

to the Paramahamsa, 'You yourself have created this disease in order to pamper the doctor's pride'?"

M: "Mahima Chakravarty believes that the Paramahamsa can cure his disease himself, if he wants to."

DOCTOR: "What? Cure that disease himself? Is that possible? We are physicians; we know what cancer is. We ourselves cannot cure it. And he to cure himself! Why, he doesn't know anything about cancer. (*To his friends*) The illness is no doubt incurable, but these gentlemen have been nursing him with sincere devotion."

M. requested the doctor to visit Sri Ramakrishna and returned home.

In the afternoon, about three o'clock, M. came to the Master and repeated the conversation he had had with Dr. Sarkar. He said to Sri Ramakrishna, "Today the doctor embarrassed me."

MASTER: "What happened?"

M: "Yesterday he heard here that you yourself had created this illness in order to pamper the doctor's pride."

MASTER: "Who made that remark?"

M: "Mahima Chakravarty."

MASTER: "What did the doctor say to you?"

M: "He described Mahima Chakravarty as 'God's Lower Third'. Now he admits that all the qualities—sattva, rajas, and tamas—exist in God. (*The Master laughs.*) Then he told me that he had waked at three in the morning and had been thinking of you ever since. When I saw him it was eight o'clock. He said to me, 'Even now the Paramahamsa is in my mind.'"

MASTER (*laughing*): "You see, he has studied English. I cannot ask him to meditate on me; but he is doing it all the same, of his own accord."

M: "He also said about you, 'I have the greatest regard for him as a man.'"

MASTER: "Did you talk of anything else?"

M: "I asked him, 'What is your suggestion today about the patient?' He said: 'Suggestion? Hang it! I shall have to go to him again myself. What else shall I suggest?' (*Sri Ramakrishna laughs.*) Further he said: 'You don't know how much money I am losing every day. Every day I miss two or three calls.'"

There were many devotees, including Narendranath, in the room. Vijaykrishna Goswami arrived and respectfully took the dust of the Master's feet. Several Brāhmo devotees came with him. Vijay had cut off his connection with the Brāhmo Samāj and was practising spiritual discipline independently. Sri Ramakrishna was very fond of him on account of his piety and devotion. Though not a disciple of the Master, Vijay held him in very high respect. He had lived in Dacca a long time. Recently he had visited many sacred places in upper India.

MAHIMA CHAKRAVARTY (*to Vijay*): "Sir, you have visited many holy places and new countries. Please tell us some of your experiences."

VIJAY: "What shall I say? I realize that everything is here where we are sitting now. This roaming about is useless. At other places I have seen two, five, ten, or twenty-five per cent of him [meaning the Master], at the most. Here alone I find the full one hundred per cent manifestation of God."

MAHIMA: "You are right, sir. Again, it is he [the Master] who makes us roam about or remain in one place."

MASTER (*to Narendra*): "See what a change has come over Vijay's mind. He is an altogether different person. He is like thick milk from which all the water has been boiled off. You see, I can recognize a paramahamsa by his neck and forehead. Yes, I can recognize a paramahamsa."

MAHIMA (*to Vijay*): "Sir, you seem to eat less now. Isn't that so?"

VIJAY: "Perhaps you are right. (*To the Master*) I heard about your illness and have come to see you. Again, in Dacca—"

MASTER: "What about Dacca?"

Vijay did not reply and was silent a few moments.

VIJAY: "It is difficult to understand him [meaning the Master] unless he reveals himself. Here alone is the one hundred per cent manifestation of God."

MASTER: "Kedar said the other day, 'At other places we don't get anything to eat, but here we get a stomachful!'"

MAHIMA: "Why a stomachful? It overflows the stomach."

VIJAY (*to the Master, with folded hands*): "I have now realized who you are. You don't have to tell me."

MASTER (*in a state of ecstasy*): "If so, then so be it!"

Saying, "Yes, I have understood", Vijay fell prostrate before the Master. He held the Master's feet on his chest and clung to them. The Master was in deep samādhi, motionless as a picture. The devotees were overwhelmed by this sight. Some burst into tears and some chanted sacred hymns. All eyes were riveted on Sri Ramakrishna. They viewed him in different ways, according to their spiritual unfoldment: some as a great devotee, some as a holy man, some as God Incarnate.

Mahimacharan sang, with tears in his eyes: "Behold, behold the embodiment of Love Divine!"

Now and then he chanted, as if enjoying a glimpse of Brahman:

> The Transcendental, beyond the One and the many, Existence-
> Knowledge-Bliss Absolute.

Navagopal was weeping. Bhupati sang:

> Hallowed be Brahman, the Absolute, the Infinite, the Fathomless!
> Higher than the highest, deeper than the deepest depths!
> Thou art the Light of Truth, the Fount of Love, the Home of
> Bliss!
> This universe with all its manifold and blessed modes
> Is but the enchanting poem of Thine inexhaustible thought;
> Its beauty overflows on every side.
>
> O Thou Poet, great and primal, in the rhythm of Thy thought
> The sun and moon arise and move toward their setting;
> The stars, shining like bits of gems, are the fair characters
> In which Thy song is written across the blue expanse of sky;

The year, with its six seasons, in tune with the happy earth,
Proclaims Thy glory to the end of time.

The colours of the flowers reveal Thy sovereign Beauty,
The waters in their stillness, Thy deep Serenity;
The thunder-clap unveils to us the terror of Thy Law.
Deep is Thine Essence, truly; how can a foolish mind perceive it?

Wondering, it meditates on Thee from yuga to yuga's end;
Millions upon millions of suns and moons and stars
Bow down to Thee, O Lord, in rapturous awe!

Beholding Thy creation, men and women weep for joy;
The gods and angels worship Thee, O All-pervading Presence!
O Thou, the Fount of Goodness, bestow on us Thy Knowledge;
Bestow on us devotion, bestow pure love and perfect peace;
And grant us shelter at Thy hallowed feet!

Bhupati sang again:

Upon the Sea of Blissful Awareness waves of ecstatic love arise:
Rapture divine! Play of God's Bliss!
Oh, how enthralling! . . .

He sang a third song:

Here vanish my fear and my delusion, my piety, rituals, and good
　　works;
Here vanish my pride of race and caste! Where am I? Where art
　　Thou, O Hari?
Thou hast stolen my life and soul, and now, O Friend, Thou dost
　　desert me:
Ah, what a fool I was to come here to the shore of this Sea of Love!
Full to the brim with heavenly bliss is filled this little soul of mine;
Premdās says: Hearken, one and all! This in truth is the way of
　　God!

After a long time Sri Ramakrishna regained consciousness of the world.

MASTER (to M.): "Something happens to me in that state of intoxication.
Now I feel ashamed of myself. In that state I feel as if I were possessed by
a ghost. I cease to be my own self. While coming down from that state I
cannot count correctly. Trying to count, I say, 'One, seven, eight', or some
such thing."

NARENDRA: "It is because everything is one."

MASTER: "No, it is beyond one and two."

MAHIMA: "Yes, you are right. 'It is neither one nor two.'"

MASTER: "There reason withers away. God cannot be realized through
scholarship. He is beyond the scriptures—the Vedas, Purānas, and Tantras.
If I see a man with even one book in his hand, I call him a rājarshi,[6] though
he is a jnāni. But the brahmarshi[7] has no outer sign whatsoever.

"Do you know the use of the scriptures? A man once wrote a letter to a
relative, asking him to send five seers of sweetmeats and a piece of cloth.

[6] A rishi, or seer, who appears with outer splendour, like a king.
[7] A seer who always dwells in Brahman-Consciousness.

The relative received the letter, read it, and remembered about the sweet-meats and the cloth. Then he threw the letter away. Of what further use was it?"

VIJAY: "I see that the sweetmeat has been sent."

MASTER: "God incarnates Himself on earth in a human body. He is, no doubt, present everywhere and in all beings, but man's longing is not satisfied unless he sees God in a human form. Man's need is not satisfied without the Divine Incarnation. Do you know what it is like? By touching any part of a cow you undoubtedly touch the cow herself. Even by touching her horns you touch the cow. But the milk comes through the cow's udder."

MAHIMA: "If a man wants milk he must put his mouth to the udder. What will he get by sucking the horns?" (*All laugh.*)

VIJAY: "But a calf at first licks other parts of the cow."

MASTER (*smiling*): "True. But seeing the calf doing so, someone perhaps puts its mouth to the udder." (*All laugh.*)

The conversation was thus going on, when Dr. Sarkar came into the room and took a seat. He said to the Master: "I woke up at three this morning, greatly worried that you might catch cold. Oh, I thought many other things about you."

MASTER: "I have been coughing and my throat is sore. In the small hours of the morning my mouth was filled with water. My whole body is aching."

DOCTOR: "Yes, I heard all about it this morning."

Mahimacharan told of his trip to various parts of the country and said that in Ceylon no man laughed. Dr. Sarkar said, "It may be so; but I shall have to inquire about it." (*All laugh.*)

The conversation turned to the duties of life.

MASTER (*to the doctor*): "Many think that the duty of a physician is a very noble one. The physician is undoubtedly a noble man if he treats his patients free, out of compassion and moved by their suffering. Then his work may be called very uplifting. But a physician becomes cruel and callous if he carries on his profession for money. It is very mean to do such things as examine urine and stool in order to earn money, like a business man carrying on his trade."

DOCTOR: "You are right. It is undoubtedly wrong for a physician to perform his duties in that spirit. But I don't like to brag before you—"

MASTER: "But the medical profession is certainly very noble if the physician devotes himself to the welfare of others in an unselfish spirit.

"Whatever may be a householder's profession, it is necessary for him to live in the company of holy men now and then. If a man loves God, he will himself seek the company of holy men. I give the illustration of the hemp-smoker. One hemp-smoker loves the company of another hemp-smoker. At the sight of a person who does not smoke, he goes away with downcast eyes or hides himself in a corner; but his joy is unbounded if he meets a hemp addict. Perhaps they embrace each other. (*All laugh.*) Again, a vulture loves the company of another vulture."

DOCTOR: "It has also been noticed that a vulture runs away for fear of a crow. In my opinion one should serve all creatures, not men alone. Often I feed the sparrows with flour. I throw small pellets of flour to them and they come in swarms. They love to eat them."

MASTER: "Bravo! That's grand. Holy men should feed other creatures. They feed ants with sugar."

DOCTOR: "Will there be no singing today?"

MASTER (to Narendra): "Why don't you sing a little?"

Narendra sang to the accompaniment of the tānpurā and other instruments:

> Sweet is Thy name, O Refuge of the humble!
> It falls like sweetest nectar on our ears
> And comforts us, Beloved of our souls!
> The priceless treasure of Thy name alone
> Is the abode of Immortality,
> And he who chants Thy name becomes immortal.
> Falling upon our ears, Thy holy name
> Instantly slays the anguish of our hearts,
> Thou Soul of our souls, and fills our hearts with bliss!

Narendra sang again:

> O Mother, make me mad with Thy love!
> What need have I of knowledge or reason?
> Make me drunk with Thy love's Wine;
> O Thou who stealest Thy bhaktas' hearts,
> Drown me deep in the Sea of Thy love!
> Here in this world, this madhouse of Thine,
> Some laugh, some weep, some dance for joy:
> Jesus, Buddha, Moses, Gaurānga,
> All are drunk with the Wine of Thy love.
> O Mother, when shall I be blessed
> By joining their blissful company?

A strange transformation came over the devotees. They all became mad, as it were, with divine ecstasy. The pundit stood up, forgetting the pride of his scholarship, and cried:

> O Mother, make me mad with Thy love!
> What need have I of knowledge or reason?

Vijay was the first on his feet, carried away by divine intoxication. Then Sri Ramakrishna stood up, forgetting all about his painful and fatal illness. The doctor, who had been sitting in front of him, also stood up. Both patient and physician forgot themselves in the spell created by Narendra's music. The younger Naren and Latu went into deep samādhi. The atmosphere of the room became electric. Everyone felt the presence of God. Dr. Sarkar, eminent scientist that he was, stood breathless, watching this strange scene. He noticed that the devotees who had gone into samādhi were utterly unconscious of the outer world. All were motionless and transfixed. After a while, as they came down a little to the plane of the relative world, some laughed and some wept. An outsider, entering the room, would have thought that a number of drunkards were assembled there.

A little later Sri Ramakrishna resumed his conversation, the devotees taking their seats. It was about eight o'clock in the evening.

MASTER: "You have just noticed the effect of divine ecstasy. What does your 'science' say about that? Do you think it is a mere hoax?"

DOCTOR (*to the Master*): "I must say that this is all natural, when so many people have experienced it. It cannot be a hoax. (*To Narendra*) When you sang the lines:

> O Mother, make me mad with Thy love!
> What need have I of knowledge or reason?

I could hardly control myself. I was about to jump to my feet. With great difficulty I suppressed my emotion. I said to myself, 'No, I must not display my feelings.'"

MASTER (*with a smile, to the doctor*): "You are unshakable and motionless, like Mount Sumeru. You are a very deep soul. Nobody could perceive the deep emotion of Rupa and Sanātana. If an elephant enters a small pool, there is a splashing of water on all sides. But this does not happen when it plunges into a big lake; hardly anyone notices it. Rādhā once said to her companion: 'Friend, you are weeping so much at our separation from Sri Krishna. But look at me. How stony my heart is! There is not a tear in my eyes.' Brindē, her friend, replied: 'Yes, your eyes are dry. But there is a deep meaning in it. A fire of grief is constantly raging in your heart because of your separation from Krishna. No sooner do the tears gather in your eyes than they are dried up in the heat of that fire.'"

DOCTOR: "Nobody can beat you in talk!" (*Laughter.*)

The conversation turned to other things. Sri Ramakrishna described to the doctor his ecstasies at Dakshineswar. He also told him how to control anger, lust, and the other passions.

DOCTOR: "I have heard the story that you were once lying on the ground unconscious in samādhi when a wicked man kicked you with his boots."

MASTER: "You must have heard it from M. The man was Chandra Haldar, a priest of the Kāli temple at Kālighāt; he often came to Mathur Babu's house. One day I was lying on the ground in an ecstatic mood. The room was dark. Chandra Haldar thought I was feigning that state in order to win Mathur's favour. He entered the room and kicked me several times with his boots. It left black marks on my body. Everybody wanted to tell Mathur Babu about it, but I forbade them."

DOCTOR: "This is also due to the will of God. Thus you have taught people how to control anger and practise forgiveness."

In the mean time Vijay had become engaged in conversation with the other devotees.

VIJAY: "I feel as if someone were always moving with me. He shows me what is happening even at a distance."

NARENDRA: "Like a guardian angel."

VIJAY: "I have seen him [meaning the Master] in Dacca. I even touched his body."

MASTER (*with a smile*): "It must have been someone else."

NARENDRA: "I too have seen him many a time. (*To Vijay*) How can I say I do not believe your words?"

THE MASTER'S TRAINING OF HIS
DISCIPLES

Monday, October 26, 1885

IT WAS ABOUT TEN O'CLOCK in the morning when M. arrived at the Śyāmpukur house on his way to Dr. Sarkar to report the Master's condition.

Dr. Sarkar had declared the illness incurable. His words cast gloom over the minds of the Master's devotees and disciples. With unflagging devotion and zeal they nursed the patient—their teacher, guide, philosopher, and friend. A band of young disciples, led by Narendra, was preparing to renounce the world and dedicate their lives to the realization of God and the service of humanity. People flocked to the Master day and night. In spite of the excruciating pain in his throat, he welcomed them all with a cheerful face. There seemed to be no limit to his solicitude for their welfare. His face beamed as he talked to them about God. Dr. Sarkar, seeing that conversation aggravated the illness, forbade him to talk to people. "You must not talk to others," the physician had said to the Master, "but you may make an exception in my case." The doctor used to spend six or seven hours in Sri Ramakrishna's company, drinking in every word that fell from his lips.

MASTER: "I am feeling much relieved. I am very well today. Is it because of the medicine? Then why shouldn't I continue it?"

M: "I am going to the doctor. I shall tell him everything. He will advise what is best."

MASTER: "I haven't seen Purna for two or three days. I am worried about him."

M. (*to Kali*): "Why don't you see Purna and ask him to come?"

KALI: "I shall go immediately."

MASTER (*to M.*): "The doctor's son is a nice boy. Please ask him to come."

M. arrived at Dr. Sarkar's house and found him with two or three friends.

DOCTOR (*to M.*): "I was talking about you just a minute ago. You said you would come at ten; I have been waiting for you an hour and a half. Your delay has made me worry about him [meaning Sri Ramakrishna]."

(*To a friend*) "Please sing that song."

886

The friend sang:

> Proclaim the glory of God's name as long as life remains in you;
> The dazzling splendour of His radiance floods the universe!
> Like nectar streams His boundless love, filling the hearts of men
>   with joy:
> The very thought of His compassion sends a thrill through every
>   limb!
> How can one fittingly describe Him? Through His abounding
>   grace
> The bitter sorrows of this life are all forgotten instantly.
>
> On every side—on land below, in sky above, beneath the seas:
> In every region of this earth—men seek Him tirelessly,
> And as they seek Him, ever ask: Where is His limit, where His
>   end?
> True Wisdom's Dwelling-place is He, the Elixir of Eternal Life,
> The Sleepless, Ever-wakeful Eye, the Pure and Stainless One:
> The vision of His face removes all trace of sorrow from our hearts.

DOCTOR (*to M.*): "Isn't it a beautiful song? How do you like that line, 'Where is His limit, where His end?' "

M: "Yes, that's a very fine line. It fills the mind with the idea of the Infinite."

DOCTOR (*tenderly, to M.*): "It is already late in the morning. Have you taken your lunch? I finish mine before ten and then begin my professional calls; otherwise I don't feel well. Look here, I have been thinking of giving a feast to you all [meaning Sri Ramakrishna's devotees] one day."

M: "That will be fine, sir."

DOCTOR: "Where shall I arrange it? Here or at the Śyāmpukur house? Whatever you suggest."

M: "It doesn't matter, sir. Wherever you arrange it we shall be very happy to dine with you."

The conversation turned to Kāli, the Divine Mother.

DOCTOR: "Kāli is an old hag of the Sonthāls."

M. burst into loud laughter and said, "Where did you get that?"

DOCTOR: "Oh, I have heard something like that." (*M. laughs.*)

They began to talk about the ecstasy that Vijay and the others had experienced the previous day in the Master's room. The doctor also had been present on the occasion.

DOCTOR: "Yes, I witnessed that ecstasy. But is excessive ecstasy good for one?"

M: "The Master says that an excess of ecstasy harms no one, if it is the result of the contemplation of God. He further says that the lustre of a gem gives light and soothes the body; it does not burn."

DOCTOR: "Oh, the lustre of a gem! That's only a reflected light."

M: "He also says that a man does not die by sinking in the Lake of Immortality. God is that Lake. A plunge in that Lake does not injure a man; on the contrary it makes him immortal. Of course, he will become immortal only if he has faith in God."

DOCTOR: "Yes, that is true."

The doctor took M. in his carriage. He had to see a few patients on the way to Syāmpukur. They continued their conversation in the carriage. Dr. Sarkar referred to Mahima Chakravarty's pride.

M: "He visits the Master. Even if he has a little pride, it will not last long. If one only sits in the Master's presence awhile, one's pride crumbles to pieces. It is because the Master himself is totally free from egotism. Pride cannot exist in the presence of humility. A celebrated man like Pundit Iswar Chandra Vidyāsāgar showed great modesty and humility in the Master's presence. The Paramahamsa visited his house; it was nine o'clock in the evening when the Master took his leave. Vidyāsāgar came all the way from the library to the gate of his compound to see him off. He himself carried the light to show the way. As the Master's carriage started off, Vidyāsāgar stood there with folded hands."

DOCTOR: "Well, what does Vidyāsāgar think of him?"

M: "That day he showed the Master great respect. But when I talked with him later, I found out that he didn't much care for what the Vaishnavas call emotion or ecstasy. He shares your views on such things."

DOCTOR: "Neither do I care very much for any such display of emotion as folding one's hands or touching others' feet with one's head. To me the head is the same as the feet. But if a man thinks differently of the feet, let him do whatever he likes."

M: "We know that you do not care for a display of feelings. Perhaps you remember that the Master now and then refers to you as a 'deep soul'. He said to you yesterday that when an elephant plunges into a small pool it makes a big splash, but when it goes into a big lake you see hardly a ripple. The elephant of emotion cannot produce any effect at all in a deep soul. The Master says that you are a 'deep soul'."

DOCTOR: "I don't deserve the compliment. After all, what is bhāva? It is only a feeling. There are other aspects of feeling, such as bhakti. When it runs to excess, some can suppress it and some cannot."

M: "Divine ecstasy may or may not be explainable; but, sir, it cannot be denied that ecstasy, or love of God, is a unique thing. I have seen in your library Stebbing's book on Darwinism. According to Stebbing the human mind is wonderful, whether it be the result of evolution or of special creation. He gives a beautiful illustration from the theory of light. Light is wonderful, whether you know the wave theory of light or not."

DOCTOR: "Yes. Have you noticed further that Stebbing accepts both Darwin and God?"

The conversation again turned to Sri Ramakrishna.

DOCTOR: "I find that he is a worshipper of the Goddess Kāli."

M: "But with him the meaning of Kāli is different. What the Vedas call the Supreme Brahman, he calls Kāli. What the Mussalmāns call Allāh and the Christians call God, he calls Kāli. He does not see many gods; he sees only one God. What the Brahmajnānis of olden times called Brahman, what the yogis call Ātman and the bhaktas call the Bhagavān, he calls Kāli.

"In Sri Ramakrishna one finds all the attitudes and ideals of religion. That is why people of all sects and creeds enjoy peace and blessedness in his presence. Who can fathom his feeling and tell us the depth of his inner experience?"

DOCTOR: " 'All things to all men.' I don't approve of it although St. Paul says it."

M: "Who can understand the state of his mind? We have heard from him that unless one is engaged in the yarn trade, one cannot tell the difference between number forty and number forty-one yarn. Only a painter can appreciate another painter. The mind of a saint is very deep. One cannot understand all the aspects of Christ unless one is Christlike. Perhaps the deep realization of the Master is what Christ meant when He said: 'Be ye perfect as your Father in Heaven is perfect.' "

DOCTOR: "What arrangements have you made about having him nursed?"

M: "At present one of the older devotees is assigned every day to look after him. It may be Girish Babu or Ram Babu or Balaram or Suresh Babu or Navagopal or Kali Babu. It is that way."

It was about one o'clock in the afternoon when the doctor and M. entered the Master's room on the second floor. Sri Ramakrishna sat there, smiling as usual, completely forgetful of the fatal illness which was eating his life away. Among the many devotees in the room were Girish, the younger Naren, and Sarat. Sometimes they were motionless, like the snake before its charmer, and sometimes they displayed great joy, like the bridal party with the bridegroom. The doctor and M. bowed low before the Master and sat on the floor. At the sight of the doctor, the Master said, laughing, "Today I have been feeling very well."

Then the Master went on with his soul-enthralling conversation.

MASTER: "What will mere scholarship accomplish without discrimination and renunciation? I go into a strange mood while thinking of the Lotus Feet of God. The cloth on my body drops to the ground and I feel something creeping up from my feet to the top of my head. In that state I regard all as mere straw. If I see a pundit without discrimination and love of God, I regard him as a bit of straw.

"One day Dr. Ramnarayan had been arguing with me, when suddenly I went into that mood. I said to him: 'What are you saying? What can you understand of God by reasoning? How little you can understand of His creation! Shame! You have the pettifogging mind of a weaver!' Seeing the state of my mind he began to weep and gently stroked my feet."

DOCTOR: "Ramnarayan did that because he is a Hindu. Besides, he is a believer in flowers and sandal-paste. He is an orthodox Hindu."

M. (to himself): "Dr. Sarkar says that he has nothing to do with gong and conch-shells!"[1]

MASTER: "Bankim[2] is one of your pundits. I met him once. I asked him, 'What is the duty of man?' And he had the impudence to say, 'Eating, sleeping, and sex gratification.' These words created in me a feeling of great

[1] These are used by the Hindus in the temple for worshipping the Deity.
[2] Bankim Chandra Chatterji, the celebrated writer of Bengal.

aversion. I said: 'What are you saying? You are very mean. What you think day and night and what you do all the time come out through your lips. If a man eats radish, he belches radish.' Then we talked about God a great deal. There was also much devotional music in the room, and I danced. Then Bankim said to me, 'Sir, please come to our house once.' 'That depends on the will of God', I replied. 'There also', he said, 'you will find devotees of God.' I laughed and said: 'What kind of devotees are they? Are they like those who said, "Gopal! Gopal!"?' "

DOCTOR: "What is the story of 'Gopal! Gopal!'?"

MASTER (*with a smile*): "There was a goldsmith who kept a jewelry shop. He looked like a great devotee, a true Vaishnava, with beads around his neck, rosary in his hand, and the holy marks on his forehead. Naturally people trusted him and came to his shop on business. They thought that, being such a pious man, he would never cheat them. Whenever a party of customers entered the shop, they would hear one of his craftsmen say, 'Kesava! Kesava!' Another would say, after a while, 'Gopal! Gopal!' Then a third would mutter, 'Hari! Hari!' Finally someone would say, 'Hara! Hara!' Now these are, as you know, different names of God. Hearing so much chanting of God's names, the customers naturally thought that this gold-smith must be a very superior person. But can you guess the goldsmith's true intention? The man who said 'Kesava! Kesava!'[3] meant to ask, '*Who are these?*—who are these customers?' The man who said 'Gopal! Gopal!' con-veyed the idea that the customers were merely *a herd of cows*. That was the estimate he formed of them after the exchange of a few words. The man who said 'Hari! Hari!' asked, '*Since they are no better than a herd of cows, then may we rob them?*' He who said 'Hara! Hara!' gave his assent, mean-ing by these words, '*Do rob by all means, since they are mere cows!*' (*All laugh.*)

"Once I went to a certain place with Mathur Babu. Many pundits came forward to argue with me. And you all know that I am a fool. (*All laugh.*) The pundits saw that strange mood of mine. When the conversation was over, they said to me: 'Sir, after hearing your words, all that we have studied before, our knowledge and scholarship, has proved to be mere spittle. Now we realize that a man does not lack wisdom if he has the grace of God. The fool becomes wise and the mute eloquent.' Therefore I say that a man does not become a scholar by the mere study of books.

"Yes, how true it is! How can a man who has the grace of God lack knowledge? Look at me. I am a fool. I do not know anything. Then who is it that utters these words? The reservoir of the Knowledge of God is inex-haustible. There are grain-dealers at Kāmārpukur. When selling paddy, one man weighs the grain on the scales and another man pushes it to him from a heap. It is the duty of the second man to keep a constant supply of grain on the scales by pushing it from the big heap. It is the same with my words. No sooner are they about to run short than the Divine Mother sends a new supply from Her inexhaustible storehouse of Knowledge.

[3] These names of God have a double meaning in Bengali. The second meaning of each word is given in italics.

"During my boyhood God manifested Himself in me. I was then eleven years old. One day, while I was walking across a paddy-field, I saw something. Later on I came to know from people that I had been unconscious, and my body totally motionless. Since that day I have been an altogether different man. I began to see another person within me. When I used to conduct the worship in the temple, my hand, instead of going toward the Deity, would very often come toward my head, and I would put flowers there. A young man who was then staying with me did not dare approach me. He would say: 'I see a light on your face. I am afraid to come very near you.'

"You know I am a fool. I know nothing. Then who is it that says all these things? I say to the Divine Mother: 'O Mother, I am the machine and Thou art the Operator. I am the house and Thou art the Indweller. I am the chariot and Thou art the Charioteer. I do as Thou makest me do; I speak as Thou makest me speak; I move as Thou makest me move. It is not I! It is not I! It is all Thou! It is all Thou!' Hers is the glory; we are only Her instruments. Once Rādhā, to prove her chastity, carried on her head a pitcher filled with water. The pitcher had a thousand holes, but not a drop of water spilled. People began to praise her, saying, 'Such a chaste woman the world will never see again!' Then Rādhā said to them: 'Why do you praise me? Say: "Glory unto Krishna! Hail Krishna!" I am only His handmaid.'

"Once in that strange mood of mine I placed my foot on Vijay's chest. You know how greatly I respect him—and I placed my foot on his body! What do you say to that?"

DOCTOR: "But now you should be careful."

MASTER (with folded hands): "What can I do? I become completely unconscious in that mood. Then I do not know at all what I am doing."

DOCTOR: "You should be careful. No use folding your hands now and expressing regret!"

MASTER: "Can I do anything *myself* in that mood? What do you think of this state? If you think it is a hoax, then I should say that your study of 'science' and all that is bosh!"

DOCTOR: "Now listen, sir! Would I come to see you so often if I thought it all a hoax? You know that I neglect many other duties in order to come here. I cannot visit many patients, for I spend six or seven hours at a stretch here."

MASTER: "Once I said to Mathur Babu: 'Don't think that I have achieved my desired end because you, a rich man, show me respect. It matters very little to me whether you obey me or not.' Of course you must remember that a mere man can do nothing. It is God alone who makes one person obey another. Man is straw and dust before the power of God."

DOCTOR: "Do you think I shall obey you because a certain fisherman[4] obeyed you? . . . Undoubtedly I show you respect; I show you respect as a man."

MASTER: "Do I ask you to show me respect?"

[4] Alluding to Mathur Babu, who belonged to the low caste of the fishermen.

GIRISH: "Does he ask you to show him respect?"

DOCTOR (to the Master): "What are you saying? Do you explain it as the will of God?"

MASTER: "What else can it be? What can a man do before the will of God? Arjuna said to Sri Krishna on the battle-field of Kurukshetra: 'I will not fight. It is impossible for me to kill my own kinsmen.' Sri Krishna replied: 'Arjuna, you will have to fight. Your very nature will make you fight.' Then Sri Krishna revealed to Arjuna that all the men on the battle-field were already dead.[5]

"Once some Sikhs came to the Kāli temple at Dakshineswar. They said: 'You see, the leaves of the aśwattha tree are moving. That too is due to the will of God.' Without His will not even a leaf can move."

DOCTOR: "If everything is done by the will of God, then why do you chatter? Why do you talk so much to bring knowledge to others?"

MASTER: "He makes me talk; therefore I talk. 'I am the machine and He is the Operator.'"

DOCTOR: "You say that you are the machine. That's all right. Or keep quiet, knowing that everything is God."

GIRISH (to the doctor): "Whatever you may think, sir, the truth is that we act because He makes us act. Can anyone take a single step against the Almighty Will?"

DOCTOR: "But God has also given us free will. I can think of God, or not, as I like."

GIRISH: "You think of God or do some good work because you like to. Really it is not you who do these things, but your liking of them that makes you do so."

DOCTOR: "Why should that be so? I do these things as my duty."

GIRISH: "Even then it is because you like to do your duty."

DOCTOR: "Suppose a child is being burnt. From a sense of duty I rush to save it."

GIRISH: "You feel happy to save the child; therefore you rush into the fire. It is your happiness that drives you to the action. A man eats opium being tempted by such relishes as puffed rice or fried potatoes." (Laughter.)

MASTER: "A man must have some kind of faith before he undertakes a work. Further, he feels joy when he thinks of it. Only then does he set about performing the work. Suppose a jar of gold coins is hidden underground. First of all a man must have faith that the jar of gold coins is there. He feels joy at the thought of the jar. Then he begins to dig. As he removes the earth he hears a metallic sound. That increases his joy. Next he sees a corner of the jar. That gives him more joy. Thus his joy is ever on the increase. Standing on the porch of the Kāli temple, I have watched the ascetics preparing their smoke of hemp. I have seen their faces beaming with joy in anticipation of the smoke."

DOCTOR: "But take the case of fire. It gives both heat and light. The light no doubt illumines objects, but the heat burns the body. Likewise, it is not

[5] Reference to the eleventh chapter of the Gītā.

an unadulterated joy that one reaps from the performance of duty. Duty has its painful side too."

M. (*to Girish*): "As the proverb goes: 'If the stomach gets food, then the back can bear a few blows from the host.' There is joy in sorrow also."

GIRISH (*to the doctor*): "Duty is dry."

DOCTOR: "Why so?"

GIRISH: "Then it is pleasant." (*All laugh.*)

M.: "Again we come to the point that one likes opium for the sake of the relishes that are served with it."

GIRISH (*to the doctor*): "Duty must be pleasant; or why do you perform it?"

DOCTOR: "The mind is inclined that way."

M. (*to Girish*): "That wretched inclination draws the mind. If you speak of the compelling power of inclination, then where is free will?"

DOCTOR: "I do not say that the will is absolutely free. Suppose a cow is tied with a rope. She is free within the length of that rope. But when she feels the pull of the rope—"

MASTER: "Jadu Mallick also gave that illustration. (*To the younger Naren*) Is it mentioned in some English book?

(*To the doctor*) "Look here. If a man truly believes that God alone does everything, that He is the Operator and man the machine, then such a man is verily liberated in life. 'Thou workest Thine own work; men only call it theirs.' Do you know what it is like? Vedānta philosophy gives an illustration. Suppose you are cooking rice in a pot, with potato, egg-plant, and other vegetables. After a while the potatoes, egg-plant, rice, and the rest begin to jump about in the pot. They seem to say with pride: 'We are moving! We are jumping!' The children see it and think the potatoes, egg-plant, and rice are alive and so they jump that way. But the elders, who know, explain to the children that the vegetables and the rice are not alive; they jump not of themselves, but because of the fire under the pot; if you remove the burning wood from the hearth, then they will move no more. Likewise the pride of man, that he is the doer, springs from ignorance. Men are powerful because of the power of God. All becomes quiet when that burning wood is taken away. The puppets dance well on the stage when pulled by a wire, but they cannot move when the wire snaps.

"A man will cherish the illusion that he is the doer as long as he has not seen God, as long as he has not touched the Philosopher's Stone. So long will he know the distinction between his good and bad actions. This awareness of distinction is due to God's māyā; and it is necessary for the purpose of running His illusory world. But a man can realize God if he takes shelter under His vidyāmāyā and follows the path of righteousness. He who knows God and realizes Him is able to go beyond māyā. He who firmly believes that God alone is the Doer and he himself a mere instrument is a jīvanmukta, a free soul though living in a body. I said this to Keshab Chandra Sen."

GIRISH (*to the doctor*): "How do you know that free will exists?"

DOCTOR: "Not by reasoning; I feel it."

GIRISH: "In that case I may say that I and others feel the reverse. We feel that we are controlled by another." (*All laugh.*)

DOCTOR: "There are two elements in duty: first, the 'oughtness' of a duty; second, the happiness, which comes as an after-effect. But at the initial stage this happiness is not the impelling motive. I noticed in my childhood the great worry of the priest at the sight of ants in the sweets offered before the Deity. He did not, at the outset, feel joy at the thought of the sweets. First of all he worried about them."

M. (*to himself*): "It is difficult to say whether one feels happiness while performing the duty or afterwards. Where is the free will of a man if he performs an action, being impelled by a feeling of happiness?"

MASTER: "What the doctor is speaking of is called love without any selfish motive. I do not want anything from Dr. Mahendra Sarkar; I do not need anything from him, but still I love to see him. This is love for love's sake. But suppose I get a little joy from it; how can I help it?

"Ahalyā once said to Rāma: 'O Rāma, I have no objection to being born even as a pig. But please grant that I may have pure love for Thy Lotus Feet. I do not want anything else.'

"Nārada went to Ayodhyā to remind Rāma that He was to kill Rāvana. At the sight of Rāma and Sītā, he began to sing their glories. Gratified at Nārada's devotion, Rāma said: 'Nārada, I am pleased with your prayer. Ask a boon.' Nārada replied, 'O Rāma, if Thou must give me a boon, then grant that I may have pure love for Thy Lotus Feet and that I may not be deluded by Thy world-bewitching māyā.' Rāma said, 'Ask something more.' 'No, Rāma,' answered Nārada, 'I do not want anything else. I want only pure love for Thy Lotus Feet, a love that seeks no return.'

"That is Dr. Sarkar's attitude. It is like seeking God alone, and not asking Him for wealth, fame, bodily comforts, or anything else. This is called pure love.

"There is an element of joy in it, no doubt; but it is not a worldly joy; it is the joy of bhakti and prema, devotion to God and ecstatic love of Him. I used to go to Sambhu Mallick's house. Once he said to me: 'You come here frequently. Yes, you come because you feel happy talking with me.' Yes, there is that element of happiness.

"But there is a state higher than this. When a man attains it, he moves about aimlessly, like a child. As the child goes along, perhaps he sees a grass-hopper and catches it. The man of that exalted mood, too, has no definite aim.

(*To the devotees*) "Don't you understand the doctor's inner feeling? It is the prayer of a devotee to God for right purpose, that he may have no inclination for evil things.

"I too passed through that state. It is called dāsya, the attitude of the servant toward his master. I used to weep so bitterly with the name of the Divine Mother on my lips that people would stand in a row watching me. When I was passing through that state, someone, in order to test me and also to cure my madness, brought a prostitute into my room. She was beautiful to look at, with pretty eyes. I cried, 'O Mother! O Mother!' and rushed out of the room. I ran to Haladhari and said to him, 'Brother, come and see who has entered my room!' I told Haladhari and everyone else about this woman. While in that state I used to weep with the name of the Mother on my lips. Weeping, I said to Her: 'O Mother, protect me! Please make me stainless. Please see that my mind is not diverted from the Real to the unreal.' (*To the doctor*) This attitude of yours is also very good. It is the attitude of a devotee, one who looks on God as his Master.

"When a man develops pure sattva, he thinks only of God. He does not enjoy anything else. Some are born with pure sattva as a result of their prārabdha karma. Through unselfish action one finally acquires pure sattva. Sattva mixed with rajas diverts the mind to various objects. From it springs the conceit of doing good to the world. To do good to the world is extremely difficult for such an insignificant creature as man. But there is no harm in doing good to others in an unselfish spirit. This is called unselfish action. It is highly beneficial for a person to try to perform such action. But by no means all succeed, for it is very difficult. Everyone must work. Only one or two can renounce action. Rarely do you find a man who has developed pure sattva. Through disinterested action sattva mixed with rajas gradually turns into pure sattva.

"No sooner does a man develop pure sattva than he realizes God, through His grace.

"Ordinary people cannot understand pure sattva. Hem once said to me: 'Well, priest! The goal of a man's life is to acquire name and fame in the world. Isn't that true?' "

Tuesday, October 27, 1885

Sri Ramakrishna was seated in his room. Narendra and other devotees were with him. The Master was conversing with them. It was about ten o'clock in the morning.

NARENDRA: "How strangely the doctor behaved yesterday!"

A DEVOTEE: "Yes, the fish swallowed the hook but the line broke."

MASTER (*smiling*): "But the hook is in its mouth. It will die and float on the water."

Narendra went out for a few minutes. Sri Ramakrishna was talking to M. about Purna.

MASTER: "The devotee looking on himself as Prakriti likes to embrace and kiss God, whom he regards as the Purusha. I am telling this just to you. Ordinary people should not hear these things."

M: "God sports in various ways. Even this illness of yours is one of His sports. Because you are ill new devotees are coming to you."

MASTER (*smiling*): "Bhupati says, 'What would people have thought of you if you had just rented a house to live in, without being ill?' Well, what has happened to the doctor?"

M: "As regards God he accepts for himself the attitude of a servant. He says, 'Thou art the Master and I am Thy servant.' But then he asks me, 'Why do you apply the idea of God to a man?' "

MASTER: "Just see! Are you going to him today?"

M: "I shall see him if it is necessary to report your condition."

MASTER: "How do you find this boy Bankim? If he cannot come here you may give him instruction. That will awaken his spiritual consciousness."

Narendra entered the room and sat near Sri Ramakrishna. Since the death of his father he had been very much worried about the family's financial condition. He now had to support his mother and brothers. Besides, he was preparing himself for his law examination. Lately he had served as a teacher in the Vidyāsāgar School at Bowbāzār. He wanted to make some arrangement for his family and thus get rid of all his worries. Sri Ramakrishna knew all this. He looked affectionately at Narendra.

MASTER (to M.): "Well, I said to Keshab, 'One should be satisfied with what comes unsought.' The son of an aristocrat does not worry about his food and drink. He gets his monthly allowance. Narendra, too, belongs to a high plane. Then why is he in such straitened circumstances? God certainly provides everything for the man who totally surrenders himself to Him."

M: "Narendra, too, will be provided for. It is not yet too late for him."

MASTER: "But a man who feels intense renunciation within doesn't calculate that way. He doesn't say to himself, 'I shall first make an arrangement for the family and then practise sādhanā.' No, he doesn't feel that way if he has developed intense dispassion. A goswāmi said in the course of his preaching, 'If a man has ten thousand rupees he can maintain himself on the income; then, free from worries, he can pray to God.'

"Keshab Sen also said something like that. He said to me: 'Sir, suppose a man wants, first of all, to make a suitable arrangement of his property and estate and then think of God; will it be all right for him to do so? Is there anything wrong about it?' I said to him: 'When a man feels utter dispassion, he looks on the world as a deep well and his relatives as venomous cobras. Then he cannot think of saving money or making arrangements about his property.' God alone is real and all else illusory. To think of the world instead of God!

"A woman was stricken with intense grief. She first tied her nose-ring in the corner of her cloth and then dropped to the ground, saying, 'Oh, friends, what a calamity has befallen me!' But she was very careful not to break the nose-ring."

All laughed. At these words Narendra felt as if struck by an arrow, and lay down on the floor. M. understood what was going through Narendra's mind and said with a smile: "What's the matter? Why are you lying down?"

The Master said to M., with a smile: "You remind me of a woman who felt ashamed of herself for sleeping with her brother-in-law and couldn't understand the conduct of those women who lived as mistresses of strangers. By way of excusing herself she said: 'After all, a brother-in-law is one's own. But even that kills me with shame. And how do these women dare to live with strangers?'"

M. himself had been leading a worldly life. Instead of being ashamed of his own conduct, he smiled at Narendra. That was why Sri Ramakrishna referred to the woman who criticized the conduct of immoral women, though she herself had illicit love for her brother-in-law.

A Vaishnava minstrel was singing downstairs. Sri Ramakrishna was pleased with his song and said that someone should give him a little money. A devotee went downstairs. The Master asked, "How much did he give the singer?" When he was told that the devotee had given only two pice, he said: "Just that much? This money is the fruit of his servitude. How much he had to flatter his master and suffer to earn it! I thought he would give at least four ānnās."

The younger Naren had promised to show Sri Ramakrishna the nature of electricity with an instrument. The instrument was exhibited.

It was about two o'clock. Sri Ramakrishna and the devotees were sitting in the room. Atul brought with him a friend who was a munsiff. Bagchi, the famous painter from Shikdārpārā, arrived. He presented the Master with several paintings. Sri Ramakrishna examined the pictures with great delight.

Bagchi had long hair like a woman's. Sri Ramakrishna said: "Many days ago a sannyāsi came to Dakshineswar who had hair nine cubits long. He used to chant the name of Rādhā. He was genuine."

A few minutes later Narendra began to sing. The songs were full of the spirit of renunciation. He sang:

> O Lord, must all my days pass by so utterly in vain?
> Down the path of hope I gaze with longing, day and night. . . .

He sang again:

> O Mother, Thou my inner Guide, ever awake within my heart;
> Day and night Thou holdest me in Thy lap.
> Why dost Thou show such tenderness to this unworthy child of
>   Thine? . . .

Then he sang:

> O gracious Lord, if like a bee
> My soul cannot imbed itself
> Deep in the Lotus of Thy Feet,
> What comfort can I find in life?
> What can I gain with wealth untold,
> Neglecting Thee, supremest Wealth?
>
> I take no pleasure in the sight
> Of the most lovely infant's face,
> If all its loveliness reveals
> No trace of Thy dear features there.
> Moonlight is meaningless to me
> As darkest night, if Thy love's moon
> Rise not in my soul's firmament.
> The purest wife's unspotted love
> Is stained, if in it is not set
> The priceless gem of love divine.
>
> O Lord, whenever doubt of Thee,
> Born of base error and neglect,
> Assails my mind, I writhe in pain
> As from a serpent's poisonous fangs!

What more, O Master, shall I say?
Thou art my heart's most precious Jewel,
The Home of Everlasting Joy.

It was half past five in the afternoon when Dr. Sarkar came to the Master's room at Śyāmpukur, felt his pulse, and prescribed the necessary medicine. Many devotees were present, including Narendra, Girish, Dr. Dukari, the younger Naren, Rakhal, M., Sarat, and Shyam Basu.

Dr. Sarkar talked a little about the Master's illness and watched him take the first dose of medicine. Then Sri Ramakrishna began to talk to Shyam Basu. Dr. Sarkar started to leave, saying, "Now that you are talking to Shyam Basu, I shall say good-bye to you."

The Master and a devotee asked the doctor if he would like to hear some songs.

DR. SARKAR (to the Master): "I should like it very much. But music makes you frisk about like a kid and cut all sorts of capers. You must suppress your emotion."

Dr. Sarkar took his seat once more, and Narendra began to sing in his sweet voice, to the accompaniment of the tānpurā and mridanga:

> This universe, wondrous and infinite,
> O Lord, is Thy handiwork;
> And the whole world is a treasure-house
> Full of Thy beauty and grace. . . .

He sang again:

> In dense darkness, O Mother, Thy formless beauty sparkles;
> Therefore the yogis meditate in a dark mountain cave.
> In the lap of boundless dark, on Mahānirvāna's waves upborne,
> Peace flows serene and inexhaustible.
> Taking the form of the Void, in the robe of darkness wrapped,
> Who art Thou, Mother, seated alone in the shrine of samādhi?
> From the Lotus of Thy fear-scattering Feet flash Thy love's lightnings;
> Thy Spirit-Face shines forth with laughter terrible and loud!

Dr. Sarkar said to M., "This song is dangerous for him." Sri Ramakrishna asked M. what the doctor had said. M. replied, "The doctor is afraid that this song may throw your mind into samādhi."

In the mean time the Master had partially lost consciousness of the outer world. Looking at the physician, he said with folded hands: "No, no. Why should I go into samādhi?" Hardly had he spoken these words when he went into a deep ecstasy. His body became motionless, his eyes fixed, his tongue speechless. He sat there like a statue cut in stone, completely unconscious of the outer world. Turned inward were his mind, ego, and all the other organs of perception. He seemed an altogether different person.

Narendra continued his songs, pouring his entire heart and soul into them:

> What matchless beauty! What a bewitching Face I behold!
> The Sovereign of my soul has entered my lowly hut;

The springs of my love are welling forth on every side.
Tell me, my Beloved! O Thou, the Lord of my heart!
What treasure shall I lay before Thy Lotus Feet?
Take Thou my life, my soul; what more can I offer Thee?
Take everything that is mine. Deign to accept my all.

Narendra continued:

O gracious Lord, if like a bee
My soul cannot imbed itself
Deep in the Lotus of Thy Feet,
What comfort can I find in life? . . .

As the doctor heard the words, "The purest wife's unspotted love", his eyes were filled with tears. He cried out, "Ah me! Ah me!"
Narendra sang again:

Oh, when will dawn the blessed day
When Love will waken in my heart?
When will my tears flow uncontrolled
As I repeat Lord Hari's name,
And all my longing be fulfilled? . . .

In the midst of the singing Sri Ramakrishna had regained consciousness of the outer world. When Narendra finished the song, the Master continued his conversation, keeping them all spellbound. The devotees looked at his face in wonder. It did not show the slightest trace of the agonizing pain of his illness. The face shone with heavenly joy.

Addressing the doctor, the Master said: "Give up this false modesty. Why should you feel shy about singing the name of God? The proverb says very truly: 'One cannot realize God if one is a victim of shame, hatred, or fear.' Give up such foolish notions as: 'I am such a great man! Shall I dance crying the name of God? What will other great men think of me on hearing of this? They may say that the doctor, poor fellow, has been dancing uttering the name of Hari, and thus pity me.' Give up all these foolish notions."

Doctor: "I never bother about what people say. I don't care a straw about their opinions."

Master: "Yes, I know of your strong feeling about that. (All laugh.)

"Go beyond knowledge and ignorance; only then can you realize God. To know many things is ignorance. Pride of scholarship is also ignorance. The unwavering conviction that God alone dwells in all beings is jnāna, knowledge. To know Him intimately is vijnāna, a richer Knowledge. If a thorn gets into your foot, a second thorn is needed to take it out. When it is out both thorns are thrown away. You have to procure the thorn of knowledge to remove the thorn of ignorance; then you must set aside both knowledge and ignorance. God is beyond both knowledge and ignorance. Once Lakshmana said to Rāma, 'Brother, how amazing it is that such a wise man as Vaśishtha wept bitterly at the death of his sons!' Rāma said: 'Brother, he who has knowledge must also have ignorance. He who has knowledge of one thing must also have knowledge of many things. He who is aware of light is also aware of darkness.' Brahman is beyond knowledge and ignorance, virtue and vice, merit and demerit, cleanliness and uncleanliness."

Sri Ramakrishna then recited the following song of Rāmprasād:

> Come, let us go for a walk, O mind, to Kāli, the Wish-fulfilling
>   Tree,
> And there beneath It gather the four fruits of life. . . .
>
> When will you learn to lie, O mind, in the abode of Blessedness,
> With Cleanliness and Defilement on either side of you?
> Only when you have found the way
> To keep your wives contentedly under a single roof,
> Will you behold the matchless form of Mother Śyāmā. . . .

SHYAM BASU: "Sir, what remains after one throws away both thorns?"

MASTER: "Nityaśuddhabodharupam—the Eternal and Ever-pure Consciousness. How can I make it clear to you? Suppose a man who has never tasted ghee asks you, 'What does ghee taste like?' Now, how can you explain that to him? At the most you can say: 'What is ghee like? It is just like ghee!' A young girl asked her friend: 'Well, friend, your husband is here. What sort of pleasure do you enjoy with him?' The friend answered: 'My dear, you will know it for yourself when you get a husband. How can I explain it to you?'

"It is said in the Purāna that Bhagavati, the Divine Mother, was once born as the daughter of King Himālaya. After Her birth She showed Her father Her many forms. The Lord of the mountains, after enjoying all these visions, said to the Divine Mother, 'May I have the vision of Brahman as It is described in the Vedas!' Then the Divine Mother answered, 'Father, if you want to have the vision of Brahman you must live in the company of holy men.'

"What Brahman is cannot be described in words. Somebody once said that everything in the world has been made impure, like food that has touched the tongue, and that Brahman alone remains undefiled. The meaning is this: All scriptures and holy books—the Vedas, the Purānas, the Tantras, and so forth—may be said to have been defiled because their contents have been uttered by the tongues of men; but what Brahman is no tongue has yet been able to describe. Therefore Brahman is still undefiled. One cannot describe in words the joy of play and communion with Satchidānanda. He alone knows, who has realized it."

Addressing Dr. Sarkar, Sri Ramakrishna continued: "Look here. One cannot attain Knowledge unless one is free from egotism. There is a saying:

> When shall I be free?
> When 'I' shall cease to be.

'I' and 'mine'—that is ignorance. 'Thou' and 'Thine'—that is Knowledge. A true devotee says: 'O God, Thou alone art the Doer; Thou alone doest all. I am a mere instrument; I do as Thou makest me do. All these—wealth, possessions, nay, the universe itself—belong to Thee. This house and these relatives are Thine alone, not mine. I am Thy servant; mine is only the right to serve Thee according to Thy bidding.'

"Those who have read a few books cannot get rid of conceit. Once I had a talk with Kalikrishna Tagore about God. At once he said, 'I know all about that.' I said to him: 'Does a man who has visited Delhi brag about it? Does a gentleman go about telling everyone that he is a gentleman?'"

SHYAM: "But Kalikrishna Tagore has great respect for you."

MASTER: "Oh, how vanity turns a person's head! There was a scavenger woman in the temple garden at Dakshineswar. And her pride! And all because of a few ornaments. One day a few men were passing her on the path and she shouted to them, 'Hey! Get out of the way, you people!' If a scavenger woman could talk that way, what can one say about the vanity of others?"

SHYAM: "Sir, if God alone does everything, how is it that man is punished for his sins?"

MASTER: "How like a goldsmith you talk!"

NARENDRA: "In other words, Shyam Babu has a calculating mind, like a goldsmith, who weighs things with his delicate balance."

MASTER: "I say: O my foolish boy, eat the mangoes and be happy. What is the use of your calculating how many hundreds of trees, how many thousands of branches, and how many millions of leaves there are in the orchard? You have come to the orchard to eat mangoes. Eat them and be contented.

(To Shyam) "You have been born in this world as a human being to worship God; therefore try to acquire love for His Lotus Feet. Why do you trouble yourself to know a hundred other things? What will you gain by discussing 'philosophy'? Look here, one ounce of liquor is enough to intoxicate you. What is the use of your trying to find out how many gallons of liquor there are in the tavern?"

DOCTOR: "Quite so. And what is more, the Wine in God's Tavern is beyond all measure. There is no limit to It."

MASTER (to Shyam): "Why don't you give your power of attorney to God? Rest all your responsibilities on Him. If you entrust an honest man with your responsibilities, will he misuse his power over you? God alone knows whether or not He will punish you for your sins."

DOCTOR: "God alone knows what is in His mind. How can a man guess it? God is beyond all our calculations."

MASTER (to Shyam): "That's the one theme of you Calcutta people. You all say, 'God is stained by the evil of inequality', because He has made one person happy and another miserable. What these rascals see in themselves they see in God, too.

"Hem used to come to the temple garden at Dakshineswar. Whenever he chanced to meet me, he would say: 'Well, priest, there is only one thing worth having in this world, and that is honour. Isn't that so?' Very few indeed say that the goal of human life is the realization of God."

SHYAM: "We hear a great deal about the subtle body. Can anyone show it to us? Can anyone demonstrate that the subtle body, when a man dies, leaves the gross body and goes away?"

MASTER: "True devotees don't care a rap about showing you these things.

What do they care whether some fool of a big man respects them or not? The desire to have a big man under their control never enters their minds."

SHYAM: "What is the distinction between the gross body and the subtle body?"

MASTER: "The body consisting of the five gross elements is called the gross body. The subtle body is made up of the mind, the ego, the discriminating faculty, and the mind-stuff. There is also a causal body, by means of which one enjoys the Bliss of God and holds communion with Him. The Tantra calls it the Bhāgavati Tanu, the Divine Body. Beyond all these is the Mahā-kārana, the Great Cause. That cannot be expressed by words.

"What is the use of merely listening to words? Do something! What will you achieve by merely repeating the word 'siddhi'? Will that intoxicate you? You will not be intoxicated even if you make a paste of siddhi and rub it all over your body. You must eat some of it. How can a man recognize yarns of different counts, such as number forty and number forty-one, unless he is in the trade? Those who trade in yarn do not find it at all difficult to describe a thread of a particular count. Therefore I say, practise a little spiritual discipline; then you will know all these—the gross, the subtle, the causal, and the Great Cause. While praying to God, ask only for love for His Lotus Feet.

"When Rāma redeemed Ahalyā[6] from the curse, He said to her, 'Ask a boon of Me.' Ahalyā said, 'O Rāma, if You deign to grant me a boon, then please fulfil my desire that I may always meditate on Your Lotus Feet, even though I may be born in a pig's body.'

"I prayed to the Divine Mother only for love. I offered flowers at Her Lotus Feet and said with folded hands: 'O Mother, here is Thy ignorance and here is Thy knowledge; take them both and give me only pure love for Thee. Here is Thy holiness and here is Thy unholiness; take them both and give me only pure love for Thee. Here is Thy virtue and here is Thy sin; here is Thy good and here is Thy evil; take them all and give me only pure love for Thee. Here is Thy dharma and here is Thy adharma; take them both and give me only pure love for Thee.'

"Dharma means good actions, like giving in charity. If you accept dharma, you have to accept adharma too. If you accept virtue, you have to accept sin. If you accept knowledge, you have to accept ignorance. If you accept holiness, you have to accept unholiness. It is like a man's being aware of light, in which case he is aware of darkness too. If a man is aware of one, he is aware of many too. If he is aware of good, he is aware of evil too.

"Blessed is the man who retains his love for the Lotus Feet of God, even though he eats pork. But if a man is attached to the world, even though he lives only on boiled vegetables and cereals, then—"

DOCTOR: "He is a wretch. But let me interrupt you here and say something. Buddha once ate pork and as a result had colic. To get rid of the pain he would take opium and thus become unconscious. Do you know the meaning of Nirvāna and such stuff? Buddha would become stupefied after

6 See foot-note, p. 699.

eating opium. He would have no consciousness of the outer world. This is what they call Nirvāna!"

All laughed to hear this novel interpretation of Nirvāna. The conversation went on.

MASTER (*to Shyam*): "There is no harm in your leading the life of a householder. But do your duties in an unselfish spirit, fixing your mind on the Lotus Feet of God. You must have noticed that a man with a carbuncle on his back speaks to others in his usual way; perhaps he attends to his daily duties also; but his mind is always on the carbuncle. It is like that.

"Live in the world like an immoral woman. Though she performs her household duties, her mind is fixed on her sweetheart. (*To the doctor*) Do you understand that?"

DOCTOR: "Never having had such an experience myself, how can I understand?"

SHYAM: "Oh, yes! You understand a little." (*All laugh.*)

MASTER: "Moreover he has had long experience in that trade. Isn't that so?" (*All laugh.*)

SHYAM: "Sir, what do you think of Theosophy?"

MASTER: "The long and short of the matter is that those who go about making disciples belong to a very inferior level. So also do those who want occult powers to walk over the Ganges and to report what a person says in a far-off country and so on. It is very hard for such people to have pure love for God."

SHYAM: "But the Theosophists have been trying to re-establish the Hindu religion."

MASTER: "I don't know much about them."

SHYAM: "You can learn from Theosophy where the soul goes after death —whether to the lunar sphere or the stellar sphere or some other region."

MASTER: "That may be. But let me tell you my own attitude. Once a man asked Hanumān, 'What day of the lunar fortnight is it?' Hanumān replied: 'I know nothing about the day of the week, the day of the lunar fortnight, the position of the stars in the sky, or any such things. On Rāma alone I meditate.' That is my attitude too."

SHYAM: "The Theosophists believe in the existence of mahātmas. Do you believe in them, sir?"

MASTER: "If you believe in my words, I say yes. But now please leave these matters alone. Come here again when I am a little better. Some way will be found for you to attain peace of mind, if you have faith in me. You must have noticed that I don't accept any gift of money or clothes. We do not take any collection here. That is why so many people come. (*Laughter.*)

(*To the doctor*) "If you won't take offense, I shall tell you something. It is this: You have had enough of such things as money, honour, lecturing, and so on. Now for a few days direct your mind to God. And come here now and then. Your spiritual feeling will be kindled by hearing words about God."

After a little while, as the doctor stood up to take his leave, Girish Chandra

Ghosh entered the room and bowed low before the Master. Dr. Sarkar was pleased to see him and took his seat again.

DOCTOR (*pointing to Girish*): "Of course he would not come as long as I was here. No sooner am I about to leave than he enters the room."

Girish and Dr. Sarkar began to talk about the Science Association established by the latter.

MASTER: "Will you take me there one day?"

DOCTOR: "If you go there you will lose all consciousness at the sight of the wondrous works of God."

MASTER: "Oh, indeed!"

DOCTOR (*to Girish*): "Whatever you may do, please do not worship him as God. You are turning the head of this good man."

GIRISH: "What else can I do? Oh, how else shall I regard a person who has taken me across this ocean of the world, and what is still more, the ocean of doubt? There is nothing in him that I do not hold sacred. Can I ever look on even his excreta as filthy?"

DOCTOR: "This question of excreta doesn't bother me. I too have no feeling of repugnance. Once a grocer's child was brought to my office for treatment. His bowels moved there. All covered their noses with cloths; but I sat by his side for half an hour without putting a handkerchief to my nose. Besides, I cannot cover my nose when the scavenger passes by me with a tub on his head. No, I cannot do that. I know very well that there is no difference between a scavenger and myself. Why should I look down on him? Can't I take the dust of his [meaning Sri Ramakrishna's] feet? Look here."

The doctor saluted Sri Ramakrishna and touched the Master's feet with his forehead.

GIRISH: "Oh, the angels are saying, 'Blessed, blessed be this auspicious moment!'"

DOCTOR: "What is there to marvel at in taking the dust of a man's feet? I can take the dust of everybody's feet. Give me, all of you, the dust of your feet."

The doctor touched the feet of all the devotees.

NARENDRA (*to the doctor*): "We think of him [meaning the Master] as a person who is like God. Do you know, sir, what it is like? There is a point between the vegetable creation and the animal creation where it is very difficult to determine whether a particular thing is a vegetable or an animal. Likewise, there is a stage between the man-world and the God-world where it is extremely hard to say whether a person is a man or God."

DOCTOR: "Well, my dear young friend, one cannot apply analogies to things divine."

NARENDRA: "I do not say that he is God. What I am saying is that he is a godlike man."

DOCTOR: "One should suppress one's feelings in such a matter. It is bad to give vent to them. Alas! No one understands my own feelings. Even my best friend thinks of me as a stern and cruel person. Even people like you will perhaps one day throw me out after beating me with your shoes."

MASTER: "Don't say such a thing! They love you so much! They await your coming as eagerly as the bridesmaids in the bridal chamber await the coming of the groom."

GIRISH: "Everyone has the greatest respect for you."

DOCTOR: "My son and even my wife think of me as a hard-hearted person. My only crime is that I do not display my feelings."

GIRISH: "In that case, sir, it would be wise for you to open the door of your heart, at least out of pity for your friends; for you see that your friends cannot otherwise understand you."

DOCTOR: "Will you believe me when I say that my feelings get worked up even more than yours? (*To Narendra*) I shed tears in solitude.

(*To Sri Ramakrishna*) "Well, may I say something? When you are in ecstasy you place your foot on others' bodies. That is not good."

MASTER: "Do you think I know at that time that I am touching another with my foot?"

DOCTOR: "You feel that it is not the right thing to do, don't you?"

MASTER: "How can I explain to you what I experience in samādhi? After coming down from that state I think, sometimes, that my illness may be due to samādhi. The thing is, the thought of God makes me mad. All this is the result of my divine madness. How can I help it?"

DOCTOR: "Now he accepts my view. He expresses regret for what he does. He is conscious that the act is sinful."

MASTER (*to Narendra*): "You are very clever. Why don't you answer? Explain it all to the doctor."

GIRISH (*to the doctor*): "Sir, you are mistaken. He is not expressing regret for touching the bodies of his devotees during samādhi. His own body is pure, untouched by any sin. That he touches others in this way is for their good. Sometimes he thinks that he may have got this illness by taking their sins upon himself.

"Think of your own case. Once you suffered from colic. Didn't you have regrets at that time for sitting up and reading till very late at night? Does that prove that reading till the late hours of the night is, in itself, a bad thing? He [meaning Sri Ramakrishna] too may be sorry that he is ill. But that does not make him feel that it is wrong on his part to touch others for their welfare."

Dr. Sarkar felt rather embarrassed and said to Girish: "I confess my defeat at your hands. Give me the dust of your feet." He saluted Girish.

DOCTOR (*to Narendra*): "Whatever else one may say about him [meaning Girish], one must admit his intellectual powers."

NARENDRA (*to the doctor*): "You may look at the thing from another standpoint. You can devote your life to scientific research without giving a thought to your health or comfort. But the Science of God is the grandest of all sciences. Isn't it natural for him to risk his health to realize Him?"

DOCTOR: "All religious reformers, including Jesus, Chaitanya, Buddha, and Mohammed, were in the end filled with egotism. They all said, 'Whatever I say is alone true.' How shocking!"

GIRISH (*to the doctor*): "Now, sir, you are committing the same mistake.

You are accusing them all of egotism. You are finding fault with them. For that very reason you too can be accused of egotism."

Dr. Sarkar remained silent.

NARENDRA (*to the doctor*): "We offer worship to him bordering on divine worship."

At these words the Master laughed like a child.

IN THE COMPANY OF DEVOTEES
AT ŚYĀMPUKUR

IT WAS ABOUT TEN O'CLOCK in the morning when M. arrived at Dr. Sarkar's house in Sānkhāritolā, Calcutta, to report Sri Ramakrishna's condition. M. and Dr. Sarkar became engaged in conversation.

DOCTOR: "You see, Dr. Behari Bhaduri always harps on the same thing. He says that Goethe's spirit came out of his body and that Goethe himself saw it. It must have been very amazing."

M: "As Sri Ramakrishna says, what shall we gain from these discussions? We have been born in this world in order to cultivate devotion to the Lotus Feet of God. He tells us the story of a man who entered an orchard to eat mangoes. But instead of eating the fruit, he took out pencil and paper and began to jot down the number of trees, branches, and leaves in the orchard. A servant saw him and asked: 'What are you doing? Why have you come here?' The man said: 'I have come here to eat mangoes. I am now counting the trees, branches, and leaves in the orchard.' Thereupon the servant replied: 'If you have come here to eat mangoes, then enjoy them. What will you gain by counting the trees, branches, and leaves?' "

DOCTOR: "I see that the Paramahamsa has been able to extract the essence."

Then Dr. Sarkar told M. many stories about his homeopathic hospital. He showed M. the list of the patients who visited the hospital every day. He further remarked that at the beginning many medical practitioners had discouraged him about homeopathy and had even written against him in magazines.

M. and Dr. Sarkar got into the doctor's carriage. The doctor visited many patients. He entered a house of the Tagore family at Pāthuriāghātā and was detained there by the head of the family. Returning to the carriage, he began to talk to M.

DOCTOR: "I was talking to that gentleman about the Paramahamsa. We also talked about Theosophy and Colonel Olcott. The Paramahamsa is angry with the gentleman. Do you know why? Because he says he knows everything."

M: "No, why should the Master be angry? I heard that they once met each other. Paramahamsadeva was talking about God. The gentleman said, 'Oh, yes! I know all that!'"

DOCTOR: "He has donated thirty-two thousand five hundred rupees to the Science Association."

They drove on, talking about Sri Ramakrishna's illness and the care that should be taken of him.

DOCTOR: "Do you intend to send him back to Dakshineswar?"

M: "No, sir. That would greatly inconvenience the devotees. They can always visit him if he is in Calcutta."

DOCTOR: "But it is very expensive here."

M: "The devotees don't mind that. All they want is to be able to serve him. As regards the expense, it must be borne whether he lives in Calcutta or at Dakshineswar. But if he goes back to Dakshineswar, the devotees won't always be able to visit him, and that will cause them great worry."

Dr. Sarkar and M. arrived at Śyāmpukur and found the Master sitting with the devotees in his room. Dr. Bhaduri also was there.

Dr. Sarkar examined the Master's pulse and inquired about his condition. The conversation turned to God.

DR. BHADURI: "Shall I tell you the truth? All this is unreal, like a dream."

DR. SARKAR: "Is everything delusion? Then whose is this delusion? And why this delusion? If all know it to be delusion, then why do they talk? I cannot believe that God is real and His creation unreal."

MASTER: "That is a good attitude. It is good to look on God as the Master and oneself as His servant. As long as a man feels the body to be real, as long as he is conscious of 'I' and 'you', it is good to keep the relationship of master and servant; it is not good to cherish the idea of 'I am He'.

"Let me tell you something else. You see the same room whether you look at it from one side or from the middle of the room."

DR. BHADURI (to Dr. Sarkar): "What I have just said you will find in the Vedānta. You must study the scriptures. Then you will understand."

DR. SARKAR: "Why so? Has he [meaning the Master] acquired all this wisdom by studying the scriptures? He too supports my view. Can't one be wise without reading the scriptures?"

MASTER: "But how many scriptures I have heard!"

DR. SARKAR: "A man may mistake the meaning if he only hears. In your case it is not mere hearing."

MASTER (to Dr. Sarkar): "I understand that you spoke of me as insane. That is why they (pointing to M. and the others) don't want to go to you."

DR. SARKAR (looking at M.): "Why should I call you [meaning the Master] insane? But I mentioned your egotism. Why do you allow people to take the dust of your feet?"

M: "Otherwise they weep."

DR. SARKAR: "That is their mistake. They should be told about it."

M: "Why should you object to their taking the dust of his feet? Doesn't God dwell in all beings?"

Dr. Sarkar: "I don't object to that. Then you must take the dust of everyone's feet."

M: "But there is a greater manifestation of God in some men than in others. There is water everywhere; but you see more of it in a lake, a river, or an ocean. Will you show the same respect to a new Bachelor of Science as you do to Faraday?"

Dr. Sarkar: "I agree with that. But why do you call him God?"

M: "Why do we salute each other? It is because God dwells in everybody's heart. You haven't given much thought to this subject."

Master (to Dr. Sarkar): "I have already told you that some people reveal more of God than others. Earth reflects the sun's rays in one way, a tree in another way, and a mirror in still another way. You see a better reflection in a mirror than in other objects. Don't you see that these devotees here are not on the same level with Prahlāda and others of his kind? Prahlāda's whole heart and soul were dedicated to God."

Dr. Sarkar did not reply. All were silent.

Master (to Dr. Sarkar): "You see, you have love for this [meaning himself]. You told me that you loved me."

Dr. Sarkar: "You are a child of nature. That is why I tell you all this. It hurts me to see people salute you by touching your feet. I say to myself, 'They are spoiling such a good man.' Keshab Sen, too, was spoiled that way by his devotees. Listen to me—"

Master: "Listen to you? You are greedy, lustful, and egotistic."

Dr. Bhaduri (to Dr. Sarkar): "That is to say, you have the traits of a jīva, an embodied being. These are his traits: lust, egotism, greed for wealth, and a hankering after name and fame. All embodied beings have these traits."

Dr. Sarkar (to the Master): "If you talk that way, I shall only examine your throat and go away. Perhaps that is what you want. In that case we should not talk about anything else. But if you want discussion, then I shall say what I think to be right."

All remained silent.

After a while the Master became engaged in conversation with Dr. Bhaduri.

Master: "Let me tell you the truth. He [meaning Dr. Sarkar] is now following the path of negation. Therefore he discriminates, following the process of 'Neti, neti', and reasons in this way: God is not the living beings; He is not the universe; He is outside the creation. But later he will follow the path of affirmation and accept everything as the manifestation of God.

"By taking off, one by one, the sheaths of a banana tree, one obtains the pith. The sheaths are one thing, and the pith is another. The sheaths are not the pith, and the pith is not the sheaths. But in the end one realizes that the pith cannot exist apart from the sheaths, and the sheaths cannot exist apart from the pith; they are part and parcel of one and the same banana tree. Likewise, it is God who has become the twenty-four cosmic principles; it is He who has become man.

(To Dr. Sarkar) "There are three kinds of devotees: superior, mediocre, and inferior. The inferior devotee says, 'God is out there.' According to him

God is different from His creation. The mediocre devotee says: 'God is the Antaryāmi, the Inner Guide. God dwells in everyone's heart.' The mediocre devotee sees God in the heart. But the superior devotee sees that God alone has become everything; He alone has become the twenty-four cosmic principles. He finds that everything, above and below, is filled with God.

"Read the Gītā, the Bhāgavata, and the Vedānta, and you will understand all this. Is not God in His creation?"

DR. SARKAR: "Not in any particular object. He is everywhere. And because He is everywhere, He cannot be sought after."

The conversation turned to other things. Sri Ramakrishna was always experiencing ecstatic moods, which the doctor said might aggravate his illness. Dr. Sarkar said to him: "You must suppress your emotion. My feelings, too, are greatly stirred up. I can dance much more than you."

THE YOUNGER NAREN (smiling): "What would you do if your emotion increased a little more?"

DR. SARKAR: "My power of control would also increase."

MASTER AND M: "You may say that now!"

M: "Can you tell us what you would do if you went into an ecstatic mood?"

The conversation turned to money.

MASTER (to Dr. Sarkar): "I don't think about it at all. You know that very well, don't you? This is not a pretence."

DR. SARKAR: "Even I have no desire for money—not to speak of yourself! My cash-box lies open."

MASTER: "Jadu Mallick, too, is absent-minded. When he takes his meals he sometimes becomes so absent-minded that he doesn't know whether the food is good or bad. When someone says to him, 'Don't eat that; it doesn't taste good', Jadu says: 'Eh? Is this food bad? Why, that's so!' "

Was the Master hinting that there was an ocean of difference between absent-mindedness due to the contemplation of God, and absent-mindedness due to preoccupation with worldly thoughts?

Pointing to Dr. Sarkar, Sri Ramakrishna said to the devotees, with a smile: "When a thing is boiled, it becomes soft. At first he was very hard. Now he is softening from inside."

DR. SARKAR: "When a thing is boiled, it begins to soften from the outside. I am afraid that won't happen to me in this birth." (All laugh.)

Dr. Sarkar was about to take his leave. He was talking to Sri Ramakrishna.

DOCTOR: "Can't you forbid people to salute you by touching your feet?"

MASTER: "Can all comprehend the Indivisible Satchidānanda?"

DR. SARKAR: "But shouldn't you tell people what is right?"

MASTER: "People have different tastes. Besides, all have not the same fitness for spiritual life."

DR. SARKAR: "How is that?"

MASTER: "Don't you know what difference in taste is? Some enjoy fish curry; some, fried fish; some, pickled fish; and again, some, the rich dish of fish pilau. Then too, there is difference in fitness. I ask people to learn to shoot at a banana tree first, then at the wick of a lamp, and then at a flying bird."

It was dusk. Sri Ramakrishna became absorbed in contemplation of God. For the time being he forgot all about his painful disease. Several intimate disciples sat near him and looked at him intently. After a long time he became aware of the outer world and said to M. in a whisper: "You see, my mind was completely merged in the Indivisible Brahman. After that I saw many things. I found that the doctor will have spiritual awakening. But it will take some time. I won't have to tell him much. I saw another person while in that mood. My mind said to me, 'Attract him too.' I shall tell you about him later."

Shyam Basu, Dr. Dukari, and a few other devotees arrived. Sri Ramakrishna talked to them.

SHYAM: "Ah, what a fine thing you said to us the other day!"

MASTER (smiling): "What was that?"

SHYAM: "What remains with a man when he goes beyond jnāna and ajnāna, knowledge and ignorance."

MASTER (smiling): "It is vijnāna, special Knowledge of God. To know many things is ignorance. To know that God dwells in all beings is knowledge. And what is vijnāna? It is to know God in a special manner, to converse with Him and feel Him to be one's own relative.

"To know that there is fire in wood is knowledge. But to make a fire with that wood, cook food with that fire, and become healthy and strong from that food is vijnāna."

SHYAM (smiling): "And about the thorn?"

MASTER (smiling): "Yes. When a thorn gets into the sole of your foot, you procure a second thorn. After taking out the first thorn with the help of the second, you throw both thorns away. Likewise, you should procure the thorn of knowledge in order to remove the thorn of ignorance. After destroying ignorance, you should discard both knowledge and ignorance. Then you attain vijnāna."

Sri Ramakrishna was pleased with Shyam Basu. He was quite an elderly person and wanted to devote his time to contemplation. This was his second visit to the Master.

MASTER (to Shyam Basu): "Give up worldly talk altogether. Don't talk about anything whatever but God. If you see a worldly person coming near you, leave the place before he arrives. You have spent your whole life in the world. You have seen that it is all hollow. Isn't that so? God alone is Substance, and all else is illusory. God alone is real, and all else has only a two-days existence. What is there in the world? The world is like a pickled hog plum: one craves for it. But what is there in a hog plum? Only skin and pit. And if you eat it you will have colic."

SHYAM: "Yes, sir. Everything you have said is true."

MASTER: "For many years you have devoted yourself to various worldly things. You will not be able to think of God and meditate on Him in this confusion of the world. A little solitude is necessary for you; otherwise your mind will not be steady. Therefore you must fix a place for meditation at least half a mile away from your house."

Shyam Basu remained silent a few moments. He appeared absorbed in thought.

MASTER (smiling): "Besides, all your teeth are gone. Why should you bother so much about the Durgā Pujā? (All laugh.) A man used to celebrate the worship of Durgā with the sacrifice of goats and with other ceremonies. He continued the worship many years and then stopped it. A friend asked him, 'Why don't you perform the Durgā Pujā any more?' 'Brother,' replied the man, 'my teeth are all gone. I have lost the power to chew goat-meat.'"

SHYAM: "Ah! How sweet these words are!"

MASTER (smiling): "This world is a mixture of sand and sugar. Like the ant, one should discard the sand and eat the sugar. He who can eat the sugar is clever indeed. Build a quiet place for thinking of God—a place for your meditation. Have it ready. I shall visit it."

SHYAM: "Sir, is there such a thing as reincarnation? Shall we be born again?"

MASTER: "Ask God about it. Pray to Him sincerely. He will tell you everything. Speak to Jadu Mallick, and he himself will tell you how many houses he has, and how many government bonds. It is not right to try to know these things at the beginning. First of all realize God; then He Himself will let you know whatever you desire."

SHYAM: "Sir, how much wrong, how many sinful things a man does in this world! Can he ever realize God?"

MASTER: "If a man practises spiritual discipline before his death and if he gives up his body praying to God and meditating on Him, when will sin touch him? It is no doubt the elephant's nature to smear his body with dust and mud, even after his bath. But he cannot do so if the māhut takes him into the stable immediately after his bath."

In spite of his serious illness the Master keenly felt the sorrow and suffering of men. Day and night he thought about their welfare. The devotees wondered at his compassion. The assurance of Sri Ramakrishna that no sin can touch a man if he gives up his body while praying to God was deeply impressed on their minds.

Friday, October 30, 1885

It was nine o'clock in the morning. Sri Ramakrishna was talking with M. in his room. No one else was present. M. was going to Dr. Sarkar to report his condition and bring him to examine the Master.

MASTER (to M., smiling): "Purna came this morning. He has such a nice nature! Manindra has an element of Prakriti, of womanliness. He has read the life of Chaitanya and understood the attitude of the gopis. He has also realized that God is Purusha and man is Prakriti, and that man should worship God as His handmaid. How remarkable!"

M: "It is true, sir."

Purna was then fifteen or sixteen years old. Sri Ramakrishna always longed to see him. But his relatives did not allow him to visit the Master. One night, before his illness, Sri Ramakrishna had been so eager to see Purna that he had suddenly left Dakshineswar and arrived at M.'s house in Calcutta. M. had brought Purna from his home to see Sri Ramakrishna. The Master had given the boy many instructions about prayer and had afterwards returned to Dakshineswar. Manindra was about the same age as Purna. The devotees addressed him as "khokā".[1] He used to dance in ecstasy when he heard the chanting of God's name.

About half past ten M. arrived at Dr. Sarkar's house. He went up to the second floor and sat in a chair on the porch adjacent to the drawing-room. In front of Dr. Sarkar was a glass bowl in which some goldfish were kept. Now and then Dr. Sarkar threw some cardamom shells into the bowl. Again, he threw pellets of flour to the sparrows. M. watched him.

DOCTOR (smiling, to M.): "You see, these goldfish are staring at me like devotees staring at God. They haven't noticed the food I have thrown into the water. Therefore I say, what will you gain by mere bhakti? You need knowledge too. (M. smiles.) Look there at the sparrows! They flew away when I threw flour pellets to them. They were frightened. They have no bhakti because they are without knowledge. They don't know that flour is their food."

Dr. Sarkar and M. entered the drawing-room. There were shelves all around filled with books. The doctor rested a little. M. looked at the books. He picked up Canon Farrar's Life of Jesus and read a few pages. Dr. Sarkar told M. how the first homeopathic hospital was started in the teeth of great opposition. He asked M. to read the letters relating to it, which had been published in the "Calcutta Journal of Medicine" in 1876. Dr. Sarkar was much devoted to homeopathy.

M. picked up another book, Munger's New Theology. Dr. Sarkar noticed it.

DOCTOR: "Munger has based his conclusions on nice argument and reasoning. It is not like your believing a thing simply because a Chaitanya or a Buddha or a Jesus Christ has said so."

M. (smiling): "Yes, we should not believe Chaitanya or Buddha; but we must believe Munger!"

DOCTOR: "Whatever you say."

M: "We must quote someone as our authority; so it is Munger." (The doctor smiles.)

Dr. Sarkar got into his carriage accompanied by M. The carriage proceeded toward Śyāmpukur. It was midday. They gossiped together. The conversation turned to Dr. Bhaduri, who had also been visiting the Master now and then.

M. (smiling): "Bhaduri said about you that you must begin all over again from the stone and brick-bat."

DR. SARKAR: "How is that?"

M: "Because you don't believe in the mahātmās, astral bodies, and so forth. Perhaps Bhaduri is a Theosophist. Further, you don't believe in the Incarnation of God. That is why he teased you, saying that when you died

[1] Baby.

this time you would certainly not be reborn as a human being. That would be far off. You wouldn't be born even as an animal or bird, or even as a tree or a plant. You would have to begin all over again, from stone and brick-bat. Then, after many, many births, you might assume a human body."

DR. SARKAR: "Goodness gracious!"

M: "Bhaduri further said that the knowledge of your physical science was a false knowledge. Such knowledge is momentary. He gave an analogy. Suppose there are two wells. The one gets its water from an underground spring. The other has no such spring and is filled with rain-water. But the water of the second well does not last a long time. The knowledge of your science is like the rain-water. It dries up."

DR. SARKAR (with a smile): "I see!"

The carriage arrived at Cornwallis Street. Dr. Sarkar picked up Dr. Pratap Mazumdar. Pratap had visited Sri Ramakrishna the previous day. They soon arrived at Śyāmpukur.

Sri Ramakrishna was sitting in his room, on the second floor, with several devotees.

DR. SARKAR (to the Master): "I see you are coughing.[2] (Smiling) But it is good to go to Kāśi." (All laugh.)

MASTER (smiling): "But that will give me liberation. I don't want liberation; I want love of God!" (All laugh.)

Pratap was Dr. Bhaduri's son-in-law. Sri Ramakrishna was speaking to Pratap in praise of his father-in-law.

MASTER (to Pratap): "Ah, what a grand person he has become! He contemplates God and observes purity in his conduct. Further, he accepts both aspects of God—personal and impersonal."

M. was very eager to mention Dr. Bhaduri's remarks about Dr. Sarkar's being born again as a stone or brick-bat. He asked the younger Naren very softly whether he remembered those remarks of Dr. Bhaduri. Sri Ramakrishna overheard this.

MASTER (to Dr. Sarkar): "Do you know what Dr. Bhaduri said about you? He said that, because you didn't believe these things, in the next cycle you would have to begin your earthly life from a stone or brick-bat." (All laugh.)

DR. SARKAR (smiling): "Suppose I begin from a stone or brick-bat, and after many births obtain a human body; but as soon as I come back to this place I shall have to begin over again from a stone or brick-bat." (The doctor and all laugh.)

The conversation turned to the Master's ecstasy in spite of his illness.

PRATAP: "Yesterday I saw you in an ecstatic mood."

MASTER: "It happened of itself; but it was not intense."

DR. SARKAR: "Ecstasy and talking are not good for you now."

MASTER (to Dr. Sarkar): "I saw you yesterday in my samādhi. I found that you are a mine of knowledge; but it is all dry knowledge. You have not tasted divine bliss. (To Pratap, referring to Dr. Sarkar) If he ever tastes divine bliss, he will see everything, above and below, filled with it. Then he

[2] The Bengali word for "coughing" is "kāśi". Kāśi is also a name for Benares.

will not say that whatever he says is right and what others say is wrong. Then he will not utter sharp, strong, pointed words."

The devotees remained silent.

Suddenly Sri Ramakrishna went into a spiritual mood and said to Dr. Sarkar: "Mahindra Babu, what is this madness of yours about money? Why such attachment to wife? Why such longing for name and fame? Give up all these, now, and direct your mind to God with whole-souled devotion. Enjoy the Bliss of God."

Dr. Sarkar sat still without uttering a word. The devotees also remained silent.

MASTER: "Nangtā used to tell me how a jnāni meditates: Everywhere is water; all the regions above and below are filled with water; man, like a fish, is swimming joyously in that water. In real meditation you will actually see all this.

"Take the case of the infinite ocean. There is no limit to its water. Suppose a pot is immersed in it: there is water both inside and outside the pot. The jnāni sees that both inside and outside there is nothing but Paramātman. Then what is this pot? It is 'I-consciousness'. Because of the pot the water appears to be divided into two parts; because of the pot you seem to perceive an inside and an outside. One feels that way as long as this pot of 'I' exists. When the 'I' disappears, what is remains. That cannot be described in words.

"Do you know another way a jnāni meditates? Think of infinite ākāśa and a bird flying there, joyfully spreading its wings. There is the Chidākāśa, and Ātman is the bird. The bird is not imprisoned in a cage; it flies in the Chidākāśa. Its joy is limitless."

The devotees listened with great attention to these words about meditation. After a time Pratap resumed the conversation.

PRATAP (to Dr. Sarkar): "When one thinks seriously, one undoubtedly sees everything as a mere shadow."

DR. SARKAR: "If you speak of a shadow, then you need three things: the sun, the object, and the shadow. How can there be any shadow without an object? And you say that God is real and the creation unreal. I say that the creation is real too."

PRATAP: "Very well. As you see a reflection in a mirror, so you see this universe in the mirror of your mind."

DR. SARKAR: "But how can there be a reflection without an object?"

NARENDRA: "Why, God is the object."

Dr. Sarkar remained silent.

MASTER (to Dr. Sarkar): "You said a very fine thing. No one else has said before that samādhi is the result of the union of the mind with God. You alone have said that.

"Shivanath said that one lost one's head by too much thinking of God. In other words, one becomes unconscious by meditating on the Universal Consciousness. Think of it! Becoming unconscious by contemplating Him who is of the very nature of Consciousness, and whose Consciousness endows the world with consciousness!

"And what does your 'science' say? This combined with this produces that; that combined with that produces this. One is more likely to lose consciousness by contemplating those things—by handling material things too much."

DR. SARKAR: "One can see God in those things."

M: "If so, one sees God more clearly in man, and still better in a great soul. In a great soul there is a greater manifestation of God."

DR. SARKAR: "Yes, in man, no doubt."

MASTER: "Losing consciousness by contemplating God—through whose Consciousness even inert matter appears to be conscious, and hands, feet, and body move! People say that the body moves of itself; but they do not know that it is God who moves it. They say that water scalds the hand. But water can by no means scald the hand; it is the heat in the water, the fire in the water, that scalds.

"Rice is boiling in a pot. Potatoes and egg-plant are also jumping about in the pot. The children say that the potatoes and egg-plant jump of themselves; they do not know that there is fire underneath. Man says that the sense-organs do their work of themselves; but he does not know that inside dwells He whose very nature is Consciousness."

Dr. Sarkar stood up. He was about to take his leave. Sri Ramakrishna also stood up.

DR. SARKAR: "People call on God when they are faced with a crisis. Is it for the mere fun of it that they say, 'O Lord! Thou, Thou!'? You speak of God because of that trouble in your throat. You have now fallen into the clutches of the cotton-carder. You had better speak to the carder. I am just quoting your own words."

MASTER: "There is nothing for me to say."

DR. SARKAR: "Why not? We lie in the lap of God. We feel free with Him. To whom should we speak about our illness if not to Him?"

MASTER: "Right you are. Once in a while I try to speak to Him about it, but I do not succeed."

DR. SARKAR: "Why should you even speak to Him? Does He not know of it?"

MASTER (smiling): "A Mussalmān, while saying his prayers, shouted: 'O Āllāh! O Āllāh!' Another person said to him: 'You are calling on Āllāh. That's all right. But why are you shouting like that? Don't you know that He hears the sound of the anklets on the feet of an ant?'

"When the mind is united with God, one sees Him very near, in one's own heart. But you must remember one thing. The more you realize this unity, the farther your mind is withdrawn from worldly things. There is the story of Vilwamangal in the Bhaktamāla. He used to visit a prostitute. One night he was very late in going to her house. He had been detained at home by the śrāddha ceremony of his father and mother. In his hands he was carrying the food offered in the ceremony, to feed his mistress. His whole soul was so set upon the woman that he was not at all conscious of his movements. He didn't even know how he was walking. There was a yogi seated on the path, meditating on God with eyes closed. Vilwamangal stepped on him. The yogi became angry, and cried out: 'What? Are you blind? I have been thinking of God, and you step on my body!' 'I beg your pardon,' said Vilwamangal, 'but may I ask you something? I have been unconscious, thinking of a prostitute, and you are conscious of the outer world though thinking of God. What kind of meditation is that?' In the end Vilwamangal renounced the world and went away in order to worship God. He said to the prostitute: 'You are my guru. You have taught me how one should yearn for God.' He addressed the prostitute as his mother and gave her up."

DR. SARKAR: "To address a woman as mother is the Tāntrik form of worship."

MASTER: "Listen to a story. There was a king who used daily to hear the *Bhāgavata* recited by a pundit. Every day, after explaining the sacred book, the pundit would say to the king, 'O King, have you understood what I have said?' And every day the king would reply, 'You had better understand it first yourself.' The pundit would return home and think: 'Why does the king talk to me that way day after day? I explain the texts to him so clearly, and he says to me, "You had better understand it first yourself." What does he mean?' The pundit used to practise spiritual discipline. A few days later he came to realize that God alone is real and everything else—house, family, wealth, friends, name, and fame—illusory. Convinced of the unreality of the world, he renounced it. As he left home he asked a man to take this message to the king: 'O King, I now understand.'

"Here is another story. A man needed a scholar of the *Bhāgavata* to expound the sacred text to him every day. But it was very difficult to procure such a scholar. After he had searched a great deal, another man came to him and said, 'Sir, I have found an excellent scholar of the *Bhāgavata*.' 'Very well,' said the man, 'bring him here.' The other man replied: 'But there is a little hitch. The scholar has a few ploughs and bullocks; he is busy with them all day. He must look after the cultivation of his land. He hasn't a moment's leisure.' Thereupon the man who required the scholar said: 'I don't want a *Bhāgavata* scholar who is burdened with ploughs and bullocks. I want a man who has leisure and can tell me about God.' (*To Dr. Sarkar*) Do you understand?"

Dr. Sarkar remained silent.

MASTER: "Shall I tell you the truth? What will you gain by mere scholarship? The pundits hear many things and know many things—the Vedas, the Purānas, the Tantras. But of what avail is mere scholarship? Discrimination and renunciation are necessary. If a man has discrimination and renunciation, then one can listen to him. But of what use are the words of a man who looks on the world as the essential thing?

"What is the lesson of the *Gītā*? It is what you get by repeating the word ten times. As you repeat 'Gītā', 'Gītā', the word becomes reversed into 'tāgi', 'tāgi'—which implies renunciation. He alone has understood the secret of the *Gītā* who has renounced his attachment to 'woman and gold' and has directed his entire love to God. It isn't necessary to read the whole of the *Gītā*. The purpose of reading the book is served if one practises renunciation."

DR. SARKAR: "A man once explained the meaning of Rādhā to me. He said to me: 'Do you know the meaning of Rādhā? Reverse the word and it becomes "dhārā."[3] That's the meaning.' (*All laugh.*) Well, let us stop here for today."

Dr. Sarkar left. M. sat near Sri Ramakrishna and repeated the conversation he had had at Dr. Sarkar's house.

M: "Dr. Sarkar was feeding the goldfish with cardamom shells and the sparrows with flour pellets. He said to me: 'Did you notice? The fish didn't see the cardamom shells and therefore went away. First of all we want knowledge, and then bhakti. Did you notice those sparrows? They too flew away when I threw the pellets of flour. They have no jnāna; therefore they have no bhakti.'"

MASTER (*smiling*): "That knowledge means the knowledge of the physical world, the knowledge of 'science'."

M: "He said further: 'Must I believe a thing simply because a Chaitanya or a Buddha or a Christ has said it? That would not be proper.' A grandson has been born to him. He praised his daughter-in-law highly. He said, 'I don't notice her at all in the house; she is so quiet and bashful.'"

MASTER: "He has been thinking of this place [meaning himself]. His faith is growing. Is it possible to get rid of egotism altogether? Such scholarship! Such fame! And he has so much money! But he doesn't show disrespect for what I say."

It was about five o'clock in the afternoon. The devotees were sitting quietly in the room. Many outsiders also were present. All sat in silence.

M. was seated very near Sri Ramakrishna. Now and then they exchanged a word or two in a low voice. The Master wanted to put on his coat. M. helped him.

MASTER (*to M.*): "You see, nowadays it is not necessary for me to meditate much. All at once I become aware of the Indivisible Brahman. Nowadays the vision of the Absolute is continuous with me."

M. did not reply. The room was full of men, all silent.

Presently Sri Ramakrishna spoke.

MASTER: "Well, all these people are sitting here without uttering a word. Their eyes are fixed on me. They are neither talking nor singing. What do they see in me?"

M. said to the Master: "Sir, they have already heard many things you have said. Now they are seeing what they can never see anywhere else—a man always blissful, of childlike nature, free from egotism, and intoxicated with divine love. The other day you were pacing the outer room of Ishan's house. We too were with you. A man came to me and said that he had never before seen such a happy person as you."

M. became silent. The room was still. A few minutes later Sri Ramakrishna spoke to M. in a whisper.

MASTER: "Well, how is the doctor coming along? Does he now receive well the ideas of this place?"

[3] The word "dhārā" does not mean anything in particular. The doctor made the statement to change the conversation.

M: "How can an effective seed fail to sprout? It must germinate somehow or other. I feel like laughing when I remember what you said the other day."

MASTER: "What was that?"

M: "You said that Jadu Mallick was so absent-minded that while taking his meals he didn't know whether a particular dish was seasoned with salt or not. If anyone pointed out to him that a dish was not salted, he would say, in a surprised voice: 'Yes? Yes? I see it is not salted.' You told this to the doctor because he had said to you that he was always absent-minded. You meant that he became absent-minded thinking of worldly things and not because of contemplation of God."

MASTER: "Will he not pay attention to what I say?"

M: "Of course he will. But he forgets many of your instructions because of his numerous duties. Today, too, he made a nice remark when he said, 'To look on a woman as mother is a spiritual discipline of the Tantra.'"

MASTER: "What did I say to that?"

M: "You told him about that *Bhāgavata* scholar who owned bullocks and ploughs. (*The Master smiles.*) Further, you told him about the king who said to the pundit of the *Bhāgavata*, 'You had better understand it yourself first.' (*The Master smiles.*)

"Then you told him about the *Gītā*, whose essence is the renunciation of 'woman and gold', renunciation of the attachment to 'woman and gold'. You said to him, 'How can a worldly man who has not renounced "woman and gold" teach others?' Perhaps he didn't understand the drift of your words. He changed the subject."

Sri Ramakrishna was thinking about the welfare of his devotees. Purna and Manindra were two of his young devotees. He sent Manindra to talk to Purna.

It was evening. A lamp was burning in Sri Ramakrishna's room. The devotees and visitors were sitting at a distance. The Master was introspective. Those in the room were also thinking of God and sat in silence.

A few minutes afterwards Narendra entered the room with a friend, whom he introduced to the Master as an author. Sri Ramakrishna talked with him about the metaphysical significance of Rādhā and Krishna. The author said that Rādhā and Krishna were the Supreme Brahman. Vishnu, Śiva, Durgā, and the other deities had sprung from them.

MASTER: "That is good. There are different aspects of Rādhā. In Her seductive aspect She was Chandrāvali. In Her aspect of love She participated in Sri Krishna's līlā at Vrindāvan. Nandaghosh, Krishna's foster-father, had the vision of the Eternal Rādhā.

"First is the seductive Rādhā, then the Rādhā of love. If you go farther, you will see the Eternal Rādhā. It is like taking off the layers of an onion one by one. First the red layers, then the pink, then the white. Afterwards you don't find any more layers. Such is the nature of the Eternal Rādhā, Rādhā the Absolute. There the discrimination following the process of 'Not this, not this' comes to an end.

"There are two aspects of Rādhā-Krishna: the Absolute and the Relative.

They are like the sun and its rays. The Absolute may be likened to the sun, and the Relative to the rays.

"A genuine bhakta dwells sometimes on the Absolute and sometimes on the Relative. Both the Absolute and the Relative belong to one and the same Reality. It is all one—neither two nor many."

AUTHOR: "Sir, why do they speak of the 'Krishna of Vrindāvan' and the 'Krishna of Mathurā'?"[4]

MASTER: "That is the view of the goswāmis. But the scholars of upper India think differently. According to these scholars there is only Krishna, and no Rādhā. The Krishna of Dwārakā is not associated with Rādhā."

AUTHOR: "Sir, Rādhā and Krishna are themselves the Supreme Brahman."

MASTER: "That is good. But you must remember that everything is possible for God. He is formless, and again He assumes forms. He is the individual and He is the universe. He is Brahman and He is Śakti. There is no end to Him, no limit. Nothing is impossible for Him. No matter how high the kites and vultures soar, they can never strike against the ceiling of the sky. If you ask me what Brahman is like, all I can say is that It cannot be described in words. Even when one has realized Brahman, one cannot describe It. If someone asks you what ghee is like, your answer will be, 'Ghee is like ghee.' The only analogy for Brahman is. Brahman. Nothing exists besides It."

Saturday, October 31, 1885

Hariballav Bose, a cousin of Balaram, came to see Sri Ramakrishna. He saluted the Master respectfully.

Hariballav was the government pleader at Cuttack. He did not approve of Balaram's visiting the Master, especially with the ladies of the family: Balaram had said to his cousin: "You had better meet him first. Then you can say whatever you like."

Presently the Master and Hariballav became engaged in conversation.

MASTER: "Can you tell me how I shall get well? Do you think this is a serious illness?"

HARIBALLAV: "Sir, the doctors can tell you better than I about that."

MASTER: "When the women take the dust of my feet, I say to myself that they are saluting God, who dwells inside me. I look at it in that way."

HARIBALLAV: "You are a holy man. All should take the dust of your feet. What harm is there in that?"

MASTER: "You may speak that way about sages like Dhruva, Prahlāda, Nārada, or Kapila; but who am I? Please come again."

HARIBALLAV: "I shall certainly come, because you attract me. You don't have to urge me."

Hariballav was about to depart. He saluted Sri Ramakrishna and was going to take the dust of the Master's feet, when Sri Ramakrishna moved

---

[4] The Krishna of Vrindāvan, where He was a cowherd boy, is always associated with Rādhā and the gopis; but the Krishna of Mathurā and Dwārakā, where He was the king, is not associated with them.

his feet away. But Hariballav persisted; he took the dust of Sri Ramakrishna's feet against the latter's wish.

When he stood up, the Master stood up too, to show him courtesy. The Master said to him: "Balaram feels unhappy because I don't go to his house. I thought of visiting you all there one day, but then I was afraid you might say to Balaram, 'Who asked him to come here?' "

HARIBALLAV: "Who has been telling you things? Please don't let such a thought enter your mind."

Hariballav departed.

MASTER (to M.): "He is a devotee of God; why else would he have forcibly taken the dust of my feet? I told you the other day that in samādhi I had seen Dr. Sarkar and another person. He is the other person. So he has come."

M: "Yes, sir. Undoubtedly he is a bhakta."

MASTER: "How guileless he is!"

M. went to Dr. Sarkar's house to report Sri Ramakrishna's condition. The doctor talked to M. about Sri Ramakrishna, Mahimacharan, and the other devotees.

DOCTOR: "Mahimacharan didn't bring the book he promised to show me. He said he had forgotten all about it. It is quite possible. I am forgetful too."

M: "He has read a great deal."

DOCTOR: "Then why is he in such a plight?"

Referring to the Master, the doctor said: "What will a man accomplish with mere bhakti? He needs jnāna too."

M: "Why, the Master says that bhakti comes after jnāna. But his conception of jnāna and bhakti is quite different from yours. When he says that one obtains bhakti after jnāna, he means that first comes the Knowledge of Reality and then bhakti; first the Knowledge of Brahman and then bhakti; first the Knowledge of God and then love for Him. When you speak of jnāna you mean the knowledge obtained through the senses. The jnāna Sri Ramakrishna speaks of cannot be verified by our standards. The Knowledge of Reality cannot be tested by the knowledge obtained through the senses. But your jnāna, the knowledge through the senses, can be verified."

The doctor remained silent. Then he referred to the subject of Divine Incarnation.

DOCTOR: "What is this idea of Divine Incarnation? What is this taking the dust of a man's feet?"

M: "Why, you say that during your experiments in the laboratory you go into ecstasy when you think of God's creation. Further, you feel the same emotion when you think of man. If that is so, why shouldn't we bow our heads before God? God dwells in the heart of man.

"According to Hinduism God dwells in all beings. You have not studied this subject much. Since God dwells in all beings, what is wrong in saluting a man?

"Sri Ramakrishna says that there is a greater manifestation of God in certain things than in others, as the sun is reflected better by water and by a mirror than by other objects. Water exists everywhere, but is most apparent in a river or lake. We bow down to God and not to man. God is God—not, man is God.

"God cannot be known through reasoning. All depends on faith. Of course, I am repeating to you what Sri Ramakrishna says."

Dr. Sarkar presented M. with one of his books, *The Physiological Basis of Psychology.* He wrote on the first page "As a token of brotherly regards."

It was about eleven o'clock in the morning. Sri Ramakrishna was sitting in his room with the devotees. He was talking to a Christian devotee named Misra. Misra was born of a Christian family in northwestern India and belonged to the Quaker sect. He was thirty-five years old. Though clad in European dress he wore the ochre cloth of a sannyāsi under his foreign clothes. Two of his brothers had died on the day fixed for the marriage of one of them, and on that very day Misra had renounced the world.

MISRA: " 'It is Rāma alone who dwells in all beings.' "

Sri Ramakrishna said to the younger Naren, within Misra's hearing: "Rāma is one, but He has a thousand names. He who is called 'God' by the Christians is addressed by the Hindus as Rāma, Krishna, Iśvara, and by other names. A lake has many ghāts. The Hindus drink water at one ghāt and call it 'jal'; the Christians at another, and call it 'water'; the Mussalmāns at a third, and call it 'pāni'. Likewise, He who is God to the Christians is Allāh to the Mussalmāns."

MISRA: "Jesus is not the son of Mary. He is God Himself. (*To the devotees*) Now he (*pointing to Sri Ramakrishna*) is as you see him—again, he is God Himself. You are not able to recognize him. I have seen him before, in visions, though I see him now directly with my eyes. I saw a garden where he was seated on a raised seat. Another person was seated on the ground, but he was not so far advanced.

"There are four door-keepers of God in this country: Tukārām in Bombay, Robert Michael in Kashmir, himself [meaning Sri Ramakrishna] in this part of the country, and another person in eastern Bengal."

MASTER: "Do you see visions?"

MISRA: "Sir, even when I lived at home I used to see light. Then I had a vision of Jesus. How can I describe that beauty? How insignificant is the beauty of a woman compared with that beauty!"

After a while Misra took off his trousers and showed the devotees the gerruā loin-cloth that he wore underneath.

Presently Sri Ramakrishna went out on the porch. Returning to the room, he said to the devotees, "I saw him [meaning Misra] standing in a heroic posture." As he uttered these words he went into samādhi. He stood facing the west.

Regaining partial consciousness, he fixed his gaze on Misra and began to laugh. Still in an ecstatic mood, he shook hands with him and laughed again. Taking him by the hands, he said, "You will get what you are seeking."

MISRA (*with folded hands*): "Since that day I have surrendered to you my mind, soul, and body."

Sri Ramakrishna was laughing, still in an ecstatic mood.

The Master resumed his seat. Misra was describing his worldly life to the devotees. He told them how his two brothers were killed when the canopy came down at the time of the marriage.

Sri Ramakrishna asked the devotees to take care of Misra.

Dr. Sarkar arrived. At the sight of him Sri Ramakrishna went into samādhi. When his ecstasy abated a little, he said, "First the bliss of divine inebriation and then the Bliss of Satchidānanda, the Cause of the cause."

DOCTOR: "Yes."

MASTER: "I am not unconscious."

The doctor realized that the Master was inebriated with divine bliss. Therefore he said, "No, no! You are quite conscious."

Sri Ramakrishna smiled and said:

> I drink no ordinary wine, but Wine of Everlasting Bliss,
> As I repeat my Mother Kāli's name;
> It so intoxicates my mind that people take me to be drunk!
> First my guru gives molasses for the making of the Wine;
> My longing is the ferment to transform it.
> Knowledge, the maker of the Wine, prepares it for me then;
> And when it is done, my mind imbibes it from the bottle of the mantra,
> Taking the Mother's name to make it pure.
> Drink of this Wine, says Rāmprasād, and the four fruits of life are yours.

As the doctor listened to the words, he too became almost ecstatic. Sri Ramakrishna again went into a deep spiritual mood and placed his foot on the doctor's lap. A few minutes later he became conscious of the outer world and withdrew his foot. He said to the doctor: "Ah, what a splendid thing you said the other day! 'We lie in the lap of God. To whom shall we speak about our illness if not to Him?' If I must pray, I shall certainly pray to Him." As Sri Ramakrishna said these words, his eyes filled with tears. Again he went into ecstasy and said to the doctor, "You are very pure; otherwise I could not have put my foot on your lap." Continuing, he said: " 'He alone has peace who has tasted the Bliss of Rāma.' What is this world? What is there in it? What is there in money, wealth, honour, or creature comforts? 'O mind, know Rāma! Whom else should you know?' "

The devotees were worried to see the Master's repeated ecstasies in this state of ill health. He said, "I shall be quiet if someone sings that song— 'The Wine of Heavenly Bliss'."

Narendra was sent for from another room. He sang in his sweet voice:

> Be drunk, O mind, be drunk with the Wine of Heavenly Bliss!
> Roll on the ground and weep, chanting Hari's sweet name!
> Fill the arching heavens with your deep lion roar,
> Singing Hari's sweet name! With both your arms upraised,
> Dance in the name of Hari and give His name to all!
> Swim day and night in the sea of the bliss of Hari's love;
> Slay desire with His name, and blessed be your life!

Master: "And that one—'Upon the Sea of Blissful Awareness'."
Narendra sang:

> Upon the Sea of Blissful Awareness waves of ecstatic love arise:
> Rapture divine! Play of God's Bliss!
> Oh, how enthralling! . . .

Narendra sang again:

> Meditate, O my mind, on the Lord Hari,
> The Stainless One, Pure Spirit through and through.
> How peerless is the light that in Him shines!
> How soul-bewitching is His wondrous form!
> How dear is He to all His devotees!
>
> Ever more beauteous in fresh-blossoming love
> That shames the splendour of a million moons,
> Like lightning gleams the glory of His form,
> Raising erect the hair for very joy.
>
> Worship His feet in the lotus of your heart;
> With mind serene and eyes made radiant
> With heavenly love, behold that matchless sight.
> Caught in the spell of His love's ecstasy,
> Immerse yourself for evermore, O mind,
> In Him who is Pure Knowledge and Pure Bliss.

Dr. Sarkar listened to the songs attentively. When the singing was over, he said, "That's a nice one—'Upon the Sea of Blissful Awareness'."

At the sight of the doctor's joy, Sri Ramakrishna said: "The son said to the father, 'Father, you taste a little wine, and after that, if you ask me to give up drinking, I shall do so.' After drinking the wine, the father said: 'Son, you may give it up. I have no objection. But I am certainly not going to give it up myself!' (*The doctor and the others laugh.*)

"The other day the Divine Mother showed me two men in a vision. He [meaning the doctor] is one. She also revealed to me that he will have much knowledge; but it is dry knowledge. (*Smiling, to the doctor*) But you will soften."

Dr. Sarkar remained silent.

Friday, November 6, 1885

It was the day of the Kāli Pujā, the worship of the Divine Mother, Sri Ramakrishna's Chosen Ideal. At about nine o'clock in the morning the Master, clad in a new cloth, stood in the south room on the second floor of his temporary residence at Śyāmpukur. He had asked M. to offer worship to Siddheśvari at Thanthaniā, in the central part of Calcutta, with flowers, green coconut, sugar, and other sweets. After bathing in the Ganges, M. had offered the worship and come barefoot to Śyāmpukur. He had brought the prasād with him. Sri Ramakrishna took off his shoes and with great reverence ate a little of the prasād and placed a little on his head.

At the Master's request M. had purchased two books of songs by Rāmprasād and Kamalākānta for Dr. Sarkar.

M: "Here are the books of songs by Rāmprasād and Kamalākānta."

MASTER: "Force songs like these on the doctor:

> How are you trying, O my mind, to know the nature of God? . . .
>
> Who is there that can understand what Mother Kāli is? . . .
>
> O mind, you do not know how to farm!
> Fallow lies the field of your life. . . .
>
> Come, let us go for a walk, O mind, to Kāli, the Wish-fulfilling Tree. . . ."

M: "Yes, sir."

Sri Ramakrishna was pacing the room with M. He had put on his slippers. In spite of his painful illness his face beamed with joy.

MASTER: "And this song is also very good: 'This world is a framework of illusion.' "

M: "Yes, sir."

Suddenly Sri Ramakrishna gave a start. He put aside his slippers and stood still. He was in deep samādhi. It was the day of the Divine Mother's worship. Was that why he frequently went into samādhi? After a long while he sighed and restrained his emotion as if with great difficulty.

It was about ten o'clock. Sri Ramakrishna was seated on his bed, leaning against the pillow. The devotees sat around him. Ram, Rakhal, Niranjan, Kalipada, M., and many others were present. Sri Ramakrishna was talking about his nephew Hriday.

MASTER: "Hriday is even now clamouring for land. He said to me one day while he was living with me at Dakshineswar, 'Give me a shawl, or I will sue you.' The Divine Mother removed him from Dakshineswar. He pestered the visitors for money. If he had stayed with me all these people could not have come. That is why the Mother removed him. R— also began to act that way. He became querulous. When he was asked to accompany me in a carriage he would hold back. He would be annoyed if the other youngsters came to me. If I went to Calcutta to see them, he would say: 'Why should you bother about them? Will they renounce the world?' If I wanted to offer refreshments to the other young boys, I would be afraid of R— and say to him, 'Take some yourself and then give it to them.' I came to know that he would not stay with me. Thereupon I said to the Divine Mother, 'Mother, don't remove him altogether, like Hriday.' Then I came to know that he was going to Vrindāvan. If R— had stayed with me at that time, all these youngsters could not have mixed with me. He left for Vrindāvan and these young boys began to visit me frequently."

R— (humbly): "Sir, that wasn't really in my mind."

RAM (to R—): "Do you think you understand your mind as well as he understands it?"

R— remained silent.

MASTER (to R—): "Why should you feel that way? I love you more than a father loves his son. . . . Now please keep quiet. . . . You no longer have that attitude."

After a time the devotees went to another room. Sri Ramakrishna sent for R— and said to him, "Did you mind what I said?"

R—: "No, sir."

Sri Ramakrishna said to M.: "It is the day of the Kāli Puja. It is good to make some arrangements for the worship. Please speak to the devotees about it."

M. went to the drawing-room and told the devotees what the Master had said. Kalipada and others busied themselves with the arrangements.

About two o'clock in the afternoon Dr. Sarkar arrived, accompanied by Professor Nilmani. The doctor listened to the report of the illness and prescribed medicine. Sri Ramakrishna said to him, "These two books have been purchased for you." M. handed him the books.

The doctor wanted to hear some songs. At the Master's bidding, M. and another devotee sang:

> How are you trying, O my mind, to know the nature of God?
> You are groping like a madman locked in a dark room. . . .

Then they sang:

> Who is there that can understand what Mother Kāli is?
> Even the six darśanas are powerless to reveal Her.
> It is She, the scriptures say, that is the Inner Self
> Of the yogi, who in Self discovers all his joy;
> She that, of Her own sweet will, inhabits every living thing.
>
> The macrocosm and microcosm rest in the Mother's womb;
> Now do you see how vast it is? In the Mulādhāra
> The yogi meditates on Her, and in the Sahasrāra:
> Who but Śiva has beheld Her as She really is?
> Within the lotus wilderness She sports beside Her Mate, the Swan.
>
> When man aspires to understand Her, Rāmprasād must smile;
> To think of knowing Her, he says, is quite as laughable
> As to imagine one can swim across the boundless sea.
> But while my mind has understood, alas! my heart has not;
> Though but a dwarf, it still would strive to make a captive of the
>   moon.

Again they sang:

> O mind, you do not know how to farm!
> Fallow lies the field of your life.
> If you had only worked it well,
> How rich a harvest you might reap! . . .

Then:

> Come, let us go for a walk, O mind, to Kāli, the Wish-fulfilling
>   Tree,
> And there beneath It gather the four fruits of life. . . .

Dr. Sarkar said to Girish, "That song of yours is very nice—the one about the vīnā, in the *Life of Buddha*."

At a hint from the Master, Girish and Kalipada sang together:

> Behold my vīnā, my dearly beloved,
> My lute of sweetest tone;
> If tenderly you play on it,
> The strings will waken, at your touch,
> To rarest melodies. . . .

They continued:

> We moan for rest, alas! but rest can never find;
> We know not whence we come, nor where we float away.
> Time and again we tread this round of smiles and tears;
> In vain we pine to know whither our pathway leads,
> And why we play this empty play. . . .

They sang again:

> Hold me fast, O Nitāi! I feel as if I shall pass away!
> Bestowing Hari's name on men,
> I raised high waves in the river of my love,
> And now upon its raging stream I am carried helplessly.
> With grief my heart is laden down;
> Alas! Nitāi, to whom shall I speak of it?
> Behold, I am swiftly borne away by the current of man's deep woe.

Then they sang:

> Jagāi! Mādhāi! Oh, come and dance,
> Chanting Hari's name with fervour! . . .

And finally:

> Come one and all! Take Rādhā's love!
> The high tide of her love flows by;
> It will not last for very long.
> Oh, come then! Come ye, one and all! . . .

Listening to these songs, two or three of the devotees—among them, Manindra and Latu—went into a spiritual mood. Latu was seated by Niranjan's side. When the singing was over, the Master spoke with the doctor. The previous day Dr. Pratap Mazumdar had prescribed nux vomica for the Master. Dr. Sarkar was annoyed to hear of it.

DOCTOR: "To give him nux vomica! Why, I am not dead yet!"

MASTER (*smiling*): "Why should you die? God forbid! May your avidyā die."

DOCTOR: "I never have any avidyā!"

Dr. Sarkar understood avidyā to mean "mistress".

MASTER (*smiling*): "Oh, no! I don't mean that! In the case of a sannyāsi, his mother, Avidyā, Ignorance, dies giving birth to a child, Viveka, Discrimination."

Hariballav arrived. Sri Ramakrishna said, "I feel very happy when I see you." Hariballav was a man of very humble nature; he sat on the bare floor and not on the mat. He began to fan the Master. He was the government lawyer at Cuttack. Professor Nilmani sat near them. Sri Ramakrishna did not want to offend him; casting his glance on the professor, he said, "Oh, what a grand day it is for me!"

A few minutes later Dr. Sarkar and Professor Nilmani took their leave. Hariballav also departed, saying that he would come again.

It is the dark night of the new moon. At seven o'clock the devotees make arrangements for the worship of Kāli in Sri Ramakrishna's room on the second floor. Flowers, sandal-paste, vilwa-leaves, red hibiscus, rice pudding, and various sweets and other articles of worship are placed in front of the Master. The devotees are sitting around him. There are present, among others, Sarat, Sashi, Ram, Girish, Chunilal, M., Rakhal, Niranjan, and the younger Naren.

Sri Ramakrishna asks a devotee to bring some incense. A few minutes later he offers all the articles to the Divine Mother. M. is seated close to him. Looking at M., he says to the devotees, "Meditate a little." The devotees close their eyes.

Presently Girish offers a garland of flowers at Sri Ramakrishna's feet. M. offers flowers and sandal-paste. Rakhal, Ram, and the other devotees follow him.

Niranjan offers a flower at Sri Ramakrishna's feet, crying: "Brahmamayi! Brahmamayi!" and prostrates himself before him, touching the Master's feet with his head. The devotees cry out, "Jai Mā!", "Hail to the Mother!"

In the twinkling of an eye Sri Ramakrishna goes into deep samādhi. An amazing transformation takes place in the Master before the very eyes of the devotees. His face shines with a heavenly light. His two hands are raised in the posture of granting boons and giving assurance to the devotees; it is the posture one sees in images of the Divine Mother. His body is motionless; he has no consciousness of the outer world. He sits facing the north. Is the Divine Mother of the Universe manifesting Herself through his person? Speechless with wonder, the devotees look intently at Sri Ramakrishna, who appears to them to be the embodiment of the Divine Mother Herself.

The devotees begin to sing hymns, one of them leading and the rest following in chorus.

Girish sings:

Who is this Woman with the thick black hair,
Shining amidst the assembly of the gods?
Who is She, whose feet are like crimson lotuses
Planted on Śiva's chest?
Who is She, whose toe-nails shine like the full moon,
Whose legs burn with the brightness of the sun?
Who is She, who now speaks soft and smiles on us,
And now fills all the quarters of the sky
With shouts of terrible laughter?

Again:

> O Mother, Saviour of the helpless, Thou the Slayer of sin!
> In Thee do the three gunas dwell—sattva, rajas, and tamas.
> Thou dost create the world; Thou dost sustain it and destroy it;
> Binding Thyself with attributes, Thou yet transcendest them;
> For Thou, O Mother, art the All. . . .

Behari sings:

> O Śyāmā, Thou who dost sit upon a corpse!
> I beg Thee, hear my heart's most fervent prayer:
> As my last breath forsakes this mortal flesh,
> Reveal Thyself within my heart!
> Then, in my mind, from forest and from grove
> I shall gather Thee red hibiscus flowers,
> And, scenting them with the sandal-paste of Love,
> Shall lay them at Thy Lotus Feet.

M. sings with the other devotees:

> O Mother, all is done after Thine own sweet will;
> Thou art in truth self-willed, Redeemer of mankind!
> Thou workest Thine own work; men only call it theirs. . . .

They sing again:

> All things are possible, O Mother, through Thy grace;
> Obstacles mountain high Thou makest to melt away.
> Thou Home of Bliss! To all Thou givest peace and joy;
> Why then should I be made to suffer fruitlessly,
> Brooding on the success or failure of my deeds?

And again:

> O Mother, ever blissful as Thou art,
> Do not deprive Thy worthless child of bliss!
> My mind knows nothing but Thy Lotus Feet.
> The King of Death scowls at me terribly;
> Tell me, Mother, what shall I say to him? . . .

They conclude:

> In dense darkness, O Mother, Thy formless beauty sparkles;
> Therefore the yogis meditate in a dark mountain cave. . . .

Gradually Sri Ramakrishna came back to the consciousness of the outer world. He asked the devotees to sing "O Mother Śyāmā, full of the waves of drunkenness divine". They sang:

> O Mother Śyāmā, full of the waves of drunkenness divine!
> Who knows how Thou dost sport in the world?
> Thy fun and frolic and Thy glances put to shame the god of
>   love. . . .

When this song was over, Sri Ramakrishna asked the devotees to sing "Behold my Mother playing with Śiva". The devotees sang:

> Behold my Mother playing with Śiva, lost in an ecstasy of joy!
> Drunk with a draught of celestial wine, She reels, and yet She
>   does not fall. . . .

Sri Ramakrishna tasted a little pudding to make the devotees happy, but immediately went into deep ecstasy.

A few minutes later the devotees prostrated themselves before the Master and went into the drawing-room. There they enjoyed the prasād.

It was nine o'clock in the evening. Sri Ramakrishna sent word to the devotees, asking them to go to Surendra's house to participate in the worship of Kāli.

They arrived at Surendra's house on Simlā Street and were received very cordially. Surendra conducted them to the drawing-room on the second floor. The house was filled with a festive atmosphere and a veritable mart of joy was created with the songs and music of the devotees. It was very late at night when they returned to their homes after enjoying the sumptuous feast given by Surendra, the Master's beloved disciple.

THE MASTER AT COSSIPORE

-1000*Wednesday, December 23, 1885*

ON FRIDAY, DECEMBER 11, Sri Ramakrishna was moved to a beautiful house at Cossipore, a suburb of Calcutta. The house was situated in a garden covering about five acres of land and abounding in fruit-trees and flowering plants. Here the final curtain fell on the Master's life.

At Cossipore he set himself with redoubled energy to the completion of the work of spiritual ministration he had begun long before at Dakshineswar. Realizing that the end of his physical life was approaching, he gave away his spiritual treasures without stint to one and all. He was like one of those fruit-sellers who bring their fruit to the market-place, bargain at first about the prices, but then toward sunset, when the market is about to close, give away the fruit indiscriminately. Here his disciples saw the greatest manifestation of his spiritual powers. Here they saw the fulfilment of his prophecies about his own end: "I shall make the whole thing public before I go." "When people in large numbers come to know and whisper about the greatness of this body, then the Mother will take it back." "The devotees will be sifted into inner and outer circles toward the end." And so on. Here he predicted that a band of young disciples, with Narendranath as their leader, would in due course renounce the world and devote themselves to the realization of God and the service of humanity.

The main building at Cossipore had two storeys, with three rooms below and two above. The Master occupied the central hall of the upper storey; a small room to the left was used at night by his attendants. To the right of the hall was an open balcony where Sri Ramakrishna sometimes sat or walked. On the ground floor, a hall just below the Master's and a small room to the right of it were used by the devotees, and a small room to the extreme left was occupied by the Holy Mother. In the garden compound were some outbuildings, two reservoirs, and pleasant walks. Sri Ramakrishna breathed more freely in the open air of the new place.

Almost all the devotees had gathered by this time. They had started coming to him in 1881. By the end of 1884 Sarat and Sashi had become known to the Master, and since their college examinations in the middle of 1885 they had been visiting him almost daily. Girish Ghosh had first met the Master in September 1884 at the Star Theatre. Since the beginning of the

931

following December he had been a constant visitor. And it was during the latter part of December 1884 that Sarada Prasanna first visited the Master at the Dakshineswar temple. Subodh and Kshirode first visited him in August 1885.

The young devotees had taken up their quarters at the garden house to tend Sri Ramakrishna, although many of them visited their own homes every now and then. The householders came to see the Master almost every day, and some of them occasionally spent the night.

On the morning of December 23 Sri Ramakrishna gave unrestrained expression to his love for the devotees. He said to Niranjan, "You are my father: I shall sit on your lap." Touching Kalipada's chest, he said, "May your inner spirit be awakened!" He stroked Kalipada's chin affectionately and said, "Whoever has sincerely called on God or performed his daily religious devotions will certainly come here." In the morning two ladies received his special blessing. In a state of samādhi he touched their hearts with his feet. They shed tears of joy. One of them said to him, weeping, "You are so kind!" His love this day really broke all bounds. He wanted to bless Gopal of Sinthi and said to a devotee, "Bring Gopal here."

It was evening. Sri Ramakrishna was absorbed in contemplation of the Mother of the Universe. After a while he began to talk very softly with some of the devotees. Kali, Chunilal, M., Navagopal, Sashi, Niranjan, and a few others were present.

MASTER (to M.): "Buy a stool for me. What will it cost?"

M: "Between two and three rupees."

MASTER: "If a small wooden seat costs only twelve ārinās, why should you have to pay so much for a stool?"

M: "Perhaps it won't cost so much."

MASTER: "Tomorrow is Thursday. The latter part of the afternoon is inauspicious. Can't you come before three o'clock?"

M: "Yes, sir. I shall."

MASTER: "Well, can you tell how long it will take me to recover from this illness?"

M: "It has been aggravated a little and will take some days."

MASTER: "How long?"

M: "Perhaps five to six months."

Hearing this, Sri Ramakrishna became impatient, like a child, and said: "So long? What do you mean?"

M: "I mean, sir, for complete recovery."

MASTER: "Oh, that! I am relieved. Can you explain one thing? How is it that in spite of all these visions, all this ecstasy and samādhi, I am so ill?"

M: "Your suffering is no doubt great; but it has a deep meaning."

MASTER: "What is it?"

M: "A change is coming over your mind. It is being directed toward the formless aspect of God. Even your 'ego of Knowledge' is vanishing."

MASTER: "That is true. My teaching of others is coming to an end. I cannot give any more instruction. I see that everything is Rāma Himself. And sometimes I say to myself, 'Whom shall I teach?' You see, because I am living in a rented house many kinds of devotees are coming here. I hope I shall not have to put up a 'signboard', like Shashadhar or Krishnaprasanna Sen,[1] announcing my lectures." (*The Master and M. laugh.*)

M: "There is yet another purpose in this illness. It is the final sifting of disciples. The devotees have achieved in these few days what they could not have realized by five years' tapasyā. Their love and devotion are growing by leaps and bounds."

MASTER: "That may be true; but Niranjan went back home. (*To Niranjan*) Please tell me how you feel."

NIRANJAN: "Formerly I loved you, no doubt, but now it is impossible for me to live without you."

M: "One day I found out how great these young men were."

MASTER: "Where?"

M: "Sir, one day I stood in a corner of the house at Śyāmpukur and watched the devotees. I clearly saw that every one of them had made his way here through almost insurmountable obstacles and given himself over to your service."

As Sri Ramakrishna listened to these words he became abstracted. He was silent a few moments. Presently he went into samādhi.

Regaining consciousness of the outer world, he said to M.: "I saw everything passing from form to formlessness. I want to tell you all the things I saw, but I cannot. Well, this tendency of mine toward the formless is only a sign of my nearing dissolution. Isn't that so?"

M. (*wonderingly*): "It may be."

MASTER: "Even now I am seeing the Formless Indivisible Satchidānanda— just like that. . . . But I have suppressed my feelings with great difficulty.

"What you said about the sifting of disciples was right: this illness is showing who belong to the inner circle and who to the outer. Those who are living here, renouncing the world, belong to the inner circle; and those who pay occasional visits and ask, 'How are you, sir?' belong to the outer circle.

"Didn't you notice Bhavanath? The other day he came to Śyāmpukur dressed as a bridegroom and asked me, 'How are you?' I haven't seen him since. I show him love for Narendra's sake, but he is not in my thought any more.

(*To M.*) "When God assumes a human body for the sake of His devotees, many of His devotees accompany Him to this earth. Some of them belong to the inner circle, some to the outer circle, and some become the suppliers of His physical needs.

"I experienced one of my first ecstasies when I was ten or eleven years old, as I was going through a meadow to the shrine of Viśālākshi. What a vision! I became completely unconscious of the outer world.

"I was twenty-two or twenty-three when the Divine Mother one day asked me in the Kāli temple, 'Do you want to be *Akshara*?' I didn't know

[1] Shashadhar and Krishnaprasanna were two well-known Hindu preachers, contemporaries of Sri Ramakrishna.

what the word meant. I asked Haladhari about it. He said, 'Kshara means jīva, living being; Akshara means Paramātman, the Supreme Soul.'

"At the hour of the evening worship in the Kāli temple I would climb to the roof of the kuthi and cry out: 'O devotees, where are you all? Come to me soon! I shall die of the company of worldly people!' I told all this to the 'Englishmen'. They said it was all an illusion of my mind. 'Perhaps it is', I said to myself, and became calm. But now it is all coming true; the devotees are coming.

"The Divine Mother also showed me in a vision the five suppliers of my needs; first, Mathur Babu, and second, Sambhu Mallick, whom I had not then met. I had a vision of a fair-skinned man with a cap on his head. Many days later, when I first met Sambhu, I recalled that vision; I realized that it was he whom I had seen in that ecstatic state. I haven't yet found out the three other suppliers of my wants. But they were all of a fair complexion. Surendra looks like one of them.

"When I attained this state of God-Consciousness, a person exactly resembling myself thoroughly shook my Idā, Pingalā, and Sushumnā nerves. He licked with his tongue each of the lotuses of the six centres, and those drooping lotuses at once turned their faces upward. And at last the Sahasrārā lotus became full-blown.

"The Divine Mother used to reveal to me the nature of the devotees before their coming. I saw with these two eyes—not in a trance—the kirtan party of Chaitanya going from the banyan-tree to the bakul-tree in the Panchavati. I saw Balaram in the procession and also, I think, yourself [meaning M.]. Chuni's spiritual consciousness and yours, too, have been awakened by frequent visits to me. In a vision I saw that Sashi and Sarat had been among the followers of Christ.

"Under the banyan-tree in the Panchavati I had a vision of a child. Hriday said to me, 'Then a son will soon be born to you.' I said to him: 'But I regard all women as mother. How can I have a son?' That child is Rakhal.

"I said to the Divine Mother, 'O Mother, since You have placed me in this condition, provide me with a rich man.' That is why Mathur served me for fourteen years.[2] And in how many different ways! At my request he arranged a special store-room for the sādhus. He provided me with carriage and palanquin. And whatever I asked him to give to anyone, he gave. The Brāhmani[3] identified him with Pratāprudra.[4]

"Vijay had a vision of this form [meaning himself]. How do you account for it? Vijay said to me, 'I touched it exactly as I am touching you now.'

"Latu counted thirty-one devotees in all. That's not many. But a few more are becoming devotees through Vijay and Kedar.

"It was revealed to me in a vision that during my last days I should have to live on pudding. During my present illness my wife was one day feeding

---

[2] From 1858 to 1871.
[3] The brāhmin woman who was one of the Master's spiritual teachers.
[4] A king of Orissa and a devoted follower of Chaitanyadeva, whom he served with the utmost love and faithfulness.

me with pudding. I burst into tears and said, 'Is this my living on pudding near the end, and so painfully?' "

It was the fourteenth day of the dark fortnight of the moon. At four o'clock in the afternoon Sri Ramakrishna was sitting in his room. He told M. that Ram Chatterji had come from the Kāli temple at Dakshineswar to inquire about his health. He asked M. whether it was now very cold at the temple garden.

Narendra arrived. Now and then the Master looked at him and smiled. It appeared to M. that that day the Master's love for his beloved disciple was boundless. He indicated to M. by a sign that Narendra had wept. Then he remained quiet. Again he indicated that Narendra had cried all the way from home.

No one spoke. Narendra broke the silence.

NARENDRA: "I have been thinking of going there today."

MASTER: "Where?"

NARENDRA: "To Dakshineswar. I intend to light a fire under the bel-tree and meditate."

MASTER: "No, the authorities of the powder-magazine will not allow it. The Panchavati is a nice place. Many sādhus have practised japa and meditation there. But it is very cold there. The place is dark, too."

Again for a few moments all sat in silence.

MASTER (to Narendra, smiling): "Won't you continue your studies?"

NARENDRA (looking at the Master and M.): "I shall feel greatly relieved if I find a medicine that will make me forget all I have studied."

The elder Gopal, who was also in the room, said, "I shall accompany Narendra."

Kalipada Ghosh had brought a box of grapes for Sri Ramakrishna; it lay beside the Master. The Master gave Narendra a few and poured the rest on the floor for the devotees to pick up.

It was evening. Narendra was sitting in a room downstairs. He was smoking and describing to M. the yearning of his soul. No one else was with them.

NARENDRA: "I was meditating here last Saturday when suddenly I felt a peculiar sensation in my heart."

M: "It was the awakening of the Kundalini."

NARENDRA: "Probably it was. I clearly perceived the Idā and the Pingalā nerves. I asked Hazra to feel my chest. Yesterday I saw him [meaning the Master] upstairs and told him about it. I said to him: 'All the others have had their realization; please give me some. All have succeeded; shall I alone remain unsatisfied?' "

M: "What did he say to you?"

NARENDRA: "He said: 'Why don't you settle your family affairs first and then come to me? You will get everything. What do you want?' I replied, 'It is my desire to remain absorbed in samādhi continually for three or four days, only once in a while coming down to the sense plane to eat a little food.' Thereupon he said to me: 'You are a very small-minded person. There is a state higher even than that. "All that exists art Thou"—it is you who sing that song.' "

M: "Yes, he always says that after coming down from samādhi one sees that it is God Himself who has become the universe, the living beings, and all that exists. The Iśvarakotis alone can attain that state. An ordinary man can at the most attain samādhi; but he cannot come down from that state."

NARENDRA: "He [the Master] said: 'Settle your family affairs and then come to me. You will attain a state higher than samādhi.' I went home this morning. My people scolded me, saying: 'Why do you wander about like a vagabond? Your law examination is near at hand and you are not paying any attention to your studies. You wander about aimlessly.' "

M: "Did your mother say anything?"

NARENDRA: "No. She was very eager to feed me. She gave me venison. I ate a little, though I didn't feel like eating meat."

M: "And then?"

NARENDRA: "I went to my study at my grandmother's. As I tried to read I was seized with a great fear, as if studying were a terrible thing. My heart struggled within me. I burst into tears: I never wept so bitterly in my life. I left my books and ran away. I ran along the streets. My shoes slipped from my feet—I didn't know where. I ran past a haystack and got hay all over me. I kept on running along the road to Cossipore."

Narendra remained silent a few minutes and then resumed.

NARENDRA: "Since reading the *Vivekachudāmani* I have felt very much depressed. In it Śankarāchārya says that only through great tapasyā and good fortune does one acquire these three things: a human birth, the desire for liberation, and refuge with a great soul. I said to myself: 'I have surely gained all these three. As a result of great tapasyā I have been born a human being; through great tapasyā, again, I have the desire for liberation; and through great tapasyā I have secured the companionship of such a great soul.' "

M: "Ah!"

NARENDRA: "I have no more taste for the world. I do not relish the company of those who live in the world—of course, with the exception of one or two devotees."

Narendra became silent again. A fire of intense renunciation was burning within him. His soul was restless for the vision of God. He resumed the conversation.

NARENDRA (to M.): "You have found peace, but my soul is restless. You are blessed indeed."

M. did not reply, but sat in silence. He said to himself, "Sri Ramakrishna said that one must pant and pine for God; only then may one have the vision of Him."

Immediately after dusk M. went upstairs. He found Sri Ramakrishna asleep.

It was about nine o'clock in the evening. Niranjan and Sashi were sitting near the Master. He was awake. Every now and then he talked of Narendra.

MASTER: "How wonderful Narendra's state of mind is! You see, this very Narendra did not believe in the forms of God. And now you see how his soul is panting for God! You know that story of the man who asked his guru how God could be realized. The guru said to him: 'Come with me. I shall show you how one can realize God.' Saying this, he took the disciple to a lake and held his head under the water. After a short time he released the disciple and asked him, 'How did you feel?' 'I was dying for a breath of air!' said the disciple.

"When the soul longs and yearns for God like that, then you will know that you do not have long to wait for His vision. The rosy colour on the eastern horizon shows that the sun will soon rise."

This day Sri Ramakrishna's illness was worse. In spite of much suffering he said many things about Narendra—though mostly by means of signs.

At night Narendra left for Dakshineswar. It was very dark, being the night of the new moon. He was accompanied by one or two devotees. M. spent the night at the Cossipore garden. He dreamt that he was seated in an assembly of sannyāsis.

Tuesday, January 5, 1886

Sri Ramakrishna was sitting on his bed and talking to M. No one else was in the room. It was about four o'clock in the afternoon.

MASTER: "If Kshirode makes a pilgrimage to Gangāsāgar, then please buy a blanket for him."

M: "Yes, sir."

Sri Ramakrishna was silent a few minutes. Then he continued.

MASTER: "Well, can you tell me what is happening to these youngsters? Some are running off to Puri and some to Gangāsāgar. All have renounced their homes. Look at Narendra! When a man is seized with the spirit of intense renunciation, he regards the world as a deep well and his relatives as venomous cobras."

M: "Yes, sir. Life in the world is full of suffering."

MASTER: "Yes, it is the suffering of hell—and that from the very moment of birth! Don't you see what a trouble one's wife and children are?"

M: "Yes, sir. You yourself said: 'These youngsters[5] have no relationship whatsoever with the world. They owe nothing to the world, nor do they expect anything from it. It is the sense of obligation that entangles a man in the world.' "

MASTER: "Don't you see how Niranjan is? His attitude toward the world is this: 'Here, take what is thine, and give me what is mine.' That is all. He has no further relationship with the world. There is nothing to pull him from behind.

" 'Woman and gold' alone is the world. Don't you see that if you have money you want to lay it by?"

M. burst out laughing. Sri Ramakrishna also laughed.

M: "One thinks a great deal before taking the money out. (*Both laugh.*)

[5] The Master had meant his young disciples.

But once you said at Dakshineswar that it is quite different if one is able to live in the world free from the three gunas."

MASTER: "Yes—like a child!"

M: "Yes, sir. But it is exceedingly difficult; it requires tremendous power." Sri Ramakrishna remained silent.

M: "Yesterday they went to Dakshineswar to meditate. I had a dream."

MASTER: "What did you dream?"

M: "I dreamt that Narendra and some others had become sannyāsis. They were sitting around a lighted fire. I too was there. They were smoking tobacco and blowing out puffs of smoke. I told them that I could smell hemp."[6]

MASTER: "Mental renunciation is the essential thing. That, too, makes one a sannyāsi."

Sri Ramakrishna kept silent a few minutes and then went on.

MASTER: "But one must set fire to one's desires. Then alone can one succeed."

M: "You said to the pundit of the Mārwāris from Burrabāzar that you had the desire for bhakti. Isn't the desire for bhakti to be counted as a desire?"

MASTER: "No, just as hinchē greens are not to be counted as greens. Hinchē restrains the secretion of bile.

"Well, all my joy, all my ecstasy—where are they now?"

M: "Perhaps you are now in the state of mind that the Gītā describes as beyond the three gunas. Sattva, rajas, and tamas are performing their own functions, and you yourself are unattached—unattached even to sattva."

MASTER: "Yes, the Divine Mother has put me into the state of a child. Tell me, won't the body live through this illness?"

The Master and M. became silent. Narendra entered the room. He was going home to settle his family affairs.

Since his father's death Narendra had been in great distress about his mother and brothers. Now and then they had been threatened with starvation. Narendra was the family's only hope: they expected him to earn money and feed them. But Narendra could not appear for his law examination; he was passing through a state of intense renunciation. He was going to Calcutta that day to make some provision for the family. A friend had agreed to lend him one hundred rupees. That would take care of the family for three months.

NARENDRA: "I am going home. (To M.) I shall visit Mahimacharan on the way. Will you come with me?"

M. did not want to go. Looking at M., Sri Ramakrishna asked Narendra, "Why?"

NARENDRA: "I am going that way; so I shall stop at Mahima's place and have a chat with him."

Sri Ramakrishna looked at Narendra intently.

NARENDRA: "A friend who comes here said he would lend me a hundred rupees. That will take care of the family for three months. I am going home to make that arrangement."

[6] Many wandering sannyāsis smoke Indian hemp.

Sri Ramakrishna remained silent and looked at M.

M. (to Narendra): "No, you go ahead. I shall go later."

Thursday, March 11, 1886

It was eight o'clock in the evening. Sri Ramakrishna was in the big hall on the second floor. Narendra, Sashi, M., Sarat, and the elder Gopal were in the room. Sri Ramakrishna was lying down. Sarat stood by his bed and fanned him. The Master was speaking about his illness.

MASTER: "If some of you go to Dakshineswar and see Bholanath, he will give you a medicinal oil and also tell you how to apply it."

THE ELDER GOPAL: "Then we shall go for the oil tomorrow morning."

M: "If someone goes this evening he can bring the oil."

SASHI: "I can go."

MASTER (pointing to Sarat): "He may go."

After a time Sarat set out for Dakshineswar to get the oil from Bholanath. The devotees, sitting around Sri Ramakrishna's bed, were silent. Suddenly the Master sat up. He spoke to Narendranath.

MASTER: "Brahman is without taint. The three gunas are in Brahman, but It is Itself untainted by them.

"You may find both good and bad smells in the air; but the air itself is unaffected.

"Sankarāchārya was going along a street in Benares. An outcaste carrying a load of meat suddenly touched him. 'What!' said Sankara. 'You have touched me!' 'Revered sir,' said the outcaste, 'I have not touched you nor have you touched me. The Ātman is above all contamination, and you are that Pure Ātman.'

"Of Brahman and māyā, the jnāni rejects māyā.

"Māyā is like a veil. You see, I hold this towel between you and the lamp. You no longer see the light of the lamp."

Sri Ramakrishna put the towel between himself and the devotees.

MASTER: "Now you cannot see my face any more. As Rāmprasād said, 'Raise the curtain, and behold!'

"The bhakta, however, does not ignore māyā. He worships Mahāmāyā. Taking refuge in Her, he says: 'O Mother, please stand aside from my path. Only if You step out of my way shall I have the Knowledge of Brahman.' The jnānis explain away all three states—waking, dream, and deep sleep. But the bhaktas accept them all. As long as there is the ego, everything else exists. So long as the 'I' exists, the bhakta sees that it is God who has become māyā, the universe, the living beings, and the twenty-four cosmic principles."

Narendra and the other devotees sat silently listening.

MASTER: "But the theory of māyā is dry. (To Narendra) Repeat what I said."

NARENDRA: "Māyā is dry."

Sri Ramakrishna affectionately stroked Narendra's face and hands, and said: "Your face and hands show that you are a bhakta. But the jnāni has different features; they are dry.

"Even after attaining jnāna, the jnāni can live in the world, retaining vidyāmāyā, that is to say, bhakti, compassion, renunciation, and such virtues. This serves him two purposes: first, the teaching of men, and second, the enjoyment of divine bliss. If a jnāni remains silent, merged in samādhi, then men's hearts will not be illumined. Therefore Śankarāchārya kept the 'ego of Knowledge'. And further, a jnāni lives as a devotee, in the company of bhaktas, in order to enjoy and drink deep of the Bliss of God.

"The 'ego of Knowledge' and the 'ego of Devotion' can do no harm; it is the 'wicked I' that is harmful. After realizing God a man becomes like a child. There is no harm in the 'ego of a child'. It is like the reflection of a face in a mirror: the reflection cannot call names. Or it is like a burnt rope, which appears to be a rope but disappears at the slightest puff. The ego that has been burnt in the fire of Knowledge cannot injure anybody. It is an ego only in name.

"Returning to the relative plane after reaching the Absolute is like coming back to this shore of a river after going to the other side. Such a return to the relative plane is for the teaching of men and for enjoyment—participation in the divine sport in the world."

Sri Ramakrishna was talking in a very low voice. Addressing the devotees, he said: "The body is so ill, but the mind is free from avidyāmāyā. Let me tell you, there is no thought in my mind of Ramlal or home or wife. But I have been worrying about Purna, that kāyastha boy. I am not in the least anxious about the others.

"It is God alone who has kept this vidyāmāyā in me, for the good of men, for the welfare of the devotees.

"But if one retains vidyāmāyā one comes back to this world. The Avatārs keep this vidyāmāyā. So long as a man has even the slightest desire, he must be born again and again. When he gets rid of all desires, then he is liberated. But the bhaktas do not seek liberation.

"If a person dies in Benares he attains liberation; he is not born again. Liberation is the goal of the jnānis."

NARENDRA: "The other day we went to visit Mahimacharan."

MASTER (smiling): "Well?"

NARENDRA: "I have never before met such a dry jnāni."

MASTER (smiling): "What was the matter?"

NARENDRA: "He asked us to sing. Gangadhar sang:

Rādhā is restored to life by hearing her Krishna's name.
She looks about; in front of her she sees a tamāla tree.

"On hearing this song, Mahimacharan said: 'Why such songs here? I don't care for love and all that nonsense. Besides, I live here with my wife and children. Why all these songs here?'"

MASTER (to M.): "Do you see how afraid he is?"

Sunday, March 14, 1886

Sri Ramakrishna sat facing the north in the large room upstairs. It was evening. He was very ill. Narendra and Rakhal were gently massaging his

feet. M: sat near by. The Master, by a sign, asked him, too, to stroke his feet. M. obeyed.

The previous Sunday the devotees had observed Sri Ramakrishna's birthday with worship and prayer. His birthday the year before had been observed at Dakshineswar with great pomp; but this year, on account of his illness, the devotees were very sad and there was no festivity at all.

The Holy Mother busied herself day and night in the Master's service. Among the young disciples, Narendra, Rakhal, Niranjan, Sarat, Sashi, Baburam, Jogin, Latu, and Kali had been staying with him at the garden house. The older devotees visited him daily, and some of them occasionally spent the night there.

That day Sri Ramakrishna was feeling very ill. At midnight the moonlight flooded the garden, but it could wake no response in the devotees' hearts. They were drowned in a sea of grief. They felt that they were living in a beautiful city besieged by a hostile army. Perfect silence reigned everywhere. Nature was still, except for the gentle rustling of the leaves at the touch of the south wind. Sri Ramakrishna lay awake. One or two devotees sat near him in silence. At times he seemed to doze.

M. was seated by his side. Sri Ramakrishna asked him by a sign to come nearer. The sight of his suffering was unbearable. In a very soft voice and with great difficulty he said to M.:

"I have gone on suffering so much for fear of making you all weep. But if you all say: 'Oh, there is so much suffering! Let the body die', then I may give up the body."

These words pierced the devotees' hearts. And he who was their father, mother, and protector had uttered these words! What could they say? All sat in silence. Some thought, "Is this another crucifixion—the sacrifice of the body for the sake of the devotees?"

It was the dead of night. Sri Ramakrishna's illness was taking a turn for the worse. The devotees wondered what was to be done. One of them left for Calcutta. That very night Girish came to the garden house with two physicians, Upendra and Navagopal.

The devotees sat near the Master. He felt a little better and said to them: "The illness is of the body. That is as it should be; I see that the body is made of the five elements."

Turning to Girish, he said: "I am seeing many forms of God. Among them I find this one also [meaning his own form]."

Monday, March 15, 1886

About seven o'clock in the morning Sri Ramakrishna felt a little better. He talked to the devotees, sometimes in a whisper, sometimes by signs. Narendra, Rakhal, Latu, M., Gopal of Sinthi, and others were in the room. They sat speechless and looked grave, thinking of the Master's suffering of the previous night.

MASTER (*to the devotees*): "Do you know what I see right now? I see that it is God Himself who has become all this. It seems to me that men and other living beings are made of leather, and that it is God Himself who, dwelling inside these leather cases, moves the hands, the feet, the heads. I had a similar vision once before, when I saw houses, gardens, roads, men, cattle—all made of One Substance; it was as if they were all made of wax.

"I see that it is God Himself who has become the block, the executioner, and the victim for the sacrifice."

As he describes this staggering experience, in which he realizes in full the identity of all within the One Being, he is overwhelmed with emotion and exclaims, "Ah! What a vision!"

Immediately Sri Ramakrishna goes into samādhi. He completely forgets his body and the outer world. The devotees are bewildered. Not knowing what to do, they sit still.

Presently the Master regains partial consciousness of the world and says: "Now I have no pain at all. I am my old self again."

The devotees are amazed to watch this state of the Master, beyond pleasure and pain, weal and woe.

He casts his glance on Latu and says: "There is Loto. He bends his head, resting it on the palm of his hand. I see that it is God Himself who rests His head on His hand."

Sri Ramakrishna looks at the devotees and his love for them wells up in a thousand streams. Like a mother showing her tenderness to her children he touches the faces and chins of Rakhal and Narendra.

A few minutes later he says to M., "If the body were to be preserved a few days more, many people would have their spirituality awakened."

He pauses a few minutes.

"But this is not to be. This time the body will not be preserved."

The devotees eagerly await the Master's next words.

"Such is not the will of God. This time the body will not be preserved, lest, finding me guileless and foolish, people should take advantage of me, and lest I, guileless and foolish as I am, should give away everything to everybody. In this Kaliyuga, you see, people are averse to meditation and japa."

RAKHAL (tenderly): "Please speak to God that He may preserve your body some time more."

MASTER: "That depends on God's will."

NARENDRA: "Your will and God's will have become one."

Sri Ramakrishna remains silent. He appears to be thinking about something.

MASTER (to Narendra, Rakhal, and the others): "And nothing will happen if I speak to God. Now I see that I and the Mother have become one. For fear of her sister-in-law, Rādhā said to Krishna, 'Please dwell in my heart.' But when, later on, she became very eager for a vision of Krishna—so eager that her heart pined and panted for her Beloved—He would not come out."

RAKHAL (in a low voice, to the devotees): "He is referring to God's Incarnation as Gaurānga."[7]

[7] According to the Bengal school of Vaishnavism Sri Krishna wanted to taste and enjoy His own sweetness as Rādhā did. But this could not be done to the fullest

The devotees sit silently in the room. Sri Ramakrishna looks at them tenderly. Then he places his hand on his heart. He is about to speak.

MASTER (*to Narendra and the others*): "There are two persons in this. One, the Divine Mother—"

He pauses. The devotees eagerly look at him to hear what he will say next.

MASTER: "Yes, one is She. And the other is Her devotee. It is the devotee who broke his arm, and it is the devotee who is now ill. Do you understand?"

The devotees sit without uttering a word.

MASTER: "Alas! To whom shall I say all this? Who will understand me?"

Pausing a few moments, he says:

"God becomes man, an Avatār, and comes to earth with His devotees. And the devotees leave the world with Him."

RAKHAL: "Therefore we pray that you may not go away and leave us behind."

Sri Ramakrishna smiles and says:

"A band of minstrels suddenly appears, dances, and sings, and it departs in the same sudden manner. They come and they return, but none recognizes them."

The Master and the devotees smile.

After a few minutes he says:

"Suffering is inevitable when one assumes a human body.

"Every now and then I say to myself, 'May I not have to come back to earth again!' But there is something else. After enjoying sumptuous feasts outside, one does not relish cheap home cooking.

"Besides, this assuming of a human body is for the sake of the devotees."

Sri Ramakrishna looks at Narendra very tenderly.

MASTER (*to Narendra*): "An outcaste was carrying a load of meat. Śankarāchārya, after bathing in the Ganges, was passing by. Suddenly the outcaste touched him. Śankara said sharply: 'What! You touched me!' 'Revered sir,' he replied, 'I have not touched you nor have you touched me. Reason with me: Are you the body, the mind, or the buddhi? Analyse what you are. You are the Pure Ātman, unattached and free, unaffected by the three gunas—sattva, rajas, and tamas.'

"Do you know what Brahman is like? It is like air. Good and bad smells are carried by the air, but the air itself is unaffected."

NARENDRA: "Yes, sir."

MASTER: "He is beyond the gunas and māyā—beyond both the 'māyā of knowledge' and the 'māyā of ignorance'. 'Woman and gold' is the 'māyā of ignorance'. Knowledge, renunciation, devotion, and other spiritual qualities are the splendours of the 'māyā of knowledge'. Śankarāchārya kept this

---

extent unless Krishna were infatuated with Himself, as Rādhā had been. Accordingly He assumed a form in which all the aspects of the Krishna of Vrindāvan and those of Rādhā coexisted; and in this aspect Krishna enjoyed His own charm and sweetness. This form is known as Sri Gaurānga, who was a blending of Rādhā and Krishna.

'māyā of knowledge'; and that you and these others feel concerned about me is also due to this 'māyā of knowledge'.

"Following the 'māyā of knowledge' step by step, one attains the Knowledge of Brahman. This 'māyā of knowledge' may be likened to the last few steps of the stairs. Next is the roof. Some, even after reaching the roof, go up and down the stairs; that is to say, some, even after realizing God, retain the 'ego of Knowledge'. They retain this in order to teach others, taste divine bliss, and sport with the devotees of God."

NARENDRA: "Some people get angry with me when I speak of renunciation."

MASTER (in a whisper): "Renunciation is necessary.

(Pointing to his different limbs) "If one thing is placed upon another, you must remove the one to get the other. Can you get the second thing without removing the first?"

NARENDRA: "True, sir."

MASTER (in a whisper, to Narendra): "When one sees everything filled with God alone, does one see anything else?"

NARENDRA: "Must one renounce the world?"

MASTER: "Didn't I say just now: 'When one sees everything filled with God alone, does one see anything else?' Does one then see any such thing as the world?

"I mean mental renunciation. Not one of those who have come here is a worldly person. Some of them had a slight desire—for instance, a fancy for woman. (Rakhal and M. smile.) And that desire has been fulfilled."

The Master looks at Narendra tenderly and becomes filled with love. Looking at the devotees, he says, "Grand!"

With a smile Narendra asks the Master, "What is grand?"

MASTER (smiling): "I see that preparations are going on for a grand renunciation."

Narendra and the devotees look silently at the Master. Rakhal resumes the conversation.

RAKHAL (smiling, to the Master): "Narendra is now beginning to understand you rather well."

Sri Ramakrishna laughs and says: "Yes, that is so. I see that many others, too, are beginning to understand. (To M.) Isn't that so?"

M: "Yes, sir."

Sri Ramakrishna turns his eyes to Narendra and M. and by a sign of his finger draws the attention of the devotees to them. He first points out Narendra and then M. Rakhal understands the Master's hint and says to him with a smile, "Don't you mean that Narendra has the attitude of a hero, and he [meaning M.] that of a handmaid of God?"

Sri Ramakrishna laughs.

NARENDRA (smiling, to Rakhal): "He [meaning M.] doesn't talk much and is bashful. Is that why you say he is a handmaid of God?"

MASTER (smiling, to Narendra): "Well, what do you think of me?"

NARENDRA: "You are a hero, a handmaid of God, and everything else."

These words fill Sri Ramakrishna with divine emotion. He places his hand on his heart and is about to say something.

He says to Narendra and the other devotees:

"I see that all things—everything that exists—have come from this."

He asks Narendra by a sign, "What did you understand?"

NARENDRA: "All created objects have come from you."

The Master's face beams with joy. He says to Rakhal, "Did you hear what he said?"

Sri Ramakrishna asks Narendra to sing. Narendra intones a hymn. His mind is full of renunciation. He sings:

> Unsteady is water on the lotus petal;
> Just as unsteady is the life of man.
> One moment with a sādhu is the boat
> That takes one across the ocean of this world. . . .

Narendra has hardly finished one or two lines, when Sri Ramakrishna says to him by a sign: "What are you singing? That is a very insignificant attitude, a very commonplace thing."

Now Narendra sings about the love of Krishna, impersonating one of His handmaids:

> How strange, O friend, are the rules of life and death!
> The Youth of Braja has fled away,
> And this poor maid of Braja soon will die.
> Mādhava is in love with other maids
> More beautiful than I.
> Alas! He has forgotten the milkman's artless daughter.
>
> Who would ever have guessed, dear friend, that He,
> A Lover so tender, so divine,
> Could be a beggar simply for outward charm?
> I was a fool not to have seen it before;
> But carried away by His beauty,
> I yearned alone to hold His two feet to my breast.
>
> Now I shall drown myself in the Jamunā's stream,
> Or take a draught of poison, friend!
> Or I shall bind a creeper round my neck,
> Or hang myself from a young tamāla tree;
> Or, failing all of these,
> Destroy my wretched self by chanting Krishna's name.

Sri Ramakrishna and the devotees are greatly moved by the song. The Master and Rakhal shed tears of love. Narendra is intoxicated with the love of the gopis of Braja for their Sweetheart, Sri Krishna, and sings:

> O Krishna! Beloved! You are mine.
> What shall I say to You, O Lord?
> What shall I ever say to You?
> Only a woman am I,
> And never fortune's favourite;
> I do not know what to say.

You are the mirror for the hand,
And You are the flower for the hair.
O Friend, I shall make a flower of You
And wear You in my hair;
Under my braids I shall hide You, Friend!
No one will see You there.

You are the betel-leaf for the lips,
The sweet collyrium for the eyes;
O Friend, with You I shall stain my lips,
With You I shall paint my eyes.

You are the sandal-paste for the body;
You are the necklace for the neck.
I shall anoint myself with You,
My fragrant Sandal-paste,
And soothe my body and my soul.
I shall wear You, my lovely Necklace,
Here about my neck,
And You will lie upon my bosom,
Close to my throbbing heart.

You are the Treasure in my body;
You are the Dweller in my house.
You are to me, O Lord,
What wings are to the flying bird,
What water is to the fish.

THE MASTER AND BUDDHA

IT WAS FIVE O'CLOCK in the afternoon. Narendra, Kali, Niranjan, and M. were talking downstairs in the Cossipore garden house.

NIRANJAN (*to M.*): "Is it true that Vidyāsāgar is going to open a new school? Why don't you try to secure employment there for Naren?"

NARENDRA: "I have had enough of service under Vidyāsāgar."

Narendra had just returned from a visit to Bodh-Gayā, where he had gone with Kali and Tarak. In that sacred place he had been absorbed in deep meditation before the image of Buddha. He had paid his respects to the Bodhi-tree, which is an offshoot of the original tree under which Buddha attained Nirvāna.

Kali said, "One day at Gayā, at Umesh Babu's house, Narendra sang many classical songs to the accompaniment of the mridanga."

Sri Ramakrishna sat on his bed in the big hall upstairs. It was evening. M. was alone in the room, fanning the Master. Latu came in a little later.

MASTER (*to M.*): "Please bring a chāddar for me and a pair of slippers."

M: "Yes, sir."

MASTER (*to Latu*): "The chāddar will cost ten ānnās, and then the slippers—what will be the total cost?"

LATU: "One rupee and ten ānnās."

Sri Ramakrishna asked M., by a sign, to note the price.

Narendra entered the room and took a seat. Sashi, Rakhal, and one or two other devotees came in. The Master asked Narendra to stroke his feet. He also asked him whether he had taken his meal.

MASTER (*smiling, to M.*): "He went there [referring to Bodh-Gayā]."

M. (*to Narendra*): "What are the doctrines of Buddha?"

NARENDRA: "He could not express in words what he had realized by his tapasyā. So people say he was an atheist."

MASTER (*by signs*): "Why atheist? He was not an atheist. He simply could not express his inner experiences in words. Do you know what 'Buddha' means? It is to become one with Bodha, Pure Intelligence, by meditating on That which is of the nature of Pure Intelligence; it is to become Pure Intelligence Itself."

NARENDRA: "Yes, sir. There are three classes of Buddhas: Buddha, Arhat, and Bodhisattva."

MASTER: "This too is a sport of God Himself, a new līlā of God.

"Why should Buddha be called an atheist? When one realizes Svarupa, the true nature of one's Self, one attains a state that is something between asti, *is*, and nāsti, *is-not*."

NARENDRA (*to M.*): "It is a state in which contradictions meet. A combination of hydrogen and oxygen produces cool water; and the same hydrogen and oxygen are used in the oxy-hydrogen blowpipe.

"In that state both activity and non-activity are possible; that is to say, one then performs unselfish action.

"Worldly people, who are engrossed in sense-objects, say that everything exists—*asti*. But the māyāvādis, the illusionists, say that nothing exists—*nāsti*. The experience of a Buddha is beyond both 'existence' and 'non-existence'."

MASTER: "This 'existence' and 'non-existence' are attributes of Prakriti. The Reality is beyond both."

The devotees remained silent a few moments.

MASTER (*to Narendra*): "What did Buddha preach?"

NARENDRA: "He did not discuss the existence or non-existence of God. But he showed compassion for others all his life.

"A hawk pounced upon a bird and was about to devour it. In order to save the bird, Buddha gave the hawk his own flesh."

Sri Ramakrishna remained silent. Narendra became more and more enthusiastic about Buddha.

NARENDA: "How great his renunciation was! Born a prince, he renounced everything! If a man has nothing, no wealth at all, what does his renunciation amount to? After attaining Buddhahood and experiencing Nirvāna, Buddha once visited his home and exhorted his wife, his son, and many others of the royal household to embrace the life of renunciation. How intense his renunciation was! But look at Vyāsa's conduct! He forbade his son Śukadeva to give up the world, saying, 'My son, practise religion as a householder.'"

Sri Ramakrishna was silent. As yet he had not uttered a word.

NARENDRA: "Buddha did not care for Śakti or any such thing. He sought only Nirvāna. Ah, how intense his dispassion was! When he sat down under the Bodhi-tree to meditate, he took this vow: 'Let my body wither away here if I do not attain Nirvāna.' Such a firm resolve!

"This body, indeed, is the great enemy. Can anything be achieved without chastising it?"

SASHI: "But it is you who say that one develops sattva by eating meat. You insist that one should eat meat."

NARENDRA: "I eat meat, no doubt, but I can also live on rice, mere rice, even without salt."

After a few minutes Sri Ramakrishna broke his silence. He asked Narendra, by a sign, whether he had seen a tuft of hair on Buddha's head.

NARENDRA: "No, sir. He seems to have a sort of crown; his head seems to be covered by strings of rudrāksha beads placed on top of one another."

MASTER: "And his eyes?"

NARENDRA: "They show that he is in samādhi."

Sri Ramakrishna again became silent. Narendra and the other devotees looked at him intently. Suddenly a smile lighted his face and he began to talk with Narendra. M. was fanning him.

MASTER (to Narendra): "Well, here you find everything—even ordinary red lentils and tamarind. Isn't that so?"

NARENDRA: "After experiencing all those states, you are now dwelling on a lower plane."

M. (to himself): "Yes, after realizing all those ideals, he is now living as a bhakta, a devotee of God."

MASTER: "Someone seems to be holding me to a lower plane."

Saying this, Sri Ramakrishna took the fan from M.'s hand and said: "As I see this fan, *directly* before me, in exactly the same manner have I seen God. And I have seen—"

With these words he placed his hand on his heart and asked Narendra, by a sign, "Can you tell me what I said?"

NARENDRA: "I have understood."

MASTER: "Tell me."

NARENDRA: "I didn't hear you well."

Sri Ramakrishna said again, by a sign, "I have seen that He and the one who dwells in my heart are one and the same Person."

NARENDRA: "Yes, yes! Soham—I am He."

MASTER: "But only a line divides the two—that I may enjoy divine bliss."

NARENDRA (to M.): "Great souls, even after their own liberation, retain the ego and experience the pleasure and pain of the body that they may help others to attain liberation.

"It is like coolie work. We perform coolie work under compulsion, but great souls do so of their own sweet pleasure."

Again all fell into silence. After a time Sri Ramakrishna resumed the conversation.

MASTER (to Narendra and the others): "The roof is clearly visible; but it is extremely hard to reach it."

NARENDRA: "Yes, sir."

MASTER: "But if someone who has already reached it drops down a rope, he can pull another person up.

"Once a sādhu from Hrishikesh came to Dakshineswar. He said to me: 'How amazing! I find five kinds of samādhi manifested in you.'

"Just as a monkey climbs a tree, jumping from one branch to another, so also does the Mahāvāyu, the Great Energy, rise in the body, jumping from one centre to another, and one goes into samādhi. One feels the rising of the Great Energy, as though it were the movement of a monkey.

"Just as a fish darts about in the water and roams in great happiness, so also does the Mahāvāyu move upward in the body, and one goes into samādhi. One feels the rising of the Great Energy, as though it were the movement of a fish.

"Like a bird hopping from one branch to another, the Mahāvāyu goes up in the tree of the body, now to this branch and now to that. One feels the rising of the Great Energy, as though it were the movement of a bird.

"Like the slow creeping of an ant, the Mahāvāyu rises from centre to centre. When it reaches the Sahasrāra one goes into samādhi. One feels the rising of the Great Energy, as though it were the movement of an ant.

"Like the wriggling of a snake, the Mahāvāyu rises in a zigzag way along the spinal column till it reaches the Sahasrāra, and one goes into samādhi. One feels the rising of the Great Energy, as though it were the movement of a snake."

RAKHAL (to the other devotees): "Let us stop here. He has already talked a great deal. It will aggravate his illness."

Monday, April 12, 1886

About five o'clock in the afternoon Sri Ramakrishna was sitting on the bed in his room in the Cossipore garden house. Sashi and M. were with him. He asked M., by a sign, to fan him. There was a fair in the neighbourhood in celebration of the last day of the Bengali year. A devotee, whom Sri Ramakrishna had sent to the fair to buy a few articles, returned.

"What have you bought?" the Master asked him.

DEVOTEE: "Candy for five pice, a spoon for two pice, and a vegetable-knife for two pice."

MASTER: "What about the penknife?"

DEVOTEE: "I couldn't get one for two pice."

MASTER (eagerly): "Go quickly and get one!"

M. was pacing the garden. Narendra and Tarak returned from Calcutta. They had visited Girish Ghosh's house and other places.

TARAK: "We have eaten a great deal of meat and other heavy stuff today."

NARENDRA: "Yes, our minds have come down a great deal. Let us practise tapasyā. (To M.) What slavery to body and mind! We are just like coolies— as if this body and mind were not ours but belonged to someone else."

In the evening lamps were lighted in the house. Sri Ramakrishna sat on his bed, facing the north. He was absorbed in contemplation of the Mother of the Universe. A few minutes later Fakir, who belonged to the priestly family of Balaram, recited the Hymn of Forgiveness addressed to the Divine Mother. Sashi, M., and two or three other devotees were in the room. After the recital Sri Ramakrishna, with folded hands, very respectfully bowed to the Deity.

M. was fanning Sri Ramakrishna. The Master said to him by signs, "Get a stone cup for me that will hold a quarter of a seer of milk—white stone." He drew the shape of the cup with his finger.

M: "Yes, sir."

MASTER: "When eating from other cups I get the smell of fish."

Tuesday, April 13, 1886

It was about eight o'clock in the morning. M. had spent the night at the garden house. After taking his bath in the Ganges he prostrated himself before Sri Ramakrishna. Ram had just come. He saluted the Master and took a seat. He had brought a garland of flowers, which he offered to the Master. Most of the devotees were downstairs; only one or two were in the Master's room.

Sri Ramakrishna was talking to Ram.

MASTER: "How do you find me?"

RAM: "In you one finds everything.

"Presently there will be a discussion about your illness."

The Master smiled and asked Ram by a sign, "Will there really be a discussion about my illness?"

Sri Ramakrishna's slippers were not comfortable. Dr. Rajendra Dutta intended to buy a new pair[1] and had asked for the measurement of his feet. The measurement was taken.

Sri Ramakrishna asked M., by a sign, about the stone cup. M. at once stood up. He wanted to go to Calcutta for the cup.

MASTER: "Don't bother about it now."

M: "Sir, these devotees are going to Calcutta. I will go with them."

M. bought the cup in Calcutta and returned to Cossipore at noon. He saluted the Master and placed the cup near him. Sri Ramakrishna took the cup in his hands and looked at it. Dr. Rajendra Dutta, Dr. Sreenath, Rakhal Haldar, and several others came in. Rakhal, Sashi, and the younger Naren were in the room. The physicians heard the report of the Master's illness. Dr. Sreenath had a copy of the *Gītā* in his hand.

DR. SREENATH (to his friends): "Everything is under the control of Prakriti. Nobody can escape the fruit of past action. This is called prārabdha."

MASTER: "Why, if one chants the name of God, meditates on Him, and takes refuge in Him—"

DR. SREENATH: "But, sir, how can one escape prārabdha, the effect of action performed in previous births?"

MASTER: "No doubt a man experiences a little of the effect; but much of it is cancelled by the power of God's name. A man was born blind of an eye. This was his punishment for a certain misdeed he had committed in his past birth, and the punishment was to remain with him for six more births. He, however, took a bath in the Ganges, which gives one liberation. This meritorious action could not cure his blindness, but it saved him from his future births."

DR. SREENATH: "But, sir, the scriptures say that nobody can escape the fruit of karma."

Dr. Sreenath was ready to argue with the Master.

MASTER (to M.): "Why don't you tell him that there is a great difference between the Iśvarakoti and an ordinary man? An Iśvarakoti cannot commit sin. Why don't you tell him that?"

M. remained silent and then said to Rakhal, "You tell him."

---

[1] These slippers given by Dr. Rajendra are now worshipped at Belur Math, the Headquarters of the Ramakrishna Math and Mission.

After a few minutes the physicians left the room. Sri Ramakrishna was talking to Rakhal Haldar.

HALDAR: "Dr. Sreenath studies Vedānta. He is a student of the *Yogavāsishtha*."

MASTER: "A householder should not hold the view that everything is illusory, like a dream."

Referring to a man named Kalidas, a devotee said, "He too discusses Vedānta, but he has lost all his money in lawsuits."

MASTER (*smiling*): "Yes, one proclaims everything to be māyā, and still one goes to court! (*To Rakhal*) Mukherji of Janai, too, talked big. But at last he came to his senses. If I were well I should have talked a little more with Dr. Sreenath. Can one obtain jnāna just by talking about it?"

HALDAR: "You are right, sir. I have seen enough of jnāna. Now all I need in order to live in the world is a little bhakti. The other day I came to you with a problem on my mind, and you solved it."

MASTER (*eagerly*): "What was it?"

HALDAR: "Sir, when that boy (*pointing to the younger Naren*) came in, you said he had controlled his passions."

MASTER: "Yes, it is true. He is totally unaffected by worldliness. He says he doesn't know what lust is. (*To M.*) Just feel my body. All the hair is standing on end."

The Master's hair actually stood on end at the thought of a pure mind totally devoid of lust. He always said that God manifests Himself where there is no lust.

Rakhal Haldar took his leave.

Sri Ramakrishna was seated with the devotees. A crazy woman had been troubling everybody in order to see the Master. She had assumed toward him the attitude of a lover and often ran into the garden house and burst into the Master's room. She had even been beaten by the devotees; but that did not stop her.

SASHI: "If she comes again I shall shove her out of the place!"

MASTER (*tenderly*): "No, no! Let her come and go away."

RAKHAL: "At the beginning I too used to feel jealous of others when they visited the Master. But he graciously revealed to me that my guru is also the Guru of the Universe. Has he taken this birth only for a few of us?"

SASHI: "I don't mean that. But why should she trouble him when he is ill? And she is such a nuisance!"

RAKHAL: "We all give him trouble. Did we all come to him after attaining perfection? Haven't we caused him suffering? How Narendra and some of the others behaved in the beginning! How they argued with him!"

SASHI: 'Whatever Narendra expressed in words he carried out in his actions."

RAKHAL: "How rude Dr. Sarkar has been to him! No one is guiltless, if it comes to that."

MASTER (*to Rakhal, tenderly*): "Will you eat something?"

RAKHAL: "Not now. Later on."

Sri Ramakrishna asked M., by a sign, whether he was going to have his meal there.

RAKHAL (*to M.*): "Please take your meal here. He is asking you to."

Sri Ramakrishna was seated completely naked. He looked like a five-year-old boy. Just then the crazy woman climbed the stairs and stood near the door.

M. (*in a low voice, to Sashi*): "Ask her to salute him and go away. Don't make any fuss."

Sashi took her downstairs.

It was the first day of the Bengali year. Many woman devotees arrived. They saluted Sri Ramakrishna and the Holy Mother. Among them were the wives of Balaram and Manomohan, and the brāhmani of Bāghbāzār. Several of them had brought their children along.

Some of the women offered flowers at the Master's feet. Two young girls, nine or ten years of age, sang a few songs.

First they sang:

> We moan for rest, alas! but rest can never find;
> We know not whence we come, nor where we float away.
> Time and again we tread this round of smiles and tears;
> In vain we pine to know whither our pathway leads,
> And why we play this empty play. . . .

Then:

> There comes Rādhā, and there see your Krishna,
> With arching eyes and the flute at His lips. . . .

And finally:

> O tongue, always repeat the name of Mother Durgā!
> Who but your Mother Durgā will save you in distress? . . .

Sri Ramakrishna said by a sign: "That's good! They are singing of the Divine Mother."

The brāhmani of Bāghbāzār had the nature of a child. Sri Ramakrishna told Rakhal, by a sign, to ask her to sing. The devotees smiled as the brāhmani sang:

> O Hari, I shall sport with You today;
> For I have found You alone in the nidhu wood. . . .

The woman devotees went downstairs.

It was afternoon. M. and a few other devotees were seated near the Master. Narendra came in. He looked, as the Master used to say, like an unsheathed sword.

Narendra sat down near the Master and within his hearing expressed his utter annoyance with women. He told the devotees what an obstacle women were in the path of God-realization.

Sri Ramakrishna made no response. He listened to Narendra.

Narendra said again: "I want peace. I do not care even for God."

Sri Ramakrishna looked at him intently without uttering a word. Now and then Narendra chanted, "Brahman is Truth, Knowledge, the Infinite."

It was eight o'clock in the evening. Sri Ramakrishna sat on his bed. A few devotees sat on the floor in front of him. Surendra arrived from his office. He carried in his hands four oranges and two garlands of flowers. Now he looked at the Master and now at the devotees. He unburdened his heart to Sri Ramakrishna.

SURENDRA (looking at M. and the others): "I have come after finishing my office work. I thought, 'What is the good of standing on two boats at the same time?' So I finished my duties first and then came here. Today is the first day of the year; it is also Tuesday, an auspicious day to worship the Divine Mother. But I didn't go to Kālighāt. I said to myself, 'It will be enough if I see him who is Kāli Herself, and who has rightly understood Kāli.'"

Sri Ramakrishna smiled.

SURENDRA: "It is said that a man should bring fruit and flowers when visiting his guru or a holy man. So I have brought these. . . . (To the Master) I am spending all this money for you. God alone knows my heart. Some people feel grieved to give away a penny; and there are people who spend a thousand rupees without feeling any hesitation. God sees the inner love of a devotee and accepts his offering."

Sri Ramakrishna said to Surendra, by a nod, that he was right.

SURENDRA: "I couldn't come here yesterday. It was the last day of the year. But I decorated your picture with flowers."

Sri Ramakrishna said to M., by a sign, "Ah, what devotion!"

SURENDRA: "As I was coming here I bought these two garlands for four ānnās."

Almost all the devotees took their leave. The Master asked M. to stroke his legs and fan him.

Friday, April 16, 1886

The moon was shining brilliantly, flooding the garden paths, the trees, and the water of the lake with its white rays. Girish, M., Latu, and a few other devotees were seated on the steps leading to the lake. The house stood to the west of the lake. A lamp burnt in the Master's room on the second floor. Sri Ramakrishna was sitting on his bed. There were several devotees in the room.

A few minutes later Girish and M. were strolling along a garden path lined with flowering plants and fruit-trees.

M: "How beautiful this moonlight is! Perhaps nature has had the same laws from time out of mind."

GIRISH: "How do you know that?"

M: "There is no change in the uniformity of nature. European scientists have been discovering new stars through the telescope. There are mountains on the moon; they have seen them."

GIRISH: "It is difficult to be sure of that. It is hard for me to believe it."

M: "Why? The mountains have been observed through the telescope."

GIRISH: "How can you be sure that they have been rightly observed? Suppose there are other things between the moon and the earth. Light passing through them may conjure up such visions."

Narendra, Rakhal, Niranjan, Sarat, Sashi, Baburam, Kali, Jogin, Latu, and a few other young devotees had been living at the Cossipore garden house in order to nurse Sri Ramakrishna. That evening Narendra, Kali, and Tarak had gone to Dakshineswar. They were going to spend the night in the Panchavati, meditating on God.

Girish, Latu, and M. went to Sri Ramakrishna's room and found him sitting on the bed. Sashi and one or two devotees had been tending the Master. Baburam, Niranjan, and Rakhal also entered the room. It was a large room. Some medicines and a few other accessories were kept near the bed. One entered the room by a door at the north end.

Since Sri Ramakrishna had to be tended all night, the devotees stayed awake by turns. The devotee who tended him fixed Sri Ramakrishna's mosquito net and then either lay on a mat on the floor or spent the night sitting up. Since Sri Ramakrishna got very little sleep on account of his illness, his attendant, too, slept very little.

That evening Sri Ramakrishna was somewhat better. The devotees saluted the Master and sat down on the floor. The Master asked M. to bring the lamp near him. He greeted Girish cordially.

MASTER (to Girish): "Are you quite well? (To Latu) Prepare a smoke for him and give him a betel-leaf."

A few minutes afterwards he asked Latu to give Girish some refreshments. Latu said that they had been sent for.

Sri Ramakrishna was sitting up. A devotee offered him some garlands of flowers. Sri Ramakrishna put them around his neck one by one. Was he thus worshipping God who dwelt in his heart? The devotees looked at him wonderingly. He took two garlands from his neck and gave them to Girish.

Every now and then Sri Ramakrishna asked whether the refreshments had been brought.

M. was fanning the Master. On the bed was a sandal-wood fan, the offering of a devotee. The Master gave it to M., who continued to fan him with it. He also gave M. two garlands.

M. had lost a son aged seven or eight about a year and a half before. The child had seen the Master many a time. Latu was telling Sri Ramakrishna about M.

LATU: "M. wept bitterly last night at the sight of some books that had belonged to his dead child. His wife is almost mad with grief. She sometimes treats her other children violently. She creates a scene at home because he spends the night here now and then."

Sri Ramakrishna seemed worried to hear of this.

GIRISH: "It is nothing to be wondered at. Even after receiving the instruction of the *Bhagavad Gītā*, Arjuna fainted from grief at the death of his son Abhimanyu."

Girish was given the refreshments on a tray. Sri Ramakrishna took a grain and Girish accepted the rest as prasād. He sat in front of the Master and began to eat. He needed water to drink. There was an earthen jug in the southeast corner of the room. It was the month of April, and the day was hot. Sri Ramakrishna said, "There is some nice water here."

The Master was so ill that he had not enough strength even to stand up. And what did the disciples see to their utter amazement? They saw him leave the bed, completely naked, and move toward the jug! He himself was going to pour the water into a tumbler. The devotees were almost frozen with fear. The Master poured the water into a glass. He poured a drop or two into his hand to see whether it was cool. He found that it was not very cool; but since nothing better could be found, he reluctantly gave it to Girish.

Girish was eating the sweets. The devotees were sitting about, and M. was fanning Sri Ramakrishna.

GIRISH (to the Master): "Deben Babu has decided to renounce the world."

On account of his illness Sri Ramakrishna could hardly talk. Touching his lips with his finger, he asked Girish, by signs, "Who will feed his wife and children?"

GIRISH: "I don't know."

The other devotees remained silent. Girish began talking again while he ate the refreshments.

GIRISH: "Sir, which is wiser—to renounce the world regretfully, or to call on God, leading a householder's life?"

MASTER (to M.): "Haven't you read the Gītā? One truly realizes God if one performs one's worldly duties in a detached spirit, if one lives in the world after realizing that everything is illusory.

"Those who regretfully renounce the world belong to an inferior class.

"Do you know what a householder jnāni is like? He is like a person living in a glass house. He can see both inside and outside."

Again there was silence in the room.

MASTER (to M.): "The refreshments are hot and good."

M. (to Girish): "Yes, they were bought from Fagu's shop. The place is famous."

MASTER (smiling): "Yes, famous."

GIRISH: "They are really nice.

(To the Master) "Sir, my mind is now on a very lofty plane. Why does it come down again?"

MASTER: "That always happens when one leads a worldly life. Sometimes the householder's mind goes up; sometimes it goes down. Sometimes he feels a great deal of devotion; sometimes he feels less. This happens because he lives in the midst of 'woman and gold'. Sometimes a householder contemplates God or chants His name, and sometimes he diverts his mind to 'woman and gold'. He is like an ordinary fly, which now sits on a sweetmeat and now on filth or rotting sores.

"But it is quite different with sannyāsis. They are able to fix their minds on God alone, completely withdrawing them from 'woman and gold'. They can enjoy the Bliss of God alone. A man of true renunciation cannot enjoy anything but God. He leaves any place where people talk of worldly things; he listens only to spiritual talk. A man of true renunciation never speaks about anything but God. The bees light only on flowers, in order to sip honey; they do not enjoy anything else."

Girish went to the small terrace to rinse his hands.

MASTER (to M.): "A man needs the grace of God to fix his whole mind on Him. Well, Girish has eaten a great many sweets. Tell him not to eat anything else tonight."

Girish returned to the room and sat in front of the Master. He was chewing a betel-leaf.

MASTER (to Girish): "Rakhal has now understood what is good and what is bad, what is real and what is unreal. He lives with his family, no doubt, but he knows what it means. He has a wife. And a son has been born to him. But he has realized that all these are illusory and impermanent. Rakhal will never be attached to the world.

"He is like a mudfish. The fish lives in the mud, but there is not the slightest trace of mud on its body."

GIRISH: "Sir, I don't understand all this. You can make everyone pure and unattached if you want to. You can make everyone good, whether he is a worldly man or a sannyāsi. The Malaya breeze, I believe, turns all trees into sandal-wood."

MASTER: "Not unless there is substance in them. There are a few trees, the cotton-tree for instance, which are not turned into sandal-wood."

GIRISH: "I don't care."

MASTER: "But this is the law."

GIRISH: "But everything about you is illegal."

The devotees were listening to this conversation in great amazement. Every now and then the fan in M.'s hand stopped moving.

MASTER: "Yes, that may be true. When the river of bhakti overflows, the land all around is flooded with water to the depth of a pole.

"When a man is inebriated with divine love, he doesn't abide by the injunctions of the Vedas. He picks durvā grass for the worship of the Deity, but he doesn't clean it. He picks whatever he lays his hands on. While gathering tulsi-leaves he even breaks the branches. Ah! What a state of mind I passed through!

(To M.) "When one develops love of God, one needs nothing else."

M: "Yes, sir."

MASTER: "But a devotee must assume toward God a particular attitude. God in His Incarnation as Rāma demonstrated śānta, dāsya, vātsalya, and sakhya. But Krishna demonstrated madhur, besides all these.

"Rādhā cherished the attitude of madhur toward Krishna. Her love was romantic. But in the case of Sītā it was the pure love of a chaste wife for her husband. There was no romance in her love.

"But all this is the līlā of God. He demonstrates different ideals to suit different times."

A crazy woman used to accompany Vijay Goswami to the Kāli temple at

Dakshineswar and sing for Sri Ramakrishna. Her songs were about Kāli. She also used to sing the songs of the Brāhmo Samāj. The devotees called her "Pāgli"[2] and tried to keep her away from the Master.

MASTER (to Girish and the others): "Pāgli cherishes the attitude of madhur toward me. One day she came to Dakshineswar. Suddenly she burst out crying. 'Why are you crying?' I asked her. And she said, 'Oh, my head is aching!' (All laugh.) Another day I was eating when she came to Dakshineswar. She suddenly said, 'Won't you be kind to me?' I had no idea of what was passing through her mind, and went on eating. Then she said, 'Why did you push me away mentally?' I asked her, 'What is your attitude?' She said, 'Madhur.' 'Ah!' I said. 'But I look on all women as manifestations of the Divine Mother. All women are mothers to me.' Thereupon she said, 'I don't know all that.' Then I called Ramlal and said to him: 'Ramlal, listen to her! What is she talking about—this "pushing away mentally"?' Even now she keeps up that attitude."

GIRISH: "Blessed indeed is Pāgli! Maybe she is crazy. Maybe she is beaten by the devotees. But she meditates on you twenty-four hours a day. No matter how she meditates on you, no harm can ever befall her.

"Sir, how can I express my own feelings about it? Think what I was before, and what I have become now by meditating on you! Formerly I was indolent; now that indolence has turned into resignation to God. Formerly I was a sinner; now I have become humble. What else can I say?"

The devotees remained silent. Rakhal expressed his sympathy for Pāgli. He said: "We all feel sorry for her. She causes so much annoyance, and for that she suffers, too."

NIRANJAN (to Rakhal): "You feel that way for her because you have a wife at home. But we could kill her."

RAKHAL (sharply): "Such bragging! How dare you utter such words before him [meaning Sri Ramakrishna]?"

MASTER (to Girish): " 'Woman and gold' alone is the world. Many people regard money as their very life-blood. But however you may show love for money, one day, perhaps, every bit of it will slip from your hand.

"In our part of the country the farmers make narrow ridges around their paddy-fields. You know what those ridges are. Some farmers make ridges with great care all the way around their fields. Such ridges are destroyed by the rush of the rain-water. But some farmers leave a part of the ridge open and put sod there. The water flows through the sod, leaving the field covered with silt after the rain. They reap a rich harvest.

"They alone make good use of their money who spend it for the worship of God or the service of holy men and devotees. Their money bears fruit.

"I cannot eat anything offered by physicians. I mean those who traffic in human suffering. Their money is blood and pus."

Sri Ramakrishna mentioned two physicians in this connection.

GIRISH: "Dr. Rajendra Dutta is a generous person. He doesn't accept a penny from anybody. He gives away money in charity."

[2] The Bengali word for "crazy woman".

It was the night of the full moon. For some time Narendra had been going to Dakshineswar daily. He spent a great deal of time in the Panchavati in meditation and contemplation. This day he returned from Dakshineswar in the evening. Tarak and Kali were with him.

It was eight o'clock in the evening. Moonlight and the south wind added to the charm of the garden house. Many of the devotees were meditating in the room downstairs. Referring to them, Narendra said to M., "They are shedding their upādhis one by one."

A few minutes later M. came into Sri Ramakrishna's room and sat down on the floor. The Master asked him to wash his towel and the spittoon. M. washed them in the reservoir.

Next morning Sri Ramakrishna sent for M. After taking his bath in the Ganges and saluting the Master, he had gone to the roof. Sri Ramakrishna asked M. to bring his grief-stricken wife to the garden house, where she could have her meal.

The Master said to M., by a sign: "Ask her to come. Let her stay here a couple of days. She may bring the baby."

M: "Yes, sir. It would be fine if she developed intense love of God."

Sri Ramakrishna again answered by signs: "Oh, grief pushes out devotion. And he was such a big boy!

"Krishnakishore had two sons. They were of the same age as Bhavanath, and each had two university degrees. They both died. And Krishnakishore, jnāni that he was, could not at first control himself. How lucky I am that I have none!

"Arjuna was a great jnāni; and Krishna was his constant companion. Nevertheless he was completely overwhelmed with grief at the death of his son Abhimanyu.

"Why doesn't Kishori come?"

A DEVOTEE: "He comes to the Ganges every day for his bath."

MASTER: "But why doesn't he come here?"

DEVOTEE: "I shall ask him to come, sir."

MASTER: "Why doesn't Harish come?"

Two young girls aged nine and ten, who belonged to M.'s family, sang several songs about the Divine Mother for the Master. They had sung for him when he had visited M.'s house at Śyāmpukur. The Master was very much pleased with their songs. After they had finished, they were sent for by the devotees to sing for them downstairs.

MASTER (to M.): "Don't teach the girls any more songs. It is different if they sing spontaneously. But they will lose their modesty by singing before anyone and everyone. It is very necessary for women to be modest."

Flowers and sandal-paste were placed before the Master in a flower-basket. He sat on his bed and worshipped himself with these offerings. Sometimes he placed flowers and sandal-paste on his head, sometimes on his throat, sometimes on his heart, and sometimes on his navel.

Manomohan of Konnagar came in and took a seat after saluting the Master. Sri Ramakrishna was still busy with the worship of his inner Self. He put a garland of flowers on his own neck. After a while he seemed to be pleased with Manomohan and gave him some flowers. M., too, received a flower.

It was about nine o'clock in the morning. The Master and M. were talking. Sashi was also in the room.

MASTER (to M.): "What were Narendra and Sashi talking about? What did they discuss?"

M. (to Sashi): "What were you talking about?"

SASHI: "Was it Niranjan that told you about it?"

MASTER: "What were you discussing? I heard 'God', 'Being', 'Non-being', and so forth."

SASHI (smiling): "Shall I call Narendra?"

MASTER: "Yes."

Narendra came in and took a seat.

MASTER (to M.): "Ask him something. (To Narendra) Tell us what you were talking about."

NARENDRA: "I have indigestion. What's there to tell you about?"

MASTER: "You will get over your indigestion."

M. (smiling): "Tell us about the experience of Buddha."

NARENDRA: "Have I become a Buddha, that you want me to talk about him?"

M: "What does Buddha say about the existence of God?"

NARENDRA: "How can you say that God exists? It is you who have created this universe. Don't you know what Berkeley says about it?"

M: "Yes, I do. According to him, esse is percipi.[3] The world exists as long as the sense-organs perceive it."

MASTER: "Nangtā used to say, 'The world exists in mind alone and disappears in mind alone.' But as long as 'I-consciousness' exists, one should assume the servant-and-master relationship with God."

NARENDRA (to M.): "How can you prove by reasoning that God exists? But if you depend on faith, then you must accept the relationship of servant and Master. And if you accept that—and you can't help it—then you must also say that God is kind.

"You think only of the suffering in the world—why do you forget that God has also given you so much happiness? How kind He is to us! He has granted us three very great things: human birth, the yearning to know God, and the companionship of a great soul."

All were silent.

MASTER (to Narendra): "I feel very clearly that there is Someone within me."

Dr. Rajendralal arrived and took a seat. He had been treating the Master with homeopathic medicine. When the talk about medicine was over, Sri Ramakrishna pointed out Manomohan to the doctor.

RAJENDRA: "He is a distant relative of mine."

[3] The existence of external objects depends on their perception.

Narendra went downstairs. He was singing to himself:

> Lord, Thou hast lifted all my sorrow with the vision of Thy face,
> And the magic of Thy beauty has bewitched my mind;
> Beholding Thee, the seven worlds forget their never-ending woe;
> What shall I say, then, of myself, a poor and lowly soul? . . .

Narendra had a little indigestion. He said to M.: "If one follows the path of bhakti, then the mind comes down a little to the body. Otherwise, who am I? Neither man nor God. I have neither pleasure nor pain."

It was about nine o'clock in the evening. Surendra and a few other devotees entered Sri Ramakrishna's room and offered him garlands of flowers. Baburam, Latu, and M. were also in the room.

Sri Ramakrishna put Surendra's garland on his own neck. All sat quietly. Suddenly the Master made a sign to Surendra to come near him. When the disciple came near the bed, Sri Ramakrishna took the garland from his neck and put it around Surendra's. Surendra saluted the Master. Sri Ramakrishna asked him, by a sign, to rub his feet. Surendra gave them a gentle massage.

Several devotees were sitting on the bank of the reservoir in the garden, singing to the accompaniment of drum and cymbals. Sri Ramakrishna sent them word through Latu to sing the name of Hari.

M., Baburam, and several others were still sitting in the Master's room. They heard the devotees singing:

> There dances my Gorā, chanting Hari's name! . . .

When the Master heard the song he made a sign to Baburam and M. to join them. He also asked them to dance.

A few minutes later Sri Ramakrishna sent another devotee to the singers to ask them to sing the following improvised lines: "Ah, my Gorā even knows how to dance!" "How can I describe my Gorā's moods?" "My Gorā dances with both his hands upraised."

The music was over. Surendra was almost in an ecstatic mood. He sang:

> Crazy is my Father,[4] crazy is my Mother,
> And I, their son, am crazy too!
> Śyāmā is my Mother's name.
> My Father strikes His cheeks and makes a hollow sound:
> Ba-ba-bom! Ba-ba-bom!
> And my Mother, drunk and reeling,
> Falls across my Father's body!
> Śyāmā's streaming tresses hang in vast disorder;
> Bees are swarming numberless
> About Her crimson Lotus Feet.
> Listen, as She dances, how Her anklets ring!

[4] Śiva.

51

THE MASTER'S LOVE FOR HIS
DEVOTEES

M. AND NARENDRA were strolling in the garden of the house at Cossipore. Narendra was very much worried because he had not yet been able to solve the financial difficulties of his family.

NARENDRA: "I don't care for the job at the Vidyāsāgar School. I have been thinking of going to Gayā. I have been told that a zemindar there needs the services of a manager for his estate. There is no such thing as God."

M. (*smiling*): "You may say that now, but later on you will talk differently. Scepticism is a stage in the path of God-realization. One must pass through stages like this and go much farther; only thus can one realize God. That is what the Master says."

NARENDRA: "Has anybody seen God as I see that tree?"

M: "Yes, our Master has seen God that way."

NARENDRA: "It may be his hallucination."

M: "Whatever a person experiences in a particular state is real for him in that state. Suppose you are dreaming that you have gone to a garden. As long as the dream lasts, the garden is real for you. But you think of it as unreal when your mind undergoes a change, as, for instance, when you awake. When your mind attains the state in which one sees God, you will know God to be real."

NARENDRA: "I want truth. The other day I had a great argument with Sri Ramakrishna himself."

M. (*smiling*): "What happened?"

NARENDRA: "He said to me, 'Some people call me God.' I replied, 'Let a thousand people call you God, but I shall certainly not call you God as long as I do not know it to be true.' He said, 'Whatever many people say is indeed truth; that is dharma.' Thereupon I replied, 'Let others proclaim a thing as truth, but I shall certainly not listen to them unless I myself realize it as truth.' "

M. (*smiling*): "Your attitude is like that of Western savants—Copernicus and Berkeley, for instance. The whole world said it was the sun that moved, but Copernicus did not listen. Everybody said the external world was real, but Berkeley paid no heed. Therefore Lewis says, 'Why was Berkeley not a philosophical Copernicus?' "

NARENDRA: "Can you give me a History of Philosophy?"

M: "By whom? Lewis?"

NARENDRA: "No, Überweg. I must read a German author."

M: "You just said, 'Has anybody seen God as I see that tree?' Suppose God comes to you as a man and says, 'I am God.' Will you believe it then? You certainly remember the story of Lazarus. After his death, Lazarus said to Abraham, 'Let me go back to the earth and tell my friends and relatives that hell and the after-life exist.' Abraham replied: 'Do you think they will believe you? They will say it is a charlatan who is telling them such things.' The Master says that God cannot be known by reasoning. By faith alone one attains everything—knowledge and super-knowledge. By faith alone one sees God and becomes intimate with Him."

It was about three o'clock in the afternoon. Sri Ramakrishna was in bed. Ramlal, who had come from Dakshineswar, was massaging his feet. Gopal of Sinthi and M. were in the room.

Sri Ramakrishna asked M. to shut the windows and massage his feet. At the Master's request Purna had come to the Cossipore garden in a hired carriage. M. was to pay the carriage hire. Sri Ramakrishna made a sign to Gopal, asking whether he had obtained the money from M. Gopal answered in the affirmative.

At nine o'clock in the evening Surendra, Ram, and the others were about to return to Calcutta. It was the sultry month of April and Sri Ramakrishna's room became very hot during the day; so Surendra had brought some straw screens to keep the room cool.

SURENDRA: "Why, nobody has hung up these straw screens. Nobody here pays attention to anything."

A DEVOTEE (smiling): "The devotees here are now in the state of Brahmajnāna. They feel, 'I am He.' The world is unreal to them. When they come down to a lower plane and regard God as the Master and themselves as His servants, they will pay attention to the service of Sri Ramakrishna." (All laugh.)

Thursday, April 22, 1886

In the evening Rakhal, Sashi, and M. were strolling in the garden at Cossipore.

M: "The Master is like a child—beyond the three gunas."

SASHI AND RAKHAL: "He himself has said that."

RAKHAL: "He sits in a tower, as it were, from which he gets all information and sees everything; but others cannot go there and reach him."

M: "He said, 'In such a state of mind one sees God constantly.' In him there is not the slightest trace of worldliness. His mind is like dry fuel, which catches fire quickly."

SASHI: "He described the different kinds of intelligence to Charu. The right intelligence is that through which one attains God; but the intelligence that enables one to become a deputy magistrate or a lawyer, or to acquire a house, is a mean intelligence. It is like thin and watery curd, which merely soaks flattened rice but does not add any flavour to it. It is not like thick, superior curd. But the intelligence through which one attains God is like thick curd."

M: "Ah, what wonderful words!"

SASHI: "Kali[1] said to the Master: 'What's the good of having joy? The Bhils are joyous. Savages are always singing and dancing in a frenzy of delight.'"

RAKHAL: "He [meaning the Master] replied to Kali: 'What do you mean? Can the Bliss of Brahman be the same as worldly pleasure? Ordinary men are satisfied with worldly pleasure. One cannot enjoy the Bliss of Brahman unless one completely rids oneself of attachment to worldly things. There is the joy of money and sense experience, and there is the Bliss of God-realization. Can the two ever be the same? The rishis enjoyed the Bliss of Brahman.'"

M: "You see, Kali nowadays meditates on Buddha; that is why he speaks of a state beyond Bliss."

RAKHAL: "Yes, Kali told the Master about Buddha. Sri Ramakrishna said to him: 'Buddha is an Incarnation of God. How can you compare him to anybody else? As he is great, so too is his teaching great.' Kali said to him: 'Everything, indeed, is the manifestation of God's Power. Both worldly pleasure and the Bliss of God are the manifestation of that Power.'"

M: "What did the Master say to that?"

RAKHAL: "He said: 'How can that be? Is the power to beget a child the same as the power through which one realizes God?'"

Sri Ramakrishna was sitting in his room on the second floor. Narendra, Rakhal, Sashi, Surendra, M., Bhavanath, and other devotees were present. Dr. Mahendra Sarkar and Dr. Rajendra Dutta were also there to examine him. His condition was growing worse.

The house-rent was between sixty and sixty-five rupees. Surendra bore most of the expenses and had rented the house in his name. The other householder devotees contributed financial help according to their power. A cook and a maid had been engaged to look after the members of the household.

MASTER (to Dr. Sarkar and the others): "The expenses are mounting."

DR. SARKAR (pointing to the devotees): "But they are ready to bear them. They do not hesitate to spend money. (To Sri Ramakrishna) Now, you see, gold is necessary."

MASTER (to Narendra): "Why don't you answer?"

Narendra remained silent. Dr. Sarkar resumed the conversation.

DR. SARKAR: "Gold is necessary, and also woman."

RAJENDRA: "Yes, his [meaning Sri Ramakrishna's] wife has been cooking his meals."

DR. SARKAR (to the Master): "Do you see?"

[1] One of the disciples of the Master, later known as Swami Abhedananda.

MASTER (*smiling*): "Yes—but very troublesome!"

DR. SARKAR: "If there were no troubles, then all would become paramahamsas."

MASTER: "If a woman touches me I fall ill. That part of my body aches as if stung by a horned fish."

DR. SARKAR: "I believe that. But how can you get along without woman?"

MASTER: "My hand gets all twisted up if I hold money in it; my breathing stops. But there is no harm in spending money to lead a spiritual life in the world—if one spends it, for instance, in the worship of God and the service of holy men and devotees.

"A man forgets God if he is entangled in the world of māyā through a woman. It is the Mother of the Universe who has assumed the form of māyā, the form of woman. One who knows this rightly does not feel like leading the life of māyā in the world. But he who truly realizes that all women are manifestations of the Divine Mother may lead a spiritual life in the world. Without realizing God one cannot truly know what a woman is."

Sri Ramakrishna had felt a slight improvement as a result of the homeopathic treatment.

RAJENDRA (*to the Master*): "After getting rid of this illness you must begin to practise medicine as a homeopath. Otherwise, what's the use of this human life?" (*All laugh.*)

NARENDRA: "Nothing like leather!"[2] (*All laugh.*)

A few minutes later the physicians took their leave. Sri Ramakrishna and M. were engaged in conversation. The Master was telling M. how he felt about woman.

MASTER (*to M.*): "They say I cannot get along without 'woman and gold'. They don't understand the state of my mind.

"If I touch a woman my hand becomes numb; it aches. If in a friendly spirit I approach a woman and begin to talk to her, I feel as if a barrier had been placed between us. It is impossible for me to cross that barrier.

"If a woman enters my room when I am alone, at once I become like a child and regard her as my mother."

As M. listened to these words, he became speechless with wonder at Sri Ramakrishna's exalted state of mind. Bhavanath and Narendra were sitting at a distance, talking together. Bhavanath had married and was trying to find a job; so he could not visit Sri Ramakrishna frequently at Cossipore. He had said to M.: "I understand that Vidyāsāgar wants to start a new school. I have to earn my livelihood. Will it be possible for me to secure a job in that school?" The Master was much worried about Bhavanath's being entangled in worldly life. Bhavanath was twenty-three or twenty-four years old.

MASTER (*to Narendra*): "Give him a lot of courage."

Narendra and Bhavanath smiled. Sri Ramakrishna said to Bhavanath, by signs: "Be a great hero. Don't forget yourself when you see her weeping behind her veil. Oh, women cry so much—even when they blow their noses! (*Narendra, Bhavanath, and M. laugh.*)

[2] To a cobbler nothing in this world is as important as leather.

"Keep your mind firm on God. He who is a hero lives with a woman but does not indulge in physical pleasures. Talk to your wife only about God."

A few minutes later Sri Ramakrishna said to Bhavanath, by a sign, "Take your meal here today."

BHAVANATH: "Yes, sir. I am quite all right. Don't worry about me."

Surendra came in and took a seat. The devotees offered garlands of flowers to the Master every evening. Sri Ramakrishna put these garlands around his neck. Surendra sat quietly in the room. Sri Ramakrishna was in a very happy mood and gave him two garlands. Surendra saluted the Master and put them around his neck.

All sat in silence and looked at Sri Ramakrishna. Surendra saluted the Master again and stood up. He was about to leave. He asked Bhavanath to hang the straw screens over the windows.

Hirananda came in with two of his friends. He was a native of Sindh, about twenty-two hundred miles from Calcutta. After finishing his college education in Calcutta in 1883, he had returned to Sindh and taken charge of editing two papers, the Sindh Times and the Sind Sudhār. While studying in Calcutta he had often visited Keshab Chandra Sen and had come to know him intimately. He had met Sri Ramakrishna at the Kāli temple at Dakshineswar and had spent an occasional night there with the Master. Hearing of Sri Ramakrishna's illness, he now came to Calcutta from Sindh to see him. The Master himself had been very eager to see Hirananda.

Sri Ramakrishna pointed to Hirananda and said to M., by signs: "A very fine boy. Do you know him?"

M: "Yes, sir."

MASTER (to Hirananda and M.): "Please talk a little. I want to hear you both."

When M. remained silent, Sri Ramakrishna asked him: "Is Narendra here? Call him."

Narendra entered the room and sat near the Master.

MASTER (to Narendra and Hirananda): "I want to hear you two talk."

Hirananda was silent a few moments and then after great hesitation began the conversation.

HIRANANDA (to Narendra): "Why does a devotee of God suffer?"

His words were sweet as nectar. Everyone in the room could feel that his heart was filled with love.

NARENDRA: "The plan of the universe is devilish. I could have created a better world."

HIRANANDA: "Can one feel happiness without misery?"

NARENDRA: "I am not making a plan for a universe, but simply giving my opinion of the present plan.

"But all these problems are solved if we have faith only in one thing, and that is pantheism. All doubts disappear if one believes that everything is God. God alone is responsible for all that happens."

HIRANANDA: "Very easy to say that."

Narendra sang Śankara's Six Stanzas on Nirvāna:

> Om. I am neither mind, intelligence, ego, nor chitta,
> Neither ears nor tongue nor the senses of smell and sight;
> Nor am I ether, earth, fire, water, or air:
> I am Pure Knowledge and Bliss: I am Śiva! I am Śiva!
>
> I am neither the prāna nor the five vital breaths,
> Neither the seven elements of the body nor its five sheaths,
> Nor hands nor feet nor tongue, nor the organs of sex and voiding:
> I am Pure Knowledge and Bliss: I am Śiva! I am Śiva!
>
> Neither loathing nor liking have I, neither greed nor delusion;
> No sense have I of ego or pride, neither dharma nor moksha;
> Neither desire of the mind nor object for its desiring:
> I am Pure Knowledge and Bliss: I am Śiva! I am Siva!
>
> Neither right nor wrongdoing am I, neither pleasure nor pain,
> Nor the mantra, the sacred place, the Vedas, the sacrifice;
> Neither the act of eating, the eater, nor the food:
> I am Pure Knowledge and Bliss: I am Śiva! I am Śiva!
>
> Death or fear I have none, nor any distinction of caste;
> Neither father nor mother nor even a birth have I;
> Neither friend nor comrade, neither disciple nor guru:
> I am Pure Knowledge and Bliss: I am Śiva! I am Śiva!
>
> I have no form or fancy; the All-pervading am I;
> Everywhere I exist, yet I am beyond the senses;
> Neither salvation am I, nor anything that may be known:
> I am Pure Knowledge and Bliss: I am Śiva! I am Śiva!

HIRANANDA: "Good!"

SRI RAMAKRISHNA (to Hirananda, by a sign): "Give him an answer."

HIRANANDA: "It is all the same, whether you look at a room from a corner or look at it from the middle. It is the same God-Consciousness that one feels, whether one says, 'O God, I am Thy servant', or, 'I am He.' One may enter a room by several doors."

All sat in silence. Hirananda said to Narendra, "Please sing some more." Narendra sang the Five Stanzas on the Kaupin:[3]

> Roaming ever in the grove of Vedānta,
> Ever pleased with his beggar's morsel,
> Ever walking with heart free from sorrow,
> Blest indeed is the wearer of the loin-cloth.
>
> Sitting at the foot of a tree for shelter,
> Using the palms of his hands for eating,
> Wrapped in a garment fine or ugly,
> Blest indeed is the wearer of the loin-cloth.
>
> Satisfied fully by the Bliss within him,
> Curbing wholly the cravings of his senses,
> Contemplating day and night the Absolute Brahman,
> Blest indeed is the wearer of the loin-cloth.

[3] The loin-cloth of the sannyāsi; it is an emblem of renunciation.

As Sri Ramakrishna heard the line, "Contemplating day and night the Absolute Brahman", he said in a very low voice, "Ah!" Then, by a sign, he said to the devotees, "This is the characteristic of the yogi."

Narendra finished the hymn:

> Witnessing the changes of mind and body,
> Naught but the Self within him beholding,
> Thinking not of outer, of inner, or of middle,
> Blest indeed is the wearer of the loin-cloth.
>
> Chanting "Brahman", the Word of redemption,
> Meditating only on "I am Brahman",
> Living on alms and wandering freely,
> Blest indeed is the wearer of the loin-cloth.

Again Narendra sang:

> Meditate on Him, the Perfect, the Embodiment of Bliss;
> Meditate on Him, the Formless, the Root of the Universe,
> The Hearer behind the ear, the Thinker behind the mind,
> The Speaker behind the tongue, Himself beyond all words:
> He is the Life of life, the Ultimate, the Adorable!

MASTER (to Narendra): "And that one—'All that exists art Thou.'"

Narendra sang:

> I have joined my heart to Thee: all that exists art Thou;
> Thee only have I found, for Thou art all that exists.
> O Lord, Beloved of my heart! Thou art the Home of all;
> Where indeed is the heart in which Thou dost not dwell?
> Thou hast entered every heart: all that exists art Thou.
> Whether sage or fool, whether Hindu or Mussalmān,
> Thou makest them as Thou wilt: all that exists art Thou.
>
> Thy presence is everywhere, whether in heaven or in Kaabā;
> Before Thee all must bow, for Thou art all that exists.
> From earth below to the highest heaven, from heaven to
>   deepest earth,
> I see Thee wherever I look: all that exists art Thou.
> Pondering, I have understood; I have seen it beyond a doubt;
> I find not a single thing that may be compared to Thee.
> To Jāfar it has been revealed that Thou art all that exists.

As the Master listened to the line, "Thou hast entered every heart", he said by a sign: "God dwells in everybody's heart. He is the Inner Guide."

As Narendra sang the line, "I see Thee wherever I look: all that exists art Thou", Hirananda said to him: "Yes, 'All that exists art Thou.' Now you say: 'Thou! Thou! Not I, but Thou!'"

NARENDRA: "Give me a one and I'll give you a million. Thou art I; I am Thou. Nothing exists but I."

Narendra recited a few verses from the Ashtāvakra Samhitā. The room again became silent.

MASTER (to Hirananda, pointing to Narendra): "He seems to be walking with an unsheathed sword in his hand. (*To M., pointing to Hirananda*) How quiet! Like a cobra, quiet before the charmer, with its hood spread."

Sri Ramakrishna fell into an inward mood. Hirananda and M. were seated near him. There was complete silence in the room. The Master's body was being racked with indescribable pain. The devotees could not bear the sight of this illness; but somehow the Master made them forget his suffering. He sat there, his face beaming as if there were no trace of illness in his throat.

The devotees had placed flowers and garlands before him as their loving offerings. He picked up a flower and touched with it first his head, then his throat, heart, and navel. To the devotees he seemed a child playing with flowers.

Sri Ramakrishna used to tell the devotees that his divine visions and moods were accompanied by the rising of a spiritual current inside his body.

Now he talked to M.

MASTER: "I don't remember when the current went up. Now I am in the mood of a child. That is why I am playing with the flowers this way. Do you know what I see now? I see my body as a frame made of bamboo strips and covered with a cloth. The frame moves. And it moves because someone dwells inside it.

"Again, I see the body to be like a pumpkin with the seeds scooped out. Inside this body there is no trace of passion or worldly attachment. It is all very clean inside, and—"

It became very painful for Sri Ramakrishna to talk further. He felt very weak. M. quickly guessed what the Master wanted to tell the devotees, and said, "And you are seeing God inside yourself."

MASTER: "Both inside and outside. The Indivisible Satchidānanda—I see It both inside and outside. It has merely assumed this sheath [meaning his body] for a support and exists both inside and outside. I clearly perceive this."

M. and Hirananda listened intently to these words about his exalted state of God-Consciousness. A few moments later Sri Ramakrishna looked at them and resumed the conversation.

MASTER: "You all seem to me to be my kinsmen. I do not look on any of you as a stranger.

"I see you all as so many sheaths,[4] and the heads are moving.

"I notice that when my mind is united with God the suffering of the body is left aside.

"Now I perceive only this: the Indivisible Satchidānanda is covered with skin, and this sore in the throat is on one side of it."

The Master again fell silent. A few minutes later he said: "The attributes of matter are superimposed on Spirit, and the attributes of Spirit are superimposed on matter. Therefore when the body is ill a man says, 'I am ill.'"

Hirananda wanted to understand what the Master had just said; so M. told him, "When hot water scalds the hand, people say that the water scalds; but the truth is that it is the heat that scalds."

HIRANANDA (*to the Master*): "Please tell us why a devotee of God suffers."

[4] Referring to their bodies.

MASTER: "It is the body that suffers."

Sri Ramakrishna seemed about to say something more. Hirananda and M. eagerly awaited his words.

Sri Ramakrishna said, "Do you understand?"

M. said to Hirananda, in a whisper: "The body suffers for the purpose of teaching men. His life is like a book of reference. In spite of so much physical suffering, his mind is one hundred per cent united with God."

HIRANANDA: "Yes, it is like Christ's crucifixion. But still the mystery remains—why should he, of all people, suffer like this?"

M: "The Master says it is the will of the Divine Mother. This is how She is sporting through his body."

The two devotees were talking in whispers. Sri Ramakrishna asked Hirananda, by a sign, what M. was talking about. Since Hirananda could not understand the sign, Sri Ramakrishna repeated it.

HIRANANDA: "He says that your illness is for the teaching of men."

MASTER: "But that's only his guess.

(To M. and Hirananda) "My mood is changing. I think that I should not say to everyone, 'May your spiritual consciousness be awakened.' People are so sinful in the Kaliyuga; if I awaken their spiritual consciousness I shall have to accept the burden of their sins."

M. (to Hirananda): "He will not awaken people's spiritual consciousness except at the right time. When a person is ready, he will awaken his spiritual consciousness."

Friday, April 23, 1886

It was Good Friday. Hirananda had taken his midday meal at the Cossipore garden house. About one o'clock in the afternoon he was stroking Sri Ramakrishna's feet. M. sat near by. Latu and one or two other devotees were going in and out of the room. It was the Master's earnest desire that Hirananda should stay for some time at the Cossipore garden house.

While massaging the Master's feet, Hirananda conversed with him. He spoke in a very sweet voice, as if trying to console a child.

HIRANANDA: "Why should you worry so much? You can enjoy peace of mind if you have faith in the physician. You are a child."

MASTER (to M.): "How can I have faith in the doctor? Dr. Sarkar said that I would not recover."

HIRANANDA: "But why should you worry so much about that? What is to happen must happen."

M. (to Hirananda, aside): "He is not worrying about himself. The preservation of his body is for the welfare of the devotees."

It was a sultry day and the room became very hot at noontime. The straw screens had been hung over the windows. Hirananda adjusted them. The Master looked at him.

MASTER (to Hirananda): "Please don't forget to send the pajamas."

Hirananda had told Sri Ramakrishna that he would feel more comfortable if he wore the pajamas used in Sindh. Sri Ramakrishna was reminding him of them.

Hirananda had not eaten well. The rice had not been well cooked. The Master felt very sorry about it and asked him again and again whether he would have some refreshments. On account of his illness he could hardly talk; but still he repeated the question. He said to Latu, "Did you too eat that rice?"

Sri Ramakrishna could hardly keep the cloth on his body. He was almost always naked, like a child. Hirananda had brought with him one or two of his Brāhmo friends. Therefore every now and then the Master pulled the cloth to his waist.

MASTER (to Hirananda): "Will you take me for an uncivilized person if I don't cover my body with my cloth?"

HIRANANDA: "What difference does that make with you? You are but a child."

MASTER (pointing to a Brāhmo devotee): "But he feels that way"

Hirananda was about to take his leave. In a very few days he was going to start for Sindh.

MASTER (to Hirananda): "Suppose you don't go to Sindh."

HIRANANDA (smiling): "But there is nobody there to do my work. I have my duties."

MASTER: "How much do you earn?"

HIRANANDA (smiling): "My work doesn't bring me a large salary."

MASTER: "Still, how much?"

Hirananda laughed.

MASTER: "Why don't you live here?"

Hirananda did not reply.

MASTER: "Suppose you give up the job."

Hirananda said nothing. He was ready to take his leave.

MASTER: "When will you see me again?"

HIRANANDA: "I shall leave for Sindh on Monday, the day after tomorrow. I shall see you that morning."

Hirananda left.

M. was seated by the Master's side.

MASTER (to M.): "He is a fine young man, isn't he?"

M: "Yes, sir. He has a very sweet nature."

MASTER: "He said that Sindh is twenty-two hundred miles from Calcutta; and he has come all that way to see me."

M: "True, sir. That would be impossible without real love."

MASTER: "He wants very much to take me to Sindh."

M: "The journey is very painful. It takes four or five days by train."

MASTER: "He has three university degrees."

M: "Yes, sir."

Sri Ramakrishna was tired. He wanted to take a little rest. He asked M. to open the shutters of the windows and spread the straw mat over his bed. M. was fanning him. Sri Ramakrishna became drowsy.

After a short nap Sri Ramakrishna said to M., "Did I sleep?"

M: "A little."

Narendra, Sarat, and M. were talking downstairs.

NARENDRA: "How amazing it is! One learns hardly anything though one reads books for many years. How can a man realize God by practising sādhanā for two or three days? Is it so easy to realize God? (*To Sarat*) You have obtained peace. M., too, has obtained it. But I have no peace."

It was afternoon. Many devotees were sitting in the Master's room. Narendra, Sarat, Sashi, Latu, Nityagopal, Girish, Ram, M., and Suresh were present.

Kedar came in. This was his first visit to the Master for some time. While staying in Dacca, in connection with his official duties, he had heard of Sri Ramakrishna's illness. On entering Sri Ramakrishna's room he took the dust of the Master's feet on his head and then joyously gave it to the others. The devotees accepted it with bowed heads. As he offered it to Sarat, the latter himself took the dust of Sri Ramakrishna's feet. M. smiled. The Master also smiled, looking at M. The devotees sat without uttering a word. Sri Ramakrishna seemed about to go into an ecstatic mood. Now and then he breathed heavily as if trying to suppress his emotion. He said to Kedar, by a sign, "Argue with Girish."

Girish said to Kedar: "Sir, I beg your pardon. At first I did not know who you were. That is why I argued with you. But now it is quite different."

Sri Ramakrishna smiled.

The Master drew Kedar's attention to Narendra and said: "He has renounced everything. (*To the devotees*) Kedar once said to Narendra, 'You may reason and argue now, but in the end you will roll on the ground, chanting Hari's name.' (*To Narendra*) Take the dust of Kedar's feet."

KEDAR (*to Narendra*): "Take the dust of his [meaning the Master's] feet. That will do."

Surendra was seated behind the other devotees. The Master looked at him with a smile and said to Kedar, "Ah, how sweet his nature is!" Kedar understood the Master's hint and went toward Surendra.

Surendra was very sensitive. Some of the devotees had been collecting funds from the householder devotees to meet the expenses of the Cossipore garden house. Surendra felt piqued at this. He was bearing most of the expenses himself.

SURENDRA (*to Kedar*): "How can I sit near all these holy people? A few days ago some of them [referring to Narendra] put on the ochre robe of the sannyāsi and went on a pilgrimage to Buddha-Gayā. They wanted to see bigger sādhus there."

Sri Ramakrishna was trying to console Surendra. He said: "You are right. They are mere children. They don't know what is good."

SURENDRA (*to Kedar*): "Doesn't our gurudeva[5] know our inner feelings? He does not care for money. It is our inner attitude that pleases him."

Sri Ramakrishna with a nod of his head approved Surendra's words.

The devotees had brought various food offerings for the Master and placed them in front of him. Sri Ramakrishna put a grain on his tongue and gave the plate to Surendra. He asked Surendra to distribute the prasād to the devotees. Surendra went downstairs with the offerings.

[5] Referring to Sri Ramakrishna.

MASTER (*to Kedar*): "You had better go downstairs and explain it all to Surendra. See that they don't get into any hot arguments."

M. was fanning Sri Ramakrishna. The Master said to him, "Won't you eat anything?" He sent M. downstairs.

It was about dusk. Girish and M. were strolling near the small reservoir in the garden.

GIRISH: "I understand that you are writing something about the Master.[6] Is it true?"

M: "Who told you that?"

GIRISH: "I have heard about it. Will you give it to me?"

M: "No, I won't part with it unless I feel it is right to do so. I am writing it for myself, not for others."

GIRISH: "What do you mean?"

M: "You may get it when I die."

It was evening. A lamp was lighted in the Master's room. Amrita Basu, a Brāhmo devotee, came in. Sri Ramakrishna had expressed his eagerness to see him. M. and a few other devotees were there. A garland of jasmine lay in front of the Master on a plantain-leaf. There was perfect silence in the room. A great yogi seemed to be silently communing with God. Every now and then the Master lifted the garland a little, as if he wanted to put it around his neck.

AMRITA (*tenderly*): "Shall I put it around your neck?"

Sri Ramakrishna accepted the garland. He had a long conversation with Amrita. When the latter was about to take his leave, the Master said, "Come again."

AMRITA: "Yes, sir. I like to come very much. But I live at a great distance; so I cannot always come."

MASTER: "Do come, and take the carriage hire from here."

The devotees were amazed at the Master's tender love for Amrita.

The next day M. came to the garden house accompanied by his wife and a son. The boy was seven years old. It was at the Master's request that he brought his wife, who was almost mad with grief owing to the death of one of her sons.

That day the Master several times allowed M.'s wife the privilege of waiting on him. Her welfare seemed to occupy his attention a great deal. In the evening the Holy Mother came to the Master's room to feed him. M.'s wife accompanied her with a lamp. The Master tenderly asked her many questions about her household. He requested her to come again to the garden house and spend a few days with the Holy Mother, not forgetting to ask her to bring her baby daughter. When the Master had finished his meal M.'s wife removed the plates. He chatted with her a few minutes.

---

[6] After Sri Ramakrishna's death M. published his notes of conversations with the Master in five volumes. *The Gospel of Sri Ramakrishna* is an English translation of these books from the original Bengali.

About nine o'clock in the evening Sri Ramakrishna was seated in his room with the devotees. He had a garland of flowers around his neck. He told M. that he had requested his wife to spend a few days at the garden house with the Holy Mother. His kindness touched M.'s heart.

M. was fanning him. The Master took the garland from his neck and said something to himself. Then in a very benign mood he gave the garland to M.

52

AFTER THE PASSING AWAY

SRI RAMAKRISHNA passed away on Sunday, August 15, 1886, plunging his devotees and disciples into a sea of grief. They were like men in a shipwreck. But a strong bond of love held them together, and they found assurance and courage in each other's company. They could not enjoy the friendship of worldly people and would talk only of their Master. "Shall we not behold him again?"—this was the one theme of their thought and the one dream of their sleep. Alone, they wept for him; walking in the streets of Calcutta, they were engrossed in the thought of him. The Master had once said to M., "It becomes difficult for me to give up the body, when I realize that after my death you will wander about weeping for me." Some of them thought: "He is no longer in this world. How surprising that we still enjoy living! We could give up our bodies if we liked, but still we do not." Time and again Sri Ramakrishna had told them that God reveals Himself to His devotees if they yearn for Him and call on Him with whole-souled devotion. He had assured them that God listens to the prayer of a sincere heart.

The young unmarried disciples of the Master, who belonged to his inner circle, had attended on him day and night at the Cossipore garden house. After his passing away most of them returned to their families against their own wills. They had not yet formally renounced the world. For a short while they kept their family names. But Sri Ramakrishna had made them renounce the world mentally. He himself had initiated several of them into the monastic life, giving them the ochre cloths of sannyāsis.

Two or three of the Master's attendants had no place to go. To them the large-hearted Surendra said: "Brothers, where will you go? Let us rent a house. You will live there and make it our Master's shrine; and we house-holders shall come there for consolation. How can we pass all our days and nights with our wives and children in the world? I used to spend a sum of money for the Master at Cossipore. I shall gladly give it now for your ex-penses." Accordingly he rented a house for them at Barānagore, in the suburbs of Calcutta, and this place became gradually transformed into a math, or monastery.

For the first few months Surendra contributed thirty rupees a month. As the other members joined the monastery one by one, he doubled his contribution, which he later increased to a hundred rupees. The monthly rent for the house was eleven rupees. The cook received six rupees a month. The rest was spent for food.

The younger Gopal brought the Master's bed and other articles of daily use from the garden house at Cossipore. The brāhmin who had been cook at Cossipore was engaged for the new monastery. The first permanent member was the elder Gopal. Sarat spent the nights there. In the beginning Sarat, Sashi, Baburam, Niranjan, and Kali used to visit the monastery every now and then, according to their convenience. Tarak, who had gone to Vrindāvan following the Master's death, returned to Calcutta after a few months and soon became a permanent member of the monastery. Rakhal, Jogin, Latu, and Kali were living at Vrindāvan with the Holy Mother when the monastery was started. Kali returned to Calcutta within a month, Rakhal after a few months, and Jogin and Latu after a year. The householder devotees frequently visited the monastic brothers and spent hours with them in meditation and study.

After a short time Narendra, Rakhal, Niranjan, Sarat, Sashi, Baburam, Jogin, Tarak, Kali, and Latu renounced the world for good. Sarada Prasanna and Subodh joined them some time later. Gangadhar, who was very much attached to Narendra, visited the math regularly. It was he who taught the brothers the hymn sung at the evening service in the Śiva temple at Benares. He had gone to Tibet to practise austerity; now, having returned, he lived at the monastery. Hari, who was at first only a visitor at the monastery, soon embraced the monastic life and thus completed the list of the Master's sannyāsi disciples.[1]

Surendra was indeed a blessed soul. It was he who laid the foundation of the great Order later associated with Sri Ramakrishna's name. His devotion and sacrifice made it possible for those earnest souls to renounce the world for the realization of God. Through him Sri Ramakrishna made it possible for them to live in the world as embodiments of his teaching, the renunciation of "woman and gold" and the realization of God.

The brothers lived at the math like orphan boys. Sometimes they would not have the money to pay their house-rent; sometimes they would have no food in the monastery. Surendra would come and settle all these things. He was the big brother of the monks. Later on, when they thought of his genuine love, the members of this first math shed tears of gratitude.

The new monastery became known among the Master's devotees as the

---

[1] The monastic names of the Master's intimate disciples who renounced the world soon after his death were as follows:

Narendra	Swami Vivekananda	Sashi	Swami Ramakrishnananda
Rakhal	Swami Brahmananda	Kali	Swami Abhedananda
Jogin	Swami Jogananda	Gangadhar	Swami Akhandananda
Niranjan	Swami Niranjanananda	Gopal (elder)	Swami Advaitananda
Latu	Swami Adbhutananda	Sarada	
Baburam	Swami Premananda	Prasanna	Swami Trigunatitananda
Tarak	Swami Shivananda	Subodh	Swami Subodhananda
Hari	Swami Turiyananda		
Sarat	Swami Saradananda		

Barānagore Math. Narendra, Rakhal, and the other young disciples were filled with intense renunciation. One day Rakhal's father came to the math and asked Rakhal to return home. "Why do you take the trouble to come here?" Rakhal said to him. "I am very happy here. Please pray to God that you may forget me and that I may forget you too." The young disciples said to each other: "We shall never return to the worldly life. The Master enjoined upon us the renunciation of 'woman and gold'. How can we go back to our families?"

Sashi had taken charge of the daily worship in the math. The Master's relics had been brought from Balaram's house and Sri Ramakrishna was worshipped daily in the worship hall. Narendra supervised the household. He was the leader of the monastery. He would often tell his brother disciples, "The selfless actions enjoined in the Gītā are worship, japa, meditation, and so on, and not worldly duties." The brothers at the math depended on him for their spiritual inspiration. He said to them, "We must practise sādhanā; otherwise we shall not be able to realize God."

He and his brother disciples, filled with an ascetic spirit, devoted themselves day and night to the practice of spiritual discipline. Their one goal in life was the realization of God. They followed to their hearts' content the injunctions prescribed in the Vedas, Purānas, and Tantras for an ascetic life. They spent their time in japa and meditation and study of the scriptures. Whenever they would fail to experience the Divine Presence, they would feel as if they were on the rack. They would practise austerity, sometimes alone under trees, sometimes in a cremation ground, sometimes on the bank of the Ganges. Again, sometimes they would spend the entire day in the meditation room of the monastery in japa and contemplation; sometimes they would gather to sing and dance in a rapture of delight. All of them, and Narendra particularly, were consumed with the desire to see God. Now and then they would say to each other, "Shall we not starve ourselves to death to see God?"

Monday, February 21, 1887

Narendra, Rakhal, Niranjan, Sarat, Sashi, Kali, Baburam, Tarak, and Sarada Prasanna were living in the monastery. All day the members had been fasting in observance of the Śivarātri.[2] Sarat, Kali, Niranjan, and Sarada were planning to go to Puri, the following Saturday, on a pilgrimage to the sacred Jagannāth. Jogin and Latu were at Vrindāvan and had not yet seen the new place.

Narendra had gone to Calcutta that morning to look after a lawsuit in which his family had been involved since the death of his father. At nine o'clock in the morning M. arrived at the math. Tarak saw him and began to sing in praise of Śiva, Rakhal joining him:

> There Śiva dances, striking both His cheeks; and they resound,
> *Ba-ba-bom!*

[2] The night of Śiva. On this day the devotees observe fast and spend the whole night in meditation, prayer, and other spiritual exercises.

Dimi-dimi-dimi! sounds His drum; a garland of skulls from His
neck is hanging!
In His matted locks the Ganges hisses; fire shoots from His mighty
trident!
Round His waist a serpent glitters, and on His brow the moon
is shining!

Rakhal and Tarak danced as they sang. Narendra had recently composed
the song.

Sashi finished the morning worship in the shrine. Sarat then sang about
Śiva to the accompaniment of the tānpurā.

Narendra had just arrived from Calcutta. He had not yet taken his bath.
Kali asked him, "What about the lawsuit?" "Why should you bother about
it?" Narendra replied sharply.

Narendra was smoking and talking to M. and the others. He said:
"Nothing can be achieved in spiritual life without the renunciation of
'woman and gold'. 'Woman' is the doorway to hell. All people are under the
control of women. The cases of Śiva and Krishna are quite different. Śiva
turned His Consort into His servant. Sri Krishna, no doubt, led a householder's life. But how unattached He was! How quickly He renounced
Vrindāvan and the gopis!"

RAKHAL: "And how He renounced Dwārakā, too, where He was king!"

Narendra took his bath in the Ganges and returned to the monastery. He
carried his wet cloth and towel in his hand. Sarada prostrated himself before
Narendra. He too had been fasting on account of the Śivarātri. He was
going to the Ganges for his bath. Narendra entered the worship room and
prostrated himself before the picture of Sri Ramakrishna, who was daily
worshipped there as the Deity. For a few minutes he was absorbed in meditation.

The devotees assembled in a room and began to converse. The talk
turned to Bhavanath. Narendra said, "People like him live like worms in
the world."

It was afternoon. Arrangements were being made to worship Śiva in the
evening. Leaves of the bel-tree were gathered for the worship. Bel-wood
was chopped for the homa.

In the evening Sashi, who was in charge of the worship at the monastery,
burnt incense before the pictures of the various gods and goddesses.

The worship of Śiva was to take place under the bel-tree in the monastery
compound. The Deity was to be worshipped four times, during the four
watches of the night. The brothers assembled under the bel-tree. Bhupati
and M. were present also. One of the young members of the math was in
charge of the worship. Kali was reading from the *Gītā*. Now and then he
argued with Narendra.

KALI: "I alone am everything. I create, preserve, and destroy."

NARENDRA: "How is it possible for me to create? Another power creates through me. Our various actions—even our thoughts—are caused by that power."

M. (to himself): "The Master used to say: 'As long as a man feels that it is he who meditates, he is under the jurisdiction of the Ādyāśakti. Śakti must be acknowledged.'"

Kali reflected in silence a few moments and then said: "The actions you are talking about are illusory. There is not even any such thing as thought. The very idea of these things makes me laugh."

NARENDRA: "The 'I' that is implied in 'I am He' is not this ego. It is that which remains after one eliminates mind, body, and so on."

After completing the recital of the Gītā, Kali chanted: "Śāntih! Śāntih! Śāntih!"

Narendra and the other devotees stood up and circled round and round the tree, singing and dancing. Now and then they chanted in chorus: "Śiva Guru! Śiva Guru!"

It was midnight, the fourteenth day of the dark fortnight of the moon. Pitch darkness filled all the quarters. Men, birds, and animals were all hushed into silence. The young sannyāsis were clad in gerruā robes. The words "Śiva Guru", chanted in their full-throated voices, rose into the infinite sky like the rumblings of rain-clouds and disappeared in the Indivisible Satchidānanda.

The worship was over. The sun, about to rise, was painting the eastern horizon crimson. In this sacred twilight, the conjunction of night and day, the holy Brāhmamuhurta, the young worshippers finished their baths in the Ganges.

It was morning. The devotees went to the shrine room, prostrated themselves before the Deity, and gradually assembled in the big hall. Narendra was clad in a new ochre cloth. The bright orange colour of his apparel blended with the celestial lustre of his face and body, every pore of which radiated a divine light. His countenance was filled with fiery brilliance and yet touched with the tenderness of love. He appeared to all as a bubble that had risen up in the Ocean of Absolute Existence and Bliss and assumed a human body to help in the propagation of his Master's message. All eyes were fixed on him. Narendra was then just twenty-four years old, the very age at which the great Chaitanya had renounced the world.

Balaram had sent fruit and sweets to the monastery for the devotees' breakfast. Rakhal, Narendra, and a few others partook of the refreshments. After eating one or two morsels some of them cried out, "Blessed indeed is Balaram!" All laughed.

Narendra now began to joke like a child. He was imitating Sri Ramakrishna. He put a sweet into his mouth and stood still, as if in samādhi. His eyes remained unwinking. A devotee stepped forward and pretended to hold him up by the hand lest he should drop to the ground. Narendra closed his eyes. A few minutes later, with the sweetmeat still in his mouth, he opened his eyes and drawled out, "I—am—all—right." All laughed loudly.

Refreshments were now given to everyone. M. looked on at this wonderful mart of happiness. The devotees shouted joyfully, "Jai Gurumahārāj!"[3]

Monday, March 25, 1887

M. arrived at the Barānagore Math to visit his brother disciples. Devendra accompanied him. M. had been coming to the monastery very frequently and now and then had spent a day or two. The previous week he had spent three days at the math. He was very eager to observe the spirit of intense renunciation of these young men.

It was evening. M. intended to spend the night in the monastery. Sashi lighted the lamp in the worship room and chanted the name of God. Next he burnt incense before all the pictures of gods and goddesses in the various rooms. The evening service began. Sashi conducted the worship. The members of the math, with M. and Devendra, stood with folded hands and sang the hymn of the ārati.

When the worship was over, Narendra and M. became engaged in conversation. Narendra was recalling his various meetings with Sri Ramakrishna.

NARENDRA: "One day, during one of my early visits, the Master in an ecstatic mood said to me, 'You have come!' 'How amazing!' I said to myself. 'It is as if he had known me a long time.' Then he said to me, 'Do you ever see light?' I replied: 'Yes, sir. Before I fall asleep I feel something like a light revolving near my forehead.' "

M: "Do you see it even now?"

NARENDRA: "I used to see it frequently. In Jadu Mallick's garden house the Master one day touched me and muttered something to himself. I became unconscious. The effect of the touch lingered with me a month, like an intoxication.

"When he heard that a proposal had been made about my marriage, he wept, holding the feet of the image of Kālī. With tears in his eyes he prayed to the Divine Mother: 'O Mother, please upset the whole thing! Don't let Narendra be drowned.'

"After my father's death my mother and my brothers were starving. When the Master met Annada Guha one day, he said to him: 'Narendra's father has died. His family is in a state of great privation. It would be good if his friends helped him now with money.'

"After Annada had left I scolded him. I said, 'Why did you say all those things to him?' Thus rebuked, he wept and said, 'Alas! for your sake I could beg from door to door.'

"He tamed us by his love. Don't you think so?"

M: "There is not the slightest doubt about it. His love was utterly unselfish."

NARENDRA: "One day when I was alone with him he said something to me. Nobody else was present. Please don't repeat it to anyone here."

M: "No, I shall not. What did he say?"

NARENDRA: "He said: 'It is not possible for me to exercise occult powers;

---

[3] Victory to the Guru!

but I shall do so through you. What do you say?' 'No,' I replied, 'you can't do that.'

"I used to laugh at his words. You must have heard all these things from him. I told him that his visions of God were all hallucinations of his mind.

"He said to me: 'I used to climb to the roof of the kuthi and cry: "O devotees, where are you all? Come to me, O devotees! I am about to die. I shall certainly die if I do not see you." And the Divine Mother told me, "The devotees will come." You see, everything is turning out to be true.'

"What else could I say? I kept quiet.

"One day he closed the door of his room and said to Devendra Babu and Girish Babu, referring to me, 'He will not keep his body if he is told who he is.' "

M: "Yes, we have heard that. Many a time he repeated the same thing to us, too. Once you came to know about your true Self in nirvikalpa samādhi at the Cossipore garden house. Isn't that true?"

NARENDRA: "Yes. In that experience I felt that I had no body. I could see only my face. The Master was in the upstairs room. I had that experience downstairs. I was weeping. I said, 'What has happened to me?' The elder Gopal went to the Master's room and said, 'Narendra is crying.'

"When I saw the Master he said to me: 'Now you have known. But I am going to keep the key with me.'

"I said to him, 'What is it that happened to me?'

"Turning to the devotees, he said: 'He will not keep his body if he knows who he is. But I have put a veil over his eyes.'

"One day he said to me, 'You can see Krishna in your heart if you want.' I replied, 'I don't believe in Krishna or any such nonsense!' (*Both M. and Narendra laugh.*)

"I have noticed a peculiar thing. Some men, objects, or places make me feel as if I had seen them before, in a previous birth. They appear familiar to me. One day I went to Sarat's house in Calcutta, on Amherst Street. Immediately I said to Sarat: 'This house seems familiar to me. It seems to me that I have known the rooms, the passages, and the rest of the house for many, many days.

"I used to follow my own whims in everything I did. The Master never interfered. You know that I became a member of the Sādhāran Brāhmo Samāj."

M: "Yes, I know that."

NARENDRA: "The Master knew that women attended the meetings of the Brāhmo Samāj. A man cannot meditate with women sitting in front of him; therefore he criticized the meditation of the Brāhmo Samāj. But he didn't object to my going there. But one day he said to me, 'Don't tell Rakhal about your being a member of the Brāhmo Samāj, or he too will feel like becoming one.' "

M: "You have greater strength of mind. That is why the Master didn't prevent your going to the Samāj."

NARENDRA: "I have attained my present state of mind as a result of much suffering and pain. You have not passed through any such suffering. I now realize that without trials and tribulations one cannot resign oneself to God and depend on Him absolutely.

"Well, X— is so modest and humble! He is totally self-effacing. Can you tell me how I can develop humility?"

M: "Speaking about your ego, the Master said, 'Whose ego is it?'"

NARENDRA: "What did he mean?"

M: "A friend one day said to Rādhikā: 'You are egotistic. That is why you insulted Krishna.' Whereupon another friend said to the first: 'Yes, Rādhikā is egotistic, no doubt. But whose ego is it?' What she meant was that Rādhā was egotistic because she regarded Krishna as her Lord. It was Krishna Himself who kept that ego in Rādhā.

"What the Master meant was that it is God alone who has kept this ego in you, so that He may accomplish many things through you."

NARENDRA: "But my ego loudly proclaims to all that I have no suffering."

M. (smiling): "You may loudly proclaim it, if that be your sweet will."

The conversation turned to other devotees.

NARENDRA: "The Master said about Vijay Goswami, 'He is knocking at the door.'"

M: "That is to say, he has not yet entered the room. At Śyāmpukur Vijay said to the Master, 'I saw you at Dacca in this tangible form, in this very body.' You were there too."

NARENDRA: "Devendra Babu and Ram Babu want to renounce the world. They are trying hard. Ram Babu told me privately that he would give up the world after two years."

M: "After two years? After making provision for his children?"

NARENDRA: "Besides, he will rent his present house and buy a small house. Other relatives will arrange his daughter's marriage."

M: "Gopal⁴ is in an exalted state of mind, isn't he?"

NARENDRA: "What do you mean?"

M: "So much emotion, so much weeping and such exaltation in the name of God!"

NARENDRA: "Does mere emotion make a man spiritually great? Youngsters like Kali, Sarat, Sashi, and Sarada are more spiritual than Gopal. How great their renunciation is! Gopal does not accept the Master, does he?"

M: "That is true. The Master remarked that Gopal did not belong to the circle of his devotees. But I saw him show great reverence for Sri Ramakrishna."

NARENDRA: "What did you see?"

M: "At that time I was just becoming acquainted with Sri Ramakrishna. One day, after the meeting of the devotees in his room had broken up, I came out and saw Gopal on the foot-path, kneeling with folded hands before the Master. The moon was shining brightly overhead. It was the red path sprinkled with brick-dust, just outside the long verandah north of the Master's room. Nobody else was there. It appeared to me that Gopal had taken shelter at Sri Ramakrishna's feet and the Master was encouraging him."

NARENDRA: "I didn't see it."

⁴ Referring to Nityagopal.

M: "Further, the Master used to say, 'Gopal is in the state of a paramahamsa.' But I also distinctly remember his forbidding Gopal to be intimate with woman devotees. Many a time he warned him about it."

NARENDRA: "Speaking to me about Gopal, the Master asked why, if Gopal was a real paramahamsa, he should hanker after money. 'He doesn't belong to this place', the Master said. 'Those who are my own will always come here.' He used to be angry with T— because he was Gopal's constant companion and didn't come to the Master more often. 'Gopal has spiritual realizations, no doubt,' the Master said to me, 'but he has attained them all of a sudden, without the necessary preparations. He is not one of my own. If he is, why haven't I wept for him?'

"Some are proclaiming Gopal as the reincarnation of Nityānanda. But times without number the Master said to me: 'In me alone are embodied Advaita, Chaitanya, and Nityānanda.[5] I am all these three.'"

Friday, April 8, 1887

About eight o'clock in the morning two devotees, one a householder and the other a monk, were conversing in a room in the Barānagore monastery, when M. came in. The devotees were of the same age—twenty-four or twenty-five years old. M. intended to spend three days at the monastery. He went to the shrine and saluted the Deity. After visiting Narendra, Rakhal, and the other brothers, he at last came into the room where the two devotees were engaged in conversation. The householder devotee wanted to renounce the world. The monk was trying to persuade him not to do so.

MONK: "Why don't you finish the few duties you have in the world? Very soon they will be left behind.

"A man was told that he would go to hell. He asked a friend, 'What is hell like?' Thereupon the friend began to draw a picture of hell on the ground with a piece of chalk. No sooner was the picture drawn than the man rolled over it and said, 'Now I have gone through hell!'"

HOUSEHOLDER: "I don't relish worldly life. Ah, how happy you are here!"

MONK: "Why don't you renounce the world, if you want to? Why do you talk about it so much? But I repeat, why don't you enjoy the fun once for all?"

Sashi finished the regular worship in the worship hall. About eleven the brothers of the math returned from the Ganges after taking their baths. They put on clean cloths, went to the shrine, prostrated themselves before the Deity, and meditated there a little while.

After the food was offered to the Deity they had their meal. M. ate with them.

It was evening. Incense was burnt before the pictures of gods and goddesses and the evening service was performed. Rakhal, Sashi, the elder Gopal, and Harish were seated in the big hall. M. also was there. Rakhal warned one of the brothers to be careful about the food to be offered to the Master in the shrine.

RAKHAL (*to Sashi and the others*): "One day I ate part of his [meaning

[5] Advaita and Nityānanda were intimate companions of Chaitanya.

the Master's] refreshments before he took them. At this he said: 'I cannot look at you. How could you do such a thing?' I burst into tears."

THE ELDER GOPAL: "One day at Cossipore I breathed hard on his food. At this he said, 'Take that food away.'"

M. and Narendra were pacing the verandah and recalling old times.

NARENDRA: "I did not believe in anything."

M: "You mean the forms of God?"

NARENDRA: "At first I did not accept most of what the Master said. One day he asked me, 'Then why do you come here?' I replied, 'I come here to see you, not to listen to you.'"

M: "What did he say to that?"

NARENDRA: "He was very much pleased."

Saturday, April 9, 1887

The members of the math were resting a little after their meal. Narendra and M. sat under a tree in the garden to the west of the monastery. It was a solitary place and no one else was present. Narendra was recounting to M. his various experiences with Sri Ramakrishna. Narendra was about twenty-four years old, and M. thirty-two.

M: "You must remember vividly your first visit to him."

NARENDRA: "Yes. It was at the temple garden at Dakshineswar, in his own room. That day I sang two songs."

Narendra sang them for M.:

> Let us go back once more, O mind, to our own abode!
> Here in this foreign land of earth
> Why should we wander aimlessly in stranger's guise?
> These living beings round about, and the five elements,
> Are strangers to you, all of them; none is your own.
> Why do you thus forget yourself,
> In love with strangers, O my mind?
> Why do you thus forget your own?
>
> Ascend the path of Truth, O mind! Unflaggingly climb,
> With Love as the lamp to light your way.
> As your provision for the journey, bring with you
> The virtues, carefully concealed; for, like two highwaymen,
> Greed and delusion wait to rob you of your wealth.
> And keep beside you constantly,
> As guards to shelter you from harm,
> Calmness of mind and self-control.
>
> Companionship with holy men will be for you
> A welcome rest-house by the road;
> There rest your weary limbs awhile, asking your way,
> If ever you should be in doubt, of him who watches there.
> If anything along the path should frighten you,
> Then loudly shout the name of the Lord;
> For He is Ruler of that road,
> And even Death must bow to Him.

*   *   *

O Lord, must all my days pass by so utterly in vain?
Down the path of hope I gaze with longing, day and night.
Thou art the Lord of all the worlds, and I but a beggar here;
How can I ask of Thee to come and dwell within my heart?
My poor heart's humble cottage door is standing open wide;
Be gracious, Lord, and enter there but once, and quench its thirst!

M: "What did he say after listening to your songs?"

NARENDRA: "He went into samādhi. He said to Ram Babu: 'Who is this boy? How well he sings!' He asked me to come again."

M: "Where did you see him next?"

NARENDRA: "At Rajmohan's house. The third visit was at Dakshineswar again. During that visit he went into samādhi and began to praise me as if I were God. He said to me, 'O Nārāyana, you have assumed this body for my sake.' But please don't tell this to anybody else."

M: "What else did he say?"

NARENDRA: "He said: 'You have assumed this body for my sake. I asked the Divine Mother, "Mother, unless I enjoy the company of some genuine devotees completely free from 'woman and gold', how shall I live on earth?"' Then he said to me, 'You came to me at night, woke me up, and said, "Here I am!"' But I did not know anything of this. I was sound asleep in our Calcutta house."

M: "In other words, you may be both present and absent at the same time. It is like God, who is both formless and endowed with form."

NARENDRA: "But you must not tell this to anyone else. At Cossipore he transmitted his power to me."

M: "Didn't it happen when you used to meditate before a lighted fire under a tree at the Cossipore garden house?"

NARENDRA: "Yes. One day, while meditating, I asked Kali to hold my hand. Kali said to me, 'When I touched your body I felt something like an electric shock coming to my body.'

"But you must not tell this to anybody here. Give me your promise."

M: "There is a special purpose in his transmission of power to you. He will accomplish much work through you. One day the Master wrote on a piece of paper, 'Naren will teach people.'"

NARENDRA: "But I said to him, 'I won't do any such thing.' Thereupon he said, 'Your very bones will do it.' He has given me charge of Sarat. Sarat is now yearning for God; the Kundalini is awakened in him."

M: "He must be careful that dead leaves do not accumulate there. Perhaps you remember what the Master used to say: 'In a lake the fish make holes so that they may rest there. But if dead leaves accumulate in the holes the fish do not go there.'"

NARENDRA: "The Master used to call me Nārāyana."

M: "Yes, I know he did."

NARENDRA: "When he was ill he would not allow me to pour water to wash his hands. At Cossipore he said: 'Now the key is in my hands. He will give up his body when he knows who he is.'"

M: "Didn't he say it when you were in nirvikalpa samādhi?"

NARENDRA: "Yes. At the time it seemed to me I had no body. I felt only my face.

"I was studying law at home to prepare for the examinations. Suddenly I said to myself, 'What am I doing?'"

M: "Didn't it happen when the Master was at Cossipore?"

NARENDRA: "Yes. Like an insane person I ran out of our house. He asked me, 'What do you want?' I replied, 'I want to remain immersed in samādhi.' He said: 'What a small mind you have! Go beyond samādhi! Samādhi is a very trifling thing.'"

M: "Yes, he used to say that vijnāna is the stage after jnāna. It is like going up and down the stairs after reaching the roof."

NARENDRA: "Kali has a craving for knowledge. I scold him for that. Is knowledge so easy to get? Let his bhakti first mature. The Master told Tarak at Dakshineswar that emotion and bhakti are by no means the last word."

M: "What other things did he say about you?"

NARENDRA: "Once I said to him, 'The forms of God and things like that, which you see in your visions, are all figments of your imagination.' He had so much faith in my words that he went to the Divine Mother in the temple and told Her what I had said to him. He asked Her, 'Are these hallucinations, then?' Afterwards he said to me, 'Mother told me that all these are real.'

"Perhaps you remember that he said to me, 'When you sing, He who dwells here (touching his heart), like a snake, hisses as it were, and then, spreading His hood, quietly holds Himself steady and listens to your music.'

"He has no doubt said many things about me; but what have I realized?"

M: "Now you have put on the garb of Śiva; you cannot touch money. Do you remember the Master's story?"

NARENDRA: "Please tell it to me."

M: "A bahurupi[6] disguised himself as Śiva and visited a house. The master of the house wanted to give him a rupee, but he did not accept it. Then the mendicant went home, removed his disguise, came back to the gentleman, and asked for the rupee. 'Why didn't you accept it before?' he was asked. He said: 'I was impersonating Śiva, a sannyāsi. I couldn't touch money at that time.'"

When Narendra heard the story he laughed a long while.

M: "You have now put on the garb of a physician, as it were. You have become the guardian of these young men. Yours is the entire responsibility. You have to bring up the brothers of the monastery."

NARENDRA: "Whatever spiritual disciplines we are practising here are in obedience to the Master's command. But it is strange that Ram Babu criticizes us for our spiritual practices. He says: 'We have seen him.[7] What need have we of any such practice?'"

M: "Let people act according to their faith."

NARENDRA: "But the Master asked us to practise sādhanā."

[6] A professional impersonator.
[7] Sri Ramakrishna.

Narendra was again telling M. about the Master's love for him.

NARENDRA: "How many times he prayed to the Divine Mother for my sake! After my father's death, when I had no food at home and my mother and sisters and brothers were starving too, the Master prayed to the Divine Mother to give me money."

M: "Yes, I know that. You once told me."

NARENDRA: "But I didn't get any money. The Master told me what the Divine Mother had said to him: 'He will get simple food and clothing. He will eat rice and dāl.'

"He loved me so much! But whenever an impure idea crept into my mind he at once knew about it. While going around with Annada, sometimes I found myself in the company of evil people. On those occasions the Master could not eat any food from my hands. He could raise his hand only a little, and could not bring it to his mouth. On one such occasion, while he was ill, he brought his hand very close to his mouth, but it did not go in. He said to me, 'You are not yet ready.'

"Now and then I feel great scepticism. At Baburam's house it seemed to me that nothing existed—as if there were no such thing as God."

M: "The Master used to say that he too had passed through that mood."

Both M. and Narendra remained silent. Then M. said: "You are all indeed blessed! You think of the Master day and night."

NARENDRA: "But how little it is! We don't yet feel like giving up the body because we haven't realized God."

It was night. Niranjan had just returned from Puri. The members of the math, and M., greeted him with great joy. Niranjan was telling them his experiences. He was then about twenty-five years old.

The evening worship was over. Some of the brothers were meditating. But many of them assembled in the big hall around Niranjan. They were talking. After nine o'clock Sashi offered food to the Deity.

The members of the math finished their supper, which consisted of home-made bread, a little vegetable, and a little hard molasses.

Saturday, May 7, 1887

It was the full-moon day of the month of Vaiśākh. Narendra and M. were seated on a couch in M.'s study in Calcutta. They were talking. Just before Narendra's arrival M. had been studying *The Merchant of Venice, Comus,* and Blackie's *Self-culture,* which he taught at school.

Narendra and the other brothers of the monastery were full of yearning for God-realization. A fire of intense renunciation raged in their hearts.

NARENDRA: "I don't care for anything. You see, I am now talking with you, but I feel like getting up this minute and running away."

Narendra sat in silence a few minutes. Then he said, "I shall fast to death for the realization of God."

M: "That is good. One can do anything for God."

NARENDRA: "But suppose I cannot control my hunger."

M: "Then eat something and begin over again."

Narendra remained silent. a few minutes.

NARENDRA: "It seems there is no God. I pray so much, but there is no reply—none whatsoever.

"How many visions I have seen! How many mantras shining in letters of gold! How many visions of the Goddess Kāli! How many other divine forms! But still I have no peace.

"Will you kindly give me six pice?"

Narendra asked for the money to pay his carriage hire to the Barānagore Math. Just then Satkari arrived in a carriage. Of the same age as Narendra, he dearly loved the members of the monastery. He lived near the math and worked in Calcutta. The carriage was his own. Narendra returned the money to M. and said that he would go with Satkari in his carriage. He asked M. to give them some refreshments.

M. accompanied the two friends to the Barānagore Math. He wanted to see how the brothers spent their time and practised sādhanā. He wanted to see how Sri Ramakrishna, the Master, was reflected in the hearts of the disciples. Niranjan was not at the math. He had gone home to visit his mother, the only relative he had in the world. Baburam, Sarat, and Kali had gone to Puri. They intended to spend a few days there.

Narendra was in charge of the members of the monastery. Prasanna[8] had been practising austere sādhanā for the past few days. Once Narendra had told him of his desire to fast to death for the realization of God. During Narendra's absence in Calcutta, Prasanna had left the monastery for an unknown destination. When Narendra heard about it, he said to the brothers, "Why did Rāja[9] allow him to go?" But Rakhal had not been in the monastery at the time, having gone to the Dakshineswar temple for a stroll.

NARENDRA: "Just let Rāja come back to the monastery! I shall scold him. Why did he allow Prasanna to go away? (To Harish) I am sure you were lecturing him then, standing with your feet apart. Couldn't you prevent his going away?"

Harish replied in a very low voice, "Brother Tarak asked him not to go, but still he went away."

NARENDRA (to M.): "You see what a lot of trouble I am in! Here, too, I am involved in a world of māyā. Who knows where this boy has gone?"

Rakhal returned from Dakshineswar. Bhavanath had accompanied him.

Narendra told Rakhal about Prasanna's going away from the monastery. Prasanna had left a letter for Narendra. This was the substance of the letter: "I am going to Vrindāvan on foot. It is very risky for me to live here. Here my mind is undergoing a change. Formerly I used to dream about my parents and other relatives. Then I dreamt of woman, the embodiment of māyā. I have suffered twice; I had to go back to my relatives at

[8] Sarada Prasanna, one of the Master's young disciples, was addressed as Prasanna by Sri Ramakrishna and his disciples.

[9] Rakhal was addressed as "Rāja" by all the brothers. "Rakhal-Rāj", the "King of the cowherd boys", is one of the names of Sri Krishna, and Sri Ramakrishna often spoke of Rakhal as one of the intimate companions of Krishna.

home. Therefore I am going far away from them. The Master once told me, 'Your people at home are apt to do anything; never trust them.' "

Rakhal said: "These are the reasons for his going away. Once he remarked: 'Narendra often goes home to look after his mother, brothers, and sisters. And he supervises the family's lawsuit. I am afraid that I too may feel like going home, following his example.' "

Narendra remained silent.

Rakhal was talking to them about making pilgrimages. He said: "We have achieved nothing by staying here. The Master always exhorted us to realize God. Have we succeeded?"

Rakhal lay down. The other devotees were either lying down or sitting.

RAKHAL: "Let us go to the Narmadā."

NARENDRA: "What will you achieve by wandering about? Can one ever attain jnāna, that you are talking about it so much?"

A DEVOTEE: "Then why have you renounced the world?"

NARENDRA: "Must we live with Shyam because we have not seen Ram? Must we go on begetting children because we have not realized God? What are you talking about?"

Narendra went out, returning after a few minutes. Rakhal was still lying down.

A member of the monastery who was also lying down said teasingly, feigning great suffering on account of his separation from God: "Ah! Please get me a knife. I have no more use for this life. I can't stand this pain any more!"

NARENDRA (feigning seriousness): "It is there. Stretch out your hand and take it."

Everybody laughed.

The conversation again turned to Prasanna.

NARENDRA: "Even here we are involved in māyā. Why have we become sannyāsis, I wonder?"

RAKHAL: "I have read in a book that sannyāsis should not live together. The author has described a city of sannyāsis."

SASHI: "I don't care about sannyās or any such thing. There is no place where I cannot live."

They were talking of Bhavanath, whose wife had been seriously ill. Narendra said to Rakhal: "I understand that his wife has been snatched from the jaws of death. Is that why he went to Dakshineswar to enjoy the fresh air?"

Ram Babu intended to build a temple in the garden at Kānkurgāchi, where some of Sri Ramakrishna's ashes were buried.

NARENDRA (to Rakhal): "Ram Babu has made M. one of the trustees of the garden."

M. (to Rakhal): "But I don't know anything about it."

It was dusk. Sashi burnt incense before the picture of Sri Ramakrishna in the worship room and then before the pictures of gods and goddesses in the other rooms.

The evening worship began. The members of the math and the other devotees stood with folded hands near the door of the shrine and witnessed the ārati. Then they all sang in chorus the following hymn to Śiva, to the accompaniment of bell and gong:

> Jaya Śiva Omkāra, Bhaja Śiva Omkāra,
> Brahmā Vishnu Sadaśiva,
> Hara Hara Hara Mahādeva!

Narendra had introduced this song for the evening worship. It is sung in the temple of Śiva in Benares.

It was eleven o'clock at night when their supper was over. The brothers prepared a bed for M., and all went to sleep.

It was midnight. M. was wide awake. He said to himself: "Everything is as it was before. The same Ayodhyā—only Rāma is not there." M. silently left his bed. It was the full-moon night of Vaiśākh, the thrice-blessed day of the Buddhists, associated with Buddha's birth, realization, and passing away. M. was walking alone on the bank of the Ganges, contemplating the Master.

It was Sunday. M. had arrived the day before and was planning to stay till Wednesday. The householder devotees generally visited the monastery on Sundays.

The *Yogavāsishtha* was being studied and explained. M. had heard a little about the teachings of this book from Sri Ramakrishna. It taught the absolute identity of Brahman and the soul, and the unreality of the world. The Master had forbidden him and the other householder devotees to practise spiritual discipline following the method of the Advaita Vedānta, since the attitude of the oneness of the soul and God is harmful for one still identified with the body. For such a devotee, the Master used to say, it was better to look on God as the Lord and oneself as His servant.

The conversation turned to the *Yogavāsishtha*.

M: "Well, how is Brahmajnāna described in the *Yogavāsishtha*?"

RAKHAL: "Hunger, thirst, pain, pleasure, and so on, are all māyā. The annihilation of the mind is the only means to the realization of Brahman."

M: "What remains after the annihilation of the mind is Brahman. Is that not true?"

RAKHAL: "Yes."

M: "Sri Ramakrishna used to say that. Nangtā taught him that way. Have you found in the book that Vaśishtha asked Rāma to lead a householder's life?"

RAKHAL: "I haven't yet found anything like that in the book. Rāma is not even admitted by the author to be an Incarnation of God."

Presently Narendra, Tarak, and another devotee returned from the bank of the Ganges. They had intended to go to Konnagar, on the other side of the river, but had been unable to find a ferry-boat. They sat down. The conversation about the *Yogavāsishtha* went on.

NARENDRA (*to M.*): "There are many nice stories in the book. Do you know the incident of Līlā?"

M: "Yes, I have read the book here and there. Līlā had attained Brahma-jnāna."

NARENDRA: "Yes. Do you remember the story of Indra and Ahalyā, and the story of how King Viduratha became a chandāla?"

M: "Yes, I remember."

NARENDRA: "What a wonderful description of the forest!"

Narendra and the other devotees were going to the Ganges to bathe. M. accompanied them. The sun was very hot; so M. took his umbrella. Sarat, a devotee from Barānagore, was going with them to take his bath. He often visited the monastery.

M. (to Sarat): "It is very hot."

NARENDRA: "Is that your excuse for taking the umbrella?"

M. laughed.

The members of the monastery were clad in gerruā.

M. (to Narendra): "It is really very hot. One is liable to get a sunstroke."

NARENDRA: "I see that your body is the obstacle in your path of renunciation. Isn't that so? I mean you, Devendra Babu—"

M. laughed and said to himself, "Is it merely the body?"

After bathing, the devotees returned to the monastery. They washed their feet and entered the worship room. Saluting the Deity, they offered flowers.

Narendra was a little late in coming to the worship room. He found that there was no flower on the tray. There were only a few bel-leaves. He sprinkled the leaves with sandal-paste and offered them to Sri Ramakrishna. He rang the bell, saluted the Deity again, and joined the other brothers in the big hall, which was known as the room of the "dānās".

The members of the math called themselves the "dānās" and the "daityas", which mean the "ghosts" and the "demons", the companions of Śiva. They took these names because of their utter indifference to worldly pleasures and relationships.

The southernmost room of the second floor was used for meditation, contemplation, and study, and was known as Kali Tapasvi's room, since Kali used to shut himself in there most of the day. North of this room was the worship room, and north of that, again, was the room where the offerings for the worship were prepared. From this room the devotees used to watch the evening worship. North of the "offering room" was the room of the "dānās", a very long hall where the members of the math used to assemble. Here the householder devotees and visitors were received. North of this hall was a small room where the devotees took their meals. East of the worship room and of Kali Tapasvi's room ran a long verandah, at the south-west corner of which was the library of a society of Barānagore. Between Kali Tapasvi's room and this library was a staircase; and north of the dining-room was another staircase, leading to the roof.

Narendra and the other members of the math often spent their evenings on this roof. There they devoted a great deal of time to discussion of the teachings of Sri Ramakrishna, Śankarāchārya, Rāmānuja, and Jesus Christ, and of Hindu philosophy, European philosophy, the Vedas, the Purānas, and the Tantras.

Narendra, who had a beautiful voice, used to sing in the room of the "dānās" and teach music to Sarat and a few others. Kali used to take lessons on the instruments. Many, many happy hours they spent together in that hall, dancing and singing.

Narendra was sitting with the devotees in the room of the "dānās". The conversation turned to religious preaching.

M. (to Narendra): "Vidyāsāgar says that he does not speak about God to anyone for fear of being caned."

NARENDRA: "For fear of being caned? What does he mean?"

M: "This is what Vidyāsāgar says: 'Suppose that after death we all go to God. The emissaries of Death will have sent Keshab Sen there too. Keshab Sen, no doubt, committed sins while he lived on earth. When that is proved, perhaps God will say, "Give him twenty-five stripes." Then suppose I am taken to God. I used to go to Keshab Sen's Brāhmo Samāj in my earthly life. I too have committed many sins; so I too am ordered to be caned. Then suppose I say to God that I acted in that sinful way because I listened to Keshab's preaching. Thereupon God will ask His emissaries to bring Keshab back. When he is brought, the Almighty Lord will say to him: "Did you really preach that way? You yourself knew nothing about spiritual matters and yet you had the hardihood to teach others about God! Emissaries! Give him twenty-five stripes more."'"

Everybody laughed.

M: "Therefore Vidyāsāgar says: 'I cannot take care of my own self; should I be foolish enough to get an additional caning for misleading others? I myself do not understand God. How shall I lecture to others about Him?'"

NARENDRA: "How has he—who could not understand God—understood other things?"

M: "What other things?"

NARENDRA: "He says that he has not understood God. But how, then, can he understand charity and doing good to others? How can he understand about the school? How can he understand about educating boys by establishing schools? How can he understand that it is right to enter the world, marry, and beget children?

"He who rightly understands one thing understands everything else."

M. (to himself): "Yes, Sri Ramakrishna, too, said that he who knows God knows everything else. Further, he said to Vidyāsāgar that leading a worldly life, establishing schools, and so on are the outcome of rajas. The Master also said that Vidyāsāgar's philanthropy was due to the influence of sattva on rajas. Such rajas is not harmful."

After their meal the brothers of the monastery rested. M. and Chunilal were conversing. Chunilal told M. of his first visit to Sri Ramakrishna at Dakshineswar. He also told him how at one time he had felt disgusted with the world, had renounced it, and had wandered about in holy places. A few minutes later Narendra came and sat by them. He asked the younger Gopal to prepare a smoke for him. The latter had been meditating. Narendra said to him: "I say! Prepare a smoke. What do you mean by this meditation?

First of all prepare yourself for spiritual life by serving God and holy men; then you will be able to meditate. First of all karma, and then meditation." Everybody laughed.

There was a big plot of wooded land to the west of the monastery compound. M. was seated alone under a tree, when suddenly Prasanna appeared. It was about three o'clock in the afternoon.

M: "Where have you been all these days? Everyone has been so worried about you. Have you seen the brothers? When did you arrive?"

PRASANNA: "Just now. Yes, I have seen them."

M: "You left a note saying that you were going to Vrindāvan. We were terribly worried about you. How far did you go?"

PRASANNA: "Only as far as Konnagar."[10]

Both of them laughed.

M: "Sit down. Tell me all about it. Where did you stop first?"

PRASANNA: "At the Dakshineswar temple garden. I spent one night there."

M. (smiling): "What is Hazra's present mood?"

PRASANNA: "Hazra asked me, 'What do you think of me?'"

Both laughed.

M. (smiling): "What did you say?"

PRASANNA: "I said nothing."

M: "Then?"

PRASANNA: "Then he asked me whether I had brought tobacco for him."

Both laughed.

PRASANNA: "He wanted me to wait on him." (Laughter.)

M: "Where did you go next?"

PRASANNA: "By degrees I got to Konnagar. I spent the night in the open. I intended to proceed farther and asked some gentlemen whether I could procure enough money there for a railway ticket to the up-country."

M: "What did they say?"

PRASANNA: "They said, 'You may get a rupee or so; but who will give you the whole fare?'"

Both laughed.

M: "What did you take with you?"

PRASANNA: "Oh, one or two pieces of cloth and a picture of the Master. I didn't show the picture to anybody."

Sashi's father came to the math. He wanted to take his son home. During Sri Ramakrishna's illness Sashi had nursed the Master for nine months with unswerving zeal. He had won a scholarship in the Entrance Examination for his academic ability and had studied up to the B.A., but he had not appeared at the examination. His father, a poor brāhmin, was a devout Hindu and spent much of his time in spiritual practice. Sashi was his eldest son. His parents had hoped that, after completing his education, he would earn money and remove the family's financial difficulties. But Sashi had renounced the world for the realization of God. Whenever he thought of his

[10] A small town only a few miles from Barānagore, on the other side of the Ganges.

father and mother he felt great anguish of heart. Many a time he said to his friends, with tears in his eyes: "I am at a loss as to my duty. Alas, I could not serve my parents; I could not be of any use to them. What great hope they placed in me! On account of our poverty my mother did not have any jewelry. I cherished the desire to buy some for her. But now all my hopes are frustrated; it is impossible for me to return home. My Master asked me to renounce 'woman and gold'. I simply cannot return home."

After Sri Ramakrishna's passing away Sashi's father had hoped that his son would come back to his family. The boy had spent a few days at home, but immediately after the establishment of the new monastery he had begun to frequent it and, after a few days, had decided to remain there as one of the members. Every now and then his father came to the monastery to persuade him to come home; but he had not succeeded.

This day, on learning that his father had come, Sashi fled the monastery by another door. He did not want to meet him.

Sashi's father knew M. They paced the upper verandah together and talked.

SASHI'S FATHER: "Who is in charge of this place? Narendra alone is the cause of all the mischief. For a while all these young men returned home and devoted themselves to their studies."

M: "There is no master here. They are all equals. What can Narendra do? Can a man renounce home against his own will? Have we householders, for instance, been able to give up our homes altogether?"

SASHI'S FATHER: "You are doing the right thing. You are serving both the world and God. Can't one practise religion after your method? That is exactly what we want Sashi to do. Let him live at home and come here too. You have no idea how much his mother weeps for him."

M. became sad and said nothing.

SASHI'S FATHER: "And if you speak of searching for holy men, I know where to find a good one. Let Sashi go to him."

Rakhal and M. were walking on the verandah to the east of Kali Tapasvi's room.

RAKHAL (earnestly): "M., let us practise sādhanā! We have renounced home for good. When someone says, 'You have not realized God by renouncing home; then why all this fuss?', Narendra gives a good retort. He says, 'Because we could not attain Ram, must we live with Shyam and beget children?' Ah! Every now and then Narendra says nice things. You had better ask him."

M: "What you say is right. I see that you too have become restless for God."

RAKHAL: "M., how can I describe the state of my mind? Today at noontime I felt great yearning for the Narmadā. M., please practise sādhanā; otherwise you will not succeed. Even Śukadeva was afraid of this world. That is why immediately after his birth he fled the world. His father asked him to wait, but he ran straight away."

M: "Yes, the Yogopanishad describes how Śukadeva fled this world of māyā. It also describes Vyāsa's conversation with Śuka. Vyāsa asked his son to practise religion in the world. But Śuka said that the one essential thing is the Lotus Feet of God. He also expressed his disgust with worldly men for getting married and living with women."

RAKHAL: "Many people think that it is enough not to look at the face of a woman. But what will you gain merely by turning your eyes to the ground at the sight of a woman? Narendra put it very well last night, when he said: 'Woman exists for a man as long as he has lust. Free from lust, one sees no difference between man and woman.'"

M: "How true it is! Children do not see the difference between man and woman."

RAKHAL: "Therefore I say that we must practise spiritual discipline. How can one attain Knowledge without going beyond māyā?

"Let's go to the big hall. Some gentlemen have come from Barānagore. Narendra is talking with them. Let's go and listen to him."

M. did not enter the room. As he was pacing outside he overheard some of the conversation.

NARENDRA: "There is no fixed time or place for the sandhyā and other devotions."

GENTLEMAN: "Sir, can one realize God through spiritual practice alone?"

NARENDRA: "Realization depends on God's grace. Sri Krishna says in the Gītā:

> The Lord, O Arjuna, dwells in the hearts of all beings, causing them, by His māyā, to revolve as if mounted on a machine. Take refuge in Him with all thy heart, O Bhārata. By His grace wilt thou attain Supreme Peace and the Eternal Abode.

"Without the grace of God mere worship and prayer do not help at all. Therefore one should take refuge in Him."

GENTLEMAN: "May we come now and then and disturb you?"

NARENDRA: "Please come whenever you like. We take our baths in the Ganges at your ghāt."

GENTLEMAN: "I don't mind that. But please see that others don't use it."

NARENDRA: "We shall not use your ghāt, if that is what you mean."

GENTLEMAN: "No, I don't mean exactly that. But if you see other people using it, then you had better not go."

It was dusk. The evening worship was over. The devotees, as usual, sang in chorus, "Jaya Śiva Omkāra". Afterwards they assembled in the room of the "dānas". M., too, was seated there. Prasanna was reading from the Guru Gītā.

Narendra sang:

> I salute the Eternal Teacher, who is the Embodiment of the Bliss
> of Brahman,
> The Essence of knowledge and liberation, the Giver of Supreme
> Joy;

Who is all-pervading, like the ākāśa, and is the goal of the Vedānta's
teachings;
Who is One, eternal, stainless, pure, and is the constant Witness
of all things;
Who dwells beyond all moods, transcending the three gunas.

Narendra sang again:

There is none higher than the Guru, none better than the Guru;
This is what Śiva has declared.
I shall sing of the blessed Guru, the Supreme Brahman;
I shall worship the blessed Guru, the Supreme Brahman;
I shall meditate on the blessed Guru, the Supreme Brahman;
I shall bow down to the blessed Guru, the Supreme Brahman.

As Narendra sang these verses from the *Guru Gītā* in his melodious voice,
the minds of the devotees became steady, like a candle-flame in a windless
place.

Rakhal was seated in Kali Tapasvi's room. Prasanna sat near him. M., too,
was there.

Rakhal had renounced the world, leaving behind his wife and child. A
fire of intense renunciation burnt day and night in his heart. He was thinking seriously of going away, by himself, to the bank of the Narmadā or
some other holy place. Still, he was trying to persuade Prasanna not to run
away from the monastery.

RAKHAL (*to Prasanna*): "Where do you want to go, running away from
here? Here you are in the company of holy men. Wouldn't it be foolish to
run away from this? Where will you find another like Narendra?"

PRASANNA: "My parents live in Calcutta. I am afraid of being drawn by
their love. That is why I want to flee to a distant place."

RAKHAL: "Can our parents love us as intensely as Gurumahārāj [mean-
ing Sri Ramakrishna] did? What have we done for him, to deserve all this
love? Why was he so eager for our welfare in body, mind, and soul? What
have we done for him, to deserve all this?"

M. (*to himself*): "Ah! Rakhal is right. Therefore a person like Sri Ramakrishna is described as the 'Ocean of Mercy without any reason'."

PRASANNA (*to Rakhal*): "Don't you yourself feel like running away from
here?"

RAKHAL: "Yes, now and then I have a fancy to spend a few days on the
bank of the Narmadā. I say to myself, 'Let me go to a place like that and
practise sādhanā in a garden.' Again, I feel a strong desire to practise the
panchatapā for three days. But I hesitate to live in a garden that belongs to
worldly people."

Tarak and Prasanna were talking in the room of the "dānas". Tarak had
lost his mother. His father, like Rakhal's father, had married a second time.
Tarak himself had married but had lost his wife. Now the monastery was
his home. He too was trying to persuade Prasanna to live there.

PRASANNA: "I have neither jnāna nor prema. What have I in the world for a support?"

TARAK: "It is no doubt difficult to attain jnāna; but how can you say you have no prema?"

PRASANNA: "I have not yet wept for God. How can I say I have prema? What have I realized in all these days?"

TARAK: "But you have seen the Master. And why do you say that you have no jnāna?"

PRASANNA: "What sort of jnāna are you talking about? Jnāna means Knowledge. Knowledge of what? Certainly of God. But I am not even sure of the existence of God."

TARAK: "Yes, that's true. According to the jnāni, there is no God."

M. (to himself): "Ah! The Master used to say that those who seek God pass through the state that Prasanna is now experiencing. In that state sometimes one doubts the very existence of God. I understand that Tarak is now reading Buddhistic philosophy. That is why he says that according to the jnāni God does not exist. But Sri Ramakrishna used to say that the jnāni and the bhakta will ultimately arrive at the same destination."

Narendra and Prasanna were talking in the meditation room. Rakhal, Harish, and the younger Gopal were seated in another part of the room. After a while the elder Gopal came in.

Narendra was reading from the *Gītā* and explaining the verses to Prasanna:

> The Lord, O Arjuna, dwells in the hearts of all beings, causing them, by His māyā, to revolve as if mounted on a machine. Take refuge in Him with all thy heart, O Bhārata. By His grace wilt thou attain Supreme Peace and the Eternal Abode. Relinquishing all dharmas, take refuge in Me alone. I shall liberate thee from all sins. Grieve not.

NARENDRA: "Did you notice what Krishna said? 'Mounted on a machine.' The Lord, by His māyā, causes all beings to revolve as if mounted on a machine. To seek to know God? You are but a worm among worms—and you to know God? Just reflect a moment: what is a man? It is said that each one of the myriads of stars that shine overhead represents a solar system. This earth of ours is a part of only one solar system, and even that is too big for us. Like an insect man walks about on this earth, which, compared to the sun, is only a tiny ball."

Narendra sang:

> We are born, O Lord, in the dust of earth,
> And our eyes are blinded by the dust;
> With dust we toy like children at play:
> O give us assurance, Thou Help of the weak!
>
> Wilt Thou cast us out of Thy lap, O Lord,
> For a single mistake? Wilt Thou turn away
> And abandon us to our helplessness?
> Oh, then we shall never be able to rise,
> But shall lie for ever dazed and undone.

Mere babes are we, Father, with baby minds;
At every step we stumble and fall.
Why, then, must Thou show us Thy terrible face?
Why, Lord, must we ever behold Thy frown?

Small are we—oh, do not be angry with us,
But tenderly speak to us when we do wrong;
For though Thou dost raise us a hundred times,
A hundred times we shall fall again!
What else can one do with a helpless mind?

Then he said to Prasanna: "Surrender yourself at His feet. Resign yourself completely to His will."

Narendra sang again in an ecstatic mood:

O Lord, I am Thy servant, I am Thy servant! Thy servant am I!
O Lord, Thou art my Master, Thou art my Master! My Master
  art Thou!
From Thee I have received two pieces of bread and a kaupin;[11]
When I sing Thy name, devotion wells up in my heart and shields
  me from harm.
Thou art the Master, the All-compassionate; this I repeat, O Lord!
Thy servant Kabir has taken refuge at Thy feet.

Narendra said to Prasanna: "Don't you remember Sri Ramakrishna's words? God is the hill of sugar and you are but an ant. One grain is enough to fill your stomach, and you think of bringing home the entire hill! Don't you remember what the Master said about Śukadeva? Even Śukadeva was a big ant at the most. That is why I scolded Kali, saying: 'You fool! Do you want to measure God with your tape and foot-rule?'

"God is the Ocean of Mercy. Be His slave and take refuge in Him. He will show compassion. Pray to Him: 'Protect me always with Thy compassionate face. Lead me from the unreal to the Real, from darkness to Light, from death to Immortality. Reveal Thyself to me and protect me always with Thy compassionate face.'"

PRASANNA: "What kind of spiritual discipline should one practise?"

NARENDRA: "Repeat His name. That's enough. Don't you remember Sri Ramakrishna's song?"

Narendra sang:

O Śyāmā, my only hope is in Thy hallowed name!
What need have I of kośā and kusi?[12] What need of smiles and
  conventions?
Thy name dissolves death's bonds, as Śiva has proclaimed,
And I myself am Śiva's servant; whom else should I obey?
O Mother, come what may, I shall repeat Thy name;
Why should I fret myself to death? To Śiva's words I cling.

[11] Loin-cloth of a monk.
[12] Metal articles used in the temple worship.

He sang again:

> Mere babes are we, Father, with baby minds;
> At every step we stumble and fall.
> Why, then, must Thou show us Thy terrible face?
> Why, Lord, must we ever behold Thy frown?

PRASANNA: "Now you are saying that there is a God. Again, it is you who say that according to Chārvāka and many other thinkers the world was self-created."

NARENDRA: "Haven't you studied chemistry? Who combines the different elements? It is a human hand that combines hydrogen, oxygen, and electricity to prepare water. Everybody admits the existence of an Intelligent Force—a Force that is the essence of Knowledge and that guides all these phenomena."

PRASANNA: "How are we to know that God is kind?"

NARENDRA: "The Vedas say, 'That which is Thy compassionate face.' John Stuart Mill said the same thing. He said, 'How much kindness must He have, who has implanted kindness in the hearts of men.' The Master used to say: 'Faith is the one essential thing. God exists. He is very near us. Through faith alone one sees Him.'"

Narendra sang:

> Where are you seeking Me, My servant? I am very close to you.
> Far away you still are seeking, though I am so very near.
> I am not in skin or hair, I am not in bones or flesh,
> Not in mosque and not in temple, not in Kāśi or Kailāś.
> Never will you come on Me in Ayodhyā or Dwārakā;
> But you will be sure to find Me if you search where faith abides.
> Not in pleasant tasks or yoga, not in vairāgya or sannyās,
> Yet I come without delaying if you only search for Me.

PRASANNA: "Sometimes you say that God does not exist, and now you are saying all these things! You are not consistent. You keep changing your opinions."

All laughed.

NARENDRA: "All right! I shall never change what I have just said. As long as one has desires and cravings, so long one doubts the existence of God. A man cherishes some desire or other. Perhaps he has the desire to study or pass the university examination or become a scholar, and so forth and so on."

Narendra sang again, in a voice choked with emotion:

> Hail to Thee, our God and Lord! Hail, Giver of every blessing!
> Hail, Thou Giver of good!
> O Redeemer from fear, from danger and suffering!
> Upholder of the worlds!
> Hail, Lord! Victory to Thee!
>
> Unfathomable and infinite, immeasurable, beyond compare,
> O God, none equals Thee!
> Lord of the Universe! O All-pervading Truth!

Thou the Ātman Supreme!
Hail, Lord! Victory to Thee!

O Thou, the All-compassionate One, adored by the whole universe,
I bow before Thy feet!
Thou art the only Refuge in life and death, O Lord;
Before Thy feet I bow!
Hail, Lord! Victory to Thee!

This is our only prayer, O Lord! What other boon can we implore?
Thus do we pray to Thee:
Grant us true wisdom here, and in the life hereafter
Reveal Thyself to us.
Hail, Lord! Victory to Thee!

Again Narendra sang, describing how very near God is to us—as near as the musk to the deer—and exhorting his brother disciples to drink deep from the cup of Divine Bliss:

Drinking the Bliss of Hari from the cup of prema,
Sādhu, be intoxicated!
Childhood you spent in crying, and youth in women's control;
Now, in your old age, full of phlegm and wind,
You wait for the funeral couch to bear you to the cremation
    ground.

Within the musk-deer's navel the fragrant musk is found;
But how can you make it understand?
Without the proper teacher to guide him on his way,
Man, too, is blindly roaming through the world,
Deluded as the foolish deer that wanders round and round the
    woods.

M. heard all this from the verandah.

Narendra got up. As he left the room he remarked, "My brain is heated by talking to these youngsters."

He met M. on the verandah and said, "Please, let us have a drink of water."

One of the members of the math said to Narendra, "Why, then, do you say that God does not exist?"

Narendra laughed.

Monday, May 9, 1887

The next morning M. was sitting alone under a tree in the garden. He said to himself: "Sri Ramakrishna has made the brothers of the monastery renounce 'woman and gold'. Ah, how eager they are to realize God! This place has become a veritable Vaikuntha, and the brothers living here are embodiments of Nārāyana. It is not many days since the Master passed away; that is why all the ideas and ideals he stood for are there, almost intact. 'The same Ayodhyā—only Rāma is not there.' The Master has made these brothers renounce their homes. Why has he kept a few in the world? Is there no way of liberation for them?"

From a room upstairs Narendra saw M. sitting alone under the tree. He came down and said with a smile, "Hello, M.! What are you doing?"

After a little conversation M. said to him: "Ah, you have such a sweet voice. Please sing a hymn."

Narendra sang the following hymn to Śiva, in which the devotee prays for forgiveness for his sins:

> Even before I saw the light of this world, my sins from previous births,
> Through which I passed because of desire for the fruit of my deeds,
> Punished me as I lay in my mother's womb.
> There I was boiled in the midst of filthy things:
> Who can describe the pain that afflicts the child in its mother's womb?
> Therefore, O Śiva! O Mahādeva! O Śambhu! forgive me, I pray, for my transgressions.
>
> In childhood my suffering never came to an end;
> My body was covered with filth and I craved for my mother's breasts.
> Over my body and limbs I had no control;
> I was pursued by troublesome flies and mosquitoes;
> Day and night I cried with the pain of many an ailment, forgetting Thee, O Śankara!
> Therefore, O Śiva! O Mahādeva! O Śambhu! forgive me, I pray, for my transgressions.
>
> In youth the venomous snakes of sound, sight, taste, touch, and smell,
> Bit into my vitals and slew my discrimination;
> I was engrossed in the pleasures of wealth, sons, and a youthful wife.
> Alas! my heart, bereft of the thought of Śiva,
> Was filled with arrogance and pride.
> Therefore, O Śiva! O Mahādeva! O Śambhu! forgive me, I pray, for my transgressions.
>
> Now in old age my senses have lost the power of proper judging and acting;
> My body, though still not wholly bereft of life,
> Is weak and senile from many afflictions, from sins and illnesses and bereavements;
> But even now my mind, instead of meditating on Śiva,
> Runs after vain desires and hollow delusions.
> Therefore, O Śiva! O Mahādeva! O Śambhu! forgive me, I pray, for my transgressions.
>
> The duties laid down in the smriti—perilous and abstruse—are now beyond me;
> How can I speak of the Vedic injunctions for brāhmins, as means for attaining Brahman?
> Never yet have I rightly grasped, through discrimination,

The meaning of hearing the scriptures from the guru and reasoning on his instruction;
How then can I speak of reflecting on Truth without interruption?
Therefore, O Śiva! O Mahādeva! O Śambhu! forgive me, I pray,
   for my transgressions

Not even once have I finished my bath before sunrise and brought
   from the Ganges
Water to bathe Thy holy image;
Never, from the deep woods, have I brought the sacred vilwa-
   leaves for Thy worship;
Nor have I gathered full-blown lotuses from the lakes,
Nor ever arranged the lights and the incense for worshipping
   Thee.
Therefore, O Śiva! O Mahādeva! O Śambhu! forgive me, I pray,
   for my transgressions.

I have not bathed Thine image with milk and honey, with butter
   and other oblations;
I have not decked it with fragrant sandal-paste;
I have not worshipped Thee with golden flowers, with incense,
   with camphor-flame and savoury offerings.
Therefore, O Śiva! O Mahādeva! O Śambhu! forgive me, I pray,
   for my transgressions.

I have not made rich gifts to the brāhmins, cherishing in my
   heart,
O Mahādeva, Thy sacred form;
I have not made in the sacred fire the million oblations of butter,
Repeating the holy mantra given to me by my guru;
Never have I done penance along the Ganges with japa and study
   of the Vedas.
Therefore, O Śiva! O Mahādeva! O Śambhu! forgive me, I pray,
   for my transgressions.

I have not sat in the lotus posture, nor have I ever controlled
The prāna along the Sushumnā, repeating the syllable Om;
Never have I suppressed the turbulent waves of my mind, nor
   merged the self-effulgent Om
In the ever shining Witness-Consciousness, whose nature is that
   of the highest Brahman;
Nor have I, in samādhi, meditated on Śankara, who dwells in
   every form as the Inner Guide.
Therefore, O Śiva! O Mahādeva! O Śambhu! forgive me, I pray,
   for my transgressions.

Never, O Śiva! have I seen Thee, the Pure, the Unattached, the
   Naked One,
Beyond the three gunas, free from delusion and darkness, absorbed
   in meditation,
And ever aware of the true nature of the world;
Nor, with a longing heart, have I meditated on Thine auspicious
   and sin-destroying form.

Therefore, O Śiva! O Mahādeva! O Śambhu! forgive me, I pray, for my transgressions.

O mind, to gain liberation, concentrate wholly on Śiva,
The sole Reality underlying the worlds, the Giver of good;
Whose head is illumined by the crescent moon and in whose hair the Ganges is hidden;
Whose fire-darting eyes consumed the god of earthly love; whose throat and ears are decked with snakes;
Whose upper garment is a comely elephant-skin.
Of what avail are all the other rituals?

O mind, of what avail are wealth or horses, elephants or a kingdom?
Of what avail the body or a house?
Know all these to be but momentary and quickly shun them;
Worship Śiva, as your guru instructs you, for the attaining of Self-Knowledge.

Day by day does man come nearer to death;
His youth wears away; the day that is gone never' returns.
Almighty Time devours everything;
Fickle as lightning is the goddess of fortune.
O Śiva! O Giver of shelter to those that come to Thee for refuge!
Protect me, who have taken refuge at Thy feet.

I salute the ever auspicious Śiva, the Home of Peace,
Who sits in the lotus posture; who has five mouths and three eyes;
Who holds in both His hands weapons and gong and drum;
Who is bedecked with many an ornament;
Whose skin is clear as crystal; who is Pārvati's Lord.

I salute the self-effulgent Guru of the gods, the Lord of Umā;
I salute the Cause of the Universe;
I salute the Lord of beasts, adorned with snakes;
I salute Śiva, whose three eyes shine like the sun, the moon, and fire;
I salute the Beloved of Krishna; I salute Śankara, who bestows boons on His devotees and gives them shelter;
I salute the auspicious Śiva.

O Śiva! White is Thy body, covered with ashes; white shine Thy teeth when Thou smilest!
White is the skull Thou holdest in Thy hand; white is Thy club, which threatens the wicked!
White is the bull on which Thou ridest; white are the rings that hang from Thine ears!
White appear Thy matted locks, covered with the foam of the Ganges;
White shines the moon on Thy forehead!
May He who is all white, all pure, bestow on me the treasure of forgiveness for my transgressions!

> O Śiva, forgive all the sins that I have committed
> With hands or feet, with words or body, with ears or eyes, with
>   mind or heart;
> Forgive my sins, those past and those that are yet to come!
> Victory unto Śiva, the Ocean of Compassion, the Great God, the
>   Abode of Blessedness!

After the hymn Narendra and M. talked again.

NARENDRA: "You may speak of leading a detached life in the world, and all that, but you will not attain anything unless you renounce 'woman and gold'. Don't you feel disgusted with your wife's body?

> Fools enjoy the contact of the body, filled with filth, peopled with worms, foul of smell by nature, made of flesh, blood, bone, and marrow; but the wise shun it.

"Vain is the life of a person who does not take delight in the teachings of Vedānta and drink the Nectar of Divine Bliss. Listen to a song."

Narendra sang:

> O man, abandon your delusion! Cast aside your wicked counsels!
> Know the Lord and free yourself from earthly suffering!
> For a few days' pleasure only, you have quite forgotten Him
> Who is the Comrade of your soul. Alas, what mockery!

"No liberation is possible for a man unless he puts on the loin-cloth of a sannyāsi. The world must be renounced."

Narendra sang from the Five Stanzas on the glory of the monk's loin-cloth:

> Roaming ever in the grove of Vedānta,
> Ever pleased with his beggar's morsel
> Ever walking with heart free from sorrow,
> Blest indeed is the wearer of the loin-cloth. . . .

Continuing, Narendra said: "Why should a man be entangled in worldliness? Why should he be ensnared by māyā? What is man's real nature? He is the blessed Śiva, the Embodiment of Bliss and Spirit."

He sang Śankarāchārya's Six Stanzas on Nirvāna:

> Om. I am neither mind, intelligence, ego, nor chitta,
> Neither ears nor tongue nor the senses of smell and sight;
> Nor am I ether, earth, fire, water, or air:
> I am Pure Knowledge and Bliss: I am Śiva! I am Śiva! . . .

Narendra recited another hymn, the Eight Stanzas on the glory of Krishna:

> I am consumed with false desires and wrapped in the sleep of lust:
> Save me, O Madhusudana!
> Thou art my only Refuge, Lord! I have no other salvation.
> I am entrapped in the mire of sin:
> O Madhusudana, redeem me!

I am ensnared in the net of love for children, wife, and home:
Save me, O Madhusudana!
I am without devotion, helpless, smitten by wrong desire,
Afflicted with grief and misery:
O Madhusudana, redeem me!

Lord, I have neither master nor place of shelter to call my own:
Save me, O Madhusudana!
Utterly wearied out am I by all this going and coming
Along the endless road of life:
O Madhusudana, redeem me!

From this hard and unavailing journey through life and death,
Save me, O Madhusudana!
Many the births that I have seen in many a bodily form,
And painful it is in the mother's womb:
O Madhusudana, redeem me!

To Thee I come for salvation out of the cycle of existence:
Save me, O Madhusudana!
For I am terrified alike of old age and of death:
I come to Thee for shelter, Lord!
O Madhusudana, redeem me!

Never a good deed have I done, but many have been my sins:
Save me, O Madhusudana!
Headlong have I fallen into the mire of worldliness;
Countless the births I have endured:
O Madhusudana, redeem me!

I have lorded it over men, but happiness is not there:
Save me, O Madhusudana!
What my words have promised, my deeds have never carried out;
Lord, I am full of wretchedness:
O Madhusudana, redeem me!

If as a man or a woman I must be born again and again—
Save me, O Madhusudana!—
May my devotion be unswerving to Thy feet, O Lord!
From the delusion of this world,
O Madhusudana, redeem me!

M. remained spellbound as he listened to these hymns sung by Narendra. He said to himself: "How intense Narendra's dispassion is! This is how he has infused the spirit of dispassion into the hearts of the other brothers of the monastery. The very contact with them awakens in the hearts of the Master's householder devotees the desire for renunciation of 'woman and gold'. Ah, how blessed are these all-renouncing brothers! Why has the Master kept us few in the world? Will he show us a way? Will he give us the spirit of renunciation, or will he delude us with worldliness?"

After the meal all were resting. The elder Gopal was copying some songs. Niranjan was on a visit to his mother. Sarat, Baburam, and Kali were in Puri.

Narendra, with one or two brothers, left for Calcutta. He had to see to his lawsuit. He was going to return in the evening; the brothers could not bear his absence.

In the afternoon Rabindra arrived, looking like a mad person. He was barefoot and had only half of his black-bordered cloth round his waist. His eyeballs were rolling like a madman's. All asked him anxiously what was the matter.

"Let me recover my breath!" he said. "I shall tell you everything presently. I am certainly not going back home; I shall stay at this very place with you all. She is certainly a traitor! Let me tell you something, friends. For her sake I gave up my habit of drinking, which I had indulged for five years. I have not taken a drop for the last eight months. And she is a traitor!"

The brothers of the math said: "Be calm, please! How did you come?"

RABINDRA: "I have come barefoot all the way from Calcutta."

The brothers asked him where he had lost the other half of his cloth.

RABINDRA: "When I was leaving her place she began to pull at my cloth. That is how half of it was torn off."

The brothers told him to bathe in the Ganges and cool off; then they would hear his story.

Rabindra belonged to a respectable kāyastha family of Calcutta. He was twenty or twenty-two years old. He had first met Sri Ramakrishna at the Dakshineswar temple and had received his special blessing. On one occasion he had spent three nights with the Master. His disposition was very sweet and tender, and the Master had loved him dearly. Once he had said to Rabindra: "You will have to wait some time; you have to go through a few more experiences. Nothing can be done now. You see, the police can't do much just when the robbers attack a house. When the plundering is almost over, the police make their arrests."

Rabindra had many virtues. He was devoted to God and to service of the poor. He had many spiritual qualities. But he had walked into the snare of a prostitute. Now, suddenly, he had discovered that the woman was being unfaithful to him. Therefore he had come to the math in this dishevelled state, resolved not to go back to the world.

A devotee accompanied Rabindra to the Ganges. It was his inmost desire that Rabindra's spiritual consciousness should be awakened in the company of these holy men. When Rabindra finished his bath, the devotee took him to the adjacent cremation ground, showed him the corpses lying about, and said: "The brothers of the math come here every now and then to meditate on God. It is a good place for meditation. Here one sees clearly that the world is impermanent."

Rabindra sat down in the cremation ground to meditate. But he could not meditate long; his mind was restless.

Rabindra and the devotee returned to the math. They went to the worship room to salute the Deity. The devotee said to him, "The brothers of the math meditate in this room."

Rabindra sat there to meditate, but could not meditate long there either.

DEVOTEE: "How do you feel? Is your mind very restless? Is that why you have got up from your seat? Perhaps you could not concentrate well."

RABINDRA: "I am sure I shall not go back to the world. But the mind is restless."

M. and Rabindra were talking. No one else was present. M. was telling him stories from the life of Buddha. At that time the members of the math regularly read the lives of Buddha and Chaitanya. M. said to Rabindra that Buddha's spiritual consciousness was first awakened by hearing a song of some heavenly maidens.

M. sang the song:

> We moan for rest, alas! but rest can never find;
> We know not whence we come, nor where we float away.
> Time and again we tread this round of smiles and tears;
> In vain we pine to know whither our pathway leads,
> And why we play this empty play. . . .

That night Narendra, Tarak, and Harish returned from Calcutta. They said, "Oh, what a big meal we had!" They had been entertained by a devotee in Calcutta.

The members of the monastery assembled in the room of the "dānās". Narendra heard Rabindra's story. He sang by way of giving instruction to him:

> O man, abandon your delusion! Cast aside your wicked counsels!
> Know the Lord and free yourself from earthly suffering!
> For a few days' pleasure only, you have quite forgotten Him
> Who is the Comrade of your soul. Alas, what mockery!

Narendra sang again:

> Drinking the Bliss of Hari from the cup of prema,
> Sādhu, be intoxicated! . . .

A few minutes later the brothers went to Kali Tapasvi's room. Girish Ghosh had just sent two of his new books to the monastery: the *Life of Buddha* and the *Life of Chaitanya*.

Since the founding of the new math Sashi had devoted himself heart and soul to the worship and service of the Master. All were amazed at his devotion. Just as he had tended Sri Ramakrishna's physical body during his illness, so now, with the same unswerving zeal, he worshipped the Master in the shrine room.

A member of the monastery was reading aloud from the lives of Buddha and Chaitanya. He was a little sarcastic while reading Chaitanya's life. Narendra snatched the book from his hand and said, "That is how you spoil a good thing!"

Narendra read the chapter describing how Chaitanya gave his love to all, from the brāhmin to the pariah.

A BROTHER: "I say that one person cannot give love to another person."

NARENDRA: "But the Master gave it to me."

BROTHER: "Well, are you sure you have it?"

NARENDRA: "What can you understand about love? You belong to the servant class. All of you must serve me and massage my feet. Don't flatter yourselves by thinking you have understood everything. Now go and prepare a smoke for me."

All laughed.

THE BROTHER: "I surely will not."

M. (to himself): "Sri Ramakrishna has transmitted mettle to all the brothers of the math. It is no monopoly of Narendra's. Is it possible to renounce 'woman and gold' without this inner fire?"

May 10, 1887

It was Tuesday, a very auspicious day for the worship of the Divine Mother. Arrangements were being made for Her special worship at the monastery.

M. was going to the Ganges to take his bath. Rabindra was walking alone on the roof. He heard Narendra singing the Six Stanzas on Nirvāna:

> Death or fear I have none, nor any distinction of caste;
> Neither father nor mother nor even a birth have I;
> Neither friend nor comrade, neither disciple nor guru:
> I am Pure Knowledge and Bliss: I am Śiva! I am Śiva!
>
> I have no form or fancy; the All-pervading am I;
> Everywhere I exist, yet I am beyond the senses;
> Neither salvation am I, nor anything that may be known:
> I am Pure Knowledge and Bliss: I am Śiva! I am Śiva!

Rabindra went to the Ganges to take his bath. Presently he returned to the monastery clad in his wet cloth.

Narendra said to M. in a whisper: "He has bathed in the Ganges. It would be good to initiate him now into sannyās."

Both Narendra and M. smiled.

Prasanna asked Rabindra to change his wet cloth and gave him a dry gerruā cloth. Narendra said to M., "Now he is going to put on the cloth of renunciation."

M. (with a smile): "What kind of renunciation?"

NARENDRA: "Why, the renunciation of 'woman and gold'."

Rabindra put on the ochre cloth and entered Kali Tapasvi's room to meditate.

Appendix A
WITH KESHAB AT DAKSHINESWAR

KESHAB CHANDRA SEN, the leader of the Brāhmo Samāj, was expected to visit Sri Ramakrishna at the temple garden at Dakshineswar. With the Master were many Brāhmo celebrities—Pratap, Trailokya, Jaygopal, and others. It was only a few days before the annual festival of the Brāhmo Samāj, and the Brāhmos were eagerly awaiting the arrival of their leader, who was to come by steamer. They were restless and talking rather noisily. Ram, Manomohan, and several other devotees of the Master were also there.

At last Keshab entered the Master's room with two fruits and a bouquet of flowers in his hands. Touching the Master's feet, he laid the offering at his side. Then he saluted Sri Ramakrishna with great reverence, bowing very low before him. Sri Ramakrishna returned in like manner his distinguished visitor's salutation. Then he laughingly began the conversation.

MASTER: "You, Keshab, want me; but your disciples don't. I was saying to them: 'Let us be restless. Then Govinda will come.' (To Keshab's disciples) See, here is your Govinda!

"We have been showing signs of restlessness all this while to set the stage for your arrival. It isn't easy to have the vision of Govinda. You must have noticed in the Krishnayātrā[1] that Nārada enters Vrindāvan and prays with great yearning: 'O Govinda! O my soul! O Life of my life!', and then Krishna comes on the stage with the cowherd boys, followed by the gopis. No one can see God without that yearning.

"Well, Keshab, say something! They are eager to hear your words."

KESHAB (humbly, with a smile): "To open my lips here would be like trying to 'sell needles to a blacksmith'."

MASTER (smiling): "But don't you know that the nature of devotees is like that of hemp-smokers? One hemp-smoker says to another, 'Please take a puff for yourself and give me one.'" (All laugh.)

It was about four o'clock in the afternoon. They heard the music from the nahabat in the temple garden.

MASTER (to Keshab and the others): "Do you hear how melodious that music is? One player is producing only a monotone on his flute, while another is creating waves of melodies in different rāgas and rāginis.[2] That is my attitude. Why should I produce only a monotone when I have an

[1] A theatrical performance depicting the life of Krishna.
[2] Modes in Indian music.

instrument with seven holes? Why should I say nothing but, 'I am He, I am He'? I want to play various melodies on my instrument with seven holes. Why should I say only, 'Brahma! Brahma!'? I want to call on God through all the moods—through śānta, dāsya, sakhya, vātsalya, and madhur. I want to make merry with God. I want to sport with God."

Keshab listened to these words with wonder in his eyes and said to the Brāhmo devotees, "I have never before heard such a wonderful and beautiful interpretation of jnāna and bhakti."

KESHAB (to the Master): "How long will you hide yourself in this way? I dare say people will be thronging here by and by in great crowds."

MASTER: "What are you talking of? I only eat and drink and sing God's name. I know nothing about gathering crowds. Hanumān once declared: 'I know nothing about the day of the week or the position of the moon and stars in the sky. I simply meditate on Rāma.' "

KESHAB: "All right, sir, I shall gather the crowd. But they all must come to your place."

MASTER: "I am the dust of the dust of everybody's feet. If anyone is gracious enough to come here, he is welcome."

KESHAB: "Whatever you may say, sir, your advent cannot be in vain."

In the mean time the devotees had arranged a kirtan. Many of them had joined it. The party started at the Panchavati and moved toward the Master's room. Hriday blew the horn, Gopidas played the drum, and two devotees played the cymbals.

Sri Ramakrishna sang:

> O man, if you would live in bliss, repeat Lord Hari's name;
> Then you will lead a life of joy and go to paradise,
> And feed upon the fruit of moksha evermore:
> Such is the glory of His name!
> I give you the name of Hari, which Śiva, God of Gods,
> Repeats aloud with His five mouths.

The Master danced with the strength of a lion and went into samādhi. Regaining consciousness of the outer world, he sat down in his room and began to talk with Keshab and the other devotees.

MASTER: "God can be realized through all paths. It is like your coming to Dakshineswar by carriage, by boat, by steamer, or on foot. You have chosen the way according to your convenience and taste; but the destination is the same. Some of you have arrived earlier than others; but all have arrived.

"The more you rid yourself of upādhis, the nearer you will feel the presence of God. Rain-water never collects on a high mound; it collects only in low land. Similarly, the water of God's grace cannot remain on the high mound of egotism. Before God one should feel lowly and poor.

"One should be extremely watchful. Even clothes create vanity. I notice that even a man suffering from an enlarged spleen sings Nidhu Babu's light songs when he is dressed up in a black-bordered cloth. There are men who spout English whenever they put on high boots. And when an unfit person puts on an ochre cloth he becomes vain; the slightest sign of indifference to him arouses his anger and pique.

"God cannot be seen without yearning of heart, and this yearning is impossible unless one has finished with the experiences of life. Those who live surrounded by 'woman and gold', and have not yet come to the end of their experiences, do not yearn for God.

"When I lived at Kāmārpukur, Hriday's son, a child four or five years old, used to spend the whole day with me. He played with his toys and almost forgot everything else. But no sooner did evening come than he would say, 'I want to go to my mother.' I would try to cajole him in various ways and would say, 'Here, I'll give you a pigeon.' But he wouldn't be consoled with such things; he would weep and cry, 'I want to go to my mother.' He didn't enjoy playing any more. I myself wept to see his state.

"One should cry for God that way, like a child. That is what it means to be restless for God. One doesn't enjoy play or food any longer. After one's experiences of the world are over, one feels this restlessness and weeps for God."

The devotees sat in silence, listening to the Master's words. When evening came, a lamp was lighted in the room. Preparations were being made for feeding Keshab and the devotees.

KESHAB (with a smile): "What? Puffed rice again today?"

MASTER (smiling): "Hriday knows."

The devotees were served first with puffed rice, and then with luchi and curries on leaf-plates. All enjoyed the meal very much. It was about ten o'clock when supper was over.

The Master went to the Panchavati with Keshab and the devotees.

MASTER (to Keshab and the others): "One can very well live in the world after realizing God. Why don't you first touch the 'granny' and then play hide-and-seek?

"After attaining God, a devotee becomes unattached to the world. He lives like a mudfish. The mudfish keeps its body unstained though it lives in mud."

About eleven o'clock the Brāhmos became eager to go home. Pratap said, "It would be nice if we could spend the night here."

MASTER (to Keshab): "Why not stay here tonight?"

KESHAB (smiling): "No, I have business to attend to. I must go."

MASTER: "Why must you, my dear sir? Can't you sleep without your fish-basket? Once a fishwife was a guest in a gardener's house. She was asked to sleep in a room full of flowers. But she couldn't get any sleep there. (All laugh.) She was restless and began to fidget about. The gardener called to her: 'Hello there! Why aren't you asleep?' 'Oh, I don't know', said the fishwife. 'There are flowers here. The smell keeps me awake. Can't you bring me my fish-basket?' She sprinkled a little water in the basket, and when she smelled the fish she fell fast asleep." (All laugh heartily.)

Keshab took a few of the flowers that he had offered at Sri Ramakrishna's feet on his arrival. He and his Brāhmo devotees cried out as they saluted the Master, "Hail, Navavidhān!" Thus they bade him adieu.

One day during the rainy season of 1881 Sri Ramakrishna and a number of devotees visited Surendra's house. It was about dusk.

The Master entered the drawing-room on the second floor, where several of Surendra's neighbours had already gathered. Keshab had also been invited but could not come. Trailokya and a few Brāhmo devotees were present. A mat covered with a white sheet was spread on the floor, and on it had been placed a beautiful carpet with a cushion. Surendra requested the Master to sit on the carpet; but Sri Ramakrishna would not listen to him and sat on the mat next to Mahendra Goswami, one of Surendra's neighbours.

MAHENDRA (to the devotees): "For several months I spent most of my time with him [meaning Sri Ramakrishna]. I have never before seen such a great man. His spiritual moods are not of the ordinary kind."

MASTER (to Mahendra): "How dare you say that? I am the most insignificant of the insignificant, the lowliest of the lowly. I am the servant of the servants of God. Krishna alone is great.

"Krishna is none other than Satchidānanda, the Indivisible Brahman. The water of the ocean looks blue from a distance. Go near it and you will find it colourless. He who is endowed with attributes is also without attributes. The Absolute and the Relative belong to the same Reality.

"Why is Krishna tribhanga, bent in three places? Because of His love for Rādhā.

"That which is Brahman is also Kāli, the Ādyaśakti, who creates, preserves, and destroys the universe. He who is Krishna is the same as Kāli. The root is one—all these are His sport and play.

"God can be seen. He can be seen through the pure mind and the pure intelligence. Through attachment to 'woman and gold' the mind becomes impure.

"The mind is everything. It is like a white cloth just returned from the laundry. It will take any colour you dye it with. Knowledge is of the mind, and ignorance is also of the mind. When you say that a certain person has become impure, you mean that impurity has coloured his mind."

Surendra approached the Master with a garland and wanted to put it around his neck. But the Master took it in his hand and threw it aside. Surendra's pride was wounded and his eyes filled with tears. He went to the west porch and sat with Ram, Manomohan, and the others. In a voice choked with sadness he said: "I am really angry. How can a poor brāhmin know the value of a thing like that? I spent a lot of money for that garland, and he refused to accept it. I was unable to control my anger and said that the other garlands were to be given away to the devotees. Now I realize it was all my fault. God cannot be bought with money; He cannot be possessed by a vain person. I have really been vain. Why should he accept my worship? I don't feel like living any more." Tears streamed down his cheeks and over his chest.

In the mean time Trailokya was singing inside the room. The Master began to dance in an ecstasy of joy. He put around his neck the garland that he had thrown aside; holding it with one hand, he swung it with the other as he danced and sang. Now Surendra's joy was unbounded. The Master had accepted his offering. Surendra said to himself, "God crushes one's pride, no doubt, but He is also the cherished treasure of the humble and lowly."

The Master now sang:

> Behold, the two brothers have come, who weep while chanting
>   Hari's name,
> The brothers who, in return for blows, offer to sinners Hari's love!
> Behold them, drunk with Hari's love, who make the world drunk
>   as well,
> Embracing everyone as brother, even the outcaste shunned by men.
> Behold, the two brothers have come, who once were Kānāi and
>   Balāi of Braja. . . .

Many of the devotees danced while Sri Ramakrishna sang this song.

When the kirtan was over, everyone sat around the Master and became engaged in pleasant conversation. Sri Ramakrishna said to Surendra, "Won't you give me something to eat?" Then he went into the inner apartments, where the ladies saluted him. After the meal Sri Ramakrishna left for Dakshineswar.

Saturday, December 3, 1881

In the afternoon Sri Ramakrishna paid a visit to his householder disciple Manomohan, at 23 Simlā Street, Calcutta. It was a small two-storey house with a courtyard. The Master was seated in the drawing-room on the first floor. Ishan of Bhawānipur asked him: "Sir, why have you renounced the world? The scriptures extol the householder's life as the best."

MASTER: "I don't know much about what is good and what is bad. I do what God makes me do and speak what He makes me speak."

ISHAN: "If everybody renounced the world, they would be acting against God's will."

MASTER: "Why should everybody renounce? On the other hand, can it be the will of God that all should revel in 'woman and gold' like dogs and jackals? Has He no other wish? Do you know what accords with His will and what is against it?

"You say that God wants everybody to lead a worldly life. But why don't you see it as God's will when your wife and children die? Why don't you see His will in poverty, when you haven't a morsel to eat?

"Māyā won't allow us to know the will of God. On account of God's māyā the unreal appears as real, and the real as unreal. The world is unreal. This moment it exists and the next it disappears. But on account of His māyā it seems to be real. It is only through His māyā that the ego seems to be the doer. Furthermore, on account of this māyā a man regards his wife and children, his brother and sister, his father and mother, his house and property, as his very own.

"There are two aspects of māyā: vidyā and avidyā. Avidyā deludes one with worldliness, and vidyā—wisdom, devotion, and the company of holy men—leads one to God.

"He who has gone beyond māyā, through the grace of God, views alike both vidyā and avidyā. Worldly life is a life of enjoyment. After all, what is there to enjoy in 'woman and gold'? As soon as a sweetmeat has gone down the throat, one doesn't remember whether it tasted sweet or sour.

"But why should everybody renounce? Is renunciation possible except in the fullness of time? The time for renunciation comes when one reaches the limit of enjoyment. Can anybody force himself into renunciation? There is a kind of renunciation known as 'monkey renunciation'. Only small-minded people cultivate it. Take the case of a fatherless boy. His poor widowed mother earns her livelihood by spinning. The boy loses his insignificant job and suddenly is seized with a fit of renunciation. He puts on the ochre cloth of a monk and goes to Benares. A few days later he writes home, 'I have secured a job for ten rupees a month.' In the mean time he tries to buy a gold ring and beautiful clothes. How can he stifle his desire for enjoyment?"

Keshab arrived with some Brāhmo devotees and respectfully saluted the Master. He took a seat on Sri Ramakrishna's left, Ram on his right. For some time a reader recited from the *Bhāgavata* and explained the text.

MASTER (*to the devotees*): "It is very difficult to do one's duty in the world. If you whirl round too fast you feel giddy and faint; but there is no such fear if you hold on to a post. Do your duty, but do not forget God.

"You may ask, 'If worldly life is so difficult, then what is the way?' The way is constant practice. At Kāmārpukur I have seen the women of the carpenter families flattening rice with a husking-machine. They are always fearful of the pestle's smashing their fingers; and at the same time they go on nursing their children and bargaining with customers. They say to the customers, 'Pay us what you owe before you leave.'

"An immoral woman goes on performing her household duties, but all the time her mind dwells on her sweetheart.

"But one needs spiritual discipline to acquire such a state of mind; one should pray to God in solitude every now and then. It is possible to perform worldly duties after obtaining love for God. If you try to break a jackfruit, your hands will be smeared with its sticky juice. But that won't happen if, beforehand, you rub them with oil."

The kirtan began. Trailokya was singing. The Master danced, Keshab and the other devotees dancing with him. Though it was winter the Master became hot and perspired. After the music he wanted something to eat. A plate of sweetmeats was sent from the inner apartments. Keshab held the plate before Sri Ramakrishna and the Master ate. When he had finished, Keshab poured water on his hands and then dried the Master's hands and face with a towel. Afterwards he began to fan the Master.

MASTER (*to Keshab and the other devotees*): "They are heroes indeed who can pray to God in the midst of their worldly activities. They are like men who strive for God-realization while carrying heavy loads on their heads. Such men are real heroes. You may say that this is extremely difficult. But is there anything, however hard, that cannot be achieved through God's grace? His grace makes even the impossible possible. If a lamp is brought into a room that has been dark a thousand years, does it illumine the room little by little? The room is lighted all at once."

These reassuring words gladdened the hearts of Keshab and the other householder devotees.

KESHAB (to Rajendra Mitra, the uncle of Ram and Manomohan): "Wouldn't it be nice if you could arrange a festival like this at your house one day?"

RAJENDRA: "Very good, I will. Well, Ram, you'll have to take charge of everything."

Sri Ramakrishna was asked to go to the inner apartments, where Manomohan's mother had prepared his meal. A glass of ice-water, of which the Master was very fond, was placed near his plate.

Keshab and the other devotees sat in the courtyard and were treated to a sumptuous feast. The Master joined them and watched them eat. He danced and sang to entertain the guests.

When it was time for Sri Ramakrishna to leave for Dakshineswar, Keshab and the other devotees took the dust of his feet and saw him off in a hired carriage.

Saturday, December 10, 1881

At Keshab's request Rajendra Mitra arranged a religious festival at his home in Calcutta and invited Sri Ramakrishna and the devotees, including the members of the Brāhmo Samāj.

Two days before, Aghorenath, a prominent member of the Brāhmo Samāj, had suddenly passed away in Lucknow. Keshab and the other Brāhmo devotees were in mourning, and Rajendra thought they could not possibly join in the festival at his house. This worried him. But Ram, the Master's devotee, said to him: "Why are you so sad? If Keshab can't come, let him stay away. Our Master will be here. He is always in communion with God. He enables one to see God. And his presence will make the festival a success."

Rajendra, accompanied by Ram and a few others, paid Keshab a visit to express their condolence for the death of Aghorenath. Keshab said to Rajendra: "Why, I haven't said I shall not join in the festival at your house. Sri Ramakrishna will be there; so how can I stay away? I am in mourning, it is true, but I shall come."

On the wall in Keshab's room hung a picture of Sri Ramakrishna absorbed in samādhi.

RAJENDRA (to Keshab): "Many people say that he (pointing to the picture) is an incarnation of Chaitanya."

KESHAB (looking at the picture): "One doesn't see such samādhi. Only men like Christ, Mohammed, and Chaitanya experienced it."

About three o'clock in the afternoon Sri Ramakrishna arrived at Manomohan's house. He rested there awhile and had some refreshments. Surendra took the Master in a carriage to the studio of the Bengal Photographer. The art of photography was explained to him, and he was shown how glass covered with silver nitrate takes the image. As the Master was being photographed he went into samādhi.

A little later Sri Ramakrishna arrived at Rajendra Mitra's house. Keshab had not yet come, and Mahendra Goswami was reading from the *Bhāgavata*. The Master conversed with the devotees.

MASTER: "Why shouldn't one be able to lead a spiritual life in the world? But it is extremely difficult. While coming here I passed over the bridge at Bāghbāzār. How many chains it is tied with! Nothing will happen if one chain is broken, for there are so many others to keep it in place. Just so, there are many ties on a worldly man. There is no way for him to get rid of them except through the grace of God.

"One need not be afraid of the world after one has had the vision of God. Both vidyā and avidyā exist in His māyā; but one becomes indifferent to them after realizing God. One understands it rightly after attaining the state of a paramahamsa. Only a swan can discard the water and drink the milk from a mixture of milk and water. A robin cannot do so."

A DEVOTEE: "Then what is the way for a householder?"

MASTER: "Faith in the guru's words. You should depend on his instruction. Do your duties in the world, holding fast to his words, like a person whirling round and holding fast to a pillar.

"One must not look on one's guru as a mere human being: it is Satchidānanda Himself who appears as the guru. When the disciple has the vision of the Ishta, through the guru's grace, he finds the guru merging in Him.

"What can one not achieve through simple faith! Once there was an annaprāsana ceremony[3] in a guru's house. His disciples volunteered, according to their powers, to supply the different articles of food. He had one disciple, a very poor widow, who owned a cow. She milked it and brought the guru a jar of milk. He had thought she would take charge of all the milk and curd for the festival. Angry at her poor offering, he threw the milk away and said to her, 'Go and drown yourself.' The widow accepted this as his command and went to the river to drown herself. But God was pleased with her guileless faith and, appearing before her, said: 'Take this pot of curd. You will never be able to empty it. The more curd you pour out, the more will come from the pot. This will satisfy your teacher.' The guru was speechless with amazement when the pot was given to him. After hearing from the widow the story of the pot, he went to the river, saying to her, 'I shall drown myself if you cannot show God to me.' God appeared then and there, but the guru could not see Him. Addressing God, the widow said, 'If my teacher gives up his body because Thou dost not reveal Thyself to him, then I too shall die.' So God appeared to the guru—but only once.

"Now you see, because of faith in her guru the disciple herself had the vision of God and also showed Him to her teacher. Therefore I say, 'Even though my guru frequents a grog-shop, still to me he is the embodiment of Eternal Bliss.'

[3] A Hindu religious ceremony in connexion with the first offering of boiled rice to a baby.

"All want to be the guru, but very few indeed want to be the disciple. But you know that rain-water doesn't collect on a high mound; it collects in low land, in a hollow.

"One should have faith in the holy name given by the guru and with it practise spiritual discipline. It is said that the pearl oyster makes itself ready for the rain that falls when the star Svāti is in the ascendant. Taking a drop of that rain, it dives into the fathomless depths of the ocean and remains there until the pearl is formed."

At the sight of the many Brāhmo devotees assembled there, the Master said: "Is the meeting of the Brāhmos a real devotional gathering or a mere show? It is very good that the Brāhmo Samāj holds regular devotions. But one must dive deep; mere ceremonial worship or lectures are of no avail. One should pray to God that one's attachment to worldly enjoyment may disappear; that one may have pure love for His Lotus Feet.

"The elephant has outer tusks and inner grinders as well. The tusks are mere ornaments; but the elephant chews its food with the grinders. The inner enjoyment of 'woman and gold' injures the growth of one's devotion.

"What will you achieve through mere public lectures? The vulture undoubtedly soars high, but its eyes are fixed on the charnel-pit. The rocket undoubtedly shoots up into the sky, but the next moment it falls to the ground.

"He who has renounced his attachment to worldly enjoyments will remember nothing but God in the hour of death. Otherwise he will think only of worldly things: wife, children, house, wealth, name and fame. Through practice a bird can be trained to repeat 'Rādhā-Krishna'; but when a cat catches it, it only squawks.

"Therefore one should constantly practise the singing of God's name and glories, and meditation and contemplation as well. And further, one should always pray that one's attachment to the world may disappear and one's love for God's Lotus Feet may grow.

"Householders devoted to God live in the world like a maidservant, who performs her duties for her master but always keeps her mind fixed on her own native village; that is to say, they do their duties in the world keeping their minds on God. Anyone leading a worldly life is sure to come in contact with its dirt; but a householder who is a true devotee of God lives like the mudfish, which, though remaining in the mud, is not stained by it.

"Brahman and Śakti are identical. One acquires love and devotion quickly by calling on God as Mother."

Saying this, the Master sang:

> High in the heaven of the Mother's feet, my mind was soaring
> like a kite,
> When came a blast of sin's rough wind that drove it swiftly toward
> the earth.
> Māyā disturbed its even flight by bearing down upon one side,
> And I could make it rise no more.
> Entangled in the twisting string of love for children and for wife,
> Alas! my kite was rent in twain.

It lost its crest of wisdom soon and downward plunged as I let it
go;
How could it hope to fly again, when all its top was torn away?
Though fastened with devotion's cord, it came to grief in playing
here;
Its six opponents[4] worsted it.
Now Nareschandra rues this game of smiles and tears, and thinks
it better
Never to have played at all.

He sang again:

O Mother, for Yaśodā Thou wouldst dance, when she called Thee
her precious "Blue Jewel":[5]
Where hast Thou hidden that lovely form, O terrible Śyāmā?
Dance that way once for me, O Mother! Throw down Thy sword
and take the flute;
Cast off Thy garland of heads, and wear Thy wild-flower garland. . . .

As Sri Ramakrishna sang, he left his seat and began to dance. The devotees, too, stood up. Every now and then the Master went into samādhi and
the devotees gazed at him intently. Dr. Dukari touched the Master's eyeballs
with his finger to test the genuineness of his samādhi. This disgusted the
devotees.

When the music and dancing were over, the devotees took their seats.
Just then Keshab arrived with some of his Brāhmo disciples. Rajendra told
him about their great joy in the Master's kirtan and requested Trailokya to
sing again. Keshab replied, "Since Sri Ramakrishna has taken his seat, the
kirtan will sound flat."

Trailokya and the Brāhmo devotees sang:

Chant, O mind, the name of Hari,
Sing aloud the name of Hari,
Praise Lord Hari's name!
And praising Hari's name, O mind,
Cross the ocean of this world.

Hari dwells in earth, in water,
Hari dwells in fire and air;
In sun and moon He dwells.
Hari's ever living presence
Fills the boundless universe.

While preparations were being made to give the guests something to eat,
Sri Ramakrishna talked with Keshab.

MASTER (*with a smile*): "Today I enjoyed very much the machine by
which a man's picture is taken. One thing I noticed was that the impression
doesn't stay on a bare piece of glass, but it remains when the glass is stained
with a black solution. In the same way, mere hearing of spiritual talk doesn't

---

[4] The six passions.
[5] A pet name of the Baby Krishna.

leave any impression. People forget it soon afterwards. But they can retain spiritual instruction if they are stained inside with earnestness and devotion."

The Master was conducted to the second floor of the house and was asked to sit on a beautiful carpet. The ladies waited on him while he ate his meal. Keshab and the other devotees were also sumptuously fed.

Sunday, January 1, 1882

Sri Ramakrishna arrived with his devotees at the house of Jnan Choudhury, in Calcutta, to join the annual festival of the Simlā Brāhmo Samāj. Keshab, Ram, Manomohan, Balaram, Kedar, Narendra, Rakhal, and other devotees were present. Narendra had met the Master only a few days before at the temple garden at Dakshineswar. He used to participate now and then in the worship of the Simlā Brāhmo Samāj and sing for the congregation.

The worship was arranged according to the usual custom of the Samāj. First the scripture was read; then Narendra sang. It was dusk. The devotees made merry. The Master looked at the householder devotees seated around him and said with a smile: "Why shouldn't it be possible for a householder to give his mind to God? But the truth is that he no longer has his mind with him. If he had it, then he could certainly offer it to God. But, alas, the mind has been mortgaged—mortgaged to 'woman and gold'. So it is necessary for him constantly to live in the company of holy men. When he gets back his own mind, then he can devote it to spiritual practice; but first it is necessary to live constantly with the guru, wait on him, and enjoy the company of spiritual people. Either he should think of God in solitude day and night, or he should live with holy men. The mind left to itself gradually dries up. Take a jar of water, for instance. If the jar is set aside, the water dries up little by little. But that will not happen if the jar is kept immersed in the Ganges.

"The iron becomes red in the furnace of a smithy. Take it out and it becomes black as before. Therefore the iron must be heated in the furnace every now and then.

"Do you know what ignorance means? It is the feeling: 'This is my house; these are my relatives; I am the doer; and the household affairs go on smoothly because I manage them.' But to feel, 'I am the servant of God, His devotee, His son'—that is a good attitude.

"The 'I' cannot be effaced altogether. You may explain it away through reasoning, but the next moment it reappears, nobody knows from where. It is like a goat that still bleats faintly and jerks its legs even after its head has been cut off.

"But the 'I' that God retains in His devotee after he has seen Him is called the 'ripe I'. It is like a sword turned into gold by touching the philosopher's stone; you cannot hurt anybody with it."

Thus the Master talked, seated in the worship hall, and Keshab and the other devotees listened with rapt attention. It was about eight o'clock in the evening. The bell rang three times for the worship.

MASTER (*to Keshab and the others*): "What's this? I see you haven't yet begun your regular worship."

Keshab: "What further worship do we need? We are having all this."

Master: "Oh no, my dear sir! Let the worship be performed according to your custom."

Keshab: "Why? We are getting on very well."

At the Master's repeated request Keshab began the worship. In the midst of it Sri Ramakrishna suddenly stood up and went into samādhi. The Brāhmo devotees sang:

> Chant, O mind, the name of Hari,
> Sing aloud the name of Hari,
> Praise Lord Hari's name!
> And praising Hari's name, O mind,
> Cross the ocean of this world. . . .

The Master still stood there absorbed in ecstasy. Keshab led him down very carefully from the temple to the courtyard. The music went on. The Master danced to the music, the devotees dancing around him.

After the refreshments Sri Ramakrishna again talked with Keshab. Soon he began to sing. Keshab sang with the Master:

> The black bee of my mind is drawn in sheer delight
> To the blue lotus flower of Mother Śyāmā's feet,
> The blue flower of the feet of Kāli, Śiva's Consort;
> Tasteless, to the bee, are the blossoms of desire.
> My Mother's feet are black, and black, too, is the bee;
> Black is made one with black! This much of the mystery
> My mortal eyes behold, then hastily retreat.
> But Kamalākānta's hopes are answered in the end;
> He swims in the Sea of Bliss, unmoved by joy or pain.

Again they sang:

> High in the heaven of the Mother's feet, my mind was soaring
>   like a kite,
> When came a blast of sin's rough wind that drove it swiftly to-
>   ward the earth. . . .

Both Keshab and the Master were in a state of divine fervour. The other devotees joined them and sang and danced till midnight.

The Master rested a few minutes and then said to Keshab: "Why did you send me presents when your son was married? What shall I do with them? Take them back."

Keshab smiled a little, and the Master continued: "Why do you write about me in your paper? You cannot make a man great by writing about him in books and magazines. If God makes a man great, then everybody knows about him even though he lives in a forest. When flowers bloom in the deep woods, the bees find them, but the flies do not. What can man do? Don't look up to him. Man is but a worm. The tongue that praises you today will abuse you tomorrow. I don't want name and fame. May I always remain the humblest of the humble and the lowliest of the lowly!"

Appendix B

A LETTER[1]

My beloved brother M.,

Three days ago I received the fourth part of the *Sri Sri Ramakrishna Kathāmrita*[2] sent by you, and today I have finished reading it. You are blessed indeed. What heavenly nectar you have sprinkled all over the country! . . . A long time ago you wanted me to set down my conversations with the Master. Now I shall try to write them for you. But I was not born under the lucky star of an M., that I might jot down the days, the dates, and the hours of my visits with the Master and note down correctly all the words uttered by his holy lips. In this letter I am giving you as many of my experiences as I remember. Very likely I shall confuse the events of one day with another—and I have forgotten many things.

It was probably during the autumn holidays of 1881 that I met Sri Ramakrishna the first time. I arrived at Dakshineswar in a country boat and, going up the steps of the landing-ghāt, asked someone where the Paramahamsa was.

"There is the Paramahamsa", was the reply. A man was pointed out on the north verandah, which faces the garden. He was sitting reclining against a bolster. He wore a black-bordered cloth. At the sight of the bolster and the black-bordered cloth I said to myself, "What kind of paramahamsa is this?"[3]

Going nearer, I found him half leaning against the bolster with his hands clasped around his drawn-up knees. Then I thought: "Evidently he is not used to pillows as gentlemen are. So perhaps he is the Paramahamsa." At his right, very near the pillow, sat a gentleman whose name, I came to know, was Rajendra Lal Mitra, later an Assistant Secretary to the Government of Bengal. A little farther off sat some others.

After a few moments the Master said to Rajendra Babu, "See whether Keshab is coming." Evidently Keshab Sen was expected that day.

Someone walked away a few steps and, coming back, said, "No, he isn't."

After a brief interval, hearing a sound outside, he said, "Please look once more."

Again someone went out and came back with the same reply.

Then Sri Ramakrishna laughed and said, quoting a popular saying, "The leaves rustle outside, and Rādhā says, 'Oh, here comes my Sweetheart!' "

[1] Written to M. by Aswini Kumar Dutta, one of the saintly patriots of Bengal.
[2] The conversations of Sri Ramakrishna in Bengali, recorded by M.
[3] A cloth with black borders, bolster, and so forth, regarded as articles of luxury, are used by householders. A paramahamsa, on the other hand, is an all-renouncing monk.

Continuing, he said: "You see, Keshab always tantalizes me like this. It is his way."

At dusk Keshab came with his party. Keshab bowed low before the Master, touching the ground with his forehead. The Master returned his salutation in the same manner.

Shortly afterwards Sri Ramakrishna said, in a state of partial consciousness: "Look! He has brought the whole Calcutta crowd. I am supposed to deliver a lecture. I won't do anything of the sort. Do it yourself if you like. Lecturing is none of my business."

Still in the ecstatic mood, he said with a divine smile: "I shall eat, drink, and be merry. I shall play and sleep. But I can't give lectures."

As Keshab Babu watched him, he became overpowered with divine emotion. Every now and then he said, "Ah me! Ah me!"

I too watched the Master and said to myself, "Can this be pretence?" I had never seen anything like it before, and you know how deep my faith is.

Coming back from samādhi, the Master said to Keshab: "Keshab, once I went to your temple. In the course of your preaching I heard you say, 'We shall dive into the river of devotion and go straight to the Ocean of Satchidānanda.' At once I looked up [at the gallery where Keshab's wife and the other ladies were sitting] and thought, 'Then what will become of these ladies?' You see, Keshab, you are householders. How can you reach the Ocean of Satchidānanda all at once? You are like a mongoose with a brick tied to its tail. When something frightens it, it runs up the wall and sits in a niche. But how can it stay there any length of time? The brick pulls it down and it falls to the floor with a thud. You may practise a little meditation, but the weight of wife and children will pull you down. You may dive into the river of devotion, but you must come up again. You will alternately dive and come up. How can you dive and disappear once for all?"

Keshab Babu said: "Can't a householder ever succeed? What about Maharshi Devendranath Tagore?"

Twice or thrice the Master repeated softly, "Devendranath Tagore— Devendra—Devendra" and bowed to him several times.

Then he said: "Let me tell you a story. A man used to celebrate the Durgā Pujā at his house with great pomp. Goats were sacrificed from sunrise to sunset. But after a few years the sacrifice was not so imposing. Then someone said to him, 'How is it, sir, that the sacrifice at your place has become such a tame affair?' 'Don't you see?' he said. 'My teeth are gone now.' Devendra is now devoted to meditation and contemplation. It is only natural that he should be, at his advanced age. But no doubt he is a great man.

"You see, as long as a man is under māyā's spell, he is like a green coconut. When you scoop out the soft kernel from a green coconut, you cannot help scraping a little of the shell at the same time. But in the case of a ripe and dry coconut, the shell and kernel are separated from each other. When you shake the fruit you can feel the kernel rattling inside. The man who is freed from māyā is like a ripe and dry coconut. He feels the soul to be separated from the body. They are no longer connected with each other.

"It is the 'I' that creates all the trouble. Won't this wretched ego ever leave a person? You see a peepal-tree growing from the rubbish of a tumble-down house. You cut it down today, but tomorrow you find a new sprout shooting up. It is the same with the ego. You may wash seven times a cup that onions have been kept in, but the wretched smell never leaves it."

In the course of the conversation he said to Keshab: "Well, Keshab, I understand that your Calcutta babus say that God does not exist. Is that true? A Calcutta babu wants to climb the stairs. He takes one step, but before taking the next he cries out: 'Oh, my side! My side!' and drops down unconscious. His relatives raise a hue and cry and send for a doctor; but before the doctor arrives the man is very likely dead. And people of such stamina say, 'There is no God'!"

After an hour or so the kirtan began. What I saw then I shall never forget either in this life or in the lives to come. Everybody danced, Keshab included. The Master was in the centre. All danced around him in a circle. During the dancing Sri Ramakrishna suddenly stood motionless, transfixed in samādhi. A long time passed this way. After hearing his words and seeing all this, I said to myself, "Yes, a paramahamsa indeed!"

Another day, probably in 1883, I visited the Master with a few young men from Srerāmpore. Looking at them, he asked, "Why have they come here?"

MYSELF: "To see you."

MASTER: "What's there to see in me? Why don't they look at the buildings and temples?"

MYSELF: "Sir, they haven't come to see those things. They have come to see you."

MASTER: "Ah! Then they must be flints. There is fire in them. You may keep a flint under water a thousand years, but the moment you strike it, sparks come out. They must be of that type. But it will be useless to try to strike fire out of me!"

At this last remark we all laughed. I do not recall now what other things he said to us that day. But it seems to me he told us about the renunciation of "woman and gold" and the impossibility of getting rid of the ego.

I visited him another day. When I bowed down to him and took a seat, he said, "Can you bring me some of that stuff—a little sour, a little sweet —that begins to fizz when you push down the cork?"

MYSELF: "Lemonade?"

MASTER: "Why don't you bring a bottle for me?"

I think I brought him a bottle. So far as I remember, I was alone with him that day. I asked him a few questions.

MYSELF: "Do you observe caste?"

MASTER: "How can I say yes? I ate curry at Keshab Sen's house. Let me tell you what once happened to me. A man with a long beard[4] brought some ice here, but I didn't feel like eating it. A little later someone brought me a piece of ice from the same man, and I ate it with great relish. You

[4] Perhaps the Master meant a Mohammedan.

see, caste restrictions fall away of themselves. As coconut and palm trees grow up, the branches drop off of themselves. Caste conventions drop off like that. But don't tear them off as those fools do [meaning the Brāhmos]."

MYSELF: "What do you think of Keshab Babu?"

MASTER: "Oh, he is a saintly man."

MYSELF: "And Trailokya Babu?"

MASTER: "A fine man. He sings very well."

MYSELF: "Shivanath Babu?"

MASTER: " . . . A very good man. But he argues."

MYSELF: "What is the difference between a Hindu and a Brāhmo?"

MASTER: "There is not much difference. In the serenade we have here, one flutist plays a single note right along, while another plays various melodies. The Brāhmos play one note, as it were; they hold to the formless aspect of God. But the Hindus bring out different melodies; that is to say, they enjoy God in His various aspects.

"The formless Deity and God with form may be likened to water and ice. The water freezes into ice. The ice melts into water through the heat of jnāna. Water takes the form of ice through the cooling influence of bhakti.

"The Reality is one. People give It various names. Take the case of a lake with four landing-ghāts on its four banks. People who draw water at one ghāt call it 'jal', and those who draw it at the second ghāt call it 'pāni'. At the third ghāt they call it 'water', and at the fourth, 'aqua'. But it is one and the same thing: water."

I told the Master that I had met Achalānanda Tirthāvadhuta of Barisāl.

MASTER: "Isn't that Ramkumar of Kotrang?"

MYSELF: "Yes, sir."

MASTER: "How did you like him?"

MYSELF: "Very much."

MASTER: "Well, whom do you like better—him or me?"

MYSELF: "Oh, can there be any comparison between you two? He is a scholar, an erudite person; but are you one?"

Sri Ramakrishna was a little puzzled at my reply and became silent. A moment later I said: "He may be a scholar, but you are full of fun! There is great fun in your company."

At this the Master laughed and said: "Well said! Well said! Right you are!"

He asked me, "Have you seen my Panchavati?"

MYSELF: "Yes, sir."

He told me a little of what he had practised there—his various religious austerities. He also told me about Nangtā.

Then I asked him, "How can I realize God?"

MASTER: "You see, He is constantly attracting us, as a magnet attracts iron. But the iron cannot come to the magnet if it is covered with dirt. When the dirt is washed away, the iron is instantly drawn to the magnet. Weep for God and the tears will wash away the dirt from your mind."

As I was writing down his words, he remarked: "Look here. Only repeating the word 'siddhi' will not produce intoxication. You must actually get some hemp, rub it in water, and then drink the solution. . . ."

Later he said: "Since you are going to lead a householder's life, create a roseate intoxication in your mind with the thought of God. You will be doing your duties, but let that pleasant intoxication remain with you. You cannot, of course, like Śukadeva, be so inebriated with the thought of God that you will lie naked and unconscious. As long as you have to live in the world, give God the power of attorney. Make over all your responsibilities to Him; let Him do as He likes. Live in the world like a maidservant in a rich man's house. She bathes her master's children, washes them, feeds them, and takes affectionate care of them in many ways, as if they were her own children; but in her heart she knows very well that they do not belong to her. No sooner is she dismissed than all is over; she has no more relationship with the children.

"Before breaking open the jack-fruit you should rub your hands with oil in order to protect them from the sticky juice. Likewise, protect yourself with the oil of devotion; then the world will not cling to you and you will not be affected by it."

All this time Sri Ramakrishna was seated on the floor. Now he got up and stretched himself on his cot.

He said to me, "Fan me a little."

I began to fan him and he was silent.

After a while he said: "Oh, it's so hot! Why don't you dip the fan in water?"

"Ah!" I said. "You have your fancies, too!"

The Master smiled and drawled out, "And—why—not?"

"Very well!" I said. "Have your full measure of them."

I cannot express in words how immensely I enjoyed his company that day.

The last time I visited him—you have mentioned it in the third part of your book[5]—I had with me the headmaster of our school, who had just then graduated. You met him the other day. As soon as Sri Ramakrishna saw him, he asked me: "Where did you pick him up? He's a fine fellow!"

Then he continued: "You are a lawyer. You are very clever. Can you give me a little of your cleverness? The other day your father came here and stayed three days."

MYSELF: "How did you find him?"

MASTER: "A nice man. But now and then he talks nonsense."

MYSELF: "Please help him get over it when you see him next."

At this Sri Ramakrishna smiled a little.

MYSELF: "Please give us a few instructions."

MASTER: "Do you know Hriday?"

MYSELF: "Your nephew? I know him only by name."

MASTER: "Hriday used to say to me: 'Uncle, please don't give out your stock of instructions all at once. Why should you repeat the same things over and over again?' I would reply: 'You fool, what's that to you? These

[5] Under May 23, 1885.

are my words and if I like I shall repeat them a hundred thousand times. You keep quiet!'"

MYSELF (*smiling*): "Exactly so!"

A little later he sat up on the bed. He repeated "Om" several times and began to sing a song whose first line is:

Dive deep, O mind, dive deep in the Ocean of God's Beauty.

Hardly had he sung one or two lines when he himself dived deep and was lost in samādhi.

When the samādhi was over, he began to pace the room and with both hands pulled up the cloth he was wearing, till it reached his waist. One end of it was trailing on the floor and the other was hanging loose.

Nudging my companion, I whispered, "See how nicely he wears his cloth!"

A moment later he threw away the cloth, with the words: "Ugh! What a nuisance! Off with it!"

He began to pace up and down the room naked. From the northern end of the room he brought an umbrella and a stick, and asked us, "Are these yours?"

Scarcely had I replied no when he said: "I knew it. I can judge a man by his stick and umbrella. They must belong to that man who was here some time ago and swallowed a lot of my words without understanding them."

A few minutes later he sat down, still naked, on the northern end of his cot, facing the west, and asked me, "Well, do you consider me ungentlemanly?"

MYSELF: "Of course not. You are a perfect gentleman. But why do you ask me that?"

MASTER: "You see, Shivanath and others don't think I am a gentleman. When they come I have to wrap a cloth or something around me. Do you know Girish Ghosh?"

MYSELF: "Which Girish Ghosh? The one who is in the theatre?"

MASTER: "Yes."

MYSELF: "I have never seen him. But I know him by reputation."

MASTER: "A good man."

MYSELF: "They say he drinks."

MASTER: "Let him! Let him! How long will he continue that? Do you know Narendra?"

MYSELF: "No, sir."

MASTER: "I wish very much that you could meet him. He has passed the B. A. examination and is unmarried."

MYSELF: "Very well, sir. I shall meet him."

MASTER: "Today there will be a kirtan at Ram Dutta's house. You may meet him there. Please go there this evening."

MYSELF: "All right."

MASTER: "Yes, do. Don't forget."

MYSELF: "It is your command. Shall I not obey it? Surely I will go."

He showed us the pictures in his room and asked me whether a picture of Buddha could be had.

MYSELF: "Very likely."

MASTER: "Please get one for me."

MYSELF: "Very well. I'll bring one when I come again."

But alas, I never returned to Dakshineswar.

That evening I went to Ram Babu's house and met Narendra. In one of the rooms the Master sat reclining against a pillow. Narendra sat at his right, and I in front.

He asked Narendra to talk with me. But Narendra said: "I have a bad headache today. I don't feel like talking."

.I replied, "Then let us put it off till another day."

And that came to pass in May or June of 1897, at Almora. The will of the Master had to be fulfilled, and it was fulfilled after twelve years. Ah, how happily I spent those few days with Swami Vivekananda at Almora! Sometimes at his house, sometimes at mine, and one day on the top of a hill with nobody accompanying us. I never met him after that. It was as if to fulfil the Master's wish that we saw each other at Almora.

I saw the Master not more than four or five times; but in that short time we became so intimate that I felt as if we had been class-mates. How much liberty I took while speaking with him! But no sooner had I left his presence than it flashed on me: "Goodness gracious! Think where I have been!" What I saw and received in those few days has sweetened my whole life. That Elysian smile of his, laden with nectar, I have locked up in the secret closet of my memory. That is the unending treasure of a hapless person like myself. A thrill of joy passes through my heart when I think how a grain of the bliss shed from that laughter has been sweetening the lives of millions, even in distant America. If that be my case, you may very well understand how lucky you are.

A CHRONOLOGY OF
SRI RAMAKRISHNA'S LIFE

1775   Birth of Khudiram.
1791   Birth of Chandra Devi.
1805   Birth of Ramkumar.
1814   Khudiram settles at Kāmārpukur.
1826   Birth of Rameswar.
1835   Khudiram's pilgrimage to Gayā.
1836   Birth of Sri Ramakrishna, February 18, about 5:15 A.M.
1843   Death of Khudiram.
1845   Sri Ramakrishna's sacred thread ceremony.
1850   Ramkumar opens his school in Calcutta.
1852   Sri Ramakrishna comes to Calcutta.
1853   Birth of the Holy Mother, December 22.
1855   Dakshineswar Kāli temple founded. Hriday at Dakshineswar. Sri Ramakrishna appointed priest of the Vishnu temple and then of the Kāli temple.
1856   Death of Ramkumar. Realization of God and first God-intoxicated state of Sri Ramakrishna.
1857   Sri Ramakrishna's treatment under Gangaprasad.
1858   Haladhari as priest at Dakshineswar. Sri Ramakrishna goes to Kāmārpukur.
1859   Sri Ramakrishna's marriage.
1860   Return to Dakshineswar. Mathur's vision.
1861   Death of Rāni Rasmani. Meeting with the Brāhmani. Tantra practice under the Brāhmani. Second divine madness.
1863   Completion of Tantra practice. Meeting with Pundit Padmalochan. Chandra Devi comes to live at Dakshineswar.
1864   Sri Ramakrishna's practice of the vātsalya bhāva under Jatadhari. Practice of the madhur bhāva. Initiation into sannyās by Totapuri.
1865   Akshay replaces Haladhari. Totapùri leaves Dakshineswar.
1866   Sri Ramakrishna in the Advaita plane for six months. Illness. Practice of Mohammedanism.
1867   Sri Ramakrishna at Kāmārpukur. Brāhmani takes leave.
1868   Pilgrimage. Meeting with Gangāmā.
1870   Tour with Mathur. Sri Ramakrishna at the Coolootola Harisabhā. Visit to Kālnā and Navadvip.
1871   Death of Mathur.
1872   The Holy Mother's first visit to Dakshineswar. The Shorasi Pujā.
1873   Death of Rameswar.
1874   The Holy Mother again at Dakshineswar.

1875 Sri Ramakrishna's first visit to Keshab Chandra Sen.

1876 Death of Chandra Devi.

1877
1878 } Intimacy with Keshab. The Holy Mother's third visit to Dakshineswar.

1879 Coming of disciples begins.

1880 Last visit to Kāmārpukur.

1881 Dismissal of Hriday. Meeting with Rakhal and Narendranath.

1882 Visit to Pundit Vidyāsāgar. The Holy Mother again at Dakshineswar.

1884 Death of Keshab. Meeting with Pundit Shashadhar. Gopāl Mā. The Holy Mother comes to live at Dakshineswar for the last time.

1885 Last visit to Pānihāti. Illness and removal to Śyāmpukur. Association with Dr. Sarkar. Removal to Cossipore.

1886 Treatment at Cossipore. Organization of disciples. Mahāsamādhi, August 16, at two minutes past 1 A.M.

GLOSSARY

abhyāsayoga Yoga, or union with God, through practice.

āchārya Religious teacher.

adharma Unrighteousness; the opposite of dharma.

Adhyātma Rāmāyana A book dealing with the life of Rāma and harmonizing the ideals of jnāna and bhakti.

Advaita Non-duality; a school of the Vedānta philosophy, declaring the oneness of God, soul, and universe.

Advaita Goswāmi An intimate companion of Sri Chaitanya.

Ādyāśakti The Primal Energy; an epithet of the Divine Mother.

āgamani A class of songs invoking Durgā, the Divine Mother.

Ahalyā The wife of the sage Gautama. Because of her misconduct she was turned into a stone by the curse of her husband. The sage, however, said that the touch of Rāma's feet would restore her human form.

ahamkāra Ego or "I-consciousness". *See* four inner organs.

Ājnā The sixth centre in the Sushumnā. *See* Kundalini.

ajnāna Ignorance, individual or cosmic, which is responsible for the non-perception of Reality.

ākāśa Ether or space; the first of the five elements evolved from Brahman. It is the subtlest form of matter, into which all the elements are ultimately resolved.

Ākbar The great Mogul Emperor of India (A.D. 1542–1605).

akshara Unchanging; also a name of Brahman.

Ālekh (*Lit.*, the Incomprehensible One) A name of God.

Amrita Immortality.

Anāhata The fourth centre in the Sushumnā. *See* Kundalini.

Anāhata Śabda Another name for Om.

Ānanda Bliss.

ānandamayakosha The sheath of bliss. *See* kosha.

Ānandamayi (*Lit.*, Full of Bliss) An epithet of the Divine Mother.

ānnā A small Indian coin, one sixteenth of a rupee.

annamayakosha The gross physical sheath. *See* kosha.

Annapurnā A name of the Divine Mother as the Giver of Food.

antaranga Belonging to the inner circle; generally used with reference to an intimate disciple.

ārati Worship of the Deity accompanied by the waving of lights.

Arjuna A hero of the *Mahābhārata* and the friend of Krishna. *See* Pāndavas.

artha Wealth, one of the four ends of human pursuit. *See* four fruits.

āsana Seat.

asat Unreal.

ashtami The eighth day of either lunar fortnight.

Ashtāvakra Samhitā A standard book on Advaita Vedānta.

āśrama Hermitage; also any one of the four stages of life: the celibate student stage, the married householder stage, the stage of retirement and contemplation, and the stage of religious mendicancy.

Assam A province in the northeast corner of India.

asti Is, or being.

asura Demon.

aśwattha The peepal-tree.

Āświn The sixth month in the Hindu calendar, falling in the autumn season.

Ātmā Self, same as Ātman.

Ātman Self or Soul; denotes also the Supreme Soul, which, according to the Advaita Vedānta, is one with the individual soul.

Ātmārāma Satisfied in the Self.

Aum Same as Om.

Avadhuta A holy man of great renunciation mentioned in the *Bhāgavata*.

Avatār   Incarnation of God.

avidyā   Ignorance, cosmic or individual, which is responsible for the non-perception of Reality.

avidyāmāyā   Māyā, or illusion causing duality, has two aspects, namely, avidyāmāyā and vidyāmāyā. Avidyā-māyā, or the "māyā of ignorance", consisting of anger, passion, and so on, entangles one in worldliness. Vidyāmāyā, or the "māyā of knowledge", consisting of kindness, purity, unselfishness, and so on, leads one to liberation. Both belong to the relative world. See māyā.

avidyāśakti   The power of ignorance.

Ayodhyā   The capital of Rāma's kingdom in northern India; the modern Oudh.

bābā   The Bengali word for father.

bābāji   A name by which holy men of the Vaishnava sect are called.

bāblā   A tree, the Indian acacia.

babu   Well-to-do gentleman; also equivalent to Mr. or Esq.

Balāi   Pet name of Balarāma, Sri Krishna's brother.

Balarāma   Sri Krishna's elder brother.

Banga   Bengal.

Bankuvihāri   A name of Sri Krishna.

Bāul   (Lit., God-intoxicated devotee) Mendicant of a Vaishnava sect.

bel   A tree whose leaves are sacred to Śiva; also the fruit of the same tree.

Bhagavad Gītā   The well-known Hindu scripture.

Bhagavān   (Lit., One endowed with the six attributes, viz. infinite treasures, strength, glory, splendour, knowledge, and renunciation) An epithet of the Godhead; also the Personal God of the devotee.

Bhāgavata   A sacred book of the Hindus, especially of the Vaishnavas, dealing with the life of Sri Krishna.

Bhagavati   The Divine Mother.

bhairava   An aspirant of the Tāntrik sect; also denotes the God Śiva, especially one of His eight frightful forms.

bhairavi   A nun of the Tāntrik sect.

bhajan   Religious music.

bhajanānanda   The bliss derived from the worship of God.

bhakta   A follower of the path of bhakti, divine love; a worshipper of the Personal God.

bhakti   Love of God; single-minded devotion to one's Chosen Ideal.

bhaktiyoga   The path of devotion, followed by dualistic worshippers.

Bharadvāja   A sage mentioned in the Purāna.

Bhārata   A name of Arjuna; also a name of India.

Bhaskarananda   A saint contemporary with Sri Ramakrishna.

bhāva   Existence; feeling; emotion; ecstasy; samādhi; also denotes any one of the five attitudes that a dualistic worshipper assumes toward God. The first of these attitudes is that of peace; assuming the other four, the devotee regards God as the Master, Child, Friend, or Beloved.

bhāvamukha   An exalted state of spiritual experience, in which the aspirant keeps his mind on the border line between the Absolute and the Relative. From this position he can contemplate the ineffable and attributeless Brahman and also participate in the activities of the relative world, seeing in it the manifestation of God alone.

bhāva samādhi   Ecstasy in which the devotee retains his ego and enjoys communion with the Personal God.

Bhavatārini   (Lit., the Saviour of the Universe) A name of the Divine Mother.

bheda   Difference.

Bhil   A savage tribe of India.

Bhishma   One of the great heroes of the war of Kurukshetra, described in the Mahābhārata.

bhoga   Enjoyment.

bhramara   The black bee.

Bibhishana   A brother of Rāvana, the monster-king of Ceylon, whom he succeeded; but, unlike him, a faithful devotee of Rāma.

Bodha   Consciousness; Absolute Knowledge.

Bodh-Gayā   A place near Gayā, where Buddha attained illumination.

Brahma   The name by which the Brāhmos invoke God.

Brahmā   The Creator God; the First Person of the Hindu Trinity, the other two being Vishnu and Śiva.

brahmachāri   A religious student devoted to the practice of spiritual discipline; a celibate belonging to the first stage of life. See four stages of life.

brahmacharya   The first of the four stages of life: the life of an unmarried student. See four stages of life.

Brahmajnāna   The Knowledge of Brahman.

Brahmajnāni   A knower of Brahman. Sri Ramakrishna used the term "modern Brahmajnānis" to denote the members of the Brāhmo Samāj.

Brahmamayi   (Lit., the Embodiment of Brahman) A name of the Divine Mother.

Brahman   The Absolute; the Supreme Reality of the Vedānta philosophy.

Brahmānanda   The bliss of communion with Brahman.

Brahmānda   (Lit., the egg of Brahmā) The universe.

Brahmāni   The Consort of Brahmā.

Brāhmani   (Lit., brāhmin woman) The brāhmin woman who taught Sri Ramakrishna the Vaishnava and Tantra disciplines, also known as the Bhairavi Brāhmani.

brahmarshi   A rishi or holy man endowed with the Knowledge of Brahman.

brāhmin   The highest caste in Hindu society.

Brāhmo   Member of the Brāhmo Samāj.

Brāhmo Sabhā   The meeting of the Brāhmos.

Brāhmo Samāj   A theistic organization of India, founded by Rājā Rammohan Roy.

Braja   Same as Vrindāvan.

Brindē   One of the gopis; also the

name of a maidservant at the Dakshineswar temple garden.

Buddha   (Lit., one who is enlightened) The founder of Buddhism.

Buddha-Gayā   Same as Bodh-Gayā.

buddhi   The intelligence or discriminating faculty. See four inner organs.

Captain   Colonel Viswanath Upadhyaya of Nepal, the Resident of the Nepalese Government in Calcutta, and a devotee of Sri Ramakrishna. The Master addressed Viswanath as "Captain".

causal body   One of the three bodies or seats of the soul, the other two being the gross body and the subtle body. It is identical with deep sleep.

chāddar   An upper garment.

Chaitanya   Spiritual Consciousness; also the name of a prophet born in A.D. 1485, who lived at Navadvip, Bengal, and emphasized the path of divine love for the realization of God; he is also known as Gaurānga, Gaur, Gorā, or Nimāi.

Chaitanyalīlā   A play by Girish Chandra Ghosh depicting the life of Sri Chaitanya.

Chaitra   The last month in the Hindu calendar, falling in the spring season.

chakkā   A vegetable curry.

chakora   A species of bird.

chakra   Any one of the six centres, or lotuses, in the Sushumnā, through which the Kundalini rises. See Kundalini.

chāmara   A fan made of a yak tail, used in the temple service.

chānābarā   A Bengali sweetmeat made of cheese, first fried in butter and then soaked in syrup.

chandāla   An untouchable.

Chandi   A sacred book of the Hindus, in which the Divine Mother is described as the Ultimate Reality.

Chandidās   The name of a Vaishnava saint.

chāndni   An open portico; the word is used in the text to denote the open portico at the Dakshineswar temple, with steps leading to the Ganges.

Chandrāvali One of the gopis of Vrindāvan.

charanāmrita The water in which the image of the Deity is bathed; it is considered very sacred.

chātak A species of bird.

chetana samādhi Communion with God in which the devotee retains "I-consciousness" and is aware of his relationship with God.

Chidākāśa The Ākāśa, or Space, of Chit, Absolute Consciousness; the All-pervading Spirit.

Chidānanda The bliss of God-Consciousness.

Chidātmā The soul as embodiment of Intelligence and Consciousness.

Chinmaya The embodiment of Spirit.

Chintāmani A mythical gem which has the power to grant its possessor whatever he may wish for; also a name of God.

Chit Consciousness.

Chitśakti The Supreme Spirit as Power.

chitta The mind-stuff. See four inner organs.

Chosen Ideal See Ishta.

daitya Demon.

dāl Lentils; also a soup made from lentils.

Dāmodara A name of Krishna.

dānā Ghost.

dandi A sect of sannayāsis who always carry a staff.

dargāh Burial place of a Mussalmān saint, considered sacred.

darśanas, the six The six systems of orthodox Hindu philosophy, namely, the Sāmkhya of Kapila, the Yoga of Patanjali, the Vaiśeshika of Kanāda, the Nyāya of Gautama, the Purva Mimāmsā of Jaimini, and the Vedānta or Uttara Mimāmsā of Vyāsa.

Dasaharā A Hindu festival.

Daśaratha The father of Rāma.

Dāśarathi A mystic poet of Bengal.

dāsya One of the five attitudes assumed by the dualistic worshipper toward his Chosen Ideal: the attitude of a servant toward his master.

Dattātreya The name of a great Hindu saint.

dayā Compassion.

Dayāmaya The Compassionate One.

Dayananda The founder of the Ārya Samāj (A.D. 1824–1883).

deva (Lit., shining one) A god.

Devaki The mother of Sri Krishna.

devarshi A godly person endowed with Supreme Knowledge; an epithet generally applied to Nārada.

devatā Deity or god.

Devendra(nath) Tagore A religious leader of Sri Ramakrishna's time; father of Rabindranath Tagore.

devotee The word is generally used in the text to denote one devoted to God, a worshipper of the Personal God, or a follower of the path of love. A devotee of Sri Ramakrishna is one who is devoted to Sri Ramakrishna and follows his teachings. The word "disciple", when used in connexion with the Master, refers to one who had been initiated into spiritual life by Sri Ramakrishna and who regarded Sri Ramakrishna as his guru.

dharma Righteousness, one of the four ends of human pursuit; generally translated as "religion", it signifies rather the inner principle of religion. See four fruits. The word is also loosely used to mean "duty".

dhoti A man's wearing-cloth.

Dhruva A saint in Hindu mythology.

Dhruva Ghāt A bathing-place on the Jamunā river at Vrindāvan.

Dolayātrā The Hindu spring festival associated with Sri Krishna.

dome One of the lowest castes among the Hindus.

Draupadi The wife of the five Pāndava brothers.

Drona One of the great military teachers in the Mahābhārata.

Dulāli One of the pet names of Rādhā.

Durgā A name of the Divine Mother.

Durgā Pujā The worship of Durgā.

durvā grass   Common grass, used in worship.

Durvāsā   A sage with a very angry disposition, described in the Purāna.

Duryodhana   One of the heroes of the *Mahābhārata*, the chief rival of the Pāndava brothers.

Dvaita   The philosophy of Dualism.

Dwāpara   The third of the four yugas or world cycles. *See* yuga.

Dwāraka   The capital of Krishna's kingdom, situated in western India; one of the four principal holy places of India, the other three being Kedārnāth, Puri, and Rāmeśwar.

ego of Knowledge (of Devotion)   The ego purified and illumined by the Knowledge (or Love) of God. Some souls, after realizing their oneness with Brahman in samādhi, come down to the plane of relative consciousness. In this state they retain a very faint feeling of ego so that they may teach spiritual knowledge to others. This ego, called by Sri Ramakrishna the "ego of Knowledge", does not altogether efface their knowledge of oneness with Brahman even in the relative state of consciousness. The bhakta, the lover of God, coming down to the relative plane after having attained samādhi, retains the "I-consciousness" by which he feels himself to be a lover, a child, or a servant of God. Sri Ramakrishna called this the "devotee ego", the "child ego", or the "servant ego".

eight fetters   Namely, hatred, shame, lineage, pride of good conduct, fear, secretiveness, caste, and grief.

eight siddhis or occult powers   Namely, the ability to make oneself small as an atom, light as air, etc.

ekādaśi   The eleventh day after the full or new moon, which a devotee spends in full or partial fasting, prayer, and worship.

ektārā   A musical instrument with one string.

"Englishman"   A term often used by Sri Ramakrishna in referring to men educated in English schools or influenced by European ideas.

esrāj   A stringed musical instrument.

ether   Ākāśa or all-pervading space.

fakir   Beggar; often a religious mendicant.

five cosmic principles   Namely, ether (ākāśa), air (vāyu), fire (agni), water (ap), and earth (kshiti).

five vital forces or prānas   Namely, prāna, apāna, samāna, vyāna, and udāna. These five names denote the five functions of the vital force, such as breathing, digesting, evacuating, etc.

four fruits   The four ends of human pursuit, namely, dharma (righteousness), artha (wealth), kāma (fulfilment of desire), and moksha (liberation).

four inner organs   The four inner organs of perception, namely, manas (mind), buddhi (the discriminating faculty), chitta (mind-stuff), and ahamkāra ("I-consciousness").

four stages of life   Namely, brahmacharya (life of unmarried student), gārhasthya (life of married householder), vānaprastha (life of retired householder), and sannyās (life of monk).

gandharva   A class of demigods who are the musicians of heaven.

Ganeśa   The god with the elephant's head; the god of success, the son of Śiva.

Gangā   The Ganges.

Gangāsāgar   The mouth of the Ganges at the Bay of Bengal, considered a sacred place by the Hindus.

gānjā   Indian hemp.

garden house   A rich man's country house set in a garden.

gārhasthya   The second of the four stages of life: the life of a married householder. *See* four stages of life.

Gaur   Short for Gaurānga.

Gaurānga   A name of Sri Chaitanya.

Gauri   (*Lit.*, of fair complexion)   A

name of the Divine Mother; also the name of a pundit devoted to Sri Ramakrishna.

Gayā   A sacred place in northern India.

Gāyatri   A sacred verse of the Vedas recited daily by Hindus of the three upper castes after they have been invested with the sacred thread; also the presiding deity of the Gāyatri.

gerruā   (*Lit.*, ochre) The ochre cloth of a monk.

ghāt   Bathing-place on a lake or river.

ghee   Butter clarified by boiling.

Ghoshpārā   A Vaishnava sect, the members of which generally indulge in questionable religious practices.

Giri   One of the ten denominations of monks belonging to the school of Śankara.

Girirāni   (*Lit.*, the Queen of the Mountain) Consort of King Himā-laya and mother of Umā.

Gītā   Same as the *Bhagavad Gītā*.

Goloka   The Celestial Abode of Vishnu.

golokdhām   A game in which the player tries to get to "heaven" by passing through different planes; on each false step he falls into a particu-lar "hell".

Gopāla   The Baby Krishna.

gopas   The cowherd boys of Vrindā-van, playmates of Sri Krishna.

gopis   The milkmaids of Vrindāvan, companions and devotees of Sri Krishna.

Gorā   A name of Sri Chaitanya.

goswāmi   Vaishnava priest.

Govardhan   A hill near Vrindāvan, which Sri Krishna lifted with His finger to protect the villagers from a deluge of rain.

Govinda(ji)   A name of Sri Krishna.

gram   A kind of bean.

Great Cause   The Ultimate Reality.

Guhaka   An untouchable who was a friend of Rāma.

guna   According to the Sāmkhya phi-losophy, Prakriti (nature), in con-trast with Purusha (soul), consists of three gunas (qualities or strands) known as sattva, rajas, and tamas. Tamas stands for inertia or dullness, rajas for activity or restlessness, and sattva for balance or wisdom.

guru(deva)   Spiritual teacher.

Gurumahārāj   A respectful way of re-ferring to the guru.

Haladhari   A priest in the temple gar-den at Dakshineswar and a cousin of Sri Ramakrishna.

Hāldārpukur   A small lake at Kāmār-pukur.

hāluā   A pudding made of farina.

Hanumān   The great monkey devotee of Rāma, mentioned in the *Rāmā-yana*.

Hara   A name of Śiva.

Hārdwār   A sacred place on the bank of the Ganges at the foot of the Himālayas.

Hari   God; a name of Vishnu, the Ideal Deity of the Vaishnavas.

Haridās   A disciple of Sri Chaitanya.

Hari Om   Sacred words by which God is often invoked.

hathayoga   A school of yoga that aims chiefly at physical health and well-being.

hathayogi   A student of hathayoga.

havishya   Food consisting of boiled rice, butter, and milk, and consid-ered very holy.

Hazra   A devotee who lived at the Dakshineswar temple garden and was of a perverse disposition. Same as Pratap Hazra.

"hero"   A religious aspirant described in the Tantra, who is permitted sex-ual intercourse under certain condi-tions.

hide-and-seek   The Indian game of hide-and-seek, in which the leader, known as the "granny", bandages the eyes of the players and hides herself. The players are supposed to find her. If any player can touch her, the bandage is removed from his eyes and he is released from the game.

hinchē   A kind of aquatic plant eaten as greens.

Hiranyakaśipu A demon king in Hindu mythology, the father of Prahlāda.

Hiranyāksha A demon in Hindu mythology.

Holy Mother The name by which Sri Ramakrishna's wife was known among his devotees.

homa A Vedic sacrifice in which oblations are offered into a fire.

Hriday Sri Ramakrishna's nephew, who served as his attendant during the period of his spiritual discipline. Also called Hridu and Hridē. He was expelled from the temple garden at Dakshineswar on account of certain of his actions which displeased the temple authorities.

Hrishikesh A village on the Ganges at the foot of the Himālayas, where sādhus practise austerities.

hubble-bubble A water-pipe for smoking.

Idā A nerve in the spinal column. See Sushumnā.

Indra The king of the gods.

Indrāni The consort of Indra.

Ishan A name of Śiva; also the name of a devotee of Sri Ramakrishna.

Ishta(deva) The Chosen Ideal, Spiritual Ideal, or Ideal Deity of the devotee.

Iśvara The Personal God.

Iśvarakoti A perfected soul born with a special spiritual message for humanity. "An Incarnation of God or one born with some of the characteristics of an Incarnation is called an Iśvarakoti." (Sri Ramakrishna)

Jadabharata A great saint in Hindu mythology.

jaḍa samādhi Communion with God in which the aspirant appears lifeless, like an inert object.

Jagadambā (Lit., the Mother of the Universe) A name of the Divine Mother.

Jagāi Jagāi and Mādhāi were two ruffians redeemed by Gaurānga.

Jagannāth The Lord of the Universe; a name of Vishnu.

Jagannāth temple The celebrated temple at Puri.

Jagaddhātri (Lit., the Bearer of the Universe) A name of the Divine Mother. In this form She is represented as riding a lion in the act of subduing an elephant.

jal The Bengali word for water.

Jamunā The sacred river Jumnā, a tributary of the Ganges.

Janaka, King One of the ideal kings in Hindu mythology and the father of Sītā. Sri Ramakrishna often described him as the ideal householder, who combined yoga with enjoyment of the world.

japa Repetition of God's name.

Jatilā and Kutilā Two trouble-makers depicted in the Bhāgavata, in the episode of Sri Krishna and the gopis of Vrindāvan.

jilipi A kind of sweetmeat.

jīva The embodied soul; a living being; an ordinary man.

jīvakoti An ordinary man.

jīvanmukta One liberated from māyā while living in the body.

jīvātmā The embodied soul.

jnāna Knowledge of God arrived at through reasoning and discrimination; also denotes the process of reasoning by which the Ultimate Truth is attained. The word is generally used to denote the knowledge by which one is aware of one's identity with Brahman.

jnānayoga The path of knowledge, consisting of discrimination, renunciation, and other disciplines.

jnāni One who follows the path of knowledge and discrimination to realize God; generally used to denote a non-dualist.

Jung Bāhādur A high official of the Mahārājā of Nepal.

"ka" The first consonant of the Sanskrit alphabet.

Kabir A medieval religious reformer, mystic, and writer of songs. He lived during the last part of the fifteenth and the early part of the sixteenth century. Born in the low caste of the weavers, he became the founder of a religious sect. On account of the breadth and universality of his teachings, he was revered by the Mohammedans and the Hindus alike.

kadamba A favourite tree of Sri Krishna.

Kaikeyi One of the wives of King Dasaratha and the mother of Bharata; through her evil machinations the king banished Rāma to the forest.

Kailās A peak of the Himālayas, regarded as the sacred Abode of Śiva.

kaivarta The fisherman caste.

Kāla A name of Śiva; black; death; time.

Kāli A name of the Divine Mother; the presiding Deity of the Dakshineswar temple. She is often referred to and addressed by Sri Ramakrishna as the Ādyāsakti, the Primal Energy.

kāliā A rich preparation of fish or meat.

Kālidāsa The great Sanskrit poet and author of Śakuntalā.

Kālighāt A section of northern Calcutta, where is situated the famous temple of Kāli.

Kāliya The name of a venomous snake subdued by Sri Krishna.

Kāliyadaman Ghāt A bathing-place on the Jamunā at Vrindāvan, where Sri Krishna subdued the snake Kāliya.

Kaliyuga One of the four yugas or cycles. See yuga.

Kalki The name of the next and last Incarnation, according to the Purāna.

kalmi An aquatic creeper with numerous ramifications.

Kalpataru The Wish-fulfilling Tree; refers to God.

kāma Fulfilment of desire, one of the four ends of human pursuit. See four fruits.

Kamalākānta A mystic poet of Bengal.

kamandalu The water-bowl of a monk.

Kāmārpukur Sri Ramakrishna's birthplace.

kāminikānchan (Lit., "woman and gold") A term used by Sri Ramakrishna to refer to lust and greed.

Kamśa Sri Krishna's uncle, the personification of evil, whom Sri Krishna ultimately killed.

Kānāi A pet name of the youthful Sri Krishna.

Kānchi A holy place in southern India.

Kapila A great sage in Hindu mythology, the reputed author of the Sāmkhya philosophy.

kārana Cause; also consecrated wine.

karma Action in general; duty; ritualistic worship.

karmayoga (Lit., union with God through action) The path by which the aspirant seeks to realize God through work without attachment; also the ritualistic worship prescribed in the scriptures for realizing God.

Karna A hero of the Mahābhārata.

kartā Doer; master.

Kartābhajā A minor Vaishnava sect which teaches that men and women should live together in the relationship of love and gradually idealize their love by looking on each other as divine.

Kārtika A son of Śiva; commander-in-chief of the army in heaven.

Kāsi Benares.

kathak A professional reciter of stories from the Purāna in an assembly.

Kātyāyani A name of the Divine Mother.

Kausalyā The mother of Rāma.

kavirāj Native physician of India.

kāyastha One of the subsidiary castes in Bengal.

Kedār(nāth) A high peak in the Himālayas; one of the four principal holy places of India, the other three being Dwārakā, Puri, and Rāmeswar.

Kesava A name of Sri Krishna.

Keshab Bhārati The monastic teacher of Sri Chaitanya.

Keshab (Chandra Sen) The celebrated Brāhmo leader (A.D. 1838–1884).

Kha (*Lit.*, ākāśa) A symbol of the All-pervading Consciousness.

khokā Baby.

kirtan Devotional music, often accompanied by dancing.

kirtani A professional woman singer of kirtan.

kośākuśi Metal articles used in worship.

kosha (*Lit.*, sheath or covering) The following are the five koshas as described in the Vedānta philosophy: (1) the annamayakosha, or gross physical sheath, made of and sustained by food; (2) the prānamayakosha, or vital sheath, consisting of the five vital forces; (3) the manomayakosha, or mental sheath; (4) the vijnānamayakosha, or sheath of intelligence; and (5) the ānandamayakosha, or sheath of bliss. These five sheaths, arranged one inside the other, cover the Soul, which is the innermost of all and untouched by the characteristics of the sheaths.

koul A worshipper of Kāli who follows the "left-hand" rituals of the Tantra.

kripāsiddha One who attains perfection through the *grace* of God and apparently without any effort.

Krishna One of the Ideal Deities of the Vaishnavas.

Krishnachaitanya A name of Sri Chaitanya.

Krishnayātrā A theatrical performance depicting the life of Sri Krishna.

kshara Changeable.

kshatriya The second or warrior caste in Hindu society.

kshir Milk thickened by boiling.

Kubir A Bengali mystic poet.

Kumāra Sambhava A famous book by Kālidāsa.

Kumāri Pujā (*Lit.*, the worship of a virgin) A ritualistic worship prescribed by the Tantra, in which a virgin is worshipped as the manifestation of the Divine Mother of the Universe.

kumbhaka Retention of breath; a process in prānāyāma, or breath-control, described in rājayoga and hathayoga.

Kumbhakarna A brother of Rāvana mentioned in the *Rāmāyana*, who slept six months at a time.

kumbhamelā An assembly of monks held every three years in one of several holy places in India.

Kundalini (*Lit.*, the Serpent Power) It is the spiritual energy lying dormant in all individuals. According to the Tantra there are six centres in the body, designated as Mulādhāra, Svādhisthāna, Manipura, Anāhata, Viśuddha, and Ājnā. These are the dynamic centres where the spiritual energy becomes vitalized and finds special expression with appropriate spiritual perception and mystic vision. These centres, placed in the Sushumnā, form the ascending steps by which the Kundalini, or spiritual energy, passes from the foot of the spine to the cerebrum. When an easy pathway is formed along the Sushumnā through these centres, and the Kundalini encounters no resistance in its movements upward and downward, then there is the Shatchakrabheda, which means, literally, the penetrating of the six chakras, or mystic centres. The Mulādhāra chakra, situated between the base of the sexual organ and the anus, is regarded as the seat of the Kundalini. The centres are metaphorically described as lotuses. The Mulādhāra is said to be a four-petalled lotus. The Svādhisthāna chakra, situated at the base of the sexual organ, is a six-petalled lotus. The Manipura, situated in the region of the navel, contains ten petals. The Anāhata, placed in the region of the heart, is a twelve-petalled lotus. The Viśuddha, at the lower end of the throat, has sixteen petals. The Ājnā, situated in the space between the eyebrows, is a two-petalled lotus. In the cerebrum there is the Sahasrāra, the thousand-petalled lotus, the abode of Śiva, which is as white as the silvery full moon, as bright as lightning, and as mild and serene as moonlight. This is the highest goal, and here the awakened spiritual energy manifests itself in its full glory and splendour.

kuthi The bungalow in the Dakshineswar temple garden, where the proprietors and their guests stayed while visiting Dakshineswar.

Lakshmana The third brother of Rāma.

Lakshmi The Consort of Vishnu and Goddess of Fortune.

līlā The divine play; the Relative. The creation is often explained by the Vaishnavas as the līlā of God, a conception that introduces elements of spontaneity and freedom into the universe. As a philosophical term, the Līlā (the Relative) is the correlative of the Nitya (the Absolute).

lotus Each of the six centres along the Sushumnā is called a lotus, since they have a form like that of a lotus blossom. See Kundalini.

luchi A thin bread made of flour and fried in butter.

M. Mahendranath Gupta, one of Sri Ramakrishna's foremost householder disciples and the recorder of *The Gospel of Sri Ramakrishna.*

Madan(a) The god of love in Hindu mythology; also a Bengali mystic and writer of songs.

Mādhāi See Jagāi.

Mādhava A name of Sri Krishna.

mādhavi A creeper.

Madhu and Kaitabha Two demons killed by the Divine Mother; the story is narrated in the *Chandi.*

madhur One of the five attitudes cherished by the Vaishnava worshipper toward his Ideal Deity, Krishna: the attitude of a wife toward her husband or of a woman toward her paramour.

Madhusudan(a) (*Lit.,* the Slayer of the demon Madhu) A name of Sri Krishna.

Mahābhārata A famous Hindu epic.

mahābhāva The most intense ecstatic love of God.

Mahādeva (*Lit.,* the Great God) A name of Śiva.

Mahā-Kāla Śiva; the Absolute.

Mahā-Kāli A name of the Divine Mother.

Mahākārana (*Lit.,* the Great Cause) The Transcendental Reality.

Mahākāśa The space of Infinity.

Mahāmāyā The Great Illusionist; a name of Kāli, the Divine Mother.

Mahānirvāna The great Nirvāna or samādhi.

Mahānirvāna Tantra A standard book on Tantra philosophy.

Maharshi (*Lit.,* a great rishi or seer of truth) An epithet often applied to Devendranath Tagore, the father of the poet Rabindranath.

Mahāshtami The second day of the worship of Durgā, the Divine Mother.

mahat The cosmic mind; a term used in the Sāmkhya philosophy, denoting the second category in the evolution of the universe.

mahātmā A high-souled person.

Mahāvāyu Cosmic Consciousness or the Life Force. The word is also used to denote a current felt in the spinal column when the Kundalini is awakened.

Mahāvir (*Lit.,* great hero) A name of Hanumān, the monkey devotee of Rāma.

māhut Elephant-driver.

Maidān A great field in Calcutta.

Malaya breeze The fragrant breeze that blows from the Malaya (Western Ghāt) Mountains.

manas Mind. See four inner organs.

Mānasoravar A sacred lake in Tibet.

Mandodari Rāvana's wife.

Manikarnikā Ghāt The famous cremation ground in Benares.

Manipura The third centre in the Sushumnā. See Kundalini.

mānjā A glue of barley and powdered

glass with which kite-strings are given a sharp cutting-edge.

manomayakosha   The mental sheath. *See* kosha.

mantra   Holy Sanskrit text; also the sacred formula used in japa.

Manu   The great Hindu lawgiver.

Manusamhitā   A book on Hindu law by Manu.

Mārhāttā   A race inhabiting the province of Bombay.

Mārwāri   An inhabitant of Mārwār, in Rājputāna, in central India.

math   Monastery.

Mathur   The son-in-law of Rāni Rasmani, and a great devotee of Sri Ramakrishna, whom he provided with all the necessities of life at the temple garden.

māyā   Ignorance obscuring the vision of God; the Cosmic Illusion on account of which the One appears as many, the Absolute as the Relative; it is also used to denote attachment.

"māyā of ignorance"   *See* avidyāmāyā.

"māyā of knowledge"   *See* avidyāmāyā.

māyāvādi   A follower of the Māyā theory of the Vedānta philosophy, according to which the world of names and forms is illusory, like a dream.

Mimāmsaka   A follower of the Purva Mimāmsā, one of the six systems of orthodox Hindu philosophy.

Mirābāi   A great medieval woman saint of the Vaishnava sect.

mlechchha   A non-Hindu, a barbarian. This is a term of reproach applied by the orthodox Hindus to foreigners, who do not conform to the established usages of Hindu religion and society. The word corresponds to the "heathen" of the Christians and the "kafir" of the Mussalmāns.

mohant   The abbot of a monastery.

moksha   Liberation or final emancipation, one of the four ends of human pursuit. *See* four fruits.

mridanga   An earthen drum used in devotional music.

mukti   Liberation from the bondage of the world, which is the goal of spiritual practice.

Mulādhāra   The first and lowest centre in the Sushumnā. *See* Kundalini.

muni   A holy man given to solitude and contemplation.

munsiff   A judicial officer.

Mussalmān   A follower of Mohammed.

Nāda   The Word-Brahman, Om.

nahabat   Music tower.

Naishādha   A famous Sanskrit treatise by Sriharsha.

Nānak   The founder of the Śikh religion and the first of the ten Gurus of the Śikhs. He was born in the Punjab in A.D. 1469 and died in 1538.

Nanda(ghosh)   Sri Krishna's foster-father.

Nandi   A follower of Śiva.

Nangtā   (*Lit.*, the Naked One) By this name Sri Ramakrishna referred to Totapuri, the sannyāsi who initiated him into monastic life and who went about naked.

Nārada   A great sage and lover of God in Hindu mythology.

Nārada Pancharātra   A scripture of the Bhakti cult.

Naralīlā   God manifesting Himself as man.

Nārāyana   A name of Vishnu.

Nārāyani   The Consort of Nārāyana; a name of the Divine Mother.

Narendra(nath)   A disciple of Sri Ramakrishna, subsequently world-famous as Swami Vivekananda.

Nareschandra   A mystic poet of Bengal.

Narmadā   A river in central India flowing into the Arabian Sea.

nātmandir   A spacious hall supported by pillars in front of a temple, meant for devotional music, religious assemblies, and the like.

Navadvip   A town in Bengal which was the birth-place of Sri Chaitanya.

Navavidhān   (*Lit.*, the New Dispensation) The name of the Brāhmo Samāj organized by Keshab Chandra Sen after his disagreement with the members of the Brāhmo Samāj.

nax   A card-game.

neem A tree with bitter leaves.

"Neti, neti" (*Lit.*, "Not this, not this") The negative process of discrimination, advocated by the followers of the non-dualistic Vedānta.

New Dispensation *See* Navavidhān.

ni The seventh note in the Indian musical scale.

Nidhu Babu A composer of light melodies.

Nidhu Grove A sacred grove in Vrindāvan, where Sri Krishna played with the gopis in His childhood.

Nidhuvan Same as Nidhu Grove.

Nikashā The mother of Rāvana.

nikunja Bower.

Nimāi A familiar name of Sri Chaitanya.

Nimāi-sannyās "Chaitanya's Renunciation"; a play describing Sri Chaitanya's embracing of the monastic life.

Niranjan(a) (*Lit.*, the Stainless One) A name of God; also one of the intimate disciples of Sri Ramakrishna.

nirguna Without attributes.

Nirguna Brahman (*Lit.*, Brahman without attributes) A term used to describe the Absolute.

Nirvāna Final absorption in Brahman, or the All-pervading Reality, by the annihilation of the individual ego.

nirvikalpa samādhi The highest state of samādhi, in which the aspirant realizes his total oneness with Brahman.

nishthā Single-minded devotion or love.

Nitāi A pet name of Nityānanda.

Nitya The Absolute.

Nitya-Kāli A name of the Divine Mother.

nityakarma Religious ceremonies which a householder must perform every day, but which are not obligatory for a sannyāsi.

Nityānanda (*Lit.*, Eternal Bliss) The name of a beloved disciple and companion of Sri Chaitanya.

nityasiddha (*Lit.*, eternally perfect) A term used by Sri Ramakrishna to describe some of his young disciples

endowed with great spiritual power.

Nrisimha (*Lit.*, Man-lion) A Divine Incarnation mentioned in the Purāna.

Nyāya Indian Logic, one of the six systems of orthodox Hindu philosophy, founded by Gautama.

Olcott, Col. One of the well-known leaders of the Theosophical Society.

Om The most sacred word of the Vedas; also written as Aum. It is a symbol of God and of Brahman.

ostād Teacher of music.

Padmalochan A great pundit of Bengal, who recognized the true significance of Sri Ramakrishna's spiritual experiences.

pāgli Mad woman.

pākhoāj A kind of double drum.

pānā Aquatic plants like algae or water hyacinths, often found covering the surface of lakes in tropical countries.

Panchadasi The name of a book on Vedānta philosophy.

panchatapā (*Lit.*, the austerity of five fires) While practising this discipline, the aspirant sits under the blazing sun, in the summer season, with four fires burning around him. Seated in the midst of these five fires he practises japa and meditation.

Panchavati A grove of five sacred trees planted by Sri Ramakrishna in the temple garden at Dakshineswar for his practice of spiritual discipline.

Pāndava(s) The five sons of Pandu: King Yudhisthira, Arjuna, Bhima, Nakula, and Sahadeva. They are some of the chief heroes of the *Mahābhārata*.

pāni Water.

Pānini A well-known Sanskrit grammar composed by Pānini.

Parabrahman The Supreme Brahman.

paramahamsa One belonging to the highest order of sannyāsis.

Paramahamsa(deva) A name for Sri Ramakrishna.

Paramātman The Supreme Soul.

Parashurāma A warrior sage in Hindu

mythology, regarded as a Divine Incarnation.

Parikshit   A king of the lunar race and grandson of Arjuna, mentioned in the *Mahābhārata*.

Pārvati   Daughter of King Himālaya; the Consort of Śiva, She is regarded as an Incarnation of the Divine Mother; one of Her names is Umā.

Pātanjala   One of the six systems of orthodox Hindu philosophy, also known as the Yoga philosophy.

Pāvhāri Bābā   An ascetic and yogi of great distinction who was a contemporary of Sri Ramakrishna.

Phalgu   A river in northern India which flows under a surface of sand.

pice   An Indian coin, one fourth of an ānnā.

Pingalā   A nerve in the spinal column. *See* Sushumnā.

Prabhās   A holy place in Kathiawar, in western India, where Sri Krishna gave up His body.

Prahlāda   A great devotee of Vishnu, whose life is described in the Purāna. While a boy, he was tortured for his piety by his father, the demon King Hiranyakaśipu. The Lord, in His Incarnation as Man-lion, slew the father.

Prakriti   Primordial Nature, which, in association with Purusha, creates the universe. It is one of the categories of the Sāmkhya philosophy.

prāna   The vital breath that sustains life in a physical body. *See* five vital forces.

prānamayakosha   The vital sheath, consisting of the five prānas. *See* kosha.

Pranava   Om.

prānāyāma   Control of breath; one of the disciplines of yoga.

prārabdha karma   The karma, or action, performed by a man is generally divided into three groups: sanchita, āgāmi, and prārabdha. The sanchita karma is the vast store of accumulated actions done in the past, the fruits of which have not yet been reaped. The āgāmi karma is the action that will be done by the individual in the future. The prārabdha karma is the action that has begun to fructify, the fruit of which is being reaped in this life. It is a part of the sanchita karma, inasmuch as this also is action done in the past. But the difference between the two is that, whereas the sanchita karma is not yet operative, the prārabdha has already begun to operate. According to the Hindus, the fruit of all karmas must be reaped by their doer, and the character and circumstances of the life of the individual are determined by his previous karmas. The prārabdha is the most effective of all karmas, because its consequences cannot be avoided in any way. The realization of God enables one to abstain from future action (āgāmi karma) and to avoid the consequences of all one's accumulated action (sanchita karma) that has not yet begun to operate; but the prārabdha, which has already begun to bear fruit, must be reaped.

prasād   Food or drink that has been offered to the Deity; also the leavings of a superior's meal. The name Prasād is short for Rāmprasād, a mystic poet of Bengal.

pravartaka   A beginner in religion.

prema   Ecstatic love, divine love of the most intense kind.

premā-bhakti   Ecstatic love of God.

Premdās   A writer of devotional songs.

pujā   Ritualistic worship.

puli   A kind of cake.

Purāna(s)   Books of Hindu mythology.

puraścharana   The repetition of the name of a deity, attended with burnt offerings, oblations, and other rites prescribed in the Vedas.

Puri   Situated in Orissa; it is one of the four principal holy places of India, the other three being Dwārakā, Kedārnāth, and Rāmeśwar; also one of the ten denominations of monks belonging to the school of Śankara.

purnajnāni   Perfect knower of Brahman.

Purusha   (*Lit.*, a man) A term of the Sāmkhya philosophy, denoting the eternal Conscious Principle; the universe evolves from the union of Prakriti and Purusha. The word also denotes the soul and the Absolute.

Qualified Non-dualism A school of Vedānta founded by Rāmānuja, according to which the soul and nature are the modes of Brahman, and the individual soul is a part of Brahman.

Rādhā Sri Krishna's most intimate companion among the gopis of Vrindāvan.

Rādhākānta (Lit., the Consort of Rādhā) A name of Sri Krishna.

Rādhākunda A place near Mathurā associated with Krishna and Rādhā.

Rādhikā Same as Rādhā.

rāga-bhakti Supreme love, making one attached only to God.

rāgas and rāginis Principal and subordinate modes in Hindu music.

Raghuvamsa The name of a Sanskrit treatise by Kālidāsa.

Raghuvir A name of Rāma; the Family Deity of Sri Ramakrishna.

Rāhu A demon in Hindu mythology, said to cause the eclipse by devouring the sun and the moon.

Rājarājeśvari (Lit., the Empress of kings) A name of the Divine Mother.

rājarshi A king who leads a saintly life; an epithet of Janaka.

rajas The principle of activity or restlessness. See guna.

rājasic Pertaining to, or possessed of, rajas.

Rājasuya The royal sacrifice, performed only by a paramount ruler.

Rājayoga The famous treatise on yoga, ascribed to Patanjali; also the yoga described in this treatise.

Rāma(chandra) The hero of the Rāmāyana, regarded by the Hindus as a Divine Incarnation.

Rāmānanda A devotee of Sri Chaitanya.

Rāmānuja A famous saint and philosopher of southern India, the founder of the school of Qualified Non-dualism (A.D. 1017-1137).

Rāmāyana A famous Hindu epic.

Rambhā The name of a celestial maiden.

Rāmeśwar Situated at the southernmost extremity of India and considered one of its four principal holy places, the other three being Dwārakā, Kedārnāth, and Puri.

Ramlal A nephew of Sri Ramakrishna and a priest in the Kāli temple at Dakshineswar.

Rāmlālā The Boy Rāma; also the metal image of Rāma worshipped by Sri Ramakrishna.

Rāmlīlā A Hindu religious festival depicting Rāma's life, which is observed annually by the Hindus of northern India.

Rāmprasād A Bengali mystic and writer of songs about the Divine Mother.

Rāni (Lit., queen) A title of honour conferred on a woman.

rasaddār Supplier of provisions.

Rasmani, Rāni A wealthy woman of the śudra caste, the foundress of the Kāli temple at Dakshineswar.

Rathayātrā The Hindu Car Festival.

Rāvana The monster-king of Ceylon, who forcibly abducted Sītā, the wife of Rama.

rishi A seer of Truth; the name is also applied to the pure souls to whom were revealed the words of the Vedas.

Rudra A manifestation of Śiva.

rudrāksha Beads made from rudrāksha pits, used in making rosaries.

Rukmini One of Sri Krishna's wives.

Rupa and Sanātana Two of the disciples of Sri Chaitanya.

sā, re, gā, mā, pā, dhā, ni The notes of the Indian musical scale, corresponding to do, re, mi, fa, sol, la, si.

sabhā Assembly.

Sachi The mother of Sri Chaitanya; also the consort of Indra.

sadguru True teacher.

sādhaka An aspirant devoted to the practice of spiritual discipline.

sādhanā Spiritual discipline.

Sādhāran Brāhmo Samāj   A branch of the Brāhmo Samāj.

sādhu   Holy man; a term generally used with reference to a monk.

sāgar   Ocean.

saguna   Endowed with attributes.

Saguna Brahman   Brahman with attributes; the Absolute conceived as the Creator, Preserver, and Destroyer of the universe; also the Personal God according to the Vedānta.

Sahaja   (Lit., simple one) The term by which a certain religious sect refers to God; also the natural state.

Sahasrāra   The thousand-petalled lotus in the cerebrum. See Kundalini.

Śaiva   A worshipper of Śiva.

sakhya   One of the five attitudes cherished by the dualistic worshipper toward his Chosen Ideal: the attitude of one friend toward another.

Śākta   A worshipper of Śakti, the Divine Mother, according to the Tantra philosophy.

Śakti   Power, generally the Creative Power of Brahman; a name of the Divine Mother.

Sakuntalā   A celebrated play by Kālidāsa.

śālagrām   A stone emblem of God worshipped by the Hindus.

samādhi   Ecstasy, trance, communion with God.

Sambhu   A name of Śiva.

Sāmkhya   One of the six systems of orthodox Hindu philosophy; founded by Kapila.

samsāra   The world.

samskāra   The tendencies inherited from previous births.

sānāi   A wind-instrument like an oboe.

Sanaka, Sanātana, Sananda, and Sanatkumāra   The first four offspring of Brahmā, the Creator, begotten of His mind; they are regarded as highly spiritual persons.

Sanātana Dharma   (Lit., the Eternal Religion) Refers to Hinduism, formulated by the rishis of the Vedas.

Sanātana Goswāmi   A disciple of Sri Chaitanya and a great saint of the Vaishnava religion.

sandesh   A Bengali sweetmeat made of cheese and sugar.

sandhyā   Devotions or ritualistic worship performed by caste Hindus every day at stated periods.

Śankara   A name of Śiva; also short for Śankarāchārya, the great Vedāntist philosopher.

Śankarāchārya   One of the greatest philosophers of India, an exponent of Advaita Vedānta (A.D. 788-820).

sannyās   The monastic life, the last of the four stages of life. See four stages of life.

sannyāsi   A Hindu monk.

śānta   One of the five attitudes cherished by the dualistic worshipper toward his Chosen Ideal. It is the attitude of peace and serenity, in contrast with the other attitudes of love, which create discontent and unrest in the minds of the devotees. Many of the Vaishnavas do not recognize the attitude of śānta, since it is not characterized by an intense love of God.

Śāntih   Peace.

Sarada Devi   The name of Sri Ramakrishna's wife, also known as the Holy Mother.

Sarasvati   The goddess of learning and music.

sāri   A woman's wearing-cloth.

Sārvabhauma   A great scholar and contemporary of Sri Chaitanya.

śāstra   Scripture; sacred book; code of laws.

Sat   Reality, Being.

Satchidānanda   (Lit., Existence-Knowledge-Bliss Absolute) A name of Brahman, the Ultimate Reality.

satrancha   An Indian game similar to backgammon or parchesi.

sattva   The principle of balance or wisdom. See guna.

sāttvic   Pertaining to, or possessed of, sattva.

Satyabhāmā   A wife of Sri Krishna.

Śavari   The daughter of a hunter, and a great devotee of Rāma.

śava-sādhanā   A Tāntrik ritual in

which a corpse (*śava*) is used by the worshipper as his seat.

savikalpa samādhi Communion with God in which the distinction between subject and object is retained.

seer A measure or weight equivalent to about two pounds.

siddha (*Lit.*, perfect or boiled) Applies both to the perfected soul and to boiled things.

Siddheśvari A name of the Divine Mother.

siddhi The eight occult powers which the yogi acquires through the practice of yoga; perfection in spiritual life; the intoxicating Indian hemp.

Śikhs A religious and martial sect of the Punjab.

Simhavāhini (*Lit.*, One whose bearer is the lion) A name of the Divine Mother.

śishya Disciple.

Sītā The wife of Rāma.

Śiva The Destroyer God; the Third Person of the Hindu Trinity, the other two being Brahmā and Vishnu.

six passions Namely, lust, anger, avarice, delusion, pride, and envy.

six systems *See* darśanas.

six treasures Namely, treasure, glory, strength, splendour, knowledge, and renunciation; these six in their entirety are the treasures of the Godhead.

smriti The law books, subsidiary to the Vedas, guiding the daily life and conduct of the Hindus.

"Soham" (*Lit.*, "I am He") One of the sacred formulas of the non-dualistic Vedāntist.

Sonthāls A savage tribe of central India.

śraddhā Faith.

śrāddha A religious ceremony in which food and drink are offered to deceased relatives.

Sri Used as a prefix to the name of a Hindu man, corresponding to Mr.

Śridāma A devotee and companion of Sri Krishna.

Śrimati A name of Rādhikā; also used as a prefix to the name of a Hindu woman, corresponding to Miss or Mrs.

Śrivās A companion of Sri Chaitanya.

śruti The Vedas.

sthita samādhi Samādhi, or communion with God, in which the aspirant is firmly established in God-Consciousness.

subādār An officer in the Indian army.

Subhadrā The sister of Sri Krishna.

subtle body One of the three bodies or seats of the soul. At death the subtle body accompanies the soul in its transmigration; during the dream state the soul identifies itself with the subtle body. *See* causal body.

Sudāma A devotee and companion of Sri Krishna.

śudra The fourth caste in Hindu society.

Śuka(deva) The narrator of the *Bhāgavata* and son of Vyāsa, regarded as one of India's ideal monks.

Sukrāchārya A holy man described in the Purāna, and the spiritual preceptor of the asuras or demons.

Śumbha and Niśumbha Two demons slain by the Divine Mother. The story is told in the *Chandi*.

Sumeru The sacred Mount Meru of Hindu mythology, around which all the planets are said to revolve.

Sushumnā Sushumnā, Idā, and Pingalā are the three prominent nādis, or nerves, among the innumerable nerves in the nervous system. Of these, again, the Sushumnā is the most important, being the point of harmony of the other two and lying, as it does, between them. The Idā is on the left side, and the Pingalā is on the right. The Sushumnā, through which the awakened spiritual energy rises, is described as the Brahmavartman or Pathway to Brahman. The Idā and Pingalā are outside the spine; the Sushumnā is situated within the spinal column and extends from the base of the spine to the brain. *See* Kundalini.

Svādhisthāna   The second centre in the Sushumnā. *See* Kundalini.

Swami   (*Lit.*, lord) A title of the monks belonging to the Vedānta school.

Swarup   A disciple of Sri Chaitanya.

swastyayana   A religious rite performed to secure welfare or avert a calamity.

Śyāmā   (*Lit.*, the Dark One) A name of Kāli, the Divine Mother.

Śyāmakunda   A place near Mathurā associated with Sri Krishna.

Śyāmalasundara   A name of Sri Krishna.

Śyāmasundar   A name of Sri Krishna.

Tagore   An aristocratic brāhmin family of Bengal.

tamāla   A tree with dark-blue leaves, a favourite tree of Sri Krishna.

tamas   The principle of inertia or dullness. *See* guna.

tāmasic   Pertaining to, or possessed of, tamas.

tānpurā   A stringed musical instrument.

Tantra   A system of religious philosophy in which the Divine Mother, or Power, is the Ultimate Reality; also the scriptures dealing with this philosophy.

Tāntrik   A follower of Tantra; also, pertaining to Tantra.

tapasyā   Religious austerity.

Tārā   (*Lit.*, Redeemer) A name of the Divine Mother.

tarpan   A ceremony in which a libation of water is made to dead relatives.

Tattvajnāna   The Knowledge of Reality.

teli   A member of the oil-man caste.

tilak   A mark of sandal-paste or other material, worn on the forehead to denote one's religious affiliation.

Tillotamā   A celestial maiden.

Totapuri   The sannyāsi who initiated Sri Ramakrishna into monastic life.

Trailanga Swami   A holy man who lived in Benares and was a contemporary of Sri Ramakrishna.

Tretāyuga   The second of the four yugas or cycles. *See* yuga.

tribhanga   (*Lit.*, bent in three places) An epithet of Sri Krishna.

Tukārām   The name of a saint of Bombay.

tulsi   A plant sacred to Vishnu.

Tulsi(dās)   A great devotee of Rāma and the writer of a life of Rāma.

Turiya   (*Lit.*, the fourth) A name of the Transcendental Brahman, which transcends and pervades the three states of waking, dream, and deep sleep.

twenty-four tattvas, or cosmic principles   According to the Sāmkhya philosophy the twenty-four tattvas, or cosmic principles, are: the five great elements in their subtle forms (ether, air, fire, water, earth); ego, or "I-consciousness"; buddhi, or intelligence; Avyakta, or the Unmanifested (in which sattva, rajas, and tamas remain in an undifferentiated state); the five organs of action (hands, feet, organ of speech, organ of generation, organ of evacuation); the five organs of knowledge (eyes, ears, nose, tongue, skin); manas, or mind; and the five sense-objects (sound, touch, form, taste, smell). They all belong to Prakriti, or Nature, and are different from Purusha, or Consciousness.

twice-born   A man belonging to the brāhmin, kshatriya (warrior), or vaisya (merchant) caste, who has his second, or spiritual, birth at the time of his investiture with the sacred thread.

Uddhava   The name of a follower of Sri Krishna.

Umā   The daughter of King Himālaya, and the Consort of Śiva; She is an Incarnation of the Divine Mother.

unmanā samādhi   Samādhi in which the functioning of the mind does not altogether stop.

upādhi   A term of the Vedānta philosophy denoting the limitations imposed upon the Self through ignorance, by which one is bound to worldly life.

Upanishad(s) The well-known scriptures of the Hindus.

upāsanā Worship.

vaidhi-bhakti Devotion to God associated with rites and ceremonies prescribed in the scriptures.

Vaidyanath A holy place in Behar.

Vaikuntha The heaven of the Vaishnavas.

vairāgya Renunciation.

Vaiśākh The first month of the Hindu calendar, falling in the summer season.

Vaiśeshika One of the six systems of orthodox Hindu philosophy, founded by Kanāda.

Vaishnava (Lit., follower of Vishnu) A member of the well-known dualistic sect of that name, generally the followers of Sri Chaitanya in Bengal and of Rāmānuja and Madhva in south India.

vaiśya The third or merchant caste in Hindu society.

Vajrāsana A centre in the Sushumnā.

Vali A king who was punished by God in His Incarnation as Vāmana, or the Dwarf, for his excessive charity and condemned to rule over the nether world.

Vāli A monkey chieftain mentioned in the Rāmāyana and killed by Rāma.

Vālmiki The author of the Rāmāyana.

vānaprastha The third of the four stages of life: the life of retirement, when husband and wife practise contemplation and other spiritual disciplines. See four stages of life.

Varuna The presiding deity of the ocean in Hindu mythology.

Vaśishtha The name of a sage mentioned in the Purāna.

Vasudeva The father of Sri Krishna.

Vasus A class of celestial beings.

vātsalya One of the five attitudes cherished by the dualistic worshipper toward his Chosen Ideal: the attitude of a mother toward her child.

Vedānta One of the six systems of orthodox Hindu philosophy, formulated by Vyāsa.

Vedāntist A follower of Vedānta.

Veda(s) The most sacred scriptures of the Hindus.

vichāra Reasoning.

Videha (Lit., detached from the body) An epithet given to King Janaka on account of the spirit of detachment he showed toward the world.

Vidura The name of a great devotee of Sri Krishna mentioned in the Mabābhārata.

vidyā Knowledge leading to liberation, i.e., to the Ultimate Reality.

vidyādhari Demigoddess.

vidyāmāyā The "māyā of knowledge." See avidyāmāyā.

Vidyāsāgar, Iswar Chandra A great educator and philanthropist of Bengal.

vidyāśakti Spiritual power.

vija mantra The sacred word with which a guru initiates his disciple.

Vijayā day The last day of the worship of Durgā, when the image is immersed in water.

vijnāna Special Knowledge of the Absolute, by which one affirms the universe and sees it as the manifestation of Brahman.

vijnānamayakosha The sheath of intelligence. See kosha.

vijnāni One endowed with vijnāna.

vilwa Same as bel.

vīnā A stringed musical instrument.

Virāt The first progeny of Brahman in Hindu cosmology; the Spirit in the form of the universe; the All-pervading Spirit.

Viśālākshi (Lit., the Large-eyed One) A name of the Divine Mother; also the name of a stream near Kāmārpukur.

Vishnu The Preserver God; the Second Person of the Hindu Trinity, the other two being Brahmā and Śiva; the Personal God of the Vaishnavas.

Viśishtādvaita The philosophy of Qualified Non-dualism.

Viśuddha   The fifth centre in the Sushumnā. *See* Kundalini.

Viśwāmitra   The name of a sage mentioned in the *Rāmāyana*. He was a companion and counsellor of Rāma. Though born a kshatriya, by dint of his austerities he was raised to the status of a brāhmin.

Viswanath   *See* Captain.

viveka   Discrimination.

Vivekachudāmani   A treatise on Vedānta by Śankara.

Vrindāvan   A town on the bank of the Jamunā river associated with Sri Krishna's childhood.

Vyāsa   The compiler of the Vedas and father of Śukadeva.

Wish-fulfilling Tree   *See* Kalpataru.

Yama   The King of Death.

Yaśodā   Sri Krishna's foster-mother.

yātrā   A country theatrical performance.

yoga   Union of the individual soul and the Universal Soul; also the method by which to realize this union.

Yogamāyā   The union of Purusha, the male principle, and Prakriti, the female principle, of Reality; also Śakti, or Divine Power.

yoga samādhi   The samādhi that results when the devotee is united with God.

Yogavāśishtha   The name of a well-known book on Vedānta.

yogi   One who practises yoga.

yogini   Woman yogi.

Yogopanishad   The name of an Upanishad.

Yudhisthira, King   One of the principal heroes of the *Mahābhārata*, known for his truthfulness, righteousness, and piety.

yuga   A cycle or world period. According to Hindu mythology the duration of the world is divided into four yugas, namely, Satya, Tretā, Dwāpara, and Kali. In the first, also known as the Golden Age, there is a great preponderance of virtue among men, but with each succeeding yuga virtue diminishes and vice increases. In the Kaliyuga there is a minimum of virtue and a great excess of vice. The world is said to be now passing through the Kaliyuga.

Yugala Murti   The conjoined figures of a pair; generally used to denote the combined figures of Rādhā and Krishna.

zemindar   Landlord.

INDEX OF SONGS AND HYMNS

INDEX